Psychobiology:
The Neuron and Behavior

Psychobiology:
The Neuron and Behavior

Katharine Blick Hoyenga
Kermit T. Hoyenga
Western Illinois University

Brooks/Cole Publishing Company
Pacific Grove, California

There is nothing either green or gray,
but thinking makes it so.
Rushton (1972)

Brooks/Cole Publishing Company
A Division of Wadsworth, Inc.
© 1988 by Wadsworth, Inc., Belmont, California, 94002. All rights
reserved. No part of this book may be reproduced, stored in a retrieval
system, or transcribed, in any form or by any means — electronic,
mechanical, photocopying, recording, or otherwise — without the prior
written permission of the publisher, Brooks/Cole Publishing Company,
Pacific Grove, California 93950, a division of Wadsworth, Inc.

Printed in the United States of America
10 9 8 7 6 5 4 3 2 1

Library of Congress Cataloging-in-Publication Data
Hoyenga, Katharine Blick.
    Psychobiology.

    Includes bibliographies and index.
    1. Psychobiology. I. Hoyenga, Kermit T.
II. Title. [DNLM: 1. Brain — physiology.
2. Neurophysiology. 3. Psychophysiology. WL 103 H868p]
QP360.H69   1987   612′.82   86-26837
ISBN 0-534-06978-9

Sponsoring Editor: *C. Deborah Laughton*
Marketing Representative: *Katie Konradt*
Editorial Assistants: *Monique Etienne and Amy Mayfield*
Production Coordinators: *Candyce Cameron and Fiorella Ljunggren*
Production Assistant: *Dorothy Bell*
Manuscript Editor: *Meredy Amyx*
Permissions Editor: *Carline Haga*
Interior and Cover Design: *Katherine Minerva*
Cover Art: *David Aguero*
Art Coordinator: *Sue C. Howard*
Interior Illustration: *Lori Heckelman and Scientific Illustrators*
Typesetting: *Progressive Typographers, Inc., Emigsville, Pennsylvania*
Cover Printing: *Phoenix Color Corporation, Long Island City, New York*
Printing and Binding: *Arcata Graphics/Fairfield, Fairfield, Pennsylvania*
(Credits continue on p. 509, following the Index.)

PREFACE

Humankind is currently challenged by two great frontiers: the exploration of space and the exploration of our own brains. Each frontier generates excitement — and also argument: the scientists involved disagree about what might be the "right" way to meet those challenges. Each exploration could dramatically change how we think about ourselves. Specifically, a new way to explore brain function has been evolving that could lead either into a blind alley — or to the conquest of this frontier.

The researchers who inaugurated the era of brain sciences used damaged brains as a compass and guide. The brain of an experimental animal was deliberately damaged in a certain way, and the behavior of that animal then systematically studied. Humans who had suffered from various kinds of damage in various parts of their brains were also examined. In both cases, scientists interpreted the behavioral deficits that were revealed as reflecting the normal function of that part of the brain in an undamaged organism.

But during the latter part of this era, scientists interested in sensory systems began using different techniques and making different assumptions about brain function. First, sensory perceptions of humans were systematically explored and related to variations in the types of physical stimuli being presented to the subjects. Whenever possible, the sensory perceptions of nonhuman animals were also explored. Somewhat later, advances in technology enabled scientists to study the responses and functions of single cells in the brain. In that way, the neural responses to various stimuli could be compared with the behavioral and verbal responses to those same stimuli.

These scientists believed that systematically exploring brain-cell responses to stimuli would uncover the "codes" used by the brain to represent various aspects of our sensory environments. Developments in information theory were used in these efforts to crack the codes: the types of information present in external stimuli were believed to be represented by certain patterns of neural activity in certain nerve cells. Once the types of codes used by the brain had been revealed, the knowledge of those codes could be applied to cells in parts of the brain not directly involved in processing sensory information. In other words, once researchers had learned to decipher the codes, they could investigate the way in which the brain coded its own internal states — its motives and emotions and memories. This research turned into the field of psychobiology.

Psychobiologists frequently describe themselves as being on a threshold of great discoveries (Dallos, 1981, pp. 343–344; Pfaffmann, Frank, & Norgren, 1979, p. 309; Price & DeSimone, 1977, p. 451). So far the single-unit approach has worked so well that scientists often describe their findings with increasing excitement. Indeed, in the next decade we may see the sensory codes cracked, or decoded. For all the senses, sensory prostheses are becoming more sophisticated not only because of the technological innovations occurring in computer chips but also because we are finding out more about our own brain's codes for various sensory events — a long way from the prostheses that simply magnified or amplified information for our failing senses. Knowledge of the biochemistry of brain events has revolutionized treatments for mental disorders. We may also be at a kind of threshold for the treatment of brains damaged by trauma, age, and senile disorders, both because of advances in brain biochemistry and because of advances in our ability to correct damage by transplants. We will be able to replace not only damaged hearts and kidneys but possibly even damaged parts of the brain.

Approach of the Text

This textbook applies psychobiological techniques and philosophies to brain function. In this approach, we emphasize research that has attempted to relate the responses of single nerve cells to perceptions and behaviors. The biochemistry of emotions and motives is also described and related to possible neural codes for various motivational and emotional states. The techniques used by sensory physiologists are being applied to the functions of other parts of the brain, located outside the sensory brain areas. The theory known as the neuron doctrine has historically been related to the idea that the brain is made up of separate cells called neurons. The doctrine has since been extended to include the idea that a useful way to approach brain function is to record the activity of just one cell (or just a few) at a time, eventually sampling many cells in a given area of the brain, recording their responses to various changes in sensory input. This approach assumes that brain events are in fact activity in a small set of cells. A change in the rate or pattern of activity of those cells, or the beginning of a response in other cells, would represent a different brain event.

Because of the historical roots of this approach — relating the activity in small groups of cells in experimental organisms to what trained human observers would report experiencing in response to similar stimulus events — mental events have become part of the theorizing and explanations used by many psychobiologists. They regard activity in a small set of cells as representing not only a brain event but also a given mental event, such as the perception of a certain color or the feeling of being hungry. Although the nature of the representational process is obviously central to such an approach to brain function, we cannot yet describe how the physiochemical events of our brains are translated into the mental states we directly experience as our consciousness. The relationship between mind and brain may be the most challenging outpost on this particular frontier of discovery. Being able someday to describe the nature of this relationship may truly revolutionize our sense of ourselves and our own brains in ways similar to the revolutions caused by Darwin, Freud, and Copernicus.

Organization of the Text

In taking this particular approach to brain function, this book covers most of the research areas in a somewhat unusual fashion. The first part describes the nature of the approach, including the techniques and implications of studying how activities in small groups of cells can be related to behavior, experiences, and perceptions. The background material required for understanding this approach is also summarized. The second part covers neural activity: how nerve cells carry information from one part of the body to another, including detailed descriptions of action and synaptic potentials. The third part explores the ways in which nerve cells code information by examining single-cell responses to various kinds of sensory stimuli. One chapter emphasizes the basic principles of sensory coding, giving examples from research in audition, somatosensory sensations, olfaction, and taste. The other chapter explores a single sensory system: vision. This discussion illustrates how the coding approach can be applied to a single type of brain function, from sensory organ to conscious and complex perceptions. Together, these two chapters represent the conceptual core of psychobiology, still the area in which most of this type of research has been done.

The last two parts represent more recent extensions of the psychobiological approach to more complex behavioral functions. For a number of reasons (documented in the introduction to the part dealing with motives and emotions), applying a sensory-coding approach has not been easy, and the approach so far has not led to the kind of advances found in the study of the sensory systems. In fact, many of the most recent and most exciting discoveries relevant to the last two parts of the book have involved biochemical rather than microrecording techniques. So both the biochemistry and the neural coding of hunger, sex, and emotions are covered in the fourth part. This is the research that has revolutionized the area of mental health and may revolutionize the treatment of eating and sexual disorders. The fifth part covers the biochemistry and neural coding of past experiences — the search for the engram, or the neural record of past experiences and memory. In fact, both the nature and location of some engrams may have been discovered. Advances in this area may lead to dramatic new treatments for brain damage and senile memory disorders such as Alzheimer's disease.

The last part returns to the issues introduced at the beginning of the text. Given all the research concerning the transmission and coding of sensory information, the changes that motives and emotions make in brain function, and the way experiences alter coding functions, what can be said about the nature of the relationship between mental and neural events? And what if the neuron doctrine does not prove to be useful — if it does not lead to important new research and theories? What other way could we approach the study of our own brain functions?

Course and Pedagogical Information

This book is designed to be used as an upper-division or graduate-level textbook for students interested in brain function. Normally students using this textbook would be expected to have a background either in biology or in physiological psychology. However, the basic biological and physiochemical knowledge needed to understand this approach to brain function is summarized in the first part; many students will probably need at least some review of these basic neuroanatomical and physiochemical elements. Also, many students have been able to use this material as their first introduction to brain function and have been able to master the fairly complex nature of brain function described here. The chapters in Parts Four and Five are relatively independent of one another and so can be assigned separately.

To aid the student-reader, the chapters within a part follow similar organizational lines. There are reviews of every main section within each chapter, as well as an end-of-chapter review. Each chapter begins with an overview that identifies and summarizes major concepts and types of research prior to a more in-depth treatment. The overview in Chapter 4 both identifies the principal aspects of synaptic functioning and reviews the major aspects of action potentials by comparing and contrasting action and synaptic potentials. Single-unit recording data are placed at the end of the chapters in Part Three, following presentation of the physiological and anatomical background required to understand that research.

Important terms and concepts are set in boldface. The single-unit research is described in some detail, whereas the research presented first in most chapters is summarized. Thus, students should be able to appreciate the difficulties involved in this type of research, the critical assumptions that have to be made but that may not necessarily be correct, and the tremendous excitement of doing research on this frontier. Can we in fact use our own minds to explore the terra incognita of our own brains, the brains that are responsible for those minds in the first place?

We would like to express our appreciation of the time and effort of our reviewers: Gary Bernston of Ohio State University, Phillip Best of the University of Virginia, Tom Brozoski of Grinnell College, Diane Crutchfield of the College of William and Mary, Eugene Eisman of the University of Wisconsin, Dennis Feeney of the University of New Mexico, David Fitzpatrick of California State University at Los Angeles, Michael Levine of the University of Illinois at Chicago, James J. Mitchell of Kansas State University, Virginia Saunders of San Francisco State University, Charles A. Sorenson of Amherst College, and Carol Van Hartesveldt of the University of Florida.

We would also like to thank the people at Brooks/Cole for all their patient time and expert attention: our manuscript editor, Meredy Amyx; our art coordinator, Suzi Howard; our book designer, Katherine Minerva; and our production editors, Candy Cameron and Fiorella Ljunggren. And special thanks to C. Deborah Laughton, who has been both a skilled professional and a personal friend to us. Good luck, C.D.L.!

Katharine Blick Hoyenga
Kermit Hoyenga

CONTENTS

Contents

Contents

PART ONE

Introduction

This book takes a psychobiological approach to the study of the relationship between the brain and the behavior of an organism such as ourselves. Some researchers who take this point of view say we study the brain to find out about ourselves. We want to find out how we see, hear, and feel — and why we do *not* directly perceive "reality," and why no two of us see, hear, and feel exactly the same things. We want to know how our brain can remember things for us — and why we sometimes do *not* remember things we *do* know. What we desire or need or feel may be related to subtle changes in the chemistry of our brains. Our approach emphasizes measuring the activity of single cells within a brain, or measuring what is called **single-unit activity.** By understanding the details of nerve cell functions and the variety of ways one cell can influence other cells, psychobiological researchers hope to be able to understand how brains — and our minds — work.

This part provides an introduction to and background for the other parts. Chapter 1 covers the techniques, assumptions, and philosophy of this way of studying the brain. Chapter 2 presents the background necessary for the other chapters: basic anatomical principles and basic chemical and physical principles.

Psychobiology:
Philosophy and Techniques

"In any search for meaning, identity, ultimate goals and values, or new ideologies, the nature of mind and its relation to physical reality becomes central and basic" (Sperry, 1969, p. 532).

We begin by discussing the philosophy and techniques of psychobiological research. The philosophy of any science determines (1) what that science deems capable of being studied, (2) how research results will be interpreted, (3) *which techniques* its scientists will use, and (4) how the results of those techniques will be interpreted. The philosophy of psychobiology is thus intimately related to the techniques used by a psychobiologist to decode the languages of the brain.

Philosophy of Psychobiology

According to Restak (1979, p. 15), **psychobiology** is *"concerned with the mind's attempt to know itself through the study of the brain."* This field evolved out of research on the sensory systems of the brain. In his book *The Psychobiology of Sensory Coding* (1973, p. 7), Uttal said of sensory research that this field represents "the analysis by man of his own intellect."

2

This emphasis represents a recent evolution. "That neurobiologists who study single nerve cells should be in a position to discuss higher functions of the brain, such as perception, is a recent, somewhat unexpected development" (Kuffler, Nicholls, & Martin, 1984, p. 3). By studying the brain — specifically, by studying the processes and functions of the nerve cells of the brain — we may come to know things that are fundamental to our understanding of ourselves, including who and what we are. We are at a threshold: "the excitement in neural science today resides in the conviction that the tools are at last in hand to explore the organ of the mind" (Kandel, 1981a, p. 11).

The Mind and the Brain

Psychobiology is concerned with the relationship between the physiological (electrical and chemical) processes of nerve cells in our brains and our own internal experiences. As Uttal points out (1973, p. 3), even though we measure overt behavior in our experiments, often what we are really concerned with is consciousness, awareness, thought, and perception. In other words, although psychobiology experimentally relates behavior to the physiological responses of nerve cells, the ultimate goal is to make inferences about mental states or perceptions and consciousness (see, for example, Kuffler, Nicholls, & Martin, 1984, p. xv).

This text is based on an adaptation of Barlow's (1972) **neuron doctrine.** The phrase *neuron doctrine* has been given two meanings. One describes the brain as consisting of individual nerve cells or **neurons.** The second is defined by Table 1-1. This set of five principles, and the six experimental methods associated with those principles, define and describe the philosophical approach of this book. Barlow's original principles described only sensations and perceptions, but we have extended his hypotheses into other types of mental events. As Barlow said (p. 371), "the central proposition is that our perceptions [and other mental events] are caused by the activity of a rather small number of neurons."

Two recent examples of research relevant to the neuron doctrine will illustrate this point. Johansson and Vallbo (1983) recorded activity in a nerve coming from sensory organs in the skin in human volunteers and were able to demonstrate that a single event, taking place in a single nerve cell, was enough to create a conscious sensation of a touch. Tolhurst, Movshon, and Dean (1983) compared the activity in single brain cells in the visual cortex of cats and monkeys to verbal reports of visual sensations in human beings. They concluded that a conscious sensation could be produced by concerted activity in only four neurons.

Table 1-1   A neuron doctrine.

Basic Principles

1. A description of the activity of a single nerve cell — its effects on other cells and other cells' influences on it — is enough for a functional understanding of the nervous system.
2. The nervous system is organized to represent events in the external world and changes in internal states with a minimum number of active nerve cells.
3. The selective responsiveness of neurons to specific external and internal events is a product of past experiences and of genetic effects during development.
4. "The activities of neurons, quite simply, *are* thought processes" (Barlow, 1972, p. 380). So conscious perceptions correspond to the activity of a small proportion of the numerous high-level neurons, the activity in each of which represents a *code* for a complex pattern of internal and external events. "The activity of each single cell is thus . . . related quite simply to our subjective experience" (p. 371).
5. A high frequency of activity in these high-level neurons corresponds to sensations of subjective certainty.

Appropriate Methods of Experimentation[1]

1. Selective and specific types of stimulation of a few candidate neurons should give rise to a specific sensation, motive, emotion, or memory.
2. The responses of the candidate neurons should change isomorphically with manipulated and controlled variations in the internal or external environment of the organism.
3. Changes in the responses of the candidate neurons in response to variations in internal or external environments should parallel the reports of human subjects subjected to equivalent variations.
4. Reduction or destruction of the candidate neurons' responses by lesion or by stimulation should decrease the organisms' responses to those same internal or external stimuli.
5. The anatomical connections of the candidate neurons should be appropriate to their hypothesized coding function.
6. Genetically produced changes in functions of candidate neurons should produce parallel changes in organisms' responses.

[1] All these methods involve manipulating or measuring a small set of neurons, the **candidate neurons.** These neurons are hypothesized to code variations in internal or external stimuli, the activity of which parallels the appropriate conscious sensation.

Psychobiology requires a multidisciplinary approach. Sir John Eccles (who later won a Nobel prize) provided the initial impetus for this approach in 1953; he summarized his work on the electrical activities of single nerve cells in a book entitled *The Neurophysiological Basis of Mind*. Mountcastle's pioneering research concerning how somatosensory information is coded by single nerve cells has also been central to the discipline of psychobiology. His work led to some revisions in our sense of reality—which he later elegantly summarized in an article entitled "The view from within: Pathways to the study of perception" (1975). Thus, psychobiology includes research in the areas of overlap among traditional psychology, neurochemistry, neurology, and neurobiology.

Philosophy and Methods of Studying the Brain

The philosophy of a science determines the methods it uses. The contrast between the methods of psychobiology and those used in traditional **physiological psychology** reflects the contrast between their philosophies. But before describing the differences, we should point out that these two disciplines have many important similarities. The present book, though emphasizing single-unit recording, depends on and summarizes what physiological research has discovered about brain functions. In fact, present-day researchers can profitably combine the techniques and philosophies of the two approaches. For example, Iwai (1985) explored the function of the brain in primates by combining psychobiology with physiological approaches to find out how one part of the brain is involved in the perception of visual patterns.

As theorists such as Webster have pointed out (1973), classic physiological psychology focused on identifying the functions of the brain (usually in behavioral terms) and on localizing those functions among the various parts of the brain. Because of this approach, physiological theorizing often used mental states as intervening variables. (**Intervening variables** refer to internal states that cannot be directly manipulated or measured. These states are presumed to *intervene* in some way between what an experimenter does to an animal and the subsequent changes in its behavior.) If, for example, destruction of one part of the brain (such as the ventromedial nucleus of the hypothalamus, as illustrated in Figure 1-1) led an animal to overeat, experimenters might infer that destroying that area of the brain somehow impaired the ability of eating to decrease an internal state of "hunger." This would be one explanation of why the brain damage had the effects it did on the experimental animals. Thus, physiological psychologists used "mental states" and a knowledge of brain structure and function to explain behavior. In contrast, one goal of psychobiology is to use a knowledge of both behavior and the brain to understand mental states or the mind.

Research often involves actively manipulating some **independent variable** (such as amount of training or type of brain damage) and measuring the effects of that manipulation on the **dependent variable** of behavior. In classic physiological psychology, the active manipulation sometimes takes the form of destroying a certain part of the brain in the experimental animals. Next, the behaviors of the experimental animals are compared with those of control animals whose brains have been left untouched, as we saw in Figure 1-1. From the results, the experimenter attempts to infer which parts of the brain are most relevant to what aspects of the animals' behaviors (see, for example, Webster, 1973).

In accordance with the neuron doctrine, psychobiologists often record the electrical activity of individual brain cells in an organism. Figure 1-2 illustrates what this type of research might involve. When psychobiologists actively manipulate independent variables, they often present and remove various types of visual or auditory or chemical stimuli while simultaneously recording the "behaviors" of one or more nerve cells. Then the researchers attempt to relate neural responses to internal, psychological experiences. If activity in a brain cell is increased by passing any red-colored object in front of the organism's eyes, then maybe activity in that cell is related to the organism's conscious sensations of "redness."

The philosophies and experimental techniques of both psychobiology and classic physiological psychology usually emphasize **reductionistic** rather than **wholistic** approaches to understanding behavior. That is, behavior is often explained by talking about the activity of nerve cells in certain areas of an organism's brain (whether tested by single-cell recordings in an area or by lesions of the area). For example, "hunger" and food-approach behaviors might be explained by saying that nerve cells in "hunger" centers of the brain became active. Of course, the activity of the nerve cells could then be reduced to physical and chemical events. If this approach were pushed to the extreme, the laws of behavior would someday be "reduced" to the laws of physics and chemistry.

The wholistic approach to behavior came out of the Gestalt tradition. It was believed to be impossible to analyze the whole—the behavior of an organism—in such a manner that the behavior could be completely described by the causal physical and chemical interactions among individual nerve cells. From that point of view, it would be impossible to explain behavior reductionistically because the whole is more than the sum of its parts. The activity of the whole brain *creates* effects that can *never* be understood by studying individual nerve cells. And, although both physiological and psychobiological approaches are reductionistic, some researchers have said that the mind may have wholistic properties. We shall introduce this concept of the mind in this chapter and describe it more fully in the last chapter.

As a reductionistic approach to the study of the mind and behavior, psychobiology emphasizes what studying the activity of individual nerve cells can tell us about ourselves. Patterns of neural activity constitute our "reality," but this reality does

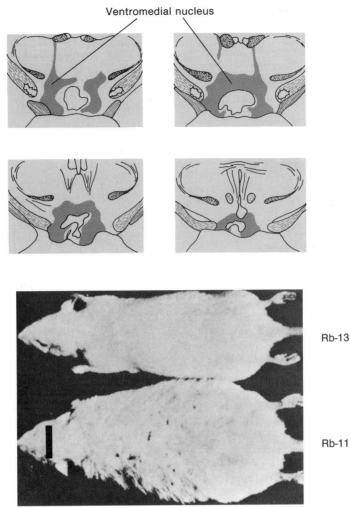

Figure 1-1 Research in physiological psychology. **a.** Diagrams show sections through a part of the brain called the ventromedial hypothalamus in rat Rb-11. The darkened area has been lesioned, and the lesion occurred in the ventromedial nucleus. **b.** The darkened bar indicates the plane of sectioning. Rat Rb-11, now obese, is photographed at autopsy, $4\frac{1}{2}$ months after the lesion. Rb-13 is a control rat.

not necessarily faithfully mimic the physics of the world outside our skins (Craik, 1943). "As we look around the room at different objects in various shapes, shades, and colors, the colors and shapes we experience, along with any associated smells and sounds, are not really out where they seem to be. . . . Instead, they are entirely inside the brain itself" (Sperry, 1969, p. 535). The implications of this distinction, the effects it can have on our concepts of ourselves and our "realities," were summarized by Mountcastle (1975, p. 109, emphasis his):

Each of us believes himself to live directly within the world that surrounds him, to sense its objects and events precisely, and to live in real and current time. I assert that these are perceptual illusions. Contrarily, each of us confronts the world from a brain linked to what is "out there" by a few million fragile sensory nerve fibers, our only information channels, our lifelines to reality. . . . Afferent nerve fibers are not high-fidelity recorders, for they accentuate certain stimulus features, neglect others. The central neuron is a story-teller . . . and it is never com-

STIMULUS   NEURAL RESPONSE

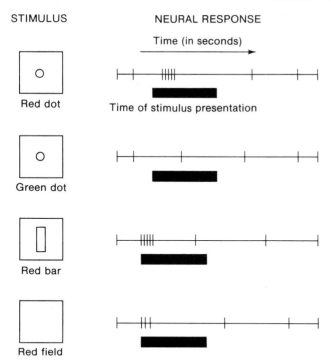

Figure 1-2   Research in psychobiology. A hypothetical nerve cell is shown responding to various visual stimuli. This cell would be a "red detector." Brain function is explored this way under the neuron doctrine. The neural response was recorded with an event recorder; the horizontal lines are the marks made by a pen as paper is moved under it at a constant speed in the direction opposite to the time indicator. The solid bar indicates when the stimulus was turned on and then off, and each "hatch mark" on the neural response record represents one "unit" of activity or a single "action potential."

pletely trustworthy. . . . *Sensation is an abstraction, not a replication, of the real world.*

Overview of the Book

The book is organized around the coding properties of individual nerve cells. How nerve cells work and how they can code information coming from external "reality" are described in Part II. This aspect of nerve cells is related to principle 1 (Table 1-1) and could be called the **communication function**: changes in the electrical activities of nerve cells enable them to communicate information from one place to another in the brain. As principle 3 and the sixth method of research (Table 1-1) imply, many of the communications among nerve cells are specified by genes (heredity).

Parts III and IV cover principles 1 and 4 of Table 1-1: the coding of external and internal states by a minimal number of neurons. Part III describes how sensory nerve cells both *select* and *code* sensory information about the external world. In Part IV, we see that some nerve cells code internal states such as hunger, and internal states can also affect the coding of external stimuli by sensory cells. How these internal states, or motives and emotions, may affect *nerve cell coding and processing of stimulus information*, both from the external world and from internal bodily functions, will be explored.

Part V is most directly concerned with principle 3: how genes and experiences interact to determine the coding characteristics of neurons. Nerve cells are changed by experience, thereby *storing information* about the world to be used at a later time. Within limits set by genetics, past experiences can change the ways nerve cells process and code incoming information. This effect literally means that two people, having different genes and different sets of past experiences, will not perceive the same situation in exactly the same way. No two of us have exactly the same set of subjective certainties.

Studying the coding properties of nerve cells may represent the mind's attempt to know itself through the study of the brain. The selection, coding, and transmission of information within the nervous system may be related to our sense of reality, to our sense of what is really "out there." The way that internal states may change the coding of neural information may be related to our desires and intentions. The way that past experiences affect coding may be part of our beliefs, of what we think to be true. Our own self-consciousness and identity are created by these coding systems, especially those found in the "highest" part of the brain, the **cerebral cortex**. The cerebral cortex does the detailed processing of information. Part of this processing may create our consciousness and our sense of who we are. By the laws of some states, people are even declared legally dead when their cortex no longer displays electrical activity.

The Mind – Body Problem

Since psychobiology studies the mind by studying the brain, how mind and body are to be defined is critically important. Before any research can be planned — or interpreted — these constructs must be identified.

Definitions of Mind, of Body, and of the Problem

Starting with Descartes and continuing with the materialism of John Locke, Western civilization's definition of mind and body created the mind – body problem. (Some Eastern philosophies, using different definitions, have not had to wrestle with this problem.) The body — the brain — is defined by its physical and chemical properties, and it is assumed to function in ways that can be predicted and explained by the laws of physics and chemistry. The mind, however, has *non*physical properties and includes the idea of mental events that have no physical substance and that cannot be physically measured. These mental events would include but would not be limited to conscious awareness of sensations, beliefs, desires, and intentions — the understanding of which is the goal of psychobiology. But just how can a physiochemical body be causally related to a nonphysical mind? This problem is aggravated by the fact that our very idea of what causation is has been derived from observations of physical events and *not* from observations of mental events, even in ourselves (but obviously our idea of causation is, itself, a mental event).

Feigl, a philosopher of science, introduced his extensive discussion (1958) of the mind–body problem with a description of its effects on science (p. 370):

> Tough-minded scientists tend to relegate the mind–body problem to the limbo of speculative metaphysics. Perhaps after trying a bit, but with questionable success to square themselves with the puzzle, they usually take one or the other of two attitudes. Either the puzzle is left to the philosophers to worry about, or else it is bluntly declared a pseudoproblem not worth pondering by anybody. Yet, the perplexities crop up again and again . . . in connection with the attempts to formulate adequately and consistently the problems, the results, and the programs of scientific inquiry.

Psychobiologists have not been able to use either of these two attitudes or "solutions" to the mind–body problem. Their goal is to learn about the mind by studying the brain. Thus, defining the brain and the mind and conceptualizing how the two are interrelated are essential parts of the neuron-doctrine approach.

Suggested Solutions to the Mind–Body Problem

The majority of suggested solutions to the mind–body problem belong to one of three different types: functionalism, dualism, and monism.

Functionalism. **Functionalism** describes both mind and body and their interactions on the basis of the *functions* of each (Fodor, 1981). This solution comes from the distinction that computer science makes between a system's hardware (what it is made of) and its software or programming. The psychology

of a computer or of a human being does not depend on what that system is made of but on how the ingredients of the system are organized by its programming. Mental states are defined by their causal relation to other mental states and to states of the body. This solution may someday prove useful, but thus far the other two solutions have been more commonly used.

Dualism. **Dualism** conceptualizes the mind and the body as entirely different kinds of events, one mental and the other physical, running in parallel to each other. Dualism thus suggests that mental events and the physical correlates of those events occur simultaneously. This approach emphasizes the difference between the essential nature and substance of mental and of brain events.

Dualism has taken several different forms, depending on how the mental and brain events are assumed to parallel each other. Some examples are illustrated in Figure 1-3. In some theories, as Figure 1-3a shows, the two types of events are assumed to have no direct effect on each other. This interpretation implies that their association is somehow fortuitous; mental and physical events do not interact. In other dualistic theories, such as the **interactionist** theories, brain and mental events *can* influence one another. In some versions of interactionist theories, the brain events cause mental events at the same time that they cause other brain events (Figure 1-3b). Here, the influence is strictly one-way: mental events do not have any direct effect on brain events. Instead, what happens in the brain (chemical and electrical events) causes both our mental events and also other brain events to occur. Mental events become an epiphenomenon — important to our conscious sense of self but not having any impact on anything in the physical world.

Some theorists use this interactive type of dualism when they say that the mind is an **emergent property** of the interactions of sufficient numbers of active brain cells (see, for example, Thompson, 1967). These theorists borrow the concept of emergence from chemistry to express a sense of faith about the future of their science. In chemistry, the properties of water were described as "emerging" from the properties of oxygen and of hydrogen. Although the properties of water could not originally be predicted from a knowledge of the properties of oxygen and hydrogen, it was assumed that with further study into the properties of molecules and into the rules of their combination, the properties of water (or of any other compound) *could* someday be predictable from the properties of its constituent elements. These theorists often imply that once enough is known about the physiochemical basis of nerve cells' activity and the way that nerve cells interact, mental events will be completely explained by the physiochemical events taking

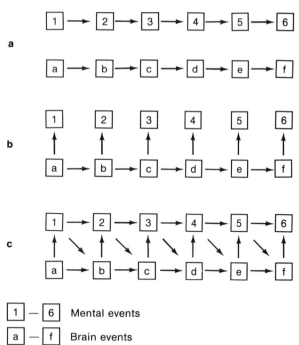

1 — 6 Mental events

a — f Brain events

Figure 1-3 There are three types of dualism, each specifying a different way in which mental events and brain events are related. **a.** Mental and brain events do not interact; mental events are just epiphenomena of brain events. **b.** Brain events cause mental events while causing other brain events, but since the action is not reciprocal, mental events are still epiphenomena. **c.** Mental events and brain events interact.

place in nerve cells. Thus, mental events — given enough research and knowledge — will eventually be reducible to physical events.

Feigl (1958) has described another way in which the concept of interactionism and emergent properties could be used: **open emergence.** In this case, "emergence" is being used to describe an **open system.** If a system is open, new laws and concepts must be added to explain events. For example, the mind may be assumed to have unique properties that are *not* reducible to physical laws. To explain behavior fully, both the laws of physics and the altogether different kinds of laws of mental events must be used. Open emergence refers to another kind of interactive dualism: not only does the brain affect the mind but the mind also has direct effects on the brain's function (Figure 1-3c).

The neurophysiologists Sperry and Eccles and the philosopher Popper (Popper & Eccles, 1977; Sperry, 1969) have all recently described an open-emergence form of interactive dualism. Sperry says (p. 533) that "the conscious properties of

cerebral activity are conceived to have analogous causal effects in brain function. . . ." Or, the "events of inner experience" have "an integral causal control role in brain function and behavior" and they are capable of "interacting at their own level with their own laws and dynamics" (Sperry, 1982, p. 1226). (But Sperry [1980, 1982] denies that he is a dualist, saying that the concept of dualism is irrelevant to his description of the emergent properties of mental events.)

"According to the dualist-interactionist philosophy presented in this book, the brain is a machine of almost infinite complexity and subtlety, and in special regions, under appropriate conditions, it is open to interaction with . . . the world of conscious experience" (Popper & Eccles, 1977, p. 226). This form of the mind–brain interaction is illustrated in Figure 1-4. "World 1" refers to the physical world, the world in which the laws of physics and chemistry can be used to explain and predict events. The brain itself is part of this physical world, and the parts of the brain most closely linked to World 2 form the **liaison brain** (part of the cerebral cortex). "World 2" refers to the world of the mind and of mental events. In Figure 1-4, the brain is assumed to affect both the "outer sense" (perceptions) and the "inner sense" (thoughts) of the mind. Perceptions, thoughts, and intentions can affect the mind's ego, and the ego can have direct, and physically measurable, effects on the liaison brain.

Monism. Some scientists prefer another solution to the mind–body problem: **monism, materialism,** or **identity** (see, for example, Feigl, 1958; Mountcastle, 1975, p. 109;

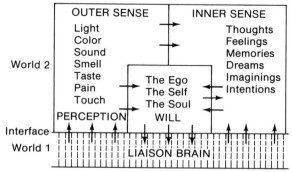

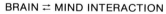

Figure 1-4 The mind–brain interaction of Popper and Eccles. The three components of World 2 (outer sense, inner sense, and the ego or self) are diagrammed with their connections to the part of the brain called the liaison brain. Cells in the liaison brain are organized into columns as indicated. World 1 is the physical brain.

Smith, 1970, p. 350; Uttal, 1973, p. 6). In this view, the mind is part of the physical and chemical properties of the brain, just as our electrical recordings of brain function are. Although the basic laws of the universe are the physical ones, mental events are the basic reality of human life (and maybe even the lives of some lower animals). Thus, not only are mental states real but they are primary to our very sense of existing. As such, mental states are just one subset (and a small one) of physical events. The physical events of the brain (ones that can be electrically recorded and chemically analyzed) and the mental events of the mind are simply two different ways of knowing and experiencing the same event. In other words, when psychobiologists study brain events, they are simultaneously (but indirectly) studying the mental events of their subjects.

Implications for Research

How mind and body are assumed to interact (or not to interact) governs the structure of research. Do we look for electrophysiological evidence of mental events? Do we conceive of those two concepts, mind and body, as referring to different kinds of worlds, following somewhat different kinds of laws? Or are the two just different labels for the same thing?

As Feigl pointed out (1958), it may be difficult empirically to distinguish monism from a carefully formulated dualism (although they could remain conceptually distinct). Attempts to prove monism empirically would begin with research seeking to establish that a given set of neural events is both *necessary* and *sufficient* for a given mental event to occur (see, for example, Uttal, 1973). Suppose that certain types of electrical activity in a certain set of nerve cells were found to occur whenever the organism's eye is exposed to a light of a certain wavelength. The researcher might be tempted to infer that that type of electrical activity is associated with the organism's sensory experience of "red," since that is what the researcher sees when he or she looks at light of that same wavelength. This inference then becomes a theory of how the mind and brain might be related. To test the theory, the researcher would have to mimic or artificially reproduce the recorded pattern of electrical activity in the *same* nerve cells in an awake, conscious organism that is capable of reporting what color sensation it is currently experiencing. To support monism, the electrical activity would have to be both necessary and sufficient to cause the internal experience of "red," no separate mental events being necessary for that experience.

Eccles describes three types of evidence that he thinks could prove that a mind separate from the brain actually does exist. First, he states that only the concept of an immaterial mind interacting with and influencing the brain can explain why our sensations of self and purpose have such unity in the face of the extensive way in which neural events are scattered among brain components. In the second type of evidence, Kornhuber (1974) electrically recorded brain activity in human volunteers, relating that activity to the time at which voluntary actions were initiated by the subjects. Just about eight-tenths of a second before the voluntary action was begun, there was widespread electrical activity in the brain, as Figure 1-5 illustrates. Eccles suggests that **readiness potentials** are evidence of the weak effects that the mind can have on the electrical activity of the brain.

The third line of evidence that Eccles cites is even more intriguing. Libet and his colleagues (Libet, 1973; Libet, Alberts, Wright, & Feinstein, 1967) studied the effects of direct brain stimulations in conscious human volunteers (who were undergoing needed brain surgery at the time). Although very low levels of brain stimulation could lead to conscious sensations if continued for several tenths of a second, the *timing* of the resulting sensations was surprising. The sensations were experimentally timed by coordinating an external event with a direct stimulation of the brain. The subject was instructed to identify the time at which the brain stimulation started, by relating that moment to the timing of the external event. The subject reported being aware of the stimulation several seconds *after* the actual time of stimulation, but the subject *timed* that sensation as occurring at the same time as did the external event that had been presented just when the brain stimulation began — several tenths of a second *before* the time of the subject's response.

Eccles says that this antedating is a "trick" that the self-conscious mind has learned to play with time. It takes time for weak stimuli such as dim lights and soft touches to build up enough brain electrical activity to lead to conscious sensations. Because of the delay, the self-conscious mind has learned to make "a time correction so that the experience will have a time sequence corresponding to the initiating stimuli, whether they be strong or weak" (Popper & Eccles, 1977, p. 364).

If Eccles is right, someday we may know all the laws of brain coding and the ways in which combinations of codes from various parts of the nervous system are integrated. However, we would also have to know the laws of mental events before we could predict behavior and mental events — and these laws would not be reducible to the laws of chemistry and physics.

There seems to be no way at present to prove the existence of mental states that either do or do not influence brain activity. The evidence that Eccles cites can provide support for such a interactionistic point of view, but the support is not conclusive (Chapter 13; Wilson, 1981). But it also seems that

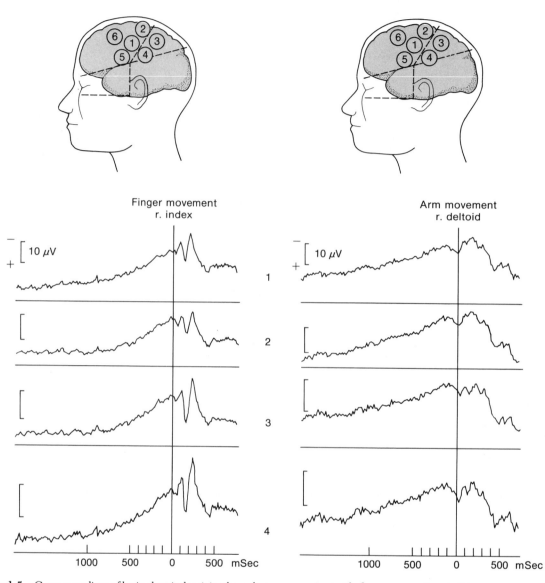

Figure 1-5 Gross recordings of brain electrical activity show changes occurring just before movements — in this case, movement of the right index finger and right arm. The electrode locations are indicated above the electrical recordings. Time 0 occurred when muscle electrical activity was first recorded. There is a consistent build-up of brain electrical activity just before the movement; Eccles calls this build-up the readiness potential.

at present we cannot prove that the concept of a mind must be used in order to explain and predict brain events completely. In fact, our own consciousness seems phenomenologically closer to the concept of independent mental states than to electrical and chemical activity in nerve cells. In this book our approach is monistic, but the idea of dualism will be broached again in the last chapter, after many different kinds of brain events have been described and explained.

Summary of the Mind–Body Problem

The mind–body problem was created when the mind was defined as being immaterial and the brain as being physical. How then can one influence the other? The suggested solutions include functionalism, various forms of dualism, and monism. In dualism, mental and physical events occur in parallel, with or without interactions between the two types of events. One type of parallelism uses the idea of open emergence, and mental events are assumed to affect physical brain events directly. In monism, brain and mental events are thought to be identical.

The problem—and the choice of solution—are centrally important to psychobiology and the neuron doctrine. Not only is understanding the mind the goal of this approach but the preferred solution often determines the type of research done.

Methods for Studying the Brain

To a large extent, the way we conceptualize minds and brains determines how we study them, and how we study them will determine what kinds of conclusions we can reach about them. This section describes some of the most commonly used physiological and behavioral techniques. However, rather than focusing on the procedural and technical details of instrumentation, we will be focusing on the strengths and weakness of each technique—and on the assumptions usually made when each physiological technique is being used to study brain function.

Physiological Methods

The most commonly used physiological methods involve (1) **lesioning** (damaging or destroying) a part of the brain and measuring the resulting changes in behavior, (2) electrically or chemically stimulating a part of the brain to see what kinds of behaviors are produced, and (3) recording from various parts of the brain when the organism is displaying various types of behaviors. Other kinds of physiological techniques have usually been limited to one or two areas of brain research and so will be discussed when the relevant topics are taken up in later chapters. We will describe various kinds of psychopharmacological procedures and chemical assays of brain tissue when we discuss emotions and memory, for example. Ways of measuring the activity levels of various areas of the brain are described in Part III.

Brain lesioning: Logic and techniques.   The logic of all types of brain lesioning studies is much the same. If a part of the brain can be identified as being a functional unit, and if that part of the brain can be completely destroyed in several experimental animals whose behaviors are subsequently extensively observed and measured, then the function of that part of the brain can be ascertained. However, this approach involves assuming that the various parts of the brain form **parallel** (separate, independent) rather than **serial** (sequential) processing systems. If one part of a parallel system is removed, only that particular parallel processing system will be affected, and the effects of its removal can be detected by observing the resulting behavioral deficits. If, however, the brain is a serial processing system, removal of any part will eliminate the whole system—without providing any information about what kinds of things the eliminated part normally does.

In some lesioning studies, the relevant part of the brain is simply removed. For example, the skull of an anesthetized experimental animal may be opened up. Then the desired part of the cortex on the top of the brain can be removed either by suction or by simply cutting and lifting it out (the brain has the consistency of tapioca pudding). In a variant on this theme, the skull is opened, and the relevant part of the cortex is isolated from the rest of the brain by cutting all its connections to the rest of the brain. The first human lobotomies used a very primitive technique similar to this to treat some mental disorders: a sharp knife was inserted through the side of the eyeball and then swung back and forth to sever the frontal lobes from the rest of the brain.

For lesions that are more precisely placed or placed more deeply in the brain, a **stereotaxic device** (see Figure 1-6) is used. The researcher looks up the coordinates of the desired part of the brain in a three-dimensional atlas of the brain (much the same way that longitude, latitude, and height or depth can be used to locate an object on, below, or above the earth). He or she places the anesthetized animal in the stereotaxic device, as illustrated, and makes a small hole at the right location in the skull.

Now the researcher inserts the electrode into the brain and makes the lesion. The electrode carrier holding the electrode to be inserted into the brain has three coordinates, corresponding to the coordinates used in the atlas. To get the tip of the electrode into the desired part of the brain, it is necessary only to match the carrier's three coordinates to the atlas's coordinates. Once the tip of the electrode has been properly inserted, a small amount of very high-frequency (radiofrequency) or direct electrical current can be passed through the two wires of the electrode, which is insulated all through its length except at its tip. The current will irreversibly destroy that part of the

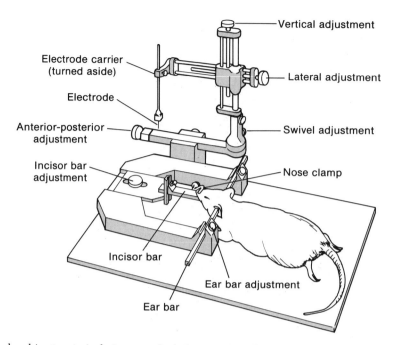

Figure 1-6 Rats are placed in stereotaxic devices to make lesions in precise brain locations or to implant gross electrodes for later brain-stimulation experiments.

brain. The more current used, and the longer the current is allowed to flow, the more brain tissue will be destroyed. Most parts of the brain are duplicated on the right and left sides; therefore, to destroy completely one functional part of the brain, both sides must be lesioned (a **bilateral lesion**) in the same relative location.

There are several major variations on this technique. Instead of using electrical current to lesion, an insulated metal tube could be inserted and the relevant part of the brain frozen. Or some chemical could be inserted through a small plastic tube called a **cannula;** the chemical would destroy the part of the brain around the end of the cannula. Finally, a **neurotoxic** chemical can be injected into some part of the animal's brain or blood stream. The toxin is specific for certain *types* of cells and can destroy cells of that type throughout the brain.

Brain lesioning: Problems. One major problem occurs when the researcher tries to decide just what a "brain part" is. In the case of lesions created by injections of neurotoxic chemicals, a **brain part** is defined biochemically as consisting of all the cells sensitive to a particular neurotoxin. Whether these cells constitute any kind of functional unit must then be dem-

onstrated. In electrical lesioning research, it is difficult to know how much damage should be done, since the appearance of one "part" of the brain often shades imperceptibly into the next. Furthermore, parts of the brain are usually not perfectly spherical, nor are they of constant shape, location, and size in all members of a species. Thus it is difficult to lesion all of one part of a brain without also destroying significant amounts of adjacent parts. Even the function of a brain "part" can vary with the heredity of the individual animal (see, for example, Donovick, Burright, & Bengelloun, 1979).

Another problem involved in any of the lesioning techniques is that when brain cells are destroyed, damage to one cell often produces damage to other cells. This effect is called **transneuronal degeneration.** Damage "crosses" from one cell to another probably because the health of a nerve cell depends on its receiving inputs regularly from other nerve cells. In any case, this means that any behavioral deficits observed after lesions could be related to the destruction of parts of the brain at some distance from the directly lesioned part.

The behavioral effects of a lesion also depend on the elapsed time between the surgery and the behavioral test (Engellenner, Goodlett, Burright, & Donovick, 1982; Isaacson, 1980; Chapter 12). Shortly after lesioning, the behavioral effects may be caused not just by damage to a certain part of the brain but also by the temporary chemical changes that damage produces in other parts of the brain. If given enough time, the brain can respond to damage by having the functions of remaining pathways changed to take over some of the functions of the damaged circuits. Nerves in pathways close to those that were damaged can sprout and form new connections, which can either reduce or increase behavioral deficits. If a part of the brain is damaged in successive stages rather than all at one time, with some time elapsing after each lesion, the resulting behavioral deficits will often be minimized.

The way that behaviors are measured after the surgery is also critically important. A given change in behavior could come from many different deficits, and to reach correct conclusions, the researcher must test all the possibilities. There's an old joke that neuroscientists frequently tell their students: unless one tested all the possibilities, one might conclude that pulling a grasshopper's legs off made it blind, since after surgery it will no longer jump in response to bright lights.

The sensitivity of a behavioral test and the particular way it is conducted may critically affect how a lesion is to be interpreted. Some persons have suffered extensive damage to their visual cortex. They will insist that they can see nothing at all, and so the usual conclusion is that destroying the visual cortex in human beings makes them blind. But one study (Weiskrantz, Warrington, Sanders, & Marshall, 1974) suggested that this conclusion might not be entirely correct. The neurologists showed one such patient slides that contained either an X or an O in various locations on the screen. The neurologists insisted that the patient point to the figure's position on the screen and identify the figure as an X or an O. The patient kept insisting that he saw nothing—but he pointed accurately and "guessed" correctly on this and other tests. If you asked such a person if he or she were blind you would come up with one conclusion—but if you actually tested the person with slides, you would have to reach a slightly different conclusion.

In another study, a patient had a part of his brain (the hippocampus) surgically lesioned on both the right and left sides to treat his epilepsy. He seems to be incapable of remembering anything that has happened to him since his surgery. After 28 years, "he still exhibits a profound . . . amnesia, and does not know where he lives, who cares for him, or what he ate at his last meal. His guesses as to the current year range from 1958 to 1993 and, when he does not stop to calculate it, he estimates his age to be 10 to 26 years less than it is" (Corkin, Sullivan, Twitchell, & Grove, 1981, p. 235).

We might be tempted to conclude that the lesions destroyed his brain's ability to store new information as memory. How-

ever, when that patient was given various perceptual-motor tasks to learn over several days, he showed a normal learning curve (Cohen & Corkin, 1981; Cohen & Squire, 1980; Milner, 1962; Nissen, Cohen & Corkin, 1981). Thus, he can still learn and later remember how to do certain kinds of tasks. However, each day he was completely unaware that he had performed the task on any previous occasion. Each day his comments sounded as if he were solving the task for the first time. Again, whether the brain's ability to store all new memories was destroyed or not depends on how the patient is tested.

The possibility always exists that what is observed after a brain lesion is not the direct effect of the lesion but is instead the animal's attempt to cope with the effect that the lesion has had on its perceptions, memories, behaviors, and so forth. If after surgery the animal runs around with head bent, the surgery could have damaged the part of its brain that controlled its neck muscles—or the animal may have been partially blinded and so it bends its head to be able to use what vision it has left.

Despite these problems, the results of lesioning experiments have contributed a great deal to our knowledge of brain structure and function. For example, these studies tell psychobiologists in which areas of the brain they should insert their electrodes to record neural activity. However, we must remember that lesions do *not* remove a function from a complete brain; they *change* the functions of whole systems, creating a "new" and possibly quite differently organized brain (Stein, Finger, & Hart, 1983).

Stimulation: Logic and techniques.   In stimulation studies, parts of the brain are stimulated while ongoing behavior is simultaneously observed. A part of the brain can be chemically stimulated or inhibited by injecting specific chemicals through a cannula implanted there. Electrical stimulation is commonly done by stereotaxically inserting one electrode onto or into the brain and placing another electrode somewhere else on or in the body. Alternatively, two electrodes could be placed close together in the same area of the brain, or one could be placed inside and the other outside a nerve cell.

Several different kinds of stimulation techniques are used. In gross stimulations, or **macrostimulations,** many nerve cells within a given area of the brain are simultaneously activated or inhibited by electrical or chemical stimulation. In **microstimulations,** one or at most a very few cells are electrically or chemically stimulated or inhibited. When one very tiny **microelectrode** or **microcannula** is inserted inside and another outside the same cell, **intracellular stimulation** is being done.

Electrical stimulation of a brain part is sometimes assumed to mimic the normal activity of that brain part. Thus, it is assumed that when a certain part of the brain is electrically stimulated, the animal will display whatever behavior is typical when that part of its brain is normally active. For example, when a certain part of the brain (the lateral hypothalamus) is lesioned, the animal stops eating. The experimenter may predict that electrical stimulation of that area of the brain will cause the animal to eat (which, in fact, it does — see Chapter 8). Whether macrochemical stimulation is assumed to activate or inhibit a part of the brain depends on whether the injected chemical is assumed to mimic the effects of some naturally occurring chemical that either activates or inhibits nerve cells in that particular region. However, it seems unlikely that electrical macrostimulation can ever mimic normal electrical activity in any part of the brain. In fact, stimulating one area of the brain can produce even greater behavioral deficits than lesioning that same area (see, for example, Solomon, Solomon, Schaaf, & Perry, 1983). The stimulation may "block" or "jam" the normal pattern of electrical activity.

Microstimulation is aiding the exploration of what certain naturally occurring *patterns* of neural activity might mean. For example, researchers can find out whether a certain pattern of activity created by means of microstimulations in a certain set of cells is both necessary and sufficient to cause a particular behavior or mental state. When chemical stimulation is done by injecting chemicals through a microcannula, the technique is called **iontophoresis** or **microiontophoresis.** Small amounts of some kind of chemical are injected onto (or sometimes into) a nerve cell. The question usually being asked is what effect that chemical has on that nerve cell.

Stimulation: Problems.   Some of the problems involved with stimulation techniques are conceptually similar to those associated with lesioning research. Since chemicals do diffuse away from the site of their injection, how can you limit macrostimulation to a "brain part"? Nerves directly stimulated may, in turn, activate other cells. Thus, the possibility always exists that the stimulation effects come from activating parts of the brain other than the "targeted" area.

Some problems either are unique to or are exaggerated by using stimulation techniques. With microstimulation, large nerve cells are much more likely to be stimulated than are small cells. Large cells have lower thresholds, and, since they are larger targets, they are more likely than small cells to be close to a microelectrode. Also, many nerve cells are too small to permit insertion of any microelectrode. Thus, our knowledge of brain codes may be subtly biased. We may know about the codes used by large cells but be unable to evoke a particular

behavior or mental event because an essential part of the code for that event involves activity in smaller, unstimulated cells.

Recording: Logic and techniques.   A third method of studying the brain is to record the electrical activity of nerve cells while simultaneously observing behavior or while presenting various kinds of stimuli to the experimental organism. Again, two electrodes are used, and the difference in the electrical activity seen by each electrode is measured by a voltmeter or current meter (just as you record the difference between the positive and negative poles of your car battery with a voltmeter).

Electrical recording can also be macro or micro. In the former, the technique is **gross recording;** both electrodes are relatively large and called **gross electrodes.** In the latter, an **extracellular microelectrode** would be inserted into the brain to record the activity of only a few nearby nerve cells. Or one microelectrode can be inserted inside a cell, as Figure 1-7 illustrates. Another electrode is placed somewhere outside that nerve cell. This **intracellular recording** is done either on nerve cells that have been removed from the animal or on nerve cells within a paralyzed and either pain-deadened or anesthetized animal.

Recording from brain parts and cells below the surface requires a stereotaxic device. Following the procedures described in the lesioning section, a stereotaxic device would be used to insert a gross electrode or a microelectrode into the target part of the brain. If the researcher were going to study the relationship between neural activity and behavior, he or she would then seal the hole in the skull with dental cement and latex. When the animal recovered from the surgery, a small electrode "driver" (a small motor attached to the electrode carrier of a stereotaxic instrument) would be used to raise and lower the electrode in order to record from brain cells.

Gross recording techniques assume that the record will reveal which parts of the brain are active during various behaviors. **Electroencephalograms (EEGs)** are electrical recordings made with gross electrodes placed either on the scalp or directly on the brain itself. The EEG might be used to find out which areas of the brain have been damaged and so are displaying abnormal types of electrical activity. Another type of gross recording, either from the surface of the brain or from a lower part of the brain, involves an **evoked potential.** This is the change in the grossly recorded electrical activity of one part of the brain, a change that is evoked by the presentation of some stimulus or by the occurrence of some response. For example, every time a light is flashed in people's eyes, positive

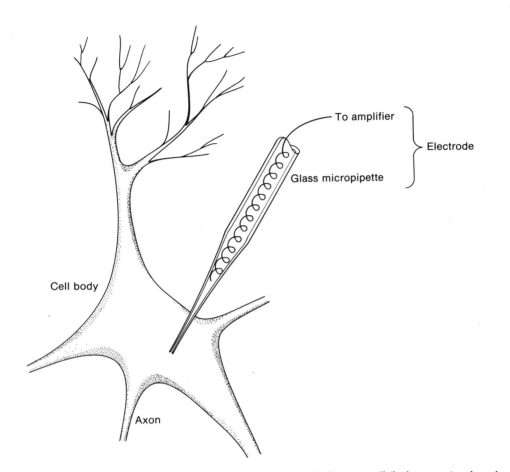

To amplifier

Electrode

Glass micropipette

Cell body

Axon

Figure 1-7 Intracellular microelectrode recording. One electrode is placed inside the nerve cell (body or axon) and another electrode (not illustrated) is placed somewhere outside the cell. Then the voltage difference or the current flow between the two electrodes can be measured and recorded.

and negative waves can be recorded from one part of their brain (see Figure 1-8).

Microelectrode recording can reveal the details of the pattern of activity and identify (by dye injection through the electrodes) which nerve cells are displaying that activity. Microelectrode recording can discover what patterns of electrical activity are being displayed by which nerve cells when the organism is exposed to certain kinds of stimuli. These patterns might constitute the **code** for that kind of stimulus information.

Recording: Problems. Interpreting records made from gross electrodes entails several problems. First, large cells will have contributed a disproportionate amount to the record.

Conclusions made from gross recordings like the EEG are largely limited to what large nerve cells are doing. They provide little or no information about the activity of smaller nerve cells.

Second, the nerve cells closest to the electrode will contribute more than will nerve cells farther away. Nevertheless, a far-away but large nerve cell might contribute just about as much as will a close but small nerve cell. Thus, the recording could reflect the activity of many nearby small cells, or the activity of a few nearby large cells, or the activity of many large cells farther from the electrode.

Third, gross recordings cannot distinguish a pattern involving stimulation of neurons progressively closer to an electrode from a pattern involving inhibition of neurons progressively

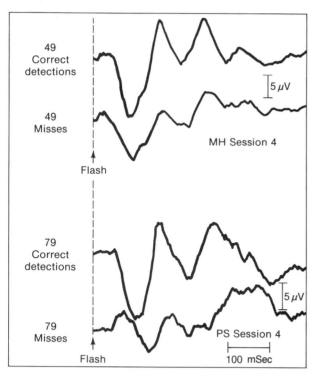

Figure 1-8 Visual evoked potentials were grossly recorded from the visual cortex of two subjects. The light was dim, and on some trials the subjects did not see it. The evoked response was smaller when the subjects did not see the light. The potentials were averaged over trials by a computer.

cells can have electrodes inserted in them, and the activity of large nerve cells is much more likely to be sampled by an extracellular microelectrode than is the activity of smaller cells. Neurons of different sizes often carry different kinds of information or carry out different kinds of information processing (Boudreau, Bradley, Beirer, Kruger, & Tsuchitani, 1971; Morest & Bohne, 1983; Liberman, 1982). So again, our knowledge of brain codes may be biased by recording only from larger cells.

Third, it is very difficult to prove that a given pattern of activity in a specified group of cells is functionally related to the observed behavior or to the mental state inferred from that behavior. Only if all the types of studies described in Table 1-1 are carried out on the same group of cells may we have confidence in our attempts to decode brain activity.

Psychological Methods

The experimenter is often forced to infer what the experimental subject's "mental state" might be, on the basis of what the experimenter would sense, feel, and perceive under similar conditions. Such inferences are likely to be fraught with error. However, we can use certain training techniques to get nonverbal animals to tell us about what they are seeing and feeling.

The physiological methods just described are used in every area of psychobiological research — and so appear in every chapter of this book. However, different behavioral techniques are used in different areas of research. The techniques necessary to get an experimental animal to tell us about what stimulus it is receiving are necessarily different from those that would tell us whether it remembered what it had seen before. Therefore, a more detailed description of each relevant behavioral technique will be given in later chapters. Here, only a brief overview of training methodology will be given.

Learning techniques.   To get experimental animals to give experimenters information about what they see, want, or remember, they are taught to make some kind of response to some kind of stimulus. One type of learning is called **classical conditioning.** Some type of innate (or already conditioned) response to a stimulus is used. For example, the innate response to a painful sensation on the hand would be to withdraw the hand. Here, the innate response or the withdrawal would be called the **unconditioned response** or **UR.** The painful stimulus would be the **unconditioned stimulus** or **US.** To create a learned association, the US is paired with some other kind of stimulus, such as the ringing of a bell. Bell

farther from the electrode. So it is often difficult to decide whether the part of the brain around the electrode is being stimulated or inhibited.

Similar problems occur when microrecording techniques are used. First, animals in whose brains single-unit activity is being recorded are often anesthetized. Anesthesia prevents pain and suffering, but it also may cause biases in recordings. For example, one anesthetic (chloral hydrate) dramatically suppresses the responses of certain serotonergic neurons (those that use serotonin as a transmitter substance) to any kind of external stimulation, such as lights or sounds (Heym, Steinfels, & Jacobs, 1984; Trulson & Trulson, 1983). The same anesthetic converts the normally excitatory effects of morphine injections on single-unit activity (in an area called the locus coeruleus) in cats to an inhibitory response (Rasmussen & Jacobs, 1985).

Second, the problem of size is even more acute with microrecordings than with gross recordings. Only large nerve ringing would be called a **conditioned stimulus** or **CS.** If the organism's paw was shocked every time a bell rang, for 40 trials, then on later trials the organism would probably withdraw its paw even if the bell were presented by itself. Withdrawal, the learned response to the bell, is a **conditioned response** or **CR,** and the bell is now a conditioned stimulus.

Two CSs can be used. If only one, say a bell, were ever paired with the pain, the bell would be a **CS+.** A second CS, say a light, that was never paired with the pain would become a **CS−.** The experimenter would alternate trials of bell-and-pain pairings with trials of presenting light alone. If the organism learned to make the CR only to the CS+ and to withhold the response to the CS−, the organism would have learned a **classically conditioned discrimination** between the two stimuli.

Two other kinds of changes in CS responses can occur in such a study: habituation and sensitization. These changes have nothing to do with pairing a CS with a US. **Habituation** would mean that whatever response is initially made to bell ringing would decrease with repeated presentations of the bell. The response might become simply orienting to and looking at the bell. When the orienting response habituated, it would no longer occur. **Sensitization** changes the response to the CS because the organism has been repeatedly exposed to an unpleasant or aversive US. The organism might make withdrawal responses to bell ringing because of sensitization, even though the bell had never been paired with the painful stimulus or US. To demonstrate sensitization, the researcher would measure the response to the CS and then repeatedly present the US all by itself. Afterwards, the response to the CS would again be measured. To show that the change in the response to the CS in a classical conditioning experiment occurs because of a learned association between a CS and a US, one must control both habituation and sensitization.

Operant conditioning is another type of learning. In operant conditioning, the organism makes a response of some sort, and then the experimenter presents that organism with some sort of stimulus that can serve either as a reward or as a punishment for having made the response. **Positive reinforcers** are defined as stimuli that, when *presented* as contingent on the organism's response, increase the organism's tendency to repeat that response. **Negative reinforcers** are stimuli whose *removal* contingent on a response increases the probability of that response. Presenting a negative reinforcer, or removing a positive reinforcer contingent on a response, suppresses that response. That procedure is called **punishment.** Giving good and poor grades to students might be described as teachers' efforts to use operant conditioning to increase students' studying responses.

If the reward or punishment is given only when a certain stimulus is present and not when that stimulus is absent, the organism is being taught to make an **operant discrimination.** A rat might be taught that depressing a lever produces a food reward if and only if there is a red light shining. If the red light is off, no lever pressing will ever receive a reward. The red light is an S^{D+}, or a positive **discriminative stimulus.** The absence of the light would be an S^{D-}, or a negative discriminative stimulus. When the rat learns to press mostly when the light is on and to inhibit pressing when the light is off, the animal has learned the operant discrimination.

Psychophysics.   Psychophysics can be used to get organisms to tell experimenters whether they can see a stimulus, how intense that stimulus is, and whether two stimuli are the same or different. As such, psychophysical techniques are used extensively in sensory psychobiological types of experiments. Human subjects can simply be trained to inform the experimenter in a consistent fashion about what they are seeing, hearing, tasting, smelling, or feeling while the experimenter systematically manipulates the stimulus parameters. Lower animals have to be taught a discrimination, either operant or classical. Then the intensity or quality of a CS+ or S^{D+} is systematically manipulated.

Some of the most productive research combines single-unit recording with psychophysics. Mountcastle and his colleagues (Mountcastle, Talbot, Sakata, & Hyvärinen, 1969) presented vibrating stimuli to the skin of both human and lower primate subjects. Thus, the conscious responses, reported verbally by the psychophysical subjects, could be directly compared with the neural response of monkeys to that same stimulus.

Measuring motives and emotions.   These types of mental events, and the behaviors associated with them, have been measured by several indirect techniques. Sometimes the psychobiological researcher simply assumes that subjecting the organism to a given set of conditions will induce in that organism a certain emotion or motive. For example, depriving organisms of food should give them a hunger motive. Exposing them to a CS+ that has been associated with a painful and frightening US should make them frightened. In human genetic research, the diagnosis made by a clinical psychologist or by a psychiatrist is assumed to provide information about the kinds of emotional and motivational problems that person has. Since the sexual motive is closely associated with sex hormones, any effect that a sex hormone has on the structure and function of nerve cells would be assumed to be related— directly or indirectly— to the sexual motive.

Summary of Methods

Following the neuron doctrine, electrical recording from a single nerve cell or from a few nerve cells might provide information about how the brain codes mental events. A given pattern of activity in a nerve coming from the eye might code for a certain color, and a burst of activity from a certain cell in the visual brain might code for a line. Activity in other cells might signal low blood sugar or a state of food deficit. Because of these ideas, this book will emphasize micro techniques. But psychobiological research could be done only after gross stimulation and lesioning research had been carried out, to indicate what parts of the brain might be more relevant to what aspects of behavior.

The behavioral techniques are used to get subjects to tell experimenters about their mental events. Human subjects are systematically trained to report their sensations. Nonverbal subjects are given classical or operant training so that the experimenter can use the trained responses to infer something about the subjects' mental events. In both cases, possible sources of bias and distortions have to be considered.

Chapter Summary

The Mind, The Body, and Research

Psychobiology is the mind's attempt to study itself through studying the brain. As such, this field of research and theory must directly confront the mind–body problem. The philosophy of psychobiology and the solution chosen to the mind–body problem then jointly determine the way in which the brain is studied.

Since this book stresses psychobiological explanations of brain function, it emphasizes microstimulation and microrecording techniques. A researcher may record from nerve cells in a conscious, behaving organism that has been trained to react in certain ways to certain stimuli (either verbally or through changes in conditioned responses). Then the responses of nerve cells are related to the behavioral responses and to the subject's inferred mental events. The researcher either looks for closed or open forms of interactions between mental and neural states or else assumes that the electrical recordings of the neural states are simply another way of examining a particular mental state.

The other techniques—lesions and macrostimulations and macrorecordings—are used to provide hypotheses about how cells in various parts of the brain might react to certain kinds of manipulations. For example, if lesioning a certain part of the brain produced an animal that overate its way to an impressive state of obesity, it could be that cells in that part of the brain react to the sight and scent of food.

The neural recordings are then used as the basis for a theory of brain/mind function. The association between a brain state and a mental or behavioral state may mean that the former is a code for the latter. However, the association could also be either fortuitous or secondary, with the most important parts of the code for that state occurring in some other cells in some other areas of the brain. In other words, to test the theory, the code must be demonstrated to be both necessary and sufficient. The most convincing way of demonstrating that any code is sufficient is, through microstimulation, to duplicate artificially that pattern of activity in an organism (human being or trained animal) capable of telling the experimenter about the mental events being evoked by that stimulation. To demonstrate that a code is necessary, those particular cells must be inhibited or destroyed and the relevant behavioral function must then be demonstrated to have been destroyed.

Back to the Basics

Anatomy and the nature of the chemical and electrical forces used by brain cells are the elements of the brain's languages. Anatomical principles define and determine which cells can "talk" to each other, and electrochemical principles describe how that "talk" can take place.

Basic Anatomic Principles

This chapter briefly reviews basic anatomy. Anatomical details of specific systems are presented in later chapters as needed. Thus, for example, sensory-system anatomy is described in Part III, and the anatomy of the motivational/emotional parts of the brain is described in Part IV.

Organization of the Nervous System

One basic principle of neural organization in vertebrates is **bilateral symmetry.** The left and right halves of the nervous system are, in large measure, mirror-image counterparts of each other. Every structure located in the left side of the brain has a mirror-image anatomical counterpart in the same area on the right side of the brain.

However, the brain is not perfectly bilaterally symmetrical. In most animals the microanatomy of the left side of the brain differs from that on the right side (Sherman, Galaburda, & Geschwind, 1982; Springer & Deutsch, 1981). Furthermore, the right and left sides of the brain may also carry out somewhat different kinds of functions. In all bilaterally symmetrical animals, the left side of the brain mostly receives information from and controls the movements of the right side of the body, whereas the right side of the brain receives information from and controls the movements of the left side of the body.

The left and right sides of the human brain may even be cognitively specialized. This division is called **lateralization** of functions. In almost all right-handed people, and in most left-handers, verbal functions are more localized to the left side of the brain, whereas nonverbal functions may be more localized to the right side. The left and right sides of the brain may have some different cognitive specializations even in species below the human on the evolutionary scale (Gaston & Gaston, 1984; Heffner & Heffner, 1984; Ifune, Vermeire, & Hamilton, 1984; Hamilton & Vermeire, 1982; Sherman, Galaburda, & Geschwind, 1982; Springer & Deutsch, 1981).

Peripheral versus central nervous system.   The nervous system is organized into the **peripheral nervous system** and the **central nervous system (CNS)**. The peripheral nervous system consists of all parts of all nerve cells that lie outside the brain and the spinal cord. Its components are largely neurons going to and from sensory organs, muscles, and glands. The CNS, as illustrated in Figure 2-1, consists of all cells and cell processes that lie within either the brain or the spinal cord.

Afferent versus efferent nerve cells.   Both the CNS and the peripheral nervous system have **afferent** and **efferent** nerve cells. Afferent nerve cells in the periphery carry information *to* the CNS, and efferent nerve cells in the periphery carry information *from* the CNS to other organs in the body, such as muscles and glands. In the periphery, **sensory** nerves coming from sensory organs are afferent, and **motor** nerves going to the muscles are efferent. Within the CNS, the terms *afferent* and *efferent* are used in reference to any given area of the brain. Nerve cell processes coming into that area are afferents; cell processes leaving that area, connecting it with other areas, are efferents.

Both the CNS and the peripheral nervous system are further subdivided on anatomical and functional criteria. The CNS is divided into the brain and the spinal cord (further divisions of the CNS will be briefly described later in this chapter). The **somatic division** of the peripheral nervous system consists of nerve cells carrying information to and from sensory organs (such as the touch and pain receptors in the skin) and information to and from the muscles attached to our skeletons (the muscles that move our arms and legs, for example). The somatic nerves carrying information from the sensory organs in the skin and in muscles to the CNS are afferent, whereas the efferent somatic nerves allow the CNS to control the activity of the skeletal muscles.

The **autonomic division** of the peripheral nervous system carries information to and from the internal organs of the body. Internal organs, or **viscera,** include the digestive system, the heart, and the various glands, such as the pancreas and the adrenal gland. The **visceral efferents** going to the internal organs allow the CNS to control the activity of those organs. Many of these visceral efferents gather together to travel in various nerve trunks, as we will describe below.

Although the **autonomic nervous system (ANS)** was originally described solely as an efferent system, there are afferents that travel in the same nerve trunks as the visceral efferents do. The visceral afferents carry information from the internal organs to the CNS, taking information about the state and functioning of the internal organs to the brain. Visceral afferents are important to the detection and coding of the internal states associated with our motives and emotions (Part V).

Sympathetic versus parasympathetic division.   The autonomic division is functionally and anatomically subdivided into the **sympathetic** and **parasympathetic** divisions (Figure 2-2). The sympathetic and parasympathetic afferents follow the same pathways as do the efferents. There are two efferent nerve cells between the CNS and the internal organs, as illustrated, but there is only one afferent. Although only one side of the body is shown in Figure 2-2, the principle of bilateral symmetry means that mirror-image structures and connections are to be found on the other side of the body.

The parasympathetic nerves are anatomically distinguished from sympathetic nerves on the basis of both where they leave the CNS and the location of the ganglia (plural of *ganglion*). (**Ganglion** refers to any collection of the cell bodies of neurons outside the CNS. The cell body is the part of the neuron that contains genetic material.) The parasympathetic nerves enter and leave the CNS either at the level of the brain itself or through the lowest sections (sacral regions) of the spinal cord. The parasympathetic nerves leaving the CNS are called the **preganglionic nerves** because they occur before ("pre") the parasympathetic ganglia. Each of the preganglionic nerves can be quite long, extending to the parasympathetic ganglia located close to the internal or **target organ**. In the ganglion, each of these nerves makes functional contact

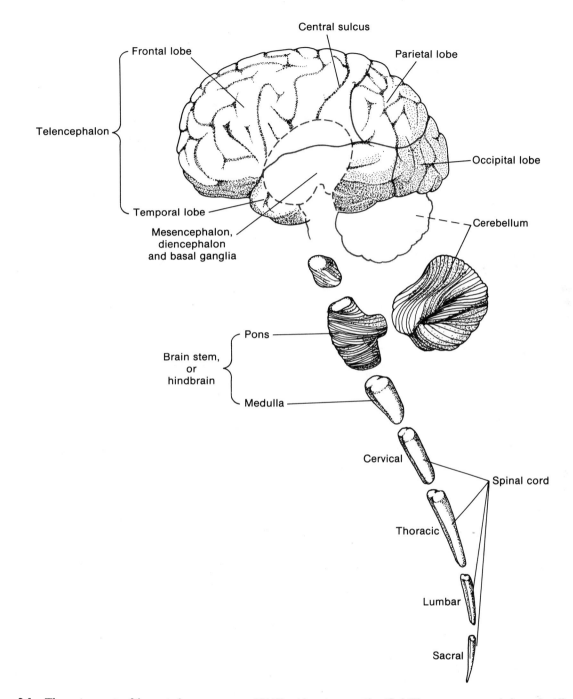

Figure 2-1   The various parts of the central nervous system (CNS), with major areas identified. The terms *mesencephalon* and *midbrain* are often used synonymously. See also Table 2-2.

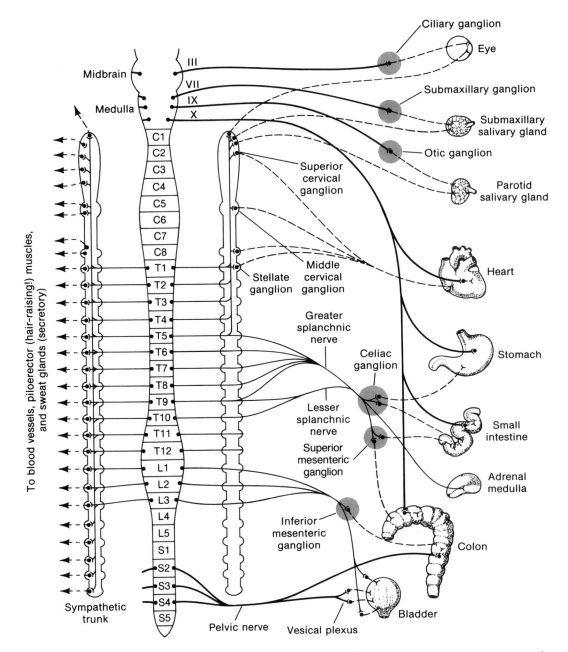

Figure 2-2 Efferent nerves of the sympathetic and parasympathetic divisions of the autonomic nervous system innervate the internal organs. Afferent neurons can also be found in the same nerve trunks. The sympathetic system is in thin lines, and the parasympathetic in thick lines. The postganglionic neurons are in broken lines. C = cervical; T = thoracic; L = lumbar; S = sacral.

with a second set of nerves—the **postganglionic** ("after" the ganglia) **nerve cells.** The *area* where a nerve cell makes functional contact with another cell is called a **synapse.** The postganglionic neurons control the activity of cells in the target organ at the synapses between those two sets of cells. The sympathetic nerves enter and leave the CNS from the middle regions of the spinal cord. The preganglionic sympathetic nerves leaving the CNS are relatively short, extending only to the sympathetic ganglia outside the spinal cord, where they make synaptic contact with the postganglionic nerves. The postganglionic nerves affect target organ activity.

Most internal organs (Figure 2-2) receive input from both the parasympathetic and sympathetic divisions (the adrenal gland is one prominent exception to this rule). However, the two divisions usually have different effects on those organs. The effects of sympathetic nerves are usually summarized by saying that their activity prepares the internal organs of the body for emergency functioning. Nerves in the parasympathetic division carry out the day-to-day "housekeeping" functions of the body. Thus, for example, activity in sympathetic nerve cells increases heart rate, whereas activity in parasympathetic nerves slows the heart. Furthermore, parasympathetic nerves act more independently of each other than do sympathetic nerves, but the sympathetic system does have subsystems specialized to respond to various types of emergencies (Wallin & Fagius, 1986).

Cranial nerves.   Some of the afferent and efferent nerve cells enter or leave the brain rather than the spinal cord. They form 12 separate nerve trunks (12 on each side) called the **cranial nerves.** Some of the cranial nerves are parasympathetic, going to and from the internal organs of the body. The **vagus,** or tenth cranial nerve, is parasympathetic; one of its target organs is the heart, and vagus activity decreases heart rate. Other cranial nerves are somatic, carrying sensory information from ears and eyes and motor information to the muscles of the facial region. The anatomy of the cranial nerves is diagrammed in Figure 2-3, and the function of each of the 12 cranial nerves is described in Table 2-1.

Anatomy of Cells in the Nervous System

Overview.   All the parts of the nervous system consist of thousands of nerve cells, as well as thousands of another type of cell called a **glial cell.** There may be between 10^{11} and 10^{12} individual nerve cells in the human brain. Each nerve cell receives information from about 1000 other nerve cells, and, in turn, each cell may have 1000 to 10,000 synapses with other cells. These numbers mean that we have more connections

Table 2-1   The cranial nerves.

Cranial Nerve	Functions
I. Olfactory	Olfaction
II. Optic	Vision
III. Oculomotor	Eye movements: control of eye muscles except the lateral rectus and superior oblique; parasympathetic: pupillary constriction and accommodation of lens in eye for near vision
IV. Trochlear	Contralateral eye movements: superior oblique muscle
V. Trigeminal	Cutaneous and proprioceptive sensations from the skin and muscles in the face area and the front part of the tongue; innervation of chewing muscles and the tensor tympani muscles in the ear
VI. Abducens	Ipsilateral eye movements: lateral rectus muscle
VII. Facial	To muscle of face and middle ear; parasympathetic: salivary gland
VIII. Vestibuloacoustic	Audition and balance
IX. Glossopharyngeal	Parasympathetic: secretions from parotid (salivary) gland; swallowing muscles; visceral sensations; taste sensations from taste buds in posterior part of the tongue; touch sensations from posterior part of the tongue
X. Vagus	Parasympathetic: innervates smooth muscles in heart, blood vessels, trachea, bronchi, esophagus, stomach, parts of intestine; controls pharynx and larynx (voice); parasympathetic: visceral sensations from pharynx, larynx, aortic body, thorax, and abdomen
XI. Spinal accessory	Innervation of trapezius and sternocleidomastoid muscles in neck
XII. Hypoglossal	Innervation of intrinsic muscles of tongue

among the nerve cells in our brains than there are stars in the galaxy! Furthermore, the cells in the various regions of the nervous system have somewhat different structures; there may be nearly 1000 different *types* of nerve cell structures. Thus, our brains represent a system of staggering complexity. Different parts of the brain are composed of various mixtures of the different kinds of nerve cells, and the kinds of interconnections formed differ from one area of the nervous system to another.

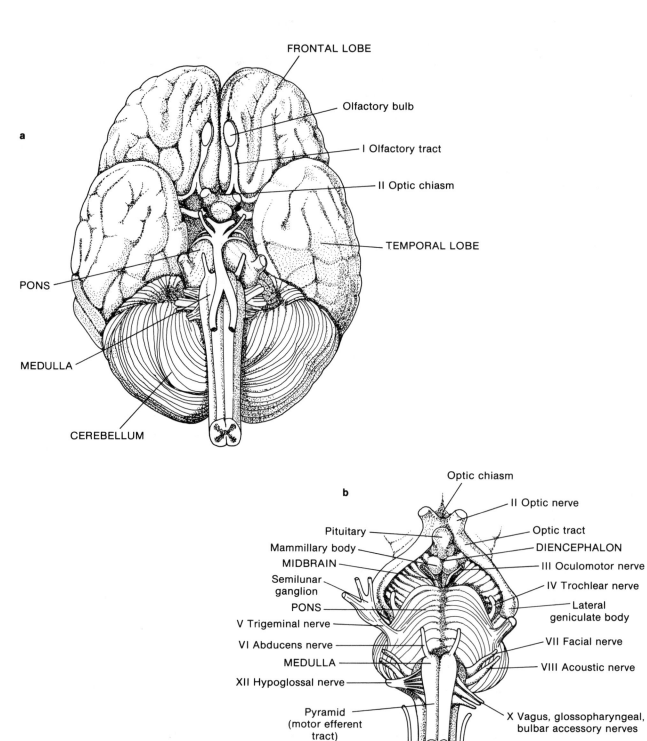

Figure 2-3 A ventral view of the brain stem shows the cranial nerves. **a.** Base of the brain. **b.** Cranial nerves. (See Tables 2-2 and 2-3 and text for explanation of terms.)

All this enables different areas of the brain to carry out different functions.

Cells in the brain share many features with other types of body cells. Nerve and glial cells have **cell bodies,** which contain the **nucleus** as well as many organelles specialized to carry out the metabolic processes of each cell. The cell nucleus contains genetic material. All cells have **membranes** separating their **cytoplasm** from **extracellular fluid.** Extracellular fluid is similar to blood plasma (except that it has no white or red blood cells); it surrounds all body cells, including nerve cells.

Nerve cells also have unique anatomical specializations for the coding and transmitting of information. As Figure 2-4 illustrates, different nerve cells have different shapes and appearances, but most (though *not* all) neurons have **dendrites** and **axons.** Dendrites are heavily branched extensions, or processes, of the cell body that usually collect and integrate information from many other nerve cells and carry that information back to the cell body. The axon, another extension of the cell body, is often smaller in diameter and is usually much less branched than are the dendrites. The part of the axon closest to the cell body is enlarged and is called the **axon hillock.** The axon carries information away from the cell body to other cells, often in other parts of the nervous system. An individual axon is also called a nerve **fiber.**

Types of glial cells.   Even more numerous than nerve cells, glial cells actually make up the bulk of our brains. The three basic divisions of glial cell types in the CNS are **astrocytes, microglia,** and **oligodendrocytes.** Astrocytes have a starlike appearance. Their functions probably include providing structural support for nerve cells, aiding in repair after injury to nerve cells, keeping nerve cells' processes organized during development and during regeneration after injury, and being involved in metabolic processes that control the composition of the extracellular fluid around the nerve cells. The microglia may proliferate and migrate to any area of the brain in which injury has occurred. The oligodendrocytes are responsible for the formation of a fatty substance called **myelin,** which surrounds the axons of some of the CNS cells. Nerve-cell axons surrounded in this fashion are said to be **myelinated.** Myelinated nerves both in the CNS and in the periphery have special transmission properties, as we will describe in Chapter 3.

The precise nature and functions of CNS glial cells are still actively being debated and researched. Glial cells have often been assumed to have merely support functions, helping to keep the extracellular fluid in a **homeostatic** or constant condition. Recently, however, researchers have suggested that glial cells may actually participate actively in the information-processing and communication functions of CNS neurons (MacVicar, 1984; Bevan & Raff, 1985). If true, this discovery could dramatically affect our assumptions about how the brain works.

In the peripheral nervous system, the glial cells are called **Schwann cells.** Schwann cells surround the axons of cells in the periphery in a variety of ways. Sometimes one Schwann cell will simply surround a single axon or group of axons in such a way that the axons become embedded within the Schwann cell. Sometimes there are several loose folds of Schwann cell membrane around a given axon. In both of these cases, the Schwann cells protect the nerve cells and electrically and chemically isolate them from each other.

In the most complex arrangement, many layers of Schwann cell membrane become tightly packed around a single axon. In the process of becoming so tightly packed around the axon, the internal cytoplasm of the Schwann cell is nearly eliminated and the composition of the Schwann cell membrane is altered. By this process, many peripheral axons get myelinated.

Neural cell bodies and organelles.   Some of the organelles found in neural cell bodies are illustrated in Figure 2-5. One important organelle is the nucleus, which contains most of the genetic material of the cell, the **chromosomes.** The **endoplasmic reticulum** (rough and smooth) is an extensive network of internal membranes involved in the synthesis of proteins and other substances, including glandular secretions. It is also part of the cellular organization of other functions carried out by the cell (somewhat different functions being localized to different areas of the cytoplasm).

Some areas of the endoplasmic reticulum are quite specialized. In nerve cells, the endoplasmic reticulum close to the nucleus is the **Nissl substance,** which has a distinctive appearance and is a site of intense protein-synthesizing activity. In other parts of the cell body and into the dendrites (but not the axons), part of the endoplasmic reticulum takes the form of a **Golgi complex.** This complex is closely associated with small, globular-shaped granules. In gland cells, the Golgi complex seems to be involved in the synthesis of the substances secreted by those cells, and the granules may be miniature storehouses. The role of the Golgi complex in nerve cells is still uncertain, but the **vesicles** found at the end of axons may be storehouses for substances secreted by active nerve cells into synapses.

The tubelike processes found in a nerve cell are **microtubules** and the thinner **neurofilaments,** both of which are important to the movement of substances to and from the cell body and to the structure of the cell.

The **mitochondria,** which contain their own genetic material, are important to cellular metabolism. They are complex

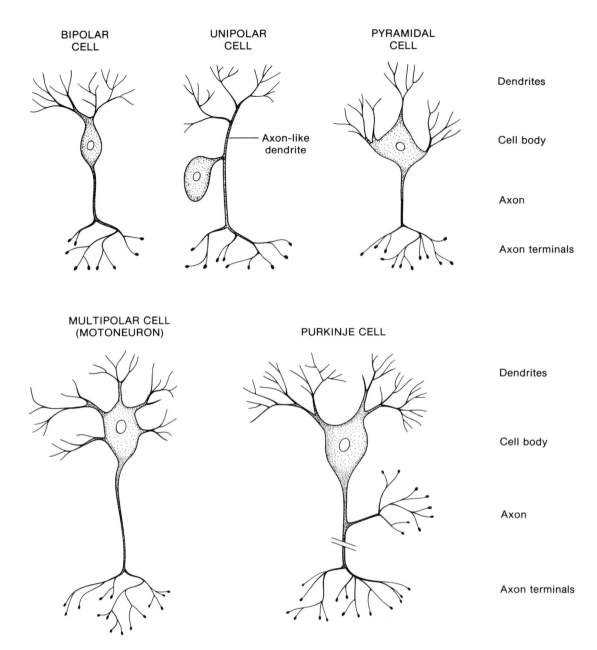

Figure 2-4 Nerve cells can have many different shapes.

organelles specialized for the production of the energy required by the cell to carry out its functions. For the nerve cell, an important source of fuel comes from molecules of **adenosine triphosphate (ATP)**. ATP is produced by the mitochondria.

Membrane. The plasma membrane surrounding the cell body, axons, and dendrites is a three-layered structure, as illustrated in Figure 2-6. The top and bottom layers consist of **lipid** (fat) molecules, oriented perpendicularly to the top and bottom and extending their hydrophobic ("water-hating")

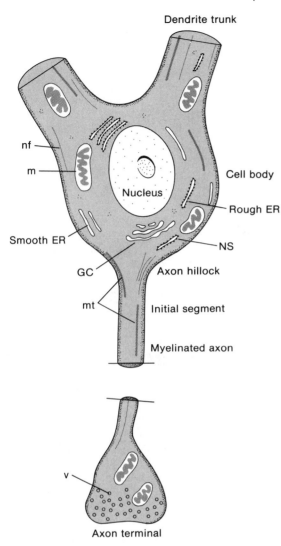

Dendrite trunk

nf

m

Nucleus

Cell body

Rough ER

Smooth ER

NS

GC

Axon hillock

mt

Initial segment

Myelinated axon

v

Axon terminal

Figure 2-5   A nerve cell's organelles include endoplasmic reticulum (ER), Golgi complex (GC), Nissl substance (NS), microtubule (mt), neurofilament (nf), vesicles (v), and mitochondria (m).

found embedded within the membrane also differ. The membranes of axons, cell bodies, and some dendrites may contain specialized proteins, ones that open "holes" or "pores" in the membrane when chemically or electrically stimulated. These particular membrane proteins make the membranes of nerve and muscle cells unique in the body by enabling them to be electrically or chemically stimulated into activity. The only other body cells that can respond this way are egg cells from the ovaries of females and, as has recently been discovered, CNS glial cells (MacVicar, 1984; Bevan & Raff, 1985).

Dendrites.   In most nerve cells, the dendrites are large, intensely branched, and specialized for carrying information back to the cell body. The main organelles of the cell body extend without any clear boundaries well into the dendrites. Depending on the nerve cell, dendrites can vary in length all the way from millimeters to feet. The dendrites of somatic afferent cells carry sensory information — pain, pressure, temperature — all the way from the toes to their cell bodies found just outside the spinal cord. In this special case, there may be an exception to the rule that only axons are myelinated: some of these sensory axonlike dendrites are surrounded by myelin.

Axons.   Axons are often smaller in diameter and less branched than are the dendrites (though in many nerve cells, axons and dendrites cannot be easily differentiated.) The axon cytoplasm is **axoplasm.** Axons are specialized for taking information away from the cell body towards other nerve cells by having the membrane proteins necessary for an **action potential.** (An action potential is a brief change in the electrical characteristics of the axonal membrane and is the way in which a nerve cell carries information from one area of the body to another.) The axon hillock usually integrates the electrical activity occurring over the cell body and dendrites and initiates the action potential. At the ends of its axon branches, the first nerve cell makes synaptic contact with the dendrites, cell body, or axon of a second nerve cell. This part of the axon is the **end foot** or **axon terminal.** Some nerve cells found in the retina of the eye have no axons, only cell bodies and dendrites.

processes into the middle layer. Various kinds of protein molecules are either partially or completely embedded within the layers. Some of these proteins also have branches that extend out into the extracellular fluid and may have important functions in the synapses.

Different parts of the nerve cells have somewhat different kinds of membranes. With certain exceptions, only the axons of cell membranes are ever myelinated. The types of proteins

Synapse.   Several different kinds of synapses, one of which is illustrated in Figure 2-7, have been found within the nervous system. All the types share certain common features. In the area of the synapse, the two nerve cells making functional contact with each other also come much closer to being in physical contact — the space between the two is decreased (and sometimes eliminated). The membranes on both sides of the synapse have a unique physical structure and unique pro-

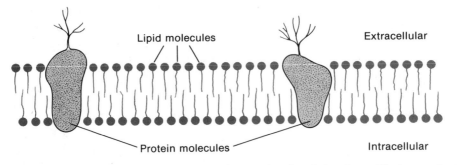

Figure 2-6 A cell membrane has three layers, with protein molecules extending though those layers. The inner and outer layers are the "heads" of lipid molecules and the inner layer contains their water-hating "tails."

teins, making it possible for information to be transmitted from one cell to another. The membrane on the first cell's side of the synapse is the **presynaptic membrane,** and the membrane on the other cell's side is the **postsynaptic membrane.**

Although there are many different subtypes, two major types of synapse are electrical and chemical. In electrical synapses, the channels or holes formed by proteins in the presynaptic membrane are physically continuous with similar channels in the postsynaptic membrane, allowing the two cells to share some cytoplasm constituents and electrical currents. Electrical types of synapses are common in invertebrates and have even been found in a few locations in the brains of higher mammals, such as the retina. Compared with chemical synapses, electrical synapses are faster but are much less flexible.

Chemical synapses, with their flexibility and their ability to be affected by the past experiences of the cells, are by far the most common types of synapse in mammals such as ourselves. In chemical synapses, the pre- and postsynaptic cells do not

actually make physical contact with each other; these synapses are one-way communicators. The small space (20 to 30 nanometers) remaining between the two cells is called the **synaptic cleft.** Both presynaptic and postsynaptic membranes are usually greatly thickened. Small organelles called **synaptic vesicles,** found just inside the presynaptic membrane, may contain the chemicals secreted by the presynaptic cell onto the postsynaptic cell to influence its activity.

Chemical synapses may be further subdivided into **Type I** and **Type II.** Type I synapses have larger synaptic clefts, have a greater area devoted to synaptic membranes, and have larger, rounder vesicles than do Type II synapses. These two types of synapse may subserve somewhat different kinds of functions (Shepherd, 1983). Type I synapses are more common on the distal parts of dendrites (the parts furthest from the cell body) and may often have an excitatory effect on the postsynaptic cell. Type II synapses are somewhat more commonly found on the proximal parts of dendrites and on the cell bodies and may often have inhibitory effects. However, these distinctions should not be pushed too far, since many synapses are hard to classify, and both Type I and Type II synapses can be either excitatory or inhibitory in effect.

Another way to classify synapses is by which parts of the cells are functionally interconnected. The "classic" type of synapse is **axodendritic:** an axon terminal of one cell forms the synapse's presynaptic membrane, and the postsynaptic membrane is part of the dendrites of a second cell. However, axons also make synaptic contact with the cell bodies (**axosomatic**) and axons (**axoaxonic**) of another cell. **Dendrodendritic** synapses, connecting the dendrites of two cells, have also been found.

Even more complex synaptic arrangements have been identified. For instance, one axon can be presynaptic to the axon of a second cell, which in turn is presynaptic to the dendrite of a third cell, in a **serial axoaxodendritic** synapse.

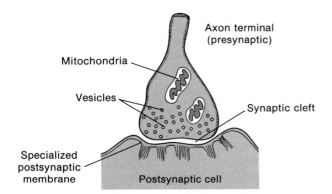

Figure 2-7 Schematic drawing of a synapse, showing some of the presynaptic and postsynaptic structures, as well as the gap or cleft between the cells.

28

Or, at one place on the membrane, one cell will be presynaptic to a second, and, just a few millimeters away, the first cell will be postsynaptic to that same second cell (a **reciprocal synapse**). In the retina of the eye, nerve cells form complex patterns of interconnections, called a **synaptic glomerulus,** in which three or more nerve cells form serial and reciprocal synapses with each other.

Gross CNS Anatomy

The names of the major subdivisions of the CNS, and the structures found in each one, are listed in Table 2-2 and illustrated in Figures 2-8 and 2-9. Fluid-filled **ventricles** (cavities) are also shown in those figures. The fourth ventricle can be seen in Figure 2-8. The third ventricle is also on the midline, lying just between the right and the left hypothalamus. Two lateral ventricles, located just below the corpus callosum, project to the right and left sides of the brain, as shown in Figure 2-9.

Cerebrospinal fluid (CSF) is found between the brain and the skull, as well as in the ventricles (Kuffler, Nicholls, & Martin, 1984; Rowland, 1981). It is also found in the spinal canal, a hollow tube in the center of the spinal cord. CSF is

Table 2-2   Subdivisions of the brain and their major structures

Subdivisions	Structures
Hindbrain:	
Myelencephalon	Medulla
Metencephalon	Pons
	Cerebellum
Midbrain:	
Mescencephalon	Tectum: superior and inferior colliculi
	Midbrain tegmentum: red nucleus, substantia nigra, nuclei of III and IV, locus coeruleus
Forebrain:	
Diencephalon	Hypothalamus
	Pituitary
	Optic tracts
	Subthalamus
	Thalamus
Telencephalon	Cerebral hemispheres
	Basal ganglia
	Rhinencephalon or limbic system

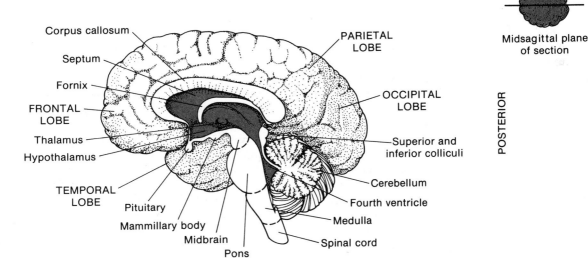

Figure 2-8   Midsagittal section (separating the brain into right and left halves) of the human brain, showing how the spinal cord and brain stem are related to the cerebellum, thalamus, and cerebral cortex.

29

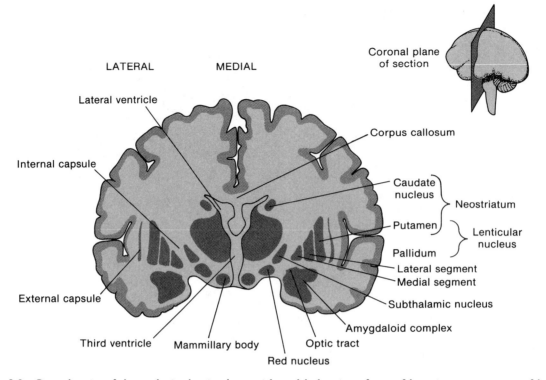

Figure 2-9 Coronal section of a human brain, showing the ventricles and the locations of some of the major motor structures of the brain. **Medial** refers to structures lying close to the midline or middle of the brain; **lateral** refers to structures lying closer to the left or right side.

secreted by the structures called **choroid plexuses,** which are capillary networks in the walls of the lateral ventricles (Rowland, 1981). Since CSF is absorbed by clusters of capillaries found between the brain and the skull, CSF continually flows through the ventricles to the spinal canal and over the surface of the brain. Hydrocephaly (literally, "water on the brain") can occur if too much CSF is secreted, if one of the canals connecting the ventricles is blocked, or if capillary absorption is impaired.

The interstitial or extracellular fluid that surrounds CNS cells and that is found in the CSF differs in composition from the blood because of a so-called **blood–brain barrier** (Fenstermacher, 1985; Rowland, 1981). For example, CSF normally has almost no protein in it. The barrier has three components: a structural component, an enzymatic component, and an active transport mechanism. Capillaries in the other parts of the body have pores through which substances pass from the blood supply to the extracellular fluid. But in the brain, the walls of the capillaries have only a very few widely scattered pores. Thus, any material entering the brain must dissolve in and diffuse through the cells forming the walls of the capillaries. These cells contain enzymes that metabolize certain

substances, preventing their transfer across the blood–brain barrier. They also have active transport mechanisms that require energy and that move specific substances such as glucose and some amino acids across the blood–brain barrier. One area of the brain, the **area postrema** in the brain stem, has no blood–brain barrier and so is directly affected by substances in the blood.

Psychobiologists make use of the CSF primarily for injections and chemical analyses. Substances injected into one of the ventricles will directly affect brain tissue since the blood–brain barrier is bypassed. The levels of various kinds of neural metabolites to be found in the CSF after doing a spinal tap can be used as a very rough index of the activity level of certain kinds of neurons in an organism's brain. The more active a certain kind of neuron is, the more of its metabolites will be found in the CSF.

The Cortex of the Cerebral Hemispheres

The layers of neural tissue surrounding the brain form the **cerebral cortex,** which is also called the **neocortex.** The cerebral cortex is one part of the brain more highly developed in human beings than in other species. Approximately 70% of all the neurons in the CNS of primates are found in the cortex. This is where the most complex processing and coding of sensory information occur. Like other sections of the nervous system, the cortex is bilaterally symmetrical.

The anatomical divisions of the cerebral cortex are indicated in Figure 2-8. They differ not only in function but in their microanatomy: the types of cells and the types of interconnections formed by those cells. The **occipital lobe** is the most **posterior** (rear) portion of the neocortex, and it processes visual information. The **temporal lobe** (see Figure 2-1) is the most **lateral** portion (on the right and left sides, just inside the ears) and is closely associated with hearing and with verbal functions (at least on the left side, for most people). The **parietal lobe** is on the **dorsal** side (the top) and carries out sensorimotor functions. The **frontal** lobe occupies the most **anterior** or frontal location in the cerebral cortex. It may be involved in the ability to plan, to organize behaviors serially, and to control emotional reactions.

Major divisions of the cortex. There are three general types of neocortex: **sensory, motor,** and **association.** The sensory areas include parts of the parietal, temporal, and occipital lobes. Classically, the sensory cortex was thought to be exclusively and uniquely devoted to the processing of sights, sounds, and skin sensations, and the motor cortex (in the frontal lobe) was considered to be devoted to the organization and coordination of movement. The association cortex was thought to *associate* the information coming from different sensory systems, giving rise to our unitary perceptions of the world.

Research has suggested that these classic divisions of function were accurate only as a first approximation. The first distinction to break down was the one between the sensory and motor divisions (see, for example, Masterton & Berkley, 1974). For example, individual nerve cells in the frontal motor cortex respond to touch and to sensations of pressure in much the same way as do individual cells in the parietal sensory cortex. Some researchers now often refer to these parts of the brain as being the **sensorimotor** cortex. Furthermore, few cells in the association cortex respond to more than one kind of sensation. Instead, many cells in the association cortex seem to respond to more *complex* kinds of sensory information. The term *association cortex* is now used to refer to areas that do not receive direct input from sensory organs and that also have no direct output to the cells in the spine that control muscles.

Organization within each division. Although all three types of cortex contain several layers of cells, as illustrated in Figure 2-10, the appearance of those layers varies among the

three types of neocortex. The differences shade gradually from one area into another in such a way that there is no clear microanatomical boundary line between adjacent areas of sensory and motor cortex, for example. In Figure 2-10, these "transitional" types of cortex are designated as Type 2 and Type 4. Some areas of the cortex also do not have all six layers clearly present.

All three types of cortex have the same general types of cells. The **pyramidal** cell, found in layers II, III, and V, is named for the triangular shape of its cell body. Its **apical** (topmost) dendrites extend into the upper cortical layers, and its **basal** (bottommost) dendrites receive input from other cells whose cell bodies are found in the same cortical layer as the pyramidal cell. The axons of the pyramidal cell connect one area of the cortex to other areas or to regions of the brain below the cortex. The **stellate** cell is circular, with starlike dendritic projections. The afferents carrying information to the cortex project to its stellate cells. In turn, the axons of a stellate cell project to other cortical layers within that cell's vicinity. Stellate cells have also been called **granule** or **basket** cells. These cells serve as local processors of the incoming or afferent information. **Fusiform** cells, found in the deepest layers of the cortex, are spindle-shaped. Their axons often project out of the cortex and their dendrites extend either to the upper layers or just up into layers V and VI.

The unit of function in all three types of cortex seems to be a vertically organized set of cells called a **column,** which extends throughout all six layers (Goldman-Rakic, 1984; Mountcastle, 1975). Each cortical area contains thousands of columns, and all the nerve cells within a column respond in similar ways to similar types of sensory input. Interactions among adjacent columns seem to be rare, and when they do occur they tend to be inhibitory. Cortical columns tend to be of the same size across species with brains of different sizes; however, species higher on the evolutionary scale have more columns in each cortical area. The functional distinctions among different types of cortex are determined by how the information coming into each part is organized into columns and how the columns are connected to other columns and to other parts of the brain.

Language and consciousness. In the human brain, the most dramatic departure from the principle of bilateral symmetry occurs in the areas involved in the production and understanding of written and spoken language. If Eccles is right about how the mind and body are related and interconnected (Chapter 1), the human form of consciousness may exhibit the same lack of symmetry.

Damage to the left side of the cerebral cortex is much more likely to impair language functions irreversibly in nearly all

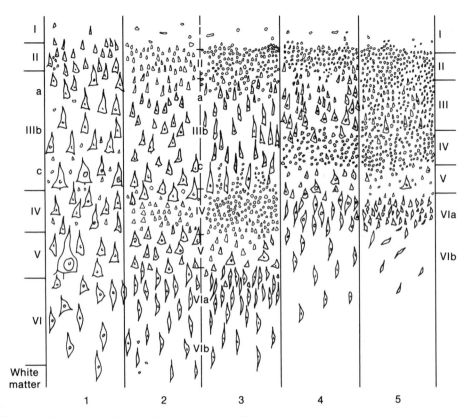

Figure 2-10   There are five fundamental types of cortical structures: Type 1 = agranular motor cortex; Type 2 = frontal homotypic or granular; Type 3 = parietal homotypical; Type 4 = polar (for example, occipital "association" cortex); Type 5 = granular koniocortex (occipital, sensory). The axons entering and leaving the cortex, many of them myelinated, form the so-called **white** (from myelin) **matter** found below the cortex.

right-handed people, and also in many left-handed people, than is damage to anatomically equivalent areas on the right side of the brain. Damage to a posterior portion of the left frontal lobe, an area now called **Broca's area,** makes speech difficult if not impossible for the afflicted person, although that person will still be capable of understanding language. This type of problem is called *motor aphasia*. A person with damage to Broca's area might respond to the question "What are you doing today?" with a one-word answer: "Working." The person might find it difficult, if not impossible, to elaborate further.

Damage to a posterior portion of the left temporal lobe, the area now called **Wernicke's area,** leaves a person able to speak but causes difficulty in understanding the written or spoken language of others. This condition is sometimes called *fluent aphasia*. A person so impaired might respond to the question of "What are you doing today?" with: "I was there and then I was here while they were there." Thus, although

people with damage to Wernicke's area can speak fluently (they can produce many words in a relatively brief period of time), the words they use are often so vague as to be meaningless. These people also may use the wrong word or wrong sound within a word, or they may make up words. Their speech may resemble that produced by schizophrenics, sometimes so much so that they are misdiagnosed.

Some researchers believe that the uniquely human type of conscious awareness may be largely localized to the left side of the brain because that is the side on which most language functions are localized (Popper & Eccles, 1977; Springer & Deutsch, 1981). Eccles describes consciousness as an emergent property (in the open sense) of nervous tissue that can carry out language functions. He writes (1982, p. 156), "The dominant linguistic hemisphere is uniquely concerned in giving conscious experiences to the subject and in mediating his willed actions." Eccles continues, "It is postulated that in normal subjects activities in the minor [right] hemisphere reach

32

consciousness mostly after transmission to the dominant hemisphere."

If Eccles is correct, we are normally consciously aware of what happens to the left side of our body (the part controlled by the right, nonverbal side of our cerebral hemispheres) only because the two halves of our brain are interconnected by large fiber tracts called the **cerebral commissures.** The largest commissure is the **corpus callosum** (see Figure 2-8). Cerebral commissures carry the information from the right to the left side of the brain, where the "conscious self" is supposedly located, so that we can be aware of the events happening on the left side of our body.

The functions that are uniquely developed in the human being—speech and self-conscious awareness—may also be uniquely lateralized. However, it is not yet possible—and may never be—to characterize adequately the nature of consciousness in nonverbal animals. Until that can be done, Eccles's idea of equating self-conscious awareness with verbal functions must remain an intriguing, but unprovable, possibility.

Sensory Pathways

Specialized sensory organs receive energy in various forms from the world around us or inside us, and that energy is converted into electrochemical activity. Each sensory organ is maximally sensitive to a certain kind of physical energy, and so each sensory organ acts like a window opening out onto the external, physical world. Information about this world is carried to the CNS on the sensory nerves of the somatic or autonomic nervous systems, including several of the cranial nerves. The information coming from all the sensory nerves passes through at least two synapses, at least one of which is in the **thalamus,** before it reaches a sensory area of the neocortex. This process means that the information is transformed in some way at least twice before it finally reaches the cortical sensory processing areas and conscious awareness.

Once the information reaches the cortex, it is again reanalyzed and reinterpreted by several different areas of the brain. The information is related to stored information (memory) and interpreted in light of the current internal state of the organism (motivation and emotions). All this processing generally proceeds from sensory cortex to association cortex and finally to other structures such as the **amygdala** and the **hippocampus** before an output "decision" is made—and the organism does something.

Each sensory pathway carries specific kinds of information. The **somatosensory** system carries information about what is happening on the surface of the body to the brain. Several different kinds of somatosensory organs are embedded in the skin. Information about balance or the position of the body in space and about rotation of the head through space comes from the **vestibular** organs, which are part of the structures found in the inner ear and include the **semicircular canals** and the **otolith** organ or "gravity detector." The sensory organs of the **visual** and **auditory** systems work on stimuli reaching our body from objects that can be at some distance from our body, so these sensory organs are **distance receptors.** The chemical senses of taste and smell, or the **gustatory** and **olfactory** senses, come from sensory organs embedded on our tongues and in our noses.

Motor Systems and Control of Movement

Motor systems work both serially and in parallel with each other. Thus, different motor areas of the brain should be visualized as different aspects of a functional unit or system. Since we do not describe motor-system anatomy elsewhere, our discussion here will involve more detail than we include in our treatment of the sensory systems.

Control of movement patterns. Figure 2-11 represents one way in which various structures in the motor system may interact to control movements in vertebrates. Movement is controlled by a hierarchical sequence of control structures, with cells in the **motor cortex** being at the middle level of the sequence. Cells in the prefrontal (anterior frontal) and parietal association cortices (plural of *cortex*) may be at the top of the hierarchy, directly related to the organism's "intention" to carry out particular movements (see Chapter 8). Next come the **basal ganglia,** which include the **caudate nucleus** (here, "nucleus" is used to designate a group of cell bodies all found in a given circumscribed area), the **putamen,** and the **pallidum** (also called the **globus pallidus**). In many organisms, the caudate and the putamen have similar structures and are collectively called the **striatum.** The basal ganglia, along with other motor structures below the level of the thalamus and in the midbrain, are often collectively referred to as the **extrapyramidal system.**

The pattern of electrical activity that will eventually determine the pattern of activity in particular muscles may be generated by either the basal ganglia or the lateral **cerebellum.** Coordinated activity, such as reaching for a food object, may depend on activity in basal ganglia cells. They may control movements whose strength and intensity vary according to the goal of the intended movement, providing the coordination necessary for continuous, slow, smooth movements. However, the various structures in the basal ganglia may have somewhat different functions (Guyton, 1981). The globus

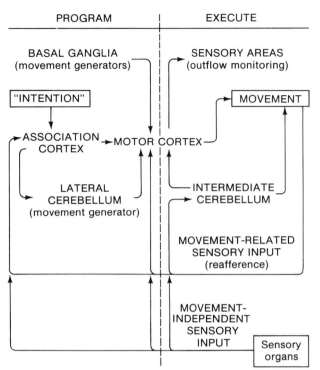

PROGRAM | EXECUTE

BASAL GANGLIA
(movement generators)

SENSORY AREAS
(outflow monitoring)

"INTENTION"

MOVEMENT

ASSOCIATION
CORTEX → MOTOR CORTEX

LATERAL
CEREBELLUM
(movement generator)

INTERMEDIATE
CEREBELLUM

MOVEMENT-RELATED
SENSORY INPUT
(reafference)

MOVEMENT-
INDEPENDENT
SENSORY
INPUT

Sensory
organs

Figure 2-11   One way in which brain structures might interact in the control of movement in a primate. The diagram is divided into programming (planning) and execution (coordination) modules. (The locations of the structures identified here are illustrated in Figures 2-1 and 2-9.)

pallidus may help to maintain muscle tone in support of intended movements. The caudate and putamen may help to control "gross intentional movements that we normally perform unconsciously" (Guyton, 1981, p. 157).

Cells in these nuclei might be especially important to initiating movements that occur without sensory guidance (Evarts, Kimura, Wurtz, & Hikosaka, 1984). Single cells in these areas can fire well before muscles begin to contract. Some of them may even fire before cells in the cerebellum and motor cortex do, so the basal ganglia can initiate commands to the motor cortex and cerebellum (DeLong, 1974; Evarts et al., 1984). Damage to the basal ganglia produces distinctive movement disorders, such as Parkinson's disease. Victims show a characteristic tremor of their limbs when resting, and their muscles are constantly rigid.

Lateral cerebellum cells may generate the patterns for movements that depend on how *long* the relevant muscles must remain contracted. For eample, the lateral cerebellum controls the coordination of voluntary movements of the eye

muscles. How long these muscles remain active determines how far the eye rotates in its socket (Kornhuber, 1974). The cerebellum is also involved in the guidance and the coordination of visually guided voluntary and learned movements. Guidance involves well-learned motor patterns during which we no longer have to think consciously and separately about each step of the motor sequence (Stein, 1986). Damage to the cerebellum impairs muscle tone, balance, the ability to coordinate movements with sensory input, and the ability to learn complex motor tasks such as diving or playing the piano.

The motor cortex receives input from the basal ganglia, the lateral cerebellum, and the sensory systems. Axons from cells in the lateral cerebellum, globus pallidus, and **substantia nigra** make synaptic contact with cells in different thalamic nuclei; in turn, axons from those thalamic cells project to (are connected to) different areas in the motor cortex. Substantia nigra cells project to the basal ganglia. Cells in the motor cortex may adjust the output of intended movement according to the conditions of the current environment, allowing motor output to be regulated by the demands and constraints of that environment.

The intermediate cerebellum receives input from the motor cortex. It projects back to the motor cortex and to the spinal and brain stem cells, which form synapses with the neurons directly controlling the muscles, the **motoneurons.** The intermediate cerebellum may shape the evolving command for movement (Ghez & Fahn, 1981).

Two aspects of motor control—outflow monitoring and reafference—represent a high level of interaction between motor and sensory systems. **Reafference** refers to sensations created in the sensory organs by the organism's own movements. For example, closing your eyes makes your visual world look dark. Self-induced sensations must be distinguished from the sensations produced by external events, such as extinguishing the lights. In **outflow monitoring,** information from motor areas is sent to the sensory areas of the brain, informing them of the types of sensations that will be produced by the forthcoming movements. Animals can use this information to distinguish between reafference and sensory stimulation coming from outside sources.

Efferent motor pathways.   The patterns for movements, once generated, are sent from the brain through the spinal cord to motoneurons. The **corticospinal tract** originates largely from pyramidal cells in layer V of the motor areas of the frontal cortex and the somatosensory areas of the parietal cortex. Cells in the motor cortex respond just prior to a movement, and their rate of firing is closely related to the actual amount of force required to make the forthcoming movement

(Evarts, 1966). Some of their axons congregate in the brain stem, in an area between the spinal cord and the medulla, forming the **pyramidal tract.** Pyramidal tract axons send out branches, or **collaterals,** to the extrapyramidal system, and they also descend in the spinal cord to form synapses with spinal sensory neurons (these axons come largely from sensory cortex cells) or with spinal **interneurons** (whose axons don't leave their own spinal area) or motoneurons. Higher organisms, such as human beings and apes, have more pyramidal axons that make direct synaptic contact with spinal motoneurons than have lower animals, giving them the ability to control individual muscles separately. Cutting the pyramidal tract in higher primates produces severe and permanent impairments in fine motor control.

The other corticospinal axons are not part of the pyramidal system. Some of these axons do not cross over to the other side of the CNS, except perhaps at their level of termination in the spinal cord. Axon collaterals from these neurons also project to the basal ganglia. Cutting these pathways produces severe deficits in the ability to stand and walk. Some cortical motor axons project to motoneurons in the cranial nerves, controlling facial muscles. Some CNS areas involved in generating movement patterns are only indirectly connected to spinal efferents. For example, cerebellar efferents make synaptic contact with cells in the **red nucleus** or the **vestibular nuclei.** Axons from these two nuclei then descend in the spinal cord. The basal ganglia affect motoneurons only very indirectly, by controlling motor cortex efferents.

The Limbic and Reticular Systems

The limbic and reticular systems of the brain are related to arousal, emotions, and motives. Details of their anatomy will be described in Part IV; here we describe only general principles of organization as proposed originally by MacLean (1970, 1975, 1985). On the basis of his interpretation of lesion data from human (accidentally damaged) and nonhuman subjects, MacLean described our brains as having three separate though highly interconnected systems. The three parts of the **triune brain** are the **reptilian system,** the **limbic system,** and the cerebral hemispheres.

The evolutionarily oldest part of our brain is the **reptilian system.** MacLean said that this system controlled reflexes and regulated instinctive and stereotypic types of behaviors and experiences. This system includes the **reticular activating system (RAS),** which receives input from the sensory systems. In turn, as Figure 2-12 shows, the RAS affects the activity of cells in other parts of the brain, including the cerebral cortex and the limbic system.

Because of its connections to the sensory channels, the RAS may be involved in the effects of arousal on the processing of sensory information—or how motives and emotions affect what we see, hear, feel, smell, and taste. Stimulation of the RAS can awaken sleeping animals and can arouse and activate an already wakened animal (French, 1957). Conversely, extensive damage to the RAS, if it occurs all at one time, can lead to a state of permanent sleep (Adametz, 1959; Lindsley, Schreiner, Knowles, & Magoun, 1950). However, as we will describe in Chapter 8, the older idea of the RAS as a homogeneous network of cells and cell processes has been abandoned. The RAS is actually a collection of nuclei (groups of cell bodies), and each nucleus subserves somewhat different arousal and motor functions. For example, there are both afferent and efferent nuclei and both sensory and motor nuclei.

The second-oldest part of our brains is the **limbic system,** or the "emotional" and "motivational" brain. The limbic system includes the structures indicated in Figure 2-12. The limbic system in lower animals, as well as in human beings, is closely interconnected with the olfactory sense (which may account for the emotional effects produced by many odors). MacLean (1970, 1975, 1985) subdivided the limbic system into three parts. One part, including the **amygdala** and the **hippocampus,** is related to the feelings and motives involved in self-preservation. Nerve cells in these areas may be "kept busy with the selfish demands of feeding, fighting, and self-protection" (1970, p. 134). The second part of the limbic system includes the **septum** and may be involved in the motives for sociability and sexuality.

The third part of the limbic system is the one that is most fully developed in mammals, especially the human mammal. It includes part of the thalamus, the interconnections of the thalamus with the **hypothalamus,** and the anterior part of the frontal cortex called the **prefrontal cortex.** The hypothalamus controls the autonomic nervous system and is involved in aggressive, sexual, emotional, and motivational (for example, hunger and thirst) types of behaviors. This third part of the limbic system is connected to the visual rather than to the olfactory system, and its evolutionary development may be closely related to three uniquely mammalian characteristics: the nursing of young, audiovocal communications between mothers and offspring, and play behaviors.

The newest and most highly evolved part of the brain is the cerebral cortex. MacLean says (1970, p. 131) that "the evolutionary development in lower animals of a respectable cortex might be regarded as Nature's attempt to provide the reptilian brain with a 'thinking cap' and emancipate it from stereotypic behavior." Since some parts of the limbic system and the RAS

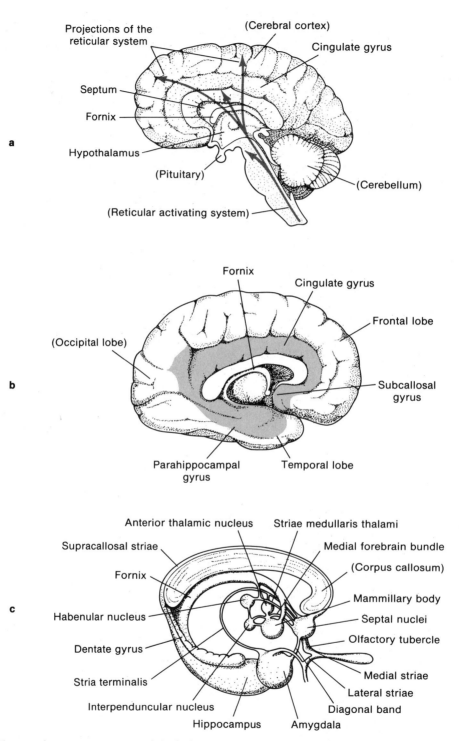

Figure 2-12   The reticular activating system and the limbic system, shown in midsagittal (**a** and **b**) and cutaway (**c**) views. All the structures not in parentheses are part of the limbic system. In **b**, the dotted sections are the limbic lobe, or primitive cortical tissue. The noncortical parts of the limbic system are shown in **c**.

are closely associated with monitoring internal states, they can provide "higher" centers of the brain with information about those states.

Summary of Anatomy

The nervous system is divided into peripheral and central divisions, each with thousands of nerve cells as well as glial cells. Each of those divisions can be further subdivided, although neither the anatomical nor the functional distinctions between the parts of the CNS can be regarded as clear cut. For example, the cerebral cortex can be divided into sensory, motor, and association cortex. Sensory pathways are the parts of the peripheral nervous system and the CNS most closely related to the transmission and analysis of sensory information. The generation of motor patterns and the transmission of motor information from one part of the body to another are done by such structures as the motor cortex, the cerebellum, the basal ganglia, the pyramidal system, and the extrapyramidal system. The parts of the CNS most closely related to motivational and emotional states are the limbic and the reticular activating system. However, all these parts of the brain work together. Thus, understanding the brain codes underlying various conscious experiences may involve translations of the *patterns* of activity in specified small groups of cells located throughout the brain.

Chemical and Electrical Forces

Much of the activity of our nerve cells can be carried out without providing the cells with any source of energy, such as ATP. Our nerve cells can maintain their ability to transmit information even if all their metabolic processes have been blocked for several hours. Here we describe the forces that the axonal membrane uses to carry out such feats.

Molecules of Matter

All substances are made up of various combinations of **atoms.** Atoms combine to form **molecules,** and **compounds** are substances composed of like molecules. In turn, all atoms are made up of elementary particles, three of which are called **neutrons, protons,** and **electrons.** The neutrons and protons are to be found in the nucleus of each atom, and the electrons circulate around the atom in "probability patterns" or "shells."

The neutron carries no electrical charge, each proton carries one positive charge, and each electron carries one negative charge. Just as two opposite poles of a magnet attract each other, the positive charge on the proton attracts the negative charge on the electron. The simplest (smallest and least heavy) atom is that of hydrogen, which has one proton in its nucleus and one electron encircling the nucleus. An atom of any substance has as many protons as electrons, making the atom electrically neutral.

Covalent bonds.   One way that atoms can combine with each other to form molecules is by forming **covalent bonds** on which the atoms of two different substances share electrons. Thus, the force holding electrons to the nucleus of the atom is then involved in holding together the various atoms of the molecule. This type of bonding is found in most organic compounds, all of which contain molecules with carbon atoms. These are the compounds out of which our body is formed.

Ionic bonds.   Other atoms form molecules by using **ionic bonds:** one atom "donates" an electron to an atom of another substance. Sodium chloride (NaCl, or salt) is an ionically bonded molecule. The sodium atom has donated one of its electrons to chlorine and so the sodium atom becomes positively charged (Na^+) and the chlorine atom becomes negatively charged (Cl^-). The two opposite charges attract each other, holding the sodium and chlorine atoms together in a molecule, as Figure 2-13 illustrates.

Solutions.   Although both covalent and ionic compounds can dissolve (go into **solution**) in solvents such as water, only

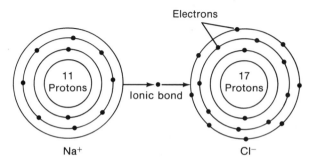

Figure 2-13   A molecule of sodium chloride (NaCl, or salt) uses ionic bonds. The sodium atom "donates" one of its electrons to chlorine, giving the sodium and chlorine atoms opposite charges (positive and negative). The opposite charges attract each other, holding the salt molecule together.

the ionic compounds form ionic solutions that can conduct electrical current. These solutions are called **electrolytes.**

To understand the forces at work on the nerve cell, it is necessary to describe the nature of ionic solutions. When salt is mixed with water, the sodium (Na^+) atoms separate from the chlorine (Cl^-) atoms because water molecules are **polar;** that is, water molecules are composed of one oxygen (O^{--}) atom plus two hydrogen (H^+) atoms. Although the compound itself is electrically neutral, both of the hydrogen atoms are attached to the same side of the oxygen atom. As Figure 2-14 illustrates, the hydrogen side of the water, or H_2O, molecule has a weak positive charge associated with it, and the oxygen side of the molecule has a weak negative charge. The oxygen side of the molecule is attracted to the positively charged Na^+ atoms and the hydrogen side is attracted to the Cl^- atoms. Consequently, water molecules "push" their way between the Na^+ and the Cl^- atoms, separating them.

When NaCl dissolves in water, each molecule has been separated into two charged particles called **ions.** The Na^+ ion, which has given up an electron to Cl^-, acquires a positive charge, since one of its positively charged protons is now left without an electron. Any positively charged ion is a **cation.** The Cl^- ion has gained an electron from Na^+ and so it now has a negative charge and is called an **anion.** Because these ions have charges associated with them, each attracts several of the polar water molecules. In fact, a Na^+ ion tends to carry around with it eight water molecules, whereas Cl^- attracts and carries four water molecules with it. This entourage of water molecules obviously changes the effective size of the ions, which is important to the ion's ability to fit through pores in the nerve cell membrane.

Ionized solutions separated by a membrane have two passive forces working on them: an **electrical force** and an os-motic or **diffusion force.** These forces, which allow an axon to function, do not require cellular energy or ATP.

Electrical Forces

Ohm's law.   Three concepts necessary to an understanding of electrical forces are illustrated in Figure 2-15, and the way in which they are interrelated is described by **Ohm's law:**

$$E = IR \qquad \text{or} \qquad I = \frac{E}{R}$$

E is voltage, the force "pushing" the current through the wires. Voltage is measured in **volts** or **millivolts** and is symbolized in the diagram by a battery. R is resistance (measured in **ohms** or in **milliohms,** as in the nervous system). R reflects the degree of difficulty that current has in flowing through wires of a certain diameter, composed of a certain substance. I is the actual flow of electrical current through the wires, measured in **amperes** or **milliamperes.** According to Ohm's law, the greater the voltage is, the more current will flow, and the greater the resistance is, the less current will flow.

A completely equivalent way of expressing Ohm's law is

$$I = Eg$$

Here, g, or **conductance,** is the inverse of resistance. In other words, since

$$g = \frac{1}{R} \qquad \text{and} \qquad I = \frac{E}{R}$$

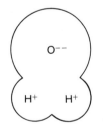

Figure 2-14   A water molecule has a polar nature. Two hydrogen (H) atoms are attached to one oxygen (O) atom to form a molecule of water. Both hydrogen atoms attach to the same side of the oxygen atom, and the hydrogen atoms have "donated" electrons to the oxygen atom. Thus the oxygen side is negatively charged, leaving the hydrogen side positively charged.

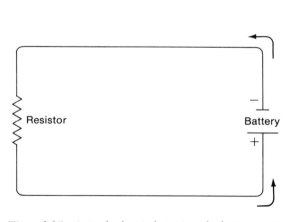

Figure 2-15   A simple electrical circuit, with a battery, a resistor, and connecting wires. Electrons "move" (by successive "bumpings") in the direction indicated by the arrows.

the second version of Ohm's law presented above converts exactly into the equivalent equation.

Batteries and voltage. The voltage of a battery is determined by the *difference* in the electrical charge between the positively charged **anode** and the negatively charged **cathode**. A voltmeter measures the voltage difference between those posts. If the anode and cathode are connected to each other through a series of wires and resistors, the voltage force will cause electrical current or electrons to flow from the cathode to the anode. The excess of electrons on the cathode repel each other at the same time that they are being attracted to the positive force on the anode. Together, these two actions constitute the electrical force.

The electrical force. Since electrical forces affect nerve membranes, we have to be able to describe how much electrical force actually exists for any ion, outside or inside the cell, at any given time. One way of doing this is to describe how much force must be exerted to "push" a certain number of ions carrying a certain amount of charge into an electrical field carrying the same kind of charge (positive or negative):

$$\text{electrical force} = z_x F E$$

This equation says that the more charges there are in a given solution of an ion, and the greater the voltage in the electrical field, the more force will have to be exerted to bring the ion up to the field. z is the amount and type of charge carried by an ion; since each Na^+ ion carries one positive charge, the z for Na^+ would be $+1$. E is the amount of voltage in the field into which the charged molecule is being "pushed." F is the Faraday number, or the amount of charge carried on a gram ion of any univalent ion. **Univalent** simply means that the ion contains only one "extra" proton or one "extra" electron. Na^+ is univalent, but calcium ions are **bivalent** (Ca^{++}), since each calcium ion has two "extra" protons and so *two* "extra" positive charges.

(A **gram ion** is a way of measuring the amount of any substance in solution. If the amount of the substance in solution is converted to gram ions, then we can compare Na^+ solutions to potassium solutions. A gram ion of a solution of any substance has the same number of charged molecules or ions in it, regardless of the substance. If we multiply this number by z, then we get the total number of charges present in a solution of any ion, even bivalent and trivalent ions.)

Capacitors. The addition of a capacitor to the electrical circuit of Figure 2-15 is shown in Figure 2-16. Physically, a

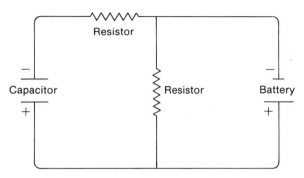

Figure 2-16   A capacitor has been added to the simple circuit of Figure 2-15. A capacitor can briefly store electrical charges.

capacitor consists of two "sheets" of some substance that has relatively low resistance (or high conductance), separated by a sheet of a substance with relatively high resistance. Substances with high electrical resistance are said to be **insulators.** To make a capacitor, you could put a sheet of paper (an insulator) between two sheets of aluminum or copper foil and roll them up.

In Figure 2-16, the capacitor has been hooked up to a battery. As before, the excess electrons will repel each other, but in this case when they leave the cathode they will accumulate on the first plate of the capacitor. The anode will attract the electrons on the second plate of the capacitor, leaving "extra" protons, or excess positive charges, behind. The "excess" electrons accumulating on the first plate will also repel electrons on the second plate. However, because the two plates of the capacitor are separated by an insulator, electrons can't actually flow across the capacitor itself. The accumulation of positive charges on the one plate and negative charges on the other plate is **capacitive current.** Accumulation is accomplished solely by the electrical forces described earlier, operating across the gap provided by the insulator. If the negative and positive plates of the capacitor were connected to each other through a resistor, current would flow through the circuit until the capacitor "ran out of" its charges. Capacitive current causes a charge to be stored on a capacitor, and discharging that store through a resistor produces **resistive current.**

The time (T) it would take a capacitor to become fully charged, and the time it would take to discharge a fully charged capacitor, depends on the **capacitance** (C) of the capacitor and the resistance (R) through which the current has to flow:

$$T = RC$$

The capacitance of a capacitor depends on two things: the size of the plates of the conductor and the distance between the plates. The larger the plates are, the more charge a capacitor can hold, and the longer it will take to charge and to discharge it. The farther apart the two plates of the conductor are, the weaker the electrical force is. The weaker the electrical force is, the fewer the charges that can be stored and the more quickly the capacitor can be charged or discharged.

The nerve cell membrane has characteristics of a leaky capacitor. Since ionized solutions exist inside the cell and in the extracellular fluid outside the cell's membrane, those solutions act like the conductor plates of a capacitor. The membrane itself is the insulator. Since it has holes in it through which current can flow, it is a leaky capacitor.

Chemical Forces

Any substance in solution is affected by the osmotic or diffusion force. Any substance has a tendency to diffuse from a region of high concentration to a region of low concentration. To measure the force that this process can exert, it is necessary to visualize what would happen if the experiment illustrated in Figure 2-17 were carried out. Suppose that you had a beaker of water separated into two halves by a sheet of some porous material. Although the pores in that material are freely permeable to water, they are too small to allow either Cl^- or Na^+ ions (with their entourage of four and eight water molecules, respectively) to get through. So this membrane is **semipermeable.** If we put a cup of salt into one side of the beaker, osmotic forces would immediately be created. These forces would be at

work on both the Na^+ and the Cl^- ions, attempting to push them from the region of high concentration—where the salt was added—to the region of low concentration on the other side of the membrane. However, the pores in the membrane are too small, and these ions can't get through. But the osmotic force is also working on the water. Water is now more concentrated on the side that has not been "diluted" with salt, and so water molecules will be forced from that side of the membrane to the other side. The amount of water on the salted side of the beaker will now begin to increase: the osmotic force is opposing the force of gravity and causing the water level to rise.

We again need a way to express the amount of force involved in such situations:

$$\text{osmotic force} = (RT) \ln\left(\frac{X_o}{X_i}\right)$$

In this equation, R is the gas constant and comes from the laws expressing the force that expanding gases can create. T is temperature, which in the brain we can also regard as a constant (though having a fever might change this!). The ln is a natural logarithm.* The X with the subscripts o and i refers to the concentrations of the substance X on either side (out and in) of the membrane. This equation says that the greater the difference between the concentrations on the two sides of the membrane, the greater the osmotic force created.

Ions and Semipermeable Membranes

The situation gets more complicated—and much closer to the conditions of the nerve cell membrane—if several different ions are put into solution on both sides of a membrane that is permeable to some but not to all of them. We will again add salt to one side of a beaker of water, but in this case the semipermeable membrane will allow water molecules *and* Cl^- ions through. The Na^+ ions, being attached to eight molecules of water, will still be too large to fit through the pores. An electrical **potential**—the difference in voltage between the inside and the outside of a cell—will be created.

Semipermeable membranes and electrical forces. In looking at how the electrical force is created by the semipermeable membrane, we will ignore water movement through the

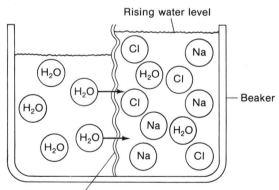

Figure 2-17 The osmotic or diffusion force. Because of the greater concentration of water (H_2O) molecules on the left side, water moves across the semipermeable membrane, against the force of gravity, causing the fluid level on the right side to rise. Na = sodium; Cl = chlorine.

* The logarithm of any number (base 10) is the number of times 10 must be multiplied by itself to equal that number; for instance, the log of 100 is 2. The ln, or natural logarithm, of a number uses the base e ($e = 2.71828$. . .), so the ln of a given number is the number of times e must be multiplied by itself to equal that number.

membrane. The osmotic force moves the negatively charged Cl^- ions from the region of high concentration, through holes in the membrane, to the region of low concentration on the other side. However, for every Cl^- ion that changes sides, one Na^+ ion will be left behind. So one side of the membrane will steadily accumulate negatively charged Cl^- ions, and the other side will have steadily more unopposed, positively charged Na^+ ions left behind.

An electrical force is created as soon as this process starts to happen. Positively charged Na^+ ions are pushed to the other side not only by osmotic forces but also by electrical forces: like Na^+ charges repel each other. The Na^+ ions are also attracted to the negatively charged Cl^- ions on the other side. However, the Na^+ ions can't get through, so these forces do not create any movement of Na^+ ions through the membrane. But these same forces affect the Cl^- ions — and, in this case, in opposite directions.

What happens will depend on how the electrical and chemical forces working on Cl^- come into balance. The osmotic forces are still working to push Cl^- from the region of high to the region of low concentration, but the electrical forces created by that diffusion will work to push Cl^- the other way. Cl^- continues to move through the membrane until the osmotic forces working on it in one direction are exactly equal to the electrical forces working on it in the other direction. Then the Cl^- ion is said to be at **equilibrium.**

The Nernst equation.   All that remains is to visualize how the electrical and chemical forces work together across a semipermeable membrane, such as the nerve membrane. The **Nernst equation** gives us a way of expressing the equilibrium just described. Since Cl^- ions continue to diffuse across the membrane until the electrical force created by the diffusion is exactly equal and opposite to the osmotic forces, we can equate the two. This can be done mathematically by using the two earlier equations for the electrical force and the osmotic force:

$$z_x FE = (RT) \ln \left(\frac{X_o}{X_i} \right)$$

Solving the equation for E produces the Nernst equation:

$$E = \frac{RT}{Fz_x} \ln \left(\frac{X_o}{X_i} \right)$$

This equation can be simplified. R, F and T are constants, and a natural logarithm can be converted to the logarithm to

the base 10 by multiplying by 2.303. The simplified equation reads:

$$E = \left(\frac{61}{z_x} \right) \log \left(\frac{X_o}{X_i} \right)$$

This equation tells us what electrical force E can be created by a given concentration force (a given difference in concentration for any ion) acting across a semipermeable membrane. It tells us what the electrical force (E) should be to exactly oppose the concentration forces observed to exist for that ion across a membrane that is permeable to it. If the electrical force calculated from the Nernst equation for an ion actually exists across a semipermeable membrane, that ion is at equilibrium.

Summary of Basic Forces

Nerve cells are active because of electrical and osmotic forces. Electrical forces are created whenever there is a difference in electrical charge between one point and another. Chemical forces are created whenever there is a difference in concentration for molecules in solution between one point and another. The nerve cell membrane is simultaneously affected by both forces. The result is described by the Nernst equation: the potential or voltage difference across a membrane that would produce an electrical force exactly equal and opposite to the osmotic force created by differences in concentration across the membrane.

The membrane is a leaky capacitor as well as a semipermeable membrane, for several reasons: (1) it separates two electrolytic solutions (extracellular fluid and cytoplasm), which can act like the two conductor plates of a capacitor; (2) the inside of the nerve cell membrane has an excess of negative charges and the outside has an excess of positive charges; (3) the membrane is permeable to some ions but not to other ions; and (4) many of the ions exist in concentrations that differ between the inside and the outside of the nerve cell membrane. Thus, electrical and chemical forces are always present at any nerve membrane.

Chapter Summary

Implications for Information Processing

Both the peripheral and the central nervous systems are made up of millions of nerve cells. Each nerve cell is surrounded by a membrane and has a cell body, dendrites, and an axon (at least, most of them do). Different kinds of nerve cells are connected to each other across synapses in different kinds of ways in the various regions of the brain. The cortex may be the "highest" processing center, where the most sophisticated and detailed processing of external (sensory) and internal (motivational and emotional) types of information are carried out. However, the most important functional distinction among different areas of the brain seems to be how nerve cells in one area are interconnected with other cells in that same area and with cells in other areas of the brain. Thus, any researcher has to know the anatomy of the brain before he or she can explore which parts of the brain may be coding which aspects of our behavior and experiences.

Neurons work because of basic electrical and chemical principles. These forces allow the nerve cell to communicate information from one point to another in the nervous system and to encode that information in various ways. To understand this, we must know how osmotic and electrical forces affect the nerve membrane and how that membrane acts like a leaky capacitor. These forces are ultimately responsible for the brain's codes.

PART TWO

The Communication Function
of Nerve Cells

One major function of nerve cells is to communicate information from one part of the body to another. For example, information about what is happening on the surface of the skin is sent to the spinal cord and then to the brain. Directions about what glands and muscles should do is carried from the CNS on efferent autonomic or somatic nerves to those organs.

The specialization of the neural membrane allows information to be conducted from one point to another. The axon carries information away from the cell body toward the area in which that nerve cell makes synaptic contact with another neuron. The **resting membrane** of the axon is ready to conduct information, and the **active membrane** is in the process of conduction. The neural membranes in the synaptic areas have a structure different from the membranes away from the synapse. Their differences allow the synaptic part of the membrane to communicate information from one nerve cell to the next. The synapse also changes the form of, or **transforms,** the information being communicated from one cell to another.

Neural membranes are specialized by their membrane proteins, for which they are coded by genes. Membrane proteins, when activated, form channels or holes through the membrane. The opening of these channels allows information to pass from point to point in the nervous system. Some enzymatic proteins regulate the flow of information from one cell to another. Which genes are active in a given cell determine its nature, making it into a nerve rather than, say, a liver cell. Thus, if genes affect behavior, they must do so by directly or indirectly affecting the specialized proteins in nerve cells. In fact, since genes code for proteins, it seems logical that the genetic background of organisms might affect the ability of their neurons to pass information from one point to another in their brains.

This part describes the properties and functions of the resting and active nerve membrane and describes how nerve cells can transmit information across a synapse. It also explains the mechanisms by which genes control nerve cell activity.

C H A P T E R

The Nerve Membrane

Following an overview, this chapter describes the resting and the active neural membrane (an active membrane is one that is currently displaying an action potential). The critical experiments are described in some detail to help you appreciate the challenge of brain research. You should clearly understand the overview before going on to later sections so that you do not get lost in the details.

Overview

Baker and his colleagues (Baker, 1966; Baker, Hodgkin, & Shaw, 1962a, 1962b) identified the elements essential to resting potentials and action potentials. As Figure 3-1 illustrates, they took a giant axon from a squid, attached it to a cannula, placed it on a rubber pad, and squeezed out its axoplasm by passing a rubber-covered roller over it several times. Then the axon was filled with a solution and suspended in a bath of some other solution. Baker and his colleagues were able to vary the solutions inside and outside the axon to see just what was

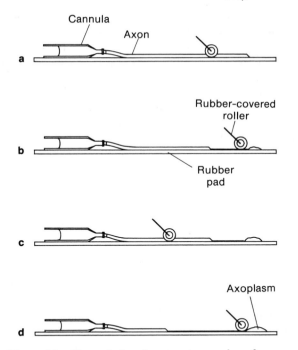

Figure 3-1   One technique for removing axoplasm from an axon. A giant axon removed from a squid is attached to a cannula and placed on a rubber pad. Passing a rubber-covered roller over it squeezes out the axoplasm.

required for that axon to generate normal resting and action potentials.

Essential Elements

All that is needed for an action potential is a nerve membrane with a resting potential, more Na^+ outside than inside, and some kind of stimulus. If an axon is suspended in sea water and a solution of ionizing K_2SO_4 (potassium sulfate) is injected into it, the inside of the axon becomes negatively charged in relation to the outside. *So all that is needed for a resting potential is a nerve cell membrane that has more K^+ inside than outside.* Stimulating any axon that has a resting potential can generate thousands of normal-looking action potentials, as long as the concentration of Na^+ (or any cation of a similar size) is much greater outside than inside.

Perhaps even more important is what is *not* needed. No external source of energy such as ATP is needed for an axonal membrane to produce resting and action potentials. Baker and his colleagues estimated that at least 95% of the axoplasm, and therefore essentially all of the axon's supply of ATP, had been successfully removed by the injections and the roller. This means that the electrical and chemical forces described in Chapter 2 are sufficient to create resting and action potentials. These forces are the **passive forces,** since they do *not* require ATP and/or cellular metabolism.

Resting Membrane

A resting membrane can be described by specifying (1) the differences in ion concentration across it, (2) the ions to which it is permeable, and (3) the electrical potential across the membrane (the difference in voltage between inside and outside).

Differences in ion concentration.   A difference in ion concentrations across a membrane is needed for a cell to transmit information. In the normal cell, both Na^+ and Cl^- are in much greater concentration outside than inside the membrane. Calcium (Ca^{++}), a bivalent cation, is also more concentrated outside than inside. But K^+ is much more concentrated inside than outside. Furthermore, negatively charged protein molecules are found only inside the membrane (in the experiments with squid axons just described, the sulfate ion — SO_4 — substituted for these protein molecules). You can think of the nerve cell as being filled with K^+ and negatively charged protein molecules, suspended in a bath of sea water (an ionized salt solution).

Permeability of the resting nerve membrane.   The resting mammalian nerve cell membrane is much more permeable to Cl^- and to K^+ than it is to Na^+, and it is impermeable to the protein molecules. (Provided that the nerve cell membrane is undamaged, the protein molecules stay inside, along with all their negative charges.) If you visualize these permeabilities as representing "holes" in the membrane, there is a Cl^- hole and a separate K^+ hole. Neither of these holes is large enough to let the fully hydrated Na^+ ion through. Thus, the resting membrane is semipermeable. As described in Chapter 2, any semipermeable membrane separating two solutions with different ion concentrations can create electrical potentials.

Electrical potential.   Since the resting membrane is more permeable to K^+ than to protein molecules, K^+ will tend to diffuse out of the cell down its **concentration gradient** (a difference in concentrations between one point and another), leaving the negatively charged protein molecules behind. Since the membrane is also more permeable to Cl^- than to Na^+, Cl^- will tend to diffuse in, down its concentration gradient, leaving some unopposed Na⁺ ions outside. Because the membrane separates excess negative charges on the inside from excess positive charges on the outside, it has a **negative potential,** or is negatively charged inside in relation to outside. The negative charge is the **resting potential.**

Action Potentials

When something happens to stimulate the nerve cell membrane, its permeabilities change. And when that happens, its electrical potential or voltage (measured in millivolts) will also change. The change in potential is the action potential. An action potential as seen by a pair of microelectrodes, one inside and one outside the cell, is illustrated in Figure 3-2.

Depolarization.   The first part of the curve is called depolarization. The membrane is losing its inside-negative potential, or is becoming **depolarized.** This change in membrane potential occurs whenever something happens to increase the permeability of the membrane to Na⁺. Then Na⁺ ions begin rushing into the neuron, down their concentration and electrical gradients. The increase of positive charges inside the membrane depolarizes it. In fact, so many Na⁺ ions rush in during **depolarization** that the membrane potential actually reverses and temporarily becomes more positive inside than outside.

Repolarization.   Next, the permeability of the membrane to K⁺ increases. K⁺ ions rush out of the cell, through the K⁺ holes, down their concentration gradient. The movement of

positively charged ions out of the cell makes the cell less positive inside. Finally, with the movement of enough K⁺ ions out of the cell, the inside once again becomes negatively charged with respect to the outside, or becomes **repolarized.** The process is **repolarization.** Eventually, the cell recovers its resting potential and even overshoots it. Any such increase in inside negativity is **hyperpolarization;** a prolonged movement of K⁺ ions out of cells causes the membrane to become **hyperpolarized.**

You should keep the following facts about resting and active membranes clearly in mind:

1. Both Na⁺ and Cl⁻ are more concentrated on the outside than on the inside, and K⁺ and the negatively charged protein molecules are more concentrated on the inside.
2. Because the resting membrane is impermeable to protein and only slightly permeable to Na⁺, a resting potential, negative on the inside with respect to the outside, is generated.
3. During an action potential, the permeabilities of the membrane first to Na⁺ and then to K⁺ are increased. The increased permeability to Na⁺ causes Na⁺ to rush in and leads to depolarization; then the increased permeability to K⁺ causes K⁺ to rush out, leading to repolarization and hyperpolarization. Very few ions have to move for these changes in potential to occur.

Properties of the Resting Nerve Membrane

The differences in ion concentrations across a nerve cell membrane vary from one species to the next, and there may also be differences within a species, depending on the location of the nerve cell. Table 3-1 presents some representative dif-

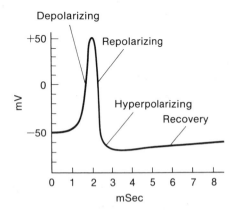

Figure 3-2 An action potential recorded by an intracellular microelectrode. The membrane potential first depolarizes and then actually reverses in polarity before normal membrane potential is restored. mV = millivolts; mSec = milliseconds.

Table 3-1   Concentration forces in a typical mammalian neuron.

	Concentrations (in millimols)		Equilibrium Potentials (in millivolts)
Ion	*Outside*	*Inside*	
K	7.15	150.00	−80.6
Cl	125.00	9.00	−70.0
Na	150.00	15.00	+61.0

ferences in concentration across a hypothetical but "typical" mammalian neuron for Na^+, Cl^- and K^+.

The Nernst Equation and Differences in Concentration

Table 3-1 also lists the equilibrium potentials of each of those three ions. The equilibrium potentials were calculated from the Nernst equation introduced in Chapter 2:

$$E = \left(\frac{61}{z_x}\right) \log \left(\frac{X_o}{X_i}\right)$$

You should insert the concentration values from Table 3-1 into this equation to see that the equilibrium values for each ion are the ones given in that table. For example, the ratio of external to internal Na is 10 ($\frac{150}{15}$) and the logarithm of 10 is 1. Multiplying that by 61 (since the z for Na^+ is $+1$) gives you the sodium equilibrium potential of $+61$ mV. (Actually **activities**—which refer to the ease with which an ion in solution can move—should be used in these equations instead of concentrations, since the activity of an ion is affected by the number of other ions in the solution.)

For this hypothetical but typical neuron, the resting membrane potential is -70 mV. Therefore, the resting membrane potential is also the Cl^- equilibrium potential. (Actual resting membrane potentials vary from -20 mV to -90 mV, but we will be using -70 mV as a "standard" reference value.) When the membrane is at rest, since the Cl^- equilibrium potential is equal to the resting membrane potential, the electrical force working to push Cl^- out is exactly equal and opposite to the chemical force working to push Cl^- in. Therefore the Cl^- ion is at equilibrium with the resting membrane potential.

Being at equilibrium does *not* mean that the ion does not pass through the membrane. It means only that when the equilibrium exists, the forces working to push that ion inside the nerve are exactly equal and opposite to the forces working to push that ion outside the nerve. If the membrane is permeable to that ion and that ion is found on both sides of the membrane, the outward movement, or **flux**, of the ion through the membrane pores will be exactly equal to the inward movement or flux of that ion. In a given period of time, if Cl^- is at equilibrium in the resting membrane, as many Cl^- ions will move out as move in.

Both Na^+ and K^+ are out of equilibrium. The membrane potential is not quite sufficiently negative on the inside (attracting the positively charged K^+ ions to the inside) to exactly oppose the concentration forces working to push K^+ out.

Thus, K^+ will be under some constant slight pressure to leak out of the cell. In order to oppose the concentration forces working to push the Na^+ ion in, the membrane should be close to 60 mV *positive* on the inside in relation to the outside. Since that is obviously not the case, Na^+ ions will be under great pressure to move inside.

Figure 3-3 depicts another way of expressing the forces at work on the resting membrane. If the two arrows for the chemical and electrical forces are pointing in opposite directions and are exactly equal in length, then in the resting membrane that particular ion is at equilibrium. If one arrow is longer than the other, that ion is not at equilibrium: there will be a steady tendency for that ion to leak in the direction indicated by the longer arrow. If both arrows are pointed in the same direction, as is the case for the Na^+ arrows, that ion is obviously far from equilibrium and will tend to move in the indicated direction. However, the degree to which the ion can move through the membrane depends not only on the relative sizes of the two forces but also on how permeable the membrane is at that time to that particular ion.

This figure can be used to visualize what would happen to the cell if ion concentrations were changed. If the internal concentration of K^+ were increased, the concentration arrow for K^+ would become longer and the tendency for K^+ to leak out of the cell would be increased. If the membrane were depolarizing, becoming less negative on the inside than usual, the electrical forces working on all the ions would suddenly change. For example, the electrical force working on Cl^- would become smaller, and the concentration force working on Cl^- would now be greater than the electrical force. If the membrane were permeable to Cl^-, there would be a net inward flux of Cl^-.

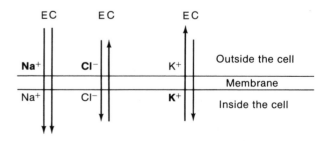

Figure 3-3 The direction and amount of electrochemical forces working across a resting membrane create a dynamic equilibrium. The names in heavy type represent the ions with the higher concentrations, and the arrows indicate the direction and relative size of the electrical and chemical forces involved. E = electrical force; C = concentration force.

Since Na$^+$ is so much out of equilibrium with the resting membrane potential, either the resting membrane is completely impermeable to Na$^+$ or some other force is at work. If neither of these possibilities were true, Na$^+$ would leak continuously into the cell and neither the resting potential nor the differences in concentration for that ion would remain at the values indicated in Table 3-1.

Permeabilities: Resting Potentials and Current Flows

The permeability of a membrane determines the degree to which substances can move from one side to the other side of that membrane. The permeability (P) of a membrane is somewhat analogous to conductance in an electrical circuit. However, P and g are *not* identical to each other. Since g is defined by E and I (voltage and current), g exists only when there is both a voltage difference between the two ends of a conductor and a flow of current through the conductor. If there is no current flowing through the membrane, there is no membrane conductance. However, P can exist — as holes in a membrane — even if there are no current flows or electrical potentials to be found across the membrane.

The Goldman equation and resting potentials.   The permeabilities of the resting membrane to the ions can be explored in several ways. One is to suspend the nerve cell in a solution in which one ion has been radioactively labeled. After a time, the cell can be removed and gently washed and the amount of radioactivity it picked up measured. Or else the nerve can be injected with some radioactively labeled ion such as K$^+$, and the amount of radioactivity it loses over time to an external solution can be measured.

When these and similar experiments were done, the mammalian membrane was found to be very permeable to Cl$^-$ and to K$^+$, but only slightly permeable to Na$^+$ (Caldwell, Hodgkin, Keynes, & Shaw, 1960; Coombs, Eccles, & Fatt, 1955; Goldman, 1943; Hodgkin & Horowicz, 1959; Keynes, 1948, 1949, 1951a, 1951b, 1979). (When similar experiments were carried out on the squid axon, it was found to be relatively impermeable to Cl$^-$ [Caldwell & Keynes, 1960].) So Cl$^-$ and K$^+$ ions pass relatively freely back and forth through the mammalian membrane. Since neither Na$^+$ nor K$^+$ is at equilibrium, there will be a steady leakage of K$^+$ out of the cell and Na$^+$ into the cell. Na$^+$ will be pushed in by the greater concentration of Na$^+$ outside and by its attraction to the negative charges on the inside.

The effects of these forces and permeabilities on the resting nerve cell membrane potential can be described by the **Gold-** man equation (or the **Goldman-Hodgkin-Katz equation** [Goldman, 1943; Hodgkin & Katz, 1949]):

$$E_m = 61 \log \frac{P_K(K^+)_o + P_{Na}(Na^+)_o + P_{Cl}(Cl^-)_i}{P_K(K^+)_i + P_{Na}(Na^+)_i + P_{Cl}(Cl^-)_o}$$

This equation describes how the membrane potential (E_m) is affected by ion concentration gradients and by ion permeabilities. The size of the membrane potential depends on the ratio of the concentration difference across the membrane for each ion (for example, K^+_{out} versus K^+_{in}), multiplied by the permeability of the membrane to that ion. Other things being equal, the more permeable the membrane is to any given ion, the more the electrical forces created by the differences in concentration for that ion will contribute to the total membrane potential.

Current flows and permeabilities.   Another equation is better than the Goldman equation for describing the changes in ion flows caused by changes in membrane permeability. This equation is derived from Ohm's law. The permeability of the membrane to an ion is equated with g or conductance. I is the net flow of ions through the membrane, analogous to the movement of electrons in Ohm's law. And the voltage force working on each ion through the membrane is the absolute value of the difference between the current membrane potential and the equilibrium potential of that ion. Table 3-1 shows that the net force working on Cl$^-$ is zero, the net force working on K$^+$ is 10.6 mV ($|-70 - (-80.6)|$), and the force working on Na$^+$ is 131 mV ($|-70 - (61)|$).

For each ion (x), Ohm's law ($I = gV$) would be

$$I_x = P_x|E_m - E_x| \tag{1}$$

The total current through the membrane would be the sum of all the net movements of each individual ion through the membrane:

$$I_m = I_{K^+} + I_{Na^+} + I_{Cl^-} \tag{2}$$

In the resting membrane, we can assume that the net current flow is zero (inward flux equal to outward flux: this is not strictly true, but it will do as a first approximation). If we insert equation 1 values for each ion into the appropriate places in equation 2, the result will be

$$0 = P_{K^+}|E_m - E_{K^+}| + P_{Na^+}|E_m - E_{Na^+}| + P_{Cl^-}|E_m - E_{Cl^-}|$$

If this equation is solved for E_m:

$$E_m = \frac{P_{K^+}(E_{K^+}) + P_{Na^+}(E_{Na^+}) + P_{Cl^-}(E_{Cl^-})}{P_{K^+} + P_{Na^+} + P_{Cl^-}}$$

The degree to which the equilibrium potential for each ion contributes to the total membrane potential is weighted by (multiplied by) the permeability of the membrane to that ion. This equation can be used to calculate the effects a change in membrane permeability — or a change in the equilibrium potential of any ion created by manipulating ion concentrations — would have on the membrane potential. If you substituted the equilibrium potentials of Table 3-1 and used $P_{K^+} = 1$, $P_{Na^+} = .08$, and $P_{Cl^-} = 2$, the membrane potential would be -70 mV. (The relative permeabilities to Cl^- and K^+ are based on those of another excitable membrane, the frog muscle membrane [Hodgkin & Horowicz, 1959]).

To test yourself, you should use the above equation to answer the following questions (you can also use Figure 3-3 to answer these questions by changing the length of the arrows appropriately whenever the condition they represent is altered):

1. Suppose that a solution of Na^+ plus some negatively charged ion were added to the solution outside the membrane (for example, add Na_2SO_4 to the outside). Assume that the membrane is impermeable to the sulfate ion. What type of effect (hyperpolarizing or depolarizing) would this have on the Na^+ equilibrium potential and on the membrane potential?
2. What effect would increasing the concentration of K^+ outside the cell (as by adding K_2SO_4 outside) have on the K^+ equilibrium potential and the membrane potential?
3. What effect would increasing the permeability of the membrane to Na^+ have on the membrane potential?
4. What effect would increasing the permeability of the membrane to K^+ have on the membrane potential?

(The answers to these questions will be found at the end of the chapter.)

Types of Membrane Channels

Membrane permeabilities have been described as channels that are pores or holes in the membrane through which ions can pass. The resting membrane has many different kinds of channels, not all of which are present in all parts of the cell. Each membrane channel is defined by *how it is activated* and by **selectivity** (that is, which ions pass most readily through that pore [Edwards, 1982; Hille, 1978]).

Types of activation.   The channels described so far have been either leakage channels or electrically gated channels. The **leakage channels** are open at a resting membrane potential and their state (open or closed) does not change when the membrane potential changes. In contrast, the permeabilities of an **electrically gated channel** change when the membrane potential changes. The electrically gated channels are probably membrane proteins that undergo changes in conformation or in three-dimensional shape when the membrane potential changes. These conformational changes either plug or open pores in the membrane for the various ions. In the resting membrane, the open K^+, Cl^-, and Na^+ channels may be leakage channels, but many of them are also electrically gated channels, some of which are open at the resting potential (Edwards, 1982; Hille, 1978). Thus, changes in membrane potential, away from its resting value, will open some channels and close others. The relative permeabilities of the membrane to Cl^-, Na^+, and K^+ simply reflect how many of the leakage channels are present and how many of the electrically gated channels are open when the membrane has a given potential difference across it.

Other channels are **chemically gated.** These channels are proteins whose three-dimensional conformation changes when some chemical attaches itself to the protein. When the protein changes its shape, channels through the membrane are either opened or closed. Some types of chemically gated channels are found only in the area of a synapse and are probably mostly closed in the resting state (Edwards, 1982; Hille, 1978). These channels would contribute very little to the resting membrane potential. Some other chemically gated channels open (or close) when the ionic concentrations inside the nerve change. And some chemically gated channels are also sensitive to the membrane potential, making them electrically as well as chemically gated.

Selectivity of channels.   One major factor determining the selectivity of any of these channels is its size relative to the size of a hydrated ion. If the ion, plus its associated water molecules, is too large to fit through the channel, that channel is relatively impermeable to that ion. In the resting membrane, the open Na^+ channels are much more permeable to Na^+ than to K^+ ions, and the reverse is true of the open K^+ channels. However, since the size distinction is relative rather than absolute, at least a few of each kind of ion are moving through the "wrong" channel at any given time. If too many of the "wrong" ions are moving through a channel, they interfere with the ability of the "right" ion to get through (too many ions are trying to get through the same channel at the same time in different directions).

But some aspects of permeability are related to something other than channel size. Membrane channels can also be specific to the type of ion—cation or anion—that is allowed through. Current theories visualize the channels as being "lined" with charged particles. If the channel is lined with positively charged particles, only anions will be allowed through.

The Na-K Pump

To account for the observed resting potentials and differences in concentration, either the membrane must be impermeable to Na^+ or there is some other force at work. Since the membrane is at least slightly permeable to Na^+, some energy-requiring force must be present in addition to the passive forces. This other force is also responsible for the lack of equilibrium of K^+ in the resting membrane.

Many membranes, including those of nerves and muscles, contain pumps. The idea of a **pump** is a way of describing a process by which membranes move substances from one side to another against their electrical or concentration gradients. Since this movement cannot be caused by passive forces, it requires cellular energy. Most pumps are membrane proteins and use ATP for their energy source. Every molecule of a substance moved through the membrane involves converting a molecule of ATP to **adenosine diphosphate (ADP)**. The cell must carry out energy-requiring metabolic processes to reconvert ADP to ATP.

The electrogenic pump.   In the nerve cell membrane, the pump most important to the resting potential is the **Na-K pump.** This pump exchanges internal Na^+ ions for external K^+ ions in a three-for-two ratio: for every three internal Na^+ ions that the pump pushes out, two external K^+ ions are pumped in. Because of this exchange ratio, the pump is **electrogenic,** which means that as it operates it produces a voltage difference across the membrane. More positive ions are pumped out than are pumped in, so if the pump were the only force at work, the membrane would become steadily more negative on the inside.

Putting this all together, we find that there is no net movement of any ion through the resting membrane. Cl^- is at equilibrium in many cells. The inward leakage of Na^+ and the outward leakage of K^+ will be exactly compensated for by the pump.

The rate of the pump.   Under normal conditions, the rate at which a pump moves ions across the membrane depends on the capacity of each pump and the number of pumps in each square micrometer of the membrane (Stevens, 1979). Operating at the maximal rate (which never occurs under resting conditions and normal ion concentrations), each pump can transport some 200 Na^+ ions and 130 K^+ ions per second. Since most neurons have between 100 and 200 sodium pumps per square micrometer, a typical small neuron has perhaps a million sodium pumps and has a total pump capacity to move about 200 million Na^+ ions per second.

Pumping rate also varies according to the conditions within the cell. The cell must be able to carry on normal metabolic activities or the pump will stop. If the cell is poisoned by some substance that prevents oxidative metabolism, the pump will stop, Na^+ will stop moving out of the cell, and the inward flux of K^+ will decrease. Figure 3-4 illustrates the effect that a

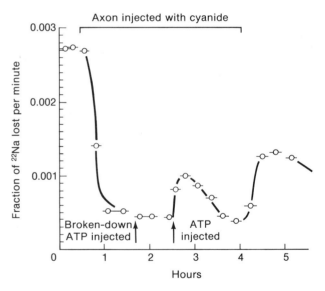

Figure 3-4   Effect of a metabolic poison on Na^+ efflux. Graph shows action of pump in an axon loaded with radioactively labeled Na (^{22}Na) and then injected with a metabolic poison that prevented ATP synthesis. At the first arrow, a control solution of ATP (broken down by boiling) was injected and had no effect. At the second arrow, ATP was injected. The poison caused the pump to stop, but an ATP injection started it up again, at least temporarily.

metabolic poison has on Na^+ **efflux** (remember that the efflux —or outward flux—of Na^+ is attributable largely to the pump). Since so much energy is required by neural pumps, the brain is one of the most metabolically active organs within the body. Because it depends on temperature-sensitive metabolic processes, the rate of the pump also varies directly with body temperature.

The pump rate also varies with ion concentrations. The greater the internal Na^+ or the external K^+ concentration, the faster the pump will work. If there is no K^+ on the outside but considerable Na^+ on the inside, the pump rate will be greatly decreased, although not always to zero (internal Na^+ may sometimes be exchanged with external Na^+) (Kennedy & De Weer, 1977).

The Resting Membrane as a K^+ Membrane

The resting membrane potential depends on (1) its relative permeability to the various ions, (2) the difference in ion concentrations across the membrane, and (3) the rate at which the Na-K pump is working. The fluids inside and outside the neuron are electrically neutral: the number of positive charges exactly equals the number of negative charges. However, there is a small excess of positive charges in the fluid layer just outside and a small excess of negative charges in the fluid layer just inside the membrane. The excess charges produce the membrane potential.

The membrane is affected more by changes in concentration of K^+ than by changes in concentration of Na^+ or Cl^-. If K^+ concentrations are changed, the membrane potential changes to a new value close to the new K^+ equilibrium potential. If Cl^- concentrations are manipulated, the membrane potential will change in the predicted direction—but only slightly and temporarily. The membrane then returns close to the K^+ equilibrium potential. The resting membrane thus acts like a K^+ membrane (Bernstein, 1902; Boyle & Conway, 1941).

There are several reasons why the membrane is more affected by changes in K^+ than by changes in Cl^- concentrations. First, some neural membranes (though not muscle membranes), such as in the squid, are more permeable to K^+ than to Cl^- (Caldwell & Keynes, 1980; Coombs, Eccles, & Fatt, 1955; Hodgkin & Horowicz, 1959). Second, although some cells do have a few Cl^- pumps (Walker & Brown, 1977), the rate at which the more numerous electrogenic Na-K pumps work will be affected by changes in K^+ and not by changes in Cl^- concentrations. Third, although electrically gated Cl^- channels are found in some neurons, they are

opened only very slowly and only with large hyperpolarizations (Chenoy-Marchais, 1982). The electrically gated K^+ channels are found in more cells, are much more numerous in all cells, and are more sensitive to slight changes in potential (Edwards, 1982; Hille, 1978).

Because of these three factors, any change that manipulations of Cl^- concentration create in the membrane potential will be immediately opposed by K^+ currents. K^+ and Cl^- currents will then continue until the *ratios* of outside to inside K^+ and Cl^- concentrations end up nearly the same as they started out—which means that the equilibrium potentials will also be the same, and the membrane potential will be back to normal. The converse is *not* true of manipulations of K^+ concentration. Cl^- may not be able to flow as freely through the membrane, and only K^+ manipulations can change membrane permeabilities (the electrically gated K^+ channels) and the rate of the electrogenic Na-K pump.

Capacitance of Nerve Membranes

The nerve cell membrane acts like a charged but leaky capacitor. It consists of two "plates" of conductive material (the thin layers of fluid on either side of the membrane) separated by an insulating material (the membrane itself). It is leaky because the membrane is permeable to some of the ions. The capacitance of a membrane determines not only how much charge it can store but also how fast the charge can be changed during stimulation—and thus how fast an action potential can travel.

Capacitance and size. One major factor determining membrane capacitance is the size of the cell. Here, we will discuss only axons, which you should visualize as being a small cylinder with extracellular fluid on the outside and axoplasm on the inside. Since capacitance depends on the size of the conductive plates, larger axons will have a larger capacitance. In fact, the capacitance of a nerve increases in direct proportion to the diameter of the axonal cylinder. Thus, larger axons can store a greater amount of charge.

Capacitance and myelin. The other major factor affecting the capacitance of a membrane is the presence of myelin. Myelin acts like an electrical insulator (fat is a good insulator both thermally and electrically). Myelin increases the distance between the axoplasm and the extracellular fluid, as Figure 3-5 illustrates. Myelin decreases the capacitance of an axon everywhere except at specialized regions that lack myelin—the **nodes of Ranvier.** Myelinated axons have less capacitance

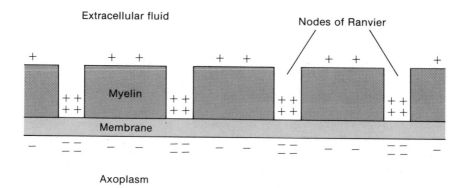

Extracellular fluid

Nodes of Ranvier

Myelin

Membrane

Axoplasm

Figure 3-5   Myelin decreases the capacitance of a nerve membrane and so decreases the number of charges stored across it.

and so store fewer charges per square centimeter than do unmyelinated axons.

Summary of the Resting Membrane

The resting membrane is a charged but leaky capacitor. Outside the membrane, in the extracellular fluid, are relatively large concentrations of Na^+ and Cl^- ions (as in sea water) and a smaller concentration of K^+ ions. Just inside the membrane is a solution with relatively smaller concentrations of Na^+ and Cl^- ions but a much greater concentration of K^+ as well as negatively charged protein ions.

The inward and outward flux of ions through the resting membrane depends on how permeable it is to each ion and how much any membrane potential differs from the equilibrium potential of that ion. The equilibrium potential for an ion is calculated with the Nernst equation: it identifies the membrane potential that must exist to create an electrical force that exactly counterbalances the concentration force created by the internal/external concentration ratio for that ion. The more permeable the membrane is to that ion, and the more any membrane potential differs from the ion's equilibrium potential, the greater the net flux (I_x) of that ion through the membrane. The total contribution of all ion equilibrium potentials and relative permeabilities to the membrane potential can be described by the Goldman and modified Ohm's equations.

An active or energy-requiring force is also present in the resting membrane: the Na-K pump. This pump exchanges three internal Na^+ ions for every two external K^+ ions and thus exactly compensates for the passive leakage of Na^+ into and K^+ out of the resting cell. A complete description of ion fluxes through the resting membrane would therefore have to include some description of the effects of the Na-K pump.

All these forces at work on the resting nerve membrane prepare it for activity. In fact, the way in which an action potential is generated and then passes down the axonal membrane can be explained by these same forces. These forces are the physical basis of mental states and the mind—though we are certainly a long way from understanding how the movements of ions can eventually be translated into a self-aware consciousness.

Properties of the Active Nerve Membrane

Together with the chapter overview, the section on techniques describes what happens to an axonal membrane when it is stimulated. A more detailed discussion of the electrical events that take place during each phase of the action potential explains the way information is communicated from one part of the body to another. We will concentrate on a "typical" axon. However, some neurons do not normally display action potentials and can communicate information only over short distances.

Techniques of Study

We will discuss the following techniques of study: (1) radioactively labeling various ions to track their movements during a series of stimulated action potentials, (2) manipulating the concentrations of the various ions on either side of the membrane, (3) electrically "solving" Ohm's equation for a nerve cell by holding voltage constant while measuring current, and (4) using various ionic poisons on an axon to see what effect they have on flows of current through a stimulated membrane.

The voltage-clamp technique has been particularly useful. Hodgkin, Huxley, and Eccles shared a Nobel prize in 1963 for their work in developing a membrane clamp. Hodgkin and Huxley (1952a, 1952b, 1952c, 1952d) worked on the squid axon. Eccles (1973/1977) concentrated on the motoneuron synapse (as already described, a motoneuron makes synaptic contact with, or **innervates,** a muscle).

Radioactive tracers.   This technique, described earlier (see Figure 3-4), has been used to study not only the resting but also the active membrane. By radioactively labeling Na^+ ions in a solution in which an axon has been suspended, researchers can measure how much radioactivity the axon acquires per **impulse** (action potential). Thus, it has been possible to demonstrate that the influx of Na^+ ions is much greater in an active neuron than in a resting neuron. Furthermore, it was possible to demonstrate that the efflux of K^+ ions is much greater in active than in resting neurons (Keynes, 1948, 1949, 1951a, 1951b).

Using radioactive tracers, experimenters have calculated how many K^+ ions leave and Na^+ ions enter the cell during a typical action potential in an axon taken from the giant squid. About 4×10^{-12} mols (gram molecules) of Na^+ enter (approximately 2×10^{12} ions) and slightly fewer K^+ leave each square centimeter of neuronal membrane during each action potential. However, this quantity is almost negligible compared with the total number of Na^+ and K^+ ions in that vicinity. Thus, except for extremely small axons that are repeatedly excited during a given period of time, we can assume that an action potential has *no* effect on ion concentrations or on the equilibrium potentials for the various ions. The radioactive tracer technique by itself does not demonstrate exactly when and why the ion fluxes are occurring.

Ion manipulations.   Another technique involves manipulating ion concentrations. The Nernst and Goldman equations are used to predict what should happen, on the basis of various theories of the ionic events during an action potential. This was done with intact squid axons and mammalian muscle cells by Hodgkin and his co-workers (Hodgkin, 1964a, 1964b, 1976; Hodgkin & Horowicz, 1959; Hodgkin & Huxley, 1952a, 1952b, 1952c, 1952d). The technique can be more rigorously applied by squeezing the axoplasm out of squid axons and replacing it with various ionic solutions (Baker, 1966; Baker, Hodgkin & Shaw, 1962a, 1962b; Chandler & Meves, 1965, 1970).

The neuron during an action potential becomes depolarized because of an inrush of positively charged Na^+ ions. If Na^+ current occurs because membrane permeability to Na^+

ions is increased by the stimulus, the height of the action potential should be directly related to the difference in Na^+ concentration across the membrane. The height of an action potential is measured by the total change in potential from resting potential to the potential observed at the top of the action potential. If the membrane becomes much more permeable to Na^+ than to any other ion during the initial part of the action potential, the Goldman equation will reduce to the Na^+ equilibrium potential. Of course, the ratio of internal to external ions determines the Na^+ equilibrium potential.

Figure 3-6 presents some effects of reducing the difference in concentration of Na^+ by replacing internal K^+ ions with Na^+ ions (Baker, Hodgkin, & Shaw, 1962a, 1962b). As more and more K^+ ions were replaced with Na^+ ions, the height of the action potential decreased. For the normal difference in Na^+ concentration across the membrane, the Na^+ equilibrium potential is positive (approximately $+61$ mV in some cells). However, if the internal concentration of Na^+ were increased, the Na^+ equilibrium potential would become less and less positive, and the height of the action potential would decrease. So, during depolarization, the neuron membrane is *seeking* the Na^+ equilibrium potential. ("Depolarization" refers to the entire upswing of the action potential, even though at the top of the action potential the membrane potential actually reverses, becoming positive on the inside in relation to the outside for a very brief period of time.)

K^+ efflux causes repolarization, or the recovery of the normal negative-inside potential. Figure 3-6 shows that shortly after the action potential, the membrane becomes even more negative than normal, or hyperpolarizes. Figure 3-6 also shows that as internal K^+ ions were replaced by Na^+ ions, not

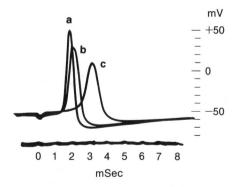

Figure 3-6   Replacing a neuron's internal K^+ with Na^+ ions affects its action potential.   **a.** Normal number of K^+ ions.   **b.** One-quarter of the K^+ ions replaced by Na^+ ions.   **c.** Half the K^+ ions replaced by Na^+ ions.

only was the height of the action potential reduced but the length and degree of hyperpolarization were also reduced. The decrease in internal K^+ makes the K^+ equilibrium potential less negative and so reduces the hyperpolarization.

Figure 3-7 shows what happens to hyperpolarization when the internal K^+ ions are replaced by glucose (the simplest sugar). When two-thirds of the K^+ ions (supplied by K_2SO_4) are replaced, there is no more hyperpolarization. Although it cannot be easily seen in Figure 3-7, the rate of repolarization is also decreased when internal K^+ is replaced by glucose. Thus, repolarization and hyperpolarization occur because K^+ ions move out and the membrane is seeking the K^+ equilibrium potential.

Voltage-clamp studies. The voltage-clamp technique can provide a detailed description of the time course and sequence of changes in membrane permeabilities during an action potential. *Two* electrodes are inserted inside a squid axon (or into any other sufficiently large neuron), and each is paired with one of two electrodes placed on the outside (Chandler & Meves, 1965, 1970; Hodgkin, 1964a, 1964b, 1976; Hodgkin & Huxley, 1952a, 1952b, 1952c, 1952d). One of these electrode pairs is used for current and one for voltage: the voltage pair measures the voltage difference across the membrane, and the current pair is used to stimulate or to pass electrical current through the membrane. Figure 3-8 is a schematic drawing of the experimental apparatus.

In voltage-clamp experiments, the current electrodes are used to change the voltage difference across the membrane to some desired value. Afterward, ions will flow through the

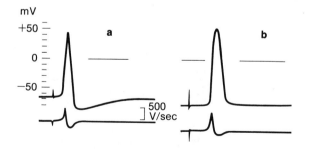

Figure 3-7   Diluting (decreasing) the level of internal potassium sulphate (K_2SO_4) by injecting isotonic glucose affects both the action and resting potentials. The upper trace is the membrane potential recorded with an intracellular microelectrode, and the lower trace is the rate of change of potential.   **a.** Isotonic K_2SO_4.   **b.** 0.33 K_2SO_4 and 0.67 isotonic glucose. Records were taken 3 to 5 minutes after changing the internal solution; the external solution was sea water throughout.

membrane because the driving force working on each ion, $|E_m - E_x|$, has been changed by the change in membrane potential. Normally, the movement of ions through the membrane changes membrane voltage. But during a voltage clamp, the voltage electrodes sense any small change in voltage. By means of the feedback amplifier, the sensed change in voltage causes the current electrodes to pass current through the membrane in the opposite direction. This current not only keeps the membrane potential constant at whatever voltage the experimenter desires but allows researchers to measure the flow of current through the membrane as a function of time elapsed since a change in membrane potential. Ohm's law can be used to convert the current flow to changes in conductance over time.

Figure 3-9 summarizes some of Hodgkin and Huxley's (1952a, 1952b, 1952c, 1952d) voltage-clamp experiments on a squid axon. Figure 3-9a shows the effects of varying the clamped voltage. A small clamped change in membrane voltage produced an inward movement of some positively charged ion through the membrane (or an outward movement of some negatively charged ion), followed by a small outward movement of some positively charged ion. As the depolarized and clamped voltage change was increased, both the first inward flow and the later outward flow increased—at least up to a point. When the membrane voltage was changed by 108 to 115 mV, only an outward current appeared. And when the membrane voltage was changed by 129 mV, then, at the time at which the inward flow of current occurred in the other records, only an outward flow of current could be seen.

These records reflect the changes in membrane permeability to Na^+ and to K^+ ions that occur as a function of the time elapsed since a stimulating depolarization. The resulting flows of current are related to the equilibrium potentials of each of those ions. The inward flow of current reverses at the 130 mV depolarization because at the membrane potential is now even more positive on the inside than the Na^+ equilibrium potential. In this situation, Na^+ moves *out* of the membrane in response to the depolarization. The inward Na^+ current (I_{Na}) seen in most of the records is followed by an outward K^+ current (I_K).

One other aspect of Figure 3-9a is important. Notice that the Na^+ current apparently "turns off," but the K^+ current continues as long as the membrane remains depolarized (at least during the time periods used by the study). The curves clearly indicate that the inward current first starts *and then stops*. Sometime during this period, the outward current starts and then continues on to the end of the recording.

In Figure 3-9b, Hodgkin and Huxley combined the voltage-clamp technique with the ion-replacement technique.

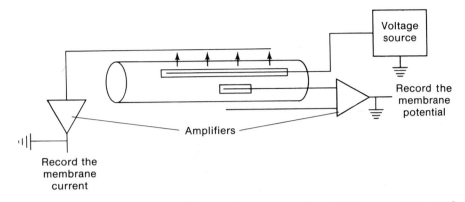

Figure 3-8 A membrane's voltage can be "clamped" by using the apparatus schematically represented in this figure. One pair of electrodes is used to both change and record the membrane potential. The other pair records membrane current and applies sufficient current in the opposite direction to keep voltage constant. The current that must be generated to keep the membrane potential constant is equal and opposite to the amount of membrane current that normally occurs after a given change in membrane potential.

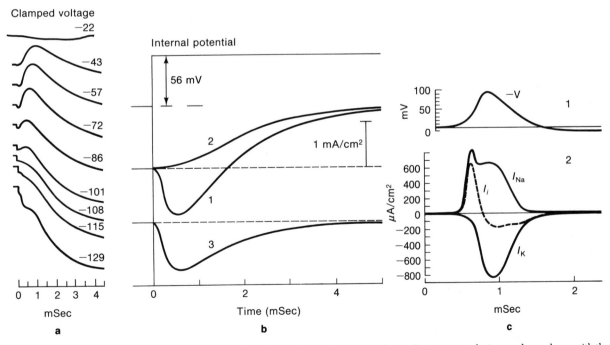

Figure 3-9 These records come from Hodgkin and Huxley's voltage-clamp research. **a.** Ionic current during a voltage clamp with the axon suspended in sea water. Inward movement of positive ions is an upward deflection. **b.** Separation of membrane current into Na and K components. (1) Current with axon in sea water $= I_{Na} + I_K$. (2) Current with most of external Na removed $= I_K$. (3) Difference between 1 and 2 $= I_{Na}$. **c.** (1) membrane potential $(-V)$. (2) ionic current (I_i), Na current (I_{Na}), and K current (I_K).

The curve in the middle, labeled 1, repeats the 57 mV depolarization curve in part a. The curve on top, labeled 2, occurred when the membrane was depolarized by 57 mV and clamped at that voltage after all the external Na^+ had been removed and replaced with an impermeable cation, choline. The bottom curve, labeled 3, is the mathematical difference between curves 1 and 2. Since no inward Na^+ current could have occurred in 2 (there was no external Na^+ to come in), the curve in 2 must represent only the outward movement of K^+. If 2, the outward movement of K^+, is subtracted from 1, 3 must be an inward movement of Na^+ that normally occurs when an unclamped axon is suspended in a sea-water solution and is depolarized by 57 mV. Again, the inward Na^+ current turns on and then turns off, despite the continued depolarization of the membrane, whereas the K^+ current continues.

Figure 3-9c shows the total flows of current through the membrane during an action potential. These flows were calculated by Hodgkin and Huxley on the basis of the current flows they observed during their membrane clamp experiments and on their mathematical theory of ionic events. The curve labeled I_i is the total change in membrane current during an action potential produced by a brief depolarizing stimulus applied to the membrane at time 0. Hodgkin and Huxley represented the later, outward flow of current as gradually ending when the membrane potential returned to normal. As the membrane potential returns to normal, membrane permeabilities should also return to normal, and the membrane would return to the state described by the Goldman equation.

Figure 3-9c also shows the separate K^+ and Na^+ currents that normally occur during an action potential. The curves labeled I_{K^+} and I_{Na^+} represent Hodgkin and Huxley's calculations for the changes in K^+ and Na^+ currents. The K^+ current is assumed to decrease gradually as the membrane potential returns to normal. This decrease would be expected, given the idea that the membrane is seeking the K^+ equilibrium potential during this hyperpolarization. As the membrane potential comes closer to the K^+ equilibrium potential, the driving force on K^+ will steadily decrease, and so the K^+ current would also be expected to decrease.

The shape of the Na^+ current curve deserves some special comment. The current first rapidly increases and then slightly decreases; then follows a slight increase before the final, slow decrease is seen. The first decrease occurs because at the height of the action potential the membrane potential is close to the equilibrium potential for Na^+ and the driving force on Na^+ has decreased. Then, as the membrane starts to repolarize (K^+ is beginning to flow rapidly out of the membrane), the membrane potential moves away from the Na^+ equilibrium potential, and the driving force on Na^+ once again increases,

temporarily increasing the Na^+ current. The explanation for the final decrease in the Na^+ current must be sought elsewhere, however. It occurs when the membrane is repolarizing and therefore the driving force on Na^+ should be steadily increasing, reaching its maximum during hyperpolarization.

All this research and theorizing and these calculations produced the curves presented in Figure 3-10. These curves describe what happens to the membrane after a brief but sufficiently depolarizing stimulus has occurred at time 0. The curve labeled E describes the changes in membrane potential. The membrane-potential curve represents the solution to Hodgkin and Huxley's theoretical equations derived to explain the action potential. That curve, and the other curves in this figure, were calculated by Huxley, using a mechanical calculator (Hodgkin, 1976). Such curves are now produced by computer simulations.

The curves labeled g_{K^+} and g_{Na^+} describe the changes in Na^+ and K^+ conductances as a function of the time elapsed since the depolarizing stimulus occurred. These conductance curves were calculated (again, laboriously by hand) from the version of Ohm's law described in the first part of this chapter. The calculations were based on the changes in membrane current observed after applying a depolarizing clamp (Figure 3-9c). These current values were then plugged into Ohm's law, along with the E_m values at various times after stimulation, to produce the conductance curves presented in Figure 3-10.

The voltage-clamp studies provided a detailed model for the nature and the timing of the permeability changes during an action potential. The initial response of the membrane to a threshold depolarization is a rapid increase in Na^+ conductance (or permeability). Next, Na^+ conductance declines at the same time that K^+ conductance is increasing. These changes in conductance therefore account for the initial inward Na^+ current that depolarizes the membrane and the subsequent outward K^+ current that repolarizes and then hyperpolarizes the membrane. These events are understood today in nearly the same way that Hodgkin and Huxley originally described them in 1952 (see Bezanilla & Armstrong, 1974).

Ionic poisons.   Three ionic poisons have been used to study action potentials. One poison is **TTX** or tetrodotoxin, a poison extracted from the ovary of a puffer fish. A second poison is **TEA,** or tetraethylammonium, which is an artificial poison. TTX attaches to and blocks the outside of the electrically gated Na^+ pore; TEA blocks the electrically gated K^+ pore. TTX seems "to enter the mouth of the sodium channel, where it sticks like a fat man caught halfway through a porthole, effectively plugging the channel" (Keynes, 1979, p. 129). The

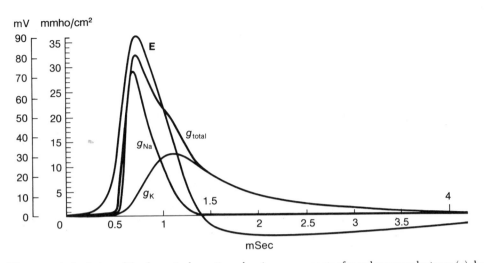

Figure 3-10 The numerical solution of the theoretical equations showing components of membrane conductance (g) during an action potential (E).

third poison is **pronase,** which attaches to the sodium channel inside the membrane. When pronase becomes so attached, the decrease in sodium permeabilities normally seen during continued depolarization no longer occurs (Armstrong, Bezanilla, & Rojas, 1973).

These poisons are applied to a stimulated nerve cell. Either the cell is voltage-clamped or the resulting changes in membrane potential are intracellularly recorded. When a TTX-poisoned nerve cell is stimulated, only K^+ current and a period of hyperpolarization are seen. When a TEA-poisoned nerve cell is stimulated, only Na^+ current is seen. In the presence of TEA, the cell depolarizes, but repolarization occurs very, very slowly (and presumably occurs because of something other than outward movement of K^+ ions). If axons have had pronase injected into them, once again the repolarization occurs much more slowly than it does in normal axons, suggesting that the decrease in sodium permeability is very important to repolarization.

A Detailed Description of Ion Movements

Knowledge of the ionic events occurring during the various phases of the action potential came from the types of experiments just described. The phases of the action potential are depolarization, repolarization, hyperpolarization, and recovery.

Depolarization. In the experiments described thus far, researchers applied a **suprathreshold** ("above" threshold) de-

polarizing electrical stimulus to the neuron membrane. In the normal actions of neurons, the threshold depolarizing stimulus is produced either by actions at the surface of a sensory receptor organ or by chemical actions across a synapse. But any type of stimulus that depolarizes a neural membrane to threshold will usually produce an action potential. Given that the stimulus is above threshold, the resulting action potential will have the same size, regardless of the size of the stimulus.

A threshold is defined both experimentally and conceptually. A 5 mV to 20 mV depolarization is often enough to trigger an action potential. However, the value of the threshold varies according to the conditions on both sides of the membrane. The **threshold** is the membrane potential at which $I_{Na^+} = I_{K^+} + I_{Cl^-}$. If the stimulus is going to trigger an action potential, it must depolarize the membrane past the threshold so that the depolarizing inward Na^+ current will be greater than the hyperpolarizing outward K^+ and inward Cl^- currents. If I_{Na^+} were less than $I_{K^+} + I_{Cl^-}$, the greater amount of hyperpolarizing K^+ and Cl^- currents would mean that the I_{Na^+} could not depolarize the membrane. Because the K^+ and Cl^- currents oppose the effects of any I_{Na^+} in the membrane potential, anything that affects I_{Cl^-} or I_{K^+} — such as changes in the K^+ or Cl^- equilibrium potentials or changes in K^+ or Cl^- permeability — will change the threshold.

Application of a suprathreshold stimulus to the membrane triggers the **Hodgkin cycle** (illustrated in Figure 3-11). First, some depolarizing stimulus increases membrane permeability to Na^+. Na^+ ions will begin to flow into the neuron, down their concentration and electrical gradients. The increase of positively charged Na$^+$ ions in the cell further depolarizes the membrane, which further increases the permeability of the membrane to Na$^+$, which further increases the inward I_{Na^+}. I_{Na^+} continues to increase until the driving force on Na$^+$ weakens (the membrane approaches the Na$^+$ equilibrium potential) and until the Na$^+$ permeability decreases, as described below.

Repolarization.   *Two* events are important for repolarization, at least in the squid giant axon: a decrease in permeability to Na$^+$ and an increase in permeability to K$^+$. Both of these events are caused by a depolarizing stimulus, just as is the case for the increase in Na$^+$ permeability. However, the events responsible for repolarization have a much slower time course than does the depolarization-induced increase in Na$^+$ permeability (see the curves in Figures 3-9 and 3-10).

The increase in K$^+$ permeability leads to an increased rate of movement of K$^+$ ions out of the cell, down their concentration and electrical gradients (the inside of the cell is now positively charged). At the peak of the action potential, the driving force working on K$^+$ ions is very large ($\approx |(+40) - (-90)|$). Any increase in K$^+$ permeability will quickly lead to an increase in I_{K^+}. The movement of positive ions out of the membrane will restore the membrane to its normal inside-negative state. The I_{K^+} continues until the membrane potential reaches the K$^+$ equilibrium potential, eliminating the driving force on K$^+$.

The depolarization-induced decrease in Na$^+$ permeability is **sodium inactivation.** When Na$^+$ pores are inactivated, the Na$^+$ ion will no longer go through. If there were no inactivation, any repolarizing effect of outward movement of K$^+$ would be opposed by an I_{Na^+}. Pronase destroys sodium inactivation and so greatly prolongs repolarization.

Both sodium inactivation and the increased K$^+$ permeability continue until the membrane is repolarized. The sodium inactivation accounts for the **absolute refractory period.** For a period of time after a depolarizing stimulus, no other depolarizing stimulus will be able to trigger an action potential. The membrane is temporarily refractory, or unexcitable. The membrane cannot be excited because the sodium pores have been inactivated and cannot be reopened by depolarization. Restoration of normal membrane potential (repolarization) is required to restore normal K$^+$ permeability and reactivate Na$^+$ pores. Because of the absolute refractory period, an action potential cannot reverse its direction in the middle of an axon. This inability is sometimes referred to as the **safety factor.**

Hyperpolarization.   During hyperpolarization, the permeability of the membrane to K$^+$ remains high (see Figure 3-10). As long as the membrane's permeability to K$^+$ continues to be higher than normal, the membrane potential will remain close to the K$^+$ equilibrium potential, as predicted by the Goldman and Ohm's equations. The membrane hyperpolarizes because although slightly more Na$^+$ ions entered than K$^+$ ions left during the action potential, some Cl$^-$ ions also entered (Caldwell & Keynes, 1960).

During hyperpolarization, the membrane is in a **relative refractory period.** (In Figures 3-9 and 3-10, the absolute refractory period fades gradually into the relative refractory period. Whether the membrane is in one state or the other is strictly a matter of degree.) The membrane is refractory for two reasons: (1) the membrane potential is further from the threshold and (2) the threshold has been increased. If a 5 mV depolarization, from -70 mV to -65 mV, is normally sufficient to trigger an action potential, then now that the membrane is around -80 mV, a larger depolarizing stimulus will be required. But even more important, the fact that the hyperpolarized membrane is now more permeable to K$^+$ than it is in the resting condition means that the threshold has been increased: even more depolarization will be required before the inward I_{Na^+} will be able to exceed the outward I_{K^+}.

Recovery of membrane potential and ion concentrations.   The membrane recovers its normal resting potential largely because K$^+$ permeability returns to its normal resting value. As this happens, the membrane potential will also return to normal because of the leakage of other ions. For example, some Cl$^-$ may leave because the hyperpolarized membrane is more negative than the Cl$^-$ equilibrium potential. By now, the Na$^+$ channels have all been reactivated and more Na$^+$ may enter. The membrane has now returned to normal permeabilities and voltage potentials.

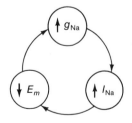

Figure 3-11   The Hodgkin cycle is responsible for the rapid depolarization occurring during the first phase of the action potential. Depolarization leads to an increase in Na$^+$ conductance, which leads to an inward Na$^+$ current, which leads to more depolarization—and so on.

The changes in Na^+ and K^+ concentrations remain after repolarization. For many larger neurons, these changes are negligibly small. But after repeated activity, or during activity in a smaller axon, these changes in concentrations would begin to affect resting and action potentials unless there were some mechanism present to restore concentrations to normal. This mechanism is the Na-K pump described earlier. As internal Na^+ and external K^+ increase, the pump increases its rate of activity, and so it restores ion concentrations to their normal levels.

But the pump is *not* required for normal action potentials to occur. Baker and his colleagues (Baker, Hodgkin & Shaw, 1961) removed the axoplasm of a giant squid axon and refilled it with various electrolytic solutions. Little if any pump activity could have remained after these procedures, and so obviously the pump is not required for the normal action potential. (However, in some cells, the pump may contribute to repolarization and hyperpolarization; see, for example, Padjen & Smith, 1983.)

Action Potentials in Other Types of Membranes

We have just described the action potentials of the squid giant axon. However, not all action potentials look alike. Action potentials in other parts of the nerve cell or in other species sometimes have distinctive differences from the squid's action potential because of having different membrane proteins (see Table 3-2).

Ca^{++} channels.   Only some parts of the nerve have fast, electrically gated Ca^{++} channels. Axons usually have only a very few of these channels. However, many of them are found in synaptic terminals (required for synaptic activity), in cell bodies (entry of Ca^{++} during neural activity regulates metabolic processes within the cell), and in some dendrites. Where present, these channels lead to distinctively shaped action potentials. Ca^{++} channels open at about the same time as do the K^+ channels, but because the Ca^{++} current is inward, down the concentration gradient of Ca^{++} ions, that current is depolarizing. The Ca^{++} current leads to a broader, more slowly depolarizing potential. In some cells, a Ca^{++} current can even produce a depolarizing "hump" in the repolarization phase and prolong repolarization (Adams, Smith, & Thompson, 1980; Barrett & Barrett, 1976; Harada & Takahashi, 1983; Horn & McAfee, 1979; Salkoff, 1983).

Some cells may have slow, electrically gated Ca^{++} channels. Brown and Griffith (1983a, 1983b) suggested that cell bodies in the hippocampus might have them. The prolonged depolarization associated with the channels could be responsible for the spontaneous, regular bursts of action potentials often observed in these cells.

Ca-activated K^+ channels.   Another kind of chemically gated channel can be found in some neuronal cell bodies and in muscle cell membranes. Internal Ca^{++} opens up a K^+ channel. Thus, if the membrane also has electrically gated Ca^{++} channels, the inrush of Ca^{++} during an action potential

Table 3-2   Some ion channels in active membrane.

Channel	How Activated	Location	Effect on E_m
Fast I_{Na}	Depolarization	All active membrane	Depolarizing
Fast I_K	Depolarization	All active membrane (except nodes of Ranvier?)	Repolarizing and hyperpolarizing
Fast I_{Ca}	Depolarization	Dendrites, cell bodies, axon terminals (e.g., dorsal root ganglion cells, hippocampus)	Depolarizing
Slow I_{Ca}	Depolarization	Cell bodies in dorsal root and hippocampus	Slow depolarization and repetitive discharge
Slow I_K (M-current)	Depolarization (blocked by muscarinic ACh action)	Cell bodies	Hyperpolarizing
Ca-activated I_K	By $[Ca]_i$	Cell bodies	Hyperpolarizing
Resting I_K	Active at resting potential (closed by serotonin)	Cell bodies and ????	Resting potential

(See text for references.)

will open the K$^+$ channels. Flow of current through these channels produces a negative potential that usually persists long after the action potential is completed (the **negative afterpotential**). If Ca^{++} is removed from the extracellular fluid, no Ca^{++} can enter, and the long-lasting negative afterpotential is eliminated (Adams, Smith, & Thompson, 1980; Barrett & Barrett, 1976; Harada & Takahashi, 1983; Krnjević, Puil, & Werman, 1978; McAfee & Yarowsky, 1979; Salkoff, 1983). This channel can also be blocked by TEA in some but *not* all neurons (MacDermott & Weight, 1982; Meech & Standen, 1975).

Ca-activated K$^+$ channels may have even more unusual properties, at least in some neuron terminals, dendrites, and cell bodies. They may also be affected by transmitter substances, making them both electrically and chemically gated. The transmitter may have an indirect effect by working on the Ca^{++} channel (Horn & McAfee, 1980) or may operate directly on the Ca-activated K$^+$ channel itself (Kehoe & Marty, 1980).

Other K$^+$ channels.   In addition to the fast, repolarizing I_K and the Ca-activated I_K, there are at least two other types of potassium channels. Because sensory and motor axons have different numbers of these channels, they respond differently to a sustained depolarizing stimulus. Sensory fibers with many K$^+$ channels fire repetitively, whereas motor fibers with only a few fire only once (Dubois, 1983).

A slow I_K was first discovered in the cell bodies of frog sympathetic ganglia (Brown & Adams, 1980). It has since been found in several other neuronal membranes (Nowak & Macdonald, 1983). This channel produces the **M-current,** which flows through a depolarization-opened K$^+$ channel, but much more slowly than does the K$^+$ current responsible for repolarization. Furthermore, as Table 3-2 indicates, the M-current can also be affected by transmitter substances: the M-current is blocked in the presence of the transmitter substance **acetylcholine (ACh).** The function of the M-current may be to control excitability and to suppress "bursting," or the clustering of action potentials (Simmons, 1985).

A third type of K$^+$ channel, found in *Aplysia* (sea snail), is open at resting membrane potentials. It is affected only slightly by changes in membrane potentials, but it is closed by another transmitter substance, **serotonin** (5-hydroxytryptamine, or **5-HT**) (Camardo, Klein, & Kandel, 1981; Siegelbaum, Camardo, & Kandel, 1982).

The effect of the pump on small axons.   Sometimes the pump contributes to changes in potential. A burst of neural activity occurring simultaneously in many small, unmyelinated axons running close together in the same nerve trunk can produce significant changes in ion concentrations inside and outside the membranes. These changes cause the Na-K pump to increase its rate of activity. Since the pump is electrogenic, the increased rate of pumping activity can sometimes be seen as a long-lasting hyperpolarization or still another kind of negative afterpotential (see, for example, Padjen & Smith, 1983). The negative afterpotential can be as great as 35 mV and can last for several minutes.

Spinal versus cortical cells.   One way to illustrate variations in action potentials is to contrast mammalian spinal cells with cortical cells. Motoneurons in the spinal cord typically have extensive, long-lasting hyperpolarizations that increase the relative refractory period and decrease the frequency of firing. The membrane of these spinal neurons has the Ca-activated K$^+$ channel. Many cortical cells lack that channel and thus have much shorter negative afterpotentials. The dendrites of spinal cells lack all electrically gated channels, but—at least in pyramidal cells—cortical dendrites can have "patches" of membrane with electrically gated Ca^{++} channels. These channels may act to increase or "boost" depolarizing or excitatory synaptic input, facilitating the spread of depolarization to the axon hillock. Action potentials recorded in the cell bodies of these cortical cells will often show depolarizing humps because the depolarization caused by dendritic Ca^{++} currents spreads to the cell body.

Changing Ideas about the Electrically Gated Ionic Channels

What causes the electrically produced changes in membrane permeability? We include some details about the nature of the most frequently studied electrically gated channels, the "fast" Na$^+$ and K$^+$ channels (see Table 3-2).

Gating currents.   Hodgkin and Huxley (1952d) originally proposed that movement of electrically charged protein molecules in the membrane caused the changes in permeability by opening and closing channels in the membrane. As the charge across the membrane changed, the orientation of these charged particles in the membrane also changed. If this were true, it should be possible to record electrically the movement of the charged particles in the membrane. The physical movement of the particles would mean that an electrical charge would not be closer to one side or the other than it had been before the shift, as Figure 3-12 illustrates. However, Hodgkin and Huxley's techniques could not reveal these electrical changes. The changes in potential produced by such movements of charged particles in the membrane were swamped by the much greater electrical changes produced by the **ionic current,** or the physical movement of ions, through membrane pores.

Later researchers were able to record the movement of charged membrane particles by eliminating ionic currents. If the Na^+ channels were blocked by TTX, the electrical changes produced by the movements of charged particles could be seen (Armstrong & Bezanilla, 1977; Keynes, 1979). These electrical changes are the **gating currents.** K^+ gating currents could be recorded only after blocking not only membrane currents but also the Na^+ gating currents. Na^+ gating currents were blocked by clamping the membrane at a slightly depolarized value (which inactivated some of the Na^+ channels) and by perfusing the squid giant axon with dibucaine (a local anesthetic) (White & Bezanilla, 1985).

The Na^+ channel.   The nature of the Na^+ channel has been explored by voltage clamps and blocking agents such as TTX and pronase. Like other channels, the Na^+ channel is probably a large protein molecule transversing the membrane. The selectivity of the Na^+ channel may be created by a narrowing of the channel close to the mouth at the outside edge. Further selectivity is created by negatively charged particles lining the channel. The gating processes evidently occur below these particles.

The number of Na^+ channels varies from cell to cell and from one location to another in the same cell. Some neurons in cold-blooded animals may have only about 3 to 13 Na^+ channels per square micrometer of membrane, whereas the giant squid axon has as many as 500 per square micrometer. Only the parts of nerve cells able to develop an action potential have electrically gated Na^+ channels. These channels may not

often be found in dendrites and they may be especially numerous in the nodes of Ranvier (between the myelinated regions of an axon) and in the axon hillock (Catterall, 1984). The density of Na^+ channels determines how many Na^+ ions will enter a patch of membrane during an action potential. Each channel can conduct as many as 100 Na^+ ions per impulse (Keynes, 1979), which means that enough Na^+ ions enter during an action potential to produce the observed change in the membrane potential.

The Na^+ channel can exist in several states. The exact number and type of states is still controversial (Armstrong & Bezanilla, 1977; Bezanilla & Armstrong, 1974, 1977; Chandler & Meves, 1970; Chiu, 1977; Edwards, 1982; Goldman, 1976; Hille, 1978). Three states that have to exist are the closed resting state in which depolarization can open the channel, the open state produced by depolarization, and the closed state called **inactivation** also produced by depolarization (see Figure 3-12). However, some researchers believe that the complexity of the shape of the curve describing the change in voltage over time when TTX and pronase are present indicates that even more states may exist.

The K^+ channel.   Much less is known about the K^+ channel. The K^+ channel may also be inactivated during depolarizations, which may have to last much longer than a normal action potential ever would (Ehrenstein & Gilbert, 1966; Stevens, 1977). Each K^+ channel may be only half as permeable to K^+ as the Na^+ channel is to Na^+ (Stevens, 1977).

The number of electrically gated K^+ channels varies from cell to cell and from one area to another. First, cell membranes that have both electrically gated Na^+ and K^+ channels may have only one K^+ channel for every ten Na^+ channels. Furthermore, the K^+ channel may not exist at the nodes of Ran-

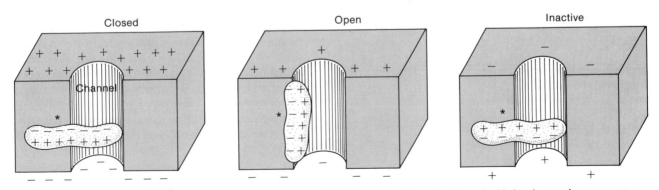

Figure 3-12   One model of how changes in membrane potential might cause protein molecules embedded in the membrane to rotate around a pivotal point (*) located on one side of a channel. The orientation of the charged particle acts as a gate that admits ions or prevents them from passing through the membrane.

vier in mammals (Kaars & Faber, 1981; Kocsis & Waxman, 1980). In these nodes, repolarization may be caused by Na$^+$ inactivation and by the movements of K$^+$ and Cl$^-$ through their leakage channels (Chiu, Ritchie, Rogart, & Stagg, 1979). However, oddly enough, the electrically gated K$^+$ channels appear to exist underneath the myelin—a place in which they could not affect membrane potentials, since no current can flow through myelin.

Summary of the Active Membrane

All that is needed for an action potential is a membrane with electrically gated channels and both concentration and electrical forces. These factors have been explored by using radioactive tracers, varying ionic concentrations, applying the voltage-clamp technique, and injecting ionic poisons.

The threshold of an axonal membrane is the potential at which the inward I_{Na^+} is equal to the outward I_{K^+} plus the inward I_{Cl^-}. If the depolarizing stimulus crosses that threshold by sufficiently increasing the permeability of the membrane to Na$^+$ with respect to its permeability to K$^+$, the I_{Na^+} can further depolarize the membrane. This change increases Na$^+$ permeability, which increases the inward, depolarizing I_{Na^+}. Depolarization also, but more slowly, increases K$^+$ permeability and eventually inactivates the Na$^+$ channel. Na$^+$ inactivation and the outward movement of K$^+$ ions through the K$^+$ channel cause repolarization and then hyperpolarization. As the membrane repolarizes, the Na$^+$ channels slowly become reactivated and the K$^+$ permeabilities return to normal. Thus, the membrane potential returns to normal voltage and to normal excitability. On a much slower time scale, the Na-K pump restores normal ion concentrations.

Other kinds of channels are also found in different species and in different areas on the same nerve cells. They can produce action potentials that look very different from those recorded in the squid giant axon.

Propagation of Action Potentials

This section describes how an action potential moves down the axon and what factors affect how fast that movement can occur.

The Nature of Propagation

Propagation refers to the movement of an action potential from one area to another on the neural membrane. Movement depends on the ability of an active (depolarized) area of the membrane to excite adjacent areas of the membrane (see Figure 3-13). Since the active membrane area is negative on the inside in relation to the outside, differences in electrical potential exist between the active area and the adjacent areas of the membrane. Positive ions will therefore tend to move from the active area to adjacent inactive areas, and negative ions will tend to move from the inactive areas to the active area. Both currents will reduce the potential difference across membrane areas adjacent to the active area, depolarizing them. When these adjacent areas are depolarized past threshold, an action potential will be generated on either side of the original active area. By this process, the action potential will move away in both directions from the point of initial stimulation.

Once this happens, the action potentials cannot reverse their direction and "go back the way they came." When an action potential has begun traveling down the membrane, the patch of membrane it just left will be first absolutely and then relatively refractory. Since these areas are temporarily unable to generate another action potential, the action potential, once generated, moves in only one direction (the safety factor).

The distinction between capacitive current and ionic (or ohmian) current is important to an understanding of propagation. **Capacitive current** changes the charge on the membrane capacitor, just as a capacitor becomes charged or discharged in an electrical circuit. **Ohmian current** is the actual movement of charges through space. In the nervous system, ohmian or ionic current is carried by the physical movement of ions. Ionic current includes the movement of charges laterally through the axoplasm and extracellular fluid, as well as the movement of charges through membrane pores.

An active area of membrane depolarizes adjacent areas of the membrane by changing capacitive charges across those membrane areas. Similarly, an electrical stimulus first changes the charge on the membrane capacitor, or depolarizes the membrane capacitor, before any ionic current through the membrane can occur. The initial parts of the curves in Figure 3-9 consist of capacitive and not ionic currents—these artificially produced capacitive currents were ignored in Hodgkin and Huxley's model of ionic currents during an action potential. Until now, we have discussed mostly ionic currents, but how fast an action potential can travel is determined largely by the rate at which capacitive charges across the membrane can be changed.

Factors Affecting the Rate of Propagation

Characteristics of the membrane called *cable properties* affect the rate of propagation, or how fast the action potential will

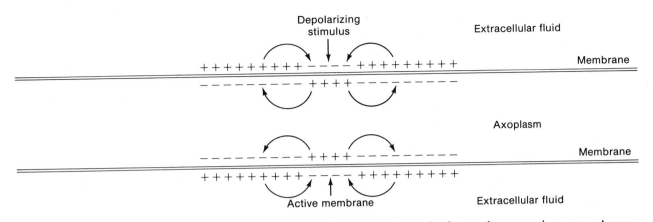

Figure 3-13 An action potential moves down the membrane. The active membrane depolarizes adjacent membrane areas. Arrows indicate the direction of cation movement; anions would move in the opposite direction. Movement of both types of ions is depolarizing to adjacent areas.

travel down the membrane. Size and myelin are the properties most important to propagation.

Size and shape of the neuron.   **Cable properties** are the electrical properties that an axon shares with an electrical cable submerged on the ocean floor. Cable properties are determined by the physical nature of the neuron, such as its diameter and whether it is myelinated. The cable properties describe how electrical forces such as resistance and capacitance affect the spread of potential changes down the membrane "cable." Here, an axon should be visualized as a long, narrow cylinder. Current can flow both down the cylinder (in the axoplasm) and through the extracellular fluid.

Some cable properties are illustrated in Figure 3-14. If an electrical stimulus is applied to a given point on a membrane (or on a cable), the electrical field generated will extend in both directions down the membrane. Suppose that the membrane has no electrically gated pores (as many dendrites have not) and that the electrical stimulus has been applied until conditions have become stable (no more change in membrane capacitive charge is occurring and all the current is ionic). How far the change in electrical potential will spread passively from the site of stimulation is determined by the **length constant** of a membrane or a cable. The greater the length constant, the further the change in electrical potential will spread down a membrane. The greater the length constant of a membrane with electrically gated pores, the faster the action potential will travel.

The length constant of a membrane is determined by the size of the axonal cylinder and by the insulative properties of the membrane. The greater the size of the cylinder (the greater the cross-sectional area of the axoplasm), the lower the resistance of the axoplasm to longitudinal spread of current. The greater the size of the cylinder, the greater the length constant and the faster the action potential will travel. The better insulated the membrane is (the fewer pores it has or the more myelin), the greater the length constant.

The time required for an active area of membrane to depolarize adjacent areas is determined by the **time constant** of the membrane. The time constant is related to the capacitive properties of the membrane: the time constant of a capacitor is two-thirds of the total time required to completely charge or to discharge a capacitor of that size (see Chapter 2). Therefore the time constant of the membrane is directly related to its capacitance and also to the resistance through which the ionic current has to flow to change the capacitive charge. Here

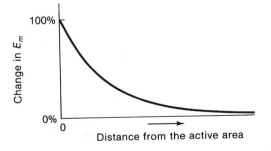

Figure 3-14 One of the cable properties of the membrane is the length constant. The further from the active area a given patch of membrane is, the less change there will be in its membrane potential. Larger axons have greater length constants.

again, the current flows longitudinally through the axoplasm and the extracellular fluid. The axoplasm's resistance decreases as a function of the square of the diameter of the axonal cylinder.

In contrast, the size of a capacitor increases as a direct function of the size of the cylinder. The larger the cylinder, the larger the plates of the capacitor, and the larger the capacitor is. Since resistance decreases with the square and capacitance increases only as a direct function of cylinder size, larger neurons—despite having more capacitance—still have a smaller time constant and so a faster rate of propagation.

The importance of axonal size is demonstrated by the squid with its giant axon. This largest of all known axons has the greatest rate of propagation of any nonmyelinated axon, a circumstance that is useful to the squid, for this large axon controls the muscles it needs to get away from its enemies.

Characteristics of the membrane. The major membrane characteristic affecting rate of propagation is its permeability, including both leakage and electrically gated channels. The more leakage channels a membrane has, the smaller its length constant will be. However, the more electrically gated Na^+ channels the membrane has per unit area, the more rapidly capacitive current can be changed into ionic current, which flows through the membrane. This relationship means that the action potential will be conducted more rapidly from one point to another. The numerous Na^+ channels found in the axon hillock give this part of the membrane a comparatively low threshold, which explains why action potentials are often generated here first.

Presence of myelin. Higher vertebrates have myelin to speed up propagation, saving both space and energy. The saving in space is truly impressive, as pointed out by Morell and Norton (1980, p. 88): "At a mammalian body temperature of 37 degrees Celsius an unmyelinated fiber would have to be several millimeters in diameter to conduct at the speed (100 meters per second) of a myelinated fiber only 20 microns, or a fiftieth of a millimeter, in diameter. To put it another way, if the human spinal cord contained only bare [unmyelinated] nerve fibers, it would have to be several yards in diameter to maintain its conduction velocities." Morell and Norton went on to describe the savings in energy. "In a frog a myelinated nerve fiber 12 microns in diameter conducts signals at a velocity of 25 meters per second. So does the unmyelinated giant axon of the squid, but it is 500 microns in diameter and uses 5,000 times as much energy."

In a myelinated axon (see Figure 3-15), only capacitive current flows across the membrane between the nodes of Ranvier (changing the charge on the membrane capacitor). In other words, ionic current can flow only at the nodes. Because myelin greatly increases the electrical resistance of the membrane, it increases the length constant and decreases the time constant of the membrane. The increase in the length constant means that the effect of a reversed membrane potential (during the action potential) will spread further down the axon, leading to a faster change in the charge at the next node. The increase in resistance also decreases membrane capacitance between the nodes, in turn decreasing the time constant. Under these circumstances, membrane capacitance between the nodes can change very rapidly.

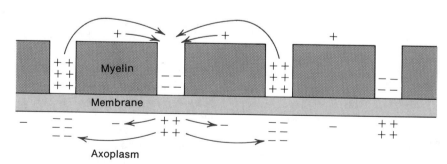

Figure 3-15 Myelin produces **saltatory conduction** in nerve membranes. The action potential "jumps" (*saltare* is Latin for "to dance") from node to node, meaning that ionic current flows through the membrane only at the nodes and then only after they have been depolarized past threshold by the longitudinal currents.

The savings in space and energy produced by the myelin come from these properties. Myelination increases the rate of conduction far more effectively per unit of space than can increasing the size of the nerve cell itself. And since ionic and leakage currents flow only at the nodes, the membrane Na-K pump must work only at the nodes. Thus, a myelinated axon can get by with far fewer pumps than it would need otherwise, and pumps are the greatest consumers of energy in neurons.

These properties of myelin may be able to explain what happens in multiple sclerosis, which spares nerve cells but destroys myelin. This effect would greatly reduce the rate of propagation of nerve cells and may contribute to the symptoms of the disease, which include visual problems, muscle weakness, lack of coordination, and spasticity. Myelin degenerates as the disease progresses. Axons first stop and then start conducting again — but this time more slowly, because there is no more myelin. The decaying myelin forms hardened plaques that eventually and permanently stop neural conduction. This sequence of stages explains why sufferers have periods of reduced symptoms, followed by stages of ever-increasing disability.

Summary of Propagation

The propagation of action potentials down an axon can be explained by the physical and electrical properties of the nerve cell. An active area of the membrane causes ionic currents to flow (positive ions from and negative ions toward that region) through the extracellular fluid and through the axoplasm. The larger the axon, the less resistance there is to this flow, and so an active area of a larger cell can depolarize adjacent membrane areas faster. Furthermore, the more Na^+ pores there are, the faster the impulse will travel. But the most important factor in speed is myelin: myelination greatly decreases membrane capacitance and so greatly speeds the rate of propagation. Not so incidentally, myelin also decreases the number of pumps a nerve cell needs, saving not only space but energy as well.

Chapter Summary

The Resting and Active Nerve Membrane

By virtue of the properties of the resting and active nerve membrane, which allow resting and action potentials, a neuron is specialized to conduct information from one point to another. All that is needed is (1) differences in concentration across the membrane, (2) an electrical potential across the membrane, and (3) electrically gated channels in the membrane.

The resting membrane has capacitive and ohmian properties. The membrane potential is negative on the inside by -40 mV to -90 mV. The membrane separates two solutions with different ion concentrations. Outside the membrane there are relatively large amounts of Na^+, Ca^{++}, and Cl^- ions and relatively few K^+ ions. Inside the nerve are far fewer Na^+, Ca^{++}, and Cl^- ions but many more K^+ ions. The resting membrane does not have perfect electrical resistance (hence its ohmian properties, or its being a leaky capacitor): it has leakage channels. There are fewer Na^+ than K^+ (and often Cl^-) leakage channels (and some of them may simply be electrically gated channels that are open at the resting potential).

The resting membrane potential depends on ratios of ion concentrations and on the permeability of the membrane. Here are the answers to the questions asked in the subsection entitled **Current flows and permeabilities.** Increasing the amount of Na^+ outside the membrane will tend to depolarize the membrane. Because the concentration forces working to push Na^+ in are increased — the E_{Na^+} is increased — some Na^+ will come in to depolarize the membrane. Increasing the amount of K^+ outside the cell will also depolarize the membrane because the decrease in E_{K^+} will decrease the concentration forces, causing K^+ to leak out steadily. With less K^+ leakage (or if the concentration outside the membrane is high enough, with some K^+ coming into the cell), the number of positive ions inside the membrane will increase. The changes in membrane potential produced by changes in Na^+ and K^+ permeability normally occur during the depolarization and repolarization phases of the action potential.

The action potential can be explained by the properties of the resting membrane. If the membrane becomes depolarized (because of an electrical or a chemical stimulus), electrically gated Na^+ channels begin to open. Then Na^+ ions start rushing into the nerve because of the forces provided by the electrical potential difference and the difference in concentration of Na^+ ions across the membrane. The entry of Na^+ ions into the nerve depolarizes the membrane and reverses the membrane potential. During this time, K^+ channels begin to open, and K^+ ions begin to leave the membrane because of the electrical and concentration forces working on the K^+ ion. The movement of K^+ ions out of the membrane acts first to repolarize and then to hyperpolarize the membrane potential. When the electrically gated channels return to their normal resting state, the membrane potential also returns to its normal resting level. The reversal of charges during the action potential causes the active area of the membrane to stimulate or to depolarize adjacent areas. This process is speeded up by increasing the size of the cell and by the presence of myelin.

The Na-K pump accounts for most of the energy used by the nerve cell. However, in most cells, the actions of the pump have little if any effect on the changes of membrane potential that occur during an action potential. Instead, the pump acts to oppose the constant leakage of ions across the membrane and to restore ion concentrations after activity by pumping Na^+ to the outside and K^+ to the inside. The presence of myelin also saves energy for nerve cells by reducing the number of pumps needed.

Later chapters discuss how action potentials are stimulated (or inhibited) outside a neurophysiologist's laboratory. The next chapter describes one normal mechanism of stimulation — the chemical events occurring at synapses.

C H A P T E R

The Nerve-Cell Synapse

Nerve cells communicate across synapses. Our thoughts must involve sequential activation of different sets of nerve cells — all by means of the synapses between them. A nerve cell can receive synaptic information from thousands of other cells. In turn, each cell can make contact with thousands of other different cells. The patterns of synaptic interconnections among neurons — the circuitry of the brain — determine the ways in which information is coded by the brain. Synapses also change the pattern of neural activity being communicated; each successive set of synapses in a sensory or motor pathway may translate the information it receives into a different kind of code.

Overview

Since most synapses in the mammalian brain are chemical, this chapter discusses only chemical synapses. If at any time you feel confused by the details of synaptic activity described later, you should return to this overview. The chapter describes synaptic events in detail, starting with presynaptic events and proceeding to the postsynaptic events found in two types of synapses. Next it discusses various synaptic elements, including brain circuitry, chemical transmitter substances, and the ways in which past activity can change a chemical synapse.

Synaptic Events

Synaptic events are illustrated in Figure 4-1. First, an action potential invades the presynaptic membrane, which can be part of the axon, cell body, or dendrites of the presynaptic cell. When the action potential invades the presynaptic membrane area, the depolarization increases the membrane's permeability to Ca^{++} as well as to Na^+ and (subsequently) to K^+. Ca^{++} rushes into the presynaptic cell, down its concentration gradient, causing the presynaptic cell to release some substance into the synaptic cleft. The mechanisms by which that substance is released from the presynaptic cell seem to be similar in all cells.

The presynaptic cell releases a **transmitter substance.** Different cells in different parts of the nervous system release different transmitter substances. Molecules of transmitter substance are probably stored in synaptic vesicles, the round or oval structures in the presynaptic cell. Some researchers believe that when the action potential increases Ca^{++} inside the presynaptic cell, it causes one or more of the synaptic vesicles to move to the inside of the presynaptic membrane, fuse to the membrane, and release their contents into the synaptic cleft. Once released, the molecules of the transmitter substance passively diffuse across the synaptic cleft to the postsynaptic membrane.

Transmitter substances have different kinds of effects, depending on what kinds of receptor are found in the postsynaptic membrane. The same transmitter substance can be excitatory at some synapses and inhibitory at other synapses, which means that different **receptor proteins** are present on different postsynaptic cells. A molecule of transmitter substance will be "recognized" by and will temporarily combine with one of the molecules of the receptor protein, which has sections extending out of the postsynaptic membrane for that purpose. Each type of receptor protein will preferentially recognize or combine with one type of transmitter substance more than any other type of transmitter, and each type of receptor produces a certain type of change in the postsynaptic cell.

Comparisons among Synaptic and Action Potentials

Synaptic transmission of information systematically differs from the transmission of information down an axon because a synapse *transforms* neural activity. In the following discussion, postsynaptic potentials will be compared with action potentials. A **postsynaptic potential** is a change in the membrane potential of the postsynaptic cell produced by the transmitter substance.

1. *A synapse is unidirectional.* If part of the membrane is depolarized to threshold, a regenerative action potential can be conducted in both directions away from the point of stimulation. A chemical synapse is unidirectional: information goes from presynaptic cell to postsynaptic cell and not vice versa. This is not to say, however, that the postsynaptic cell has no effect on the presynaptic cell. In fact, the effects that postsynaptic events have on the presynaptic cell allow the synapse to be changed by its previous activity.

2. *Synaptic events can either depolarize or hyperpolarize the postsynaptic cell.* An action potential always has the same form and appearance as long as the stimulus producing the action potential is above threshold. But electrical activity in the presynaptic cell can either depolarize (excite) or hyperpolarize (inhibit) the activity of the postsynaptic cell. The depolarizing postsynaptic potentials are called **excitatory postsynaptic potentials,** or **epsps.** Hyperpolarizing potentials are **inhibitory postsynaptic potentials,** or **ipsps.**

3. *A synapse changes the pattern of electrical activity.* As long as the cell is healthy and the rate at which it is being stimulated does not exceed its absolute refractory period, the pattern of action potentials created on the cell membrane will faithfully mimic the pattern of stimulations. This is not the case for the synapse. The postsynaptic distribution of action potentials in time can be very different from the pattern that occurred in the presynaptic cell.

4. *Synapses insert delays into the transmission of information.* An action potential is completed in 2 to 4 milliseconds (mSec), and it can travel extremely rapidly, whereas in chemical synapses, events take place comparatively slowly. In a chemical synapse, the space between the presynaptic and postsynaptic membranes varies from 150 (nerve–nerve synapses) to 500 (nerve–muscle synapses) angstroms wide. Even "fast" synaptic events may take 0.5 mSec for the transmitter to be secreted and for it to diffuse across the gap to the postsynaptic

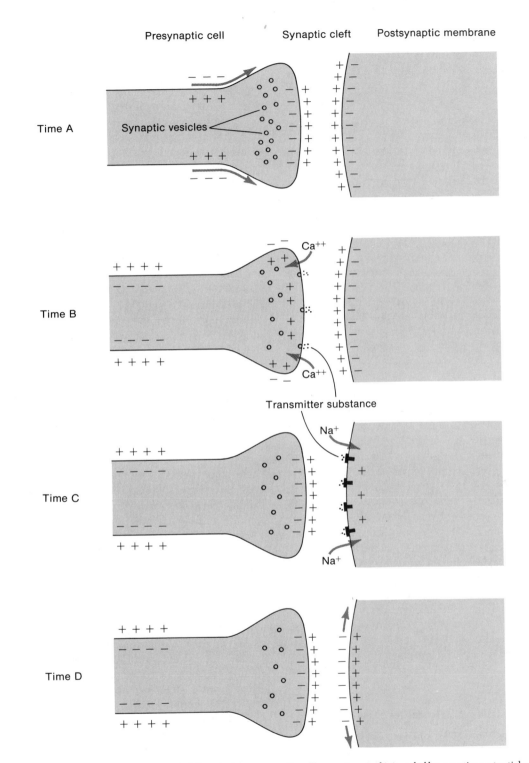

Figure 4-1 Four phases of a synaptic event. At Time A, the presynaptic cell's axon terminal is invaded by an action potential, as indicated by the arrows and the reversal of charges across the membrane. The presynaptic cell releases a transmitter substance (Time B), which diffuses across the synaptic cleft (Time C). At Time D, an action potential is conducted in both directions away from the postsynaptic area, as indicated by the arrows.

cell. In that same time, an action potential can have traveled more than 12 millimeters, or 250,000 to 625,000 times as far. Some synapses are even slower, taking many minutes to develop fully.

5. *Synapses are blocked by different agents.* Action potentials can be blocked by ionic poisons such as TTX, whereas the effects of the transmitter on the postsynaptic cell are blocked by agents specific to a particular receptor protein. For example, synapses that have a certain kind of acetylcholine (ACh) receptor can be blocked by curare. (Curare is based on a poison discovered by Native South Americans. It blocks the types of synapses found between neurons and skeletal muscles and so paralyzes the organism.)

6. *Synapses are subject to changes over time.* The size of the action potential is constant, but postsynaptic potentials vary in size. If the stimulation is above threshold, and if the time between stimulations is longer than the absolute refractory period, action potentials can be generated repeatedly. Each action potential will have the same shape and size as preceding potentials (though in very small axons, the change in internal and external ion concentrations could eventually change the potential). In contrast, synaptic potentials can be temporarily decreased by repeated stimulations, especially high-frequency stimulations that cause **fatigue.** But with different parameters of stimulation, repeated stimulations will temporarily increase the size of the postsynaptic potentials.

7. *Synaptic potentials are graded.* Action potentials are all-or-none types of events, but the size of the postsynaptic potentials, and the number of action potentials generated in the postsynaptic cell when a depolarizing stimulus exceeds the threshold, depend on the timing and the number of presynaptic events. If the stimulus to the axon is above threshold, an action potential is always generated. But a single presynaptic action potential is seldom enough to produce an action potential in the postsynaptic cell. Instead, several presynaptic action potentials occurring in a given period of time can have a summative effect on the postsynaptic membrane, called **temporal summation.** Whereas action potentials are all-or-none, synaptic potentials are **graded.** (In computer language, action potentials are digital events and synaptic potentials are analog events.)

Types of Effects of Transmitter Substances

There are four *types* of effects (discovered so far) that the transmitter substance can have on the postsynaptic membrane.

1. *Controlling chemically gated channels.* The simplest synapse involves chemically gated channels. When the transmitter substance combines with a receptor protein, specialized channels or pores in the postsynaptic membrane are opened. In many excitatory synapses, the transmitter will open Na^+ channels. Or the transmitter substance may *close* channels. The type of channel affected—for example, Na^+ versus K^+—determines the effect on the postsynaptic membrane.

2. *Effects of neuromodulators.* More than one type of transmitter substance may be released at a synapse by the same presynaptic nerve. One of these substances will often be a **neuromodulator,** which affects the way the postsynaptic membrane responds to the "true" transmitter. The neuromodulator may facilitate or inhibit the effect of the "true" transmitter, as by changing the way a transmitter binds to its receptor.

3. *Controlling electrically gated channels.* Some channels are both electrically and chemically gated (Chapter 3). The transmitter substance can modulate the electrical response of the postsynaptic membrane to other types of synaptic input. This type of effect may be important to the sophisticated ways in which synapses encode and transform information.

4. *Changing the rate of the Na-K pump.* The Na-K pump is electrogenic. If the transmitter substance affected the enzymes controlling the rate at which the pump worked, the transmitter substance could change membrane potential without having any effect on membrane permeability.

Techniques of Study

Many of the methods used to study action potentials have also been used to study synaptic potentials. Researchers manipulate internal and external ion concentrations to study the nature of synaptic ionic events. For example, if the transmitter substance increased the permeability of the postsynaptic membrane to K^+, changing the concentrations of K^+ inside or outside the membrane would change the size of the postsynaptic potential. The voltage-clamp technique had to be adapted to the size of mammalian cell bodies, which are considerably smaller than the squid axon (Eccles, 1973/1977). Instead of two separate electrodes, a single microelectrode is usually inserted into the cell body. It contains two separate channels or barrels, which can be activated separately for either stimulation or recording. Other researchers have inserted electrodes into both the presynaptic and the postsynaptic cell (Faber & Korn, 1982; Korn, Mallet, Triller, & Faber, 1982; Triller & Korn, 1982). The detailed timing of the presynaptic and postsynaptic electrical changes can then be simultaneously measured.

Microiontophoresis has been used extensively to study synapses. Passing charged ions out through a tiny, hollow glass electrode causes very small amounts of some chemical to be deposited around the tip. If the tip faces the postsynaptic membrane, tiny amounts of a chemical hypothesized to be the transmitter substance can be deposited on the postsynaptic membrane to see if the effects are similar to those produced by presynaptic stimulation. Either substances that act like or facilitate the supposed transmitter, the **agonists,** or substances that block or decrease the supposed transmitter, the **antagonists,** can be deposited on the postsynaptic membrane.

Rapid progress in microscopic techniques has provided fascinating new information. Two views of presynaptic and postsynaptic membranes seen through an electron microscope are presented in Figure 4-2. In an exciting new technique, a synapse during various stages of stimulation can be flash-frozen and then broken apart in a vacuum. The membranes tend to split in half in such a way that either the top layer of the presynaptic cell membrane can be viewed from the inside (the **P face**) or the bottom layer of the postsynaptic cell membrane can be viewed from the outside (the **E face**). The membrane can then be examined under an electron microscope (see, for example, Figure 4-5).

Summary of Overview

To find out how a transmitter substance is released from the presynaptic cell, researchers have manipulated ion concentrations, particularly extracellular concentrations of Ca^{++}, and have inserted electrodes inside the presynaptic cell. The molecules of transmitter substance carry the information from the presynaptic cell to the postsynaptic cell. By using the voltage-clamp technique and by manipulating ion concentrations, researchers have found out why some synapses are hyperpolarizing and some are depolarizing. In addition, the microiontophoretic applications of various substances onto the postsynaptic membrane have provided evidence about which transmitter substances might be used at which synapses.

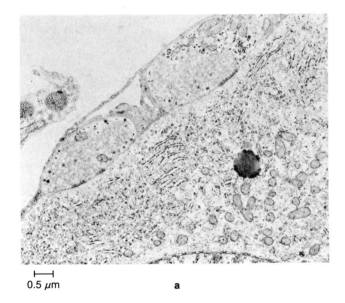

0.5 μm   **a**

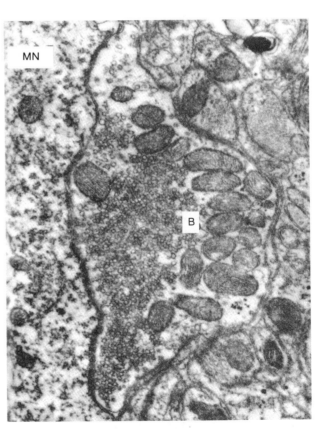

b

Figure 4-2   Two views of a synapse as seen through an electron microscope.   **a.** A ganglion cell with the outlines of two synaptic boutons separated by a triangular depression, which is bridged by a thin Schwann-cell covering.   **b.** A large bouton (B) or axon terminal forms a synapse with the surface of a motoneuron (MN).

Presynaptic Events

Although different kinds of postsynaptic events occur in different synapses, presynaptic events are very similar. This section describes the events occurring between the depolarization of the presynaptic nerve terminal membrane and the release of transmitter molecules into the synaptic cleft.

Molecular Events Preceding Transmitter Release

Obviously, having an action potential invade the presynaptic nerve terminal leads to the release of transmitter substance. However, it is not so obvious just what about that action potential causes this to happen.

Changes in Na^+ and K^+ are not necessary. Katz and Miledi (1967a) used the axoaxonic giant synapse in the squid to study presynaptic events. They dissected it out and implanted one or more microelectrodes within the presynaptic neuron for stimulation and for microiontophoretic injections of various substances. Another microelectrode was implanted first in or near the postsynaptic membrane and then in or near the presynaptic cell to record alternately the presynaptic and postsynaptic potentials.

To study the role of Na^+ and K^+, Katz and Miledi added either TEA or TTX to the solution perfusing the giant synapse. As TTX gradually took effect, the size of the presynaptic action potential triggered by above-threshold presynaptic depolarizations gradually decreased. The size of the postsynaptic depolarization also decreased. However, Katz and Miledi found that the inrush of Na^+ was not necessary for release of the transmitter substance. When they increased the size of the presynaptic depolarizing stimulus, the size of the postsynaptic potential also increased. This happened even though Na^+ currents had now been completely eliminated by the TTX (the depolarization here is supplied solely by the experimenters' presynaptic electrode). When TEA was used to block g_{K^+}, the presynaptic action potential was prolonged, but once again transmitter substance was still released.

The inrush of Ca^{++} is necessary for transmitter release. Katz and Miledi (1967a, 1967b) showed that depolarization increased the permeability of the membrane to Ca^{++}. The increase in $g_{Ca^{++}}$ during an action potential allows Ca^{++} to rush in, down its concentration gradient. This inrush of Ca^{++} *is* necessary for the release of transmitter substance. Increasing the external concentration of Ca^{++} increases transmitter release. A brief iontophoretic injection of Ca^{++} facili-

tates transmitter release as long as the injection occurs just before the presynaptic depolarization.

Other treatments that change Ca^{++} also affect transmitter secretion in predictable fashions. For example, magnesium interferes with Ca^{++}'s ability to combine with other molecules, whereas manganese blocks Ca^{++} channels in nerve membranes. Katz and Miledi found that iontophoretic injections of Mg^{++} inhibited transmitter release only if an injection occurred just before the depolarizing stimulation.

Llinás (1982) used voltage-clamp techniques on the giant synapse of the squid to investigate Ca^{++} currents. At least a 15 mV depolarization is required before any Ca^{++} current can be detected. Once the current begins to flow, it increases slowly with time. Maximal Ca^{++} current is seen with a depolarization of 60 mV. Still further increase in the depolarization *decreases* the Ca^{++} current — as would be expected if the membrane potential were now approaching the Ca^{++} equilibrium potential and thus the driving force on Ca^{++} would be decreasing. The result of one such experiment is illustrated in Figure 4-3. A large part of the synaptic delay can be attributed to the time required for depolarization to open the Ca^{++} channels because the postsynaptic potential begins very shortly after the Ca^{++} current begins.

How Ca^{++} activates transmitter release is currently unknown. But the presence of four Ca^{++} ions seems to be required for each secretion event. The transmitter release may be related to the inhibitory effect that Ca^{++} has on an intracellular enzyme called **ATPase** (adenosine 5′-triphosphatase) (Vizi, 1978). Since ATPase catalyzes the formation of ADP from ATP (the cell's energy source), Ca^{++} may inhibit processes that normally occur because of ATP. One possibility is that the Ca^{++} inhibition of ATPase causes an increase in the permeability of the presynaptic membrane to transmitter substances.

Vesicles and Quanta

Figure 4-4 is a microscopic look at presynaptic structures. Mitochondria are common, as are the round or oval structures called vesicles. Since vesicles are seen only in presynaptic terminals of chemical synapses, they may store transmitter molecules. Ca^{++} somehow causes these vesicles to move and fuse to the intracellular side of the presynaptic membrane. These vesicles extrude their contents into the synaptic cleft by a process called **exocytosis**: the vesicle walls contract, forcing the molecules of transmitter substance out through an opening in the membrane. The empty vesicle is then hypothesized to break away from the presynaptic membrane to be refilled and reused. Heuser (1978) cited Marchbanks's estimate that 20

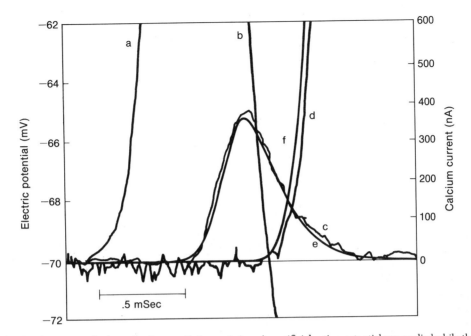

Figure 4-3 Calcium has a crucial role to play in synaptic transmission. An artificial action potential was applied while the flow of various ions across the presynaptic membrane was blocked by drugs. First Na$^+$ and K$^+$ were blocked, and then a Ca-blocker was added. On the graph, only the initial depolarization (**a**) and repolarization (**b**) of the action potential are visible. The difference between the currents measured with and without the Ca-blocker corresponds to the Ca^{++} current alone. (**c**) The postsynaptic response to the transmitter (**d**) begins soon after the Ca^{++} current. The graph also shows the Ca^{++} current (**e**) and the postsynaptic response (**f**) predicted by Llinás's (1982) model of synaptic transmission. nA = nanoamperes.

minutes of walking is enough to completely recycle all the vesicles in the synapses between the motoneurons and the leg muscles they innervate.

Does one vesicle hold one quantum of transmitter substance? Fatt and Katz (1952) discovered that transmitter substance was released in discrete "packets" of molecules. They recorded spontaneous postsynaptic activity at the frog synapse between a motoneuron and a muscle cell (the **neuro-muscular synapse**). Without any presynaptic depolarization, the muscle cell membrane shows small (0.5 to 1.0 mV), random depolarizations. These depolarizations are **miniature end-plate potentials,** or **miniature epps** (the postsynaptic muscle cell membrane is called an **end plate**). Each miniature epp may represent the release of one packet, or **quantum,** of transmitter substance. Since each packet of transmitter substance contains approximately the same number of molecules (several thousand), one vesicle may contain one quantum of transmitter substance. If this is the case, any increase in depolarization would cause still more vesicles to release their quanta (plural of *quantum*) into the cleft.

Later research (see reviews in Kandel, 1976, 1981c; Kuno, 1971) has mathematically described these miniature epps:

$$m = np$$

In this equation, n is the number of quanta (or vesicles) in a synapse and p is the probability of release of any one of them. Thus m is the quantal content of a synaptic event or the average number of quanta released. Since a is the number of molecules of transmitter substance in a quantum, the total number of molecules released for any given synaptic event would equal am. Variations in synaptic activity can be described by a, n, or p.

The number of quanta released per presynaptic action potential varies tremendously. For neuromuscular synapses, m may be from 100 to 200. m may range all the way down to a value of 1 for other synapses, such as some of those found on motoneurons in the spinal cord (Eccles, 1973/1977; Kuno, 1971) and those seen on a certain cell (the Mauthner cell) of the goldfish (Faber & Korn, 1982; Korn et al., 1982; Triller & Korn, 1982).

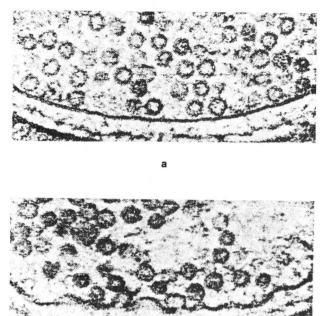

a

b

Figure 4-4   High-magnification views of quick-frozen nerve terminals from a frog neuromuscular junction show synaptic changes in vesicles. In the absence of stimulation (**a**), a number of synaptic vesicles lie very close to the presynaptic membrane, but the membrane itself is "unperturbed." After one stimulus (**b**), the vesicles that were close to the presynaptic membrane disappear. At this time, changes occur in the membrane, presumably as a result of the collapse of synaptic vesicles after exocytosis.

Does presynaptic activity change the appearance of presynaptic vesicles?   Heuser (1978) and Kuno (1971) reviewed some of the evidence supporting vesicular release of transmitter substance. When synapses become fatigued by repeated stimulations, each presynaptic impulse produces much smaller epsps. When a synapse has been fatigued and that synapse is examined under a microscope, the synaptic vesicles seem to have been depleted. If the venom from a black widow spider is applied to the synaptic area during stimulation, eventually the spontaneous miniature epsps disappear, and then synaptic vesicles can no longer be seen.

The most impressive correlation between presynaptic vesicles and the release of transmitter substance comes from the freeze-fracture studies of synaptic events. Heuser, Reese, Dennis, Jan, Jan, and Evans (1979) provided some remarkable pictures of how the presynaptic nerve changes following stimulation. They used the quick-freezing technique to prepare synaptic material. The membranes were quick-frozen during the act of exocytosis, then freeze-fractured, and finally their appearance under an electron microscope was compared with that of unstimulated terminals. (The researchers used a chemical to increase the number of quanta discharged per impulse in order to magnify the effects of stimulation.)

Two freeze-fractured terminals are shown in Figure 4-5. Part 4-5a is the presynaptic membrane of an unstimulated nerve terminal that has been broken in half between its layers and the result viewed from the inside. This figure shows what the outer most layer of an inactive presynaptic nerve membrane looks like. The synaptic area is the slight ridge surrounded by large particles of some sort. Figure 4-5b is the presynaptic membrane of a stimulated terminal. This neuron was given one stimulus 5 mSec before freezing; the membrane was quick-frozen at the time of maximal postsynaptic depolarization. The circles presumably represent openings in the membrane or places in which vesicles have fused with the membrane and extruded their contents. The indentations, therefore, indicate active zones. Nerve terminals that were stimulated 3 mSec or less before freezing — ones that were not in the act of exocytosis at the time of freezing — do not show such active zones.

Heuser and his colleagues (1979) estimated that one vesicle undergoes exocytosis for each quantum of discharged transmitter substance. Furthermore, each vesicle seems to act independently of all other vesicles. This research corroborates the physiological measurements of postsynaptic potentials, which had also indicated that quanta were released independently.

Nonvesicular Release?

On the basis of the research summarized above, most neurophysiologists believe that transmitter release is associated with the synaptic vesicles. But this belief is not universally shared. Tauc (1982) reviewed evidence suggesting that some transmitter substance may come directly from the cytoplasm of the cell. The molecules of transmitter substance in vesicles and in the cytoplasm can be manipulated separately and one made distinguishable from the other by radioactively labeling only one pool. Although the transmitter substance that is released spontaneously (miniature epps, or **mepps,** appear in the absence of presynaptic depolarization) apparently comes from the cytoplasm, the transmitter substance that is released by a presynaptic action potential seems to come from vesicles (Carroll & Aspry, 1980).

Dunant and Israël (1985) claim that even evoked release comes from the cytoplasm. They studied the **cholinergic**

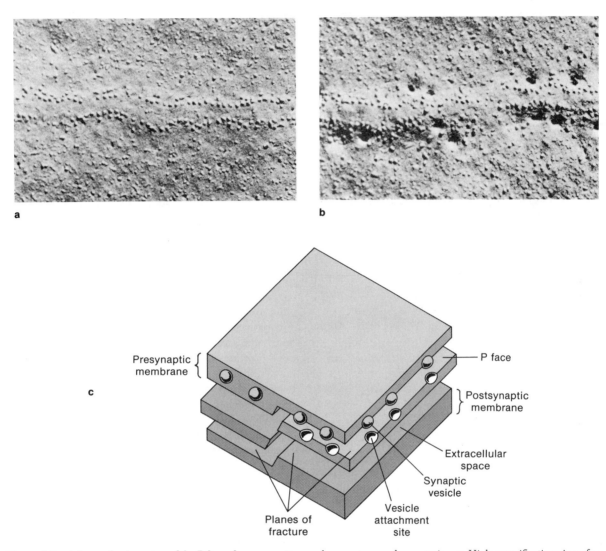

a

b

c

Presynaptic membrane

P face

Postsynaptic membrane

Extracellular space

Synaptic vesicle

Vesicle attachment site

Planes of fracture

Figure 4-5 A freeze-fracture view of the P face of a presynaptic membrane may reveal exocytosis. **a.** High-magnification view of one active zone (the slight ridge bordered by parallel rows of large intramembrane particles) from a frog motor nerve terminal, which was given one stimulus 3 mSec before being quick-frozen. By this time, the action potential had presumably arrived at the terminal, but that did not change the appearance of the active zone. **b.** An active zone given one stimulus 5 mSec before being frozen. Between 3 and 5 mSec following stimulation, the terminal begins to discharge transmitter quanta, and at this time certain changes in the postsynaptic membrane appear. These changes may occur because channels into the underlying vesicles are opening. The darkened indentation represents vesicle openings in the membrane. **c.** Illustration of freeze-fracture. (Magnification = 143,000×)

(using acetylcholine, or ACh, as a transmitter) synapse made by nerve terminals on the electric organ of the saltwater *Torpedo* fish. Even when repeatedly stimulated, the terminal showed no decrease in the number of vesicles. Only after several minutes of stimulation could any change be seen in any vesicles. In fact, even when the presynaptic cell terminal was totally emptied of its vesicles, if ACh was injected in the presynaptic terminal, a subsequent injection of Ca^{++} caused that ACh to be released. What had been identified by other researchers as fusion of the vesicles to the presynaptic membrane (Figure 4-5) was found to occur *after* the release of ACh. Dunant and Isräel suggested that large intramembrane particles may be associated with ACh release; the particles may be channels opened by Ca^{++}. Release of ACh from several particles could be synchronized, producing the mepps. Vesicles may simply store ACh and accumulate Ca^{++} after presynaptic activity, thus terminating that activity.

Summary of Presynaptic Events

Presynaptic events producing the release of transmitter substance from nerve terminals are common to most synapses. The inward movement of Ca^{++}, normally caused by a depolarization-induced increase in membrane permeability to Ca^{++}, is necessary. The method by which Ca^{++} leads to transmitter release is currently unknown but may involve ATPase. Most researchers also believe that the Ca^{++}-triggered events cause synaptic vesicles to move to and fuse to the presynaptic membrane. Then, by a process of exocytosis, each vesicle releases its quantum of transmitter-substance molecules into the cleft. However, transmitter may be released by the cytoplasm instead of by vesicles.

Postsynaptic Events at Fast Synapses

This section and the next distinguish between the activities of fast and slow synapses. The latency of a postsynaptic effect in a "fast" synapse is around 0.5 mSec, and the effect lasts from 2 to 4 mSec. In a "slow" synapse, the latency of the postsynaptic effect ranges from 100 mSec to 5 seconds (sec), and the duration of the effect ranges from seconds to minutes (Hartzell, 1981). The time difference between fast and slow synaptic events implies that different kinds of processes are involved (Hartzell, 1981; Greengard, 1976, 1978a, 1978b; Greengard & Kebabian, 1974).

Excitatory Synapses

Several types of fast excitatory or depolarizing synapses have been studied. They include the neuromuscular synapses that produce the depolarizing end-plate potential, or epp. Excitatory postsynaptic potentials, or epsps (nerve–nerve synapses), have been investigated by studying the excitatory synapses between the preganglionic and postganglionic neurons of the autonomic nervous system, the giant synapses found in some invertebrates, and some vertebrate spinal synapses.

Nicotinic cholinergic synapses.   The neuromuscular synapses and most preganglionic-postganglionic synapses are cholinergic, which means that they all use ACh as their transmitter substance. But there are different kinds of cholinergic receptor proteins in the nervous system. If the postsynaptic receptor protein can combine with both ACh and nicotine, this synapses is **nicotinic** as well as cholinergic.

In fast cholinergic nicotinic synapses, the postsynaptic activity begins after ACh molecules diffuse across the synaptic cleft. They diffuse down their concentration gradient: just after release, the concentration of ACh is much greater in the region of the presynaptic than the postsynaptic membrane. Once ACh reaches the postsynaptic membrane, one or more of these molecules temporarily combine with the receptor proteins on the postsynaptic membrane, as Figure 4-6 illustrates. The receptor molecule is a large protein spanning the width of the postsynaptic membrane. Each molecule of receptor protein "recognizes" one or more molecules of transmitter substance. The analogy of a key fitting into a specific lock is often used to describe the recognition process.

A receptor protein will combine with substances other than transmitter substances. In some synapses, the receptor protein may combine more easily with one of these other substances than it does with the transmitter. If the combination results in the same postsynaptic effects as does the combination of the receptor with the transmitter substance, the substance is an agonist. Nicotine is sometimes said to be an ACh agonist because it first activates (before it blocks) nicotinic synapses. Sometimes the combination of one of these other substances with the receptor blocks the ability of the transmitter itself to combine with the receptor. If the combination of this other substance with the receptor does not produce changes in membrane potential, the substance is an antagonist. Other antagonists may break up or inactivate molecules of the transmitter substance. Thus, an antagonist prevents the synapse from working normally.

Changes in permeability.   When ACh combines with its receptor molecule, the permeability of the postsynaptic membrane increases (its resistance) has decreased. Specifically, the permeabilities to both Na^+ and K^+ are increased. The postsynaptic membrane depolarizes during epps or epsps largely because of the inrush of Na^+ ions. However, the membrane does not reverse in polarity (become positive on the inside) as it does during the action potential. The epp and epsp also involve a simultaneous increase in g_{K^+}, and the outflow of K^+ opposes the effect of the Na^+ current on the membrane potential.

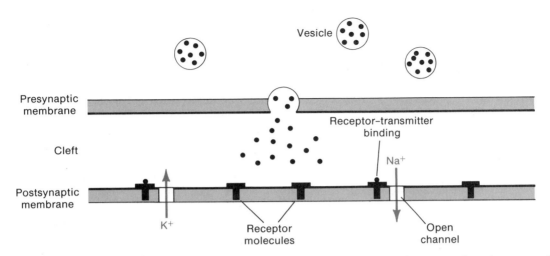

Figure 4-6 Once a molecule of transmitter substance has combined with a receptor molecule, pores or channels are opened in the postsynaptic membrane, changing its resistance (or permeability).

Changes in potential. Figure 4-7 shows the flows of current and the changes in potential associated with an epp or epsp. The attachment of ACh to postsynaptic membrane receptors causes a rapid increase in flow of current through the

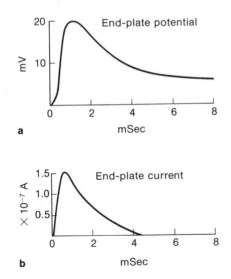

Figure 4-7 a. When the end plate of a muscle membrane is stimulated, the end-plate potential changes and current flows through the membrane. The ordinate is the change in membrane potential from resting levels, measured in mV; the abscissa is the time in mSec from the onset of the epp. **b.** The end-plate current, showing the time course of the current flow responsible for the end-plate potential. A = Amperes.

membrane (largely Na^+ flowing in). Then, as the channels opened by the ACh molecules close, the membrane resistance increases and the current flow declines (Stevens, 1977). The changes in membrane potential of the epp or epsp are a result of these current flows. In this figure, the epp is a 20 mV depolarization. Once the flow of current through the membrane decreases, the membrane gradually drifts back to its resting potential.

The ionic basis of the epp and epsp. The epp or epsp comes from a temporary increase in g_{K+} and g_{Na+}. The results of a voltage-clamp experiment are presented in Figure 4-8 (Weight & Votava, 1970). The postsynaptic membrane potential was changed by passing various amounts and types (depolarizing or hyperpolarizing) of current through an intracellular electrode. With no postsynaptic current flow, the epsp was a normal depolarizing potential. As the postsynaptic membrane was hyperpolarized, the epsp got larger. If the postsynaptic membrane was depolarized, the epsp got smaller and finally reversed to become a hyperpolarizing potential.

The potential at which the epsp reversed from depolarizing to hyperpolarizing (about -14 mV) is the **reversal potential** for the epsp or epp. It could also be called the **equilibrium potential,** or E_{epsp} and E_{epp}. The fact that the E_{epp} is about halfway between E_{Na+} and E_{K+} suggests that the membrane during an epp goes toward a point about halfway between the equilibrium potentials of Na^+ and of K^+, regardless of what the potential on the postsynaptic membrane was at the start of the epp. This value for the equilibrium potential suggests that an

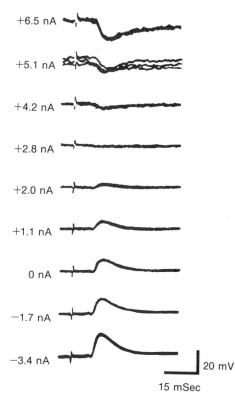

Figure 4-8   A voltage-clamp experiment shows the amplitude of a fast epsp as a function of depolarizing (+) and hyperpolarizing (−) currents, indicated in nanoamperes (nA). Presynaptic cells received a single 0.5 mSec stimulus, which caused an epsp in a ganglion cell. The epsp increased with hyperpolarization and decreased with depolarization, ultimately reversing to become a hyperpolarizing potential.

Events occurring at single postsynaptic channels.   Some experiments recorded currents flowing through single channels in the postsynaptic membrane. One way to do this is to record the membrane's spontaneous activity, or "noise," during the continuous infusion of very tiny amounts of ACh into the synaptic area (Katz & Miledi, 1970, 1972). The noise is assumed to result from the openings and closings of individual postsynaptic membrane channels. By measuring and quantifying the noise, Katz and Miledi estimated that the combination of one or two molecules of transmitter substance with one receptor protein opened one channel. Enough positive ions entered through that channel to produce about a 0.3 μV (microvolt) change in the postsynaptic potential.

Figure 4-9 shows that this type of membrane noise, involving a tiny change in potential, was increased by infusing the area around the membrane with ACh. Some spontaneous miniature epps are also shown. Since the average miniature epp (assumed to result from the release of one quantum of transmitter substance) was a few thousand times larger (0.7 mV) than the average depolarization produced by the noise, there must be a few thousand transmitter molecules in a quantum.

Another way to record the single-channel events is to use a microelectrode so tiny and placed so close to the postsynaptic membrane that it records only from a patch of membrane small enough to contain just one receptor protein (see, for example, Neher & Sakmann, 1976). The time a single postsynaptic channel remains open can be estimated, as Figure 4-10 illustrates. The average channel-open time when ACh combines with its receptor is about 1 mSec. However, the average channel-open times vary with different agonists. Some ACh agonists, such as carbachol, have shorter channel-open times than others, such as suberyldicholine (used in Figure 4-10).

epp or epsp involves an increase in permeability to both K$^+$ and Na$^+$.

Another way to study the ionic basis of the epp or epsp is to vary ion concentrations across the postsynaptic membrane. For example, increasing extracellular Na$^+$ increases E_{Na^+} and thus increases the size of the depolarizing epp. Changing K$^+$ concentrations also has the predicted effects on the epp, but variations in Cl$^-$ usually have little or no effect (Eccles, 1973/1977; Kandel, 1981b; Weight, 1974).

Not all excitatory synapses are alike. In some excitatory synapses, only g_{Na^+} may be increased, and in still other synapses, g_{Cl^-} may also be increased (Gage, 1974; Weight, 1974). The E_{epsps} can also vary (Gage, 1976).

Summary of fast excitatory postsynaptic events.   The combination of one or two molecules of ACh with a receptor opens one pore or channel in the postsynaptic membrane. The channel remains open for about 1 mSec, and in that time about 12,000 ions enter the cell, leading to the 0.3 μV change in potential (Kuffler & Yoshikami, 1975; Lester, 1977). The additive effects of having many such events (the number equal to the number of molecules in a quantum of transmitter substance) all occurring at the same time produces the larger potential change of the miniature epp. The release of more than one quantum by a presynaptic action potential produces the 10 to 30 mV epp (see reviews in Gage, 1976, and in Peper, Bradley, & Dreyer, 1982).

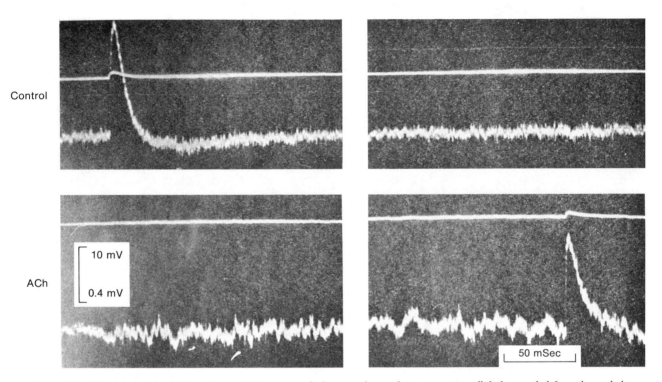

Figure 4-9   Membrane potentials from the end-plate region of a frog muscle membrane were intracellularly recorded. In each panel, the upper trace was recorded on a low-amplification channel (10 mV scale); the lower trace was simultaneously recorded on a high-amplification channel (0.4 mV scale). The upper two records are controls; the lower two show membrane noise during application of ACh. In the lower records, the upward displacement of the upper trace shows the ACh-induced depolarization. Two spontaneous miniature epps are visible.

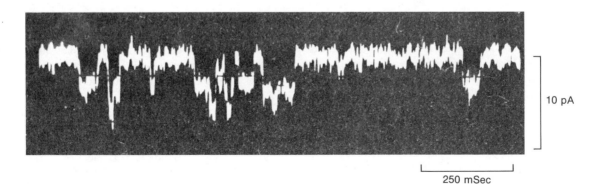

Figure 4-10   Individual channel openings and closings can be visualized by recording current flow through a tiny patch of membrane — approximately 10 μm^2 (micromillimeters) of a frog muscle membrane. The downward deflections of the record represent inward current, measured in picoamperes (pA). The membrane was stimulated with an ACh agonist.

The nature of the nicotinic postsynaptic receptor. In the following discussion, we will describe a "typical" nicotinic receptor. However, the nicotinic receptors found on muscles are probably different from those found on nerve cells: they have different agonists and antagonists (Patrick & Heinemann, 1982).

Normally, the neuromuscular cholinergic receptors occur only in the end-plate area. Figure 4-11 shows which areas of a muscle cell membrane are normally sensitive to ACh. Figure 4-12 compares the appearance of neuromuscular synapses to synapses between two neurons. (The function of acetylcholinesterase will be described later.) The photomicrograph in Figure 4-12 depicts the cholinergic axon terminals innervating another nerve cell. The receptors are found only immediately under the axon terminals, or **boutons.** Figures 4-11 and 4-12 show that the sensitivity of the muscle cell membrane to ACh, and thus the presence of ACh receptors, extends throughout the area of the muscle membrane that lies just under the elongated presynaptic axon terminals.

The structure of cholinergic nicotinic receptors has been described (Conti-Tronconi, Gotti, Hunkapiller, & Raftery, 1982; Gage, 1974; Patrick & Heinemann, 1982; Schwartz, 1981). The receptor complex probably consists of two portions, a **binding component** and an **ionophore component.** The binding component attaches to ACh molecules, and the ionophore component is the channel through which the ions flow. The receptor (in at least some nicotinic synapses) may have two ACh binding sites. Each receptor consists of four different proteins (one protein occurs twice, making five molecules in all) arranged in a 90 angstrom circle around a central pit (the ionophore?).

The ionophore component has been the subject of some controversy. Some researchers have suggested that there may be separate K$^+$ and Na$^+$ channels or ionophores, each activated by a separate transmitter-substance–receptor-molecule combination (Eccles, 1966, 1973/1977; Gage, 1974; Gage & Armstrong, 1968; Maeno, 1966). However, there is probably only one ACh-gated channel through which both Na$^+$ and K$^+$ flow (though in opposite directions!) during epps and epsps (Gage, 1976; Kordaŝ, 1969; Peper, Bradley & Dreyer, 1982).

Inhibitory Synapses

Hyperpolarizing changes in the postsynaptic membrane. Much of our knowledge about inhibitory synapses came from the pioneering work of Eccles (see his summary in Eccles, 1973/1977). This work was done with the inhibitory synapses on the cat spinal motoneuron and with the inhibitory synapses on the pyramidal cells in the hippocampus (part of the limbic system).

In some fast inhibitory synapses, the postsynaptic membrane is hyperpolarized. The hyperpolarizing potential is an inhibitory postsynaptic potential (ipsp). Often when a molecule of the inhibitory transmitter substance combines with its receptor protein on the postsynaptic membrane, there is an increase in permeability to both K$^+$ and Cl$^-$. Since K$^+$ is normally not at equilibrium, K$^+$ will flow out of the cell, but there will be little movement of Cl$^-$ ions. The increase in g_{K+} and I_{K+} will hyperpolarize the membrane, just as it does in the hyperpolarizing phase of the action potential.

The time course of the current flows and the potential changes during an ipsp are illustrated in Figure 4-13. The combination of transmitter with the receptor temporarily opens channels in the postsynaptic membrane, causing outward K$^+$ current and hyperpolarization. After the channels close, the hyperpolarization gradually decreases and the membrane potential goes back to the resting level.

The ionic basis of the ipsp. The ionic events of the ipsp were studied with the voltage-clamp technique beginning in the 1950s. The research was done by Eccles and his colleagues, who were thus the first researchers to use the voltage-clamp technique in the CNS. The ipsp changes when the postsynaptic potential changes, as Figure 4-14 illustrates. With a normal resting potential of -74 mV, the normal hyperpolarizing ipsp is seen. When the postsynaptic membrane is increasingly depolarized before the ipsp is evoked, the ipsp gets progressively larger. But when the postsynaptic membrane is hyperpolarized, the ipsp gets smaller and can even reverse, becoming a **depolarizing ipsp.**

The reversal potential for the hyperpolarizing ipsp is about -82 mV. The reversal potential is also the equilibrium potential for the ipsp, or the E_{ipsp}. Since the E_{ipsp} is about halfway between the E_{K+} and E_{Cl-}, the inhibitory transmitter may open both K$^+$ and Cl$^-$ channels. During the ipsp, the membrane is seeking a value between the equilibrium potentials of K$^+$ and Cl$^-$.

Equilibrium potentials can also be changed by manipulating ion concentrations. Varying Cl$^-$ levels inside or outside produces predictable variations in the ipsp in both the motoneuron and the hippocampal pyramidal cell (Allen, Eccles, Nicoll, Oshima, & Rubia, 1977; Coombs, Eccles, & Fatt, 1955; Eccles, 1973/1977). For these synapses, there is no direct evidence for the involvement of K$^+$ ions, although the direction and magnitude of the ipsps would be difficult to explain without them.

Not all inhibitory synapses involve the same ionic channels.

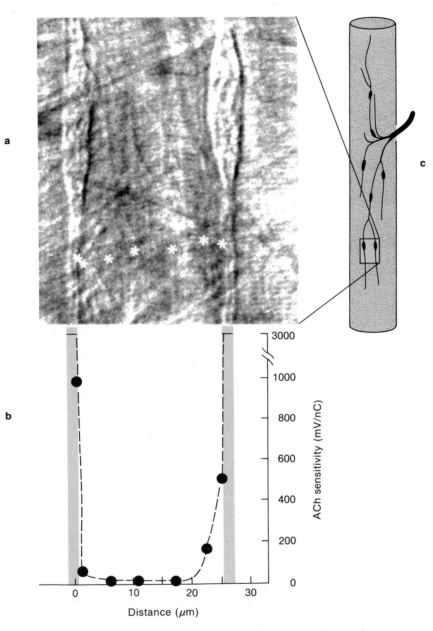

Figure 4-11 The ACh sensitivity of the membrane decreases sharply with increasing distance from a neuromuscular synapse in a frog. **a.** Micrograph of part of two nerve terminals, as indicated in the sketch to the right. Each terminal's Schwann cell appears as a thickening of the terminal in the upper part of the micrograph. **b.** The ACh sensitivity of the membrane (measured in mV of change in membrane potential against a standard or reference voltage change: nC) varies according to the position of a micropipette containing ACh. The horizontal scales in a and b are identical, and the points in b correspond to the locations of the asterisks in a. The anatomical location of the area in the photograph is shown in the drawing at the right.

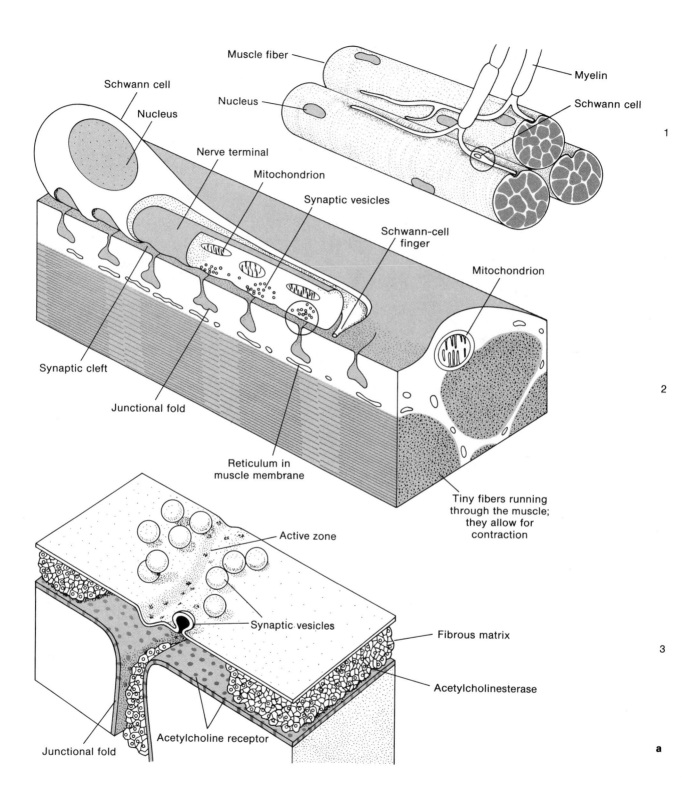

Muscle fiber

Myelin

Schwann cell

Nucleus

Nucleus

Schwann cell

1

Schwann cell

Nucleus

Nerve terminal

Mitochondrion

Synaptic vesicles

Schwann-cell finger

Mitochondrion

Synaptic cleft

Junctional fold

Reticulum in muscle membrane

Tiny fibers running through the muscle; they allow for contraction

2

Active zone

Synaptic vesicles

Fibrous matrix

3

Acetylcholinesterase

Junctional fold

Acetylcholine receptor

a

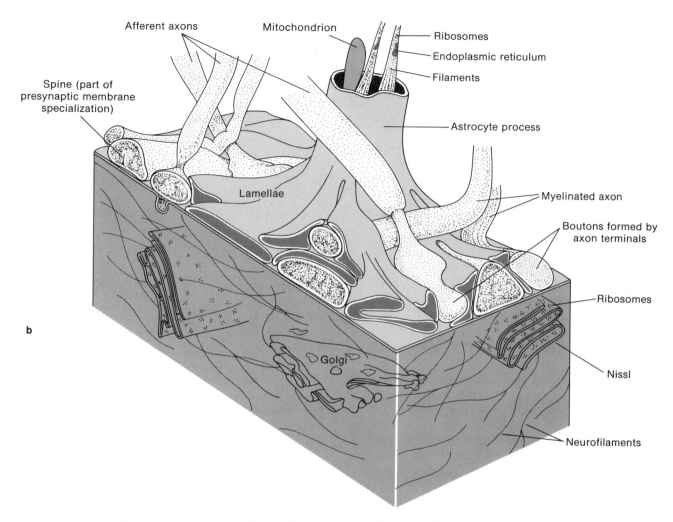

Afferent axons   Mitochondrion   Ribosomes
Endoplasmic reticulum
Filaments

Spine (part of presynaptic membrane specialization)

Astrocyte process

Lamellae

Myelinated axon

Boutons formed by axon terminals

b

Ribosomes

Golgi

Nissl

Neurofilaments

Figure 4-12 **a.** The nerve–muscle synapse of a frog. The slender terminal branches of the axon of a motoneuron lack the fatty myelin present around the rest of the axon and lie in gutterlike depressions in the muscle cell membrane (1). Each terminal region is covered by a Schwann cell embracing it with fingerlike processes, subdividing it into from 300 to 1000 regularly spaced compartments (2). ACh is destroyed by molecules of acetylcholinesterase enzyme (balls), which are found in the fibrous matrix filling the cleft and lining the junctional folds (3). **b.** A synapse between two nerve cells (the postsynaptic cell is a motoneuron). Golgi apparatus actually should be more centrally located. Spines (upper right) were encountered only on dendrites and not on cell bodies.

Sometimes only the permeability to K^+ or only the permeability to Cl^- is increased. During ipsps involving only increases in permeability to Cl^- and occurring at a normal postsynaptic resting potential, there is often no change in potential observed. To see the effect of an inhibitory transmitter requires depolarizing the postsynaptic membrane; a hyperpolarizing ipsp can then be seen. If intracellular Cl^- is increased, the ipsp also becomes depolarizing (Faber & Korn, 1982).

In some synapses, the ipsp involves only increases in Cl^- permeability. Since the ipsp is still hyperpolarizing even in these synapses, Cl^- could not be at equilibrium with the resting membrane. In fact, in several different electrically excitable cells ranging from some nerve cells in *Aplysia* (Russell & Brown, 1972) to the giant axons of the crayfish and the heart muscle of a frog (Walker & Brown, 1977), Cl^- pumps have been found. In a hyperpolarizing, increased g_{Cl^-} ipsp, presumably Cl^- is actively transported out of the cell. The ipsp increase in permeability to Cl^- could produce a hyperpolarizing

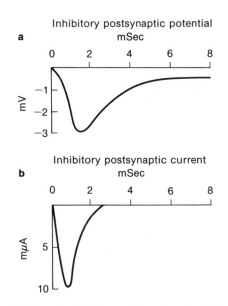

Figure 4-13 **a.** An inhibitory postsynaptic potential in a motoneuron. The ordinate is the change in membrane potential from the resting level, in mV; the abscissa is the time from the onset of the ipsp, in mSec. **b.** The inhibitory postsynaptic current, indicating the time course of the flows of current responsible for the ipsp. $m\mu A$ = millimicroamperes.

movement of Cl^- into the cell. Other cells presumably have *inward* Cl^- pumps, because ipsps in them are depolarizing and are associated with an outward movement of Cl^- (Bührle & Sonnhof, 1985; Scholfield, 1978).

The inhibitory receptor. There may be some important differences in structure and function between excitatory and inhibitory receptors. The channel-open times may be longer for at least some inhibitory synapses. Faber and Korn (1982) calculated the average channel-open time for the ipsp on the goldfish Mauthner cell to be 7.15 mSec. Gold and Martin (1982) looked at the ipsps in the Müller cells in the brain stem reticular formation of lampreys and found that the channel-open time varied from 29 to 35 mSec.

Why are ipsps inhibitory? All ipsps tend to inhibit action potentials in the postsynaptic membrane. This is true even for the ipsps that involve no change in membrane potential (those having increased g_{Cl^-} when Cl^- is at equilibrium with the resting membrane). The inhibitory effect of a hyperpolarizing ipsp is easy to visualize: the ipsp moves the membrane potential farther away from the threshold for an action potential, subtracting from and thus reducing the effects of any depolarizing excitatory inputs.

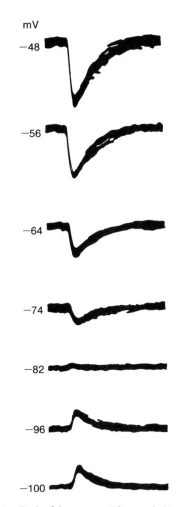

Figure 4-14 Each of these potentials recorded intracellularly from a motoneuron represents the summation of about forty trials. The potentials were caused by direct inhibitory synaptic input. Through a steady background current applied with one barrel of a double microelectrode, the membrane potential was changed to the voltage indicated on each record. The normal membrane potential was −74 mV. Hyperpolarization is indicated by a downward movement of the traces.

But an ipsp is inhibitory mostly because it increases the membrane's permeability. An increase in permeability acts to short-circuit the membrane and decreases the effects of any Na^+ currents. For example, as long as the permeability of the membrane to Cl^- is above normal, any attempt to depolarize the membrane will cause an increased flow of Cl^- into the membrane. Cl^- current will oppose the depolarizing effect of any excitatory input. Similarly, not only will an increase in K^+ permeability hyperpolarize the membrane but the increased flow of K^+ out of the membrane will oppose the depolarizing effects of any increase in g_{Na^+}. This short-circuiting effect may also explain why cells with a depolarizing, Cl-dependent ipsp are inhibitory (Scholfield, 1978). A depolarizing ipsp is still inhibitory because the relatively large increase in g_{Cl^-} acts to clamp the membrane at E_{Cl^-}, opposing any more depolarization (Bührle & Sonnhof, 1985).

Most ipsps are inhibitory for two reasons:

1. If the ipsp is hyperpolarizing, the potential of the postsynaptic membrane is moved farther from the threshold for stimulating an action potential.
2. The increase in permeability to K^+ and/or Cl^- will act to short-circuit the postsynaptic membrane and to oppose any excitatory effect of increased g_{Na^+}. Since the threshold of a membrane has already been defined as that potential at which $I_{K^+} = I_{Na^+}$, speaking of an ipsp's short-circuiting effect is equivalent to saying that the ipsp increases the threshold.

Synaptic Inactivation

A molecule of a transmitter substance combines with its receptor molecule only for a brief period. The gates are also open only for a brief time. The duration of current in an epp or an epsp is determined by how long the gates remain open. Gate-closing times determine the duration of postsynaptic potentials because by the time the gates close, the transmitter substance has already left its receptor and been removed from the synapse (see, for example, Peper, Bradley, & Dreyer, 1982; Stevens, 1977). The removal of transmitter substances *at either fast or slow synapses* is accomplished by three mechanisms:

1. diffusion of transmitter away from synaptic cleft
2. breakdown of transmitter by inactivating enzymes
3. reuptake of transmitter into presynaptic cell or into glial cells.

Cholinergic synapses. The duration of the effect of ACh on the postsynaptic membrane is limited by diffusion and by the enzyme **acetylcholinesterase (AChE).** AChE inactivates ACh by breaking it into acetate and choline, neither of which can combine with a postsynaptic receptor. Thus, once an ACh molecule breaks off from the receptor molecule, it may encounter a molecule of AChE instead of another receptor. Because of AChE, the concentration of ACh in the cleft decreases within microseconds (Kuffler & Yoshikami, 1975; Peper, Bradley, & Dreyer, 1982). Some of the acetate and choline diffuses out of the cleft into the rest of the extracellular fluid, but some of the choline is taken back up into the presynaptic cell by a pump in the presynaptic membrane, recombined with acetate, and reused.

AChE can be found in various locations. In the neuromuscular synapse, AChE molecules are associated with the loose matrix of fibers filling the synaptic cleft (Lester, 1977). Many of the ACh molecules released from the presynaptic vesicles would be broken down and inactivated before they could reach the postsynaptic membrane. In nicotinic synapses between nerve cells, the AChE molecules appear to be located in the postsynaptic membrane (Fossier, Baux, & Tauc, 1983). Molecules of AChE are interspersed between receptor molecules. Together, ACh receptors and AChE molecules occupy 25% of the surface of the postsynaptic membrane (Gage, 1976).

Other types of synapses.   Other synapses have different inactivating enzymes. But in these synapses, the major mechanism for removing transmitter substance from the cleft is **reuptake** into the presynaptic cell. Transport mechanisms for molecules of transmitter substance are found in the presynaptic membrane. In an energy-requiring process, these mechanisms take molecules of transmitter substance from the cleft back into the presynaptic cell, where the transmitter substance can presumably be placed back into synaptic vesicles and reused. This type of inactivating event is best understood for **aminergic** synapses, synapses that use a **biogenic amine** (neurally active substances made from an amino acid) as a transmitter.

Summary of Fast Postsynaptic Events

Fast synapses have receptor proteins with a binding component and an ionophore component. The binding component attaches preferentially to certain transmitter substances. The ionophore component varies. In most (but not all) excitatory synapses, the ionophores allow Na^+ and K^+ ions to pass through. Because of the inrush of Na^+, the membrane becomes depolarized. In inhibitory synapses, the ionophores allow K^+ and/or Cl^- ions through. The outward flow of K^+ or the inward movement of Cl^- hyperpolarizes and inhibits the postsynaptic membrane. However, ipsps can be inhibitory even during depolarization because of the short-circuiting (causing an increase in the threshold) produced by the increased permeability to K^+ and/or Cl^-.

The duration of any of these postsynaptic events at both fast and slow synapses is determined by the duration of gate opening. Transmitter molecules are removed extremely rapidly by diffusion, by being pumped back into the presynaptic membrane (especially in aminergic synapses), and by inactivating enzymes (especially in cholinergic synapses).

Postsynaptic Events at Slow Synapses

Slow synapses produce changes in postsynaptic enzyme activities rather than in postsynaptic ionophores. However, not all slow synapses have the same types of postsynaptic events (Hartzell, 1981; Kehoe & Marty, 1980; Libet, 1979). Whatever their mechanism, slow synapses are common in the CNS and may be more common than fast synapses in the brain itself (Greengard, 1976, 1978a, 1978b; Greengard & Kebabian, 1974; Hartzell, 1981; Iversen, 1984; Nathanson, 1977). Most CNS transmitters (some exceptions are glutamate, gamma-amino butyric acid [GABA], and glycine) may be used primarily in slow synapses. However, the same transmitter can be used in both fast and slow types of postsynaptic activities; acetylcholine is one example (Patrick & Heinemann, 1982). A nicotinic receptor is used at fast synapses, but at slow synapses the cholinergic receptor has different agonists as well as different kinds of postsynaptic effects. Since muscarine, a drug extracted from a mushroom (*Amanita muscaria*), also attaches to this receptor, it is a **muscarinic receptor.**

Cyclase Receptors and Enzymatic Reactions

How slow synapses work is still being actively researched. One hypothesis of slow synaptic activity is generally accepted as being true for at least some slow synapses (see, for example, Kuffler, Nicholls, & Martin, 1984; Schwartz, 1981; Shepherd, 1983). Greengard's original work in this area (Greengard, 1976, 1978a, 1978b; Greengard & Kebabian, 1974) was based on Sutherland's description of a second-messenger system.

The second-messenger system and adenylate cyclase. Sutherland and his colleagues (Sutherland, Øye, & Butcher, 1965) proposed that hormones affect body cells by activating an **adenylate cyclase.** An activated adenylate cyclase is an **enzymatic** protein, a protein that regulates metabolic processes. In particular, in some cells the activated adenylate cyclase serves as an enzyme or a catalyst for changing ATP to **cyclic adenosine monophosphate,** or **cAMP.** The cAMP is the **second messenger** (the hormone itself was the first messenger), producing the ultimate effects on the body cells.

Adenylate cyclase receptors and protein kinase. The slow synapses whose properties have been most thoroughly investigated are found between target organs and sympathetic postganglionic neurons. The postsynaptic receptor found in the membranes of the target organs has at least three components:

1. a **binding protein,** which attaches to a molecule of transmitter substance (in this case, norepinephrine)
2. a **regulatory protein,** which attaches to **guanine triphosphate (GTP)**; GTP regulates the activity of the receptor
3. an **enzymatic protein,** which activates an adenylate cyclase enzyme and thus serves as a transducer.

A molecule of transmitter would activate an adenylate cyclase, producing a molecule of the second messenger (cAMP, for instance). In other synapses, the transmitter may *decrease* adenylate cyclase levels. If a cell had both types of synapse present, the decreasing adenylate cyclase synapse would directly control the effects of the increasing adenylate cyclase synapse.

The next steps involve a **protein kinase.** The second messenger would activate a protein kinase, which is an enzyme for phosphorylation reactions. In **phosphorylation,** a phosphate ion (PO_4) is attached to some molecule, such as a protein molecule. A phosphorylated protein may change other reactions in the body cell, including but probably not limited to changes in membrane resistance, changes in the activity of genes in the nucleus, and changes in the rate of metabolic reactions in the cell. These reactions are illustrated in Figure 4-15. In the discussion of slow synaptic potentials, we will limit ourselves to the changes in membrane potentials and permeabilities.

Other second messengers. In other cells, there may be a different kind of receptor, associated with a different kind of second messenger. Although Greengard suggests that in some of these synapses a **guanylate cyclase** may be associated with the binding site, the guanylate cyclase may only regulate the receptor activity. Transmitter-induced changes in postsynaptic intracellular levels of "free" Ca^{++} could mean that Ca^{++} is a second messenger. Ca^{++} could affect phospholipids (complex molecules consisting of fats — or lipids — and phosphate molecules) that form the membrane and, by doing so, could change membrane conductances (Iversen, 1984). Ca^{++} may be released from intracellular stores (**mobilized**) by a reaction between a transmitter molecule and an enzymatic receptor. The activated enzyme might break down one of the lipid components of the membrane, and one product of the breakdown could catalyze the Ca^{++} mobilization (Michell, Kirk, Jones, Downes, & Creba, 1981).

Evidence indicating slow synaptic activity. Greengard (1978a) listed some of the experiments that would be relevant to these proposed types of slow synaptic activity. Some of them appear in Table 4-1. For only a few synapses, largely in inver-

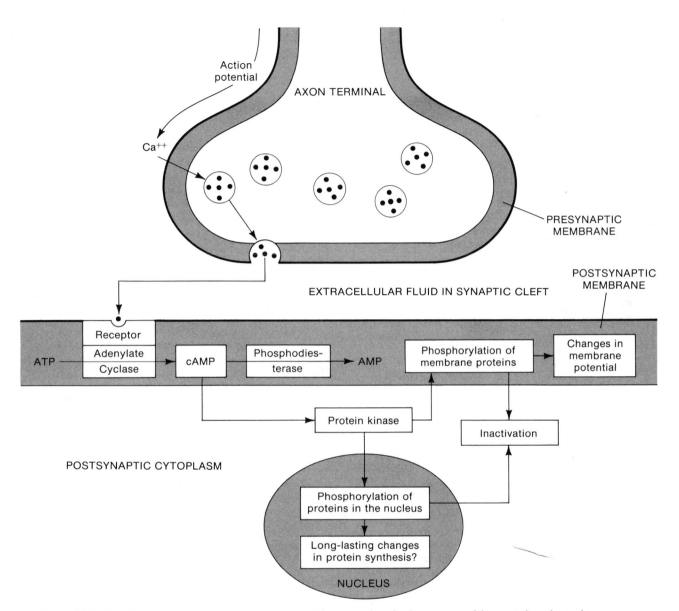

Figure 4-15 Possible postsynaptic events at a slow synapse. The arrows describe the sequence of the events hypothesized to occur at a slow synapse. All the metabolic reactions make this synapse slow in comparison with fast synaptic events.

tebrates, have any of these experiments actually been carried out; for no synapse have all been done. For example, injections of cAMP or **cGMP (cyclic guanine monophosphate,** another possible second messenger) into the cell (criterion 6 in the table) should duplicate the effect of the transmitter substance on the postsynaptic membrane. The **serotonergic** (using serotonin, or 5-HT, as a transmitter substance) synapses in the sea snail *Aplysia* respond the same way to intracellular postsynaptic injections of cAMP as to injections of 5-HT into the synaptic cleft (Camardo, Klein, & Kandel, 1981; Deterre, Paupardin-Tritsch, Bockaert, & Gerschenfeld, 1981; Klein & Kandel, 1980; Siegelbaum, Camardo, & Kandel, 1982).

Table 4-1   Some criteria for evaluating
a possible slow synapse.

Criterion	References
1. Electrical stimulation of the presynaptic neurons should increase the levels of the cyclic nucleotide found in the postsynaptic neurons. (See Figure 4-15.)	See reviews in Greengard, 1978a, and Nathanson, 1977.
2. Levels of the cyclic nucleotide should increase when the hypothesized neurotransmitter is placed into that part of the brain (in vivo or in vitro).	See reviews in Greengard, 1978a, and Nathanson, 1977.
3. A neurotransmitter-sensitive adenylate or guanylate cyclase should be present in the postsynaptic cell.	See reviews in Greengard, 1978a, and Nathanson, 1977.
4. The cyclic nucleotide levels should increase in the postsynaptic cells when the presynaptic cells are electrically stimulated.	See reviews in Greengard, 1978a, and Nathanson, 1977.
5. The cyclic nucleotide levels should increase in the postsynaptic cells when they are stimulated by the appropriate transmitter substance.	See reviews in Greengard, 1978a, and Nathanson, 1977.
6. Injections of cAMP or cGMP should mimic the physiological effects of synaptic and neurotransmitter stimulation in the postsynaptic cell.	Snail: de Peyer, Cachelin, Levitan, & Reuter, 1982; Deterre, Paupardin-Tritsch, Bockaert, & Gerschenfeld, 1981; Levitan, de Peyer, Cachelin, & Reuter, 1982. Nudibranch photoreceptor: Alkon, Acosta-Urquidi, Olds, Kuzma, & Neary, 1983.
7. Injections of protein kinase inhibitors should block the effect of presynaptic stimulation.	Serotonergic synapses in *Aplysia*: Adams & Levitan, 1982; Lemos, Novak-Hofer, & Levitan, 1981.
8. Synaptic activity should lead to the phosphorylation of some synaptic protein.	Serotonergic synapses in *Aplysia*: Lemos, Novak-Hofer, & Levitan, 1982. Rat brain stem (nucleus of cranial nerve VII): Dolphin & Greengard, 1981.

Decreases in Membrane Permeability

The transmitter substance at a slow synapse can produce a *decrease* in membrane permeability to one or more of the major ions. So far, only slow synapses have ever been found to produce decreases in permeability or conductance.

Decrease in K^+ conductance and excitation.   Some slow epsps involve an *increase* in membrane resistance. If membrane permeability to K^+ were decreased, K^+ leakage out of the cell would be decreased. The decreased rate of loss of positive ions would cause the membrane to depolarize. If the depolarization reached threshold, an action potential would be generated.

One example of this type of effect involves muscarinic slow synapses, some of which may be found in the sympathetic ganglia between the preganglionic and the postganglionic neurons. (Most of the cholinergic synapses are nicotinic and thus involve increases in the permeability of the postsynaptic membrane.) When frog muscarinic synapses were studied, the results were interpreted as showing that both ACh and cGMP depolarize the cell by *decreasing* K^+ conductance (Greengard, 1978a; Brown & Adams, 1980; Weight & Votava, 1970). The type of channel involved in this effect may be similar to the M-current channel described earlier (Brown & Adams, 1980; Nowak & Macdonald, 1983). (However, it has not yet been conclusively demonstrated that adenylate cyclase is involved in this action.)

Figure 4-16 shows how this particular slow epsp varies with changes in the membrane potential. (The membrane potential was changed by applying a constant current across the membrane.) This figure should be compared with Figure 4-8 to see how the slow synapse differs from the fast one. The reversal potential for the slow epsp, or the slow E_{epsp}, was about -88 mV, which is also the K^+ equilibrium potential for that cell. This correspondence suggests that the epsp occurs because of a decrease in K^+ permeability.

Hyperpolarization and decreases in conductance.   Slow synapses could hyperpolarize by decreasing membrane permeability. A decrease in membrane Na^+ permeability would decrease the rate at which Na^+ leaks in. If that slow influx of positive ions were reduced, the membrane would tend to hyperpolarize. However, a substance might also decrease postsynaptic conductance only indirectly, by decreasing the presynaptic release of some transmitter that increases conductance.

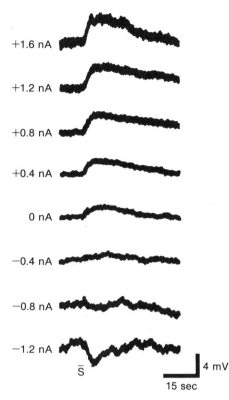

+1.6 nA

+1.2 nA

+0.8 nA

+0.4 nA

0 nA

−0.4 nA

−0.8 nA

−1.2 nA

$\bar{S}$

4 mV

15 sec

Figure 4-16   The amplitude of a slow epsp varies as a function of depolarizing (+) and hyperpolarizing (−) currents, with the currents indicated in nanoamperes. The resting membrane potential was −65 mV. The fast epsp was blocked by nicotine to record the slow epsp in isolation. Stimulation began 10 seconds after the beginning of each record. The period of stimulation is indicated by the line labeled S under the bottom record. Note that the slow epsp reversed with hyperpolarizing current, the opposite of the fast epsp depicted in Figure 4-8.

In one example of the conductance-decreasing effect, Marshall and Engberg (1979) found that iontophoresing the transmitter **norepinephrine (NE;** also called **noradrenaline)** onto cat motoneurons produced an increase in membrane resistance. The size of the associated hyperpolarization *increased* when the membrane had previously been hyperpolarized and decreased when the membrane had been depolarized. On the basis of this finding, the researchers suggested that NE may nonspecifically decrease the permeability of the cell to both Na^+ and K^+ (but they also pointed out that increasing the rate of Na-K pump activity could produce hyperpolarization).

Increases in Membrane Permeability

Like fast synapses, slow synaptic events can produce an increase in membrane conductance. The same ions implicated in fast ipsps and epsps could also be involved in the conductance-increasing slow synapses.

Several slow synapses involving an increase in membrane permeability have been found. In one snail neuron, injections of protein kinase enhanced the Ca-activated K^+ conductance (de Peyer et al., 1982; Levitan et al., 1982). In some mammalian cells, such as the cholinergic sympathetic postganglionic cells and some **noradrenergic** (using NE as a transmitter) synapses in the brain stem, the transmitter substance hyperpolarizes by *opening* the Ca-activated K^+ channel (Aghajanian & VanderMaelen, 1982; Cole & Shinnick-Gallagher, 1984).

Possible Effects on the Na-K Pump

The slow synapse may affect the Na-K pump. Since the pump is electrogenic, the rate at which it works will affect membrane potential. In particular, increasing the pump rate hyperpolarizes the membrane (De Weer, 1975; Koike, Mano, Okada, & Oshima, 1972).

In several active membranes, transmitter substances have been shown to affect — directly or indirectly the rate at which the Na-K pump works. In muscle cells of rats, at least when those cells are suffering from the effects of low potassium, NE suppresses the pump rate (Akaike, 1981). In the normal muscle cells of frogs, NE increases the pump rate (Koketsu & Ohta, 1976). Thus, transmitter-activated adenylate cyclase could change membrane potential by changing the pump rate.

Interactions of Fast and Slow Synapses

The sympathetic ganglion.   One set of synapses in vertebrates may involve both slow and fast effects, as well as excitatory and inhibitory effects (see reviews in Horn & Dodd, 1983; McAfee, Henon, Whiting, Horn, Yarowsky, & Turner, 1980; Simmons, 1985). Some possibilities are presented in Figure 4-17, which shows how slow and fast synapses can interact within a single ganglion. This is a very simple microcircuit, showing how slow synapse activity is anatomically in a position to modulate the postsynaptic effects of ionophores.

Several different transmitters appear in this ganglion in addition to the cholinergic fast synapse described earlier. Furthermore, exactly *which* transmitters appear here varies from one species to the next (Simmons, 1985). (The transmitter substances mentioned here will be more fully described in the

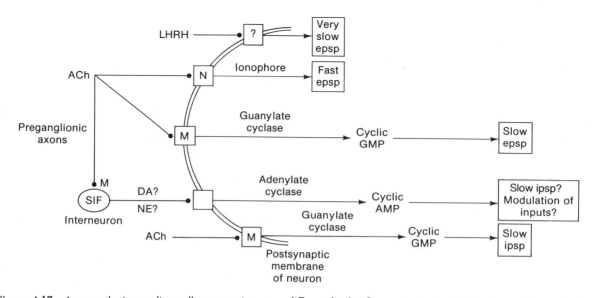

Figure 4-17 A sympathetic ganglion cell may receive many different kinds of synaptic input. ACh is released by terminals of preganglionic fibers onto ganglion cells and acts on nicotinic receptors for fast epsps and on muscarinic receptors for slow epsps. ACh may also affect dopaminergic or noradrenergic interneurons (the SIF, or small-intensely-fluorescent, cells). The dopamine or norepinephrine from these cells may elicit the slow ipsps or may modulate other inputs. Alternatively, ACh may affect a muscarinic receptor directly on the ganglion cells to produce the slow ipsps. N = nicotinic; M = muscarinic.

next section.) Some of the muscarinic synapses may be excitatory (frog: Brown & Adams, 1980) and some may be inhibitory (rabbits: Cole & Shinnick-Gallagher, 1984; frog: Horn & Dodd, 1981). One slow synapse found in the frog may use a substance very similar to **luteinizing hormone-releasing hormone (LHRH)** as a transmitter. This peptide hormone is normally secreted by the hypothalamus onto the pituitary (Jan, Jan, & Kuffler, 1979; Jan, Jan, & Brownfield, 1980). Many other peptides, including cholecystokinin, bombesin, **substance P,** and **somatostatin,** are also found in the sympathetic ganglia of several species (Kessler, Adler, & Black, 1983; Simmons, 1985). These peptides may be all associated with slow epsps.

However, there is still extensive disagreement about the nature and function of many of these ganglionic synapses, especially those associated with a slow ipsp. Greengard (1978a) suggested that an interneuron made synaptic contact with the postganglionic neuron to cause the slow ipsp. He thought that this synapse used **dopamine (DA)** as a transmitter and had an adenylate cyclase receptor. But Libet (1979) argues that in the rabbit, the **dopaminergic** (using DA as a transmitter) synapse shown in Figure 4-17 produces a modulatory effect on the postsynaptic membrane instead of a slow ipsp. Horn and Dodd (1981, 1983) suggest that the slow ipsp

might come from a direct, muscarinic synapse of the preganglionic fiber onto the postganglionic cell, as also illustrated in Figure 4-17. Another possibility is that injections of cAMP may break down, attach to, and activate specific **adenosine receptors** to produce the ipsp (Henon & McAfee, 1983; Brown, Caulfield, & Kirby, 1979; Snyder, Katims, Annau, Bruns, & Daly, 1981). Even this "simple" connection between pre- and postganglionic cells offers many opportunities for this microcircuit to change the information going to the internal organs.

Channels that are both chemically and electrically gated. Some channels are both electrically and chemically gated and so represent another way fast and slow synaptic activities can interact. For example, Horn and McAfee (1979, 1980) suggest that NE may inhibit an electrically gated Ca^{++} channel in frog sympathetic ganglia. NE would reduce the Ca^{++} "hump" that follows the peak of the action potential in those neurons and would also reduce the prolonged negative afterpotential associated with the Ca-activated K^+ current. Other examples of such channels include

1. the inhibitory effect of NE on Ca-activated K^+ channels in hippocampal cells (Madison & Nicoll, 1982)

2. the inhibitory effects of ACh on the M-current in both hippocampal cells (Cole & Nicoll, 1983) and sympathetic postganglionic cells (Nowak & Macdonald, 1983).

These synaptic interactions greatly enrich the possible ways in which information can be encoded and transformed. For example, stimulating the NE adenylate-cyclase receptor in the hippocampus would increase the number of action potentials evoked by any excitatory, fast synaptic activity. As we pointed out in Chapter 3, the M-current is thought of as a "braking" current (Simmons, 1985). In this case, ACh would increase the excitability of the postsynaptic cell by blocking the M-current.

Comparisons between Fast and Slow Synapses

The differences between the types of effects associated with fast and slow synapses must be important to their interactions. These differences determine the ways in which the nervous system can code information.

Increases versus decreases in permeability.   Because only slow synapses decrease permeability, comparing the postsynaptic effects of decreased permeability with those of increased permeability might give us some clues as to why the CNS has so many slow synapses. For example, suppose that one area of the postsynaptic membrane is being inhibited by a fast synapse at the same time that an adjacent area is receiving excitatory input. Because of the increase in membrane permeability to K^+ or to Cl^-, some of the flow of current through the membrane will go through the inhibited membrane patch—

shorting out the membrane—instead of going through the patch of membrane beneath the excitatory synapse (Figure 4-18). At the same time that inward Na^+ current at the excitatory synapses is depolarizing the membrane, the outward K^+ current at the inhibitory synapse will be opposing that depolarization.

Even conductance-increasing epsps short out the effects of adjacent synapses (see Zieglgänsberger & Champagnat, 1979). For example, an action potential in the area of an excitatory synapse is small compared with the action potential away from the synapse (Figure 4-19). The increased permeability to K^+ associated with the excitatory transmitter ionophore explains why. The ACh channel is seven times more permeable to Na^+ than is the electrically gated channel and so shorts out the action potential in the synaptic area (Gage, 1976).

Conductance-decreasing slow synapses do *not* affect adjacent synaptic activity. They affect only the membrane in the synaptic area. Since the passive spread of any change in membrane potential is directly related to the resistance of that membrane (its length constant), the spread of changes in membrane potential will be more extensive around resistance-increasing than resistance-decreasing synapses. Some types of information processing or coding used by the brain may require the wide spread of slow synaptic effects, some may require the short-circuiting effects of fast synapses, and many codes probably require the interaction of both types.

Ionophores versus transducers.   A major difference between slow and fast synapses is directly related to the types of

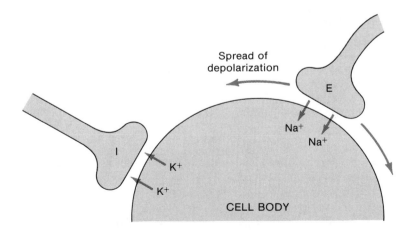

Figure 4-18   The short-circuiting effect of fast ipsps (from I) on epsps (from E). When the wave of depolarization reaches the membrane area being inhibited at I, the outflow of K^+ will oppose the depolarization, effectively short-circuiting it.

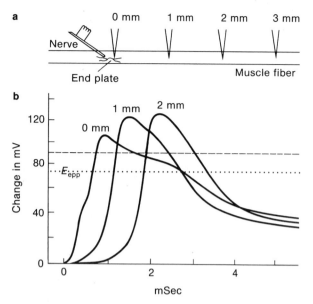

Figure 4-19   Synaptic activity can short out an action potential.   **a.** Action potentials were evoked by a single nerve impulse and were recorded at 0, 1, and 2 mm from the synaptic area on the muscle membrane.   **b.** The broken line is at zero membrane potential; the resting membrane potential was −90 mV. The dotted line is the equilibrium potential for the endplate potential (E_{epp}).

receptor each uses. Fast synapses have receptors associated with ionophores, whereas slow synapses have a **transducer** type of receptor. If a synapse uses a transducer, more than just the membrane potential can be changed. Proteins in other parts of the cell can be phosphorylated, possibly producing long-term effects on cellular metabolism as well as the shorter-term effects on the membrane potential. There is even the possibility that proteins in the nucleus could be phosphorylated by slow synaptic activities. Phosphorylation could change how the genetic code of the cell is being read and so could have permanent effects on cell structure or function. In certain CNS synapses, this change in gene expression might be one possible basis for memory (Chapter 11).

Fast versus slow time scales.   Fast synapses, by definition, have short-lasting effects on neuron excitability. Slow potentials can modulate the activity of a postsynaptic cell for several seconds. Thus, fast synapses seem designed for rapid communication of information, and slow synapses seem better able to modify rates and patterns of neural activity. Slow epsps can cause a small, fast epsp to produce a burst of action potentials

rather than just one; slow ipsps can inhibit repetitive firing. These are examples of how slow synaptic activity can modify the pattern of neural activity being passed across a fast synapse (Horn & Dodd, 1983).

Summary of Slow Postsynaptic Events

Slow synapses use enzymatic receptors or transducers and a second-messenger system. The second messenger may be Ca^{++} or cAMP. The transmitter substance may activate an adenylate cyclase enzyme, changing ATP into cAMP. cAMP activates a protein kinase, which then phosphorylates cellular proteins, possibly including membrane channel proteins. Ca^{++} could affect membrane phospholipids after being mobilized by a breakdown product from a membrane lipid.

The postsynaptic membrane potential is then changed. The membrane may be hyperpolarized or inhibited because of a decreased permeability to Na^+, an increased permeability to K^+, or an increased rate of activity in the Na-K pump. The membrane may be depolarized or excited because of a decreased permeability to K^+, an increased permeability to Na^+, or a decreased rate of activity in the Na-K pump. Not all these events have yet been experimentally demonstrated.

The interactions among, and differences between, the postsynaptic effects of slow and fast synapses presumably explain why the nervous system has both types. Only slow synapses involve a decrease in membrane permeability, and so only in slow synapses does synaptic activity *not* tend to short out the effects of adjacent synaptic activity. Also, slow synapses can have effects on the postsynaptic cell other than those on membrane potential — effects that may eventually be used to explain information coding and long-term memory. Slow synaptic events are currently the focus of an extremely active and exciting area of research.

Transmitter Substances: Location, Function, and Metabolism

Many transmitter substances have already been mentioned: dopamine, acetylcholine, norepinephrine, substance P, and serotonin (5-HT). We are ready for a more systematic description of these and other substances, specifying their nature, synthesis, and distribution. This knowledge is extremely important to a biochemical analysis of brain–behavior relationships, including drug effects and genetic abnormalities. The biochemistry of behavior will be described in much more detail in later chapters covering motives and emotions; here we will only summarize the general nature of these transmitters.

General Principles

There is some logic and order regarding which transmitters are used in which areas of the brain. We might ask further why we have so many transmitters with so many different kinds of postsynaptic effects in our brains. The reason for having at least two types—fast and slow—has just been discussed. In addition, Evarts (1985) described what he thought was the function of such diversity in the CNS. Fast synapses appear wherever fast responding might be necessary, such as in the sensory cortex and basal ganglia. Cells using the biogenic amines (DA, NE, or 5-HT) as transmitters for slow synapses have relatively low spontaneous rates of firing and only slowly change their firing rate after receiving afferent input. These aminergic synapses may set the synaptic **gain**—increasing or decreasing the effect—of fast synaptic input. Motives and emotions may involve changing the rate of firing of aminergic neurons (see Chapters 8, 9, and 10). Cholinergic cells innervating muscarinic receptors create much longer-lasting postsynaptic effects, and these neurons may fire only at critical times, such as when an event is to be remembered (see Chapter 11).

Relevant types of research.   To prove that any given transmitter substance is actually being used at any given synapse, certain kinds of research must be carried out.

1. Research must show that the chemical is contained within the presynaptic terminal, both in synaptic vesicles and in the cytoplasm. The inactivating enzymes and some type of reuptake mechanism should also be present in the presynaptic cell.
2. Research must demonstrate that stimulation releases the chemical at the right time, in response to the right stimuli. Thus, presynaptic depolarization should increase the release of transmitter, and the release ought to be inhibited when extracellular Ca^{++} is reduced or extracellular magnesium is increased.
3. A given amount of presynaptic activity should release the number of molecules required for the amount of postsynaptic activity recorded.
4. The changes in the postsynaptic membrane that occur during synaptic activity should be precisely mimicked by iontophoretic injections of the supposed transmitter onto that membrane.

These steps require a detailed analysis of quantal events at the synapse. Microiontophoresis of exceedingly small and known amounts of the chemical onto the postsynaptic membrane should exactly mimic the effects of the quantal release. If the synaptic activity increases the permeability of the postsynaptic membrane to Cl^-, that effect should also be produced by the experimental injections. For slow synapses, iontophoresis should produce not only the changes in membrane permeability but also the increases in Ca^{++} or cAMP levels, activation of a protein kinase, and increased phosphorylation.

Since these research projects involve so many technical difficulties, the transmitter substance has not been conclusively established for any synapse. Still, there is good evidence that ACh is the transmitter at the neuromuscular synapse. The major transmitters for the autonomic nervous system (ACh and NE) are also fairly well established. Some doubt should be reserved about everything else described in this section.

One transmitter per cell?   Some substances released by presynaptic terminals may function as neuromodulators and not as true transmitter substances. Furthermore, some presynaptic terminals may release *both* a transmitter substance and a neuromodulator, or even more than one transmitter substance. Despite this complication, all the axon terminals coming from the same cell release the same transmitter substance(s) (and modulators?). This principle is **Dale's law,** giving credit to Sir Henry Dale's research, carried out in the early 1930s; but Eccles actually presented this as a principle of synaptic activity in 1957 (Schwartz, 1981).

Same transmitter, different effects.   ACh is excitatory at the preganglionic-postganglionic synapses of the parasympathetic and sympathetic systems, but it is usually inhibitory at the synapse between the postganglionic neurons and their target organs. However, some of the amino acid transmitters seem to have only inhibitory and others only excitatory effects. A transmitter such as ACh may be associated with an ionophore (nicotinic) at some synapses, and at other synapses it is associated with a transducer (muscarinic). *Since the effect of a transmitter is determined by the receptor,* the *same* cell often has different effects at different synapses.

The Transmitters and Neuromodulators

This section provides the background for the biochemical analyses of motives, emotions, and memory discussed in later chapters. The data are summarized in Tables 4-2 and 4-3 and in Figures 4-20 and 4-21. References for the material in Table 4-3 are in the preceding two sections as well as this section.

Table 4-2 Location and effect of transmitter substances.

Transmitter	Blocker	Receptor Type	Receptor Location
Fast Synapses			
Acetylcholine	Hexamethonium	Nicotinic ionophore: (g_K and g_{Na} $\uparrow$); depolarizing; can also hyperpolarize	Neuromuscular; superior cervical ganglion; hippocampus; parasympathetic target organs and postganglionic cells; spinal cord interneurons; substantia nigra
GABA	Picrotoxin, penicillin	A receptor, ionophore; $g_{Cl}\uparrow$; depolarizing or hyperpolarizing	Hypothalamus; cerebral cortex; substantia nigra; dorsal raphe; caudate; cerebellar Purkinje; spinal interneurons
GABA		B receptor: block electrically gated Ca^{++} channels? $\uparrow K^+$	Presynaptic inhibition in spinal cord and cuneate nucleus; hippocampus
Glutamate		Ionophore; depolarizing; $\uparrow g_{Ca}$?	Hippocampus; temporal cortex
Slow Synapses			
Serotonin	Lysergic acid diethylamide (LSD)?	Receptor 1, $\uparrow$cAMP? and $\downarrow$cAMP?; inhibitors?	Facial motor nucleus; reticular neurons; motoneurons; cerebellar Purkinje; granule cells; pyriform cortex; frontal cortex; hippocampus
Serotonin	LSD	Receptor 2; Ca^{++}?: excitatory?	Cerebral cortical Betz cells; caudate-putamen; frontal cortex; cingulate gyrus; nucleus accumbens; amygdala; hippocampus; reticular cells; lateral geniculate; optic tectum
Dopamine	Chlorpromazine	D-1 receptor, cAMP: inhibitory; $\uparrow Ca^{++}$-activated K^+ current	Superior cervical postganglionic; striatum; hippocampus; limbic cortex
		D-2 receptor: depolarizing but inhibitory; inhibition of cAMP	Median eminence of pituitary; hippocampus; striatum and limbic structures, esp. frontal cortex
Norepinephrine	Propranolol	Beta-receptor, cAMP; postsynaptic: ($\uparrow g_{Na}$ or g_{Ca}?; blocking Ca^{++}-activated K^+?); increases effects of inputs	Cerebellar Purkinje; hippocampus; hypothalamus; cerebral cortex; spinal motoneurons; cat salivary gland
		presynaptic: inhibitory	Hypothalamus
	Phentolamine	Alpha-receptor, cGMP?; Alpha$_1$: $\uparrow g_K$, depolarizing; increases effect of excitatory input	Superior cervical ganglion; sympathetic preganglionic presynaptic; hippocampus; cerebral cortex; lateral geniculate; dorsal raphe; spinal motoneurons
		Alpha$_2$; presynaptic: inhibitory; $\downarrow$cAMP?	
		Alpha$_2$; autoreceptors: inhibitory; $\uparrow g_K$?	Locus coeruleus

Table 4-2 *(continued)*

Transmitter	Blocker	Receptor Type	Receptor Location
Acetylcholine	Atropine	Muscarinic receptor: ($\uparrow$cGMP?; $\downarrow$cAMP?); blocking the M-current? hyperpolarizing or depolarizing	Sympathetic postganglionic; parasympathetic target organs; hippocampus; cortex; interneurons in spinal cord; substantia nigra
Histamine	Diphenhydramine	H_1 receptor; Ca^{++}?	Hippocampus; cerebral cortex; striatum
Histamine	Metiamide	H_2 receptor; cAMP?; $\downarrow Ca^{++}$-activated K^+	Hippocampus; cerebral cortex; striatum

Acetylcholine. ACh is synthesized by nerve cells from choline circulating in the blood stream. Once choline is transported into the nerve cell, it is attached to acetyl coenzyme A, forming ACh. ACh is broken down by acetylcholinesterase (AChE).

ACh is a major transmitter in the peripheral nervous system. As indicated in Table 4-2, nicotinic receptors are found largely in the peripheral nervous system, although the CNS also has such receptors in areas such as the hippocampus, striatum, and cortex (Clarke, Pert, & Pert, 1984; Krnjević, 1975). The CNS receptors may explain some of the stimulatory and addictive effects of nicotine. The nicotinic receptors can be either excitatory or inhibitory.

Muscarinic receptors are found throughout the nervous system. CNS cholinergic neurons are depicted in Figure 4-20 and some synapses are also listed in Table 4-2. The largest input to the cerebral cortex comes from the **nucleus basalis of Meynert,** an area of the brain stem that degenerates in the form of senility known as **Alzheimer's disease** (Cuello & Sofroniew, 1984).

Some neurons in the basal ganglia may be cholinergic interneurons or **intrinsic neurons** (short neurons whose dendrites and axons are all contained within a small area). As described in Chapter 2, basal ganglia are large collections of neurons deep within the cerebral cortex associated with the control of movement. Because of this location of ACh neurons, choline

Table 4-3 Synthesis and metabolism of transmitter substances.

Transmitter	Blood Precursor	Synthesizing Enzyme(s)	Degrading Enzyme(s)	Metabolic Products
Acetylcholine (ACh)	Choline	Choline acetyltransferase	AChE	Acetate and choline
Dopamine (DA)	Tyrosine	Tyrosine hydroxylase	COMT, MAO: types A and B	Homovanillic acid (HVA)
Norepinephrine (NE)	Tyrosine	Tyrosine hydroxylase, dopamine β-hydroxylase	COMT, type A MAO	3-methoxy-4-hydroxy-phenylglycol (MHPG)
Serotonin (5-HT)	Tryptophan	Tryptophan hydroxylase	COMT, type A MAO	5-hydroxyindolacetic acid (5-HIAA)
Histamine	Histidine	Histidine decarboxylase	?	?

ACh = acetylcholine
AChE = acetylcholinesterase
COMT = catechol-3-O-methyltransferase (outside neurons)
MAO = monoamine oxidase (inside neurons)
NE = norepinephrine

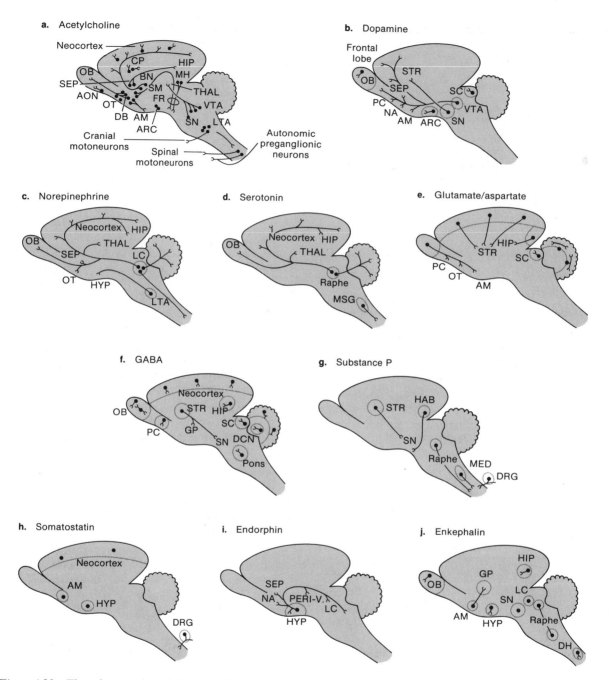

Figure 4-20 These diagrams show the locations of neurons containing the various transmitters used by the mammalian brain, regardless of receptor type. AM = amygdala; AON = anterior olfactory nucleus; ARC = arcuate nucleus; BN = nucleus basalis; CP = caudate-putamen; DB = dorsal horn; DRG = dorsal root ganglion; EPN = endopeduncular nucleus; FR = fasciculus retroflexus; GP = globus pallidus; HAB = habenula; HIP = hippocampus; HYP = hypothalamus; IP = nucleus interpeduncularis; LC = locus coeruleus; LTA = lateral tegmental area; MEF = medulla; MH = medial habenula; MSG = medullary serotonin group; NA = nucleus accumbens; OB = olfactory bulb; OT = olfactory tubercle; PC = pyriform cortex; PERI-V. = periventricular gray; SC = superior colliculus; SEP = septum; SM = stria medullaris; SN = substantia nigra; STR = striatum; THAL = thalamus; VTA = ventral tegmental area.

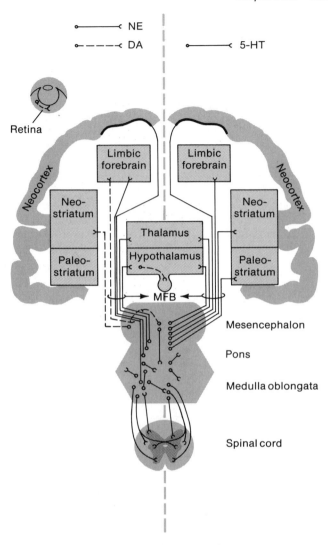

Figure 4-21 Highly simplified schematic drawing of the main monoamine neuron systems in the human central nervous system. NE = norepinephrine; DA = dopamine; 5-HT = serotonin; MFB = medial forebrain bundle.

— the ACh precursor — has been fed to some people suffering from some types of movement disorders (for example, tardive dyskinesia) because the problem seemed to involve an ACh deficiency. The treatment often seems to help, but the patients complain about ending up smelling "fishy" from the choline (Gelenberg, Wojcik, & Growdon, 1979).

Biogenic amines. The biogenic amines are closely related to one or more of the amino acids (proteins are long chains of amino acids). The biogenic amines include NE, DA, 5-HT, and **histamine.** NE and DA are also referred to as **catecholamines,** and synapses using these transmitters are aminergic. Serotonin (5-HT) is an **indoleamine.** The amines are synthesized from amino acids circulating in the blood stream (see Table 4-3). Since these amino acids are found in foodstuffs, diet may affect brain biogenic amine levels. The biogenic amines are inactivated by the enzymes indicated in Table 4-3. There is a possibility that all aminergic synapses may use an enzymatic receptor.

NE and DA neurons have some similar properties. Neither DA nor NE neurons have very many "normal" synaptic terminals (NE terminals may have even fewer than DA terminals do) (Moore & Bloom, 1978, 1979; Oades, 1985). Instead, the axons have areas of "swelling" called **varicosities** (see Figure 4-29). Varicosities may broadly distribute DA and NE among the cells of the target organs. Iontophoresis of NE or DA typically inhibits the spontaneous firing rates of cells (Moore & Bloom, 1978, 1979; Segal, 1985) but both also tend to be associated with increased behavioral activity and with alertness.

Although intracellular recordings during iontophoresis of DA sometimes show a depolarization, especially in the striatum, the spontaneous firing rates of these cells are inhibited by both depolarization and hyperpolarization (Moore & Bloom, 1978, 1979). DA may affect two types of receptors, a depolarizing one on the dendrites (D-2 receptor?) and a hyperpolarizing one closer to the axon hillock (D-1 receptor) (Bernardi, Cherubini, Marciani, Mercuri, & Stanzione, 1982; Herrling & Hull, 1980). Of the different types of DA receptors, only those known as D-1 and D-2 (each with different agonists and antagonists) have been extensively studied. Activating the D-1 receptors increases cAMP, but activating the D-2 receptors may *decrease* cAMP levels (Iversen, 1975; Kebabian & Calne, 1979; Stoof & Kebabian, 1981). The locations of these receptors as described in Table 4-2 are probable but not certain.

Some of the neural responses to DA may be affected by changes in the internal state of the organism. For example, in the absence of female sex hormones (subjects were female rats whose ovaries had been removed), microiontophoresis of DA inhibited 98% of the DA-responsive cells. After an injection of an estrogen, 89% of the DA-sensitive cells were now *excited* by DA (Arnauld, Dufy, Pestre, & Vincent, 1981).

The CNS neurons using DA are described in Figures 4-20 and 4-21 and in Table 4-2. Dopaminergic neurons tend to be discretely activated and have well-organized axon pathways that affect specific cells in the target neuron groups (Moore & Bloom, 1978, 1979). The dopaminergic projections to the cortex tend to terminate on discrete sets of cells. The projections extend mainly to cells in the top cortical layers (Bunney & Aghajanian, 1976a & 1976b). Some intrinsic neurons in two sensory systems (the olfactory system and the visual system) and perhaps some interneurons in sympathetic ganglia may also be dopaminergic (Libet, 1979; Greengard, 1978a). But the limbic and motor systems involve the most extensive DA activity. For example, some types of schizophrenia may involve DA abnormalities (see Chapter 10). Also, in Parkinson's disease (Chapter 2), the dopaminergic substantia nigra neurons projecting to the basal ganglia may have degenerated. This movement disorder is often treated with high doses of oral *l*-DOPA, which is converted into dopamine.

Both NE and DA are synthesized from tyrosine (Table 4-3), and so neurons that contain NE also have rather high levels of DA. NE is the transmitter substance between the postganglionic sympathetic neuron and the target organ. NE synapses may also modulate activity in the primarily cholinergic sympathetic ganglia (Brown & Caulfield, 1979; Horn & McAfee, 1979).

In the CNS, a major source of noradrenergic axons is the **locus coeruleus.** As Figure 4-20 shows, the locus coeruleus can affect activity in almost every region of the CNS. The NE projections to the cortex run parallel to the surface, largely in the lower cortical layers, and they are widely and diffusely distributed (Bunney & Aghajanian, 1976b). So NE cells tend *not* to have anatomically organized, discrete projections; instead, the axons of each cell project diffusely to many other cells throughout the brain (Beaudet & Descarries, 1978; Moore & Bloom, 1979; Segal, 1985). Like the noradrenergic sympathetic system, the brain NE system acts as a unit instead of in separately activated subsections.

Oades (1985) has related NE and DA activity to arousal and attention, respectively. Since NE synapses are distributed very diffusely across the cortex, and since DA cortical projections are more localized, activity in NE cells may increase the effects of external stimuli on the brain (alertness, arousal). Even though NE usually inhibits spontaneous firing rates at beta adrenergic synapses (see Table 4-2), it may actually *increase* the effects of input from other excitatory or inhibitory synapses (Moore & Bloom, 1978, 1979; Segal, 1985). DA activity may allow the brain to switch processing from one stimulus to another and thus facilitate the input of certain information into certain parts of the brain (specific attention).

Some CNS cells contain the enzyme necessary to convert NE into **epinephrine** (phenylethanolamine N-methyltransferase). These neurons are concentrated in the pons, medulla, and hypothalamus. Epinephrine may be a transmitter in these areas.

Serotonin is synthesized from **tryptophan.** Serotonergic cell bodies are found in the **raphe nuclei** in the brain stem. Their axons go throughout the brain and spinal cord. Activities in the raphe nuclei cells change systemically with changes in arousal level and with the sleep–waking cycle (see Chapter 8). According to Peroutka, Lebovitz, and Snyder (1981), there may be two types of serotonin receptors. The one with largely inhibitory effects may be associated with an adenylate cyclase, and the excitatory one could be associated with a Ca^{++} second-messenger system.

Histamine is synthesized from histadine and is extensively used as a transmitter by invertebrates. In vertebrates, as Table 4-2 indicates, there may be two types of histamine receptors, one associated with cAMP and one associated with Ca^{++}.

GABA.   Gamma-amino butyric acid, or **GABA,** is an amino acid synthesized within body and brain cells. Its receptors may be associated strictly with ionophores. It is largely an inhibitory, hyperpolarizing transmitter used by intrinsic neurons (see Figure 4-20), although it may have a depolarizing action at some synapses (Kuffler & Nicholls, 1976). GABA receptors may be linked to changes in anxiety states (Snyder, 1984; Chapter 10).

Other amino acids.   Amino acids other than GABA are also probably transmitter substances or neuromodulators (Bennett, Mulder, & Snyder, 1974; Davidson, 1976; Schwartz, 1981). **Glutamate** is a fast excitatory transmitter in the CNS. For example, infusions of glutamate first depolarize and then hyperpolarize the pyramidal cells found in the hippocampus. Both effects may be related to the effect of glutamate on Ca^{++} permeability. The initial depolarization would be caused by Ca^{++} rushing in, and the hyperpolarization would be caused by opening the Ca-activated K^+ channel and letting K^+ ions leave (Nicoll & Alger, 1981).

Glycine and **aspartate** may be transmitters or neuromodulators. Glycine may be a major transmitter in the pons, medulla, and spinal cord (McBride, Flint, Ciancone, & Murphy, 1983). Glycine is an inhibitory transmitter in the spinal cord (Zieglgänsberger & Champagnat, 1979).

Peptides as transmitters.   Probably the most exciting area of research on transmitter substances today involves the roles of peptides. A **peptide** is a small chain of amino acids, and so a peptide transmitter substance would be a larger molecule than any of those discussed up to this point. There is a large number of possible biologically active peptides (Bloom, 1981; Kelly, 1982; Snyder, 1980; Hökfelt, Johansson, Ljungdahl, Lundberg, & Schultzberg, 1980). The CNS distribution of some of them is illustrated in Figure 4-20. Most often the peptides are neuromodulators and not transmitter substances.

Many peptides originally discovered in the viscera have also been found in the brain. Visceral peptides may therefore be transmitters or neuromodulators. For example, **somatostatin** inhibits the secretion of growth hormones (**somatotropic** hormones) from the pituitary. This peptide is found in the viscera as well as in the brain and spinal cord. Injections of somatostatin can depress motor activity.

Two of the other major peptides affect pain coding. Substance P may be used in the first synapses between pain afferents and spinal neurons. The **endorphins** block the transmission of pain to the brain. They were discovered in researching the effects of morphine on the brain (Snyder, 1980). To have the effects it does, morphine must combine with receptors. Discovery of these receptors initiated the search for endogenous (naturally occurring) morphinelike substances: if there is a receptor, there must be a naturally occurring substance that normally combines with that receptor. When these substances were discovered, they were called *endorphins* (for *endo*genous mo*rphine*like substances).

Since then, many different endorphins and their receptors have been found. Most of them — like morphine — decrease sensitivity to pain. The endorphins that have been studied most extensively are **leu-enkephalin, met-enkephalin,** and **β-endorphin.** However, all the endorphins so far discovered have the leu-enkephalin or met-enkephalin sequence of amino acids in their structure. There are at least three types of **opioid receptors** (for endorphins): **delta, mu,** and **kappa** (Morley, Levine, Yim, & Lowy, 1983) (and probably more). The delta receptors are located mostly in the limbic system and the spinal cord, whereas the mu receptors are found in the cerebral cortex, hippocampus, hypothalamus, and thalamus. The kappa receptors are found in the thalamus and hypothalamus. The mu and kappa receptors may be associated with sensations of pain and hunger, and the delta receptors may be associated with emotional reactions and experiences. Some receptors may be presynaptic, regulating the release of other transmitters (Mulder, Wardeh, Hogenboom, & Frankhuyzen, 1984).

The endorphins may most often be neuromodulators. For example, enkephalins may moderate the cAMP response to the "true" transmitters by affecting the GTP regulatory protein subunit (Collier, 1980; Hökfelt et al., 1980; Rodbell, 1980; Zieglgänsberger & Bayerl, 1976). However, met-enkephalin hyperpolarizes locus coeruleus neurons, and the hyperpolarization involves an increase in K^+ conductance (Pepper & Henderson, 1980; Williams, Egan, & North, 1982); this suggests that the endorphin may be acting like a transmitter at this synapse. Furthermore, both morphine and enkephalin hyperpolarize spinal sensory neurons carrying pain information, and this hyperpolarization is also associated with an increased g_{K+} (Yoshimura & North, 1983).

Many of the peptide hormones found in the body have also been found in the brain. Some neurons that secrete one or another of the peptides have also been identified. Hoebel (1985) has suggested that these be called **integrative peptides** because their effect on the brain is often complementary to their effect on the rest of the body. For example, angiotensin levels in the blood increase when the organism has been deprived of water. Angiotensin acts to conserve water in the organism by increasing water reabsorption from the urine by the kidneys. At the same time, angiotensin stimulates certain brain cells and the animal begins to drink. Angiotensin may be secreted by neurons found in the **subfornical** organ, which protrudes into the third ventricle (and thus lacks a blood–brain barrier). Angiotensin may be carried by CSF to hypothalamic cells. Cholecystokinin (CCK) is also found both in the gut and in neurons; its injection into either the blood or the hypothalamus can suppress food intake.

Summary of Types of Transmitter Substances

Most of the transmitter substances are small, simple molecules. They are manufactured by nerve cells from precursors found in the blood stream, although some of the amino acids may be transported directly into the cell and used as transmitters without modification. Whether a transmitter substance is excitatory or inhibitory and whether it produces slow or fast changes in postsynaptic potential depend on the nature of the receptor rather than the nature of the transmitter substance itself. More than one substance may be liberated by a presynaptic terminal.

The large number of transmitter substances used by the brain must be related to the great variety of postsynaptic effects that can be produced. For a nerve cell to receive different *kinds* of input from different axon terminals, it must have different kinds of postsynaptic receptors. The coding characteristics of that cell may require that it receive fast ipsps from one type of afferent (for instance, an intrinsic neuron), slow ipsps from another, and slow and fast epsps from still other afferents. To control its rate of firing, it will need receptor proteins that will control the Ca-activated K^+ channel and the M-current. The richness and flexibility of neural coding characteristics, especially in mammals, require a plurality of transmitters.

Information Processing and Types of Synaptic Circuits

What any given nerve cell will do depends on the total synaptic input to that neuron. The synapses made on a motoneuron in the spinal cord of a cat are illustrated in Figure 4-22.

Interaction of Graded Synaptic Potentials

Whether a postsynaptic membrane develops one or more action potentials in any given period of time depends on the total number of ipsps and epsps occurring on its cell body, dendrites, and axon hillock. Since, unlike the action potential, synaptic potentials are graded—increasing in size with increases in the number of quanta released—postsynaptic potentials can add together.

Spatial and temporal summation.   The depolarizations produced by several epsps all occurring at the same time can have an additive effect on the amount of depolarization seen in the postsynaptic cell; this effect is called **spatial summation.** The more excitatory synapses active at any given time on any given postsynaptic cell, the more that cell will be depolarized. In addition, since each epsp lasts for several milliseconds, epsps can sum over time. This, as already described, is temporal summation. The more excitatory synapses are active within the time that an epsp lasts, the more depolarized the postsynaptic membrane will be. Ipsps also sum spatially and temporally.

Interactions of ipsps and epsps on a single postsynaptic cell.   Perhaps the best illustration of how ipsps and epsps work together in affecting the excitability of the postsynaptic cell can be found in the work of Eccles and his colleagues on the motoneuron in the cat spinal cord (Eccles, 1973/1977; Curtis & Eccles, 1959; Coombs, Eccles, & Fatt, 1955). The motoneuron receives excitatory and inhibitory inputs from different cells. The excitatory input comes from afferents that

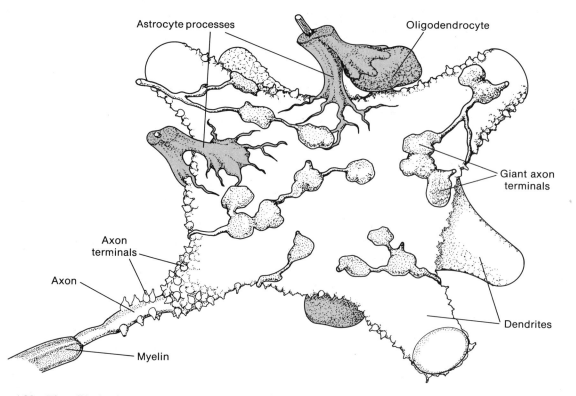

Figure 4-22   The cell body of a motoneuron is covered with synapses. Its dendrites are covered with axon terminals at all distances from the cell body. Notice that astrocytic processes cover some of the oligodendrocytic surface as well as the surface of the motoneuron. Note also that there are axon terminals on the initial, unmyelinated segment of the axon.

are excited by the stretching of a muscle. These afferents make direct excitatory contact with the motoneuron innervating that same muscle, in turn triggering one of the **monosynaptic** (one-synapse) spinal reflexes, the **stretch** or **kneejerk reflex.** Stretching the muscle excites the chain of neurons controlling that reflex, causing the stretched muscle to contract. This reflex helps maintain posture (and provides useful information about the state of the CNS to doctors, who therefore go around pounding on their patients' kneecaps with rubber hammers).

As Figure 4-23 shows, the inhibitory input comes from interneurons. One particular interneuron is a **Renshaw cell,** named by Eccles after the man who first discovered it: Birdsey Renshaw (Eccles, Fatt, & Koketsu, 1954; Eccles, 1973/1977). The Renshaw cell is excited by collateral branches from motoneurons and in turn it inhibits both many motoneurons and also the interneurons connected to muscles antagonistic in effect to those muscles innervated by the motoneuron that excited the Renshaw cell. In other words, a Renshaw cell excited by a **flexor muscle** (a muscle that moves

a limb closer to the body) will inhibit interneurons connected to **extensor muscles** (muscles that move a limb away from the body). Another inhibitory interneuron is excited by afferents coming from opposing muscles: if the motoneuron innervates an extensor muscle, the interneuron is excited by afferents from a flexor muscle. Because of these reflexive connections, contraction of the extensor will not be opposed by simultaneous contraction of the flexors—and vice versa.

Eccles and his colleagues recorded from a motoneuron during stimulation of its excitatory and inhibitory afferents. Both ipsps and epsps could be observed, separately and together, on the same motoneuron. Figure 4-24 shows that if an epsp depolarization reaches the threshold, a spike or action potential is generated. However, a subthreshold stimulation produces a subthreshold depolarization, an epsp without an action potential. When both excitatory and inhibitory synapses onto the same motoneuron are simultaneously activated, the hyperpolarization of the ipsp subtracts from the epsp, producing a smaller depolarization.

Figure 4-25 illustrates more interactions between ipsps and epsps. In the first and last frames of Figure 4-25a there are records of ipsps and epsps ocurring by themselves in a motoneuron in which the epsps were below threshold. In the middle records, the effect of an ipsp on the epsp is illustrated, with the tracing of an isolated epsp being added to each record to illustrate the degree to which the inhibitory input reduced the depolarization. Figure 4-25b shows the records of the stimulation (upper line) and the effect of that stimulation on the excitability of a different postsynaptic membrane receiving above-threshold synaptic inputs. The action potentials generated in frames 2 and 5 have been suppressed by ipsps in the third and fourth frames. Figure 4-25c ilustrates the recording arrangement.

Whether a postsynaptic cell has an action potential depends on its synaptic input summed over space and time. The summation depends on the length and time constants of that membrane (Chapter 3).

Convergence, Divergence, and Synaptic Efficacy

Synaptic efficacy refers to how large an epsp is for a given synaptic input (Kuno, 1971). Synaptic efficacy depends on the number of different fibers converging on the neuron, the location of the presynaptic terminals, and the *am* (as defined in the section "Presynaptic Events" in this chapter, *am* refers to the amount of transmitter released).

Location of the synapse.   Figure 4-25c illustrates typical locations of inhibitory and excitatory synapses. The inhibitory

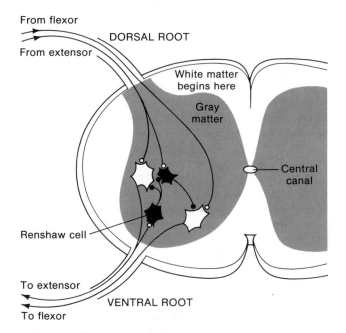

Figure 4-23   Inputs to motoneurons innervating flexor and extensor muscles. The motoneurons are shown in a cross section of the right half of the spinal cord. The white matter takes its characteristic appearance because of the myelin on the axons traveling up and down the outer edges of the cord. Renshaw cells are inhibitory interneurons excited by axon collaterals from motoneurons. The central canal contains cerebrospinal fluid.

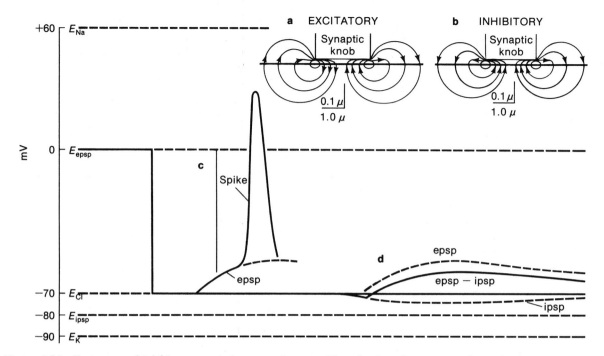

Figure 4-24 Excitatory and inhibitory synaptic inputs can interact with each other. An ipsp can subtract from the depolarization produced by an epsp.

synapses tend to be on the cell body, and the excitatory synapses are on the dendrites. The difference in synaptic location may explain the different time courses and effects of ipsps and epsps. The closer a synapse is to the axon hillock (the part of the neuron with the lowest threshold), the more effect that particular synapse will have on the firing rate of the postsynaptic cell. The changes in electrical potential created postsynaptically will be less likely to spread to the axon hillock, the farther away that synapse is located. The size of the area to which the changes in potential will spread is determined by the length constants of the nerve membrane, or by how far membrane depolarization (or hyperpolarization) will spread from the synapse and how much change in potential will occur at any given point.

The dendrites and cell bodies, as we have said, often have no (or only a few) electrically gated channels. Having a few of these channels might not be enough to allow an action potential, but it might be enough to "boost" or amplify the changes in membrane potential produced by a synapse, allowing for a greater spread of current away from the synapse.

Convergence and divergence. Most synaptic circuits involve both divergence and convergence. In **convergence,** many different kinds of cells make synaptic contact with the same postsynaptic cell. The **convergence ratio** is the number of presynaptic fibers coming into a given area of the brain, divided either by the number of postsynaptic axons leaving that area or by the total number of cells being innervated by those fibers. The greater the convergence ratio, the greater the synaptic efficacy. In **divergence,** one presynaptic cell makes synaptic contact with many different postsynaptic cells, allowing the information being carried by any one presynaptic cell to be dispersed among many different cells.

Amount of transmitter released. The amount of transmitter released by the presynaptic cells depends on the properties of those cells. am depends on the average size of the presynaptic terminals, the number of quanta released per action potential ($m = np$), and how many synapses a given presynaptic terminal makes with a given postsynaptic membrane. The more synapses, the greater the synaptic efficacy. Activity in one synapse is seldom enough to excite a postsynaptic cell without simultaneous input from other excitatory synapses. But in some synapses (such as some neuromuscular synapses), one presynaptic cell may form so many synapses with the postsynaptic cell that activity in that one presynaptic cell is sufficient.

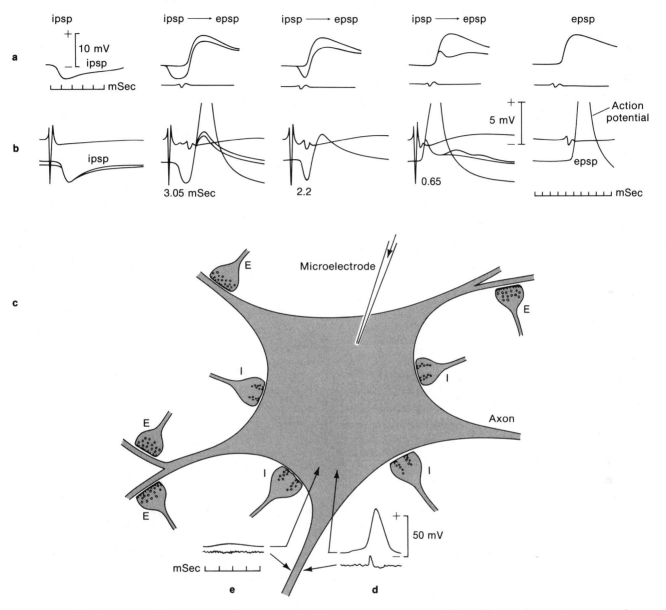

Figure 4-25 Summary of the interactions of excitatory and inhibitory synaptic inputs.   **a.** Effects of ipsps and epsps shown separately and together.   **b.** Records of stimulation and its effects on excitability of different postsynaptic membranes.   **c.** The excitatory (E) and inhibitory (I) synapses are shown with characteristic histological features. See text for further description.

Presynaptic Inhibition and Facilitation

Presynaptic inhibition and facilitation usually occur across an axoaxonic synapse, as Figure 4-26a illustrates. Sometimes activity in axon 1 will facilitate the effect that axon 2 has on the postsynaptic membrane of cell 3. This is **presynaptic facilitation.** In other synapses, cell 1 activity inhibits the effect that axon 2 has on the postsynaptic cell 3: **presynaptic inhibition.**

The way in which activity in cell 1 can affect the release of transmitter substance by cell 2 is still under investigation. Presynaptic inhibition often involves a small depolarization in the axon terminal of cell 2 (Kennedy, Calabrese, & Wine, 1974). This might mean that the depolarization invading the axon terminal of cell 2 would be short-circuited in the region of the axoaxonic synapse with cell 1, decreasing the size of the action

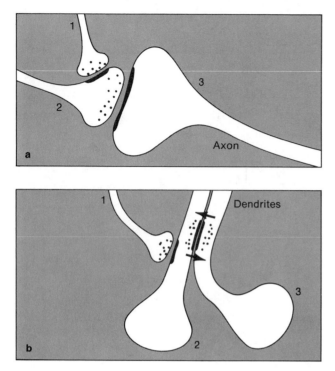

Figure 4-26   Various types of elements can occur in synaptic circuits.   **a.** The arrangement used by presynaptic facilitation or inhibition; note the axoaxonic synapse.   **b.** One type of reciprocal synapse.

potential and decreasing the amount of transmitter substance released by cell 2.

The transmitter released by cell 1 onto cell 2 may increase the permeability of the axon terminal to Cl^-. This action could be depolarizing if there were an inward Cl^- pump. An increase in g_{Cl^-} would lead to a depolarizing outward flow of Cl^- (Eccles, 1977; Weight, 1974). Arguing by analogy, then, presynaptic facilitation could involve hyperpolarizing the presynaptic terminal of cell 2, increasing the size of the action potential and increasing the amount of transmitter released.

There are other possibilities. The synapses that either facilitate or inhibit the action of other synapses often occur between the axon of one cell (cell 1) and the dendrites of another (cell 2). In turn, those dendrites make a reciprocal kind of dendro-dendritic synapse with cell 3 (as illustrated in Figure 4-26b). Here, depolarization of cell 2 by cell 1 would add to and facilitate any depolarization produced by the dendrodendritic synapse. Hyperpolarization of cell 2 by cell 1 would inhibit the effect of the dendrodendritic synapse.

Both presynaptic facilitation and inhibition may sometimes use Ca^{++} channels. For example, Horn and McAfee (1979)

speculated that the release of NE by axoaxonic synapses may block Ca^{++} channels, reducing the amount of Ca^{++} coming into cell 2 during its action potential. Since the release of transmitter depends on the entry of Ca^{++}, this action of NE would inhibit the synapse between cells 2 and 3. Presynaptic facilitation may directly affect Ca^{++} channels (Klein & Kandel, 1980; Siegelbaum, Camardo, & Kandel, 1982) or may indirectly affect Ca^{++} channels through the effects of serotonin on a K^+ channel (see Table 3-2). Serotonin closes this channel. When it is closed, the action potential is prolonged, increasing the amount of Ca^{++} entering. If cell 1 secreted serotonin onto cell 2, and if serotonin—as just described—increased the entry of Ca^{++}, the amount of transmitter substance released by cell 2 onto cell 3 would be increased.

Several different types of transmitter substance are found in axoaxonic synapses. According to Eccles (1973/1977), the transmitter substance for presynaptic inhibition is often GABA. There are also mu types of opioid receptors on the terminals of the types of afferents that carry pain information into the CNS.

Synaptic Interactions without Action Potentials

In some areas of the CNS, such as the retina of the eye, cells synaptically interact without action potentials. The cells involved often lack true axons. These forms of interaction often involve synapses among dendritelike processes. The synaptic patterns are often serial or reciprocal (Chapter 2). Thus, several nerve cells may interact within the same network of complex synaptic patterns.

These cells without axons (to be discussed later) often do not spontaneously show action potentials. However, they may have electrically gated channels, which would serve to amplify the change in membrane potential created at a synapse, increasing the spread of membrane potential changes more than if only the cable properties of the membrane were involved (length constant). These channels may also play a role in adaptation to constantly present stimuli.

Summary: One Type of Microcircuit

Putting all this information together tells us how the brain may process information. Any given area of the brain uses all these principles: spatial and temporal summation; convergence, divergence, and synaptic efficacy; presynaptic facilitation and inhibition. Studying a given area of the brain in depth, with both microelectrode recordings and microanatomical techniques, will allow us to draw a **microcircuit** map, indicating

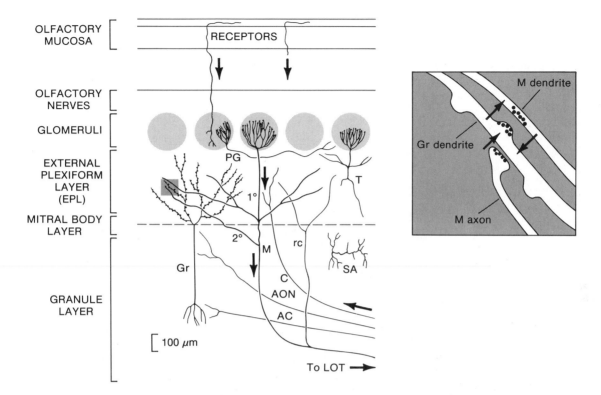

Figure 4-27 Microcircuit of the mammalian olfactory bulb (the inset presents an enlarged view of the boxed area).
Inputs: Afferent fibers (above) from olfactory receptors; central fibers (below) from three sources: centrifugal fibers (c) from the nucleus of the horizontal limb of the diagonal band; ipsilateral fibers from the anterior olfactory nucleus (AON); contralateral fibers from the anterior commissure (AC).
Principal neurons: Mitral cell (M), with primary (1°) and secondary (2°) dendrites and recurrent axon collateral (rc); tufted cell (T).
Intrinsic neurons: Periglomerular short-axon cell (PG); deep short-axon cell (SA); granule cell (Gr). LOT = lateral olfactory tract.

how nerve cells in a given area make synaptic contact with each other (Shepherd, 1978). Figure 4-17 of a sympathetic ganglion is one example of a microcircuit. Other microcircuits will be described in later chapters in association with their function (for example, learning, in Chapter 11).

One microcircuit is described here both as an example and as a summary. The circuit in Figure 4-27 comes from the olfactory bulb, a relay station linking the olfactory receptors in the nose to the CNS. Both convergence and divergence occur in the connection of the olfactory receptors with the mitral cells, allowing for variations in synaptic efficacy and for spatial and temporal summation of input. Reciprocal synapses (two-way synapses) are found both between mitral and periglomerular cell dendrites and also between the dendrites of mitral cells and granule cells. Both dendrodendritic and axoaxonic synapses are found between mitral and granule cells. The centrifugal fibers coming from the CNS control release of

transmitter from granule cells (GABA: Jahr & Nicoll, 1982). Understanding these synaptic events will enable us to see how olfactory information is coded.

Sensory input may be centrifugally controlled because CNS fibers presynaptically inhibit or facilitate other synapses. According to Jahr and Nicoll's analysis of these circuits (1982, p. 229): "noradrenaline [norepinephrine] and enkephalin block GABA release from granule cells, whereas glutamate enhances GABA release. The granule cell, then, is the final common pathway on which the centrifugal fibres and their transmitter candidates exert presynaptic control and thereby modulate the flow of information through the olfactory bulb." One major function of this particular microcircuit is to make it possible for the brain to regulate — and perhaps select — its own sensory input.

Some Mechanisms of Synaptic Modulation

Synaptic events can change. Here we describe some of the mechanisms by which synapses can be changed either by their own levels of past activity or by exogenously applied (swallowed or injected) drugs.

Availability of Inactivating and Synthesizing Enzymes

Several major mechanisms by which synaptic activity can be modulated or changed are illustrated in Figure 4-28. Although the figure shows a noradrenergic synapse, presumably very similar types of mechanisms exist for the other aminergic synapses. One major modulatory mechanism is the availability of

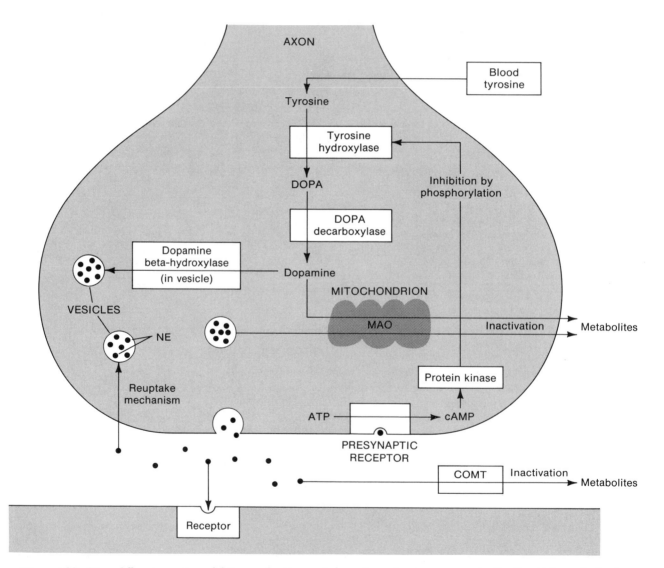

Figure 4-28   Many different synaptic modulation mechanisms control noradrenergic synapses. *am* varies directly with increasing levels of presynaptic dopamine beta-hydroxylase and varies inversely with increasing levels of MAO in mitochondria. See text for explanation and description of processes. MAO = monoamine oxidase; COMT = catechol-3-O-methyltransferase.

the inactivating and synthesizing enzymes. As Figure 4-28 shows, the more dopamine beta-hydroxylase is available, the more NE will be stored in the vesicles, thus potentially increasing *am*. But the more **monoamine oxidase (MAO)** is present, the smaller *am* will be. Synaptic activity may inhibit a synthesizing enzyme (tyrosine hydroxylase) and so decrease NE levels. This inhibition occurs when a presynaptic receptor is activated by a molecule of transmitter substance. One major class of drugs used to treat depression is MAO inhibitors. By inhibiting MAO, these drugs increase the amount of NE available for release.

Active Transport

The active transport of the transmitter substance back into the presynaptic cell limits the duration of the epsps at an aminergic synapse. This process is affected by exogenous drugs and by past synaptic activity. For example, the greater the level of NE in the cleft — the greater the synaptic activity has been — the more rapidly NE is actively transported back into the presynaptic cell. The tricyclics, a class of drugs commonly used to treat depression, block NE uptake, as does caffeine.

Both the presynaptic receptors and the reuptake mechanism thus create a **negative feedback loop** — that is, a loop in which the output of a system inhibits the process that creates the output. For example, heat produced by a furnace affects a thermostat that, when the heat rises enough, will turn off the furnace. The more active a synaptic system, the less NE will be manufactured and the more rapidly it will be transported back into the presynaptic cell once released. Both effects attenuate future synaptic activity. Negative feedback loops allow the output of a system such as a synapse to be carefully regulated.

In cholinergic synapses, the presynaptic choline reuptake system is also part of a negative feedback loop (Gilad, Rabey, & Shenkman, 1983; Kuhar & Murrin, 1978). An increase in reuptake capacity is associated with an increased capacity for ACh synthesis. Conversely, an increase in synaptic activity decreases uptake and thus presumably suppresses ACh synthesis: another negative feedback loop.

Presynaptic Receptors and Autoreceptors

As shown in both Figure 4-28 and Figure 4-29, presynaptic membranes also have receptors (see also Table 4-2). For NE synapses, the presynaptic receptors all seem to be of one certain type: **alpha$_2$**. (Postsynaptic NE receptors may also be alpha$_2$; other postsynaptic receptors are **alpha$_1$**, **beta$_1$**, and **beta$_2$** [Aghajanian & VanderMaelen, 1982; Maggi, U'Pri-

chard, & Enna, 1980; Westfall, 1977; Young & Kuhar, 1980].) In Figure 4-29, mechanism 1 shows that the presynaptic receptor may have excitatory or inhibitory effects on the presynaptic cell, although inhibitory effects are more common. In Figure 4-28, activating the presynaptic receptor can have enzymatic effects on the presynaptic cell similar to those found postsynaptically in slow synapses. Activating presynaptic receptors can also suppress the transmitter release mechanism.

Many cells also have **autoreceptors.** An autoreceptor is any receptor anywhere on a cell that responds to the transmitter released by that cell. Many autoreceptors are also presynaptic receptors, being located only in the presynaptic membrane. However, some presynaptic receptors may respond to transmitter substances other than the one secreted by that particular cell and thus are *not* autoreceptors. In some cases, autoreceptors combine with the transmitter substance as it is released by that same cell. Researchers believe that many dendrites and axon terminals may have autoreceptors. The effect on neuron activity is usually inhibitory (hyperpolarizing?), creating a very powerful negative feedback loop.

Figure 4-29 (mechanism 4) and Figure 4-30 show a variety of presynaptic receptors and autoreceptors. Some blood-borne transmitters may regulate noradrenergic activity and transmitter release through autoreceptors. In sympathetic ganglia, presynaptic noradrenergic receptors may regulate the release of ACh (Christ & Nishi, 1971; Dun & Karczmar, 1977; Kobayashi & Libet, 1970). The noradrenergic receptor may inhibit Ca^{++} channels in the presynaptic cell (Horn & McAfee, 1980; Westfall, 1977).

Changes in Postsynaptic Receptor Availability or Sensitivity

Synaptic activity and drugs can change the number or sensitivity of the postsynaptic receptors. Most often, extensive synaptic activity decreases the number of the postsynaptic receptors. Called **down regulation** (Maggi, U'Prichard, & Enna, 1980; Schwartz & Kellar, 1983), this process occurs in all types of synapses, although in cholinergic synapses continued stimulation by an agonist first decreases and then increases the number of postsynaptic receptors (Schwartz & Kellar, 1983).

Conversely, a decrease in synaptic activity increases the number or sensitivity of the postsynaptic receptors (Maggi, U'Prichard, & Enna, 1980; Schwartz & Kellar, 1983; Staunton, Magistretti, Koob, Shoemaker, & Bloom, 1982). This process is **denervation supersensitivity.** For example, cutting the axon of a motoneuron causes that axon to degenerate. The muscle fibers normally innervated by that motoneuron

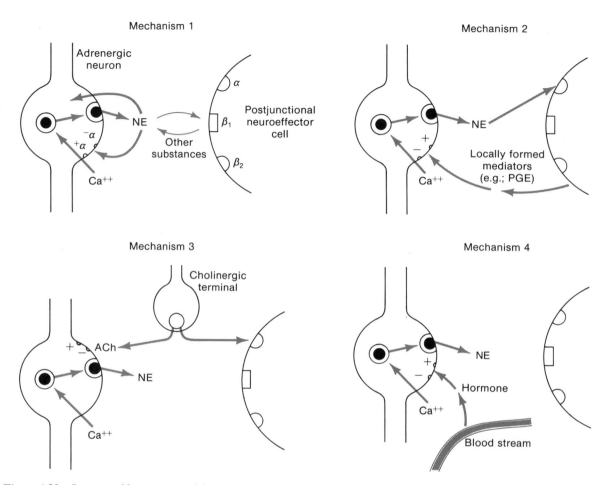

Figure 4-29 Some possible synaptic modulation mechanisms used by noradrenergic synapses. The + or − sign above the receptors indicates the effect that receptor activation has on that neuron. The presynaptic receptors are alpha (α) types, and the postsynaptic receptors are either alpha or beta (β) types. PGE = prostaglandins.

then develop new ACh receptors all over their membranes, the receptors no longer being limited to just the synaptic area. Because of the great increase in the number of ACh receptors, the muscle becomes supersensitive to small amounts of circulating ACh.

Prostaglandins, Neuromodulators, and Hormones

The effects of substances other than "true" transmitters on the synapse are illustrated in Figure 4-29 and Figure 4-30. In Figure 4-29, mechanism 2 and mechanism 4 both involve such effects: the first from substances released by the postsynaptic cell and the second from substances reaching the presynaptic cell from the blood stream or extracellular fluid. (Mechanism 3 in Figure 4-29 involves presynaptic facilitation or inhibition.) Other peptides such as substance P and somato-

statin may modulate synaptic activity by increasing or decreasing synthesizing enzyme levels in the presynaptic cells (Kessler, Adler, & Black, 1983). Figure 4-30 summarizes the ways in which the activity of a peripheral sympathetic neuron can be modulated.

The various **prostaglandins** are lipids that were first discovered to affect contraction in smooth muscles (for example, intestinal muscles). Prostaglandins are released by synaptic stimulation, but it is still unclear whether they come from the postsynaptic cell, as illustrated in Figure 4-30, or from the presynaptic cell (Westfall, 1977). Some types of prostaglandins may be part of a negative feedback loop, inhibiting further release of transmitter substance. Other types of prostaglandins may enhance the response of the postsynaptic cell to the transmitter substance.

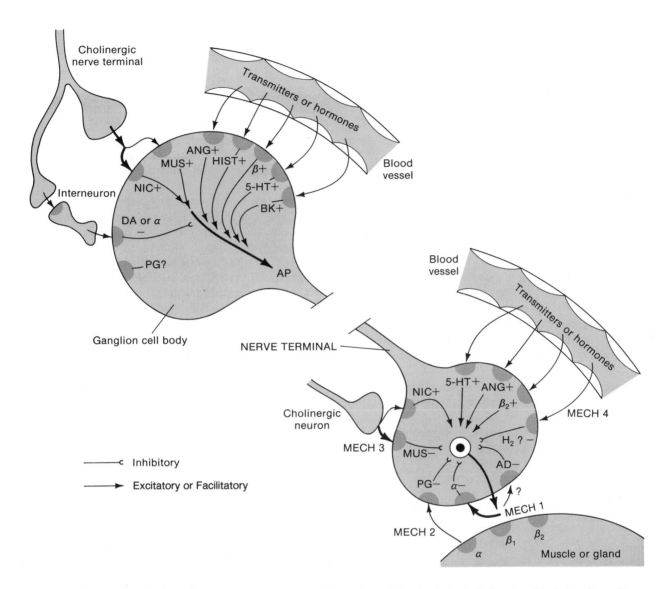

Figure 4-30 In a peripheral noradrenergic neuron, synaptic activity can be modulated at the level of either the cell body (ganglion cell) or the nerve terminal. MUS = muscarinic receptor; NIC = nicotinic receptor; ANG = angiotensin; HIST = histamine, β = beta adrenergic; H_2 = histamine receptor; 5-HT = 5-hydroxytryptamine (serotonin); AD = adenosine; BK = bradykinin; α = alpha adrenergic; PG = prostaglandin; + = excitatory or facilitatory response; − = inhibitory response; AP = action potential. See text for further description.

Other Changes That Depend on the Frequency of Synaptic Activity

Some types of changes are modulated precisely by how much synaptic activity has gone on before, and how long ago. Some of these changes *increase* synaptic activity. They have been used as models of how the synapse can "remember" past activity.

Posttetanic potentiation. The first mechanism to be discovered was **posttetanic potentiation (PTP)**. If the presynaptic neuron is stimulated repeatedly with very strong and very high-frequency electrical impulses (a **tetanizing stimulation**), the epp or epsp following a subthreshold test stimulus is increased. The increase lasts from several seconds to several minutes. PTP may come from an accumulation of Ca^{++}

within the presynaptic nerve. If Ca^{++} were increased presynaptically, more transmitter would be released per **impulse** (action potential) (Landau, Smolinsky, & Lass, 1973; Weight, 1974; Wilson & Skirboll, 1974; Zucker & Lara-Estrella, 1983).

Facilitation.   **Frequency facilitation** is an increase in the epsp or epp response to a subthreshold stimulation seen after one conditioning stimulus has been applied to the presynaptic nerve. The increased response to the second or test stimulus declines as the interval between the two stimulations increases, up to 200 mSec. The probability of release of transmitter is increased by the conditioning stimulus (Weight, 1974). The effect probably involves presynaptic Ca^{++} (Landau, Smolinsky, & Lass, 1973).

Depression.   **Depression** follows the period of frequency facilitation. After a conditioning stimulus, there is a period of facilitation followed by a period of depression of transmitter release. The depression lasts from one to ten seconds, depending on the conditioning stimuli. Frequency depression may represent fatigue, or depletion of transmitter (Weight, 1974).

Long-term potentiation.   After a period of brief, intense tetanic stimulation of hippocampal afferents, the synapses of those axons with the hippocampal neurons are facilitated or potentiated. Unlike PTP, **long-term potentiation (LTP)** lasts for hours or even weeks (Stringer & Guyenet, 1983; see Chapter 11).

Summary of Synaptic Modulation

Activity across a given synapse is unlikely to be exactly the same for any two stimulations. Some changes are caused by negative feedback loops: synaptic activity inhibits future activity across the same synapse. The uptake mechanism, the presynaptic receptor, the autoreceptor, and the down regulation of the postsynaptic receptor are all inhibited by prior synaptic activity. This inhibition may account for frequency depression. Synaptic activity may be temporarily facilitated by past activity: PTP, LTP, and frequency facilitation. This last type of effect may eventually provide models about how synapses can "remember" what has happened to them.

Chapter Summary

The Synapse and Transmission of Information

The synaptic transmission of information depends on both presynaptic and postsynaptic events. The presynaptic neuron releases transmitter substance into the synaptic cleft. The release process involves the entry of Ca^{++} into the presynaptic cell, which causes one or more quanta of transmitter substance to be released. The transmitter molecules diffuse across the cleft and combine with specialized receptor proteins on the postsynaptic membrane.

Different types of receptor proteins have different effects on the postsynaptic cell membrane. Some receptor proteins are associated with ionophores or membrane channels. If the ionophore allows K^+ or Cl^- through, the postsynaptic cell is hyperpolarized and inhibited. If the ionophore allows K^+ and Na^+ through, the cell is depolarized and excited. Some receptor proteins are associated with enzymes. Enzyme activation triggers a series of reactions leading to phosphorylation of a membrane protein and usually either hyperpolarization or depolarization.

Synaptic activity is controlled and modulated by a variety of mechanisms. For cholinergic synapses, the duration of synaptic activity is limited by the amount of AChE present. For aminergic synapses, active transport of amine back into the presynaptic terminal limits synaptic activity. Since the rate of active transport can be varied, this mechanism can also be used to modulate synaptic activity. Other modulatory mechanisms include presynaptic receptors, autoreceptors, increases or decreases in the availability of synthesizing and degrading enzymes, increases and decreases in the probability of release of transmitter, and the modulatory effect that hormones and neuromodulators have on synaptic function.

The synapse not only transmits information but *transforms* it. Our phenomenological reality — our sensations of events inside and outside our skin, and our memories of things past — is therefore *not* a faithful replica of "real-world" events. Very literally, our reality is created by our brain circuits.

C H A P T E R

Genetics and the Nerve Cell

Our behavior and brains are products of the continuing interaction between the environment that surrounds us and our **chromosomes,** the hereditary material with which we started life. The **genes** found on the chromosomes can affect the communication function of nerve cells: different types of heredity can influence the ways in which axons and synapses pass information from one point to another.

The research and principles described in this chapter are directly relevant to principle 3 of the neuron doctrine and to the sixth method of experimentation (see Table 1-1). Thus, this chapter will complete our description of the basic elements from which brain circuits and brain codes are formed.

Overview

The chromosomes in humans give us our special species identity, both in appearance and in behavior. And yet because of evolutionary continuity, up to 99% of the genes active in humans may be identical to those active in our closest relatives, the chimpanzees — though that small difference in gene activity can mean a large difference in genetic products (Plomin, DeFries, & McClearn, 1980).

Human Chromosomes

Humans have 46 chromosomes, arranged in 23 pairs, as Figure 5-1 illustrates. If an organism's chromosomes have been arranged into pairs, based on size and physical appearance, the resulting display is the organism's **karyotype.** One pair is the pair of **sex chromosomes.** This pair consists of either two **X chromosomes** (in mammalian females) or one X and one **Y chromosome** (in mammalian males). Since the X is much larger than the Y chromosome and contains many more genes, that pair is mismatched in size in the male. The other 22 chromosome pairs are the **autosomes.**

In humans, as in all other species that reproduce sexually, one member of each pair comes from the paternal side and one from the maternal side. Each sexually reproducing organism is the product of hereditary traits received from both the father and mother. In members of both sexes, one chromosome of each of their autosome pairs came from the father and one from the mother. One of the mammalian female's X chromosomes also came from her father and one from her mother. The mammalian male's X chromosome came from his mother and his Y chromosome from his father (since mothers do not have any Y chromosomes to pass on to anyone).

Each chromosome contains many genes, usually estimated to be in the thousands for humans. The gene is the unit of heredity. Each functional gene codes for a single protein, and the proteins collectively determine the structure and functions of each body cell in an organism.

The protein can be either an enzymatic protein or a structural protein; that is, the gene can contain the hereditary code for a protein that, once manufactured, serves as an enzyme, regulating the rate of metabolic reactions in the cell. Or the gene can code for a structural protein that eventually becomes part of the cell wall or of the membrane of an intracellular organelle. In either case, the kinds of reactions the cell carries out, and the structure and appearance of the cell, are deter-

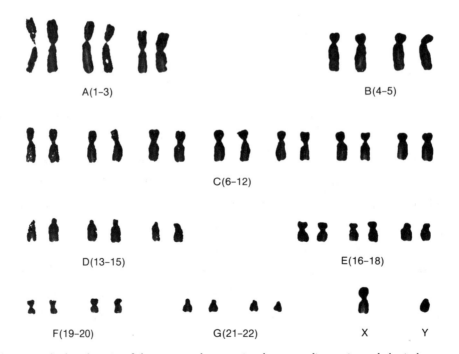

A(1–3)   B(4–5)

C(6–12)

D(13–15)   E(16–18)

F(19–20)   G(21–22)   X   Y

Figure 5-1   A karyotype displays the pairs of chromosomes by arranging them according to size and physical appearance. Each pair is given a letter-number "name." This karyotype came from a human male: note the Y chromosome.

mined by which genes are actively producing proteins in that cell.

Effects of Genes on the Brain and Behavior

In the area of genetic research, psychobiologists, like other psychologists, are most interested in the ways in which the heredity of an organism can affect behavior. A psychobiologist might first study the link between a given gene or set of genes and the functioning of nerve cells and then study the link between the nerve cell and the behavior of the organism. This chapter concentrates on the first relationship. Later chapters explore how genetically affected neural activity might be related to sexual behaviors, emotional problems, learning, and hunger.

Since each cell in the body contains exactly the same hereditary material, the different appearance and function of the various types of body cells need an explanation. For example, since a nerve cell looks different from a red blood cell and carries out different kinds of metabolic processes, different proteins must be manufactured by those cell types. And if this is so, only a few genes must be active in each type of body cell. The genes coding for structural or enzymatic proteins not needed by a particular type of cell are **repressed**: the protein for which they are the code is not being manufactured by the cell. Repression occurs early during development, when body tissues became organized into the various organs (Brown, 1981; Caplan & Ordahl, 1978; Stent, 1964). An alternative to the theory of genetic repression proposes that all genes are always active, but the factor controlling which genetic products become functional proteins operated at some level other than that of the genes themselves (Davidson & Britten, 1979).

Regardless of the reason, many of the active genes and/or proteins found in nerve cells are unique to that type of cell. If those particular genes were somehow altered—as by a mutation—the proteins normally appearing in brain cells would not appear or would have different properties. If the gene involved were the one coding for a protein that forms part of the electrically gated Na^+ pore, the axons of nerve cells would not function normally. If the gene involved coded for part of a chemically gated pore or for a transmitter-synthesizing enzyme, the way the synapse operates would be changed.

This chapter concentrates on the genes coding for proteins important to nerve-cell membranes. It surveys the types of research that are used to demonstrate genetic effects on nerve cells and behavior. A description of basic genetic principles provides the necessary background for further discussion. Finally, it treats the ways in which genes and their protein-products can affect the functioning of nerve cells.

Genetic Types of Research

This section provides only a general background. A reader interested in a more detailed explanation of behavioral genetics, including the mathematical statistics associated with that research, should consult the Plomin, DeFries, & McClearn book *Behavioral Genetics: A Primer* (1980) for a readable yet sophisticated introduction to this topic. A higher-level discussion can be found in Fuller and Thompson's *Foundations of Behavior Genetics* (1978). A fascinating description of how genes affect the functioning of various types of nerve cells appears in Pak and Pinto's review (1976). The following discussion draws heavily on those sources.

Purposes of Genetic Research

The purpose of genetic research might seem obvious: to assess the "nature" part of the nature/nurture controversy. However, a single-unit approach to behavior adds other purposes to the obvious one.

Hereditary aspects of behavior. One major purpose of genetic research is to establish the degree to which hereditary influences can affect the behavior of the organism. Is a given rat emotional or easily frightened in part because of the genes it inherited from its parents? Do some mice overeat their way into obesity in part because of genes?

Using one or more of the research techniques to be described, we *can* determine the degree to which individual differences among organisms living in a given environment can be attributed to differences among their genes. When researchers do so, what they have measured is **heritability.** In other words, of the differences in a given trait among a given group of individuals, heritability is the proportion that can be attributed to differences in their genes.

Other trait differences among organisms in a group can be attributed to differences in their developmental and current environments. This influence is **environmentality** (Fuller & Thompson, 1978). In addition, genes and environments might interact. For example, organisms with different genes might react differently to changes in rearing environments. Together these factors would explain why organisms differ from one another. A major purpose of genetic research is to evaluate the genetic component of this explanation.

A specific example will make things clearer. Suppose that only some organisms in a given group had a gene for obesity, the presence of which tended to increase food intake. Further suppose that some of these organisms, as well as some organisms without that particular gene, were exposed to an environment with abundant supplies of sweet-tasting and fatty foods. Animals tend to overeat when sweet-tasting and fatty foods are freely available. Suppose the tendency to overeat such foods were greatly exaggerated in the organisms possessing the obesity gene. The differences among all those organisms in the average amount of food eaten per day (not to mention amount of body fat) could be attributed to differences in their heredities, in their environments, and in the interaction of their heredities with their environments.

Researchers assume that differences among individuals in groups such as these can be usefully expressed as **variance.** Variance is the average degree to which individuals *in a given group* differ from each other with respect to some particular characteristic. One way of calculating a type of variance score is to calculate the group's average score on a certain trait, such as IQ. Then each individual's IQ score would be subtracted from the group's average to find that individual's **deviation score.** The absolute values (ignoring the sign) of all the deviation scores would be added together and divided by the number of people in the group to find the average deviation score.

The variance defined this way would be small if the members of the group were homogeneous, differing little from each other. For example, the variance in the IQ scores among club members restricting their membership to geniuses would be relatively small. Variance is large if the members of the groups are heterogeneous. The variance in IQ scores among all the people living in any town would be relatively large, since that group would probably include retarded as well as very bright people.

Using the concept of variance, we can express the relationship between heritability and behavior in a simple equation. First, assume that there is no interaction between the genes possessed by a particular group of organisms and the environments experienced by that group: all organisms, regardless of their genetics, would be assumed to react the same way to the same environments. If so, and if V_G refers to variance (individual differences) attributable to genetic differences, and if V_P refers to the total variability among members of a certain group in trait scores, then for that trait,

$$\text{heritability} = \frac{V_G}{V_P}$$

In an exactly parallel fashion, if V_E refers to variance attributable to environmental differences, then

$$\text{environmentality} = \frac{V_E}{V_P}$$

Genetic research tries to measure heritability by estimating V_G relative to V_P.

Defining heritability in this way sets limits on what the purposes of genetic research can be. In the types of research described above, heritability could be defined *only* for a group of organisms having a certain range of genetic differences, and then *only* for the range of possible environments actually experienced by members of that group. If either the genetic differences or the environmental differences among those organisms were changed, the heritability of the trait in question would also be changed. Thus, genetic research can find out *only* about the heritability for a given group of organisms having a given set of possible genes and environments.

Some specific examples illustrate this important point. If organisms had absolutely identical heredities (as is true of mammalian identical twins and is nearly true of some highly inbred strains of laboratory mice and fruit flies), no differences among them could be attributed to genetic factors. As defined, heritability is the proportion of variance attributable to genetic differences. If all members of the group had the same genes ($V_G = 0$), heritability would have to be 0, and any differences observed among organisms of those strains would have to be attributed to differences in their environments. However, that would *not* mean that the genes those organisms share are having no effect on their body appearance or their behaviors.

Alternatively, suppose that a group of genetically disparate organisms could be raised in absolutely identical environments (which is impossible, though it can be closely approximated by closely controlled laboratory conditions). Any differences among those organisms would have to be attributed to differences in their heredities. Again, that would *not* mean that their common environments had no effect on their behaviors. For example, if they were isolated from all contact with other organisms of their own species, their emotions and motives would have been strongly affected. But since there are no environmental differences among them, all differences that do exist have to be attributed to genetic factors ($V_P = V_G$), and heritability would be equal to 1.

Genetic research is therefore limited to estimating the heritabilities of various traits among given groups of organisms. However, groups of humans will differ from each other not only in the range of genetic differences found both between *and* within the groups but also in the environmental differences found between *and* within the groups. Consequently, genetic research can precisely determine the relative contributions of genes and environment to IQ scores only for a given group of people in whom the genetic and environmental variations are well measured. Even so, any conclusion *cannot* be generalized to any other groups having different environments or genes.

Regulation of neural activity by genetic expression.   We suggested earlier that phosphorylation of proteins during slow synaptic activity might affect the activity of genes in the nucleus. The protein-product of these genes could then affect the future activity of that cell. Regulating which genes are expressed in nerve cells allows those cells to adapt to future changes in function or input (Thoenen & Edgar, 1982). For example, agonists that stimulate cells in a sympathetic ganglion can increase, within 48 hours, cellular levels of the enzyme (tyrosine hydroxylase) involved in the manufacture of their transmitter substance, NE.

But this is not the only way in which genetic expression may be involved in neural activity. During fetal development, which genes are active presumably determines what transmitter substance will be manufactured by the cell and what types of synapses will be formed with what types of other cells. Since there are not enough genes to specify exactly all the synaptic connections to be formed among all the cells, the genes must instead specify *rules* for making connections. Developing cells then interact with each other to determine which of their genes will be activated and thus which synapses will be formed and which transmitter substances will be manufactured.

By studying neural processes during fetal development, we can not only discover the ways in which some genes are activated and others repressed but also learn about the molecular basis of neural activity. For example, one experimenter cultured fetal nerve cells either with or without a drug that prevents protein synthesis (O'Dowd, 1983). At certain periods in development, the appearance of electrically gated Na^+ channels could be blocked without affecting the electrically gated K^+ channels. Thus, each channel is under the control of different genes, and each gene is expressed at different developmental times.

Some of the rules governing the development of nerve cells in the ANS have been discovered through this type of research (Patterson, Potter, & Furshpan, 1981). Immature ANS sympathetic cells can manufacture both NE and ACh. (If left alone, most of these sympathetic postganglionic cells would develop into noradrenergic neurons, but a few would develop into cholinergic neurons innervating certain blood vessels and sweat glands.) When samples of these immature cells are studied in a culture medium, they can be "persuaded" to go either way by varying the conditions under which they are cultured and whether the cells are electrically stimulated into activity. Studying the ways in which the activity of nerve cells affects

the expression of their genes will tell us more about genes, about nerve cells, and eventually about behavior.

Research Techniques

Heritability is studied in several different ways. Because of ethical considerations, the most powerful techniques cannot be used with humans. Interpreting research done with humans will therefore always entail more doubt than will better-controlled research done with other animals.

Selective breeding.   **Selective breeding** was an early technique, practiced long before the existence of genes was even suspected. Most of the animals we have domesticated have been subjected to selective breeding for hundreds of their generations. Today we have many distinct strains of horses, cows, cats, and dogs, each strain with somewhat different physical and behavioral characteristics. Selective breeding involves systematically mating only those males and females having a high level of some trait and/or mating only those having a low level of the same trait. If a trait can selectively be bred for — or against — by such methods, the trait has a genetic component. Two different strains of animals could be produced by such a breeding program. One strain would have a much higher level of the trait than would the other, and both strains would differ from the parent strain.

The results of a breeding study are illustrated in Figure 5-2. The trait studied was "emotionality," here defined and measured by the level of activity in an open field. An **open field** is a square or rectangular box that is marked off into squares by lines on its floor or by the placement of photocells on its walls. The more lines an organism crosses in a given, standardized period of time, the greater its level of activity is assumed to be. Inactive mice are assumed to be **emotional** because frightened mice go to a corner and "hide"; more active mice are assumed to be less emotional. The systematic mating of active males with active females and inactive males with inactive females produced two different strains. In another breeding program, involving rats, the resulting strains have "bred true" for hundreds of generations. These strains still exist today as **Maudsley reactive** (emotional: frequently defecating in the open field) and **nonreactive** (nonemotional: seldom defecating in the open field) rats.

Selective breeding has produced strains of experimental animals that differ in learning, in emotional responsiveness, in motives, and in sensory responses (DeFries & Plomin, 1978; Fuller & Thompson, 1978; Plomin, DeFries, & McClearn, 1980). The effects of heredity on motivational and emotional

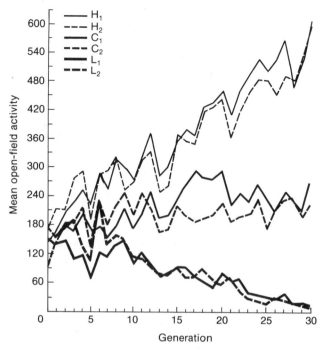

Figure 5-2 The amount of activity displayed in an open field can be selectively bred for or against. Two lines (future strains) of mice were selected for high levels of open-field activity (H_1 and H_2), and two were selected for low levels of open-field activity (L_1 and L_2). Two lines were randomly mated to serve as controls (C_1 and C_2).

aspects of neural coding, as well as its relationship to the effects of experience on neural coding, will be covered in some detail in later chapters.

Heritability can be measured through selective breeding. For a given selection criterion (for example, how active a mouse must be before it is selected for breeding into the active strain), the greater the degree to which the two strains come to differ from the parental strain, the higher the heritability will be.

Strain comparisons.   Another way of estimating heritability is to compare different strains of animals on a given trait or characteristic. To create the most powerful test, the different strains should be raised in as controlled an environment as possible (to reduce variance attributable to environmental differences). Animals of the two strains should also be mated or **crossed** with each other, producing what is called an F_1 generation. The F_1 generation is then tested. Trait differences among strains raised in nearly identical environments would be attributed to genetic differences.

Family resemblances.   The more closely related two family members are to each other, the more genes they are likely to share. Therefore, if trait similarity among family members tends to parallel the estimated genetic similarity, the trait in question may have some genetic basis. For example, if father and son are more similar to each other in a behavioral trait than are an uncle and that son, maybe the greater number of genes shared by father and son accounts for their greater behavioral similarity. However, family members also tend to share similar environments, so the greater similarity among more closely related family members should probably be called **familiality,** which would represent shared genes (V_G) as well as shared environments (V_E).

Studies of human families can mathematically estimate heritability. The genes shared by pairs of family members can be probabilistically related to trait resemblances. For example, a parent and his or her child, or two siblings, are, on the average, expected to share half their genes in common. Half-siblings would, on the average, share only a quarter of their genes. The more the trait resemblances paralleled the degree of genetic similarity, the greater the familiality would be. Family studies can also investigate the way in which traits such as retardation or color blindness tend to "run in families." By looking at the family tree and seeing which relatives do and do not have the trait in question, a researcher can estimate the genetic basis of the trait. This process is often called a **pedigree analysis.**

Family studies are also done with nonhuman animals. Strains of animals that differ in some trait can be bred in various patterns. For example, the similarity of offspring all having both the same mother and the same father can be compared with that of offspring having the same mother but different fathers. Once again, the greater the degree to which behavioral similarities parallel the average genetic similarities, the greater the estimated heritability of the trait.

Twin studies.   Identical human twins share *all* their genes, whereas fraternal twins, like any other sibling pair, share only half of their genes, on the average. If identical twins are more similar to each other in some trait than are fraternal twins, the trait may have some genetic basis. Furthermore, if it can be demonstrated that identical twins do *not* have environments that are any more similar than the environments shared by fraternal twin pairs, the greater degree of similarity between identical twins in comparison with fraternal twins can directly estimate the heritability of the trait in question (Plomin, DeFries; & McClearn, 1980).

Something like twin studies can be carried out in nonhuman animals as well. Pairs of animals in highly inbred strains tend to have nearly identical genes. The similarity among pairs of animals from the same inbred strain could be compared with the similarity among pairs of animals each from a different strain — all being raised in the same controlled environment — to estimate heritability.

Adoption studies.   The most powerful studies of humans control for the effect of environmental similarities. The similarities between adopted children and their natural parents are measured in comparison with their similarities to their adopted parents. In the first case, only genes and not environments are shared, and in the second case, only environments and not genes are shared. This type of research pits variance attributable to genes directly against variance attributable to environment. Such studies can also be done with identical twins adopted into different foster families.

A version of the adoption study can be carried out in animals using the routine controls for environmental factors. Offspring are **cross-fostered:** the offspring from one mother are raised by another mother, either from the same or from a different strain, as illustrated in Figure 5-3. Such a study can separate the effects of shared genes from the postnatal effects of being reared by a mother of a given strain.

The prenatal environment can also be controlled in animal "adoption" research. One control for prenatal environment is to cross two different strains. For example, Maudsley reactive fathers might be mated to Maudsley nonreactive mothers and reactive mothers mated to nonreactive fathers. This procedure is called a **diallel cross.** All offspring have half reactive and half nonreactive genes, but half come from a reactive uterine environment and half from a nonreactive uterine environment. If all the resulting offspring are cross-fostered to the same strain of mothers to control for postnatal environment, then the effects of genetics on the trait can be rather precisely estimated (see, for example, Joffe, 1965a, 1965b).

Another control for the prenatal environment has a decidedly "science fiction" flavor to it. It involves ovary transplants. The eggs developing in the ovaries of one mother are re-moved, ovary and all, and implanted in another mother whose ovaries have also been removed. This second female is then mated. Experimenters can thereby separate the effects of genes from the effects of prenatal environment.

A molecular lesion technique.   One technique of genetic research is particularly relevant to a single-unit approach. It involves inducing a change in a specified gene and measuring the physiological and behavioral effects of that change. This whole process is called the **molecular lesion technique.** As described in Pak and Pinto's review (1976), organisms like fruit flies or *Paramecia* are exposed to some chemical mutagen that induces a change in one or more genes (often just one). Then the organism is examined physically and behaviorally. It is also examined genetically to see, for example, on which one of the fly's four pairs of chromosomes the mutated gene might be found. By relating the effects the mutated gene has on the nervous system to the effects it has on behavior, geneticists can use the molecular lesion technique to study the relationships among genes, brain cells, and behaviors.

This genetic technique has been used to analyze which parts of the brain are involved in which behaviors (Hall, 1977) and to analyze how genes code for various sensory functions (Ready, Hanson, & Benzer, 1976). Eventually researchers hope to be able to interrelate genes, neural physiology, and behavior. *Paramecia*, fruit flies, and mice have all been used in research.

Selective mutations.   The mutations most useful to the neuron doctrine are those that change the way nerve cells function. *Paramecia* have been subjected to mutagens that alter their behavior. **Receptor potentials** (changes in the membrane potential of a sensory receptor organ), action potentials, synaptic potentials, and the membrane proteins involved in channel gating have all been studied in these mutated organisms (Kung, Chang, Satow, Van Houten, & Hansma, 1975, p. 899). For example, one genetic mutation in *Paramecia* affects an electrically gated channel and offers a chance to understand the molecular basis of the action potential. Another single gene, which probably came from a "natural" mutation in humans, codes for a single protein that produces color blindness. Analyses of the vision of people possessing that gene have contributed greatly to our understanding of color vision. By studying the ways in which the altered genes affect both nerve cells and behaviors, researchers may someday find a complete reductionistic explanation of behavior.

In one fascinating example of the molecular lesion technique, *Paramecia* were exposed to a powerful mutagen and

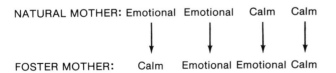

NATURAL MOTHER: Emotional   Emotional   Calm   Calm

FOSTER MOTHER: Calm   Emotional   Emotional   Calm

Figure 5-3   In a cross-fostering study, the offspring of one group of female subjects are given to another group of female subjects to raise. To separate genetic from postnatal effects, some offspring of each strain are given to a genetically similar and some to a genetically dissimilar mother.

then induced to reproduce asexually. *Paramecia* are covered with cilia, which usually propel them in a spiralling forward direction. When disturbed or exposed to various solutions, the *Paramecium* exhibits avoidance reactions: the cilia beat synchronously in the opposite direction, and the animal moves backward for a body length or more before moving forward again. Exposing a large group of *Paramecia* to a mutagen produced many different kinds of mutants with abnormal avoidance reactions (Kung et al., 1975). Studying how a change in a single gene can produce these behavioral effects constitutes a very promising area of research.

Summary of Types of Genetic Research

Genetic researchers use several kinds of techniques to analyze the genetic basis for any given type of behavior. Heritability can be estimated from selective breeding, from strain comparisons, and from family resemblances. When these techniques are combined with proper controls — as with cross-fostering in animals or adoption studies in humans — they can provide powerful genetic tools for the analysis of the brain and behavior.

Genetic research attempts to analyze brain function from a certain point of view. Knowing how genes work, and knowing the heritability of a certain trait, can provide clues about how brain states may be related to behavioral characteristics. Studying how neural activity changes genetic activity can provide information both about genes and about the molecular basis of various types of neural activity. Even more important, by using the molecular lesion technique, researchers eventually may fully trace the links among a gene, a protein, the activity of nerve cells, and behavior — and, by inference, a mental state. Although this has not yet been done for any given gene, the promise is there.

Basic Genetic Principles

This section describes how genes code for proteins, how they interact with each other to produce variability in traits, and how the operation of genes is regulated during development and by the activities of the adult cell.

Genes, Chromosomes, and Proteins

Chromosomes contain thousands of genes. Each gene is a code for a structural or enzymatic protein or for a set of functionally related enzymatic proteins. Which genes are active or are being decoded determines the structure and function of a cell.

The chemical nature of genes and proteins. Chromosomes consist of molecules of **deoxyribonucleic acid (DNA)**. Each DNA molecule has two strands of DNA, each composed of alternating groups of phosphoric acid and sugar molecules (see Figure 5-4). Nucleic acids (complex organic compounds containing nitrogen), or **nucleotides,** are attached to the side of each of these strands. Nucleotides are also sometimes referred to as **bases.** Four nucleotides, or bases, are found in DNA: adenine, thymine, guanine, and cytosine.

The two strands of DNA are twisted around each other in a double helix, as discovered by Watson and Crick (1953a, 1953b) (see Figure 5-5). The two strands are attached but held a fixed distance from each other by pairs of corresponding nucleotides: adenine always pairs with thymine, and guanine always pairs with cytosine. Because of this pairing of nucleotides, one strand of DNA is said to be **complementary** to the other strand.

DNA molecules code for protein molecules. A single DNA molecule contains several thousand genes and runs the length of a chromosome. The genetic message is contained in the sequence of the nucleotides found in each gene. Each sequence of three nucleotides, or **triplet,** codes a given amino acid, as indicated in Table 5-1. A triplet of nucleotides is a **codon.** Some triplets code for the ending or for the beginning of a coding sequence: these are the **stop** and **start** codons. Some amino acids are coded for by more than one triplet. For example, three adenines in a row code for the amino acid phenylalanine, but so does the triplet of adenine, adenine, and guanine. Since proteins are chains of amino acids, the chains of nucleotides in a gene code for the chain of amino acids in a protein molecule and for the beginning and end of that chain.

There may be no more than 150,000 functional genes (genes coding for a protein) in mammals. The number could be as small as 30,000 — even though mammals have enough DNA to code for more than 3 million proteins. Much of the "unused" DNA is found in long noncoding sequences, or **introns.** The function of introns is currently being debated; bacteria seem to do quite well without them. Introns may increase the rate of evolution or may just be an evolutionary by-product.

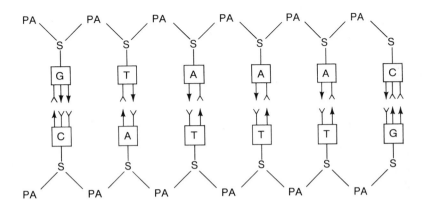

Figure 5-4   A DNA molecule is constructed from phosphate, sugar, and nucleic acids. PA = phosphoric acid; S = sugar; A = adenine; T = thymine; G = guanine; C = cytosine.

Other DNA is used for purposes other than that of coding for proteins. It may be used to regulate the activity of other genes, to act as "spacing" material between functional genes, and to code for **ribonucleic acid (RNA)**. Still other DNA occurs in very repetitive sequences; only some of this may function as codes for proteins. The repetitive DNA and RNA may play a role in genetic regulation (Davidson & Britten, 1979).

Transcription and translation.   The way in which genetic information is translated into protein molecules is illustrated in Figure 5-6. **Transcription** is the process of taking the genetic code from a gene in a DNA molecule and transferring it to a molecule of **messenger** ribonucleic acid (**messenger** RNA). **Translation** is the process of using the information from messenger RNA to create a **polypeptide chain** (a chain of amino acids) from it.

Transcription and translation require three different kinds of RNA. RNA also consists of a sequence of nucleotides: uracil (replacing the thymine of the DNA molecule), guanine, cytosine, and adenine. The messenger RNA takes the genetic code

out of the nucleus and into the cytoplasm of the cell where the protein is manufactured. The **ribosomal RNA** is found in the ribosomes, the cellular organelles in which the protein synthesis takes place. A sequence of three nucleotides in a **transfer RNA** molecule "recognizes" a specific amino acid molecule and transports it to a ribosome to be attached to a growing chain of amino acids.

In transcription, first the two strands of DNA separate. One strand, the **coding strand,** is used as the template for creating a strand of messenger RNA (only one DNA strand is used for coding: Hayashi, Hayashi, & Spiegelman, 1963). The messenger RNA is complementary to the DNA coding strand, in exactly the same way that the other strand of DNA, which is not used for coding, is complementary to the coding strand (see Figure 5-4). Thus, a guanine on the DNA results in a cytosine on the RNA, and vice versa. But since thymine in the DNA is replaced by uracil in RNA, adenosine in the DNA codes for uracil in the RNA molecule, whereas thymine in the DNA codes for adenosine in the RNA.

The molecule of RNA complementary to the DNA coding

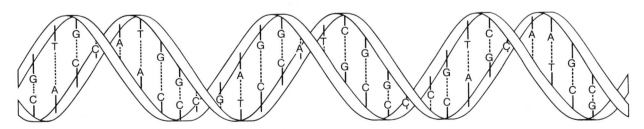

Figure 5-5   The double helix form of the two strands of the DNA molecule. The two strands are opposite in polarity, or complementary to each other, meaning that — for example — every guanine found on one strand is associated with a cytosine on the other. A = adenine; T = thymine; G = guanine; C = cytosine. For replication of DNA or production of RNA the two strands are separated at the broken lines.

Table 5-1 The genetic code.

First Letter	Second Letter				Third Letter
	A	G	T	C	
A	Phe	Ser	Tyr	Cys	A
	Phe	Ser	Tyr	Cys	G
	Leu	Ser	stop	stop	T
	Leu	Ser	stop	Try	C
G	Leu	Pro	His	Arg	A
	Leu	Pro	His	Arg	G
	Leu	Pro	Gln	Arg	T
	Leu	Pro	Gln	Arg	C
T	Ile	Thr	Asn	Ser	A
	Ile	Thr	Asn	Ser	G
	Ile	Thr	Lys	Arg	T
	start, Met	Thr	Lys	Arg	C
C	Val	Ala	Asp	Gly	A
	Val	Ala	Asp	Gly	G
	Val	Ala	Glu	Gly	T
	Val	Ala	Glu	Gly	C

NOTE: Each amino acid is coded by a triplet of three bases, or nucleotides, as shown in the table, which is a compact way of setting out the 64 possible triplets.

The four bases are denoted by the letters A, G, T, and C. In DNA the four bases are: A = Adenine; G = Guanine; T = Thymine; C = Cytosine.

The 20 amino acids are identified as follows:

Ala = Alanine
Arg = Arginine
Asn = Asparagine
Asp = Aspartic acid
Cys = Cysteine
Glu = Glutamic acid
Gln = Glutamine
Gly = Glycine
His = Histidine
Ile = Isoleucine

Leu = Leucine
Lys = Lysine
Met = Methionine
Phe = Phenylalanine
Pro = Proline
Ser = Serine
Thr = Threonine
Try = Tryptophan
Tyr = Tyrosine
Val = Valine

strand does not leave the nucleus in its original form. The DNA in most animals, including humans, contains long sequences of nucleotides that do code for amino acids, interspersed with introns. Thus, each functional gene, coding for a single protein, contains multiple coding sequences separated from each other by these noncoding introns (Chambon, 1981). Before the messenger RNA leaves the nucleus, evidently these introns are split out of the messenger RNA. Later, the coding sequences are spliced together.

Once the splitting and splicing are completed, the mature messenger RNA leaves the nucleus to serve as the template for a protein molecule. Several ribosomes attach themselves to the messenger RNA chain. A chain of amino acids develops from each ribosome. Transfer RNA carries the appropriate amino acid molecule to the ribosome and attaches itself to the complementary triplet or codon on the messenger RNA, and then its amino acid molecule is attached to the end of the growing chain. When the stop codon is reached, the chain breaks off from the ribosome. This polypeptide chain may sometimes be broken down by cells into smaller functional chains. For example, one very long polypeptide is the "parent" molecule for enzymes regulating adrenal activity as well as for the various endorphins.

Genetic Interactions

The genetic material of each **eukaryotic cell** (a cell that has separate and distinct nuclei; since bacteria don't have nuclei, they are **prokaryotic cells**) is contained in pairs of chromosomes. There can be interactions between two genes located at analogous places on a pair of chromosomes. Genes located at different places — and even on different chromosomes — can also interact.

Pairs of genes at a locus. Genes occupying **homologous** places (the same relative position) on each one of a pair of chromosomes (see Figure 5-1) are said to be occupying the same **locus**. If each coding strand of DNA on the two homologous loci (plural of *locus*) of the paired chromosomes contains the *same* sequence of nucleotides and thus codes for the *same* protein, the organism is **homozygous** at that particular locus. If, however, the nucleotide sequences at the homologous loci on the matching pair of chromosomes are different, each coding for a different protein, the organism is **heterozygous** at that locus. These relationships are illustrated in Figure 5-7.

Most gene pairs in most mammals are homozygous. Ayala (1978) has estimated that only about 6.7% of the loci of humans are, on the average, heterozygous. Nevertheless, in different individuals of any species, more than one alternative gene exists for any one homologous locus. Genes that can occupy the same locus are **alleles** of each other. At least one-third of the loci in humans may have two or more alleles (though each individual could have, at most, two alleles — one on each of the homologous chromosome pair) (Hopkinson & Harris, 1971). All the alleles at a given locus code for proteins having a similar function. One allele may code for the protein producing blue eyes, for example, and another allele may code for the protein producing brown eyes.

In an organism heterozygous for a given locus, different alleles may interact in a **dominant – recessive** relationship.

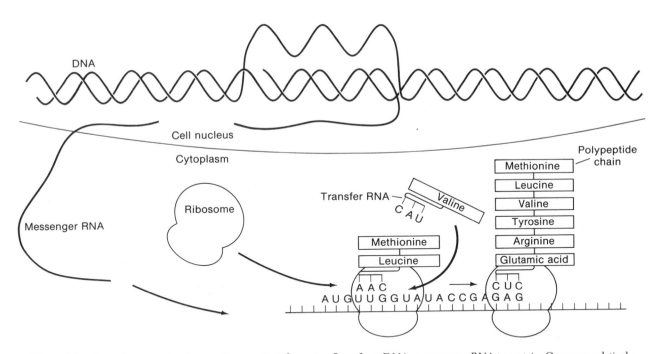

Figure 5-6 According to molecular genetics, genetic information flows from DNA to messenger RNA to protein. Genes are relatively short segments of the long DNA molecules. The DNA code is expressed in two steps: first the sequence of nucleotide bases in the coding strand of the DNA double helix is transcribed onto a single complementary strand of messenger RNA (except that thymine is replaced by the closely related uracil [U]). The messenger RNA is then translated into protein; the complementary molecules of transfer RNA add amino acids one by one to the growing peptide chain as the ribosome moves along the messenger RNA strand. Each of the 20 amino acids found in proteins is specified by a codon of three RNA bases. A = adenine; C = cytosine; G = guanine.

This relationship was discovered by Austrian monk Gregor Mendel in his work on pea plants during the mid-1800s. If one allele is dominant over the other, a heterozygous individual will express only the dominant gene. The protein coded by the

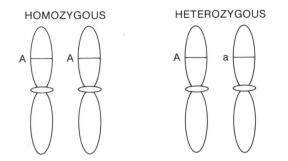

Figure 5-7 A represents a protein coded for by a gene at one locus; *a* represents a slightly different protein coded by an allelic gene at that same locus. In an organism homozygous at a given locus, both genes code for the same protein. In an organism that is heterozygous at that locus, each gene codes for a different but related protein.

recessive gene will not be manufactured. In fact, if a gene is recessive to all other possible alleles occupying that locus, the protein for which that recessive gene was a code will appear in an organism only if the organism is homozygous at that locus and both genes are the same recessive allele.

Mendel's work with peas can illustrate this important concept. Mendel found that the allele coding for roundness in peas is dominant over the allele coding for wrinkles (see the discussion in Plomin, DeFries, & McClearn, 1980). He started with two inbred strains of peas that were homozygous at that location: in one strain, both alleles coded for wrinkles, and in the other strain, both alleles coded for roundness. Table 5-2 shows his results. When he crossed wrinkled peas with round peas, each member of the resulting F_1 generation had one chromosome from the wrinkled parent and one from the round parent, making them all heterozygous at that locus. Since all the F_1 generation produced round peas, roundness is dominant over wrinkles.

Demonstrating this point requires crossing the members of the F_1 generation. When the F_1 generation is crossed, producing the F_2 generation, once again the offspring get one chro-

Table 5-2 Dominant and recessive traits in the F_2 generation of the F_1 cross.

F_1 Generation			F_2 Generation		
Parent	RR		Parent	RW	
WW	RW	RW	RW	RR	RW
	RW	RW		RW	WW
All round			$\frac{3}{4}$ round, $\frac{1}{4}$ wrinkled		

R = round
W = wrinkled

mosome of that particular pair from each parent. *Which* gene they get from each parent is randomly determined. Thus, on the average, one would expect one-fourth of the offspring to have two round genes, one-fourth to have two wrinkled genes, and one-half to be heterozygous, with one round and one wrinkled gene. If roundness is dominant, one-fourth of the offspring would be expected to produce wrinkled peas and three-fourths to produce round peas, as Table 5-2 illustrates. That is exactly what Mendel found.

When a dominant–recessive relationship does exist even partially, the distinction between a **genotype** and a **phenotype** becomes very important. The genotype of an individual refers to her or his genetic composition, whereas the phenotype refers to the observable, measurable characteristics. If the individual is heterozygous, part of the genotype—the recessive gene—will not be visible in the phenotype. Organisms' observable characteristics—like those of the peas in the F_1 generation—are not a perfect reflection of their genetic characteristics.

Other interactions between genes at a given locus are possible. For example, a gene may be dominant over one allele at that locus but recessive to another. Furthermore, often dominance is not complete and the recessive gene is partially or weakly expressed. Another possibility is that pairs of genes at a given locus may have an **additive** relationship. That is, the effects of the two genes simply combine so that if, for example, one allele produces a certain protein, twice as much of that protein might appear in the homozygous as in the heterozygous state.

Interactions among genes at different loci. The interactions of genes are not limited to those occupying the same locus. **Epistasis** refers to interactions among genes at different loci. For example, a person's score on an IQ test is thought to

be a **polygenic** trait, representing the additive effects of many different genes at many different loci. In one type of model, the more "good" genes a person has, the higher his or her IQ test score will be, so that "IQ" genes simply add to produce the final product or phenotype. The combination of a given allele at locus 1 and another allele at locus 2 could also affect the phenotype in a nonadditive fashion. The locus 2 allele may inhibit the function of the locus 1 allele or it may magnify the effects of the locus 1 allele on the phenotype.

Continuous versus discontinuous traits. Most of the behavioral characteristics of organisms vary along a continuum. IQ test scores, for example, can theoretically vary from near 0 to more than 200 (a level at which measurements become unreliable). The continuous nature of such phenotypic characteristics often implies that if they do have a genetic basis, they are being affected by many different genes across many different loci rather than by just one **major gene.** However, when we analyze the ways in which we measure behavior, we often find out that we were measuring some heterogeneous amalgam of individual behavioral characteristics. For example, an IQ score can be seen as a combination of many different and separate cognitive skills. In other words, the apparently continuous nature of such behaviors may be an artifact of the way we measure them. In this case, major genes, as opposed to the additive effects of many different genes, might code for individual behavioral "units."

Many complex traits are not phenotypically continuous the way IQ test scores are. That is, the trait either exists or does not exist. Examples of dichotomously classified behaviors might include the shape of peas, juvenile diabetes, or the set of behaviors that leads to a diagnosis of schizophrenia—delusions, hallucinations, and incoherent speech. Behavioral geneticists often use psychiatric diagnoses, though recognizing all the problems and potential errors this entails, to classify people as either having or not having a certain disorder. Such classifications depend critically on the diagnostic criteria being used: a different set of criteria could well lead to classifying people differently.

The heritability of dichotomously classified behaviors is often explained by a **polygenic threshold model of heritability.** The trait is assumed to be affected by many different genes; each gene at each locus, by itself, has only minor effects on the trait. The effects of the relevant genes across all the various loci combine (usually additive combinations are assumed) to form a dimension of **liability** or **likelihood.** The more of those genes an organism has, the greater his or her likelihood or liability of displaying that trait. Environmental factors are also assumed to affect liability. If a threshold does exist, when the liability exceeds that threshold, the individual will display that particular trait.

Expressivity and penetrance.   An individual's phenotype can also differ greatly from his or her genotype because some of his or her genes have either more or less of an effect on the phenotype in comparison with that same gene in other individuals. Traits that do not appear in the phenotype of all organisms having the same genotype are said to be **incompletely penetrant.** If this is the case, some people with a given genotype will express a particular characteristic and some will not. The greater the proportion of the people with that genotype who do express the trait, the greater the **penetrance** of that gene. A gene may vary in penetrance because of epistatic effects or because of environmental effects.

In addition, a major gene can also sometimes produce a continuous effect on a trait. Traits that can appear in varying degrees, rather than on an all-or-nothing basis, are said to have **variable expressivity.** Any such trait is expressed to different degrees in different people having exactly the same genotype. Once again, phenotypes presumably vary because other genes

that various individuals have also affect that trait and because of the environments of those individuals: people with alcoholic genotypes won't become alcoholics unless they drink alcohol!

Genetic Variability

These genetic principles can be used to explain the mechanism and function of genetic variability. Genetic variability also creates behavioral variability.

Sexual reproduction.   Sexual reproduction causes genetic variability in plants and animals. In sexual reproduction, the **gametes** (sperm) from the male combine with the gamete (egg) from the female to form the **zygote** (the fetus at the beginning of its development). The way in which gametes are formed by the parents is illustrated in Figure 5-8. (Remember that similar events will occur for the other 22 pairs in the human.) In the first phase of either mitosis or meiosis, homologous chromosomes are paired, coming into close proximity to each other. In **mitosis,** each chromosome doubles or replicates itself. After the cell divides, each daughter cell will have

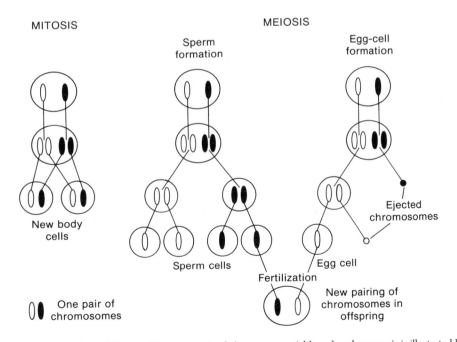

Figure 5-8   Mitosis and meiosis have different effects on a pair of chromosomes (although only one pair is illustrated here, you should remember that humans have 23 pairs). Mitosis produces diploid cells (all chromosomes are paired), whereas meiosis produces haploid cells (only one member of each chromosome pair is present).

exactly the same number and types of chromosomes as did the parent cell.

In **meiosis,** the paired chromosomes also first replicate themselves. But then different events occur in sperm and egg formation. In sperm formation, the cell with the paired, replicated chromosomes splits to form two daughter cells, each having only one of every duplicated homologous pair of chromosomes. Then each of those cells splits in such a way that each of the resulting four sperm cells has *one* chromosome from each of the replicated pairs of the parent cell. In egg formation, the "extra" chromosomes are simply ejected so that each egg also ends up with one and only one of each of the parent's replicated chromosome pairs. Thus, the gametes (egg and sperm cells) become **haploid** (having only one member of each pair of homologous chromosomes), whereas the parent cells were **diploid** (all chromosomes existing in pairs).

The events depicted in Figure 5-8 occur independently for every chromosome pair. Thus, each gamete has a different, randomly selected group of chromosomes. And since zygotes are the random product of the formation of two such gametes (sperm and egg), no two people in the world will ever be genetically identical (unless they are identical twins, formed from the splitting of a single zygote). (If there are 100,000 gene loci in humans, and if, on the average, 6700 of those are heterozygous [6.7% heterozygosity], one individual could potentially produce 10^{2017} different gametes—but only 10^{80} atoms are estimated to exist in the entire known universe! [Ayala, 1978].)

Another source of variability related to sexual reproduction can be found in the genetic material of the mitochondria (the "energy factories" of the cell) (Goodenough & Levine, 1970; Grivell, 1983). Mitochondria have a single chromosome, a double strand of DNA, wound in the shape of a helix. Unlike nuclear DNA, each strand of mitochondrial DNA separately codes for different proteins, which are used largely within the mitochondria themselves. Since egg cells contain mitochondria and sperm cells do not, in sexually reproducing species there will be a separate maternal influence on the mitochondria—and thus the activity—of the cells in the offspring.

Cross-over and introns.   Even more genetic variability can be created by cross-over. **Cross-over** occurs during meiosis when two members of a chromosome pair are lined up during the process of replication. At this time, they may come into contact with each other, break, and exchange segments, leading to a reshuffling of the genetic information. Chromosomes containing gene sequences not found in either parent are created. If this happens during meiosis, the altered chromosomes

are passed on to the next generation. Not only new chromosomes but new proteins can be created by cross-over.

One type of cross-over is illustrated in Figure 5-9. The most common form is equal cross-over, in which the members of a chromosome pair exchange homologous segments. If the organism is heterozygous at one or more of the crossed-over loci, a new chromosome, containing different genes, will be created and can be passed on to offspring.

Even more dramatic changes can occur. Unequal cross-over can occur when nonhomologous segments are exchanged. In **insertion,** a sequence of nucleotides is inserted into the homologous chromosome, creating one chromosome longer and another shorter than either parent chromosome. **Deletion** is the removal from one chromosome of genetic material, which may then be inserted into the homologous chromosome—or even into an entirely different chromosome. In **inversion,** a deleted sequence is inserted back into the same or into another chromosome—in reverse order. Chromosome breakage can even lead to **chromosomal abnormalities.** The chromosomes fail to separate and so one gamete has three copies (**trisomy**) of that particular chromosome and the other gamete has only one (**monosomy**).

Cross-over may be facilitated by introns. The increase in the length of the DNA chain caused by introns also increases the rate of cross-over. Furthermore, breakage is more likely to occur in the longer intron than in the shorter coding sequence. If breakage and homologous cross-over occur in the introns of a heterozygous gene pair, then the resulting split and spliced messenger RNA transcribed from that altered gene will code for an entirely new and different protein not found in either parent. If the cross-over occurred in the middle of a coding sequence, then the resulting sequence would probably have been nonsense, since a codon would usually have been split.

Mutation.   The ultimate source of genetic variability is, of course, mutation. When a mutation occurs, one or more of the nucleotides in a DNA molecule are changed. If this happens in a coding sequence, the changed codon might specify a different amino acid. The resulting protein would have a different amino acid in it and so would probably have a somewhat changed structure and function.

Mutations are relatively rare. They may occur only about once in a billion DNA replications. Still, in a population of several million individuals, there will probably be a few mutations per generation in nearly every allele appearing in that population. If the mutation occurs in a gamete, the change will be passed on to the next generation.

Mutations are the ultimate source of variability for evolutionary change in a species. Sexual reproduction can produce

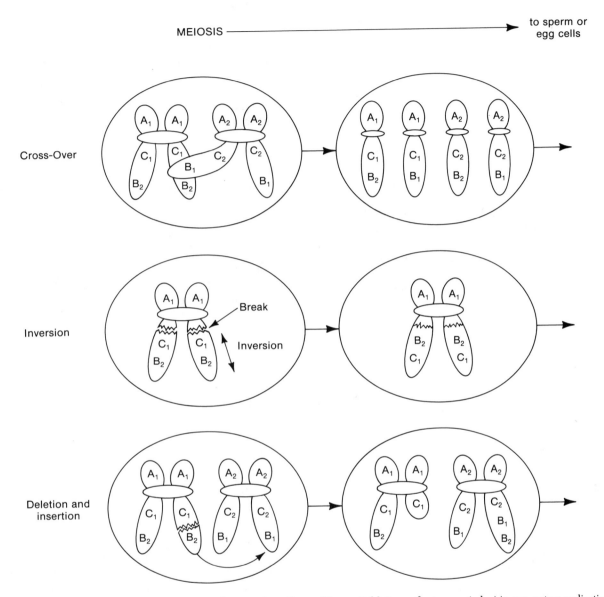

Figure 5-9 Genetic variability can be created in a variety of ways. The capital letters refer to genetic loci in one or two replicating chromosomes. The numerical subscripts refer to allelic genes at those loci. See text for further description.

new combinations of chromosomes, and cross-over (especially unequal cross-over) can produce new and different amino acid chains, but only mutations change the amino acids within a chain. Most mutations are undoubtedly disadvantageous— they do not facilitate survival or reproduction—but the ones that are advantageous will tend to spread throughout a population, changing the characteristics of that species. Through accumulated, random, but selected for ("survival of the fittest") mutations, a species gradually changes and evolves.

Genetic Regulation

This last principle of genetics describes how different genes can be expressed in the various body cells of a single organism.

The phenotype of a *cell* differs according to which of its genes were activated during its development and which are active at the present.

Operon model.

The operon model is one explanation for how such regulation could take place (Brown, 1981; Caplan & Ordahl, 1978; Davidson & Britten, 1979; Plomin, DeFries, & McClearn, 1980; Stent, 1964; Thoenen & Edgar, 1982). In this model, sequences of nucleotides that code for a protein are called **structural genes.** Several closely related (in DNA location and protein function) structural genes are associated with a given **operator gene.** The operator gene is a short segment of DNA that serves as a type of on/off switch: when the switch is on, the DNA is transcribed into messenger RNA, and when it is off, the DNA is not transcribed. The combination of one or more structural genes and their associated operator gene is an **operon.**

Regulator genes code for a short protein molecule that can bind with a certain operon. If the binding causes the operon to be turned off, the protein molecule is called a **repressor.** The repressor will thus shut down or **repress** the structural genes associated with that operator gene. The repressor itself may be inactivated by some metabolite, which could be (1) coded for by other genes, (2) a product of some metabolic process, or (3) a protein phosphorylated by slow synaptic activity. Once the repressor combines with that metabolite, the operator will no longer be inhibited by the repressor, and the structural genes can then be transcribed into messenger RNA.

Genetic regulation during fetal development.

Irreversible gene repression allows zygotic tissue to differentiate into mature cells. A metabolite coming from other cells might permanently repress some genes coding for enzymes used only in the liver, for example, allowing other genes to be expressed so that the tissue can differentiate into nervous tissue (Caplan & Ordahl, 1978). Depolarization and the entry of Ca^{++} into a developing sympathetic neuron permanently represses the genes associated with the ACh enzymes. This effect permits the genes associated with the NE enzymes to be expressed and allows the cell to differentiate into a noradrenergic neuron (Black, 1982; Patterson, Potter, & Furshpan, 1981).

Other types of regulation.

Each step of transcription and translation is regulated by enzymes. Cellular levels of these enzymes could regulate the amount and types of proteins produced by a cell. For example, one set of enzymes splits large polypeptide molecules into smaller, functional protein molecules. Which of these enzymes are present, and in what quantity, could determine where the larger molecule is split and therefore which proteins are produced in which cells.

Many different cells may produce exactly the same large polypeptide. If different cells, located in different organs, have different splitting enzymes in them, the resulting proteins will also differ from organ to organ. For example, different opioid peptides are found at various locations in the brain because each location has different splitting enzymes (Marx, 1983).

Summary of Genetic Principles

The chromosomes carry the units of heredity, the genes. Each gene codes for a structural or enzymatic protein. The protein is produced by transcription (transferring the genetic code onto a messenger RNA molecule) and translation (the ribosome's reading the genetic code of the messenger RNA molecule and building a chain of amino acids from that information).

In sexually reproducing species, chromosomes come in homologous pairs (the diploid number). Genes at a homologous locus on each of the pairs can code either for the same protein or for a slightly different protein having the same type of function in the cell. If the genes are the same, the organism is homozygous at that locus; if different, the organism is heterozygous. Humans may be heterozygous at about 6.7% of their loci, on the average. At least 30% of human loci have two or more alleles associated with them.

Genes can interact. Some of the possible forms of interaction are a dominant–recessive relationship, additive interactions, and epistatic interactions.

Genetic variability occurs among organisms and within the same organism. Genetic differences among organisms can be created by sexual reproduction, cross-over, and mutations. Genetic differences within an organism, or phenotypic differences among cells in different organs, are created by genetic regulation. One model for this regulation is the operon, although other types of regulation are possible.

Effects of Genes on Neurons

The protein-product of genes can have several different types of effects on neurons:

1. indirect effects on neural function

2. effects on the nerve membrane by a gene coding for an electrically activated membrane channel
3. effects on a synapse, such as a gene's changing the level and type of transmitter present in the presynaptic cell or the type of receptor on the postsynaptic cell
4. effects on the three-dimensional structure of nerve cells and their patterns of interconnections by genes coding for structural and enzymatic proteins.

Some very interesting research has been carried out with genetic mutations in the fruit fly, *Drosophila* (Pak & Pinto, 1976; Plomin, DeFries, & McClearn, 1980). The fruit fly has only four pairs of chromosomes, and the genes on most of them have been identified and mapped. The variety of behavioral mutants that have been produced offer great promise for a genetic analysis of behavior. One mutant is called *drop dead*: it walks and flies for a couple of days — and then suddenly drops on its back and dies. One is called *fruitless* because the male courts both females and other males but doesn't copulate with either. Another male can't separate from the female after copulation and so is called *stuck*. Still another mutation (*norp*A) involves a protein found in light receptor cells in the fruit fly's eye. Because of this mutation, the receptor cells do not depolarize in response to light and the animal is blind (Pak, Ostroy, Deland, & Wu, 1976).

By examining these and other mutants, researchers may someday identify the complete path from gene to behavior. First they would pinpoint the chromosomal location and sequence of nucleotides of the gene. Second, they would describe the sequence of amino acids and the three-dimensional structure of the protein and define the role it plays in cellular functioning. In particular, the role of the altered protein (the one coded by the mutant gene) would be studied chemically and electrophysiologically in nerve cells, by the techniques described in earlier chapters, to see just how neural functioning was altered. For example, how does the mutated protein block membrane depolarization in the *norp*A eye? The alteration of neural functioning could then be directly related to the observed behavioral alterations.

Indirect Effects

Indirect effects of gene-products on nerve cell functions are of interest for two reasons. First, if a protein-product affects the brain, it is important to establish whether the effect occurs because the protein is an integral part of nerve cells or whether the protein affects another body organ that in turn affects the brain. Indirect effects are also important in their own right.

Hormonal levels.   A given gene might be expressed only in some organ other than the brain, thus only indirectly affecting the brain itself. One good example (see also Chapter 9) is the effects that the genes of the X and Y chromosomes have on the brain. The sex-determining genes may or may not directly affect brain structure and function, but they *do* affect the structure and function of the gonads (testes and ovaries). And the sex hormones secreted by the gonads do have direct and permanent effects on neural structure and function.

Genes also affect the adrenal gland, whose hormones then affect the brain. One genetic abnormality in humans causes the cortex (outside portion) of the adrenal gland to secrete large quantities of sex hormones instead of its usual hormone (glucocorticoids). In a developing embryo, the high levels of sex hormones affect the structure of nerve cells in the fetal brain in ways similar to the effects that normal levels of sex hormones have. This abnormality is the adrenogenital syndrome; genetic females with this syndrome may develop a "male" brain (Chapter 9). In another example, two inbred mice strains differ in the level of one of the adrenal enzymes responsible for the synthesis of catecholamines (Ciaranello, Lipsky, & Axelrod, 1974). As we will describe in Chapter 11, the adrenal hormones have indirect effects on brain function in the adult.

Metabolism in other tissues.   Some genetic effects can be even more indirect. For example, some genes associated with obesity in laboratory rodents may have indirect effects on the brain by changing the metabolism of body fat organs. A signal that normally is sent out by rapidly growing **white fat** (the kind of fat that makes organisms look obese) may be absent in the genetically obese rodent. If so, an increase in white fat would not be able to inhibit hunger and the organism would keep on eating (Chapter 8).

If the metabolism of glial cells is affected, nerve cells will also be affected. One of the functions of glial cells is to regulate the level of electrolytes in the extracellular fluid around the nerve cells. Any gene that impaired glial cells' ability to carry out this function — such as a mutation that eliminated one of the pumps in the glial cell membrane — would dramatically affect neural activity.

Genetic Effects on the Structure of the Axonal Membrane

Most of the research concerning the genes coding for cell membrane structures was carried out by selective mutations.

In some of these animals, the mutated gene coded for a protein in the nerve cell membrane.

The *pawn*.   The *pawn* is a mutant *Paramecium* that cannot move backwards. Some description of the behavior of *Paramecia* is necessary to understand how the mutated gene causes that particular behavioral deficit. When a *Paramecium* is exposed to some type of substance that it normally avoids, such as a solution containing a high quantity of barium ions, the membrane covering its body (a single cell) depolarizes, and action potentials are generated. Unlike the action potentials associated with squid axons or with mammalian nerve cells, the depolarization phase in the *Paramecium* is caused only by inflow of Ca^{++} ions. Then, as in other excitable membranes, repolarization occurs because of an outward K^+ current. The increase in intracellular Ca^{++} causes the cilia covering the *Paramecium*'s body to reverse their swimming pattern, propelling it backwards for a brief time.

The *pawn* has no action potentials in a barium solution, so it has no inrush of Ca^{++} (Kung et al., 1975; Schein, Bennett, & Katz, 1976). Without the Ca^{++}, the cilia don't reverse, and the animal doesn't avoid the substance. The mutant gene may code for a protein that lines the wall of the electrically gated Ca^{++} channel, or it may affect the number of channels present or the gate itself.

***Drosophila*.**   Certain fluit fly mutants provide an opportunity to study another type of membrane channel (Jan, Jan, & Dennis, 1977; Salkoff, 1983; Salkoff & Wyman, 1981; Tanouye, Ferrus, & Fujita, 1981; Wu, Ganetzky, Haugland, & Liu, 1983). There are several forms of the mutant, all exhibiting a similar behavior. While under ether anesthesia, normal flies are immobile or shake their legs only slightly. *Shaker* and *Eag* mutants shake their legs vigorously.

The mutant genes code for proteins affecting the action potential. When the muscle cell membranes of the mutants were examined electrophysiologically, researchers found that the action potential lasts longer in the mutant, leading to greater presynaptic entry of Ca^{++}, which causes more transmitter to be released. Presumably the action potential is also prolonged at the neuromuscular junction, so that the effect of the motoneuron on the muscle is greatly accentuated—and the animal shakes its legs instead of remaining quiet.

The muscle action potential is abnormal because of a change in K^+ channels. Evidently the mutants have poorly functioning (or nonfunctioning) electrically gated K^+ channels. The *Shaker* mutation seems primarily to affect the fast K^+ channel, whereas the *Eag* mutation has a greater effect on a slower K^+ channel (Wu et al., 1983). When these channels

are impaired, repolarization is delayed. In support of this explanation, normal fruit flies can be made to act like mutants by giving them drugs that block the electrically gated K^+ channel. Also, voltage-clamp studies on mutant membranes show that the outward K^+ current is absent. The mutated codons may have affected an amino acid that forms part of a K^+ channel protein.

Conduction velocity in mice.   It has been possible to change genetically the rate at which axons conduct action potentials. Hegmann (1975) has carried out a selective breeding program in which the character bred for and against was the rate at which neurons going to some of the muscles in the leg conducted action potentials. With each generation, male and female mice with the highest conduction velocity were mated for the high line; for the low line, the slowest-conducting brothers and sisters were mated. In one study, Hegmann continued selective breeding for 13 successive generations.

The experiments produced different strains of mice with different conduction velocities. Analyses of crosses among the various strains suggested that the alleles that increase conduction velocity tended to be dominant. The way in which the gene works to change conduction velocity has not yet been established (changes in the resistance of the membrane or changes in the size of the axons are likely possibilities). Some of the behavioral effects associated with altered conduction velocity have been explored (Hegmann, 1979). The strains with high conduction velocity have faster leg withdrawal reflexes—and are *less* active and display more defecation in the open-field measure of emotionality. Exactly why faster conduction velocity might be associated with difference in open-field behaviors is not yet clear.

Dystrophic mice.   Muscular dystrophy in humans affects their muscles and their motoneurons in such a way that eventually the muscle tissue wastes away. To understand the molecular basis of this genetic disorder, researchers have created mutant dystrophic mice. Although these mice probably do *not* have the same abnormal genes and protein as do dystrophic humans, the mice can provide clues about what could be happening to the human victim—and they also provide information about how excitable membranes work.

These mice show disturbances in both muscle (Adrian & Bryant, 1974; Kerr & Sperelakis, 1983; Sellin & Sperelakis, 1978) and motoneuron function (Jaros & Jenkison, 1983). Motoneurons are more affected than are sensory neurons. Fewer than normal of the dystrophic neurons are myelinated, and when they are myelinated, the nodes of Ranvier are wider than normal. The membrane of the muscle cell shows even more profound disturbances: it may be abnormally permeable to Na^+, resulting in a reduced resting membrane potential and in a reduced action potential because of an intracellular accumulation of Na^+. Permeability to Cl^- and K^+ may also be altered. However, the effects that occur in the muscles of affected animals may be secondary to the effects that occur in the motoneurons (Plomin, DeFries & McClearn, 1980).

Genetic Effects on Synaptic Activity

Genes can directly affect synaptic activity by several mechanisms. The most relevant genes either code for the enzymes that synthesize or degrade the transmitter substances or code for receptor proteins. These enzymes and proteins may be the most likely loci for the genetic basis of human emotional disorders such as depression and schizophrenia.

Nevertheless, relatively little has been done at the molecular level. Instead, researchers have concentrated on the genetic basis for the overall level of transmitter substances in various parts of the brain. However, separating genetic effects on membranes from genetic effects on synaptic activity is somewhat artificial since, as we have already pointed out, the altered electrically gated K^+ channels in the *Shaker* and *Eag* mutants affect transmitter release.

Absolute levels of transmitters, receptors, and associated enzymes.   Research on absolute levels of transmitters, receptors, and associated enzymes will be covered in detail in later chapters (for instance, genes and transmitters in emotional disorders are discussed in Chapter 10). Here we present only a few examples of this research.

Narcolepsy is a disorder in which the affected person spontaneously falls asleep. All such people have these attacks and often have attacks of cataplexy during which they experience motor inhibition and may fall to the ground (D. D. Kelly, 1981b). An animal model of narcolepsy has been created by breeding for this syndrome in dogs. The gene, which is recessive and autosomal, increases the level of dopamine in the brain. Its protein-product may affect enzymatic activity, receptor sensitivity, or DA reuptake (Mefford, Baker, Boehme, Foutz, Ciaranello, Barchas, & Dement, 1983). It is not yet clear how changes in DA might be related to sleep and motor inhibition.

Other experimenters selectively bred mice for long and for short periods of sleep in response to an injection of alcohol. Compared with short periods, long sleep times are associated with a higher level of the enzyme responsible for converting DA to NE (dopamine-β-hydroxylase) in the blood stream (and presumably in the brain) (Horowitz, Dendel, Allan, & Major, 1982).

Strains of mutant fruit flies have genetically altered levels of enzymes required for the synthesis of transmitter substances in their brains (Livingstone & Tempel, 1983). One interesting example is the *Ddc* (dopa decarboxylase) mutation, which shows decreased levels of dopamine and serotonin synthesis. *Ddc* mutants also show deficits in learning that are quite likely to be related to their transmitter deficits.

Different strains of mice have reliable differences in behaviors and in levels of brain enzymes (Tiplady, Killian, & Mandel, 1976; Tunnicliff, Wimer, & Wimer, 1973; Will, 1977). For example, strains of mice selected to have high or low blood pressure also have, respectively, high or low levels of norepinephrine in their brains. In addition, the strains differ in aggressiveness, level of activity, and learning performances. At least two genes may be involved in this control of NE levels: one autosomal and one on the X chromosome (Schlager, Freeman, & El Seoudy, 1983).

Responses to environmental changes.   Probably the most intriguing genetic effects on enzyme levels have to do with the ways in which these levels change in response to certain kinds of experiences. One set of genes controls basal levels of enzymes and a *separate* set of genes regulates *changes* in enzyme levels caused by exposure to stressors such as pain or cold. Genetic control of responses to stress may provide the best model for emotional disorders in humans (Stolk & Nisula, 1979).

Genetic Effects on Neural Structure and Patterns of Interconnections

Genes also affect how a nerve cell looks when examined under a microscope and which nerve cells form synaptic connections. Most of these effects occur during fetal development, but nerve cells can form new connections throughout life. Regardless of the timing of the effect, the proteins coded for by the genes are part of the way in which the growth of nerve cells and the connections among types of nerve cells are specified.

Pak and Pinto's review (1976) of this area of research provides many intriguing examples of genetically specified connections. The genes producing the albino mutations in species such as cats and mice (and including the genes producing the Siamese coat-color pattern) affect neural connections in the visual system. The retinal-thalamic connections are all "miswired" in these animals. This fascinating research will be described in more detail in Chapter 12. In the mouse *staggerer* mutant—so named because of its characteristic staggering gait—the spines on Purkinje cells in the cerebellum fail to develop. Thus, there is little or no synaptic input to the cerebellum in these mice. The *weaver* mice show similar disorders of gait, and the connections to the cerebellum are also disordered in this mutant (Goodman, Kuhar, Hester, & Snyder, 1983).

The structure and numbers of various types of cells are genetically controlled. One inbred mouse strain has an abnormally large number of dopamine-containing neurons in the midbrain (Fink & Reis, 1981). Another strain of mice carries genes that increase the number of axons belonging to each noradrenergic locus coeruleus cell (Levitt & Noebels, 1981). Genetically controlled changes in neuron numbers could well have behavioral implications. For example, the strain of mice having more dopamine cells also shows more exploratory activity. Furthermore, both learning ability in mice and proneness to seizure in gerbils are correlated with genetically controlled changes in the appearance of hippocampal cells (Paul, Fried, Watanabe, Forsythe, & Scheibel, 1981; Schwegler & Lipp, 1981; Schwegler, Lipp, Van der Loos, & Buselmaier, 1981). The ways in which these genetically produced changes in neuron number may be related to learning and memory will be discussed in Chapter 11.

Summary of the Effects of Genes on Nerve Cells

Genes affect the structure and function of nerve cells either directly or indirectly. The indirect effects occur through genetic influences on other organs, and these organs in turn produce hormones or metabolites that affect the brain. The direct effects are even more intriguing and relevant to a single-unit approach to behavior, for single-cell mutations have been identified that affect electrically gated channels. The basal enzyme levels and the change in levels in response to experience are also under genetic control. The genes affecting basal levels and responses to stress are probably different ones. The structure, numbers, and patterns of synaptic connections of cells in the brain are genetically controlled. Future research will be directed toward filling in the missing steps—by showing exactly how the protein-product of the gene affects neural function and how the differences in neural functions are related to differences in behavior.

Chapter Summary

Genes and Communication of Information

Each chromosome contains thousands of genes, and each gene is a code for a protein. The protein codes are nucleotide triplets, and each triplet, or codon, is a code for an amino acid. A sequence of triplets codes for a sequence of amino acids in a protein. The intervening steps involve messenger RNA, which takes the genetic code transcribed from the DNA in the cell nucleus to the cytoplasm, where the code is read and translated into a protein by ribosomes. In addition, some DNA simply codes for transfer and ribosomal RNA.

In sexually reproducing species, the chromosomes come in homologous pairs. Genes at homologous loci on the paired chromosomes can interact. Genes at different loci, and on different chromosomes, also interact. These interactions cause the phenotypes of individuals to differ from their genotypes.

Genetic variability is the basis for a genetic analysis of behaviors. This variability is created by sexual reproduction, cross-over, mutation, and, within cells, genetic regulation. Genetic mutations can affect the ways in which nerve cells conduct information down their axons or transmit it from one cell to another. Levels of transmitter substances are also genetically controlled, both during the fetal development of the organism and during adulthood.

The communication of information in the nervous system occurs through action and synaptic potentials—and both of these communicative functions are related to genetic activity in ways that are just being explored.

PART THREE

The Coding Function of Nerve Cells

This part is the conceptual core of this book. The neuron doctrine (Table 1-1) emphasizes the cellular basis of behavior and the mental events inferred from those behaviors. Most of our knowledge and hypotheses about how brain cells might code information has come from studying the sensory systems.

Such an approach has far-reaching implications for conceptualizing brain and mental events. First, our sensory organs are windows through which we perceive the world around us. What we consciously experience as being real and physically present is determined by the types of physical stimuli to which our sensory organs can respond. And we do not phenomenologically experience many types of physical energies as being "real" because of the limitations of those organs. For example, some species can directly perceive heat waves and electrical fields. We know that such types of physical energy are "real" only because of specialized measuring instruments that convert heat or electrical energy into a form of energy to which our sensory organs can respond.

Second, even when we do have windows onto the world of a certain type of physical energy, those windows are not transparent. Even of the forms of energy that we can directly perceive, our sensory organs are more sensitive to some than to other types of stimulation. Our ears can respond only to a limited range of sound wave frequencies. The optical apparatus of our eyes allows some light wavelengths to pass more freely through than other wavelengths. Only certain types of airborne molecules cause a sensation of odor.

Third, once the energy passes through the filter of our sensory organs, the information in the energy is coded by our sensory systems. At least, some of it is coded. Some aspects of the information are ignored, and some types of information are even created literally out of nothing by these coding functions. This latter aspect of coding produces **sensory illusions**. They would be called hallucinations, except that all normal organisms of a given species perceive exactly the same information — even though it isn't "real." Furthermore, each synapse in the sensory systems *recodes* the information. What this means is that we literally do *not* consciously perceive the world. What we perceive is our own brain codes — and the information contained in those codes is the end product of filtering and recoding.

Fourth, even though the filtering and recoding change the information, our evolutionary history ensures that our perceptual codes will provide a workable model of the world. If they did not, we would not have survived and reproduced. Thus, because of evolutionary continuity, analyzing how other organisms solved coding problems will provide useful hypotheses about how our brains solved similar problems. For example, receptors for transmitter substances might have evolved from the receptors that unicellular organisms use to detect chemicals in their environment.

Information that was useful to survival might be exaggerated in our sensory systems, and information that was not so useful might have dropped out of our coding systems over generations of evolution. We humans have very boring codes for olfactory perceptions compared with the rich and varied codes used by lower organisms. Olfactory information is much more important to those animals than it is to us. They use the information to locate predators, prey, and sexually receptive organisms of the opposite sex. Can you imagine what your perceptual world might be like if you could directly perceive how all other people smelled (and not just those who haven't bathed recently), and through their odors discern their emotional state?

We present a detailed analysis of the coding systems used by the various sensory systems. Chapter 6 emphasizes the similarities in the coding schemes used across different sensory systems. The material is organized by types of code and types of filter instead of by types of sensory system. By analyzing a single sensory system, Chapter 7 demonstrates how our sensory experiences are turned into a unified perception of the world. We chose the visual system because the most is known about that system. Once we know something about how the brain is likely to encode various types of information, we can use this knowledge to understand how motives, emotions, and memories of past experiences can change the codes.

CHAPTER

Principles of Sensory Coding

In the course of evolution, all the sensory systems faced similar problems. And to a large extent, they all used similar solutions. Although these similarities will be emphasized in this chapter, the differences should not be ignored. Some of the differences in sensory systems among species will also be described. For example, responses of taste afferents to substances on the tongue show consistent differences across species (Iwasaki & Sato, 1984; Pfaffmann, Frank, Bartoshuk, & Snell, 1976). Our dinner might not taste the same to us as it does to our cat.

Overview

First, all sensory systems must convert physical energy to ion movements and changes in membrane potential. Second, all must take the information contained in the physical energy and code it in such a way that sensations and perceptions occur. In other words, the five sensory systems described in this chapter must take the energy forms listed on the left in

Table 6-1 Transduction and sensations in the sensory systems.

Type of Physical Energy	Sensory System and Receptors	Conscious Perceptions
Airborne water- or lipid-soluble molecules	Hair cells in olfactory epithelium	Various odors
Water-soluble molecule	Taste cells in tongue	
NaCl (cations)		Salty
Acids (hydrogen ions)		Sour
An organic molecule such as quinine		Bitter
Sugar molecule		Sweet
Air molecule vibration	Hair cells in cochlea	
Vibration amplitude		Loudness
Vibration frequency		Pitch
Skin sensations	Somatosensory organs: Ruffini ending, hair receptor, Pacinian corpuscle, Meissner's corpuscle	Vibration
Pressure	Meissner corpuscle, Pacinian corpuscle, Merkel disks	Pressure
Touch	Hair receptor, Merkel disks, Meissner corpuscle	Touch
Rate of movement of air molecules	Free nerve endings	Hot, cold
Tissue damage	Free nerve endings	Pain

Table 6-1 and transform them into the perceptions listed on the right (vision is covered in Chapter 7). These processes must be faithful enough that the percept is, for the most part, **isomorphic** with the "real-world" energy forms. ("Isomorphic" means having variations in physical energy that match variations in biophysical energy or neural activity.)

Principles of Coding and Transduction

To be useful, conscious perceptions must be isomorphic with important variations in physical energies inside and outside the organism. Thus, all sensory systems follow very similar laws of psychophysics. **Psychophysics** is the branch of behavioral science that studies how variations in conscious perceptions are related to variations in physical energies. The details of that relationship provide clues to sensory coding mechanisms.

All sensory systems **transduce** or transform a certain type of physical energy into a form of energy that can affect ion movements and membrane potentials. One type of chemical transduction has already been discussed: the chemical energy of transmitter substances is transduced to electrical energy by synaptic receptors. Our chemical senses, which include the olfactory (smell) and gustatory (taste) systems, may follow processes of transduction similar to those used by the synapse. Other senses, such as the auditory and many somatosensory receptors, transduce mechanical energy into electrochemical energy.

All sensory systems must encode the information. The amount of physical energy present—such as the number of airborne molecules or the amplitude of vibration in air molecules caused by sound waves—gives rise to feelings of varying intensity of stimulation. Variations in the frequency of vibration or in the types of molecules in the air create sensations of different *kinds* of stimuli; for example, sound as opposed to scent. Moreover, developmental experiences can alter the coding used by a sensory system (Chapter 12).

All sensory systems show habituation, adaptation, and centrifugal control. Habituation occurs in sensory systems just as it does in behavior (Chapter 1): the neural responses to a repeating stimulus often decrease over trials. **Adaptation** is a decrease in neural response to a continuously present stimulus. **Centrifugal control** describes the effects that "higher" centers of the brain have on the transmission and coding of information by "lower" sensory areas. Signals going from "higher" to "lower" areas of the brain are **centrifugal,** whereas **centripetal** refers to information going from "lower" to "higher" centers. The brain controls its own input through centrifugal fibers.

At least some of the neurons in all sensory systems show **spontaneous activity.** They are continuously active in the absence of sensory input. (The sensory receptors themselves may not be spontaneously active.) The nature of the spontaneous activity may differ across brain areas. For example, sensory neurons show an essentially random distribution of action potentials over time, but neurons in the reticular activating system (RAS) show "waves" of greater and lesser activity. Waves of depolarization may be spontaneously generated in those neurons (Nakahama, Yamamoto, Aya, Shima, & Fujii, 1983).

Experimental Problems

For a variety of reasons, more is known about vision than about any of the four sensory systems described in this chapter. For the chemical senses, the problem is the physical nature of the stimuli themselves. For example, in audition, the relationship between intensity and frequency of vibration on the one hand, and between loudness and pitch on the other, was clearly understood at the beginning of sensory coding research (though there *is* some overlap in loudness and pitch perceptions). But what are the relevant dimensions of substances that can be tasted and smelled? Some chemical substances normally found inside the body are monitored by specialized internal chemoreceptors. Although **interoceptors** respond to changes in internal chemistry, we have not yet identified which one (or more) out of all the chemical changes is critically important to various motives and emotions.

The responses of somatosensory and auditory receptors have only rarely been directly recorded. Although the receptor organs can be clearly identified (for instance, eye and ear) in most sensory systems, there is a great variety of structures embedded in the skin. It has never been clear which of those structures are and which are not sensory receptors. Only in the last few years has it been possible to make intracellular recordings from individual receptors in the ear, and only intracellular recordings can provide a detailed picture of ionic currents and membrane potential changes. These problems are just now being partially overcome, and so the next few years in research should be exciting.

Psychophysics

Psychophysical experiments are critically important to cracking the brain codes for sensory experiences. They give the neural scientists the information they need about how mental events vary when physical energies outside and inside the organism are varied. Most psychophysical experiments are performed on human subjects, who can be given verbal instructions about how to describe their mental events. (However, even human subjects need to be extensively trained before their psychophysical data are reliable and consistent.) Most of the experiments in neural recording are done on lower

animals. But there are no guarantees that different organisms encode physical energies the same way; thus psychophysical experiments done on lower organisms and neural recordings done on human subjects are of critical importance.

This section discusses several kinds of psychophysical experiments. First we consider the relevant physical aspects of the stimuli that can activate the various sensory organs. Then we describe human psychophysical techniques, followed by an account of how psychophysics is done in lower animals.

The Physics of Sensory Stimuli

Table 6-1 summarizes some of the physics of sensory stimuli. Sensory receptors respond either to chemical or to mechanical types of energy. **Chemoreceptors** include the taste and olfactory receptors, as well as the visual receptors (Chapter 7) and some of the interoceptors monitoring internal chemicals relevant to motives and emotions (Part IV). The **mechanoreceptors** include most of the somatosensory receptors, as well as auditory receptors and other interoceptors.

The chemoreceptors are stimulated by various chemicals (chemical energy). As the table indicates, the cation part of ionizing salts may stimulate salt taste receptors. Although anions may also have an effect, it may be inhibitory. Acids produce a sour taste, perhaps because of the hydrogen ions produced by acids ionizing in solution. Bitter and sweet tastes are produced by more complex molecules, presumably ones having a particular size and shape. The early research on olfaction by Amoore (1965) suggested that the three-dimensional size, shape, and perhaps electrical charge of molecules may allow them to excite specific receptors in the nasal epithelium. The concentration of molecules in air or the saliva is related to the intensity of the resulting smell or taste. Some interoceptors sense and respond to changes in body temperature (Nelson & Prosser, 1981) and others respond to blood levels of glucose and to the concentration of solutes in the blood.

Sound waves are created by vibrating objects. As the object, such as a string in a piano, moves back and forth, it first compresses and then creates vacuum (suction) pressure on the air molecules around it. The movement of the object is converted into waves of compression and rarefaction (expansion) in the air molecules. These waves spread outward from the object in much the same way that something thrown into a pool of quiet water creates outward-spreading waves.

The nature of the resulting waves determines how they are perceived. The greater the distance through which the object moves in its vibrations, the greater the amplitude of the resulting sound waves. The faster the object moves back and forth, the greater the frequency of the sound waves, or the more of them that occur in a certain period of time. Observers' judgments of loudness are most strongly affected by the amplitude of the sound wave, although frequency can also affect perceived loudness (we perceive as softer those frequencies to which we are less sensitive). Similarly, observers judge pitch to be most consistently related to the frequency of the sound wave, although amplitude can also affect perception of pitch. If the object vibrates at a constant rate, observers will hear a pure tone. If various parts of the object vibrate at different frequencies, complex tones are heard. As Figure 6-1 illustrates, the ear does a **Fourier analysis** on any sound. A Fou-

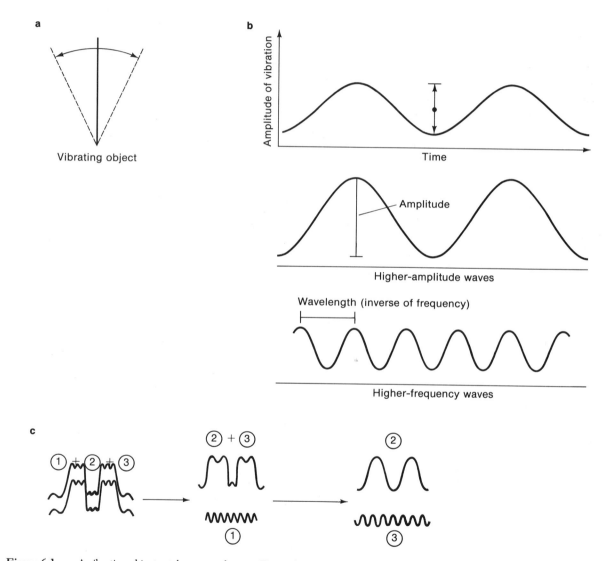

Figure 6-1   **a.** A vibrating object produces sound waves. Forward movement of the object causes compression and backward movement, rarefaction.   **b.** These waves can differ in amplitude and in frequency. The greater the distance over which the object moves back and forth, the greater the amplitude of the resulting wave. The more rapidly the object vibrates, the shorter the resulting wavelength, or the greater the frequency of the waves.   **c.** The ear does a Fourier analysis of complex sounds. The sound is broken down into its component sine wave frequencies. A special structure in the ear, the basilar membrane, would be vibrating in three places in response to the original complex sound. Each place of vibration would correspond to a frequency of one of the three component sine waves (numbered 1, 2, and 3).

rier analysis breaks down any complex but repetitive pattern into its component parts, weighting each component by the amount it contributes to the complex whole. If the sound frequencies randomly change, or many frequencies are present, observers will hear only noises.

Other types of mechanical energy are transduced by some interoceptors and some somatosensory receptors. Touch receptors respond to any physical event that moves skin hairs or deforms the skin layers. For warmth and cold receptors, somehow the physical nature of heat must be converted to a change in membrane potential. One interoceptor is a **baroceptor,** which responds to changes in blood pressure (usually measured in milligrams, or mg). Internal and **cutaneous** (in the skin) pain receptors are apparently excited by any stimulus — mechanical, chemical, or thermal — that threatens or produces tissue damage. The exact physical aspects of the stimuli that are transduced into pain are at present unknown.

Absolute Thresholds

One of the three major types of psychophysical experiments measures just how little physical energy of each type is required for some type of sensation. The smallest amount of physical energy that can be detected by a sensory system is its **absolute threshold.**

Threshold measurement.   In psychophysical threshold experiments with human subjects, the amount of energy in a stimulus is varied across trials. For example, a different amplitude of a certain frequency tone may be presented on each trial. The energy (amplitude, for instance) used for each trial may be varied in a continuous fashion: the energy is increased or decreased in small steps over successive trials. Or the amount of energy can be randomly varied over trials (within limits, of course). For each trial, subjects are asked to indicate whether they can detect the presence of the stimulus, usually by saying yes or no. The lowest level of energy used for any trial will be one that is never detected by the subject, and the highest level will be one that is always detected.

Despite its name, the threshold is not an absolute. A psychophysical threshold is depicted in Figure 6-2. The probability that a subject will detect the presence of a stimulus increases continuously, in an S-shaped curve, as a function of the intensity of the stimulus actually present. The absolute threshold refers to the intensity of stimulus that is detected 50% of the time by that subject. (Actually, the intensity that is detected 75% of the time is averaged with the intensity detected 25% of the time, but the result is close to the 50% point.)

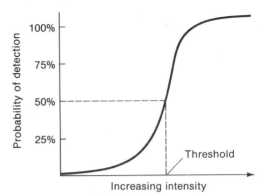

Figure 6-2   This curve might come from a psychophysical experiment studying absolute thresholds. As the intensity of the stimulus increases, the subject's probability of detecting it also increases. This curve could also represent results from a difference threshold experiment if the abscissa were re-labeled: magnitude of the difference between comparison and standard stimuli.

The threshold measured this way will vary with the response biases of the observers. Some observers may be biased toward saying no, for example. A mathematical procedure derived from Signal Detection Theory (Tanner & Swets, 1954; Swets, Tanner, & Birdsall, 1961) can be used to control for the effects of response biases. Use of this procedure gives the researcher separate probabilistic measures of response biases and the sensitivity of the sensory system.

Some thresholds.   Absolute thresholds vary across sensory systems, species, types of sensations, and the part of the body receiving those stimulations. For example, a male moth may be able to detect and respond appropriately to as few as 200 molecules of a substance emitted by a female moth. Human olfactory systems are not nearly so sensitive.

Even within the area of chemical sensitivities, the average threshold of a given species for a given stimulus varies from one type of stimulus to the next, as Table 6-2 indicates. Humans are most sensitive to the bitter taste of quinine and the scent of musk and are least sensitive to the taste of sucrose and the unique odor of ether. Humans are most sensitive to sweet tastes on the tip of the tongue and to bitter tastes toward the base of the tongue (but see Collings, 1974). Sensitivity to salty and sour tastes may be greatest along the sides of the tongue.

Human mechanoreceptors may be relatively more sensitive than human chemoreceptors. Auditory systems can detect an amplitude of vibration so small that the round window (at the entrance to the inner ear) moves only one-tenth the diameter

Table 6-2   Human sensory thresholds for some tastes and odors.

Taste		Smell	
Substance	Threshold (mg/liter H$_2$O)	Substance	Threshold (mg/liter air)
Hydrochloric acid	32.850	Artificial musk	.00004
		Butyric acid	.00900
Formic acid	82.800	Carbon tetra-chloride	4.53300
Sodium chloride	585.000		
Sucrose	3420.000	Chloroform	3.30000
Sodium sac-charin	4.186	Ethyl acetate	.68600
		Ethyl ether	5.83300
Quinine sulfate	3.376	Ethyl mercaptan	.04600
Caffeine	135.800	Methyl salicylate	.10000
		Propyl mercaptan	.00600
		Valeric acid	.02900
		Amyl acetate	.03900

of a hydrogen ion. (But with the better measuring techniques currently in use, the estimate may have to be revised upwards: Dallos, 1981). As little as 5 mg of pressure may be detectable on the most sensitive areas of the human skin, such as the face. The least sensitive parts of the body, such as the big toe, may require from 140 mg (in females) to 350 mg (in males) of pressure to be detectable (Weinstein, 1968).

Difference Thresholds and Estimations of Magnitude

Difference thresholds and estimations of magnitude are theoretically related. The **difference threshold** is the amount of change in a stimulus that is just detectable. The difference threshold can refer to the intensity or to the quality of a stimulus. In audition, the difference thresholds for both loudness and pitch can be separately measured. **Magnitude estimations** are defined by the type of experiment used to produce them: subjects are exposed to varying intensities of stimulation and asked to rate how intense each stimulus seems to them in relation to a "standard" intensity.

Techniques of measurement.   In psychophysical experiments concerned with the difference thresholds of human subjects, several procedures can be used, but all lead to similar results and conclusions. The subject is first given one stimulus, called a standard. That subject is then exposed to a series of trials on which the standard is presented, followed by a comparison stimulus. The subject may be asked to judge whether the comparison stimulus is the same as or different from the standard or to say whether it is louder (higher, heavier, harder,

more intense) or softer (lower, lighter, softer, less intense) than the standard. Over trials, the comparison stimulus either becomes steadily more intense, becomes steadily less intense, or randomly varies in intensity.

The results of such an experiment can again be seen in Figure 6-2. But now the ordinate should read "Probability of detection of difference" and the abscissa should read "Increasing difference between standard and comparison." Once again the threshold is not an absolute; it is the difference between the comparison and the standard that is detectable 50% of the time (or the average between those detected 75% and 25% of the time). Here also the use of Signal Detection procedures can control for the effects of response biases.

Magnitude-estimation experiments also use a standard stimulus. The standard is assigned a particular numerical value, such as 1 or 100. The subject is then given a random series of stimuli differing in intensity and is instructed to assign numbers to them according to their perceived intensities relative to the standard. For example, a smell judged to be twice as intense as a standard with a value of 1 should be rated 2. The ratings for each stimulus intensity are then averaged to arrive at its magnitude estimation.

Some difference thresholds.   For all sensory systems, the difference threshold increases as the intensity of the standard increases. E. H. Weber first described this relationship in the nineteenth century; in 1860, Gustav Fechner formalized it in a law that has become known as **Weber's law** (see Uttal, 1973, and Somjen, 1972/1975):

$$\frac{\Delta I}{I} = k$$

ΔI is the difference threshold, or the **just-noticeable difference (jnd)**. I is the intensity of the standard stimulus.

According to this law, the increment in intensity that is just detectable (50% of the time) is a constant proportion of the intensity of the standard. For example, suppose adding one lighted candle to a room containing ten lighted candles produces a detectable increase in brightness. Then if the room has a hundred candles in it, ten would have to be added for the increment in brightness to be detected. In a darkened room we can easily detect a dim light, but in a brightly lighted room we would not be able to see the difference that same dim light would make in the perceived brightness.

Weber's law is not an exact description of all difference thresholds, but it is a useful summary (Brown & Deffenbacher, 1979; Somjen, 1972/1975; Uttal, 1973). Throughout most of the intensity scale, Weber's law is accurate. The relationship breaks down for the weakest-intensity stimuli, where the jnd does not tend to increase as much as the law would predict for increases in *I*. The relationship may also break down at the very highest levels of stimulation, where again the jnd may not increase rapidly enough.

Jnds vary according to species, the part of the body receiving stimulation, and the sensory system. In humans, the difference thresholds tend to be relatively small for brightness, loudness, and vibration frequency on the skin and relatively large for taste, temperature, and pain. This means that the auditory system is much more sensitive to small differences in loudness than the somatosensory system is to small differences in the intensity of some painful stimulus.

Relationships between jnds and estimations of magnitude.   Fechner used the Weber's law he formalized to derive an equation specifying how psychological intensity varied as a function of physical intensity. Fechner assumed that all jnds were psychologically. equal: one just-perceived increment in intensity would be psychologically equal to all other just-perceived increments in intensity (Somjen, 1972/1975; Uttal, 1973). Given that, the following equation would be true:

$$\text{Psi} = k \cdot \log I$$

In this equation, Psi is the psychological intensity, and *I* is the intensity of physical stimulus. The equation states that judged magnitude is related to the logarithm of physical magnitude. This equation is the **Weber-Fechner law.**

However, Stevens (1961, 1962, 1970) later made a different assumption. A just-noticeable increment in intensity was assumed to increase in perceived size as the physical intensity of the standard was increased. This assumption produced **Stevens' power law:**

$$\text{Psi} = k \, (I)^n$$

Psi and *I* again refer to psychological and physical intensity, but now the perceived magnitude of the stimulus is assumed to be a power function of the physical magnitude of that same stimulus.

Some logarithmic and power functions are illustrated in Figure 6-3 (*X* instead of *I* is used to refer to stimulus intensity in those functions). As part a shows, logarithmic relationships between physical intensity and perceived magnitude are characterized by **compression:** the perceived magnitude does not increase as fast as does the physical intensity of the stimulus. Part b shows that power functions, depending on the size of the exponent (*n*), can show either compression or **amplifica-**

tion. In amplification, the judged magnitude increases faster than does physical magnitude. Part c shows that with the proper choice of an exponent, a power function can be made nearly indistinguishable from a logarithmic function. As Somjen (1972/1975) and Uttal (1973) pointed out, this similarity may explain why neural scientists found logarithmic functions in their neural recordings before 1960 and found power functions after 1960.

Figure 6-3d shows how the exponent of the power function varies across sensory systems. Rather large changes in intensity produce only small changes in psychological magnitude throughout most of the scale; the exponent for that scale is .33. But for electric shock to the skin, a small amount of pain goes a long way. Small changes in the physical magnitude of the stimulus produce large changes in perceptions. The exponent for that scale is 3.5. More colloquially, we can perceive many different brightnesses, but pain seems to come in only a few quantities: a little, a lot, and much too much!

Exponents also vary within sensory systems. Although the exponents for sugar (sucrose) and salt are above 1.0, as Table 6-3 shows, the exponents for acid are below 1.0. There are also consistent individual differences in taste exponents, suggesting some real perceptual differences among people (Borg, Diamant, Ström, & Zotterman, 1967).

Judged Similarities among Stimuli

Observers can also be trained to judge the degrees of similarity and difference among various stimuli. Amoore's classic research (1965) on odors provides one good example. His panel of 29 judges were given 7 compounds to serve as standards, representing 7 different kinds of odors: ethereal, camphoraceous, musky, floral, minty, pungent, and putrid. These compounds were adjusted to be of the same psychological intensity. Then 40 other odors were presented. Each judge's task was to rate how similar the test odor was to each of the standards.

Amoore wanted to find the primary odors. Amoore found an interesting relationship when he related the results of this psychophysical procedure to the chemical analyses of the size and shapes of the 40 odor molecules. For ethereal, camphoraceous, musky, floral, and minty scents, there was a very good match between the size and shape of the molecules and their judged similarity to the standard odors. In another measure of similarity, subjects were asked to select which adjectives from a list of 146 went with each odor (Dravnieks, 1982). The degree to which the same adjectives were used could reflect the psychological similarity among the odors.

Similarities can also be measured with **cross-modal matching.** Is a bright light more similar to a loud sound or to a

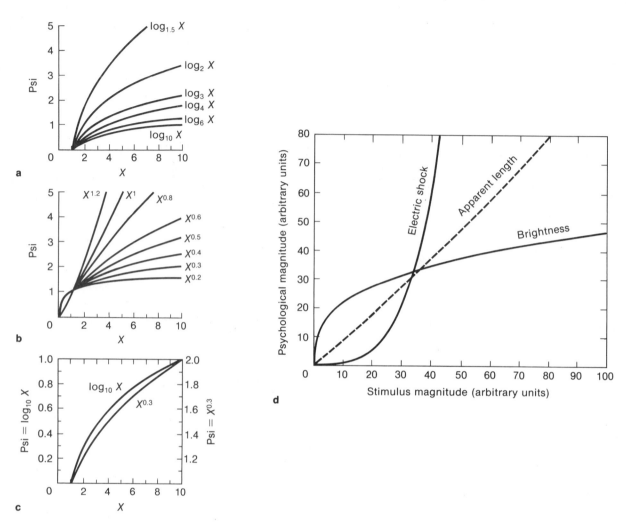

Figure 6-3 Some possible psychophysical functions. **a.** What Psi would be, according to Fechner, for X taken to various logarithmic bases, if $k = 1$. **b.** What Psi would be, according to Stevens, for X taken to various powers, again when $k = 1$. **c.** Psi for one logarithmic function compared with Psi for one power function; the curves are very similar. **d.** The exponent of Stevens' power function varies across different sensory systems. See text for further explanation.

high-frequency sound? Either trained or untrained observers are asked to make such judgments. Aspects of sensation that use similar types of neural codes might be perceived as being more similar to each other than aspects using different neural codes.

Psychophysics in Lower Animals

A nonverbal organism can be trained to tell an experimenter when a stimulus is present or whether one stimulus is different from another.

Discrimination experiments. An experimenter can use either operant or respondent training procedures (Chapter 1). Blough's pioneering study (1955) used operant discrimination procedures to measure absolute visual thresholds in pigeons. The pigeons' task was to peck key A (an elevator-type push button) whenever a light was present and key B whenever the light was absent. Pecks on the wrong key were never reinforced. Once the pigeons had learned the discrimination, pecks on key A steadily decreased the intensity of the stimulus light and pecks on key B increased it. To keep the pigeons working, Blough occasionally presented bright lights so that

Table 6-3   Stevens' power exponents for some sensory systems.

Continuum	Measured Exponent	Stimulus Condition
Loudness	0.67	3000-hertz tone
Brightness	0.33	Small target in dark
Brightness	0.5	Very brief flash
Smell	0.6	Heptane
Taste	1.3	Sucrose
Taste	1.4	Salt
Temperature	1.0	Cold on arm
Temperature	1.5	Warmth on arm
Vibration	0.95	60 hertz on finger
Vibration	0.6	250 hertz on finger
Duration	1.1	White noise stimuli
Finger span	1.3	Thickness of blocks
Pressure on palm	1.1	Static force on skin
Heaviness	1.45	Lifted weights
Force of handgrip	1.7	Hand dynamometer
Vocal effort	1.1	Vocal sound pressure
Electric shock	3.5	Current through fingers
Tactile roughness	1.5	Rubbing emery cloths
Tactile hardness	0.8	Squeezing rubber
Visual length	1.0	Projected line
Visual area	0.7	Projected square
Angular acceleration	1.41	5-second stimulus

pecks on key A could be reinforced and presented complete blackouts so that pecks on key B could be reinforced. The level of illumination maintained on the stimulus light indicate the pigeon's absolute brightness threshold.

A learned discrimination can also be used to measure difference thresholds. A louder–softer discrimination might be used. Then the two stimuli could be made steadily more similar to each other across trials by decreasing the intensity of the comparison stimulus in relation to the standard until the discrimination broke down and the animal began responding randomly. The difference between the stimuli at the time of random responding might reflect the difference threshold.

Generalization experiments.   Another type of psychophysical experiment uses discrimination training to produce results similar to those obtained in an experiment with judged similarity. Animals are taught to make a particular conditioned response to a particular stimulus. Then other stimuli, varying from the training stimulus along some particular dimension, are presented, usually in random order. The animal's tendency to respond, or rate of responding, to each of those test stimuli is measured.

This procedure generates a **generalization gradient,** which is a plot of how response rate varies when systematic changes are made in the stimulus. The rate of responding to each of the test stimuli might be a measure of how similar the organism perceives each of those stimuli to be to the original training stimulus. There are some problems with this assumption, however. The shape of a generalization curve—how response rate varies according to changes in the stimulus—depends on which training and testing procedures are used. Do the training and testing procedures then affect perceived similarities?

An interesting variant of generalization procedures can be used for odors and tastes. The original training involves a **conditioned aversion** (Halpern & Tapper, 1971; Pritchard & Scott, 1982b), in which an organism is exposed to a given taste or odor and is then made violently ill by a drug injection or by irradiation. On the next day, the organism is tested with various odors or tastes. The degree to which the organism shows rejection of or aversion to those stimuli may reflect their perceived similarity to the training taste or odor.

Summary of Psychophysics

Psychophysical experiments indirectly explore mental events by measuring changes in behaviors in certain systematic ways. In absolute-threshold experiments, the degree of stimulus energy that can just be detected 50% of the time tells experimenters how much stimulation in the external world is required for a human subject to report having a certain conscious sensory experience. Likewise, in difference threshold experiments, the difference between two stimuli that can just be detected 50% of the time tells experimenters about how variations in physical events may produce variations in mental events. Magnitude-estimation experiments are directed toward exploring that same relationship. Psychophysical measures of stimulus similarity may provide clues about neural coding. The variations on these procedures used in nonhuman animals give us an inferential window on the mental world of nonverbal organisms.

Transduction by Receptors

All receptor organs are specialized to transform energy from one type into another. How they might go about their task is described in this section, first in general principles and then in terms of specific receptors.

Anatomy of Receptors

As Figure 6-4 illustrates, chemoreceptors and mechanoreceptors convert chemical or mechanical energy into movements of ions through membranes. Chemoreceptors may be similar to transmitter receptors on membranes: a molecule of some chemical is "recognized" and binds to the receptor molecule. The activated receptor then directly or indirectly opens a membrane channel, causing depolarization by an influx of Na^+ ions. Pressure on the skin might exert pressure on the membrane of a mechanoreceptor organ embedded in the skin. This pressure might "stretch" the membrane and increase the size of its pores, just as stretching an elastic fabric will increase the size of any holes in it. Ions, probably Na^+, would flow in.

Chemoreceptors.   The **papillae** illustrated in Figures 6-5 and 6-6 are found on the surface of the tongue. Each papilla contains from 1 to 15 taste buds (Arvidson & Friberg, 1980). In turn, each taste bud may have from 30 to 50 individual taste cells. Each neuron innervates from 1 to 9 taste buds within a papilla. A neuron may also innervate taste buds in adjacent papillae (Beidler, 1969, 1975; Pfaffmann, Frank, & Norgren, 1979).

Gustatory and olfactory receptors, depicted in Figures 6-5, 6-6, and 6-7, have many similarities in appearance and function. First, there are hairlike extensions found on the top of both the taste buds in the papilla and the olfactory receptors situated in the olfactory epithelium (see Figures 6-5 and 6-7).

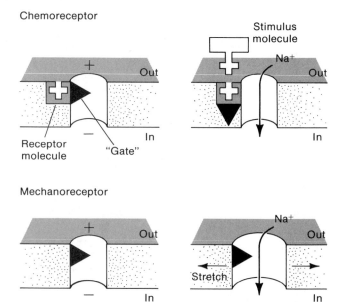

Figure 6-4   There are several models of how sensory receptors might work. In chemoreceptors, specialized receptor molecules combine with stimulus molecules, and the combination opens the gate for Na^+ current. In mechanoreceptors, stretch may physically enlarge the Na^+ pores, thereby increasing the inward Na^+ current.

Also, both types of receptors are continually being regenerated. A gustatory cell in a taste bud lasts only 10 days before being replaced with a new one. Olfactory cells may last 60 days before degenerating and being replaced.

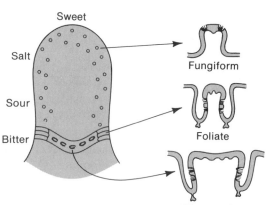

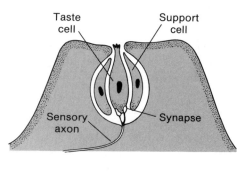

Figure 6-5   The various papillae have differing anatomies and are found on different parts of the tongue. The taste buds are found either on the top or on the sides of the papilla.

a

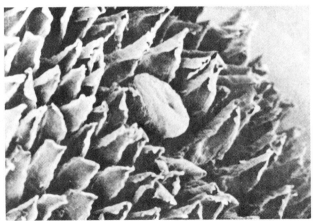

c

b

Figure 6-6 Various types of papilla. **a.** Foliate papillae in the rabbit's tongue. **b.** Circumvallate papillae in the dog's tongue. **c.** Several filliform papillae (leaflike) and one fungiform papilla in the rabbit's tongue.

There are also important differences between these receptors. First, the projections on the sensory surface of each cell are true cilia in olfactory cells but are just peglike projections of membrane and cytoplasm in the taste pore. Some of the projections found in the taste pores may actually come from supporting cells and not from the taste receptors themselves (Shepherd, 1983). Also, taste cells have no axons; they make synaptic contact with neurons going into the CNS in cranial nerves VII and IX. These neurons postsynaptic to the taste cells are the **primary afferents** (the first nerve cell between

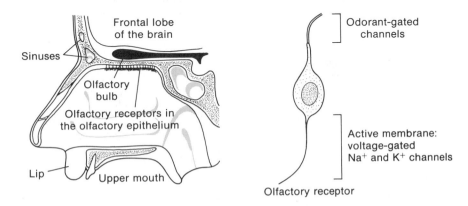

Figure 6-7 Anatomy of olfaction. The olfactory receptors are located in the roof of the nasal cavity. The cell bodies of the receptors are embedded in the olfactory epithelium, which is covered by mucus. Each olfactory receptor cell has membrane areas that respond to airborne molecules (odorant-gated channels) and active membrane areas (voltage-gated K^+ and Na^+ channels), which may act to boost the signal and/or which may allow adaptation to occur.

HAIRY SKIN GLABROUS (hairless) SKIN

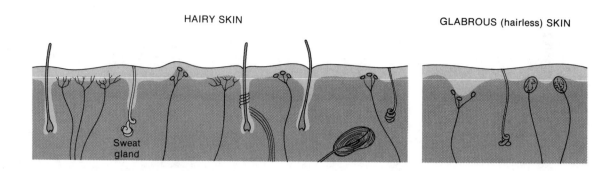

Sweat gland

	Free Nerve Endings	Merkel Disks in Pincus Domes (Ruffini Endings)	Hair Follicle Endings	Pacinian Corpuscle	Merkel Disks	Meissner Corpuscles
Adaptation	Very slow	Slow	Rapid	Very rapid	Slow	Rapid
Fiber type						
A-alpha	———	———	———	———	———	———
A-beta	———	Pressure; hair displacement; vibration (<10–2800 Hz)	Light touch; vibration (30–40 Hz)	In joints, signal joint position; in skin, signal pressure, vibration (250–300 Hz)	Touch, pressure	Touch, vibration
A-delta	Lower threshold, fast pain; cold; strong pressure	———	Touch from movement of downy hairs	———	———	———
C	Higher threshold, burning pain; slow pain; warmth; hair movement	———	———	———	———	———

Figure 6-8 Somatosensory receptors are found in the hairy and glabrous (nonhairy) skin and in muscles. The inset describes some characteristics of the various fiber types. Contracting of either type of muscle fiber is controlled by the CNS, but the **extrafusal** fibers are for

the receptor organ and the CNS). Olfactory cells do have axons. As Figure 6-7 shows, their axons penetrate the bone above the olfactory epithelium and make synaptic contact with cells in the olfactory bulb above. Since olfactory cells have axons, they are the only true nerve cell that regenerates.

Mechanoreceptors. Figure 6-8 illustrates some of the cutaneous (skin) and muscle mechanoreceptors and the primary afferents that carry their information to the CNS. The figure lists which type of physical stimulation is assumed to change the membrane potential of each organ. Temperature and pain may be transduced mechanically or chemically: neither possibility has yet been rejected.

A more complex mechanoreceptor is illustrated in Figures 6-9 through 6-13: the outer, middle, and inner ears of the auditory system. In order to explain how sound waves are converted into mechanical deformations of auditory hair cell membranes, we must describe the mechanical functions of these structures. First, waves of rarefaction and condensation

in air molecules create pressure waves at the eardrum, or **tympanic membrane,** illustrated in Figure 6-9. The resulting vibrations of the eardrum are translated into rotating movements of the three ear bones found in the middle ear: the **stapes** (stirrup), **incus** (anvil), and **malleus** (hammer). Because of the way the middle-ear bones are interconnected, they act like a lever system, amplifying the movements of the eardrum. They convert greater amplitude but less forceful vibrations on the eardrum to more forceful but smaller amplitude vibrations on the surface of the **oval window** at the entry to the inner ear. Going from the larger eardrum to the smaller oval window also increases the force of the vibration. Since the inner ear is filled with fluid, this conversion process recovers most of the energy normally lost when vibrations in the air are transferred to vibrations in fluid (it is harder to vibrate water than air).

The **eustachian tube** connects the middle ear to the oral cavity. It equalizes air pressure on either side of the eardrum, except when mucus plugs the tube, such as when you have a

MUSCLE RECEPTORS

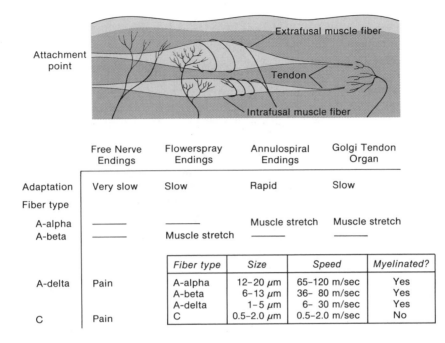

	Free Nerve Endings	Flowerspray Endings	Annulospiral Endings	Golgi Tendon Organ
Adaptation	Very slow	Slow	Rapid	Slow
Fiber type				
A-alpha	———		Muscle stretch	Muscle stretch
A-beta	———	Muscle stretch	———	———
A-delta	Pain			
C	Pain			

Fiber type	Size	Speed	Myelinated?
A-alpha	12–20 μm	65–120 m/sec	Yes
A-beta	6–13 μm	36– 80 m/sec	Yes
A-delta	1–5 μm	6– 30 m/sec	Yes
C	0.5–2.0 μm	0.5–2.0 m/sec	No

limb movement, whereas the **intrafusal** fibers control the sensitivity of the muscle to stretch stimuli. Thus, if the intrafusal fibers are shortened, then the muscle will be extremely sensitive to stretch types of stimuli. The muscle receptor information is important to the control of posture and movement. See text for further description of the other somatosensory receptors.

cold. If the eustachian tube is plugged when you are in an airplane, the difference in air pressure between the outer and middle ear can lead to pain and can damage the eardrum. Either yawning or chewing gum while the plane is gaining altitude can sometimes break the plug, equalize the pressure, prevent pain and damage, and restore hearing to normal levels of sensitivity.

The vibrations are transferred to the fluid-filled **cochlea,** or inner ear. As Figures 6-9 and 6-10 indicate, the cochlea is a tubular structure, divided in half lengthwise by a structure called the **basilar membrane.** This membrane separates the lower from the upper halves of the tube all the way from the basal region of the cochlea (near the oval and round windows) to near the apex. However, perhaps to save space (*not* just to make things hard for students to visualize), this tube is curled up on itself, much like one of those New Year's Eve noise-makers that uncurl when blown into.

The basilar membrane ends just in front of the apex, at a region called the **helicotrema.** An opening there allows the fluid beneath the membrane to mix with the fluid on top of the membrane. Thus, the **scala vestibuli** on top of the basilar membrane and the **scala tympani** beneath the membrane contain the same fluid, **perilymph.**

The **Organ of Corti,** illustrated in Figure 6-11, includes all the structures lying between the basilar and tectorial membranes. The **inner** and **outer hair cells** are the receptor organs. As Figures 6-11 and 6-12 show, at each turn of the cochlea there are three rows of outer hair cells and one row of inner hair cells. The tectorial membrane lying over the hairs of those cells (see Figure 6-12c) may be important to transduction. At least the longest hairs of the outer hair cells, and probably all their hairs, are actually embedded in the gelatinous **tectorial membrane.** The hairs of the inner cells may not be embedded (Steel, 1983). The very thin **Reissner's membrane** creates another compartment in the cochlea. **Endolymph** is found in this compartment, the **scala media.** The **cortilymph** may contain a fluid different in composition from either endolymph or perilymph.

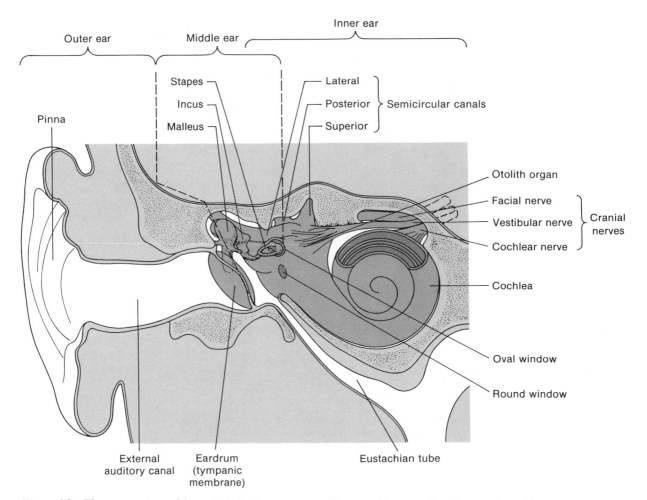

Figure 6-9 The gross anatomy of the ear includes the outer ear, middle ear, and inner ear. In addition to the cochlea, sensory receptors for gravity and rotation are also found in the inner ear; for example, the otolith organ.

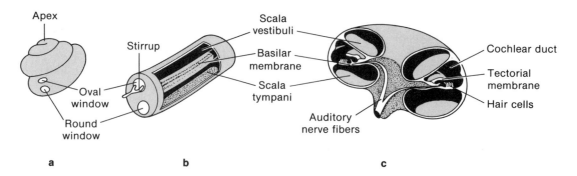

Figure 6-10 The anatomy of the cochlea is complex. **a.** Coiled structure of the cochlea. **b.** Cutaway view of a portion of that structure as it would look uncoiled. **c.** Cross-sectional view of a coiled cochlea.

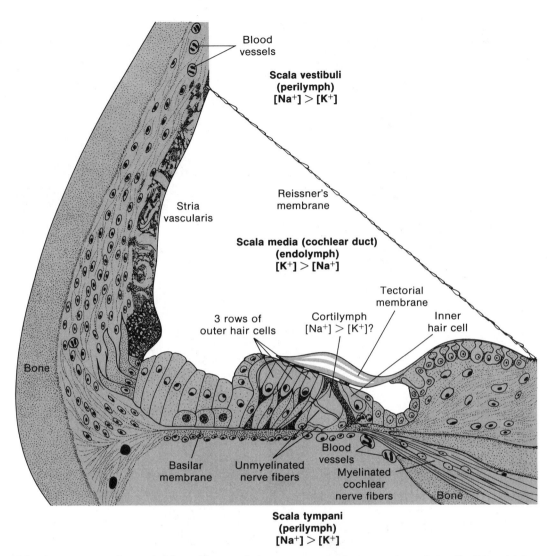

Figure 6-11 A cross section of one coil of the cochlea reveals the sensory organs, the inner and outer hair cells. Although it is not clearly shown, many researchers believe that the tips of the hairs of the outer cells are embedded in the tectorial membrane, whereas the hairs of the inner cells are free standing.

The hair cells do not have axons but serve as presynaptic membranes to dendrites of the auditory neurons or primary afferents (in cranial nerve VIII). However, 95% of the fibers in the auditory nerve come from the inner hair cells, and the auditory fibers that do come from the outer hair cells are the smallest ones and are often unmyelinated (Dallos, 1981; Liberman, 1982; Morest & Bohne, 1983). Each sensory fiber innervating an inner hair cell goes to one and only one receptor (with rare exceptions), and each inner hair cell is innervated by 20 to 25 different fibers (Liberman, 1982). Each

sensory fiber attached to outer hair cells innervates dozens of those cells (Morest & Bohne, 1983).

The manner in which vibrations of the ear bones create vibrations of the basilar membrane, deforming hair cells, is illustrated in Figure 6-13 (also refer to Figures 6-9 and 6-10). A wave of compression causes the stapes to press in on the oval window membrane. Since fluid is largely incompressible, and since the fluid in the cochlea is completely surrounded by bone, the pressure wave pushes out on the membrane of the round window found just below. Also note that the oval win-

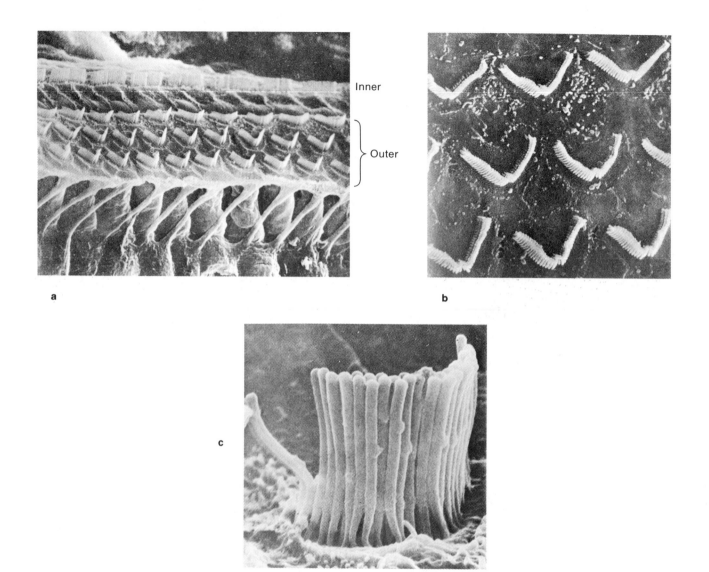

Figure 6-12 Scanning electron micrographs of auditory hair cells. **a.** The one row of inner and the three rows of outer hair cells in the guinea pig. **b.** The typical W-pattern of hairs on outer hair cells in the part of the Organ of Corti closest to the heliocotrema (guinea pig). **c.** Hairs on an outer hair cell in a rhesus monkey. Observe the smooth rounded tips and the rounded lumps on the hairs.

dow opens into the scala vestibuli, while the round window separates the scala tympani from the middle ear. Thus, a wave of condensation pushes the basilar membrane down. A wave of rarefaction pulls the oval window out and pulls the basilar membrane up. Since the basilar membrane and the tectorial membrane are separately attached to the bone, the up-and-down movement causes the tectorial membrane to move back and fourth across the tops of the hairs.

Sound waves of different frequencies have maximal effects at different places on the basilar membrane. High-frequency sound waves have the greatest effect on the basal region of the basilar membrane, the part closest to the oval and round windows. The lowest-frequency sound waves cause the entire basilar membrane to vibrate, but the amplitude of vibration is greatest at the apex. Between the basal and apical regions, the lower the frequency of vibration, the closer the region of maximal vibration is to the apex.

One way to visualize this process is to think about the effects

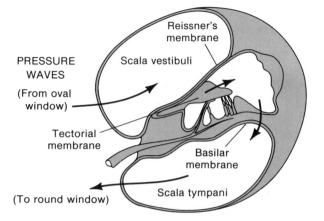

Figure 6-13 Directions of forces acting on inner ear structures during a wave of compression.

that vibration or pressure waves at the oval window would have on the basilar membrane stretched out between the base and the apex of the cochlea. Waves are set up in the cochlear fluid and they travel down the basilar membrane; the phenomenon of **traveling waves** was discovered by Békésy (1956).

Békésy used cochlea from cadavers to demonstrate the traveling wave. By injecting gold flakes into the cochlea, and by watching their movements through a surgically created window into the cochlea, he was able to see the movement of the basilar membrane. The basilar membrane vibrates at the frequency of stimulation, and the place at which maximal vibration occurs varies systematically according to the frequency of stimulation because of the increasing stiffness of that membrane from the basal region to the apex. If a curve is drawn connecting the points of maximal displacement (summing the traveling waves measured at each of several different times from the start of stimulation), the resulting **envelopes** of vibration for the various frequencies have maxima at different distances from the oval window. Thus, different frequencies maximally stimulate different hair cells.

The other mechanoreceptor of the inner ear is the **vestibular apparatus,** which consists of a globular structure, the **otolith organ,** and three loops of **semicircular canals** (see Figure 6-9). The sensory receptors in these structures look similar to the auditory hair cell and are also thought to be excited by having their hairs bent. The hair bending occurs in the otolith organ when head position changes in relation to gravity, and so these hairs might be called **gravity detectors.** Since the hairs are bent in the semicircular canals by movement of the head, which causes the fluid in the canals to move, the semicircular canals detect rotation. Together, these structures provide organisms with their sense of balance.

Concepts of Transduction

All receptors conform to certain principles of transduction.

Adequate stimulus. The **adequate stimulus** for any given receptor organ is the type of stimulation to which that organ is most sensitive. This does *not* mean that the organ responds only to that and to no other type of stimulation, but only that each receptor is characterized by its own special sensitivities to physical energies. For example, the adequate stimulus for the cochlea is vibration of air molecules eventuating in movement of the hairs on the hair cells. However, a constant change of pressure between outer and middle ears, created by the absorption of air by the middle ear when the eustachian tube is blocked, can create a constant ringing sound (as well as decreased sensitivities to real sounds).

Amplification, adaptation, and compression. Most of the receptors amplify threshold amounts of energy (Koshland, Goldbeter, & Stock, 1982; Russo & Koshland, 1983). For example, the outer and middle ears amplify the vibration energy by increasing the vibration force transmitted to the hair cells in the cochlea. Thus, the absolute threshold of the receptors is decreased (or their sensitivity increased). Other sensory systems show amplification at other levels. In these cases, as described earlier, the power function relating physical energy to perceived intensity has an exponent greater than one.

If this were the only mechanism operating, amplification would swamp the system when it was subjected to higher levels of energy. But receptors — as well as some cells at higher levels of sensory processing — also show compression and adaptation (Koshland, Goldbeter, & Stock, 1982; Russo & Koshland, 1983). In compression, ever-increasing amounts of stimulus energy produce smaller amounts of change in the output of the receptor organ. In psychophysical terms, the power function would have an exponent less than one. Both adaptation and compression increase the sensitivity of the transduction mechanism to small increases in stimulus energy above the threshold level. (However, since all stages of the sensory system show adaptation, this process will be discussed separately in the last section of this chapter.)

Three stages of transduction. The following discussion is based on Uttal's description (1973) of three stages of transduction. In the first stage, **nonneural stimulus modifications,** the chemical or mechanical physical energy is amplified or altered in some way *without* changing the nature of the energy involved: vibrations remain vibrations and chemicals remain chemicals. The second and third stages involve changes in the membrane. The second stage is the **primary sensory action:** energy is actually transformed from one type into another. Receptors transform mechanical or chemical energy into changes of membrane permeability and ion movements. The third stage involves **changes in membrane potential and creation of action potentials.** For receptor organs that lack axons (auditory hair cells and taste cells), the final stage of transduction will not be complete until action potentials are created in the primary afferents. For all types of receptors, **generator potentials** are the changes in membrane potential produced during this last stage of transduction. These potentials "generate" the action potentials either directly, by means of electrically gated Na^+ pores, or indirectly, across a synapse.

Receptor cells that lack axons (auditory hair cells and taste cells) were once thought not to be able to have action potentials (Russell, 1983; Sato, 1980). But this is not true (Hudspeth & Corey, 1977; Kashiwayanagi, Miyake, & Kurihara, 1983; Lewis & Hudspeth, 1983; Roper, 1983). Electrically gated Na^+ and Ca^{++} channels and even action potentials have been seen in taste cells. When vestibular hair cells in the frog were mechanically or electrically stimulated, both electrically gated channels and some action potentials were found. Furthermore, those cells have not only an electrically gated Ca^{++} channel but also a fast K^+ channel and a Ca-activated K^+ channel. The electrically gated Ca^{++} channels may be required for the release of transmitter substances from receptors onto afferent nerves. The other electrically gated channels may allow for adaptation.

Transduction in Chemoreceptors

There are several hypotheses about transduction in chemoreceptors. They are based on experimentation, often intracellular recordings, but there is no generally accepted model of transduction in chemoreceptors. In fact, different gustatory and olfactory cells may use entirely different mechanisms of transduction.

Olfactory transduction.   The first stage of transduction starts when an organism inhales odorous molecules. They are absorbed into the mucus covering the mucous membrane, where they diffuse to the olfactory receptor cilia. Because of the physical nature of odorous molecules, the mucus, and the mucous membrane, the various odor molecules diffuse differently across the olfactory epithelium in such a way that different odors contact different receptor cells (Getchell, Margolis, & Getchell, 1984; Price, 1984). The molecules may then be adsorbed into the membrane (which would mean they would

have to be soluble in lipids), or they may bind to some type of receptor molecules.

Two lines of evidence indicate that receptor molecules may be involved. First, the membranes of these cells do contain types of protein unique to them. Second, genetic research implies that olfactory receptor proteins exist. Different people can be "smell-blind" or anosmic, to different kinds of substances, implying that various single genes code for various olfactory receptor protein molecules (Amoore, 1969). However, the genes could also affect the pattern of neural connections made within the CNS.

If receptor molecules are involved, the second stage of transduction would begin with the binding. For example, Ash (1968) found that using odors to stimulate tissue taken from the olfactory epithelium of rabbits produced certain molecular changes, as if an odor molecule combined with a membrane receptor. Another study added homogenates (tissue put through a blender) of rat olfactory epithelium to a membrane that had been artificially created (Vodyanoy & Murphy, 1983). The olfactory homogenate caused channels to form in the artificial membrane. When that membrane was stimulated by odors, new channels opened and stayed open for approximately 42 seconds. The new channels seemed to be selective to K^+: they were blocked by a K^+-channel blocking chemical. Some of the K^+ channels may be activated by Ca^{++} (Getchell, 1986). If these results can be generalized to living membranes, then when an odor molecule combines with a membrane receptor protein, K^+ channels are opened. These channels are normally found in the cilia and in the membrane of olfactory cells closest to the cilia (Adamek, Gesteland, Mair, & Oakley, 1984; Getchell, 1986).

The third stage of transduction can be best studied with intracellular electrodes. Getchell (1977) recorded from 14 olfactory receptor cells in the salamander. The resting potentials ranged from -20 to -60 mV, with an average of -33 mV. These cells depolarized by 4 to 8 mV when stimulated by odor molecules. The action potentials often superimposed on this depolarization were from 10 to 50 mV in amplitude. When odor molecules interact with receptor proteins, a series of chemical reactions is initiated, reactions very similar to those found postsynaptically in slow synapses. cAMP would then open the K^+ channel (Getchell, 1986). However, in order for the *increase* in K^+ conductance found with the artificial membranes to cause the depolarization recorded by Getchell, the concentrations of K^+ inside and outside the olfactory cell would have to be atypical — and that does not seem to be the case.

Both intracellular and extracellular recordings have shown that most olfactory cells depolarize in response to more than one type of odorous molecule (Getchell, 1977; Revial, Sicard, Duchamp, & Holley, 1982). But some cells are inhibited by odors (Getchell, 1986). Each receptor cell has a maximum response to one or a few similar odors and smaller responses to other odors. Thus, each cell has a **best odor:** a type of odorous molecule that is the adequate stimulus for that cell. In addition, because of the physical properties of the mucus and mucous membrane, different odors affect different cells. But the ability of each cell to respond to many different molecules implies that if there are receptor proteins, each cell has several different kinds.

Gustatory transduction. The first stage of nonneural modification in taste is similar to that of olfaction. Molecules of the substances are dissolved in saliva. Then either they are adsorbed into taste cell membranes or they bind to receptor proteins.

Some research implies that specific taste receptor proteins may exist. First, some people have hereditary "taste blindness" for some bitter-tasting substances such as phenylthiocarbamide, but these people can still taste the bitter sensations produced by other substances (Price & DeSimone, 1977). "Taste-blind" people also perceive low concentrations of saccharin and sucrose as being less sweet than do other people (Bartoshuk, 1979). Second, placing a substance that destroys proteins on the tongues of frogs also eliminates the responses to water and to one type of salt ($CaCl_2$). However, responses to NaCl are not affected, suggesting that maybe only some taste responses involve specific receptor proteins (Kitada, 1984).

Some receptor proteins may have been identified. One team of researchers used homogenates of cow and pig tongues and subjected the homogenates to various kinds of fractionation procedures to isolate receptor proteins (Dastoli, Lopiekes, & Doig, 1968; Dastoli & Price, 1966; see also review in Price & DeSimone, 1977). One protein isolated from the tips of tongues reacted to (combined with) substances that tasted sweet and only to such substances. In fact, the strength of the binding of that protein to sweet-tasting substances was directly related to the psychophysically judged sweetness of each substance. The other protein isolated from the base of the tongue reacted only to bitter-tasting substances. The locations of these proteins correspond to psychophysical localizations of taste sensations on the tongue.

One receptor protein, one that transduces some salty sensations, may be linked to an active transport mechanism. The presence of a Na^+ ion outside the receptor membrane activates an active transport process. The transport of Na^+ to the inside would depolarize the cell (Heck, Mierson, & DeSimone, 1984).

Are the taste cells in a bud, and all the buds in a single papilla, sensitive to only one of the four basic taste substances (sour, sweet, bitter, and salty)? Békésy's early research (1964, 1966) indicated that that might be the case, leading one recent review to state: "for the remainder of this review it will be assumed that there are not less than four primary tastes, and that there are receptors specific for each" (Price & DeSimone, 1977). But this may not be true. Other researchers who chemically stimulated single papillae in humans have found that a single papilla can react to all four of the basic taste substances (Arvidson & Friberg, 1980). Different amino acids also have unique tastes—unique both with respect to each other and with respect to the four basic tastes—a finding suggesting that there may be several amino acid receptors in addition to the four already described (Pritchard & Scott, 1982a, 1982b). Also, there is probably more than one type of sweet receptor, each one responding to different types of substances (Jakinovich, 1983).

Intracellular recordings reveal the second phase of transduction. The results of the first intracellular recordings published in 1961 (Kimura & Beidler) were confirmed and extended by later research (Akaike, Noma, & Sato, 1976; Ozeki, 1971; Price & DeSimone, 1977; Sato, 1980). Resting membrane potentials range from -10 to -50 mV. Each cell responds to more than one taste stimulus, although each cell tends to have a **best taste** producing the largest response. The cells either depolarize or hyperpolarize, with up to a 40 mV change in membrane potential. The change in potential occurs relatively slowly and also declines very slowly with continued stimulation. Hyperpolarization has been observed only in certain kinds of taste cells: cells that depolarize in response to salt may hyperpolarize in response to water, and vice versa. The depolarization in response to salty, sour, and sweet-tasting substances is associated with a decrease in membrane resistance, and the decrease (though not the depolarization) is largest for salty stimuli. The depolarization produced by bitter substances is associated with an *increase* in membrane resistance.

There are several possible explanations. Salts may depolarize because an increase in anions outside the membrane will depolarize any membrane. The depolarization may activate electrically gated K^+, Ca^{++}, or Na^+ channels as it does in nerve membranes. Sweet and sour molecules may combine with receptor proteins, although hydrogen ions may also have an effect. Bitter substances may depolarize by *decreasing* K^+ conductance, perhaps through a process that involves a receptor protein and cAMP (as it does in slow synapses).

Generator potentials increase the amount of transmitter substance released by the taste cells onto the primary afferents.

Action potentials travel on these afferents to the olfactory lobe of the brain. The transmitter substance involved in the synapse between taste cell and primary afferent is probably one or more of the biogenic amines, perhaps 5-HT (Price & DeSimone, 1977).

Interoceptors.   Even less is known about the various interoceptors. Interoceptors sensitive to the level of carbon dioxide in the blood are important to the control of respiration. Both the intestine (Mei, 1978) and the liver (Niijima, 1969) have receptors that respond specifically to glucose. The intestine also has several receptors, each type responding to only one amino acid (Jeanningros, 1982). These receptors might be important to hunger, but the method of transduction is unknown.

Transduction in Mechanoreceptors

Just two mechanoreceptors will be discussed here: the Pacinian corpuscle and the auditory hair cell. Other mechanoreceptors found in muscles and tendons are important to the control of movement. The stretch receptors in the stomach may communicate information about stomach distention (such as occurs after overeating) to the brain cells concerned with eating (Paintal, 1954).

The Pacinian corpuscle.   Much of the research on transduction in the Pacinian corpuscle was done by Loewenstein (1959, 1960; Loewenstein & Rathkamp, 1958). It is largely thanks to him that we know as much as we do about the Pacinian corpuscle, a mechanoreceptor found in the skin and illustrated in Figure 6-14 (see also Figure 6-8).

Transduction starts with the onionlike layers surrounding the bare nerve endings found inside the corpuscle. These layers physically change the nature of the pressure stimulus in such a way that pressure is transmitted to the bare nerve ending only at the onset and offset of the pressure. Consequently the bare nerve ending does not respond to constant pressure.

The other two stages are neural. The second phase of transduction takes place in the bare nerve ending itself. Theoretically, the pressure deforms the membrane of the bare nerve ending, increasing membrane permeability in some mechanical fashion. The third phase of transduction begins with the depolarizing movement of ions (presumably Na^+ rushing in). The depolarization spreads passively down the bare nerve ending. If the depolarization at the first node of Ranvier (the nerve is myelinated nearly to the boundary of the capsule) is above threshold, one or more action potentials will be generated.

The other mechanoreceptors in the skin probably have similar transduction mechanisms. Differences in the size and shapes of the capsules surrounding the bare nerve endings may account for the different sensitivities of these organs to types of touch, pressure, and vibration. For example, the Merkel disk may change the form of the applied pressure but it is not necessary for transduction (Gottschaldt & Vahle-Hinz, 1981).

Transduction in the ear.   The first phase of transduction has already been described. The nonneural modifications consist of all the things that happen to the vibration between when the eardrum moves and when the stereocilia on hair cells become bent. Which frequencies of vibration are passed through most forcefully depends on the size and shape of the structures in the middle and inner ear. Among different species (though *not* within a species), organisms with larger eardrums are less capable of hearing the higher-frequency vibrations (Heffner, 1983). Because of the size and shape of the ear bones and eardrum, human ears pass sound of 3000 cycles per second (cps) more readily than other frequencies.

The effects of different frequencies of stimulation vary along the length of the basilar membrane: different frequencies maximally stimulate different hair cells. In fact, the ear performs Fourier analyses (see Figure 6-1), changing the *time* of arrival of a sound wave into the *place* of maximal vibration on the basilar membrane. Each sine wave component of a complex tone (for example, each pure tone in a chord) will affect a unique set of hair cells. Each of these sets will be stimulated according to the amount of energy (amplitude of the sound wave) devoted to that particular sine wave in the chord, since membrane movement is proportional to the wave amplitude.

Since 1977, researchers have used intracellular recordings to investigate the second phase of transduction (Dallos,

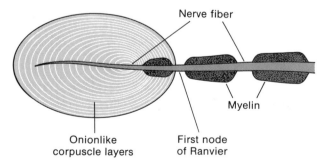

Figure 6-14   The Pacinian corpuscle is a mechanoreceptor. Sufficient pressure or vibration applied to its onionlike layers will produce action potentials at the first node of Ranvier.

Santos-Sacchi, & Flock, 1982; Russell, 1983; Russell & Sellick, 1977, 1978, & 1983; Sellick & Russell, 1980; Nuttall, Brown, Masta, & Lawrence, 1981; Tanaka, Asanuma, & Yanagisawa, 1980). Hudspeth and his colleagues (Corey & Hudspeth, 1979a, 1979b; Hudspeth, 1983, 1985; Hudspeth & Corey, 1977; Hudspeth & Jacobs, 1979) also used micromanipulators to bend hairs on vestibular receptors during intracellular recordings. Auditory hair cells are assumed to be similar to vestibular hair cells.

Inner versus outer hair cells.   Although each inner or outer hair cell is excited by more than one frequency of stimulation, because of the traveling wave, each is maximally excited by only one frequency (the traveling wave). The more a sound stimulus differs from that **best** or **characteristic frequency**, the less the cell depolarizes.

Inner hair cells (whose primary afferents make up the bulk of the auditory nerve) have resting potentials between -20 and -90 mV, with -30 mV being the most common. These hair cells depolarize in response to sound pressure or to having their hairs bent in one certain direction. (Vestibular cells will hyperpolarize when their hairs are bent in the opposite direction.) The depolarization can range from less than 1 mV up to 25 mV. Low-frequency tones cause depolarization during the movement of fluid past the hairs (the **velocity** response), which occurs when the basilar membrane moves upward towards the scala vestibuli (during rarefaction) (Russell & Sellick, 1983; Nuttall et al., 1981). For higher-frequency tones, hair cells may be depolarized when the basilar membrane moves downward toward the scala tympani (during compression) (Sokolich, Hamernick, Zwislocki, & Schmiedt, 1976). In this case, the cells may be excited when their stereocilia are bent by movement of the tectorial membrane (the **displacement** response) (Sellick & Russell, 1980).

Intracellular recordings show how outer hair cells differ from inner hair cells (Dallos, Santos-Sacchi, & Flock, 1982; Russell & Sellick, 1983). Outer hair cells have larger resting membrane potentials (a median of -71 mV) but smaller receptor potentials (up to 15 mV). Only outer hair cells hyperpolarize in response to sounds that differ greatly from their best frequency. At all frequencies, outer hair cells respond to displacement rather than to the velocity of basilar membrane movement. In fact, passive current spread from the outer hair cells may cause the inner hair cells to depolarize during the high-frequency stimulations. Since responses of outer hair cells are delayed (by 90°, which corresponds to half of a compression or rarefaction wave) relative to the inner hair cell responses, passive current spread from outer hair cells would

therefore stimulate inner hair cells "out of phase" or during condensation.

Thus, the active stimulation (as opposed to the effects of passive current spread) of both inner and outer hair cells may occur during rarefaction or upward movement of the basilar membrane. During low-frequency stimulations, these depolarizations are separate and discrete (the **ac response**), one depolarization appearing for each wave of rarefaction. During high-frequency stimulations (about 5 kHz), the cells show waves of less and more intense depolarization in phase with the stimulus, but the cells remain depolarized as long as the stimulus continues (the **dc response**) (Russell & Sellick, 1983).

Causes of changes in membrane permeability and potentials.   Davis (1965) proposed that the movement of hairs relative to the top of the hair cell decreased the resistance of the hair cell membrane. The decrease would produce an increase in the flow of ions through the membrane—possibly by mechanically changing the size of the pores—and the flow of current would depolarize the basal end of the hair cell.

The recent intracellular recordings have supported Davis's theory (Corey & Hudspeth, 1979; Hudspeth, 1985; Russell, 1983; Valli, Zucca, & Casella, 1979). Hudspeth and his colleagues have found tiny filaments extending between the hairs. Movement of the basilar membrane would change the angle of these filaments relative to their connections to hairs, possibly opening some gate in the hairs. If the resulting ion movement through the hair membrane were depolarizing, the depolarization would passively spread from the hairs to the cell body. In fact, the depolarization of inner hair cells *is* associated with an increase in permeability, and the channels seem to be K^+ channels, possibly Ca-activated (Tanaka, Asanuma, & Yanagisawa, 1980). The inflow of K^+ ions would be depolarizing because of the high concentration of K^+ in the endolymph (see Figure 6-11). This process takes place extremely rapidly, within a few microseconds (μsec).

Depolarization of the inner hair cell would increase the release of transmitter onto auditory nerve cells because of the electrically gated Ca^{++} channels. The transmitter substance may be an amino acid (Dallos, 1981). Transmitter release would depolarize auditory nerve cell dendrites and increase the rate of action potentials in their axons. Since inner hair cells during low-frequency stimulations usually depolarize only in response to rarefaction, action potentials would be generated largely in that phase. However, as pointed out, for frequencies above 5 kHz, hair cells may stimulate the auditory nerve more uniformly throughout the sound (Russell & Sellick, 1978, 1983).

Summary of Transduction

The adequate stimulus for receptors varies not only among sensory systems but within a sensory system. Chemoreceptors respond to various types of molecules, but different olfactory and gustatory cells may be maximally sensitive to different molecules. Hair cells often respond to many different frequencies, but each has its characteristic or best frequency.

Receptors also show amplification. The amplification may be mechanical, as in mechanoreceptors (such as the ear bones and eardrum). The amplification may also be selective: the middle ear amplifies some frequencies more than other frequencies.

The three phases of transduction are found in all sensory receptors. For chemoreceptors, the nonneural phase starts with the inhaling or ingesting of the molecules, which then go into solution. For mechanoreceptors, the changes are all mechanical ones, as in the lever action of the middle ear bones. The second phase of transduction, in which one type of energy is converted into changes in membrane permeability, is either chemically produced (chemoreceptors) or mechanically produced (mechanoreceptors). The change in permeability leads to changes in ionic current; the currents cause changes in membrane potential. If the depolarization is large enough, action potentials are generated either in the receptor cell itself (somatosensory mechanoreceptors and olfactory cells) or in the primary afferent innervating the receptor (auditory hair cells and taste cells).

Coding Principles

If sensory stimuli speak the language of physicists, how are the syllables of action and synaptic potentials translated into the words of the language describing those physical stimuli? In other words, what are the rules of syntax and grammar governing how the brain uses its syllables and words as a code for internal and external events? The coding strategy of research owes much to the ideas of Somjen (1972/1975) and Uttal (1969, 1973). Our description of the principles of coding is based on what they wrote.

The Concept of Coding

The concept of coding encompasses how aspects of sensory stimulation are converted into patterns of activity in sensory neurons. These patterns of activity—by some process not yet completely conceptualized—are converted into the mental events of sensations and perceptions.

Signs versus codes.   Some patterns of sensory activity may be artifacts or spurious associates of the transduction process. Such patterns would *not* be a code for any aspect of sensory stimulation. Uttal (1969) labels this kind of pattern a **sign,** distinguishing it from a true **code.** A sign is any dimension of neural activity that is *not* transmitted to "higher" sensory processing areas of the brain.

At the level of the cortex, a sign would be any dimension of neural activity that is *neither necessary nor sufficient* for any behavioral or inferred mental event. To prove that a pattern is *necessary,* systematic variations in the pattern must always parallel systemic variations in the physical stimulus at *all* levels of sensory processing. Only if all the studies done at all levels of that sensory system found the same variations in activity, systematically related to variations in the physical stimulus, should we be willing to believe that a given pattern is necessary and thus part of a code.

To prove that a pattern is *sufficient,* artificial duplication of that pattern, as by electrical stimulation of one or more nerves, must cause the same sensory experience as the physical stimulus itself did. Therefore to prove that a neural pattern is sufficient requires an organism that can accurately describe his or her mental experiences either verbally or through changes in trained discriminative responses.

Each successive processing station may use a different code for the same aspects of sensory stimulation. Thus, as sensory information ascends the CNS, the sequence of nuclei may be visualized as transforming and combining the syllables of neural activity into different patterns, patterns that cortical cells eventually interpret as words or primitive units of sensation.

Parallel and serial processing.   For years, researchers assumed that the brain processed sensory information only in a serial fashion. Sensory information was thought to ascend through successively "higher" levels of processing, involving increasingly more complex codes. This type of strictly sequential or **serial processing** does occur, but **parallel processing,** sending information simultaneously to several areas of the brain, may be even more common. A sensory nucleus may send slightly different aspects of information simultaneously to different areas, and many times it would be difficult to conceptualize any of that information as representing either less or more complex analyses of the stimulus input.

Anatomy of Coding

Only basic principles of anatomy are covered here. This section should be used as a reference for the rest of this chapter.

Somatosensory system. Figure 6-15 shows how somatosensory information has been classically divided on functional and anatomical bases into two pathways (Guyton, 1981; Martin, 1981). One similarity between them is that the sensation from one side of the body goes to the **contralateral** (opposite) side of the brain. Another is that there are at least two synapses between the sensory organ and the first cortical cell. Both divisions project into the thalamus before they ascend to the cortex, and both are joined by cutaneous sensations from the facial nerve before they reach the thalamus.

The two pathways differ functionally in what is coded and in the types of codes used. The **spinothalamic pathway** carries pain, temperature, and some touch sensation. The **lemniscal** or **dorsal column system** carries more information about deep cutaneous sensations, fine touch, kinesthesia, and proprioceptive (skeletomuscle) sensations. The spinothalamic system codes primarily for which type of sensation has occurred (for example, pain versus temperature), whereas the lemniscal system emphasizes information about the location and amount of stimulation.

There are also important anatomical differences. The spinothalamic afferents make synaptic contact with cells in the **substantia gelatinosa** just after entering the spinal cord. The second-order neuron immediately crosses the cord before ascending in the white (myelinated) matter of the cord. The lemniscal primary afferents may not make synaptic contact with cells in the spinal cord. These sensory axons ascend directly in the dorsal columns, often on the same side of the spinal cord (no crossing). The lemniscal system crosses after a synapse in the **cuneate** (upper-body information) or **gracile** (lower-body information) nuclei. Although Figure 6-15 shows both systems with input into the RAS, the lemniscal system input, if it exists at all, is much weaker than that of the spinothalamic system.

The anatomy of pain differs in some respects from that of the other somatosensory inputs. For example, as Figure 6-15 shows, some primary afferents of the spinothalamic type may form synapses with cells in the dorsal horn of the spinal cord; axons of the dorsal-horn cells then ascend in the dorsal col-

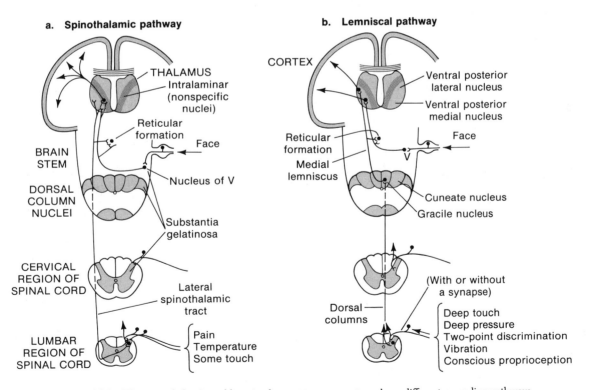

Figure 6-15   The spinothalamic and lemniscal somatosensory systems have different ascending pathways.

umns of the cord. Dennis and Melzack (1977) have argued that these particular axons may carry pain information. Some pain afferents may also enter the spinal cord through the ventral roots (Chung, Lee, Endo, & Coggeshall, 1983), long thought to contain only efferent axons. Pain sensation from the internal organs travels on autonomic sensory nerves to the CNS.

The somatosensory thalamus and cortex are illustrated in Figure 6-16a and b. Each area receives different kinds of stimuli: area 3a of the cortex receives information from receptors in muscles, joints, and tendons; areas 3b and 1 receive information largely from surface skin receptors; and area 2 receives information from joint and deep tissue receptors (Kaas, Nelson, Sur, Lin, & Merzenich, 1979; Merzenich & Kaas, 1980; Mountcastle, 1975; Sur, Wall, & Kaas, 1981). In all these areas, the body surface is mapped onto the cortical surface in a point-to-point fashion. Area 5 carries out higher-level somatosensory processes. The posterior parietal cortex may also have some somatosensory functions. Figure 6-16a (part 1) also shows a body map in the early view of cortical organization, presented for reference so that results of earlier experiments, using earlier landmarks, can be compared with later experiments.

The output from somatosensory cortex is organized by layers. All somatosensory areas are interconnected by projections from the primary somatosensory cortex (3b and 1) (Jones, Burton, & Porter, 1975; Jones, Coulter, & Hendry, 1978). Some cortical output descends to lower sensory areas; in addition, analogous areas on both sides of the brain are interconnected in a highly organized fashion by fibers passing through the commissures such as the corpus callosum.

Olfactory and gustatory systems. The anatomy of the taste system is presented in Figures 6-17 and 6-18. Figure 6-17 shows the location of the cortical taste area in relation to the cortical somatosensory areas. Touch and temperature information from the tongue are sent to areas 3a and 1, while taste information is projected to a special cortical taste area. Taste information is sent to the thalamus before going on to the cortex and is also sent to many structures of the limbic system.

As Figure 6-18 shows, olfactory information is sent to even more structures of the limbic system. Olfactory information, unlike other types of sensory information, does *not* pass through the thalamus before going to the cortex (Tanabe, Yarita, Iino, Ooshima, & Takagi, 1975). The olfactory cortical areas in the rodent include the anterior olfactory cortex, the pyriform cortex, the olfactory tubercle, the amygdala, and the transitional entorhinal cortex (Shepherd, 1983). In the primate, olfactory information is sent to part of the neocortex called the **prefrontal cortex,** located just anterior to the taste area and just below the motor-sensory area I (MsI) (see Figure 6-19) (Tanabe et al., 1975). Figure 6-18 also shows some of the olfactory centrifugal connections: cells in the brain stem and septum send axons to the olfactory bulb.

Auditory system. As Figure 6-20 shows, auditory information extensively crosses and recrosses at all levels of the auditory system. There is also a variety of pathways to the cortex, some more direct than others. This is parallel processing: different nuclei carry out different kinds of processing on the same sensory information, and then all the nuclei forward that information to the cortex. In addition, there are centrifugal

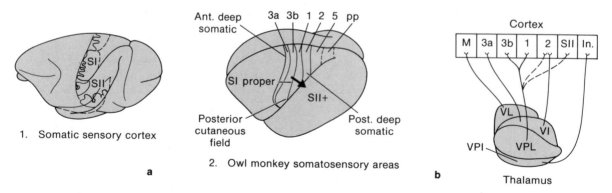

1. Somatic sensory cortex

2. Owl monkey somatosensory areas

a   b

Figure 6-16   a. Traditional (1) and current (2) views of the primate parietal somatosensory cortex. The traditional view had only two divisions. In view 2, the anterior deep somatic field (3a), the SI proper (3b), the posterior cutaneous field (area 1), and the posterior deep fields (area 2) all have separate representations of the body surface. Area 5 and posterior parietal cortex (PP) may also be involved. **b.** Some of the connections between cortex and thalamus, with dashed lines representing weaker connections. VPL = ventral posterior lateral; VPI = ventral posterior inferior; VI = ventral intermediate; VL = ventrolateral; M = motor cortex; In = insular cortex.

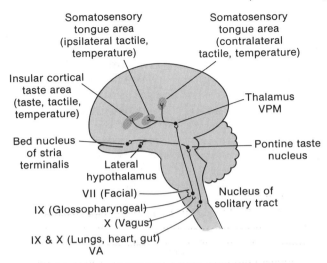

Figure 6-17 Taste pathways in the primate CNS. VA = visceral afferents; VPM = ventral posterior medial nucleus of the thalamus.

fibers going from the superior olivary region to the cochlea: the **olivo-cochlear bundle.**

Figure 6-21 illustrates the cortical auditory areas. In each area, the basilar membrane is mapped onto the surface of the cortex. Thus, information coming from hair cells located in the basal region of the cochlea is sent to the areas labeled B, and information coming from apical hair cells is sent to the areas labeled A. The earlier views of cortical organization of the auditory areas are presented so that earlier and later research can be compared.

Types of Code

The kinds of code described in this section are the basis for the single-unit approach to studying the brain. Researchers first discovered coding by recording sensory responses and later applied the same approach to motives, emotions, learning, and memory. In reading about the kinds of codes used by sensory systems, you should remember that most of the studies used anesthetics, which might create unknown biases in coding responses to stimuli (Chapter 1).

Place versus pattern codes in individual fibers. Activity in individual nerve fibers codes for certain aspects of stimulation. Either the fact of activity in a given nerve cell or the pattern of its activity may be a code for the presence of certain characteristics in the physical stimuli. These coding characteristics are either place or pattern codes, respectively.

A **place code** indicates by the location of the activated nerve cell what kind of stimulus has occurred. In other words, if the stimulation of a particular nerve cell depends on which sort of physical energy has been applied, then the code is a place code. The use of place codes is also indicated by the phrase **labeled line,** which implies that all the neurons from receptor to cortex are place-coding some specific aspect of a stimulus. For example, if a certain cell in a cutaneous nerve is active, the fact of its being active may be signaling the occur-

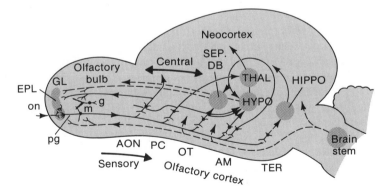

Figure 6-18 The central olfactory pathway in the rodent is connected to limbic structures. Primates have the limbic structures, but they are not so heavily interconnected with the olfactory system as they are in lower animals. Abbreviations for olfactory bulb: on = olfactory nerves; pg = periglomerular cell; m = mitral cell; g = granule cell; GL = glomerular layer; EPL = external plexiform layer. Abbreviations for olfactory cortex: AON = anterior olfactory cortex; PC = pyriform cortex; OT = olfactory tubercle; AM = amygdala; TER = transitional entorhinal cortex. Abbreviations for limbic regions: SEP-DB = region of septum and diagonal band; HYPO = hypothalamus; THAL = thalamus; HIPPO = hippocampus.

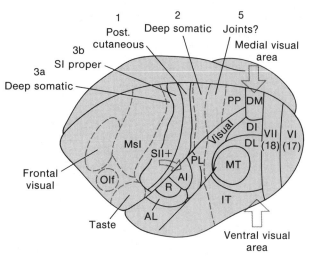

Figure 6-19 Summary of sensory subdivisions of the neocortex in a primate. Many of these subdivisions are in areas previously called "association cortex." AL = anterior lateral auditory field; DI = dorsointermediate visual area; DL = dorsolateral visual area; DM = dorsomedial visual cortex; IT = inferior temporal visual area; MT = middle temporal visual area; MsI = motor-sensory area I; PL = posterior lateral auditory field; R = rostral auditory field; VI = visual area I; VII = visual area II; other abbreviations as in Figure 6-16.

rence of painful stimulation to higher levels of sensory processing. Activity in a *different* cell may be a code for touch. No matter how that particular cell is activated — by touch or by an experimenter's electrical stimulation — the resulting sensation will be the same.

Pattern codes signal sensations by the *way* in which a given cell has been activated. A single auditory neuron may signal that a soft sound has occurred by a low rate of firing, and that *same* auditory neuron may signal that a loud sound has occurred by firing at a high rate. Or one neuron may signal the presence of one type of stimulus by increasing its firing rate above the level of spontaneous activity, and it may signal the presence of a different type of stimulus by decreasing its firing rate below the spontaneous level.

There are many possible patterns codes that could be used. The simplest (for researchers, anyway) is rate of firing. For example, the intensity of a stimulus is often coded by rate of firing. But *changes* in the pattern of activity during stimulation could also be codes (Klemm & Sherry, 1982; Nakahama et al., 1983). For example, in recording from individual somatosensory cells, Mountcastle et al. (1969) discovered that increasing intensity of pressure on the skin did not cause any consistent

increase in firing rate; instead, the firing pattern consistently became more regular.

Patterns of activity are also relevant to synaptic responses. Segundo, Moore, Stensaas, and Bullock (1963) showed that the output of a postsynaptic cell changed when the *pattern* of presynaptic stimulation was changed, even when the average rate was kept constant. The pattern of preganglionic neural activity may even determine *which* transmitter the presynaptic neuron uses to produce a particular enzymatic reaction in the postganglionic sympathetic neurons (Ip & Zigmond, 1984).

Since synapses can change an input pattern, synapses can recode information. For example, NE modulates the response of pyramidal cells in the hippocampus to any synaptic input (Madison & Nicoll, 1982). ACh can inhibit an electrically activated K^+ current at muscarinic receptors (the M-current). Since the M-current normally decreases the depolarizing effects of any increase in g_{Na^+} (the K^+ current tends to hyperpolarize), blocking the M-current increases the postsynaptic cell's tendency to respond to any steady input with a rhythmic, repetitive pattern of discharges (Brown & Adams, 1980).

A given cell can simultaneously signal several types of information to higher sensory levels. The fact that one certain cell instead of another is active may be a place code for one aspect of information, and the way it is active may be a pattern code for another type of information.

Three levels of place coding. Place codes have three levels representing progressively higher degrees of abstraction. At the lowest level, place codes occur **between modalities.** (A sensory **modality** is the type of sensation, such as auditory or visual.) A between-modality place code means that the occurrence of sound instead of light is signaled by activity in the auditory instead of the optic nerve. Electrical stimulation of the auditory nerve produces sensations of sounds in people, and stimulation of the optic nerve produces sensations of light. At the second level, **quality coding within a modality** is often (but not always) coded by a type of place code. For example, whether a high- or a middle-frequency sound has occurred is coded by which hair cell in the inner ear has been most strongly stimulated. Different hair cells respond to different frequencies.

Feature detection is the highest level of place coding. A given cell changes its rate of firing from spontaneous levels if and only if stimulation having a given feature (the **trigger feature**) is present. An example of a feature detector would be a cell in your brain that would fire only if your grandmother's face were projected onto your retina. Feature detectors were first discovered in the visual system: the frog's brain has "bug

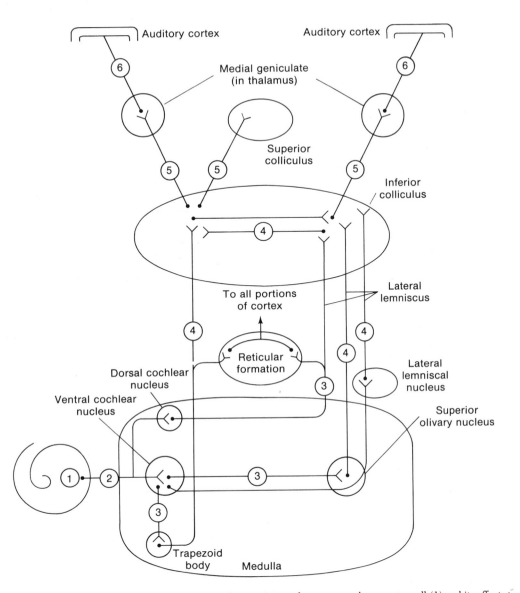

Figure 6-20 Schematic drawing of the afferent auditory pathways. A stimulus occurs at the receptor cell (1) and its effects travel from neuron to neuron in turn, following one or more of the various routes indicated by the neurons numbered from 1 to 5, in sequence. Even if the shortest possible route is taken, the auditory information must affect at least five different cells on its way to the cortex.

detectors." These cells fire only if a small dark spot is moved across the retina (Lettvin, Maturana, McCulloch, & Pitts, 1959).

Across-fiber pattern codes.   Another type of coding is used by the chemosensory systems and — maybe — the somatosensory system. In **across-fiber pattern codes,** activity in a single nerve cell, by itself, contains no useful information. The information about sensations is in the *total pattern* of activity across a set of sensory neurons. If the neuron doctrine is true, this type of code would require recoding in higher-level sensory cells. Higher-order nerve cells would have to integrate the rate of activity across at least hundreds of different cells, using that information to signal which type of stimulus had occurred.

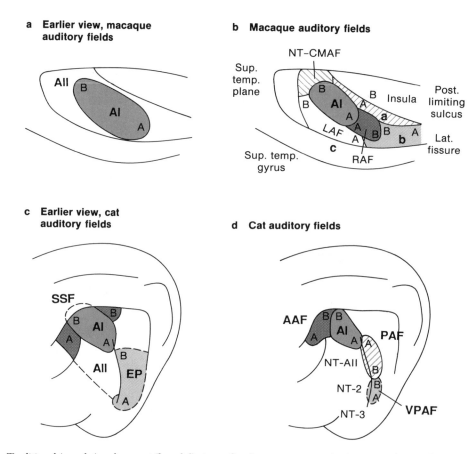

a Earlier view, macaque auditory fields

b Macaque auditory fields

c Earlier view, cat auditory fields

d Cat auditory fields

Figure 6-21 Traditional (**a** and **c**) and current (**b** and **d**) views of auditory cortex organization in monkeys and in carnivores differ. The apex (A) and the base (B) of the cochlea are indicated in all figures. In the traditional view, only primary (AI) and secondary (AII) fields were described. AI was later redefined and five other areas added. AI = primary auditory cortex; LAF = lateral auditory field; RAF = rostrolateral auditory field; (in part **b**) a, b, and c = other fibers organized by stimulus tone pitch; NT-CMAF = nontopographic (not organized by stimulus pitch) caudomedial auditory field; olf = olfactory.

We will now describe how sensory neurons signal (1) *what* type of stimulus has occurred (within modalities), (2) *how much* stimulation has occurred, (3) *where* the stimulus was (in three-dimensional space or on the body), and (4) *when* the stimulus occurred.

Codes for Quality of Stimulus within a Modality

The code for quality of stimulus is usually changed by every synapse that the information crosses on its way to the cortex. For example, consistent changes in coding mechanisms occur across processing levels in both the olfactory system (Duchamp, 1982; Tanabe, Iino, & Takagi, 1975) and the gustatory system (Doetsch & Erickson, 1970). When higher levels

of processing are compared with lower levels, researchers commonly find that the higher level of processing includes more specific responses and more inhibitory actions among responses to different stimuli being presented at the same time (Duchamp, 1982; Erulkar, 1972; Katsuki, 1961; Martin & Dickson, 1983; Mountcastle & Powell, 1959; Tanabe, Iino, & Takagi, 1975). Although these differences should be kept in mind, the following discussion will emphasize similarities in coding not only across synaptic levels but also across species.

Across-fiber pattern code in the chemical senses. Many researchers have found evidence indicating that the chemical senses may use an across-fiber pattern code for stimulus quality (taste: Schiffman & Falkenberg, 1968; Doetsch & Erickson,

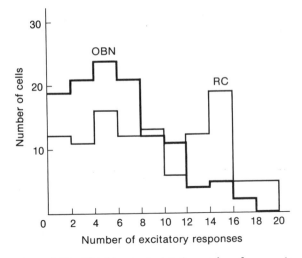

Figure 6-22 This histograph plots the number of neurons in the olfactory bulb (heavy lines) according to the number of different odors to which each neuron responded. For comparison, similar data from receptor cells (light lines) are presented. OBN = olfactory bulb neurons; RC = receptor cells.

1970; Oakley & Benjamin, 1966; Pfaffmann, 1959; Pfaffmann et al., 1976; Pritchard & Scott, 1982a, 1982b; Yamamoto, Yuyama, Kato, & Kawamura, 1984, 1984a, & 1984b; see also review by Yamamoto, 1984; olfaction: Haberly, 1985; Revial et al., 1982; Duchamp, 1982; Tanabe, Iino, & Takagi, 1975; Nemitz & Goldberg, 1983).

Although chemical receptors have a best taste and a best odor, each also has nearly as intense a response to several other chemical substances that, to a human psychophysical observer, do not smell or taste similar. Figure 6-22 compares the number of odors eliciting a strong response in each olfactory receptor with the number of odors to which each olfactory bulb neuron responds. The higher-level neuron is more selective, but both respond to many totally different odors. Figures 6-23 and 6-24 show that taste neurons (innervating the taste buds) have similar response characteristics. Although each cell has a best taste, most respond to more than one primary taste substance, especially when higher concentrations are used in the stimulating solutions. So even though the concept of a best taste and a best odor might imply some type of place code for type of taste and type of odor, the best taste of a taste neuron is *not* defined as the substance that elicits at least some response in the lowest possible concentration (the absolute threshold or the adequate stimulus). Instead, the best taste is the substance that elicits the highest rate of response in that cell regardless of concentration.

The form that such an across-fiber pattern code could take has been explored for taste cells. Schiffman and Falkenberg (1968) mathematically analyzed information from recordings of single nerve cells' responses. The information needed for their type of analysis comes from the responses of many different sensory afferents to many different types of stimuli. The mathematical analysis finds dimensions for sensory systems in which the dimensions are unknown prior to the analysis. The

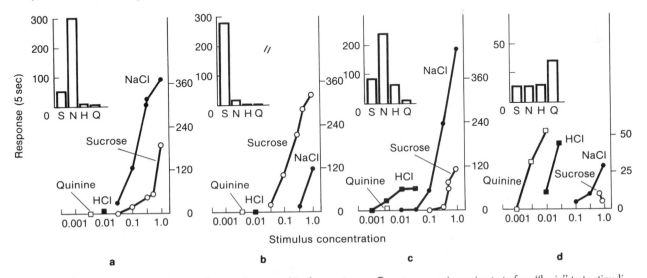

Figure 6-23 **a, b.** Responses (in impulses per five seconds) of two primary afferent neurons in a primate to four "basic" taste stimuli. **c, d.** Response of two other neurons (note lower scale values in **d**). The inset is a response histogram profile for 0.5 sucrose (S), 0.3 NaCl (N), 0.01 HCl (H), and 0.003 quinine hydrochloride (Q).

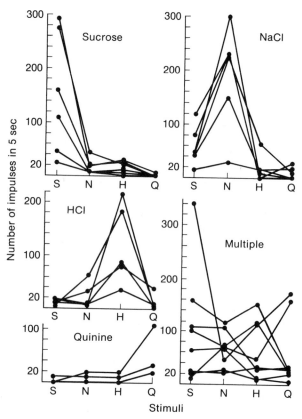

Figure 6-24 Composite of responses of several cells, each of which responds best to sucrose, NaCl, HCl, or quinine, respectively. One multiple-response class of cells, showing the averaged responses of eight different cells, is also presented.

analysis uses degrees of similarity and degrees of difference among types of cell response to various types of stimuli to place each cell and each stimulus in an *n*-dimensional (at least two-dimensional) space. The distance between any two responses or any two types of stimuli corresponds to their relative degree of similarity or difference. So both responses and stimuli are mapped onto those dimensions so that the similarity among cells and among sensations can be visualized simultaneously. In other words, the analysis is a procedure for detecting natural groupings in data when neither the identity nor the number of subgroups in that set of data is known beforehand.

To illustrate their technique, the researchers applied the analysis to data taken from individual visual receptor cells being stimulated by different colors. Their analysis showed that one visual dimension was intensity. Two other dimensions could not be labeled but were obviously related to color. When a line was drawn through where the colors were located

in that two-dimensional space, it accurately reproduced the spectrum, as Figure 6-25 illustrates. Thus, different sets of visual cells respond to different colors.

The taste dimensions produced by this type of analysis are shown in Figures 6-26 and 6-27. Types of taste stimuli form clusters in two-dimensional space (even though the dimensions have no obvious labels), but individual nerve cells do *not* form clusters. Since cells don't cluster, there are no "salt" taste cells in the same sense that there are "red" visual cells. This finding provides strong evidence for an across-fiber pattern code for taste quality. In addition, the type of code shows some changes across levels of synaptic processing, as Figure 6-27 shows.

Some relatively pure pattern and place coding could exist in taste cells (Yamamoto et al., 1984, 1985a, 1985b). Some of the relevant data come from afferent responses to sweet tastes. Sweet cells may have some elements of an individual pattern code, since only best-taste sweet cells respond during continued stimulation with rhythmical changes in firing rate (Ogawa, Sato, & Yamashita, 1973; Scott & Erickson, 1971). Also, sweet tastes cannot be mapped onto the same dimensions

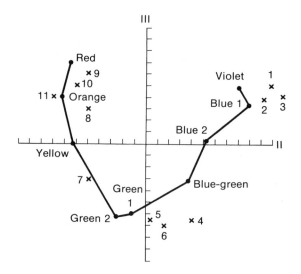

Figure 6-25 An across-fiber pattern code, as analyzed by Schiffman and Falkenberg's technique, would look like this if the responses of visual receptor cells to various colors of lights were plotted. Small X's are neurons and dots are visual stimuli. No attempt was made to name the two dimensions pictured, other than to say that they are of different sensory qualities; dimension I (not shown) was intensity. All the stimuli could be joined by a line reproducing the visual spectrum of colors, and the neurons (except for 7) fell into three distinct clusters or types corresponding to violet-blue, green, and red-orange.

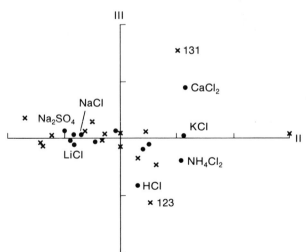

Figure 6-26   Erickson's data of rat taste neurons' responses to various taste substances are replotted according to Schiffman and Falkenberg's technique. The x's and dots are as in Figure 6-25. Only a few stimuli and neurons were labeled, to avoid cluttering. Here, the neurons do not fall into distinct clusters.

used for the other primary tastes. Finally, the response rate of at least one type of sweet-best primary afferent in rats to various substances closely parallels the human psychophysical ratings of sweetness (Pfaffmann et al., 1976). These findings imply "sweet" place and pattern codes.

Other research suggests that an across-fiber pattern code may not be found in all levels of processing or all species. The higher one goes in a chemosensory system, the fewer different substances a given cell responds to. In a given array of 20 different stimulant substances, the modal number to which a given receptor cell may respond is 15 or 16. An olfactory bulb cell may respond to only 5 or 6 (see Figure 6-22). At the level of the cortex, 40% to 50% of the cells may respond to only one odor (Tanabe, Iino, & Takagi, 1975; Yamamoto, 1984). Both excitatory and inhibitory responses to the same taste can be found, with NaCl most often producing excitatory responses and sucrose most often producing inhibitory responses (Pfaffmann, Frank, & Norgren, 1979). The responses of taste afferents in hamsters are more selective than those found in the rat (Smith, Van Buskirk, Travers, & Bieber, 1983a, 1983b).

"Whether one chooses to accept a labeled line [place code] or an across-fiber pattern interpretation depends on whether one believes that activity in a single neuron type represents, in and of itself, a single taste quality. Unless this point is experimentally testable, the distinction between these two theoretical approaches is primarily a philosophical one" (Smith et al.,

1983b, p. 557). However, in other sensory systems, some of the appropriate tests *have* been carried out.

Place codes in the somatosensory system.   Type of sensation within the somatosensory system is coded by a place code. As Table 6-4 describes, different types of sensations are produced when fibers connected to different types of cutaneous receptor organs are stimulated. In fact, although individual cutaneous nerve fibers do sometimes respond to several different types of cutaneous sensation, highly selective fibers have been found in several species (Burgess & Perl, 1967; Casey & Morrow, 1983; Iriuchijima & Zotterman, 1960). But most conclusively, some studies have stimulated and recorded from individual cutaneous peripheral nerve fibers in awake, conscious human volunteers. These studies confirmed that activity in different nerve fibers gives rise to different kinds of sensations. Thus, there is a true place code for at least some stimulus qualities within the somatosensory system.

A pattern code for vibration frequency and for pain may be superimposed upon this place code. Although the presence of vibration (as opposed to touch or pain) is coded for by which receptor and therefore which fiber has been stimulated, the *rate* of the vibration may be encoded by the pattern of the response. Both primary afferent and cortical cells responding to a vibratory stimulus show clusters of action potentials at the frequency of the vibratory stimulus. Work done with human volunteers shows that only repetitive stimulation of the unmyelinated afferents at a rate of 3 per second can evoke pain (Mayer & Price, 1982).

Place and pattern codes for auditory frequencies.   Both place and pattern codes are used by the auditory system for frequency. For lower frequencies (less than 5 kHz), the depolarization in the hair cell, its release of transmitter substance, and the action potentials in the auditory nerve occur only during the rarefactory phase (Galambos & Davis, 1943; Erulkar, 1972; Uttal, 1973).

Phase-locked firing (Rose, Brugge, Anderson, & Hind, 1967) is shown in Figure 6-28. If a neuron responded with a burst of action potentials to each rarefaction, the number of bursts per second would accurately reflect the number of cycles per second in the sound wave. If the neuron could not respond to every cycle (because of its absolute refractory period), it would still tend to fire only during rarefactions. Some higher-order cell could sum the activities of many of these sensory neurons. Thus the number of bursts per second across a set of neurons—no one of which fired for each rarefaction—would still accurately reflect the stimulating frequency.

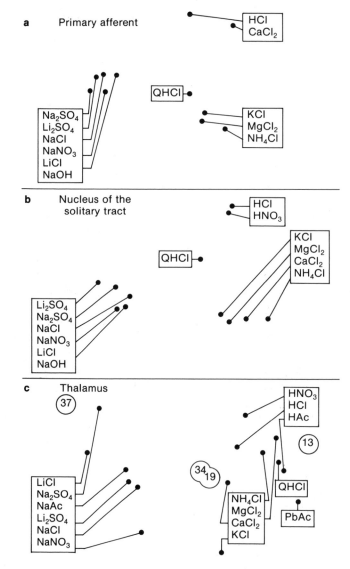

Figure 6-27   Taste stimuli can be arranged in a two-dimensional space at each of the three different levels of taste processing. The circled numbers in the thalamus graph represent neurons; note that neuronal positions don't overlap with stimulus positions, indicating that there is no unique cell or set of cells that responds to any specific stimulus.

This is the **volley theory** of sound-frequency coding (Wever, 1949).

For higher-frequency sounds, hair cell depolarization, release of transmitter substance, and auditory nerve action potentials occur during both rarefaction and condensation. The only frequency-related information available comes from which hair cell and therefore which auditory nerve cell has

been excited. Some **tuning curves** of neurons at various levels of the auditory system are presented in Figure 6-29. A tuning curve measures the threshold sensitivity of an afferent to various frequencies. Each cell has its own adequate stimulus or characteristic frequency. Frequency could be place coded for these sounds.

To prove that lower-frequency sounds are coded by pattern

Table 6-4 Human peripheral somatosensory nerve sensations.

Fiber Type	Receptive Field	Adaptation	Receptor	Conscious Sensation
Skin Sensations				
A beta	Small, sharp	Fast	Meissner corpuscles	Low-frequency vibration, texture
A beta	Large, obscure borders	Fast	Pacinian corpuscle	High-frequency vibration
A beta	Small, sharp borders	Slow	Merkel disks	Pressure, texture
A beta	Large, obscure borders	Slow	Ruffini endings	No conscious sensation
A delta	In hairs	Fast	Free endings	Touch
A delta	Large	Slow	Free endings	Pain
A delta	Large	Slow	Free endings	Cold
C	Large	Slow	Free endings	Burning pain, itch
C	Large	Slow	Free endings	Warmth
Proprioceptive Sensations				
A alpha	In a joint	Slow	Ruffini endings	Joint position
A alpha	In a joint	Fast	Pacinian-like	Extreme joint position
A alpha	In a tendon	Slow	Ruffini-like	Limb movement and position
A alpha	In a muscle spindle	Fast	Annulospiral	Limb movement and position
A beta	In a muscle spindle	Fast	Flower-spray	Limb movement and position

NOTE: A beta are large and myelinated afferents.
A alpha are the largest myelinated afferents.
A delta are the smallest myelinated afferents.
C fibers are small, unmyelinated afferents.

while higher-frequency sounds are coded by place, researchers must electrically stimulate auditory neurons in an awake human subject (Merzenich, Michelson, Pettit, Schindler, & Reid, 1973; Simmons, Epley, Lummis, Guttman, Frishkopf, Harmon, & Zwicker, 1965; Tong, Clark, Blamey, Busby, & Dowell, 1982). In designing an auditory prosthesis, surgeons and researchers have implanted electrodes onto deaf persons'

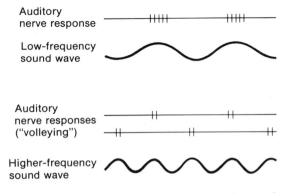

Figure 6-28 Phase-locked firing can be recorded in peripheral auditory neurons in response to sound stimuli whose frequency is below 5 kHz. The neuron fires only during the rarefaction phases. Even if the neuron does not fire for every cycle, it still tends to respond only during rarefaction.

auditory nerves. Stimulation parameters were systematically varied while each subject reported what she or he heard. There are large individual differences, but somewhere between 300 and 600 Hz, the frequency of the electrical stimulation determined what pitch was heard: the more rapid the stimulation, the higher the perceived pitch. Above that point, changes in the frequency of stimulation did not change the perceived pitch. Instead, changing the *position* of the stimulating electrodes changed which pitch was heard.

The pitch pattern code for low frequencies is recoded at some synapse on the way to the cortex. Since no phase-locked firing is seen in cortical cells, a place code would have to be used for all frequencies (Brugge & Merzenich, 1973; Merzenich, Knight, & Roth, 1975; Knight, 1977; Uttal, 1973). Supporting this conclusion is the fact that in human volunteers only the place and not the frequency of cortical stimulation determines which pitch is perceived (Dobelle, Mladejovsky, Stensaas, & Smith, 1973).

Coding in the auditory system has two — possibly related — mysteries: what is the function of the outer hair cells and why is the basilar membrane tuning curve broader than the tuning curve for the auditory hair cells (Johnstone, 1981)? Figure 6-30 illustrates the latter problem. The loudness and pitch of a tone stimulus are varied. The amplitude of movement of the basilar membrane at a given location is compared with the

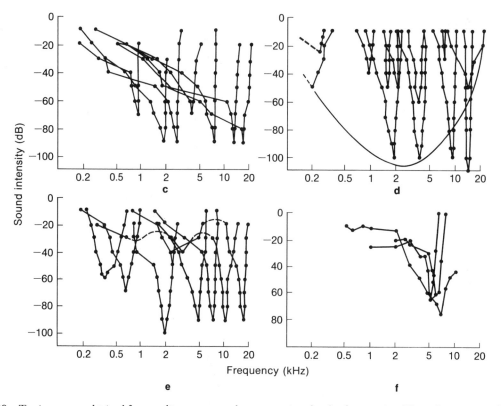

Figure 6-29 Tuning curves obtained from auditory neurons change at various levels of processing. The ordinate is sound intensity in decibels, and the abscissa is the frequency of the stimulus tone. **a, b.** From primary afferents. **c.** From the cochlear nerve. **d.** From the inferior colliculus. **e.** From the trapezoid body. **f.** From the geniculate.

amplitude of response of an inner hair cell at the same location. The tuning curve of the hair cell is much sharper than the basilar membrane tuning curve (Evans & Wilson, 1975). Better agreement between basilar membrane and hair cell tuning curves can be produced with better measuring techniques (Khanna & Leonard, 1982; Rhode, 1978), but some discrepancy still remains. What sharpens the tuning curves for hair cells?

Although there are three times as many outer as inner hair cells, they are innervated by only 5% of the primary afferents.

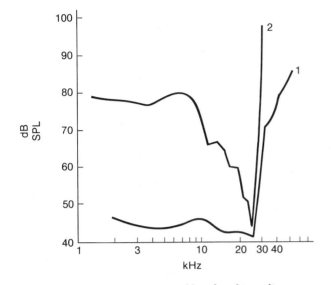

Figure 6-30   One perplexing problem found in auditory research. The narrow curve (2) is a tuning curve from a primary afferent; the broad curve (1) is a tuning curve for one point on the basilar membrane. How can the broad basilar membrane curve cause the narrow neural curve? SPL = sound pressure level.

So what do the outer hair cells do? Outer hair cells do not contribute to intensity or frequency discrimination (Nienhuys & Clark, 1978; Prosen, Moody, Stebbins, & Hawkins, 1981). But when outer hair cells are removed by exposure to drugs or to loud sounds, the threshold of neurons innervating inner hair cells is greatly increased (Dallos & Harris, 1978; Rebillard, Ryals, & Rubel, 1982; Ryan, Dallos, & McGee, 1979). Thus, one obvious suggestion is that the outer hair cells are responsible for the sharp tuning and sensitivity of the inner hair cells.

Outer hair cells may mechanically affect inner hair cells. Since outer hair cell cilia are embedded in the tectorial membrane, the way that membrane moves could be altered by these cells. On the basis of their study of hair cells in the vestibular apparatus, Orman and Flock (1983) suggested that auditory hair cells have musclelike contractile abilities. Later, Brownell, Bader, Bertrand, and de Ribeaupierre (1985) studied individual outer hair cells in isolation. They found that depolarizing stimuli caused the cells to shorten, and hyperpolarizing stimulation caused them to lengthen. If these changes occur during sound-induced depolarizations and hyperpolarizations, outer hair cells could affect the way the inner hair cells get stimulated (Hudspeth, 1985; Zwislocki, 1980; Zwislocki & Kletsky, 1979; Flock, Flock, & Ulfendahl, 1986; Gitter, Zenner, & Frömter, 1986; Kiang, Liberman, Sewell, & Guinan, 1986).

There are other possibilities. Passive current spread from outer to inner hair cells could change the frequency selectivity of the inner hair cells. The sharp tuning of inner hair cells could also be caused by electrically gated pores, which, if present, would change the rate of depolarization and repolarization in the inner hair cell membranes (Lewis & Hudspeth, 1983). The hairs themselves may vary in stiffness and so respond more selectively to frequency than the basilar membrane does (Flock & Strelioff, 1984).

Common Codes for Intensity of Stimulus

Most sensory systems share a common solution to the problem of coding stimulus intensity: a pattern code.

Chemical senses.   The code for intensity may be rate of firing. For both chemical systems, the primary afferents have firing rates that closely parallel the concentrations of stimulating substances (Nemitz & Goldberg, 1983; Oakley & Benjamin, 1966; Pfaffmann, 1959; Pritchard & Scott, 1982a, 1982b; Sato, 1980; Revial et al., 1982; Yamamoto, 1984). The intensity-response rate function for some "salty" and "bitter" cortical cells matches Stevens' power law, with an exponent of about 0.4. Firing rates of primary afferents also closely parallel the psychophysically rated intensity of a stimulus (Borg et al., 1967).

Some intensity codes for taste cells and afferents are illustrated in Figure 6-31. Pfaffmann et al. (1976) suggested that the code for taste intensity in the primary afferent could be rate of activity in the "multiple sensitivity fibers" that responded equally to all primary taste substances. In some cells, a *decrease* in firing rate may code an increase in intensity of odor (Duchamp, 1982).

Somatosensory system.   The Pacinian corpuscle may also use a pattern code for intensity. The greater the pressure exerted on the wall of a corpuscle, the more its membrane depolarizes. Greater depolarizations produce more action potentials per second at the first node of Ranvier.

Data from human subjects confirm the pattern code for intensity. In most—but *not* all—cases, the number of action potentials per second in the primary afferent is a power function (Stevens' law) of the magnitude of stimulus and is also directly related to the judged intensity of the stimulation (Vallbo, Hagbarth, Torebjörk, & Wallin, 1979; Järvilehto, 1977; Torebjörk & Ochoa, 1980). This correspondence suggests that the compression responsible for this power function is a property of receptor organs and not higher neural centers.

Some exceptions to the power function may occur: in some

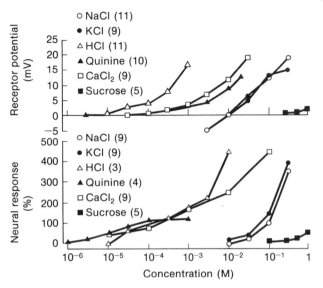

Figure 6-31   Concentration of taste stimulus is directly related to magnitude of response in both the taste receptor (upper graph) and primary afferent (lower graph: percent of baseline firing rate) in the frog. Each point represents the average of several experiments; the number of experiments is indicated in parentheses after each stimulus label. Concentration seems to be pattern coded by amount of change in potential and by response rate.

cases intensity is place coded. For example, in the human somatosensory system, some afferents have a very high threshold (Johansson & Vallbo, 1983; Vallbo et al., 1979). The firing of these fibers could be a place code for very intense stimulation. Studies done on human volunteers have shown that intensity of pain is coded both by frequency of firing and by the number of fibers activated (Mayer & Price, 1982).

The biochemistry of pain-intensity coding has been extensively studied in the search for new drugs for the treatment of pain. Substance P may be the transmitter substance between the primary afferent and the first spinal cord cell (Hökfelt et al., 1980; Iversen, 1982; Lembeck, Donnerer, & Colpaert, 1981; Piercey, Schroeder, Folkers, Xu, & Horig, 1981). In some rats and human beings who have a hereditary inability to sense pain, the level of substance P in the spinal cord is greatly reduced (Pearson, Brandeis, & Cuello, 1982; Scaravilli, 1983). (In other people, lack of sensitivity to pain is related to deficiencies in the number of small myelinated and unmyelinated cutaneous fibers, presumably the ones that carry pain sensations to the CNS [Dyck, Mellinger, Reagan, Horowitz, McDonald, Litchy, Daube, Fealey, Go, Kao, Brimijoin, & Lambert, 1983].) An endorphin may be the transmitter sub-

stance for some centrifugal control of pain at the spinal level (Bloom, 1981; Hökfelt et al., 1980; Snyder, 1980; see the next section of this chapter). This may explain why opiates can relieve pain.

Opiate drugs also act on brain cells to decrease the intensity of painful sensations. When electrically stimulated, some areas of the midbrain, such as the **periaqueductal gray** and the **periventricular gray** areas, decrease sensations of pain (Watkins & Mayer, 1982). Most interesting, the rate of firing of cells in these areas is increased by opiates. And the degree to which these drugs suppress sensations of pain is closely correlated with their effect on the rate of neural activity in these same areas (Terman, Shavit, Lewis, Cannon, & Liebeskind, 1984). These cells may be part of a CNS centrifugal pain-control system, as the next section will describe.

Coding for loudness.   In the auditory system, several codes for amplitude of stimulation may be used (Galambos & Davis, 1943; Brugge & Merzenich, 1973). Figure 6-32 comes from one of the first single-unit recording experiments carried out on a sensory system. The greater the amplitude of the stimulating sound wave, the more frequently the primary afferent neurons fire. In addition, the probability of an action potential during the rarefaction phase increases with amplitude, a response that would represent another type of pattern code for

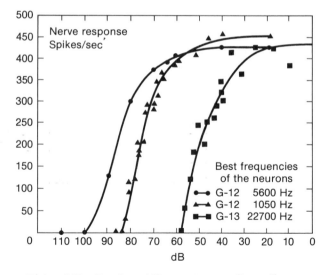

Figure 6-32   For three different primary auditory afferents, nerve firing rate increases with increases in sound intensity. The points on the graph were determined by counting the responses occurring during the first 0.1 second and multiplying by 10. Intensity seems to be pattern coded by rate.

loudness. Finally, there are high-threshold afferents in the auditory nerve, and their firing may be a place code for a very intense stimulus.

Figure 6-33 illustrates how all these codes for loudness — if, in fact, they are true codes — become recoded into a place code in the cortex. The responses of six cells in the auditory cortex to sounds of different amplitude were recorded. Each cell responded maximally to only one amplitude (Brugge & Merzenich, 1973). Cortical cells may have a best loudness, just as they have a best frequency.

Receptive Fields and Lateral Inhibition

The **receptive field** for any set of neurons, or for any receptor, primary afferent, or cortical cell, is the location in space or on the body that, when stimulated, changes the rate of firing of that particular cell. Each such receptive field of a dorsal root is called a **dermatome.** Each dorsal root, or collection of neurons entering the CNS between certain spinal vertebra, collects all the sensory afferents coming from a given dermatome or strip of skin on the body.

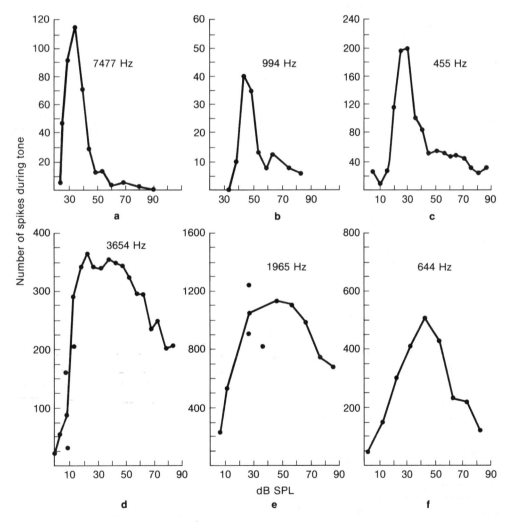

Figure 6-33   The responses of six cortical neurons, each to its best-frequency tone, vary according to sound amplitude. The ordinate is the total number of responses evoked by a tone for a given number of stimulus trials. Loudness may be recoded from a pattern to a place code by cortical cells. SPL = sound pressure level.

At the level of a single neuron, different types of somato-sensory afferent have different receptive field sizes (Johansson & Vallbo, 1983). The receptive fields are often irregularly shaped. Neurons connected to Meissner corpuscles and to Merkel disks often have small receptive fields with sharp borders. Such neurons respond only to stimulation of the skin within their receptive fields and do not respond to any stimulus even slightly outside those fields. Other somatosensory afferents connected to Pacinian corpuscles and Ruffini endings have larger receptive fields with indistinct borders. The firing rate of these cells gradually decreases as the stimulus is moved farther from their receptive fields.

A receptive field can have two different definitions in the auditory system. One is the area on the basilar membrane, vibration of which changes the activity of that nerve cell. This definition can be translated into the tuning curves. The second definition is the area in space from which a sound can excite a particular cell. In the auditory system of owls, for example, there are neurons that have well-defined receptive fields in this latter sense. They fire only when a sound source is located at a given point in the space around the owl and do not fire for any other sound location (Knudsen & Konishi, 1978; Knudsen, Konishi, & Pettigrew, 1977).

Receptive fields often have lateral inhibition, especially for cells located above the level of the primary afferent. **Lateral inhibition** means that stimulation of the center of a receptive field has a different effect on firing rate from that of stimulation in the periphery of that field. In a **center-surround** somato-sensory receptive field, touch applied to the center of the field may increase firing rate, but touch applied to the periphery of that field would inhibit that same cell (Mountcastle & Powell, 1959).

Lateral inhibition is found in all sensory systems. Some higher-order neurons in the taste and olfactory systems are excited by some substances and inhibited by others (Duchamp, 1982; Pfaffmann et al., 1979; Tanabe, Iino, & Takagi, 1975; Nemitz & Goldberg, 1983). Presumably, these higher-order cells receive excitatory input from some receptors (or from some papillae) and inhibitory input from adjacent receptors. Cells in the higher auditory centers are usually affected by sounds presented to either ear. **EE cells** are excited by similar sounds presented to either ear, and **EI cells** are excited by a sound presented to one ear and inhibited when that same sound is presented to the other ear (Erulkar, 1972). Cochlear nucleus cells with low rates of spontaneous activity are inhibited by frequencies outside the tuning curves of each of those cells (Martin & Dickson, 1983).

Theorists generally assume that lateral inhibition serves to increase the sharpness of the coding for stimulus quality, in-tensity, or location. To state it another way, lateral inhibition is assumed to decrease difference thresholds, making the nervous system—and the organism—more sensitive to small differences between and among stimuli.

Coding for Spatial Location of the Stimulus

The coding of spatial location is relevant only to the somatosensory and auditory systems. The codes for the source of an odor are probably the changes in intensity that occur when the position of the nose is changed (literally sniffing out the odor's location). The place on the body at which a touch or a pain occurred is coded largely by which cell is activated. Each cell responds only to stimulation of its receptive field on a certain part of the body. Painful sensations cannot be precisely localized unless touch and pressure receptors are stimulated simultaneously. Apparently activity in the dorsal column system is being used to locate sensations carried by the spinothalamic system (Guyton, 1981).

Coding for the spatial location of a sound source demands more sophistication. Much of this type of coding—though not all—depends on having two ears, one on each side of the head (Erulkar, 1972). The same sound reaching each ear has a different intensity and arrives at a different time or at a different phase of the auditory wave. Sound coming from the source illustrated in Figure 6-34 will arrive first at the left ear and will be louder at that ear, and, at least at the moment illustrated, the rarefaction phase will be stimulating the left ear at the same time as the condensation phase is stimulating the right ear. Cells in the superior olivary nucleus and in the inferior colliculus of mammals may code for the spatial location of a sound

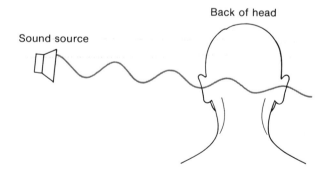

Figure 6-34 The first step of coding for spatial location of a sound source in the auditory system. Compared with the waves arriving at the left ear, those arriving at the right ear are of lower amplitude (coming from farther away) and often arrive during a different phase of the wave.

source (Erulkar, 1972; Kuwada, Yin, & Wickesberg, 1979; Rose, Gross, Geisler, & Hind, 1966).

Phase and loudness difference between the ears may be used to create the receptive fields of some auditory cells that respond only to a given location of a sound source (Erulkar, 1972). For higher-frequency tones, loudness differences between the two ears would be the most accurate source of spatial information, and EI cells are sensitive to loudness differences between the two ears. Some cells in the olivary region and inferior colliculus may have a best loudness difference, responding maximally to a given loudness difference and to a given spatial location of a sound source. For lower-frequency tones, since the phases are further apart in time, phase differences could be used to code location of sound. EE cells are sensitive to the phase differences in sound waves arriving at each ear. Some of these cells have a "best phase difference," corresponding to a given spatial location of a sound source.

Columnar Organization and Feature Detectors

By the time the sensory information has reached the cortex, the information is organized into columns (Chapter 2). Many cells respond only to a certain aspect of stimulation (feature detection). If a microelectrode perpendicular to the cortical surface is inserted gradually while the organism is being exposed to various stimuli, each cell encountered during the penetration of that column will respond to similar aspects of stimulation.

Not much work has been done on the spatial organization of the chemical senses. However, Pfaffmann et al. (1979) did note that best-taste cortical neurons tend to be "spatially segregated," and Yamamoto et al. (1985b) found that cells responding to sucrose, salt, and quinine were spatially separated, although cells responding to acid were evenly distributed across the cortex. However, Haberly (1985) indicated that cells all over the olfactory cortex responded to each odor with no evidence of segregation.

Somatosensory columns and feature detectors. The columns in the somatosensory cortex are organized by type of sensation and receptive field (Mountcastle, 1975; Sur, Wall, & Kaas, 1981). All cells in a column respond to the same type of stimulation—in this study, only to touch or only to pressure—and they all tend to have overlapping receptive fields. In addition, within area 3b, the skin surface is mapped twice. One map comes from slowly adapting and another from rapidly adapting types of receptor organ. For organisms that have whiskers (such as rats), there is a column of cells associated with each whisker. Bending one whisker excites all cells in its column or **whisker barrel** (Ito & Seo, 1983).

Cortical and thalamic stimulations carried out in awake human patients (undergoing brain surgery for problems such as Parkinson's disease or brain tumors) show that human cortex is organized the same way. Sensory information is clustered, and cells in a given area of both the cortex and the thalamus respond to only one type of stimulation (Bates, 1973; Libet, 1973; Libet, Alberts, Wright, Lewis, & Feinstein, 1975). Stimulation of a given area of cortex in human beings can produce certain kinds of recognizable sensations such as a temperature or a pressure.

The somatosensory cortex also has feature detectors. Some cells in primates respond specifically to movement of a surface across the skin, provided that the surface has a given texture and moves at a given rate of speed and sometimes in a given direction (Darian-Smith, Sugitani, Heywood, Karita, & Goodwin, 1982). In the human studies mentioned above, cortical stimulations sometimes resulted in very complex types of natural sensations. Examples include how a ball feels rolling on the surface of the skin, how talcum powder feels when it is sprinkled on the skin, and a sensation of hand raising. Mountcastle (1975) also found cells in areas 5 and 7 that were activated in awake, behaving monkeys prior to movement only if the movement was for a given goal and purpose, such as reaching for food when hungry (see Chapter 8). These might be "motivated, intentional movement detectors."

Auditory columns and feature detectors. All auditory cortex cells in a column tend to have the same best frequency. The best-frequency columns are arranged so that columns with the same best frequency are located side by side, in an **isofrequency band** (Knight, 1977; Merzenich, Knight, & Roth, 1975). The isofrequency bands are arranged in an orderly fashion in each auditory cortical area, as schematically illustrated in Figure 6-35. In addition, as illustrated, EE and EI (**binaural**) bands occur at right angles to the isofrequency bands (Middlebrooks, Dykes, & Merzenich, 1980). Finally, individual columns of cells can also have the same **best delay time** (difference between times of arrival at each ear) (Brugge & Merzenich, 1973). However, how delay time organization might be related to frequency and binaural organization is not yet known.

Some cells respond to highly specific sound characteristics. For example, some cortical cells respond only to a certain direction of change in frequency (Whitfield & Evans, 1965) (upward and downward scale detectors?). Cortical cells may respond only to certain loudnesses or phase delays (Brugge & Merzenich, 1973; Knudsen, Konishi, & Pettigrew, 1977)

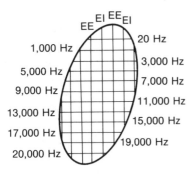

Figure 6-35 The auditory cortex might be columnarly organized in this way, as viewed on the surface of the cortex. Horizontal rows of columns respond to similar frequencies, with different rows responding to systematically different frequencies. Columns are vertically organized across the surface according to whether cells in that column are excited by stimuli at both ears (EE) or are excited by stimuli presented to one ear and inhibited by similar stimuli presented to the other (EI).

(loudness and spatial location detectors?). Some collicular and cortical cells may respond only to moving sound sources (Erulkar, 1972; Rose et al., 1966; Sovijari & Hyvärinen, 1974). In monkeys some cells have been found that respond only to the sounds made by other monkeys (Glass & Wollberg, 1983).

Illusions (or Hallucinations) because of Coding Mechanisms

Since neural codes always represent an abstraction from and not a faithful replica of stimulation parameters, we all suffer from certain illusions. Because of the across-fiber pattern code, a salty substance can have a different taste when the concentration changes (Dzendolet & Meiselman, 1967). The way a substance tastes also changes with time elapsed since the stimulation started: a substance may start out sweet, become sour, and then turn salty (Doetsch & Erickson, 1970). Human volunteers say that a painful stimulation is less intense if pressure or vibration is applied to an adjacent area of the skin. They have the illusory perception that the pain has lessened (Hagbarth, 1983).

At this point, you should review the mind–body problem discussed in Chapter 1. At least one interpretation of Libet's research (Libet, 1973; Libet et al., 1967; see Chapter 1) is that because of the way the cortex codes the time of stimulation, people can suffer a curious illusion. Cortical stimulation *perceived* as beginning at the same time skin stimulation commenced actually started *before* the skin stimulation.

Another type of cutaneous stimulation may make subjects feel that their limbs are bent at impossible angles — or subjects may even feel they have more than one arm on a side (Craske, 1977; Goodwin, McCloskey, & Matthews, 1972). When a vibratory stimulus is applied to a flexor muscle or tendon, the sensations coming from the muscle receptors reflexly cause that muscle to contract. But when movement is prevented by restraints, the subjects experience illusions of movement and position ("My muscle is contracted; therefore my arm must have moved."). If a speaker or a light is in physical contact with the arm involved in the illusory movement, the subject will also perceive the light or sound as moving (Lackner & Shenker, 1985).

As we pointed out, activity in the dorsal column system may aid in the localization of pain, and visceral pain is transmitted to the CNS along autonomic sensory neurons (Guyton, 1981). Visceral pain is often localized by the somatosensory primary afferents that enter the spinal cord at the same level as do the autonomic sensory neurons. Thus, heart attack victims suffer from the illusion that the pain is coming from their shoulder and the upper part of an arm. These are the dermatomal areas innervated by the somatosensory afferents entering the spinal cord at the same level as do the visceral afferents from the heart.

The auditory system produces some fascinating illusions. If earphones are used to present sound to the two ears in such a way that the two ears receive sounds that do not differ in phase or loudness, the sound seems to come from inside the head (Brown & Deffenbacher, 1979; Erulkar, 1972). Pulsating a noise at a certain frequency can produce the illusion of a pure tone accompanying that noise—and the tone perceived matches the frequency of noise pulsation (Johnstone, 1981; Merzenich et al., 1973). This is the case even if the noise contained no energy at the particular frequency of the illusory tone. If two tones of different frequencies are presented, the person will perceive a third tone whose frequency is the difference between the frequencies of the other two tones. Thus, a 200 Hz tone combined with a 300 Hz tone will produce an illusory 100 Hz tone. In both cases, the brain appears to misinterpret a pulsating intensity code as a phase-locked (pattern) code for a tone of that frequency.

Summary and Implications of Coding Principles

Quality of sensation is often place coded by which nerve cell has been activated, and intensity of sensation is often pattern coded by rate of firing. But there are exceptions. In the lower-frequency ranges, frequency of sound waves may be pattern coded by phase-locked firing. High-threshold fibers may place-code for intense stimulation in both the auditory and the somatosensory systems. The chemical senses appear to use an across-fiber pattern code for stimulus quality. Spatial location (regardless of how it is defined) is place coded in both the somatosensory and auditory systems. Lateral inhibition may enhance the sensitivity of the sensory system, making nerve cells more responsive to small changes in stimulus intensity, location, and quality. The cortex is columnarly organized for intensity, quality, and spatial location.

Feature detection comes close to the interface between neural events and mental events. Does activity in a certain feature detector cause the conscious perception of a certain stimulus? If so, how? Or if activity in several feature detectors occurring simultaneously is required for a conscious perception, how does the integration across nerve cells occur? Some special types of coding responses, occurring in certain parts of the brain, seem to lead to conscious sensations, whereas other coding responses do not. We are often unaware of the signals being sent to our brains from the sensory receptors embedded in our muscles. What makes the difference? The feature detectors still fire when the organism is unconscious or anesthetized, but there is obviously no conscious perception in these cases. What has changed in the brain to explain the disconnection of coding from perceptual responses? The research on feature detection comes closest to telling us what the brain's coding system might be—and yet at the same time it raises intriguing questions that have no obvious answers.

Since "the central neuron is a story-teller with regard to the nerve fibers, and it is never completely trustworthy, allowing distortions of quality and measure" (Mountcastle, 1975, p. 109), we suffer from various illusions. Presumably, all the illusions to which we are subject can eventually be related to the ways in which our nervous systems code sensory information.

Adaptation and Centrifugal Control

Adaptation and centrifugal control change the sensory input to the cortex. Centrifugal control may contribute to adaptation and may also be used to change how a certain type of sensory information affects the sensory neurons, an effect that we might call **attention**. Adaptation and centrifugal control also allow sensory systems to compensate for the amplification produced by receptors.

Rapidly and Slowly Adapting Receptors

Some sensory adaptation occurs at the receptor level. In **slowly adapting receptors,** the stimulus-evoked change in membrane potential drifts slowly back to resting levels even though the stimulation continues. In **rapidly adapting receptors,** the stimulus-evoked change in potential quickly returns to resting levels. Slowly adapting receptors may be specialized for signaling the intensity and presence of stimuli, whereas the rapidly adapting receptors may specialize in signaling *changes* in stimulation.

The somatosensory system has both kinds of receptors. The large myelinated afferents are connected to either slowly or rapidly adapting receptors (see Table 6-3 and Figure 6-8). However, the receptors connected to smaller myelinated neurons and to unmyelinated neurons tend to adapt slowly. For example, although perceived intensity of a painful stimulus does decrease despite the continuation of the stimulus, the decrease occurs very slowly and is never complete. In contrast, the pressure sensations carried by larger neurons communicate information to the brain only when the intensity or type of pressure changes. We lose awareness of any constantly present, unchanging pressure sensation—such as the pressure being exerted right now by the contact of your body with the chair or bed.

Chemoreceptors adapt slowly. Figure 6-36 shows the adaptation of receptor potential responses to four taste stimuli in frogs. The adaptation is not complete even after 30 minutes. Ozeki (1971) observed that adaptation to salt or sucrose occurs more rapidly than does adaptation to sour or bitter-tasting solutions. In his review of olfactory receptor cells, Getchell (1986) pointed out that the most common pattern of response to odors is an initial burst followed by a steady low-frequency discharge that lasts as long as the odor stimulation does. But our conscious awareness of the taste or odor of something adapts even more rapidly and completely than does the taste cell, implying that adaptation also takes place in "higher" sensory levels.

Chemoreceptors also show cross-adaptation (Duchamp, 1982; Doetsch & Erickson, 1970; Price & DeSimone, 1977; Scott & Erickson, 1971; Sato, 1980). **Cross-adaptation** occurs when presentation of one stimulus changes the reaction of a receptor or neuron to, or the psychophysical judgment of, a different stimulus. For example, stimulation with NaCl decreases receptor responses not only to that solution but to all other solutions that also taste salty. Cross-adaptation may be caused by differing rates of adaptation. One type of receptor stimulated by a substance may adapt more rapidly than another type of receptor stimulated by the same substance so that what

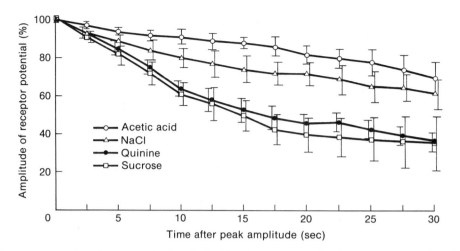

Figure 6-36 Receptor potentials in frog taste cells adapt slowly. The abscissa is time after the receptor potential reached its maximum amplitude (at time 0 sec); the ordinate is the amplitude of receptor potentials, measured as a percentage of their peak amplitude. Each point represents an average obtained from testing from five to seven taste cells. The vertical bars are the standard errors of the means.

has just been tasted or scented affects the perceived taste or scent of the next substance.

Auditory adaptation is unusual: a constantly present sound is *not* a constant energy source. Sound waves consist of alternating periods of rarefaction and condensation. Hudspeth's work with the vestibular hair (see, for example, Hudspeth & Jacobs, 1979) implies that the hair cell membrane may remain depolarized as long as the hair remains bent in the critical direction—something that would never occur during sound stimulation.

Mechanisms of Adaptation

Some adaptation occurs at the receptor level and some must occur at higher levels of sensory processing. Each level may use different mechanisms or have different ways of decreasing its output to a certain input.

Since receptor adaptation depends on how a receptor transduces energy, mechanoreceptors and chemoreceptors work differently. Mechanoreceptors adapt by mechanical as well as chemical processes. The Pacinian corpuscle is a rapidly adapting receptor, but if the onionlike layers of corpuscle are removed, the neural membrane itself adapts slowly (Shepherd, 1983). The Pacinian corpuscle adapts rapidly because the onionlike layers surrounding it mechanically adjust themselves to a constantly present pressure. After the adjustment, the pressure is no longer transmitted to the membrane inside. The chemical components of adaptation probably involve the electrically gated and Ca-activated K^+ channels (Swerup, 1983). Opening these channels repolarizes the membrane. Chemo-

receptors might use a synaptic modulation mechanism for adaptation (Chapter 3). For example, if transduction involves an intracellular enzyme, the enzyme may become depleted with continued stimulation (an effect similar to synaptic fatigue).

Central synapses adapt either by using a synaptic modulation mechanism or by presynaptic inhibition (Chapter 4). For example, interneurons within any sensory processing area might be excited by the stimulus and in turn presynaptically inhibit the synapses that pass that information on to higher areas. Because of adaptation in the CNS, the higher one goes in a system such as the auditory system, the more likely one is to find cells that fire only to the onset—or only at the offset—of a stimulus (Somjen, 1972/1975). *Sensory systems are specialized for communicating information about changes in stimulation, and some of these systems totally ignore constantly present stimulation.*

Sometimes sensory neurons at higher levels show an increased or sensitized response to stimulation. For example, Ogawa, Sato, and Yamashita (1973) recorded from taste afferents during repeated presentations of the same taste stimulus, with three or more minutes occurring between successive stimulations. Stimulus repetition often increased responses to some of the taste substances.

Centrifugal Systems

Centrifugal pathways are found in every sensory system, including the interoceptors. Receptors sensitive to increases in blood pressure are located in the aorta. When stimulated, they initiate a reflexive decrease in heart rate. Their ability to respond to increases in blood pressure is controlled by cells in the hypothalamus. This centrifugal feedback prevents a decrease in heart rate during exercise (Hockman & Talesnik, 1971). Few of these systems have been investigated in any detail, but two that have will be used as examples.

An auditory centrifugal system.   Axons from the superior olivary region in the brain stem descend in the auditory nerve to hair cells in the cochlea (Somjen, 1972/1975). These axons project to the cochlea either on the same side or on the opposite side of the brain. The latter, the **crossed olivo-cochlear bundle (COCB),** seems to be more important. These axons fire in response to auditory stimuli and have a best frequency. Destroying these fibers does not affect the organism's ability to hear when tested in a quiet environment, but when the environment is noisy, destruction of the COCB greatly impairs the ability to discriminate between two sounds (Dewson, 1968).

How the COCB affects hair cells is still being debated. The olivo-cochlear bundle is probably presynaptic to the outer hair cells (see, for example, Warr & Guinan, 1979), but it may also form synapses with the neurons innervating the outer hair cells (Bodian, 1978). The COCB may form synapses with inner hair cell primary afferents (Warr & Guinan, 1979), although Bodian (1978, p. 4586) said that there were no "morphological signs of synaptic junctions" in that region. In any case, the most important interactions seem to be those occurring between outer hair cells and the COCB.

Stimulating the COCB decreases afferent responses to sound stimulation. When he recorded single auditory neuron responses to sounds, Wiederhold (1970) found that stimulating the COCB just before sound stimulation decreased the responses of primary afferents. The suppressing effect of COCB stimulation was greatest when the afferent was being stimulated with its best frequency, and the effect of COCB stimulation was also greatest for cells whose best frequency was between 10 and 15 kHz.

Recent studies have explored the physiological basis for this effect. Desmedt and Robertson (1975) found that changing Cl^- concentrations around the hair cells systematically changed the effects of COCB stimulation on those cells, and Mountain (1980) found that COCB stimulation hyperpolarizes outer hair cell membranes. The transmitter substance used by the COCB is ACh, which may hyperpolarize by increasing the membrane's permeability to Cl^-. Mountain (1980) proposed that this hyperpolarization uses a second messenger to change the stiffness of the hair cells. This hypothesis fits with what we discussed previously, in that the contraction of outer hair cell cilia (Kiang et al., 1986; Orman

& Flock, 1983) may alter the way inner hair cells get stimulated. Infusing ACh onto isolated outer hair cells does cause them to shorten (Brownell et al., 1985). Furthermore, intracellular recordings from inner hair cells have confirmed that COCB stimulation blocks their response to auditory stimulation but has no effect by itself on their membrane potentials (Brown, Nuttall, & Masta, 1983). The effect of either sound or COCB stimulation on outer hair cell cilia may change the inner hair cell's response to sound, thereby changing primary afferent activity, which comes mostly from inner hair cells.

Centrifugal control of pain input.   Interest in the centrifugal control of pain was sparked by a theory proposed by Melzack and Wall (Melzack & Wall, 1965; Dennis & Melzack, 1977). In human volunteers, the rated intensity of a painful stimulation is *decreased* if other receptors, innervated by the larger-diameter, myelinated fibers, are stimulated at the same time (Hagbarth, 1983). Melzack and Wall turned this observation into the **Gate-Control Theory of Pain.** Particular types of spinal cord synaptic connections were hypothesized. Specifically, activity in larger-diameter afferents would presynaptically inhibit the first synapse that the primary pain afferents made with spinal cord cells. Thus, activity in larger-diameter afferents would "close the gate," keeping pain information from entering the spinal cord. Later research has found that CNS centrifugal axons also inhibit pain afferents (Watkins & Mayer, 1982; Terman et al., 1984). Although the circuitry involved is probably *not* as hypothesized by the Gate-Control Theory, researchers still propose that pain transmission is controlled at the level of the first synapse by other somatosensory afferents and by CNS efferents.

Some, but not all, kinds of stress can affect the CNS so as to produce **analgesia,** or reduced sensitivity to pain. For example, exposing the feet of a rat to a painful electrical shock decreases the rat's responses to later painful shocks (Watkins & Mayer, 1982; Terman et al., 1984). Some cells in the periaqueductal gray area send their axons to the **rostral ventral medulla.** Some medullary cells respond to painful stimuli, and the pain responses are inhibited by injections of morphine either directly into the periaqueductal gray or into the blood stream (Fields & Heinricher, 1985). Furthermore, some of these medullary cells send their axons to the spinal cord and so may be the cells responsible for some forms of analgesia. As Figure 6-37 illustrates, some of these analgesic treatments probably have their effects by stimulating an interneuron in the spinal cord. The interneuron would use an endorphin as a neuromodulator to regulate the responses of spinal cord pain-sensitive afferents.

Other analgesic treatments do not involve that type of inter-

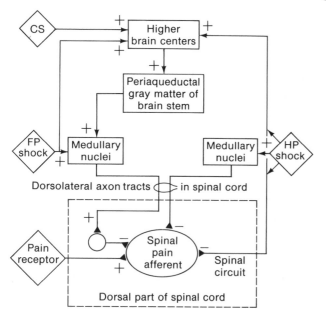

Figure 6-37   Some of the efferent pain control pathways. The pathways activated by a shock to the front paws (FP) of a rat, or by a classically conditioned CS, exert their efferent control eventually through an opioid interneuron in the spinal cord. Shock to the hind paw (HP) does not involve endorphins.

shock, being held immobile, being forced to swim in cold water, and being given an injection of insulin.

Outflow Monitoring

Outflow monitoring is a special type of centrifugal control. As discussed in Chapter 2, it can explain how organisms distinguish between reafference (motor-produced sensations) and the same sensations produced by external stimuli. In outflow monitoring, information is sent to sensory areas of the brain just before a movement occurs, informing them of the type of sensations that are likely to be produced by the movement. Several primitive organisms such as electric fish and crayfish use outflow monitoring to distinguish between self-induced and externally-elicited sensations (Bell, 1981; Krasne & Bryan, 1973; Zipser & Bennett, 1976). Mountcastle (1975, p. 129, emphasis his) identified outflow monitoring in primates: some cortical cells are activated "as if they are alerted in *anticipation of a movement about to be effected.*" Mountcastle (1975; Mountcastle, Lynch, Georgopoulos, Sakata, & Acuna, 1975) discovered cells in area 5 that might receive input from motor areas of the cortex just prior to movement.

Later researchers have found similar types of cells in area 5 and have also proved that these cells can be activated in the total absence of normal sensory input; that is, although these cells are responding to types of sensory input, the input does *not* come from sensory organs. These cells were still active even when the limb was **deafferented** by cutting all the dorsal roots carrying sensory afferents from that limb to the spinal cord (Bioulac & Lamarre, 1979; Seal, Gross, & Bioulac, 1982). Although other interpretations are possible, the activity in these area-5 cells may represent efferent copies of movement-produced sensations. The relevant neural interconnections do exist in the cortex (Jones, Coulter, & Hendry, 1978).

Outflow monitoring may cause some illusions. The illusory movements of a limb in space described earlier may be caused by outflow monitoring. In another illusion, human subjects are seated in a darkened room and told to look straight ahead at a luminescent piece of plastic. They are then told to describe any changes that occur in a sound whose stationary source is in front of them but invisible in the dark. Under these conditions, the subjects will often report that the sound moves. The movement is an illusion.

Apparently, each illusory movement occurs just after the subject's head moves. The illusion is attenuated when the subject's head is stabilized (Hoyenga & Wallace, 1982). When a subject's head is not stabilized, the tension in the neck muscles spontaneously changes because of fatigue, altering the position of the head. The subject is not aware of these

neuron and so do not involve endogenous opiates. The non-opiate forms of analgesia use both centrifugal axons and also intrinsic circuits within the spinal cord, as illustrated. As we said earlier, electrical stimulation of certain parts of the brain, such as the periaqueductal gray and the periventricular gray areas, can cause analgesia.

Whether the stress-induced analgesia involves endorphins depends on several treatment parameters (Watkins & Mayer, 1982; Terman et al., 1984), including whether the stimulus was a CS or a US (see Figure 6-37) and whether a shock of long or short duration was used to create the analgesia. For example, using shocks of short rather than long duration involves nonopiate circuits. In addition, the nature of the analgesia depends on heredity; different strains of rats differ in the degree to which footshock-induced analgesia depends on endogenous opiates (Urca, Segev, & Sarne, 1985).

Some stressful treatments induce analgesia through hormone secretions. Removal of the pituitary (which controls hormone secretions) decreases or eliminates this analgesia (Watkins & Mayer, 1982). Some forms of analgesia involve adrenal hormones (Terman et al., 1984). Hormonal analgesic treatments include (for rats, at least) acupuncture, prolonged fatigue-induced tension changes but only of the need to move his or her head to maintain a straight-ahead fixation. Since the subject is outflow-monitoring voluntary neck movements, presumably information about the movement is sent to the auditory centers analyzing the position of the sound in space. Subjects appear to be unconsciously telling themselves: "Since I have had to move my head, the sound source must also have moved."

Summary and Implications for Coding and Perception

Both adaptation and centrifugal control increase sensitivity. Adaptation decreases responses to constantly present stimuli and therefore exaggerates responding to stimulus change. Centrifugal fibers may increase sensory responses to stimuli to which the organism is attending and decrease responses to stimuli that are being ignored. At an even more speculative level, centrifugal systems may be involved not only in illusions but also in certain types of psychopathology such as glove anesthesia or psychogenic deafness, in which physiologically undamaged people report that they can feel nothing on a hand or hear nothing.

Chapter Summary

The Codes of the Brain

By analyzing the ways in which sensory systems respond to the various aspects of the physical sensory world, researchers are discovering the ways in which the brain codes information. The search for brain codes begins with psychophysics, which explores how variations in the physical parameters of stimulation lead to variations in conscious experiences. This research measures absolute thresholds, difference thresholds, magnitude estimations, and perceived similarities among stimuli in both human and — with special techniques — nonhuman subjects.

All receptors are windows on the physical energies existing in the world around us. Receptors take certain types of energy and transform them into energies used by the nervous system. The three phases of transduction are the nonneural phase, the actual process of transduction, and the changes in membrane potential and the action potentials in the primary afferent. Mechanoreceptors carry out the second phase by changes in membrane permeability created mechanically by the physical energy. Chemoreceptors may act like postsynaptic receptor proteins.

Sensory systems use different codes to represent the various aspects of the physical sensory world. Pattern codes, or changes in the activity of a given cell, are often used to code intensity of stimulus. Place codes, or activation of a certain cell by a particular aspect of sensory stimulation, are often used to represent the type of sensation occurring both between and within modalities. Because of receptive fields, the place of stimulation is also coded by a type of place code. Feature detectors represent the highest, most abstract form of place coding. These cells are found in the cortex (and in some "lower" centers). The chemical senses, at least at "lower" levels, may code type of sensation by an across-fiber pattern code.

Since none of these coding mechanisms involves a completely accurate representation of information about the real-world stimulus, we are all subject to certain illusions. Adaptation and centrifugal control further change the sensory information that reaches the cortex and may cause further illusions. An ignored stimulus is no longer sensed, a constantly present stimulus "disappears," and a stationary sound source "moves." Our very sense of reality is an illusion: we are aware only of what our sensory cells tell us.

CHAPTER

Vision

In 1972, Weiskrantz pointed out that "of the three million or so nerve fibres that stream into the primate brain, about two million originate in the eyes. Of these fibres, about one-and-a-half million are in the geniculo-striate system [which directly connects the eye with the cortex, and so] about half, therefore, of all the inputs to the brain are fibres of retinal origin having relatively direct and concentrated access to the cerebral cortex" (p. 427). This gives some idea of the importance of visual information to the primate brain.

Overview

Much of the research described here began with the work of six scientists. In 1967, three of those scientists were given the

Nobel Prize in physiology or medicine for their work in vision. George Wald showed how important the pigments found in the retinal receptor cells were for color perception. Ragnar Granit pioneered research into how the retina processes and encodes information about visual stimuli. Haldan Keffler Hartline discovered inhibitory processes in the retina.

In 1981, three more scientists whose work has been seminal for the field of vision received the Nobel Prize. David H. Hubel and Torsten N. Wiesel discovered the coding mechanisms used by the visual cortex. Roger W. Sperry worked on patients whose left and right hemispheres had been surgically disconnected (usually for treatment of epilepsy) to show how important the communication between the hemispheres is. Since our perceptions of our visual worlds are unitary (not split down the middle), the hemispheres communicate before conscious perception occurs.

This chapter applies the principles of sensory processing to vision. We emphasize vision in primates, especially the human primate. First we discuss the psychophysics of light, followed by a description of primate visual anatomy and then transduction in the mammalian visual system. The coding sections describe how different populations of visual cells code the intensity, wavelength, and spatial features of visual stimuli. The last section describes how adaptation and centrifugal control affect perception: even if the world remains the same, our perceptions of it do not.

Throughout, we will describe the ways in which coding mechanisms determine — and distort — visual perception. For example, all we human primates suffer from the very curious illusion that a roughly equal mixture of red and green lights looks just like a pure yellow light does! Why can't we see what reddish green really looks like?

The Psychophysics of Light

Psychophysical research has given us the information we need to interpret the patterns of electrical activity recorded from individual cells in the visual system. Absolute and difference thresholds describe the sensitivity of the system, and judgments of magnitude and similarity supply information about possible coding mechanisms.

Nature of Light

The physics of light is more complicated than the physics of any other stimulus energy to which our sensory organs are sensitive. Light energy has the properties both of a particle and of a wave and so some physicists have described light as "wavicles." But it is sometimes useful (if not completely accurate) to talk about light particles emitted by glowing objects, and at other times it is useful to talk about light waves radiating from those objects. We will describe the transduction and perceived brightness of light in terms of particles and the color perceptions of light in terms of wavelengths.

Psychophysics of Detection and Brightness

Light as photons of energy.   Glowing objects emit particles or **photons** of light. Generally, the more photons of light enter the retina within a given brief time period, the brighter we perceive the radiating object to be. But most of the objects we see don't emit light. We see them because of the light they reflect back to our eye, light that originally came from the sun or a light bulb. **Illuminance** describes the amount of light striking an object or a surface, and **luminance** is the amount of light reflected by the surface back to our eyes. **Reflectance** combines these two concepts: it refers to the proportion of light reflected back by an illuminated surface. White or shiny objects have a high reflectance, whereas black objects have a low reflectance (which is why white clothes are cooler and dark clothes are warmer).

Absolute thresholds.   The absolute sensitivity of the visual system is close to the theoretical maximum. For example, Hecht, Shlaer, and Pirenne (1942) calculated that in a light flash detected 50% of the time, only 6 to 9 photons actually reached the light-sensitive part of the eyeball. Since the flash covered an area containing 350 to 500 individual receptor cells, one photon of light must be enough to excite one receptor. Summed across 6 to 9 receptors, this excitation produces a sensation. The calculation was subsequently confirmed by intracellular recordings in individual light receptor cells in the retina. (The **retina** is the part of the eyeball in which light-sensitive receptor cells are located.)

Other psychophysical experiments measure **acuity,** which describes how sensitive we are to variations in brightness across our retinas. One way of measuring acuity is find out how thin a line can be seen. The thinner the line that can be detected, the greater the eye's acuity. An experimenter can also test acuity by measuring how much change in luminance, in what size space, is required for the subject to detect the variation. One stimulus used for this purpose is presented in Figure 7-1. As you can test for yourself, our eyes are most sensitive to luminance variations in medium-width bands. We are less sensitive to luminance changes in narrower or broader bands. That is to say, we are most sensitive to moderate **spatial frequencies** and are less sensitive to lower or higher spatial frequencies (broader and narrower bands).

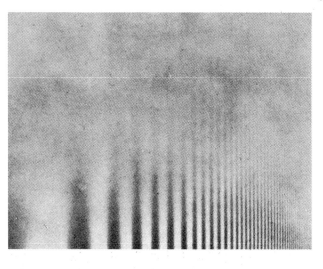

a

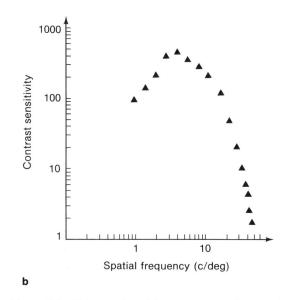

b

Figure 7-1 This test of spatial acuity measures how much change in luminance is required for the eye to detect the change as a function of the distance over which the change occurs. **a.** The width of the vertical dark and light bands decreases from the left to the right; the amount of change in luminance varies from less than 1% at the top to about 30% at the bottom. The objective contrast is the same across the figure, yet the spatial frequencies in the middle appear most distinctly: the dark lines appear taller at the center. **b.** Graph shows how acuity varies according to the spatial frequency of the stimulus (measured in number of cycles per degree, which corresponds to the narrowness of each bar).

Adaptation affects both the absolute and acuity thresholds. An eye that has been in darkness for an hour or more is maximally sensitive to light. **Dark adaptation** is the increase in sensitivity as a function of the time spent in the dark. Although sensitivity increases, acuity decreases: in the dark, you are sensitive to light but you cannot see the fine details of your visual world. Conversely, on going from a darker to a brighter area, vision is impaired for a few minutes. The adjustment to a more luminous surrounding or background is **light adaptation**. During light adaptation, there is a decrease in sensitivity, but acuity is restored.

Effect of wavelength and retinal location on absolute and difference thresholds.   Both acuity and sensitivity vary with retinal location. You have the greatest acuity for objects you are looking directly at, but your sensitivity is greatest just to one side or another of that point. Thus, in the dark, you are most able to detect a very dim light (except for the longest wavelengths: see Figure 7-2) by looking just to the side of where you think it is. In lighted conditions, you are best able to see a very fine line by looking directly at it.

Absolute threshold and perceived brightness depend on both wavelength and retinal location, as Figure 7-2 shows. When the observer is focusing directly on the light, the lowest thresholds are for wavelengths in the range from 550 to 600 mμ *(millimicrons*)* — yellow. However, when the observer is

---

* Now often called *nanometers*, or *nm*.

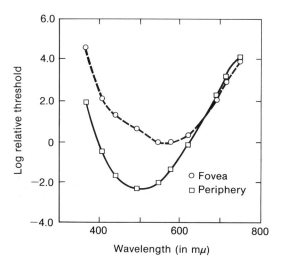

Figure 7-2 Absolute threshold varies according to retinal location and to the wavelength of the light stimulus to be detected.

looking to one side or another of the light source so that photons from the light source fall on the edges of the retina, thresholds are lowest for 500 mμ (green) wavelengths. The explanation of these effects is that our retinas contain two different types of receptor, which occur in varying densities across the retina, as Figure 7-3 shows. **Cones,** which are most concentrated in the center of the retina, provide the greatest acuity and are collectively most sensitive to 600 mμ light. **Rods,** the other receptor type, are more sensitive to light (especially to green) and are most dense 20° away from the center.

Difference thresholds and estimations of magnitude. Psychophysical experiments have demonstrated that the power function exponent for light intensity (.33) is smaller than that for any other sensory system (see Figure 6-3). Accordingly, we are more sensitive to changes in intensity in the visual system than in any other sensory system.

Psychophysics of Color

Lights of different wavelengths are perceived as being of different colors. If rays of white light are passed through a prism that unequally bends rays of different wavelengths, the result is the color spectrum. Water droplets in the air do the same thing to produce a rainbow after a shower.

Perception of color. The color spectrum tells us several important things about vision. First, as you view a color spectrum under normal daylight conditions, the yellow light looks the brightest, even though its physical intensity may be no different from that of any other wavelength. Second, color sensations are not on a perceptual continuum as the perceived pitches of sound frequencies are. Successively lower sound wavelengths (higher frequencies) form a perceptual continuum for us—a scale. We say that some notes are higher and some lower than others. This is not the case with light wavelengths: blue doesn't seem "higher" than red, for example. Third, wavelengths from 700 to 640 look similar to each other (all red), but then there is an abrupt change to orange, followed closely by another abrupt change to yellow. These perceptual discontinuities are reflected in the difference-threshold curve of Figure 7-4.

Some colors, such as violet and brown and the metallic colors (for example, silver and gold), are not found in the spectrum. These **extraspectral** colors can be perceived only with special light sources and special kinds of reflective surface. Gold is perceived when a reddish yellow surface has highlights. Brown is perceived when yellowish red is surrounded by a lighter surface. So, as Land demonstrated (1959, 1974), when lights are presented in complex patterns, colors other than the spectral hues can be seen.

Additive mixtures. Mixing visual wavelengths produces different perceptual experiences from those generated by mixing auditory wavelengths. A combination of tones produces the sensation of a chord (or discord, depending on the degree of difference between the tones), but the combination will be perceived as a mixture. In **additive mixtures,** different wavelengths of light are combined to produce a given perception. Mixing just three lights in varying proportions (red, blue, and yellow are often used) can produce all the colors of the visual spectrum. Combining any different wavelengths—as long as

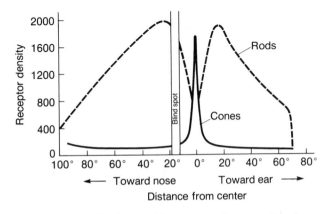

Figure 7-3   The density of the two types of receptors (number per 0.0069 square millimeter) is plotted as a function of retinal location. There are no receptors in the area (blind spot) where neural axons gather to leave the retina.

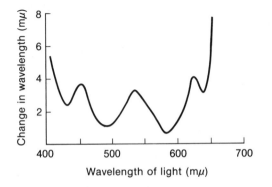

Figure 7-4   Difference thresholds vary according to spectral location. Our perception of color varies with the wavelength of the light stimulus. See text for implications.

they are taken from different areas of the spectrum — will produce a sensation of white or gray, depending on the intensity of the light source.

But not all mixtures are perceived as such. We perceive greenish yellow to be a mixture of green and yellow lights, and greenish blue is perceived as a mixture of green and blue. And yet a mixture of red and green lights looks like yellow instead of "reddish green." We have no idea what yellowish blue light really looks like (we see white). The codes used by the visual system for wavelength can provide some possible explanations of these perceptual phenomena.

Subtractive mixtures.   The color of visible objects depends on which wavelengths are reflected by those objects and which are absorbed or **subtracted** from the spectrum. White objects reflect all wavelengths relatively equally — which is why they look white to us. Black objects tend to absorb all wavelengths equally. A blue object looks as it does because it absorbs all wavelengths *except* blue.

When you mix colors as in pigments of paint, you use the **subtractive** laws of color mixing. For example, if you mixed yellow and blue paint and used the mixture to paint an object, the mixed yellow and blue will absorb all light wavelengths *but* those in the green range (the yellow pigment absorbs blue wavelengths and the blue pigment absorbs yellow and red wavelengths). The painted object will look like what is left: green.

Summary of Psychophysics

Light has the properties both of particles and of energy waves. Absolute thresholds and luminous intensities are described in terms of light particles (photons) and color perceptions are described in terms of wavelengths. Vision is an extremely sensitive sensory system in the primate. But both sensitivity and acuity vary (inversely) with dark or light adaptation. The way in which the primate retina codes wavelength produces conscious sensations of color — but wavelength does not relate in any direct fashion to color sensations, demonstrating that color is something that exists only in our brains, not in light sources and objects.

Anatomy of the Visual System

Visual anatomy starts with the retina and ends with the visual cortex. All parts are organized in a beautifully systematic man-

ner. Since the retina is part of the brain, the complexity of its anatomy will be no surprise.

Retinal Anatomy

Figure 7-5 shows the location of the retina. Light waves (or photons) enter the eye through the **cornea,** pass first through the **aqueous humor** (a clear, watery fluid) and then through the **lens.** After the lens, the light waves must pass through the **vitreous humor** (a mostly clear, gelatinous substance) before reaching the retina at the back of the eye, where the light-sensitive cells are found.

Different parts of the cornea bend the various wavelengths to a different degree. The edges of the cornea bend all light waves more than does its center, and the difference between the degree of edge and center bending is greatest for the shortest wavelengths. These optical phenomena produce **spherical aberrations,** which cause some blurring of the image. If the light is a mixture of wavelengths, **chromatic aberrations** (colored blurs) will also occur because when the other wavelengths are in focus on the retina, the blue light waves will come to a focus in front of the retina.

By controlling the iris and the lens, we control certain aspects of the light striking our retinas. The **iris,** located just in front of the lens, gives our eyes their color. In bright conditions, the iris is contracted, the **pupil** appears small — and the aberrations are reduced because light no longer passes through the cornea's edges. Under dim conditions, the pupil enlarges to let all available light in — and the resulting images of objects

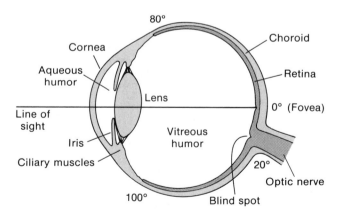

Figure 7-5   Cutaway view of the right eyeball as seen from the top or bottom (see Figure 7-11). "Line of sight" refers to the path taken by light waves from an object on which the eye is directly focusing. The image of that object will then fall at 0°, or in the fovea.

are somewhat fuzzy because of the aberrations. The thickness of the lens is controlled by contractions of the surrounding **ciliary muscles.** By varying the thickness of the lens, we control the degree to which it bends light waves as we focus either on near or on far objects.

Gross anatomy of the retina.   The thickness of the layers of retinal nerve cells varies from one area to another. For example, there is no retina at the **blind spot,** where the nerves leave the eyeball (see Figure 7-5), and the retina is quite thin in the area of the **fovea.** When we look directly at an object, its visual image is projected to our fovea.* As Figure 7-6 shows, the retina is thinner in the foveal region because the cell bodies and axons of some of the cells have been pushed aside. The light-sensitive layer of the retina is located at the very back of the eye, farthest from the light entry point. The biochemistry of the light receptors requires that they be placed close to the heavily vascularized **choroid** and the **pigmented epithelium.**

Microanatomy of the retina.   The microanatomy of the primate retina is presented in Figures 7-7 and 7-8. Five general types of cells have been identified, each having several different subtypes. The five types illustrated in Figure 7-7 are **receptors** (rods and three different kinds of cones), **horizontal cells, bipolar cells** (for example, midget, rod, and flat), **amacrine cells,** and **ganglion cells** (for example, midget and diffuse). Light must pass through the ganglion cell and the bipolar layers to reach the receptors. The primate retina has both vertical and horizontal neural connections (Dowling & Boycott, 1966; Boycott & Dowling, 1969; Boycott & Kolb, 1973; Kolb, 1970). The **vertical connections** process information as it goes from the outer layer of the eye (the receptor cells) to the layer next to the vitreous humor. The **horizontal connections** process information within a given layer.

In primates, vertical processing begins with the receptors, the rods and cones. The rods are connected to the **rod bipolars** and the cones are connected either to **midget bipolars** or to **flat midget bipolars** (not illustrated). **Flat cone bipolars** and **diffuse cone bipolars** are also connected exclusively to cones. Each midget bipolar makes contact with only one cone; both are most dense in the fovea. However, each cone innervates at least one of each type of midget bipolar, as well as several flat cone bipolars. The flat cone bipolars connect with

---

* In organisms with poor color vision, the analogous area is called the *area centralis.* To avoid confusion, we will use *fovea* to refer to the part of the retina where images of objects being directly looked at are focused.

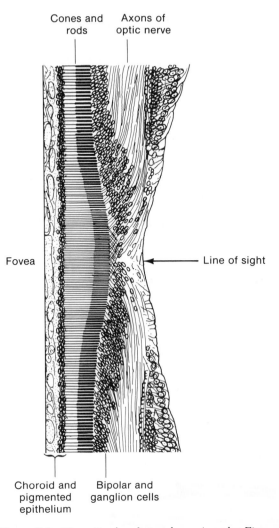

Figure 7-6   The retina has distinct layers (see also Figure 7-5). The structures depicted here are explained in the text and are pictured in more detail in Figure 7-7 and 7-8. Light enters from the left.

about six cones, and a rod bipolar makes contact with from one to four rods. Thus, the receptor–bipolar connections are characterized by extensive convergence and divergence, except in the foveal region.

The bipolars pass the visual information on to the ganglion cells. The midget ganglion cells receive information from the midget bipolars, and the diffuse ganglion cells collect information from all types of bipolars. The information then passes out of the retina on ganglion cell axons. The ganglion cell axons collectively form the **optic nerve.**

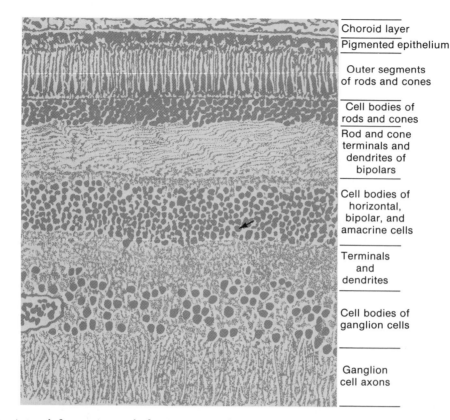

Choroid layer
Pigmented epithelium
Outer segments of rods and cones
Cell bodies of rods and cones
Rod and cone terminals and dendrites of bipolars
Cell bodies of horizontal, bipolar, and amacrine cells
Terminals and dendrites
Cell bodies of ganglion cells
Ganglion cell axons

Figure 7-7   Drawing made from a micrograph of a primate retina, shown in cross section. See text for explanations and see Figure 7-8 for a schematic diagram of cells and connections. The arrow points to a displaced ganglion cell. The ganglion cell layer has a blood vessel with red blood cells in it.

Horizontal processing occurs through the electrical connections among receptors and the synaptic interconnections among horizontal and amacrine cells. In the primate, there may be cone–cone and rod–cone electrical synapses, but no rod–rod connections have been seen (Nelson, 1977; Raviola & Gilula, 1973). Horizontal cells interconnect receptors, and the amacrine cells interconnect bipolars where they form synapses with ganglion cells. In the fovea, a horizontal cell connects about six cones; in the peripheral retina, a horizontal cell connects from 30 to 40 cones. And from four to six horizontal cells may make contact with the same cone.

Horizontal cells in primates have both axons and dendrites. The dendrites make contact exclusively with cones and the axon terminals contact with rods (Boycott & Kolb, 1973; Kolb, 1970). The axon connecting the terminals with the cell body and its dendrites may be too small to carry impulses. If so, the axon terminals and the dendrites may independently process rod and cone information, respectively. The axonlike inter-

connection may serve only a metabolic and not an information-processing function (Nelson, Lützow, Kolb, & Gouras, 1975; Rodieck, 1973).

There are at least two other types of cells to be found in the primate retina, ones whose functions are less well understood. The **interplexiform cells** are a centrifugal, vertical processing system. They look similar to the amacrines and are found in the same retinal layer, but the interplexiform cells send processes back to the outer layer, thus sending information to bipolar and horizontal cells. These cells receive their major input from amacrine cells (Dowling & Ehinger, 1975). A **biplexiform cell** is found in the ganglion cell layer, and its axon also exits the eye in the optic nerve. But this cell receives input not only from amacrines and bipolars but also directly from rods (Mariani, 1982).

The primate retina is simplified in comparison with the retinas of many lower animals. In the frog, for example, horizontal cells are connected not only to receptors but to bipolars.

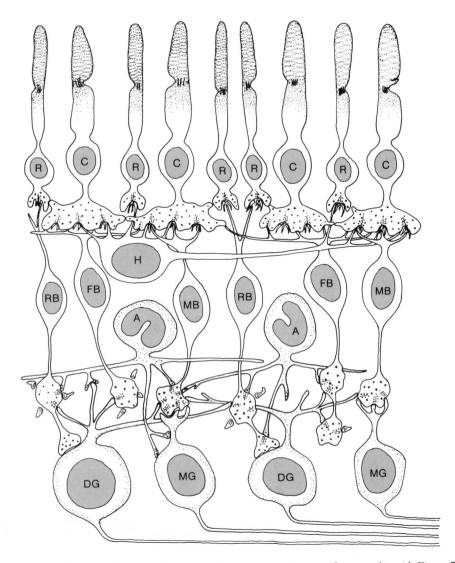

Figure 7-8   Summary of cell types and synaptic interconnections in a primate retina. Compare this with Figure 7-7 and see text for details. R = rod; C = cone; MB = midget bipolar; RB = rod bipolar; FB = flat bipolar; H = horizontal cell; A = amacrine cell; MG = midget ganglion; DG = diffuse ganglion.

In lower species, the amacrine cell layer is also more complex and there are no direct bipolar–ganglion cell synapses. The types of electrical synapse found among receptors vary from species to species. For example, the cone interconnections found in turtles differ from those in fishes (Baylor & Hodgkin, 1973; Detwiler, Hodgkin, & McNaughton, 1978; Fuortes, Schwartz, & Simon, 1973; Scholes, 1975; Schwartz, 1975b). Retinas in these species do more processing of visual information than do retinas in primates, including the rate and direc-

tion of object movement—something the primate retina does not do.

The color perceptions of a species depend on how many different types of cone that species has, how many of each type, and how the cones are connected to the rest of the CNS. Some species, including human are **trichromats,** having three different kinds of cone. Some species have only two, and others have four or five different kinds of cone. For example, the goldfish has four different color receptors, including one

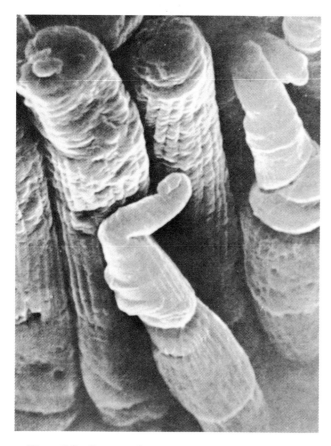

Figure 7-9 Scanning electron micrograph of rods and cones in a mud puppy (a type of salamander). See Figure 7-10 for labels of parts.

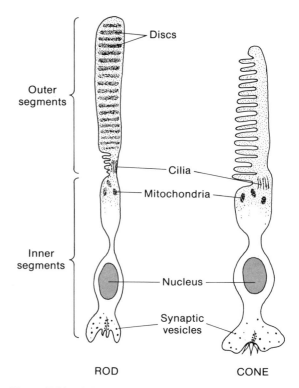

Figure 7-10 Schematic diagram of a rod and a cone. The light-sensitive elements for transduction are in the outer segments, the folds of the cone and the discs of the rod cell.

sensitive to ultraviolet (Neumeyer, 1985). Although rats and cats have three types of cone, their color vision is very weak because they have only a few cones of each type (Cicerone, 1976; De Valois & Abramov, 1966; Ringo, Wolbarsht, Wagner, Crocker, & Amthor, 1977).

Anatomy of rods and cones. Figure 7-9 is a scanning electron micrograph of rods and cones, and Figure 7-10 presents schematic diagrams of a rod and cone. The absorption of light and the transduction of light energy into electrophysiological energy take place in the outer segment. The inner segment contains the cell bodies of the receptors. The receptor terminal is the area of synaptic contact of receptors with bipolars, horizontal cells, and other receptors.

Central Pathways

The central pathways of vision are shown in Figures 7-11 through 7-13. The visual world, or **visual field,** is mapped onto the retina, the lateral geniculate, and the visual cortex (see Figure 7-11). The axons of the ganglion cells travel in the optic nerve to the **optic chiasm.** There are no synapses there, but half the optic nerve fibers cross in such a way that the nerve fibers carrying information from the left visual field travel in the **optic tract** to the right **lateral geniculate.** Conversely, nerve fibers carrying information from the right visual field travel in the left optic tract to the left lateral geniculate. The ganglion-cell axons form synapses with geniculate cells, and the axons of geniculate neurons travel through the **optic radiations** to the left and right visual cortex. Thus, the visual system also follows the rule of crossing illustrated in the somatosensory system (see Figure 6-15): information from the left side of the visual world is sent to the right hemisphere, and vice versa.

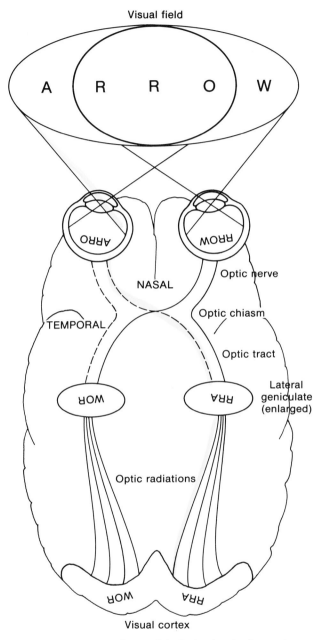

Visual field

A R R O W

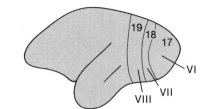

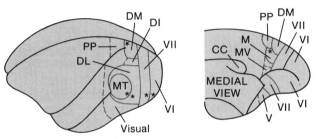

a. Marmoset visual areas

19 18 17
VI
VIII VII

b. Owl monkey visual areas

DM DI
PP VII
DL
MT
VI
Visual

PP DM
VII
M VI
CC MV
MEDIAL VIEW
VII VI
V

Figure 7-12 Traditional (a) and current (b) views differ on how the visual cortex in primates is organized. Areas 17, 18, and 19 have commonly been considered to be three separate representations of the visual field. **a.** the first (VI) and second (VII) visual areas correspond to areas 17 and 18. **b.** "Area 19" and adjoining cortex have a number of visual areas, including the dorsolateral (DL), dorsointermediate (DI), dorsomedial (DM), medial (M), middle temporal (MT), posterior parietal (PP), and ventral (V) visual areas. A medial ventral (MV) visual area is implied by patterns of cortical projections. CC = corpus callosum. Asterisks mark the location of the fovea in those areas that have been mapped.

Figure 7-12 shows the cortical areas that receive direct or indirect visual information. It includes both a traditional and a current view of primate visual or **striate cortex** organization. "Area 17" has also been called the *primary visual cortex*. In the new system, this area is **Visual Area I**. Similarly, "area 18" became **Visual Area II**. In each area, either the left or right side of the visual world is mapped in a point-for-point fashion onto the surface of the cortex.

Figure 7-13 shows other visual cortical connections. The **superior colliculus** receives information both directly from the retina and from the visual cortex. The nuclei responsible for ocular movements (movements of the eye in its socket) are controlled by the superior colliculus. There are also indirect visual pathways. The superior colliculus projects to a part of the thalamus called the **pulvinar**, and various areas of the pulvinar project to various visual areas in the primate cortex.

Figure 7-11 Ventral view of the brain, showing how various parts of the visual field are mapped onto the structures of the visual pathway. The image of the object is reversed (left for right) and inverted (upside down) by the cornea and lens. The axons in the nasal half of the optic nerve cross at the optic chiasm, but those in the temporal half do not cross. Thus, the left side of the visual field is sent to the right lateral geniculate and cortex.

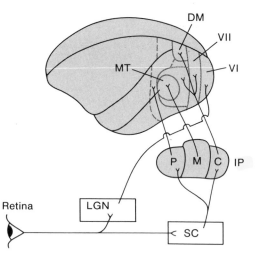

Figure 7-13   The thalamocortical connections of the visual system in monkeys are both topographic (having retina mapped onto structure) and reciprocal (having both afferent and centrifugal connections). Posterior (P), medial (M), and central (C) divisions of the inferior pulvinar complex (IP) of the thalamus are shown. LGN = lateral geniculate nucleus; SC = superior colliculus; VI = Visual Area I; VII = Visual Area II; DM = dorsomedial visual area; MT = middle temporal visual area.

Besides the connections shown, the lateral geniculate may project directly to Visual Area II, as well as to Visual Area I.

X-, Y-, and W-Cells in Cat Visual Systems

One classification system cuts across levels of visual processing. Visual sensory cells of cats have been divided into **X-cells, Y-cells,** and **W-cells.** This tripartite division has proven useful in research on both ganglion and geniculate cells (see the references for Table 7-1 in the *Credits* section at the back of the book). Although all the original work on the X-, Y-, and W-cell system was done in cats, the distinctions among those cell types may closely parallel a phasic–tonic classification imposed on the ganglion and geniculate cells in the primate visual system. For example, under most (though *not* all) conditions, cat X-cells are **tonic,** responding to an appropriate light stimulus as long as the stimulus is present. Y-cells are **phasic,** responding only to the onset or offset of an appropriate light stimulus. In fact, some researchers (for example, Malpeli, Schiller, & Colby, 1981) have used the cat classification system in primates.

However, Sherman (1985) and Rowe & Stone (1977) have suggested that although the phasic and tonic responses of X- and Y-cells are typical of them, these responses should *not* be used as part of their definitions. In addition, X- and Y-cells' responses to the speed and direction of moving stimuli are part of the differentiating characteristics of cat X-, Y-, and W-cells, but these responses are not seen in primate ganglion cells. Primate cells differentially responsive to movement are found only at the cortical level.

The defining characteristic of X- versus Y-cells is whether they show *linear* or *nonlinear* summation within their receptive fields. X-cells show some linear effects. When their responses are studied with a spatial acuity test like that in Figure 7-1, the cell may be excited whenever a light bar covers the center of its receptive field and be inhibited whenever a dark bar is over the center. If the receptive field is covered half by a dark bar and half by a light bar, the cell does not respond, as though it linearly summed the excitatory and inhibitory effects. Y-cells combine input from different parts of their receptive fields in a nonlinear fashion. The combination often produces a rate of output greater (or less) than would be predicted simply from summing individual excitatory and inhibitory effects.

Table 7-1 describes other properties of X-, Y-, and W-cells. For example, only Y-cells show a **periphery effect,** in which stimuli well outside the receptive field of a cell nevertheless affect its responses. The three types of cells also have distinctive anatomies, whether they are found in the retina, the geniculate, or the cortex, as Figures 7-14, 7-15, and 7-16 show. The differences in anatomy presumably correlate with functional differences.

Summary of Anatomy

The visual system is highly organized. The retina has separate layers of cells performing vertical and horizontal processing of visual information. The information leaves the retina on the axons of retinal ganglion cells, traveling through the optic nerve, the optic chiasm, and the optic tract to the lateral geniculate. From there, the information is projected to various cortical areas. In addition to this direct pathway, there are several indirect pathways, not all of which go to the cortex. Finally, there are different kinds of pathways, working in parallel, each separately carrying different kinds of information to the visual cortex. Examples of this are the cat's system of X-, Y-, and W-cell pathways and the primate's tonic–phasic distinction.

Table 7-1 Types of retinal ganglion and geniculate cells in cats.

Characteristics	Type of cell		
	X	Y	W
Receptive field size	Small	Large	Largest
Summation	Linear	Nonlinear	Mixed
Periphery effect	Usually none	Yes	None
Axon speed	Slow	Fast	Very slow
Soma size	Medium	Large	Small
Proportion of population	40%	<10%	50–55%
Location of receptive field	"Fovea" (area centralis)	"Fovea"; relatively more in periphery	Horizontal streak through "fovea"
Central projection	LGN and Area I	LGN, SC, Areas I, II, and III *(Eye/headmovement coordination)*	LGN, SC, Areas I, II, and III
Response to a constant stimulus	Tonic; transient during light adaptation	Phasic or transient; tonic after dark adaptation	Phasic or tonic
Receptive field	Off- or on-centers and opponent surround; no directional sensitivity	Off- or on-centers and opponent surround; no directional sensitivity	Some spatial opponent; some directional sensitivity
Spontaneous activity	More	More	Less
Receptor type	Some cones only	Rods and cones	Rods and cones
Best speed of stimulus movement	Slower targets	Faster targets	Some effect
Spatial frequency sensitivity	High frequencies	Low frequencies	Relatively insensitive
Color coding	Yes	No	Some
Ultimately connected to which type of cortical cell	Mostly simple; some complex	Complex	
Function (??)	Fine-detail stereopsis *Color*	Spatial form analysis; motion detection *Gross-features*	Direction coding

LGN = lateral geniculate
  SC = superior colliculus

Transduction

Transduction in the visual system is very different from transduction in any other sensory system. By definition, the process of transduction is not complete until action potentials are generated in true axons, which only ganglion cells have.

Overview

The first phase of transduction starts when the light waves strike the cornea and concludes when the light photons are absorbed by specialized **pigments** (pigmented or colored protein molecules found in the receptors. The vertical processing within the retina—and the second phase of transduction—begins with the receptor cells. When a photon of light is absorbed by a light-sensitive molecule, a series of molecular processes is initiated that researchers describe as a **cascade.*** At the end of this process, the permeability of the rod membrane to Na^+ is *decreased*, and therefore the third phase of transduction begins with the receptor membrane *hyperpolarizing* (at least in vertebrates). This step, which makes visual transduction unique, was discovered by Tomita (Tomita, 1965; Toyoda, Nosaki, & Tomita, 1969). The hyperpolarization of the receptor membrane (since the visual system evidently did not repeal the laws of synaptic processing—just those of transduction) causes a receptor to *decrease* its rate of transmitter output.

The next two types of cells in the vertical processing chain respond to this hyperpolarization. The bipolar and the gan-

* *Cascade* describes a series of actions that have an increasing number of active parts in successive stages.

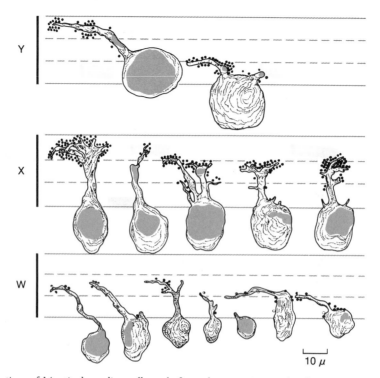

Figure 7-14 Reconstructions of 14 retinal ganglion cells made from electron micrographs of cat retinas, shown grouped by cell type. Black dots represent synaptic contacts; shading indicates that a portion of the cell was missing from the serial sections used for the reconstructions.

glion cells either hyperpolarize or depolarize in response to light. But in the ganglion cell, if the depolarization reaches threshold, an action potential is generated and the visual information leaves the retina.

The horizontal processors modify the process of transduction at every synapse. The first stage of horizontal processing occurs at the electrical synapses between receptors, spreading hyperpolarization among adjacent receptors. Next, the horizontal cells hyperpolarize in response to light and then the amacrines depolarize. (In some species, amacrine cells may also be hyperpolarized by a light stimulus.) Amacrines also show something resembling an action potential, the function of which is unclear since these cells lack axons (see Figure 7-8).

Phase I: Nonneural Changes

Nonneural changes come largely from the optics of the eye. Because the cornea, the lens, and the humors are not completely transparent, they absorb some photons of light, which therefore never reach the retina. The other types of retinal cells are also likely to absorb photons before they can reach the receptors, especially energy from the short-wavelength end of the spectrum. Also, some light waves are scattered, because the structures of the eye — and the humors — do not have a uniform density. The scattered light waves don't reach the retina. The effect of these noneural changes is shown in Figure 7-17.

The major nonneural modifications have already been mentioned. The cornea and lens of the eye not only focus the image on the retina but invert it. Other nonneural modifications involve the effect of pupil size on the number of photons entering the eye and on spherical and chromatic aberrations, as shown in Figure 7-18. The thickness of the lens affects the degree to which the light waves are bent.

Phase II: Changes in Receptor Permeability

The second phase of transduction begins with the absorption of one or more photons of light by a light-sensitive pigment and ends with a change in membrane permeability.

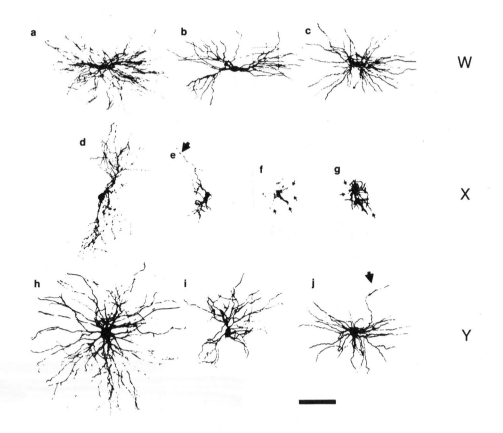

Figure 7-15 Drawings of W = (**a**–**c**), X = (**d**–**g**), and Y = (**h**–**j**) cells from the cat lateral geniculate nucleus. Cells **a**, **d**, and **h** are from adults; cells **b**, **c**, **e**–**g**, **i**, and **j** are from 3- to 4-week-old kitten. W-cells: note the horizontal orientation of the dendritic trees. X-cells: note the vertical orientation of the dendritic trees of the adult; the kitten X-cells were morphologically immature. The arrows in both **j** and **e** indicate the axon. The small arrows in **f** and **g** indicate terminal swellings on the ends of the dendrites. Y-cell: the adult cell had large cell bodies and thick, radially oriented dendrites. Scale bar = 100 μm for all drawings.

Rhodopsin and photoisomerization. The outer segments of rods and cones contain a light-sensitive pigment. The pigment in rods, **rhodopsin,** is a combination of a colorless protein called **opsin** and a purple-colored molecule called **11-*cis*-retinal.** The 11-*cis*-retinal is manufactured from vitamin A. It has its characteristic purple color because it absorbs mostly light in the green part of the spectrum, reflecting red and blue wavelengths. The cones also have 11-*cis*-retinal, but in them the molecule is associated with three different kinds of opsins, in three different kinds of cones; the opsin in a cone determines its wavelength sensitivity. The cone pigments are **photopsins** or **iodopsins.** The rest of this section describes rods and rhodopsin, but transduction in cones must be very similar.

Rhodopsin molecules are embedded in the disc membranes of rods. Figure 7-19 illustrates one way the molecule might be embedded. These molecules may constitute up to 98% of the protein in those membranes (Miljanich, Schwartz, & Dratz, 1980). When a photon of light strikes a molecule of rhodopsin, the molecule is **photoisomerized,** changing its three-dimensional shape. Specifically, light changes rhodopsin from the *cis* to the *trans* isomer. (An **isomer** is a molecule having the same chemical composition but a different three-dimensional shape.) The *trans* isomer is longer, so light "straightens" the rhodopsin molecule.

After the rhodopsin has been "straightened," its component parts are then exposed to the actions of various enzymes. In one of those enzymatically produced changes, the molecule loses its purple color, so light is said to **bleach** rhodopsin. At several stages of this process, if a second light photon is absorbed, the rhodopsin may go back to its original, light-sensitive *cis* isomer. At the end of this process, rhodopsin breaks up

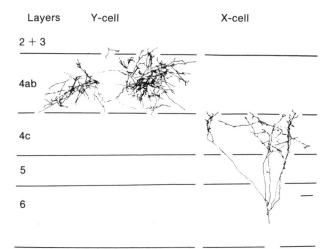

Layers	Y-cell	X-cell
2 + 3		
4ab		
4c		
5		
6		

Figure 7-16 These two axon terminal trees found in the cortex of a cat come from cells located in the lateral geniculate. The Y-cell's terminal ramified (branched) entirely within layer 4ab, whereas the X-cell's terminal ramified entirely within layer 4c. Thus, X- and Y-cell axons terminate in different cortical layers.

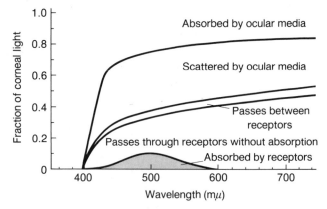

Figure 7-17 The effects of all the nonneural modifications of light made by the eye. The illustration is based on the assumption that 10% of the light of 500 mμ wavelength that strikes the cornea gets absorbed by the visual receptors.

into separate retinal and opsin molecules. The receptor must then go through a series of energy-requiring stages to reconstitute (or reassemble) the rhodopsin molecule back into its light-sensitive form.

Light-initiated chemical reactions. Sometime before the bleaching stage, a critical reaction is initiated, triggering a cascade of molecular reactions that eventually change the membrane's permeability. The process is a cascade because one photon isomerizes one molecule of rhodopsin. It in turn is a catalyst for other reactions affecting thousands of intracellular molecules. These critical reactions may be terminated by the phosphorylation of the rhodopsin molecule, with either ATP or GTP serving as the source of the phosphorus (Kühn, 1978; Paulsen & Bentrop, 1983).

Figure 7-20 presents some possible reactions. The possibility most strongly supported by recent evidence is a *light-evoked decrease in cGMP* (Fesenko, Kolesnikov, & Lyubarsky, 1985; Woodruff & Bownds, 1979; Woodruff, Bownds, Green,

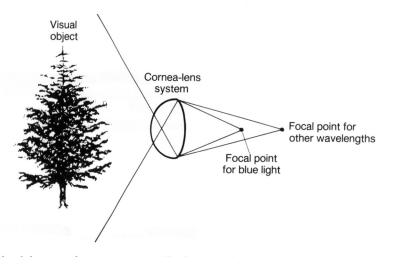

Figure 7-18 Spherical and chromatic aberrations are caused by the cornea-lens system's bending of some wavelengths more sharply than other wavelengths. So if one is focusing on a green part of an object, the blue parts may be slightly blurry or hazy.

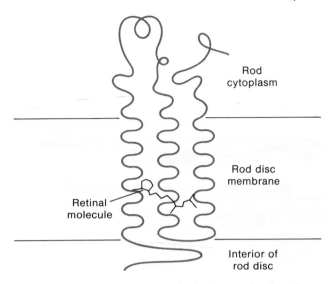

Figure 7-19 One possible way the rhodopsin molecule might be embedded in the rod disc membrane. The light-sensitive portion is the retinal molecule, which goes from a *cis* to a *trans* isomer upon light absorption. Only three of the nine helical segments (Nathans, Thomas, & Hogness, 1986) of the molecule are shown.

Morrisey, & Shedlovsky, 1977; Vuong, Chabre, & Stryer, 1984; Yau & Nakatani, 1984). Within 100 to 300 mSec after exposure to light, the cGMP content of frog rod outer segments is decreased by from 1000 to 2000 molecules. Probably somewhere between 1.5×10^6 (or 3.3% of the supply) and 5×10^4 (or .1%) molecules of cGMP are degraded per molecule of bleached rhodopsin. This cascade represents considerable amplification of the light signal.

In this model, one rhodopsin isomer may activate a cGMP **phosphodiesterase (PDE)**. Although not illustrated, the mechanism by which isomerized rhodopsin activates PDE may itself involve one or more steps (O'Brien, 1982). The PDE then breaks down cGMP, decreasing cGMP levels in the retina. A decrease in cGMP would decrease the phosphorylation of some membrane protein. (Since cGMP normally phosphorylates membrane proteins—as in slow synapses—reducing cGMP would reduce phosphorylation.) Reducing phosphorylation decreases the membrane's permeability to Na^+. This model is supported by the fact that increasing the level of cGMP in rods by means of intracellular injections—just the opposite of what light does to cGMP levels—rapidly increases Na^+ permeability (Bownds, 1980; Lipton, 1983; Lipton, Rasmussen, & Dowling, 1977; Miller & Nicol,

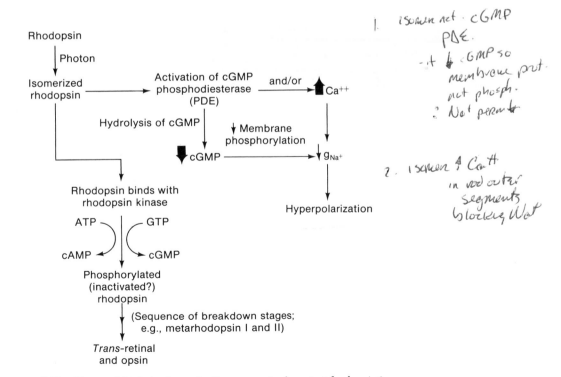

Figure 7-20 Two models of visual transduction summarized; see text for description.

1979). Injections of PDE rapidly hyperpolarize rods (Clack, Oakley, & Stein, 1983).

The other possibility illustrated in Figure 7-20 is that an isomer of rhodopsin *increases Ca++ levels within the rod outer segments* and Ca++ blocks Na+ permeability (Gold & Korenbrot, 1980; Lipson, Ostroy, & Dowling, 1977; Yoshikami & Hagins, 1980; Yoshikami, George, & Hagins, 1980). To test this theory, researchers turned individual rods inside out in order to chemically stimulate the inside of the membrane. cGMP injections rapidly increased permeability to Na+, but similar injections of Ca++ had no effect. So internal Ca++ may have no direct effects on membrane permeability (Fesenko, Kolesnikov, & Lyubarsky, 1985).

However, Ca++ may modulate the effects of cGMP on the membrane. Both *increases* in Ca++ and *decreases* in cGMP augment the light-evoked response of the other type of molecule (George & Hagins, 1983; Lolley & Racz, 1982). The decrease in cGMP may cause internal Ca++ to increase. Several models of possible interactions between intracellular Ca++ and cGMP were described by Lipton, Rasmussen, and Dowling (1977). For example, the decrease in cGMP may be responsible for transduction, whereas the secondary increases in Ca++ may lead to light adaptation.

Summary of phase II.   Regardless of details, two steps are clear: (1) a photon of light isomerizes a molecule of rhodopsin, and (2) this isomerization produces molecular changes causing the closure of from 100 to 300 Na+ channels in a rod's outer segment membrane.

Phase III: Changes in Membrane Potentials

Phase III of transduction begins with the hyperpolarization of the receptor cell membrane and includes changes in the membrane potentials of horizontal cells, bipolar cells, and amacrine cells. Phase III ends with membrane potential changes and action potentials in the ganglion cells.

Hyperpolarization and dark current in rods.   One model for rod hyperpolarization by light (Korenbrot, 1985) is illustrated in Figure 7-21. First, at the left-hand side an unstimulated rod is shown. In the dark, rods maintain a uniform membrane potential of from 35 to 45 mV, negative on the inside. Since E_{Na} is +5 to +10 mV and E_K is approximately −60 to 65 mV, positive charges flow out of the outer segment, along the rod, and back into the rod in the inner segment. This is the **dark current.** The disequilibriums of K+ and Na+ concentrations are maintained by Na-K pumps found only in the inner

segments. Also, the inner segment's membrane is impermeable to Na+. Thus, K+ flows out of the inner segment, down its electrochemical gradient. The dark current in the inner segment is carried by K+ ions, but the dark current of the outer segment is carried by Na+. Na+ enters the outer membrane — which is highly permeable to that ion — down the Na+ electrochemical gradient.

As the right-hand side of Figure 7-21 shows, exposure to light decreases the Na+ permeability of the outer segment, decreases the inward Na+ current, and decreases the dark current. (Ca++ is illustrated as moving out during light exposure.) The outer segment hyperpolarizes, and this change in potential spreads passively to the inner segment and the synaptic area. Hyperpolarization of the synapse *decreases* the rate at which the rod secretes transmitter substance onto bipolars and horizontal cells.

Although chemically gated (by cGMP) hyperpolarization is probably the major mechanism regulating membrane potential, rod membranes have electrically gated channels as well. Depolarization may open and hyperpolarization close K+ and Ca++ channels in the membrane (Fain, Quandt, & Gerschenfeld, 1977; Korenbrot, 1985; one of the K+ channels may be calcium activated). A Na+ channel may be *opened* by hyperpolarization, thus opposing the effects of the light stimulus itself (Fain, Quandt, Bastian, & Gerschenfeld, 1978). The hyperpolarization-induced closure of the Ca++ channel is probably responsible for the light-evoked decrease in transmitter secretion. The electrically gated Na+ channel may be involved in adaptation.

Receptor responses at thresholds.   Cones are less sensitive to small amounts of light than rods are, but cones have a faster (shorter latency) response and a faster recovery to normal potentials once the light stimulus is removed (Baylor & Hodgkin, 1973; Fain, 1975b; Schwartz, 1975a, 1975b). At the absolute threshold of individual cones, the response to a photon of light may be a $25 \mu V$ hyperpolarization. A 35 to 70 μV hyperpolarization is required for an animal (a turtle) to be able to detect the light (Dvorak, Granda, & Maxwell, 1980; Lamb & Simon, 1977). Cones are even more sensitive to light increments: at the difference threshold, the response of a cone to an increment of one photon of light is a further 5 to 10 μV increment in hyperpolarization (Fain, Granda, & Maxwell, 1977).

Baylor, Lamb, and Yau (1979b) studied rod responses to single photons of light. Tiny pieces from a toad retina were placed in a microscope and a single outer segment was gently sucked up into a pipette. Thus, the researchers isolated and recorded from a single outer segment. When this outer seg-

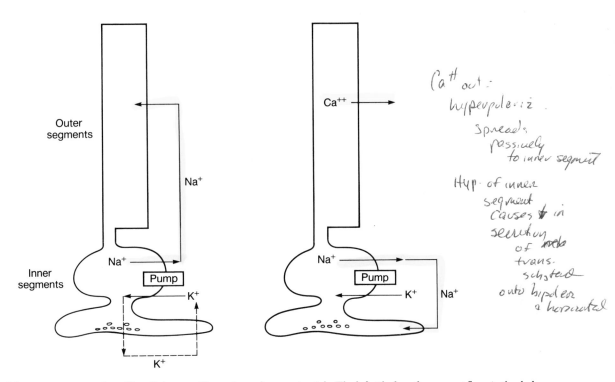

Labels in figure:
Outer segments
Inner segments
Na⁺
Na⁺ → Pump
K⁺
K⁺
Ca⁺⁺ →
Na⁺ → Pump
K⁺   Na⁺

Handwritten notes (right margin):
Ca⁺⁺ out:
hyperpolariz.
spreads
passively
to inner segment
Hyp. of inner
segment
causes ↓ in
secretion
of neuro
trans.
schifted
onto bipolar
& horizontal

Figure 7-21 Schematic representation of how light may affect rod membrane potentials. The left side describes current flows in the dark, and the right side shows what light does to those currents. It also illustrates dark current.

ment was exposed to a series of dim flashes, sometimes a change in membrane current could be seen and sometimes no change would be detected.

The responses of a single segment to forty consecutive flashes of dim light are presented in Figure 7-22. A detectable response was called a "success." In Figure 7-23, the proportion of successes in a series of light stimulations was plotted as a function of different intensities of stimulus. This figure thus represents a psychophysical absolute-threshold curve for a sensory receptor. The curve came from theoretical equations based on the assumption that an elementary electrical event (the amount by which current was changed during the "success" responses) came from a single photoisomerization. The good fit between the curve and the data points suggests that rods do reliably detect a single photon of absorbed light.

Because receptors have electrical synapses between them, hyperpolarization in one receptor hyperpolarizes adjacent receptors (in the turtle: Baylor, Fuortes, & O'Bryan, 1971). For example, from 85% to 90% of the response recorded in a single rod may come across the electrical synapses from the responses of adjacent rods (Fain, 1975b). Thus, the electrical synapses increase the voltage changes evoked by light and decrease the absolute threshold (Copenhagen & Owen, 1976).

A model of retinal responses to light. Figure 7-24 shows how retinal cells respond to light. The "spot" condition refers to stimulating the center of a receptive field with a tiny spot of light. The "annulus" condition refers to stimulating the receptive field of a cell with a ring, or annulus, of light. Thus, the annulus stimulates only the peripheral, or **surround,** portion and not the **center,** or central portion, of a receptive field. The type of response made by each retinal cell to center or surround stimulation, including the action potentials in amacrine and ganglion cells, is summarized by that figure.

One model of how various cells in a primate retina may respond to light is presented in Figures 7-25 and 7-26. First look at the activity of the various cells in the dark. Rods and the various kinds of cone may use different transmitter substances (probably amino acids: Slaughter & Miller, 1983; Waloga & Pak, 1976). In the dark, the relatively depolarized receptors secrete excitatory transmitter substances onto horizontal cells, keeping them depolarized in the dark.

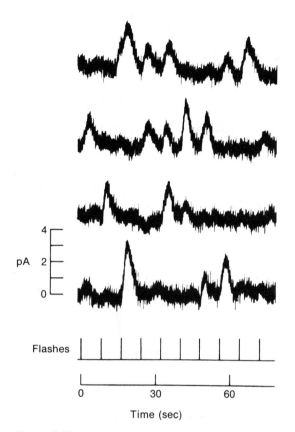

Figure 7-22 An outer rod segment responds to a series of forty consecutive flashes of dim light. The flashes lasted 20 mSec and were delivered at the times indicated below the tracings. The amplitude of the response is measured in picoamperes (pA).

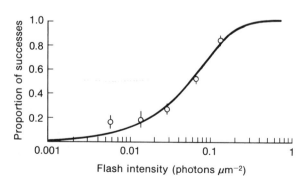

Figure 7-23 The proportion of responses in Figure 7-22 that exceeded a certain size (detection) was plotted at each of five different light-stimulus intensities on a logarithmic scale. The bars are ±1 standard deviation, estimated from the numbers of "successful detections" and "failures."

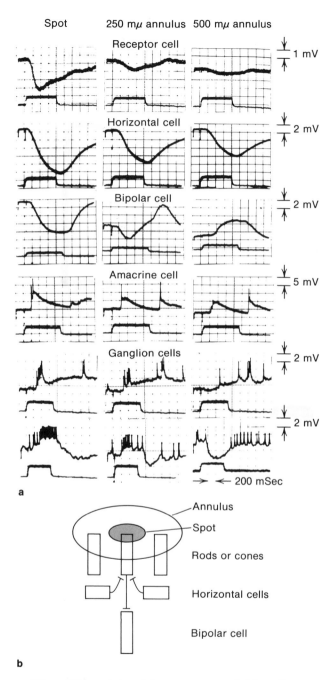

Figure 7-24 **a.** Intracellular responses recorded from all types of retinal cells in a mud puppy (a salamander). **b.** Responses both to a spot and to an annulus (ring-shaped stimulus) were recorded. In each recording, the lower trace indicates stimulus onset and offset. Note that some cells had an opponent type of receptive field, responding one way to a spot and another way to an annulus. Only ganglion cells had trains of action potentials; amacrines seemed to have only one transient action potential; none of the other cells did.

1. LIGHT hyperpol. receptors so they stop secreting ~~excis~~ -excitating trans

2. In turn excited horiz & bipolars are suppressed ∴ they can't release inhib. trans-

The transmitter substance secreted by a single receptor may be either excitatory or inhibitory in its effects on a bipolar, depending on which chemically activated channels the bipolar has. So some bipolars are relatively depolarized and some are hyperpolarized in the dark. In this model, all bipolar transmitter substance(s?) are assumed to be excitatory to the postsynaptic membranes of amacrines and ganglion cells. Thus, the bipolars that are depolarized in the dark depolarize the amacrines and ganglion cells to which they are connected, whereas the hyperpolarized bipolars have their transmitter secretion inhibited.

Next look at what exposure to light does to horizontal and bipolar cells. Since the secretion of excitatory transmitters by the receptors onto the horizontals is suppressed by light, so *horizontal cells are hyperpolarized by light*. In turn, their release of an inhibitory, hyperpolarizing transmitter onto the rods and cones is suppressed by the light-evoked hyperpolarization. (GABA may be the transmitter substance: Lam, Lasater, & Naka, 1978; Murakami, Shimoda, Nakatani, Miyachi, & Watanabe, 1982a, 1982b). So if horizontal cells are hyperpolarized by electrical stimulation, nearby cones are depolarized (Baylor, Fuortes, and O'Bryan, 1971). Since receptors hyperpolarize in response to light, light-activated *horizontal cells laterally inhibit* (depolarize) adjacent rods (probably from the axon terminals in primates) and cones (from the dendrites).

Bipolars have a center-surround type of receptive field, and in the centers of their receptive fields they are either hyperpolarized or depolarized by light. Some bipolars receive excitatory transmitter in the dark; these bipolars hyperpolarize in response to the light-evoked decrease in transmitter secretion. Since light decreases the rate at which the other bipolars receive an inhibitory transmitter substance, they are depolarized by light. If the cell hyperpolarizes in response to a light spot on the center of its receptive field — because of the responses of rods and cones to which that cell is directly connected — that cell is said to have an **off-center receptive field.** If the cell depolarizes in response to a light spot centered on its receptive field, it has an **on-center receptive field.**

Horizontal cells cause bipolars to be affected by receptors to which they are not directly connected (see Figure 7-24). Because of the inhibitory nature of the horizontal cell, an annulus centered on the periphery of a bipolar receptive field stimulates the horizontal cells and inhibits any light-evoked responses of the rods and cones in the center of the field. The horizontal cells excited by the annulus would inhibit the rods or cones in the center of the receptive field, the receptors to which the bipolar is directly connected. In some cells (and in some species), not only may annular stimulation inhibit responses to spot stimulation of the center but the annulus may by itself produce the opposite potential. The annulus is stimulating the surround part of the bipolar receptive field. The

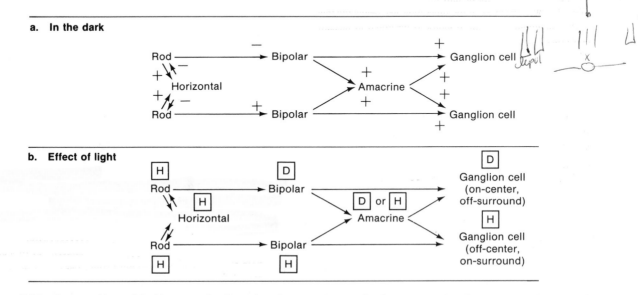

Figure 7-25 One possible model of how retinal cells work: rod system. See text for description and explanations. **a.** The types of transmitter each cell type secretes. **b.** What happens during light stimulation. Plus (+) = excitatory transmitter; minus (−) = inhibitory transmitter; H = hyperpolarized by light; D = depolarized by light. NOTE: Amacrines may presynaptically inhibit bipolar–ganglion synapse.

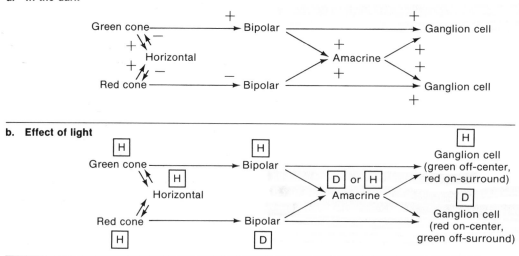

Figure 7-26 One possible model of how retinal cells work: cone system. See Figure 7-25 for explanation of symbols.

horizontal cells may laterally inhibit either the same or a different type of cone from those found in the receptive field center.

There are several kinds of ganglion cell. As we mentioned previously, some are phasic and some are tonic. Furthermore, *some are hyperpolarized and some depolarized* by light. Cells depolarized by light are **on cells**. **Off cells** are inhibited by light but often exhibit a burst of action potentials when the light is turned off. Some cells are excited by small spots of light in the center of their receptive fields and are also excited by the *removal* of light from the surround part of their fields. These particular cells are also inhibited by light in their surrounds, presumably because of horizontal cells. These are the **on-center, off-surround** cells (Kuffler, 1952). Other cells are excited by the removal of a small spot of light from their receptive field centers or by the presentation of light to their surrounds. These are **off-center, on-surround** cells.

Amacrines can depolarize or hyperpolarize and also have center-surround receptive fields. Amacrines may presynaptically inhibit the bipolar–ganglion cell synapse and also make direct inhibitory synaptic contact with bipolars and ganglion cells. There are several kinds of amacrine cell (based on responses to light and connections made to other cells). Each type may use a different kind of transmitter substance. GABA, glycine, dopamine, and ACh have all been suggested (Frumkes, Miller, Slaughter, & Dacheux, 1981; Ikeda & Sheardown, 1982; Iuvone, Galli, Garrison-Gund, & Neff, 1978; Miller, Dacheux, & Frumkes, 1977). Amacrines may

decrease any response to constantly present light: activating amarcrines may inhibit all output from the retina.

Summary of Transduction

Transduction begins with a photon of light passing through the cornea. The optical characteristics of the cornea, lens, iris, and aqueous and vitreous humors modify the light before it reaches the retina. Once a photon of light is absorbed by a molecule of rhodopsin (or an iodopsin), the form of the energy is changed from light to chemical. The rhodopsin isomerizes, and one of the isomers triggers a cascade of chemical reactions that decreases the membrane's permeability to Na^+. The resulting hyperpolarization inhibits transmitter release.

The effect on the other retinal cells depends on which kinds of transmitter receptors they have. Horizontal cells are hyperpolarized by light; they then laterally inhibit adjacent receptors, and that inhibition is responsible for — or creates — the surround parts of the receptive fields of bipolars, amacrines, and ganglion cells. Without horizontal cells, there would be no opponent surrounds in the receptor fields of these other retinal cells. Bipolars and ganglion cells are either depolarized or hyperpolarized by light. Amacrines, at least in primates, may be depolarized by light and may inhibit the flow of information out of the retina.

Subcortical Coding

Our visual world is constructed by the coding processes of our visual brains. Because the coding rules used by retinal ganglion cells and lateral geniculate cells in primates seem similar (Sherman & Spear, 1982; Wiesel & Hubel, 1966), they will be discussed separately from cortical coding mechanisms. A pattern code is usually used for variations in photon density over time, and a place code is used for variations over space. Wavelength is coded by both place and a type of place-pattern code. In many cases, separate populations of cells are being used to code for different aspects of visual stimulation.

Brightness Coding in the Retina and Geniculate

Increasing the number of photons per unit of time and space increases the perceived brightness of a stimulus. Up to a point, the more photons absorbed by a receptor, the greater will be the change in its membrane current and the more hyperpolarized that membrane becomes. But after that point, the receptor response **saturates.** Increasing the intensity of a light will no longer increase hyperpolarization, since the membrane is already maximally hyperpolarized. Instead, more intense lights lead to a longer-lasting hyperpolarization. The other retinal cells that do not have action potentials (horizontals, bipolars) also tend to show graded responses to variations in stimulus photon density. The more photons, the greater the change in membrane potential.

However, amacrines, ganglion cells, and lateral geniculate cells have a different response pattern. The phasic cells often respond strongly to light onset (or offset) and do not show a very well-sustained response to a sustained light stimulus. The on types of tonic cells show a burst of action potentials at light onset, declining to a steady rate maintained throughout the stimulation. Intensity may be coded by the number of action potentials in the on or off burst of the phasic cells and by the number of action potentials either at the peak onset response or during the sustained response of the tonic cells.

These responses can be plotted according to the intensity of the stimulus. Figure 7-27 illustrates one possible relationship. Although this recording comes from a horseshoe crab, the responses are similar to those of some tonic ganglion cells (Sherman & Spear, 1982; Wiesel & Hubel, 1966). The way steady-state responses are related to the intensity of the stimulus implies a complex coding function.

To complicate matters further, many ganglion cells are stimulated by light of one wavelength and are inhibited by light from another region of the wavelength spectrum. These cells are **chromatically opponent.** As Figure 7-26 shows, if a

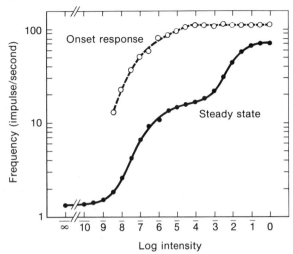

Figure 7-27   The number of action potentials in the onset response or in the steady response varies according to the intensity of the stimulus. The nerve cell's response is plotted as a function of the log of light intensity. The steady-state response was the mean firing rate during the last five seconds of the ten-second flash stimulus; the onset response was the highest frequency of firing during the early part of the record. There was no onset response for low intensities.

bipolar or ganglion cell responds to any given wavelength (for example, red or green) in the center of its receptive field, that response comes directly from cones in that part of its field. But the chromatically opponent responses may follow an indirect route from cone to horizontal to bipolar. Because of these patterns of interconnection, most chromatically opponent cells are **spatially opponent** as well, having surround responses opposite to their center responses. Therefore, activity in such cells is ambiguous. An increase in the number of action potentials in the on-burst, for example, could mean either that a large light (of the on-center wavelength) got brighter or that a small spot of light got closer to the receptive field center. Or it could mean that the wavelength of the light was changed, becoming closer to the excitatory region of the spectrum. Only about 37% of the retinal ganglion cells are less ambiguous, responding only to changes in light intensity over time or space but not to changes in wavelength (Gouras & Zrenner, 1981). These less ambiguous cells are spatially but not chromatically opponent and could therefore code for brightness.

Coding of Spatial Location and Lateral Inhibition

A faithful image of the light patterns in our visual world is reproduced on our retina (though inverted and reversed). But the responses of our retinal and geniculate cells are not so faithful.

Receptive fields.   We'll first consider how the location of a light spot in the visual field is coded. Spatial localization is coded by which receptor — located in which part of the retina — is excited by light. Since the image of the visual world is focused on the retina, the location of each light spot in the visual field will correspond to a unique retinal location, stimulating a unique group of receptors. In turn, bipolar cells, ganglion cells, and lateral geniculate cells whose receptive fields include that location will also respond to that spot. Thus, which cells are activated can serve as a code for where on the retina (and thus where in the visual field) the spot of light is located.

A more complex visual stimulus creates a pattern of light across the retina. A pattern produces areas of lesser and greater stimulation (from less and more luminant parts of the stimulus) in receptors. The degree to which a light pattern can produce spatial variations in rod and cone activity depends largely on two factors: receptive field size and receptor density.

First, acuity depends on the receptive field size of a geniculate or ganglion cell. The fewer receptors connected to ganglion cells in any area of the retina, the more sensitive that area of the retina can be to spatial differences in photon absorption. For example, if all receptors were connected to a single ganglion cell, that cell could never signal differences in the luminance of one area compared to another. The larger the receptive fields of ganglion cells (or the greater the convergence of receptors to the ganglion cells in a given area of the retina), the lower will be the spatial acuity of that retinal area. Although summation — which increases receptive field size — decreases acuity, it increases sensitivity.

Second, the density of rods and cones at a particular place on the retina determines acuity and sensitivity. The more receptors there are per unit area, the greater the degree to which spatial differences in image brightness can be coded by differences in responses among adjacent rods and cones. Putting this all together, we have the greatest acuity for images projected onto our fovea where the cones are most dense and receptive field centers smallest. We have the greatest sensitivity for images projected just outside our fovea where receptive field centers are largest and the rods are most dense.

X-, Y-, and W-cells and spatial coding.   The X-, Y-, and W-cells in the cat visual system have different functions with regard to spatial coding (Sherman & Spear, 1982; Sherman, 1985). As Table 7-1 indicates X-cells may encode the fine

spatial details of a visual stimulus. These cells have small receptive fields, they are concentrated in the area centralis (corresponding to the fovea in primates), and they can sum stimuli linearly within their receptive fields. Y-cells may encode the overall form of a stimulus pattern: they sum stimuli nonlinearly within their receptive fields and they show the periphery effect. The periphery effect may come from amacrine cells with very large receptive fields. Less is known about W-cells, but they may carry the information needed by higher centers for coding and perceiving movement.

Lateral inhibition and Mach bands.   In 1959, Ratliff and Hartline showed how the responses of receptors are affected by spatial variations in luminance — producing some surprises. The *Limulus*, or horseshoe crab, has two compound eyes (one on each side of its head). Each eye has about 1000 separate light-sensitive structures called **ommatidia.** Each ommatidium has its own lens and set of receptor cells arranged in a circle. The photoreceptor cells are electrically coupled with the dendrites of a type of cell called an **eccentric cell,** which is also found in each ommatidium. The axon of the eccentric cell carries the visual information out of the ommatidium and gives off collaterals that form inhibitory synapses with axons from other ommatidia. Although the vertebrate eye is certainly not arranged that way, the inhibitory collaterals may have effects on visual processing similar to the effects that horizontal cells have. The way the crab eye responds to variations in brightness may tell us something about what horizontal cells do to perceptions of brightness in primates.

Figure 7-28 comes from Ratliff and Hartline's experiments. They recorded the number of action potentials (impulses) per second from the axon of one eccentric cell as they moved a certain visual stimulus past the front of the eye. The stimulus, as illustrated, consisted of a dark and a light region, with a sharp edge between the two. In the top curve, lateral inhibition (the effects of the axon collaterals) was eliminated by using a small mask to prevent light from reaching any ommatidium other than the one from which they were recording.

In the lower part of Figure 7-28, the mask was removed in order to reveal the effects of lateral inhibition. As the light part of the pattern was moved across the test receptor or the ommatidium being recorded from, a high rate of firing occurred. However, the firing was being inhibited by the axon collaterals of adjacent ommatidia, which were also being stimulated by the bright part of the pattern. When the dark edge approached the test ommatidium, its firing rate increased. Since the dark part of the visual stimulus was now over ommatidia adjacent to the right side, they no longer laterally inhibited the test receptor. When the edge passed to the left of the test receptor, it was

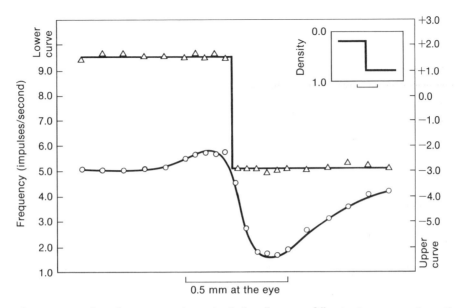

Figure 7-28 A single receptor in a *Limulus* eye responds to a simple "step" pattern of illumination across various retinal locations. The stimulus is shown in the insert. The upper (rectilinear) graph shows the frequency of discharge of the test receptor when a mask confined the stimulus to the test receptor (scale of ordinate on the right). The lower (curvilinear) graph is the frequency of discharge from the same test receptor after the mask was removed and adjacent receptors were also affected by the stimulus when it was moved to the various positions. The major point of this figure is that the *forms* of the two curves differ; the absolute magnitude of response is not really relevant.

now exposed to darkness. In addition, it was still being laterally inhibited by ommatidia to the left of it, since those ommatidia were still exposed to the bright part of the pattern. When the pattern was moved still further, no nearby ommatidia were stimulated, so there was no lateral inhibition and the firing rate of the test receptor returned to baseline.

To help you conceptualize what lateral inhibition does to perception, consider that the lower part of Figure 7-28 could be duplicated if the visual stimulus were stationary and recordings were made simultaneously from different ommatidia across the eye. The lower axis would then reflect the retinal positions of the receptors. In both cases, the dark edge creates an increment in firing rate above that produced when all ommatidia in an area are equally stimulated, and the light edge creates a suppression in firing rate below that produced when all receptors are less stimulated. Thus, lateral inhibition may have the effect of enhancing the appearance of edges in our visual world. Edges may be so perceptually salient to us because the responses of our visual system exaggerate the effects of spatial changes in luminance.

Another possible perceptual consequence of lateral inhibition is presented in Figure 7-29. This figure contains a stimulus with a dark area, a light area, and a luminance gradient between them. But if you look at it, you can see two bands. A bright band is located just inside the light area, and a dark band is located just inside the dimmer area. These are **Mach bands.** They don't exist—except in your mind. The bands do not correspond to any objective variations in luminance. These light and dark bands were first reported more than 100 years ago by Austrian physicist, philosopher, and psychologist Ernst Mach (Ratliff, 1972).

Now compare Figures 7-28 and 7-29. Note that the bright Mach band roughly corresponds to the area of maximal firing rate and the dim Mach band corresponds to the area of minimal firing rate. Thus, lateral inhibition may exaggerate differences in luminance between adjacent areas of the retina and may produce Mach bands. In the vertebrate retina, presumably the lateral inhibition comes from the horizontal cells.

The only problem with this otherwise very satisfying explanation is that Mach bands are not produced by sharp edges (as in Figure 7-28), only by gradients of brightness between a bright and a dark area (as in Figure 7-29). So lateral inhibition may account for edge enhancement as seen in the recordings from ommatidia and in perceptual studies with human subjects, but something else may be required to explain Mach bands (Ratliff, Milkman, & Rennert, 1983).

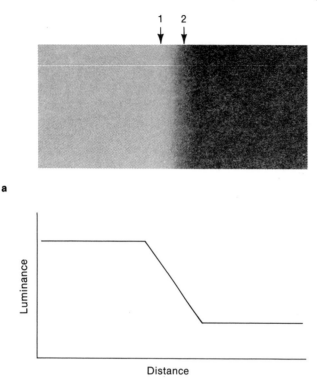

a

b

Figure 7-29   a. Mach bands. Illusory bands of first brightness (1) and then darkness (2) appear when the eye is exposed to a stimulus consisting of a dark region close to a high-luminance region, with a luminance gradient between them. **b.** Luminance gradient. See text for implications.

Wavelength Coding in the Retina and Geniculate

For us to perceive differences among wavelengths, our visual system must respond differentially to those wavelengths. Young (1802) proposed that the eye had three "resonators," each capable of being stimulated by different wavelengths. In 1866, Helmholtz (1866/1962) expanded on Young's ideas, and the result became known as the **Young-Helmholtz trichromatic theory of color vision.** Hurvich and Jameson (1956; Jameson & Hurvich, 1955) expanded upon and quantified a theory proposed in the late 1800s by Hering (1964). They suggested that some cells in the visual system are excited by one wavelength and inhibited by another. Their proposal became known as the **opponent-process theory of color vision.**

In a way, both theories are correct. At the level of the receptors, the differential responses occur because different cones contain different pigments that are maximally sensitive to different wavelengths. After the receptor level, the coding changes. Different cells are still activated by different wavelengths (a place code), but the same cell also responds in an opponent fashion to different wavelengths (a pattern code).

Trichromacy and three types of cones. In many primates, each of the three kinds of cone contains a different pigment maximally sensitive to different wavelengths. These primates are trichromats. Figure 7-30 presents curves representing the spectral sensitivity of those pigments in one human observer. Those curves were determined psychophysically but correspond closely to actual measurements of peak absorption by pigments in a variety of trichromatic species, including humans (Bowmaker, 1981; Granit, 1968; Nathans, Piantanida, Eddy, Shows, & Hogness, 1986; Nathans, Thomas, & Hogness, 1986). Although each type of cone pigment is maximally sensitive to a different wavelength, each absorbs light throughout a broad spectral region. So although the "red" cone pigment is most sensitive to the 580 mμ wavelength (yellowish green), it also absorbs light from 690 to 470 mμ. The "green" cone is most sensitive to green lights of about 540 mμ, and the "blue" cone is most sensitive to blue lights of about 440 mμ. This also means that normal trichromats must have at least three color-coding genes, one for each type of pigment found in each type of cone.

The spectral sensitivities illustrated in Figure 7-30 may not present the complete story. The subject illustrated in that figure was three times more sensitive to blue light than the average primate trichromat (Wald, 1964). Furthermore, studies of pigments have found three **families,** as opposed to three individual types (see, for example, Bowmaker, 1981; Nathans et al., 1986; Nathans, Thomas, & Hogness, 1986). That is, the red cone family contains three pigments with peak sensitivities of 555, 561, and 565 mμ. The green cone family may have two types of pigment, one sensitive to 528–529 mμ and another sensitive to 533–534 mμ. In fact, although people have just one "blue" and one "red" gene, nearly everyone may have two "green" genes, each coding for a slightly different green-sensitive pigment. Too few blue cones were found to be certain of the results. Figure 7-31 shows that red and green cones are most concentrated in the center of the fovea (at 0° eccentricity) and blue cones are most concentrated at the edges of the fovea (at about 1.5° eccentricity).

Together, these two figures explain several aspects of our visual experiences. First, we are less sensitive to blue light than to any other wavelength. Not only is the blue pigment less absolutely sensitive to light than are the other two pigments but we have fewer blue cones than we do red and green cones.

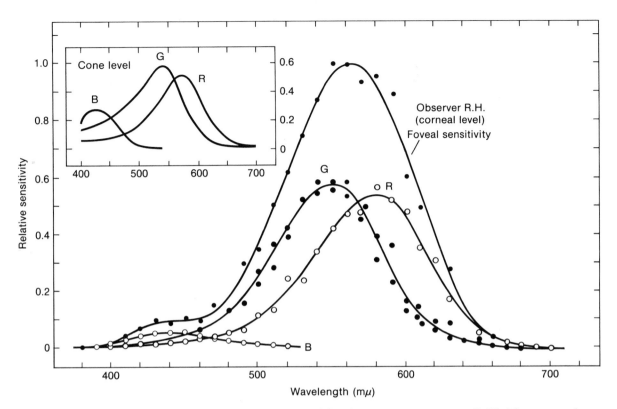

Figure 7-30 Sensitivities of the individual cones, compared to total foveal sensitivity, in one person (R.H.). The main graph shows measurements at the level of the cornea; the inset shows the corresponding curves measured at the level of the cones. This is a particularly blue-sensitive observer; the average observer is only about one-third as sensitive to blue.

Add this fact to that of the greater absorption of blue light by the ocular media, and it explains why blue can never appear as bright to us as do red and green.

Second, mixtures of red, blue, and green light can reproduce all the other colors in the visual spectrum. (The red cone, although maximally sensitive to yellow light, is still more sensitive to red light than is any other cone type.) Since all that we ever see is mixtures of the outputs of red, blue, and green cones, mixtures of those three lights can reproduce all our other spectral color sensations.

Nontrichromatic color perceptions. However, not all species are trichromatic. Some turtles may have five types of cones, making them **pentachromats** (Daw, 1973). Hummingbirds and goldfish can see near-ultraviolet wavelengths (Goldsmith, 1980; Neumeyer, 1985). We primate trichromats have no idea, of course, what color ultraviolet light is. Thus, these organisms live in a world that possesses "a richness that lies beyond our ken" (Goldsmith, 1980, p. 788).

The richness of birds' and reptiles' color perceptions compared to ours probably means that our primate color vision is a recent evolutionary development. Early mammals were largely nocturnal (active only at night), and color vision—being useless for them—degenerated. When our ancestors once more became diurnal (active during the day), color vision reevolved, but incompletely. Thus, our poorer color perceptions, compared with birds', reflects a retina less highly evolved for daytime living.

Some people have defective color vision. For example, **monochromats** can see only black, white, and shades of gray. They may have only rods, or rods and one defective type of cone (containing rhodopsin) (Alpern, Falls, & Lee, 1960). Other individuals have two normal and at least one defective pigment. The abnormal pigment does not absorb the wavelength appropriate for that cone. These individuals are **anomalous trichromats.**

Color-blind dichromats may totally lack one pigment (Nathans et al., 1986; Rushton, 1972, 1975; Wald, 1964,

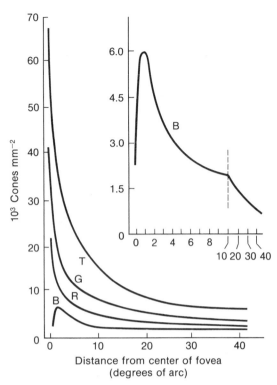

Figure 7-31   The estimated densities of red (R), green (G), and blue (B) cones vary systematically across the retina. The total (T) cone density at each retinal location is also indicated. The inset is an enlarged view of blue cone densities; the dashed line indicates a change of scale on its abscissa.

1965). **Protanopes** lack the red cone pigment, and **deuteranopes** lack the green cone pigment. Both abnormalities are caused by recessive X-linked genes (many more men than women have these defects). A third type of color blindness is coded by an autosomal gene: **tritanopes** may lack the pigment normally found in blue cones. Alternatively, dichromats may have three pigments, but one would be defective. If so, the defective pigments may be the same ones that the anomalous trichromats have. But in color blindness, the defective pigment would be even less sensitive to light than in the anomalous trichromats (Frome, Piantanida, & Kelly, 1982).

What colors these people see is determined by what pigments they have. All the spectral colors that dichromats are capable of perceiving can be reproduced by mixing only two wavelengths of light — which isn't surprising, since they have only two types of pigments. Both protanopes and deuteranopes are unable to distinguish red from green light and so are red–green blind. The protanope differs from the deuteran-ope, however, in being considerably less sensitive to long-wavelength (red) lights. Although the deuteranope doesn't perceive long-wavelength lights as being red, he or she can detect them. The protanope, lacking the red pigment, cannot see red lights at all unless they are very bright. The tritanope is blue–yellow blind, being unable to distinguish between those two wavelengths. Monochromats are totally color blind: all their receptors contain the same pigment and thus cannot respond differentially to different wavelengths.

Opponent color coding.   Bipolars, ganglion cells, and geniculate cells apparently share similar coding mechanisms. According to Gouras and Zrenner (1981), 59% of retinal ganglion cells show at least some color opponency (35% do not and 4% of the cells were unclassifiable). Thus, 59% are hyperpolarized by one wavelength and depolarized by another wavelength. These same cells also have an opponent, center-surround receptive field. The center and surround usually have different color sensitivities. A **red on-center, green off-surround** cell is excited by red light on the center of its receptive field and is inhibited by green light (an annulus) on its surround.

These cells are classified by their color opponency and receptive field characteristics. There are red and green types of on-center cells (with green and red off-surrounds, respectively). There are also red and green off-center cells (with green and red on-surrounds). **Blue on-center, yellow off-surround** types of cells are found, but there are no blue off-center cells.

Opponent cells may combine two codes for color. Color is place coded by whether the firing rate of a red–green or a blue–yellow cell was changed by the stimulation. An opponent type of pattern code occurs when the same cell has a different kind of response to increases and decreases in wavelength. The red–green system receives opponent inputs from red and green cones, whereas the blue–yellow system may receive input from blue cones, on the one hand, and, on the other, from both green and red cones combined for the opponent yellow input. The opponent-surround response for various ganglion cells may be mediated either by horizontal cells or by amacrines (Gouras & Zrenner, 1981).

A theory of color vision and color blindness.   The place and pattern coding of color can explain color perceptions. For example, a protanope sees all wavelengths above about 493 mμ as being yellow and all wavelengths below that point as being blue (Wald, 1964). Wavelengths in the region of 493 mμ are perceived as white, gray, or black, depending on luminous intensity. A deuteranope has similar color experiences, except that his or her gray range is around 497 mμ. A tritanope, who sees red and green normally, perceives both yellow and blue wavelengths as being colorless.

Suppose these people have normal numbers of cones, normally connected to opponent ganglion cells, but one of their cone types contains an abnormal pigment. The pigment may be relatively normal in sensitivity but abnormal in wavelength absorption: the red cone in the protanope may contain the green pigment. Or the pigment may be very insensitive, as well as having abnormal wavelength absorbency (see, for example, Frome, Piantanida, & Kelly, 1982). But recent data suggest that the red cone in the protanope may have green pigment, the green cone in the deuteranope may have red pigment, and the blue cone in the tritanope may have green or red pigment (or both) (Nathans et al., 1986; Nathans, Thomas, & Hogness, 1986). How would their opponent ganglion cells respond?

For the protanope and deuteranope, the red–green opponent system is disabled or inoperative. A red on-center, green off-surround ganglion cell would never be differentially excited by different wavelengths. Both green and red lights would have exactly the same effects on the red excitatory and the green inhibitory input—since both inputs come from cones containing the same pigment. The protanope and deuteranope can see blue and yellow colors normally, since the blue–yellow opponent system would still be functioning.

One difference between protanopes and deuteranopes would be the point on the spectrum perceived as being colorless. This point represents the place at which the remaining two pigments are equally sensitive to that wavelength, producing a white, gray, or black sensation. At this point, all the cones will be equally stimulated, and he or she will see colorless light—just as normal trichromats do when all their cones are equally stimulated.

The tritanope's blue–yellow opponent system is inoperative. If the blue process comes from cones containing the same pigment(s) as does the yellow process, blue–yellow opponent ganglion cells will never be able to respond differentially to different wavelengths. Thus, the tritanope will see red and green, and his or her gray region on the spectrum will correspond to the wavelength to which the green and red pigments are equally sensitive.

This model can explain "color blindness" in the normal trichromat. Any wavelengths that have equivalent effects on any opponent system cannot be distinguished. Since yellow light and equal amounts of green plus red light have equivalent effects on both the red–green and the blue–yellow opponent systems, trichromats cannot distinguish between those two visual experiences. Trichromats are "blind" to reddish green.

Similarly, trichromats are "blind" to yellowish blue, since they can't distinguish that combination from green light. The combination of any pair of opponently coded colors cannot be perceived. Although this model might not be correct, it is important that you understand the implications for color perception of a combined place-pattern code for wavelength.

To test yourself, try to imagine what the visual experiences of the following imaginary organism might be like (maybe it is a visitor from Andromeda). It has four kinds of cones in its retina, and the opponent coding is red–blue and green–yellow. How many colors would have to be mixed to reproduce its visual spectrum? What colors could it see that we can't—and vice versa? One possible answer appears later.

Summary of Subcortical Coding

Intensity coding uses receptor potential size and rate of activity in certain cells (brightness cells?) at higher levels. Coding of spatial location is affected by lateral inhibition and by the inverse relationship between retinal acuity and sensitivity. Place codes are used for spatial location, and lateral inhibition sharpens the coding. Wavelength coding uses a place code at the receptor level, since the three types of cones in humans are maximally sensitive to different wavelengths. From bipolars on, wavelength coding is opponent, a combination of place and pattern. One set of cells responds in one way to green and another way to red light, and another set of cells is excited by blue and inhibited by yellow. Because of these coding mechanisms, we perceive Mach bands as being real, and we perceive reddish green light to be the same as yellow light.

Cortical Coding Mechanisms and Feature Detectors

Wiesel and Hubel's research on cortical coding mechanisms won them the Nobel Prize in 1981. The idea of feature detectors implied that somehow a cell or small set of cells can signal the presence of a certain stimulus feature and create conscious awareness. Hubel and Wiesel also discovered both the columnar and the **laminar** (layered) organizations of the visual cortex, as illustrated in Figure 7-32. Cells in different cortical layers not only often have different receptive field characteristics but also have different shapes and different axonal projections. For example, cells in layers II and III project to other areas of the cortex. Although we will use Hubel and Wiesel's

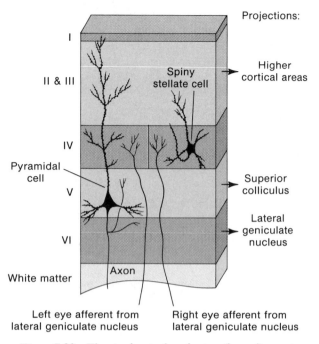

Projections:

Higher cortical areas

Superior colliculus

Lateral geniculate nucleus

Figure 7-32 The visual cortex has a laminar (layered) organization. Visual afferents go to, and cortical efferents come from, certain specific layers.

ideas to organize the data on receptive field characteristics of cortical cells, we will also present other ideas, with other implications. But regardless of whose ideas about coding eventually prove to be true, it is clear that different populations of cortical cells are devoted to processing different kinds of visual information.

Receptive Field Characteristics

Table 7-2 is one way of classifying characteristics of cortical receptive fields. Some words of caution are in order. First, the classification comes largely from Hubel and Wiesel (Hubel, 1982; Hubel & Wiesel, 1959, 1962, 1965, 1974a, 1974b, 1977; Hubel, Wiesel, & Stryker, 1977). This classification is widely used in research on the cat and monkey visual cortex, but it has not gone without challenge (see, for example, Henry, 1977). De Valois and De Valois (1980), for instance, have suggested that the visual system may not code information in this way; we will describe their research shortly.

Therefore, this table of receptive-field characteristics should be read as a theory instead of as a list of known properties. Rowe and Stone's discussion (1977) of the "naming of neurones" is as pertinent to classifying characteristics of cortical receptive fields as it is to the X-, Y-, and W-cell classification system. Rowe and Stone suggested that a classification should be based on as many features of a cell as possible and the result should be used only as a hypothesis, to be tested and refined (or discarded) by future research. Cells have multiple

Table 7-2 Receptive fields of primate cortical cells.

Receptive Field Type	Color Response	Binocularity	Sensitivity (Direction and Speed)	Location	
				Retina	Cortex
Uniform	Some chromatically tuned Some chromatically opponent Some luminosity	Mostly monocular (70%)	Slow speed	More in fovea	17, IVc
Center-surround	Some chromatically opponent Some double-opponent Some luminosity	All(?) monocular		More in fovea	17, IVc
Simple	Some chromatically opponent Some double opponent No luminosity	Mostly monocular (51%–80%)	Slower speeds at right angles to orientation	More outside	17, 18, IVb, VI?
Hypercomplex I (simple end-stoppered)	Mostly luminosity Some chromatically tuned	Many binocular	Only few respond to stationary line	Mostly outside fovea	17, 18, 19, all layers except I and IV
Hypercomplex II (complex end-stoppered)	Mostly luminosity Some chromatically tuned		Only few respond to to stationary line	Mostly outside fovea	17, 18, 19, all layers except I and IV

response characteristics and should *not* be defined by only one (Finlay, Schiller, & Volman, 1976; Pribram, Lassonde, & Ptito, 1981).

Center-surround and uniform receptive fields. Some cortical cells have receptive-field characteristics similar to those of ganglion and geniculate cells (Dow & Gouras, 1973; Michael, 1978a; Poggio, Baker, Mansfield, Sillito, & Grigg, 1975). Some cortical cells are spatially opponent with **center-surround** types of receptive fields. However, some are not spatially opponent, having **uniform** receptive fields. These two types of cells are found only in the primate and not in the cat cortex, and even in the primate cortex they seem to be limited to layer IV of Visual Area I. Since this layer contains the cells on which most of the geniculate axons terminate, it is not surprising that their receptive-field characteristics are so similar to those of the axons from which they receive their input.

Simple cells. The receptive fields of center-surround and **simple** cells are illustrated in Figure 7-33. Figure 7-34 presents Hubel and Wiesel's idea that axons from center-surround cells project to simple cells to create their receptive-field characteristics. The receptive fields of simple cells can be mapped with small spots of light and have distinct excitatory and inhibitory regions. A stimulus covering all of the excitatory but none of the inhibitory region will most strongly excite such a cell. One spot of light in an excitatory region would not be enough to elicit a response. Consequently, these cells are most strongly excited by bars and by edges, *provided* that the bar or edge has a certain orientation (such as horizontal, vertical, or oblique) *and* that the edge is located in a particular part of the retina (or in a particular part of the visual field). Although simple cells will respond to moving edges (if the movement is at right angles of the orientation of their edges), they respond best to stationary edges. Simple cells are sometimes called **edge detectors.**

Complex cells. As Figure 7-35 illustrates, the receptive fields of **complex** cells cannot be mapped with spots of light. They do not have discrete excitatory and inhibitory regions. Instead, complex cells respond best to moving bars and edges, provided that the bar or edge has a certain orientation and the movement is in a certain direction (usually at right angles to the edge orientation). Complex cells don't respond well to stationary edges or bars.

Hypercomplex cells? Figure 7-36 illustrates how the receptive-field properties of **hypercomplex I** cells might differ

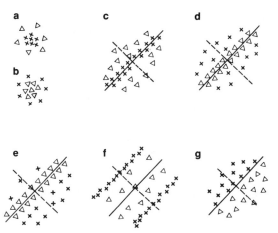

Figure 7-33 Common arrangements of lateral geniculate (a and b) and cortical (c–g) receptive fields. **a.** On-center receptive field. **b.** Off-center receptive field. **c–g.** Cortical receptive fields whose axes are shown by continuous lines through the centers of the fields; in the figure, these axes are all oblique, but these axes do occur in all orientations. $\triangle$ = areas giving inhibitory or off-responses; X = areas giving excitatory or on-responses.

from those of simple and complex cells. Hypercomplex cells may be **end-stoppered:** the length as well as the orientation and movement of the edge may be important. Edges that are "too long" produce inhibition, decreasing or eliminating the response. **Hypercomplex II** cells may respond to either of two different orientations or edges, 90° apart.

Whether hypercomplex cell types exist is being debated. Hubel and Wiesel (for example, Hubel, 1982) talk about their being special types of simple and complex cells, as do Henry (1977) and Rose (1974). What was called *hypercomplex I and II cells* are now called *end-stoppered simple and complex cells.* But Michael (1979) has found evidence that the hypercomplex cells in monkey cortex are *not* simply end-stoppered complex or simple cells. Michael showed that the inhibitory regions are also sensitive to edge orientation. Maximal inhibition is produced by lines in the inhibitory area having the same orientation as do the moving lines that maximally excite the cell when they are in the center of its receptive field.

Orientation columns. As Figure 7-37 illustrates, if an electrode records from successively encountered cells as it descends perpendicularly to the surface, simple and complex cells in all the layers tend to respond to edges and bars that have the same orientation and that occupy the same part of the

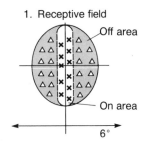

1. Receptive field

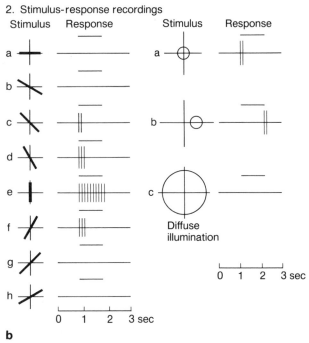

2. Stimulus-response recordings

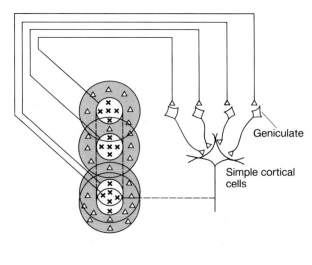

B

Geniculate

Simple cortical cells

Figure 7-34 One model of a receptive field of a simple cell in Visual Area I. **a.** A receptive field (1) and a series of recordings of that cell's responses to various visual stimuli (2). In contrast to a vertical bar, a small spot in the receptive field center produces only a weak response (record a). A small spot in the inhibitory "flanks" or off areas (record b) produces a weak inhibitory response. Diffuse light (record c) is ineffective. **b.** Hubel and Wiesel's model. A simple neuron receives excitatory connections from four or more cells in the lateral geniculate that have similar center-surround organizations and similar receptive-field locations, only slightly displaced along a vertical line. Thus, the cortical cell has an elongated on region that can be maximally stimulated by a bar of light. Δ = areas giving inhibitory or off-responses; X = areas giving excitatory or on-responses.

visual field. If the electrode penetrates the cortex obliquely, successively deeper cells tend to have slightly different orientations.

Hubel and Wiesel proposed that cells are organized into columns according to their orientation selectivities. All cells within a column have similar orientation selectivities; adjacent columns have slightly different orientation selectivities. A set of columns contains all possible orientations for a given area of the retina. This set of columns is **hypercolumn,** or **cortical module.** Adjacent hypercolumns analyze for all possible edge

orientations in adjacent retinal areas. Thus, the retina is mapped onto the cortex by a series of hypercolumns. The average receptive-field size of cells in a hypercolumn increases with the distance of their receptive fields from the fovea.

Researchers can explore cortical organization by distinguishing active from less active cells. One way to do this is to use **2-[^{14}C]deoxy-D-glucose (2-DG).** The 2-DG compound is a radioactively labeled glucose analog; once absorbed into brain cells, it cannot be metabolized. Because of its glucose, the 2-DG is assumed to be taken up or absorbed by brain cells

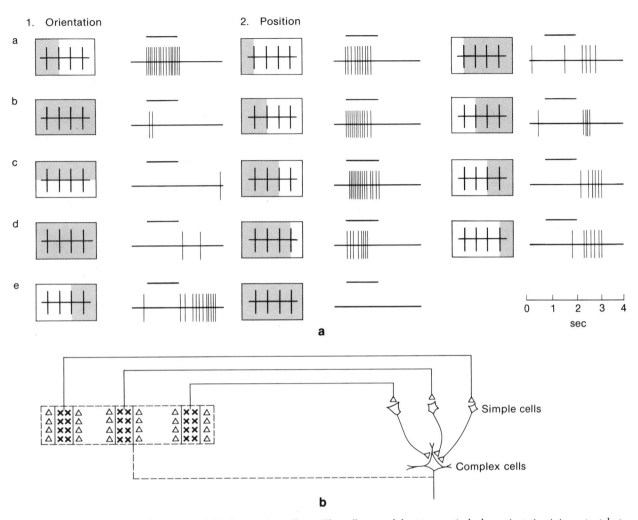

Figure 7-35 One model of a receptive field of a complex cell. **a.** The cell responds best to a vertical edge; orientation is important, but position within the field is not critical. 1. Orientation: with light on the left and dark on the right (record a), there is an on-response; with light on the right (record e), there is an off-response. 2. Position: The position of the edge in the field is also relevant, and illuminating the entire receptive field (record e) produces no response. The timing of the stimulus is indicated by a bar above the records. **b.** Hubel and Wiesel's model. A complex cell receives excitatory connections from several simple cortical cells with a vertical axis of orientation, a central excitatory zone, and two flanking inhibitory zones; they would also have retinal locations slightly displaced from each other along a horizontal line in the retina. △ = areas giving inhibitory or off-responses; X = areas giving excitatory or on-responses.

in direct proportion to their degree of activity. Thus, more active cells become more radioactively labeled. Alternatively, a researcher could selectively stain for a particular enzyme: **cytochrome oxidase.** The more active cells are, the more of this enzyme they have.

An animal is injected with 2-DG just before an experiment starts. Then it is anesthetized and a particular visual pattern is presented to one or both eyes. Finally the animal is given a drug overdose and its brain sectioned. The sections are exam-

ined for patterns of radioactivity. As Figure 7-38 illustrates, a pattern projected onto the retina is reproduced in the pattern of radioactivity found in layer IV of Visual Area I.

The 2-DG method was also used to visualize orientation columns (Hubel, Wiesel, & Stryker, 1977). Anesthetized monkeys were injected with 2-DG and then had their retinas stimulated with moving lines, all having the same orientation. Thus, if the moving lines were all vertical, vertical edge detectors would be more active and would become more radioac-

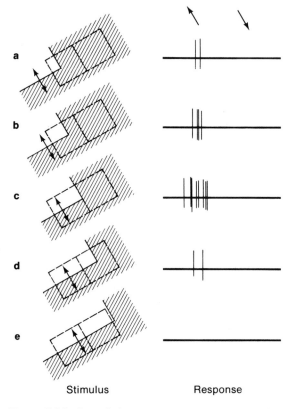

Figure 7-36 Records from a possible hypercomplex cell in Visual Area II. The stimulus was an edge oriented at 2:00, with dark below, terminated on the right by a second edge intersecting the first at 90°. **a–c.** What happens with up-and-down movement across varying portions of the cell's receptive field. **d–e.** What happens when the stimulus is moved across all of the receptive field and varying parts of the cell's antagonistic surround. Each record sweep lasted two seconds.

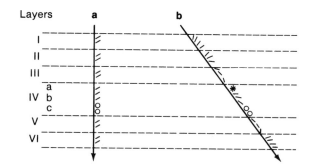

Figure 7-37 Schematic illustration of orientation columns in monkey cortex. **a.** An electrode tract (the arrows) made perpendicular to the surface will encounter simple, complex, and hypercomplex cells, all with the same preferred edge orientation. **b.** Oblique electrode tracts will, at different depths, encounter cells with different preferred orientations, and the preferred orientations will sometimes change in a very regular fashion (except for the break at *), suggesting that the oblique tract is paralleling a hypercolumn. The only exception occurs in layer IVc, where uniform and center-surround receptive fields are found.

tively labeled than any other kind of edge detector. Figure 7-39 presents some of the results. In Figure 7-39a, the brain was sectioned perpendicularly to the surface, and horizontal columns appeared. Figure 7-39b presents a brain section taken parallel to the surface, where the columns for vertical edge detectors appear as spots and stripes.

Ocular dominance columns. **Ocular dominance** is also organized into columns. "Ocular dominance" describes the degree to which cells are influenced by one eye more than by the other. Ocular dominance varies considerably from one cell to the next (except that all cells in layer IV may be monocular). Some **binocular** cells are nearly equally sensitive to input

from both eyes. Other cells are more **monocular,** being much more sensitive to input from either the left or the right eye. Cells within a column are usually dominated by only one eye, and so these cells form an **ocular dominance column.** Severing the corpus callosum greatly reduces some kinds of binocular interactions among cortical cells, at least in cats (Harvey, 1980; Payne, Elberger, Berman, & Murphy, 1980).

Ocular dominance columns can be made visible by staining for cytochrome oxidase. Suppose that visual stimulation is limited to only one eye, but that eye is stimulated with all orientations. Then a series of either left or right ocular dominance columns will appear in a section cut perpendicular to the surface of the cortex. When the brain is sliced in the coronal plane (see Figure 2-9 and Figure 7-40b), the columns appear as stripes. Thus, the visual cortex has both orientation and ocular dominance columns. Hubel and Wiesel suggested that the stripes of orientation columns are perpendicular to the ocular dominance columns. A right-eye-dominant orientation hypercolumn would be adjacent to a left-eye-dominant orientation hypercolumn.

Some spots of cortex (as seen on the surface after a 2-DG injection) are more active than the rest of the cortex, regardless of which eye is stimulated or what kind of line stimulus is used. These areas are **blobs.** The cytochrome oxidase measuring technique confirms that blobs are more metabolically active than the rest of the cortex. Blob cells might have center-

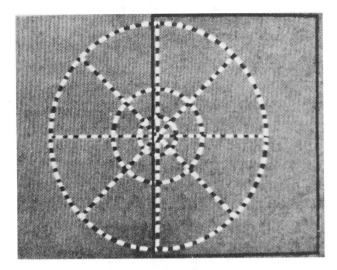

a

b

Figure 7-38 The visual field is mapped onto the cortex. **a.** One of the visual stimuli used in the experiment. **b.** Pattern of activation on the visual cortex produced by that stimulus, as revealed by the 2-DG method. This is the pattern of radioactivity from a single flat-mounted section of brain tissue, mostly from layers 4b and 4c. The blackened segments correspond to portions of ocular dominance strips, since only one eye was stimulated. About half of the total surface area of the primate Visual Area I can be seen.

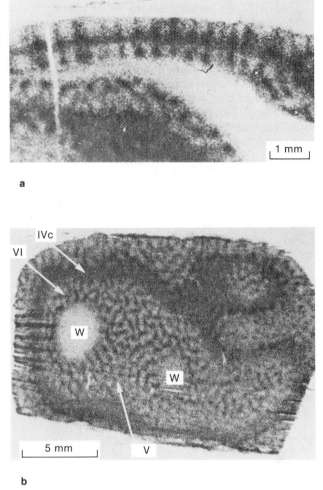

a

b

Figure 7-39 **a.** Pattern of radioactive label from the 2-DG method in monkey Visual Area I. The brain slice was taken perpendicular to the surface, and the dark areas are the areas of radioactive label or high cellular activity. The monkey was stimulated with moving vertical, irregularly spaced white stripes presented across the whole visual field to both eyes for 45 minutes. The labeled regions or columns extend through the full thickness of the cortex. Layer IVc, located at mid-depth, is uniformly labeled because there are no orientation-specific cells there. **b.** Tangential section from the same area, same type of experiment. The section grazes white matter (W) in two places; surrounding these are the densely labeled orientation columns of layer VI. Layer V is lightly labeled, and layer IVc is uniformly labeled, with no columns. (The dense bands at the extreme left are artifacts.)

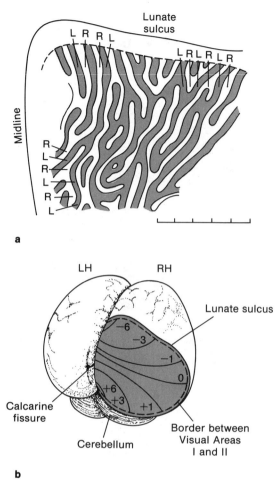

a

b

Figure 7-40   a. Reconstruction of the banding pattern made by ocular dominance columns, indicating the eye preference of columns. The left-eye (contralateral) ocular dominance columns have been shaded, and the dashed line is the border between Visual Areas I and II (see Figure 7-12). **b.** Anatomy of this primate visual cortex, for reference. The horizontal meridian (O) and the horizontal lines 1, 3, and 6 degrees above (+) and below (−) the meridian are shown. LH = left hemisphere; RH = right hemisphere.

surround or uniform receptive fields and may all be chromatically opponent (Hubel & Livingstone, 1981, 1982; Humphrey & Hendrickson, 1983; Horton & Hubel, 1981). **Interblob** cells are orientation sensitive, but not many are chromatically opponent. Visual Area I blobs are connected to metabolically active stripes in Visual Area II. Conversely, the interblob regions of Area I are connected to interstripe areas of Area II (Livingstone & Hubel, 1983).

Spatial Frequency Detectors

Cortical cells may respond to particular spatial frequencies as well as to (or instead of) bar orientations (Campbell & Robson, 1968; De Valois & De Valois, 1980; Enroth-Cugell & Robson, 1966; Schiller, Finlay, & Volman, 1976a, 1976b, 1976c, & 1976d; Finlay, Schiller, & Volman, 1976; Sherman & Spear, 1982). In other words, cells are assumed to encode the visual world in terms of patterns of dark and bright bands, as illustrated in Figure 7-1. The visual system may perform Fourier analyses on the spatial frequencies found in visual patterns. As described in Chapter 6, the ear does a Fourier analysis on any sound, breaking complex sounds down into their sine-wave components.

Fourier analyses in the visual system.   In the visual system, sine waves vary in amplitude across distance instead of across time. Figure 7-1 may represent the basic unit for vision just as a pure tone represents an auditory unit. Within its visual field, each cell would be maximally sensitive to a certain spatial frequency and to a certain orientation of that frequency. Figure 7-41 illustrates a Fourier analysis of one complex visual waveform. The amplitude of a visual spatial frequency is the difference between the most and least luminous parts of the sine wave, divided by the average luminance of the wave. If the amplitude is equal to 1, the **contrast** is maximal. Visual contrast is thus analogous to sound-wave amplitude. The **frequency** of a visual pattern is the inverse of the retinal distance taken up by one full cycle of the sine wave. The **frequency spectra** describe the contrasts present in each one of the sine-wave frequency components of the complex pattern.

Evidence for spatial frequency filters.   One way of testing for spatial frequency analyses (the cells doing such analyses are called **filters**) is to compare responses to bars and to sine-wave gratings. If cells are bar detectors, both cells and psychophysical responses should be more sensitive to variations in bar dimensions than to variations in sine waves.

Some cortical cells may be filters. Researchers have found some neurons in the visual cortex of both cat and monkey that are more selective for spatial frequencies than for bar width (Albrecht, De Valois, & Thorell, 1980). That is, both the optimal bar width and the optimal spatial frequency for each cell were determined. Responses decreased more markedly with changes from the optimal frequency than with changes in bar width. When the responses of human psychophysical observers were tested, again subjects were found to be more sensitive (having a lower absolute threshold) to sine waves than to bars (Watson, Barlow, & Robson, 1983). Furthermore, organisms injected with 2-DG were exposed to various spatial

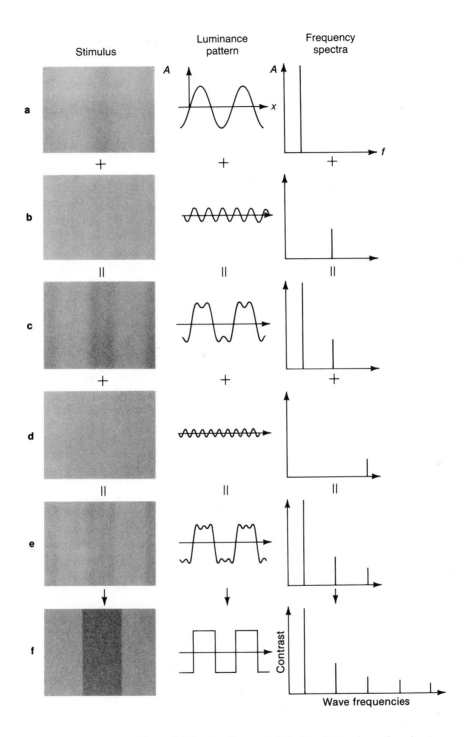

Figure 7-41 Fourier analyses can be done on visual stimuli. The stimuli are to the left; the middle column shows luminance varying over spatial position in the form of sine waves; the right column has the corresponding frequency spectra (see text). **a.** A single sine wave. **b.** A wave with 3× the frequency. **c.** The sum of a + b. **d.** A sine at 5× the frequency. **e.** The sum of c + d. **f.** From adding waves at 7, 9, and 11× first frequency.

frequencies and then their brains were examined (Tootell, Silverman, & De Valois, 1981). Spatial frequency columns were clearly visible on the surface of the occipital cortex.

The eye can also be exposed to complex patterns (such as plaids). The experimenter can then analyze to which aspects of those patterns the cells respond (De Valois, De Valois, & Yund, 1979). Cells responded more to the Fourier components than to the edges of plaid and checkerboard patterns.

Orientation analyses versus spatial frequency filters.
Both orientation and spatial frequency analyses can be studied in the same nerve cells (Pribram, Lassonde, & Ptito, 1981; Schiller, Finlay, & Yolman, 1976c). Simple cells were found to be slightly more selective for spatial frequencies (more sharply tuned) than were complex cells. However, some cells changed their responding when the orientation of an edge or bar was changed. The same cells had *no* detectable change in response when the spatial frequencies of a sine-wave stimulus in their preferred orientation were changed.

Separate populations of cells may carry out orientation and spatial frequency analyses. Spatial frequency columns may intersect in an orderly fashion with orientation columns (Tootell, Silverman, & De Valois, 1981). Edge detectors may be used for in-focus foveal vision, whereas spatial frequency analyzers may code stimuli with blurred, out-of-focus edges. Thus, even stimuli out of focus would provide spatial information to the brain.

Binocularity and Perception in Three-Dimensional Space

We live in a three-dimensional world and we have phenomenological experiences of depth known as **stereoscopic vision.** An illusion of three-dimensional space can be created by presenting a stimulus to both left and right eyes (with a device called a **stereoscope**). The stimulus presented to one eye is displaced sideways in relation to its position in the other eye, causing the same features of the stimulus to activate slightly different (though adjacent) locations in the left and right retinas. When present, this **retinal** or **binocular disparity** creates **stereoscopic depth perception.**

Stereoscopic displacement causes a uniform perception — one involving a phenomenological sensation of three dimensions — instead of two different, competing images. This effect has to mean that the information from those left and right retinal cells in adjacent retinal locations eventually converges on the *same* central cell. In the primate, the convergence occurs only at the cortical level. Convergence is par-

tially under genetic control; people in a few families do not see a three-dimensional world in a stereoscope.

Furthermore, although having both a left and a right visual cortex may be sufficient for stereoscopic depth perception, it is not necessary — at least in cats. Given special treatment after surgery (amphetamine injections and visual experiences; see Chapter 12), cats can display depth perception even after bilateral visual cortical lesions (Feeney & Hovda, 1985; Hovda & Feeney, 1985; Hovda, Sutton, & Feeney, 1985). However, this may not be true for primates; for example, total visual cortical lesions destroy a primate's capacity for form vision, but a cat subjected to those lesions can still perform visual pattern discriminations (Sherman, 1985).

Binocular disparity detectors.   Visual Area II (or area 18: see Figure 7-12) may have cells specialized to detect degree of binocular disparity (Hubel and Wiesel, 1970; Tootell, Silverman, De Valois, & Jacobs, 1983). The middle temporal visual area of monkeys might have similar neurons (Maunsell & Van Essen, 1983). Different cells respond to various degrees of displacement of the pattern projected to the left and right eyes, something that normally occurs when objects lie either in front of or behind an object on which we are focusing. Retinal disparity might help us focus and might also cause our phenomenological experience of the world to be three-dimensional.

Stereoscopic movement.   Some cells respond to movement in three-dimensional space (Cynader & Regan, 1978). In Visual Area II of the cat, cells are narrowly tuned for movement in space. Some cells respond only on the movement of objects that would hit or narrowly miss the head. Other cells respond best to objects moving across the visual field at a certain distance from where the animal is focusing. These cells are organized into clusters (columns?).

Color Coding

Table 7-2 summarizes information about cortical color-coding mechanisms. The center-surround and uniform receptive field types of cortical cells might specialize in color analyses; their responses would convey less ambiguous information about color. Responses of simple and complex cells vary not only with wavelength but also with the spatial characteristics of the stimulus (orientation, direction of movement, spatial frequency).

Michael (1981) discovered that color cells in primate Area I are columnarly organized. All the chromatically sensitive cells in a column respond to the same color. The simple and complex cells in one column, for example, have excitatory input from red cones and inhibitory input from green cones in the centers of their receptive fields. The hypercomplex cells in that same column are spectrally tuned, responding more to green edges than to edges of any other wavelength. Other columns lack color sensitivity. Michael may have recorded from color-sensitive cells in blobs (the intensely active cortical columns), which seem to be specialized for color processing (Horton & Hedley-Whyte, 1984; Hubel & Livingstone, 1983). Blobs are larger in humans than in other primates, and blob cells may be directly connected to geniculate cells.

Zeki (1980, 1983) recorded the color responses of cells in the **lunate sulcus** (anterior to primary visual areas: see Figure 7-40). Some of his results are presented in Figure 7-42. He found some very unusual cells. One was excited by blue and inhibited by red, another was excited by green and inhibited by purple, and a third was excited by red and inhibited by blue. All these cells were in one column. Many cells were narrowly tuned; they had narrow **action spectra),** responding to only a few wavelengths. The histogram shows that many different kinds of color cells were found. These cells also show **color constancy:** their responses to an object of a given color

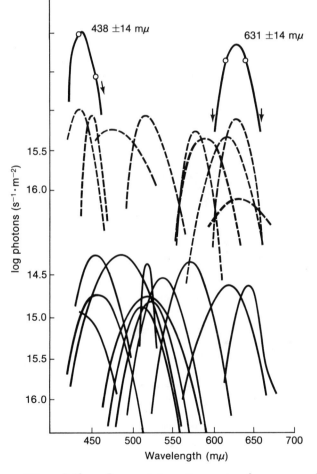

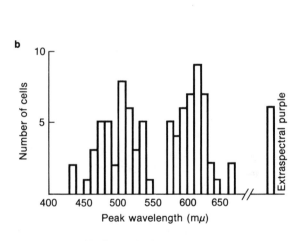

Figure 7-42   a. Representative action spectra of some narrow-band cells in primate Visual Area IV (outside 17, 18, and 19). Action spectra come from measuring the threshold intensity of every wavelength to which the cell responds. In the upper two spectra, arrows indicate that there was no response to those wavelengths. The discontinuous lines are from cells inhibited and the continuous lines from cells excited by light.   **b.** Histogram of this distribution of types of action spectra. Even purple-sensitive cells were found (purple is not in the spectrum)!

change only slightly when the color of the light source is changed.

Zeki (1983) duplicated some of Land's perceptual conditions (1974), which involved a complex array of multicolored rectangles. For example, a red square was placed in the center of the receptive field of a cortical cell and the whole display of different-colored rectangles was illuminated by a red light. The red square was perceived by a human observer as being a "washed-out" red. Then blue and green light were added to the display, and that red square was now perceived as a vivid red. A red-sensitive cell from Visual Area I responded to the first stimulus but not to the second; a color-coding red cell from the lunate sulcus did not respond to the first stimulus but responded vigorously to the second. Thus these responses corresponded closely to the consciously perceived colors. For these cells, just as in our perceptions, an apple remains "red" when seen under either bluish or yellowish light. These cells may receive input from many different Area I cells, with varying proportions of excitatory and inhibitory interconnections causing the great selectivity for wavelength. Cells with color constancy may be color feature detectors.

Some Higher-Level Feature Detectors

Place cells in the hippocampus. Some hippocampal cells —perhaps nearly 55%—respond only to complex features of a particular place in space (McNaughton, Barnes, & O'Keefe, 1983; O'Keefe, 1979). They respond to many different kinds of sensory input, but they seem to be most sensitive to visual inputs. "A place cell is a cell which constructs the notion of a place in an environment by connecting together several multi-sensory inputs, each of which can be perceived when the animal is in a particular part of an environment" (O'Keefe, 1979, p. 425).

As Figure 7-43 shows, one cell responded most vigorously when the animal's head was in a given part—or place in space—on that elevated maze. Other hippocampal cells responded when the animal's head was in other locations in the

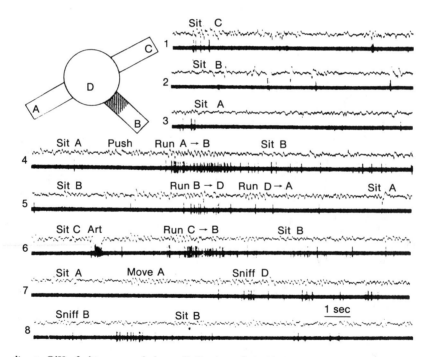

Figure 7-43 According to O'Keefe, hippocampal place cells fire (records 1–8) whenever the animal is occupying a given location in a maze (the ABCD structure, viewed from above). The rat in this experiment had been made hungry and thirsty, and he had been trained to run to a small porcelain dish wherever it was placed on this maze. The maze was elevated off the floor and had no walls so as to maximize the amount of spatial information present. The bottom trace in each record indicates when each cell responded; in these records there may be two cells that are responding to the same location in the maze. The top trace is the slow-wave activity recorded from the microelectrode. The area shaded in the maze marks where the rat's head was during maximal firing of this cell or cells. The behavior described at the beginning of each record continues throughout that record. ART: artifact caused by vigorous headshake; in 7 and 8, the part of the maze labeled B had been removed and an arm novel to the rat had been put in its place.

maze. Some cells responded specifically when the animal was in that maze and did not find what it expected to (the dish with food or water in it had been removed). O'Keefe calls these **"misplace"** cells. And many cells responded to more than one set of place cues.

Research with human subjects. Stimulating various areas in the human visual system reveals some complex coding properties of groups of cells. Some of the most systematic work was done by Penfield (1947). He stimulated sensory cortex in humans undergoing brain surgery for epilepsy. Stimulations of visual cortex produced sensations of flashing, dancing, colored lights. However, these types of sensation may be possible only from brains altered by brain damage and frequent epileptic seizures.

Brindley and Lewin (1968) placed small, gross electrodes on the occipital cortex of a blind woman to provide the data needed for a visual prosthesis. Stimulation through a single electrode usually caused a sensation of a tiny spot of white light at a certain visual field position, but sometimes several spots or even a "cloud" were seen. The small spots are **phosphenes.** Increasing the intensity of the stimulating current increased the perceived brightness of the phosphenes. No colors and no complex sensations were evoked, although they can be evoked by optic tract stimulation (Tasker, Organ, & Hawrylyshyn, 1980).

Receptive fields of human cells have also been mapped (Marg, 1973; Marg, Adams, & Rutkin, 1968; Wilson, Babb, Halgren, & Crandall, 1983). The cells mapped were probably in Visual Areas I, II, and III. Circular, simple, and complex types of receptive field were found. The human cells were sensitive to movement but, unlike those of the monkey, were not sensitive to the direction or rate of movement.

Temporal cortex. The primate temporal cortex does some complex visual coding and projects the results to areas in the limbic system. Some temporal cells respond to hands or respond only if the stimulus is three dimensional (Gross, Rocha-Miranda, & Bender, 1972). In monkeys, some temporal cells respond to facial types of stimulus (Perrett, Rolls, & Caan, 1982; Perrett, Smith, Potter, Mistlin, Head, Milner, & Jeeves, 1984, 1985). In the experiments of Perrett and associates, some cells responded more strongly to some parts (such as the eyes) than to other parts of faces. Some cells would respond to almost any face but did not respond to any of the other complex visual stimuli that were tried, including things like food, other parts of the body, scenic photographs, a football, and a colored plastic bag. Some facial cells responded only to a *particular* face, such as the face of the primates' caretaker. Many of these cells were also sensitive to facial expressions of various

emotions. Face-sensitive cells tended to occur together in clusters.

The existence of such cells suggests that socially living species may have one or more cortical areas devoted to processing faces. **Prosopagnosia,** an inability to recognize faces of familiar people, occurs after some bilateral lesions in the occipital-temporal region of humans (Damasio, 1985; Grüsser, 1984; Jeeves, 1984; Tranel & Damasio, 1985). Although many of the people who suffer from this disorder have defects in a variety of perceptual and linguistic areas, a few seem to have all their abilities intact *except for* the ability to recognize faces as being familiar — including their own face. Such people may learn to identify friends and family members only by reference to such features as length of legs and color of hair. Some of them also show difficulties in recognizing other types of "faces"; one bird-watching expert could no longer differentiate among many of the similar bird species. The question now is whether prosopagnosia involves damage to brain areas specialized for processing facial features.

Summary of Cortical Coding

Cells in the visual cortex can have complex types of receptive fields. Some cells analyze for two-dimensional spatial characteristics, including rate and direction of movement. Still other cells, sensitive to degree of binocular disparity, may code for stereoscopic vision and for movement in three-dimensional space. Other cells are more sensitive to changes in wavelength than to changes in the spatial characteristics of the visual stimuli; these might be specialized for color perception. Some cells show even more dramatic selectivities, being more strongly excited by faces or by a given place in space than by any other type of patterned visual stimulation tested.

Adaptation and Centrifugal Control

The transmission of visual information changes constantly. The changes occur when centrifugal activity from higher visual areas alters the response characteristics of cells in other visual areas or when cells adapt.

Stabilized Retinal Images

The cortex (and consciousness) ignores a constant pattern of light on the retina. At the cortical level, tonic cells are rare: simple or complex cells may fire tonically to a constantly moving stimulus but not to a stationary stimulus. These cells respond only to appropriate *changes* in their receptive fields. Most cortical cells adapt extremely rapidly to a completely stationary stimulus.

Adaptation can dramatically affect perceptions. Under normal conditions, the visual cortex is never exposed to a constant pattern of stimulation across the retina because our eyes are constantly moving. Unconscious eye movements cause whatever we are looking at to jiggle constantly across our retinas. To find out what would happen if these eye movements did not occur, experimenters have used a tiny projector mounted onto contact lenses to project a stimulus to a constant retinal location regardless of eye movements. More recently, researchers have used light beams, mirrors, and computers to allow the projection system to compensate immediately and perfectly for any eye movements. These research techniques produce a **stabilized retinal image,** which disappears from perceptions within seconds. Any constant pattern of stimulation across retinal receptors quickly fails to stimulate any cortical cells—and so conscious sensations disappear.

When a complex image is stabilized on the retina, it disappears in pieces. If the image is a word such as BEER, the subject may see PEER, PEEP, BEE, and then BE. A facial profile may disappear and reappear in meaningful pieces, leaving only eyes or only mouth and chin visible. And color disappears from the image the most rapidly of all, leaving only sensations of differing regions of brightness. Since edges and colors disappear separately, wavelength and spatial information must adapt separately (Pritchard, 1961).

The separate disappearance of colors and boundaries has been used to create very unusual sensations (Crane & Piantanida, 1983). When one side of the visual field is green and the other is red, stabilization of the image causes the boundary to disappear and some observers see "reddish green"! Subjects knew that the image was colored, but they were unable to name or to describe the color, except as reddish green.

If this unusual color sensation can be duplicated in other subjects, we can speculate about its implications. Maybe the human cortex never lost its color processing abilities when our ancestors' habits changed from diurnal to nocturnal. When we once again became diurnal, our eyes reevolved color receptors, but this time with fewer cone types. Thus, although our eye may be unable to transmit a unique "reddish green" signal, our brains may have retained the ability to decode such a signal.

Light and Dark Adaptation

Retinal coding characteristics—both sensitivity and acuity—change as a function of time elapsed since a change in background illumination occurred. Although light adaptation occurs relatively rapidly, dark adaptation will take at least 30 minutes to complete, depending on the intensity and duration of exposure to the previous background illumination. Dark adaptation consists of at least two different sets of processes: **fast adaptation** and **slow adaptation.** Each phase uses different kinds of neural and chemical mechanisms (Virsu, 1978). The slow phase is **receptoral adaptation;** the fast phase involves **network adaptation,** which may be the reverse of one of the light-adaptation processes.

Receptoral adaptation.   Single receptor cells adapt to a constantly present background level of illumination (light adaptation). Hyperpolarization of a receptor reaches a maximum shortly after light onset and then, after 50 to 100 mSec, it declines (Baylor & Hodgkin, 1974). The decline is associated with an increase in sensitivity (Fain, 1976) and allows receptors to respond to a greater range of brightness. Light adaptation involves several processes occurring nearly simultaneously (Baylor, Hodgkin, & Lamb, 1974; Normann & Perlman, 1979a, 1979b), including (1) effects of the ion channels that are opened by hyperpolarization and that then act to depolarize (or reduce the hyperpolarization of) the membrane (Fain et al., 1978), (2) the inhibitory (depolarizing) feedback from horizontal cells, and (3) changes in Ca^{++} or in bleached rhodopsin that affect membrane potential.

Receptors adapt to darkness by means of two separate processes. One depends on how much light-sensitive pigment has been bleached prior to light offset (Virsu, 1978). If the adapting light had a high intensity, the presence of the bleached pigment during dark adaptation will keep the membrane hyperpolarized. The receptor adapts to darkness by regenerating the bleached pigment and thus decreasing hyperpolarization. This process is **photochemical** adaptation. The receptors also show adaptation unrelated to bleached pigment, possible because of intracellular changes, such as changes in levels of Ca^{++}.

Because of the effects of bleached pigment, the adaptation of a receptor to steady background lights is similar to the first phase of dark adaptation just after exposure to a very intense light (Baylor & Hodgkin, 1974; Lamb, 1981). The aftereffects of light and the effects of background illumination levels may have similar (but not identical) hyperpolarizing effects on the receptor membrane (Baylor, Lamb, & Yau, 1979a; Lamb & Simon, 1977). For example, both light and the bleaching of rhodopsin decrease the dark current (Albani & Yoshikami, 1980). The similarity is also seen psychophysically, leading Rushton (1965) to describe the aftereffects of bright light as being **"dark light."**

Dark and light adaptation in retinal output.   Dark and light adaptation affect the responses of all types of retinal cells and thus the output of the whole retina. Figure 7-44 shows how dark adaptation affects the retinal sensitivity of any organism having both rods and cones. This type of curve plots the absolute sensitivity of the whole organism (through psychophysics) or of the retina (by recording responses of ganglion cells) as a function of time. The first part of the dark-adaptation curve is dominated by cone responses, which have a shorter latency than do rod responses. However, after about 5 minutes or so, the sensitivity of cones stops increasing, but rod sensitivity continues to increase. After that point, rods are more sensitive than cones, and so they determine the absolute sensitivity of the retina. The change in the curve at that point is the **rod–cone break.**

Both retinal responses and perceptions change during dark adaptation. After the rod–cone break, the brightest part of the spectrum shifts from about 555 (the greatest area of cone sensitivity) to about 500 μm (the greatest area of rod sensitivity) (see Figure 7-2). At some point after the rod–cone break, lateral inhibition weakens (Barlow, Fitzhugh, & Kuffler, 1957) and the surround parts of the receptive fields also weaken, leaving only the strong center response. Acuity decreases because of the loss of lateral inhibition and because of the shift from cones to rods (foveal ganglion cells have the smallest receptive fields — one cone).

Fast and slow adaptation.   Figure 7-45 defines network (fast) and receptoral (slow) dark adaptation. Figure 7-45a comes from a retina isolated from the choroid so that the bleached rhodopsin could not be regenerated. Figure 7-45b comes from an intact retina, one in which bleached pigment

can be regenerated. In both cases, the retinas were exposed to a background of a given luminous intensity before dark adaptation was begun (the light was turned off). The electrical responses of rat retinas to flashes of light were recorded as a function both of time in the dark and of the luminous intensity of the prior background. The sensitivity of the retina was defined as a detectable change in one part of the grossly recorded electrical response of the retina (this evoked potential is the **electroretinogram,** and the part of the evoked activity used for this curve is the **b-wave**).*

The curves should be examined one piece at a time. First, look at the bold solid lines for the log threshold in parts a and b. This curve shows how the difference threshold increases as a function of the background luminance, illustrating Weber's law for vision. The dashed-line curve plots the amount of rhodopsin that had been bleached after exposure to backgrounds of various intensities. Up to log 4 background, there is no measurable amount of rhodopsin bleached (what rhodopsin had been bleached was too small and too quickly regenerated to be measured). After that point, increasing background illuminance increased the amount of bleached rhodopsin present in the retina.

The series of curves drawn with the X's and the fine lines are dark-adaptation curves. With dim adapting intensities, dark adaptation is extremely rapid, taking only seconds to complete. During this rapid phase, the increase in sensitivity as a function of time in the dark is exponential. However, when measurable amounts of pigment *had* been bleached, dark adaptation occurs in two distinguishable phases: fast and slow. The more pigment that had been bleached, the quicker the fast phase ends. The slow phase is linear, and complete adaptation may take two to three hours.

Since the slow phase of dark adaptation depends on the regeneration of bleached pigment, it cannot occur if the retina is isolated from the choroid (compare part a with part b). However, some mechanism other than just pigment regeneration is involved. Although dark adaptation can take up to three hours, pigment regeneration is complete in 30 minutes (Pöppel, Held, & Dowling, 1977). Also, much of receptoral or slow adaptation occurs even without significant pigment bleaching, presumably because of changes in the second-messenger system used for transduction (Virsu, 1978).

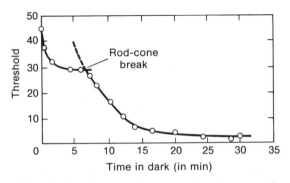

Figure 7-44   Dark adaptation curve, showing how visual sensitivity (the inverse of the threshold intensity) increases as a function of the time spent in the dark.

* Dowling (Dowling, 1967a; Weinstein, Hobson, & Dowling, 1967) says these curves come from an all-rod retina. However, rat retinas also have cones. Nevertheless, all that fact may mean is that the curve applies separately to adaptation in cones as well as in rods (Dowling, 1967b). Cones would also show both phases or types of dark adaptation.

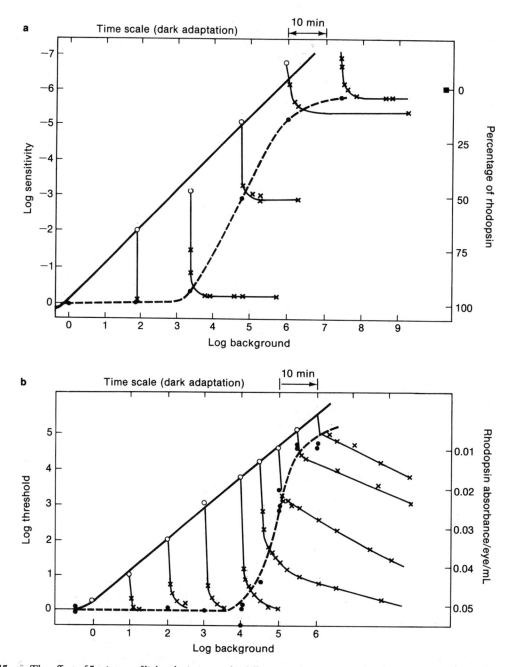

Figure 7-45 **a.** The effect of 5 minutes of light adaptation on the difference threshold (○), rhodopsin content (●), and dark adaptation (X, fine lines) in a retina isolated from the pigmented epithelium in which no pigment regeneration can occur (in rat). The criterion response for threshold measurement was a 20 μV change in potential. **b.** The same response in an intact eye. After exposure to more intense adapting lights (abscissa), intense stimuli (left ordinate) are required for a response (difference or increment threshold). Once the light is removed, sensitivity rapidly increases. If the adapting lights were dim, recovery is complete; after intense adapting lights — and significant amounts of bleached rhodopsin — the recovery is never complete in the isolated retina (a). Recovering occurs, but at a slower rate, in the intact retina (b).

Some fast adaptation might be explained by synaptic reorganization. Amacrine activity may drop out if these cells are no longer receiving suprathreshold levels of stimulation. If so, amacrines could no longer be inhibiting ganglion-cell responses to light flashes. But the major part of fast adaptation probably comes from changes in extracellular ion concentrations (for example, Ca^{++} or K^+) in the inner plexiform layer. These ion concentrations might take an appreciable amount of time to be restored to normal, accounting for the "slowness" of fast adaptation.

Afterimages and dark light.   You can sometimes see dark light. After exposure to a flash intense enough to bleach pigment, you will see a dark spot—corresponding to the retinal location of the flash—if you look at a white wall. This is a **negative afterimage.** But if you look at a dark surface, you will see a bright spot: **positive afterimage.** The luminance of the background determines whether you see a positive or negative afterimage. Any colors appearing in the flash also appear in a positive afterimage, but in a negative afterimage the opponent colors appear. On a white background, a red flash will produce a dim green afterimage.

Afterimages may occur because the brain is interpreting the effects of dark light—bleached pigment—the same way it would interpret the effects of light on the receptors (Adelson, 1982; Long & Beaton, 1982). Thus, looking at a dark background, which doesn't stimulate retinal cells, will allow the cells still being stimulated by dark light to produce the sensation of a positive afterimage. But since those cells are being stimulated by dark light—just as if they were light adapted—they will not show as much of an increase in response when the eye is turned toward a bright background. The suppressed response of that part of the retina and those particular cones will produce the sensations of a negative afterimage and complimentary colors.

You may have noticed that afterimages do not last as long as does the slow phase of dark adaptation. Dark light is essentially a stabilized retinal image (eye movements do not affect which receptors are being hyperpolarized by bleached pigment) and so quickly disappears. However, changing the background against which the afterimage is being viewed can restore the image.

Illusions and adaptation.   Since different aspects of visual stimuli are coded by different cortical cells, adaptation can produce some interesting illusions. For example, exposure to a pattern moving in one direction during adaptation can produce an illusion of movement in the reverse direction when a stationary pattern is viewed. Watching the scenery out of a train window for a while; when the train stops, the scenery appears to be moving in the opposite direction! Presumably cells responsive to movement in one direction adapt, and so when stimulation ceases, the spontaneous activity of opposite-direction coding cells produces illusory movement in the opposite direction (Barlow, 1972).

Centrifugal Connections and Effects

Centrifugal projections occur throughout the visual system. Lower animals have centrifugal projections to the retina, but they have not been found so far in mammals (Rodieck, 1973). In the primate retina, the interplexiform cells project centrifugally from the inner to the outer layers. Both complex and simple cortical cells project back to the geniculate; cortical-geniculate connections are found on about half of the geniculate cells in primates, 40% of which are excitatory (McClurkin & Marrocco, 1984). These cortical connections affect the spatial coding properties of the geniculate cells. Cortical complex cells and geniculate Y-cells in cats also project to the colliculus (Finlay, Schiller, & Volman, 1976; Singer, Tretter, & Cynader, 1975). These connections may aid the colliculus in its processing of spatial information and movement.

These pathways affect cortical responses to visual input. Horn and Hill (1969) reported that the receptive fields of some cortical cells tilt when the body is tilted. Since the cortex probably does not receive direct vestibular input, vestibular information must be sent to lower visual centers. Thus, at least some cortical cells have a "plastic" or changeable receptive field. The vestibular information coming from body tilt presumably suppresses some cortical inputs and facilitates others so that the "tilted" receptive field occurs.

Some movement-sensitive cortical cells respond whether the movement comes from the eye's motion in relation to a stimulus or from the passing of a stimulus across a stationary background. However, some cells respond only when a stimulus is moving across a stationary background and are inhibited by eye movement, presumably because of information from eye-movement centers. These cells could distinguish between the effects of eye movement (reafference) and the real movement of an object in space (Bridgeman, 1973). Similar effects were seen for the phosphenes produced by electrical stimulation in the cortex of humans: during voluntary eye movements, the phosphenes moved with the eyes, but during involuntary movements, the phosphenes remained fixed in perceptual space (Brindley & Lewin, 1968).

The colliculus seems specialized for the type of processing that requires differentiating between real and self-induced movement (reafference). This differentiation must involve outflow monitoring (Guthrie, Porter, & Sparks, 1983). For example, some collicular cells receive centrifugal signals that suppress their activity during voluntary eye movements (Robinson & Wurtz, 1976). And some cortical cells seem to be excited by efference copies of signals going to the muscles controlling eye movements (Toyama, Komatsu, & Shibuki, 1984).

Outflow monitoring may cause an illusion called the **autokinetic effect** (Hoyenga & Wallace, 1978, 1979, 1982; Wallace & Hoyenga, 1975, 1978a, 1978b). Human observers told to focus on a pin-point of light in a dark room often perceive the light to move — though it is completely stationary. This illusion is caused by eye movements. Subjects are unaware of the effects that their involuntary eye movements have on target fixation. What they *are* aware of is that after involuntary, unconscious eye movement, the retinal location of the target changed. Then they initiate voluntary, correcting eye movements. Because voluntary eye movements are outflow monitored, the spot is seen as having moved. Subjects appear to be telling themselves: "I am moving my eyes, therefore the visual target must have moved."

Summary of Adaptation and Centrifugal Control

Both adaptation and centrifugal activity change coding responses to visual stimuli. An image totally stabilized on the retina literally disappears from consciousness. Light adaptation and the network phase of dark adaptation are inversely related: synaptic reorganization and changes in ion concentrations around receptors and synapses change sensitivity. The receptoral phase of dark adaptation occurs only after significant amounts of pigment bleaching, and this phase is caused by the effects of second-messenger metabolism and the photochemical regeneration of pigment (removal of dark light).

Centrifugal activity in the mammalian visual system has been identified, but its function has not yet been well characterized. Visual cells also show evidence of outflow monitoring: sensory cells are affected by motor signals prior to the sending of those signals to the muscles.

Chapter Summary
Visual Codes

Light has both wave and particle properties. The wave properties govern wavelength coding and color perception, and parti-

cle properties or photons are largely responsible for brightness perceptions and spatial coding. Different populations of cells, starting at the level of the retina, apparently process different aspects of visual information. During all processes, the information present in the external world is modified.

The process starts with transduction. Receptor hyperpolarization decreases the rate of transmitter release by receptors. This decrease affects all the other cells in the retina, both the vertical processors (bipolar and ganglion cells) and the horizontal processors (horizontal and amacrine cells). Information leaves the retina as patterns of action potentials in the axons of specific retinal ganglion cells.

Luminance is largely pattern coded. Receptor cells have a greater change in membrane potential after a greater absorption of photons by their pigment molecules. Some ganglion cells and cortical cells do not respond to changes in spatial or wavelength properties and so may code perceptual brightness.

Spatial coding includes the detection of light on a particular place on the retina, the detection of changes in light in a particular place on the retina, and the detection and identification of patterns. During changes in retinal location and in adaptation, acuity is inversely related to sensitivity. In the cortex, populations of cells seem to be specialized for responding to edge and bar orientations, particular directions and speeds of movements, and particular spatial frequencies. A separate population of cells is sensitive to retinal disparity, providing one basis for stereoscopic vision and for analysis of movement in three-dimensional space. Centrifugal activity from motor areas of the cortex may allow some cells to distinguish between self-induced and real-object movement.

A separate population of cells codes wavelength information. Starting at the receptor level, there are three types of cones, and wavelength is place coded. At the next level, there are two types of opponent systems (red–green and blue–yellow), each cell responding in one way to one wavelength and giving the opposite response to other wavelengths (a combination place and pattern code). Some cortical cells respond uniquely to color. And in "higher" cortical centers, cells may be even more selective for wavelength responses.

Wavelength codes produce our own unique color experiences. Organisms with different types and numbers of cones, or with different opponencies, will have different kinds of color experiences. That hypothetical organism described at the end of the subcortical coding section would probably have color experiences very different from those of us primate trichromats. The color spectrum and difference thresholds of Figure 7-3 would be very different. The colors seen by that organism could be reproduced only by mixing *four* different wavelengths. That organism could see reddish green and yellowish blue, but it would *not* be able to see reddish blue (purple) or yellowish green (presumably the first would look gray and the second would look red).

Coding characteristics of the visual system provide us with information about how our brains affect our perceptual realities. We see bands of light and darkness that don't exist. We see movement where there is none (as in the train effect and in autokinetic movement). We see colors that aren't there and don't see colors that are there. In fact, color is solely a property of our brains and is not part of physical reality: "There is nothing either green or grey but thinking makes it so" (Rushton, 1972, p. 29P).

PART FOUR

The Coding of Internal Motivational and Emotional States

The effect of internal states on interoceptors may be part of the neural code for motives and emotions. We assume that neurons signal the changes in internal states (for example, activity in glands or changes in blood levels of such things as hormones, glucose, and insulin) caused by an emotion or motive. These signals affect how other cells code external stimuli and thus what kind of response the organism will make. But our understanding of motivational and emotional coding is not nearly as advanced as our grasp of sensory coding, for several reasons. One is that the psychology of motives and emotions is plagued with considerably more disagreement about definitions and relevant variables than is the psychology of sensations. To discover how motives and emotions are coded, we must first resolve the problem of what they are.

It is easy to agree on definitions of visual and auditory stimuli, but definitions of events that produce motives and emotions have so far eluded consensus. Nevertheless, some aspects of emotions and motives are generally agreed upon.

The psychology of motives involves specific characteristics of behaviors, characteristics for which the theories of motives hope to provide explanations. The motivationally relevant aspects of behavior include **arousal and energization** and **choice.**

The arousal and energization aspects of behavior can be measured by the intensity, vigor, and probability of occurrence of a given type of response to a given situation. Motives are used to explain why behaviors occur with a given intensity at a given time — and to predict how behaviors will vary in intensity from one time to another and from one organism to another. Specifically, variations in the vigor and frequency of eating behavior would be assumed to be relevant to an internal state of hunger produced by food deprivation.

Motives can cause both **behavioral arousal** and **neural activation** (changes in some neural activity). There may be several different kinds of arousal (Routtenberg, 1968, 1971), two of which may be **deficit** or **aversive arousal** and **incen-**

tive arousal. Deficit arousal and activation are caused by deprivation, pain, or an unpleasant emotional state. Incentive arousal is elicited by the stimuli (sight, scent) coming from some type of goal object or incentive, such as food or the presence of a sexually receptive member of the opposite sex. Deficit and incentive arousal are negative and positive reinforcers, respectively (Chapter 1). In some areas of the brain, these two states may differentially affect neural activity (see, for example, Roos, Rydenhag, & Andersson, 1983).

Both aversive and incentive arousal have **nonspecific** and **specific** components. The codes for nonspecific arousal include the responses of those neurons that are activated by a variety of deficits, emotions, pains, *and* incentives. The codes for specific arousal are those neural responses that differentiate among those states. If a neuron shows the *same* pattern of activity in response to food deprivation, pain, and the sight of a willing sexual partner, that neuron could be coding for nonspecific arousal. But if a neuron shows a certain pattern of activity *only* in the presence of food deprivation, or *only* when food is seen, that pattern of activity in that neuron might be part of a code for that specific type of arousal (see, for example, Diamond & Weinberger, 1984).

Arousal can also involve **selective attention.** Having a certain type of internal state, the organism becomes selectively attentive to its environment. Some types of stimuli are more likely to attract attention and to produce specific and nonspecific arousal than are other types of stimuli. A starving organism is more likely to pay attention to, and be aroused by, the sight, sound, and scent of food than by the sight, sound, and scent of an organism of the opposite sex. The organism is focusing its attention largely on the relevant stimulus, ignoring others.

Motives are also used to explain and predict choice. Suppose that a male rat were given a choice between a sexually receptive female rat and the opportunity to eat a chocolate chip cookie (rats like them as much as people do). Further suppose that on one day the rat chose the female, but the next day the rat chose the cookie. You might be tempted to explain the variation by saying that on the first day, the sexual motive was stronger than the hunger motive, but on the second day, the hunger motive was stronger. You would also predict that organisms who had gone without food for two days would more frequently respond to the food than to the sexual incentive. This is the **directing function** of motivation.

Reinforcement affects behavior that involves making a choice. Operant conditioning presents reinforcers contingent on behaviors. Whether a given reward will work, producing change in operant behaviors, depends on the motivational state of the organism. Food is a much more effective reinforcer for a hungry organism than for an organism whose stomach is currently distended with food.

If talking about motives could do no better than this by way of explaining and predicting behavior, discussing motives would add almost nothing to our explanations of behavior—you might just as well talk just about intensity and choice and skip the concept of motivation. However, if a given experimental manipulation created simultaneous changes in several different behaviors, using a motivational concept would make the explanations much simpler. Depriving a rat of food might simultaneously increase its reactivity to stimulus change, its rate of running in an activity wheel, the specific and nonspecific arousal elicited by presenting food, the likelihood that it will choose food over any other possible reward, and its rate of eating that food. We might explain why this rat did all those things, and predict that similarly treated rats would do similar things, by saying that hunger caused these behaviors. Using emotional states could similarly simplify explanations. We could use the concept of anger to summarize and predict the diverse behaviors that both frustration and pain can elicit.

A second reason why the coding of emotional and motivational states is difficult to explore is that these states are removed from both the input and the output. The input conditions for sensory coding—the physical sensory stimuli—can be well defined. But what might be the adequate stimulus for hunger? Where would you look? Which of the many changes that food deprivation produces in the body might be relevant to the neural codes? And, to make matters even more difficult, 24 hours of food deprivation will produce different levels of hunger, depending on the organism's activity levels, the temperature of the surrounding environment, and the organism's weight compared to "normal." Twenty-four hours of food deprivation will produce no hunger (that is, no food consumption) in organisms made artificially fat beforehand and will produce little hunger if organisms remain inactive in a hot environment during deprivation.

Motivational output is also hard to define. The output for sensory coding is, at least in some sense, experiencing a given perception. The output of a motivational condition is arousal and choice. For both kinds of output, phenomenological experiences have to be inferred from the behaviors of subjects. But the way motives are behaviorally measured requires a psychobiologist to know where in the nervous system the choice and vigor of motor output are triggered and controlled in order to be certain that similar outputs are involved in motivational states. Once that location has been established, the physiological changes produced by motives and emotions can be related to the activity of output neurons.

A third problem concerns the location of the emotional and

motivationally relevant neurons. In the sensory systems, researchers record from the nerve cells directly connected with the relevant sensory organ. But where are the motivational transducers? What cells are directly connected to them?

Research efforts have so far concentrated on the areas of the brain that lesion and stimulation studies have indicated might be relevant to motives. For example, lesions in a certain area of the hypothalamus produce **aphagia** (not eating), and lesions in another area of the hypothalamus produce **hyperphagia** (excessive eating). Rats will learn to perform operant responses such as lever pressing when the only reward for doing so is a short burst of electrical stimulation through an implanted gross electrode to a certain part of their brains. This is **self-stimulation** behavior. Having discovered the anatomy of reinforcement, researchers can record the responses of single cells in the identified areas during self-stimulation, hunger, or eating. For example, gross electrodes in the lateral hypothalamus will support self-stimulation, and the way that cells in this area respond to taste stimuli depends on the motivational state of the animal.

Using lesion and gross-stimulation studies to guide the placement of microelectrodes for single-unit research (recording single-unit activity) means that those studies will suffer from some of the problems of the gross techniques described in Chapter 1. Most of the data we have may not have come from the nerve cells most critically important to various motives, and the cells most important to various emotions may not yet have been identified.

We can list the types of neural response that are probably most relevant to motivational and emotional states:

1. The change in neural activity must parallel some relevant change in the internal environment, either one associated with nonspecific or specific arousal or one associated with satiety.

2. The neural change must be shown to be relevant to the ways in which motivational and emotional states change neural responses to stimuli in the external environment (for instance, attention).

3. The neural change must be shown to be relevant to the neural codes involved in the appropriate motor responses (such as invigoration and choice).

4. The neural change associated with satiety must be related to the neural change associated with reinforcement.

The next three chapters explore those four relationships. Chapter 8 describes the effects of nonspecific arousal and specific homeostatic motives, Chapter 9 is concerned with the sexual motive, and Chapter 10 discusses emotions. Throughout, you should remember that motivational and emotional neural codes may not exist as distinguishable patterns of activity in a certain key set of cells. Instead, motives and emotions may only change sensory and output coding. Motives and emotions would then just be part of the *relationship* between, on the one hand, the environmental events (sensory coding) that arouse motives and emotions and, on the other hand, the ways in which behavior (output coding) is affected by those events (G. P. Smith, 1982). Or, as Norgren and Grill (1982, p. 125) point out, although our conscious awareness of ourselves and our behaviors includes the concepts of motives and emotions, it does not necessarily follow that our brain has unique and distinguishable codes for those same concepts.

Effects of Hunger, Thirst, and Arousal on Nerve Cells

Some motives and their associated behaviors can be viewed as the final resort of the nervous system when **homeostasis** is threatened. ("Homeostasis" refers to keeping bodily internal conditions within a certain narrow range.) Internal responses are the first line of defense. For example, suppose that an organism were exposed to a hot environment and the internal body temperature started to rise above the homeostatic range. Internal responses such as increasing vasodilation and sweating in the skin would occur first. Only when the internal responses failed to keep the body temperature within certain narrow limits would the appropriate motives be aroused, energizing appropriate behaviors such as seeking shade or getting wet to increase evaporation.

Overview

There are two major ideas about the psychology of motives: **drive theories** and **incentive theories** (Hoyenga & Hoyenga, 1984; Pfaff, 1982). Although all theories of motivation have both drive and incentive aspects (emphasizing the roles of both internal states and external stimuli, respectively), theories do differ in the amount of emphasis given to each aspect. Many theorists, such as Hull (1943), claim that motives are **drives,** or internal states of tension created by homeostatic disruption. Tension goads and energizes the organism into behavior—specifically, into a search for whatever it is that would rectify the homeostatic disruption. Food would, of course, rectify a disruption created by food deprivation. Alternatively, motives may act like **incentives,** external or environmental stimuli, the perception of which creates a motive or incentive arousal in the organism. The motive can be either to approach and attain or to avoid and escape that stimulus (choice and energization).

This chapter starts out with a general discussion of how arousal might affect brain codes and then goes on to specific arousal and specific motives. Although the last two sections are the ones most relevant to the neuron doctrine, that research cannot be interpreted without the background provided by the other sections. Some candidate codes for hunger and thirst will be explored, along with possible codes for reinforcement. Can the neuron doctrine be extended to explain how the internal states associated with motives and emotions are coded?

Command Cells and Motives

Using single-unit research to analyze motivation means that the behavioral output must be identified. Motivated behavior appears to be goal directed and spontaneous, occurring under the control of motives and emotions inside the organism and not being reflexly elicited by identifiable external stimuli. This apparent spontaneity may be an emergent phenomenon, arising out of complex combinations of reflexes (Teitelbaum, Schallert, & Whishaw, 1983), just as many researchers believe that self-conscious awareness is an emergent property of sufficiently complex circuits. Motor output is organized and given an appearance of spontaneity by the organism's "intention" to respond, an internal state that organizes reflexes in the context of a particular motive.

Invertebrate Command Cells

The concept of **command cells** evolved from work done with invertebrates. The nervous systems of these organisms, including mollusks such as *Aplysia* and *Pleurobranchae*, are so simple that individual cells can be labeled and correctly identified from one organism to the next. Thus, a command cell found in one organism can be identified and studied in all other organisms of that species, greatly facilitating single-unit research.

Definitions of command cells.   Kandel (1976) describes invertebrate command cells as those whose stimulation can trigger complete motor sequences. Stimulation of one cell in the crayfish, for example, produces a complete escape response involving movement of eye stalks, antennae, swimmerets (leglike structures), and tail. Command cells control a complete sequence of complex behaviors relevant to a given, motivated act. Although more than one cell can evoke a given behavioral sequence, the sequences often differ in their details, so each command cell may be associated with a unique motivated behavior pattern.

Shepherd (1983) identifies two types of command cells. When **trigger** cells are stimulated, a motor sequence is elicited that outlasts the stimulation period. Activity in this type of cell precedes a behavioral sequence. **Gating** types of command neurons affect a behavioral sequence by *remaining* active throughout the movement. Since the behavioral effects of these command cells stop when their activity stops, they serve as "gates" for motor output. Gating command cells may control posture or rhythmic types of motor activity, such as continuing swimming movements in swimmerets.

For a cell to be correctly classified as a command neuron, it must meet three criteria: it must be necessary, sufficient, and appropriate to the observed behavioral sequence (Parsons, ter Maat, & Pinsker, 1983). The criteria are defined as follows:

1. A cell is *necessary* if the associated behavioral sequence is absent or severely disrupted when the cell is prevented from firing (by destruction or hyperpolarization).
2. A cell is *sufficient* if the associated behavioral sequence is evoked when it is stimulated in an intact, behaving animal.
3. A cell is *appropriate* if during its electrical activity it varies isomorphically with variations in the behavioral sequence.

Command cells and motivation.   For cells whose activity varies according to the motivational state of the organism, studying how their activities are related to activities in command cells may provide hypotheses about how a vertebrate brain may code motivational states (Gillette, Kovac, & Davis, 1982; Kandel, 1976; Kupfermann & Weiss, 1982). Since activity in command cells immediately and necessarily precedes activity in motor cells, a command cell might be the motivational analog to feature detectors in the sensory systems. Both command cells and feature detectors have complex trigger features, responding only when a complex combination of circumstances is present. Activity in command cells might reflect the "intention" (in higher organisms, a decision) to make a certain type of response, relevant to a certain type of goal object; if so, this activity might be the endpoint of internal, motivational types of coding processes.

Possible Command Systems in Primates

In higher organisms, a small set of cells, a **command system,** might be necessary, sufficient, and appropriate to a behavioral act. The act could be either innate or learned. In the latter case, an act might be defined by its effects on the environment rather than by the exact pattern of muscular activity. Some provocative research has been carried out in primates.

Command systems in the association cortex of primates. Mountcastle (1975; Mountcastle et al., 1975) described cells in the primate parietal association cortex that had properties very similar to those of the invertebrate command cells. Parietal cells would thus be at the top of the motor command hierarchy (representing the "intention" to move? see Chapter 2). As Mountcastle said (Mountcastle et al., 1975, p. 871), "This general command function is exercised in a holistic fashion. It relates to acts aimed at general behavioral goals and not to the details of muscular contraction during execution."

Mountcastle's monkeys were trained to reach out and either press a panel or pull a lever within a specified period of time after a signal. In some cases, the signal told the monkey which lever to press, of the two mounted at eye level. In other research, the panel to be pressed was rotated between trials so that the monkey had to make different arm movements on each trial. After training was completed, the monkey's head was held in a fixed position during future trials. A micromanipulator, mounted above a hole in the skull, drove a microelectrode into various areas of the monkey's parietal cortex.

Mountcastle and his co-workers found two types of cell that might belong to a command system. Cells of the first type discharged at high rates whenever the animal reached into the immediate space surrounding it. Their pattern of activity was unrelated to the direction of the intended movement and so did not depend on which muscles were going to be active during the movement. Cells of the second type fired whenever the animal manipulated an object within that space. However, both cells fired *only* when the movement or manipulation occurred for a specific motive. Similar movements and manip-

ulations that occurred when the animal was angry, or when the arm or hand was passively manipulated by the experimenter, did not evoke activity in these parietal cells. Some of the hand-manipulation neurons were active whenever the animal was manipulating something to get food or water, or when that animal was grooming another monkey, but those neurons were not activated by apparently identical hand movements that occurred during aggression.

Some parietal cells might be part of a command system for visual tracking and visual fixation. Mountcastle and his colleagues found that these cells fire only when the animal is visually tracking or fixating on an object of interest to it at the moment. The fixating cells fire maximally when the desired object is located within arm's reach. "Such a [fixation] cell may, for example, be completely silent as the animal explores his environment visually, fixating in sequence on experimenter, instruments, books, etc., to be followed immediately by intense discharge on fixation of a food object presented within arm's length" (Mountcastle et al., 1975, p. 887).

Preparation for movement. Subsequent research has confirmed many of Mountcastle's observations (Bioulac & Lamarre, 1979; Burbaud, Gross, & Bioulac, 1985; Seal, Gross, & Bioulac, 1982). Neurons in the parietal cortex become active 200 to 300 mSec before complex movements occur, and their activity is not caused by any sensory input. "This activity may correspond to higher central processes. . . . [These cells] may play a part in the build up of 'a command message' eventually expressed at the level of the motor cortex" (Burbaud, Gross, & Bioulac, 1985, p. 346). Thus, activity in this command system might precede (and facilitate?) the "generalized activation" that can be recorded in motor-cortex neurons approximately 100 mSec prior to a response (Kwan, Mackay, Murphy, & Wong, 1985). These command-system cells are, in fact, directly connected to motor-cortex cells (Zarzecki, Strick, & Asanuma, 1978).

Command cells are conditional. Since they fire only during a *particular* motivational set, they must receive at least indirect input from motivational and emotional types of internal bodily states. Mogenson, Jones, and Yim (1980, p. 89) suggested that activity in limbic system structures can have tonic effects on some motor-system neurons.

In contrast, prefrontal cortex neurons (anterior to motor cortex) might be part of a motor preparation system. Cells in this area also fire before a movement, but, unlike those of command-system cells, their activity patterns can be closely related to the nature of the forthcoming movement (Kubota & Funahashi, 1982; Niki & Watanabe, 1979; Wise & Mauritz, 1985). When Penfield and Boldrey (1937) stimulated various brain areas in humans, some frontal stimulations evoked a feeling of "a desire to move."

Summary of Command Cells

The concept of command cells evolved from work on invertebrates. A command cell is necessary, sufficient, and relevant to a complex behavior pattern. Command systems may be found in primates: activity in these cells may correspond to an "intention" to respond and is not related to the motor details of the intended response. These details are supplied and coordinated by "lower" motor centers such as the motor cortex, the basal ganglia, and the cerebellum (Chapter 2). Since activity in primate command cells depends on motivational states, these cells may be analogous to feature detectors in the sensory cortex.

Effects of Level of Nonspecific Arousal on Neural Responses

Many motives and emotions increase general level of arousal. This section describes the neural and synaptic responses associated with levels of nonspecific arousal on the continuum ranging from deep sleep to paniclike levels of waking arousal. These responses can then be compared with the neural responses associated with motives (this chapter and the next) and emotions (Chapter 10). Any commonalities would be most parsimoniously attributed to the nonspecific neural correlates of various levels of arousal rather than to the specific neural correlates of some specified emotion or motive.

Behavioral arousal and cortical activation usually occur together. Arousal invigorates behavior, as measured by the rate, intensity, latency (inversely), or forcefulness of responses. Sometimes the aroused organism does not move, as when frightened organisms freeze. But even in this case, muscles are being strongly stimulated (tense muscles) and there are internal signs of arousal (for example, an elevated heart rate). Cortical activation is a particular kind of electrical activity occurring in the cortex. The EEG, recorded from gross electrodes on the scalp or cortex, normally changes when behavioral arousal changes. As Figure 8-1 shows, the states of alertness and drowsiness are associated with characteristic differences in the EEG record. Waves of electrical activity at 8 to 13 cycles per second (cps) are called **alpha waves.** The alpha waves come from the synchronized excitatory and inhibitory post-synaptic potentials of cortical cells. Activation is a pattern of low-voltage, fast, and random gross potentials, or **desynchronization.** Single-unit recordings show that increasing cortical activation is associated with an increase in the average interval between the action potentials of cortical cells; the variability of their firing rate also decreases (Webb, 1976a, 1976b).

This section concentrates on two areas of research. In the first, activities in brain-stem cells are recorded and related to nonspecific changes in arousal level. The second type analyzes sensory coding changes during both nonspecific and specific changes in arousal level, including selective attention. The

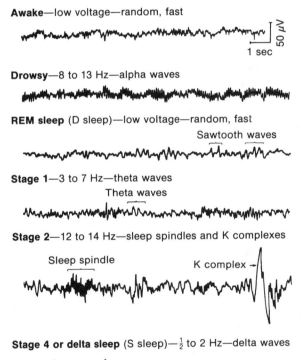

Figure 8-1 If the electroencephalogram of a human subject is recorded during sleep, the record goes through characteristic changes during the various stages of sleep. Stage 3 sleep (not illustrated) is intermediate between Stages 2 and 4 in characteristics. REM sleep can be recognized by the tonic inhibition of motoneurons and muscles, with phasic eye movements and muscle twitches being superimposed on that chronic inhibition.

ultimate goal here is to understand how changes in level of specific arousal may be coded and also how changes in both nonspecific arousal and arousal specific to some homeostatic motive change the way the brain responds to sensory input. However, sleep, like the hunger and thirst motives, may also be a homeostatic mechanism. Deprivation of a certain kind of sleep causes that particular kind to increase temporarily during the next sleep period. Total sleep deprivation can cause severe behavioral and physical pathology and even death (Rechtschaffen, Gilliland, Bergmann, & Winter, 1983; Vertes, 1984).

Stages of Sleep

Levels of arousal and arousability change systematically during the stages of sleep. The deeper the stage of sleep—or the larger the amplitude of the EEG waves (see Figure 8-1)—the harder it is to arouse the organism. Stage 1 sleep involves **theta waves** (3 to 7 cps). In Stage 2 sleep, **sleep spindles** and **K complexes** are seen (as in Figure 8-1), and in Stage 4 sleep, **delta waves** ($\frac{1}{2}$ to 2 cps) are seen. However, the stage of **rapid-eye-movement (REM)** sleep is very different from the others. It is characterized by low-voltage, fast-activity EEGs and rhythmic, rapid movements of the eyes. Although the organism can spontaneously awaken during REM sleep (as in Figure 8-2), the organism can be quite difficult to awaken.

Characteristics of the various sleep stages.   The stages of sleep occurring during the night in a normal person are presented in Figure 8-2. Normal sleep has cycles that vary in duration as the night proceeds. Stage 1 REM sleep differs from Stage 1 **non–rapid-eye-movement (NREM) sleep** in several respects. For example, only REM sleep has rapid eye movements and inhibition of motor neurons.

Dream recall is more likely for a person awakened during REM than during any other stage of sleep. Dreams recalled from NREM sleep stages are "more poorly recalled, more similar to waking thought, less vivid and visual, more conceptual and plausible, under greater volitional control, less emotional, and more pleasant" than REM dreams (D. D. Kelly, 1981a, p. 479). The only exception is that most genuine **nightmares** occur during Stages 3 and 4 of NREM sleep (D. D. Kelly, 1981a, 1981b). In a true nightmare (as opposed to a "bad dream"), people experience labored breathing, partial paralysis, and extreme anxiety. There is usually no well-structured dream activity but only vague impressions of things like having rocks or a demon on the chest. Similar phenomena in children are called **night terrors.**

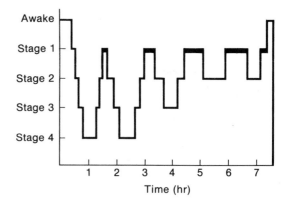

Figure 8-2   A typical night's pattern of sleep stages in a young adult human. Stage 1 REM sleep can be distinguished from Stage 1 NREM sleep only by criteria other than the electroencephalogram (see Figure 8-1). REM sleep is indicated by a dark bar. The first REM period is usually short, but later periods tend to be progressively longer. Stages 3 and 4 dominate the NREM period during the early part of the night but may not occur later on; the duration of Stage 2 NREM sleep increases progressively through the night. In this example, because the morning awakening interrupted the last REM period, the likelihood of dream recall is good; if NREM sleep had intervened between REM sleep and awakening, the chance of dream recall would be greatly reduced.

Anatomy and functions of sleep effects.   Figures 8-3 and 8-4 present the anatomy of sleep and arousal. The structures in Figure 8-3 labeled with an S are those that might be active in promoting sleep. Lesions of these structures often produce insomnia. The structures labeled with an A are associated with either behavioral arousal or REM sleep. Lesions of those structures often make the animal difficult to arouse. High-frequency electrical stimulation of those structures can produce cortical activation in a drowsy animal and REM electrical activity in a sleeping animal, and can even awaken a sleeping animal.

High-frequency electrical stimulation of a neural structure can sometimes produce activation even though low-frequency stimulation of that same area produces sleep. For example, in Figure 8-3, the intralaminar thalamic nuclei are labeled with both an S and an A. The dual effect of electrical stimulation can also be seen in the caudal reticular area. Figure 8-3 shows only the pontine reticular area, the area in which high-frequency stimulation can most easily evoke activation. The reticular activating system, or **reticular formation (RF),** also extends caudally into the medullary or bulbar brain stem and rostrally into the midbrain region.

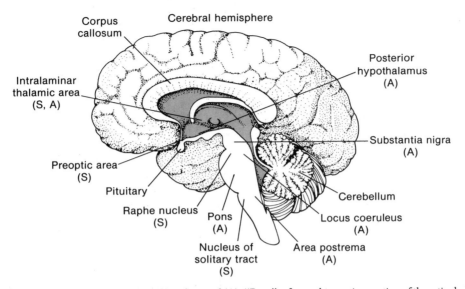

Figure 8-3 Many areas of the brain control sleep (S) and arousal (A). "Pons" refers to the pontine portion of the reticular formation. The reticular formation extends rostrally into the midbrain and caudally into the medulla. Stimulation of the intralaminar thalamic nuclei (which may also be a part of the reticular formation) can produce either relaxation and analgesia (low-amplitude, low-frequency stimulation) or arousal and anxiety (increased amplitude, higher frequency). The nucleus of the solitary tract receives parasympathetic afferent information via cranial nerves X and IX, whereas the area postrema is very sensitive to blood-borne substances since there is no blood–brain barrier (Chapter 2) at that point.

The opposite effects of the two rates of stimulation just described presumably reflect the activation of different neuronal systems. One difference would be size, since larger neurons with shorter absolute and relative refractory periods are better able to follow high-frequency stimulations (fire for every stimulation) than are smaller neurons. Instead of being stimulated, normal activity in the smaller neurons would be blocked. If present, certain electrically gated channels—such as the K^+ channels, which control the rate of repolarization—could also determine whether a neuron could or could not follow high-frequency stimulations.

In Figure 8-4, some of the areas of the brain associated with various phenomena of REM sleep are pointed out (Vertes, 1984). A theta rhythm in a limbic area, the hippocampus, is seen during both waking arousal and REM sleep. Waking hippocampal theta is associated with movements in the rat and dog, with attention in the cat, and with nonspecific arousal in the rabbit. The theta rhythm may be controlled by the RPO, one of the pontine nuclei. This nucleus activates the cells in the medial septal region that actually generate the theta rhythm.

Although three events listed in Figure 8-4 are present tonically throughout REM sleep, muscle twitches, increases in heart and respiratory rate, eye movements, and ponto-geni-

culo-occipital spikes (**PGO spikes**) occur phasically and in synchrony (Vertes, 1984). The muscle twitches associated with REM sleep (the myoclonic twitches) may be controlled by another pontine nucleus (RPC) and by the gigantocellular nucleus in the pons (NGC: large cell bodies). PGO spikes can be recorded through gross electrodes in animals and have similar characteristics in each of those three structures. PGO spikes appear during REM sleep and may be generated in the **X area** of the pons. Some PGO waves are closely related to the timing of eye movements both during REM sleep and during waking. The pontine nuclei (pontis oralis and pontis caudalis) are part of the pontine reticular formation.

Some RF pathways are shown in Figures 8-5 and 8-6. The RF has both ascending and descending pathways. As Figure 8-5 shows, sometimes both axons come from the same nerve cell. Some descending pathways are excitatory to motoneurons, a fact that may explain the increase in muscle tension associated with behavioral arousal and with the muscle twitches of REM sleep. Other descending pathways are inhibitory and may also be active during REM sleep, producing muscle atonia (relaxation) or sleep "paralysis."

The ascending pathways affect cortical activity. Hobson and McCarley (1977) have proposed that part of the pontine RF is responsible for causing dream images. They suggested

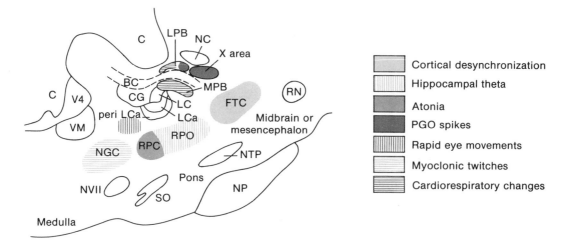

Figure 8-4 A schematic parasagittal section through the brain stem of the cat (pons and medulla as seen at approximately 3.0 mm lateral to the midline) shows the locations of cell groups involved in controlling the major events of REM sleep. With the exception of the periabducens area (cross-hatched region of the dorsal pontomedullar RF), which is medial to the plane of section, each of the areas shown is located approximately at the sagittal plane shown. BC = brachium conjunctivum; C = cerebellum; CG = central gray; DLT = dorsolateral tegmental nucleus; FTC = central tegmental field; LC = locus coeruleus; LCa = locus coeruleus, pars alpha; LPB = lateral parabrachial nucleus; MPB = medial parabrachial nucleus; NC = cuneform nucleus; NGC = nucleus gigantocellularis; NP = nucleus of the pons; NTP = pontine tegmental nucleus; N VII = nucleus of the facial nerve; peri LCa = peri-locus coeruleus, pars alpha; RN = red nucleus; RPC = nucleus pontis caudalis; RPO = nucleus pontis oralis; SO = superior olive; VM = medial vestibular nucleus; V4 = fourth ventricle.

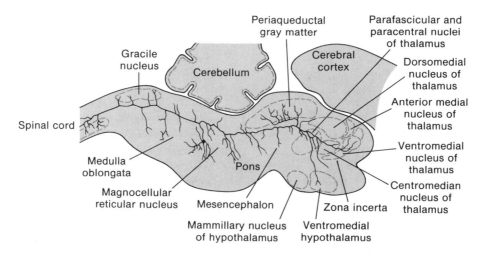

Figure 8-5 Sagittal section from the brain of a 2-day-old rat, showing a single large reticular cell. Its axons have both ascending and descending collaterals. The descending segment gives off many collaterals to the adjacent reticular formation, to the gracile nucleus (somatosensory), and to the ventral nuclei of the spinal cord. The ascending segment gives off collaterals to the reticular formation and to many other structures of the brain, including the ventromedial hypothalamus (see discussion of hunger).

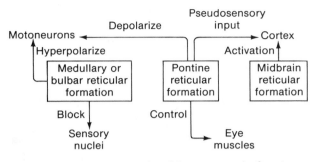

Figure 8-6   This theoretical model summarizes the functions of some of the reticular nuclei.

that efferents from the RF induce activity in sensory cortical cells. If the brain interpreted the activity in sensory neurons as having come from external stimuli, the result would be dream images.

Activity in some RF neurons may be responsible for many of the effects that motivational and emotional arousal has on sensory processing. Although not shown in Figure 8-6, since the RF receives input from all the sensory systems, it can be activated by any external event. However, spinothalamic and olfactory inputs are particularly well represented. The RF sends axons not only to the cortex but also to limbic-system structures and the hypothalamus, the structures most involved in emotions and motives.

Sleep may have homeostatic functions (Vertes, 1984). During NREM, most brain cells fire at slower rates, and protein synthesis and secretion of growth hormone are increased. Strenuous activity before sleep increases the amount of NREM sleep. REM sleep may serve to ameliorate some of the adverse effects of NREM sleep: more deaths occur at night than during the day (Vertes, 1984). Furthermore, defects in REM structures that normally act to ameliorate otherwise fatal NREM sleep effects may cause the Oriental Nightmare Death Syndrome (most people who die during nightmares are Asian) and the sudden infant death syndrome. As we mentioned earlier, deprivation of REM or NREM sleep can cause injury and death (Rechtshaffen et al., 1983; Vertes, 1984).

Biochemistry of sleep and arousal.   The catecholamines may act synergistically with regard to sleep, and 5-HT may be a part of NREM sleep, whereas ACH may be involved in REM sleep. NE agonists facilitate and antagonists inhibit arousal and REM sleep (Monti, 1982, 1983). But depleting NE does not decrease cortical activation (Vertes, 1984). DA agonists in small doses decrease and in large doses increase arousal. Furthermore, blocking both NE and DA receptors

simultaneously greatly decreases arousal (Monti, 1982). 5-HT is important to NREM sleep: injecting the 5-HT precursor, 5-hydroxy-tryptophan, into the blood stream or 5-HT itself into the cerebral ventricles induces sleep and cortical synchronization, and drugs inhibiting 5-HT synthesis suppress sleep. ACh agonists injected directly into the pons of cats cause the cortical activation and the paralysis of REM sleep (D. D. Kelly, 1981a).

Single-Unit Recordings during Sleep and Arousal

Single-unit research has explored the codes for sleep stages and arousal levels. Some cells are devoted to muscle control and others may be responsible for some of the effects that a change in arousal levels has on stimulus codes.

Cells affecting motoneurons.   Organisms are paralyzed during REM sleep because the motoneurons of the spinal cord and the cranial nerves become hyperpolarized (Chase, Chandler, & Nakamura, 1980; Chandler, Chase, & Nakamura, 1980; Chandler, Nakamura, & Chase, 1980; Chase & Morales, 1983; Glenn & Dement, 1981). Oddly enough, stimulation of the pontine RF during waking excites motoneurons, whereas stimulation from the same electrode in the same place when the organism is sleeping causes hyperpolarization (Chandler, Nakamura, & Chase, 1980). The pontine RF (ventral to the LC, the LCa, and peri LCa of Figure 8-4) tonically excites medullary RF cells throughout REM sleep, and, in turn, medullary cells inhibit motoneurons (Chase, Enomoto, Murakami, Nakamura, & Taira, 1981), causing the paralysis of REM sleep. Instead of running and jumping, muscles only twitch, and people dream about being unable to move or being unable to escape from something. Cats in whom these areas of the brain are defective display flight, attack, and running during REM sleep.

Mesencephalic RF cells and sleep cycles.   Many mesencephalic RF cells are most active during arousal and REM sleep and are considerably less active during NREM sleep. This pattern was first discovered by Moruzzi and his associates (see, for example, Mollica, Moruzzi, & Naquet, 1953) and later demonstrated in freely moving rats (Komisaruk & Olds, 1968; Vertes, 1979). Machne and his co-workers (Machne, Calma, and Magoun, 1955), working with paralyzed cats, found that many RF cells increase their activity both during naturally produced arousal (painful stimulation) and when the RF is electrically stimulated. Injecting caffeine into anesthetized rats also causes an increase in the firing rates of mesencephalic reticular neurons (Chou, Khan, Forde, & Hirsh, 1985). Interestingly enough, if the rats have been preadapted by being given caffeine water to drink for two weeks prior to single-unit recording, these cells no longer respond to low doses of caffeine. The energizing effect of caffeine upon motor activity is also attentuated by caffeine adaptation.

But these mesencephalic cells are probably not responsible for switching from NREM to REM sleep (Vertes, 1984) or for coding arousal level. For example, if an animal is focusing attention on some stimulus, RF firing rates may *decrease* temporarily (Kasamatusu, 1970). These cells may simply be responsible for triggering REM desynchronization (see Figure 8-4) since their activity increases just *before* cortical activation is seen (Steriade, Oakson, & Robert, 1982).

Arousal: Noradrenergic, serotonergic, and dopaminergic cells.   The RF is not a uniform structure: cells of a specific type are gathered together in nuclei (collections of cell bodies) located throughout its extent. Each nucleus has somewhat different changes in activity during the stages of sleep and changes in the organism's level of arousal.

Many noradrenergic reticular cells (see Figure 8-7) originate in the areas labeled A5, A7, A2, and A1. Their axons in the ventral bundle project to structures in the lower brain stem, the hypothalamus, the preoptic area, and the septum. The locus coeruleus (LC; A6 in Figure 8-7a) projects largely in the dorsal bundle to the entire cortex and to many limbic structures. The adrenergic types of cells illustrated in Figure 8-8 overlap NE cells in origin and projection, so epinephrine may also be important to activation and arousal.

Changes in the arousal level of a waking animal are directly related to the firing rates of many NE cells. Both aversive arousal (fear, anxiety, and pain) and incentive arousal (food presentation) can increase the activity of LC cells in both rats and monkeys, species in which most LC cells are noradrenergic (Aston-Jones & Bloom, 1981a, 1981b; Foote, Aston-Jones, & Bloom, 1980). LC activity might allow the organism to be vigilant, and it may help the organism to respond to stress appropriately (Aston-Jones, 1985; Jacobs, 1986; Segal, 1985). However, LC cells do not respond to sensory stimuli when the animal is asleep, and the lowest level of activity found in these cells occurs during REM sleep (Aston-Jones & Bloom, 1981a; Steinfels, Heym, Strecker, & Jacobs, 1983; Trulson, & Jacobs, 1979; Trulson & Trulson, 1983). Thus, LC neurons are not involved in any REM-sleep event and are probably more important to phasic or stimulus-induced, generalized arousal than to sleep stages and events (Vertes, 1984).

The serotonergic cells of the raphe nuclei are illustrated in Figure 8-9. As Figure 8-10 shows, the firing rate of some 5-HT raphe cells is also directly related to level of arousal

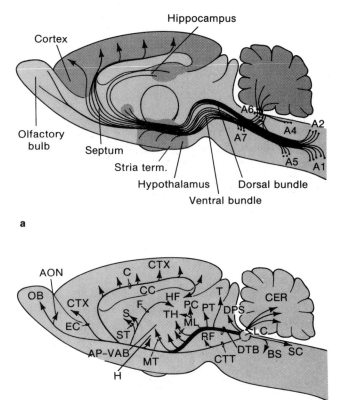

Figure 8-7   Sagittal projections of the ascending norepinephrine (NE) pathways in the rat brain.   **a.** Stippling indicates major nerve terminal areas. One major NE pathway arises from cells in the medulla and pons (A1, A2, A5, and A7) and passes through the ventral tegmental area before continuing in the **medial forebrain bundle.** These fibers innervate the lower brain stem, hypothalamus, preoptic area, and septum.   **a, b.** The other major pathway arises from the locus coeruleus (A6) and passes the other pathway dorsally but later joins the medial forebrain bundle and enters the hypothalamus intermingled with fibers from the ventral bundle and with dopaminergic fibers. A6 neurons project diffusely throughout the telencephalon, including the cortex. AON = anterior olfactory nucleus; AP-VAB = ansa peduncularis-ventral amygdaloid bundle system; BS = brain stem nuclei; C = cingulum; CC = corpus callosum; CER = cerebellum; CTT = central tegmental tract; CTX = cerebral neocortex; DPS = dorsal periventricular system; DTB = dorsal catecholamine bundle; EC = external capsule; F = fornix; H = hypothalamus; HF = hippocampal formation; LC = locus coeruleus; ML = medial lemniscus; MT = mamillothalamic tract; OB = olfactory bulb; PC = posterior commissure; PT = pretectal area; RF = reticular formation; S = septal area; SC = spinal cord; ST = stria terminalis; T = tectum; TH = thalamus.

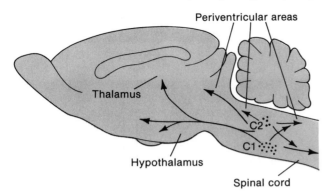

Figure 8-8 A sagittal section from the rat brain shows the ascending adrenergic pathways. They overlap extensively with the noradrenergic pathways, and so adrenergic cells might have similar types of effect on the brain.

(Trulson & Jacobs, 1979). However, these cells are probably not part of any arousal code. 5-HT raphe neurons in freely moving cats do continue to respond to external stimuli even during sleep (Trulson, Crisp, & Trulson, 1984; Trulson & Trulson, 1983; Steinfels et al., 1983). Like NE cells, 5-HT cells fire at their lowest rates during REM sleep (Aston-Jones & Bloom, 1981a; Trulson & Jacobs, 1979; Trulson, Crisp, & Trulson, 1984). As we pointed out earlier, injections of 5-HT can induce sleep, and *increases* in 5-HT are associated with *decreases* in motivated behaviors. Because of these data, Trul-

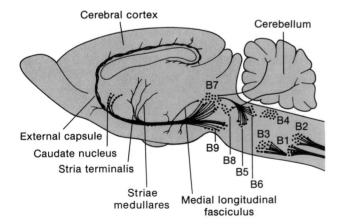

Figure 8-9 The main serotonin pathways in the rat brain. The clusters of serotonergic neurons are often found along the raphe nuclei. Electrical stimulation of the raphe nuclei inhibits cells whose axons form the spinothalamic tract; thus, serotonergic cells control the input of sensory information at the level of the spinal cord.

son and Jacobs (1979) suggested that 5-HT cells may increase their firing rates during waking arousal because they are part of a compensatory system whose function is to prevent over-arousal.

The dopaminergic reticular cells are illustrated in Figure 8-11. One important group of DA cells originates in the substantia nigra (see A9 in Figure 8-11) and extends to the striatum (the **nigrostriatal** projection). The **ventral tegmental** A10 axons project throughout the hypothalamus, the limbic system, and the cerebral cortex. Unlike that of NA and 5-HT cells, the firing rate of some brain-stem DA cells does not change during many spontaneous variations in arousal (Trulson, 1985). Ventral tegmental cells (including the substantia nigra) show no change in firing rate on going from quiet waking to NREM sleep, and their rate increases only slightly with high levels of arousal. These cells are also unaffected by conditions that normally change deficit or incentive arousal, such as hunger or the sight of food (Trulson, Crisp, & Trulson, 1983; Trulson & Preussler, 1984).

However, in freely moving cats a few DA cells do show an excitatory response to sights and sounds when single-unit activity is summed over a period of seconds (Trulson, 1985). These responses to external sensory stimuli become strongly inhibitory when the animal pays attention to them, and the responses are suppressed during sleep (Steinfels et al., 1983). As we suggested earlier (Chapter 4), activity levels in aminergic cells may change only slowly in response to excitatory types of input. Also, manipulations of DA levels affect sleep and arousal.

One study compared midbrain DA and non-DA cells (Miller, Farber, Gatz, Roffwarg, & German, 1983). Although the non-DA cells in the substantia nigra and nearby regions were dramatically more active during arousal and REM sleep than during quiet waking or NREM sleep, the DA cells (including A10 cells projecting to limbic and cortical regions) showed no such changes in firing rate. So the effects of DA agonists and antagonists on arousal and activation may not involve substantia nigra cells, at least if the relevant pattern code is overall rate of firing.

Activity in DA cells may specifically reflect *conditioned* arousal or attention evoked by a specific stimulus. Most DA cells are inactive in the awake, behaving rat, so one study used a DA blocker to inhibit presynaptic DA receptors in order to identify DA cells by the increase in spontaneous rate of activity (the DA blocker also *reduced* behavioral activity levels) (Miller, Sanghera, & German, 1981). Some DA cells changed firing rate in response to an S[D] or a CS. Both cues were used to signal a milk-chocolate reward for hungry rats. In the A9 region, five cells decreased and three increased their firing rates in response to these stimuli. In A10, most cells

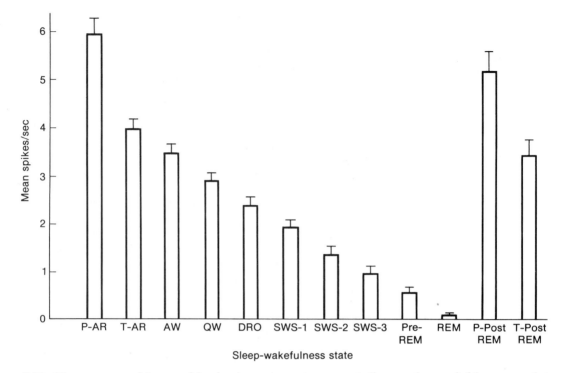

Figure 8-10 The spontaneous firing rate of dorsal raphe neurons varies systematically across sleep – wakefulness – arousal states; their firing rate seems to be directly related to the animal's level of arousal. P-AR = phasic arousal, stimulus evoked; T-AR = tonic arousal; AW = active waking; QW = quiet waking, DRO = drowsy; SWS-1 = early slow-wave sleep; SWS-2 = middle slow-wave sleep; SWS-3 = late slow-wave sleep; Pre-REM = 60 seconds before REM started; REM = rapid-eye-movement sleep; P-Post REM = one second after REM ended; T-Post REM = 10 seconds after REM. Vertical bars are standard errors of the mean.

increased, but most unresponsive cells were also found in A10 (A10 = ventral tegmentum; A9 = substantia nigra). Trulson and his co-workers (Trulson, Crisp, & Trulson, 1983; Trulson & Preussler, 1984) also found that a conditioned anxiety state increased firing rates.

Many pontine RF cells are cholinergic (D. D. Kelly, 1981a). These cells branch extensively throughout the reticular system, spinal cord, thalamus, and hypothalamus. Once it was suggested that the ACh RF cells may be coding for — and thus causing — REM sleep. Although the gigantocellular (cholinergic?) pontine RF cells (NGC in Figure 8-4) do increase their firing rates during the transition from NREM to REM sleep, their firing pattern during REM sleep is phasic, as opposed to the tonic pattern required by that suggestion. The phasic bursts of firing occur during specific movements in an awake animal and during muscle twitches in REM sleep (Hobson, McCarley, Freedman, & Pivik, 1974; Siegel, 1979).

Codes for arousal and sleep. The cells responsible for triggering either REM or NREM sleep have not been identified. Furthermore, any hypothesized code for sleep and arousal must recognize the differences among cells found even within a given area. For example, Chu and Bloom (1973) found that the activity of some LC cells in the cat increased (non-NE cells?) and that of some decreased (NE cells?) on going from waking to NREM sleep. Hobson, McCarley, and Wyzinski (1975) suggested that the increased-rate cells might trigger NREM sleep.

In conclusion, single-unit studies during the sleep – wakefulness cycle and during stimulus-evoked changes in arousal level suggest that activity in some groups of RF cells might be one aspect of the brain's code for nonspecific arousal and/or part of the reasons for the effects that arousal has on stimulus processing. But to demonstrate that this is a code and not just a sign, the change in cell activity must be functionally related to the behavioral effects of arousal. Relating activity in

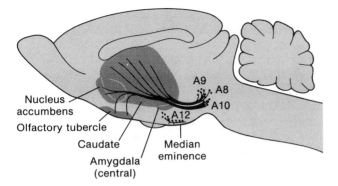

Figure 8-11   The sagittal projection of the ascending dopa- mine (DA) pathways in the rat brain includes three groups of cells. The cell bodies of the DA = containing neurons include a group in the substantia nigra (A9), a more caudal group (A8), and a third, ventral group that surrounds the tegmental group (A10). Axons from A9 and A8 ascend in the internal capsule, passing through the globus pallidus to terminate in the caudate- putamen; they are part of the nigrostriatal projection. Axons from A10 terminate in the basal telencephalon, including the nucleus accumbens and olfactory tubercle; these are the meso- limbic fibers. Other DA fibers (not shown) terminate in the frontal and cingulate cortex.

various RF cell groups to arousal-evoked changes in sensory coding is a first step in this direction.

Arousal and Responses in the Sensory Systems

Shifts in attention are associated with shifts in patterns of neural activity. For example, dogs conditioned to attend to visual or auditory stimuli show suppressions of grossly re- corded cortical evoked activity in response to the attended stimulus and an increase in the potentials evoked by an irrele- vant stimulus (Young, Ellison, & Feeney, 1971). Thus, it is not surprising that phasic changes of arousal affect spontane- ous and evoked activity in sensory cells. In fact, single-unit responses to stimuli are more reliable and consistent in the awake, attentive subject than in inattentive, sleeping, or anes- thetized subjects.

Effect of arousal on sensory coding.   One early study showed how single-unit activity in RF cells might be related to sensory processing. Goodman (1968) recorded **multiple- unit activity** (simultaneous activity of several cells) in the mesencephalic RF of monkeys. The monkeys had been trained to press a bar in response to a visual stimulus to obtain

water. The shortest reaction times occurred only during mod- erate RF firing rates; both faster and slower RF firing rates always meant longer reaction times. In this experiment, mod- erate levels of EEG activation (arousal?) were associated with the most efficient behaviors.

Arousal and the visual system of mammals.   In cats, the firing rates of cells in the lateral geniculate and optic tract vary with the sleep–wakefulness cycle. Geniculate cells began re- sponding more to diffuse light when the cat was awakened (Hubel, 1960; Livingstone & Hubel, 1981). However, both the response to an excitatory center *and* the inhibitory re- sponse to the surround were increased after awakening. Lat- eral geniculate cells are tonically depolarized during REM sleep and are hyperpolarized during NREM sleep (Hirsch, Fourment, & Marc, 1983). The hyperpolarization may ex- plain why excitatory effects of input to the lateral geniculate are inhibited during sleep.

Cells in the visual cortex are also more responsive to visual stimuli when animals are awake and attentive. Along with increased responsiveness, Visual Area I cells become *more* selective in their responses to changes in stimuli when the cat is phasically aroused (Hubel, 1959; Livingstone & Hubel, 1981). The visually responsive neurons of the inferotemporal cortex in primates may become completely unresponsive to visual stimuli when the EEG goes from desynchronized to synchronized (awake to sleeping) (Gross, Rocha-Miranda, & Bender, 1972). And when a primate is attending to a visual stimulus, the visually evoked activity of cells in its inferotem- poral and prefrontal cortex is altered (Mikami, Ito, & Kubota, 1982; Moran & DeSimone, 1985).

Arousal and the auditory system.   Auditory cells are also affected both by tonic changes in level of nonspecific arousal and by phasic changes or attention. Brugge and Merzenich (1973) found that cortical cells in primates become less re- sponsive to tones when the EEGs are synchronized (that is, during sleep). The cells became even less responsive during REM sleep. Presentation of an aversive CS changes tone- evoked activities in auditory cortex cells. The tone-evoked activity of some nerve cells is increased and that of others is decreased during the CS (Kitzes, Farley, & Starr, 1978).

When primates are attending to tones, cellular responses to those stimuli become more selective and more reliable (Bea- ton & Miller, 1985; Benson & Hienz, 1978; Hocherman, Benson, Goldstein, Heffner, & Hienz, 1976; Miller, Sutton, Pfingst, Ryan, Beaton, & Gourevitch, 1972). For example, cells in the auditory cortex become even more responsive to tones after the animal has been given operant training in tone discriminations. Responsiveness increases still more when the trained animal is actually performing the task it was trained to do — as opposed to just sitting around in its home cage listening to tones. Similar effects of training can be seen in inferior colliculi and medial geniculate cells (Ryan, 1975).

Arousal and signal-to-noise ratio.   The effects just described may occur because both nonspecific arousal and attention increase the **signal-to-noise ratio** of stimulus processing. Spontaneous background activity is the "noise" and evoked activity is the signal. Behavioral arousal and cortical activation increase the size of the "signal" in relation to the "noise." Arousal therefore makes the organism more responsive to sensory input, and paying attention to a particular type of input would further increase responsiveness. For example, both amphetamine and caffeine increase arousal and attention, and both drugs also increase the effect of mesencephalic RF stimulation upon cortical cell activity. In addition, even in the absence of arousal, these drugs increase the signal-to-noise ratio of sensory processing in cortical nerve cells (Arushanian & Belozertsev, 1978).

NE and the locus coeruleus.   Changes in signal-to-noise ratio may be specifically associated with activity in the NE, LC cells. Many of the effects of arousal on sensory processing can be duplicated by stimulating the LC. For example, Livingstone and Hubel (1981) found that spontaneous or phasic arousal and LC stimulation had exactly the same effects on visual cells. Also, microiontophoretic injections of NE onto cerebellar, cortical, and collicular cells cause changes in them identical to those caused by LC stimulation or stimulus-evoked arousal (Moises, Woodward, Hoffer, & Freedman, 1979; Sato & Kayama, 1983; Segal, 1985; Waterhouse & Woodward, 1980; Woodward, Moises, Waterhouse, Hoffer, & Freedman, 1979). NE by itself causes hyperpolarization, but neurons given any of these treatments have larger excitatory *and* larger inhibitory responses to sensory stimuli. Similarly, LC stimulation inhibits cells in the hippocampus through NE synapses. When subthreshold LC stimulation preceded the presentation of a tone, a CS^+ for food, the response to the tone was increased (Segal & Bloom, 1976). So NE increases the signal-to-noise ratio of any type of sensory-evoked activity.

NE may produce these effects because it blocks Ca-activated K^+ channels. By doing so, NE selectively increases hippocampal cell responses to strong inputs and decreases responses to weaker synaptic inputs (Madison & Nicoll, 1982).

Thus, if the effects of weaker inputs are called "noise," NE increased the signal-to-noise ratio in these cells.

As we pointed out before, the LC might be associated largely with nonspecific arousal. LC cells are activated by painful stimuli or during states of fear and anxiety. However, in awake, spontaneously behaving rats and monkeys, these cells also respond to visual, auditory, and nonnoxious somatosensory stimuli (Foote, Aston-Jones, & Bloom, 1980). LC responses to these sensory stimuli are indirect, implying that considerable processing of the stimulus information occurs before activity in LC cells is affected by those stimuli (Aston-Jones, Ennis, Pieribone, Nickell, & Shipley, 1986). The responsiveness of LC cells to various stimuli seems to reflect how responsive the animal is to those same stimuli. If the animal stops paying attention to a stimulus, LC cells stop responding to it. The more arousing the stimulus is, the greater its effect on LC activity.

Both incentive and noxious arousal can affect LC cells. For example, LC cells in monkeys are most strongly stimulated by the sight of a preferred food or of an unfamiliar person entering the room. This nonspecific phasic arousal and the associated activity in LC cells may explain why aversive stimuli and positive incentives both can increase the signal-to-noise ratio in sensory cells.

Summary of Arousal Effects

Spontaneous changes in arousal and arousability are paralleled by changes in various RF cell activity, suggesting that cells in some of these nuclei might be part of the brain's codes for specific and nonspecific, phasic and tonic, arousal and attention. For example, LC stimulation, NE application, and spontaneous arousal all increase the signal-to-noise ratio in sensory cells. Sensory cells become more responsive to appropriate stimuli and may even become more selective in their responses.

We now know which cells respond in what ways to specific and nonspecific arousals. What we do not know yet is whether these responses are signs or codes. For example, DA agonists and antagonists do affect sleep and arousal, but since some DA cells are not affected by either sleep stage, aversive drives, or incentive arousal, their activity may not be part of a code for nonspecific arousal. The 5-HT raphe cells have been theoretically related to NREM sleep because of the effects of 5-HT agonists and antagonists, but many raphe cells are not more active in NREM sleep than in waking. However, the pattern of their activity rather than just its rate could be related to an NREM sleep code.

Consequently, future studies will have to focus on the pattern and variability in responses. As Evarts (1967) discovered, the cells that are most active during waking tend to decrease activity when the animal falls asleep, whereas the least active cells tend to *increase* in activity at that time. Thus, the variability in activity decreases from waking to sleep. We don't know whether average rate of activity, variability in rate, or rate pattern is most important to the relationship between RF activity and motivated behaviors.

Single-unit activity in RF cells might be related to motivational effects. For example, some RF activity is related to changes in sensory coding. Comparing RF activity with activity in command cells and with more aspects of behavior would be useful. Until this has been done, we have not proved that any single-unit activity in RF cells is related to the code for either the nonspecific or specific arousal aspects of emotions and motives.

Basic Physiology of Two Homeostatic Motives

Some of the basic physiology of hunger and thirst will be covered in this section. The research on transmitters and food intake might someday lead to the ideal antiobesity pill.

Hunger

Food deprivation (hunger) and eating (satiety) affect many areas of the body and brain. Just as the brain processes external sensory information in parallel systems, it may also process internal motivational information in multiple interdependent but parallel systems.

Hunger: Internal changes caused by food deprivation. Figure 8-12 summarizes some changes that occur in the body in the **postabsorptive** (deprived) state (Booth, 1981; Friedman & Stricker, 1976; Grossman, 1979). Blood glucose may drop slightly. Increased sympathetic activity stimulates both **glycogenolysis** (breakdown of glycogen into glucose) in the liver and **lipolysis** (breakdown of fatty tissue into glycerol and **free fatty acids**). The liver converts the free fatty acids into ketone bodies, used as fuel by the brain and muscles. Sympathetic nerves stimulate the pancreas to secrete **glucagon** and the adrenal medulla to secrete epinephrine, which inhibits the entry of glucose into body cells. Thus, food deprivation increases blood levels of glucagon, epinephrine, glycerol, free fatty acids, and ketones and decreases blood levels of glucose.

The idea that glucose levels, or rate of absorption of glucose into body cells, affects hunger and intake of food is the **glucostatic theory,** usually attributed to Mayer (Hoyenga & Hoyenga, 1984). Le Magnen (1983) has argued that the small drop in blood glucose that occurs just before eating begins is *the* stimulus triggering eating in the food-deprived state. Campfield and his colleagues (Campfield, Brandon, & Smith, 1985) also continuously monitored blood glucose in rats and found a drop about 12 minutes prior to the rat's beginning to eat. If 10% glucose was infused into the veins to prevent the drop in glucose, the subsequent meal was delayed.

The physiological effects of food deprivation interact with each other. Epinephrine inhibits **lipogenesis** (formation of new fatty tissue) by adipose tissue and opposes both the secretion and the effects of **insulin.** Insulin normally facilitates the entry of glucose into body cells and stimulates lipogenesis in adipose (fatty) tissue. Glucagon increases the mobilization of

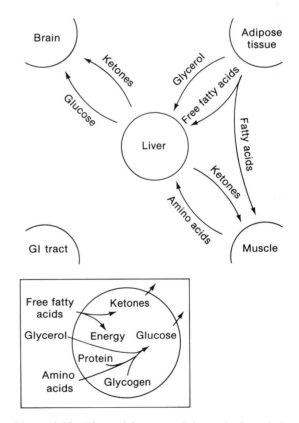

Figure 8-12   The mobilization and dispersal of metabolic fuels in the postabsorptive (deprived) state. Because the liver plays such an important role in controlling these pathways, the insert shows the pattern of activity in the liver.

liver glycogen and free fatty acids from adipose tissue. Glucagon also facilitates the production of new glucose from glycerol (from breakdown of adipose tissue) and from amino acids (from breakdown of muscle). These events help supply the organism's needs for fuels, and some of them could be the hunger stimuli transduced directly or indirectly by brain motivational cells.

Satiety: Internal responses to eating.   Figure 8-13 summarizes some of the changes caused by eating, when the organism is in a **postprandial** (after-meal) state. Digestion increases blood glucose. This effect triggers an increase in insulin, which, by stimulating glucose entry into cells, keeps blood glucose levels from rising too much above normal. Insulin also stimulates lipogenesis in adipose tissue. Interestingly enough, insulin increases even before food is placed in the mouth — a **cephalic response** (literally, a response "in the head") to food, which might increase the amount of food eaten (Geiselman & Novin, 1982; Louis-Sylvestre, 1984).

Changes in insulin level because of diabetes affect food intake by changing glucose levels. In the juvenile form of diabetes, the pancreas secretes little or no insulin. Without insulin, no glucose can move into body cells, and the diabetic is chronically hungry. Brain cells can absorb glucose without insulin, but insulin and glucose do have direct effects on some brain-cell activity. Thus, an absence of insulin could mimic part of the brain's code for food deprivation and the mental state of hunger. In the adult form of diabetes (often associated with obesity), cell insulin receptors develop "resistance." This effect is similar to the decreased sensitivity to transmitters that postsynaptic receptors display after synaptic overactivity: down regulation of receptors. In fact, the insulin receptor may be a protein kinase (Roth & Cassell, 1983), which is also a postsynaptic receptor (Chapter 4). Injections of relatively high doses of insulin will lead to eating, possibly because the insulin causes a drop in blood glucose; chronic injections of insulin can produce obesity in experimental animals.

Specialized cells in the gut are activated by food. Neurosecretory cells secrete hormones into the gut and into the blood stream. One of these hormones, **cholecystokinin (CCK)**, may be a satiety stimulus. However, CCK is released by the upper part of the intestine, and that part of the gut may *not* be required for satiety (Koopmans, 1981). Stomach afferents, including the gastric stretch receptors, send information along the parasympathetic vagus afferents to the **solitary tract** in the brain stem.

Parasympathetic efferents stimulate the liver, pancreas, and adrenal medulla. Parasympathetic afferents may carry the information back to the brain. The liver increases **glycogenesis**

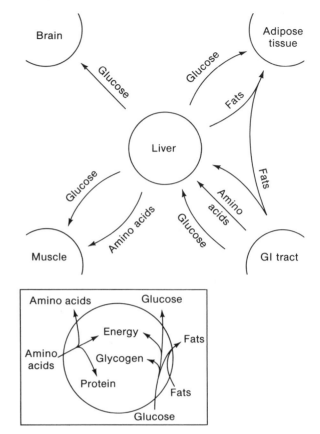

Figure 8-13   How metabolic fuels are handled in the postprandial (after-meal) state. The fuels originate in the GI (gastrointestinal) tract. Again, the liver's role is highlighted in the inset.

(formation of glycogen from glucose), pancreatic secretion of insulin is increased, and the secretion of norepinephrine is inhibited.

In the postprandial state, the body is storing nutrients. Although glycogen in the liver acts as a small "emergency" source of glucose, the major storehouse is adipose tissue. Adipose cells are gathered in fatty organs. The size of each cell and the number of cells in each organ can increase to enlarge storage capacity, if necessary; the result can be obesity.

Fat stores may also indirectly provide satiety stimuli. Kennedy (1953) proposed a **lipostatic theory** in which changes in body fat levels affect food intake and hunger. Adipose cells may send hormonal stimuli (insulin?) to the brain, signaling their size and number. Surgical removal of adipose tissue, which should decrease the hormonal stimulus for eating, causes animals to eat less, even when tempted with a highly preferred food (Faust, Johnson, & Hirsch, 1977). Furthermore, hunger (as measured by food intake) is much more closely related to the total loss of fat in the body than to the time since the last meal (see, for example, Neuringer & Campell, 1983).

Brown adipose tissue.   Until this point, when we discussed fat cells we were talking about *white* fat cells. But another type of adipose tissue may also provide satiety stimuli. Unlike white fat, it appears brownish under the microscope because of its dense concentration of mitochondria. This is brown fat, or **brown adipose tissue (BAT),** a tissue specialized for production of heat (Hoyenga & Hoyenga, 1982, 1984). When stimulated by the sympathetic nervous system or by norepinephrine, its heat production increases. Exposure to cold activates BAT, and adaptation to a cold environment increases its size and thermogenic capacity. Researchers have suggested that at least some BAT exists in all mammals, including the adult human. BAT organs are found around the cervical spinal cord, between the shoulder blades, in the armpit region, in the chest cavity, and around the kidneys.

BAT is stimulated by eating (Glick, 1982; Himms-Hagen, Triandafillou, & Gwilliam, 1981; Rothwell & Stock, 1979, 1983; Trayhurn, Goodbody, & James, 1982; but see Hervey & Tobin, 1983). BAT may have originally evolved as an adaptation to cold environments and later become adapted for use during overeating. Eating stimulates brown fat either through the sympathetic nervous system or by circulating NE. Even eating a single meal causes a quick increase in BAT thermogenesis (Glick, 1982; Glick, Teague, & Bray, 1981). In this case, the heat production is termed **dietary thermogenesis (DIT).** During DIT, food energy is converted into heat and dissipated rather than being stored as lipid in white fat cells. Because the BAT in an organism can grow whenever that organism consistently overeats, BAT thermogenesis may moderate the obesity-inducing effects of overindulgence.

BAT may send direct or indirect thermogenic stimuli to the brain. This possibility updates Brobeck's (1948) **thermostatic theory,** according to which animals use food intake to regulate body (especially brain) temperature. Rats of different genetic backgrounds, given different diets, all eat enough to maintain a comparatively constant daily level of DIT (Jenkins & Hershberger, 1978). Also, the larger the meal, the more BAT thermogenesis occurs (Glick, 1982). The rate of BAT thermogenesis may be a satiety stimulus for the brain because of heat receptors either in the brain or in BAT, the information being carried to the brain by autonomic afferents.

The hypothalamus and hunger.   Many areas of the brain, especially the hypothalamus and structures in the limbic sys-

tem, are involved in hunger and satiety. The research we will describe here used gross stimulation and lesion techniques. Two hypothalamic areas have been extensively studied: the ventromedial and the lateral regions (Grossman, 1979; Keesey & Powley, 1975; Nisbett, 1972; Panksepp, 1974; Powley, 1977; Sclafani & Kluge, 1974). The human hypothalamus is illustrated in Figure 8-14.

The **ventromedial region of the hypothalamus (VMH)** contains cells that may be part of a satiety system. VMH stimulation causes an animal to drop any food from its mouth: the animal does not begin to eat again until the stimulation ends. Conversely, bilateral lesions in the ventromedial nucleus impair satiety. The relevant lesions may have destroyed neurons outside the ventromedial nucleus itself (Gold, 1973). However, it now seems as though much of the earlier research were confounded; the studies with negative results used male rats, whereas the studies that used females got positive results: VMH lesions reliably cause obesity in females (King & Frohman, 1986). (Similarly, the specific association of obesity with damage to the ventral noradrenergic bundle, which passes close to the VMH on its way to the lateral perifornical area, has also been challenged: Peters, Gunion, & Wellman, 1979).

Animals with a damaged VMH begin eating one long meal shortly after surgery (at least, the females do) and continue to eat somewhat more frequently and in much larger meals than normal for several weeks. During the period of overeating, the animals are described as showing **dynamic hyperphagia.** Once the animals have eaten themselves into obesity, the hyperphagia decreases and body weight levels stabilize at a new, considerably higher level. The animals are now in a **static** phase.

Both static- and dynamic-phase animals overreact to stimuli. Both are oversensitive to the taste of food. Dynamics will eat even more if they are offered something like chocolate chip cookies, and static animals will lose weight if bitter quinine is added to their food. Furthermore, environmental stimuli such as being touched, which does not produce emotional responses in normal rats, causes VMH rats (rats with VMH lesions) to become anxious or aggressive. The obesity comes largely from overeating, but VMH lesions also cause changes in levels of insulin. Basal (between-meal) levels of insulin, secretion of insulin in response to eating, and even the cephalic insulin response are all increased, shifting metabolism toward storage of calories as fat.

VMH lesions produce degenerative changes in brown fat, and the degeneration may be more extensive in females (Hogan, Coscina, & Himms-Hagen, 1982; Seydoux, Rohner-Jeanrenaud, Assimacopoulos-Jeannet, Jeanrenaud, & Girardier, 1981). The change in BAT after VMH lesions may be a

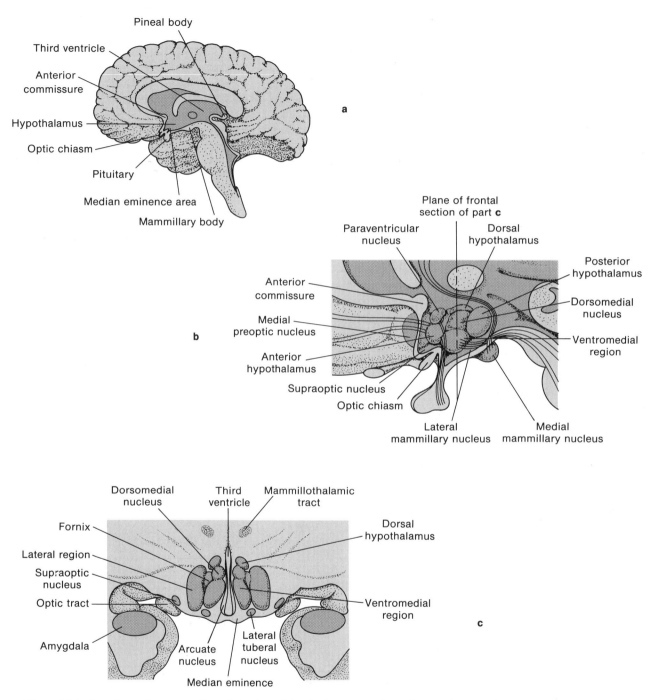

Figure 8-14 Location and structure of hypothalamic nuclei in the human. **a.** Sagittal view. **b.** Magnified sagittal view. **c.** Coronal (frontal) view of the hypothalamus at the level of the plane shown in b.

form of transneuronal degeneration. Stimulating the VMH activates BAT (Perkins, Rothwell, Stock, & Stone, 1981; Shimazu & Takahashi, 1980). Since changes in BAT affect DIT, VMH animals gain weight even when restricted to normal amounts of food, and females gain much more weight after VMH damage than males do (some males do not gain at all) (Hoyenga & Hoyenga, 1982; King & Frohman, 1986).

The **lateral region of the hypothalamus (LH)** contains cells that may be part of a hunger system. Stimulating the LH causes eating, even in satiated rats. Bilateral lesions of the LH cause aphagia, **adipsia** (lack of drinking), and, eventually, death from starvation. However, if after surgery the animals are given direct stomach injections of food and water and good nursing care, they will eventually begin to eat within 5 to 30 days (Teitelbaum & Epstein, 1962; Teitelbaum & Stellar, 1954). (See Chapter 12 for a discussion of recovery from brain damage.)

The animals still show some interesting deficits after "recovery" (Grossman, 1979; Stricker & Zigmond, 1976; Teitelbaum, Schallert, & Whishaw, 1983). If the animals are given only normal rat chow, they remain skinnier than normal, especially the males (Hoyenga & Hoyenga, 1982). LH animals (animals with LH lesions) still will not eat in response to insulin and they will not drink when dehydrated. They are "finicky" eaters, rejecting even slightly bitter food. LH rats also show **sensory neglect;** they ignore a variety of external stimuli, not just food stimuli (Feeney & Wier, 1979; Levitt & Teitelbaum, 1975; Marshall, 1978; Teitelbaum, Schallert, & Whishaw, 1983; Wolgin & Teitelbaum, 1978).

LH and VMH: Theories of hunger control. One theory claims that all organisms may have a **set point** for body weight (Keesey & Powley, 1975; Nisbett, 1972; Sclafani & Kluge, 1974). A set point in the brain is analogous to a thermostat. If body weight falls below the set point, certain brain cells are activated to produce hunger. If body weight is increased above the set point (as by chronic insulin injections), hunger will be inhibited until the level of body weight falls back toward normal. Thus, organisms made artificially obese do not eat until their body weight returns close to normal.

LH and VMH neurons may regulate set-point level. For example, if animals are made obese *before* they are given VMH lesions, they are *not* hyperphagic after surgery. Instead, they eat just enough to maintain that higher-than-normal body weight. Conversely, if animals are starved *before* they are given LH lesions, they do *not* show aphagia after the surgery. They eat just enough food to maintain that lower-than-normal level of body weight. Thus, damage to LH cells, which would obviously decrease their activity, may reset the set point down-ward; damage to VMH cells would reset the set point upward.

The results of LH and VMH lesions and stimulations can also be explained by a drive theory of motivation. Food deprivation disrupts homeostasis and organisms are compelled to search for food. Cells in the LH and VMH sense (transduce?) internal states, such as the states that are created by a change in the level of glucose and/or a change in the size and number of fat cells. VMH cell activity would inhibit and LH cell activity would evoke that drive.

An incentive theory can also fit the data. Activity in VMH cells would normally *inhibit* the incentive arousal evoked by the sight and smell of food. Activity in VMH cells would literally make food smell and taste less palatable to an organism; the organism would be less aroused by food and therefore less likely to eat. VMH cells would be activated by satiety stimuli. Conversely, activity in LH cells might make eating more reinforcing to the animal or might increase the incentive arousal evoked by food. LH cells would be activated by hunger *and* by food stimuli, and VMH cells should inhibit LH cells.

Lesions would affect the incentive value of food. Lesions of the LH would mean that food deprivation would no longer increase the incentive arousal evoked by food. In fact, the ability to be aroused by the sight of food when deprived of food seems to be drastically damaged in LH-lesioned cats (Wolgin & Teitelbaum, 1978). Damage to the VMH would mean that increases in body weight would be much less able to inhibit the incentive value of food. With VMH damage, satiety would no longer make food taste less pleasant and so the organism would continue to eat. This theory thus explains why LH-lesioned animals react less to all kinds of external stimuli and VMH-lesioned animals tend to overreact. Amphetamine, which increases arousal, also increases eating in LH-lesioned animals (it increases blood glucose and inhibits eating in intact animals: Wolgin & Teitelbaum, 1978). Figure 8-15, which presents one model of the hypothalamic control of hunger, summarizes many of these results.

DA, hunger, and the hypothalamus. DA agonists and antagonists have inconsistent effects on eating, as Table 8-1 indicates. Stricker and Zigmond (1976) say that LH lesions cause aphagia because the DA hunger circuits passing through the LH have been destroyed. Using an incentive-arousal theory, these researchers say that because a decrease in brain DA levels impairs organisms' ability to become normally aroused by stimuli, LH-lesioned rats are not aroused by food or by hunger.

Eating does affect brain DA levels. Eating increases DA metabolites in rat brains (Heffner, Hartman, & Seiden, 1980), which means that DA neurons have been stimulated. The

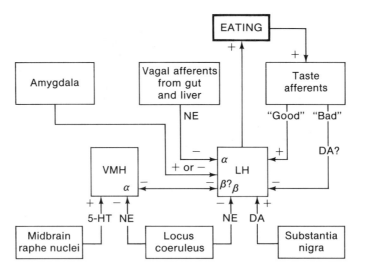

Figure 8-15 One possible model of the biochemistry and anatomy of eating and hunger. The arrows are not necessarily direct connections; for example, the connections from the LH to eating behavior probably involve many of the brain areas illustrated in Figures 8-7, 8-8, 8-9, and 8-11. "Good" and "bad" tastes are shown as having opposite effects on the LH; they probably are modulated by the animal's state of hunger (see text). 5-HT = serotonin; NE = norepinephrine; DA = dopamine; α = alpha-noradrenergic receptor; β = beta-noradrenergic receptor; plus (+) = excites; minus (−) = inhibits.

increase in DA is specific to eating and is not caused by food deprivation. Conversely, DA antagonists suppress the intake of highly palatable foods by both control and VMH-lesioned rats. These DA blockers may inhibit the incentive arousal normally experienced during eating (Xenakis & Sclafani, 1982) (it's not fun any more?).

Stricker and Zigmond's theory is supported by the effects of injecting chemical toxins (6-hydroxydopamine, or **6-OHDA**) into the brain to destroy DA and NE cells. Injections of 6-OHDA make rats act much like LH-lesioned animals, including showing sensory neglect. Aphagia occurs even when the animals are pretreated with a drug that prevents damage to NE cells so that only the DA cells are destroyed. Stricker and Zigmond also point out that strongly arousing stimuli, including handling, tail pinch, and amphetamine, can evoke feeding in either DA-depleted or LH-lesioned rats or cats (Wolgin & Teitelbaum, 1978). Animals treated with 6-OHDA or having LH lesions recover because the remaining DA neurons gradually become more effective: the number of postsynaptic receptors and levels of DA synthesizing enzymes both increase.

If Stricker and Zigmond are correct, the effects that prelesion starvation or forced feeding have on eating after LH and VMH lesions can be given an interpretation other than the set-point one. Since deprivation and overeating change brain amine levels (see Chapter 10), prelesion starvation may "preadapt" neurons, facilitating recovery after LH lesions. In other

words, the presurgical starvation of LH-lesioned rats would increase the effectiveness of all the deficit-signaling neuron circuits, decreasing recovery time. Many of the necessary changes in the remaining neurons would have already occurred during the starvation period. Similarly, a prelesion overfeeding would strongly stimulate satiety cells in to-be-VMH-lesioned subjects, changing enzyme and receptor levels, again facilitating recovery.

But the DA hypothesis is not completely consistent with all the data. First, as Table 8-1 indicates, DA agonists and antagonists do not have consistent effects on food intake in normal organisms. Some of the inconsistencies may be related to the type of food being offered. DA and agonists may specifically increase protein and might even suppress carbohydrate intake (Leibowitz, Weiss, Yee, & Tretter, 1985). Second, there are behavioral and physiological differences between LH-lesioned and DA-depleted rats. LH-lesioned rats show much less depletion of levels of DA in their brains than is usually seen after injecting the amount of 6-OHDA required to affect eating. Furthermore, smaller LH lesions can produce aphagia and adipsia without the arousal deficits caused by DA depletion (Grossman, 1979). DA agonists can restore eating in animals treated with 6-OHDA, but these agonists do *not* restore eating in LH-lesioned rats (Ljungberg & Ungerstedt, 1976). Third, the substantia nigra is one major source of DA fibers passing through the LH, and damage to that pathway alone, sparing

Table 8-1   Effects of various transmitters on eating and drinking.

Transmitter	Effect	Comments
Endorphin	Increases eating and drinking; opiate blockers (naloxone) increase self-stimulation in LH and suppress the facilitating effect that hunger has on self-stimulation	Opioid receptors; enhanced reinforcer effectiveness in part by activating NE neurons; increase intake especially of fat and protein; may suppress carbohydrate intake
GABA	In nigrostriatal tract, decreases eating	Decreases DA
	Injected into the raphe, increases eating	May increase endorphin release by stimulating DA; or works through serotonin
Prostaglandins	Decrease eating	
Satiety neuropeptides: somatostatin, neurotensin, vasoactive inhibitory peptide (VIP)	Decrease eating	Released by gut and also found in brain
Pancreatic polypeptides: neuropeptide Y, peptide YY	Increase eating	Effect may be specific to carbohydrates
Endogenous antianxiety substances	Increase eating	Increase endorphins?
Bombesin	Suppresses feeding	Present in brain; binds to receptors: systemic or LH injections work
CCK	Decreases eating	Systemic or brain injections; found in gut and in limbic system
		Brain has receptors; CCK is released by CAs; levels in VMH and LH are increased by meals in both lean and obese mice and rats
Norepinephrine	Increases dietary thermogenesis and suppresses food intake	Beta and alpha$_2$ receptors; probably peripheral effects
	Increases eating	Alpha$_2$ receptor; in paraventricular nucleus of hypothalamus; specific to carbohydrate intake
	Decreases eating	Beta receptors in brain
	Increases consumption of familiar (as opposed to unfamiliar) foods	Effects of injections into the amygdala
	Depletion of NE	Impairs taste-aversion learning
Epinephrine	Decreases eating	
Dopamine		
agonists	Increase or decrease eating	Facilitates gnawing, release of endorphins? Dopamine depletion in nigrostriatal tract decreases eating and DA agonists restore; DA depletion in VMH leads to hyperphagia
antagonists	Increase or decrease eating	Suppress intake of highly palatable carbohydrate; increase intake of and preference for protein
Serotonin	Injected into the medial hypothalamus, decreases eating	Selectively suppress carbohydrate intake

  CA = catecholamine
 CCK = cholecystokinin
  DA = dopamine
GABA = gamma-amino butyric acid
  LH = lateral hypothalamus
  NE = norepinephrine
 VMH = ventromedial hypothalamus

the LH, can cause the characteristic sensory neglect (Feeney & Wier, 1979). However, as we described earlier, the activity of substantia nigra cells is not increased by feeding, satiety, or glucose injections in cats or rats.

NE, hunger, and the hypothalamus. Leibowitz (1976, 1985; Leibowitz et al., 1985; Weiss & Leibowitz, 1985) suggested that eating occurs when alpha-adrenergic receptors are stimulated, and eating is suppressed when beta-adrenergic receptors are stimulated. However, the effect of alpha- or beta-agonists and antagonists may depend on the brain region involved (see Figure 8-15), how good the food tastes, and how hungry the animal is (Antelman & Caggiula, 1977; Margules, 1970a, 1970b; Margules & Dragovich, 1983). Alpha-adrenergic stimulation of eating may involve the paraventricular hypothalamic nucleus and may appear only when high-carbohydrate foods are offered and not when high-fat or high-protein foods are offered (Leibowitz et al., 1985).

Noradrenergic neurons regulate hunger and eating. NE infused specifically into the VMH produces eating (alpha-receptors?), whereas NE infused into the LH decreases the food intake (beta-receptors?) of hungry animals (Matthews, Booth, & Stolerman, 1978; Myers & McCaleb, 1980). However, NE placed directly onto certain LH cells inhibits them through an **alpha-adrenergic receptor** (Shimizu, Oomura, Novin, Grijalva, & Cooper, 1983). As we will describe, blood glucose inhibits these cells because of afferents innervating alpha receptors.

Hunger and satiety can change brain NE levels. Food deprivation decreases NE levels in the hypothalamus of rats (Glick, Waters, & Milloy, 1973), and eating increases the activity of the catecholaminergic axons coming from the solitary-tract nucleus (Margules & Lichtensteiger, 1978). Feeding also causes noradrenergic activity in the VMH of rats (Martin & Myers, 1975). However, the stimulus that has these effects on the VMH and LH may be the smell instead of the taste of food (Myers, McCaleb, & Hughes, 1979).

A recent study related the ability of drugs to bind to brain receptors to their ability to suppress eating (Paul, Hulihan-Giblin, & Skolnick, 1982; see also Kolata, 1982, for quotes from those authors). Receptors specific for amphetamine, a highly effective appetite suppressant in normal organisms, were concentrated in the hypothalamus and brain stem. These receptors may be presynaptic and may act to decrease NE release at alpha-adrenergic synapses. The number of these receptors in the brain decreases when animals are deprived of food for several days, and the decrease would act to increase the amount of NE released at appetite-increasing alpha-adrenergic synapses. This type of research holds out the hope of finding a drug to treat obesity, one that specifically binds to those receptors and lacks the ability of amphetamines to produce addiction and psychosis.

Serotonin. Any treatment that increases 5-HT or activates 5-HT receptors suppresses eating, and 5-HT antagonists increase eating (Blundell, 1977; Gibbons, Barr, Bridger, & Leibowitz, 1981; Table 8-1). However, depleting brain 5-HT levels by lesions (such as raphe lesions) or by drug treatment does *not* cause any consistent changes in body weight (Baez, Browning, & Cusatis, 1980; Coscina & Stancer, 1977). These negative results suggest that 5-HT neurons may play only a limited role in appetite and hunger. For example, depleting 5-HT selectively increases intake of sweet solutions (Ellison, 1977). This fact supports Wurtman's idea (1983) that 5-HT *selectively* suppresses appetite for carbohydrates (for example, cakes and cookies) but has little effect on the desire for fats or proteins.

Endorphins. Two theories of hunger and appetite have emphasized endorphins. Margules (1978, 1979) proposed that brain endorphin systems evolved to control "bodily resources and energy in anticipation of famine." Morley (Morley, 1980; Morley & Levine, 1982; Morley et al., 1983) suggested that endorphins tonically "induce" ingestive behaviors. This tonic influence is "held in check" by the monoamines and neuropeptides. These theorists summarized the evidence that opiate antagonists reduce and agonists increase intake of food as well as water (see also Table 8-1; Cooper, 1983; McLean & Hoebel, 1982; Sanger, 1981; Tepperman, Hirst, & Gowdey, 1981).

Although eating and deprivation do affect brain endorphin levels, the effects are inconsistent and so do not strongly support these theories. For example, only water and *not* food deprivation increases hypothalamic levels of one endorphin, **dynorphin,** and pituitary levels of dynorphin are *decreased* by deprivation (Reid, Konecka, Przewlocki, Millan, Millan, & Herz, 1982; Przewlocki, Laśon, Konecka, Gramsch, Herz, & Reid, 1983). Food deprivation may decrease hypothalamic but not pituitary levels of another endorphin, beta-endorphin (Gambert, Garthwaite, Pontzer, & Hagen, 1980). When nondeprived rats ate a highly palatable food, the concentration of beta-endorphin but not dynorphin was decreased, so beta-endorphin may be used up during eating. Probably different endorphins are involved in appetite (eating) and in hunger (food deprivation), and endorphins may specifically increase intake only of fat and protein (Leibowitz et al., 1985).

Other possible transmitters. The effects of other transmitter substances are also summarized in Table 8-1. The effects of microinjections depend on their location (for instance, GABA: Kelly, Alheid, Newberg, & Grossman, 1977). CCK can inhibit eating, and food deprivation may increase CCK receptors in the olfactory bulb and hypothalamus, an effect that may be related to disuse up regulation of postsynaptic receptors (Saito, Williams, & Goldfine, 1981b). But since Koopmans (1981) was unable to demonstrate that any hormone coming from the intestines, including CCK, had any effect on food intake, the CCK producing these effects may be a neuromodulator secreted by brain cells, perhaps by DA cells (Hökfelt et al., 1980). And in fact, Schick, Yaksh, and Go (1986) were able to demonstrate that eating does cause some cells in the hypothalamus to release CCK (in cats).

Thus, increasing activity in 5-HT cells should decrease the intake of, and appetite for, carbohydrates. DA may control protein intake, NE along with 5-HT may control carbohydrate intake, and endorphins may control protein and fat intake.

Dietary control of transmitters. Since many of the transmitters are manufactured from essential amino acids — ones that must come from eating — the type of food eaten may affect brain levels of transmitters (Anderson & Johnston, 1983; Fernstrom, 1981; Wurtman & Fernstrom, 1975). For example, giving animals a protein-free, high-carbohydrate meal increases brain levels of tryptophan and 5-HT. Normally

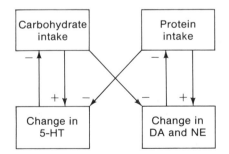

Figure 8-16 Model illustrating possible specific effects of the type of food eaten on the levels of various brain transmitters. In turn, various types of brain transmitter levels affect which type of food is preferred at any given moment. 5-HT = serotonin; DA = dopamine; NE = norepinephrine.

tryptophan competes with other amino acids to cross the blood–brain barrier. Eating a protein-free meal high in carbohydrates increases insulin, which increases the ratio of tryptophan to the other amino acids and thus facilitates the active transport of tryptophan across the blood–brain barrier. Eating pure tryptophan also increases brain 5-HT. If 5-HT selectively decreases carbohydrate intake, the effect of diet upon transmitters sets up the feedback loops illustrated in Figure 8-16.

Diet also affects other transmitters. Tyrosine levels in the diet affect brain NE, DA, and epinephrine levels. If dietary tyrosine changes NE and DA hunger-regulating neurons, the other feedback loops illustrated in Figure 8-16 might also occur. Dietary choline levels change brain choline and ACh levels, a fact that has been used occasionally to treat various kinds of movement and senile disorders related to ACh deficiencies.

Thirst

Just as it does with hunger, the brain has several thirst systems, or several separate populations of "thirst" cells, all operating in parallel (Andersson, 1978; Epstein, 1982; Fitzsimons, 1971; Rolls, Wood, & Rolls, 1980).

Two types of thirst. The two types of thirst are **osmotic** and **hypovolemic** (lowering of blood volume). Water deprivation causes both an increase in the osmotic pressure of the blood and a slight decrease in blood volume. However, normal daily consumption of water, especially in rats and primates, is governed primarily by osmotic changes, with volemic changes contributing much less — only about 20% to 26% of the rat's drinking (Rolls, Wood, & Rolls, 1980). Blocking either osmotically evoked *or* volemically evoked drinking by itself has no effect on water intake, but blocking both decreases water intake by about 70%.

An increase in the osmotic pressure of the blood — usually caused by an increase in concentration of Na^+ — stimulates osmotic receptors, or **osmoreceptors,** in the brain and periphery. At first, it was thought that these receptors were responding to Na^+ ions in the extracellular fluid. Later, researchers demonstrated that an increase in the osmotic pressure of the blood and extracellular fluid drew water out of cells, and that it was this water movement to which the (now misnamed) osmoreceptors responded (Rolls, Wood, & Rolls, 1980). The peripheral receptors are in the stomach, gut, and liver.

Hypovolemic thirst is also called extracellular thirst, since drinking is evoked by a drop in levels of extracellular fluid. Both water deprivation and blood loss can cause this kind of thirst. **Baroreceptors** (pressure receptors) are found near the heart (atrium, arotic artery, and pulmonary veins). Loss of pressure stimulates those receptors and causes drinking and hypothalamic secretion of **antidiuretic hormone (ADH),** also called **vasopressin.** ADH increases water reabsorption in the kidney, thus decreasing urine output (urine output is **diuresis**). Loss of pressure also stimulates baroreceptors in the kidney. The kidney then secretes renin into the blood, where it is converted first into angiotensin I and then into **angiotensin II.** Angiotensin II has several homeostatic effects, including contraction of arterial muscles (to maintain blood pressure), secretion of ADH, and stimulation of drinking. Angiotension receptors have been found in the brain, especially in the **subfornical organ** located on the most dorsal and anterior part of the wall of the third ventricle.

Satiety is produced by a combination of sensory input from taste cells (water receptors) and osmoreceptors in the gut and liver. How important each of these factors is varies from species to species (Rolls, Wood, & Rolls, 1980).

Control of diuresis and drinking.   Since LH lesions lead to adipsia as well as aphagia, LH cells (or axons passing through the LH) may control water intake. Osmoreceptors are found in the **preoptic area,** the **supraoptic nucleus,** and the LH. When the osmotic pressure of their blood is increased, animals with preoptic lesions do not drink as much as they did before. The parts of the hypothalamus lining the third ventricle may have both osmoreceptors and angiotensin receptors. These parts include the **periventricular nucleus of the preoptic area,** the **organum vasculosum of the lamina terminalis (OVLT),** and the subfornical organ.

Thirst transmitters.   The catecholamines, the endorphins, and ACh all affect drinking. Injecting ACh into the hypothalamus (especially the subfornical organ) elicits drinking (Routtenberg, 1972), so ACh may be important to osmotic drinking. Injections of 6-OHDA produce adipsia as well as aphagia, and how long the adipsia lasts is closely related to the degree of DA depletion (Grossman, 1979). Periodic presentation of water to water-deprived rats increases NE levels in the pons-medulla and DA levels in the caudate. But this effect seems more closely related to the rats' *expectancies* of drinking than to drinking per se. For example, the first presentation of water to deprived rats did *not* affect transmitters. The presentation of water in rats trained to expect it, even though they did not get to drink it, *did* increase catecholamine levels (Emmett-Og-

lesby, Lewy, Albert, & Seiden, 1978). Also, as we have mentioned, water deprivation increases hypothalamic but decreases pituitary dynorphin levels, and opiate agonists increase drinking.

Summary of Physiology

The physiologies of thirst and hunger, both deficit and satiety signals, are another example of parallel processing by the brain. Several signals, including blood glucose levels and hormonal stimuli from fat stores, are probably used as food-deficit stimuli. The areas around the LH and VMH, as well as limbic-system structures, contain cells (or axons from cells) that process those hunger stimuli. At least two types of signal are used to signal water deficits: osmotic and hypovolemic. Each motive has effects on multiple parallel receptor systems, both central and peripheral. The water- and food-deficit signals may directly or indirectly affect cells that have a direct input to a command system; if so, this activity may be a cellular correlate of the drive concept. Or the deficit signals may affect the way nerve cells using various transmitter substances respond to external and internal stimuli, thus affecting incentive arousal. Both probably occur.

Genetics of Hunger

There are major-gene obesities in rodents, but the genetic basis for overeating in humans is considerably more uncertain. However, recent reviews and recent data suggest that human obesity has a strong genetic basis (Bray, 1981; Bouchard, Savard, Després, Tremblay, & Leblanc, 1985; Stunkard, Foch, & Hrubec, 1986; Stunkard, Sørensen, Hanis, Teasdale, Chakraborty, Schull, & Schulsinger, 1986). There could be a hereditary defect in BAT that decreases dietary as well as cold-stimulated thermogenesis and so increases the tendency to store calories as fat, as opposed to burning them off as heat (Hoyenga & Hoyenga, 1982).

The Genetics of Overeating

First, the genetic basis of hyperphagia was explored. Next, three possible relationships between genes and food-seeking behaviors were explored. One was that the gene proteins affect some peripheral tissue, such as fat, and behavior is affected only indirectly through autonomic afferents or blood hormone levels. Second, the gene proteins could change the metabolism of some transmitter used by the feeding circuitry of the brain. Third, the gene proteins could act during fetal development to change the structure and interconnections of nerve cells in the feeding circuit.

Animal breeding studies.   Animals have been selectively bred for fast and for slow growth rates. Mice selected over several generations for high juvenile growth rates typically became obese adults (McCarthy, 1979). The obesity came from an increased efficiency in storing calories as fat (lower BAT thermogenesis?), a decreased activity level, and an increase in meal size. Meal size and energy efficiency were controlled by separate genes and so could be separately selected for or against. One study looked at the VMH of chickens bred for high and low growth rates (Burkhart, Cherry, Van Krey, & Siegel, 1983). Again, the high-rate line produced obese adult chickens and the low-rate line produced lean adults. VMH lesions produced obesity only in the low-growth-rate line, so the genes in the high line may have damaged the VMH.

Types of genetic obesity in rodents.   The gene or genes promoting obesity may have evolved when a species was exposed to a food-poor environment. Genes promoting obesity in a food-rich environment also increase that organism's chances of surviving in a food-poor environment or in times of famine. In other words, organisms genetically predisposed to obesity when food is plentiful are more likely to survive a famine, not simply because they have more fat to live off but because they have different metabolic adaptations to starvation.

These metabolic adaptations have been studied in several strains of rodents. Some rodent strains spontaneously develop obesity; this trait probably involves several genes. In other strains, a single recessive gene causes obesity in the homozygous rodent (Bray & York, 1979; Coleman, 1978). Three recessive gene strains are the *fa/fa* mutation in rats (the **fatty Zucker** rat), the *ob/ob* mutation in mice, and the diabetic-obese mutation in mice, the *db/db* mutation. In these strains, the heterozygous animal (for example, the *Fa/fa* rat) does not become obese but may show some increased resistance to starvation over the homozygous, dominant-gene *(Fa/Fa)* animal (Hoyenga & Hoyenga, 1982). Not only are the homozygous recessive rodents hyperphagic but they cannot tolerate cold (they die). They also very efficiently turn calories into fat. All this could be explained by their having less or more poorly

functioning BAT. (The same may be true of some obesities in humans, especially in females: Hoyenga & Hoyenga, 1982.)

Peripheral defects in genetically obese rodents.   Obese rodents have more numerous and larger white fat cells than do their lean relatives (Bray & York, 1979). The genetically obese rodents may have stronger and more frequent stimuli coming from their enlarged fat stores. For example, NE levels in sympathetically innervated tissue, including the heart, white fat, *and BAT*, are significantly lower in Zucker obese than in lean rats (Levin, Triscari, & Sullivan, 1981). The sympathetic nervous system — the source of that NE — is chronically suppressed, suggesting that the parts of the brain controlling that system are also suppressed. In contrast, levels of the enzyme causing lipogenesis in white fat tissue (lipoprotein lipase) are not altered by the Zucker gene (Quig, Layman, Bechtel, & Hackler, 1983).

Changes in BAT in genetically obese rodents.   The three recessive-gene obese strains of rodents have defects in BAT. One defect is in the sympathetic, beta-adrenergic control of BAT metabolism and thermogenesis. The BAT of a Zucker rat has fewer beta-adrenergic binding sites or receptors (Levin, Comai, O'Brien, & Sullivan, 1982). Normally injections of beta-adrenergic agonists stimulate adenylate cyclase activity in BAT. However, as one would predict from the decrease in number of receptors, these injections in *ob/ob* mice cause only two-thirds the increase seen in lean controls (Bégin-Heick & Heick, 1982). In addition, BAT mitochondria are defective in *ob/ob* and *db/db* mice (Goodbody & Trayhurn, 1981; Himms-Hagen & Desautels, 1978). Some of the BAT defects found in obese rodents can be normalized by food restriction. For example, food deprivation increases thermogenesis in the BAT of *ob/ob* mice (Himms-Hagen, 1985).

Deficiencies in beta-adrenergic receptors and in mitochondria may explain why the BAT of Zucker rats does not respond normally to overeating (Triandafillou & Himms-Hagen, 1983). BAT grows less during overeating in the homozygous recessive rodents than in the lean controls. Less of the food the genetically obese rodents eat is burned off, leaving more for storage in white adipose tissue. If any one of these BAT metabolic defects is the one directly related to the obesity gene, the hyperphagia associated with this gene would be secondary, possibly related to the reduced thermogenesis.

Central transmitter changes in genetically obese rodents.   CCK receptors have been identified and localized to the olfactory bulb, limbic system, and parts of the cortex (Van Dijk, Gillessen, Möhler, & Richards, 1981; see Table 8-2).

The increased numbers of CCK receptors found in obese mice might be causally related to their decreased levels of cortical CCK (CCK inhibits appetite) because of up regulation of unused postsynaptic receptors. In Zucker obese rats, however, *higher* levels of CCK were found in the ventromedial, dorsal medial, and anterior hypothalamus than in lean rats. This discrepancy in the outcomes of research with rats and mice might represent a species difference or an anatomical difference; the rat study examined only the hypothalamus and the mouse study looked only at the cortex. Hyperphagic obesity in VMH mice increases CCK receptors (Saito, Williams, Waxler, & Goldfine, 1982).

Although the reduced levels of DA and 5-HT may not be relevant, the increase in hypothalamic NE is consistent across strains. The sex difference in hypothalamic NE levels in *ob/ob* mice may be part of the reason why females become fatter than males (Hoyenga & Hoyenga, 1982). Since stimulation of alpha-receptors can stimulate eating (especially of highly palatable carbohydrates), the increased levels of NE could be related to hyperphagia.

The pattern of results listed in Table 8-2 makes the relationship between genetic obesity and brain transmitters very unclear. The decreased sensitivity of the *ob/ob* mouse to peripherally injected CCK, combined with the increased number of CCK receptors, is inconsistent with any direct role for changes in this peptide. Also, brain endorphin levels in these rodents are not abnormal—only pituitary levels are changed —and yet obese rodents respond to agonists and antagonists as though they had higher-than-normal levels of brain endorphin

receptors. Even the changes in NE may have only indirect effects, secondary to the effects of changes in size of white fat cells or BAT thermogenesis.

Changes in cell structure in genetically obese rodents. The *ob/ob* genes may alter the structure of hypothalamic neurons. VMH but not LH cells in the obese mouse have a smaller average cell-body size (Bereiter & Jeanrenaud, 1979). Furthermore, the dendrites of both VMH and LH neurons have a different kind of spatial distribution (Bereiter & Jeanrenaud, 1980) in the *ob/ob* rodent. The changes probably are caused by (or cause) changes in the types of information coming into the VMH and LH.

Implications. Most of the differences between the brains of genetically obese rodents and their lean controls can be related to brain areas and transmitter substances already identified as being important to deficit or to satiety stimuli. However, in the research on the obese rodents, cause and effect are still uncertain. Almost all the research has been done on rodents that had already developed obesity, and so whether the neural effects are primary or secondary cannot yet be determined.

Taste Preferences

Obviously, if the rewarding effects of taste were genetically altered, food intake would be affected. In incentive theories, the taste of food is the most important factor in food intake, and

Table 8-2 Central transmitter levels in genetically obese rodents.

Transmitter	Effect	References
CCK	Levels decreased in *ob/ob*	Straus & Yalow, 1979
	Increased number of receptors in *ob/ob*	Saito, Williams, & Goldfine, 1981a
	Ob/ob less sensitive to anorexic effects of peripheral injections	McLaughlin & Baile, 1981
Catecholamines	Elevated hypothalamic NE in all three strains, especially in LH and especially in female *ob/ob*	Kuprys & Oltmans, 1982; Lorden, 1979; Levin & Sullivan, 1979; Oltmans, 1983; Orosco, Jacquot, & Cohen, 1981
	Reduced DA & 5-HT levels in *fa/fa*	Finkelstein, Chance, & Fischer, 1982; Levin & Sullivan, 1979; Oltmans, 1983
	More appetite-suppressing effects of amphetamine	Grinker, Drewnoski, Enn, & Kissileff, 1980
Endorphins	Higher levels in pituitary in *ob/ob* and *fa/fa*, especially in females	Deutch & Martin, 1982; Ferguson-Segall, Flynn, Walker, & Margules, 1982; Gibson, Liotta, & Krieger, 1981; Govoni & Yang, 1981; Margules, Moisset, Lewis, Shibuya, & Pert, 1978
	Food intake more sensitive to agonists and antagonists	Ferguson-Segall et al., 1982

even though drive theories claim that food deprivation is the most important factor in food intake, they do not overlook the role played by the taste of the food.

Genetically obese rodents.   Despite earlier negative reports (see review in Bray, 1979), genetically obese *ob/ob* mice and Zucker rats apparently do show an exaggerated preference for fat (Anderson, Leprohon, Chambers, & Coscina, 1979; Castonguay, Hartman, Fitzpatrick, & Stern, 1982; Mayer, Dickie, Bates, & Vitale, 1951; Romsos, Chee, & Bergen, 1982; Romsos & Ferguson, 1982). They also tend to avoid carbohydrates. Both of these effects could reflect the increase in endorphins in these rodents (Tables 8-1 and 8-2), except that the increase is limited to the pituitary. Another possibility is that the responses of taste neurons could have been changed. Or else dietary preferences of the genetically obese rodent could be caused by altered metabolism. For example, eating carbohydrates might make these animals feel sick (because of their insulin resistance), and so they learn to avoid that type of food.

Breeding studies.   Taste preferences can be changed by selective breeding. Alcohol intake — and thus presumably the reinforcing effect of the taste of alcohol — is heritable. Strains also consistently differ in their intake of sour and salty solutions (Fuller & Thompson, 1978). This section describes the heritability of preferences for sweets.

Genes affect responses to sweet-tasting substances in humans and in rats. Humans differ from one another in how sweet they perceive solutions to be. Humans who perceive solutions of sucrose and saccharin to be abnormally sweet cannot detect the bitter taste of a certain substance (Bartoshuk, 1979; Gent & Bartoshuk, 1983). Obviously the phenomenological response to sucrose and saccharin in rats can't be measured, but the tendency to drink sweet solutions in large quantities can be bred for and against (Nachman, 1959). The trait is polygenic and the heritability is high (Fuller & Thompson, 1978).

The most intriguing strains of rats were bred for self-stimulation and not for the intake of sweet solutions (Cohen, Lieblich, & Ganchrow, 1982; Ganchrow, Lieblich, & Cohen, 1981; Lieblich, Cohen, & Beiles, 1978; Lieblich, Cohen, Ganchrow, Blass, & Bergmann, 1983; Moreau, Cohen, & Lieblich, 1984). Lieblich and colleagues selected animals for breeding according to whether their brothers and sisters showed high or low rates of self-stimulation when the electrodes had been placed into their LH. Six generations of selection produced two high (LC1-high and LC2-high) and two low self-stimulating strains (LC1-low and LC2-low) of ani-

mals. The researchers were therefore breeding for the ability to be reinforced by LH stimulation.

Animals from the four strains were tested to see what other behaviors covaried with rate of self-stimulation. For example, LH stimulation can increase eating, but it is especially effective in animals of a high strain (LC2-high: 41.7% ate in response to LH stimulation) in comparison with the animals of the corresponding low strain (LC2-low: 5.5% ate in response to LH stimulation). Animals in that same high strain also drink more saccharin than do animals in the corresponding low strain. Furthermore, not only do the females in both the LC2-high and LC2-low strains show more self-stimulation than do the males of the corresponding strains but the LC2-high females also drink more saccharin. And drinking saccharin in great quantities causes an elevation of brain opiate levels *only* in the LC2-high females.

This line of research holds out great promise. Since consumption of saccharin is associated with high rates of self-stimulation in only one of the two strains, the two strains can be compared physiologically and behaviorally to explore the genetic-biochemical reasons for their differences. For example, just how do the structure and biochemistry of cells in the LH areas differ among those four strains? Does ingestion of saccharin produce higher rates of activity in LH neurons in the LC2-high strain than in any of the other three strains?

Summary of Genetics

The heterogeneity among the strains of genetically obese animals (including obese humans) means that each gene or set of genes undoubtedly involves a different pathway from its protein to eating behavior and body weight. Although both the amount of food eaten and the type of food preferred are clearly heritable, whether the genetic effects are exerted directly on brain cells or indirectly though effects on other parts of the body cannot yet be determined. The genetic basis of both BAT activation and the effects of sweet tastes on the activity of neurons in the LH and VMH is a promising area for future research.

Neural Coding of Hunger, Thirst, and Motivationally Relevant Stimuli

The data and theories we have described make specific predictions about single-unit activity. Research on sleep and arousal suggested that ACh cells might be related to the effects that food and deprivation have on levels of nonspecific arousal. Stricker and Zigmond's theory (1976) predicts that eating, especially eating highly preferred and incentive-arousing food, should increase activity in DA neurons. Since LH and VMH lesions consistently affect food intake, activity in cells in those areas should be changed by food deprivation and by eating. According to Leibowitz's theory (1976, 1985; Leibowitz et al., 1985; Weiss & Leibowitz, 1985), cells with alpha-receptors should react to eating and food deprivation differently from cells with beta-receptors. According to Wurtman (1983), 5-HT cells should respond specifically to activity in sweet-taste sensory receptors. Thirst stimuli and drinking should affect the firing rates of cells in the LH, preoptic and supraoptic nuclei, and the periventricular area.

Neurons outside the Hypothalamus

Few researchers have motivationally studied cells outside the hypothalamic area, but we will discuss some examples of their work.

DA versus NE cells.   The DA substantia nigra cells do *not* increase their firing rate in response to motivational stimuli such as eating, hunger, glucose injections, or type of diet (Strecker, Steinfels, & Jacobs, 1983; Trulson, Crisp, & Trulson, 1983). This fact creates problems for a theory of a DA feeding circuit, unless a pattern code other than rate can be documented in these cells. The NE locus coeruleus cells *are* strongly stimulated by incentive types of arousal (seeing a preferred food) (Foote, Aston-Jones, & Bloom, 1980). The widespread effects of NE cells on limbic and cortical cells may explain why incentive arousal increases signal-to-noise ratios.

Cellular activity in freely behaving subjects.   Komisaruk and Olds (1968) recorded from cells in a freely behaving rat's hypothalamus, preoptic area, midbrain reticular system, and hippocampus. Some cells responded nonspecifically to any shift in arousal, but others were more specific. The stimuli eliciting specific neural activity included those produced by the rat's actively wiggling its whiskers, exploring, moving, or manipulating some object.

Mink, Sinnamon, and Adams (1983) measured single-unit activity in the rat forebrain during three types of motivated behaviors: sexual stimulation, thirst, and escape from aversive stimuli. The responses specific to sexual stimulation were concentrated in the medial preoptic area, and the responses to drinking when thirsty were concentrated in the lateral septum and the lateral preoptic area. The latter area also contained

neurons specifically responding to any stimulus eliciting an escape response.

Both specific and nonspecific neurons were found in both sets of data. Perhaps the nonspecific neurons are related to the general-arousal component of motives and emotions, whereas the specific neurons are more relevant to the choice of which behavior is performed and what goal object is preferred. For example, the response to drinking occurred in nuclei that, when lesioned, affect drinking behavior and responses to thirst stimuli.

Thirst Stimuli and Neural Responses

The ways in which the thirst stimuli interact in affecting single-unit activity in the hypothalamus might tell us something about brain codes for thirst.

Osmotic pressure and angiotensin.   Cells responsive to osmotic pressure, blood volume, and angiotensin are found in the supraoptic and paraventricular nuclei of the hypothalamus (Epstein, 1982; Hayward, 1977). These cells secrete ADH (vasopressin) into the pituitary, as Figure 8-17 illustrates. Their axons extend into the pituitary, and ADH is released from the pituitary whenever these cells are stimulated. The same cell may respond to osmotic stimuli, to angiotensin, and to ACh (Akaishi & Negoro, 1983). However, the osmotic effects on paraventricular firing rates may come indirectly by way of other cells (Vincent, Arnauld, & Bioulac, 1972). These cells thus can integrate all thirst stimuli prior to secretion of ADH.

Activity in some of these cells may affect the thirst motive. Water deprivation causes an increase in the activity (measured by the 2-DG technique) of paraventricular but not of supraoptic cells (Sutherland, Martin, McQueen, & Fink, 1983). When animals were given only salt water to drink (which made them very thirsty), paraventricular activity increased. Allowing the animals to drink plain water brought the activity of those cells back to control levels (Dyball & Pountney, 1973).

Nonsecretory cells in the hypothalamus also respond to osmotic stimuli. Lesions in the LH or the lateral preoptic area decrease drinking after water deprivation. Injecting salt solutions directly into the lateral preoptic area causes drinking, and injections of plain water suppress drinking in thirsty rats (Blass & Epstein, 1971). The LH also has cells with osmoreceptors, as shown by microiontophoresing salt and sucrose directly onto cell membranes (Oomura, Ono, Ooyama, & Wayner, 1969).

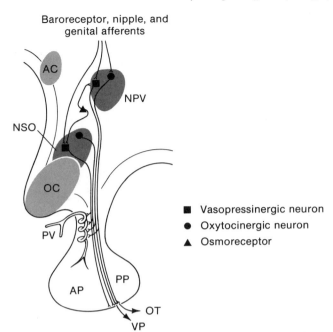

Baroreceptor, nipple, and
genital afferents

■ Vasopressinergic neuron
● Oxytocinergic neuron
▲ Osmoreceptor

Figure 8-17 Some of the hypothalamic **magnocellular** (large-cell) neuroendocrine cells are involved in thirst and the control of the body's water balance. The two types of neurons that secrete the peptides vasopressin and **oxytocin** (for delivery of milk and contractions of the uterus) lie scattered in the supraoptic (NSO) and paraventricular (VPV) nuclei and also in the internuclear zone (not illustrated). These peptides are released into the portal and systemic blood stream under the influence of specific osmotic, volemic, and external stimuli. The osmoreceptor cells called the **neurons of Verney** provide excitatory input to the vasopressinergic cells. Other excitatory input for these cells arises from afferents of cranial nerves IX and X, and from baroreceptors, chemoreceptors, and atrial volume receptors. Also see text. AC = anterior commissure; AP = anterior pituitary; NPV = paraventricular nucleus; NSO = supraoptic nucleus; OC = optic chiasm, OT = oxytocin, PP = posterior pituitary; PV = portal vessels; VP = vasopressin.

Stimuli from drinking.   Two hypothalamic regions have cells responding to thirst stimuli. Cells in the supraoptic nucleus respond in the same way to solutions in the mouth as to solutions injected into the blood stream (Nicolaïdis, 1969; Vincent, Arnauld, & Bioulac, 1972). Thus, if a cell is excited by salt in the blood, it will be inhibited when the organism drinks water. Lateral preoptic cells receive information from osmoreceptors in both the mouth and the stomach. Their firing rate changes proportionately when the osmotic pressure

of the blood is increased by sucrose or salt injections (Sessler & Salhi, 1983).

LH osmosensitive neurons have some very thought-provoking responses. Some of them are excited not only by osmotic stimuli but also by other mildly arousing sensory stimuli (Vincent, Arnauld, & Bioulac, 1972). They might be responding to the nonspecific arousal components of thirst. Some of these particular cells are also excited by drinking, and thus might be responding to the arousal aspects of incentive stimuli. Other LH cells are *inhibited* by drinking. So even within the LH, cells are heterogeneous: some are excited by both incentive and aversive arousal, and some have specific responses to drinking.

Hunger Stimuli and Hypothalamic Neural Responses

Almost from the first days of single-unit recording in the hypothalamus, the effects both of food deprivation and of glucose injections have been explored. However, care must be taken to distinguish between osmoreceptors and glucosensitive cells in the LH (few osmoreceptors are found in the VMH: Oomura, Ono, & Ooyama, 1969). Osmoreceptors increase their firing when glucose is injected into the carotid artery or directly onto the cell, apparently because the osmotic effect of glucose pulls water out of the cell. The true glucoreceptor cells respond only to glucose and not to any other osmotic stimulus (Oomura, Ono, & Ooyama, 1969; Oomura, Ooyama, Sugimori, Nakamura, & Yamada, 1974).

Glucose receptors and glucosensitive hypothalamic cells.   Some early studies found that after food deprivation, the overall activity of VMH neurons tended to be less than that of LH neurons. Glucose injections reversed that pattern by increasing VMH and decreasing LH activity (Anand, Chhina, Sharma, Dua, & Singh, 1964; Chhina, Anand, Singh, & Rao, 1971). The researchers ruled out any indirect effects from peripheral glucoreceptors. Furthermore, when slices of hypothalamic tissue were studied, most of the VMH cells were excited and the LH cells inhibited when glucose was added to the dish containing the tissue slice (Fukuda, Ono, Nishino, & Sasaki, 1984). Finally, direct injections of glucose into the VMH suppress eating (Panksepp & Meeker, 1976), as one would expect if VMH activity inhibited food intake or the incentive value of food.

Some VMH cells probably have true glucose receptors, whereas LH cells lack specific glucose receptors and so are just glucosensitive (Oomura et al., 1974; Oomura, 1976). For example, not only do injections of female sex hormones suppress eating in female rats but this hormone also increases the neural inhibition caused by applications of NE to VMH glucoreceptor cells (Kow & Pfaff, 1985b). As Figure 8-18 illustrates, when glucose is attached to a receptor, the neuron depolarizes. Depolarization could come from direct changes in membrane permeability or from changes in the metabolic processes in that cell. In either case, insulin facilitates the effect of glucose on VMH cells (see Figure 8-19).

The VMH cells with glucoreceptors also respond to hormones, body temperature, and brain temperature and could therefore respond to dietary thermogenic signals. Nearly all VMH cells that responded to glucose (with an increase in firing rate) also responded to warming the scrotal area or the preoptic area of the brain (Nakayama & Imai-Matsumura, 1984; Nakayama, 1986). Almost equal numbers were excited and inhibited by these thermal stimuli, but if a cell responded in one way to scrotal warming, it almost always responded in the same way to preoptic warming.

When glucose is microinfused onto LH neurons, the resulting hyperpolarization is not associated with any change in membrane resistance. These cells respond in a similar way to *any* osmotic stimulus. Furthermore, use of metabolic inhibitors such as ouabain prevents glucose from hyperpolarizing LH cells. Oomura and his colleagues have suggested that glucose acts osmotically to increase the activity of the Na-K pump, which then leads to hyperpolarization. LH cells are depolarized by insulin; glucose opposes this effect (Figure 8-19).

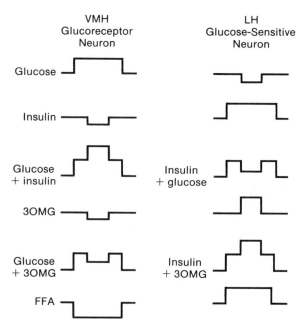

Figure 8-19   Summary of some of the effects of glucose, insulin, glucose analogs, FFA, and their interaction, on LH and VMH neurons. An upward deflection indicates an increase in firing rate, and a downward deflection, an inhibition. 3OMG = 3-O-methyl-glucose, a glucose analog that can compete with glucose.

LH glucosensitive neurons also respond to several other food-related agents. Many of these neurons are inhibited not only by glucose but also by warming of the body (Nakayama & Imai-Matsumura, 1984; Nakayama, 1986). These neurons are also inhibited when the thalamic taste nucleus is electrically stimulated (Emmers, 1969). Oomura and his colleagues carried out the most systematic research on these cells; some of their results are summarized in Tables 8-3 and 8-4 and in Figure 8-19. Microinfusions of free fatty acids (FFA) onto the cells stimulates them (Oomura, Nakamura, Sugimori, & Yamada, 1975). Stimulating liver glucoreceptors has the same inhibitory effect as direct injection of glucose onto the LH cells, and the afferents from the liver glucoreceptors work through LH alpha-adrenergic receptors (Miyahara & Oomura, 1982; Shimizu et al., 1983).

However, these alpha-receptor effects are *not* consistent with the alpha-adrenergic mediated *increases* in eating described earlier. The inconsistencies still have not been well explained. Until they are, the alpha-adrenergic effects on eating probably should *not* be attributed to LH cell activity. Instead, since direct injections of NE into the paraventricular

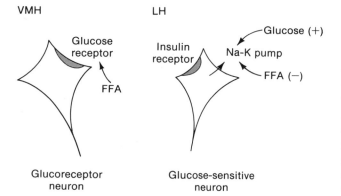

Figure 8-18   Oomura's (1976) model has glucoreceptor neurons in the VMH and glucose-sensitive neurons in the LH. The glucoreceptor neuron has glucose receptors in its membrane; FFA (free fatty acids) inhibit the firing of this type of cell by blocking the glucose receptor. The glucose-sensitive neuron has insulin receptors in its membrane; the rate of the Na-K pump is accelerated by glucose but is slowed by FFA.

Table 8-3 Effects of free fatty acids and sucrose on glucose-sensitive (mostly inhibitory) and glucose-insensitive LH cells.

Glucose		Type of Effect	FFA	Sucrose
↑	29	↑	11	4
		↓	8	2
		None	9	2
None	68	↑	6	0
		↓	8	0
		None	35	15
↓	43	↑	22	0
		↓	4	2
		None	15	8

nucleus increase eating, activity in the latter area may be responsible for most of the alpha-adrenergic eating effects (Leibowitz et al., 1985).

One recent study explicitly compared food-related response of glucose-sensitive and glucose-insensitive LH neurons (Aou, Oomura, Lénárd, Nishino, Inokuchi, Minami, & Misaki, 1984). Monkeys were trained to press a lever in the presence of a light cue to obtain food. Thirty presses for each reward were required; the availability of reward was signaled by a tone. A greater proportion of glucose-sensitive than of glucose-insensitive LH cells responded to this task. Most changes in firing rate occurred during the bar pressing and food consumption phases, and most cells *decreased* their firing rate at these times (this response is similar to the effects of glucose on these cells). Compared with cells in the prefrontal

Table 8-4 Effects of free fatty acids and sucrose on VMH cells that do not have glucose receptors and on those that do have receptors (mostly excitatory in effect).

Glucose		Type of Effect	FFA	Sucrose
↑	42	↑	9	0
		↓	18	0
		None	15	7
None	73	↑	2	0
		↓	10	0
		None	40	8
↓	7	↑	4	0
		↓	1	0
		None	2	3

cortex (described previously), fewer LH cells responded to the light and sound cues, and the cue-related responses were similar in both glucose-sensitive and -insensitive types of LH cell: increases in firing — especially in response to the light — were common.

The other research done on the VMH and LH cells has typically not identified them as glucosensitive or as having glucoreceptors. Thus, we can only speculate about how these types of cells would respond to the motivational types of manipulation described next.

Interactions between the VMH and LH. If a hunger stimulus has one effect on LH neurons, that same stimulus has the *opposite* effect on VMH neurons. This principle has been found to be true for food deprivation, intestinal food injections, a drop in blood glucose, glucose added to a culture dish, stomach distention, anorexic drugs, and the sight of food (Anand & Pillai, 1967; Fukuda et al., 1984; Khanna, Nayar, & Anand, 1972; Myers & McCaleb, 1980). For example, Oomura and his colleagues (Oomura, Kimura, Ooyama, Maeno, Iki, & Kuniyoshi, 1964; Oomura, Ooyama, Yamamoto, & Naka, 1967) recorded from LH and VMH neurons simultaneously during various hunger manipulations. Whenever firing rates of neurons in one area increased, neurons in the other decreased their firing rates. But when only a few VMH neurons were directly electrically stimulated — eliminating the possible contaminating effects of general arousal level — VMH stimulation more often *excited* than inhibited most LH cells (Van Atta & Sutin, 1971). Thus, cells in the VMH and LH respond in opposite ways to motivational inputs, but they are not interconnected in any directly inhibitory fashion.

Arousal and emotional stimuli. Stimulating limbic system structures affects LH single-unit activity. Some LH neurons are excited and others inhibited by stimulating the amygdala, the striatum, the septum, the hippocampus, the preoptic area, or the frontal cortex (Ono, Oomura, Sugimori, Nakamura, Shimizu, Kita, & Ishibashi, 1976; Van Atta & Sutin, 1971). Most LH cells could be driven from more than one limbic-system structure. If so, the same neurons could respond the same way or in opposite ways to the stimulations. With intracellular recording, amygdala stimulation was found to cause an epsp followed by a prolonged ipsp in the same cell (Oomura, Ono, & Ooyama, 1970). Thus, LH cells may integrate stimuli from limbic-emotional areas of the brain.

Changes in level of arousal also affect the firing rates of VMH and LH neurons. However, the effect of arousal is determined by how food-deprived the animal is. Figures 8-20 and 8-21 show how changes in the arousal of a hungry animal (the shift from sleep to wakefulness) affect activity in five LH and in four VMH neurons, respectively. As arousal increases, single-unit activity in LH neurons tends to increase and that in VMH neurons decreases. But these effects of arousal are seen *only* when the animal is hungry: the effects are absent or even *reversed* in satiated animals. Figure 8-22 shows how activity in one VMH neuron and one LH neuron changes from sleep to wakefulness when the cat is either hungry or satiated. Arousal does not affect LH activity in a satiated cat, and satiation attenuates the suppressing effects of arousal on the VMH cell.

Figure 8-23 summarizes these effects, showing what proportion of neurons exhibited what types of effect. Most of these neurons reacted to changes in arousal *only* when the organism was food deprived, as though hunger increased reactivity to stimuli in nerve cells as well as in the behavior of intact organisms (Hoyenga & Hoyenga, 1984). Hungry animals tend to be more reactive to external stimuli, especially unexpected or food-related stimuli, than are nonhungry animals.

Stimuli from the digestive system.   Consistently with their role in hunger and appetite, the VMH and LH also receive information from internal digestive organs. The information comes from neurons in the nucleus of the solitary tract in the brain stem (see Figure 8-3), which receives afferents from vagal parasympathetic sensory neurons.

LH and VMH cells receive information from the stomach and liver. VMH and LH activity changes when amino acids are infused into the intestine (Jeanningros, 1982). Injecting food directly into the intestine increases NE **turnover**[*] in the LH but decreases NE turnover in the VMH (Myers & McCaleb, 1980). Both these effects imply that there are NE afferents to these hypothalamic areas. Stimulating stomach stretch receptors (which happens when we eat too much) increases single-unit activity in the VMH and decreases activity in the

---

[*] "Turnover" refers to both synthesis and degradation of a transmitter substance and so reflects the amount of activity that has been occurring in NE synapses.

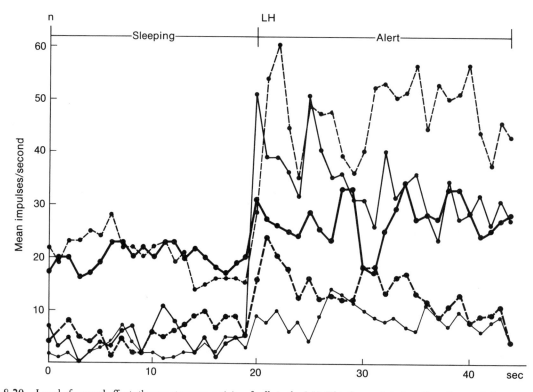

Figure 8-20   Level of arousal affects the spontaneous activity of cells in the LH. This figure plots the effect of arousal changes on activity in five LH cells in hungry cats; each neuron was recorded in a different animal.

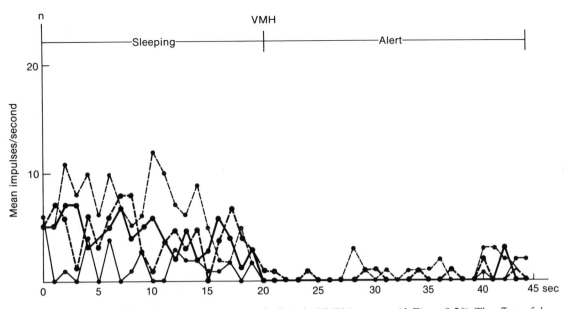

Figure 8-21 Level of arousal affects the spontaneous activity of cells in the VMH (compare with Figure 8-20). The effects of changes in arousal on the spontaneous activity of four VMH cells are plotted; each neuron was recorded in a different hungry cat.

LH (Anand & Pillai, 1967). Activation of glucoreceptors in the liver by glucose injections inhibits many LH neurons, probably through alpha-adrenergic postsynaptic receptors (Miyahara & Oomura, 1982; Schmitt, 1973; Shimizu et al., 1983).

Effects of transmitters on LH cells. The effects of transmitters other than NE on LH and VMH activity are all consistent with their effects on hunger and satiety (see Table 8-1). NE inhibits LH neurons through alpha-receptors. ACh excites LH cells but inhibits VMH cells (Hayward, 1977). Fenfluramine (a 5-HT agonist and carbohydrate appetite suppressant) increases activity in VMH cells and decreases activity in LH cells (Khanna, Nayar, & Anand, 1972). Since CCK changes associated with hunger stimuli are found mostly in the cortex and not in the hypothalamus, it is not surprising that microinjections of CCK have no consistent effect on either the VMH or the LH neurons. CCK does tend to excite some cortical cells (Ishibashi, Oomura, Okajima, & Shibata, 1979).

Whereas endorphins tend to increase food intake, intravenous injections of morphine tend to excite VMH neurons and inhibit LH neurons. These effects are opposite to what would have been expected (Kerr, Triplett, & Beeler, 1974). Maybe endorphin, like NE, acts on some part of the brain other than the hypothalamus.

Effects of the sight, smell, and taste of food on neural responses. Some of the first behavioral research done in this area related LH activity to food-related behavior. Hamburg (1971) found that LH cells were *inhibited* by food-related stimuli in freely moving rats. The inhibition lasted as long as the animal continued to eat and as long as food was present. However, if the food dish was removed, even though the animal continued to chew what food remained in its mouth, the LH unit activity increased again. Most of the LH cells inhibited by sight of the food dish were also inhibited by VMH stimulation.

Similarly, Ono and his colleagues (Ono et al., 1976; Sasaki, Ono, Muramoto, Nishino, & Fukuda, 1984) found that all LH neurons in a monkey that responded to food-motivated behavior were inhibited during the period just before the monkey pressed a bar to obtain food. However, Oomura and colleagues (Oomura, Ooyama, Naka, Yamamoto, Ono, & Kobayashi, 1969) recorded from several LH neurons in freely moving but food-deprived rats and found that their firing rate *increased* when the animal began searching or reaching for food. But only one LH cell of 63 was excited, whereas 29 were inhibited, during actual ingestion of food. The effect of going from sleep to food seeking on three of these cells is illustrated in Figure 8-24. So attending to food-related stimuli may, like glucose, inhibit LH cells, but looking for food cues may excite

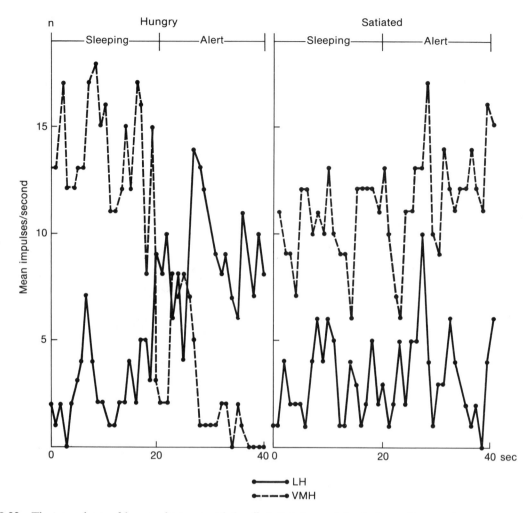

Figure 8-22 The internal state of the animal interacts with the effects that changes in level of arousal have on the spontaneous activity of LH and VMH neurons. Changes in level of arousal have no effect on LH or VMH activity in satiated cats.

those cells. Or perhaps different populations of cells are involved in inhibitory versus excitatory responses to motivational stimuli.

As this research implies, the LH receives indirect information from visual, gustatory, and olfactory afferents. The information crosses several synapses before reaching the LH. For example, using odors or electrodes to stimulate the olfactory bulb or tract increases activity in many LH cells (Scott & Pfaffman, 1967). In contrast, Emmers (1969) found that stimulating the thalamic taste nucleus usually *inhibits* LH cells.

Some LH cells respond to taste stimuli applied to the

tongue, but a mixture of excitatory and inhibitory responses is seen. Norgren (1970) found that some LH cells in rats responded (with either excitation or inhibition) specifically to sucrose alone or to water alone, and some responded to both. Ono, Sasaki, Nakamura, and Norgren (1985) recorded from LH cells in unanesthetized rats that had been trained to lick a spout to receive glucose. Slightly more LH cells were excited than were inhibited (61 versus 54) by glucose on the tongue.

Some taste-sensitive cells also respond to visual and auditory cues. Some of the taste-sensitive LH cells respond in the same way both to taste and to just the *sight* of food, although

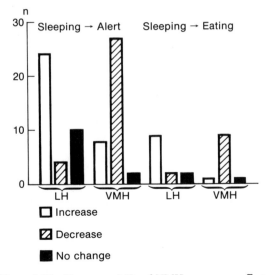

Figure 8-23   How many LH and VMH neurons are affected and in what way when hungry cats go from sleep either to the alert state or to eating? The ordinate indicates the number of neurons within a population that responded in a particular manner. Open bars = frequency increase; cross-hatched bars = frequency decrease; stippled bars = no change in frequency of firing.

the sight of food can also activate LH cells that do not respond to taste stimuli (Aleksanyan, Burešová, & Bureš, 1976; Burton, Rolls, & Mora, 1976; Rolls, Burton, & Mora, 1976). Activity in the visual LH neurons precedes the animal's responses to food, suggesting that the activity in these LH cells could be presynaptic to command cells (Rolls, Sanghera, & Roper-Hall, 1979).

These changes are specific with regard both to hunger and to food stimuli. For example, for the visual cells, no change in firing rate occurs when the animal looks at nonfood objects or when the animal eats in the dark. Also, neither arousal nor motor movements, nor even the movements associated with swallowing and chewing, can produce these effects (Rolls, Sanghera, & Roper-Hall, 1979). Both visual and gustatory LH neurons are also affected by the motivational condition of the animal. These cells respond to their respective stimuli only if the animal is food-deprived (Burton, Rolls, & Mora, 1976). Only LH cells responding specifically to sucrose or to water on the tongue were affected by deprivation. Food deprivation increased the number of cells responding to sucrose, and satiation increased the number of cells responding to water alone (Norgren, 1970). LH cells that respond to saccharin in the

mouth quit responding after the animal had been given an aversion to saccharin (Aleksanyan, Burešová, & Bureš, 1976). That same aversion *increased* VMH cells' responses to saccharin.

Summary of Neural Coding

Cells in the paraventricular and supraoptic nuclei secrete ADH in response to thirst stimuli: hypovolemia, angiotensin, and increases in osmotic pressure. However, they probably do not have osmoreceptors in their membranes, and although they respond to thirst stimuli, their relationship to thirst and to drinking is incompletely explored. (Some alpha-adrenergic receptor paraventricular neurons may also be involved in hunger.) Preoptic, periventricular, and lateral hypothalamic cells also respond to osmotic stimuli. Their activity may be directly related to thirst motivation and to drinking.

Arousal, hunger, and emotional stimuli affect VMH and LH neurons. Stimulation of limbic-system structures changes LH activity. VMH and LH activity depends on the level of arousal; their arousal responses are exaggerated by food deprivation. Hunger stimuli have mostly reciprocal types of effect on VMH and LH neurons (though exceptions were noted). Being food-deprived increases LH but decreases VMH nerve-cell activity, and glucose increases VMH and decreases LH activity. Some stimulation of VMH mostly excites LH cells, the reciprocal relationship between VMH and LH activity can probably be explained by these areas' receiving reciprocal types of input, which therefore induce reciprocal patterns of activity.

LH and VMH cells respond to motivational stimuli in ways predictable from the effects that stimulating these areas have on food intake. VMH cells are excited by satiety stimuli, such as glucose, glucose combined with insulin, stomach distention, fenfluramine, and body and brain warming. Some VMH cells are inhibited by hunger-related stimuli, such as FFA. LH cells are inhibited by stimuli related to the cessation of eating, such as glucose, fenfluramine, and stomach distention; LH cells are excited by hunger-related stimuli, such as FFA and insulin. LH cells also respond to the taste, smell, and sight of food. Although the LH responses can be either excitatory or inhibitory, both types of response, as well as responses to changes in arousal, are increased by food deprivation. A conditioned food aversion suppresses responses.

Perhaps the heterogeneity of the data could be simplified by hypothesizing at least two separate populations of cells in the

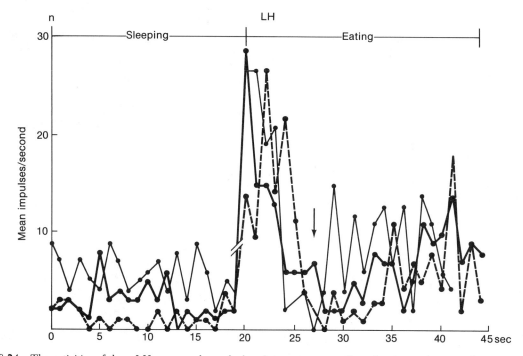

Figure 8-24 The activities of three LH neurons changed when hungry cats went from sleeping to the state of eating. Firing rates characteristic of the alert state (including searching and reaching for food) are eliminated by placing food in the cage directly in front of the animal (an action indicated by the arrow). Each neuron was recorded in a different animal.

LH: first-order neurons whose activity is affected by food-related stimuli, and second-order neurons that respond to the first-order cells. Some of the first-order cells probably integrate the food-related stimuli, including extracellular glucose levels and the activity from liver and gut receptors. These neurons may also receive input from the RF and from the limbic system. This input would allow nonspecific arousal and emotional states to affect the way that food-deficit signals are integrated by those first-order LH cells.

The first-order LH cells may then affect second-order LH neurons. The responses of these cells to food-related stimuli may be contingent on the nutritional state of the animal. In other words, the first-order LH cells receive many (or all) of the deficit signals, and their integration of these signals serves as a *gate*, determining whether visual and taste stimuli will excite or inhibit the second-order cells. In turn, these second-order cells may determine if those visual and taste stimuli will be incentives, will excite command cells, and will act as reinforcers for the animal.

Before one can conclude that LH activity is relevant to hunger motivation, the relationship between activity in LH cells and the reinforcing effects that food or satiety stimuli have on hungry organisms has to be established. Showing that the sight of food changes LH activity does not prove that this change in activity is part of the code for the reinforcing effects of those stimuli on the organism. We now turn to research relevant to this relationship.

Effects of Motivational States on Reinforcement

This final section of the chapter explores some implications of Olds and Milner's discovery in 1954 that electrical stimulation of various parts of the brain was reinforcing. Animals will learn to perform a variety of arbitrarily chosen responses, such as pressing a lever, when the only reward for doing so is a brief burst of low-current electrical stimulation delivered through a gross electrode to some part of their brain (self-stimulation). This phenomenon has been demonstrated in rats, cats, monkeys, dolphins, dogs, and humans (Olds & Fobes, 1981). Other parts of the brain will support **escape behavior.** Animals will learn an arbitrary response to get the brain stimulation turned *off.* And many parts of the brain do both: low levels of current support self-stimulation and higher or more prolonged levels of current produce escape behavior.

As reviewed in Olds and Fobes (1981), the areas of the brain that support self-stimulation include parts of the limbic system, such as the limbic cortex, parts of the thalamus, and parts of the RF. However, the structure that produces some of the highest rates of self-stimulation is the **medial forebrain bundle (MFB).** Rates of up to 5000 presses per hour for MFB stimulation have been reported. Animals will press continuously at this rate until they are physically exhausted; after sleeping, the animal will return to self-stimulation (Olds, 1958b). The MFB passes through the preoptic nucleus and the LH. Some of its axons are dopaminergic or noradrenergic, coming from the substantia nigra, the locus coeruleus, and other places (see Figures 8-7 and 8-8 and Figure 8-25).

The phenomenological states associated with self-stimulation can be explored in humans. Some people have had electrodes implanted either during brain surgery or in preparation for brain surgery as part of treating a problem like epilepsy or some emotional disorder (Bishop, Elder, & Heath, 1963; Heath, 1963; 1972). These subjects either were stimulated by the experimenter or were given their own button that controlled the stimulation. Valenstein (1973, p. 73) quotes some of Heath's subjects about how they *felt* during the brain stimulation: "I feel good. I don't know why, I just suddenly felt good." "It's like I had something lined up for Saturday night . . . a girl." "I'm feeling fine . . . feel like I could clean up the whole hospital." Sexual types of sensation may occur with self-stimulation near the septal area (Heath, 1963). Other subjects said that stimulation made them "feel great," or they said that it got rid of "bad" thoughts. One person described his situation as that of having a "happy button" to press. However, the most intense pleasure was usually experienced by patients who had been in unpleasant emotional or physical states at the time of the stimulation. Patients who were feeling good generally experienced only mild sensations of pleasure (Valenstein, 1973).

This section explores self-stimulation from an incentive point of view. Motives may affect behavior largely because of the effects they have on neurons that process external stimuli. The internal state of the animal will determine the degree to which food—or brain stimulation—can serve as a positive incentive (producing both specific and nonspecific arousal) and reinforcer. The incentive-arousal properties of stimuli would be determined jointly by learning, by the internal state

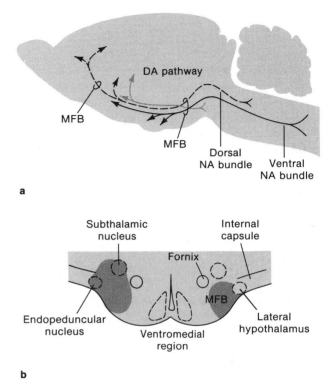

Figure 8-25   a. Sagittal view of the rat brain, showing some of the major noradrenergic and dopaminergic pathways.   **b.** A cross-sectional view at the hypothalamic level. Many of these cells' axons are in the MFB, a major brain structure that supports self-stimulation when electrodes are implanted in it.

of the organism, and by intrinsic properties of the stimulus. In other words, food is reinforcing because some food tastes good, either intrinsically (such as sweets) or because of learning. Food is *not* reinforcing *just* because it can reduce the organism's hunger. But the positive incentive-reinforcing aspects of food—how good it tastes—are increased by hunger.

Three types of studies will be discussed. (The effects of learning will be covered in the last two chapters.) If specific motivational states act as gates, determining the degree to which specific stimuli have positive incentive-reinforcing properties, then the ways in which hunger changes sensory responses to specific types of external stimulus are relevant. Second, the ways in which hunger and thirst affect the reinforcing effects of brain stimulation can add supporting data. Finally, the ways in which cells in various areas of the brain respond during self-stimulation are just beginning to be explored.

Hunger and Sensory Coding

Theorists have speculated about how the internal state of the animal affects sensory coding and the reinforcing effects of stimuli. As Pfaffman and his colleagues said, "Our evidence is clear that for taste there is an identified linkage in the anatomy and physiology of *information processing* and *motivation of behavior*" (Pfaffmann, Norgren, & Grill, 1977, p. 30, emphases theirs).

Cabanac (1979) reviewed data relevant to the brain codes for reinforcement. The reinforcing value of taste and the pleasurability ratings humans assign to taste stimuli vary according to the degree of hunger present. For humans, for example, drinking 50 grams of glucose in a 200 milliliter solution makes sweet solutions sampled later taste less pleasant—but only if the glucose was actually swallowed. If the solution is only sampled and then spit out, the rated pleasantness of sweet solutions tasted 45 to 60 minutes later is unchanged. Drinking a salty solution makes salty stimuli more unpleasant. These effects are specific, since the rated pleasantness of salt solutions is unchanged by drinking glucose, and vice versa. Furthermore, food restriction increases the rated pleasantness of sweet solutions (Cabanac, 1979), and going on a nearly salt-free diet increases the rated pleasantness of salty foods (Bertino, Beauchamp, Riskey, & Engelman, 1981).

Activity in taste afferents.   Taste-driven neural activity is affected by hunger stimuli at several levels of the brain, starting from the primary sensory afferents and extending at least up to the hypothalamic level. As we have already described, hypothalamic neural responses to taste stimuli are usually increased by hunger (Aleksanyan, Burešová, & Bureš, 1976; Burton, Rolls, & Mora, 1976), and the taste-sensitive cells are likely to be in the area of the LH transversed by the MFB (Norgren, 1970).

Activity in the solitary tract nucleus—the first taste synapse—is affected by gastric distention and is centrifugally controlled by the LH (Glenn & Erickson, 1976; Matsuo, Shimizu, & Kusano, 1984). Neural responses to solutions placed on rats' tongues were usually suppressed within minutes of an injection into the stomach, whether the injection was simply of air or of a salt solution. Responses to sucrose were most suppressed, and responses to bitter tastes were *not* affected. Gastric distention may cause these changes by indirect input either to the solitary tract nucleus or to the receptor cells themselves. Furthermore, gross electrode LH stimulation activates solitary tract neurons. When the LH was given one "conditioning" stimulus just before electrical stimulation of a rat's tongue, gustatory solitary tract neurons were facilitated, responding more than to taste stimuli alone, by 30% to 80%, for 50 to 150 mSec. Neurons responding to pressure or temperature changes on the tongue were *suppressed* by this same "conditioning" LH stimulation.

Contreras (1977) depleted the sodium stores of rats by feeding them a salt-free diet. Although the neural responses to low concentrations of salt applied to the tongue were not affected by salt deprivation, deprivation did *decrease* the neural response to greater concentrations, especially for the neurons for which NaCl is the best taste. The variability in the spontaneous firing rate was also increased by salt deprivation. Thus, neurons in sodium-deprived rats are less sensitive to NaCl, a condition that may explain why those rats avidly eat even the most concentrated salt solutions.

Olfactory afferents and hunger.   Mitral-layer cells in the olfactory bulb of rats respond both to nonspecific arousal and to food deprivation and satiety (Pager, 1974; Pager, Giachetti, Holley, & Le Magnen, 1972). The mitral cells receive input from MFB efferents. Cells in this layer are active only if the animal is both food deprived *and* being stimulated with food odors. If the animal is satiated, these cells are mostly inhibited by any type of odor; they are also inhibited in either satiated or hungry animals stimulated with nonfood odors. The only exception to this pattern was that the first few trials of each session elicited largely excitatory effects, which may reflect nonspecific arousal effects. Both specific and nonspecific effects are produced by efferents from the MFB, since cutting those fibers eliminated both deprivation and arousal effects on the first trials.

Thus, changes in the internal state change olfactory and gustatory coding. These changes may affect neurons in such a way that their activity acts as a gate for the effects of sensations, determining the degree to which they can produce incentive arousal and reinforcement.

Motives and Self-Stimulation

Following an overview, we will present specific studies on motives and self-stimulation.

Background.   Olds and Fobes's (1981) review of this area described how the reinforcing effects of brain stimulation can be affected by motivational states. Gross stimulation through electrodes implanted in the MFB, at the level of the LH, can produce eating as well as support self-stimulation. This type of eating is often called **stimulus-bound.** It occurs at the onset of stimulation and stops promptly when the stimulation ceases.

Both stimulus-bound eating *and* the reinforcing effects of that stimulation can be increased by any treatment that normally increases food consumption. Thus, both self-stimulation and stimulus-bound eating are increased by insulin injections, by food deprivation, and by lesions of the VMH. Conversely, treatments that decrease eating, such as some appetite suppressants, forced-feeding obesity, and stomach distention, decrease both self-stimulation and stimulus-bound eating. Similar parallels were found by Olds and Fobes (1981) for stimulus-bound drinking and treatments that affect water consumption.

Given this type of evidence, it seems reasonable to assume that these treatments have similar effects on eating or drinking and self-stimulation because they affect the way the brain normally responds to reinforcing stimuli. Food deprivation would increase the sensitivity of cells stimulated by "good" tastes, cells that are also activated by reinforcing brain stimulation. But there are some problems with this apparent convergence between stimulus-bound behavior and self-stimulation (see review of Olds & Fobes, 1981). The same electrode can elicit eating at one time, drinking at another, chewing at still another, and maybe nonspecific exploration at still another time. This variability argues against the excitement of any specific motivational cells.

Furthermore, either specific or nonspecific arousal could have parallel effects on stimulus-bound behavior and on self-stimulation behavior even if there were no motivationally specific effects. For example, sedative drugs decrease eating *and* self-stimulation, probably because they suppress all activity. The stimulant amphetamine can increase both self-stimulation *and* the degree to which animals will work to turn that same stimulation *off* (Hoebel, 1979). (Amphetamine depresses eating in normal rats but increases eating in LH aphagics.) The amphetamine effect on self-stimulation in intact rats is often attributed to the increase in gross activity levels. A rat made more active by amphetamine is more like to stumble over the lever, accidentally pressing it.

Effects of hunger versus sex hormones.   Both hunger and the male sex hormone, androgen, affect self-stimulation. Olds (1958a) found that self-stimulation at some electrode sites could be increased by hunger. Self-stimulation through *different* electrodes was decreased by castration (removal of testes) and restored when the animal was given a replacement injection of androgen. Self-stimulation at sites that were increased by hunger tended to be *decreased* by male sex hormones, and vice versa. Similarly, Hoebel (1979) found that with electrode locations that produced stimulus-bound eating, hunger increased self-stimulation, whereas satiation increased escape

behavior. Conversely, with electrodes producing stimulus-bound sexual activity, ejaculation decreased self-stimulation and increased escape behavior.

Self-stimulation thresholds.   Do self-stimulation thresholds reflect the excitability of reward neurons in the brain? Much of the research done in the area represented by this question has assumed that self-stimulation thresholds reflect the thresholds of the neurons involved in reinforcement. Treatments that lower the self-stimulation threshold or that increase the rate at which self-stimulation occurs are thus assumed to work by changing the excitability of reward neurons.

One impressive study compared the effects of LH stimulation with those produced by stimulation in brain escape area. Naturally occurring behaviors were recorded in freely moving rats (Stellar, Brooks, & Mills, 1979). The rats were presented with a variety of stimuli, some of which (such as sugar water or a sexual odor) elicited approach behaviors and some of which (such as footshock or an aversive odor) elicited escape behaviors. If the LH was stimulated, approach behaviors were increased and escape behaviors suppressed. If the escape area of the brain was stimulated, exactly the opposite occurred: approach behaviors were decreased and escape behaviors facilitated. Thus, "pleasurable" and "aversive" brain stimulations seemed to add to or subtract from the effects of naturally occurring environmental stimulations. The fact that brain and environmental stimulations can combine in their effects on behavior could mean that the excitability of nerve cells affected by sugar water or footshock was increased by the appropriate brain stimulations.

As we have said, good taste sensations, such as sweets, affect the excitability of LH neurons (though both inhibitory and excitatory effects have been found). We also described how breeding for high and low rates of LH self-stimulation produced, in at least the LC2 strain, a correlated high or low preference for saccharine solutions. Did the breeding program change the excitability of LH taste and self-stimulation neurons? Since the LC2-high strain was also more sensitive to pain and to brain-stimulation-induced analgesia (Chapter 6), the LC2 breeding program may have affected some NE and 5-HT reward and punishment circuits in the brain (Moreau, Cohen, & Lieblich, 1984).

Along this line, Phillips and Mogenson (1968) simultaneously measured self-stimulation and stimulus-bound drinking. Animals were allowed free access to various solutions during LH self-stimulation. If the solution available to them was quinine water, both self-stimulation and stimulus-bound drinking were suppressed. But if the solution was saccharin, both were facilitated. Cutting the taste nerves — even though that operation produced aphagia and adipsia—*increased* self-stimulation (Jacquin, Harris, & Zeigler, 1982).

This result might be explained by postulating separate populations of cells. One might be tonically inhibited by taste afferents (to explain the effect on self-stimulation). The other might be phasically excited by taste afferents (to explain the effects that good taste sensations have on the amount of food eaten and on self-stimulation). Other research has also found at least two different populations of self-stimulation and hunger-sensitive cells (Atrens, Williams, Brady, & Hunt, 1982).

Neural Responses to Self-Stimulation

If hunger does affect excitability of cells in the self-stimulation circuit, it is important to identify *which* cells might be involved; these cells may be part of the brain codes for "pleasure." Self-stimulation in the MFB seems to involve different processes from self-stimulation in some of the limbic structures. Self-stimulation in the MFB is associated with hyperactivity, high rates of self-stimulation, lack of satiation (no decline in self-stimulation over time), and sometimes stimulus-bound behaviors. In contrast, self-stimulation in

structures such as the septum, the amygdala, and the hippocampus is associated with hypoactivity, usually lower rates of self-stimulation, satiation, and behaviors evoked by the *termination* of the stimulation (Olds, 1958b; Rolls; 1971a). So, as would be expected, *only* MFB or LH stimulation and not limbic stimulation increases the activity of RF neurons (Rolls, 1971a; Routtenberg & Huang, 1968).

MFB self-stimulation.   The MFB and the LH are interconnected. Collaterals from MFB axons form synapses with LH neurons, and LH axons enter the MFB (see Figure 8-25).

Gallistel, Shizgal, and Yeomans (1981) proposed the model of MFB self-stimulation in Figure 8-26. In the first stage, the relevant axons in the MFB are stimulated. Research on the electrical properties of the neurons associated with self-stimulation indicates that the first-stage axons are small and myelinated and are neither NA nor DA cells. These first-stage axons may actually come from the cell bodies of neurons found in the LH (Velley, Chaminade, Roy, Kempf, & Cardo, 1983). If true, this would mean that at least some LH cells are critically important to the self-stimulation effects—and, by extension, to the rewarding and incentive properties of external stimuli.

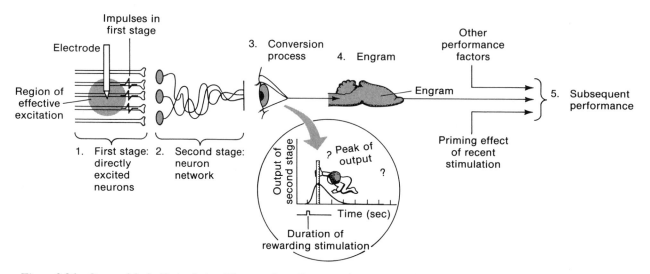

Figure 8-26   One model of self-stimulation. The rewarding effect occurs by stages numbered as follows: 1. Stimulating pulses of current produce successive volleys of impulses in reward-relevant axons. 2. A postsynaptic network (of unknown complexity) carries out spatial and temporal summation. 3. The transient output of this network is seen by a conversion process (represented by the little person), which translates some aspect of the network signal, such as its peak, into an engram—a memory record of the reward. 4. This record, together with the priming effect of recent stimulation and many other factors such as the internal state of motivation, determines the speed (vigor, rate) of the responses. For simplicity, the priming pathway is not shown; it would have a directly stimulated first stage and an integrator, but no engram-forming stage.

According to this model, the second stage critically involves a neural network that spatially and temporally sums neural activity. A conversion process translates the summed electrical activity into "pleasure" and provides an **engram,** or memory of that stimulation, to influence future behavior. **Priming effect** refers to giving the animal a "taste" of the reinforcing brain stimulation just before placing it in the task situation; this energizes its behavior (like priming a pump).

Although the first stage may not use DA or NE, the second-stage integrator may involve DA synapses. In one supportive study, a graft of embryonic substantia nigra tissue was placed above the striatum of animals in which the nigrostriatal pathway on that side of the brain had been destroyed by injections of 6-OHDA (Fray, Dunnett, Iversen, Björklund, & Stenevi, 1983). Axons from the embryonic tissue grew into and reinnervated at least parts of the striatum. After allowing time for reinnervation, these researchers placed self-stimulation electrodes in that brain implant. The electrode would support self-stimulation only if its tip were correctly located in the implant *and* if axons from the implant had reinnervated at least some striatal cells. So DA neurons isolated from their usual inputs can still support self-stimulation.

MFB stimulation changes neural activities in at least four different areas of the brain: the MFB itself, the RF, some limbic-system structures, and the prefrontal and cingulate cortex (Ito, 1972; Ito & Olds, 1971; Olds, 1974a, 1974b; Rolls, 1971a, 1971b, 1972; Rolls & Cooper, 1973; Sinnamon, Cromarty, & Miller, 1979). This type of data gives some clues about where the code for reinforcement and incentives might be in the brain. However—with few exceptions—what else stimulates those same neurons has not been determined, even though these studies could eventually reveal what codes are being used for motives, incentives, and reinforcement.

Possible incentive codes.   Some researchers have examined cells whose firing rates were affected by rewarding brain stimulation and have found that many of the neurons excited by reinforcing brain stimulation are also excited by aversive or unpleasant brain stimulation (Keene, 1973a, 1973b, 1975). The only exceptions discovered so far include two parts of the thalamus and the pallidum. For example, activity in RF neurons might be related to the hyperactivity and arousal associated with MFB stimulation. Rolls (1971a, 1971b, 1977) studied RF responses to external, stimulus-evoked variations in level of arousal. Those RF cells increased their activity during MFB stimulation and also whenever stimuli such as pinching or odors produced EEG activation (the animals were anesthetized). This is probably nonspecific arousal and so is unrelated to the specific rewarding effects of MFB stimulation.

Other studies explored what kinds of natural stimulations normally excited the cells that were affected by reinforcing brain stimulation. Komisaruk and Olds (1968) implanted microelectrodes in freely moving rats to determine what types of behavior were reliably associated with the increases in neural activity recorded by those electrodes. They also measured the degree to which self-stimulation would occur through those same electrodes. One neuron in the preoptic area responded only when the animal actively wiggled its whiskers. This electrode also supported one of the highest self-stimulation scores observed in the study. Another preoptic neuron was excited during any kind of exploratory locomotor behavior. Stimulation through this electrode produced stimulus-bound eating as well as self-stimulation. A midbrain reticular neuron was excited whenever the animal was directing its behavior toward any kind of stimulus—pleasant or unpleasant—in its environment. This electrode did *not* support self-stimulation. Similarly, Norgren (1970) found that if an electrode was close to an LH cell responding to sucrose on the tongue, that electrode supported self-stimulation.

Kanki, Martin, and Sinnamon (1983) measured the activity of neurons in the cingulate (limbic) region of the cortex during self-stimulation, orienting/exploratory behavior, and saccharin drinking. The animals oriented toward (looked and sniffed at) visual, olfactory, or tactile stimuli. Most commonly, all three stimuli depressed the activity in cingulate cells: of the 43 neurons showing change in activity, 32 were inhibited. In particular, if a neuron was inhibited during saccharin consumption, it was also inhibited by MFB stimulation.

In this study, both rewarding brain stimulation and the natural reward of saccharin had the same effect on the neurons. Nonetheless, one cannot conclude that those were "reward" neurons. First, their decrease in activity could be a sign and not a code for reward. After all, some neurons showed an increase rather than a decrease in activity during saccharin consumption. Second, since neurons in the same area were inhibited both by brain stimulation and by orienting behaviors, nonspecific arousal rather than specific reinforcing effects may be involved.

Rolls (1971a, 1971b) found that LH cells affected by MFB stimulation might be part of a more specific code for food reinforcement arousal. LH cells were usually inhibited by MFB, paralleling the inhibitory effects that glucose often has on those cells. Most of the LH neurons inhibited by food ingestion are also inhibited by MFB stimulation. These same neurons tend to be *excited* by rewarding nucleus accumbens stimulation (Sasaki et al., 1984).

However, if the stimulating electrode is placed in a more posterior position in the MFB-LH area, both excitatory and inhibitory LH responses to rewarding brain stimulation were seen (Ono et al., 1985). But even in this case, the same neurons tended to respond in the same way to food ingestions; out of 96 cells responding, 72 had the same kind of response (inhibitory or excitatory) to food ingestion as to rewarding brain stimulation. In addition, some of the responsive neurons also responded in the same way (85 out of 111) to a tone signaling the occurrence of that particular reward. Still, many neurons (61.1%) responded to the rewards but *not* to the tones, so the reward responses cannot be attributed to nonspecific arousal effects.

Rolls (1977) summarized research done in his laboratory on self-stimulation and LH cells. Some cells responded only to certain reinforcers and not to others, and both natural and brain-stimulation reinforcers could increase the activity of the *same* brain cell. This research comes very close to identifying the possible brain codes for reinforcement.

Summary of Motives and Reinforcement

Incentive stimuli often cause arousal (both specific and nonspecific) as well as reinforcement. Activity in the brain changes when the deficit state of the organism is changed. Hunger changes activity in olfactory and taste afferents and probably increases the excitability of the first-stage self-stimulation neurons. In some cases, natural reinforcers have effects on neural activity similar to those produced by self-stimulation.

Although we are getting close to the neural code for reinforcement, we do not know what the phenomenological experiences are of animals who are self-stimulating. It may not be what we would call "pleasure." For example, one human subject said he self-stimulated because it made him almost remember something, and he kept hitting the button in an effort to find out what that something was (Heath, 1963). Furthermore, since reinforcing types of stimulation in different areas of the brain produce different patterns of brain neural activity, different phenomenological experiences could be involved. Activity in *no* single structure—defined either anatomically or biochemically—has been shown to be both necessary and sufficient for all kinds of reinforcement. There may be no one single reward circuit and no one set of cells activated by *all* types of rewards. Yet the promise is there; the next few years' research should be exciting.

Chapter Summary

The Effects of Motives on Coding

As the internal state of the animal changes, neurons in certain parts of the brain also change their activity. The internal state of the animal can be changed by arousing the animal, by genetic manipulations, by food and water deprivation, or by giving a deprived animal food to eat or water to drink. *All* these changes in internal state have been related to changes in the biochemistry or activity of cells in areas of the brain assumed to be involved in emotions and motives: the RF, the hypothalamus, and structures of the limbic system. Both specific and nonspecific effects have been seen. The code for internal states may be the average rate of activity or an increase in variability.

However, we have very little idea yet of either how these changes are brought about or how they relate to brain codes for internal states and for the incentive-reinforcing effects of stimuli. Certainly it is possible to show that both nonspecific increases in arousal and the specific changes in internal states caused by deprivation can change the responses of sensory neurons to sensory stimulation. Thus, motives alter the way that information gets into the system.

The VMH and LH areas of the hypothalamus have received more attention than other areas of the brain. In particular, the LH area seems to receive much of the motivationally relevant information, both for thirst and for hunger, including information from the VMH. For example, the complex analysis of visual information carried out by the amygdala may feed into the LH to enable those cells to respond to the sight of food, especially if the LH deficit cells have increased the excitability of the LH visual cells. The biochemistry and structure of LH cells are changed by obesity genes. In one strain of rats, LH self-stimulation is associated with an increased saccharin intake.

LH cells have several different kinds of receptors (Antelman & Caggiula, 1977; Leibowitz et al., 1985; Margules, 1970a, 1970b; Margules & Dragovich, 1973). Stimulation of the alpha-receptors in the LH may suppress all eating, whereas stimulation of paraventricular alpha-receptors may specifically increase carbohydrate intake. Information from the liver glucoreceptors affects LH glucosensitive neurons through alpha-receptors. LH beta-receptors may suppress food intake, and blocking LH dopamine receptors may increase protein intake specifically.

If the neuron doctrine of Chapter 1 is correct for motivational codes, the activity of small sets of LH cells may be a critical part of subjective experiences of hunger and thirst.

Some LH cells increase and some decrease their activity during eating. Identifying the glucosensitivity of these cells, relating them to reward cells and to VMH stimulation, would be useful. Some (the same?) LH cells may integrate this activity and regulate the tonic effects of the limbic system on motor pathways.

However, nonmotivational aspects of RF, LH, and VMH activity should not be overlooked in this analysis. Many RF cells are active *only* during motoneuron activity, suggesting that some of the changes in RF activity are artifacts of changes in muscle tension (see review in Siegel, 1979). LH stimulation increases stomach acid, decreases blood glucose, and increases insulin secretion. VMH stimulation increases glucose and glycerol in the blood, suppresses insulin secretion, and increases lipolysis in white adipose tissue but causes lipogenesis and increased thermogenesis in brown adipose tissue. Some of the changes in LH and VMH neural activity, and the effects of stimulating and lesioning those structures, may be secondary to these effects. If the LH is involved in increasing food intake, it is also involved — either directly or through the VMH — in physiological adaptations to hunger that indirectly affect food intake.

The internal state of the animal may affect neural reactivity and the reactivity of the intact, behaving animal. For example, the arousal-induced changes in the neural activity in the LH and VMH are exaggerated by food deprivation. Some neurons in the LH increase in activity when the animals wakes up, but *only* if the animal is hungry. Some (or the same?) neurons that respond to the taste or sight of food also do so only when the animal is hungry. On the behavioral level, hunger does not increase the activity of rats in a quiet environment (Hoyenga & Hoyenga, 1984): hungry animals are not necessarily more restless. But hunger does increase animals' *reactivity*. A hungry animal is more aroused by both by food and by nonfood stimuli.

The combination of certain external stimuli and certain internal states could evoke both nonspecific and specific types of arousal. The nonspecific arousal recorded throughout the RF and in the locus coeruleus could increase sensory responses to many different kinds of stimulus and could also increase the excitability of the descending RF motor tracts. Choice-making behavior might be related to specific arousal. Some changes in internal state could specifically increase certain neural responses to specific types of external stimulus, and these neural responses may have input to command-system cells.

C H A P T E R

Sex Hormones: Reproductive Motives and Behaviors

The concepts of sexual motivations and behaviors may be limited to the sexual act itself, but the concepts of reproductive motives and behaviors are much broader in scope. Reproductive behaviors include all behaviors that facilitate reproduction. Thus, for example, reproductive behaviors could include any that increase attractiveness to the opposite sex or the ability to rear offspring successfully.

Overview

First we describe the ways in which sex hormones may affect nerve cells. Both the structure and the function of a nerve cell can be changed by its prior or present exposure to sex hormones. Genes determine (1) gender, and thus which hormones are in greatest supply (male or female types); (2) the organism's sensitivity to sex hormones; and (3) at least some of the cellular reactions to sex hormones.

Describing hormone-sensitive, **sexually dimorphic** behaviors provides a background for the last two sections. "Sexually dimorphic" refers to any characteristic—of behavior, neural anatomy, appearance, or physiology—that differs between the sexes. If one behavior occurs more frequently in one gender than in the other, or if that behavior is evoked by different stimuli in the two genders, the behavior is sexually dimorphic. Sexually dimorphic behaviors are **masculine** or **feminine,** depending on the gender in which they occur more often. Thus, sexually dimorphic does not necessarily mean that the behavior or characteristic is exclusive to a gender, just that its expression varies according to gender.

According to the neuron doctrine of Chapter 1, sexually dimorphic behaviors must be directly related to dimorphic neuron structure. Sexually dimorphic neuron structure and function can be absolute (a given structure is found only in one gender) or comparative (one type of structure is found more often, *on the average*, in one gender than in the other). Most sexually dimorphic characteristics are also **hormone sensitive.** Their form or frequency depends on the organism's hormone levels. A brief description of hormone-sensitive, sexually dimorphic behaviors provides the background for the effects that sex hormones have on nerve cells.

The last two sections of this chapter describe the effects of sex hormones on development and on adult organisms. The sex hormones present during the **perinatal** period (just before and just after birth) can change neural structures and interconnections. In adults, sex hormones can affect the electrical and secretory activity of nerve cells. Both effects are *not* limited just to the parts of the brain controlling sexual behaviors. The concept of reproductive behaviors corresponds to the generalized actions of sex hormones.

However, we cannot yet conclusively relate the effects of sex hormones on the brain to specific sex differences in behavior. For example, the VMH is sexually dimorphic and it also controls sexually dimorphic physiologies and behaviors: ovulation, energy balance, aggression, and sexual behavior. It does not seem likely that the *same* neurons are involved in all these motives and behaviors, but the relevant research has not been done. Researchers who have implanted electrodes in the VMH of their subjects tend to manipulate *only* hunger variables or *only* sexual variables (for an exception, see Kow & Pfaff, 1985b). So we do not know whether sex hormones might affect the way in which VMH cells respond to satiety stimuli. But since sex hormones affect food intake and fat storage (Hoyenga & Hoyenga, 1982), maybe some of the same cells *are* involved.

This chapter concentrates on mammals, especially primates. Gender is determined by different mechanisms in nonmammalian species and there are species-specific effects of sex hormones on nerve cells. For example, if a fetal mammal has two of the same type of sex chromosome present (two X's),

that organism develops as a female. But if a bird's egg has two of the same type of sex chromosomes present (two Z's), that egg develops into a male bird.

Types of Sex Hormone and Effects

Some sex-hormone effects were first discovered in sexual accessory organs such as the uterus and the prostate gland. Much later, researchers discovered that sex hormones also affect brain cells and that the types of effect were not always similar to those found in the sexual organs. This section surveys types of effect, with emphasis on the brain.

Types of Sex Hormone and Metabolic Pathways

Both genders have all three types of sex hormone (androgen, estrogen, and progestin) circulating through their bodies. Although the concentration of sex hormones is sexually dimorphic, the overlap between the genders is not surprising, given the close chemical relationships among the hormones and their interconversion in body tissues.

Male and female hormones. The hormones found in greater concentration in the male than in the female are the class of hormones known as **androgens,** or "male" sex hormones. Some specific members of this class having androgenic types of effect on body cells are **testosterone, dihydrotestosterone,** and **androstenedione.**

The two feminine types of hormone are usually found at higher levels in females than in males. The class of hormones known as **estrogens** includes **estradiol** and **estrone.** These hormones cause the wall of the uterus to become thicker. **Progestins** cause the wall of the uterus to become secretory during the last part of the menstrual cycle or during pregnancy. One progestin is the naturally occurring **progesterone.**

Metabolism of the hormones. The metabolic pathways of the sex hormones are illustrated in Figure 9-1. The sequence starts with cholesterol. Some progestins, including progesterone, can be changed into androgens. Testosterone can be changed into either dihydrotestosterone or estradiol. The first testosterone reaction is catalyzed by a **5-alpha-reductase** enzyme: testosterone is **reduced** (a hydrogen ion is added) by that **reducing enzyme.** The second testosterone reaction is catalyzed by an **aromatizing enzyme:** testosterone is **aromatized** (converted into an aromatic ring-type structure) into estradiol. Many tissues of the body, including some neurons,

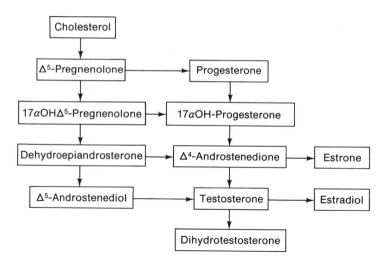

Figure 9-1 The metabolic pathways of the sex hormones show how the sex hormones can be interconverted. The "parent" molecule of all of them is cholesterol.

have the enzymes necessary to convert testosterone into dihydrotestosterone or estradiol.

Sources of the sex hormones. Sex hormones come from two glands in the body: the **gonads** (testes and ovaries) and the adrenal cortex. The testes secrete mostly androgens and only some female hormones. However, the same is also true of the adrenal cortex: among the sex hormones, mostly androgen is secreted. The ovaries secrete mostly estrogens and progestins, although they also secrete androgens. About half of the androgens in a human female come from her ovaries and the other half from the cortex of her adrenal gland (Hoyenga & Hoyenga, 1979).

Sex differences in the hormones. Since the circulating levels of sex hormones vary from hour to hour, from day to day, and from season to season in adults of both genders, we cannot make any simple statements about the level of any given sex hormone in males compared with females. The level of estrogen in adult human males ranges from 2% to 30% of the level found in females, and androgens in females vary from 6% to 20% of the males' levels (Money, 1980). After menopause (when the ovaries quit functioning), primate females may have less estrogen than males of the same age. Females of all species have more progesterone between the age of puberty and the age of menopause than males ever have.

The sexual dimorphisms in prenatal and **neonatal** (just after birth) hormone levels are species specific. Before birth,

primate females have more estradiol than males do (Resko, Ploem, & Stadelmann, 1975; Reyes, Boroditsky, Winter, & Faiman, 1974). In rats, prenatal levels of estrogen may not be sexually dimorphic, and both sexes have a brief surge of estradiol the first day after birth (Corbier, Roffi, Rhoda, & Kerdelhué, 1984; Döhler & Wuttke, 1975; Habert & Picon, 1984). Neither males nor females have large amounts of progesterone during these periods, but rat and primate females may have more than males do (Hagemenas & Kittinger, 1972; Döhler & Wuttke, 1975; Shapiro, Goldman, Bongiovanni, & Marino, 1976; Tapanainen, Huhtaniemi, Koivisto, Kujansuu, Tuimala, & Vihko, 1984; Weisz & Ward, 1980).

Not only are prenatal and neonatal levels of testosterone sexually dimorphic but the dimorphism may be related to sexual dimorphisms in brain anatomy and function. Prenatal males have significantly higher levels of testosterone than do females in species including the rat, mouse, hamster, rhesus monkey, and humans (Pang & Tang, 1984; Resko, Ellinwood, Pasztor, & Buhl, 1980; Slob, Ooms, & Vreeburg, 1980; Tapanainen et al., 1984). Furthermore, males have more testosterone in the neonatal period as well, at least up to the seventh month in humans (Corbier, Kerdelhué, Picon, & Roffi, 1978; Forest, Cathiard, & Bertrand, 1973; Maccoby, Doering, Jacklin, & Kraemer, 1979; Robinson & Bridson, 1978; Slob, Ooms, & Vreeburg, 1980). The neonatal period is part of the sensitive period for hormone effects on the rat brain, and neonatal hormones could also affect the primate brain.

Hormones and Sexual Development

In order to appreciate the implications of sex-hormone effects on body cells, you must understand what they do. The sexually dimorphic developmental stages are outlined in Table 9-1. In every stage except puberty, you have to add something to get masculine development. The fetus will develop in the feminine direction if *nothing* is added. Thus—although there are some exceptions to this—fetuses are inherently feminine: masculinity must be actively induced. Consequently, many more things go wrong with masculine than with feminine development.

The Y chromosome and the fetal gonad.   In the first stage, the fetal gonad develops into either ovaries or testes. Some gene on the Y chromosome causes the outer, or **cortical,** portions of the fetal gonads to degenerate and the inner, or **medullary,** portions to differentiate into two testes. Without a Y, the cortical portions of the gonads differentiate into two ovaries.

Sex hormones and the internal and external sex organs.   Once ovaries or testes have differentiated, the direct effect of the sex chromosomes is ended. Sexual development after that point is determined by the presence or absence of male hormones. If testes differentiated, the internal and external organs differentiate in the male direction. The testes secrete testosterone, causing the potential male internal organs, the **Wolffian structures,** to develop into vas deferens, ejaculatory duct, and seminal vesicles. A *different* hormone, the **Mullerian inhibitory substance (MIS),** secreted by different testicular cells, causes the potential female internal organs, the **Mullerian structures,** to degenerate. Androgens later cause the male external organs to develop into a penis and scrotal sacs.

If ovaries instead of testes had differentiated, the fetus would lack both androgens and MIS. Without androgens, the Wolffian structures degenerate. Without MIS, the Mullerian structures develop into the uterus, fallopian tubes, and upper portion of the vagina. Later, with no androgens present, the external sex organs develop into a clitoris, labia, and lower portion of the vagina.

Sex hormones and the brain.   Some brain structures differentiate during and after the time that the testes in fetal males secrete their hormones. In humans, this time is mostly well before birth, but in rats, brain development continues for at least ten days after birth. Sex hormones affect nerve-cell development, and all three types of sex hormones may have their own unique effects on the brain.

Different types of effects are given different labels. Increasing the frequency of some masculine characteristic would be a

Table 9-1   Sex hormones and stages of sexual development.

Stage	Male	Female
Fetal Development		
Gonadal	Presence of Y chromosomes causes medulla of fetal gonads to develop into testes	In the absence of Y chromosome, the cortex of the fetal gonads develop into ovaries
Internal sex organs	Androgens from testes cause Wolffian structures to develop into male internal sex organs	In the absence of androgens, the Wolffian structures degenerate
	MIS from the testes cause the Mullerian organs to degenerate	In the absence of MIS, the Mullerian structures develop into female internal organs
External sex organs	Androgens from the testes cause external genitals to differentiate into penis and scrotal sacs	In absence of androgens, the external genitals differentiate into clitoris, labia, and lower third of vagina
Brain organization	Androgens from the testes lead to masculinization and defeminization of brain and behavior	The absence of androgens leads to feminization and demasculinization of brain and behavior
Puberty		
Growth of gonads and the adrenal glands	Development of secondary sex characteristics, activational effects on the brain, adult sex hormone levels	Same types of effects as in the male

MIS = Mullerian Inhibiting Substance

masculinizing effect. For example, if androgens before birth increase the adult organism's aggression, the effect is masculinizing, since males are normally more aggressive than females. Conversely, an effect that *decreases* the frequency of some masculine characteristic is **demasculinizing.** Increasing the frequency of some feminine characteristic is **feminizing,** and decreasing the frequency of such a characteristic is **defeminizing.**

Puberty and the sex hormones.   Between the perinatal period and puberty, the gonads are relatively quiescent. At puberty, the gonads secrete sex hormones in large quantities. The cortex of the adrenal gland also increases its output of hormones, including the sex hormones. The **secondary sexual characteristics** develop under the influence of these hormones. In humans, males develop muscles, facial and chest hair appears, the Adam's apple enlarges (the voice changes), and the penis grows. Females develop body fat, especially over the hips (giving females their characteristic shape and skin texture), and females also develop breasts.

Hormone cycles appear at puberty. In males, androgen levels vary over the day (highest during the morning), over the month, and over the season (highest in early fall) (Hoyenga & Hoyenga, 1979, 1984). The hormone cycle in the primate female, the **menstrual cycle,** is associated with periods of uterine bleeding. Lower females have an **estrous cycle.** In lower animals, sexual behaviors vary with the seasonal changes in hormones (males and females) and with the menstrual or estrous cycle (in females).

Throughout these cycles, gonadal secretion is controlled by the pituitary and three areas of the hypothalamus. These nuclei secrete a peptide called luteinizing hormone-releasing hormone (LHRH) into the portal vein system that carries hormones from the hypothalamus to the posterior pituitary, where the peptide stimulates the posterior pituitary cells to secrete the **gonadotropic hormones** into the blood stream (Negro-Vilar & Ojeda, 1981). The gonadotropic hormones are **luteinizing hormone (LH)** and **follicle-stimulating hormone (FSH).** These hormones travel to the gonads, where they increase the rate of secretion of sex hormones.

In males, LH stimulates the testes to secrete testosterone, whereas FSH stimulates spermatogenesis (the development of sperm). A **negative-feedback loop** characterizes the relationship between testosterone levels in males and the release of pituitary hormones. As Figure 9-2 illustrates, rising levels of sex hormones inhibit the pituitary. This effect is exerted directly by sex hormones on pituitary cells. There are also indirect effects of sex hormones, LH, and FSH on the hypothalamic cells that secrete LHRH. A rise in sex hormones *suppresses* LH secretion, which then leads to secretion of *less* testosterone.

The estrous cycle in female rats is four to five days long. It is divided into four phases (Figure 9-3): **proestrus** (one day), **estrus** (one to two days), **metestrus** (one day), and **diestrus** (one to two days). Both estrogen and progesterone are high during proestrus, and sexual interest is greatest during estrus. Thus, in species such as the rat, a castrated female's sexual interest in a male can be maximized by giving her several daily estrogen injections, followed by a progestin injection. Such a pattern of treatments resembles the natural, estrus-inducing pattern. The hormones are lowest and sexual behavior is suppressed during diestrus and metestrus because of a delayed effect of the earlier progesterone peak.

The primate's menstrual cycle is illustrated in Figure 9-4. Estrogen levels steadily increase during the **follicular phase** (the first part of the cycle) because egg follicles in the ovaries are developing and increasing their output of estrogen. For most of the cycle, hormone secretion in females is under the same type of negative-feedback control as that described for males. However, close to ovulation, estrogen reaches a critical level. Then the release of LH and FSH from the pituitary is stimulated instead of being inhibited: a **positive-feedback loop** (Negro-Vilar & Ojeda, 1981). Increases in estrogen thus lead to increases in FSH and LH.

When LH reaches a critical level in primates, at least one egg (and usually only one) is released from one of the developing follicles. After **ovulation,** the follicular secretion of estrogen drops below the critical level required for the positive-feedback effect. Under the influence of LH, the follicle left behind turns itself into a minigland called the **corpus luteum** ("yellow body"). During the **luteal phase** of the cycle, the corpus luteum, under the influence of FSH, secretes high levels of estrogen and progesterone. Under the influence of estrogen and progesterone, the wall of the uterus builds up to prepare for the implantation of a fertilized egg. Without fertilization—and a hormone secreted by a fertilized egg—the corpus luteum degenerates, sex-hormone levels drop, and the wall of the uterus sloughs off as menstrual blood during the **menstrual phase** of the cycle. Since progesterone surges occur *before* ovulation in rats but *after* ovulation in primates, it is not surprising that progesterone usually does not facilitate sexual interest and behaviors in primate females.

Normally only females show the positive-feedback effect exerted by sufficiently high levels of estrogens. In species such as rats, the brains of males lack the capacity for a positive-feedback effect. In primates, including the human, positive feedback is inhibited by testosterone. Normally, only castrated

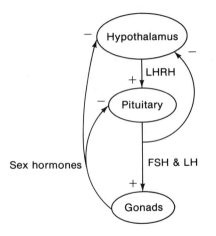

Figure 9-2 Negative-feedback loops act to maintain homeostatic conditions. In such a loop, increased activity in the output organs (here, an increased secretion of sex hormones by the gonads) suppresses the mechanism that turns those output organs on (here, the hypothalamus and pituitary).

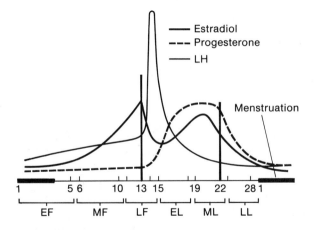

Figure 9-4 Example of the hormonal changes in a primate's menstrual cycle. The length of each phase is shown for a "standard" 28-day cycle in humans. EF, MF, LF = early, mid-, and late follicular phases; EL, ML, LL = early, mid-, and late luteal phases. The follicle containing a developing egg grows during the follicular phases, and the empty egg follicle, the corpus luteum, secretes its sex hormones during the luteal phase.

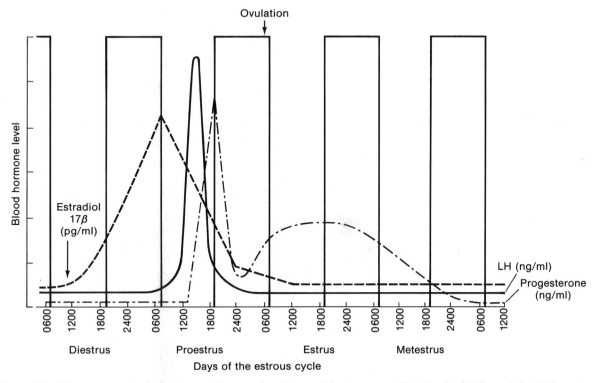

Figure 9-3 The estrous cycle of a female rat. The time of ovulation and the variations in blood levels of 17β estradiol, LH (luteinizing hormone), and progesterone are indicated. The late proestrus period is characterized by declining levels of hormones and the animal's sexual receptivity. The metestrus and early diestrus periods are characterized by low plasma hormone levels and sexual nonreceptivity. pg = picograms; ng = nanograms.

males can show the large surge of LH and FSH after estrogen injections.

Organizational versus Activational Effects of Sex Hormones

Sex hormones can have two different types of effect. One occurs during the perinatal period and the other after puberty.

Organizational effects. Sex hormones *before and just after birth* (neonatal effects are greater than prenatal effects in some rodents) can have *permanent* effects on the *structure and function* of a *developing* organ. This is an **organizational effect.** The development of Wolffian structures and a penis are examples of organizational effects: once the organ completes its process of differentiation, the hormone's effect cannot be reversed. Even surgery cannot change a penis into anything but an approximation of a clitoris. Cells in the adrenal gland, liver, and brain show organizational effects; the structure and function of cells in these organs are permanently sexually dimorphic (Bardin & Catterall, 1981; Kine, Vinson, Major, & Kilpatrick, 1980).

The nature of the organizational effects of androgens and estrogens can be described in five general principles.

1. Although an organizational effect cannot be reversed, its effect on behavior *can* often be altered by changing hormone levels or the environment (as we will discuss later). For example, removing neonatal androgens by castrating newborn male rats increases female types of sexual behavior in those males *only* if they are later exposed to other males. Thus, even with sexually dimorphic brains, if adult males and females are given the same levels of hormones, a sexually dimorphic brain may not cause behaviors to be sexually dimorphic.

2. The sexes have different sex-hormone levels during the perinatal period: male levels of hormones cause both masculinization and defeminization. In the first case, male levels of fetal sex hormones masculinize the brain and behavior by increasing masculine types of brain structure and behaviors. At the same time, male levels of hormones defeminize by decreasing the probability that feminine brain structures and behaviors will develop. Specifically, the fetal male has more androgens than does the fetal female because of the high levels of androgens secreted by the fetal testes during certain stages of fetal development. Removing fetal androgens would demasculinize and feminize the brain and behavior of a male rat. For example, if a male rat were castrated immediately after birth, he would be expected to be demasculinized (for exam-

ple, his aggression would be decreased) and feminized (for example, his infant-caretaking behavior would be increased).

3. The perinatal androgens secreted by fetal male testes may be masculinizing and defeminizing through two separate metabolic pathways. First, brain cells aromatize testosterone to estradiol, and experimental injections of estradiol into neonatal rats are more powerful in their *masculinizing* effects on the brain than is testosterone itself. Thus, as originally suggested by McDonald (Doughty & McDonald, 1974), male rats may be normally masculinized and defeminized by a *female* sex hormone, estradiol. Second, testosterone is also reduced to dihydrotestosterone by some brain cells and by most of the androgen-sensitive cells in the rest of the body. This conversion may be relatively more important for brain masculinization in species such as primates, hamsters, guinea pigs, mice, and ferrets than it is in rats (Goy, 1981; Hutchison & Steimer, 1984; Martin & Baum, 1986; Toran-Allerand, 1984).

4. Feminizing and demasculinizing the brains and behaviors of female animals may require normal female levels of sex hormones. During fetal development, both male and female animals have high levels of estrogens circulating throughout their bodies; most of this hormone comes from the mother, crossing over in the placenta to the fetus. Protein molecules that attach to estrogen molecules are found at higher levels in the circulation of fetal female rats than in male rats. These molecules may act to preserve the estrogens, preventing their excretion and thus allowing them to cross the blood–brain barrier to affect the brains of females. Normal types of feminine brain structures and behaviors in females may require normal levels of estrogens to be present in the perinatal period (Döhler, 1986).

5. The details of feminizing, masculinizing, defeminizing, and demasculinizing effects may depend on when the hormone appears and in which part of the brain and whether the external structure or the internal physiology of the cell is more affected (Goy & McEwen, 1980). For example, male rats and dogs may be mostly masculinized before birth, but defeminization may occur mostly after birth (Baum, 1979; Davis, Chaptal, & McEwen, 1979). Injecting estrogens into the preoptic region of the brain of a female rat may be masculinizing, whereas similar injections into the ventromedial region may be defeminizing (Nordeen & Yahr, 1982, 1983). Perinatal androgens and estrogens may have permanent effects on fetal brain cells such that their shape and their patterns of synaptic interconnection depend on which hormone was present during fetal development. These hormones may also have permanent effects on brain-cell metabolism such that, for example, estrogen masculinizes the brains of rats by increasing

the sensitivity of their adult brain cells to the actions of testosterone.

Perinatal progesterone has mixed effects. In male rats, neonatal progesterone injections may interfere with the masculinizing and defeminizing effects of estradiol (Reddy, Rajan, & Daly, 1980). These injections also cause pyramidal cells in the rat cerebral cortex to increase their branching and can produce a heavier brain (Menzies, Drysdale, & Waite, 1982). In humans, progestin pills given to pregnant females, because of progestin conversion into testosterone, can sometimes have masculinizing effects (Hoyenga & Hoyenga, 1979). The human brain may still be somewhat hormone sensitive even after birth: higher *neonatal* levels of progesterone in humans are related to happy/excited moods, a lack of timidity, and either high (males) or low (females) scores on measures of muscular strength from six months to three years after birth (Marcus, Maccoby, Jacklin, & Doering, 1985; Jacklin, Maccoby, & Doering, 1983; Jacklin, Maccoby, Doering, & King, 1984). But since in lower animals neither gender has much perinatal progesterone, and since in humans neonatal progesterone levels are not sexually dimorphic, these effects may be irrelevant to normal brain masculinization or feminization.

Activational effects.

Sex hormones have *temporary and reversible* effects on the *function* of an already fully *developed* organ. These **activational effects** would normally occur only *after puberty*. Sex hormones affect the uterus in a temporary and reversible fashion: the same effects recur in each hormone cycle. Sex hormones change enzyme levels in the sex organs and in the adrenal glands, kidney, brain, and liver (Bardin & Catterall, 1981). In each case, the effect appears whenever a critical level of the right hormone is present, and the effect disappears or reverses itself when the hormone is removed.

Comparison of organizational and activational effects.

The terms *organizational* and *activational* actually refer to a continuum of possible effects rather than a dichotomy. In fact, the brain has periods of varying *sensitivity* to various types of effects of sex hormones. Developing organs remain at least somewhat sensitive to hormones even after fetal development is completed. Effects similar to those produced by small hormone injections during the sensitive period can be produced later, but only by using either higher doses of the same hormones or more prolonged treatments. For example, the human brain may still be slightly hormone sensitive right after birth (Marcus et al., 1984; Jacklin et al., 1983; Jacklin et al., 1984).

The surge of sex hormones at puberty may have relatively permanent or organizational-like effects on the brain, the body, and behavior. For example, in humans, the growth of body hair, penises, and breasts is a relatively permanent effect of puberty; removing the gonads later in life will have only slight effects on these sexually dimorphic body characteristics. Such organizational-like effects have been described for organs such as the liver (Pak, Tsim, & Cheny, 1985) and the hypothalamic area of the brain in rats (Anderson, 1982; Terasawa & Timiras, 1968). Some behaviors are also durably affected by pubertal sex hormones in rats, including sexual behaviors (Dunlap, Gerall, & Carlton, 1978; Gerall, Dunlap, & Hendricks, 1973; Hendricks & Duffy, 1974; Hendricks & Weltin, 1976) and activity levels (Slob, Huizer, & van der Werff ten Bosch, 1986). Even sex-role traits in humans may depend on what levels of sex hormones are present at the time of puberty (Imperato-McGinley, Peterson, & Gautier, 1984).

Three types of behaviors.

One system for classifying hormone-sensitive behaviors is described in Table 9-2. This system uses the distinction between organizational and activational effects (based on Baum, 1979, and on Goy & McEwen, 1980). The behaviors are classified according to whether certain hormones must be present or absent, and at what time, for the behavior to be fully expressed.

Sensitivity to perinatal or postpubertal sex-hormone levels differentiates the behavior types. **Type I behaviors** are sensitive to organizational hormone levels. Masculine Type I behaviors are increased by the presence of masculinizing hormones, and feminine behaviors are suppressed by masculinizing hormones. **Type II traits** are insensitive to organizational hormone levels but require either male or female adult activational hormones in order to be fully expressed. **Type III traits** are sensitive to organizational hormones but are either suppressed by, or are insensitive to, activational sex hormones. Some types of play behavior are sensitive to (increased by) perinatal androgens but are suppressed by the pubertal surge of hormones. Type III traits are apparently less frequently found than are Type I or II traits, but researchers have also less often looked for them.

Not all sexual behaviors are Type I. Masculine types of sexual behavior include **mounting** a receptive female. The female indicates her receptivity by a **lordosis** posture: all four of her legs are spread, bracing her for the male to mount her from the rear; her back is swayed and her tail is bent out of the male's way. When the female assumes the lordosis posture, the male mounts, engages in **intromission** (insertion of penis), and eventually **ejaculates.** Mounting is a Type I behavior in

Table 9-2 Hormone-sensitive behaviors defined according to hormone effects.

Behavior Type	Organizational Effects of Masculinizing Hormones[a]	Activational Effects of All Three Sex Hormones	Examples
Type I	Sensitive to perinatal hormones		Some types of aggression
	Increased by hormones	Increased by appropriate activational sex hormone(s)	Intromission and ejaculation
			Mounting in most species
	Decreased by hormones	Increased by appropriate activational sex hormone(s)	Lordosis in most species, including rodents, ruminants, and some carnivores
Type II	Not sensitive to perinatal hormones	Increased by appropriate activational sex hormone(s)	Mounting in mice and in some strains of rats
			Lordosis in primates, ferrets and marmosets; sexual interest in humans
Type III	Sensitive to perinatal hormones	Either suppressed by, or insensitive to, activational hormones	
	Increased by hormones		Rough-and-tumble play
	Decreased by hormones		Active-avoidance performances in rodents

[a] Masculinizing hormones include testosterone in all species and estradiol in rodents; progesterone normally seems to be at too low a level during the perinatal period to exert any significant organizational effects.

most species, except possibly for some strains of rats (Whalen, Edwards, Luttge, & Robertson, 1969) and mice (Young, 1982). Lordosis may be a Type I behavior except in primates (Goy, 1981).

Cellular Actions of Sex Hormones

Researchers have discovered how activational sex hormones affect brain and body cells and thus most types of behaviors (Table 9-2). The idea that sex hormones exert their organizational effects on the brain and Types I and II behaviors through similar types of mechanisms is plausible but unestablished.

The "classic" model. The classic model of steroid hormone action on cells is presented in Figure 9-5. Sex hormones are carried in the blood to the target cells by protein hormone receptors to which they are attached, usually rather "loosely." Then the sex hormones (as well as other steroid hormones) passively diffuse across the wall of a cell, down their concentration gradient (Chan & O'Malley, 1976; Goy & McEwen, 1980; Pfaff & McEwen, 1983; Pimentel, 1978a, 1978b). Once in the cytoplasm, a hormone molecule encounters a hormone-receptor molecule. Each of the three sex hormones has its own receptor protein. The hormone-receptor complex is then **translocated** into the nucleus.

Two types of **genomic** (gene) effects occur in the nucleus: transductional and translational (Chan & O'Malley, 1976;

Goy & McEwen, 1980; Pfaff & McEwen, 1983; Pimentel, 1978a, 1978b). The hormone-receptor complex may attach to specific sites on the DNA and thereby derepress a DNA coding sequence, leading to the manufacture of a new messenger RNA sequence. The new RNA sequence would move out to the cytoplasm for the synthesis of a new protein (see, for example, Kaye, 1983). In other cases, the hormone-receptor complex may **repress** genes (turn them off) decreasing the level of some protein. The hormone-receptor complex may have translational effects. The cutting and splicing (activation) of a nuclear RNA sequence may be controlled by sex hormones. Again, new proteins affecting the structure and function of the cell would appear, effects that may change the frequencies of sexually dimorphic behaviors.

Genomic effects can be identified by certain characteristics. The effect requires at least minutes and maybe hours to take place, and the effect may last for many hours — even many hours after a sex hormone such as estrogen has left the cell (Tam, Haché, & Deeley, 1986). Drugs that inhibit RNA synthesis or protein synthesis inhibit genomic effects of sex steroids on their target cells. These drugs also inhibit the corresponding sexually dimorphic behaviors, such as estradiol-induced lordosis or the delayed, progesterone-induced suppression of lordosis (Etgen, 1984). Also, if cells in a target organ are exposed to sex hormones, their receptors should be translocated to the nucleus. In other words, according to the classic model, the level of receptors in the cytoplasm should decrease and that in the nucleus should increase. This cytoplasmic

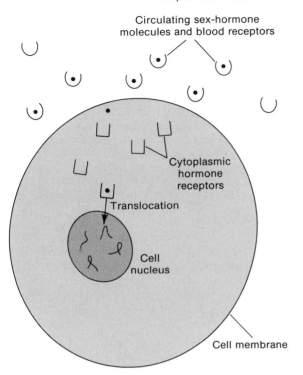

Circulating sex-hormone
molecules and blood receptors

Cytoplasmic
hormone
receptors

Translocation

Cell
nucleus

Cell membrane

Figure 9-5 The "classic" model of the cellular effects of sex hormones. Sex hormone molecules are carried to target cells by blood receptors in the blood stream. After the hormones pass through the cell's membrane, they combine with cytoplasmic hormone receptors and get translocated to the nucleus, where the activity of specific genes is then changed.

depletion of hormone receptors can be measured. Later, new receptors are manufactured to replenish the levels in the cytoplasm.

We should mention that the classic model of genomic hormone effects has been challenged (for example, Clark, 1984; King & Greene, 1984; Schrader, 1984; Welshons, Lieberman, & Gorski, 1984). According to new models and results of research, there are few—if any—cytoplasmic hormone receptors. Instead, there are two types of nuclear receptors: **unoccupied** and **occupied** by a hormone molecule. The cytoplasmic receptors found by other researchers are attributed to artifacts of the methods used for analyzing and preserving cells. However, these newer ideas will not change the basic facts of genomic effects: only occupied receptors in the nucleus can affect genes, and the process takes a significant amount of time to complete.

Nontraditional types of activational effects on target cells. There may be specific hormone receptors not only in the cytoplasm (or just in the nucleus) but also in the membrane of target cells in the brain and body. Cells in the uterus, for example, may have estrogen receptors on their membranes (Pietras & Szego, 1977). A hormone molecule would affect the cell by combining with membrane receptors. The hormone–membrane-receptor complex could then have effects on membrane permeability and currents similar to those produced on a postsynaptic membrane after slow synaptic actions (Chapter 4). These effects would take place faster than those caused by genomic activation (Koenig, Goldstone, & Lu, 1983). Alternatively, hormones could diffuse into cells and directly affect metabolic processes.

Genomic versus membrane effects and sexual behavior. Several lines of research have shown that hormones do affect target-cell metabolism *without* changing genetic activity (Baulieu, 1978). For example, Dufy and his colleagues (Dufy, Vincent, Fleury, Du Pasquier, Gourdji, & Tixier-Vidal, 1979) injected estradiol directly onto the membrane of a pituitary cell. A series of action potentials and an increase in membrane resistance occurred within a minute. These action potentials varied with external Ca^{++} levels and so were probably Ca^{++} spikes. The spikes occurred just after an increase in membrane resistance. Thus, estradiol could be having effects on cell membranes similar to those observed in the postsynaptic membranes of slow synapses involving Ca^{++} as the second messenger.

Some of the sexual characteristics already described can be related to genomic and membrane types of effect (Moss & Dudley, 1984). The facilitative effect of estrogen both on lordosis and on LH and FSH secretion (positive-feedback effect) may involve a genomic process. On the other hand, the negative-feedback process between gonadal and pituitary hormone levels may be carried out at the membrane level.

Summary of Cellular Effects

There are sexually dimorphic hormone levels, just as there are sexually dimorphic patterns of reproductive behaviors. But there is much overlap between the sexes in both. Both brain and body tissue interconvert the three types of sex hormones.

The sex hormones exert both organizational (during perinatal development) and activational (after puberty) effects. Organizational sex hormones permanently affect the structure and function of developing internal and external sex organs and brain cells and also the frequency of some sexually dimorphic behaviors. The activational effects on brain cells and some sexually dimorphic behaviors—and possibly the organizational effects—are caused by the sex hormone's passing through the cell wall, attaching to specific hormone receptors (either in the cytoplasm or nucleus), repressing or activating specific genes in the nucleus, and suppressing old proteins or producing new ones. These changes in protein levels would permanently affect the structure and interconnections of those cells (organizational) or influence their rates of activity (activational). However, sometimes activational sex hormones have "nontraditional" or nongenomic effects. The activity of some nerve cells can be changed in too short a time to allow for any change in gene-protein activity.

Hormone Receptors in the Brain

Target cells for sex hormones have specific hormone receptors. Stumpf and Sar (1976, 1978) explored the distribution of estrogen, androgen, progestin, and corticosteroid (another steroid secreted by the adrenal cortex) receptor sites in the mammalian brain. Although there is overlap, each hormone has its own specific distribution pattern, one that is shared by many mammalian species. Sex-hormone receptors are most likely to be found in the hypothalamus, pituitary, and limbic system (see Table 9-3). Measuring cytoplasmic receptors or unoccupied nuclear receptors establishes whether the cell *could* be genomically affected by sex hormones, but measuring the number of nuclear (or occupied) receptors shows that the cell *is* being affected by the sex hormone.

Receptors and Sexual Behavior

Estradiol (**E**) injections increase the number of occupied nuclear E receptors in many of those brain areas. In the rodent, the increase in the number of occupied E receptors in the mediobasal hypothalamus (including the VMH) normally reaches a maximum just before the surge of progesterone (**P**) that elicits maximal sexual behaviors. One genomic effect of E may be to increase the number of P receptors.

Progesterone affects sexual interest and activity in many nonprimates. In fact, the level of P receptors often increases just when the animal's sexual interest does (Brown & Blaus-

Table 9-3   The anatomy of sexual behaviors.

Area	Function	References
Medial preoptic and anterior hypothalamus (including suprachiasmatic nucleus)	Positive feedback effects of estrogens on LHRH in rats (ovulation & estrus); controls male sexual behavior (testosterone or estradiol); activity in these cells inhibits lordosis (estradiol inhibits neurons here)	Christensen & Clemens, 1974 Goodman, 1978; Nordeen & Yahr, 1982; Pfaff, 1980
Mediobasal hypothalamus (e.g., VMH, arcuate & dorsomedial n.)	Estrogen and progesterone facilitate female sexual interest; arcuate secretes LHRH; negative feedback effects of sex hormones on LHRH secretion; positive feedback effects of estrogens on LHRH in primates	Krey, Butler, & Knobil, 1975; McEwen, 1981; Nordeen & Yahr, 1982; Rainbow, Parsons, & McEwen, 1982; Rubin & Barfield, 1983
Medial anterior hypothalamus	Activity in these cells facilitates lordosis in rats	Pfaff, 1980
Dopaminergic arcuate	These neurons secrete dopamine into median eminence to inhibit prolactin secretion	Demarest, McKay, Riegle, & Moore, 1981
Amygdala	Neuronal activity facilitates positive feedback effects of estrogen in female rats; neuronal activity facilitates mounting in male rats	Kendrick, 1983a; 1983b; Nishizuka & Arai, 1981a, 1981b
Midbrain central gray	Stimulation can facilitate lordosis in the female rat; controls secretion of LH and FSH	Sakuma & Pfaff, 1979; Haskins & Moss, 1983

LHRH = luteinizing hormone-releasing hormone
VMH = ventromedial hypothalamus
LH = luteinizing hormone
FSH = follicle-stimulating hormone

tein, 1984). Although E increases both sexual interest and the number of P receptors (occupied + unoccupied), these two effects may not be directly related since the receptor increase also occurs in sexually unreceptive animals (Barfield, Glaser, Rubin, & Etgen, 1984). P injections first cause an early increase in **receptivity** or lordosis; this rapid effect may involve membrane or cyclic nucleotide effects (Barfield et al., 1984). Later, that same P injection will cause both an increase in occupied P receptors and an increase in "invitational" or **proceptivity** behaviors, in which the female actively solicits the attention of males. A second, delayed injection of P suppresses sexual interest and may do so by decreasing the number of occupied E receptors in the mediobasal hypothalamus (Okulicz, Evans, & Leavitt, 1981). Thus, only the delayed inhibitory and proceptivity effects involve genomic activation (Barfield et al., 1984; Etgen, 1984).

Changes in E and P receptors parallel changes in sexual behaviors. But that parallelism does not prove that the one *causes* the other. The receptor changes may be more directly related to other types of behaviors sensitive to sex-hormone levels, such as aggression and nest building.

Researchers locating hormone receptors have encountered several technical difficulties. The research involves injecting radioactively labeled sex hormones into the blood stream or brain. Areas of the animal's brain are examined post mortem for radioactivity. But recent research that uses the newly developed and more sophisticated technologies finds receptor distribution patterns that differ slightly from those in earlier studies. Also, it is easier to interpret studies that clearly differentiate between unoccupied (cytoplasmic or nuclear) and occupied receptors. Furthermore, the number and location of hormone receptors is affected by both perinatal and adult levels of sex hormones; these should be specified and controlled by the researcher. Finally, the time between a sex-hormone injection and receptor measurement may affect receptor measurement. For example, sex differences in receptor numbers may reverse with time after a hormone injection (Nordeen & Yahr, 1983).

Estrogen Receptors

E receptors specifically attach to estrogens, especially to E. Androgens such as testosterone (**T**) do not attach well to E receptors (Attardi & Ohno, 1976; Westley & Salaman, 1976).

Activational effects of sex hormones. E receptor levels are affected by activational hormone levels. As the classic model of hormone action predicts, within 48 hours after an E injection, brain cytoplasmic (or unoccupied nuclear) E receptors are depleted and occupied nuclear receptors are increased.

Because T is aromatized into E, T injections can have exactly the same effects on E receptors as E injections do. As we pointed out before, P injections decrease occupied E receptors (Okulicz, Evans, & Leavitt, 1981). However, P injections may not affect levels of unoccupied brain E receptors (Schwartz, Blaustein, & Wade, 1979).

Location of estrogen receptors. The anatomical distribution of E receptors is similar in rats, mice, and primates (Sheridan & Weaker, 1982; Stumpf & Sar, 1978; Warembourg, 1977). In the adult female squirrel monkey (which had normal perinatal hormones and was ovariectomized six days before the experiment), E receptors are found in the hypothalamus and pituitary, as Figure 9-6 illustrates (see also Table 9-3). E receptors are also found in some limbic-system structures and in some parts of the thalamus, the colliculus, the RF, and the spinal cord. The greatest density of E receptors in the adult is found in the areas of the brain that control sexual behaviors and pituitary secretion of LH and FSH. These include the pituitary, the preoptic/anterior hypothalamus, the medial basal hypothalamus, the medial amygdala, and the midbrain central gray (see Table 9-3).

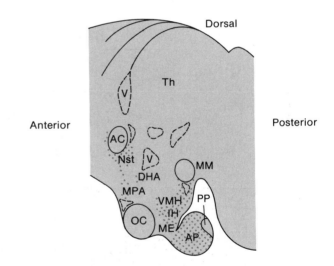

Figure 9-6 Estrogen-concentrating cells (indicated by dots) are found in the hypothalamus and pituitary, as seen in a sagittal section of an ovariectomized monkey. AC = anterior commissure; AP = anterior pituitary; DHA = dorsal hypothalamic area; IH = nucleus infundibularis; ME = median eminence; MM = mammilary body; MPA = medial preoptic area; Nst = nucleus of the stria terminalis; OC = optic chiasm; PP = posterior pituitary; Th = thalamus; V = ventricle; VMH = ventromedial hypothalamus.

Estrogen receptors during development. Similar receptors, in similar brain areas, are seen in perinatal and adult rats and mice (Attardi & Ohno, 1976; Dudley, 1981; Reddy, Rajan, & Daly, 1980; MacLusky, Lieberburg, & McEwen, 1979; Vito & Fox, 1982). The one dramatic exception is that the perinatal but not the adult rodent cortex has E receptors. These receptors are not found to any great extent in an occupied nuclear form in cortical cells, suggesting that E may not have genomic effects on cortical-cell development—which makes the reason for having cortical E receptors, and having them only during development, pretty much a mystery.

Figure 9-7 shows how the concentration of E, T, and P receptors changes during early development in the rat. Not all brain areas show the same developmental pattern (MacLusky, Lieberburg, & McEwen, 1979). (The other receptors in that figure will be discussed later in this section.) The number of E receptors increases sharply just before birth and remains at high levels for at least 21 days after birth. Thus, the number of E receptors is high during the time the rat brain is most sensitive to the masculinizing and defeminizing effects of E.

Sex differences in adult E receptors. When the number of estrogen receptors is averaged over all areas of the hypothalamus and/or pituitary, researchers do not find any sex differences in the number of E receptors. However, the kinetics of those receptors *are* sexually dimorphic. In the pituitary, the rate of replenishing E-depleted unoccupied E receptors is lower in the normal female rat than in the normal male. The female rat given a neonatal injection of T also has slower replenishment (Cidlowski & Muldoon, 1976). Thus, replenishment rate is dimorphic and organized by perinatal hormones.

The ability of E injections to increase occupied E receptors in the VMH may be permanently suppressed by giving females perinatal E injections. Normal adult males also do not show the E-induced increase in VMH E receptors (Parsons, Rainbow, & McEwen, 1984). For this reason, after injections of radioactively labeled E, in some areas of the hypothalamus more occupied E receptors are found in normal females or in males castrated at birth than in normal males or females neonatally masculinized by T injections (DeBold, 1978; Marrone

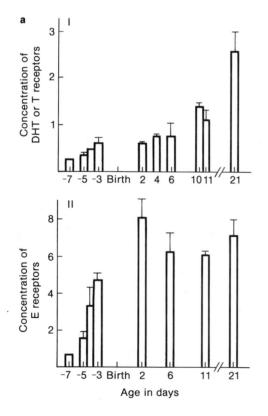

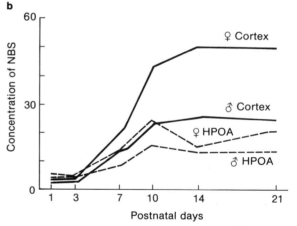

Figure 9-7   a. Development of androgen and estrogen receptors in the rat hypothalamus. The horizontal axis represents the age of the animal in days. The vertical axis is the concentration, as measured by radioactively labeled ($[^3H]$) hormones, $[^3H]$dihydrotestosterone, $[^3H]$testosterone (both in I), and $[^3H]$estradiol (in II), measured in moles of radioactivity bound per milligram of tissue $\times 10^{17}$. **b.** Sex differences in the postnatal development of occupied nuclear progestin receptors (NBS) in the hypothalamic-preoptic area and the cerebral cortex. DHT = dihydrotestosterone; E = estradiol; NBS = number of binding sites or receptors; T = testosterone; HPOA = hypothalamic-preoptic area.

& Feder, 1977; Olsen & Whalen, 1980; Whalen & Massicci, 1975). But this may be true only if at least 60 minutes have elapsed between when E is injected and when the animal is euthanized (Nordeen & Yahr, 1983). Thus, even though males and females might have equal numbers of unoccupied receptors in some areas of their brains, the receptors' ability to be occupied and therefore to produce changes in protein synthesis is lower in many areas of the male than of the female brain.

Furthermore, when hypothalamic nuclei from adults are examined individually, sex differences in receptor levels *can* be found (see Figure 9-8). In the medial preoptic nucleus— part of the positive-feedback loop—male rats may have half as many E receptors as females do. This dimorphism may be the reason the male rat brain cannot show positive-feedback effects. The mediobasal regions of the hypothalamus (including the VMH) also have more unoccupied E receptors in normal females than either in males or in females given neonatal masculinizing hormone treatments (Nordeen & Yahr, 1983). Defeminizing perinatal hormone treatments permanently decreased adult levels of occupied E receptors in both the preoptic area and the mediobasal hypothalamus (measured 60 minutes after an E injection).

All these sex differences cannot by themselves fully account for sex differences in sexual behaviors. For example, neonatally castrated males and normal females have equal numbers of occupied nuclear receptors after E injections. Nevertheless, females still show more lordosis than males do.

Androgen Receptors

Although T itself does not bind to the E receptor, T can be metabolized to E. Thus, the aromatized metabolites of radioactively labeled T would bind to E receptors, which would mean that both they and the androgen receptors would get radioactively labeled after T injections. In fact, Westley and Salaman (1976) were able to demonstrate that the testicular T (coming from testes) in rat males produced occupied nuclear E receptors in the hypothalamus. Also, E itself can bind to the androgen receptor.

More than one type of androgen receptor? Sheridan (1983) suggested that there are at least three kinds of androgen receptors. Type T binds more readily and closely to T than to dihydrotestosterone (**DHT**). But T is also reduced to DHT, which may have its own receptors. DHT receptors bind better to DHT than to T. Type DHT+T receptors bind to both steroids equally. Sheridan suggested that Type DHT+T does *not* have genomic effects.

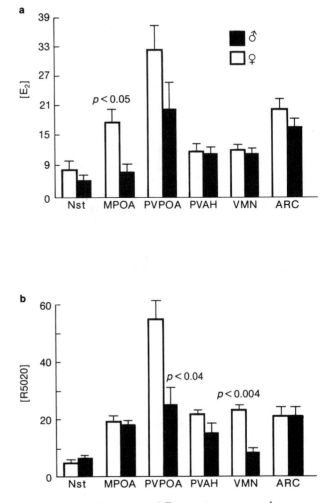

Figure 9-8 There are sex differences in estrogen and progestin receptor levels in hypothalamic nuclei of adult rats. The rats were gonadectomized (had gonads removed) at least one week and not more than three weeks before the measurement. Hormone receptor levels were measured by the binding of [³H]estradiol (**a**) and of [³H]R5020, a synthetic progestin (**b**). Measurements of progestin receptors were done in rats given estrogen treatment; the researchers said that most of the neural actions of progestin require estrogen "priming," as does the progestin receptor. Significant sex differences were seen in estrogen receptor levels in the medial preoptic area. Sex differences in progestin receptors were seen in one of the preoptic areas, the cortex (Figure 9-7), and the ventromedial hypothalamus. Nst = nucleus of the stria terminalis; MPOA = medial preoptic area; PVPOA = periventricular region of the preoptic area; PVAH = periventricular portion of the anterior hypothalamus; VMN = ventromedial nucleus; ARC = arcuate nucleus (see also Table 9-3).

Anatomical distribution of androgen receptors.   Injecting radioactively labeled T labels many of the same areas of the brain as do similar radioactive E injections. There are, however, some differences (androgen receptors?). For example, T produces more labeling than E does in the sensory and motor areas of the brain (Stumpf & Sar, 1978).

Researchers can experimentally differentiate among the E and androgen receptors. They may label different parts of the T molecule (so that only DHT or only E metabolites retain the label). They can also inject radioactively labeled DHT that cannot be aromatized, or inject unlabeled E before the T injection so that the E receptors are already occupied. Comparing the results produced by these techniques allows Type T and Type DHT receptors to be distinguished from each other and from E receptors.

T receptors are found in only a few areas, but DHT receptors are widespread, especially in primates (Michael & Rees, 1982; Rees & Michael, 1983; Sheridan, 1983; Sheridan & Weaker, 1982; Stumpf & Sar, 1976). For example, in rodents, there are just a few spinal motoneurons with T receptors—although there are more of them in males than in females. But nearly all spinal neurons in both genders have DHT receptors (Breedlove & Arnold, 1983). There are also DHT receptors in many motor areas of the brain stem, although species differ in *which* motor areas have them. DHT receptors in the primate are found in a variety of sensory and motor areas, including the RF and the structures listed in Table 9-4. Thus, "the high levels of testosterone [in males] are seemingly acting on a few very discrete populations of neurons whereas the low levels of DHT may be acting very diffusely throughout the nervous system" (Sheridan, 1983, p. 176). In addition, the further up the phylogenetic scale, the more CNS areas have DHT receptors.

Developmental changes.   Figure 9-7 shows the developmental changes in androgen receptors (measured with both T and DHT) in the rat (Attardi & Ohno, 1976). Androgen receptors increase throughout development. This means that there are both androgen and E receptors in the brain during the sensitive period.

Enzymes and organizing effects of T.   The masculinizing and defeminizing effects of T will depend not only on which hormone receptors are present in which parts of the brain but on which enzymes (the reducing or the aromatizing enzymes) are present in those areas. For example, T cannot masculinize by conversion to E even in areas with E receptors if those same areas lack the aromatizing enzyme. Some areas of the brain

Table 9-4   The location of androgen receptors in the primate brain (as measured after DHT injections).

Amygdaloid nuclei(n): pars basal, central, cortical lateral medial and posterior	Paraventricular n.
	Periventricular hypothalamus
	Piriform cortex
Anterior hypothalamus	Preoptic: suprachiasmatic,
Arcuate n.	medial and lateral
Periventricular n.	Reticular n.
Cingulate cortex	Lateral septum
Medial habenula	Supramammillary n.
Hippocampus	Suprarhinal cortex
Interhemispheric cortex	Diagonal tract (Broca)
Interstitial stria terminalis n.	Ventromedial hypothalamus
Lateral hypothalamus	Zona incerta
Medial thalamus: pars medial and lateral n.	

may have T receptors and so may be directly affected by testosterone through those receptors. For example, adult male rats have more T receptors in their medial preoptic area than females do (Jacobson, Arnold, & Gorski, 1982).

Which enzyme is present in which areas determines whether E or DHT is masculinizing and defeminizing (Jenkins & Hall, 1977; Lieberburg & McEwen, 1977; Schindler, 1976; Selmanoff, Brodkin, Weiner, & Siiteri, 1977; Sholl, Goy, & Uno, 1982). Where the reducing enzyme is present, DHT could be masculinizing. For example, human brains show more conversion of T to DHT in the hypothalamus than in the cortex, and more conversion in male than in female brains. DHT is formed throughout the perinatal rodent brain, but in preadult rats, more DHT is formed in female than in male pituitaries (McEwen, 1978).

When the aromatizing enzyme is present, E could be the masculinizing hormone. Little aromatizing activity is found in the human brain, and then only in the hypothalamus, temporal lobe, and amygdala. The aromatizing enzyme is not present in the cortex or in the pituitary of either sex in rats (McEwen, 1978), but there may be sex differences (see Table 9-5). Thus, T from neonatal testes binds to E receptors in the amygdala and hypothalamus of neonatal rat brains but *not* to those in the cortex—since the cortex lacks the aromatizing enzyme (Westley & Salaman, 1977).

Depending on which enzymes and receptors are present, some brain areas may be masculinized and defeminized by DHT, some by T, and some by E. Compared with rodents, primates may use more DHT and T pathways.

Table 9-5 Location of aromatizing and reducing enzymes in the brains of male and female rats (see also Figure 9-6 and Tables 9-3 and 9-4).

	Male	*Female*	*Combined*
Brain area			$\bar{x} \pm$ SEM
Aromatizing activity			
MPN-AHN	30.4	12.6	21.5 ± 8.8
MBH	5.1	3.6	4.4 ± 0.5
LPN	2.7	1.3	2.0 ± 0.8
Am	2.0	1.1	1.6 ± 0.5
LHN	1.0	0.6	0.8 ± 0.2
Reducing activity			
LHN	17.0	17.4	17.2 ± 5.9
MPN-AHN	14.6	11.1	12.9 ± 3.7
LPN	13.0	10.5	11.7 ± 2.0
Am	4.8	3.6	4.2 ± 1.1
MBH	1.6	0.8	1.2 ± 0.4

MPN-AHN = medial preoptic nucleus – anterior hypothalamic nucleus
MBH = medial basal hypothalamus
LPN = lateral preoptic nucleus
Am = amygdala
LHN = lateral hypothalamic nucleus
SEM = standard error of the sample mean (the population mean is likely to be located in that range)

Progesterone Receptors

Progesterone receptors bind only to P and not to androgens or E (Blaustein & Feder, 1979; Moguilewsky & Raynaud, 1979). P also causes a depletion of its own unoccupied receptors (Schwartz et al., 1979).

Anatomical location of progesterone receptors. There is more than one type of brain P receptor. In both immature and adult (castrated) rats, E increases the number of P receptors from 12 to 72 hours after an injection (Blaustein & Feder, 1979; Moguilewsky & Raynaud, 1979; Schwartz, Blaustein, & Wade, 1979). The increase occurs at a time when a P injection will facilitate receptivity. However, this type of E-dependent P receptor is found only in the uterus, pituitary, preoptic area, and hypothalamus.

The P receptors found in other parts of the brain, as illustrated in Figure 9-9, are not affected by E injections (rats and guinea pigs). This means that some effects of P on brain function and behavior may require prior exposure to E (such as sexual receptivity) and some may not.

Species differ in P receptor types and locations. Figure 9-9 contrasts P receptors in rat and primate brains. Although the rat has P receptors in the cortex, amygdala, and midbrain, P receptors in the female monkey are restricted to the hypothalamus and preoptic areas (MacLusky, Lieberburg, Krey, & McEwen, 1980). Also, the E effect on P receptors is much greater in the rat than in the primate hypothalamus, and the P receptor in the primate preoptic area is not sensitive to E. This difference may explain why P facilitates sexual receptivity in female rodents but not in primates; in fact, P sometimes decreases the female primate's attractiveness to the male (Baum, 1979; Hoyenga & Hoyenga, 1979).

Sex differences in progesterone receptors. The level of P receptors is sexually dimorphic (more in females) only after the animals have been primed with very high levels of E (Etgen, 1985). These differences are shown in Figure 9-8. Without that priming, the absolute levels of receptors, or their response to E, may *not* be either sexually dimorphic or affected by perinatal hormone levels (Etgen, 1981; Kirchhoff, Grünke, & Ghraf, 1983). However, the E-sensitive P receptors may be more sensitive to low levels of E in females than in males (Blaustein, Ryer, & Feder, 1980), a possibility that could explain why P implanted in the VMH will stimulate lordosis only in female and not in male rats.

Summary of Hormone Receptors

All three types of sex hormone have at least one receptor specific to that hormone; androgens and P may have more than one type. Whether a brain cell possesses a certain receptor (and, for T effects, the relevant enzymes) determines whether that cell can be organizationally or activationally affected by sex hormones.

There are more species differences in androgen and P receptor types and functions than in E receptors, but E receptors may be more sexually dimorphic. More of the primate brain may be affected by DHT than is the case for lower species. Organizational sex hormones may regulate the metabolic activity of E receptors and the number, sensitivity, and brain location of all the receptors. In certain areas of the brain, the E receptors in males may be less able to be occupied and thus have less effect on specific protein synthesis than in females.

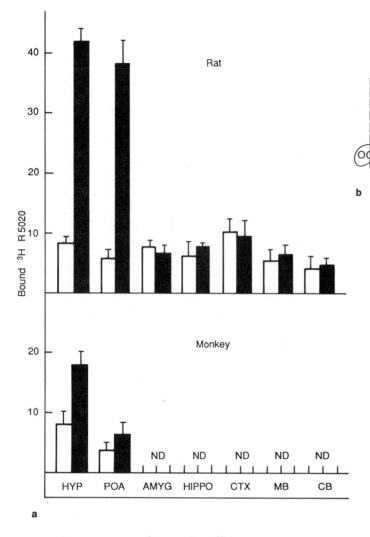

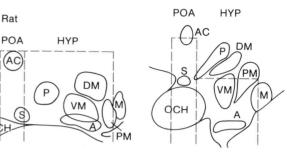

Figure 9-9 **a.** Effects of estrogen treatment on the distribution of cytosol [³H]R5020-binding (an artificial progestin) sites contrasted in rat and monkey brains. Ovariectomized rats and monkeys were given control treatments (☐) or estrogen treatments (■). These results are the average (± the standard error of the mean) of four rats and three monkeys. AMYG = amygdala; CB = cerebellum; CTX = cortex – cingulate and parietal; HIPPO = hippocampus; HYP = hypothalamus; MB = midbrain; ND = none detected; POA = preoptic area. **b.** Anatomy of the preoptic and hypothalamic areas studied. A = arcuate; AC = anterior commissure; DM = dorsomedial n. of the hypothalamus (H); M = mammillary body; OCH = optic chiasm; P = paraventricular n. of H; PM = posterior n. of H; S = suprachiasmatic n.; VM = ventromedial n. of H.

The Genetics of Sexual Differentiation and Reproductive Behaviors

A gene on the Y chromosome controls gonadal development. Other genes, both autosomal and **X-linked** (the gene is found on the X chromosome), control the activity of this gene and also control the hormone sensitivity of brain and body cells. Some theorists have suggested that familial factors, perhaps even genetic ones, may affect the development of homosexuality in humans (Pillard & Weinrich, 1986).

Genes That Cause Testes

Some gene, either one on the Y chromosome or an autosomal gene controlled by a Y-chromosome gene, causes testes to develop in the fetus. If the developing mammal has a Y chromosome, it will almost always develop testes, regardless of how many X chromosomes are also present.

H-Y antigen and testes. A protein found in the membranes of all cells in males but not in females is called **H-Y antigen.** This protein was once hypothesized to cause testes to develop in XY mammals (Bühler, 1980; Müller & Schindler, 1983; Ohno, 1979, 1980; Short, 1978; Wachtel, 1977). However, males of one strain of mice develop testes in the presence of a Y chromosome even though mice of this strain do *not* have any H-Y antigen protein (McLaren, Simpson, Tomonari, Chandler, & Hogg, 1984). Thus, some gene found on the Y chromosome causes testes to develop, but this gene is *not* the gene that codes for H-Y antigen (Kolata, 1986; Mittwoch, 1986). Instead, the H-Y antigen protein may be necessary for normal spermatogenesis (Burgoyne, Levy, & McLaren, 1986).

Three or four genes?   Several genes may be required for testes to develop normally in mammals that have a Y chromosome. One gene may code for the testes-causing protein and another would code for the protein required for this testes-causing protein to be able to attach to the membranes of fetal gonadal cells, causing them to turn into testicular cells. A third gene, the H-Y antigen gene, may have to be present or the testes will be unable to carry on spermatogenesis after puberty. Other genes may act as regulatory or repressor genes, increasing or decreasing the activities of still other genes before birth and/or after puberty.

Sexual anomalies.   Because there are so many genes that have to be functioning normally in order for normal testes to develop, it is not surprising that anomalous sexual development often occurs in human and nonhuman mammals (Ohno, 1979, 1980). A **sexual anomaly** is said to occur whenever the sex chromosomes do not match the gonads in some mammal, presumably because of some inherent defect or mutation in the genes described above. For example, some people are XX in karyotype but still develop testes; the testes-determining gene in these people may have been transposed either to an X chromosome or to an autosome. Some humans can be XY and yet not have testes, a condition that reflects another possible defect in the testes-determining gene.

Another anomaly occurs in cattle. A **freemartin** is an XX cow with testes. She was born **co-twin** (sharing a placenta) with a male. A freemartin has H-Y antigen present in her body tissues in addition to the Y-determining gene product that causes testes to develop.

X-Inactivation

The X chromosome is much larger than the Y chromosome and thus contains far more genetic material. To equalize the genetic material across the sexes, **X-inactivation** evolved in female mammals. Early in fetal development, one X chromosome is inactivated in every cell (Gartler & Riggs, 1983). Every cell descended from one of these cells has the *same* X chromosome inactivated. Since which X is inactivated in which fetal cell is largely random, different body tissues, descended from different fetal cell lines, will have different X chromosomes active.

Normal males do not inactivate their X, but males and females with more-than-normal numbers of X chromosomes (for instance, XXY males and XXX females) will inactivate all but one. The only exceptions occur in the gonads. Normal males inactivate their one X and during meiosis females reactivate their inactivated X (Gartler & Riggs, 1983).

Females as genetic mosaics.   Normal mammalian females are therefore **genetic mosaics,** with different chromosomes active in different body cells. The genetic variability in females exceeds that of males, with some interesting consequences. For example, some coat-color genes in cats, such as the ones for orange and black, are X-linked. Nearly all calicos are females. The different splotches of color on their fur represent areas in which different X chromosomes are active. The only male calicos also have two X's and are therefore usually sterile.

Possessing a deleterious gene that is both X-linked and recessive has different implications for males and for females. Males will be more likely to express the problem fully, since females are more likely to have the normal, dominant gene on their second X. But heterozygous females may partially express the deleterious gene because of X inactivation. Some forms of color blindness are X-linked and recessive. Heterozygous females have patches of color blindness on their retinas (Born, Grützner, & Hemminger, 1976). Another X-linked trait in mice depletes myelin in the CNS. The distribution of myelin in the optic nerves of heterozygous females shows a mosaic pattern, with normal tissue randomly interspersed with abnormal tissue (Skoff & Montgomery, 1981).

Characteristics of inactivation.   The inactivation may not be complete or completely random. For example, not all genes on the inactivated X are suppressed. Since female mammals with too many X's have abnormal ovaries, the inactivation must not be complete. Also, there are some X-linked genes that are active on *both* X's of heterozygous females (Migeon, Shapiro, Norum, Mohandas, Axelman, & Dabora, 1982; Shapiro, Mohandas, Weiss, & Romeo, 1979).

There are also limits to randomness. Perhaps the inactivation process itself may be random, but a selection process may cause cells with a "bad" (deleterious) gene to be preferentially destroyed (Luzzatto, Usanga, Bienzle, Esan, & Fasuan, 1979). In some organisms, the paternal X chromosome is preferentially deactivated (Rastan, Kaufman, Handyside, & Lyon, 1980).

Androgen-Insensitivity Syndrome

The X chromosome contains a gene regulating the androgen receptor (receptors?). If this gene has been damaged or destroyed, the organism has defective androgen receptors (Attardi, Geller, & Ohno, 1976; Ohno, 1979; Wieland, Fox, & Savakis, 1978). The problem may go undetected in female humans, although such females will have scanty body hair (androgens cause growth of axillary and pubic hair in both genders). The sexual development of males will be severely disrupted.

Sexual development of *tfm* mutant mice and rats. The *tfm** mutant male mouse and rat lack androgen receptors and so develop vagina, clitoris, and mammary glands. In the absence of androgen receptors, male organs fail to develop. However, since their testes are functional and secrete MIS, these mutants have neither Wolffian *nor* Mullerian organs.

Their behaviors present intriguing puzzles (Ohno, 1979; Olsen & Whalen, 1981; Shapiro & Goldman, 1979). The *tfm* male rats do show some female kinds of behavior, such as a female-type avidity for saccharin, but these males do *not* display much lordosis. However, they do display high levels of lordosis if they have been castrated right after birth. Apparently the aromatization of testicular T in these *tfm* mutant males is enough to defeminize their brains with respect to sexual behavior but not with respect to degree of preference for saccharin. Perhaps saccharin preferences have a different defeminizing threshold, or perhaps saccharin preferences and lordosis are defeminized by different kinds of androgen receptors or enzymes.

Sexual development of androgen-insensitive humans. XY people with androgen-insensitivity syndrome develop similarly to the *tfm* mutant rodent: they lack male or female internal sex organs and have external female sex organs. Since these people look female at birth, the problem often goes undiscovered until puberty (they don't menstruate). They are usually raised as females and apparently develop normal female behavior and identity (Hoyenga & Hoyenga, 1979). For example, maternal interests and behaviors and sexual interest and behaviors — except for a reduced sensitivity of the clitoris — are at normal female levels (Vague, 1983).

Enzyme Deficits

The genes coding for one or more of the enzymes that metabolize testosterone can be defective. In one syndrome, the reducing enzyme is defective. Humans with this problem are not normally masculinized. Since external sexual organs appear to be more sensitive to DHT than to T (the reverse may be true for the Wolffian structures), XY people with this deficit are born with only small penises, their testes are undescended, and they may have partially fused labia.

At puberty, the much higher levels of T can further masculinize their external genitals and cause the testes to descend. Some of these people are raised as females but decide to change their identity to male when they develop a penis at puberty. However, the degree to which people with this disorder can change their sexual identity at puberty is currently being debated (Ehrhardt, 1979; Hoyenga & Hoyenga, 1979; Peterson, Imperato-McGinley, Gautier, & Sturla, 1979).

Organisms can also inherit abnormally high or low levels of sex hormones because one or more of the synthesizing enzymes is defective. In people with the adrenogenital disorder, the enzyme that allows corticosteroids to be synthesized by the adrenal gland is defective. Under these conditions, the adrenal gland secretes extremely high levels of androgen. XX adrenogenital female humans usually have enlarged clitorises and a somewhat masculinized and defeminized brain (Hoyenga & Hoyenga, 1979; see also next section and Chapter 5).

Behavioral Sensitivity to Sex Hormones

Genes affect the degree to which behavior can be organized or activated by sex hormones. Probably several gene loci are involved, each with varying amounts of heterozygosity. The genetically controlled effects cannot usually be related to a single receptor or protein-product.

Genes affect the hormone sensitivity of sexual behaviors as well as the broadly defined reproductive behaviors, including activity levels (Broida & Svare, 1983), aggression (Fuller & Thompson, 1978; Selmanoff, Goldman, Maxson, & Ginsburg, 1977; Shrenker & Maxson, 1982), and nest building (Schneider, Lynch, & Gundaker, 1983; Schneider, Lynch, Possidente, & Hegmann, 1982). Here we will concentrate on the genetic basis of sexual behaviors per se.

Activational hormone sensitivity. Animals of species including guinea pigs, rats, mice, quail, and chickens have been selectively bred for sexual behavior (see review in Fuller & Thompson, 1978). Different strains can be created, with one strain showing high and another low levels of sexual behavior. These breeding programs seem to lead to different levels of tissue hormone sensitivity. The strains do not have different levels or types of sex hormones (but see Benoff, Siegel, & Van Krey, 1978).

Organisms of different strains show reliable differences in the frequency or intensity of sexual behaviors even when all

---

* *Tfm* mutants are those having the testicular feminizing genes, also called *androgen insensitivity*.

have been castrated and injected with exactly the same replacement doses of sex hormones. But it is unclear just what the molecular-neural basis for these genetic effects is. Efforts to demonstrate strain differences in number of receptors or amount of aromatizing enzyme have so far proved unsuccessful (for example, see Van Krey, Siegel, Balander, & Benoff, 1983).

One breeding program analyzed the components of sexual behavior in female guinea pigs in some detail (Goy & Jakway, 1959; Goy & Young, 1957). Different components were controlled by different genes. Some strains were comparatively unresponsive to sex hormones, but when sexual behaviors were elicited by extremely high doses of hormones, those behaviors were frequent and intense. Other strains were more sensitive to hormones, but their sexual behaviors were less intense and frequent. Lordosis itself seems to be under the control of two separate sets of genes: the presence versus the absence of one gene determines whether a female will show lordosis after stimulation, and the presence versus the absence of a second gene determines how long a female will display lordosis under appropriate stimulation by hormones and males.

Organizational hormone sensitivity.   Strains differ in sensitivity to organizing hormone effects. Reproductive behav-

iors, such as aggression, are affected (Vale, Ray, & Vale, 1972). Vale, Ray, and Vale (1973) found that females from different strains of mice were differentially sensitive to the effects of neonatal T or E treatment. Some strains showed little masculinization or defeminization, as Table 9-6 shows (although this result varies according to both strain and type of hormone treatment: E versus T). Genomic stimulation may be part of some of the organizational effects of sex hormones on sexual behaviors.

Summary of Genetics

Given all the genes that must be present and normal for sexual development to proceed normally, the variety of abnormalities that occur is unsurprising. The normal testes-differentiating effects of a Y chromosome apparently require three or four genes, only one of which may be on the Y chromosome. If any one of them is abnormal, testes may fail to differentiate in XY organisms or may differentiate in XX organisms. For androgens to have normal organizational and activational effects, all the synthesizing enzymes, metabolizing enzymes, and hormone receptors must be normal.

Other genes affect neuronal sensitivity to sex hormones indirectly. Presumably these genes are activated by the geno-

Table 9-6   Interactive effects of genes and neonatal hormone treatments on sexual behavior in female mice.

	Male Sexual Behaviors					*Female Sexual Behaviors*		
	Neonatal treatment					*Neonatal treatment*		
Strains	*TP Female*	*Oil Female*	*EB Female*	*Oil Male*	*Strains*	*TP Female*	*Oil Female*	*EB Female*
Mean number of approaches to a female					*Mean number of times approached by a male*			
a	21.00(19)[a]	4.80(12)	2.05(6)	35.80(18)	a	12.75(15)	17.05(20)	8.95(18)
b	12.55(16)	8.75(17)	34.85(20)	34.00(19)	b	5.00(17)	16.20(20)	11.10(20)
c	22.05(20)	15.00(15)	25.95(18)	27.85(20)	c	18.95(18)	32.15(20)	11.50(18)
Mean number of mounts of a female					*Mean number of times mounted by the male without intromission*			
a	.65(4)	.05(1)	.00(0)	1.15(8)	a	5.00(9)	6.00(18)	6.70(10)
b	3.25(4)	.00(0)	.00(0)	1.70(5)	b	3.65(10)	11.10(19)	25.00(19)
c	3.15(6)	1.55(6)	1.12(4)	4.05(16)	c	4.80(15)	8.55(19)	24.75(20)
					Mean number of times mounted by the male with intromission			
					a	1.60(4)	10.15(14)	.50(1)
					b	1.17(3)	12.15(17)	.20(1)
					c	5.60(10)	4.10(12)	3.00(5)

[a] Number of animals in each group appear in parentheses.

mic effects of occupied hormone receptors. Thus, different strains of animals show different levels of sensitivity to the organizational or activational effects of sex hormones on sexual behavior.

The next section describes hormone-sensitive, sexually dimorphic reproductive behaviors. Many of these behaviors also show an interaction between hormone effects and genotypes.

The Hormone-Sensitive, Sexually Dimorphic Behaviors

Although only sexually dimorphic behaviors are hormone sensitive, the converse is not true: some sexually dimorphic behaviors are solely a product of sex differences in developmental experiences. A behavior is **hormone sensitive** if the frequency with which it is displayed changes when either perinatal or activational sex hormone levels (or both) are changed. Both human and nonhuman data are surveyed; the major conclusions and references are listed in Table 9-7. This research provides a background for the next two sections. Knowing *which* behaviors are hormone sensitive, and in what ways, will enable you to think about the implications of why hormones affect the structure and function of nerve cells.

Techniques and Problems

The most sophisticated methods obviously cannot be used with human subjects. Human fetuses or adults cannot be as-

Table 9-7   Hormone-sensitive behaviors in mammals.

Type of Behavior	Organizational	Activational	Species	References
Sexual Behaviors				
Mounting	+	++	Most strains of rats and mice	1, 2, 3, 14
	++	++	Ewes, guinea pigs, dogs, hamsters	1, 2, 14
	++	—	Juvenile primates	17
	+?	+	Adult primates	1, 2, 5, 14, 16, 17
Lordosis	++	++	Rats	1, 2, 14
	+	++	Hamsters	1, 2, 3, 14
	0	+	Primates	3, 5, 6, 14, 17
	0	++	Ferrets, Japanese quail	3, 5, 6, 14
Partner choice	+	0	Dogs, rodents, ferrets	4, 7, 14, 20, 21
	+?	0	Human	4, 8, 10, 12, 14
"Sex drive"	+?	+	Human	3, 4, 8, 10, 12
Gender Identity				
Identity as a male or female	++	0?	Human	18 (but see 19)
Social Behaviors and Motives				
Aggression				
Shock-elicited	+	+	Rat	1, 2, 3
Isolation-induced	++	++	Mouse	1, 2, 3
Intrasexual	++	++	Rat, mouse, hamster	3, 13
Dominance	++	+	Rat, primate	2, 3, 13
Intrasexual and dominance	+?	+?	Human	3, 4, 8, 9, 10
Nurturance behaviors				
Parental behaviors	?	+?	Primates	3
All types	+	+	Rats, mice	3
Nest building	+	?	Rabbits	3
Pup retrieval	+	+	Rats	3
Grooming	+	+?	Rats, primates	4
Grooming, doll play, and attraction to infants	+	+?	Human	3, 8, 10, 11
Play				
Rough and tumble	++	+	Rodents, primates	2, 3
	+	?	Humans	3, 4, 8, 10

Table 9-7 *(continued)*

Type of Behavior	Organizational	Activational	Species	References
Responses to Sensory Stimuli				
Shock sensitivity	?	+	Rodents, human	1, 7, 15
Olfactory sensitivity	?	+	Rodents, human	1, 2, 3, 7, 15
Taste sensitivity and	++	+	Rodents	1, 2, 3, 4, 7
preferences	?	+	Human	3, 7
Exploratory tendencies	+	+	Rats	3, 4
Visual and auditory sensitivity	?	+	Human	15
Energy Balance				
Activity levels	++	++	Rodents	1, 2, 3, 4
	+	?	Human, primates	3, 8, 10
Body size	++	++	Many species, including primates	1, 2, 3, 4
Propensity to obesity	+	+	Many species, perhaps including humans	4
Life Span	+	+	Rodents, human	2, 3
Learning Performance				
Active avoidance	+	0	Rodents	1, 2, 3
Passive avoidance	?	+?	Rodents	1, 2, 3
Maze learning	+	+?	Rodents	1, 2, 3
Taste aversion	?	+	Rodents	1, 2, 3
Performance on "aptitude tests"	0?	+	Human	3, 4, 8, 10
Lateralization of the Brain	+?	+?	Human	1, 2, 3, 10

+ = Behavior is somewhat sensitive to appropriate hormone manipulations
++ = Behavior is very sensitive to appropriate hormone manipulations
0 = Behavior is not sensitive to hormone manipulations
? = No work done
+? or 0? = Some effects of hormone manipulations reported, but results are inconsistent across studies (see text for further description of effects)
— = Little or no research has been done

References (extensively modified from a table in Beatty, 1979):
1. See references on pp. 13–73 of Goy & McEwen, 1980, especially Tables 1 & 2
2. See references in Beatty, 1979
3. See references in tables of Hoyenga & Hoyenga, 1979
4. See references in Hoyenga & Hoyenga, 1982
5. Phoenix, Jensen, & Chambers, 1983
6. Johnson & Phoenix, 1978
7. See references in Gandelman, 1983
8. See references in Ehrhardt & Meyer-Bahlburg, 1981
9. See references in Meyer-Bahlburg & Ehrhardt, 1982
10. See references in Hines, 1982
11. Goldberg, Blumberg, & Kriger, 1982
12. See references in Bancroft, 1981
13. See references in Bouissou, 1983
14. See references in Baum, 1979
15. See references in Parlee, 1983
16. Phoenix & Chambers, 1982
17. Goy, 1981
18. Money & Ehrhardt, 1972; Ehrhardt, 1979
19. Peterson, Imperato-McGinley, Gautier, & Sturla, 1979
20. Beach, Johnson, Anisko, & Dunbar, 1977
21. Martin & Baum, 1986

signed to groups and given varying amounts of sex hormones, as researchers have done with other animals.

Human research. Experimenters studying humans must depend on "accidents of nature." Some people have been exposed to abnormal levels and types of sex hormones. In some cases, the children's mothers were given sex hormones during pregnancy in an effort to prevent spontaneous abortions. In other cases, some genetic abnormality causes a hormonal abnormality, such as those in androgen-insensitive and adrenogenital people.

A completely adequate control group cannot be found. Obviously, people in the "experimental" group with the hormone abnormality differ from genetically and hormonally normal people in many ways, not just in prenatal hormone levels. Factors that should be controlled for—but seldom can be—include socioeconomic status, age, the type and severity of problems during their mother's pregnancy with them, the effects of having abnormal genitals, and, most important, postnatal environments. For example, in one study involving identical male twins, one twin had his penis burned off in a circumcision accident. This twin was then castrated and raised as a female. Throughout prepubertal development, the male and female identical twins were compared, showing the important effects of postnatal environments on sexually dimorphic behaviors (Money & Ehrhardt, 1972).

Experimenters concerned with the activational effects of sex hormones on human behavior usually try to relate naturally occurring variations in hormone level to variations in behavior. People's hormone levels vary daily and across seasons, and researchers have attempted to correlate the changes with changes in behavior. A classic example of this approach is to relate the hormonal changes of the female menstrual cycle to behavioral changes. Since people differ from one another in hormone levels, researchers have also attempted to relate their differences to behavioral differences. Do men who score above average in testosterone level also score above average in level of aggressiveness? Some researchers gave humans sex hormones (for instance, the birth control pill) and looked for changes in behavior. But since this type of research is correlational, it is difficult to be certain that a change in behavior, associated with some change in hormone, is actually *caused* by the hormone. In correlational research, the relationship could go the other way: the behavior might have caused the hormone changes.

Nonhuman research. The research done on nonhumans can be much better controlled, leading to more reliable conclusions that hormonal changes cause behavioral changes.

However, these conclusions should not then be uncritically generalized to humans.

In the nonhuman research on organizational hormones, females may be given T or E injections during the perinatal period, or males may be castrated neonatally. Then the behaviors of these groups are compared with those of control animals given sham injections or sham operations. Since perinatal hormones permanently change the structure and function of the ovaries and testes, all animals should have their gonads removed and be injected with the *same* sex hormones before testing. However, the adrenal output of sex hormones may also be changed by perinatal hormones, and the metabolism of sex hormones in the liver may have been permanently affected. Thus, it is difficult to be absolutely certain that all groups have exactly the same activational levels of sex hormones at the time of testing.

To study the activational effects of hormones, organisms have their gonads removed (by castration or gonadectomy) and are given either control or sex-hormone injections. Then the behaviors of the various groups are compared. The major problem here is that the timing can be critical. For example, in rats, P enhances receptivity when given at certain times after E treatment and inhibits receptivity when given at other times.

Interpreting hormone–brain–behavior relationships. Sex hormones can affect the brain either directly or indirectly. Direct effects would include organizing effects on cell structure and interconnections and activational effects on neural activity. However, the effect could also be indirect, mediated by the environment (see review in Moore, 1985). For example, female rats lick the anogenital region of their male offspring more often than they do their female offspring. This sexually differentiating response depends on what levels of sex hormones were present in the offspring during the critical neonatal period; in turn, the anogenital licking increases the likelihood of male types of sexual behavior as adults (Moore, 1982, 1984). Female primates also treat male and female offspring differentially (Fairbanks & McGuire, 1985; Jensen, Bobbitt, & Gordon, 1967; Mitchell, 1968; Mitchell & Brandt, 1970). Thus, sex differences in perinatal hormone levels could cause sex differences in developmental experiences, and the differences in experiences may be the direct cause of sexual dimorphisms in brain and behavior.

Environmental experiences can cause metabolic changes that directly affect the hormone–brain–behavior relationships. For example, winning a tennis or a wrestling match or graduating from medical school can cause T levels to rise temporarily in male humans (Elias, 1981; Mazur & Lamb, 1980). In turn, the T increase will increase brain aromatizing enzyme levels (Hutchison & Steimer, 1984). The presence of sex differences in cortical cell shapes in adult rats depends on the rearing environment; sex differences may appear only if both sexes are reared in a complex, stimulating environment and not when the rearing environment is impoverished (Juraska, 1984; Chapter 12).

The relative sensitivity of the brain–behavior response to activational hormones depends on environmental factors. The sensitivity of some strains of male and female rats to estrogenic effects on lordosis depends on what time of day the test is given (Söderstein, 1984). Female rats will mount other females in response to T injections, but having had prior experience with mounting increases the sensitivity of that behavior to T (De Jonge & Van de Poll, 1984). In primate males, the relationship between sexual interest and T depends on the social rank a male holds. Dominant males may never totally lose sexual interest even after castration, and subordinate males may never display sexual behavior even if high doses of T are given to them (Keverne, Eberhart, Yodyingyuad, & Abbott, 1984).

Sexual Behaviors

Not surprisingly, most sexual behaviors are both sexually dimorphic and hormone sensitive. But, as Table 9-7 shows, mounting behavior in rats and mice appears to be less sensitive (in some strains, totally insensitive) to perinatal hormones than it is in other species (Goy & McEwen, 1980; Young, 1982). In these less sensitive strains, females may be normally somewhat masculinized before birth by exposure to their brothers' androgens, crossing over through the amniotic fluid (Baum, 1979).

Some of the brain regions organized by perinatal sex hormones have been identified (Nordeen & Yahr, 1982). Implanting E in the preoptic area of female rats is masculinizing (and eliminates the positive-feedback effect of E on LH). Implanting E into the VMH of female rats is defeminizing. The preoptic area is critical for male types of sexual behavior, and the VMH is important for female types of sexual behavior (Table 9-3). But very unexpectedly, if neonatal hormone implants are placed on only one side of the hypothalamus, masculinization is maximized if the implants are made on the right-hand as opposed to the left-hand side of the brain. Conversely, defeminization is maximized by left-side implants. The sensitivity periods of the left and right sides of the brain may be somewhat different (Nordeen & Yahr, 1982).

In rodents, dogs, and ferrets, choice of sexual partner depends on organizational but not on activational levels of sex hormones present during the critical periods. If females are perinatally masculinized by androgens and estrogens, they will often prefer sexually receptive females to males as sexual partners. Although castrating an adult of these species greatly reduces all interest in any sexual activity, partner preference is *not* affected.

In humans, the data are often contradictory, making human sexual behavior difficult to categorize. As we pointed out previously, there may be a familial component to partner preference, but even if this component is replicated by future researchers, the roles of genes versus hormones versus environments still need to be specified. For example, some researchers have also suggested that level of perinatal T may affect partner preference, but the data of other researchers are inconsistent with such an effect. Humans that have been castrated — had their gonads removed — at some time after puberty are sometimes less sexually interested and active than are hormonally normal humans, but any decline in sexual behavior occurring after castration is variable, slow, and almost always incomplete.

Activational T may facilitate female sexual interest in rats, lower primates, and humans (De Jonge & Van de Poll, 1984; Hoyenga & Hoyenga, 1979, 1984; Table 9-7 references). Treating female rats with T specifically increases proceptive or invitational types of sexual behavior and increases their preference for a sexually active male over a sexually active female in a choice situation. In the human female, both her adrenal androgens and her average level of T may be important to her sexual motivation (Persky, Dreisbach, Miller, O'Brien, Khan, Lief, Charney, & Strauss, 1982). T has been successfully used to enhance sexual motivation in human females (Sherwin, Gelfand, & Brender, 1985).

Which hormones have masculinizing effects on mounting varies from one species to another. As a general rule, if the region of the brain controlling a certain behavior is masculinized by E or T, that behavior will be activated by both hormones, but not by DHT, in the adult. If DHT is perinatally masculinizing, masculine behaviors will also be activated by DHT. However, in some species in which perinatal E is masculinizing and defeminizing, DHT can activate many components of male sexual behaviors in males castrated as adults (Olsen & Whalen, 1984).

Social Motives and Emotions

Although reproduction obviously takes two organisms, sexual activity is usually considered separately from other forms of social behaviors. Fewer experiments have been done in this area than in that of the social-sexual motive.

Aggression may be Type I (sensitive to both organizational and activational hormone levels) in all species (with the possible exception of humans). Nevertheless, different kinds of aggression are differentially sensitive to perinatal and activational sex hormone levels. Organizational and activational T — with or without aromatization to E — either increases the frequency with which aggressive actions are displayed or increases the ease with which appropriate environmental stimuli (threat, for example) can evoke these behaviors. Even in this respect, however, there are great differences among species and genetically based differences within a species. Some scanty data suggest that aggression in humans might be increased by masculinizing hormones both before birth and after puberty.

Nurturance also appears to be Type I in most species, but the data are less convincing. For example, retrieval of straying pups but not nest-building propensities appears to be sensitive to perinatal hormones in rats. In humans, playing with dolls and preference for infants rather than older children may be suppressed by prenatal androgens or by artificial progestins that have masculinizing side effects. Females' interest in infants may increase after puberty.

Both aggression and nurturance can be affected by uterine position. In both male and female mice, the level of aggressive and parental behaviors depends, in part, on whether the subject was next to two males or to two females in the uterus (vom Saal, 1981; 1983).

In most species, **rough-and-tumble play** appears to be Type III (sensitive to organizational hormones but suppressed by activational hormones). Rough-and-tumble play is a masculine behavior. When female rats, monkeys, or humans are exposed to high levels of perinatal androgens, estrogens, or masculinizing progestins, they display more rough-and-tumble play as adolescents. This type of play is suppressed by puberty. Even in adult nonhuman primate males, it occurs most frequently during the time of the year when T levels are lowest.

Responses to Sensory Stimuli

If the sexual motive acts more like an incentive than a drive, sensory coding of sexual types of stimulus, especially olfactory and somatosensory, should be hormone sensitive. Table 9-7 indicates that sensory sensitivities and preferences are sensitive to activational hormone levels, and many are also sensitive to organizational hormone levels. For example, females of many species have a greater preference for sweet-tasting solutions than males do. This preference can be defeminized by perinatal T (but *not* E) injections in female rats. Gonadectomizing an adult female rat also reduces her intake of sweet solutions. Thus, cells in the sensory areas of Table 9-7 should be sensi-

tive to hormones; we will discuss this evidence in the last section.

Hunger and Food Intake

Energy-balance mechanisms are sexually dimorphic and hormone sensitive. Males are larger than females because of both perinatal and activational androgen effects. Female rats are more active. Activity in rats can be defeminized by perinatal T injections and activated by E. Females of many species, including the human, show a greater propensity toward obesity than males do. In many species, this tendency includes the obesity produced by lesions of the VMH. In lower animals, the development of obesity has been shown to be hormone sensitive. Even in humans, progestins — either produced during the luteal phase of the cycle or ingested as part of a birth control pill — increase food intake (see Table 9-7 references).

Learning: Motives and Emotions?

The research that explores the possibility of sex differences in the performance of various learned tasks has generated a great deal of controversy. Female rats are better than males at active avoidance, whereas males are better at passive avoidance, maze learning, and **taste-aversion** tasks (males stay away from tastes associated with illness longer than females do). There are also consistently sexually dimorphic performances on "aptitude" tests in humans. Males get high average scores on math and on **spatial tasks** (measuring the ability to visualize in three-dimensional space), but if there is any sex-related difference in performances on verbal tasks, females get slightly higher average scores.

But there are several reasons why it is premature to discuss the hormone sensitivity of these behaviors. First, in lower animals, sex differences in performance may not reflect any differences in cognitive capacity but may simply reflect differences in activity levels, stimulus reactions, exploratory behaviors, or motives. We have argued elsewhere (Hoyenga & Hoyenga, 1979) that the sex difference in rat maze-learning performances reflects female exploratory tendencies — which lead them to "explore" errors more often — and not sex differences in "spatial abilities."

The differences should *not* be overinterpreted. Variability in scores is very great compared to the size of the sex differences on intellectual tasks. That means that the sex difference has little practical or personal significance (although from the point of view of hormonal effects on the brain, these differences may have considerable theoretical importance). With few exceptions, in neither human nor nonhuman is there any clear indication of what neural structures are involved, so the psychobiology of sex hormones and learning performances is still in the future.

There are only two possible exceptions. One might be in the organization of functions within the brain and how this organization might be affected by sex hormones both before birth and during puberty (later in this chapter). These factors *might* have some effect on math and spatial performances. However, the relationship between organization and cognitive abilities depends not only on gender but on the subject's hand preference *and* the hand preferences of his or her relatives (Harshman, Hampson, & Berenbaum, 1983). Second, as we will describe, sex hormones affect hippocampal neurons, and the hippocampus seems to be importantly involved in several types of learning and memory (Chapters 11 and 12; see also Figure 9-9 and Table 9-4).

Summary of Sexually Dimorphic, Hormone-Sensitive Behaviors

Since the sexes have different reproductive roles, evolution has made those role behaviors sensitive to hormone levels. Role behaviors include sexual behaviors, social behaviors, stimulus sensitivities and preferences, energy balance, and performances on various types of learning task. The next two sections look at how sex hormones affect individual cells in specific areas of the brain. The goal of this research, past and future, is to be able to relate the behaviors described in this section to the effects of sex hormones on the structures and activities of single cells.

Organizational Effects on the Brain

Sex hormones have organizational effects on Type I and III behaviors (Table 9-2). Hormones also have specific and permanent effects on neural anatomy and physiology; some of those effects are listed in Table 9-8. How organizational effects on brain and on behavior might be interrelated is not yet clear—with one or two intriguing exceptions.

Mechanisms and Locations of Effects

Perinatal hormones may have classic, genomic types of effect on brain cells. During the sensitive period, new proteins would permanently affect the structure and function of these cells. In

Table 9-8   Effects of perinatal hormones on brain cells.

1. Increase in number of nerve cells in a given nucleus
2. Increase in size of the cell body
3. Changes in cellular organelles
4. Increase in length and branching of dendritic trees
5. Change in shape of the dendritic tree
6. Increase in number of spines on dendrites
7. Increase in number of different kinds of synapse in an area
8. Change in location of synapses
9. Increase in number of organelles in synaptic region
10. Increase in density of afferent inputs to a region
11. Increase in volume of some brain area

fact, drugs that inhibit protein synthesis do block the masculinizing and defeminizing effects of neonatal T or E in rats (Goy & McEwen, 1980). Sex hormones do affect protein synthesis in the developing rat and human brain. Different neonatal hormones lead to the synthesis of different proteins in various regions of the developing brain (ter Haar & MacKinnon, 1973; Hall & Jenkins, 1982).

Organizational effects on proteins.   Sex differences in perinatal hormones can lead to permanent sex differences in brain proteins. Litteria (see Litteria, 1977) has carried out an extensive program of research. She has demonstrated how changes in the neonatal hormonal environment can permanently suppress protein synthesis in the limbic and hypothalamic areas of the adult rat brain. In fact, the protein content of neural membranes is sexually dimorphic throughout the brain (Angelbeck & DuBrul, 1983; Montero, Guillamón, Azuara, Ambrosio, Segovia, & Orensanz, 1983). These proteins could be either structural or enzymatic. As we will describe, transmitter metabolism is permanently changed by the effects of perinatal sex hormones on enzymatic proteins.

Neonatal sex hormones have temporary effects on transmitter levels during fetal development, presumably by activating genes for the relevant enzymatic proteins. For example, there is more serotonin (5-HT) synthesis in the brains of neonatal females than in male rats. Giving females injections of T blocks this period of increased 5-HT synthesis, thereby defeminizing this aspect of developing brain function (Giulian, Pohorecky, & McEwen, 1973; Hardin, 1973; Ladosky & Gaziri, 1970). Castration of males and E treatment of females defeminize neonatal levels of NE and demasculinize the level of the inactivating enzyme, MAO. That is, NE is higher in females, so decreasing NE is defeminizing. Since MAO levels are higher in males, a decrease is demasculinizing (Gaziri &

Ladosky, 1973; Wilson & Agrawal, 1979). This means that masculinization and defeminization may be an indirect effect of sex hormones: changes in transmitter levels during the sensitive period may directly affect neural structure and metabolism.

The adult levels of some brain metabolic enzymes also depend on neonatal sex hormones. For example, some hypothalamic enzyme levels are both sexually dimorphic and sensitive to perinatal hormone levels (Luine, Khylchevskaya, & McEwen, 1975; Packman, Boshans, & Bragdon, 1977). Thus, the metabolic rates in some areas of the adult brain are sexually dimorphic because of sex differences in neonatal hormone levels.

Neuronal growth and sex hormones.   Toran-Allerand (1976, 1980; Toran-Allerand, Hashimoto, Greenough, & Saltarelli, 1983) has shown how sex hormones affect the growth pattern of neonatal nerve cells. She cultured samples of cells from the hypothalamus and preoptic area of newborn

mice and varied the sex-hormone content of the culture medium. Figure 9-10 presents one example of what she and her colleagues have found. In the presence of E (but *not* T), the branching pattern of dendrites is extensively increased, suggesting that E promotes the growth of dendrites.

Her research program provided several ideas about how sex hormones organize the brain. First, in mice, the effect is specific to E. DHT has no effect, and T affects dendritic branching *only* if E is also present in the culture medium. Second, only some nerve cells are stimulated by E. Other nerve cells from the same region are not affected. Third, the primary effect of E is to induce new dendritic branches.

Neonatal hormones may stimulate the growth of dendrites from some hormone-sensitive cells. During brain development, nerve-cell processes compete with one another for synaptic endings. The presence of E could give certain types of nerve cell a developmental edge in this competition. Without E, those cells would lose their edge and different synaptic connections would be formed. For example, Arai and Matsu-

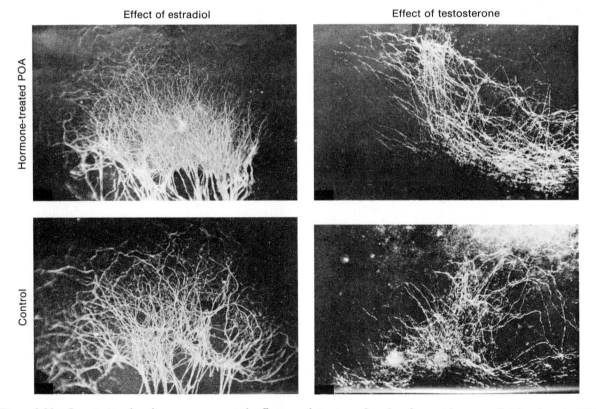

Figure 9-10   Organizational sex hormones permanently affect neural structures. Samples of neonatal mouse cells taken from the POA (preoptic area) were cultured in various media. The bottom row of photographs shows neural tissue without hormone treatment. The top row shows the effect of estradiol (left) and testosterone (right). Note that testosterone by itself has no effect.

moto (1978) showed that E injections increase the rate of synapse formation in the arcuate nucleus during the neonatal period in female rats.

Effects on behavior.   In some cases, the brain cells involved in organizational effects are known. In the zebra finch, only the male sings. Arnold (1980) has shown that the area of the brain controlling singing is much larger in the male than in the female. If the female is given E on the first day of life, her song centers are masculinized, and if she is given T injections as an adult, she will sing.

Sexual behavior is also dimorphic in rats, and one recent study—sounding as if it came from the pages of a science-fiction magazine—also specifically relates brain area to behavior. Arendash and Gorski (1982) transplanted the preoptic area from neonatal male rats to neonatal female rats. The transplants grew and established neural connections with their host brains. The females with the transplants showed more lordosis in response to minimal doses of E and more mounting in response to T injections as adults than did the controls given sham operations. The authors explained the change in lordosis as a "side effect" of the transplant's increasing the total number of E receptors in that area of the brain and thus increasing sensitivity to minimal doses of E. The effect on mounting was attributed to giving these females a partially masculinized preoptic area that facilitated masculine types of sexual behavior (Table 9-3).

Table 9-3 summarizes reproductive brain anatomy, relating structure to function. You should look back at that table during the next sections to formulate your own ideas about how neural effects of hormones are to be related to behavioral effects.

Biochemical Effects of Sex Hormones

The levels of transmitter substances found in various parts of the brain are often sexually dimorphic. The nature of the dimorphism depends on which transmitter is being studied.

Biogenic amines.   The biogenic amines are the transmitters most likely to show organizational hormone effects. Many catecholaminergic (NE and DA) cells in the brain have receptors for one or more of the sex hormones (Heritage, Stumpf, Sar, & Grant, 1980; Sar & Stumpf, 1981) and so can respond to more than one hormone. Other cells with E or DHT receptors receive massive input from these nerve terminals, another type of interaction.

Table 9-9 summarizes some of the effects of perinatal sex hormones on biogenic amines. Both the direction of the sex

difference and the role played by neonatal hormones—if any has been demonstrated—are also listed. *Increasing* the level of some transmitter normally found at *higher* levels in the *male* brain is *masculinization. Decreasing* the level of some transmitter normally found at *higher* levels in the *female* brain is *defeminization.* Usually only T effects have been tested, but presumably E would have similar effects, at least in rat brains. The levels of inactivating enzymes, such as COMT and MAO, may be permanently affected by T. COMT may be one of the protein enzymes produced by genomic organizational hormone effects in the hypothalamus of developing organisms (Ladosky, Figueirêdo, & Schneider, 1984). Sex differences in, and organizational effects on, COMT levels are illustrated in Figure 9-11.

The levels of NE found in the brain may be inversely related to masculine sexual behaviors. Drugs that stimulate NE receptors also inhibit masculine types of sexual behaviors in male rats; the receptor involved may be an alpha$_2$ (Rodriguez, Castro, Hernandez, & Mas, 1984). This research is consistent with the organizational effects of T on NE levels in females, but it is *inconsistent* with the sex differences in NE levels (Table 9-9). Possibly NE receptors have different effects on masculine sexual behaviors in different brain areas or different receptors.

DA levels can be masculinized and 5-HT levels defeminized in perinatal female rats. In both genders, DA facilitates and 5-HT inhibits masculine types of sexual behaviors, and DA inhibits lordosis. Thus, the sex differences and organizational effects of sex hormones on those two transmitters are as expected (Hull, Nishita, Bitran, & Dalterio, 1984).

Other transmitter substances.   Table 9-9 lists sex differences and effects of perinatal sex hormones on transmitter substances other than the amines. For example, cholinergic receptors may be permanently increased (masculinized) by prenatal hormones, as may levels of substance P.

Adult E injections have sexually dimorphic effects on cholinergic receptors, presumably related to sex differences in organizational hormone levels (see Figure 9-12). In females, estradiol injections significantly increase cholinergic receptors in the medial basal hypothalamus and decrease them in the preoptic area. In the male, only cortical cholinergic receptors are affected. The genomic induction of muscarinic receptors by E in the VMH of females is closely associated with the effect of E on lordosis. Contrary to what was seen in females, E injections given to males cause neither lordosis nor any change in the number of muscarinic receptors (Rainbow et al., 1984). Infusing muscarinic agonists into the hypothalamus and

Table 9-9 Effects of perinatal manipulations of sex hormone levels on transmitter metabolism in the adult.

Sex Differences and Transmitter	Effects of Perinatal Sex Hormones	References
Biogenic Amines		
More hypothalamic MAO in males	Testosterone masculinizes	Gaziri & Ladosky, 1973
More hypothalamic COMT in females	Testosterone defeminizes	Ladosky & Schneider, 1981; Ladosky, Figueirêdo, & Schneider, 1984
Tuberoinfundibular DA activity higher in females	Testosterone defeminizes	Demarest, McKay, Riegle, & Moore, 1981
DA levels in caudate, arcuate, and median eminence higher in males	Testosterone masculinizes	Crowley, O'Donohue, & Jacobowitz, 1978
NE levels higher in several hypothalamic areas in males	Testosterone in females *decreases* NE levels	Barraclough, Lookingland, & Wise, 1984; Crowley, O'Donohue, & Jacobowitz, 1978
5-HT in forebrain, midbrain, and hypothalamus higher in neonatal female	Testosterone and DHT defeminize; estrogens feminize	Guilian, Pohorecky, & McEwen, 1973; Ladosky & Gaziri, 1970
5-HT levels higher in female anterior hypothalamus and arcuate–median eminence in adults	Not tested	Renner, Biegon, & Luine, 1985
5-HT receptors in hypothalamus and preoptic area increased by activational estrogen only in females	Not yet tested	McEwen, Biegon, Fischette, Luine, Parsons, & Rainbow, 1984
Acetylcholine		
More synthesizing and degrading enzymes in preoptic-suprachiasmatic areas in the female	Testosterone defeminizes (but so does neonatal castration of the male)	Libertun, Timiras, & Kragt, 1973
Activational estradiol injections: increase muscarinic receptors in preoptic nucleus and VMH only in females but not in castrated males; decrease muscarinic receptors only in males	Not yet tested	Dohanich, Witcher, Weaver, & Clemens, 1982; McEwen et al., 1984; Rainbow, Snyder, Berck, & McEwen, 1984
Synthesizing and degrading enzymes in diagonal band lower in males and increased by activational estrogen injections only in females	Not yet tested	McEwen et al., 1984
More nicotinic receptors in amygdala of male mouse	Testosterone and estradiol masculinize	Arimatsu, 1983; Arimatsu, Seto, & Amano, 1981
Peptides		
Anterior pituitaries of adult males contain more substance P	Testosterone masculinizes	Yoshikawa & Hong, 1983

NOTE: Except where noted, all the subjects were rats; DHT = dihydrotestosterone; COMT and MAO are synthesizing and degrading enzymes (see Table 4-3); 5-HT = serotonin; DA = dopamine; NE = norepinephrine; VMH = ventromedial nucleus of the hypothalamus.

preoptic areas of castrated, E-primed female rats stimulates lordosis (Dohanich, Barr, Witcher, & Clemens, 1984).

Causes of effects. Although the effects of organizational sex hormones are reliable, the details of how hormones cause these effects are still being explored. Enzyme levels, number of synapses, presynaptic release mechanisms, and uptake mechanisms all could be affected.

Morphological Effects of Sex Hormones: Sex Differences in Neuron Structure

There are sex differences in the *structure* of many nerve cells. In many—though not all—cases, these sexually dimorphic structures depend on organizational hormone levels. Figure 9-13 is a diagram of a "representative" nerve cell showing synaptic types to help you visualize some of these effects.

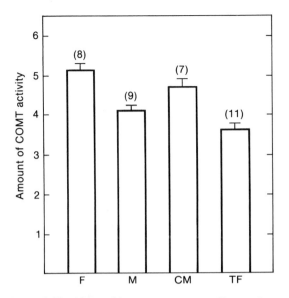

Figure 9-11 Neonatal hormone treatment affects rat hypothalamic catecholamine-O-methyltransferase (COMT) activity 12 days after birth. The data are reported as the mean ±SEM for the number of animals given in parentheses above each bar. F = intact female rats; M = intact male rats; CM = male rats castrated at birth; TF = female rats treated with 30 μg testosterone propionate at birth. Differences were significant ($P < 0.01$) for F versus M and CM versus TF but not for M versus TF or F versus CM.

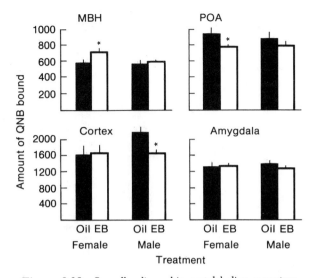

Figure 9-12 Sexually dimorphic acetylcholine receptors. ACh receptors were measured by the specific binding of [³H]quinuclidinyl benzilate (QNB) in the medial basal hypothalamus (MBH), medial proptic area (POA), parietal cortex, and amygdala of adult female and male rats. Gonadectomized animals (those with gonads removed) were injected either with estradiol benzoate (EB: a long-acting form of estradiol) or a control substance (sesame seed oil) at 72, 48, and 24 hours before measurements were taken. The * marks a significant difference between the effects of EB and oil; oil-treatment males also had significantly more receptors in the cortex than did the oil-treated females.

Often only dendritic spine or shaft types of synapse are sexually dimorphic and sensitive to perinatal hormone levels. These sexually dimorphic neurons have so far been found only in areas of the brain that, when lesioned or stimulated, change reproductive behaviors, including energy balance, aggression, and nurturance.

The hypothalamus and preoptic area. Table 9-10 summarizes sex differences in the structures and interconnections of nerve cells. This research began with Raisman and Field (1973), the first researchers to report sex differences of this type. Because of its importance to sexual behavior and to the control of pituitary hormones, most researchers have concentrated on the hypothalamus. Figure 9-14 summarizes some of the sexually dimorphic interconnections of the arcuate nucleus described in Table 9-10. Females have comparatively more dendritic spine synapses and males more somatic synapses. These patterns can be defeminized and masculinized by neonatal injections of T. Thus, a brain area important to LHRH synthesis also has sexually dimorphic synaptic connections with the rest of the brain.

Table 9-10 describes how synapses in the suprachiasmatic nucleus are sexually dimorphic, but the role of perinatal sex hormones was not examined. This nucleus is important to sexual behaviors and positive-feedback loops (Table 9-3). Males have more dendritic spine types of synapse, and, on the basis of microscopic appearances, males have more excitatory and females more inhibitory types of synapse, as Figure 9-15 shows.

The preoptic area is very dimorphic. Sex differences in the number of cells found in the preoptic area have been seen not only in rats but also in primates—though *not* in mice (Table 9-10). One part of this area stains very darkly, and that part is four or five times larger in male rats than in females. This is the **Sexually Dimorphic Nucleus of the Preoptic Area (SDN-POA).** The SDN-POA has a dense concentration of cells, and there are more cells in males than in females. By examining this area, researchers can readily classify brain slices as coming from males or females. Sexual dimorphism in analogous darkly staining areas have been seen in guinea pigs,

Table 9-10 Morphological effects of perinatal sex hormones on brain and neuron structure.

Brain Site	Sex Differences	Effects of Sex Hormones	References
Arcuate	Females have more axodendritic spine synapses and fewer axosomatic synapses (rat)	Spine synapses defeminized and axosomatic synapses masculinized by testosterone	Matsumoto & Arai, 1980, 1981a
Suprachiasmatic	More axodendritic spine synapses and more excitatory(?) synapses in males (rat); no sex difference in size or in number of cells (rat and human); shape was spherical in males and elongated in females (human)	?	Güldner, 1982; Swaab, Fliers, & Partiman, 1985
Preoptic	Of the afferents not coming from the amygdala, a greater proportion end on spines rather than shafts (see Figure 9-13) in the adult female (rat)	Defeminized by testosterone	Raisman & Field, 1973
	Spatial pattern of dendritic branching is dimorphic (rat)	Masculinized and defeminized by testosterone	Greenough, Carter, Steerman, & DeVoogd, 1977
	Neurons in males have more dendritic branches and dendritic spines (primate)	?	Ayoub, Greenough, & Juraska, 1983
Periventricular nucleus of preoptic region	More dopaminergic afferents and cell bodies in female (rat)	Defeminized by testosterone	Simerly, Swanson, Handa, & Gorski, 1985
Hypothalamus	More glucocorticoid receptors in males (rat) (glucocorticoid is a stress hormone secreted by adrenal cortex: Chapter 10)	?	Turner & Weaver, 1985
Sexually dimorphic nucleus (in medial preoptic area)	Five times larger (more cells?) in male rats but not in male mice; 2.5 times larger, with 2.2 times as many cells, in male humans	Completely masculinized by prenatal plus postnatal testosterone or estrogens in rats; humans not tested	Döhler, Coquelin, Davis, Hines, Shryne, & Gorski, 1982; Döhler, Hines, Coquelin, Davis, Shryne, & Gorski, 1982; Gorski, Harlan, & Christensen, 1977; Jacobson, Shryne, Shapiro, & Gorski, 1980; Swaab & Fliers, 1985; Young, 1982
Ventromedial n.	Larger in males (more cells?) in the dorsomedial subdivision; males had more shaft and spine synapses (rat)	Neonatal castration of males decreased size of nucleus; no effect of testosterone injections on neonatal (5-day-old) females	Matsumoto & Arai, 1983a, 1983b
	More long-latency connections between VMH and central gray in females (rat)	Defeminized by testosterone	Sakuma, 1984
Amygdala (Medial)	More synapses in the male, mostly because of dendritic shaft synapses (rat)	Masculinized by testosterone or estrogen	Nishizuka & Arai, 1981a, 1981b
	Larger in area in males (larger cell bodies and dendritic fields?) (rat)	Masculinized by estrogen	Mizukami, Nishizuka, & Arai, 1983
	Nucleus of cells is larger in females (greater protein synthetic activity?) (primate)	Various during the estrous cycle	Bubenik & Brown, 1973

Table 9-10   (*continued*)

Brain Site	Sex Differences	Effects of Sex Hormones	References
Lateral septum	Receives more vasopressinergic afferents from suprachias-matic nucleus in males (rat)	Masculinized by testosterone	De Vries, Best, & Sluiter, 1983; De Vries, Buijs, & Swaab, 1981
Hippocampus	More glucocorticoid receptors in females (glucocorticoid is a hormone secreted by the adrenal cortex) (rat)	?	Turner & Weaver, 1981, 1985
	Fewer granule cells and lower granule-cell density in females (mice)	?	Wimer & Wimer, 1985
Locus coeruleus	More loss of cells with age in males (human)	?	Wree, Braak, Schleicher, & Zilles, 1980
Cortex	Greater percentage of gray matter (unmyelinated processes and cell bodies in female) (human)	?	Gur, Gur, Obrist, Hunger-buhler, Younkin, Rosen, Skolnick, & Reivich, 1982
Spinal cord	Motoneurons innervating muscles for intromission and ejaculation diminished or absent in females (rat)	Masculinized by testosterone but *not* by estrogens	Breedlove & Arnold, 1981; Breedlove, Jacobson, Gorski, & Arnold, 1982; Jordan, Breedlove, & Arnold, 1982
Sympathetic system	More preganglionic axons coming from spinal cord and more postganglionic neurons in males (rat and cat)	Masculinized by testosterone and estrogen	Henry & Calaresu, 1972; Wright & Smolen, 1983a, 1983b
Effect of Lesions			
Septal lesions	A transient hyperemotionality and aggressiveness (but only at certain ages) only in females (rat)	Defeminized by testosterone or estrogens	Iovino, Monteleone, Barone, & Steardo, 1983; Phillips & Deol, 1973
VMH lesions	More obesity in females (several species)	Defeminized by testosterone	Valenstein, 1968; see also references in Hoyenga & Hoyenga, 1982
LH lesions	More loss of weight in males (rat)	?	See references in Hoyenga & Hoyenga, 1982
Caudate lesions	Impair 2-way avoidance only in males (rat)	?	See references in Beatty, 1979
Destruction of septal ACh input to hippocampus	Sympathetic NE axons sprout into hippocampus: sprouting is stronger in females (rat)	Defeminized by testosterone	Loy & Milner, 1980, 1983
Lateralization Effects			
Cortical thickness	Thicker on right side in males; thicker on left side in females (rat)	Neonatal castration masculin-ized females' brains and feminized at least the anterior two-thirds of males' brains	Diamond, Dowling, & Johnson, 1981; Diamond, 1984
Cortical transmitters	Levels more similar on the two sides in females than in males (rat)	?	Denenberg & Rosen, 1983
DA levels in nucleus	Levels somewhat more lateralized (more on right side) in male than in female rats when both were handled	?	Camp, Robinson, & Becker, 1984

(*continued*)

Table 9-10   (continued)

Brain Site	Sex Differences	Effects of Sex Hormones	References
	by the experimenter during the neonatal period; no lateralization in nonhandled rats of either gender		
Left versus right spatial movement preferences	Early handling lateralizes males' brains; early handling *de*lateralizes females' brains (rat)	?	Sherman, Garbanati, Rosen, Hofmann, Yutzey, & Denenberg, 1983
	Females have a stronger turning preference than males do, and *only* in females is this preference related to lateralization of DA levels (DA is higher in striatum of side contralateral to preferred turning direction) (rat)	?	Dark, Ellman, Peeke, Galin, & Reus, 1984; Zimmerberg, Glick, & Jerussi, 1974
Hippocampal thickness	Thicker on right side for males of some ages; thicker on left side of 90-day-old females (rat)	Not affected by neonatal removal of ovaries	Diamond, Murphy, Akiyama, & Johnson, 1982
Blood flow	Greater lateralization of blood flow in female than in male right-handed humans	?	Gur et al., 1982
Corpus callosum	The posterior part is larger in females (more axons?) (human)	?	Holloway & de Lacoste, 1986; de Lacoste-Utamsing & Holloway, 1982; but see Weber & Weis, 1986; Witelson, 1985
Subcortical transmitter levels	Females are more lateralized in striatal NE levels (more on left side) (rat)	?	Dark et al., 1984
Left versus right brain damage	In males, left posterior lesions damage verbal more than nonverbal functions, whereas right lesions damage nonverbal more than verbal; speech functions more localized in the left hemisphere of females, spread out more diffusely in left hemisphere of males; vocabulary decreased after left or right anterior or posterior lesions in females but only after left damage in males (human)	?	Inglis & Lawson, 1982; Inglis, Ruckman, Lawson, Mac-Lean, & Monga, 1982; Kimura, 1983, 1985; McGlone, 1980

? = effect of perinatal hormones not yet established
VMH = ventromedial hypothalamus
 LH = lateral hypothalamus
ACh = acetylcholine
 DA = dopamine

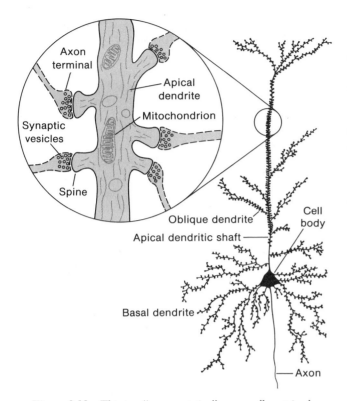

Figure 9-13 This is a "representative" nerve cell, a stained pyramidal neuron whose cell body is in layer 5 of the cortex. The enlargement on the right side of the figure presents a segment of the apical shaft as it might appear in an electron microscope. At higher magnifications (30,000 to 40,000 power), dark projections from the dendrites appear: these are spines. Synapses on the cell body do not have spines.

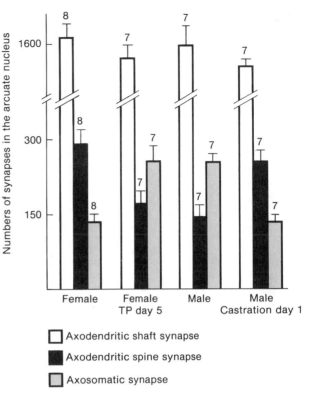

Figure 9-14 This graph summarizes some of the sexually dimorphic interconnections of the arcuate nucleus. The ordinate is the number of axodendritic shaft, axodendritic spine, or axosomatic synapses per field of 18,000 μm^2 in the normal male and female, the neonatally androgen-treated female given injections of TP (testosterone propionate, a long-acting form of T) on day 5, and neonatally castrated male rats. The vertical bars indicate standard errors of the mean, and the number above each bar is the number of subjects in the group.

hamsters, mice, gerbils, and humans (Bleier, Byne, & Siggelkow, 1982; Commins & Yahr, 1984a; Swaab & Fliers, 1985). However, the dimorphism in mice is quite subtle (Blier, Byne, & Siggelkow, 1982; Young, 1982).

The size of the SDN-POA in rats is sensitive to neonatal hormones (see Figure 9-16). Prolonged T or E treatment completely masculinizes this area in females. The *tfm* male, despite not having androgen receptors, still has a normal male-sized SDN-POA. Females given perinatal injections of an artificial estrogen (diethylstilbestrol, or DES) develop a male-sized SDN-POA (Döhler, Coquelin, Davis, Hines, Shryne, & Gorski, 1984). Therefore, T aromatization and E cause masculinization in this area.

The SDN-POA becomes sexually dimorphic shortly after birth, although the dimorphism may be prenatally triggered.

Just before birth, the volume of the SDN-POA is identical in males and females. The SDN-POA continues to grow after birth, but only in males, leading to a steadily increasing sex difference (Jacobson, Shryne, Shapiro, & Gorski, 1980). However, not only does complete masculinization of this area in females require prenatal treatments but prenatal treatments can suppress the neonatal growth of this area in males. Stressing the pregnant female rat suppresses male sexual behaviors in her male offspring. In one case, pregnant females were stressed three times a day during the latter part of their pregnancy by exposure to restraint, heat, and bright lights (Anderson, Rhees, & Fleming, 1985). When the male offspring were examined 20 and 60 days after birth, the size of the SDN-POA of stressed males was 50% smaller than that in controls.

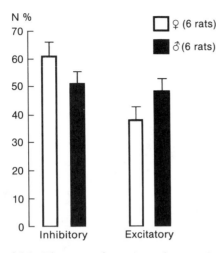

Figure 9-15 The types of synapse in the suprachiasmatic nucleus of the rat are sexually dimorphic. The suprachiasmatic neurons in the female receive relatively more inhibitory than excitatory input, whereas the reverse is true for the male.

The neonatal E that normal females have (as described earlier) may be required for normal female growth of the SDN-POA. When female rats were given daily injections of an E antagonist for the five days after birth, not only was lordosis decreased but the SDN-POA was also reduced in size (Hancke & Döhler, 1984). Similarly, castrating the female at birth leads to a reduced SDN-POA in comparison with untreated controls (Handa, Corbier, Shryne, Schoonmaker, & Gorski, 1985). Thus, normal female levels of perinatal estrogen are required for normal female development here as well as in sexually dimorphic brain lateralization in rats (Table 9-10).

We do not yet know what this means. Although lesions of the SDN-POA in male gerbils disrupts mounting (Commins & Yahr, 1984b), similar lesions in male rats do not disrupt male sexual behaviors (Arendash & Gorski, 1983; Gorski, 1984). Also, the size of the SDN-POA does not seem to be related in any simple way to any sexual behavior. For example, even though females treated with androgen on day 4 and neonatally castrated males (Figure 9-16) have the same size SDN-POA, *only* neonatally castrated males show high levels of lordosis and positive-feedback effects of E.

Sex differences in this area have also been electrophysiologically explored. Dyer, MacLeod, and Ellendorff (1976) recorded single-unit activity in the preoptic and the anterior hypothalamic areas of normal male and female rats as well as neonatally castrated males and females neonatally treated with T. Some cells in the preoptic region project to the mediobasal hypothalamus; more of these cells receive an input from the amygdala in males than in females. Giving T to neonatal females increases the input the amygdala has to these cells. Preoptic cells that did not project to the mediobasal area also fired twice as fast in normal females and neonatally castrated males as did the same type of cell in normal males and females given neonatal T.

Akema and Kawakami (1982) found sex differences in the effects of medial preoptic stimulation on arcuate cells and in the effects of hippocampal stimulation on preoptic cells. Stimulating the preoptic area affected more arcuate cells in females (50%) than in males (<33%). Also, more preoptic cells responded to hippocampal stimulation in proestrous females (>50%) than in males (≈30%). However, since the responsiveness of preoptic cells was decreased in diestrus, these synapses are sensitive to both activational and organizational hormones. But to be able to relate these connections to sex differences in hormone control or behavior, the recordings have to be done in freely moving animals whose behaviors can be observed.

Other areas of the brain and spinal cord. The limbic system and peripheral nervous system also have sexually dimorphic aspects (see Table 9-10). The motoneurons with T receptors control mounting and intromission, and their numbers are reduced or absent in females. But the reasons for sex differences in the other motoneurons and in the sympathetic nervous system are, at present, unknown.

The effects of sex hormones on the amygdala can be seen in Figure 9-17. Neurons here receive more synapses, especially dendritic shaft synapse, in males than in females. Earlier we discussed how the growth of the shaft synapse is specifically stimulated by E. Neonatal castration of males reduces their synapses to the female level, whereas neonatal androgen treatment of females increases their synapses to the male level. The rat amygdala has P receptors (Figure 9-9) and DHT receptors (Table 9-4), it has sexually dimorphic levels of T aromatizing and reducing enzymes (Table 9-5) and nicotinic receptors (Table 9-9), and it is related to positive-feedback effects and mounting behaviors (Table 9-3).

Sensory pathways can also be sexually dimorphic. One sex difference is found in the lateral geniculate of squirrel monkeys (Jacobs, 1983). Most squirrel monkeys have poorer color vision than do humans. Males are all protanopes (having a red-pigment deficit), and only some females have good trichromatic vision. During the recording of single-unit activity in the lateral geniculate, more chromatically opponent cells were found in females (21.5%) than in males (14%). Three

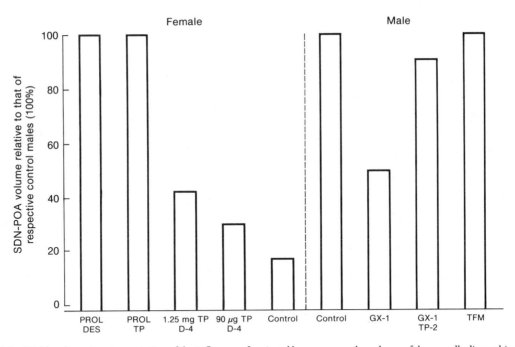

Figure 9-16 Highly schematic representation of the influence of perinatal hormones on the volume of the sexually dimorphic nucleus of the preoptic area (SDN-POA). SDN-POA volume in males with the testicular feminizing genes *(tfm)* or in males whose testes were removed on day 1 (GX-1), with and without treatment with testosterone propionate on day 2 (TP-2), and that of females injected with different doses of TP on day 4 (D-4), or after prolonged treatment with TP (PROL TP) or diethylstilbestrol (PROL DES, a type of estrogen), is compared with that of control males and females. The volumes are expressed as a percentage of that in control males. See text for further description and implications.

females — but no male — had as many as 61% to 78% of their cells chromatically opponent. Furthermore, of the chromatically opponent cells, more of them in females than in males were red–green opponent (for females, red–green = 49; blue–yellow = 54; for males, red–green = 1; blue–yellow = 85).

One controversial type of sex difference is the way in which functions, structures, and metabolic processes are organized in the brain. Sex differences have been found in both rats and humans. Although the differences have usually been summarized by saying that the male brain is more lateralized than the female brain, Table 9-9 shows that this is not strictly true; sex differences in brain organization are much more complicated than that.

Some of these organizational differences have been related to behavioral differences. In rats, there is a more lateralized turning preference in females than in males (males more frequently switch preference between right and left sides). The more consistent female side preference may be related to the lateralization of DA in some female brain areas. Sex differ-

ences in behavioral asymmetry tests are common in rats, such as rotations induced by amphetamine (which increases release of DA) and turning to the right versus the left during pinching of the tail (Camp, Robinson, & Becker, 1984). However, sometimes males and sometimes females are more behaviorally asymmetric.

Summary of Organizational Effects

The levels and types of sex hormones present during the time in which the brain is being formed affect the metabolism, structure, and function of the brain. Since the sexes differ in perinatal sex hormones, the brain is also sexually dimorphic. The differences have been best documented in the hypothalamus and the spinal cord; they are probably related to sex differences in sexual behavior and positive-feedback effects. However, sex differences have also been seen in certain limbic-system structures and the sympathetic nervous system,

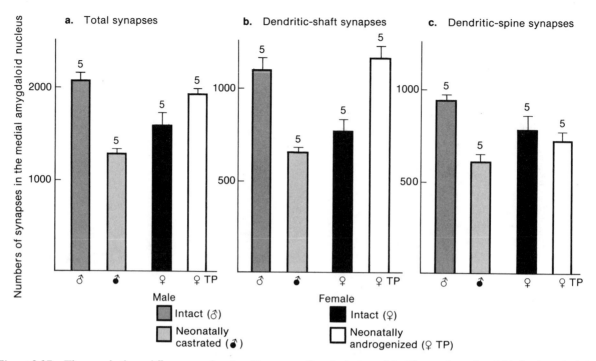

Figure 9-17 There are both sex differences and perinatal hormone effects in the amygdala. The numbers of total (a), dendritic shaft (b), and dendritic spine synapses (c) per field of 10,000 μm^2 in the middle part of the medial amygdaloid nucleus (AMN) of adult rats are plotted. Males have more of all types of synapse, but neonatal castration decreases synaptic numbers in males, and an injection of testosterone propionate (TP) on day 5 increases the number in females. The bars are standard errors of the mean, and the number above each is the number of subjects in the group.

differences that are probably more related to sex differences in reproductive behaviors (Table 9-7) than to mounting and lordosis. In relating sexually dimorphic brain structures to sexually dimorphic behaviors, you must remember that behavior and brain structures are also affected by environmental experiences. Thus, sex differences in behavior depend not just on the brain but also on sex differences in past experiences and current environments — including activational hormone levels.

Activational Effects on Neural Activity

Up to the present time, it has been difficult to relate the effects of sex hormones on neural activity to the effects of those same hormones on behavior. Pfaff's work is therefore exceptional.

Mechanisms of Effects

Activational sex hormones have genomic effects and can also affect neural activity without changing protein synthesis (see

review by Pfaff & McEwen, 1983; McEwen, 1981). In addition, in at least two cases, sex hormones after puberty can still have organizational-like effects on neurons. One occurs after brain damage, and the second shows how sex hormones can affect neural structure even in a normal adult.

Patterns of regeneration after brain damage. After brain damage, the neurons in areas adjacent to the damaged one can sprout new axonal processes. This regrowth can reinnervate parts of the brain that lost their connections in the lesion (Chapter 12): sprouting axons reinnervate a region denervated by brain damage. A neuron with a severed axon may regenerate a new one.

Sex hormones affect both regeneration processes. When the **hypoglossal** nerve (the twelfth cranial nerve; see Figure 2-3) is cut, the cell body regenerates a new axon, reinnervating the tongue. The regenerating axons reach the tongue more quickly in normal males than in females or castrated males (Yu, 1982). When the connections between the arcuate and the mediobasal hypothalamus are cut, many dendritic shaft and spine synapses in the arcuate are eliminated. Giving castrated, lesioned females E injections increases both types of synapse (Matsumoto & Arai, 1981b). Lesioning the septal area causes its connections to the hippocampus to degenerate. However, adjacent sympathetic axons—which normally innervate the blood vessels in that area—sprout into the denervated hippocampus and reinnervate some of its cells. More reinnervation occurs in adult female rats than in males (Loy & Milner, 1980, 1983). Either sex hormones activationally affect regenerating fibers or else the sexual dimorphisms in neural structures and interconnections due to perinatal hormones affect reinnervation.

Activational sex hormones and neural structure. Activational hormones affect the structure and number of neurons even in *adult* brains. Commins and Yahr (1984a) found that the cross-sectional size of one brain area in gerbils varied with activational hormone levels. Also, the surge in hormones at puberty increases the number of dendritic spines (and their synapses?) on preoptic neurons in female rats (Anderson, 1982).

Normally there are more vasopressinergic neurons coming from the suprachiasmatic nucleus to the lateral septum in males than in females. Both male and female hormones increase the number of neurons secreting ADH (vasopressin, or VP). Castrating adult males decreases the number of these neurons; paradoxically, so does castrating females (Södersten, Henning, Melin, & Ludin, 1983). Injections of ADH directly into female brains inhibits their sexual behavior (Södersten et al., 1983), whereas ADH facilitates mounting after castration in male rats (De Vries, Buijs, & Sluiter, 1984).

In canaries, the size of the area controlling singing is larger in the male than in the female; only the male sings. This telencephalic area is affected by organizational hormones, but activational hormones also have an effect (Bottjer & Arnold, 1984; Nottebohm, 1981). The size of the nucleus in males increases in spring (when singing also increases), and T injections also increase its size in the female canary. T probably increases size by increasing dendritic growth and the number of afferent terminals. Nottebohm (Goldman & Nottebohm, 1983; Kolata, 1984; Paton & Nottebohm, 1984) recently reported that T actually increases the *number* of cells present in that area of the brain. He said this was the first discovery of a case in which the number of brain cells present in the adult actually increased, as opposed to dying with age.

Sex differences in effects of sex hormones on hippocampal activity. Sex differences in the effects of sex hormones on neural activity are seldom systematically explored. Teyler,

Vardaris, Lewis, and Rawitch (1980) put brain slices taken from the hippocampal region of male and female rats into a culturing medium. The slices from female rats were taken during either proestrus or diestrus. Either T or E was added to the medium, and then microelectrodes recorded the pyramidal-cell response to stimulation of hippocampal afferents.

As Figure 9-18 shows, the change in electrical activity produced by sex hormones depends on the type of hormone, the sex of the animal, and the stage of the estrous cycle. Overall, E has much stronger excitatory effects than T—but only in males. These sexually dimorphic responses can be changed by manipulating activational hormone levels. For example, castrated male rats, treated for seven days with E injections, subsequently show a female pattern of hippocampal responses (Foy, Chiaia, & Teyler, 1984). Since the hippocampus is involved in learning and memory (Chapters 11 and 12), and since learning performances are sensitive to activational hormones (Table 9-7), hippocampal sex differences may be related to sex differences in learning performances.

Systemic versus microiontophoretic injections of E. When E is injected into the blood stream (a **systemic** injection), excitatory and inhibitory long-latency and short-latency effects are all seen. For example, Yagi (1973) found that systemic E changed neural firing patterns in the preoptic and hypothalamic areas within 15 to 16 minutes after the injection. Although these effects are too fast to be genomic, many could be indirect rather than direct. If E inhibited an inhibitory interneuron, then another neuron might be disinhibited, causing an increased firing rate.

Effects on the membrane. Microiontophoretic injections of E or T directly onto the membranes of some cells can elicit extremely rapid changes in firing rate. For example, Yamada and Nishida (1978) found latencies ranging from 3 to 20 seconds! These changes must come from direct effects of the hormone on the neural membrane, with or without membrane hormone receptors. We have already described the effects of E on pituitary cell membranes. Within a minute after application, E produced a Ca-dependent action potential and an increase in membrane resistance.

Kendrick and Drewett (1979) described another membrane effect. They examined the refractory periods of neurons that projected from the amygdala to the preoptic-anterior hypothalamic area in male rats. The rats were either intact, castrated at least 8 weeks before the experiment, or castrated but treated with T daily for 18 to 22 days before the experiment. The neurons of rats exposed to T had significantly shorter absolute refractory periods. Thus, T had a direct effect

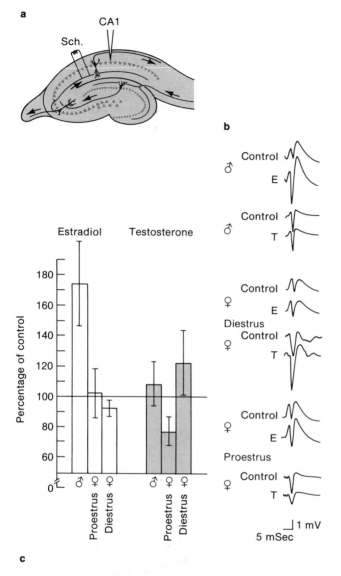

on the membrane of these cells. (As Chapter 3 said, the absolute refractory period depends on Na-inactivation, so T may affect this process.)

Effects on synapses.   Sex hormones also have a variety of effects on synaptic activity. For example, both E and P inhibit the presynaptic uptake of NE, and P increases the spontaneous release of NE (Janowsky & Davis, 1970). More examples of the activational effects of sex hormones on neural activity are described in the next section.

Sex Hormones and Transmitter Substances

Table 9-11 describes some of the effects sex hormones have on transmitter substances. The mechanisms for the effects are usually unknown, often unexplored.

Effects of transmitter substances on sex hormones.   The relationship between hormones and transmitters is a two-way street. Research in this area has had to explore a continuing interaction — making causal statements difficult.

First, transmitter substances control sex-hormone levels and receptors. The pituitary is controlled by neural as well as endocrine activity. For example, DA inhibits prolactin release. The level of sex hormones may then affect hormone receptors, or perhaps transmitter substances can directly control receptors. DA agonists increase the uptake of E in the brain and pituitary of female — but not of male — rats, so DA may control E receptors only in females (Woolley, Hope, Gietzen, Thompson, & Conway, 1982).

Two recent reviews described the effects of transmitters on hormone receptors and metabolism (Cardinali, Vacas, Ritta, & Gejman, 1983; Nock & Feder, 1981). First, neural activity and thus transmitter substances can affect the rate at which E receptors are renewed after being occupied. Second, neural activity can affect whether T is converted into E or into DHT. Third, neural activity can affect the degree to which E increases the number of P receptors. Fourth, neural activity can affect the degree to which protein synthesis can be induced by sex hormones.

Effects of sex hormones on transmitter substances.   Any or all of the following effects could produce the hormone responses described in Table 9-11:

1. hormone activation of the neurons secreting a particular transmitter substance

Figure 9-18   One example of sex differences in brain electrical activity.   **a.** Diagram of a transverse hippocampal slice, such as the ones used in this experiment. Stimulating electrodes were placed on the Schaffer (Sch.) collaterals, which make monosynaptic contact with the cell bodies of pyramidal cells in the CA1 area, where the recording micropipettes were placed.   **b.** Representative evoked or field potentials from the hippocampal slices, both from the control period and after administration of either estradiol (E) or testosterone (T). Slices from both proestrous (high-hormone) and diestrous females were studied.   **c.** Bar graph summarizes the major results; the bars are standard errors of the mean. See text for further description.

Table 9-11 Activational effects of sex hormones and transmitter levels and turnover (in rats).

Type of Effect on Transmitter	Effect of Sex Hormones	References
MAO	Higher levels in females; E increases the type of MAO called B but decreases Type A	Chevillard, Barden, & Saavedra, 1981; Robinson, Sourkes, Nies, Harris, Spector, Bartlett, & Kaye, 1977
Level and turnover of transmitters	Overall synthesis or turnover of DA, NE, & 5-HT are inhibited by T, though some areas, such as DA in the median eminence, may show an increased turnover	Engel, Ahlenius, Almgren, Carlsson, Larsson, & Södersten, 1979; Simpkins, Kalra, & Kalra, 1983
	E may increase DA levels in striatum and 5-HT levels in raphe and substantia nigra; P increases 5-HT levels in ventral tegmental area	Crowley, O'Donohue, Muth, & Jacobowitz, 1979; Di Paolo, Bédard, Dupont, Poyet, & Labrie, 1982; Di Paolo, Daigle, Picard, & Barden, 1983
	E may inhibit GABA transmission	Pfaff & McEwen, 1983
	Removal of T (gonadectomy) may increase number of dopaminergic afferents to periventricular nucleus	Simerly, Swanson, Handa, & Gorski, 1985
	E increases glutamic acid levels in MBH and amygdala	Mansky & Wuttke, 1983
	Males have more pituitary enkephalin, but castration of both sexes reduces dynorphin levels	Hong, Yoshikawa, & Lamartiniere, 1982
	ACh activity higher during diestrus (inhibited by E?)	Libertun, Timiras, & Kragt, 1973
Transmitter uptake	Pretreatment with E increases NE uptake; concurrent treatment with E specifically inhibits NE uptake; addition of P to E inhibits uptake of 5-HT and DA as well	Endersby & Wilson, 1974; Ghraf, Michel, Hiemke, & Knuppen, 1983
Transmitter release	E leads to increased release of NE and DA from hypothalamus	Paul, Axelrod, Saavedra, & Skolnick, 1979
	DA and NE release from striatum not affected by T but increased by E and P	Becker & Ramirez, 1981
Transmitter binding	NE and DA binding affinity decreased by E and increased by DHT	Inaba & Kamata, 1979; Wilkinson, Bhanot, Wilkinson, & Brawer, 1983
	ACh receptors have greater binding in females, especially during proestrus	Avissar, Egozi, & Sokolovsky, 1981; Miller, 1983
Number of receptors	E increases density of muscarinic ACh receptors in VMH	Pfaff & McEwen, 1983
	E first reduces and then increases 5-HT receptors; details depend on gender, brain location, and type of receptor (e.g., receptor 1 5-HT$_1$ decrease and receptor 2 5-HT$_2$ increase in cortex); P may also increase receptor 2 5-HT$_2$ and decrease receptor 1 levels in cortex	Biegon & McEwen, 1982; Biegon, Reches, Snyder, & McEwen, 1983; Fischette, Biegon, & McEwen, 1983
	E decreases cortical beta-NE receptors	Biegon et al., 1983; Fischette, Biegon, & McEwen, 1983
	DA receptors in striatum increased by relatively high, prolonged exposure to E; lower and/or acute doses may have opposite effects; may also be two types of DA receptors; effect of E is facilitated by E-induced increase in prolactin in females, and in males, the increase of DA receptors occurs *only* if prolactin levels increase first	Chiodo & Caggiula, 1983; Di Paolo et al., 1982; Di Paolo, Poyet, & Labrie, 1982; Gordon & Perry, 1983; Hruska, 1986; Hruska, Ludmer, Pitman, De Ryck, & Silbergeld, 1982; Hruska & Pitman, 1982; Miller, 1983

(continued)

Table 9-11 *(continued)*

Type of Effect on Transmitter	Effect of Sex Hormones	References
	Prolonged E treatment increases opiate and benzo-diazepine receptors in the hypothalamus	Wilkinson et al., 1983
	The sexually dimorphic region of the preoptic area contains more opiate receptors in females than in males; the sex difference is absent during proestrus and is greatest during diestrus	Hammer, 1984
	GABA receptors increased by P in caudate and cortex and by E in those areas plus hippocampus and olfactory bulb	Maggi & Perez, 1984

DA = dopamine
NE = norepinephrine
5-HT = serotonin
MBH = mediobasal hypothalamus
MAO = monoamine oxidase
E = estrogen
P = progestin
T = testosterone
DHT = dihydrotestosterone

2. hormone effects on the karyotype influencing the level of manufacturing enzymes, inactivating enzymes, and hormone receptors
3. hormone effects on membrane or cytoplasm affecting their protein content, the number of receptors, or the degree of binding of transmitter to receptor, or changing the level of enzymes involved in slow synaptic activity.

Many of these effects are indirect, crossing one or more synapses (Ondo, Mansky, & Wuttke, 1982). For example, E changes the activity of ACh neurons in the striatum only indirectly, by influencing DA neuron activity (Euvrard, Labrie, & Boissier, 1979).

With regard to the effects of sex hormones on transmitter substances, although catecholamine activity is most consistently found to be affected by sex hormones, the levels of most if not all transmitters are sexually dimorphic and affected by sex hormones. For example, ACh levels in the hypothalamus in rats change with the estrous cycle in such a way that whether males or females have the greater ACh levels depends on the stage of estrous in which the females were measured (Egozi, Kloof, & Sokolovsky, 1986). Some effects of hormones on transmitter levels were discovered by chemically analyzing the whole brains of subjects, but more useful and recent research has involved measuring transmitter activity in specific and separate brain areas.

The major transmitters all affect sexual behaviors. DA facilitates, and NE and 5-HT inhibit, mounting. Lordosis is facili-tated by ACh (muscarinic receptors) and perhaps by NE, and is inhibited by both DA and 5-HT (Carter & Davis, 1977; Clark, Smith, & Davidson, 1984; Clemens, Humphrys, & Dohanich, 1980; Dohanich et al., 1984; Everitt, Fuxe, Hök-felt, & Jonsson, 1975; Hull et al., 1984; Rodreguez et al., 1984).

Sex hormones control both the number of transmitter receptors and the degree to which these receptors bind to transmitter molecules. Probably the best documented—but most controversial—effect is that of E on DA receptors. E decreases the number of postsynaptic DA receptors and perhaps decreases the extent to which these receptors bind to DA (references in Table 9-11). As will be described shortly, this effect of E may explain why human females develop DA-deficiency movement disorders more often than males (Miller, 1983). But this effect of E could be secondary to its effect on prolactin; the E-induced increase in prolactin may cause the decrease in DA receptors.

Figure 9-19 provides another example of how sex hormones affect receptors. The effect of E on the number of 5-HT receptors varies according to brain area and gender. Particularly dramatic sex differences are seen in the dorsal raphe nucleus. E slightly decreases 5-HT receptors in females but greatly increases their number in males. As Table 9-3 shows, the significant hormonal effects on 5-HT receptors in the mediolateral preoptic area, the anterior hypothalamus, the arcuate, and the central gray could all be related to sex differences in mounting, lordosis, or positive-feedback effects.

310

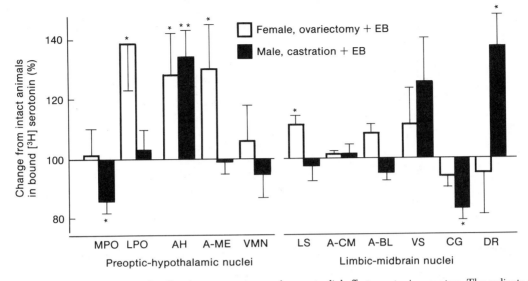

Figure 9-19 Sex hormones activationally affect hormone receptors; here, estradiol affects serotonin receptors. The ordinate measures serotonin receptors (radioactively labeled by [³H]serotonin) in the preoptic, hypothalamic, and limbic–midbrain nuclei of castrated and hormone-treated rats. MPO = medial preoptic area; LPO = lateral preoptic area; AH = anterior hypothalamic nucleus; A-ME = arcuate-median eminence; VMN = ventromedial nucleus of the hypothalamus; LS = lateral septum; ACM = corticomedial amygdala; ABL = basolateral amygdala; VS = part of the hippocampus; CG = central gray; DR = dorsal raphe nucleus; * and ** = significant hormone effects.

Single-Unit Recording: Effects of Sex Hormones on Neural Activity

Single-unit recordings often suffer from being unable to determine whether the effects of sex hormones are direct or indirect. This section looks first at effects of sex hormones on spontaneous activity and second at how sex hormones modulate sensory coding. The latter is most important to our frame of reference: changes in internal state, including the level of sex hormones, change how sensory stimuli are processed.

Effects of hormones on levels of activity in CNS neurons. Sex hormones have widely generalized effects on neural activity. High intravenous doses of E can increase glucose utilization in most areas of the brain (Namba & Sokoloff, 1984). Table 9-12 describes some of the single-unit-recording research, identifying which studies used microiontophoretic injections. The other studies recorded changes in single-unit activity either after systemic injections of hormones or associated with estrous-cycle changes in hormone levels.

Cells in the hypothalamus, preoptic area, and limbic system are most likely to be sensitive to sex hormones. Sometimes systemic T and E have similar effects, suggesting that T is being aromatized to E to produce these effects. Other parts of

the brain are affected by both E and either T or DHT, and sometimes the effects are not the same. In these areas, some neurons may have E and some T/DHT types of hormone receptor. Many of the shorter-latency effects of E and T observed after systemic injections must be indirect. The longer-latency effects could be genomic, the new protein having excitatory or inhibitory effects on the membrane.

Comparing the effects of systemic injections to those of microiontophoretic injections can tell us what the systemic injections are doing. Cells in the septal area, preoptic area, midbrain central gray, hippocampus, and anterior hypothalamus respond to microiontophoretic E injections. One study found that *the only response of septal, preoptic, and anterior hypothalamic neurons was inhibition*, as Figure 9-20 illustrates (Yamada & Nishida, 1978). However, Haskins and Moss (1984) found mostly excitatory effects of E on specially selected preoptic-septal and midbrain central gray neurons (see Table 9-12). The responses to T have been mostly *excitatory*. Outside the hypothalamus, few responsive neurons are found (Kelly et al., 1977).

E, DA, and movement disorders. The effects of hormones on neural activity have been related to movement disorders. Female rats are more sensitive to the effects of amphet-

Table 9-12   Activational effects of sex hormones on neuron activity (spontaneous and evoked by brain stimulation).

Area	Effect	References
Hypothalamus		
Mediobasal	Microiontophoretic E inhibits, but only in males (rat)	Yamada & Nishida, 1978
	Systemic P increases single-unit activity; increase in single-unit activity closely parallels correlated releases of LH (monkey)	Yeoman & Terasawa, 1984
Anterior hypothalamus	Long-term E depresses spontaneous activity (rat)	Lincoln, 1967
	Microiontophoresed T excited cells in males —and E had no effect on those particular cells; microiontophoresed E inhibited some cells in this area in females (rat)	Yamada, 1979; Yamada & Nishida, 1978
Arcuate	E increases sensitivity to medial preoptic stimulation and increases activity (rat)	Kubo, Gorski, & Kawakami, 1975
Lateral	Systemic T and E have similar effects: mostly increases in firing rates (rat)	Lincoln, 1967; Orsini, 1982
	Microiontophoretic E and T excited 13 cells, inhibited 9, but 11 cells were specifically excited only by T	Orsini, Barone, Armstrong, & Wayner, 1985
All areas	P inhibits (rat)	Barraclough & Cross, 1963; Ramirez, Komisaruk, Whitmoyer, & Sawyer, 1967
Medial preoptic area	T increases responsiveness to lateral septal stimulation (rat)	Kendrick, 1983a
	T decreases refractory period of cells projecting to MFB but not those projecting to lateral septum (rat)	Kendrick, 1983b
	Transitory increase or long-lasting decrease in firing rates after intravenous E (rat)	Yagi, 1973
	Microiontophoretic E inhibits in females during most—but not all—of the estrous cycle; removal of ovaries reduces E responsiveness in females; microiontophoretic T excites cells in males; E has no effect on the cells excited by T (rat)	Kelly, Moss, & Dudley, 1976, 1977, 1978; Kelly, Moss, Dudley, & Fawcett, 1977; Yamada, 1979; Yamada & Nishida, 1978
	T mostly increases spontaneous activity (rat)	Pfaff & Pfaffmann, 1969
	Long-term E may decrease spontaneous activity (rat)	Lincoln, 1967
	A few cells projecting to arcuate – median eminence inhibited by microiontophoresed E (rat)	Kelly, Moss, & Dudley, 1977
Medial preoptic + anterior area (combined)	Spontaneous activity higher during proestrus (E?) (rat)	Dyer, Pritchett, & Cross, 1972; Moss & Law, 1971
Medial preoptic + septal area (combined)	E mostly increases spontaneous activity, and mostly during proestrus-estrus; only neurons that responded to vaginal stimulation and not to somatosensory stimulation were studied (rat)	Haskins & Moss, 1983
Septal area	Long-term E inhibits (rat)	Lincoln, 1967
	Microiontophoretic E inhibits in intact female during most, but not all, of the	Kelly, Moss, & Dudley, 1976, 1977, 1978; Yamada, 1979; Yamada & Nishida, 1978

Table 9-12   *(continued)*

Area	Effect	References
	estrous cycle of an intact female; ovariectomy inhibits; T excites cells in the male (rat)	
Medulla	E increases activity in anesthetized female (rat)	Kow & Pfaff, 1982
	Mostly decreases (4 out of 5 cells tested) in spontaneous activity seen after T treatment in males (rat)	Pfaff & Pfaffman, 1969
	Microiontophoretic E mostly facilitated firing (rat)	Kawakami & Ohno, 1981
Amygdala	T decreases refractory period of neurons projecting to medial preoptic – anterior hypothalamic area; DHT has no effect but E has a similar effect (rat)	Kendrick & Drewett, 1979, 1980
Substantia nigra – caudate	E increases spontaneous activity in caudate and *decreases* number of cells affected by DA; changes DA effect from inhibition to excitation in females; E increases some and decreases some spontaneously activity levels of two different sets of substantia nigra neurons (rat)	Arnauld et al., 1981
Midbrain central gray	E usually excites these neurons during metestrus; few effects of E during proestrus-estrus (rat)	Haskins & Moss, 1983
Hippocampus	E strongly excites only male neurons in cultured hippocampal slices; T slightly excites male and diestrous female neurons (rat) (see Figure 9-18)	Teyler et al., 1980

NOTE: For abbreviations, see Table 9-10; for sexual anatomy, see Table 9-3.

amine than males are. The increase of behavioral activity levels seen after amphetamine injections occurs at lower doses in females than in males. Females also display more intense **stereotypy** ("compulsive" gnawing, chewing, licking), and they do more turning in circles (**"rotational behavior"**) (Robinson, Becker, & Presty, 1982; Savageau & Beatty, 1981). Amphetamine affects DA synapses in the striatum (Hruska & Silbergeld, 1980), and activational sex hormones change the postsynaptic effects of DA. The adenylate cyclase response is increased by E and inhibited by T (Barr, Ahn, & Makman, 1983).

Behavioral responses to DA injections into the dorsal part of the rat striatum, and of amphetamine into the ventral part, are modulated by E (Joyce, Montero, Van Hartesveldt, 1984). Unilateral injections of DA elicit turnings and rotations to the opposite side. This effect is *suppressed* by E, probably through E receptor-mediated, nongenomic membrane effects. Injecting amphetamine bilaterally increases activity. Removal of the ovaries from females leads to a decline in amphetamine-mediated increases in activity; an E injection increases the response. This effect may be genomic.

Single-unit recordings may be able to elucidate the cellular basis of these effects. DA iontophoresed onto caudate neurons usually inhibits most of them (86%) (Arnauld et al., 1981). (The caudate is innervated by the DA substantia nigra or A9 group of cells.) When E was injected, the number of spontaneously active striate cells increased from 25% to 87% within two to six hours. However, E *decreased* the number of cells responding to iontophoresed DA; the cells that did respond were now *excited* instead of inhibited. Removal of the pituitary caused the E effects to vanish (effects mediated by prolactin?).

Thus E may moderate activity level, stereotypy, and rotational behavior. These effects of E are mediated by the release of **prolactin** in males but not in females. (Prolactin is a pitui-

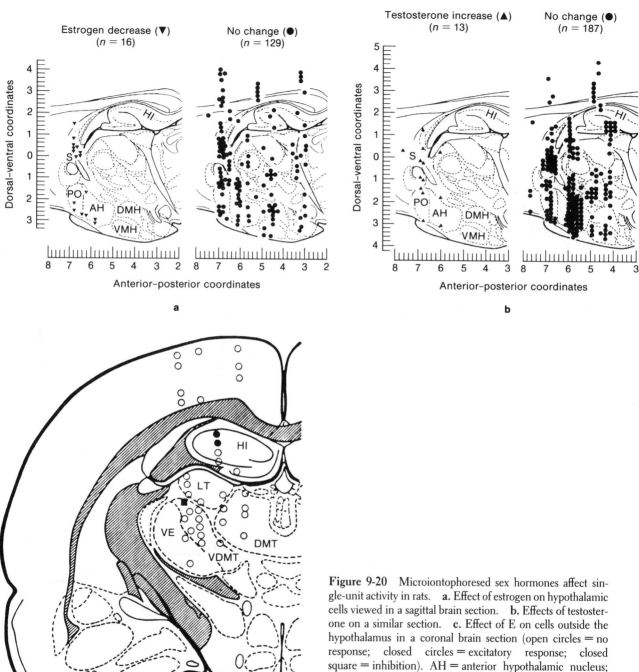

Figure 9-20 Microiontophoresed sex hormones affect single-unit activity in rats. **a.** Effect of estrogen on hypothalamic cells viewed in a sagittal brain section. **b.** Effects of testosterone on a similar section. **c.** Effect of E on cells outside the hypothalamus in a coronal brain section (open circles = no response; closed circles = excitatory response; closed square = inhibition). AH = anterior hypothalamic nucleus; DMH = dorsomedial hypothalamic nucleus; DMT = dorsomedial thalamic nucleus; HI = hippocampus; PO = preoptic nucleus; S = septum; LT = lateral thalamic nucleus; VDMT = ventral dorsomedial thalamic nucleus; VE = ventral thalamic nucleus; VMH = ventromedial hypothalamic nucleus.

tary hormone that facilitates milk production in lactating females; stress also increases secretion of prolactin.) The stimulating effect of E on DA-induced behaviors and striatal cells may explain why some female humans develop movement disorders when E levels are high, as they are during pregnancy or when taking birth control pills. Also, damage to the DA neurons causes movement disorders (Chapter 2). Therefore, the E-induced decrease in DA receptors (at physiological or normal levels: Table 9-11) and the conversion of normally inhibitory DA responses into excitatory ones may explain why human females are more likely than males to develop movement disorders when taking DA-receptor blocking drugs for treatment of schizophrenia.

Effects of sex hormones on sensory neurons. The coding of vaginal or flank stimulation by somatosensory neurons is hormone sensitive. These stimuli normally occur when a male mounts a receptive female. A female will sometimes, because of high hormone levels, respond to those stimuli as though they were pleasurable. The same female, at a low-hormone part of her cycle, will respond to those same stimuli as though they were aversive—she might then attack the offending male. Thus, sex hormones would seem to have an important effect on the way the brain codes those particular somatosensory stimuli.

Hormones affect peripheral nerves. Pfaff (1980) reviewed work done in his laboratory measuring peripheral nerve responses to stimulation of the flanks and genitals of female rats. The receptive field of a multiaxon bundle was larger after treatment with E. This effect occurred even after the connections between the nerve and the CNS had been cut, so the hormone directly affected either the peripheral nerves or the sensory receptors. The mechanoreptive neurons innervating the face of the rat also have enlarged receptive fields after treatment with E. In this experiment, the effect was seen at the single-neuron level and occurred only in rapidly adapting mechanoreceptor neurons (Bereiter & Barker, 1980). How these effects occur is still unknown (Bereiter, Stanford, & Barker, 1980).

E modulates somatosensory-evoked activity in the brain stem. Most E-sensitive cells respond to more than one type of stimulus (visual, auditory, vaginal). In rats, neurons that respond to these sensations, particularly to sexual types of somatosensory stimulus, are excited by E; the reverse seems to be true in cats (Alcaraz, Guzmán-Flores, Salas, & Beyer, 1969; Haskins & Moss, 1984; Kow & Pfaff, 1982; Sakuma & Pfaff, 1980). For example, in freely moving, unanesthetized rats, E increases the number of nerve cells responding to sexual stimulations, and if a neuron does respond to sexual stimulations, E also tends to increase its spontaneous firing rate.

E changes somatosensory responses in the preoptic areas and hypothalamus. In the anterior and medial hypothalamus, E nonspecifically increases the proportion of responses that are excitatory, to all types of stimulation, but E specifically *decreases* the number of *inhibitory responses* to vaginal stimulation (cat: Alcaraz et al., 1969). Lincoln and Cross (1967) demonstrated the importance of using EEG recordings to differentiate between the effects of specific and nonspecific arousal. In the rat, most of the cells in the hypothalamus (lateral and anterior) and septum that were excited by pain, cold, or vaginal stimulation were responding to nonspecific arousal. An estrogen decreased these effects, as though the hormone were suppressing responses to many external stimuli. However, E also *increased* the responsiveness of preoptic nerve cells to vaginal stimulation, an effect that was *not* associated with changes in arousal.

Sex hormones affect olfactory coding. This relationship may explain why the menstrual cycle changes olfactory sensitivity in humans (Table 9-1). The effect begins at the level of the olfactory bulb. The responses of mitral cells in female rats, activated specifically by the odor of male urine, are increased at estrus (Magnavacca & Chanel, 1979). Pfaff and Gregory (1971), however, were unable to find any effect.

Sex hormones change hypothalamic responses to odor. The proportion of hypothalamic cells excited by odors is nearly doubled in the high-E portion of the estrous cycle (Barraclough & Cross, 1963). Injecting T directly into the preoptic area of castrated male rats increased the excitatory responses of those cells to olfactory-bulb stimulation. Although E and T increase the excitability of preoptic neurons, T does not increase the specificity of responding. So T may not change sensory coding (Pfaff and Gregory, 1971; Pfaff & Pfaffman, 1969).

Sex hormones affect taste receptors. T injections given to either male or female rats increase the rate of taste-bud development (Cano, Machado, Roza, & Rodrigues-Echandia, 1982). Furthermore, T treatment changes transmitter levels in these cells, possibly explaining why sex hormones activationally affect taste sensitivity and preferences (Table 9-7).

In conclusion, sex hormones may serve **gating functions.** Hormones affect the excitability of certain sensory neurons *and* the way somatosensory neurons code sexual stimuli. Organisms' reactions to those stimuli therefore depend on their level of sex hormones.

A Paradigmatic Research Program: Pfaff and Lordosis

Pfaff and his colleagues have carried out a systematic program of research that has documented the neural and hormonal basis of lordosis in rodents. Their work allows an unusual opportunity to relate single-unit recordings to behavior. Pfaff's book (1980) is highly recommended.

Spinal control of the lordosis reflex.   Pfaff believes that lordosis is a reflex, controlled by the nature of the connections made between specific sensory neurons and specific motoneurons at the level of the spinal cord. However, a rat whose brain has been disconnected from her spinal cord will not show lordosis. Thus, descending fibers must exert a tonic influence on the spinal interneurons connecting the sensory neurons and motoneurons. Only when this tonic influence is excitatory—as it is during the high-hormone phases of her estrous cycle—will the lordosis reflex be elicited.

Figure 9-21 shows the continual interplay between the stimuli and responses involved in this spinal reflex. The stimuli come from the male's actions, and the female's responses affect what the male does next. The stimuli are olfactory and somatosensory, although the olfactory stimuli aren't indicated in that figure. If she is in estrus, male odors elicit invitational behavior from her. The somatosensory stimuli most relevant to the female's responses involve stimulation first to her flanks and back, and then to her groin, rump, and flanks. Pfaff says that Ruffini endings are the receptors most important for lor-

dosis. If the female assumes the lordosis posture in response to these stimuli, she receives vaginal stimulation. As we have just pointed out, sensory responses to touch and odor are both sensitive to activational hormone levels.

Ascending sensory pathways, descending motor pathways, and the effects of E.   In Figure 9-22, the pathways above the spinal-cord level all have nonspecific effects on lordosis. The ascending sensory pathways are not illustrated in that figure, but sexually relevant types of stimulus ascend to the medullary RF and to the central gray, producing a nonspecific excitatory effect. Cells in the mesencephalic or midbrain central gray and RF excite cells in the medullary RF. These latter cells have axons that descend in the spinal cord to tonically excite the lordosis-relevant interneurons in the spinal cord. Some of the cells have E receptors, as indicated by the black dots in that figure. Thus, E mostly excites central gray cells, leading to tonic excitation of spinal-cord "lordosis" interneurons.

E has its most important effects on cells in the hypothalamic/preoptic region. Cells in the medial anterior hypothalamus and VMH are excited by E (indirectly?) and, in turn, some of these cells excite the midbrain cells that indirectly

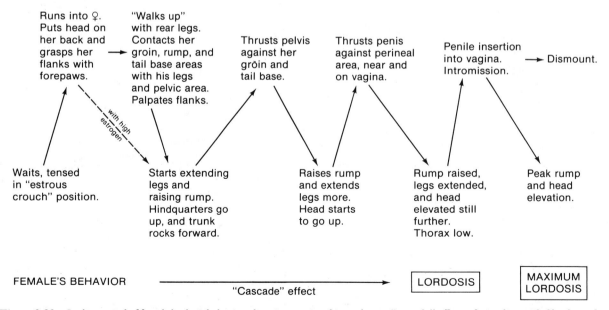

Figure 9-21   In the control of female lordosis behavior, there is a continual interplay, or "cascade" effect, of stimuli provided by the male on the female's responses. These reflexes in the female are controlled at the spinal level, with a gating effect exerted by descending hormone-sensitive brain neurons.

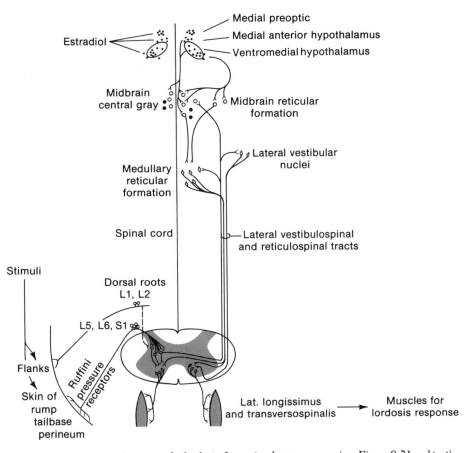

Figure 9-22 Summary of the basic neural circuitry for lordosis, from stimulus to response (see Figure 9-21 and text), and including the effect of estrogen. The black dots indicate neurons with hormone receptors; other cells are indicated by empty circles and triangles. In lordosis, stimuli, responses, circuitry, and hormone effects are all bilateral, and are shown here on just one side for convenience. See text for discussion of the neural-hormonal control of lordosis. L = lumbar region of the spinal cord; S = sacral region: Chapter 2. (See also Figure 9-6.)

facilitate lordosis (Morrell & Pfaff, 1982; Pfaff, 1980). Some cells in the preoptic area inhibit some of the VMH cells. Preoptic stimulation inhibits lordosis, and lesions of this area facilitate lordosis. Predictably, E inhibits preoptic cells and so facilitates lordosis. Because of the time required for genomic activation of E-sensitive cells, the hypothalamic effect on lordosis is delayed in comparison with the midbrain effect (Pfaff, 1980). Stimulation of the central gray can immediately increase, and lesions immediately eliminate, lordosis. The facilitating effects of VMH stimulation and lesioning are delayed by several hours.

The ways in which VMH neural activity might be affected by E are being explored by Pfaff and his colleagues. The VMH has two populations of cells. Activity of the first rapidly suppresses lordosis (membrane effects?); activity in the second set will eventually facilitate lordosis through genomic effects (Kow, Harlan, Shivers, & Pfaff, 1985). The effect of E on neural activity was studied in brain slices taken from the VMH of gonadectomized female rats (Kow & Pfaff, 1985b). Some slices were treated with E, and the researchers found that although E had no effect on the spontaneous firing rates of VMH neurons, E selectively facilitated excitatory responses to ACh, inhibitory responses to 5-HT, and both excitatory and inhibitory responses to NE. The inhibitory responses to DA and GABA were *not* affected by E treatment. These results parallel the effects those particular transmitters have on lordosis: ACh facilitates and 5-HT inhibits it. Thus, E could selectively gate input to VMH neurons.

Go back to Tables 9-7 through 9-12 to see to what extent Pfaff's model can account for the observed effects of E on neural responses and transmitter substances. You should also note that the sensory effects of E are not yet incorporated into his model (though they are described in his book), because it is still unclear where and how these effects take place. Nevertheless, their importance is potentially greater than that of the effects that are better understood.

Neural Activity during Sexual Behavior

What parts of the brain are activated by sexual behaviors? T affects self-stimulation in certain areas of the male rat brain (see, for example, Hoebel, 1979; Chapter 8). Similarly, self-stimulation in female rats varies according to their estrous cycle: LH self-stimulation is increased at estrus (Prescott, 1966). So the pleasurable sensations associated with sexual activity should have hormone-sensitive neural correlates.

Gross activity.   Michael and co-workers (Holbrooke & Michael, 1980; Michael, Holbrooke, & Weller, 1977) used gross electrodes to record from the female cat brain during sexual activity. The VMH shows the most consistent changes with sexual behavior and with E treatment. The VMH EEG flattens during E treatment and during intromission — with or without E treatment. This change may explain the female's affective responses (pleasure?) to sex.

Two people had electrodes implanted in their brains as part of their treatment. A male was being treated for epilepsy, depression, and homosexuality; a mildly retarded female was being treated just for epilepsy. Activity in various parts of their brains was recorded during sexual arousal and orgasm (Heath, 1972). The male said that he was sexually aroused by stimulation of the nucleus accumbens (described by Heath as "septal" — actually adjacent to septum; see Table 9-9). The female had arousal and orgasm induced by injections of ACh into the septal area of her brain. (ACh increases lordosis in rodents.) For both subjects, sexual arousal and orgasm were associated with nucleus accumbens spike and slow-wave activity and superimposed fast activity. According to Heath, this type of nucleus accumbens activity is the "pleasure response."

Single-unit recordings.   It is difficult to do single-unit recordings in awake animals displaying sexual behavior: the vigor of that behavior produces noise in the recordings. Nevertheless, researchers have found some cells that respond specifically to sexually arousing stimuli. Some olfactory bulb and preoptic cells respond more to sexually relevant than to sex-

ually irrelevant odors (urine from the opposite sex, as opposed to same sex; urine from receptive, as opposed to unreceptive, females) (Mink, Sinnamon, & Adams, 1983; Pfaff & Gregory, 1971; Pfaff and Pfaffmann, 1969).

T also affects the MFB neurons that support self-stimulation. Orsini (1982) found that T or E usually increased the firing rate of LH cells in male rats. T also increased the activity of cells in the part of the preoptic area transversed by the MFB (Pfaff & Pfaffman, 1969), which may explain why T can increase some self-stimulation in male rats.

Oomura, Yoshimatsu, and Aou (1983) recorded from the medial preoptic and hypothalamic areas during sexual behavior in the male monkey. Activity in medial preoptic nerve cells was closely related to sexual arousal. Activity in these cells decreased when a female was presented and stayed at low levels during the sexual refractory period after ejaculation. However, some preoptic neurons increased in activity just before actual contact with the female. Activity in these neurons might be related to the parasympathetic control of penile erection. Dorsomedial hypothalamic neurons were associated with the motor responses of sexual activity (Oomura, Yoshimatsu, & Aou, 1983). Some of these neurons had increases in activity restricted to intromission and thrusting. This finding is consistent with research showing that ejaculation can be elicited by dorsomedial but not by preoptic stimulation and that preoptic lesions specifically impair males' ability to become sexually excited by a female.

Summary of Activational Effects

Sex hormones affect neural activity both because of genomic activation and because of shorter-latency effects on the membrane. Cells in the preoptic area, hypothalamus, and some limbic-system structures are particularly likely to be affected. Some cells are excited and some inhibited. The effects may be direct if the neuron has hormone receptors or if research shows that microiontophoresed hormone quickly affects neural activity. In many if not most cases, the effect is more indirect, with hormone-sensitive cell activity affecting activity in other cells throughout the limbic system. Synaptic receptors, spontaneous activity, and sensory evoked responses are all affected by sex hormones. Again, the effects could be direct or indirect.

In contrast to the research relating neuronal activity to food deficits, the work to date on activational effects of sex hormones provides little support for the neuron doctrine. Cells all over the CNS are directly or indirectly affected by sex hormones and sexual activity. Cells in the LH of males may be related to the effects of T on self-stimulation and on responses to sexual odors. The septal region and nucleus accumbens may be related to sexual "pleasure" in male and female humans, but in female cats, the VMH has been implicated. The VMH also seems to control lordosis in female rodents. Preoptic-area neurons not only have hormone receptors but respond to sexual odors in male rodents and may be related to sexual arousal in male primates. Systematic programs of research such as Pfaff's, and single-unit recordings of hormone-sensitive responses to sensory stimuli, offer the most promise for eventually relating activity in small sets of nerve cells to sexual motivation and reproductive behaviors.

Chapter Summary

Neural Coding of Sexually Dimorphic Behaviors

Reproductive behaviors and motives include most or all of the sexually dimorphic behaviors. Some causes of sexual dimorphisms are the sex chromosomes and the sex hormones, both organizational and activational. But past experiences and current environment also exert powerful influences on these behaviors (Hoyenga & Hoyenga, 1979).

For a male or female to show normal levels and types of sexually dimorphic behaviors, including mounting and lordosis, both sex chromosomes and sex hormones must be normal during fetal development. Three or four chromosomes determine the gender of the gonad, and one of these probably codes for the H-Y antigen protein. After this time, sex hormones determine the gender of the brain and the other body organs. If the genes coding for the androgen receptors and for the enzymes that transform testosterone (T) into either estradiol (E) or dihydrotestosterone (DHT) are all present, the male brain and body can be normally masculinized and defeminized. Without any one of these, and for the normal female who lacks the testicular androgens, the brain and body are demasculinized and feminized. Sex hormones organizationally affect the structure of nerve cells, the patterns of interconnections, and brain metabolism, making them sexually dimorphic.

After puberty, the sex hormones have activational effects. Circulating hormones have several effects on nerve cells: average level of activity; membrane characteristics; responses of cells to stimulation of other parts of the brain; responses of cells to various kinds of sensory stimulus; and transmitter-substance metabolism, turnover, and receptors. These effects are not limited to the hypothalamic nuclei controlling sexual behavior and pituitary hormone secretion. Thus, activational effects might be part of the reason for sexual dimorphisms in reproductive behaviors, including nurturance, aggression, and energy balance.

Except for Pfaff's research, we are a long way from being able to apply the neuron doctrine (Table 1-1) to organizational and activational effects of sex hormones.

CHAPTER

The Psychobiology of Emotions and Curiosity

Each emotion can be both defined and differentiated from other emotions by four characteristics: (1) its *arousal* level, (2) its *internal responses*, (3) the *behavioral reactions*, and (4) the *specific "emotional" phenomenological sensations* (Hoyenga & Hoyenga, 1984). For example, any given emotion may have little or no arousal or a great deal of arousal; one emotion may be associated with a specific set of behaviors and another may have no observable behavioral reaction.

Each of these four characteristics presents unique problems for the psychobiology of emotions. Since the behavioral responses to emotional states are often learned, a subject's past experiences can complicate research on the psychobiology of emotions. For example, learning (such as learning to hide one's emotions) can change emotional expressions. A second example concerns the **phenomenological aspects** of emotion, the conscious sensations uniquely associated with each emotional state, which so far can be studied only in humans. Only the human subject can *verbally* report what emotional state she or he may be experiencing. But what is actually being directly studied is a behavioral response — a verbal report — and not a phenomenological experience. Since emotions are literally "loaded with affect," verbal reports of emotions can be distorted by subjects' desires to "look good," to "be normal," or to conform to the experimenter's expectations and so win his or her approval.

Overview

Because of the problems associated with measuring and categorizing emotions, we cover only a few areas of research. To a large extent, the areas discussed will be limited to those in which neural correlates have been explored. We start with a brief review of the physiological aspects of emotions, covering the peripheral nervous system and the anatomy of the limbic system. This will be followed by a summary of the findings and a discussion of the implications of genetic research.

Emotional states are associated with specific biochemical and neural activity in limbic-system areas of the brain. Emotional states may cause biochemical changes, and, in turn, the biochemical changes affect phenomenological experiences and behaviors. Only a few studies have recorded from single cells while experimental animals were exposed to various emotion-producing stimuli, including drugs. This research will be described in the last section, relating single-unit activity to emotions and emotional responses.

The Biology of Emotions: A Survey

The biology of emotions is largely the biology of the adrenal gland, the autonomic nervous system, and the limbic system. Any change in the phenomenological and behavioral expressions of an emotion involves changes in one or more of these systems. For example, an organism experiencing a certain emotion has certain internal responses, which may produce unique and externally observable effects. An angry cat will lay back its ears and spit at you, and an angry person will have furrowed brow, curled lips, and a reddened face. These **emotional expressions** arise directly from the effects that emotional states have on the ANS, the adrenal gland, and the muscles of facial expression. But there is considerable disagreement about how closely specific changes in these systems are related to specific phenomenological experiences.

The Issue of Specificity and the Role of Visceral Afferents

The issue of specificity is concerned with the degree to which internal responses have a separate pattern for each emotion, each uniquely associated with a different emotional state (Candland, 1977; Hoyenga & Hoyenga, 1984). The issue was created early in the twentieth century by conflict between the **James-Lange** and the **Cannon-Bard** theories of emotions and later revived by the publications of Schachter's theory. This issue is illustrated in Figure 10-1.

The James-Lange theory of emotions states that an external stimulus elicits behavioral and internal responses unique to that type of stimulus (Hoyenga & Hoyenga, 1984). The ability of a given stimulus to evoke these two types of response could be either innate or learned. For example, the sight of a bear would innately elicit activity in the sympathetic nervous system, but whether one runs from or is frozen by that sight can be changed by learning. In turn, these external and internal responses cause the phenomenological sensations. In other words, having an elevated heart rate and running would cause fear, as opposed to fear's causing the elevated heart rate and the running.

Cannon and Bard (the Cannon-Bard theory) disagreed. They believed that peripheral reactions vary little among emotional states (Hoyenga & Hoyenga, 1984). Thus, there are no specific peripheral reactions to cause different phenomenological states. They also believed that viscera have too few afferents to be able to affect CNS cells directly. This would mean that we are insufficiently sensitive to our viscera for their state to produce any phenomenological effect.

The Cannon-Bard theory states that the first response of the nervous system to an emotional stimulus — such as the sight of a bear — takes place in the cortex. If the cortex encodes this stimulus pattern as being an emotional one, the cortex stops inhibiting the thalamus. Once the thalamus is freed from inhibition, it simultaneously activates the peripheral nervous system and the emotional areas of the CNS. Only the latter would be critical for a phenomenological emotional experience, but different peripheral responses could parallel some emotional states.

Schachter believed that peripheral reactions are exactly the same for all emotional states (Hoyenga & Hoyenga, 1984). He believed that only one peripheral reaction — something called "diffuse arousal" — occurs during *any* emotional state. But Schachter did believe that we are sufficiently sensitive to the state of our viscera for this diffuse arousal to affect us. In fact, unless we are consciously aware of being aroused, we would not experience any emotional state.

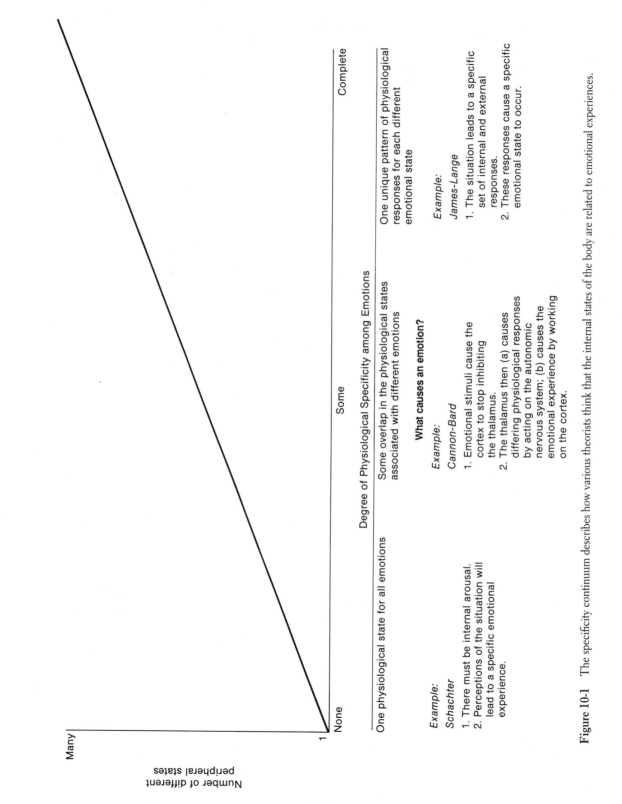

Figure 10-1 The specificity continuum describes how various theorists think that the internal states of the body are related to emotional experiences.

Schachter said that external stimuli evoke both diffuse arousal and a particular set of cognitive expectancies and beliefs. Together, the arousal and the cognitions cause phenomenological experiences. Seeing a bear in our path would evoke arousal, and we would also interpret the sight of the bear as being frightening. Together, these two components of any emotional state—arousal and cognition—would cause a specific emotional experience: for example, "I must be frightened." If that same arousal were evoked in the presence of a comedy film, we would interpret the resulting state as being amusement instead of fright.

The contrasts among these theories include disagreements not only about specificity but also about visceral afferents. The James-Lange and Schachter theories say that these afferents are required for an emotional experience (for different reasons), but the Cannon-Bard theory disagrees. We will discuss these issues.

The Autonomic Nervous System

The anatomy of the parasympathetic and sympathetic efferent divisions of the ANS were presented in Figure 2-2. The sympathetic-division efferents tend to act in concert, whereas parasympathetic efferents are more discretely activated (although there may be more specificity in sympathetic responses than has been believed: Wallin & Fagius, 1986). Contrary to claims of no specificity, the *pattern* of their activity changes when emotional states change. These changes, perhaps coded by ANS afferents or signaled by hormones, may affect our emotional experiences (for references, see the reviews of Fehr & Stern, 1970; Hoyenga & Hoyenga, 1984; Reisenzein, 1983; Tarpy, 1977).

Parasympathetic emotions.   States of quiet emotional pleasure are perhaps uniquely and specifically associated with sympathetic suppression and an increase in some specific parasympathetic efferent activity (Hoyenga & Hoyenga, 1984). These emotions include the pleasure of being groomed by another member of your species. When a human interacts with his or her pet, the human's heart rate slows as he or she pets the animal, and the animal's heart rate slows because it is getting petted. Having a full stomach can also produce quiet pleasure and parasympathetic activity.

Facial expressions.   One experiment related facial expressions in humans to ANS activity (Ekman, Levenson, & Friesen, 1983). Two types of subjects were used: trained actors and scientists studying the face. Six different emotions were stud-

ied: surprise, disgust, sadness, anger, fear, and happiness. Each emotion was elicited in two ways. In one, the subject was told to produce a certain facial expression by following a detailed description of which muscles to contract and by viewing the result in a mirror. In the second, the subject was asked to relive some situation in her or his past life in which that particular emotion had occurred. The ANS responses to each emotion were measured indirectly by using finger temperatures (peripheral vasoconstriction), heart rate, muscle tension, and skin resistance.

The data from this experiment are relevant to both major issues. First, different patterns of ANS activity were elicited by different emotions. For example, heart rate increased more in fear and anger than in happiness (not too surprising). Second, placing facial muscles into specific patterns elicited specific emotions *and* patterns of ANS activity. In either case, the effects were specific and varied according to emotional states.

Earlier research also showed that assuming certain emotional expressions can change phenomenological experiences (see references in Ekman & Oster, 1979). For example, smiling, combined with slow, deep, rhythmic breathing, can relieve anxiety and depression. The mechanism for these effects may involve CNS afferents from muscles or blood vessels, outflow monitoring of efferent signals to the facial muscles, or the effects of facial muscle contractions on blood flow to the brain (Zajonc, 1985).

The Adrenal Glands

There are two adrenal glands, each one located above a kidney. The medulla is controlled by the sympathetic nervous system, as Figure 2-2 shows. The sympathetic efferents stimulate the medulla to secrete mostly epinephrine (E), but also some small amounts of norepinephrine (NE), into the blood stream. Medulla enzymes can be regulated by activity levels in the sympathetic efferents (LaGamma, Adler, & Black, 1984), implying that different patterns of sympathetic activity could cause different and specific patterns of hormone release.

The adrenal cortex is controlled by the pituitary, as Figure 10-2 shows. **Adrenocortico***tropic* **hormone (ACTH)** is secreted by the pituitary and stimulates the release of glucocorticoids from the adrenal cortex. The **glucocorticoids** are steroidal hormones that inhibit inflammation and control blood glucose levels, as well as other things. They include cortisol and corticosterone. (Some sex hormones are also cortical steroids: Chapter 9.) The glucocorticoids participate in negative-feedback loops at the pituitary and hypothalamic levels; they inhibit pituitary release of ACTH and also inhibit the synthesis and release of the **corticotropin-releasing factor (CRF)** by hypothalamic cells. Thus, under normal conditions, these negative-feedback loops keep the levels of glucocorticoids, ACTH, and CRF relatively constant.

Arousal and stress.   The arousal caused by some emotional states is accompanied by increased activity in both the adrenal medulla and cortex (Hoyenga & Hoyenga, 1984). Being angry or frightened increases the level of E and NE in the blood stream, which stimulates the viscera in the same way as do the sympathetic efferents (which secrete most of the NE). High, prolonged arousal increases both glucocorticoid and ACTH levels in the blood, and so emotional stress "breaks" negative-feedback loops. The increased ACTH strongly stimulates the adrenal cortex. The glucocorticoids can affect brain-cell activity (Chapter 9), and they also help the body to cope with deleterious effects of stress (Selye, 1976/1978, 1980).

Different ways of causing pain-induced stress in rats produce "different psychological, neurochemical, and endocrinological consequences" (Terman et al., 1984, p. 1274). For example, the analgesic effects of giving rats a footshock every 5 seconds, for 20 minutes, involve the adrenal gland (Chapter 6). Analgesia from prolonged footshock does *not* involve the adrenal.

Evidence for adrenal specificity.   Some types of adrenal response occur with some degree of emotional specificity. For example, only adrenaline (largely from the adrenal medulla) and not noradrenaline levels (largely from the sympathetic

efferents) are increased in human males by the stress of taking various memory and speed tests (Faucheux, Bourlière, Baulon, & Dupuis, 1981). Injecting lactate into the blood of human subjects, especially in people who suffer from panic attacks, specifically evokes anxiety and feelings of panic rather than any other emotion (see review in Hoyenga & Hoyenga, 1984; Rainey, Frohman, Freedman, Pohl, Ettedgui, & Williams, 1984; Lapierre, Knott, & Gray, 1984). Lactate is produced by exercising muscles in a metabolic process facilitated by adrenal medulla hormones.

Limbic System

Papez (1937) and MacLean (1970, 1975, 1985) developed the modern concept of a limbic system (Candland, 1977; Tarpy, 1977). The limbic system and associated structures (see Figure 2-12) have been extensively studied by physiological psychologists. Lesions in, or gross stimulations of, these structures can change the internal emotional reactions and the emotional behaviors of experimental animals. But sometimes the results depend on the species being studied. For example, septal lesions temporarily cause increased irritability in rats (and septal stimulation can reduce at least some forms of aggression). The lesion effect, called **septal rage**, does not appear in monkeys, guinea pigs, or hamsters (Moyer, 1976). Many of these structures will also support self-stimulation or escape behaviors (Chapter 8). If activity in some or all of these

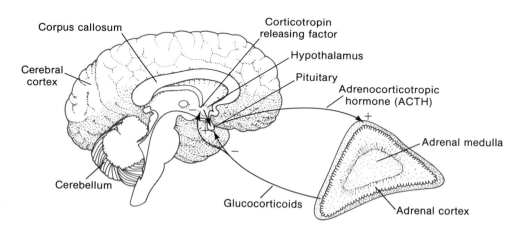

Figure 10-2   A negative-feedback system controls the levels of pituitary, hypothalamic, and adrenal hormones. The human brain is illustrated in a sagittal section. Corticotropin-releasing factor, secreted by the hypothalamus, stimulates secretion of ACTH (adrenocorticotropic hormone) into the blood by the pituitary. ACTH stimulates the secretion of the corticosteroids by the adrenal cortex into the bloodstream. In turn, the adrenal steroids inhibit both the hypothalamic and the pituitary secretion of hormones. This is another example of a negative-feedback loop, and it works much like the one described for sex hormones (see Chapter 9).

structures codes emotional experiences, it also may be part of the phenomenology of pleasure and pain.

Lesions in human subjects also cause abnormal emotions. For example, Zeman and King (1958) described a series of patients having damage to their septum and adjacent structures. These patients were irritable and frequently became enraged. Malamud (1967) studied 18 patients, all having damage to limbic-system structures. Many of them were incorrectly diagnosed by psychiatrists as being anxious, depressed, or schizophrenic.

Lilly, Cummings, Benson, and Frankel (1983) described 12 patients who had damage to both left and right temporal lobes (and presumably at least some damage to the underlying structures, including the amygdala and hippocampus). Most of these people had at least some symptoms of the **Klüver-Bucy** syndrome, named for research originally done with lesioned monkeys (Klüver & Bucy, 1939). The patients were abnormally compliant, apathetic, and unable to recognize friends. They constantly explored their environment — often by placing objects in their mouths — and ate inappropriate objects such as shoe polish, feces, and tea bags. They showed alterations in sexual behavior, including inappropriate sexual invitations, exposure of their genitals, and constant masturbation. These people often seemed demented.

Summary of Biology

The biology of emotions includes both peripheral and central structures. The adrenal gland, both the cortex and the medulla, and the visceral afferents and efferents are part of the peripheral response to emotional states. The major issues are peripheral specificity and the role of the autonomic afferents. Some research suggests that peripheral activity can affect phenomenological experiences. The research that involved lesioning or stimulating CNS structures defined the limbic system. It now remains for psychobiological research to explore how these nerve cells may code the various emotional states — and how these cells could produce emotional phenomenological experiences.

Genetics of Emotions

Research concerned with the genetics of emotions faces several problems. First, genes can have more than one kind of effect. For example, the genes could affect either the *threshold*

for an emotional response or the *likelihood* of an emotional response to a certain situation. Some animals are more likely than others to react aggressively to strong threatening signals (olfactory and visual) coming from other members of their own species. Some — because of their genes — have a lower threshold and so require less intense or prolonged threat signals in order to react aggressively.

Second, emotions of the same name are often given different definitions. Even when investigators use the same label for a state, such as "aggression" or "fear," the emotion is then often tested in different situations, with different behavioral scoring criteria. Researchers measuring aggression in one laboratory may not measure the same sets of behaviors — and therefore the same sets of genes — as researchers in another.

Third, terms like *aggression* and *fear* are often interpreted broadly even though the relevant genes are studied narrowly, by using narrow selection criteria for breeding. A given strain of rats may be labeled "emotional." The term usually implies that those rats have a low threshold, reacting with high levels of nonspecific arousal to even weak anxiety- and fear-arousing stimuli. But that strain of rats may have come from a breeding program that selected animals according to how many times they defecated in an unfamiliar, open-field area (prolific defecators are said to be emotional). Unless the "emotional" strain proves to be more highly aroused and fearful in many anxiety-arousing situations, the genes involved might be changing food intake rather than emotionality (think about it).

This section describes the genetic basis of behavior *patterns*. Later sections describe the genetic basis for transmitter metabolism when each transmitter is discussed. In only one case have genes, transmitters, and particular neurons been linked: that case is described at the end of this section.

Inheritance of Temperament and Emotionality

Geneticists have investigated mostly anger and fear. Emotions such as those associated with curiosity and exploration are also receiving attention. Few other emotions have been systematically studied.

Aggression. Family studies, strain studies, and selective-breeding programs have all found a genetic basis for **intermale aggression** (aggression among male *or female* adults of the same species). The species studied range from roosters to rodents (see references in Fuller & Thompson, 1978). Researchers found that at least one strain of mice was aggressive in a wide variety of situations because of a single, autosomal recessive gene (although a more complex genetic model could not be ruled out) (Kessler, Elliott, Orenberg, & Barchas,

1977). However, the degree of intermale aggression depends not only on genes but also on prenatal environment, social experiences, and the type of testing situation used (Simon, 1979).

Different types of aggression are probably controlled by different sets of genes, and any given set may affect more than just aggression. Some of these effects may come from genes that have multiple effects on organisms' biological systems (Fuller & Thompson, 1978). Rodents from aggressive strains are more active, are superior at maze learning, are more reinforced by the opportunity to display aggression, and are sometimes more successful in mating. Strains of rats consistently differ from each other in mouse killing, a type of **predatory aggression** (Walsh, 1982). Strains of mice also differ from each other in males' tendencies to kill infant mice (Svare & Broida, 1982).

Male and female mice may have different genes for aggression. A Y-chromosome gene may affect aggression in some strains of mice (Hoyenga & Hoyenga, 1984). Obviously, this gene would never affect aggressiveness in females. When only male mice are subjected to selective breeding, their female relatives are also aggressive (Fuller & Thompson, 1978). However, when only females are selectively bred, their male relatives do not show any consistent change in aggression (Hyde & Ebert, 1976; Hyde & Sawyer, 1979). Intermale aggression and **maternal aggression** (aggression displayed in defense of young) may have a similar genetic basis in females. Females bred to attack other females are also very aggressive in defense of their offspring.

Some researchers have explored the way in which genes affect aggression (Fuller & Thompson, 1978; Simon, 1979). Some genes affect the sensitivity of the nerve cells controlling aggression to the organizational and activational effects of androgens. In other cases (or the same case, because of organizational effects of androgens on transmitter substances?), strains differing in aggressiveness reliably differ in brain levels of transmitter substances (summarized in the next section). But since these strains differ in other behaviors as well, the transmitter differences could be related to behaviors other than aggression.

Flynn and his colleagues have provided some of the background needed by future genetic researchers (see summary of Adamec & Stark-Adamec, 1983). In cats, a connection between the amygdala and the VMH (see Figure 2-12) controls defensive behaviors and the ability to inhibit aggression. A circuit between the amygdala and the ventral part of the hippocampus facilitates aggression. The LH might have a type of command-system function. Some cats are more defensive and others more aggressive. These tendencies are directly related to differences in excitabilities (as assessed by electrical stimulation of the amygdala) of the defensive and aggressive circuits, respectively.

As Simon theorized (1979), the organism's genes may affect aggression only by influencing how its brain processes sensory information. For example, a stimulus could be coded as a "threat" in some animals instead of as a neutral stimulus. A genetic analysis of the activational and organizational effects of sex hormones on the sensory coding of threat-type stimuli would be important. Also, we should study single-unit responses to aggressive stimuli in strains differing in aggressiveness.

Not much evidence suggests any genetic basis for aggression in humans. Some researchers have looked for Y-linked effects by comparing XYY males with genetically normal males and by comparing males (XY) with females (XX). The results suggested that Y-chromosome genes could impair impulse control. Having poor impulse control could, under some circumstances, increase impulsive types of aggression (such as barroom fights) (see reviews in Hoyenga & Hoyenga, 1979, 1984).

Adoption studies of criminal behavior (see review in Fuller & Thompson, 1978) have shown that having a criminal natural father *plus* a criminal adoptive father may increase criminality, especially in sons. Cadoret and her colleagues (see, for example, Cadoret, Cain, & Crowe, 1983) also studied adoptive children and pointed out that "the increase in the number of antisocial behaviors due to both genetic and environmental factors acting together is far greater than the predicted increase from either factor acting alone" (p. 301). Whatever the nature of the effect, criminal tendencies increase *only* if the rearing environment also somehow encourages those tendencies.

Neurosis, temperament, and emotionality.   Emotionality in lower animals is studied largely with the open-field apparatus. Family studies, strain studies, and selective-breeding studies have all found a hereditary basis for open-field behavior. Heritability for this trait may be close to .25 (Fuller & Thompson, 1978; Plomin, DeFries, & McClearn, 1980). For example, one genetic program used open-field activity levels as the basis for selection in mice (DeFries, Gervais, & Thomas, 1978). Figure 5-2 shows the results of one such study. The open-field activities of those strains were inversely related to their frequency of defecation. Both behaviors may reflect the same trait and the same set of genes.

Another breeding program used open-field defecation as the basis for selection in rats. This program produced the Maudsley reactive (**MR**) strain, characterized by frequent defecation and low activity, and the Maudsley nonreactive

(MNR) strain (Broadhurst, 1975). Other differences between the strains in emotional characteristics suggest that they may really differ in levels of "emotionality." For example, MR rats have lower NE levels in their blood, adrenal, heart, and hypothalamus (Blizard, 1981). The selective-breeding program produced a marked suppression of the MR sympathetic system, including hypothalamic control of that system.

Other emotional traits in animals also have some hereditary basis (Fuller & Thompson, 1978). These traits include responses to a stressful stimulus (see also Driscoll, Martin, Kugler, & Baettig, 1983), reactivity to threatening stimuli in dogs, and spontaneous activity in fruit flies. In most of these behaviors, the genes interact with the environment. A given gene may be expressed only if the organism was reared in, or is tested in, a certain environment. Another gene may increase or decrease an organism's susceptibility to certain types of early experiences. Most of these traits are probably polygenic.

A variety of human emotional or **temperamental traits** have at least a small genetic component (Ahern, Johnson, Wilson, McClearn, & Vandenberg, 1982; Fuller & Thompson, 1978; Plomin et al., 1980). The trait dimension of **extroversion–introversion** has the strongest genetic basis. An extrovert is outgoing and social, does not react much to stress, and gives up easily; an introvert is the opposite. Estimates of the heritability of extroversion range between .4 and .7.

Human neuroses may also have some genetic basis, as twin, adoption, and family-history studies have demonstrated (Fuller & Thompson, 1978; Noyes, Clancy, Crowe, Hoenk, & Slymen, 1978; Torgersen, 1983). Heritability estimates for neurosis often depend on such factors as gender and how severe the neurosis is. Alcoholism also occurs in the families of neurotics, either because neuroticism genes also affect the likelihood of alcoholism or because of **assortative mating.** People with psychological problems tend to marry each other (Merikangas, 1982). If potential neurotics married potential alcoholics, both traits would appear in the same families even if totally different sets of genes were involved.

Schizophrenia and Affective Disorders

The emotional problems of humans are extensively studied because of their social importance. Both genetic and biochemical research has been done, but the relationship between gene and biochemistry has not yet been discovered. The biochemistry will be described in the next section.

Clinical descriptions of the emotional disorders. Schizophrenia is characterized by defects in emotions as well

as in thinking patterns. Emotionally, the schizophrenic can have **flattened affect** (showing blunted or absent emotional responses to situations such as death) as well as **inappropriate affect** (laughing during a funeral, crying during a funny movie). Their thought patterns are typically severely disordered. They show unusual, even bizarre associations to thoughts and ideas, they speak in a "word salad" that typically makes no sense to their listeners, and they make up new "words."

There are probably several kinds of schizophrenia. For example, there may be two somewhat independent sets of symptoms (Crow, 1980, 1985). The **positive symptoms** are hallucinations, delusions, disordered thinking, and excitement. The **negative symptoms** may include chronic cognitive deficits, poverty of speech, the inability to relate to people, and flattened or bizarre emotional responses. **Paranoid schizophrenia**—dominated by delusions of persecution—may represent a third type (Kendler & Davis, 1981).

Gender also affects the course and symptoms of the illness. Symptoms in males commonly develop during adolescence, whereas in females they develop later in life (Gottesman & Shields, 1982). Symptoms and developmental correlates are also sexually dimorphic (Mednick, Schulsinger, Teasdale, Schulsinger, Venables, & Rock, 1978). An atypically early age of onset in mothers means that their female offspring are at even greater risk for developing schizophrenia than is usual for a daughter of a schizophrenic mother. Parental separations and possession of an ANS that recovers rapidly from its stress responses (a condition that is increased by prenatal and birth complications) increase the likelihood of schizophrenia only in males. Male schizophrenics are more often withdrawn, and female schizophrenics are more socially "active" (often "promiscuous").

Affective disorders include **bipolar disorder** and **unipolar disorder.** In unipolar disorder, the person suffers from severe and recurrent periods of depression. Major or psychotic depression differs from that experienced by normal people (as in normal reactions to grief) in that perceptions of reality are distorted. The depressed person may feel extremely guilty over something that was in no way his or her fault, such as the attack on the marine base in Beirut. In bipolar disorder, or **manic-depressive disorder,** the person alternates between periods of mania, periods of severely distressed, depressed mood, and periods of relative normality. A person who is depressed may be diagnosed as bipolar if some of his or her family members were manic. In these cases, the person will often develop mania later. The sex ratio is about even for bipolar disorder, but more females than males develop unipolar disorder.

Twin, family-history, and adoption studies. Table 10-1 summarizes some twin and family-history studies of schizophrenia and affective disorders. The evidence for a genetic basis is usually called "overwhelming." Adoption studies confirm these conclusions. For example, the risk of developing schizophrenia is the same whether the child is reared with the affected parent or is reared by nonschizophrenic foster parents (see references listed for Table 10-1).

The statistics in Table 10-1 show that not all people genetically at risk will develop the disorder and that not all people who develop the disorder were genetically at risk. The people most at risk might be children with a monozygotic twin with a disorder, or children who have both a parent *and* a sibling with the disorder. Even in these cases, most of the people at risk do not develop the disorder. Thus, the environment experienced by the child must be equally important, if not more so. But being raised by a schizophrenic or affectively disordered parent is evidently *not* an environment that increases the likelihood of these disorders.

Some people develop these emotional disorders in the total absence of any family history of the disease. They may have had a spontaneous genetic mutation, or their disorder may have been entirely environmentally caused. Another possibility is that the diagnostic criteria used can affect estimates of heritability. The reasons for this are not clear, but if a very strict diagnostic criterion is used, heritability estimates are lower (Abrams & Taylor, 1983).

More than one type of each disorder? As Table 10-1 indicates, there is a range of values for "risk" in each family subgroup. Each disorder may involve several different subtypes, such as positive and negative symptoms. Each subtype may have a somewhat different genetic basis and heritability. However, Tsuang, Winokur, and Crowe's data (1980) suggested that paranoid versus nonparanoid subtypes did not "breed true" in families.

Attempts have been made to classify schizophrenics according to biological differences among them. For example, schizophrenics differ from normal people in brain levels of NE and in degree of brain lateralization (as described in the next section). So far, none of the classification schema have been clinically or genetically useful. They do not predict behavioral symptoms, prognosis, the relative effectiveness of different treatments, or the degree of genetic basis for the disorder (see, for example, Wyatt, Potkin, Kleinman, Weinberger, Luchins, & Jeste, 1981). However, because of the importance of such a system, attempts are still being made. For example, the schizophrenia with the least intellectual impairment may have the strongest genetic basis (Owens, Johnstone, Crow, Frith, Jagoe, & Kreel, 1985).

Table 10-1   Risks for emotional disorders among relatives of an "index" case.

			Affective Disorder	
Relationship	Schizophrenia[a]	Genetic Relatedness	Bipolar[b]	Unipolar[b]
Parents	4.2–4.4	50%	15–41	12–23
Monozygous twin	40.0–50.0	100%	11–25	20–27
Dizygous twin	9.0–15.0	50%	3–4	4–14
Sibs (neither parent affected)	6.7–10.0	50%	—[c]	18
Sibs (one parent affected)	12.5–13.8	50%	—[c]	37
All sibs	7.5–8.5	50%	17–42	11–21
Children	9.7–12.3	50%	16–25	17–26
Children (both parents affected)	35.0–46.3	50%	—[c]	—[c]
Half-sibs	3.2	25%	3	5
Aunts and uncles	1.7–2.0	25%	3	5
Nephews and nieces	2.3–3.0	25%	3	5
Grandchildren	2.6–2.8	25%	3	5
First cousins	1.7–2.9	12.5%	—[c]	—[c]
General population	0.85–1.0		1	2–10
Spouse	2.0			

[a] Rounded to nearest tenth of a percent.

[b] Rounded to nearest percent.

[c] No research.

The affective disorders have subtypes other than bipolar and unipolar. Akiskal (1983) said there may be as many as 20 different types, including neurotic depression and bereavement. Depue and Monroe (1978) proposed five different categories of bipolar disorder, as well as several categories for unipolar disorder, each with a somewhat different genetic basis. For example, the type of depression that occurs before age 20 is linked to a greatly increased risk of depression among the person's relatives (Weissman, Wickramaratne, Merikangas, Leckman, Prusoff, Caruso, Kidd, & Gammon, 1984).

One classification schema is described in Figure 10-3. Distinctions among unipolar disorders are based on (1) early (before age 40) versus late age of onset of depression, (2) whether other family members have alcoholism as well as depression, and (3) whether any family history of disorder is present (Mendlewicz & Baron, 1981; Winokur, 1982). The tendency for alcoholism and depression to appear in the same families (these families are said to display **depressive spectrum disease**) may represent multiple effects of the same gene or assortative mating effects.

A Link with Genes: Dopamine Neurons, "Curiosity," and Schizophrenia

Reis, Fink, and their colleagues carried out a systematic research program to explore one genetic-neural-behavioral link in rats and mice (Baker, Joh, Ruggiero, & Reis, 1983; Fink & Reis, 1981; Fink & Smith, 1979a, 1979b; Ross, Judd, Pickel, Joh, & Reis, 1976). Curiosity and exploration in rats, measured by the amount of exploratory activity occurring in an open-roofed box, are directly related to brain DA levels. If brain levels of DA are decreased by 6-OHDA injections, all types of curiosity behaviors occur less frequently. Injecting a

DA precursor (L-dopa) into the blood restores exploratory behaviors to normal levels in the 6-OHDA-treated rats.

Genes control the number of DA neurons in the brain. The BALB/cJ strain of mice has more midbrain DA neurons (for example, in the substantia nigra) than other strains do. The BALB/cJ strain also has twice as many DA neurons projecting to the preoptic area and to the mediobasal region of the hypothalamus as does the CBA/J strain. Mice of the BALB/cJ strain show more exploratory behaviors. Thus, the two lines of research — biochemical and genetic — converge in suggesting that a gene carried by mice in the BALB/cJ strain increases the number of DA neurons in the brain and that because of this increase, these mice are more curious.

This research may have implications for schizophrenia. As we will describe, one biochemical model for schizophrenia suggests that DA neurons in a schizophrenic's brain are overactive. High doses of the DA-agonist amphetamine produces what looks like paranoid schizophrenia in humans. Mice of the BALB/cJ strain also react more to injections of amphetamine, showing more activity and stereotypy. Furthermore, in humans schizophrenia may be inversely related to a trait called **stimulus seeking.** This trait can be measured in humans by a score on a paper-and-pencil test. Scores on this test are related to such curiosity and stimulus-seeking behaviors as jumping out of airplanes (with a parachute) (Hoyenga & Hoyenga, 1984; Zuckerman, 1984). Schizophrenics tend to get very low scores on this test.

The relationship between DA neurons and curiosity may be indirect or even fortuitous. Other behaviors and emotions may be more directly related to DA activity. Furthermore, in some rats, NE neurons may affect the activity levels seen in curiosity tests, whereas DA levels may affect other types of curiosity (Skolnick & Daly, 1974).

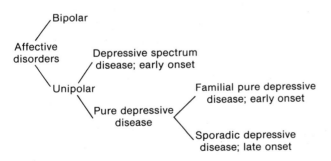

Figure 10-3 Winokur's hypothesis involves several subtypes of depression. "Familial" means that the patient has family members with depression, whereas "sporadic" means that no other family member is or has been clinically depressed. See text for further explanation.

Summary of Genetics

There is little doubt that genes and the proteins for which they code affect the activity of nerve cells. This relationship has been shown for open-field emotionality and aggression in nonhumans and for neuroticism, extroversion – introversion, and major emotional disorders in humans. The nature of these relationships remains an exciting frontier for research. Why estimates of heritability might depend on the stringency of diagnostic criteria used is unknown. Genes may provide only a generalized risk, and the details of the symptoms may be determined by environment.

Effects of Stress on Brain Transmitter Levels

Diathesis-stress models are used to explain why most people who inherit a susceptibility to an emotional disorder do not develop that disorder. The genetic susceptibility or **diathesis** is expressed only when the person—and her or his brain-transmitter metabolic pathways—are subjected to some kind of stress. As a first step, we will describe the effects that stress has on transmitter levels and turnover.

Background and a Model

We describe one model in this section and also point out some problems that a diathesis-stress model faces.

Stress and emotional disorders.   Figure 10-4 presents a diathesis-stress model for emotional disorders. The model postulates an ongoing cycle: perceiving some event as threatening triggers the cycle. An event perceived as threatening is one kind of **stressor,** and an organism reacting to that threat is said to be experiencing **stress.** Other stressors are events that in some way stimulate pain receptors or damage the body, such as extreme cold. Some events, such as pain, are innately threatening, whereas others are so perceived only because of having had certain kinds of experience in the past.

Perceiving threat or damage leads to behavioral and ANS **coping responses.** These include escape attempts, sympathetic activation, and activity in the adrenal cortex and medulla, all of which are related to neural CNS activity. **Stress responses** include both behavioral and physiological coping responses. Although these responses tend to ameliorate damage, high levels of stress responses can become stressors in and of themselves.

If coping responses failed to eliminate the stressor, the cycle and the CNS activity would continue, eventually producing changes in transmitter metabolism and perhaps a depletion of transmitter levels. Those effects could intensify the phenomenological emotional experience and thus change how the stressor was perceived. Not only would the neural pathways directly activated by the stressor change but interconnected pathways would also change.

Synapses in the directly and indirectly activated pathways would usually adapt to a continuously present stressor or habituate to a continually repeated one. Both processes use synaptic modulation mechanisms and both "dampen" or modulate the CNS responses to the stressor. For example, adaptation decreases the number of NE beta-adrenergic receptors in the hypothalamus, cortex, and brain stem (Stone, 1983; Stone &

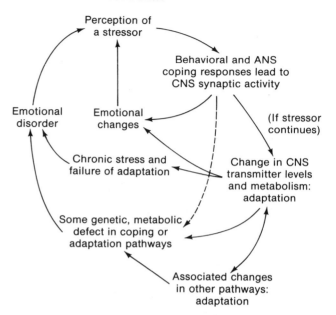

Figure 10-4   Our version of a diathesis-stress model of emotional disorders. See text for a description of the events depicted in this model. The dotted line represents a possible but somewhat less likely connection between events.

Platt, 1982). An emotional disorder occurs when adaptation fails or becomes "exhausted."

Suppose a certain genetic liability or diathesis gene modified one or more of the elements along an adaptation pathway. The modification might be in synaptic interconnections, numbers of cells, numbers of axon collaterals, basal levels of transmitters, or responses of transmitter synthesis and inactivation enzymes to stress (Stolk & Nisula, 1979). Because of the gene, habituation or adaptation would not be as complete or as rapid as it would be without the gene. Less-than-optimal adaptation may cause an emotional disorder. That disorder would change the person's perceptions even more radically. Even common objects or events would be misperceived.

Some potential problems with diathesis-stress models. First, the research documenting a link between stress and emotional problems in humans is weak. As noted in the review of Anisman and Zacharko (1982), most studies suffer from grave procedural flaws, many of which are unavoidable in human research. Second, most of the work on the biochemistry of stress has been done on animals. The behavioral and emotional consequences of such stress could well be quite different in humans. In human work, we can study only associations between brain transmitters and mental states: we cannot make causal statements.

Since the diathesis has already been documented in the genetics section, the rest of this section and the next sections provide data relevant to the stress part of diathesis-stress models. We describe the effects of stress on the brain transmitters most closely related to the biochemistry of emotional disorders.

Stress-Induced Changes in Brain Transmitters

Stressors affect brain transmitter levels and metabolism. Many transmitter systems are affected, at least indirectly. However, the degree to which those changes occur depends on several factors.

Types of stress and brain transmitters. The effects of stress on transmitters are summarized in Table 10-2. Many stressors, ranging from uncontrollable shock to social isolation and deprivation procedures, affect transmitter metabolism and levels. One stressor emphasized in the table is that of uncontrollable shock: there is no possible behavioral coping response. Only animals subjected to uncontrollable shock develop behavioral deficits that in some ways resemble those displayed by many depressed humans: suppression of activity (lack of motivation?), learning and memory impairments, and distorted responses to stimuli (Maier & Seligman, 1976).

Most of the studies listed in the table under "uncontrollable shock" used at least three different groups of subjects. Members of one group were shocked but were also given an opportunity to control the shock. For example, as Figure 10-5 illustrates, the avoidance-escape group could turn a wheel to turn off the shock (escape); if it continued to turn the wheel, that prevented future shocks (avoidance). A second group was **yoked** to the first. Any member of this group received the same number, pattern, and duration of shocks as an animal in the avoidance-escape group received. For the yoked animal, turning the wheel had no effect on its getting shocked, so this second animal was exposed to **unavoidable** or **uncontrollable** shock. The third, control group of animals never received any shock.

The transmitter changes in all three groups tell us about the effects of stress on the brain (Maier, 1984). Most important are the brain transmitter changes found in the uncontrollable group; these are caused not by shock per se but by an inability to control that shock—an inability to cope. Sometimes the avoidance-escape group differed from both the yoked and the control groups. The effects are summarized in Table 10-2

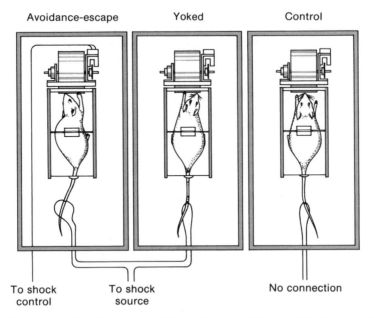

Figure 10-5 Groups used to compare the effects of controllable and uncontrollable shock. Left: an avoidance-escape animal, whose wheel is wired to the shock controller. Center: a yoked animal. Its tail electrodes are wired in series with the avoidance-escape subject, and so it receives exactly the same shock. But its wheel turning has no effect on that shock. Right: an unshocked control animal.

Table 10-2 Effects of stress on brain transmitters in mice and rats.

Type of Stress	Nature of Effect	References
Uncontrollable shock[a]	5-HT levels in LC decreased	Weiss, Goodman, Losito, Corrigan, Charry, & Bailey, 1981
	Decreased release of 5-HT onto cortex and depletion of 5-HT in septum and anterior cortex for at least 5 days after stress	Petty & Sherman, 1982, 1983; Sherman & Petty, 1982
	Decreased number of 5-HT presynaptic receptors for afferents to cortex	Sherman & Petty, 1984
	NE levels decreased in anterior cortex, hypothalamus, and LC (LC depletion highly correlated with stress-induced inactivity) because of increased turnover or release of NE	Swenson & Vogel, 1983; Weiss, Glazer, Pohorecky, Bailey & Schneider, 1979; Weiss et al., 1981
	Cortical ACh muscarinic receptors increased	Cherek, Lane, Freeman, & Smith, 1980
	Decreased self-stimulation in MFB and nAcc but not in substantia nigra (DA depletion?)	Zacharko, Bowers, Kokkinidis, and Anisman, 1983
	One type of DA receptor increased in frontal cortex; other DA receptors in other brain areas decreased	Cherek et al., 1980
	Increased DA levels in hypothalamus (trend in same direction in brain stem)	Weiss et al., 1979
Adaptation to uncontrolled stress	Repeated stressors increase tyrosine hydroxylase	Stone & McCarty, 1983; Weiss et al., 1979
	Repeated stressors reduce beta-NE receptors in hypothalamus, brain stem, and cerebral cortex (correlates with stress resistance, especially in hypothalamus)	Stone & Platt, 1982
	Repeated stressors decrease the NE response to current stress	Stone & McCarty, 1983
Exposure to one five-minute footshock	Beta-endorphin decrease in hypothalamus and pituitary, and increase in bloodstream	Millan, Przewlocki, Jericz, Gramsch, Höllt, & Herz, 1981
Controlling shock	DA levels in anterior cortex increased	Weiss et al., 1981
	5-HT levels in brain stem (except for LC) decreased	Weiss et al., 1981
	NE levels in hippocampus decrease	Swenson & Vogel, 1983
Exposure to stimuli previously associated with shock, or reintroduction of mild stressor	Depletion of hypothalamic NE	Anisman & Sklar, 1979, 1981
	Increased cortical ACh muscarinic receptors (up regulation?), and increased release of NE (whole brain)	Lane, Sands, Smith, & Cherek, 1980; Cassens, Kuruc, Roffman, Orsulak, & Schildkraut, 1981
	Increased release of DA, but *only* from afferents to frontal cortex (A10 group of cells)	Herman, Guillonneau, Dantzer, Scatton, Semerdjian-Rouquier, & Le Moal, 1982
Social isolation	Decreased NE release, which leads to an increase in postsynaptic alpha-NE receptors in the striatum	De Ceballos, Guisado, Sanchez-Blazquez, Garzon, & Del Rio, 1983
	Decreased NE levels in hippocampus and cortex	Anisman & Sklar, 1981
	Decrease in DA and 5-HT turnover	Dourish, Davis, Dyck, Jones, & Boulton, 1982
	Decreased activity in A10 neurons projecting to frontal cortex; enhanced activity in DA neurons projecting to nAcc and striatum; *enhanced* response to stress in A10 neurons projecting to cortex	Blanc, Hervé, Simon, Lisoprawski, Glowinski, & Tassin, 1980
Deprivation	Food deprivation (chronic but intermittent) decreases beta-NE receptors in cortex but not in hypothalamus or brain stem	Stone, 1983
	Periodic water deprivation increases NE turnover in pons-medulla and DA turnover in caudate	Emmett-Oglesby et al., 1978

Table 10-2 *(continued)*

Type of Stress	Nature of Effect	References
"Psychological stress"	Exposure to sight, sound, and smell of another rat being shocked causes NE release in hypothalamus and amygdala and NE depletion in the amygdala	Iimori, Tanaka, Kohno, Ida, Nakagawa, Hoaki, Tsuda, & Nagasaki, 1982

DA = dopamine
NE = norepinephrine
5-HT = serotonin
LC = locus coeruleus
MFB = medial forebrain bundle
nAcc = nucleus accumbens
[a] These effects are not seen when the animal can avoid the shock.

under the "controlling shock" category. In this case, the change in brain transmitter might be directly related to the brain circuits activated first by *learning* how to control the shock and then by *performing* the escape-avoidance response.

Changes in NE. Since some theorists think that at least some kinds of depression may involve abnormally low NE activity, stress-induced changes in NE are important to diath-

esis-stress models of depression. Soon after a stressor begins, the synthesis and use of NE increase in several areas of the brain. Some of these changes are illustrated in Figures 10-6 and 10-7. Even stimuli previously paired with shock, when later presented without shock, can increase NE utilization (Cassens et al., 1981). According to Anisman and Zacharko (1982), if the stressor is controllable, the rate at which NE is secreted or utilized is not excessive and the increased rate of

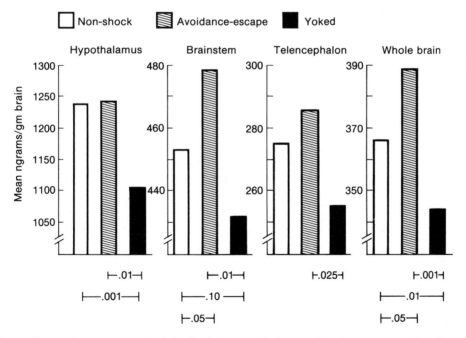

Figure 10-6 Stress affects endogenous norepinephrine levels in several brain areas. The three groups used are those shown in Figure 10-5. The subjects were exposed to their respective conditions for 20 hours prior to being euthanized for brain biochemical measurements. The results are based on groups of 21 animals each. The numbers at the bottom of the figure are the probability levels for the significance of differences between various pairs of groups. ngrams = nanograms.

333

synthesis is able to keep up with the demand. However, if the stressor is uncontrollable, the rate of utilization exceeds the rate of synthesis and brain NE levels become depleted.

NE depletion may cause an animal to become abnormally inactive or "apathetic." In Weiss's work with rats (Weiss et al., 1979; Weiss et al., 1981), NE depletion is directly related to subsequent inactivity. The relationship between depletion and inactivity is especially strong in the locus coeruleus. The degree of LC NE depletion is highly correlated (+.70) with the degree of suppression of activity seen after stress. Furthermore, injecting alpha$_2$-adrenergic agonists directly into the LC increases activity and can also completely reverse the effects of stress (Simson, Weiss, Hoffman, & Ambrose, 1986; Weiss, Simson, Hoffman, Ambrose, Cooper, & Webster, 1986).

The experiment illustrated in Figure 10-8 used drugs to relate NE depletion to inactivity. The top group in that figure was given no active drug (a placebo was substituted) and was exposed to unavoidable shock before being tested in the shuttle-box avoidance task. In this task, to avoid shock the rat had to move from one side of a rectangular box to the other. The activity of the placebo — unavoidable-shock group was suppressed: both escape and avoidance behaviors were suppressed. These rats also had long response latencies. But the group given unavoidable shock and also given an MAO inhibitor at the same time, to prevent the breakdown and hence the depletion of NE, showed *no* suppression of activity.

Serotonin. Theorists have also related 5-HT depletion to depression. 5-HT levels change during and after exposure to a stressor, and the changes persist long after the stressor is gone (Petty & Sherman, 1982). The animals who show the least change in depressionlike behaviors after stress also show the least change in 5-HT utilization (Petty & Sherman, 1983).

Dopamine. DA responses to stress have been explored largely because of research and theories relating abnormally high DA activity to schizophrenia (discussed in the next section). Although many early studies did not find reliable stress-

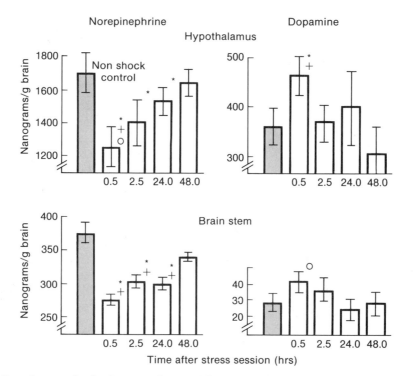

Figure 10-7   The effect of stress on levels of norepinephrine and dopamine in the hypothalamus and the brain stem of rats varies as a function of the time elapsing since exposure to uncontrollable shock. The results at each time point are based on eight subjects. Asterisk (*) = significant difference from nonshock control; plus (+) = significant difference from 48-hour group; o = significant difference from 24-hour group.

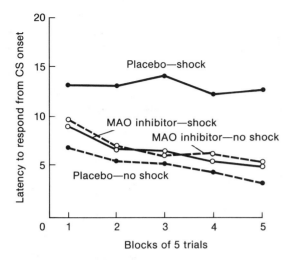

Figure 10-8 The stress-induced depletion of brain norepinephrine may be directly related to the subsequent behavioral inactivity. This figure shows the mean latency (in seconds) to cross a hurdle in an avoidance-escape test. One group received a MAO inhibitor before a session of inescapable shock, which was later followed by the shuttle-box avoidance-escape test. A second group received the MAO inhibitor without the shock session (MAO inhibitor—no shock). A third group received only a placebo injection (placebo—shock). Comparing that group with the fourth group, which received only the placebo and no shock session, shows how inescapable shock usually suppresses activity, including avoidance and escape responding.

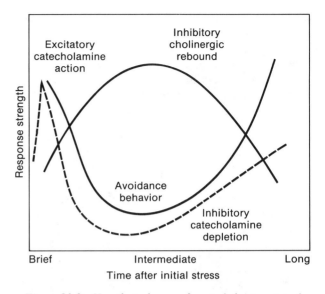

Figure 10-9 Hypothetical curves for catecholaminergic and cholinergic changes after stress and their effects on avoidance behavior. Note that immediately after stress starts, catecholamine activity shows a transient increase and then, because of depletion, falls below baseline. Cholinergic activity increases steadily, reaching a maximum at the intermediate time interval.

induced DA changes in rats, two groups of French researchers did succeed (Herman et al., 1982; Hervé, Tassin, Barthelemy, Blanc, Lavielle, & Glowinski, 1979; Lavielle, Tassin, Thierry, Blanc, Hervé, Barthelemy, & Glowinski, 1978).

The A10 neurons projecting to the frontal cortex are particularly susceptible to stress. Both increased DA utilization and synthesis occur following stress. Furthermore, only the A10 cortical group of neurons was activated by a stimulus that had previously been paired with shock. Also, some DA receptors —including those used by the A10 projections to the frontal cortex—change only in response to uncontrollable shock; no changes are seen if the shock was controllable.

Acetylcholine. Stressors, especially if uncontrollable, also affect ACh levels (Anisman & Zacharko, 1982; Glavin, 1985). Figure 10-9 shows some hypothetical curves describing the time course of ACh and NE changes (Anisman, 1975). ACh levels *increase*. Since brain ACh usually inhibits activity, the changes in ACh, which occur after NE has reached its

lowest point, may be another reason for the inactivity seen after stress.

Factors Affecting Stress Responses

Individuals differ in stress responses, including *which* CNS pathways are most affected by a stressor, the *degree* to which each of those pathways is activated, and the degree to which it can *adapt* to stress (Gilad, Rabey, & Shenkman, 1983; Keim & Sigg, 1976). If we can identify them, the factors responsible for these individual differences should be found to directly affect the degree to which stress changes brain transmitter levels. And—if a diathesis-stress model is appropriate—the likelihood of developing an emotional disorder would also be affected.

Controllability. We have said that one important factor involved in stress-induced changes in brain transmitters is stressor controllability. If the stressor is controllable, the brain transmitter changes often do not occur. Also, people who feel in control of their lives are less likely to develop depression (Hoyenga & Hoyenga, 1984). Thus, the syndrome of **learned helplessness** (as we will explain shortly, this is Seligman's name for the effects of uncontrollable stress) may be a model for stress-induced depression in humans (Maier, 1984).

Prior stress.   Another factor is prior exposure to stress. Long-term synaptic modifications change the way neural pathways will respond to a stressor (adaptation). Figure 10-10 shows how prior exposure to a stressor affects tyrosine hydrox-

ylase levels. As shown in Figure 10-10c, prior exposure to shock (though not to swimming) increases tyrosine hydroxylase levels, presumably meaning an increased capacity to synthesize NE. Certainly prior exposure to stress prevents the NE depletion usually caused by exposure to uncontrollable shocks (Figure 10-10a). Stone and McCarty (1983) found that the amount of increase in tyrosine hydroxylase after stress was

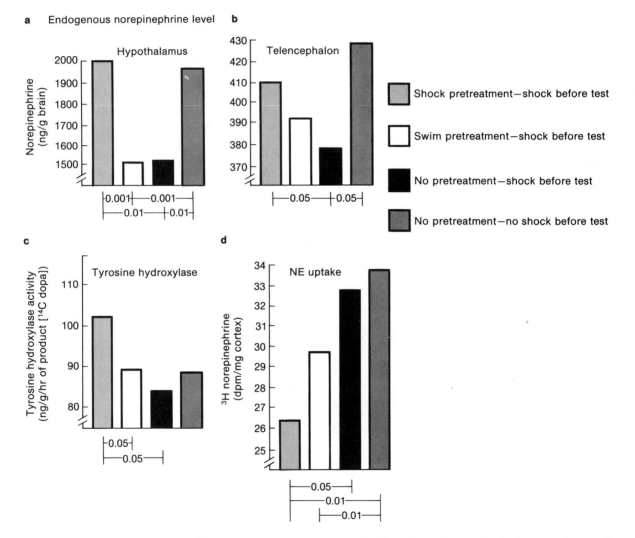

Figure 10-10   Prior exposure to stress affects current stress responses in rats. This figure shows the mean levels of norepinephrine in the hypothalamus (**a**) and telencephalon (**b**), as well as mean tyrosine hydroxylase activity (**c**) and norepinephrine uptake in the cortex (**d**) after stress. The first three groups were given a pretreatment stress before the current uncontrollable shock stress. The pretreatment was five days of either exposure to shock or immersion in cold water. The third group was given no pretreatment before the current stress, and the fourth group was a control. Prior shock exposure inhibits NE depletion (**a, b**), increases the level of the synthesizing enzyme (**c**), and decreases NE uptake (**d**), which presumably reflects an adaptive change. The numbers at the bottom are probability levels for significance of differences.

inversely related to the NE changes caused by a current stress. Prior stress decreases responses to current stressors. If these adaptive responses are exhausted by chronic stress, or genetically impaired, extensive changes in transmitter levels could lead to an emotional disorder.

However, Anisman and Sklar (1979, 1981) suggested that prior exposure to uncontrollable shock sometimes sensitizes brain NE circuits instead of causing adaptation. If this is true, subsequent exposure to even a mild stressor would substantially deplete NE.

Brown (1979) demonstrated that humans may vary in their responses to stress because they have experienced different stressors early in life. Brown found that women who had lost a parent early in life were more susceptible to depression later in life. Depression occurred *only* in a woman who encountered another severe stress later in life. In a sense, the early stress increased these women's susceptibility to later stress in a way similar to those in which genes might work.

The present environment is also important. Some reviews have concluded that experiencing stress can either precipitate, or increase the likelihood of, major emotional disorders such as schizophrenia and depression (Billings & Moos, 1984; Lloyd, 1980; Lukoff, Synder, Ventura, & Nuechterlein, 1984). The degree to which a person perceives a given stimulus as threatening, and how long the threat is perceived to last, will be affected by that individual's past experiences with similar stimuli and how much success she or he had in coping with them. The extent to which people see themselves as being able to cope with present stressors will be affected by their past experiences, and their perceived coping ability may best predict their current stress responses.

Uterine environment.   The early developmental and uterine environments are critically important. Certain events occurring during fetal development affect adaptation pathways in ways similar to genetic effects. For example, stressing a female rat during her pregnancy permanently alters the stress responses of her offspring (Peters, 1982, 1986). These offspring have a *greater* corticosterone response to stress, but their brain amine levels change *less* than do those of rats not prenatally stressed. Other researchers have found that emotional responses can be affected by prenatal stress in both rats (Joffe, 1969) and humans (Stott, 1973, 1977; Stott & Latchford, 1976).

Social factors.   Being socially isolated before stress exposure increases the degree to which stress depletes hypothalamic NE levels in rats (Anisman & Sklar, 1981). Being raised in an enriched environment, one with other members of the same species and objects with which to play, attenuates the degree of NE depletion caused by stress in comparison with the degree seen when rats are reared in social isolation in bare laboratory cages (Glavin, 1985).

Social isolation also increases human susceptibility to depression. Some women who had experienced the early death of a parent also encountered severe stress as an adult. Still, they did *not* become depressed if they had a husband or close friend to help them cope (Brown, 1979; Campbell, Cope, & Teasdale, 1983).

Stress: A Model for Depression

One major problem with Weiss's research on uncontrollable shock and subsequent inactivity as a model of depression is that both inactivity and the depletion of brain NE are *temporary*. The effects may last only for minutes, rarely as long as a day. But human depression and other behavioral deficits caused by uncontrollable shock can last much longer.

Genetic susceptibility to stress.   Certain people could become clinically depressed after stress because of some genetic defect in their transmitter synthesis and depletion pathways. Some evidence for this hypothesis exists in the literature on animals. For example, some strains of mice are much more likely than other strains to have durable response suppression (lasting five days or more) after stress. This durability may be related to differences in their NE biochemistry (Anisman, Grimmer, Irwin, Remington, & Sklar, 1979). Also, strains of rodents with the greatest adaptive, stress-induced increase in tyrosine hydroxylase have the *least* NE depletion in response to a current stressor (Stone & McCarty, 1983). Among rats, individual differences in stress-induced suppression of behavior are correlated with the amount of decrease in brain 5-HT levels caused by that stress (Petty & Sherman, 1983): the most inactive (depressed?) rats have the greatest fall in 5-HT levels.

Types of procedure and duration of effects.   Alternatively, which procedures are used in an uncontrollable shock treatment may determine how long the changes last. When sessions of shorter duration are used (one hour, as opposed to Weiss's 20 hours) and shocks at a lower level than those of Weiss are given, the behavioral changes last much *longer* than a day and are far more pervasive. These particular shock parameters cause abnormalities not only in activity levels but also in learning, perception, motivation, and emotional responses (Jackson, Alexander, & Maier, 1980; Maier & Seligman, 1976; Terman et al., 1984).

Seligman calls these more durable effects learned helplessness. This syndrome has been used as a model for human depressions (see reviews in Hoyenga & Hoyenga, 1984; Maier, 1984). Antidepressant drugs not only relieve depression but reverse the behavioral deficits caused by exposure to uncontrollable shock. Furthermore, in both human depression and learned helplessness, a single dose of an antidepressant drug has no effect; the benefit comes only after ten days of drug use (Sherman & Petty, 1980; Sherman, Sacquitne, & Petty, 1982). These drugs, as we will describe, increase NE and 5-HT release.

Sensitization and other transmitters.   Anisman and Sklar (1979, 1981) suggested that prior exposure to uncontrollable shock can sometimes sensitize brain NE circuits. Even though the NE depletions are temporary, behavioral deficits in response to a subsequent stressor could occur as long as the circuits remain "sensitized." Another possibility is that other transmitters may be responsible for the more durable effects. Petty and Sherman (1982) found that 5-HT depletions can last for at least five days after stress.

Stress: A Model for Schizophrenia

One model for schizophrenia is chronic amphetamine intake. Stress, schizophrenic diathesis, and amphetamine abuse may all induce DA overactivity.

In animals, the effects of amphetamines depend on dosage. Low doses of amphetamines cause increases in activity, and higher doses cause an initial period of hyperactivity, a subsequent period of stereotypy, and then a third period of hyperactivity (Kokkinidis & Anisman, 1980; Rebec & Bashore, 1982). Rotational behavior (turning in circles) can also be elicited by high doses (Robinson, Becker, & Presty, 1982). These behavioral responses are usually explained by amphetamine stimulation of DA release. However, the drug also stimulates NE release, which may be responsible for some of the changes in activity level (Ögren, Archer, & Johansson, 1983).

Paranoia and stereotypy.   Several parallels exist between the paranoid state induced in humans by amphetamine abuse and amphetamine-induced stereotypy in nonhumans. In humans, chronic amphetamine abuse can lead to such changes in brain biochemistry that each future abuse of the drug will trigger an emotional disorder clinically indistinguishable from paranoid schizophrenia. Animals also become more sensitive to the behavioral effects of amphetamine after prior drug exposure. Even a single prior exposure can significantly increase amphetamine-elicited circling, especially in female rats (Robinson, Becker, & Presty, 1982) (see Tables 9-8, 9-9, 9-10, and 9-11). The fact that stereotypy comes from DA activity in the striatum is consistent with the idea that schizophrenia involves DA overactivity. The NE circuits of the brain are also sensitized by chronic use of amphetamine, and paranoid schizophrenics may have high levels of NE as well as DA activity. Thus, amphetamine stereotypy has been used as an animal model for paranoid schizophrenia.

Stress and reactions to amphetamine.   Stress increases stereotypy after an amphetamine injection in rats, providing more evidence for a diathesis-stress DA model of schizophrenia. Prior exposure to a mild stressor such as tail pinch can sensitize rats to later effects of amphetamine, and vice versa (Antelman, Eichler, Black, & Kocan, 1980). Exposure to uncontrollable shocks can similarly sensitize the animal to amphetamine. In this study, prior exposure to an equal but controllable shock did *not* produce sensitization (MacLennan & Maier, 1983). Thus, uncontrollable stress increases the sensitivity of the DA system to amphetamine and also increases stereotypy and circling.

Summary of Stress Effects

Stress changes transmitter levels and biochemistry. The stress responses caused by uncontrollable shocks may be related both to depression (suppression of NE and 5-HT levels) and to schizophrenia (increase of DA activity). These pathways can adapt to repeated stress, restoring brain homeostasis. If some of the adaptational changes are inadequate (because of certain genes, chronic stress, or certain early experiences), an emotional disorder could occur.

The Biochemistry of Some Emotions

Any event that stimulates cells in the limbic system affects many transmitter substances. Some of the changes are secondary, occurring because of a change in another system. So when researchers look at the changes in brain chemistry associated with various emotional states and disorders, it is difficult to know which are primary and which secondary. And which changes are most closely related to the emotional mental events?

There is also little reason to expect that a given emotional experience or drug will cause similar changes in *all* the circuits in which that particular transmitter takes part. For example, cholinergic circuits in one part of the brain could be activated while those in another part could be inhibited by an emotional experience. A drug induces both primary and secondary changes on different types of transmitters. Drugs can also have a variety of effects on synapses using the *same* transmitter, depending, in part, on how long the drug had been given and which brain circuit is being examined.

Remembering a few general principles will help in the interpretation of this section. NE and DA usually facilitate behaviors, although the neural effect of DA is usually inhibitory and NE has mixed effects on neural activity, depending on which receptor is involved and the nature of other inputs. ACh and 5-HT usually inhibit behavioral activity, although ACh has mixed neural effects, and 5-HT usually inhibits spontaneous activity in neurons. GABA may be strictly an inhibitory transmitter. Both the DA and NE pathways affect sensory input and self-stimulation. Reducing 5-HT — as by lesioning the raphe nuclei — increases emotional reactivity. Disorders in *DA* pathways have been related to *schizophrenia*, those in *GABAergic* pathways to *anxiety*, and those in *NE/5-HT* pathways to the *affective disorders*.

Although both NE and DA activate behavior, they operate according to different principles (Chapter 4). The DA system is somewhat more systematically organized and has more discrete effects on target cells. The NE system is diffuse and may act more as a unit to affect cells throughout the brain (Moore & Bloom, 1978, 1979). Thus, NE activity could be more closely related to nonspecific arousal, and DA neurons may be more closely related to selective attention and response choice (Oades, 1985). Moreover, NE and DA neurons are mutually inhibitory (see, for example, Maj, Mogilnicka, & Kordecka, 1979).

The ventral tegmentum and the locus coeruleus may be particularly important. The DA pathway most important to emotions may be the A10 group of cells in the ventral tegmentum that project to limbic-system structures and limbic cortex. Of limbic structures, the nucleus accumbens and the **prefrontal cortex** have received the most attention. The largely noradrenergic LC projects to most of the brain; its activity increases the signal-to-noise ratio of stimulus processing (Chapter 8).

Aggression and Anger

Different kinds of aggression have different physiological as well as genetic correlates (although the two have not yet been directly related). Terminology here derives from Moyer, 1976. Intermale, predatory, and maternal aggression have al-

ready been defined. **Fear-induced aggression** is almost always preceded by an attempt to escape from some threatening situation and is always accompanied by high levels of sympathetic activity. **Irritable aggression** describes an attack that occurs before the animal has made any attempt to escape from some irritating stimulus. However, much aggression research uses shock-elicited intermale attacks, which have elements of fear-induced, intermale, and irritable aggressions. **Sex-related aggression** refers to attacks by males on females, including rape. We have added **infanticide** to Moyer's list.

Aggression and brain transmitters in lower animals. Table 10-3 summarizes some of the physiological research. Since the nature of the relationships between transmitter and aggression is often unknown, you should use that table just as a reference, a summary, or a source of hypotheses. For example, does 5-HT specifically inhibit aggression or nonspecifically inhibit all types of activity? Do DA and NE agonists facilitate aggression specifically or just all forms of active behavior? Does GABA inhibit cells in an aggression command system, or does GABA inhibit the DA neurons that facilitate aggressive actions?

The various kinds of aggression are often associated with different patterns of brain transmitter levels. Some of these patterns might be related to organizational and activational effects of androgens on brain transmitter levels. Intermale, irritable, sex-related, and infanticide types of aggression are all sensitive to androgen levels (Chapter 9 and Table 10-3). Even the aggression elicited by brain stimulation can be facilitated by activational androgens (Bermond, Mos, Meelis, van der Poel, & Kruk, 1982; Inselman-Temkin & Flynn, 1973).

Transmitters have overlapping effects on different kinds of aggression. High levels of 5-HT inhibit both predatory and intermale types of aggression (Ellison, 1977; Pucilowski & Kostowski, 1983). Several areas of the limbic system participate in aggression, but the amygdala and hypothalamus are involved in most kinds. Some overlap may come from the multiple effects of social-isolation stress, which changes brain transmitter levels (Table 10-2) and increases aggression in some strains of rodents.

Humans. Levels of serotonergic metabolites in the cerebrospinal fluid (CSF) may reflect 5-HT activity in the brain. Low CSF levels of 5-HT metabolites have been linked to high levels of aggression and impulsivity (Goodwin & Post, 1983; van Praag, 1982). Human males with the XYY chromosome pattern not only have lower than normal levels of brain 5-HT but may have higher levels of irritable or impulsive aggression

Table 10-3 Physiological substrates of different kinds of aggression.

Type	Neural Circuits Involved	Biochemistry and Endocrinology[a]
Predatory	LH, midbrain, amygdala, hippocampus	Facilitated by ACh(?) in the LH; inhibited by catecholamines in the amygdala; frog killing in rats is not affected by T; 5-HT may inhibit mouse killing in rats (Gibbons, Barr, Bridger, & Leibowitz, 1979; Pucilowski & Kostowski, 1983)
Intermale	Anterior hypothalamus	Increased by organizational and activational androgens (or the estrogen metabolites of T) (Moyer, 1976)
	Septal area	Decreased by ACTH and (in some strains) progesterone and estradiol (only in intact male mice) (Moyer, 1976)
		Decreased by ACh (Moyer, 1976)
		Higher NE levels in isolation-induced aggression in mice (Tizabi, Massari, & Jacobowitz, 1980)
		Lower GABA levels in aggressive strains of mice (Earley & Leonard, 1977, 1978)
	Whole brain	Stimulation of alpha-NE receptors increases (Charney, Menkes, & Heninger, 1981)
		Aggressive strains of mice have more tyrosine hydroxylase (Ciaranello, Barchas, Kessler, & Barchas, 1972; Ciaranello, Lipsky, & Axelrod, 1974; Tiplady, Killian, & Mandel, 1976)
	Limbic system, striatum, and diencephalon	GABA inhibits (Potegal, Perumal, Barkai, Cannova, & Blau, 1982)
	Afferent from dorsal raphe to amygdala	Fewer present in genetically aggressive strains; 5-HT inhibits (Pucilowski & Kostowski, 1983)
	Dopaminergic neurons	Isolation-induced aggressiveness is associated with an increase in DA uptake (Hadfield, 1983)
		Greater number present in genetically aggressive mouse strain, BALB/cJ (see the genetics section of this chapter for references)
		Dopamine agonists facilitate (Pucilowski & Kostowski, 1983)
Fear-induced	Hypothalamus, amygdala, hippocampus, midbrain	Inconclusive
Irritable	Anterior and medial hypothalamus, ventromedial hypothalamus, cingulus, olfactory bulbs, amygdala, septum	Facilitated by androgens; associated with a high NE/5-HT ratio (Bernard & Paolino, 1974)
Maternal	Unknown	Increased by prolactin?
Sex-related	Unknown	Any treatment that increases sexual activity increases this form of aggression
Infanticide	Olfactory bulbs, lateral septum, nucleus accumbens, medial hypothalamus, dorsal and medial raphe nuclei	Inhibited by organizational androgens and stimulated by activational androgens in mice (Svare & Broida, 1982; vom Saal, 1983); lesions in these areas also increase killing of young (Albert & Walsh, 1984)

ACh = acetylcholine
ACTH = adrenocorticotropic hormone
DA = dopamine
GABA = gamma-amino butyric acid
LH = lateral hypothalamus
NE = norepinephrine
T = testosterone
5-HT = serotonin
[a] See also references cited by Moyer, 1976.

(Bioulac, Benezech, Renaud, Noel, & Roche, 1980). Thus, 5-HT neurons may inhibit aggression in humans as well.

Platelet MAO Activity and Emotions

As Table 10-4 shows, MAO activity in blood platelets and blood serum may be altered in people with certain emotional dispositions and disorders (Buchsbaum, Coursey, & Murphy, 1980; Fowler, Tipton, MacKay, & Youdim, 1982; Table 10-4). For example, low levels of MAO are found more often in people who get high scores on a test that measures stimulus-seeking tendencies than in people who get low scores. The other traits and emotions listed in Table 10-4 may be either directly or indirectly related to either MAO levels and/or stimulus-seeking or curiosity behaviors. This does *not* mean, of course, that changes in MAO *cause* changes in emotions, only that there is a relationship. Such a relationship could be spurious or could represent only signs of the main causal events.

Platelet MAO activity and emotional traits.   Table 10-5 lists the traits that Redmond, Murphy, & Baulu (1979) found to be significantly related to platelet MAO activity in rhesus monkeys. Age had to be controlled for, since both behavior and MAO activity vary with age. Gender is also relevant. Low-MAO males are very socially active (and curious?), but low-MAO females only receive more grooming from other monkeys (largely from females).

Similar relationships have been found in humans (Buchsbaum, Coursey, & Murphy, 1980; Fowler et al., 1982; Murphy, Belmaker, Buchsbaum, Martin, Ciaranello, & Wyatt, 1977; Schooler, Zahn, Murphy, & Buchsbaum, 1978; Shekim, Hodges, Horwitz, Glaser, Davis, & Bylund, 1984; Zuckerman, 1984; Table 10-4). Low-MAO males may have more psychopathic traits than others and get into more trouble with the law. They also tend to be users of drugs, including alcohol and cigarettes. In children, both low and high MAO levels are related to impulsivity; these children react quickly, making more mistakes on a matching task than do children with moderate MAO levels.

Platelet MAO activity and emotional disorders.   The families of people with lower-than-normal levels of platelet MAO activity have significantly more suicides, suicide attempts, and alcoholism. In one study, people with low MAO were identified and followed up two years later (Coursey, Buchsbaum, & Murphy, 1982). The low-MAO subjects had more job instability, and low-MAO students had fallen behind in school. They also reported more emotional problems in their families, including depression, alcoholism, suicide attempts, use of drugs, and psychiatric hospitalization.

Surprisingly, low levels of MAO have sometimes been found in schizophrenics as well as in depressed people. However, the effect is not large and is not consistently found (Buchsbaum, Coursey, & Murphy, 1980; Fowler et al., 1982; Wyatt et al., 1981). Maybe only some schizophrenics, such as paranoids or those having hallucinations, or those with chronic rather than acute forms, have low MAO. Or the low MAO levels may simply be caused by the antipsychotic drugs given to most of the investigated schizophrenics (Maj, Ariano, Pirozzi, Salvati, & Kemali, 1984). Also, MAO levels are more variable in bipolar than in unipolar patients or in healthy controls (Edwards, Spiker, Kupfer, Foster, Neil, & Abrams, 1978). One study found that *all* the relatives of bipolar patients that had both low platelet MAO activity *and* an abnormal Na^+-Na^+ transport across cell membranes had some kind of emotional problem (Dorus, Pandey, Shaughnessy, & Davis, 1979).

One interesting idea is that different subgroups of people with emotional problems can be created on the basis of platelet MAO activity and on evoked-potential recordings (Haier, Buchsbaum, Murphy, Gottesman, & Coursey, 1980). Overall, those with schizophrenia tend to have augmenting cortical evoked potentials, regardless of MAO levels. But affective disorders seem to be most likely to occur in the augmenters who have low MAO (66%) and in the reducers who have high MAO (77%). The other two groups are much less likely to have an affective disorder (36% and 40%).

Anxiety

Some physiological correlates of anxiety appear in Table 10-4. Most of the research exploring the neural basis of anxiety has concentrated on antianxiety drugs or on the LC. Drugs that alleviate anxiety bind to a specific part of brain GABA receptors, suggesting that there may be some kind of endogenous antianxiety substance produced in the brain that normally binds to that receptor. Activity in the noradrenergic LC may be part of an anxiety code.

Benzodiazepines, anxiety, and GABA receptors.   The **benzodiazepine** types of antianxiety drugs (for example, Valium®) have largely replaced other types (Tallman et al., 1980). Although benzodiazepines produce less physical addiction than do the earlier drugs, they still can cause psychological dependence and physical withdrawal symptoms. The benzodiazepines, which include diazepam, reduce behavioral and sympathetic signs of fear in lower animals as well as in humans.

Table 10-4 Biological traits and behaviors associated with a sensation-seeking trait.

Biological Correlates	Human Behaviors Associated with the Biological Correlates in Column 1	Associated Behaviors in Nonhumans	Species
Psychophysiological			
+ Orienting reflex	+ Attention − Anxiety	+ Rearing, interrupting of ongoing behavior	Rodents
− Startle reflex	+ High arousal in chronic anxiety	− Serotonin levels	Rats
+ Augmenting of evoked potential	+ Manic-depressive disorder + Drug use + Delinquency	+ Explorativeness + Activity + Aggressiveness + Emotional reactivity to novel stimuli	Cats
Biochemical			
+ Testosterone	+ Sexual arousability (both sexes) + Sociability + Dominance + Activity	+ Sexual arousal + Aggressiveness + Dominance	Male rats Varied
Bioamines and neuroregulators			
− MAO (platelets and plasma)	− Manic-depressive disorder − Sociability − Criminal behavior	− Sociability − Agonistic behaviors (sexual and aggressive) − Play behavior − Dominance	Monkeys
− DBH (plasma and serum) (Serum)	− The trait of anxiety + A state of anxiety − Augmenting of EP[a]		
− NE (CSF) (+0) MHPG (urinary) (NE metabolite)	+ Bipolar (manic state) − Bipolar (depressive state)	*NE (brain)* + Activity + Arousability + Activity + Explorativeness + Fear (high levels) + Sexual behavior + Appetite (+0) Intracranial self-stimulation *Brain serotonin*	Rats Rats, monkeys Rats
0 5-HIAA(CSF) (Serotonin metabolite)	− Suicidal disposition − Aggressive behavior − Augmenting of EP[a]	+ Behavioral inhibition in novel environments − Startle, OR − Behavioral reactivity to novel cues − Consummatory behaviors − Sexual behavior	Rats

Table 10-4 *(continued)*

Biological Correlates	Human Behaviors Associated with the Biological Correlates in Column 1	Associated Behaviors in Nonhumans	Species
	Low-moderate levels of release of brain dopamine related to:		
0 HVA (CSF)	+ Euphoria	+ Activity (low-intermediate levels)	Rats
(Dopamine metabolite)	+ Sociability	− Activity (high levels)	
	High or chronic levels of release related to:	+ Sexual behavior ♂	
	+ Anxiety	− Sexual behavior ♀	
	− Euphoria	+ Intracranial self-stimulation	Rats
	− Sociability		
	− Augmenting of EP[a]		
(−0)endorphins (CSF)	− Augmenting of EP[a]		

MAO = monoamine oxidase   5-HIAA = 5-hydroxyindolacetic acid
NE = norepinephrine   OR = orienting response
DBH = dopamine beta hydroxylase   CSF = cerebrospinal fluid
MHPG = 3-methoxy-4-hyphoxyphenylglycol   ♂ = males
HVA = homovanillic acid   ♀ = females

NOTE: −, +, 0 in column 1 signify negative, positive, and no (zero) correlation with sensation seeking; (+0) signifies mixed results. −, +, 0 in columns 2 and 3 signify negative, positive, and no (zero) correlation with corresponding biological trait in column 1.
[a] The evoked potential gets steadily larger as stimulus intensity is increased.

All benzodiazepines so far tested facilitate GABA receptor activity. This may be the way the drugs relieve anxiety. Only 20% to 30% of all the brain benzodiazepine receptors need to be occupied for the drug to have its antianxiety effect (Paul & Skolnick, 1982; Tallman et al., 1980). Alcohol too has antianxiety effects and probably has been used for that purpose since the dawn of humankind. Alcohol also potentiates the inhibitory effects of GABA on cortical neurons (Nestoros, 1980).

The GABA-receptor complex is genetically controlled and consists of the benzodiazepine receptor, a GABA receptor, and a Cl⁻ ionophore (Gavish & Snyder, 1981; Paul & Skolnick, 1982). Either the frequency or duration of Cl⁻ channel openings caused by GABA is increased if the benzodiazepine receptor is occupied by an antianxiety drug (Study & Barker, 1981). Rats of the Maudsley reactive strain (anxious?) have fewer benzodiazepine receptors in their hippocampus, hypothalamus, midbrain, and medulla/pons than do nonreactive strain rats (Robertson, Martin, & Candy, 1978).

Since benzodiazepine receptors were found, researchers have searched for **endogenous ligands,** substances found in the brain that normally bind to those receptors. Rats exposed to an anxiety-arousing situation have a decreased level of benzodiazepine binding to brain receptors, which may mean that some endogenous ligand was occupying those receptors (Lippa, Klepner, Yunger, Sano, Smith, & Beer, 1978; Table 10-2). The search may recently have succeeded (Sangameswaran & De Blas, 1985; Stephenson, 1986).

Table 10-5 Partial correlations between platelet MAO activity and behavior in rhesus monkeys, controlling for the effects of age on MAO activity.

Behavior	Males	Females
Playing	−0.71[a]	0.26
Receiving grooming	−0.21	−0.41[a]
Self-grooming	0.69[a]	0.33
Acting dominant-aggressive	−0.55[a]	−0.14
Having social contact	−0.54[a]	−0.18
Spending time alone	0.59[a]	0.45[a]

[a] Effects are statistically significant.

As might be expected, the story of anxiety is not that simple. The benzodiazepines may have other effects on neural membranes. For example, Carlen, Gurevich, and Polc (1983) found that one benzodiazepine caused hyperpolarization by increasing the Ca-activated K^+ channel in guinea pig hippocampus neurons. And a new antianxiety drug, **buspirone** (chemically unrelated to the benzodiazepines), relieves anxiety but does *not* bind to benzodiazepine receptors (Goldberg & Finnerty, 1979; Riblet, Allen, Hyslop, Taylor, & Wilderman, 1980). We will shortly discuss a possible explanation for this.

LC, NE, and anxiety.   Redmond and Huang (1979) proposed that an increase in LC activity causes anxiety. Low-intensity stimulation of that area produces behaviors in monkeys that resemble the behavioral effects of anxiety in humans. Beta-blockers (which block beta-adrenergic receptors) decrease anxiety in humans and also decrease the behavioral effects of LC stimulation in monkeys. Monkeys with bilateral LC lesions do not look anxious even in threatening situations. A drug called **yohimbine** increases LC activity by blocking alpha-adrenergic presynaptic receptors (Costa, Guidotti, & Toffano, 1978; Paul & Skolnick, 1982; Tallman et al., 1980). Yohimbine also increases anxiety in human volunteers. A drug called **clonidine** not only prevents the anxiety-inducing effect of yohimbine but also stimulates some alpha-adrenergic presynaptic receptors (Charney, Heninger, & Redmond, 1983). (See also Table 10-4.) Some data inconsistent with this hypothesis come from single-unit recording studies that are described in the next section.

DA and anxiety.   DA may be related to anxiety states (Taylor, Riblet, Stanton, Eison, Eison, & Temple, 1982; Table 10-4). The benzodiazepines may facilitate the GABA neurons that inhibit DA systems. (Note: The authors of the study said "activate" DA systems, but that language is inconsistent with GABA's usual effects, as well as with the research cited below.) Figure 10-11 describes the multiple effects that DA agonists can have, depending on which DA receptors, innervated by which group of neurons (A10 and others), are most affected. Maybe buspirone acts on one of these other pathways.

The A10 group is important to this model. The stress-induced activity of the A10 group projecting to the frontal cortex is specifically blocked by benzodiazepines (Fadda, Argiolas, Melis, Tissari, Onali, & Gessa, 1978; Lavielle et al., 1978). That is, the effect is specific with respect to both that group of cells and that class of drugs. Other DA neurons and other types of drugs are not involved in that blocking action.

Schizophrenia

Until recently, the **dopamine hypothesis** of schizophrenia dominated research, theorizing, and treatment (Berger, 1981; Haracz, 1982). According to this hypothesis, schizophrenics have a functional overactivity in a DA brain system, either because of increased DA release or because of having an abnormally large number of DA receptors. Also remember that stress increases DA activity.

Early researchers thought the problem might be found in the nigrostriatal synapses, but later researchers focused on the connections made by the ventral tegmental DA neurons (A10) with limbic-system structures and the limbic cortex. Despite the strong evidence in favor of such a hypothesis — which will be summarized below — researchers and theorists now seem to be favoring the idea that schizophrenia represents several different disorders, each with a different genetic basis, etiology, and prognosis. Transmitters other than DA are altered in schizophrenia, though we do not know yet whether any of the changes are causal or secondary.

One classification system.   The system for classifying schizophrenic symptoms described in Table 10-6 is based on one originally suggested by Crow (1980), expanded by Seidman (1983) and Haracz (1982), and recently revised by Crow (1985). Paranoid schizophrenics (people with delusional systems) may represent another functional class. This classification is highly speculative, but it usefully organizes the discussion. One major problem concerns its relationship to genetic diathesis. Although belonging to separate categories would imply the involvement of somewhat different genes, so far most research has found that all types occur in the same families (Gottesman & Shields, 1976). However, an absence of negative symptoms may be associated with a positive family history (Owens et al., 1985).

The positive and negative symptoms are hypothesized to come from different kinds of dysfunction. The negative symptoms may appear when there is extensive, though usually diffuse, damage to the brain. This is often assessed by measuring sizes of ventricles in living brains through special X-ray techniques; some schizophrenics with marked cognitive impairments have either abnormally small or abnormally large ventricles (Owens et al., 1985). The positive symptoms may be caused by overactivity in limbic-system DA neurons, although one kind of generalized brain dysfunction may accompany the positive symptoms: some schizophrenics may have unusual brain lateralization of functions, as Flor-Henry (1979) has proposed.

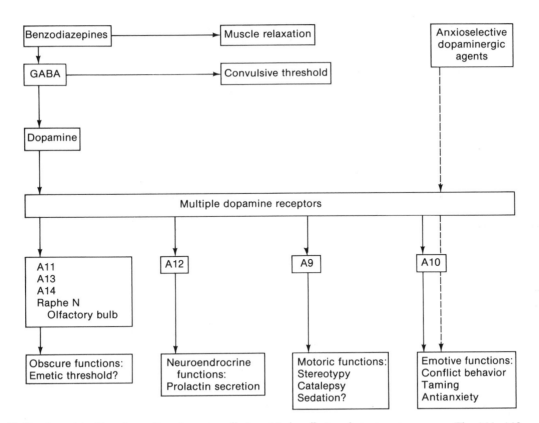

Figure 10-11 A model of how benzodiazepines may affect anxiety by affecting dopaminergic neurons. The A11, A13, and A14 dopaminergic cells are located in the hypothalamus. The A12 group is part of the hypthalamus-pituitary pathway. The A9 cells belong to the nigrostriatal pathway. The A10 cells are most relevant to anxiety, and they terminate in limbic and cortical areas (for example, nucleus accumbens, olfactory tubercle, septum, amygdala, cingulate cortex, entorhinal cortex, and frontal cortex). Emetic = vomiting; anxiolysis = decreasing anxiety.

Positive symptoms and the A10 group of dopaminergic neurons. The positive symptoms of schizophrenics might come from overactivity in the A10 group of neurons whose synapses have the D-2 receptor types. Three lines of evidence can be cited in support of this hypothesis. First, only some schizophrenics respond to the antischizophrenic drugs, or **neuroleptics.** The clinical effectiveness of a neuroleptic is highly correlated with its ability to block DA receptors (Creese, Burt, & Snyder, 1976; Seeman & Lee, 1975). But these drugs work primarily on the positive symptoms. If negative symptoms exist in the same patient, they are largely unaffected by the drug. The positive symptoms are made much worse by giving these patients DA agonists such as amphetamines. Second, the relationship between plasma prolactin levels and psychosis scores (Table 10-6) is consistent with DA overactivity. Prolactin release is controlled by DA: DA inhibits cells that release a prolactin inhibitory factor.

Third, some evidence for DA overactivity was found when the brains of schizophrenics were analyzed at autopsy. The most exciting finding was a greater-than-normal number of DA D-2 receptors. Although some researchers found this receptor increase in schizophrenics who had not been given drugs, other researchers suggested that the effect was an artifact, caused by long-term neuroleptic use (Haracz, 1982; Kato & Ban, 1982; Mackay et al., 1982). However, another group of researchers measured D-2 receptors in living human beings and found that schizophrenics — both *with* and *without* any history of drug use — have more of these receptors in their caudate nuclei than do normal volunteers (Wong, Wagner, Tune, Dannals, Pearlson, Links, Tamminga, Broussolle, Ravert, Wilson, Toung, Malat, Williams, O'Tuama, Snyder, Kuhar, & Gjedde, 1986).

As Table 10-7 describes, long-term neuroleptic use changes brain receptors. Most of these changes are probably

Table 10-6 Psychobiology of types of schizophrenia and symptoms.

A. *Positive Symptoms* (reactive: episodic, acute, affective changes)
  1. Good premorbid adjustment with episodes of disordered thinking, excitement, overactivity, mood lability, and hallucinations — and sometimes delusions.
  2. Limbic, midbrain, and upper brain stem dysfunction.
  3. Excessive subcortical arousal: symptoms result from the attempt of the cortex to deal with that arousal.
  4. Lateralization changes occur (greater dysfunction in left than in right hemisphere).
  5. Excess dopaminergic activity in caudate and in nucleus accumbens (Mackay, Iversen, Rosser, Spokes, Bird, Arregui, Creese, & Snyder, 1982).
  6. The nucleus accumbens "filter" is disordered? (Stevens, 1973)
  7. Decreased platelet MAO activity.
  8. Plasma prolactin levels correlated with psychosis scores (reflecting dopaminergic overactivity?).
  9. Psychosis is made worse by dopaminergic agonists.
  10. More of a peptide (a potential transmitter) in the amygdala, which receives a "substantial" dopaminergic innervation (Roberts, Ferrier, Lee, Crow, Johnstone, Owens, Bacarese-Hamilton, McGregor, O'Shaughnessey, Polak, & Bloom, 1983).
  11. Reduction of the number of afferent axons to the substantia nigra and shrinkage of cells in the A10 group (Bogerts, Häntsch, & Herzer, 1983).
B. *Negative Symptoms* (process: chronic, nuclear)
  1. Poor premorbid adjustment and cognitive dysfunctions, social maladjustments, blunted affect.
  2. Frontal lobe pathology and reduced neural activity (Ingvar, 1982).
  3. Widespread, diffuse damage to the brain.
  4. Enlarged ventricles.
  5. Poorer reactions to neuroleptics (dopamine receptor blockers), poorer prognosis (Wyatt et al., 1981).
  6. Psychosis may be relieved by dopamine agonists.
  7. Low cerebrospinal levels of dopamine metabolites (van Kammen, Mann, Sternberg, Scheinin, Ninan, Marder, van Kammen, Rieder, & Linnoila, 1983).
  8. Impairment of eye tracking performance is found both in them and in their nonpsychotic relatives (gene effects?) (Iacono, 1983).
  9. Childhood neurological symptoms (Fish, 1977).
  10. Reductions of brain peptides in areas *not* innervated densely by dopaminergic afferents (Roberts et al., 1983).
C. *Paranoid Symptoms*
  1. Little evidence of brain damage.
  2. Decreased platelet MAO activity(?) (Kendler & Davis, 1981; Wyatt et al., 1981).
  3. Higher norepinephrine levels in limbic forebrain (including the septum and the nucleus accumbens) (Kendler & Davis, 1981; Wyatt et al., 1981).

NOTE: Positive symptoms may be followed by the development of negative symptoms, and both can be present in the same person. However, negative symptoms can occur in the absence of positive symptoms.

up and down regulation caused by drug-elicited decreases or increases in synaptic activity. Both the sensitivity and the number of DA receptors increase with neuroleptic drug use (Rupniak, Jenner, & Marsden, 1983; Wyatt et al., 1981). If the positive symptoms of schizophrenia are associated with DA overactivity, and if neuroleptic use were suddenly discontinued, the increased sensitivity of DA receptors should promptly cause a psychosis — which has happened (Chouinard & Jones, 1980; Witschy, Malone, & Holden, 1984).

Some DA abnormalities are *not* caused by neuroleptics. Even among long-term drug-treated schizophrenics, there are two groups of DA receptor abnormalities (Seeman, Ulpian, Bergeron, Riederer, Jellinger, Gabriel, Reynolds, & Tourtel-

Table 10-7 Effect of long-term neuroleptic treatment on transmitter receptors.

Transmitter	Receptor Type	Location	Effect
Dopamine	D_2	Striatum	Increase
		Mesolimbic	Increase
	D_1	Striatum	Unknown
		Mesolimbic	Unknown
Serotonin	2	Frontal cortex	No change
Histamine	H_1	Striatum	Increase
	H_2	Cortex	No change
Norepinephrine	Alpha	Cortex	No change
GABA		Striatum	Increase

lotte, 1984). The brains of one group may have only 25% more D-2 receptors than control brains, whereas another group has 2.3 *times* as many receptors. This difference between the groups presumably cannot be attributed to neuroleptic use. Schizophrenics' brains also have greater-than-normal amounts of DA in the caudate and nucleus accumbens, which cannot be attributed to drug use (Mackay et al., 1982).

One basic problem with the DA hypothesis of positive symptoms remains. The neuroleptics immediately block DA receptors, but changes in symptoms start gradually and are not complete for 10 to 20 days or more. Also, as Table 10-7 shows, DA receptors in most parts of the brain adapt to the neuroleptics, and yet the ability of neuroleptics to relieve the positive symptoms does not adapt. (The adaptation may explain why many people after long-term neuroleptic use develop movement disorders — tardive dyskinesia — which may be caused by DA hyperactivity. This side effect is particularly common in females, perhaps because of estrogenic effects on striatal DA activity: Tables 9-10 and 9-11).

The problem of adaptation focused attention on the DA innervation of the frontal cortex. These DA neurons show much less adaptation. A subgroup of these A10 neurons, one with a high spontaneous firing rate, does not have autoreceptors (Shepard & German, 1984; White & Wang, 1984). Autoreceptors are also increased by neuroleptic use; activating these receptors *decreases* neural activity. The lack of autoreceptors may explain why some of the A10 cells do not adapt and also suggests that defects in *these* cells could be important to schizophrenia.

A10 cells have other unusual properties. The A10 group is separately controlled by a specific set of genes (Roffler-Tarlov & Graybiel, 1984). Only A10 cells are suppressed by social isolation, and only these cells show the isolation-enhanced stress DA activity (Blanc et al., 1980). Destroying the A10 group of cells produces problems in attention, decreases in affective responses and social interactions, and cognitive deficits (Bannon, Reinhard, Bunney, & Roth, 1982; Brozoski, Brown, Rosvold, & Goldman, 1979; Simon, Scatton, & Le Moal, 1980). Defects in the A10 cells could explain both positive and negative symptoms: positive by overactivity and negative by damage.

Negative symptoms.   The schizophrenics with enlarged ventricles — reflecting diffuse brain damage (Table 10-1) — are seldom helped by neuroleptics. The low CSF levels of the DA metabolite, homovanillic acid, also imply a diffuse loss of brain cells, including DA cells. When brain activity is examined, as by using 2-DG to measure metabolic rate, schizophrenics with negative symptoms have much less activity in their frontal lobes than do normal people or people with affec-

tive disorders. In fact, Sulkowski (1983) pointed out several parallels between the negative symptoms of schizophrenia and the symptoms displayed by people who have had traumatic or surgical damage to their frontal lobes (such as by frontal lobotomy).

What causes the diffuse brain damage? Since these symptoms may have some genetic basis, genes may confer some vulnerability to brain damage. The damage may even, in some people at least, be caused by a virus (Torrey, Yolken, & Winfrey, 1982).

Stimulus processing in schizophrenics.   Stevens (1973) suggested that abnormal DA input to the nucleus accumbens might distort perceptions of the sensory world. That nucleus acts like a "filter" or "gate" between emotional types of sensory input, plus memory input from the hippocampus, and the output of the nucleus accumbens to other limbic regions. DA modulates the activity of the filter; abnormal DA levels, receptors, or responses could "derange" the filter, producing abnormal responses to stimuli and to memories.

Disordered stimulus processing may be the first stage of the disorder. The rest of the symptoms may come from the person's attempt to cope with that initial problem (Chapman, 1966). Schizophrenics do have disordered stimulus processing (Iacono, 1983; Venables, 1981). For example, schizophrenics show little evidence of sensory adaptation (Freedman, Adler, Waldo, Pachtman, & Franks, 1983). Also, as we pointed out before, the number of dopaminergic neurons is directly related to curiosity in mice, and schizophrenia is inversely related to stimulus-seeking tendencies in humans. Given that someone suffers from strange sensations (hallucinations), then either withdrawal (negative symptoms) or bizarre explanations for those sensations (delusions) might be a sensible way of coping. When emotionally normal people are made deaf by hypnosis — so they don't know why they can't hear — they become paranoid (Zimbardo, Andersen, & Kabat, 1981).

Affective Disorders

According to the **biogenic amine hypotheses,** abnormalities in either NE or 5-HT or both would cause effective disorders (Garver & Davis, 1979). These hypotheses would fit the diathesis-stress model because stress decreases both NE and 5-HT levels. However, research does not consistently support any current version of any biogenic amine hypothesis.

Depression was first related to underactivity of NE neurons and then to underactivity of 5-HT neurons. The manic phase of bipolar disorder was said to be caused by NE overactivity. Attention has recently shifted to receptors; some types of NE receptor may be oversensitive and others undersensitive in depressed people (Leonard, 1982). Or low 5-HT might predispose the person to bipolar disorder, and fluctuations of NE would produce the cyclical mood changes (Prange, Wilson, Lynn, Alltop, & Stikeleather, 1974). Defects in 5-HT neurons might also be specifically related to suicides. People with low 5-HT may be a specific subgroup of depressives particularly likely to commit suicide (Åsberg, Thorén, Träskman, Bertilsson, & Ringberger, 1976; Goodwin & Post, 1983; van Praag, 1982).

Biogenic amine levels.   The CSF and brain levels (measured at autopsy) of NE and 5-HT and their metabolites in depressed people have not always supported the biogenic amine hypotheses (Lingjaerde, 1983). For example, a recent large study on CSF transmitter metabolites looked at 151 people with affective disorders (Koslow, Maas, Bowden, Davis, Hanin, & Javaid, 1983). CSF levels of an NE metabolite were increased!

Some subtypes of depression may involve disorders in one or more of the biogenic amine systems. For example, Garver and Davis (1979) hypothesized two types of depression, one with low NE levels in brain and CSF and the other with low levels of 5-HT. Figures 10-12 and 10-13 present some supportive results (Sedvall, Fyrö, Gullberg, Nybäck, Wiesel, & Wode-Helgodt, 1980). People with a family history of emotional disorders had more variable levels of CSF metabolites (5-HIAA is a metabolite of 5-HT, and HVA, or homovanillic acid, is a metabolite of DA). In particular, some (but not all) of the people with a family history of depression had low 5-HIAA and low HVA levels (some of those with a family history of schizophrenia had high levels of those metabolites). Also, learned helplessness, an animal model of depression, seems to be most closely related to a decrease in the number of 5-HT cortical presynaptic autoreceptors (Sherman & Petty, 1984).

Long-term effects of antidepressants and the treatment of depression.   Most of the drugs first used to treat depression increased synaptic NE levels (Garver & Davis, 1979; Lingjaerde, 1983). This effect was produced either by inhibiting brain MAO activity (using the **MAO inhibitors**) or by blocking the reuptake of NE and 5-HT back into the presynaptic ending (using the **tricyclics**). However, these effects were immediate, whereas the relief of depression took from 10 to 14 days to occur. Also, some "atypical" antidepressants were clinically effective but did not block reuptake of either transmitter. Furthermore, long-term treatment with these drugs produces a variety of changes in transmitter metabolism and receptors throughout the brain, many of which probably represent adaptive rather than therapeutic changes.

Effects of chronic treatment with tricyclics, MAO inhibi-

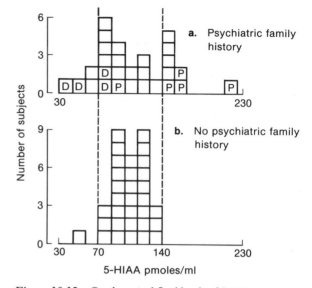

Figure 10-12   Cerebrospinal fluid levels of S-HIAA (a serotonin metabolite, and an indirect measure of brain serotonin levels) in two groups of subjects. Both high and low levels may be associated with an increased diathesis. Low levels may be associated specifically with depression. P = healthy subjects with family members who have been treated specifically for psychotic schizophrenia; D = healthy subjects with relatives who have been treated specifically for depression; empty boxes = healthy subjects either with family histories of problems other than depression or schizophrenia (**a**) or with no family history of any kind of psychiatric disorder; (**b**) pmoles = picomoles.

tors, and the "atypical" drugs are presented in Table 10-8 (number of receptors) and Table 10-9 (receptor sensitivity, measured by neural activity). The variability in results may come, at least in part, from using different treatment and test parameters: the effects of chronic drug use depend on both the time between drug injections and the time between the last injection and the test (Post, 1980).

There are consistencies as well as inconsistencies. For example, the efficacy of the NE adenylate cyclase receptor is increased by four different antidepressants and is changed in the same way by therapeutic electroconvulsive shock treatments (Menkes, Rasenick, Wheeler, & Bitensky, 1983). The presynaptic NE alpha$_2$ receptor also fairly consistently becomes desensitized (Charney, Heninger, & Sternberg, 1983; marked with a ‡ in Table 10-8). Although the activity of 5-HT is often increased by drug therapy and so may be suppressed in depression (Blier & de Montigny, 1983; de Montigny, 1984; de Montigny & Aghajanian, 1978), some drugs that are clinically effective do *not* affect 5-HT receptors (Anderson, 1983).

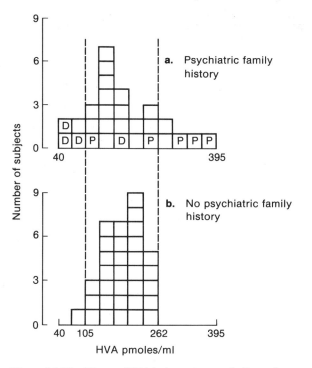

Figure 10-13 The way HVA (a dopamine metabolite, and an indirect measure of brain dopamine levels) measured in the cerebrospinal fluid is distributed in healthy subjects may be related to the family's history of emotional problems. Low HVA levels may be associated with depression and high levels with schizophrenia. P = subjects with family members who have been treated specifically for psychotic schizophrenia; D = subjects with relatives who have been treated specifically for depression; shaded boxes = same as in Figure 10-12; pmoles = picomoles.

Because of the way antidepressants affect receptors, other theorists reversed the biogenic amine hypotheses. For example, depressed people may have *too many* beta-adrenergic receptors. If so, the decrease in beta receptors caused by the antidepressant drugs would be the therapeutic effect (perhaps caused indirectly through serotonergic neurons) (Charney, Heninger, & Sternberg, 1983; Janowsky, Okada, Manier, Applegate, Sulser, & Steranka, 1982; Kato & Ban, 1982). Adaptation to stress also decreases the same receptors, implying that depressed people have faulty adaptation systems. But not all clinically effective antidepressants have this beta-adrenergic effect (Sethy & Harris, 1982).

There are other possibilities. Stone (1983) suggested that the output of neurons controlled by beta-adrenergic receptors in depression-prone people is too low to meet the demands of stress. Both past experience with stress (which protects against

current stress in this model) and effective antidepressant treatment cause a prolonged increase in postsynaptic beta-adrenergic receptors, an increase that Stone says causes a trophic or growth response in those neurons. The growth increases their total output (for instance, the number of other neurons controlled by a particular neuron) and the efficacy of output (amount of response to a given amount of NE). The decline in beta-receptors reflects this increased efficiency.

However, any NE effect could be secondary to a serotonergic effect. Table 10-10 documents some of the evidence in favor of an abnormally low level of serotonergic neurons in depression. Because of the interaction of 5-HT and NE neurons, beta-adrenergic receptors would be increased by depression, and antidepressants would normalize those receptors. Depressed people do have fewer imipramine binding sites, suggesting that they may have fewer serotonergic neurons. And since there are specific imipramine binding sites in various parts of the limbic system, there may be some type of endogenously produced substance with antidepressant effects (analogous to what was found after the discovery of brain opiate receptors).

Of course, there is always a possibility that all these changes and correlations are only signs of emotional disorder and are not causally related to any symptoms. Still, we will eventually have to explain why changes in NE and 5-HT activity are so commonly found in people with affective disorders.

Bipolar disorder and mania. Less effort has gone into exploring the biochemistry of these disorders because a very good treatment already exists: lithium. But the treatment has so many effects, it is difficult to determine which are relevant. Lithium may affect every transmitter system in the brain. For example, lithium affects GABA, ACh, NE-induced inhibitory responses, and intracellular Ca^{++} levels. Any of these could be relevant to manic states (Berrettini, Nurnberger, Hare, Simmons-Alling, Gershon, & Post, 1983; Dubovsky & Franks, 1983; Schultz, Siggins, Schocker, Türck, & Bloom, 1981; Tollefson & Senogles, 1982).

Manic-depressive illnesses may involve an abnormal Na^+-Na^+ transport mechanism across the cell membrane. The transport mechanism is abnormal regardless of the patient's mood, suggesting that it could be part of the cause (Dorus, Pandey, Shaughnessy, Gaviria, Val, Ericksen, & Davis, 1979; Ostrow, Halaris, DeMet, Gibbons, & Davis, 1982).

Another possibility involves fluctuating NE levels. NE levels fluctuate with manic and depressive mood states and return to normal when the mood returns to normal (Koslow et al., 1983; Ostrow et al., 1982). In addition, yohimbine, which blocks alpha₂ adrenergic receptors, can trigger manic symptoms (Price, Charney, & Heninger, 1984). Since these recep-

Table 10-8 Receptor binding changes (number of receptors?) after long-term antidepressant treatment.

Antidepressant Category	Brain Region	Drugs	Receptors Labeled†					
			$NE(\alpha)$	$NE(\beta)$	$5\text{-}HT_1$	$5\text{-}HT_2$	ACh	DA
Tricyclic drugs	Cerebellum	Imipramine	···	0	···	···	···	···
		Amitriptyline	0	···	···	···	0	···
		Desipramine	···	↓	···	···	···	···
	Cerebral cortex	Imipramine	0↓‡	↓	↓	↓	0	···
		Clomipramine	···	↓	0	0	···	···
		Amitriptyline	0	↓	0	↓	0	···
		Doxepin	···	↓	···	···	···	···
		Desipramine	0	↓	0↓	0↓	0	···
		Nortriptyline	···	↓	···	···	···	···
	Hippocampus	Imipramine	···	↓	↓	···	···	···
		Amitriptyline	↑↓‡	···	···	···	↑	···
		Desipramine	···	0↓	0	···	···	···
	Striatum	Imipramine	↓	↓	↓	···	0	0
		Amitriptyline	↓‡	···	···	···	···	0
		Desipramine	···	0	0	···	0	0
	Whole brain	Imipramine	0	↓	↓§	···	···	···
		Amitriptyline	↑	···	↓§	···	↑	0
		Desipramine	···	↓	↓§	···	···	···
		Doxepin	···	↓	···	···	···	···
	Limbic forebrain	Desipramine	↑‡	···	···	···	···	···
	Amygdala	Amitriptyline	↓‡	···	···	···	···	···
	Locus coeruleus	Amitriptyline	↓‡	···	···	···	···	···
	Hypothalamus	Amitriptyline	↓‡	···	···	···	···	···
"Atypical" drugs	Cerebral cortex	Mianserin	···	0	···	···	···	···
		Iprindole	0↑‡	↓	0	↓	0	···
		Zimelidine	···	···	0↑‖	···	···	···
		Trazodone	···	↓	···	···	···	···
		Bupropion	···	↓	···	···	···	···
	Hypothalamus	Zimelidine	···	···	↓↑‖	···	···	···
	Striatum	Iprindole	···	···	···	···	···	0

Table 10-8 (continued)

Antidepressant Category	Brain Region	Drugs	Receptors Labeled†					
			NE(α)	NE(β)	5-HT₁	5-HT₂	ACh	DA
	Whole brain	Iprindole	· · ·	↓	· · ·	· · ·	· · ·	· · ·
MAOIs	Cerebral cortex	Phenelzine	· · ·	↓	· · ·	· · ·	· · ·	· · ·
		Tranylcypromine	· · ·	↓	· · ·	↓	· · ·	· · ·
		Clorgyline	0↓‡	↓	↓	· · ·	· · ·	· · ·
		Pargyline	0	0↓	↓	↓	0	· · ·
		Deprenaline	· · ·	· · ·	0	· · ·	· · ·	· · ·
		Nialamide	· · ·	↓	↓	· · ·	· · ·	· · ·
	Striatum	Pargyline	· · ·	· · ·	· · ·	· · ·	· · ·	0
ECT	Cerebral cortex	· · ·	0	↓	0	↑	· · ·	· · ·
	Striatum	· · ·	· · ·	· · ·	· · ·	· · ·	· · ·	0

MAOI indicates monoamine oxidase inhibitor, ECT, electroconvulsive therapy. Unless indicated otherwise, at least 15 hours was allowed between final administration and euthanasia of the animals.

† NE indicates norepinephrine receptor site; 5-HT₁ and 5-HT₂, serotonin receptor sites labeled with tritiated serotonin and tritiated spiperone, respectively; ACh, acetylcholine; and DA, dopamine.

‡ The change in binding was seen when α_2 receptors were labeled with tritiated clonidine.

§ The measurements were made 30 to 180 minutes after the last injection.

‖ Long-term zimelidine administration caused an induction of low-affinity sites for tritiated serotonin in cortex and hypothalamus while reducing affinity sites in hypothalamus only.

tors *inhibit* NE release, yohimbine increases NE release. (However, some of these changes in NE activity could come from mood-induced changes in activity levels instead of *causing* the changes in mood levels.)

Summary of the Biochemistry of Emotions

The possibilities for future research and breakthroughs are tremendous. Behaviors associated with anxiety, aggression, and anger are also associated with particular patterns of transmitter activity. GABAergic synapses — either directly or indirectly because of their effect on DA or NE activity — may be related to anxiety. 5-HT activity inhibits several forms of aggression, and NE and DA activity increase several forms. But whether the effects are specific or nonspecific is still uncertain.

MAO activity in platelets may reflect transmitter levels and mood states. Low MAO activity has been related to antisocial behavior and drug use in humans. Some forms of schizophrenia and affective disorder may be exaggerated — or the diath-

eses increased — in low-MAO individuals. The platelet MAO activity could also be secondary to emotional stress experiences (stress decreases MAO levels) instead of causing emotional changes.

The major disorders of mood could involve changes in transmitter activity. The positive symptoms of schizophrenia may reflect DA overactivity, perhaps in the A10 group of neurons projecting to the frontal cortex. This overactivity could be caused by a combination of stress and having certain genes specific to the A10 group. The negative symptoms may come from diffuse brain damage, perhaps including the A10 projection. Some types of affective disorder may be related to low NE activity, particularly of the alpha₂ autoreceptor. Another type may have defective beta-receptor adaptations to stress, and a third may have low 5-HT, especially in suicide-prone people and manic depressives.

Changes in phenomenological experiences of mood, as indirectly measured by self-reports and by clinical diagnoses, are associated with changes in transmitter substances. The next section looks at the neural activity itself.

Table 10-9 Changes in sensitivity of receptors after long-term antidepressant treatment.

Antidepressant Category	Brain Region	Drugs	NE (Subtype)	5-HT	ACh	GABA	DA	Glutamate
Tricylic and "atypical" drugs	Hippocampus	Imipramine	$0(\beta)$	↑	0	0	· · ·	· · ·
		Clomipramine	0	↑	0	0	· · ·	· · ·
		Amitriptyline	0	↑	· · ·	0	· · ·	· · ·
		Desipramine	0	↑	· · ·	0	· · ·	· · ·
		Iprindole	0	↑	· · ·	0	· · ·	· · ·
		Zimelidine	0	0	· · ·	0	· · ·	· · ·
	Amygdala	Imipramine	↑†	· · ·	· · ·	· · ·	· · ·	· · ·
		Desipramine	↑	· · ·	· · ·	· · ·	· · ·	· · ·
		Iprindole	↑	↑	· · ·	· · ·	· · ·	· · ·
	Cingulate cortex	Clomipramine	$\downarrow(\beta)$	0	· · ·	0	· · ·	· · ·
		Desipramine	↓	· · ·	· · ·	0	· · ·	· · ·
		Maprotiline	↓	· · ·	· · ·	0	· · ·	· · ·
	Somatosensory cortex	Imipramine	· · ·	· · ·	↕	· · ·	· · ·	0
		Viloxazine	· · ·	· · ·	↕	· · ·	· · ·	0
	Dorsal lateral geniculate	Imipramine	$\uparrow(\alpha_1)$	↑	0	· · ·	· · ·	· · ·
		Clomipramine	↑	0	· · ·	· · ·	· · ·	· · ·
		Amitriptyline	↑	↑	0	· · ·	· · ·	· · ·
		Desipramine	↑	↑	0	· · ·	· · ·	· · ·
		Iprindole	↑	↑	0	· · ·	· · ·	· · ·
	Ventral lateral geniculate	Imipramine	· · ·	↑	· · ·	0	· · ·	· · ·
		Clomipramine	· · ·	↑	· · ·	0	· · ·	· · ·
		Amitriptyline	· · ·	↑	· · ·	0	· · ·	· · ·
		Desipramine	· · ·	↑	· · ·	0	· · ·	· · ·
		Iprindole	· · ·	↑	· · ·	0	· · ·	· · ·
	Substantia nigra	Imipramine	· · ·	· · ·	· · ·	· · ·	↓	· · ·
		Amitriptyline	· · ·	· · ·	· · ·	· · ·	↓	· · ·
		Iprindole	· · ·	· · ·	· · ·	· · ·	↓	· · ·
	Dorsal raphe nucleus	Imipramine	· · ·	0	· · ·	· · ·	· · ·	· · ·
		Desipramine	· · ·	0	· · ·	· · ·	· · ·	· · ·

352

Table 10-9   (continued)

Antidepressant Category	Brain Region	Drugs	NE (Subtype)	5-HT	ACh	GABA	DA	Glutamate
		Iprindole	⋯	0	⋯	⋯	⋯	⋯
	Locus coeruleus	Imipramine	↓(α_2)	⋯	⋯	⋯	⋯	⋯
		Clomipramine	0	⋯	⋯	⋯	⋯	⋯
		Desipramine	↓	⋯	⋯	⋯	⋯	⋯
	Cerebellum	Desipramine	↓(β)	⋯	⋯	0	⋯	⋯
	Facial motor nucleus	Imipramine	↑(α_1)	↑	⋯	⋯	⋯	0
		Amitriptyline	↑	↑	⋯	⋯	⋯	⋯
		Desipramine	↑	↑	⋯	⋯	⋯	⋯
		Iprindole	↑	↑	⋯	⋯	⋯	⋯
MAOI	Cingulate cortex	Tranylcypromine	↓(β)	⋯	⋯	0	⋯	⋯
		Clorgyline	⋯	↓	⋯	⋯	⋯	⋯
ECT	Hippocampus		⋯	0(β)	↑	⋯	0	⋯	⋯
	Substantia nigra		⋯	⋯	⋯	⋯	⋯	↓	⋯

MAOI indicates monoamine oxidase inhibitor; ECT, electroconvulsive therapy; NE, norepinephrine; 5-HT, serotonin; ACh, acetylcholine; GABA, γ-aminobutyric acid; and DA, dopamine. Experiments typically were conducted 24 hours or more after the last administration except in the locus coeruleus, where they were performed at 12 to 18 hours.

† The NE receptor seems to have neither α nor β characteristics.

‡ A predominantly excitatory response to ACh was converted to a depressant response with long-term treatment.

Single-Unit Studies

Whatever the effects of the mood-altering drugs, since they affect behavior and consciousness, they must also affect neural activity. This is the field of research most relevant to the neuron doctrine of Table 1-1. In fact, we will be able to understand the therapeutic action of drugs only when we can directly relate the activity of a distinct group of neurons to a given change in a specific emotional state (as assessed by verbal reports, clinical diagnoses, or behaviors of specifically trained animals).

Comparatively little research has been done in this area, for several reasons. First, there are technical difficulties. Emotional states often involve vigorous physical activity, which makes single-unit recording difficult. Emotions may take time to develop, and it is difficult to record from a single cell for a long period of time. Second, it is difficult to be sure a lower animal is experiencing any phenomenological state, from hunger to depression, shared by humans. Therefore, single-cell activity in lower animals may not be relevant to what we

humans understand as being emotions. Third, it is difficult to know how to interpret the results. For example, emotional activity must be differentiated from the sensory activity directly elicited by the emotional stimulus and from the motor activity that occurs afterwards.

This section illustrates these problems with some recordings from DA and limbic-system neurons. For example, how the LC is related to anxiety can be evaluated with single-unit research. Some researchers have explored effects of antidepressant and neuroleptic drugs on neural activity: if the nerve cells changed by those drugs can be identified, the neurons associated with the emotional problem might also be found. Finally, a model system—an emotion in a much simpler animal—will be described.

Limbic-System Activity

Many limbic structures receive dopaminergic input from all the mesencephalic DA nuclei, and these cells do respond to

Table 10-10 Extent to which blocking serotonin uptake presynaptically may be the critical effect of antidepressants.

Effect	References
NE and 5-HT·Interaction	
Serotonin suppresses beta-adrenergic receptors in rats	Stockmeier, Martino, & Kellar, 1985
Norepinephrine, acting through alpha receptors, excites 5-HT raphe neurons in mice	Trulson & Crisp, 1984
Imipramine Binding Sites	
Humans: highest density in hypothalamus; high density in substantia nigra, mammillary body, limbic cortex, amygdala, and basal ganglia	Langer, Javoy-Agid, Raisman, Briley, & Agid, 1981
Rats: hypothalamus, amygdala, globus pallidus, raphe, locus coeruleus, central gray	Palkovits, Raisman, Briley, & Langer, 1981; Rainbow, Biegon, & McEwen, 1982
As related to 5-HT uptake system	Briley, Langer, & Sette, 1981
Fewer imipramine binding sites in depressed or suicidal patients	
In blood platelets	Meltzer, Arora, Baber, & Tricou, 1981; Paul, Rehavi, Skolnick, Ballenger, & Goodwin, 1981
In the brain (frontal and occipital cortex, hippocampus)	Perry, Marshall, Blessed, Tomlinson, & Perry, 1983; Stanley, Virgilio, & Gershon, 1982
Less 5-HT uptake in platelets	Coppen, Swade, & Wood, 1978; Meltzer et al., 1981
Effect of Antidepressant Treatments on 5-HT Uptake	
Some inhibit the binding of imipramine and thus inhibit 5-HT uptake	Briley, Langer, & Sette, 1981; Langer et al., 1981
Long-term treatments normalize number of 5-HT binding sites	Suranyi-Cadotte, Wood, Nair, & Schwartz, 1982
ECS and long-term antidepressant drug use decrease imipramine binding sites in rats	Langer, Zarifian, Briley, Raisman, & Sechter, 1982
Brain 5-HT Levels Depressed in People with Affective Disorders	
CSF levels low in some patients	Goodwin & Post, 1983
Depletion of plasma tryptophan (and also brain tryptophan?) by eating a tryptophan-free meal elevates depression test scores and leads to performance deficits in human males	Young, Smith, Pihl, & Ervin, 1985
ECS and long-term antidepressant use block inhibitory effects of 5-HT autoreceptors in mice	Goodwin, De Souza, & Green, 1985

potentially emotion-producing stimuli. For example, activity in dopaminergic substantia nigra neurons in the rat is increased by light flashes and is either increased or decreased by olfactory stimuli (Chiodo, Antelman, Caggiula, & Lineberry, 1980).

Some limbic-system neurons may selectively respond only to emotionally arousing types of stimulus. Some preoptic, septal, and stria terminalis neurons in rats are excited by several aversive stimuli, including being grabbed by the experimenter (Minki, Sinnamon, & Adams, 1983). Cells in the amygdala of the rat are affected by immobilization (remember that stress, probably including immobilization stress, increases DA release here) (Henke, 1983, 1984). Some amygdala cells are

excited, some are inhibited, and some respond just to the presentation of a stimulus previously associated with immobilization stress. In cats, raphe neurons show changes in firing rate that closely parallel the cat's level of arousal, including the effects of a novel, arousing stimulus (Trulson & Jacobs, 1979). Furthermore, buspirone — the antianxiety drug that does not affect GABA receptors — suppresses the activity of serotonergic raphe neurons in rats and cats (VanderMaelen, Matheson, Wilderman, & Patterson, 1986; Trulson & Henderson, 1984). And finally, some DA ventral tegmental cells increase their firing rates during a signal previously paired with shock (Trulson & Preussler, 1984).

This research shows promise, but not enough has yet been

done to find out how emotional states are coded. All these responses could be related to nonspecific arousal.

The Locus Coeruleus and Anxiety

The physiological and biochemical research implicating the locus coeruleus in anxiety was summarized in the previous section (Redmond & Huang, 1979). Activity in single LC cells can parallel anxiety levels. For example, some antianxiety drugs inhibit the firing rate of LC neurons, and drugs that increase anxiety increase LC firing rate (Mason & Fibiger, 1979; Redmond & Huang, 1979). Activity in these cells is increased by any painful or aversive stimulation (Cedarbaum & Aghajanian, 1978).

Not all research supports this theory. First, the clinically effective antianxiety drug buspirone *increases* LC nerve-cell activity in mice (Trulson & Henderson, 1984). This effect of buspirone is specific to the LC cells themselves and is not an indirect effect coming from changes in other cell activities. Second, some LC cells may respond more to novelty or to nonspecific arousal level than specifically to anxiety. Any complex, arousing stimulus, including the presentation of food, increases LC activity in both rats and monkeys (Aston-Jones & Bloom, 1981b; Foote, Aston-Jones, & Bloom, 1980; Mason & Fibiger, 1979; Aston-Jones, 1985; Jacobs, 1986; Chapter 7). Chu and Bloom (1973, p. 910) suggested that "LC neurons become relatively inactive once the cat begins to ignore its surroundings." For example, LC activity in rats decreases during grooming and when drinking a sweetened water (Aston-Jones & Bloom, 1981a, 1981b).

Some of these effects were reinterpreted to be consistent with the LC-anxiety theory of Redmond and Huang (1979). Thus, Grant and Redmond said (1984, p. 707), "Food presentation by the experimenter could constitute an implied threat of punishment or deprivation, as food consumption by an inferior ranking primate in the presence of a high ranking one in a macaque social group usually involves a direct or indirect threat of attack." They supported this interpretation by pointing out that in their research, the stimuli that elicited the strongest LC responses were all social threat signals, such as staring directly into the monkey's eyes.

Perhaps different levels of LC activity are associated with different emotional states. Perhaps chronic or unusually high levels of LC activity could be more specifically associated with the phenomenology of anxiety. Low levels of LC activity might reflect interest or attention to external stimuli produced by mildly arousing motivational or emotional states. This suggestion is consistent with the fact that LC activity enhances stimulus processing throughout the brain by increasing signal-to-noise ratios (Chapter 8). This processing might become overactive in anxiety attacks and in paranoid schizophrenia.

Drug Effects

The single-unit approach can also be applied to the effects of drug therapy on emotional disorders. By studying how cells respond to short-and long-term treatment with those drugs, we may find some clues as to how those disorders are coded.

Antidepressants.   Shortly after an antidepressant is injected into the bloodstream of a rat, the firing rate of raphe neurons decreases (Scuvée-Moreau & Dresse, 1979; Sheard, Zolovick, & Aghajanian, 1972). This effect is attributed to stimulation of inhibitory autoreceptors on dendrites. The receptors may be activated by 5-HT coming from axon collaterals or from dendrodentric synapses. The antidepressants stimulate the autoreceptors by increasing the levels of 5-HT in the synapse (remember that these drugs immediately block reuptake). The effect is reasonably specific. Cells outside the raphe show no such consistent response to antidepressants.

The change in raphe activity cannot be directly related to the effects of these drugs on moods, since raphe activity changes immediately and moods do not. However, the suppression of raphe activity is only temporary. The return to normal levels of spontaneous activity occurs at about the time the drug would have its clinical effects on depression (Blier & de Montigny, 1983).

Both chronic and acute antidepressant drug injections inhibit LC activity in rats (Scuvée-Moreau & Dresse, 1979; Svensson & Usdin, 1978). Once again, the immediate inhibition is explained by blockage of NE reuptake at autoreceptor synapses. Chronic treatment also causes inhibition, although not to the degree that acute treatment does. The authors suggested that the "stabilization" of LC firing rate after chronic drug treatment may be related to the effect of the particular drug on mood.

Chronic antidepressant treatment of rats also changes the activity of cells postsynaptic to the LC cells (Huang, 1979; Huang, Maas, & Hu, 1980), including those in the hippocampus. A single dose of the drug produces an immediate but transient decrease in hippocampal firing rate, which is consistent with the inhibitory effects of NE and with the idea that the drug increases synaptic levels of NE by blocking reuptake.

Chronic treatment with an antidepressant produces a tonic *increase* in the spontaneous firing rate of hippocampal cells. The effect of LC stimulation on hippocampal firing rate is not affected by this chronic drug treatment. This difference suggests that the tonic change in hippocampal activity occurs because of the tonic decrease in LC activity described above. Not only do the changes closely parallel one another in time course but the changes also occur close to the time that the drug treatment would begin to have its effects on mood in depressed humans.

Both lithium and an antidepressant (imipramine) affect the NE synapse between LC cells and cerebellar Purkinje cells. Acute imipramine treatment increases the suppression of Purkinje activity caused by LC stimulation or by iontophoretic NE. Acute lithium has the opposite effect. Chronic treatment with either drug has an effect exactly opposite to that of acute treatment with that drug (Schultz et al., 1981). The chronic neural changes might be related to the therapeutic effects of those drugs, especially if similar effects occurred at limbic-system NE synapses.

Amphetamines.   Because of the amphetamine-stereotypy model of paranoid schizophrenia and the DA movement disorders, researchers have studied the cellular effects of amphetamines on limbic cells. Although the stereotypy is assumed to come from increased release of DA by substantia nigra neurons onto striatal neurons, amphetamine *decreases* the spontaneous rate of activity in the substantia nigra. These cells in the motor system may provide a model for the effect of amphetamine on limbic system cells.

One possible reason for this effect can be seen in Figure 10-14. Bunney and Aghajanian (1976a, 1976b, 1978) hypothesized a neural negative-feedback loop between the striatum and the substantia nigra. Amphetamine inhibits the cholinergic interneurons in rats (Groves, 1977), presumably by increasing synaptic levels of the inhibitory transmitter, DA. Inhibition is enhanced by chronic amphetamine infusions and is blocked by neuroleptics, or DA-receptor-blocking drugs. This pattern of synaptic activity may cause the behavioral effects of amphetamine treatment.

The striatum is part of a neural negative-feedback loop. Cholinergic striatum interneurons excite GABAergic neurons, which inhibit the substantia nigra neurons. Microiontophoretic application of amphetamine directly onto nigra neurons does not cause any significant slowing of activity in rats, and destroying the striatum eliminates the effect of systemic amphetamine (Bunney & Aghajanian, 1976a). Thus, amphetamine has these effects because of the negative-feedback loop and not because of DA autoreceptors on substantia nigra neurons (also illustrated in that figure).

Amphetamine affects other neurons as well. For example, amphetamine does have an effect on nigra autoreceptors (Antelman & Chiodo, 1981). These receptors usually show adaptation (desensitization) to chronic drug treatment, but they

can also become sensitized, depending on the time between sequential drug injections. These changes in the autoreceptors would change nigral cell activity. Amphetamine also affects cells innervated by DA or NE neurons (Groves, 1977). For example, an amphetamine injection increases reticular activity. The injection will have even stronger stimulating effects if the organism has received prior injections, which would explain the hyperarousal associated with amphetamine abuse.

Finally, amphetamine alters cell responses to LC activity. One model for these effects can be found in the cerebellar Purkinje neurons. Acute amphetamine injections decrease spontaneous activity in these neurons innervated by the LC (rat: Freedman & Marwaha, 1980; Marwaha, Hoffer, Pittman, & Freedman, 1980). The synapse between the LC axons and the Purkinje cells must have changed, since similar changes in activity were seen after microinjections of NE and after stimulating the LC. Acute amphetamine therefore increases Purkinje cell responses to both excitatory and inhibitory afferents. Thus, amphetamine causes an enhancement of the signal-to-noise ratio similar to that produced by NE or by LC stimulation.

After administering amphetamines to rats daily for 21 days, Marwaha and colleagues found that the spontaneous activity of Purkinje cells was decreased; each injection caused an even greater suppression in firing rate. A beta-blocker returned Purkinje firing rates to normal. The authors suggested that chronic amphetamine treatment facilitates the effect of NE, possibly by increasing the sensitivity or number of beta-receptors. This increase could cause oversensitivity to external stimuli. Since these effects occurred in younger but not older animals, the increase in receptors may explain why susceptibility to schizophrenia decreases with age (after puberty).

Neuroleptic drugs.   Chronic and acute treatments with the neuroleptic drugs in rats have opposite effects on spontaneous activity in the A9 and A10 cells (Bunney, 1984; Bunney & Grace, 1978). Although acute injections increase activity in already active cells and stimulate cells that were previously inactive, chronic treatment almost totally eliminates spontaneous activity. This inhibition of A9 and A10 activity occurs at about the same time that the neuroleptic suppresses symptoms. Since destroying the caudate prevents the effect of chronic treatment on A9 cells, feedback pathways between striatum and nigra are involved in the suppression caused by chronic neuroleptic treatment (Figure 10-14). Bunney and Grace hypothesized an excitatory neural feedback pathway, which could involve nonGABAergic feedback neurons. Stimulating this feedback pathway could cause the excitatory effects of a single drug treatment.

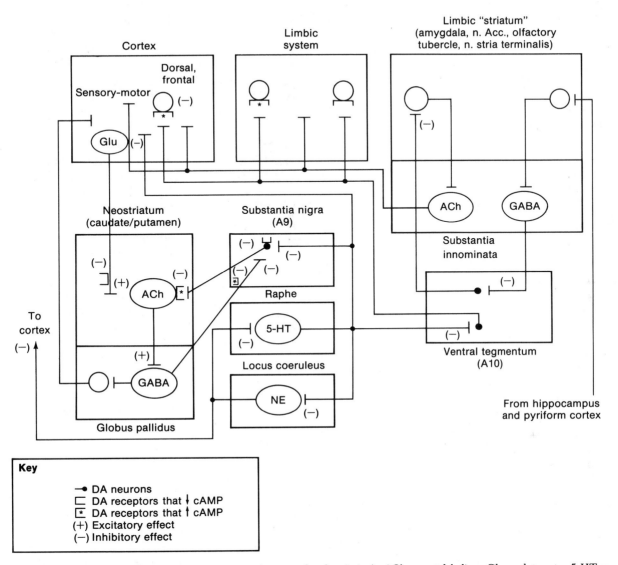

Figure 10-14 Model of dopaminergic connections (see text for description). ACh = acetylcholine; Glu = glutamate; 5-HT = serotonin; n. Acc. = nucleus accumbens; NE = norepinephrine.

Chronic drug treatment could further increase the effectiveness of that feedback pathway. The nigra cells would become chronically depolarized and so could not fire (Na⁺ channels would remain inactivated). Possibly an increase of extracellular K⁺ coming from neural activity produces the chronic depolarization. In this state, inhibitory hyperpolarizing transmitters actually *increase* substantia nigra activity.

The chronic suppression of nigra activity might be related to why many people develop DA-related tardive dyskinesias

(uncontrollable movements, especially of the face muscles and tongue) after chronic intake of neuroleptics. Parkinson's disease (damage to nigra) also involves a dyskinesia (tremor), although obviously the two dyskinesias are not identical.

Chronic neuroleptic treatment affects A9 and A10 neurons differently in the rat (White & Wang, 1983a, 1983b). The projections of A10 neurons to the dorsal frontal cortex and to the nucleus accumbens are illustrated in Figure 10-14. A subset of rapidly firing A10 neurons that has few if any autoreceptors projects exclusively to the cortex (Shepard & German, 1984; White & Wang, 1984). This is probably the A10 group whose firing rate is chronically suppressed sooner and more completely by neuroleptic treatment. Lacking autoreceptors, the neurons would show less adaptation, and so the drug remains clinically effective despite long-term use and adaptation in other DA neurons.

Other drugs do not have these chronic effects (White & Wang, 1983a, 1983b). The "atypical" neuroleptics — those that do not have movement side effects — also chronically suppress only A10 and not A9 neurons in rats. But chronic treatment either with morphine or with an antidepressant *increases* the number of spontaneously active A9 and A10 cells, suggesting that suppression is unique to neuroleptics. Furthermore, a drug that causes movement disorders but has no antipsychotic activity decreases spontaneous activity only in A9 and not in A10 cells. Thus, as the biochemistry suggests, A10 neurons may be uniquely related both to schizophrenia and to neuroleptic effects.

Effects of the Glucocorticoids

One way to establish that peripheral responses affect CNS emotional coding is to look for effects of peripheral hormones such as ACTH, CRF, and the glucocorticoids (secreted by the adrenal cortex during stress) on limbic-neuron activity. These hormones, unlike those secreted by the adrenal medulla, do cross the blood–brain barrier. Once in the brain, they combine with cellular receptors for genomic effects (Vidal, Jordan, & Zieglgänsberger, 1986), and they may affect membrane potentials directly and quickly (Meyer, 1985). Glucocorticoids also affect behavior — increasing the rate of extinction of a learned response, for example (de Wied, Bohus, Gispen, Urban, & van Wimersma Greidanus, 1976).

Hippocampus.   Cells in the hippocampus have more cytosol (or unoccupied?) glucocorticoid receptors in female than in male rats. This sex difference may be related to some of the sex differences in emotional and/or learning responses (Chapter 9). Hippocampal activity changes after peripheral injections of these hormones. For example, corticosterone injected into the freely moving rat usually *decreases* hippocampal cell activity within 10 to 40 minutes after the injection, perhaps by hyperpolarizing pyramidal cells (Pfaff, Silva, & Weiss, 1971; Vidal, Jordon, & Zieglgänsberger, 1986). The effect may last for more than two hours.

Hippocampal cells also react to pituitary ACTH and to hypothalamic CRF. Peripheral injections of ACTH *increase* hippocampal unit activity within 3 to 10 minutes of the injection, and the effect lasts for 25 to 50 minutes (Pfaff, Silva, &

Weiss, 1971). When rat hippocampal slices are perfused with CRF, the frequency of discharge is *increased* (Aldenhoff, Gruol, Rivier, Vale, & Siggins, 1983). Since these infusions also decrease the size of negative afterpotentials, the authors suggested that CRF might antagonize a Ca-activated K^+ channel; this channel would have been partially open at rest as well as during the afterhyperpolarizations.

Other limbic areas.   Cells in the preoptic area, hypothalamus, septum, central gray, and midbrain reticular formation respond to microiontophoresed cortisol in rats (Avanzino, Celasco, Cogo, Ermirio, & Ruggeri, 1983; Kelly, Moss, & Dudley, 1977; Papir-Kricheli & Feldman, 1981, 1983). Fewer preoptic than septal or medial basal hypothalamic cells respond, but the nature of the preoptic response depends on the female estrous cycle. Inhibitory responses are much more common than excitatory responses in all these areas, and the inhibitory effects last longer. Since these cells either have sex-hormone receptors or are part of the system controlling lordosis, the overlap between cortisol and sex-hormone effects may affect sexually dimorphic emotional responses.

Implications.   Some of the effects of glucocorticoids may occur through cytosol receptors, since they occur in areas of the brain that have receptors (such as the hippocampus) and since the latencies are in the range for genomic effects of hormones. The effects discovered through microiontophoresis occur too rapidly to be genomic effects and so reflect changes in membrane excitability or permeability. Some of them, as in the preoptic area, hypothalamus, and possibly the septum and hippocampus, may be part of the negative-feedback loop between glucocorticoids and the pituitary. However, effects of the glucocorticoids on neurons in these as well as other areas could affect neural coding of emotions. Corticosterone increases the rate of extinction (frustration?) of various learned responses even when implanted directly into the brain (de Wied et al., 1976).

Aplysia: A Model for the Cellular Basis of Anxiety?

Although one could not expect a simple organism to model all aspects of anxiety displayed in higher organisms, some behavioral effects of anxiety seen in humans also occur in the sea snail, *Aplysia.* The cellular basis for these effects has been identified (Kandel, 1976, 1983; Siegelbaum, Camardo, & Kandel, 1982; Walters, Carew, & Kandel, 1979). This type of research can provide models for interpreting the results of single-unit recordings done in anxious animals of other species.

Two kinds of anxiety.   The procedure used to create anxiety in *Aplysia* parallels those used to explore stressor effects on transmitter levels and those used in learned helplessness — which also involves anxiety in its initial stages. The organism is given a series of uncontrollable shocks. The treatment effects are measured by how much the organism moves in response to a glass probe applied to its "tail" end. One full step of an *Aplysia* in response to a probe is illustrated in Figure 10-15.

The uncontrollable shocks are presented in two different paradigms, as Figure 10-16 illustrates. The procedure called **sensitization** involves a series of uncontrollable shocks applied to the head. The **aversive conditioning** procedure is classical conditioning. The CS is a drop of shrimp juice applied to the head (an olfactory stimulus); the US is a shock to the head.

Aversive conditioning (signaled anxiety)

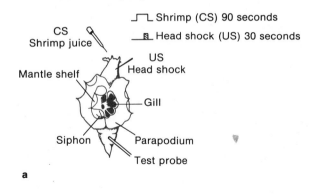

a

Sensitization (unsignaled anxiety)

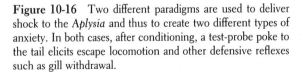

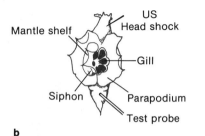

b

Figure 10-16   Two different paradigms are used to deliver shock to the *Aplysia* and thus to create two different types of anxiety. In both cases, after conditioning, a test-probe poke to the tail elicits escape locomotion and other defensive reflexes such as gill withdrawal.

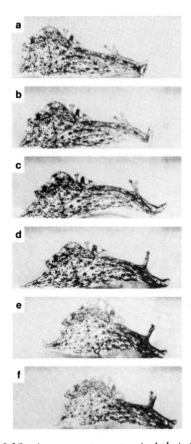

Figure 10-15   A movement sequence in *Aplysia* (¼ life size). First comes the elevation and extension of the head (**a, b**); then the midbody is arched (**c, d**). Finally the tail is retracted (**e, f**). Movements are scored in terms of tail retractions because they are discrete and easily observed.

The effects of both procedures on responses to the test probe are presented in Figure 10-17. The classically conditioned animal shows a reduced tendency to move when the shrimp juice is not there and an exaggerated tendency to move when the CS is present. The sensitized animal shows an exaggerated tendency to move either with or without shrimp juice (a novel stimulus to that animal) during the test.

The effects of sensitization depend on how many days the animal is subjected to the uncontrollable headshocks. Ten days of training produce a durable increase in responsiveness. This animal also begins to show changes in its home-cage behaviors, including restlessness, loss of appetite, and repeated attempts to escape from the cage. Consequently, Kandel (1983) suggests that sensitization may correspond to chronic anxiety in humans, whereas the effects of classical conditioning might correspond to something he calls *anticipatory anxiety*. He describes the latter as being triggered by a real or imagined danger signal.

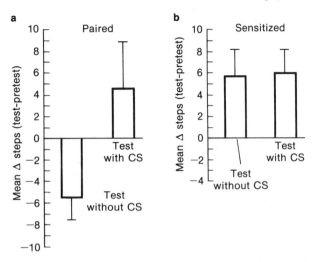

Figure 10-17 The two shock procedures illustrated in Figure 10-16 have different effects on movement responses. The ordinate measures the difference (Δ) between test scores (number of movements) and scores on a pretest. The test probe eliciting movement was administered once in the absence and once in the presence of the CS. Zero on the scale thus means that there was no difference between test and pretest scores. Paired animals showed significantly more escape locomotion after training than before, but only in the presence of the CS. Sensitized animals took significantly more steps than they did before training during both the presence and absence of the CS (a stimulus they had never experienced before). Thus, a conditioned animal might be said to have **anticipatory anxiety**, whereas the sensitized animal might be said to have **chronic anxiety**.

Studying the cellular and biochemical basis of these types of anxiety in *Aplysia* might lead to hypotheses for testing in humans. In particular, the ways in which past experiences affect current "anxietylike" behaviors in *Aplysia*, by changing neural responses to stimuli, can provide very interesting ideas about similar relationships in vertebrates.

Anatomy and biochemistry of anxiety in *Aplysia*. Figure 10-18 presents the anatomy of sensitization in *Aplysia* (neurons in this organism can be identified and numbered). The shock to the head excites a sensory neuron, which in turn excites a facilitory interneuron: this latter neuron is identified with "defensive arousal" or fear. The interneuron then presynaptically facilitates (1) the synapse between the sensory neuron in the siphon skin (stimulated by the test probe) and the excitatory interneuron and (2) the synapse between that interneuron and the motoneuron that produces movement.

The transmitter for both presynaptic excitatory effects is 5-HT. The 5-HT receptor is associated with an adenylate cyclase. 5-HT receptor activation phosphorylates a protein associated with a K$^+$ channel. Phosphorylation closes the K$^+$ channel, prolonging the depolarization associated with an action potential in the axon terminals. Prolonging action potentials increases the time during which Ca^{++} can flow in. The resulting increase in intracellular Ca^{++} increases the release of transmitter substance: presynaptic facilitation and sensitization.

Long-term sensitization causes morphological changes in these same synapses, as Figure 10-19 illustrates. With daily exposure to uncontrollable shocks and to the effects of 5-HT on the axon terminals of those synapses, the number of active transmitter-release sites in those terminals is actually increased (Bailey & Chen, 1983). Cyclic AMP (increased by 5-HT) might activate a gene coding for a regulatory subunit (such as the GMP subunit that controls enzymatic receptors: Chapter 4) of the K$^+$ channel. When this regulatory subunit is manufactured (by genetic derepression), both the K$^+$ channel and the number of transmitter-release sites might be durably altered.

Figure 10-20 shows what the anatomy of the conditioned response might be like in *Aplysia*. A 5-HT neuron is hypothesized to be activated by the US. This neuron in turn presynaptically facilitates the synapse between the CS sensory neuron and the 5-HT facilitory interneuron described above. At both presynaptic sites, 5-HT could have short-term effects on the K$^+$ channel and long-term effects on release sites. The major difference from sensitization is that the CS increases "anxiety" after being paired with the US.

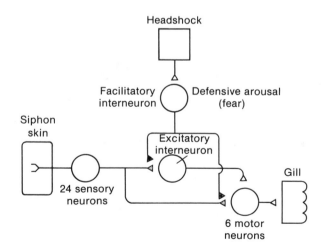

Figure 10-18 Anatomy of the sensitization of the gill-withdrawal reflex in *Aplysia*. The interneurons and the motor cells are all uniquely identified cells in this organism. See text for further description.

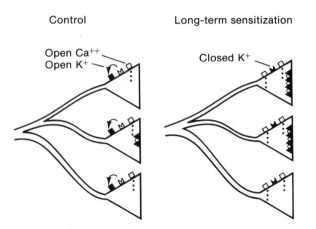

Figure 10-19 Long-term sensitization produces long-term changes in the synapses illustrated in Figure 10-18. In the experimental animals, serotonin closes the K^+ channel, increasing the Ca^{++} current, as the text describes. With sufficient numbers of conditioning sessions, both that K^+ channel and the number of transmitter-release sites might be durably changed, producing durable changes in conditioned behaviors.

Summary of Neurons and Emotions

The activity of limbic-system neurons is changed by a variety of emotionally relevant procedures, including presentation of emotional stimuli, injections of mood-altering drugs, and microiontophoresis of glucocorticoids. Some of the research has shown how various drugs affect activity in limbic cells and so has provided ideas about how the emotion changed by the drugs might be coded.

An *Aplysia* becomes chronically sensitized or "anxious" because of repeated exposure to uncontrollable shocks. Both short-term and long-term sensitization cause an increased responsiveness to certain external stimuli, such as a test probe applied to the tail. Long-term sensitization also causes a chronic increase in activity, similar to anxiety effects. However, a series of uncontrollable shocks induces a period of decreased activity in higher organisms, an effect that does not seem to occur in *Aplysia*, perhaps because of its much simpler nervous system. Nevertheless, these types of synaptic changes suggest an interesting way to approach the neural code of emotions.

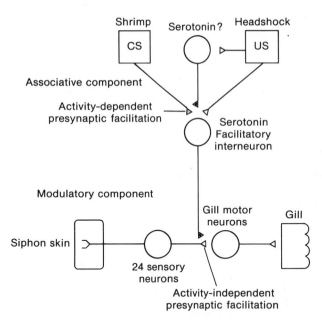

Figure 10-20 According to one model of the anatomy of a conditioned response in *Aplysia*, this form of learning involves two components: an associative component, which accounts for the timing effect of pairing a CS with a US, and a modulatory component, which affects behavior. Presynaptic facilitation, the mechanism responsible for sensitization (Figures 10-18 and 10-19), may also be used in both components of this type of learning to modulate the strength of a particular neural connection. But the two components would have different kinds of presynaptic facilitation, as illustrated. Activity-dependent presynaptic facilitation could provide the associative and temporal specificity, and conventional presynaptic facilitation could provide the modulatory component responsible for enhancing response strength.

Chapter Summary

The Coding of Emotional States

Both the CNS and the periphery are involved in emotional states. For example, anger and aggression have some genetic basis. They are also associated with certain patterns of transmitter levels in the CNS (many of which are also linked to aggressive genes in rodents). They produce sympathetic activity and activation of the adrenal medulla and cortex.

Similar relationships exist for anxiety. Anxiety causes an increase in E, NE, and corticosteroids. The corticosteroids have central as well as peripheral effects. In addition, the genes for anxiety might decrease the number of benzodiazepine receptors to be found in the brain. Anxiety-arousing stimuli —

including uncontrollable shock—increase DA and NE activity in the brain. The antianxiety drugs may potentiate the inhibitory effects of GABA on these circuits, thus decreasing anxiety and also decreasing the release of DA and NE, preventing depletion. In *Aplysia*, the anxiety may be associated first with presynaptic facilitation and then with morphological changes in synapses among sensory neurons, interneurons, and motoneurons.

Depression may be related to both stress and genes in humans, and at least one animal model of depression (learned helplessness) gives stress a major role. Stress depletes brain amines, particularly NE and 5-HT, and their depletion may contribute to depressed moods. Depletion may be durable if some experientially induced or genetically induced defect in the metabolic adaptation pathways is present.

Schizophrenia has been related both to DA and to brain damage. Stress may also play a role because stress sensitizes organisms to the effects of amphetamine (a model of paranoid schizophrenia) and increases DA release. The release of both DA and NE by amphetamine is sensitized by prior exposure to amphetamines, and overactivity in both amines has been related to paranoid schizophrenia. The projection of the dopaminergic A10 neurons to the frontal lobes may be involved in both the positive and negative symptoms of schizophrenia. This pathway may become periodically overactive in some people, producing the positive symptoms. The A10 neurons show less adaptation, just as the clinical effects of the neuroleptics on the positive symptoms don't adapt. Only A10 activity is tonically suppressed by chronic use of the "atypical" but clinically effective neuroleptics. The A10 neurons may be damaged in people with negative symptoms. These people show symptoms associated both with frontal-lobe damage and with damage to the A10 projection system. The symptoms in these people are often *improved* by amphetamine and are unaffected or even made worse by neuroleptics.

However, all these relationships do not prove that any given transmitter disorder *causes* an emotional disorder. Any change in any group of neurons will affect the activities of many other groups.

The mind–body problem is acute in the area of emotions. The introduction to this chapter described how the mind–body problem afflicts much of the research concerned with emotions (Chapter 1: the mystery of the relationship between neurons and biochemistry, on the one hand, and phenomenological experiences, on the other). The neuron doctrine will go through its severest test in the area of codes for emotions. From the point of view of monism and the neuron doctrine, the disordered thoughts and emotions of emotionally disturbed patients *are* the patterns of synaptic and biochemical activity of a few neurons. It should be possible to explore these patterns through chemical techniques and single-unit recordings in animal models of disorder and in animals treated with the drugs.

However, in dualism, the emotions are something separate from the neural activity, and the emotions are often claimed to result from the *pattern* of activity in a large number of neurons, activated and inhibited, throughout the limbic system. If this is so, one major principle of the neuron doctrine will be invalidated: the idea that phenomenological experiences depend on activity in a very small number of neurons. Future research may be able to decide the issue if it can identify which cells code for emotions.

PART FIVE

Effects of Experience on Brain Coding Mechanisms

The two chapters in this part describe the effects of experience on brain cells and synapses. But first, some important concepts need to be defined. Because definitions for these terms are often debated (and are quite debatable), our definitions are just hypotheses, designed to organize ideas.

Definitions and Concepts

Learning and memory have to be defined both behaviorally and neurophysiologically. **Behavioral learning** is the effect that certain types of *current* experiences have on behaviors. We assume that **behavioral memory** involves the effects of past events (seconds or years ago) on current behaviors: the person "remembers" past experiences, and the memories influence present behaviors. **Neurophysiological learning and memory** are the effects of learning or experience on nerve cells and synapses, effects presumed to be responsible for learned changes in behavior. Neurophysiologically, we will arbitrarily describe the changes in neural activity and synaptic processes that occur in the process of conditioning or training as being **learning**. We will use **"memory"** to refer to neural changes that last *beyond* the immediate training period, from seconds to years.

But sometimes conditioning trails are spread out over time, rather than occurring in one contiguous block of time (**distributed versus massed practice**). In the context of distributed practice, the term *learning* will be used to refer to synaptic and neural changes that cumulate as a direct function of the number of past trials (at least as long as behavior still is changing). The term *memory* refers to changes that last from one trial to the next and those that endure for some time after the completion of the last trial. Either **memory trace** or **engram** is used to refer to the physical changes that experience induces in the interconnections among nerve cells. Neurophysiological memory and learning are closely interrelated and may actually involve the same kinds of synaptic-neural changes.

Many definitions of learning state that the kinds of experience necessary for learning are associative and that the changes in behavior are adaptive. ("**Associative**" means that the change in behavior occurred because the animal associated two stimuli, or a stimulus with a response, or a stimulus with a reinforcer. The pairing of stimuli, or stimuli with responses, is assumed to be necessary.) However, we do not use those definitions because we believe that both *non*adaptive changes in behavior and changes that occur without associations are also due to learning.

Like sensations, perceptions, motives, and emotions, learning and memory cannot be directly measured but must be inferred from specific changes in behaviors. These aspects of behavior can then be correlated with neurophysiological measures of learning and memory. But the only way to prove that a given neural or synaptic change is responsible for behavioral learning and memory is to artificially induce that change and *then* measure behavior. Only for certain experientially produced changes in hippocampal neurons have we even come close to providing this proof. So although other data may have a fascinating potential, they are only sources of hypotheses and not proof.

Past experiences are assumed to alter the relationship between the input of some environmental stimulus and the output of some command system. Alteration can be caused by one or more of the following mechanisms:

1. changes in the coding process itself at some higher levels of sensory input
2. a wider distribution of the coded information in such a way that cells not normally affected by such input do become responsive
3. changes in the probability with which a given set of command cells will be activated.

Since in Chapter 8 we described motives using words and concepts that are very similar to the words and concepts used here to describe learning, we may hypothesize that past experiences may have effects on neural coding similar to the effects of internal states. Because of this overlap in terminology and concept, any way of distinguishing between motivational and experiential effects on the brain becomes very important. But some of the more common distinctions are not being used in this book. One distinction states that motivational effects are transient, whereas experiential effects are more enduring. However, learned anxiety can have durable effects on the synaptic activity in *Aplysia*. Furthermore, schizophrenia has durable effects on behavior, and that emotional/cognitive disorder has experiential as well as genetic determinants. A second common distinction differentiates *associative* (exper-

iential) and *nonassociative* (motivational) effects. But motivational states can be learned (for example, acquired anxiety), and some experientially produced changes in neural processing occur without associative training.

We use different criteria to distinguish among motivational, experiential, and interactive effects. As described in Part IV, motivational and emotional processes may involve brain codes for internal states. Now the neural effects of experience will be described as changes in synaptic effectiveness or connections. Given this distinction, motivational and experiential processes can interact. There can be acquired changes in the coding of internal states. Also, the codes for the currently existing internal states will profoundly affect the likelihood that a given set of experiences will produce a synaptic change: motives and arousal level can have a dramatic impact on both learned responses and neural memory codes.

The coding of internal states and changes in synaptic effectiveness are both likely to change the way external sensory information is coded. The presence of a given code for an internal state — implying some change in bodily conditions — can change the way that external stimuli are coded. For example, some cells in the lateral hypothalamus respond to the sight and taste of food, but *only* when the body is in a state of food deprivation (Chapter 8). Similarly, the way some cells code sensory information are likely to be changed by experientially produced changes in synaptic effectiveness (Chapter 12). Both changes could affect how coded information is distributed in the brain and the likelihood of activation of any given set of command cells.

The Neuron Doctrine and Memory

According to the neuron doctrine of Chapter 1, the specificity of stored information is achieved by changing synaptic connections among a certain small set of neurons. Changes in a different set would code for a slightly different aspect of the learned and remembered experience. This model, to be explored in the next two chapters, makes certain predictions:

1. *Arousal*. At least moderate levels of arousal, peripheral NE injections, or reticular stimulation can facilitate both neurophysiological and behavioral memory by facilitating relevant neural changes (Davis & Squire, 1984; McGaugh, Martinez, Jensen, Hannan, Vasquez, Messing, Liang, Brewton, & Spiehler, 1982).
2. *The nature of the change*. The relevant neurophysiological memory changes may involve potentiation of existing synapses, "unmasking" of previously ineffective synapses, or

formation of new synapses (Wall, 1977). A useful model might be the "anxiety"-induced changes in the 5-HT presynaptic connection with a sensory neuron axon terminal in *Aplysia* (Chapter 10). Memory formation would begin with short-term effects on some channel protein, such as the K^+ channel. Long-term effects would involve changes in synaptic morphology (such as an increased number of release sites). Morphological changes would require protein synthesis and so could be inhibited by any substance that interferes with that synthesis (Davis & Squire, 1984).

3. *Anatomy*. It is quite likely that hippocampal neurons facilitate the synaptic changes associated with at least certain types of learning and memory. However, the relevant synapses are located elsewhere, perhaps in the midbrain or brain stem (Meyer, 1984). The hippocampus may also facilitate memory retrieval. The cortex may participate only by coding the to-be-remembered stimuli and by interpreting retrieved memory codes associated with the act of recall (Meyer, 1984). These memory codes would be generated by the altered synapses after appropriate input (internal or external stimuli). In general, the structures most generally thought to be directly involved in the formation of memory traces are the cerebellum, hippocampus, amygdala, and cerebral cortex (Thompson, 1986). Neurons that change their activity during a learning experience are found not only in those structures but also in the thalamus,

hypothalamus, mesencephalon, and reticular formation (John, Tang, Brill, Young, & Ono, 1986). Neurons in the prefrontal cortex also seem to be involved in one type of memory (Fuster, 1984; Watanabe, 1986a, 1986b).

One current alternative to these hypotheses states that memories are immediately and permanently formed just after a training trial. The cellular basis of such an effect is unclear. Theorists holding this position (for example, Lewis, 1979; Riccio & Richardson, 1984) suggest that treatments that improve or disrupt performances on retention tests do so by affecting memory **retrieval** processes. The theories claim that nothing done immediately after training would affect the formation of memory traces. Thus, we will call such theories **retrieval-deficit theories.**

Chapter 11 describes some research programs that systematically explored the cellular, physiological, or biochemical correlates of learning. That research has suffered from several conceptual and technical problems, so only a sampling—to demonstrate what the approach may eventually be able to offer—will be presented.

Chapter 12 describes how experiences change information-coding and nerve-cell structures (**morphological changes**) in the brain. The way that nerve cells code sensory input can be permanently altered by experience, especially by early experiences.

11

Changes in Neural Activity
Associated with Learning and Memory

The question of how the brain "remembers" past experiences has preoccupied researchers since physiological brain research began. Because the answer seemed so close but still so tantalizingly out of reach, one of our graduate-school professors used to say that the field is one into which "only geniuses or idiots" go. But now the feeling has shifted to one of great excitement. Researchers have been able to put together enough pieces of the puzzle so that at last a clear picture is beginning to emerge: some of the work done by the "geniuses and idiots" is beginning to reveal "the biological residue of memory [that comes] from a lifetime of experience" (Thompson, 1986, p. 941).

Overview

Richard R. Thompson has done some important and fascinating single-unit memory research. He describes his research as a search for the engram. But as he said, because of conceptual and experimental difficulties, "the nature of the engram has proved to be among the most baffling questions in science" (Thompson, in collaboration with McCormick, Lavond, Clark, Kettner, & Mauk, 1983, p. 167).

Conceptual and Experimental Difficulties

One major experimental difficulty was a direct by-product of traditional physiological approaches. To analyze brain codes for past experiences, researchers must first know where to place their electrodes. Although lesion and gross-stimulation experiments have been able to identify some areas of the brain relevant to motives and to emotions, the same has not been true of learning and memory. With a few exceptions, lesioning research has suggested that damage to almost any area of the brain affects at least certain kinds of learning and memory.

There are also conceptual difficulties. For a past experience to be recalled and to affect future behavior, some aspects of that experience must have been coded, the code must have been stored in some way within the nervous system, and then the code must have been retrieved at an appropriate time. An analogy might be a library where books are coded, placed on the shelves according to the code, and then retrieved by use of that code. Brain lesions can cause retrieval failures, meaning that animals act as if they did not remember a prior experience. The failure could mean that either **input, storage,** or **retrieval** mechanisms have gone awry—but it is difficult to establish *which* of the three might have been damaged.

Another problem is that some theories have assumed that the physiological basis of memory changes over time. **Short-term memory** is often described as the change in neural activity occurring within seconds of the experience; the memory then fades rapidly with time. **Long-term memory** would last for hours or even years. Researchers often assume that short-term and long-term memories involve different types of synaptic changes occurring in the same or even in different parts of the brain. It is also common to assume that the short-term changes have to endure for a certain critical period of time to induce the type of change responsible for long-term memories. The process of changing short-term into long-term memories is **consolidation.**

Both short-term and long-term memories would be tested by presenting some cue for recall. Records of the resulting neural activity could be compared with the activity observed in some control condition. Would the retrieval type of activity for long-term memories be exactly the same as that associated with the retrieval of information from some short-term memory store? Or does the process of consolidation permanently change the electrical activity codes associated with retrieval?

To attribute a lesion effect to destruction of a memory—or to attribute a change in neural responses to a synapse critically altered by that experience—researchers must control for changes in sensory processing, motives, emotions, and motor output (Gabriel, Foster, Orona, Saltwick, & Stanton, 1980). In single-unit recordings, the effects of experience on the "memory synapses" must be differentiated from nonspecific and specific arousal effects and from attention. But if appropriate control procedures are used, then, as Thompson points out (Thompson et al., 1983, p. 177), "Electrophysiological recording of neural activity is at present the only technique that can provide such information" about the neural codes for learning and memory.

Types of Memory Research Covered

Only a few types of study can be covered while doing justice to their implications. The first section covers some of the biochemistry of learning and memory, including an overview of drugs that facilitate and impair memory. The genetic basis of learning and memory is relevant because genes can sometimes be related to brain chemistry.

The next section describes two types of research that recorded changes in single-nerve-cell activity during or after learning. The changes did not appear in control groups. First, to show how an intensive investigation of a single part of the brain can provide ideas about learning codes, we will describe neural changes in the hippocampus occurring during a variety of learning experiences. The second type of research records from many different areas of the brain during one specific type of learning experience to show how various parts of the brain may cooperate in the coding of learning and memory.

The last section describes two examples of the model-systems approach to learning and memory. Some researchers have suggested that the effects of experience ought to be first studied extensively in systems simpler than the whole vertebrate brain. This approach would provide ideas about how and in what ways experience might change neural responses. One such system is hippocampal long-term potentiation (Chapter 4). Another model system can be found in the nervous system of invertebrates. We already discussed one such model: anxiety in the *Aplysia.* This chapter will provide examples of what types of knowledge can potentially be gained by using each of several different kinds of approach.

The Biochemistry of Learning and Memory

Some of the major techniques used in the past 30 years to explore the biochemistry of learning and memory have produced knowledge that is essential to the task of discovering neural codes for memory by the use of single-unit recording techniques. Psychobiological research has shown how a certain treatment can change not only performances on a memory-retention test but also brains. And in at least a few cases, researchers have been able to demonstrate that a given change in certain synapses is directly related to the change in behavior. With a few exceptions, these studies were done on rats.

This section describes one way of searching for the memory trace: what researchers have discovered about how to improve memory and how to cause amnesia (loss of memory) and then what changes in the brain occur during learning and memory. Last, we will discuss how genetically determined brain chemistry might be related to individual differences in learning ability and memory.

Agents That Affect Retention Performance

Performances on retention tests can be degraded because of deficits in motives or perceptions, but in many cases it seems that memories have been changed. **Amnesic** agents interfere with memory. Other treatments improve retention performance—even if one of the amnesic agents has also been used.

Paradigms and assumptions.   Many amnesic treatments can be applied at a discrete point in time relative to when the organism was trained. If the amnesic agent is applied before training is begun, any retention deficit associated with that treatment could be caused by agent-induced problems in either input, retention (memory trace), or retrieval. The treatment could also be given during the retention interval, either after training was complete or after every training trial. Suppose a deficit were found when retention was tested sometime later. The deficit could have occurred either because the treatment affected the memory trace or because it affected the organism's ability to retrieve previously learned information. Finally, if the agent is applied just before a retention test, hours or days after learning, any amnesic effects observed would be attributed deficits in retrieval caused by the treatment.

The experimenter can determine just how and in what way retention performances are being affected by comparing the effects of treatments given at different times in different groups of subjects. For example, suppose that a researcher found that amnesia was induced *either* when the treatment

was given just before training *or* when it was given just before the retention test. However, there was *no* amnesia when the treatment was applied to animals on *both* occasions rather than just on one or the other. Given this pattern of results, the experimenter might conclude that the treatment produced a unique brain state or a unique set of internal cues. If that state or those cues were present during the learning experience, the organism would be able to retrieve learned information only if that state were also present during the recall period (Riccio & Richardson, 1984). In **state-dependent** or **cue-dependent** learning, anything that causes different external or internal cues in the learning and test situations impairs retrieval performances.

If a treatment presented just after training completely disrupts retention, the treatment may have destroyed the memory trace. If so, the information should be irretrievable, and the organism should be unable to recall what it had previously learned, regardless of the circumstances. In some cases there is no spontaneous recovery: the organism may never be able to perform the previously learned task, no matter how long the experimenter waits before giving the test. But if the experimenter gives the animal a certain treatment, it may then be able to remember. The amnesia was only temporary.

It is really impossible to state categorically that any treatment causes permanent amnesia. The possibility always exists that another type of treatment—one not yet tried—may lead to a "return" of the memory. If memory does return (the treatment alleviated the retrieval difficulties), the information must have been stored somewhere in the brain. The information seems literally to have been "gone but not forgotten."

ECS.   The first treatment found to influence retention performance was **electroconvulsive shock,** or **ECS** (Duncan, 1949; McGaugh & Herz, 1972). ECS refers to an amnesic treatment in which high levels of electrical current are passed through the whole brain through electrodes placed on the ears or on the corneas of the eyes. Unless the animal is also given a paralytic agent, this current will produce generalized convulsions. However, neither brain seizures nor behavioral convulsions are necessary for an ECS to cause amnesia. The amnesic effects of ECS might be responsible for its therapeutic effects on depressed humans (Meyer, 1984).

Duncan (1949) discovered the amnesic effects of ECS. He gave each of his rats 18 active avoidance trials, one trial per day. An ECS was given after every trial. Different groups of animals were given an ECS at different times after each daily trial. Figure 11-1 demonstrates, the sooner the ECS was given after each trial, the poorer the performance, as measured by the number of correct responses or "anticipatory runs." **Ret-**

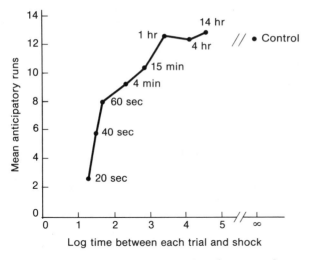

Figure 11-1 Retrograde amnesia gradient for groups of rats given multiple trials. The sooner after each trial an ECS was given (the times shown in the graph), the fewer correct responses (anticipatory runs) were made. Each point on the graph represents a different group of subjects; each group was given 18 trials of active avoidance training, with an ECS after each trial.

rograde amnesia gradient refers to this graded effect that the amount of time between training and the ECS treatment has on learning. This is one of the most frequently replicated findings of physiological psychology. Most amnesic agents will produce a similar gradient if the time elapsed between training and the treatment is varied.

However, Duncan's results could reflect a "punishment" gradient. The sooner after a trial an aversive ECS is presented, the more punishment-induced suppression of behavior would be expected. In an effort to control for this possibility, researchers have used tasks that can be learned in a single trial. Furthermore, tasks that involved punishment were used so that any possible punishing effects of an ECS would add to the effects of punishment rather than suppressing performances.

Rats when placed upon a small pedestal for the first time promptly step off it. In training, they are given a severe footshock when they step down, and the next time they are placed on that pedestal, they do not step down so promptly. This is a **one-trial passive-avoidance task.** A single ECS can be given immediately after the footshock in the one learning trial. When an ECS-treated animal is placed on the pedestal one or two days later, it will again promptly step down. Thus, a short-latency step-down response on the retention test demonstrates amnesia for the previous training. A retrograde amnesia gradient for this type of task is presented in Figure 11-2.

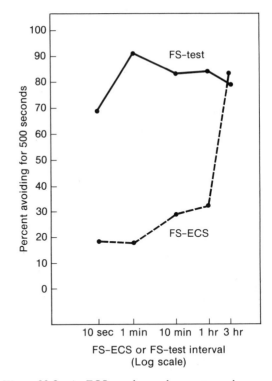

Figure 11-2 An ECS can also produce a retrograde amnesia gradient for rats given a one-trial passive-avoidance training experience. (See the text for description of the task.) For the FS–ECS graph, the time between the footshock (FS) and the subsequent ECS was varied over groups; for the FS–test graph, the time between training and the retention test was varied.

An ECS causes amnesia only when given early in the retention period. If an ECS is given just before training, just before the retention test, or just before both periods, it has no consistent effect on retention performance (McGaugh & Herz, 1972). There also may be no amnesia if the ECS is delayed for more than an hour after training. Depending on training and treatment parameters, sometimes a delay of just over 5 seconds between training and ECS will eliminate the amnesic effects of that treatment (McGaugh & Herz, 1972). The fact that the critical time between training and ECS can vary in different situations may mean that different training parameters produce somewhat different kinds — or levels — of memory.

The amnesia produced by the ECS can take some time to develop. Miller and Springer (1971) tested retention performance on a one-trial passive-avoidance task at various times after training. All the animals had received an ECS immediately after the training trial. As Figure 11-3 shows, the animals had good retention when tested 15 minutes after the training–

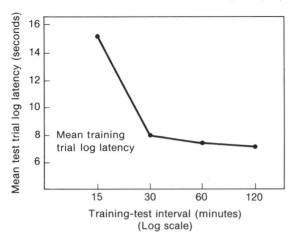

Figure 11-3 The amnesia produced by an ECS may take time to develop. These are the mean test trial latencies (in log sec) as a function of the time between the training and the test trial (min). All animals received one-trial passive-avoidance training followed immediately by an ECS.

ECS experience but were amnesic within 30 minutes. An appropriate control group demonstrated good retention a day after learning even when an ECS was given 15 minutes before the retention test. Thus, the ECS given just after training does not immediately disrupt the ability to retrieve previously learned information.

Two types of effect are incompatible with the neuron doctrine of memory presented in the introduction to this unit. As the retrieval-deficit theories predict, the ECS may not wipe out the memory trace. Retention performances can be improved, even in ECS-treated animals (Dunn, 1980; Lewis, 1979). The animal can be reminded of its prior experiences by shocking it in a different apparatus (the **reminder effect**), or it can be given an injection of physostigmine (an AChase inhibitor or anticholinesterase), ACTH, antidiuretic hormone (vasopressin), cortisol, or amphetamine. If retention performances can be improved by *any* treatment, we would have to conclude that an ECS affects retrieval rather than the memory trace itself. Also, under certain circumstances, an ECS treatment can cause amnesia for a task that was learned days before the treatment.

Meyer (1972) was the first to demonstrate this kind of amnesia. He trained rats in a series of three discriminated-choice tasks, some using food and some using avoidance incentives. The animal had to learn which way to go in a modified T-maze to get food or to avoid shock. The types of training and the sequences given to various groups are outlined in Figure 11-4. All groups were given an ECS immediately after the

third task. As Figure 11-4 shows, if the last task of the series was the only one of the three to reinforce correct responses with food, animals remembered both of the two previously learned shock-avoidance tasks. But if a previously learned task had also involved food reinforcement, an ECS given after the third task caused amnesia for that task learned days earlier! A similar effect was seen if the third task was learned for a shock-avoidance reward: earlier tasks were forgotten, but only if they had involved a shock-reduction reward.

This effect may be related to the reminder effect. Both may involve cue-dependent effects on memory retrieval. An animal is exposed to a cue that reminds it of some previously learned task. Afterwards, it is given an ECS treatment. Even if that task had been learned several days previously, the animal may display amnesia for the task. For example, Lewis, Bregman, & Mahan (1972) found that a single ECS given seven days after extensive maze training for a food reward could cause amnesia for that training. The ECS was given immediately after the animals had been "reminded" of the training. Among the reminders used were just being taken into the room in which the maze was located and being placed in the start box of the maze.

Lewis (1979) turned these and similar observations into a retrieval-deficit theory of ECS effects (which he also applied to the effects of other amnesic agents). Although memory is permanently formed immediately after training, shortly after training *and* after a reminder experience that memory would be in an active state. If an ECS were given when the memory was still active, it would interfere with later attempts to retrieve that memory from its permanent store. The memory would still be in the brain, but the animal would be unable to retrieve it.

An alternative hypothesis is more consistent with the neuron doctrine. Just after a training trial the long-term synaptic changes may not yet be complete. An amnesic treatment given during this time may disrupt the process so that only some aspects of the memory become permanently coded. Agents such as reminders or injections of amphetamine can facilitate a partial memory, just as they facilitate memory in nonamnesic animals (as we discuss later in this section; see also Davis & Squire, 1984). The amnesic gradient thus reflects a susceptibility-to-disruptions gradient of the underlying synaptic changes. The retention gradient *after* the amnesic treatment may reflect the residual synaptic changes, triggered by training, that remain after the ECS. These residual effects would fade with time because the durable synaptic changes did not have enough time to become fully stabilized. The residual effects might be similar to the short-term changes in a membrane channel described in the *Aplysia* model of anxiety.

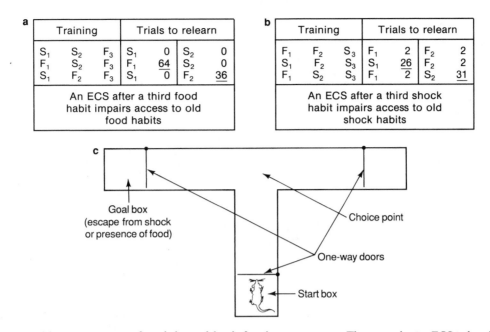

Training			Trials to relearn			
S_1	S_2	F_3	S_1	0	S_2	0
F_1	S_2	F_3	F_1	64	S_2	0
S_1	F_2	F_3	S_1	0	F_2	36

An ECS after a third food habit impairs access to old food habits

Training			Trials to relearn			
F_1	F_2	S_3	F_1	2	F_2	2
S_1	F_2	S_3	S_1	26	F_2	2
F_1	S_2	S_3	F_1	2	S_2	31

An ECS after a third shock habit impairs access to old shock habits

Figure 11-4 An ECS can cause amnesia for tasks learned days before the treatment. **a.** There are selective ECS-induced impairments, as measured by the number of trials required for relearning, for first or second tasks learned under hunger motivation. These impairments occur when the third problem in a three-problem series is also learned under hunger motivation and is followed by an ECS. **b.** Similar deficits appear for first or second tasks learned under conditions of shock-avoidance motivation, when the third trial, followed by the ECS, also involved shock motivation. **c.** Schematic of one type of T-maze, as seen from above.

The amnesic effects of a very delayed ECS may mean that ECS cues combine with the cue-dependent process of retrieval. The reactivated memories (reminder effects) become reencoded to include ECS stimuli (Riccio & Richardson, 1984). In the absence of a pretrial ECS, subsequent retrieval-test performances would be impaired because the memory code generated during retrieval attempts now includes ECS stimuli. Thus, the memory for the task after the reminder and subsequent ECS now includes stimuli different from those associated with the training and test situations.

Brain stimulation. Discrete stimulation of specific areas of the brain through implanted gross electrodes also causes amnesic effects similar to those seen after an ECS (Kesner, 1982; McGaugh & Herz, 1972). Such amnesic effects are most likely to be seen with stimulation of limbic areas of the brain, including the hippocampus, the caudate, the substantia nigra, the thalamus, the midbrain reticular formation (MRF), the lateral hypothalamus (LH), and the amygdala (Kesner, 1982; Lewis, 1979). For example, animals will have amnesia for a task if their caudate is stimulated just after training. A retrograde amnesia gradient will appear if the training–stimulation interval is varied.

The amnesic effects of brain stimulation depend on the type of task, the amount and type of reward being offered, and the brain area being stimulated (Kesner, 1982). For example, posttrial stimulation of the ventral part of the hippocampus can produce amnesia for an appetitively motivated task but not for an aversively (shock-avoidance) motivated task. But posttrial caudate stimulation can cause amnesia for both tasks.

More systematic studies of brain area and type of task need to be carried out. Researchers cannot yet confidently predict when stimulating a given area will produce amnesia, on the basis of any analysis of what that brain area is doing throughout the learning of any particular task. However, Kesner (1982) suggested that which area is involved depends on the age of the memory and the type of task. The MRF may be involved in the initial stages of memory formation, especially for aversive experiences. The hippocampus may be important to the formation of durable synaptic changes (consolidation) for both appetitive and aversive experiences. Amygdala and caudate stimulation may affect memories that involve either aversive experiences or very intense or large food rewards; the LH might be important to food-related memories.

Brain stimulation-induced amnesia also shows the reminder effect and a retrograde amnesia gradient (DeVietti & Kirkpatrick, 1976; Kesner, 1982; Lewis, 1979). If stimulating a particular area of the brain just after training produces amnesia for a particular type of task, that stimulation will also produce amnesia if given shortly after a reminder treatment. And if the time between cue presentation and stimulation of the amygdala is varied, a typical retrograde amnesia gradient appears.

Thus, brain stimulation and ECS can have similar effects. They may disrupt retrieval alone. Or they may disrupt the formation of long-term synaptic changes as well as disrupting retrieval because they change the nature of the encoded information during the reminder effect.

Antibiotics. Research with antibiotics began by assuming that consolidation involved protein synthesis. Memory may involve a change in the type or functioning of synapses either because a unique protein was synthesized or because a permanent change occurred in the rate of synthesis of membrane receptor proteins. Antibiotics inhibit protein synthesis (an effect that is fatal to bacteria). If protein synthesis is required, and if animals are injected with high doses of such drugs either before or immediately after training, they should be unable to remember their experiences when tested a day or so later.

Most antibiotic injections that inhibit whole-brain protein synthesis by 80% to 90% will produce amnesia. These treatments also produce amnesia gradients, and the amnesia also takes time to develop (Barraco & Stettner, 1976; Davis & Squire, 1984; Dunn, 1980; Eisenstein, Altman, Barraco, Barraco, & Lovell, 1983; Lewis, 1979). For amnesia to occur, the drug must usually be injected some time during the period that starts several hours before training and continues throughout training. Furthermore, if the animals are tested at various times after treatment and training, antibiotic-injected animals perform normally for several hours before their performance begins to deteriorate in comparison with that of trained but uninjected controls. The degree to which protein synthesis is inhibited may be related to the degree of amnesia produced (see review by Davis & Squire, 1984). The results of contradictory studies (see, for example, Rainbow, Hoffman & Flexner, 1980) may depend on side effects specific to task and treatment (Davis & Squire, 1984).

The amnesic effects of these drugs can be reversed (Dunn, 1980; Lewis, 1979). Reminder cues will reverse the deficit, and sometimes the subject's memory will even recover spontaneously. Arousal can also improve retention performance, whether the arousal is produced by pretest footshock or by peripheral injections of ACTH or amphetamine. Intracerebral injections of amphetamines or DA (but *not* NE) will also induce recovery from antibiotic-induced amnesia (Altman &

Quartermain, 1983), as will injections of substance P (Schlesinger, Lipsitz, Peck, & Pelleymounter, 1983).

Perhaps retrieval is blocked by antibiotics because these drugs affect brain electrical activity and hence memory retrieval codes. The drugs could also change transmitter synthesis and degradation. Maybe antibiotic-induced amnesia is related to an increase in brain NE levels (discussed later in this section). Recovery would occur because these transmitter changes are reversed by shock or amphetamines. Alternatively, the improved retention performances may simply reflect arousal-induced facilitation of antibiotic-weakened memories (Davis & Squire, 1984).

The antibiotic **puromycin** produces effects that no other antibiotic does. Puromycin blocks protein synthesis by masquerading as a transfer RNA molecule attached to an amino acid. The puromycin molecule becomes incorporated into a growing chain of amino acids, as Figure 11-5 illustrates. The synthesis breaks off at that point, forming a peptidyl-puromycin complex, which disrupts mitochondria and produces abnormal electrical activity, especially in the hippocampus.

Researchers have discovered that when puromycin has been injected immediately before or after training, none of the treatments that reverse other amnesias will reverse the puromycin-induced amnesia. Perhaps puromycin causes irreversible amnesia by acting on ACh synapses, maybe in the hippocampus (Barraco & Frank, 1983). These particular synapses may be importantly involved in regulating the durable synaptic changes occurring elsewhere in the brain, at least for certain kinds of tasks. Abnormal activity in these ACh hippocampal synapses during consolidation could permanently disrupt the memory code, making it irretrievable.

Puromycin will also cause amnesia when injected into the cortex from one to thirty days after training, depending on the location of the injection (e.g., Flexner, Church, Flexner, & Rainbow, 1984). No other antibiotic yet tested will do the same. This delayed amnesia *is* reversible. Saline injections onto the cortex of amnesic animals improves their retention performances. The amnesic effects of puromycin are prevented if the drug is injected simultaneously with another antibiotic, **cycloheximide.** This second antibiotic prevents peptidyl-puromycin fragments from forming, and the saline injections remove those fragments from the brain. Thus, perhaps *retrieval* is being blocked by those fragments. The fragments may be activating adenosine receptors on inhibitory interneurons (Dunn, 1980).

Facilitating retention. The ways in which retention or retrieval can be blocked have provided us with information regarding the biochemistry of learning and memory. The ways

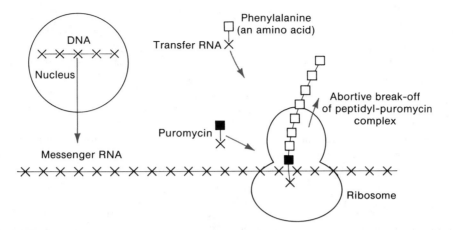

Figure 11-5 Puromycin inhibits protein synthesis because the three-dimensional shape of the puromycin molecule closely resembles the shape of the molecule formed by the combination of phenylalanine and its transfer RNA molecule. The puromycin molecule is therefore incorporated into the growing peptide chain in place of phenylalanine. But since other amino acids cannot be attached to puromycin, the growing peptide chain prematurely breaks off the ribosome in the form of a peptidyl-puromycin complex.

in which retention performances can be *improved* will supply still more relevant information (Dunn, 1980).

Injecting certain drugs into the blood stream immediately after training (or even during training) can increase retention performances. These drugs include moderate doses of stimulants such as strychnine, nicotine, and caffeine (McGaugh & Herz, 1972). Injections of the arousal/stress hormones such as ACTH, cortisol, and corticosterone can also have this effect (Gold & Zornetzer, 1983). As we describe next, peripheral injections of NE agonists can also facilitate retention performances. However, the effect these injections have critically depends on the strain of rodent being tested (see, for example, Bovet, Bovet-Nitti, & Oliverio, 1969).

Brain stimulation can improve as well as disrupt retention (Kesner, 1982). For example, posttrial MRF stimulation through implanted electrodes facilitates active-avoidance learning and retention performance in test animals, compared with implanted but unstimulated controls. In turn, the implanted controls are inferior to unimplanted controls. The stimulation may compensate for the debilitating effects of the small lesions caused by implanting the electrode. Posttrial hippocampal stimulation has similar effects.

The facilitating effects of posttrial stimulation depend on the task. LH stimulation can improve the retention performances of passive-avoidance and T-maze-learning tasks, but it does not affect the memory for a taste associated with illness. (In a conditioned-aversion task, animals are given a novel but good-tasting substance to eat or drink and are then made ill, as by irradiation or lithium injections. After recovery, the animals

will now avoid that substance, as though they now had an aversion to it.)

Landfield (1977) stimulated the septum at either high or low frequencies for 20 minutes immediately after training in a passive- or active-avoidance task. Low-frequency septal stimulation evokes a hippocampal theta rhythm, but high-frequency stimulation blocks that rhythm. Low-frequency stimulation produced more rapid learning than did the high-frequency posttrial septal stimulation. The low-frequency group also performed better on the active-avoidance retention test than did the implanted, unstimulated controls. Therefore, having a theta rhythm on the hippocampus after training meant there would be better recall two days later.

Brain Transmitters and Learning

Other posttrial treatments change transmitter levels in the brain. If memory involves changes in synaptic activity, finding out which type of transmitter substance is involved might provide clues about which synapses are involved. (If you have trouble in this section, you should briefly review Chapter 4.)

NE and E: Central versus peripheral effects. Both central and peripheral changes in norepinephrine (NE) and epinephrine (E) affect retention performance. (Peripheral E comes largely from the adrenal medulla. Some peripheral NE comes from the adrenal but most comes from activity in the sympathetic postganglionic axon terminals.) Since neither NE nor E cross the blood–brain barrier, any effect that changes in peripheral E and NE levels have on memory would have to come either from changes in internal organs signaled by activity in sympathetic afferents or from indirect effects of sympathetic activity on the diameter of cerebral blood vessels or on cerebral metabolism. In both cases, brain neuron activity would be affected. Any change in neural activity could affect memory processing in those neurons or in other neurons to which they are connected.

The level of E in the bloodstream immediately after training has a curvilinear effect on the retention performance of a variety of aversive (punished) or appetitive (food-rewarded) tasks (Gold, McCarty, & Sternberg, 1982; McGaugh et al., 1982). Moderate levels of E facilitate performance, but both lower and higher levels are consistently associated with poorer performances. Furthermore, there is a temporal gradient: the shorter the period between training and an injection of E, the greater the effect. If a drug that decreases the level of NE peripherally is injected at least two hours before training is begun, the abnormally low level of E caused by the drug induces amnesia for an avoidance response. The amnesia can be blocked by peripheral injections either of DA or of NE, as long as the injections are given within 10 to 15 minutes after training (Palfai & Walsh, 1979).

Some of the effects of various other memory manipulations depend on activity in the adrenal medulla and thus also depend on peripheral E levels. For example, removing the adrenal gland (and E) prevents the usual memory-enhancing effects of posttrial peripheral amphetamine injections (Gold & Zornetzer, 1983). Removing the adrenal gland also prevents the normally amnesic effects of posttraining amygdala stimulation. But if E is injected just before amygdala stimulation in animals without adrenal glands, the amnesic effect of that stimulation is restored (Liang, Bennett, & McGaugh, 1985).

One way to explore the role of central NE levels in memory is to lesion the locus coeruleus. However, such lesions do *not* affect the learning of simple active- or passive-avoidance tasks, conditioned aversions, or bar pressing for food (Sessions, Kant & Koob, 1976). NE depletion may produce learning deficits only on more complex tasks such as maze learning (Leconte & Hennevin, 1981).

Oddly enough, unilateral LC lesions made either before or immediately after training prolong the time during which posttrial ECS treatments can impair retention performances even on simple tasks. In fact, the time can be prolonged up to 14 days (Prado de Carvalho & Zornetzer, 1981). Animals with bilateral LC lesions showed normal learning but abnormally rapid forgetting. Thus, LC NE activity may be involved in the processes triggered by training that make it possible for normal retrieval to occur one or several days later, especially for more complex tasks.

Drug manipulations of CNS NE levels also affect retention performances. Gold and Zornetzer's research (1983) found that good retention might be associated with an optimal amount of central NE activity, the optimum being a moderate *decrease* from normal NE levels, as long as the decrease occurs just after training. For example, a 20% decrease in brain NE that occurred just after training produced good retention on a one-trial passive-avoidance task. Such a decrease occurs normally in the brain when subjects are exposed either to a high level of shock punishment or to a low level of shock combined with a peripheral E injection. Poorer retention performances occurred if there were no change in NE levels (low shock levels) or if there were a 40% decrease in brain NE levels (high shock combined with peripheral E injections). Research that has not found any effect of brain levels of NE on retention performance usually did not look for curvilinear effects (for example, Palfai, Brown, & Walsh, 1978).

We know that increases in brain NE levels can cause amnesia. NE injected into the amygdala immediately after training can cause amnesia, and NE injected into the amygdala just before a retention test can interfere with retrieval processes (Ellis, 1985). However, simultaneously injecting a beta-blocking drug prevents the NE-induced amnesia (Kesner & Ellis, 1983). Injecting an alpha-antagonist also prevents the amnesic effects of electrical brain stimulation, antibiotics, and brain seizures (Gold & Sternberg, 1978). All these amnesic treatments greatly increase the level of NE in the brain — an increase that in itself causes amnesia.

Brain NE levels interact with the amnesic effects of delayed cortical injections of puromycin (Church, Flexner, Flexner, & Rainbow, 1985; Flexner, Flexner, & Church, 1983; Flexner et al., 1984). As more time passes after training, more widespread injections of puromycin into the cortex must be used in order to cause amnesia. Within a day after training, temporal-hippocampal injections of puromycin can cause a (reversible) retention deficit. With further delays, puromycin must be injected onto the cortex as well as into the hippocampal area. Thus, over time, the memory may spread out over the brain. However, if NE synthesis is inhibited or if CNS beta-adrenergic receptors are blocked, memory does not spread. Inhibiting peripheral beta-adrenergic receptors does *not* have this effect, so it depends on CNS and not peripheral NE levels. As long as NE synthesis is blocked, puromycin injections limited to the temporal-hippocampal region will still produce amnesia even up to three months after training. The memory will spread within a month after NE synthesis returns to normal or within 60 to 90 days after the beta-adrenergic receptors are blocked (Flexner et. al., 1984).

In summary, both central and peripheral amine levels affect the brain changes triggered by training. The effects of both may be curvilinear, and some effects may be specific to certain areas of the brain. Central and peripheral NE effects may also be somewhat interchangeable. For example, neither a large depletion of central nor a depletion of peripheral NE levels was able by itself to cause amnesia. Amnesia was produced only when *both* treatments were combined (Roberts & Fibiger, 1977). Since the LC is physiologically and functionally similar to the peripheral sympathetic system, both systems may work in concert.

Dopamine.   Increasing brain DA levels sometimes improves retention performances. DA brain injections can reverse the amnesic effect of an antibiotic (Altman & Quartermain, 1983). DA injections into the caudate immediately after training can produce a long-term facilitation of performance. This effect is unique to the caudate, not being produced by DA injections into the amygdala, and is also unique to DA, not being produced by NE injections into the caudate (Kesner & Ellis, 1983). DA agonists injected into the hippocampus immediately after training improve retention performances, whereas injecting DA antagonists impairs retention (Grecksch & Matthies, 1982). Thus, DA input to the caudate and hippocampus may be part of a memory-processing system.

Serotonin.   Serotonin has received less attention than other transmitters. In a variety of treatments and tasks, hippocampal

5-HT levels are higher in those animals with good retention than in those animals with poorer retention or with amnesia (Dunn, 1980). However, these 5-HT effects may not be specific to memory, involving arousal, motivation, or nonspecific sensory processing instead (Gold & Zornetzer, 1983).

Acetylcholine.   Acetylcholine (ACh) has received experimental and theoretical attention from two sources. The memory deficits associated with aging have been attributed to ACh deficiencies, and drugs that affect ACh levels have consistent and strong effects on retention.

The effect of any cholinergic drug on retention depends on the type of organism, the dosage given, the degree of training, the time between training and drug administration, and the time between training and test (Deutsch, 1971; Gold & Zornetzer, 1983; Stanes, Brown, & Singer, 1976). Figure 11-6 illustrates one possible explanation for these effects, showing retention in a fast learner and in a slow learner. In fact, there is considerable evidence that differences in ACh metabolism or neural activity may be closely related to individual differences in learning and retention (Kammerer, Rauca, & Matthies, 1982; Lössner, Jork, Krug, & Matthies, 1982; Raaijmakers, 1982; Rauca, Kammerer, & Matthies, 1980). Innate differences in learning ability may be reflected not only in how much ACh activity occurs at various times after training but also in how long each phase lasts (Figure 11-6).

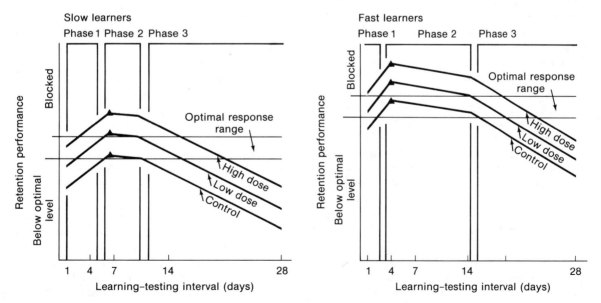

Figure 11-6   The effect of increasing cholinergic activity on retention depends on individual differences in learning performance, the dosages used, and the time between training, treatment, and testing. This is one model of synaptic transmission showing the effect of physostigmine (an anticholinesterase, which therefore increases synaptic levels of acetylcholine) on retention. See text for further description.

These theoretical curves can be experimentally tested by using injections of ACh agonists and antagonists. High doses of **physostigmine** (an AChase antagonist, which increases synaptic levels of ACh) given during Phase I (Figure 11-6) improves the performance of slow learners that have lower levels of cholinergic activity. That same treatment will impair the performance of faster learners with higher levels of cholinergic activity. However, two to eight days after training, some forgetting has occurred and cholinergic activity has decreased. At this time, large ACh injections improve the performances of both fast and slow learners.

The cholinergic septal input into the hippocampus may be affected by these ACh manipulations. The effects of posttraining systemic injections of cholinergic drugs can be mimicked by injecting the drugs directly into the hippocampus (Kesner, 1982). On some days rats were given a retention test and hippocampal injections of a muscarinic antagonist (scopolamine). On those days, their retention performances were consistently poorer (Brito, Davis, Stopp, & Stanton, 1983).

All these findings indicate that changing cholinergic activity reliably affects retention performance. Both the retention deficits and the memory-facilitating effects are temporary—as would be the case if the drugs affected retrieval by affecting cholinergic synapses at the time of the test. The formation of the memory trace may also be sensitive to ACh levels. If injections of a cholinergic agonist into the ventricles are begun shortly after training and continued for several hours, the retention performances of poorly trained mice show improvement even up to one week after the injections (Flood, Smith, & Cherkin, 1984).

Aging and certain diseases associated with senility can produce memory deficits. For example, Alzheimer's disease affects more than 100,000 Americans per year (Wurtman, 1985; Chapter 12). The disease begins with an inability to remember a familiar word or something that has just happened. It ends with a complete inability to speak, think, or act, and eventually—inevitably—in death. At autopsies, the brains of these people show systematic abnormalities in structures within and outside neurons (for example, neurofibrillary "tangles"). There is at least some genetic basis for some forms of the disease. For example, many Down's syndrome people develop the disease in their thirties (Gottfries, 1985; Hardy et al., 1985).

Some of the memory deficits of senility may be caused by the cell death and cholinergic deficiencies found in the aging and senile brain (Bartus, Dean, Beer, & Lippa, 1982; Davis & Yamamura, 1978; Chapter 12). Although several structures of the brain become damaged during the course of Alzheimer's disease, the nucleus basalis (also called the basal nucleus of Meynert) may be the focus of some of the most critical destruction. Basalis neurons innervate much of the cerebral cortex and receive input from almost all the limbic structures of the brain (Irle & Markowitsch, 1986). Because basalis neurons are cholinergic, the effects of basalis damage in Alzheimer's disease is consistent with the generalized effects of ACh upon memory processes and with the weak but sometimes therapeutic effects of cholinergic agonists on the memory deficits seen in Alzheimer's victims (Wurtman, 1985).

These effects have been modeled with lower animals. In one study, monkeys were tested for their ability to remember which one of nine stimuli had just been presented up to 30 seconds earlier. Young monkeys do better on this task than older monkeys do. ACh agonists given to young monkeys in low doses produce no effect, moderate doses produce some improvement in performance, and high doses cause performance deficits. In contrast, older monkeys show continued improvement even when given the highest doses of the ACh agonists (Bartus, 1979).

Peptides.   Peptides can either facilitate or impair memory. Posttrial injections of vasopressin and moderate doses of either ACTH or opiate agonists often facilitate memory. Posttrial injections of oxytocin, high doses of ACTH, and naloxone (an antiopiate) impair retention performances (Gold & Zornetzer, 1983).

Interpretation of the effects.   Most treatments that affect brain transmitter levels also affect retention performances. But we do not know yet *where* these effects are taking place, or even if they do occur just in a given region. We also do not know if they are specific to memory, as opposed to the effects of nonspecific arousal on brain activity.

Any explanation of these effects has to include a description of what normally activates the nerve cells using those transmitters and what effects activity in these cells usually has on brain processes (Chapter 4, Chapter 8). The noradrenergic LC neurons tend to be activated as a unit, having widespread, simultaneous effects throughout the brain. The more aroused the animal is, the more activity LC cells show (Aston-Jones & Bloom, 1981a, 1981b; Aston-Jones, 1985; Aston-Jones et al., 1986; Jacobs, 1986; Segal, 1985). Activity in these cells increases the signal-to-noise ratio of sensory cells (Chapter 8). The serotonergic raphe neuron activity is also directly related to arousal level, and the usual effect of 5-HT on neurons is inhibitory (Trulson & Jacobs, 1979). Activity in these neurons may act as a brake, preventing overarousal. However, the fact that the drug buspirone reduces not only anxiety but raphe activity as well (Trulson & Trulson, 1986) seems inconsistent with this hypothesis, unless serotonergic activity is assumed to be specifically responsible for the inhibitions of behavior associated with anxiety states. If this assumption proves to be correct, buspirone would alleviate some of the effects of anxiety because it inhibited the inhibitory serotonergic activity.

DA neurons may be involved in self-stimulation and therefore may be part of the effect of reinforcement on learning. DA activity may also be related to specific attention. The firing rate of substantia nigra neurons is not changed by sleep stage or by generalized arousal (Miller et al., 1983; Trulson, Crisp, & Trulson, 1983). However, their responsiveness to external stimuli is greater during quiet waking and is blocked during sleep (Steinfels et al., 1983). Also, some DA cells are affected (either excited or inhibited) by food-related CSs or discriminative stimuli (Miller, Sanghera, & German, 1981).

Activity in DA, 5-HT, and NE cells may regulate specific arousal, nonspecific arousal, and the effects of reinforcement —effects that *modulate* memory but that may not be necessary to its *formation*. To the extent that the hippocampus is also modulatory in its function (Isaacson, 1980), then to that extent changing the activity of its ACh afferents will also modulate memory-trace formation. Some of the effects described above may be only secondary. For example, DA injections may have the effects they do because DA neurons affect NE or ACh neurons.

Biochemical Changes Associated with Learning

During and after learning experiences, experimenters can find changes in RNA levels and types, in protein synthesis, and in the types of proteins present in the brain (Dunn, 1980; Gaito, 1976). But how to interpret these changes is far from obvious. Are these changes specific to the learning process? The increase in protein synthesis may be a nonspecific effect of the increased neural activity caused by sensory input, motivational arousal, and motor output. If there are changes specific to learning, are they specific to certain types of learning? And if there is specificity, is the specificity conferred by the type of protein synthesized or by where in the brain the increase in protein synthesis takes place? Also, some memory traces can be formed even when 90% of the protein synthesis is inhibited (although retrieval after this may require special treatments).

There are two ways to demonstrate specificity. One involves analyzing brain changes in RNA and protein levels during and after particular kinds of learning experience. Another involves looking for a particular type of protein that may have been synthesized and injecting that protein into another animal to test its effects on an "untrained" brain. (Other kinds

of experiences also cause morphological changes in brain cells; they will be covered in the next chapter.)

Changes in RNA and protein levels associated with training. Table 11-1 presents Rose's criteria for evaluating this research. If all these criteria could be met for any given biochemical change associated with experience, we would have good reason for believing that we had found the biochemical change critical to that experience. However, we have not yet even come close. All these studies have been carried out — but each type with different species, with different types of learning experience, and in different areas of the brain.

Protein phosphorylation is receiving attention because it may be involved in slow synaptic activity (see Chapter 4). Not only membrane permeability but also genomic activity may be changed by protein phosphorylation. Changes in protein phosphorylation do occur during learning and they do meet some of Rose's criteria for specificity: a specific type of change (Goelet, Castellucci, Schacher, & Kandel, 1986; Perumal, Gispen, Glassman, & Wilson, 1977; Morgan & Routtenberg, 1981), occurring specifically in trained as opposed to control groups of animals (Gispen, Perumal, Wilson, & Glassman,

Table 11-1   Criteria for demonstrating that a biochemical change is necessary and sufficient for memory formation.

1. It must have neuroanatomically localized changes in level or rate during memory formation.
2. It must have a time course that matches the time course of one specific phase of memory formation.
3. It must not be nonspecifically associated with stress, motor activity, or any other necessary but insufficient sensory, motivational, or motor changes taking place during learning and memory formation.
4. The biochemical change should be inhibited whenever the memory formation is being inhibited.
5. When the part of the brain showing the change is removed, then memory formation or memory recall must be inhibited.
6. The part of the brain showing the biochemical change must also show electrophysical changes when memory is being formed or memory is being recalled.
7. The extent of the change should be related to the strength of memory formation.
8. The change should affect synaptic activity in some detectable fashion.
9. If a single type of change corresponds to many different kinds of memory formation, then the specificity of the change must be created by *where* it occurs, rather than by *what* occurs.
10. If the biochemical change can be artificially induced, then performance on the relevant task should improve.

1977). Protein phosphorylation may affect long-term memory through a genomic process, but so far there is little evidence that phosphorylation regulates protein synthesis (Hunt, 1983).

The research team of Hydén has explored experientially produced changes in hippocampal proteins (Hydén, 1978; Hydén, Lange, & Perrin, 1977). Rats were tested to determine which paw each preferred for reaching into a tube for food. Then the subjects were forced to use the nonpreferred paw, a switch that seems to be a difficult task for rats. During and after learning, proteins and RNAs in several areas of the brain, including the hippocampus, were changed. The changes were biochemically assessed in brain slices taken immediately after a day's training trials.

Different kinds of changes occur in hippocampal and cortical proteins, as Figures 11-7 and 11-8 show. The hippocampal protein changes occur early in training and then disappear with more training. Changes in cortical protein composition are also temporary, but they occur later in training. Hydén and his colleagues interpret the hippocampal data as meaning that learning activates the genes of hippocampal cells, leading to a synthesis of some new protein. This new protein then changes the synaptic connections among the cells, after which time the new protein is no longer visible in the biochemical assays.

Changes in hippocampal protein synthesis during training may vary from subject to subject. Variability may be directly related to differences in learning and retention performances (Salganik, Parvez, Tomsons, & Shumskaya, 1983). Fast-learning rats had a higher level of hippocampal RNA synthesis before learning and a greater increase after learning than slow-learning rats did.

Interanimal transfer.   Research in the transfer of memory from one animal to another began in the 1960s, was the subject of a great deal of experimentation and controversy, and then faded (Smith, 1974). In 1976 Gaito described such research as "the only viable research program" (p. 482) for investigating the biochemistry of memory, but little research of this type has been done since then.

Animals were trained on some type of task and then their brains were ground up. Either the brain material was injected whole into naive recipients or some fraction (containing just RNA or just protein) of the brain was injected into recipients. Then the recipients were tested on some task to see if receiving a brain extract from trained donors would facilitate learning. This type of research first used worms but then shifted to rats and mice. Some control donors were given pseudoconditioning procedures before their brain (or an extract) was injected into a recipient, and some control recipients received brain extracts from untrained donors.

Although there were frequent failures to replicate, the sub-jects receiving the extracts from trained brains often showed significantly faster learning than did any other recipient group (see references and review of Smith, 1974). The positive effects could be seen even in well-controlled double-blind experiments. Positive effects were most likely to appear if the task was simple, if the donors had been overtrained on the task, and if only simple chemical procedures were carried out on the brain extract prior to injecting it into the donors.

Possibly the most controversial research came from Ungar's laboratory (Ungar, 1972, 1974). Ungar wanted to identify specific proteins created by experience. He exposed rats to various types of training, subjected their brain extracts to various biochemical procedures, and then tested the extracts by injecting them into the gut cavity of naive recipients. He wanted to see which type of extract could produce behaviors in recipients similar to those of the donors. Ungar identified what he claimed were the peptides involved in dark avoidance (**scotophobin** peptide), sound habituation, blue avoidance, green avoidance, and changes in swimming behavior (the latter three from goldfish). However, the effects of these peptides were often found to be unreliable (see, for example, Misslin, Ropartz, Ungerer, & Mandel, 1978). Even when positive effects of scotophobin were seen, they were probably caused by the protein affecting hormone levels rather than by specific changes in specific synapses (Satake & Morton, 1979).

Nevertheless, memory-protein research is still going on. Specific transfer effects have been found for conditioned aversions (Scrima, Corey, & Choo, 1982), passive avoidance (Tozzi, Sale, & Angelucci, 1980), and discriminated approach (RNA extract: Oden, Clohisy, & Francois, 1982). The transfer effects were behaviorally specific, suggesting that the extract had specific effects on cellular activity in recipient brains.

Interanimal transfer also shows the reminder effect (Tozzi, Sale, & Angelucci, 1980). The recipients were given their own passive avoidance training—though with a very weak shock—48 hours after they had received an extract from the brains of donors trained in passive avoidance. The recipients were repeatedly tested 48, 96, and 192 hours after their weak training shock. Only weakly trained recipients who received trained brain extract showed avoidance in the 48-hour test. Neither totally naive recipients nor weakly trained recipients of untrained brains showed avoidance, so the weak training acted like a "reminder."

Genetics of Learning and Memory

Another way to study the biochemistry of learning and memory is to combine the genetic and biochemical approaches. If some type of biochemistry or neural anatomy can be shown to

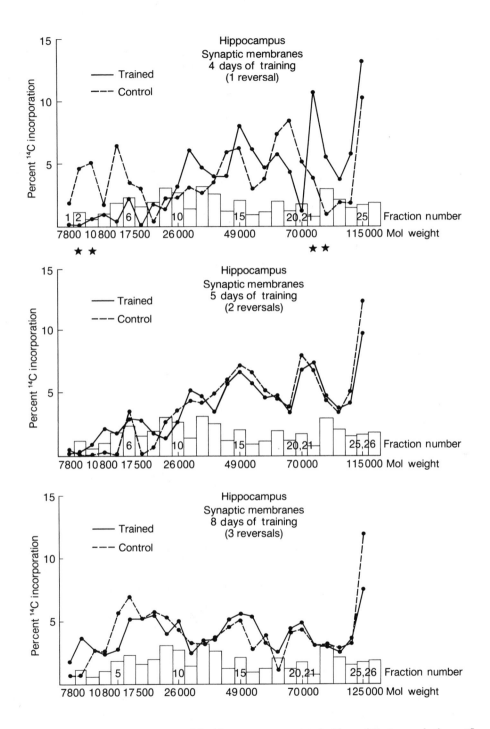

Figure 11-7 Changes in the protein composition of the hippocampus associated with conditioning are both specific and temporary. Protein composition was measured by radioactive incorporation (the height of each column indicates the relative amount of each type of protein) into protein molecules of various molecular weights. The stars designate where significant differences were found between the levels of protein contained in trained and in control hippocampi. Only proteins above 70,000 and below 115,000 molecular weight were increased after training, and then only early in the series of conditioned reversals of paw preference.

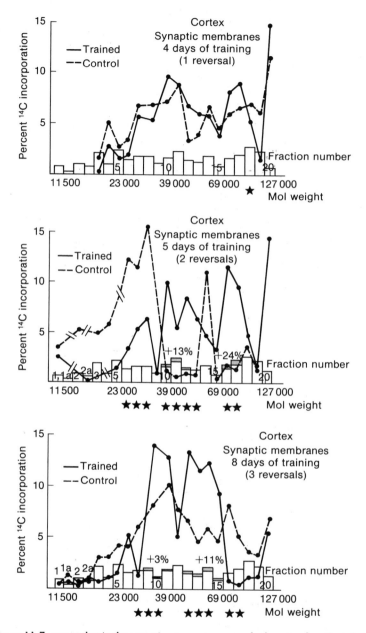

Figure 11-8 Same as Figure 11-7, except that in the sensorimotor cortex not only the rate of synthesis but also the *amount* of certain proteins is changed (the extensions on top of some bars, some of which have percent increases written above them).

correlate highly with the differences among strains in learning performances, that biochemical or anatomical correlate might be part of the brain code for learning.

Types of genetic research. Considerable attention has been paid both to interstrain differences in learning and to attempts to breed selectively for or against good learning performances. The strains of mice that tend to be good at maze learning also tend to be good at active-avoidance learning (Bovet, Bovet-Nitti, & Oliverio, 1969). However, some strains of rodents are good at some tasks and poor at others (Fuller & Thompson, 1978; Plomin, De Fries, & McClearn, 1980). Thus, we do not have an "IQ" test for rodents.

The biochemistry of fast and slow learners.   Will's review of the literature (1977) suggested that the most reliable learning-related differences among strains were found for ACh levels. This finding is consistent with the effects of cholinergic manipulations on retention-test performances. Furthermore, individual differences in ACh baseline activity and in learning-induced changes in activity do exist and are associated with differences in learning and retention performances (Kammerer, Rauca, & Matthies, 1982; Lössner et al., 1982; Raaijmakers, 1982; Rauca, Kammerer, & Matthies, 1980). Individual differences in hippocampal protein synthesis may also be related to memory (Salganik et al., 1983).

There are interesting relationships to be found among genes, learning, and hippocampal damage. Damage to the hippocampus *improves* two-way avoidance learning. The animal is placed in a rectangular box and has to learn that whatever side of the box it is on when the signal is given, it must promptly go to the other or get shocked. This task is difficult for most animals; to master the task, the animals have to learn that even if they have just received a shock on the side of the box opposite to where they are now, that side is still where they have to go to avoid another shock. Without a hippocampus, these animals may not be able to encode the spatial location of their last shock (O'Keefe, 1979; Chapter 7), and so they may have less tendency to avoid those places. Some mice and rats that are genetically poor at avoidance learning have *more* **mossy-fiber terminals** (endings of the axons of dentate granule cells) making synaptic contact in the layer of hippocampal cells (Schwegler & Lipp, 1981, 1983; Schwegler et al., 1981; if you need to review the anatomy, look ahead to Figure 11-10). Rodents that are poor at two-way avoidance learning may have more hippocampal spatial coding than do those that are better at learning that task.

The link between the number of mossy-fiber terminals and avoidance performance was dramatically supported by Schwegler and Lipp in 1983. The mossy-fiber terminals that most reliably differentiated among fast and slow avoidance-learning strains were those that formed synapses with the basal dendrites of the pyramidal cells. An association between the number of terminals and learning performances was found for two strains of rats selectively bred for good and poor performance at this active-avoidance task. It was *also* found for seven strains of mice that reliably differed in performance and for a group of randomly bred mice. In the latter group of mice, the correlation between the number of mossy-fiber terminals and the avoidance performance was −.80. For the seven strains of mice, the correlation was −.90.

The differences in performance between fast and slow learners were analyzed in some detail. Inadequate coping responses, including freezing, were the types of behavior most strongly related both to slow learning and to the number of mossy-fiber terminals on the basal dendrites. Correlating or manipulating the biochemistry of this region across strains and relating the effects to learning performances would be very useful.

However, the association between number of terminals and avoidance-learning performances may be fortuitous rather than causal. Some rats were bred for high- and low-excitability thresholds (HET and LET). Excitability thresholds were measured by the thresholds for a muscular contraction; the stimulus was a shock applied to the skin. The HET strain was good at avoidance and also had a large number of mossy-fiber terminals (Dimitrieva, Gozzo, Dimitriev, & Ammassari-Teule, 1984). Thus, having a low number of such fibers may be sufficient for good avoidance learning, but it may not be necessary.

Another promising line of research involves genetically analyzing learning deficiencies in fruit flies (see, for example, Kyriacou & Hall, 1984; Quinn, Sziber, & Booker, 1979). These animals can be avoidance trained by pairing a particular odor with shock. Several mutations of the same X-linked gene affect memories for this task. The *amnesiac* forgets the training abnormally rapidly, and the *dunce* and *rutabaga* can't learn at all. These mutations affect cAMP metabolism. Exploring the molecular relationships among genes, gene protein-products, cAMP metabolism, nerve activity, and learning may prove very fruitful (no pun intended).

Summary of Biochemistry

ECS, brain stimulation, and antibiotic treatments all produce amnesia or facilitation gradients. They may affect either the retrieval process itself or both the memory trace and the stimuli associated with retrieval efforts. Any theory of how the brain codes past experience — or how past experiences change the way the brain codes environmental or internal stimuli — will have to include either of these explanations, or some other, for these effects. But a generally accepted theory of biochemical coding is not yet available.

Brain transmitters obviously have to be involved. ACH, NE, and E all affect the ability to retrieve previously acquired information. Both very high and very low levels of NE may impair retention. The effects could be nonspecific, similar to the effects of nonspecific arousal on neural coding mechanisms and signal-to-noise ratios. The amnesic effects of some antibiotics may be secondary to the effects these drugs have on CNS levels of E and NE. This explanation of amnesia treatments may not be true of the amnesia produced by posttraining puromycin injections. Optimal levels of ACh activity are also associated with better retrieval capabilities. Strain differences in retention performances are correlated with ACh differences, including septal input to the hippocampus. The memory deficits of aging and senility may be caused by ACh deficiencies in the hippocampus.

Levels and types of brain protein and RNA are changed during learning experiences. But the changes may not be specific to memory. Although proteins are changed by learning experiences, and antibiotics can prevent retrieval, neither effect proves that specific proteins are manufactured because of specific experiences.

Genetic approaches hold out more hope, especially if strain differences in synaptic patterns can be specifically related to strain differences in learning performances on a specific task. An increase in mossy-fiber terminals on the basal dendrites of hippocampal pyramidal cells is associated with inadequate coping responses in an active-avoidance task, leading to poorer learning. But this relationship is not always seen.

All the research in this area provides information relevant to a theory of memory, and these data are uninterpretable without a theory. Thus, the research suffers from a problem opposite to the one created by the model-systems paradigm to be discussed in the last section of this chapter. In model systems, the changes associated with experience can be identified and localized, but they may not be relevant to learning in vertebrates. In contrast, the biochemical research is certainly relevant to learning in higher animals, but since it cannot be localized, it cannot be directly related to the neuron doctrine. As we will show in the next section, some of the same problems affect the interpretation of single-unit recordings made during learning. However, we must emphasize that the data of this section will have to be considered by any theory trying to explain learning and memory.

Single-Unit Activity during Learning

There are many areas of the brain that, if damaged, cause changes in the way a learned task is performed or changes in the rate and mechanics of how new learning is acquired. But the effect of the damage often depends on the age of the organism, whether the damage was done all at once or in stages (Chapter 12), the type of task, and the species involved. For example, although bilateral destruction of the hippocampus in humans impairs memory (see Chapter 1), similar damage in lower animals is usually interpreted as producing deficits in

arousal, attention, or response inhibition. Both this and the next section describe how hippocampal activity has been related to learning and memory.

General Background

To explore the neural basis of memory you could record intensively from a single brain structure during many types of learning. Or else you would record extensively from many different brain areas during the learning and performance of a given type of task. In either case, special control groups are required for the results to be interpretable.

Types of control group.   Appropriate controls for classical conditioning are necessary, and their nature is well established. The associative or experimental group not only could learn a CR but could habituate or be sensitized. To separate the neural effects of habituation and sensitization from the neural effects produced by learning a conditioned response, a control group would be habituated to the CS or sensitized to the US but not exposed to pairings of CS and US. Another control group would have just as much experience with the CS and the US as would the experimental group, but in the control group these two stimuli would be randomly presented and not paired (the US occurs at random times before and after the CS). This is a **pseudoconditioning control group.** For the experimental group, a US always follows every CS, and so it receives **associative conditioning.**

Use of a discrimination procedure can provide even more control. Only one of two different stimuli would be paired with the US (CS+). The second stimulus (CS−) would never be paired with the US. If cells change their responses to the CS+, *but not to the CS−*, the response change to the CS+ would be specific to the learned association.

Controls are also needed for operant conditioning of a response. If a discriminative stimulus is used, and if the task involves escape or avoidance, the experimental group not only will learn the conditioned response but could also be habituated or sensitized. Therefore, a control group might be presented with the discriminative stimulis and the aversive stimulus but not be allowed to escape or to avoid that aversive stimulus. This latter control, however, is the same procedure used in stress research (Chapter 10) to produce learned helplessness. Thus, any differences between the neural activity of the experimental and control groups would be caused by their different experiences, but the difference could come either from what the experimental group learns *or* from what the control group learns (or both).

Some operant-conditioning tasks use appetitive rewards. If the task uses a discriminative stimulus and a food reward, an appropriate control might be similar to the one described above. Each control animal would be yoked to an experimental animal, receiving rewards and stimuli at the same times, but the control animal would not have to perform any response to get that reward. Another control might be the use of a discrimination procedure in which one stimulus signals the availability of a reward and a second indicates that the reward is not currently available. Changes in neural responses to both stimuli are recorded to see how activity and inhibition of responding are separately coded.

Sensory and motor cells.   Both sensory and motor-cortex cells can be changed by experience, as Table 11-2 shows. For example, Woody and Engel (1972) classically conditioned cats either to blink their eyes (US was a tap to the eyeball) or to twitch their noses (US was a puff of air to the nose). After this experience, the relevant motor neurons in the cortex had a lower threshold of response to microstimulation. Thus, the threshold of motor neurons was decreased by classical conditioning experiences that stimulated those cells.

Cells in the sensory cortex, especially the "association" cortex, also show experientially induced changes. The changes can involve either an increase in firing rate (number of action potentials per unit of time), a decrease in rate, or a change in pattern. For example, in one study, cats were given discriminated classical conditioning trials. One complex visual stimulus was paired with shock and another one was not. Some cells in the visual association cortex (areas 2 and 3) changed their reponses to shock and visual stimuli, either decreasing or increasing their normal response to a particular stimulus (De Toledo-Morrell, Hoeppner, & Morrell, 1979). However, no cell in the visual cortex changed its response to *both* stimuli. The cells that changed their responses to the CS+ tended to be those cells that also responded to the shock before conditioning. The cells whose responses to the CS− changed were those that did *not* initially respond to the shock stimulus. Thus, the CS+ and the CS− seem to be coded by *separate* sensory cells in the cortex.

Table 11-2   Some examples of changes in single-unit activity that occur during operant conditioning.

Area	Type of Effect	References
Frontal cortex	Attention to cue signaling response to be made changes single-unit activity	Kubota, Tonoike, & Mikami, 1980; Ito, 1982
	Some cells respond selectively when the organism has to remember which of two stimuli had been presented in order to respond correctly several minutes later	Fuster, 1984; Watanabe, 1986a, 1986b
Basal nucleus of Meynert	The firing rates of many of these neurons change during a short-term memory task, and their change in activity may be essential to the memory coding of frontal cells	Rigdon & Pirch, 1986
Temporal cortex	Neurons respond specifically to cues involved in visual discrimination and other cells respond specifically when the organism is "remembering" a cue	Fuster & Jervey, 1982; Mikami & Kubota, 1982
Sensory cortex	The activity of cells in the auditory cortex varies according to which response was to be made and were changed by association with reinforcement	Vaadia, Gottlieb, & Abeles, 1982; Beaton & Miller, 1975
Motor cortex	The relationship of some single-unit activity to specific movements was changed by training or by association with reinforcement	Burnod, Maton, & Calvet, 1982
Lateral hypothalamus	Neurons would come to respond to a cue associated with food and would come to stop responding if a food cue was associated with food that could never be consumed	Mora, Rolls, & Burton, 1976

Hippocampus

Researchers turned their attention to the hippocampus because lesioning it interfered with certain kinds of learning and memory (see, for example, Uretsky & McClearn, 1969). To provide the necessary background, we will summarize some anatomy and some theoretical interpretations of the effects of hippocampal lesions.

Anatomy.   The anatomy of the hippocampus is presented in Figures 11-9 and 11-10. Figure 11-9 shows how the hippocampus is situated in the human brain in relation to other limbic structures. Figure 11-10 shows the microanatomy of a slice taken from a rat hippocampus. This slice is taken perpendicularly to the long axis of the hippocampus, as shown in Figure 11-10. (You can also look ahead at another hippocampal slice in Figure 11-16.)

The hippocampus has three major and several minor inputs. The first comes from the **entorhinal** cortex lying just to the side of the hippocampus. As Figure 11-10 shows, axons from the entorhinal cortex are **perforant fibers,** which form synapses with the granule cells in the **dentate gyrus.** The perforant fibers may use glutamate as their transmitter substance and may provide information about the relative novelty of a given stimulus to the hippocampus (Deadwyler, West, & Robinson, 1981). The second major input is the **fornix,** which contains not only the major efferent output from the hippocampus but the cholinergic afferent input coming from the **medial septum.** These afferents also innervate the granule cells. The input from the medial septum may provide the hippocampus with information about a stimulus whose significance to the organism has changed because of experience (Deadwyler, West, & Robinson, 1981). Third, axons from **hippocampal pyramidal cells** cross over (forming the **commissural fibers**) to form synapses with cells in the contralateral hippocampus. Granule cells also receive NE input from the LC, 5-HT input from the raphe nuclei, and probably DA input from the tegmentum (Schröder, Kammerer, & Matthies, 1982).

Some microcircuits within the hippocampus are also illustrated in Figure 11-10. Granule cells pass the incoming information (using aspartate?) onto pyramidal cells in area CA_3. Granule-cell axons are **mossy fibers** and their terminals are the mossy fiber terminals. Earlier we pointed out that the number of the terminals present in the rat was inversely related to its speed of avoidance learning (Schwegler & Lipp, 1981, 1983; Schwegler et al., 1981). Granule cells pass information to the pyramidal cells in areas CA_3 to CA_1. Within the hippo-

campus, information is transformed not only by which connections are made but also by activity in hippocampal interneurons, the basket cells. These cells have inhibitory effects and probably use GABA. The pyramidal-cell axons project out of the hippocampus (using glutamate or aspartate?) to the **lateral septum.**

Interpretation of lesion effects.   Every few years or so, there seems to be a new theory of hippocampal function based largely on the behavioral deficits observed after hippocampal lesions. Sometimes one gets the impression that because of the difficulties of interpreting lesion research, specifically memory research, researchers are forced into acting like the blind men examining the elephant: whether the elephant is seen to be more like a rope or more like a tree trunk depends on what part of the elephant a particular researcher is concentrating on.

Several theories are now being evaluated. Activity in the hippocampus may enable the animal to "tune out" or to ignore "irrelevant" stimuli (Moore, 1979; Solomon, 1979). Another possibility is that the hippocampus is somehow involved in coding an animal's position in space. For example, spatial memory becomes severely impaired with age in some rats, and only the rats that show the impairment have also suffered a loss of synaptic input to their hippocampus (Geinisman, De Toledo-Morrell, & Morrell, 1986). In his review and theory of hippocampal functioning, Solomon (1979) points out that hippocampal lesions typically impair task performances only if the task has a spatial component. Thus, classical conditioning is not impaired, but the ability of organisms to find their way through a complex maze is impaired after hippocampal damage. (However, stimulating the hippocampus can severely disrupt classical conditioning, as though a malfunctioning hippocampus were worse than no hippocampus at all: Thompson, Berger, Berry, Hoehler, Kettner, & Weisz, 1980). Some cells in the hippocampus also react as though they were spatial feature detectors (Chapter 7; McNaughton, Barnes, & O'Keefe, 1983; O'Keefe, 1976, 1979; O'Keefe & Nadel, 1978).

But the hippocampus is involved in more than just spatial coding. Although damage to the hippocampus does not impair classical conditioning (except under very special conditions, as we shall describe), classical-conditioning procedures produce reliable and often dramatic changes in hippocampal neural activity (Solomon, 1979). Even more important, hippocampal lesions cause severe and permanent deficits in humans' ability to remember what has happened to them (at least the lesions impair their ability to be consciously aware of their past experiences). However, the same has not been true of the animal

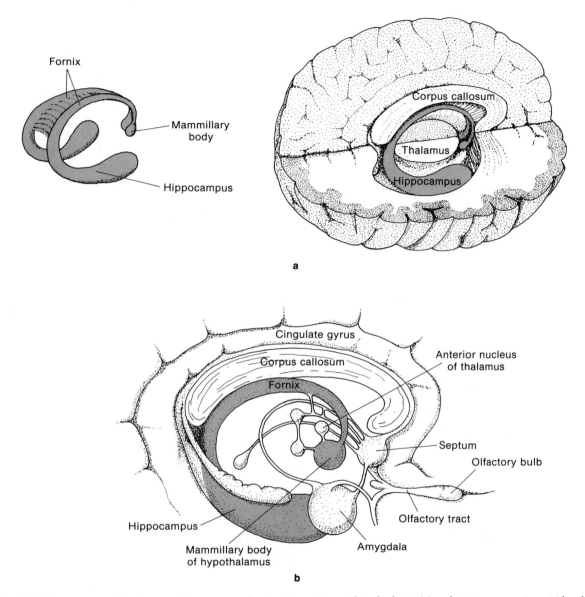

Figure 11-9 Anatomy of the human hippocampus, showing its position within the brain (**a**) and its interconnections with other limbic-system structures (**b**).

lesion effects — until recently. For example, some researchers have found that hippocampal plus amygdala damage in primates can cause memory deficits very similar to those seen in hippocampally damaged humans, when the primates are tested with tasks similar to those given to humans (Zola-Morgan, Squire, & Mishkin, 1982).

Another set of researchers devised a very clever way of training rats to remember a sequence of stimuli (Kesner & Novak, 1982). These researchers would then be able to compare the effects of hippocampal lesions in rats with the inability of hippocampally lesioned humans to remember recent events (ones presented just seconds before). Rats were trained in an

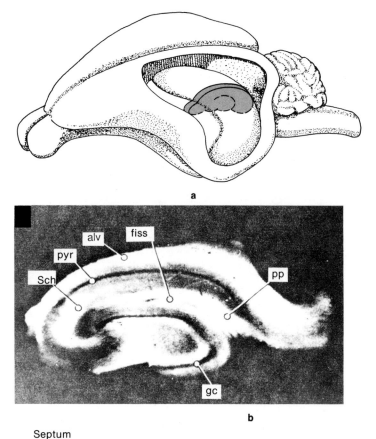

Figure 11-10 **a, b.** Position of the hippocampus in the brain of a rat (**a**) and some of the internal circuits of that hippocampus (**a, b**). There are three major inputs: from the entorhinal cortex via perforant fibers, from the medial septum via the fornix, and from the contralateral hippocampus via commissural fibers. **b.** An actual slice from a rat hippocampus, taken from slab shown in a. fiss = hippocampal fissure; gc = granule cell layer; pp = perforant path fibers; pyr = pyramidal cell layer; Sch = Schaffer collateral fibers. **c.** A slice similar to the one shown in **a** and **b**. (1) entorhinal cortical output fibers traverse ("perforate") the surrounding cortex to terminate on granule cells in the dentate gyrus; (2) dentate granule cells' short axons (the "mossy fibers") connect to the closest part of the hippocampal pyramidal cell fields (CA$_4$); (3) some CA$_4$ pyramidal fibers project back to granule cells and also connect to other pyramidal cells; (4) pyramidal cell axons project to the lateral septum through the fornix; (5) **Schaffer collaterals** from pyramidal cells connect to apical dendrites of other pyramidal cells both ipsilaterally and contralaterally (through a commissure; connection is not shown); (6) CA$_1$ cells project to a nearby cortical area called the *subiculum*; (7) subiculum cells also project to the septum through the fornix.

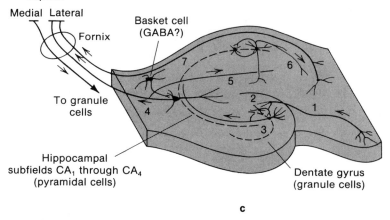

eight-arm radial maze and forced to enter each arm in a particular sequence on each trial. Then, at the end of each trial, they were presented with two arms (the rest were closed). To get rewarded, the rats had to pick which one of those two had been seen *least* recently. To test memories for more recent versus more distant events, test trials consisted of choices between arm 1 and arm 2 (most distant), between 4 and 5, and between 7 and 8 (most recent). In addition, on some trials a delay of 10 seconds was inserted between presentation and "recall" (choice). A delay has a very debilitating effect on the memory of hippocampally damaged humans.

The results appear in Figure 11-11. Part **a** shows the effects of delay on the recall of the nonlesioned control rats. These curves parallel the effects that delay has on the recall of normal humans. Without a delay, normal subjects—both rat and human—recall the first and last pairs best. But hippocampally lesioned rats (part **b**) can recall the last pair but not the first pair—which is what happens to humans with hippocampal damage. With a delay (part **c**), hippocampal rats do not even remember the last pair. Although this task obviously has a large spatial component, the time between the presentation and the test is also critical to performance deficits. This observation is not consistent with an exclusively spatial theory of hippocampal functioning, but it *is* consistent with the effect of hippocampal damage in humans.

Although spatial cues may be important to hippocampal neurons, these cells also process information about recently presented stimuli—both spatial and nonspatial. Therefore, tasks requiring the animal to remember recently presented stimuli should be the ones associated with changes in the activity of hippocampal neurons.

Olds's research. Olds and his colleagues pioneered the field of single-unit recording in awake, behaving animals (Hirano, Best, & Olds, 1970; Olds, Disterhoft, Segal, Kornblith, & Hirsh, 1972; Segal & Olds, 1972). He and some of his colleagues explored single-unit changes during learning (see, for example, Disterhoft & Segal, 1978; Segal, 1973), especially in the hippocampus.

One technique introduced by these researchers was to record from cells all over the brain, looking for the cells that showed the shortest-latency conditioned responses to the CS. These would be the cells, they hypothesized, that would be "'at the site' of the conditioning" (other researchers have disagreed with that analysis). Olds and colleagues compared neural responses to the CS during a pseudoconditioning pretraining control period with the responses seen after conditioning. The rat was conditioned to expect and to eat food that was presented immediately after a CS+, but food was never presented after a CS−.

Short-latency responses to the CS+ were found in many areas of the brain (though not in all). Both the excitatory and inhibitory responses were not seen during the control trials, but only after conditioning. However, only a few cells in each area showed such changes. Short-latency excitatory conditioned responses were seen in CA$_3$ pyramidal cells. These

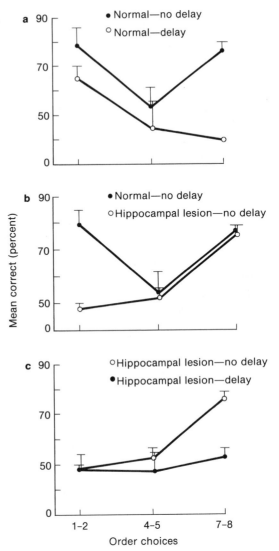

Figure 11-11 Rats with hippocampal lesions can show memory deficits similar to those found in hippocampally lesioned humans. See text for description of experiment and discussion of results.

conditioned responses were specific, since these cells responded significantly more to the CS+ than to the CS− or to a novel stimulus. In animals given extinction trials (the CS+ was no longer paired with food), the hippocampal responses to the CS+ decreased but did not return to control levels (Hirano et al., 1970; Olds et al., 1972). In addition, when the significance of the cues was reversed—the previous CS− was now paired with food—hippocampal responses changed. Thus, these cells may code for recent experiences and not for experiences occurring further in the past (Disterhoft & Segal, 1978).

The researchers also systematically examined which hippocampal cells showed these conditioned changes. The responses of all cells to the CS+ were recorded both before and after conditioning. During learning, the granule cells showed the earliest conditioned change. However, those cells responded equally to the CS+ and the CS−. These dentate granule cells were excited by a CS associated with food and were inhibited by a CS associated with shock (Segal, Disterhoft, & Olds, 1972).

Pyramidal cells showed a conditioned change in activity only during later conditioning trials. The CA₃ cells showed conditioned responses somewhat before the CA₁ cells. In pyramidal cells, there was a greater excitatory response to the CS+ than to the CS−, and these cells were excited both by shock and by food CSs. This pattern of changes over conditioning trials suggests that there is some type of sequential processing of the experience codes within the hippocampus itself.

Finally, cellular responses in the entorhinal cortex were also changed by conditioning. The conditioned responses persisted for some time after each trial. Segal (1973) suggested that a persistent change in entorhinal cellular activity increases hippocampal CS+ responses. He demonstrated that having a short period between trials—thus starting a second trial when entorhinal activity from the first trial was still continuing—increased the degree to which conditioned changes could be seen in the hippocampus. In fact, Fifková and Van Harreveld (1978), using a task similar to that used by Olds and his colleagues, found that two hours of training increased the size of dentate layer spines receiving a perforant input. This increase was not seen in the pseudoconditioned control animals and it was specific to the perforant input.

Gabriel's work.   Gabriel and his colleagues recorded from many different areas of the brain, including the hippocampus, during and after operant conditioning (Gabriel, Foster, & Orona, 1980; Gabriel et al., 1980; Orona & Gabriel, 1983a, 1983b). The subjects were rabbits and the task was escape/avoidance. The CSs were tones, one of which (the CS+) was followed within five seconds by footshock. The rabbit could terminate the footshock by moving; moving during the CS+ would prevent the shock (avoidance).

Whether cells show discriminative or nondiscriminative responses, and whether the responses to the CSs occur early or late in training, is assumed to reflect the type of processing being carried out. Some areas of the cortex show early but

nondiscriminative (equal responses to CS+ and to CS−) responses. The animal may be learning that stimuli of that modality are relevant. Later in training, because responses to the CS− decrease, specific responses appear in the cortex. This change in cortical responses occurs at the time behaviors are beginning to change: the animals are beginning to learn.

Once the code has been acquired—a differential response is made by cortical cells and the animals have learned to avoid—the code is **relegated** to certain subcortical nuclei. Specifically, cingulate cortical cells relegate the code to the anterioventral (AV) thalamic nucleus. This means that the cells in the AV nucleus begin to show discriminative responses: the responses to the CS+ increase. Relegation frees the cortical cells from having to process this information so they can then process information about other situations and other tasks, such as reversal of the significance of the CS+ and the CS−. The process of relegation may be part of forming long-term memories of what happened during this learning task. The relegated information is fed back to the superficial layers of the cortex, informing those cells that relegation has taken place.

According to these researchers, the hippocampus plays several vital roles in these processes. First, the hippocampus is one of the first structures to show discriminative activity. It is hypothesized to receive that information from the cortex. Later, the subcortical cells showing discriminative activity also send their information to the hippocampus. The hippocampus uses this information to construct detailed models of the stimuli and of their significance (the models are the short-latency CS responses discovered by Olds and his associates). The hippocampal model of stimulus significance also involves coding (which may involve spatial cues) of *where* the animal learned the association. (The animal can thus compensate for any effects of changes in location. After hippocampal lesions, moving the animal to a different room causes severe disruptions in the performance of this task.)

Once the models are constructed by the hippocampus, it controls the response. The CS− activates the hippocampus, which acts to inhibit the response. The CS+ inhibits the hippocampus—which then shows a theta rhythm—and the response is allowed to occur. (As described in Chapter 8, "theta" refers to 10–12 Hz regular EEG activity in the hippocampus.) Gabriel and his colleagues recorded bursts of single-unit activity in the hippocampus that occurred at 10–12 Hz: a burst of theta activity. Theta and nontheta activity are illustrated in Figure 11-12.

Thetalike bursts sent from the hippocampus to the subcortical nuclei would facilitate relegation. They would also cause changes in coded activity when the significance of the cues is changed (extinction) or reversed. Thus, the hippocampus may

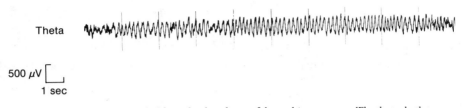

Desynchronized

Theta

500 μV

1 sec

Figure 11-12 Patterns of electrical activity recorded from the dorsal part of the rat hippocampus. The theta rhythm may occur when the hippocampus is being inhibited, and the rhythm may also be part of the relegation process (see text).

control learned behavior by "remembering" just presented cues; it also may participate in the construction of long-term memories.

Changes in internal state: Learning and hippocampal activity. Two types of research illustrate how changes in hippocampal activity and changes in rate of learning can be manipulated by the same changes in internal state. One such state is sleep. A tone CS+ was presented by itself for several trials for one group of rats, then the tone was paired with shock for all rats, and finally the tone was again presented by itself (extinction) (Best & Best, 1976). Presenting the CS by itself for several trials before the conditioning trials begin decreases the rate of learning: this is **latent inhibition.**

Activity in pyramidal hippocampal cells parallels behavioral changes. Conditioning produced a large increase in the hippocampal rate of response and extinction produced a decrease back to control levels. Furthermore, prior CS-alone trials caused latent inhibition in both behavioral and hippocampal responses.

Sometimes the CS presentations occurred when the animal was sleeping. Hippocampal cells in sleeping animals showed much less conditioning. During adaptation (presenting the CS by itself before conditioning), cells in sleeping animals started responding *less* to the CS. Thus, inhibition was increased during conditioning in sleeping animals—an unusual type of latent-inhibition effect. The effect of sleep may occur because granule cells either are tonically inhibited during the waking state and are disinhibited by the CS or are tonically excited during slow-wave sleep, which the CS temporarily interrupts (Winson & Abzug, 1977).

Bloch and his colleagues (Bloch & Laroche, 1981; Laroche & Bloch, 1982; Laroch, Falcou, & Bloch, 1983) investigated the effects of reticular stimulation on experientially induced changes in hippocampal activity in rats. They pointed out that research done both in their laboratory and in other laboratories

has shown that stimulating the midbrain reticular formation after each trial produces behavioral arousal and facilitates behavioral learning and retention (see the section entitled "The Biochemistry of Learning and Memory").

These researchers used a tone CS and a shock US. They gave half the animals a low-level MRF stimulation for 90 seconds, starting 10 seconds after *each* conditioning trial. They recorded from hippocampal pyramidal and granule cells during training and during a retention test given 16 days after the training. **Multiunit activity** (recorded from several cells simultaneously through a single extracellular electrode) in the hippocampus was increased during conditioning. Animals with MRF stimulation showed faster conditioning, more evidence of retention 16 days later, and more hippocampal multiunit activity. Both granule and pyramidal cells showed these effects.

This research shows that changes in hippocampal activity during sleep and arousal are closely related to learning and retention. But since behavior and hippocampal activity were not recorded from the same animals, hippocampal activity could not be directly related to behavioral changes.

Eyelid Conditioning

The second type of research records extensively from many parts of the brain during a single type of learning task. In the task to be described here, a tone is usually used as the CS and a puff of air to the eye is the US. The air puff elicits not only eyelid closure but also movement of the nictitating membrane (at least in rabbits and cats, which have that structure in their eyes). Conditioning is considered to have occurred when the nictitating membrane and eyelid responses begin to appear during conditioning trials after the CS but before the US is presented.

Thompson and his colleagues have extensively studied the neural changes associated with this task (Berger & Thompson,

1978a, 1978b; Patterson, Berger, & Thompson, 1979). Their work has been recently summarized (Berger, Clark, & Thompson, 1980; Thompson et al., 1980; Thompson et al., 1983). Most of their work was done with rabbits, but similar results are seen in cats.

Changes in the sensory and motor pathways. To explore the changes in sensory pathways caused by conditioning, researchers taught animals to perform a psychophysical detection task with a conditioned nictitating membrane response (Chapter 6). When a constant-intensity white noise was presented at threshold levels, it would be detected (responded to) 50% of the time (by definition). During these trials, multiunit recordings were taken from various brain structures. The trials on which the animal detected the stimulus were averaged and compared with trials on which the animal did not detect the stimulus. As Figure 11-13 shows, the behaviors of sensory cells were affected only by the stimulus, *not* by detection. Only behavior (by definition) and hippocampal single-unit activity were different during detection and nondetection trials. Therefore hippocampal activity could be part of the memory code for that task.

Association-cortex cells are also changed by conditioning. Rabbits were given a series of tone–air-puff conditioning trials (Kraus & Disterhoft, 1982). Conditioning CS caused both increases and decreases in single-unit response rate to the CS, but the response to the US was not changed by conditioning. The change in the CS response was strongest just after the conditioned behavioral response first appeared, and then it tended to decrease with further training. This type of effect, when observed by Gabriel, was attributed to relegation.

Thompson argued that the unconditioned reflex pathways are not essential to the CR. He described research in which animals were injected with morphine. The drug immediately and completely abolished the CR but had no effect on the UR.

However, motor pathways are certainly relevant. To demonstrate this, researchers classically conditioned a nictitating membrane response by pairing a tone CS with a brain-stimulus US. In this research, the US was stimulation to the motor area controlling the nictitating membrane (in the brain stem, close to the abducens nucleus) (Martin, Land, & Thompson, 1980). Only some rabbits acquired a CR. Later, all rabbits — both learners and nonlearners — were given further conditioning trials with an air-puff US. The animals that had learned with the brain-stimulation US showed much earlier and greater increases in abducens neural activity than did the prior nonlearners. There could have been some intrinsic difference in neural excitability causing the differences in ability to acquire a CR with a brain-stimulation US. The researchers sug-

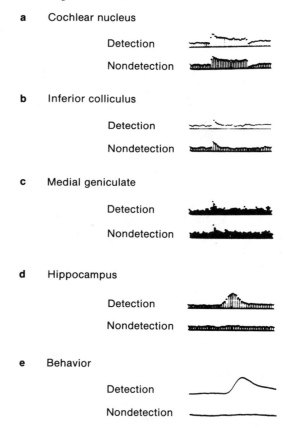

Figure 11-13 These records compare multiunit responses (recorded from several cells simultaneously) from auditory neurons with those from hippocampal neurons during a psychophysical absolute-detection experiment for a noise stimulus. In all cases, the intensity of the sound is constant and identical in both the trials on which the animal did behaviorally detect the stimulus and the trials on which it did not. **a–d.** Average poststimulus histograms (averaged over successive 15 mSec time periods: how many responses occurred at each latency after the stimulus, averaged over 200–300 trials). **e.** Average nictitating membrane response for detection (upper trace) versus nondetection (lower trace) trials. Note that the behavioral response and the hippocampal response are both clearly present on detection trials and completely absent on nondetection trials; responses from auditory neurons are present and identical on detection and nondetection trials.

gested that these results reflected differences in the excitability of interneurons rather than in the motoneurons themselves.

The hippocampus. As Figure 11-13 shows, hippocampal activity changes during behavioral detection trials as though that activity were part of the engram for that task. Multiunit recordings of pyramidal hippocampal activity during nictitating-membrane-conditioning trials support this idea (Thompson et al., 1983). Similar changes in hippocampal activity occurred during a classically conditioned leg flexion (the US was shock to the hind leg). These changes closely parallel behavior. First, changes in hippocampal activity are one of the first signs of learning to be seen anywhere in the nervous system. Some multiunit recordings of pyramidal cells are presented in Figure 11-14. Hippocampal activity precedes and parallels the behavioral responses, both the CR and the UR. The activity in the hippocampus seems to predict the shape of the conditioned response.

Conditioning increases not only the multiunit response to the CS but the response to the US. Any procedure that changes the rate of behavioral conditioning, such as changing the interval between trials, has identical effects on the rate of hippocampal conditioning. Most dramatically, the animal's rate of learning could be predicted by the hippocampal activity during the first few US presentations. The animals that learned the most quickly showed greatly increased multiunit activity in response to the US over the first few trials. Animals that learned slowly showed either unchanged or decreased hippocampal single-unit responses to the US over this period (Berry & Thompson, 1978).

Hippocampal activity during conditioning is quite different from association-cortex activity. In the cortex, the neural changes occur on later conditioning trials than do the changes in the hippocampus. Furthermore, conditioning produces no change in the cortical-cell responses to the US, whereas conditioning increases hippocampal-cell responses to the US— particularly in the fast learners.

The changes in hippocampal activity are not only intrinsic to that structure, they are associative. Although the output areas, such as the lateral septal region, may show conditioned responses similar to those of the hippocampus, input areas (the medial septal nucleus and the entorhinal cortex) do not show similar changes during conditioning (Berger & Thompson, 1978b; Thompson et al., 1980). And Figure 11-14 shows that the changes in hippocampal activity come from the association of the CS with the US by comparing responses in conditioned and control subjects. Comparing the first with the last block of US-alone trials, we can see that the response of the nictitating membrane is, if anything, larger, but there is no change in hippocampal single-unit activity. The same is true for the CS-alone trials: no change in hippocampal activity. Thus, cells within the hippocampus itself are processing associative information.

Thompson and his co-workers identified which cells in the

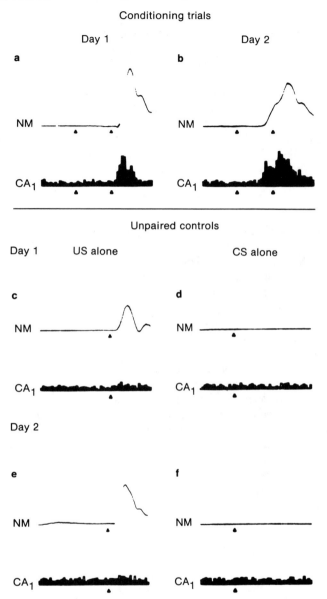

Figure 11-14 Hippocampal activity is changed by conditioning. These are examples of behavioral nictitating membrane (NM) responses (averaged over eight trials) and associated multiunit histograms (see caption for Figure 11-13) of hippocampal activity for conditioning trials and unpaired control trials. Upper trace: average NM response for one block of eight trials. Lower trace: hippocampal single-unit response poststimulus histogram for one block of eight trials. **a, b.** The first marker is for tone onset and the second marker for air-puff onset. **c–f.** The marker is for stimulus (CS or US) presentation. Hippocampal activity was recorded from the CA_1 region.

hippocampus showed these changes (Berger, Rinaldi, Weisz, & Thompson, 1983; Berger & Thompson, 1978a, 1978b, & 1978c). The individual cells whose activities closely paralleled the amplitude and latency of the nictitating response were all identified as pyramidal cells. Other cells acquired an inhibitory response to the CS during the conditioning trials. Those cells could be interneurons, such as the basket cells. Some nonpyramidal cells had a conditioned increase in rate, and some of them responded rhythmically, with bursts paralleling the theta rhythm. This rhythm may be the hippocampal activity associated with consolidation. Some cells not identified could have been "place" detectors.

The cerebellum.   The hippocampus may process (and "remember") just-presented stimuli and facilitate consolidation into long-term storage. However, another structure may actually contain the long-term memory trace: the cerebellum (McCormick & Thompson, 1984; Thompson et al., 1983; Yeo, Hardiman, & Glickstein, 1984). In Chapter 2, we described the cerebellum and its input and output nuclei as being necessary for memories for complex motor-skills learning, a category that seems to include the eyelid response.

Figure 11-15 presents some multiunit recordings of cerebellar activity taken during conditioning. The cerebellar neurons clearly distinguished between detection and nondetection trials in the psychophysical studies described earlier. Here, the earliest latency response is *not* signal dependent, showing no difference between detection and nondetection

trials. However, later activity clearly discriminates between those trials, being present on detection and absent on nondetection trials.

During conditioning, as Figure 11-15 shows, the shortest-latency multiunit cerebellar response was clearly related to the CS. It was evoked first by the CS and then by the US, and it did not change over trials. However, longer-latency CS responses, occurring just before the US was to be presented, increased over trials, closely modeling the conditioned nictitating-membrane response. Thus, whereas hippocampal activity models both the CR and the UR, late cerebellar activity models only the CR.

To verify this role for the cerebellum, researchers lesioned parts of either the left or right cerebellum. In one experiment, certain nuclei (dentate and interpositus) in the left cerebellum were lesioned and the left eye was conditioned. All this research has shown that although the UR reflex was unaffected, the CR was completely and permanently abolished (Desmond & Moore, 1982; Lavond, McCormick, & Thompson, 1984; McCormick & Thompson, 1984; Yeo, Hardiman, & Glickstein, 1984). Animals given left-eye conditioning could relearn a CR only if the conditioning were shifted to the right eye. Thus, multiunit activity in the cerebellum might reflect the changed effectiveness of some synapse affecting both the CR and cerebellar cells. The engram may be in cerebellar nuclei. As the researchers point out, "We have succeeded in localizing the essential memory trace circuit for the learned response, and it is extraordinarily localized" (Lavond, McCormick, & Thompson, 1984, p. 108).

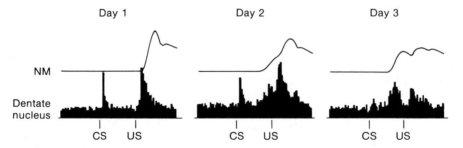

Figure 11-15   The cerebellum is changed by conditioning. This shows the change of multiunit activity (see caption for Figure 11-14) in the dentate nucleus of the left cerebellum (the side on which the US was presented) over the course of conditioning. Each record— nictitating membrane (NM) above and multiunit histogram below—is the average of an entire day's training trials. On day 1, the animal showed no learned responses, and the recording showed only stimulus-evoked responses. On day 2, the animal began to learn, and a model of the learned NM response developed. On day 3, the learned NM response was well developed, as was the neural model in the cerebellum, but there did not appear to be any neural model of the reflex NM response or UR.

Summary of Learning and Neural Activity

We examined learning and neural activity from two perspectives: (1) an intensive analysis of one structure during different kinds of learning, and (2) an extensive analysis of different structures during one kind of learning.

The effects of damage to the hippocampus have not yet been adequately conceptualized. Its damage in humans prevents them from being consciously aware of anything that has happened since the time of the damage. A similar type of deficit may be detected in lower animals if they are trained to perform similar types of task. Hippocampal damage also affects performances on other tasks, such as spatial ones, and some hippocampal pyramidal cells may be feature detectors for a given "place in space."

Regardless of how the lesion and sensory data are interpreted, cells in the hippocampus are changed by classical and operant conditioning. Changes in hippocampal responses to the CS occur early in conditioning, they are short-latency responses, and they discriminate between the CS+ and a CS−. The hippocampus could be analyzing trial stimuli according to recently constructed models of stimulus significance. New stimuli are compared with the models, and a response is either facilitated or inhibited.

The hippocampus may also affect consolidation — or relegation, in Gabriel's theory. Hippocampal activity may facilitate the ability of other brain areas to have changes in synaptic morphology or to construct more long-term models of stimulus significance. This theory of hippocampal function would be consistent with the amnesia displayed by humans after damage to their hippocampus. Thompson suggests that the cerebellum might be one of these other brain areas, especially for conditioned motor responses.

Model Systems

The **model-systems approach** to memory reduces the complexity of the system being studied. Reducing the number of connections that could possibly be changed by an experience permits the connections that are changed — and how they are changed — to be more easily identified.

One model system pairs stimulation of individual brain cells (the US) with a prior external stimulus (the CS) to see if the pairing changes responses to the CS (see, for example, Bureš

& Burešová, 1967; see also Doty's review, 1969). This pairing shows which cells have **plastic** (changeable) responses but does not necessarily tell us anything about memory per se. The changes could be effects of nonspecific arousal, for example.

We will be describing two other types of model system. One uses just part of the nervous system, preferably a brain slice studied in vitro (in a culture dish) (Schwartzkroin, 1975). Slices of hippocampus have been used to study the synaptic basis for long-term potentiation. Another way to simplify is to study the synaptic basis of memory in an invertebrate with only a limited number of cells.

Hippocampal Potentiation

As little as 30 seconds of high-frequency stimulation (greater than 10 Hz) of presynaptic neurons increases the amplitude of the hippocampal postsynaptic response. The increase can last for several hours — or even for several days, if several series of stimuli are given (Chapter 4). Although this phenomenon has been most often studied in the hippocampus, where it is strongest, it can be observed in many CNS areas. For example, long-term potentiation can also appear in the nuclei associated with the cerebellum (Racine, Wilson, Gingell, & Sunderland, 1986). However, the phenomenon does seem to be stronger in the limbic system than in the rest of the brain (Brown & McAfee, 1982; Racine, Milgram, & Hafner, 1983; Teyler & Discenna, 1984). Because in this section we discuss only the hippocampus, we will call the phenomenon **long-term hippocampal potentiation (LTHP).**

Several hippocampal pathways can develop LTHP. Blish and Gardner-Medwin (1973) first discovered LTHP in unanesthetized (but numbed) rabbits by stimulating the perforant path. Since then, LTHP has been demonstrated for commissural, septal, and Schaffer collateral input into pyramidal cells (Bliss & Dolphin, 1982; Racine, Milgram, & Hafner, 1983).

A diagram of the type of hippocampal slice often used to study LTHP is presented in Figure 11-16. (You should also look back at Figures 11-9 and 11-10.) To study LTHP, the researcher inserts stimulating electrodes onto the perforant path, the commissural path, or the Schaffer collateral path. Extracellular single-unit or multiunit recording electrodes are placed in either the granule-cell layer or the CA_1 pyramidal layer.

Relevance of LTHP to memory.   Some critics point out that the LTHP involves unnatural patterns of stimulation in order to occur, a comment that reveals how the model-systems approach suffers from a "relevance gap." But some evidence

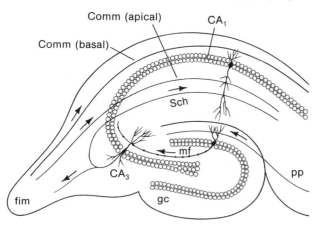

Figure 11-16 The hippocampal slice is often used in a model-systems approach to long-term potentiation. CA_1, CA_3 = pyramidal cell fields CA_1 and CA_3; comm = commissural fibers; fim = fimbria, to fornix: gc = granule cells of dentate gyrus; mf = mossy fibers; pp = perforant path; Sch = Schaffer collaterals. See also Figure 11-10 and text discussion of that figure.

shows that LTHP is probably directly relevant to learning and memory. If so, then being able to explain LTHP would also provide reductionistic explanations for at least some forms of learning and memory.

First, animals that show good or poor retention performances also differ in LTHP. One group of albino rats was inbred for seven generations to produce a group of animals that were poor not only in active-avoidance learning but also in maze learning. These animals also showed little posttetanic potentiation, which might mean that they would show little LTHP (Izquierdo, Orsingher, & Ogura, 1972). Even more impressively, Barnes (1979) compared aged with young rats. As we noted earlier, aged rats with memory problems have fewer synapses in the hippocampus than do either young rats or old rats with no impairment (Geinisman, De Toledo-Morrell, & Morrell, 1986). Barnes found that aged rats had both poor spatial memory and much less durable LTHP in comparison with the younger rats. In fact, both within and between groups, the durability of LTHP was negatively correlated with the number of spatial errors made (the correlations ranged from −.43 to −.64).

Second, learning may cause changes in LTHP. One group of researchers tested the ability of perforant-path stimulation to be used as a CS in an active-avoidance task in rats (Reymann, Rüthrich, Lindenau, Ott, & Matthies, 1982). They found that only frequencies that produce LTHP could be successfully used as CSs; if the stimuli in each stimulation series were

spread out more over time, they did not produce LTHP and were ineffective as CSs. Learning also produces LTHP-like changes in the excitability of cells in the hippocampus and in the number of postsynaptic receptors (Lynch & Baudry, 1984; Segal, 1977; Rüthrich, Matthies, & Ott, 1982). For example, Laroche, Bergis, and Bloch (1983) subjected rats to classical conditioning, but only one group received reticular stimulation immediately after each trial. LTHP was induced two days after the end of conditioning. The amount of LTHP produced was increased by the prior classical conditioning trials, and the reticular stimulation not only enhanced the conditioning but also increased the amount of LTHP that could be induced.

Third, LTHP affects later learning. In one experiment, rabbits were implanted with chronic electrodes both in the perforant path for stimulation and in the dentate gyrus for recording (Berger, 1984). Some of these rabbits were given LTHP stimulations and then all were given discriminated classical conditioning trials. The LTHP group learned significantly faster than did the other group. Also, LTHP can enhance discriminability of a brain CS (Skelton, Miller, & Phillips, 1985). Gross stimulation of the perforant path was used as a CS for a food-rewarded operant in rats. Prior LTHP of that pathway significantly increased the subsequent rate of learning. This last type of research comes closest to satisfying the memory-code criterion (criterion 1, Table 11-1) that specifies that the hypothesized neural-synaptic change must be induced and then shown to affect learning/memory performances.

Synaptic properties of LTHP. We conclude from the evidence just cited that the research exploring the synaptic basis of the LTHP is relevant to at least some memory codes. Researchers often compare LTHP effects to the theoretical model of memory suggested by Hebb—the **Hebb synapse** (Figure 11-17). For a memory trace to be formed, the *same* neuron has to be postsynaptic to both the CS- and US-activated neurons. If the CS input synapse were active just before or at the time that the US activated the neuron, the combined effect of pre- and postsynaptic activity would increase the "strength" of the CS synapse onto that neuron. With enough CS-US pairings, the CS synapse would become strong enough to activate the output neuron by itself.

However, the Hebb model may not be true for the synaptic changes occurring during LTHP. First, the postsynaptic cells do not have to be activated for LTHP to develop (McNaughton, Douglas, & Goddard, 1978). This study used perforant-path stimulation and measured extracellular epsps and spike potentials in granule cells. The high-frequency stimulation required for LTHP shows a threshold-current-level effect, although posttetanic potentiation for the same pathway

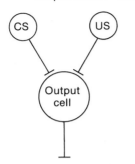

Figure 11-17   The Hebb synapse, a model for the change that occurs in synaptic connections because of learning/memory. If the CS-activated neuron affects the output neuron just before or just at the time the US-activated neuron does, then the CS-neuron synapse onto the output cell will be strengthened.

did not. This finding suggests that the two phenomena do not share the same cellular mechanism. However, when the granule cells were inhibited either chemically or by stimulation of an inhibitory pathway, high-current stimulations produced LTHP even *in the absence* of postsynaptic cell activity.

Second, the LTHP is specific to the synapses actually stimulated. To show this, one set of stimulating electrodes is placed on the basal commissural fibers and another set on the apical commissural/Schaffer collateral fibers. The recording electrode is placed in the CA_1 hippocampal region. High-frequency stimulation is applied to either set of stimulating electrodes, and later, hippocampal responses to stimulation of first one and then the other set are tested. LTHP is reliably demonstrated for the pathway subjected to high-frequency stimulation. The second pathway is *not* facilitated and may even be depressed for a prolonged period of time (Abraham & Goddard, 1983; Anderson, Sundberg, Sveen, & Wigström, 1977; Lynch, Dunwiddie, & Gribkoff, 1977). LTHP is specific to the synapses subjected to high-frequency stimulation and does not generalize even to other inputs to the same set of (and perhaps even the identical) neurons.

Third, there is an associative component to LTHP. Two different sets of stimulating electrodes are placed at different locations (on different axons) along the perforant path and both are stimulated. Later, both can be tested with a single pulse and the granule-cell response recorded. Below-threshold intensities of stimulation produce no LTHP in either pathway, but if below-threshold stimulation were used in both pathways concurrently, then LTHP was produced in both inputs to the granule cells (McNaughton, Douglas, & Goddard, 1978).

Other hippocampal inputs also have an associative component. Below-threshold high-frequency stimulation of both api-cal and basal commissural input pathways to the CA_1 pyramidal region simultaneously produced LTHP even when neither stimulation alone was effective (Barrionuevo & Brown, 1983). Even more impressively, Levy and Steward (1979) found that the crossed entorhinal input to the contralateral hippocampus would *not* produce LTHP. However, when that same stimulation was paired with stimulation of the ipsilateral entorhinal input to the same hippocampus, the crossed input showed a durable LTHP.

Thus, even though the LTHP is specific to the pathways subjected to high-frequency stimulation, LTHP can be produced by below-threshold stimulation of one pathway paired with simultaneous stimulation of another input to the same set of cells. This effect may be caused by a spread of activity among the cells because of increased extracellular K^+ (Konnerth, Heinemann, & Yaari, 1984). The spread would produce LTHP even if the same neurons were not activated by both inputs. Alternatively, both inputs could converge onto exactly the same neurons, and the simultaneous activation of both inputs might change the postsynaptic membrane, even in the absence of postsynaptic action potentials.

The possible biochemistry of LTHP.   Monoaminergic pathways are involved. If hippocampi are depleted of monoamines, or if a beta-adrenergic blocking drug is used, LTHP is reduced (Bliss & Dolphin, 1982; Chepkova & Skrebitsky, 1982). Infusion of NE into a hippocampal slice facilitates LTHP (Hopkins & Johnston, 1984). NE also increases hippocampal responses to CSs (Segal & Bloom, 1976). The serotonergic raphe, the noradrenergic LC, and the dopaminergic tegmental neurons all facilitate granule-cell responses to stimulation of afferent pathways (Assaf, Mason, & Miller, 1979; Assaf & Miller, 1978; Gribkoff & Ashe, 1984). Thus, the amines modulate LTHP just as they modulate memory-trace formation in the intact animal.

Both Ca^{++} and protein phosphorylation are also involved. One study inserted microelectrodes into Ca_1 pyramidal cells and stimulating electrodes onto the Schaffer/commissural-fiber input to those cells. If a drug that inactivated free intracellular Ca^{++} was injected into a cell, that cell no longer showed LTHP (Lynch, Larson, Kelso, Barrionuevo, & Schottler, 1983). Furthermore, increased phosphorylation of a synaptic protein is correlated with the level of LTHP shown by hippocampal slices. Phosphorylation of this protein was prevented if the slice was kept in a Ca^{++} - free medium (Browning, Dunwiddie, Bennett, Gispen, & Lynch, 1979). The change in protein phosphorylation occurred within five seconds after the high-frequency stimulation.

Finally, morphological changes in the postsynaptic membranes have been found after LTHP. Fifková and Van Harreveld (1975) found significant "swelling" of the postsynaptic granule-cell dendritic spines within two minutes of high-frequency stimulation of the entorhinal area. The effect persisted for at least 60 minutes. (These were the shortest and longest times tested.) Lee, Schottler, Oliver, and Lynch (1980) found an increase in the number of shaft types of synapse after LTHP, although these researchers did not find "swelling." However, another research team has also found increases in certain kinds of synapses after LTHP (Desmond, & Levy, 1983, 1986a, 1986b). The changes in postsynaptic membrane may explain why the number of glutamate receptors on pyramidal cells increases after high-frequency stimulation of the Schaffer collaterals (Baudry, Oliver, Creager, Wieraszko, & Lynch, 1980; Lynch & Baudry, 1984). (The amino acid glutamate may be the major excitatory transmitter in the CNS of mammals.)

All these facts could be incorporated into a model of the synaptic basis of memory. There are both specific and associational constraints on LTHP, and the effect is modulated by aminergic input. Changes in the postsynaptic membrane, including phosphorylation and changes in synaptic architecture, may be one synaptic basis of memory.

Learning and Memory in Invertebrates

Various types of snail have been used as research subjects. Learning and memory in snails are not necessarily irrelevant to mammals, although they may seem so. Given the evolutionary continuity between the neurons of snails and mammals (though there certainly are differences), the way experiences affect neural and synaptic events in snails can supply useful hypotheses about how experience may affect synapses in mammals.

Aplysia.   The sea snail *Aplysia* shows adaptation, sensitization, and classical conditioning. This organism can also show discriminated classical conditioning (Carew, Hawkins, & Kandel, 1983). Kandel (1983) uses sensitization and conditioned fear in *Aplysia* as models for unsignaled and signaled anxiety in humans (Chapter 10).

Classical conditioning requires an overlap in activity in two or more neurons. Here, the overlap includes activity in the sensory neuron activated by the CS and the activity in the US-activated neuron that presynaptically facilitates the sensory-neuron–interneuron synapse. The output of the interneuron leads to a response and it also presynaptically facili-

tates a sensory-neuron–motoneuron synapse. Refer back to Figure 10-20 for an illustration of the synaptic connections involved. In fact, the CS can be dispensed with. If the cells activated by the CS are electrically stimulated just before the US occurs (shock to the animal's tail), that synapse is facilitated more than if the US were delivered by itself or if the cell stimulation and the US were presented randomly in time (Hawkins, Abrams, Carew, & Kandel, 1983; Walters & Byrne, 1983).

The biochemical and morphological basis of this change has been explored. Again, the Hebb type of synapse does not seem to be involved. Stimulating the "facilitory interneuron" in the absence of a US is not enough to produce conditioning. However, Kandel and his colleagues suggest that the critical changes may begin with the influx of Ca^{++} associated with activity in the CS neuron. This influx may interact with the US-stimulated, 5-HT-sensitive adenylate cyclase in the terminals of that neuron. If these two events overlap in time, first K^+ channels would be inhibited and then a long-term structural change would occur in the presynaptic membrane. The mutually facilitative effects of the adenylate cyclase and the increase in the intracellular Ca^{++} levels would produce these changes. Drugs that block protein or RNA synthesis also prevent long-lasting synaptic changes but have no effect on the short-term changes; the same drugs have parallel effects on long-term versus short-term memories when given to mammals (Montarolo, Goelet, Castellucci, Morgan, Kandel, & Schacher, 1986).

Hermissenda.   Another type of marine snail, the *Hermissenda*, can also be classically conditioned (Alkon, 1979, 1982–1983, 1984; Alkon, Lederhendler, & Shoukimas, 1982). The conditioning is based on two of the organism's natural responses to stimuli. Normally it approaches light because the organisms on which it feeds are found in the upper, brighter layers of the sea. It also freezes in response to being vibrated. When the sea is turbulent, it attaches itself more firmly to whatever surface it is on to prevent being bounced about and damaged against rocks. But if a flash of light is paired with turbulence or vibration, it learns to stop approaching the light.

The synaptic connections involved in the original responses and in the conditioned changes are indicated in Figure 11-18. The organism has two types of photoreceptor, A and B. Activity in the A type of photoreceptor normally excites an interneuron, which excites the motoneuron controlling the approach muscles. (Light normally leads to approach.) Vibration excites the hair cells, an activity that will eventually lead the organism to inhibit locomotion. However, the hair cells also have an excitatory input into photoreceptor type B, and type B normally (weakly) has the effect of inhibiting locomotion.

If activity in B is associated closely in time with activity in the hair cells, the membrane of the B photoreceptor is durably changed. Regenerative interactions between the Ca^{++} and K^+ currents in the B cell membrane occur. Simultaneously occurring light-evoked activity and hair-cell input to that photoreceptor lead to a long-lasting reduction in one type of K^+ current. When that current is reduced, the depolarization produced by light in B is increased in size and duration, and so B now has a much stronger inhibitory effect on A.

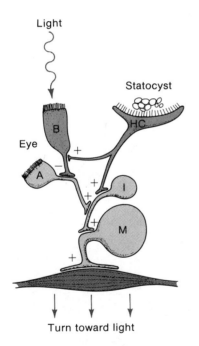

Figure 11-18   A model for learning in an invertebrate has the visual pathway interacting with the statocyst pathway to produce learning. The type B photoreceptor (B) causes monosynaptic inhibition of the medial type A photoreceptor (A). The A photoreceptor causes monosynaptic excitation of ipsilateral interneurons (I), which are also excited by ipsilateral hair cells (HC). Ipsilateral hair-cell impulses cause a transient inhibition (not shown here) and a long-lasting synaptic excitation of type B photoreceptor. Net excitation of this pathway causes movement towards light through a motoneuron (M).

Summary of Model Systems

A study of model systems holds out great promise for discovering how synapses are durably modified by experiences. In both the hippocampal LTHP model and the conditioned snail model of memory in intact higher animals, durable synaptic modifications may occur by slow synaptic mechanisms involving the Ca^{++} second-messenger system and protein phosphorylation.

The nearly simultaneous interaction of two inputs is important to both model systems. Simultaneous below-threshold stimulations of two input pathways to the same set of cells can cause LTHP in both. Similarly, activity in one sensory cell occurring simultaneously with activity in a second neuron may regeneratively interact to change the membrane properties of that cell *(Hermissenda)* or the degree to which presynaptic activity in that cell can evoke a response in the postsynaptic cell *(Aplysia)*.

These results should not be uncritically generalized to learning in the intact vertebrate. The complexity of possible interconnections may create a *qualitatively* different learning process (though that does not seem too likely at the moment). Although the hippocampus participates in classical conditioning, its presence is not essential to it. Thus, the role of LTHP is still uncertain. If the hippocampus has only a modulatory role, LTHP would also have only a modulatory role in forming the memory trace elsewhere in the brain.

Chapter Summary

Neural Codes and Learning

Research in the area of neural codes and learning continues to generate enthusiasm — but remarkably few widely accepted conclusions. Many correlates of learning and retention have been discovered. Cells in many different parts of the brain show changes in firing patterns closely related to conditioned changes in behavior. Conditioned changes in brain-stem neural activity may be fed back to the cortex. Consistent with this possibility, changes in protein are seen first in the hippocampus and then in the cortex. Either the memory trace itself or retrieval from that trace is affected by ECS, antibiotics, brain stimulation, manipulations of transmitter metabolism, and genetically based differences in transmitter metabolism and synaptic interconnections. Many of these effects, and a durable long-term potentiation, occur in the hippocampus.

Most of this literature has been interpreted as though the memory trace involved a particular type of neural code. But it is also possible that past experiences do not have a code of their own. Past experiences may change the way in which current stimuli are encoded, including the stimuli produced by changes in internal states. Past experiences could also change the likelihood of activation of a given type of command system —as opposed to a command system for another kind of behavior—in a variety of situations.

Changes in sensory coding could occur whenever stimulus pathways are activated. They might be especially likely to occur if the stimuli were frequently repeated and/or if specific and nonspecific arousal were present (NE, DA, and 5-HT effects) during that time. The change in coding might involve a change in synaptic efficacy similar to those observed in invertebrates. This idea is explored in the next chapter, which describes how past experiences change the way sensory input is coded.

C H A P T E R

12

Effect of Developmental Experiences
on Coding

The brain changes because of experience. Our brains today are not the same as they were yesterday. In Chapter 11 we described some of the variables affecting brain changes.

We discuss three questions in this chapter. First, are the anatomy and biochemistry of the brain especially sensitive to experiences occurring during early development? In other words, do young organisms with different developmental environments and experiences grow up to have systematically different brains? Second, how do the effects of developmental experiences on the brain differ from those of specialized training? Are different kinds of memory trace involved? Third, is the code used by sensory nerve cells affected by developmental experiences? If so, organisms with different developmental environments would not perceive any current environment in quite the same way.

Overview

The first section will review the effects of **environmental enrichment.** Organisms are reared in an environment much more complex than the usual laboratory environment. When enriched-environment organisms are compared with organisms reared under standard laboratory conditions, differences in both brains and behaviors can be found. But since ordinary laboratory conditions are impoverished in comparison with the variety and types of stimulation available to organisms developing in their natural environments, any difference between groups remains somewhat ambiguous. Does enrichment increase brain development beyond its normal range, or do ordinary laboratory conditions cause defective brain development?

Environmental enrichment involves exposing organisms to many different kinds of stimuli. Some researchers have looked at the implications of exposing organisms to only *one* type of stimulation. The second and third sections of this chapter discuss the effects of systematically varying somatosensory, auditory, or visual stimuli; the latter has produced especially exciting results.

Last, we discuss developmental and lesion-induced synaptogenesis. Many learning theories predict that training will be found to cause changes in synaptic connections, and many developmental theories take the position that different developmental environments produce systematic differences in the patterns of synaptic interconnections. An area of research into a process called **synaptogenesis** specifically examines how new synapses are created during development or after damage; despite the name of the process, research in this area also examines how synapses disappear with age.

This chapter thus focuses on the effects experience has on sensory coding and synaptic interconnections. The data not only will tell us how our experiences affect our perceptions but also will provide models for how learning experiences may affect the brain. The material in this chapter reflects the complexity of stimulus processing in our brains. Our brains have more synapses than could possibly be specified by our genes. Thus, some brain "wiring" requires exposure to normal environments during development so that our brains can "learn" how to process the kinds of stimulus with which we will have to deal for the rest of our lives (Hirsch, 1985). Not only children's bodies but their brains have to learn the skills needed by adults.

Aspects of brain anatomy that can be changed by experience are said to be **plastic.** Because of the brain's complexity, plasticity may be greatest during early development to ensure that only the most appropriate neural connections and coding responses remain in the adult. However, the brain does not lose its **plasticity** (its ability to be changed by experience)

once growth is complete. Some vestiges of the developmental plasticity remain and may be triggered by brain damage. As the last chapter will show, the adult brain changes during learning, and that form of plasticity remains throughout the organism's life.

Environmental Enrichment and Deprivation

We might have called this section "How to Grow Different Kinds of Brains." Organisms exposed to environmental enrichment develop larger brains than others and brains with different biochemistries and microanatomies (Bennett, 1976; Greenough, 1975, 1976). These effects can be produced even when exposure to the enriched environment is limited to two hours a day (for a 30-day period). The effects on brain structure and biochemistry last as long as the organisms are kept in the enriched environment — and some of the effects persist for some time even if the organisms are removed from that environment. These results may reflect the complex memory traces formed during the enrichment (Greenough, 1975, 1976).

Techniques

The way that research is done in the area of enrichment varies from one laboratory to the next. However, most of this research uses rats, and so you may assume that the animal subjects were rats unless we specify otherwise. Findings may differ from laboratory to laboratory, probably because they use different strains of animals and different kinds of "enriched" environments. The degree to which enrichment produces its effects can also be enhanced or decreased by the use of certain techniques, and different researchers use different techniques.

Types of environment and types of control group.   Researchers have used many different kinds of control groups. Hebb, who began this work in 1947, compared the behaviors of rats home-reared as pets with those of rats reared in the laboratory (Greenough, 1976). Rosenzweig, Bennett, Diamond and their coworkers continued the work in the 1970s by comparing the effects of rearing in different kinds of laboratory environments. Two control conditions were used in addition to an enriched-environment condition. First, animals in the **impoverished control** condition were socially isolated and raised in small, featureless cages. The cage walls were opaque to limit visual stimulation. Variations in sound level were sometimes limited. Second, animals in the **social control** group were reared together in large cages, but the cages had none of the complex objects found in the enriched environment. This group controlled for the effects of social stimulation.

Three enriched laboratory environments are shown in Figure 12-1. Young animals are placed in an environment with not only many different objects but also some other animals of the same age. The objects in the environment may be changed daily to provide further variety. However, as the figure shows, the size and nature of the objects placed in the enriched environment can vary widely. Figure 12-1b shows some "observer cages." Rats were placed in those cages to see whether merely observing—as opposed to actively exploring—the complex environment would reproduce the effects of enrichment (it didn't work: Ferchmin, Bennett, & Rosenzweig, 1975).

On most measures of brain and behavior, the social group falls somewhere between the isolated and the enriched groups (Greenough, 1975, 1976; Uphouse, 1980). But, as we noted before, the interpretation of these effects is far from obvious. Social animals may be suffering from stimulus deprivation, and the impoverished animals may suffer from both stimulus and social deprivation. When each group was compared with the social controls, it was apparent that enrichment and impoverishment have different *kinds* of effects on the brain. The effects of enrichment versus those of impoverishment are "not necessarily equal and opposite in direction," as Uphouse (1980, p. 230) pointed out. The safest conclusion may be that developmental environments affect brains and behavior.

Treatments that affect the size of enrichment effects.   Animals must actively and directly interact with the

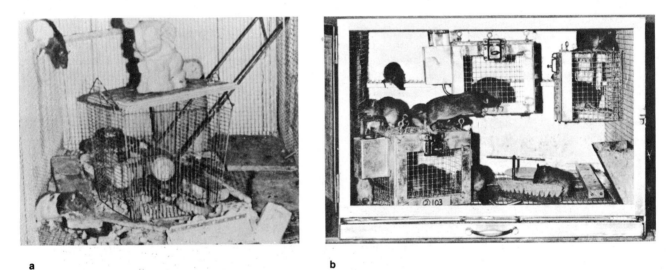

a   b

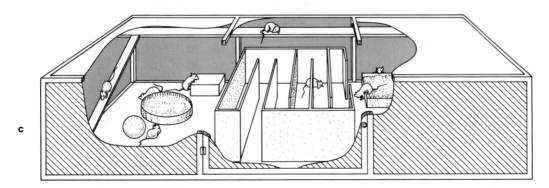

c

Figure 12-1   Three types of situation used to enrich the environments of developing rats. See text for further details.

complex environment. The animals raised in the observation cages of Figure 12-1b did not show any enrichment effects on brain weight. When those animals were later tested, their exploratory behaviors were not only lower than those of the enriched group but were also somewhat lower than those of the impoverished group (Ferchmin, Bennett, & Rosenzweig, 1975).

Social stimulation may also be necessary. Rosenzweig and Bennett (1972) found that when rats were placed by themselves in the enriched environment for the two hours a day (for a 30-day period), their brain weights and biochemistries differed little from those of their isolated controls. However, if the rat were given a stimulating drug (methamphetamine) each day just before being placed in the enriched environment, its brain became significantly heavier than that of its control. Thus, the stimulant drug could substitute for social interactions: both conditions increase the degree to which the organism actively interacts or plays with the objects in the complex environment.

Stimulants can also add to social-stimulation effects. Drugged and socially stimulated animals show larger changes in brain chemistry and weight than are seen after social stimulation alone (Bennett, Rosenzweig, & Wu, 1973). Stimulants like metrazol and amphetamines produce these effects, but other stimulants like strychnine do not (however, all these drugs facilitate retention performances: Chapter 11). Depressants such as phenobarbital attenuate enrichment effects, at least on brain weight.

Just as NE affects memory-trace formation (Chapter 11), NE activity may regulate environmental-enrichment effects. Injecting an alpha-adrenergic agonist (presynaptically inhibits NE synapses) immediately after a two-hour daily experience with an enriched environment *reduces* or even eliminates the effects of enrichment on brain weight (Mirmiran & Uylings, 1983; Pearlman, 1983). Other research done by Mirmiran and colleagues (Brenner, Mirmiran, Uylings, & Van der Gugten, 1983; Mirmiran, Van den Dungen, & Uylings, 1982; Mirmiran & Uylings, 1983) also show how important NE is to the enrichment effect. The NE activity that occurs during REM sleep may be required for enrichment to affect the brain. If NE is depleted by drugs (subcutaneous 6-OHDA injections) before enrichment, the effects are much weaker. Thus, as in the formation of memory traces after training, a moderate (as opposed to low or high) level of brain NE may maximally facilitate the experience-induced effects.

Age is also important. Generally, greater effects—both in behavior and the brain—are seen with younger animals. Younger animals also require shorter exposures to the enriched environment for maximal changes (Greenough,

1976; Katz & Davies, 1983; Uphouse, 1980). However, there may be qualitative as well as quantitative effects of age. For example, stimulants do not increase the enrichment effect in adult rats as they do in younger rats (Bennett, Rosenzweig, & Wu, 1973). Stimulants may not increase exploration and play in adult animals. Still, environmental enrichment can cause changes in microanatomy and in learning performances in adult, middle-aged, or even very old rats and mice (Green, Greenough, & Schlumpf, 1983; Juraska, Greenough, Elliot, Mack, & Berkowitz, 1980; Warren, Zerweck, & Anthony, 1982).

The age-related effects of enrichment can be used to illustrate critical and sensitive periods. A **critical period** is a certain time in development during which a certain experience must occur. If the experience occurs earlier or later, *it will not have any effect* on the brain or behavior. A **sensitive period** is a developmental period during which a certain experience can have its *greatest* effect. If delayed, the experience might have to last longer or be more intense to have similar effects. Most of the age-related enrichment effects seem to reflect sensitive rather than critical periods. However, any age-related *qualitative* differences in effects would reflect a critical period.

Many enrichment techniques may vary in effectiveness because of the way they affect play. **Play and exploration** may be the critical components of environmental enrichment (Ferchmin, Eterović, & Levin, 1980; Hoyenga & Hoyenga, 1984). Animals exposed in groups to complex environments play more than do animals in the social or impoverished groups. Injections of stimulants before the experience increase the frequency of play. Merely observing the complex environment does not involve play. Young animals play more than adults do. Environmental enrichment and juvenile play often do have the same beneficial effects on adaptive behavior in the adult, including problem solving (Fagan, 1981; Hoyenga & Hoyenga, 1984; P. K. Smith, 1982).

Effects on Behavior

Activity and exploration.   Rodents' activity is measured in a variety of ways, with no guarantee of equivalence. The methods include measuring movement in the home cage, the activity displayed in a large, empty box (the open-field measure), and the number of revolutions per day or per hour in an activity wheel. Exploration can also be measured in a large box; various objects are placed in the box to be explored.

Although developmental enrichment affects levels of activity, the type of effect varies from one experiment to the next. For example, open-field or cage activity may be either increased or decreased (Crnic, 1983; Einon, 1980; Engellenner et al., 1982; Manosevitz & Joel, 1973; Smith, 1972). The reasons for the variability are not yet established.

The effects of enrichment on exploratory tendencies interact with the effects of repeated experiences with the exploratory environment. Animals raised in an enriched environment are more likely than impoverished controls to show a decrease in exploration from the first to the second time they are placed in an exploratory chamber (see, for example, Ferchmin, Eterović, & Levin, 1980; Manosevitz & Joel, 1973). The decrease could mean that the enriched rats and mice become more easily "bored" with the exploratory apparatus because they have become accustomed to high levels of stimulation.

Learning. Not all types of task performance are improved by being reared in a complex environment. But the enriched group performs consistently better in complex mazes than does either the impoverished or the social control group (Bennett, 1976; Greenough, 1975, 1976). The changes in activity (variable) and exploration cannot account for the effect of enrichment on maze learning (Smith, 1972). Even in cats, the ability to learn a maze is improved by being reared in an enriched environment (Cornwell & Overman, 1981). Perhaps only complex learning tasks "push" the capacity of the brain enough so that the increased brain "processing capacity" of the enriched group can be demonstrated in learning tasks.

Other types of learning are sometimes improved by enrichment. These effects are variable but can include improvement in a motor-skills task (Ferchmin & Eterović, 1977; Warren, Zerweck, & Anthony, 1982) and in avoidance (Crnic, 1983; Ferchmin, Eterović, & Levin, 1980).

Memory. If enrichment increases the number of memory traces in the brain, perhaps enrichment would have its most intriguing effects on memory. As Chapter 11 described, amnesic agents such as posttrial ECS impair retrieval performances. Amnesic effects can be moderated by developmental enrichment. For example, in a one-trial, step-down passive-avoidance task, the enriched group showed a typical retrograde amnesia gradient when the time between training and the ECS was varied (Gardner, Boitano, Mancino, D'Amico, & Gardner, 1975). However, an ECS given either 10 or 60 seconds after the trial produced equal amnesic effects in the impoverished group. This result implies that whatever processes occur after a trial, they are taking longer to complete in the isolated than in the enriched group.

The time allowed between the trials of a complex learning task differentially affects the learning rates of enriched, impoverished, and social groups (Greenough, Wood, & Madden,

1972). As Figure 12-2 shows, the three groups were exposed either to **massed** (30 seconds between trials) or to **spaced** (2 hours between trials) training trials on a complex maze. Animals from the enriched group showed equally good performance under both spaced and massed conditions, whereas animals from the impoverished group showed equally poor (and significantly poorer) performance under both conditions. However, the social group did significantly better (fewer errors) under the spaced than under the massed condition. Thus, since the social rearing made these animals sensitive to the amount of time between trials, perhaps rearing conditions affect memory processing speed.

Finally, posttrial injections of cholinergic drugs have different effects on animals from enriched and impoverished environments (Greenough, Yuwiler, & Dollinger, 1973). Animals were injected after each day's training session with eserine, which inhibits acetylcholinesterase (AChE), thereby increasing synaptic ACh levels. As Figure 12-3 shows, different doses had different effects on the groups. Specifically, only the

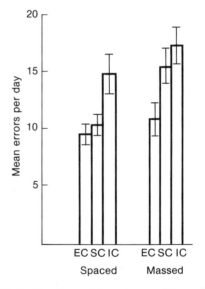

Figure 12-2 Developmental rearing conditions affect the way in which massed versus spaced practice trials change the rate of learning. In this case, 30 seconds elapsed between trials in massed practice; in spaced practice, there were 2 hours between trials. This figure shows the mean daily learning errors, averaged across 3 days of maze training, as a function of rearing condition and distribution of practice (spaced versus massed). The brackets at the top of the bars are standard errors of means. EC = enriched; SC = social; IC = impoverished (see text for further description of these groups).

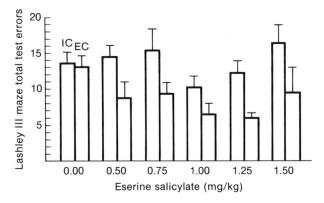

Figure 12-3   The developmental environment affects the relationship between memory-active drugs and learning-memory performances. This figure shows the mean total errors, averaged over three test trials in a maze, as a function of rearing condition and drug dosage. The test trials were given 48 hours after an eserine injection (which increases synaptic ACh levels). The brackets indicate standard errors of the mean. See text for implications. IC = impoverished; EC = enriched.

enriched animals showed improved learning at lower doses, and only the impoverished animals showed *no* improvement at the highest doses. If posttrial injections of eserine affect memory processing, the developmental environment affects memory-trace formation.

Effects on Gross Anatomy and Biochemistry

Environmental enrichment increases whole brain weight. This effect is not secondary to an increase in body weight, since enriched animals eat less and weigh less than do the impoverished animals (Greenough, 1976). Cortical weight is most affected, although other parts of the brain show some effect.

Cortex.   Cortical thickness is increased in the enriched animals in comparison with their controls, and the effect is largest in the occipital cortex—even in blinded animals (Bennett, 1976; Greenough, 1975, 1976). The impoverished rats have the thinnest and lightest cortex. The increase in weight and thickness comes primarily from increases in the number of glial cells and secondarily from an increase in size of neural cell body. The increase in glial cells may be caused by increased cortical activity.

In this regard, the results of examining the parietal area of Einstein's brain are of great interest. The most dramatic difference between his brain and 11 "controls" was the increased ratio of glial cells to neurons found in Einstein's brain (Diamond, Scheibel, Murphy, & Harvey, 1985). Given the support function of glial cells, not only could an increased glial/neuron ratio reflect increased neural activity in the past but a greater ratio would support greater levels of neuronal activity in the present.

The increased glial/neural ratio persists even after the enriched animals are placed in an impoverished environment (see Figure 12-4). **Persistence** is measured by how much of the original difference between the brains of the enriched group and those of the isolated controls (EC − IC) remains after the enriched animals have been placed in isolation for varying periods of time. The weight of the occipital cortex and the ratio of cortical weight to total brain weight are both increased by enrichment. The effects can last up to 47 days after enrichment is ended (following longer periods of enrichment) (Bennett, Rosenzweig, Diamond, Morimoto, & Hebert, 1974). The fact that cortical changes eventually disappear may reflect either disuse atrophy or some process similar to that of relegation observed with single-unit recordings during learning (Chapter 11).

Cholinergic enzymes are also sensitive to developmental experiences. Enrichment decreases the amount of AChE per unit of brain weight or cortex weight. However, enrichment *increases* the amount of **cholinesterase (ChE)** activity per unit of brain weight (Rosenzweig, Bennett, & Diamond, 1972; Bennett, Rosenzweig, & Wu, 1973). Although AChE is found mainly in nerve cells, ChE is found primarily in glial cells. The number of glial cells is increased, and thus ChE is also increased. And since mostly neural size, and *not* numbers, is increased, the absolute amount of AChE will change very little. But the increase in cortical weight (because of the glial cells) means that the AChE per unit of cortical weight will decrease.

The persistence of cholinergic enzyme changes is illustrated in Figure 12-5. The isolated brain has greater AChE levels per unit of brain weight than does the brain from the enriched rat, and the ratio of cortical AChE activity to subcortical AChE activity is larger in isolated controls. "Persistence" again refers to how much of the original EC − IC difference remains at varying times after the animals from the EC group were placed in isolation. Even after 47 days, the AChE activity in occipital cortex regressed only slightly.

Protein synthesis is also affected by rearing environments. There are more different *types* of RNA and proteins found in enriched brains than in control brains (Uphouse, 1980). There is also a greater ratio of RNA to DNA: the enriched animals have more RNA (Bennett, 1976). More neurons have high levels of RNA (Warren, Zerweck, & Anthony, 1982:

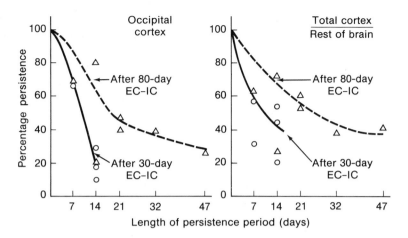

Figure 12-4 Persistence of changes in brain weight. The effects of environmental enrichment on gross brain anatomy can persist for many days even after the animals have been placed in impoverished conditions (EC − IC). The degree of persistence (see text for definition of term) is related to how long the enrichment period lasted.

mice). Thus, the brains of animals exposed to enrichment show higher levels of protein synthesis and probably synthesis of more different kinds of protein. The increase in protein synthesis may reflect genomic effects of experience.

Other brain structures. Although enrichment can affect other parts of the brain, the effects seem to be smaller and less reliable than the cortical effects. For example, Rosenzweig and Bennett's research group usually find the subcortex to be heavier in isolated than in enriched brains. Other researchers,

using other strains, found the subcortex from enriched animals to be heavier (Ferchmin & Eterović, 1977; Ferchmin, Eterović, & Levin, 1980). Also, although some investigators have not found any enrichment effect on the corpus callosum, one team found that enrichment increased the thickness of that structure (more axons?) (Walsh, Cummins, Budtz-Olsen, & Torok, 1972).

The hippocampus is frequently examined, but only a few, variable effects of rearing environment are found. Some researchers found cross-sectional brain slices from the hippo-

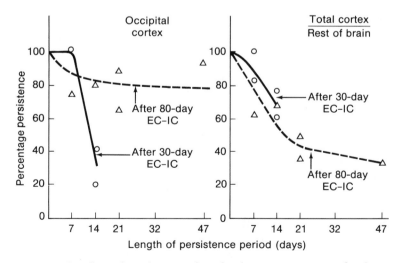

Figure 12-5 AChE persistence. The effects of enrichment on brain biochemistry persist even after the animals have been placed in isolated conditions. Again, the degree of persistence is related to the length of the prior enrichment period.

campus of enriched animals to be larger or thicker (Katz & Davies, 1983; Walsh, Budtz-Olsen, Penny, & Cummins, 1969). Other researchers have not been able to replicate those findings (Jones & Smith, 1980). The types of glial cells found there may be affected by developmental experiences (Walsh et al., 1969). As we will see, the neurons in the hippocampus *are* sensitive to enrichment, but the changes occur in microanatomy and not gross anatomy.

Microanatomy: Enrichment versus Special Training

Changes in microanatomy and in interconnections among nerve cells are far more important to the neuron doctrine than are gross changes. Microanatomical research also compares enrichment-versus-impoverishment effects with effects of special training. (Only the original and not the more recent enrichment research included training sessions: Bennett, 1976; Greenough, 1975, 1976.) Specialized training has effects of its own on microanatomy, effects that are not always the same as those seen after enrichment. Therefore, the effects of task training and the effects of enrichment probably involve somewhat different kinds of processing into memory traces (durable synaptic-neural changes). Presumably this difference in effects simply reflects the differences in what the organism has learned during its exposure to these two situations.

Effects of enrichment on cortical-cell microanatomy. Cortical cells from enriched rats have more dendritic branches than do those of either the isolated or the social control groups (animals in the social group are more similar to isolated than to enriched animals in this respect) (Bennett, 1976; Greenough, 1975, 1976). Some ways of studying the effects of experience are illustrated in Figures 12-6 and 12-7. After euthanasia, animals' brains are stained and sliced. Then the slices are placed under a microscope and examined until an entire cell, or at least most of a cell, can be seen. The researcher draws that cell on a sheet of paper by using a projection of the view from the microscope.

The drawings are then analyzed. The cell drawing may be placed in the middle of a series of concentric rings, as shown in Figure 12-6. Figure 12-7 shows how a hippocampal granule cell is analyzed. Various aspects of the dendritic trees are tabulated. The researcher can count the number of spines and the number of dendritic branchings and measure the length of each branch. Typically, these counts are done separately for apical and basal dendrites. Sometimes **oblique** and **terminal** dendrites are also separately analyzed.

Some typical effects of experience on microanatomy are illustrated in Figures 12-8 and 12-9 (Bennett, 1976; Greenough, 1975, 1976; Walsh, 1981). Enriched animals have more dendritic branching. The effects of experience are greatest for the basal dendrites, for the third-, fourth-, and fifth-order branchings in Figure 12-8, and for the second-, third-, and fourth-order branchings in Figure 12-9. Differences in dendritic branching may mean differences in synaptic interconnections. The basal dendrites may receive input from nearby neurons, whereas the apical dendrites may receive input from sensory neurons and from the other hemisphere via the callosum. The pyramidal cells from enriched rats may therefore have more synaptic inputs from nearby neurons.

The cells in enriched animals have more spines, and the synaptic area of the synapses is larger, especially in layer IV (Globus, Rosenzweig, Bennett, & Diamond, 1973; Walsh, 1981; West & Greenough, 1972). Because of these changes in spines, it is not surprising that enrichment leads to an increase in the number of synapses per neuron (Turner & Greenough, 1985). Even in tropical fish, social stimulation—compared with impoverishment and social isolation—increases the number of dendritic spines in their visual brains (Coss & Globus, 1978). Changes in spines are particularly intriguing because of the spine changes caused by LTHP (Chapter 11; Fifková & Van Harreveld, 1978). Perhaps in both cases, memory processing is associated with spine changes.

Cells are not equally affected by environmental enrichment. The effects are strongest for cells in the visual cortex, weaker in the auditory cortex, and absent in the parietal and frontal cortex. The visual cortex may be particularly susceptible, since visual stimuli differ the most between the complex and the social environments. Cells in layers II, IV, and V (these layers include both sensory input and efferent cells) are more affected by experience than are cells in other layers.

Gender—probably because of the effects of perinatal hormones on the brain (Chapter 9)—interacts with the effects of enrichment on brain microanatomy. In Figure 12-9, enrichment has been found to increase the number of dendritic branches of cells in the occipital cortex less in female than in male rats (this sex difference could also be interpreted as meaning that females are less vulnerable to the debilitating effects of isolation: Juraska, 1984). However, Figure 12-10 shows that in the hippocampus, the microanatomy of dentate granule cells was affected more by developmental environment in females than in males (Juraska, Fitch, Henderson, & Rivers, 1985). Presumably these gender differences in the responses of microanatomy to enrichment are paralleled by differences in behavioral responses. However, no cause-and-effect statements are yet warranted because, just as was true for

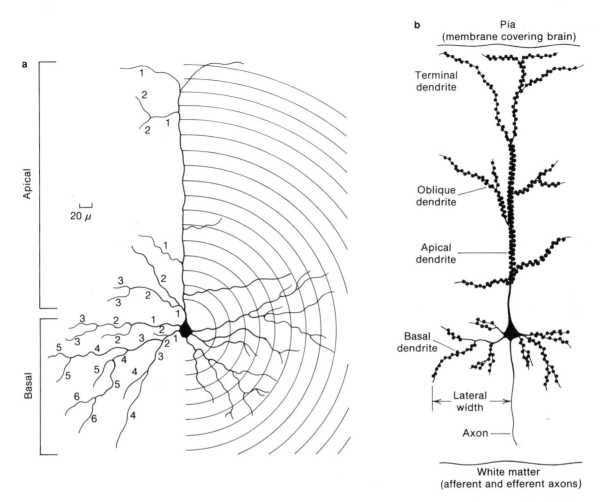

Figure 12-6 One way of analyzing brain microanatomy to detect any effect of developmental rearing conditions. **a. Dendritic extent** is estimated from the intersections between dendrites and a concentric-ring overlay. To measure branching pattern and dendritic length, the dendrites are grouped and counted in terms of how far away each branch is from the cell body (order of branching). **b.** The number of spines are counted for each different kind of dendrite. **Lateral width** is the distance between the axon and the extent of the basal dendrites.

the anatomy change, either males are affected more (spatial memory), females are affected more (gross activity) (Einon, 1980), or there are no sex differences in enrichment effects on behavior (Tees, Midgley, & Bruinsma, 1980).

Somewhat different effects occur when older rats are exposed to enrichment. Environmental enrichment can change the shapes of nerve cells in both adult (145 days of age) and middle-aged (450 days of age) rats (Green, Greenough, & Schlumpf, 1983; Juraska et al., 1980). In young (just past weaning, or 23 to 26 days of age) rats, enrichment increases the *number* of higher-order branchings of *basal* dendrites. But in adult rats, enrichment increases mainly the *length* of the branches and the terminal dendrites, and the effects are seen in

both apical and basal dendrites. These age differences may be caused by differences in the ways the rats interact with the complex environments (young rats play more) or by differences in how a young as opposed to an older brain reacts to stimulation.

Effects of special training on cortical-cell microanatomy. Giving an adult animal training on a series of learning tasks causes the microanatomy of its brain to change in comparison with the brains of food- or water-deprived and handled control animals (Greenough, 1975, 1976). In one experiment, the trained rats were given a series of visual-discrimination problems to solve, with a water reward. This experience increased

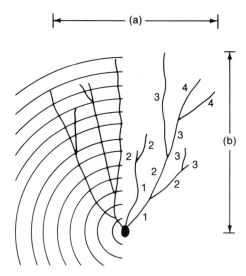

Figure 12-7 The scoring procedure used to analyze the effect of developmental environments on a hippocampal granule cell. The right side of the figure shows the order of each dendritic branch. The left side shows how dendrites intersect with the overlay of concentric rings, each ring spaced at 20 μm intervals. The lateral spread of the dendrites is (**a**), and the height or vertical spread is (**b**), measured perpendicularly to the width.

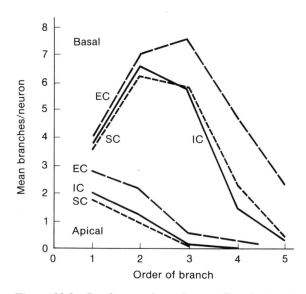

Figure 12-8 Developmental enrichment affects brain microanatomy. The average number of branches at each order (see Figure 12-6) away from the cell body and from the apical dendrites was calculated for a sample of pyramidal neurons from layer V of the occipital cortex of rats reared in various environments. EC rats differed significantly from the other groups in basal orders 3, 4, and 5, and from SC animals in apical orders 1 and 2. Similar effects were seen in other pyramidal cells and in stellate cells from layer IV. EC = enriched; SC = social; IC = impoverished.

the branching of the *apical* dendrites in layer V but not in layer IV of the visual cortex. So specific training affects apical dendrites, whereas environmental enrichment affects basal dendrites and the input from sensory cells and cells of the corpus callosum.

A pair of studies directly contrasted enrichment and learning effects on the microanatomy of the visual cortex (Greenough, Juraska, & Volkmar, 1979; Juraska et al., 1980). Apical dendrite branchings in both layers IV and V were increased after exposure to a series of complex maze-learning problems. The maze training, unlike the enrichment exposure, did *not* affect the stellate cells. Although there were some effects of maze training on the basal dendrites, the apical dendrites were most affected, again in contrast to the effects of enrichment. Furthermore, the training effects were generally smaller than the enrichment effects. Thus, we cannot assume that enrichment produces exactly the same synaptic-neural changes as does training.

Two other studies limited training to only one hemisphere so that the effects could be seen in a single animal by comparing right to left cortex. In one experiment, rats were trained to reach down a tube for food (Greenough, Larson, & Withers, 1985). In the sensorimotor cortex, cells in the hemisphere

opposite the trained paw had larger apical dendritic fields. In another study, rats had their corpus callosums severed and were later given maze training with one eye occluded (Chang & Greenough, 1982). Again, the occipital-cortex cells on the trained side had larger distal apical dendrites. These studies document the specificity of the training effect; using each animal as its own control rules out nonspecific effects of motives, hormones, and emotions.

Enrichment and the microanatomy of cells outside the cortex. The microanatomy of cells outside the cortex is also affected by environmental enrichment. They include two brain areas that single-unit recordings showed were involved in learning: the cerebellum and the hippocampus. For example, social rearing increases the number of dendritic branches in the cerebellar Purkinje cell of the monkey (Floeter & Greenough, 1979). And we already mentioned the study that found gender effects (Juraska et al., 1985). Female enriched rats had more dendrites per hippocampal dentate granule cell than did female isolates. Males showed little effect of rearing

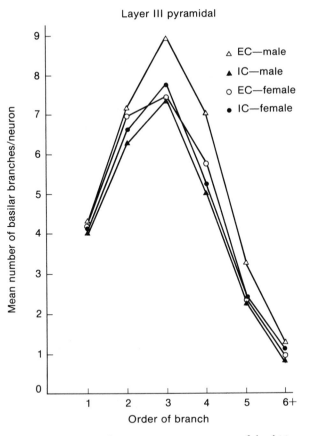

Figure 12-9 Enrichment increases some types of dendritic branching. This figure shows the mean number of branches per neuron by order of branch, for different rearing environments. The layer III pyramidal cells of the occipital cortex were affected by rearing conditions more in males than in females. EC = enriched; IC = impoverished.

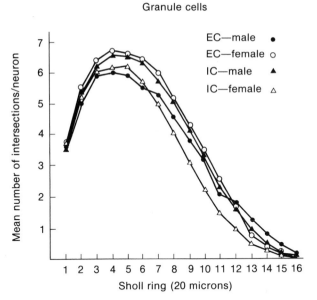

Figure 12-10 Granule cells from the hippocampus. This graph shows the mean number of dendritic intersections with the concentric rings (Figure 12-7) for rats exposed to various developmental environments. Experience can be seen to have larger effects upon branching in females than in males. EC = enriched; IC = impoverished.

Summary of Environmental Enrichment

Organisms reared in an enriched environment have brains that differ from those of organisms reared either in total isolation or in a social group. The "enriched brain" is heavier and has a thicker cortex and more glial cells (the increase in DNA, the increase in ChE, and the decrease in AChE). It also synthesizes more and different kinds of proteins. The microanatomy of nerve cells is also changed, with "enriched cells" having more of certain kinds of dendrites and more and larger synapses. Other areas of the brain may also be affected by rearing environment, especially the hippocampus. Some of these effects can be duplicated with older subjects and by using specialized training as opposed to enrichment. There are, however, differences between young and old (for example, in the hippocampus) and between training and enrichment (for example, in apical versus basal dendrites).

How should we interpret these effects? The brain from the enriched rat may be the "normal" one, and brains from social and isolated controls may show the detrimental effects of environmental deficiencies. Specifically, the deficient environments might not stimulate enough play behaviors. Another

conditions and so isolated males had more dendrites than did isolated females, but enriched females had more dendrites than did enriched males.

Another hippocampal study compared isolated versus enriched dendritic branching in two different age groups of rats (Fiala, Joyce, & Greenough, 1978). A group of young rats (23 to 26 days of age) was placed in a complex environment for four weeks. Another group of older rats (145 days at the start) was placed in the complex environment for 12 weeks. Figure 12-10 shows that cells from enriched rats had more lower-order dendritic branching and had wider dendritic fields. But these enrichment effects were seen *only* in the younger rats.

possibility—not necessarily incompatible with the first—is that enriched animals learn more than do their controls, causing the differences observed in their brains. It certainly seems to be true that enriched and impoverished brains process information differently immediately after a training trial.

Both hypotheses predict that the enriched animals should show more adaptive behaviors, at least in some situations. Just as specialized training can increase adaptive behaviors, so can developmental enrichment. Although there are overlaps between these two effects, there are also differences: there may be qualitatively different kinds of memories involved. When we look at nerve cells from enriched brains, are we seeing at least one kind of memory?

Effects of Stimulation during Development

The differences between the synaptic interconnections of enriched and control animals may reflect what those animals have learned. If so, there are many different types of stimulus that the enriched animals *could* have learned about. The rest of this chapter discusses the changes in sensory coding and in brain anatomy and biochemistry produced by manipulating just one type of sensory stimulus. The olfactory, somatosensory, and auditory systems are covered in this section, and vision is in the next.

Olfactory

The physiology, anatomy, and coding responses of olfactory cells are just beginning to be related to stimuli present during development. Raising rats in a deodorized environment leads to their having smaller mitral cells in the olfactory bulbs (Benson, Ryugo, & Hinds, 1980; Laing, Panhuber, Pittman, Willcox, & Eagleson, 1985). Conversely, raising rats in the presence of a very strong odor changes cellular responses to that odor, though in a very complex fashion (Coopersmith & Leon, 1984; Eckert & Schmidt, 1985; Wilson, Sullivan, & Leon, 1985). Perhaps because of the changes, rats are behaviorally more sensitive to an odor with which they have been reared, and they are less sensitive to odors in general if they have been reared in a deodorized environment (Laing & Panhuber, 1980). Furthermore, in preference tests, rats favor the odor with which they were reared (Laing & Panhuber, 1978). Thus, olfactory coding in an adult depends in part on the odors to which olfactory neurons are exposed during development.

Somatosensory

Removing a whisker from a neonatal rodent causes permanent changes in the brain. If a whisker is removed early in a mouse's life, of course the whisker cortical cells will stop receiving any type of sensory input from that whisker. A pair of comprehensive studies will illustrate what conclusions can be drawn from such research (Jeanmonod, Rice, & Van der Loos, 1981; Simons, Durham, & Woolsey, 1984).

One row of whisker follicles (termed *row C*) was destroyed in mice either on the day of birth or on one of several varying days afterward. Figure 12-11 presents the data from the study by Jeanmonod, Rice, and Van der Loos, and Figure 12-12 shows Nissl-stained brain sections taken from mice in which whisker follicles had been destroyed at varying periods of time after birth. As can be seen most dramatically in Figure 12-12c (destruction at day 1), removal of a whisker follicle prevents the normal development of the cortical barrel normally associated with that follicle. The barrels normally associated with the row-C whiskers have completely disappeared.

The day on which the whisker follicles are destroyed determines the nature of the cortical effect. If a row of follicles is destroyed on the day of birth, regeneration and sprouting of peripheral nerves will reinnervate the central nerves connected to the row-C barrel cells in the cortex. Thus, the barrels will survive, though in altered form. Delaying the destruction until day 1 may mean that it is too late for much peripheral sprouting and regeneration. In that case, all the central cells normally connected to the row-C whisker afferents would either degenerate or become connected to the barrel cells in row B or D (Simons, Durham, & Woolsey, 1984). Delaying the destruction even longer can prevent all central changes.

Neural responses are also changed. The Simons, Durham, & Woolsey (1984) study recorded from single cells in rats and mice after similar neonatal treatment ("whiskerectomies"). They found that the cells in abnormally enlarged barrels responded to adjacent whiskers instead of to stimulation of the area from which the whisker had been removed. These effects of whisker destruction have to cross at least three synapses to affect cortical cells. Therefore, normal activity in peripheral afferents is required for normal cortical development in the somatosensory system.

Other experimenters gave kittens operant-discrimination training using somatosensory stimuli (Spinelli & Jensen, 1979). Starting at various times after eye opening, each kitten was given eight minutes a day of discriminated avoidance training. Between training periods, the kittens were kept in a normal laboratory environment. During training, a kitten was suspended in a sling with goggles over its eyes. Stimulating

Barrelfield configurations		P_0	P_1	P_2	P_3	P_4	P_5	P_6	$P_{8,10}$	Animals with each configuration
Thin barrellike territory **BLT**		7	1							8
Broad barrellike territory **BLT**	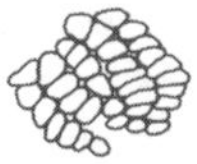	12	2							14
Barrelless territory **BLS**		1	5							6
Ill-defined barrellike territory **IDB**			1	11	1					13
Poorly defined barrels **PDB**	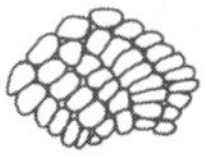			1	11	3				15
Sharply defined, sometimes small, barrels **SDB**					1	5	8	2		16
Normal-looking barrelfields **NLB**				1	1	4	2	1	5	14
Small barrels (few whiskers) **SMB**	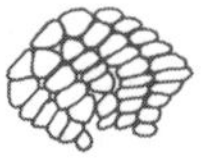	1	1	1	3	1				7
Disruption of barrels of neighboring rows* (more whiskers)	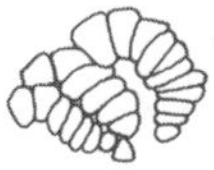	5	4	2	2					13
Animals for each day of lesion		26	14	16	19	13	10	3	5	106 Total

Figure 12-11 Removing a row (row C) of whisker follicles in neonatal mice permanently changes somatosensory barrels in the cortex. The nature of the change depends on the mouse's age when the whiskers were removed. For each lesion day (P0, or day of birth; P1, or postnatal day 1, on the top), the number of barrelfield configurations is indicated and illustrated. The boxed numbers indicate which type of effect most commonly occurred after whisker removal or lesions made on that particular day. The heavy line divides two groups: those showing day-of-lesion effects (above) and those showing the effect of number of whiskers removed (below). "Normal-looking barrelfields" were found in both groups. * = row D whiskers inadvertently damaged.

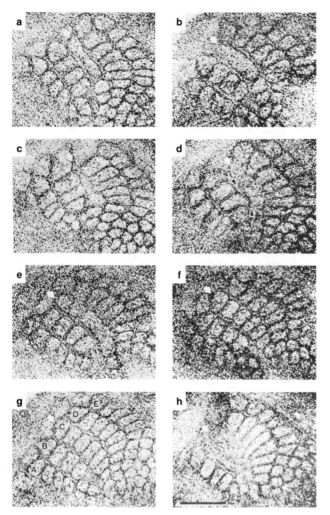

Figure 12-12 Photomicrographs of 40 μm thick brain sections taken from the right somatosensory cortex of 12-day-old mice, summarizing the effects of neonatally removing the C whisker now. The white arrows point to the areas affected. The bar in **h** represents 500 μm for all photographs. **a.** Lesion at P0 (day of birth): thin barrellike territory (see Figure 12-11). **b.** Lesion at P0: broad barrellike territory. **c.** Lesion at P1: barrelless territory. Note that the fifth barrel in row C and the barrels in rows B and D "compensate" for the loss of C (see Figure 12-11). **d.** Lesion at P2: ill-defined barrellike territory. The black arrowheads point to barrel fragments on the border toward row B. The white arrowhead points to the most obvious of the poorly defined strands of neurons belonging to barrel D1. **e.** Lesion at P3: poorly defined barrels (see Figure 12-11). **f.** Lesion at P5: sharply defined barrels. **g.** Normal field, taken from a control animal. **h.** Lesion at P1: disruption of barrels of neighboring row B, in addition to row C. See text for implications.

electrodes were attached with rubber bands to both forearms, but only one forearm was ever shocked. Whenever the kitten allowed that particular forearm to drop, the arm was shocked; at the same time, either vertical or horizontal lines (in different kittens) were projected into one eye. As long as that forearm was held up, the kitten was not shocked, and the other visual stimulus was projected into the *opposite* eye. This training continued for about ten weeks.

After the training period, the kitten was anesthetized and single-cell responses in the forearm area of its somatosensory cortex, the cells that had been activated by the shock, were recorded. Those cells were compared with cells in the contralateral somatosensory cortex and with cells recorded from yoked control animals (for whom the visual stimuli and shock had been randomly paired). When the responses to cutaneous stimulation of somatosensory cells that had *not* been stimulated by training (in the hemisphere that had not been stimulated) were compared with the responses of cells in the stimulated hemisphere, the researchers found that more cells responded to stimulation of that part of the kitten's skin on the stimulated than on the nonstimulated side. This training-induced increase in the responsiveness of the somatosensory cells was produced by only from 10 to 29 minutes of shock (summed over all training trials)!

Shock-trained somatosensory cells also responded differently to other types of stimuli. Although about 25% of the cells on both the trained and untrained sides responded to auditory stimuli, 75% of the trained but only 30% of the untrained cells responded to visual stimuli. Furthermore, the eye that had received the visual stimulus associated with the shock was also the eye that controlled most of the somatosensory cells—and those cells were also most sensitive to the line orientation (either vertical or horizontal) of that particular stimulus.

Not all kittens showed these effects equally. The kittens that learned the behavioral response the most quickly also showed the most dramatic changes in neural coding. The kitten that was oldest at the time the training began showed the fewest changes in coding. Somatosensory cells in the yoked controls responded similarly, but to a much lesser degree than trained cells.

This study shows how specialized training can change cortical coding characteristics. The training may also have affected the way the kittens perceived the somatosensory and visual stimuli. The relationship observed between speed of learning and the amount of coding change suggests that this would be the case. But did fast learning cause greater coding changes? Or did the coding changes enable the kittens to learn faster?

Although this research suggests that most kinds of somatosensory plasticity may fade with maturity, adult brains can also be changed. A raccoon that had lost its right forelimb some time prior to its capture was studied electrophysiologically (Rasmusson, Turnbull, & Leech, 1985). Neurons in the area that normally responds to forelimb stimulation responded either to stimulation of the stump or to stimulation of the hindpaw on the same side of the body. Therefore, a very large area, even in the adult cortex, can show plasticity after peripheral nerve damage. Studies of this type will provide the information we need to help people who have suffered such damage accidentally.

Auditory

Only rarely have changes in auditory coding been found after manipulating the auditory developmental environment. The largely negative results may reflect differences in the ways in which the auditory system, in comparison with the other sensory systems, codes the quality and quantity of stimulation. But most of the negative results came from studies using simple auditory stimuli, aspects of which are well coded in the cochlea (frequency and amplitude). More complex aspects of stimuli that are discretely coded only at the level of the colliculus or tectum might show experiential changes—as we now describe.

Auditory coding for complex stimuli is sensitive to developmental experiences. Tees (1967) raised rats with ear plugs and then tested their ability to learn auditory discriminations. Deprived rats learned the discriminations as well as the nondeprived rats. However, the deprived rats were less able to distinguish one auditory *pattern* (a particular sequence of high and low tones) from another.

Instead of depriving subjects, one set of researchers varied the types of auditory stimulus to which the rats were exposed during development (Clopton & Winfield, 1976). Young rats were exposed to one of two different patterns of sound for five hours a day throughout the first four months of their lives. The pattern used was note scales. One group was exposed to an upward scale, interspersed with noise. The other group was exposed to a downward scale, the notes also being interspersed with noise. A third group was not exposed to any unusual auditory stimulation. When the researchers recorded from inferior colliculus cells, they found that pattern coding differed according to rearing conditions. Specifically, the number of cells responding to the upward pattern was greatly increased in the rats that had been exposed to that pattern during development.

Another set of researchers (Sanes & Constantine-Paton, 1983, 1985) exposed mouse pups to unusual auditory stimulation. Mice were exposed to loud clicks for 24 hours a day, until 19 or 24 days after birth, starting at 8 days of age. The tuning curves of inferior colliculus cells were affected. Cells that normally respond to frequencies contained in the click sound showed rather dramatically broader, less discriminative tuning curves. Thus, those cells responded to more frequencies than did the analogous cells in the control mice.

Plasticity is not limited to the developmental period. Adult male rats were exposed to either 24 hours of silence or 24 hours of repetitive tones (Rees, Güldner, & Aitkin, 1985). The rats exposed to tones had larger synapses in their ventral cochlear nucleus. So even adult auditory systems can be changed.

Knudsen (1983) changed the way in which auditory neurons in the barn owl code the spatial location of the sound source. Normally cells in the tectum of barn owls respond to both auditory and visual stimuli—but only when the noisy object is in the right visual location. In other words, that cell will respond to a visual stimulus in a particular spatial position, and that same cell also responds to an auditory stimulus—but only when the visual and auditory stimuli are in exactly the same place in space.

Knudsen inserted an ear plug into only one ear of young barn owls. Since intensity differences between the ears are one cue for locating a sound source (Chapter 6), spatial coding would be affected. Later, he found that tectal cells had compensated for the plug. The auditory and visual maps of space, in the presence of the plug, were in perfect register. But when the plug was removed, a cell responded to visual stimuli from one place in space and to sounds coming from an entirely different place in space! Thus the auditory receptive fields of those cells were changed so that the code for auditory "place in space" came into registration with the visual map code.

Summary of Developmental Effects

Cortical cells are the ones most dramatically changed by environmental enrichment. Although parietal cells are not much affected by enrichment, changing the somatosensory input to the parietal cortex (by removal of a whisker or by shocking the animal in a training task) does change these cells. The auditory cortex cells are only slightly affected by enrichment, and most of the research looking for changes in auditory coding as a function of complex variations in auditory development have examined the colliculus. Tuning curves and codes for spatial location may be changed by exposing young organisms to unusual kinds of auditory stimulation. So the way sensory cells code information can be permanently altered during development. This possibility raises interesting questions about just what "reality" is. Each of us, having had different developmental experiences, may perceive a different "reality."

Binocular versus Monocular Visual Deprivation

We learn to see. Although mammals can see at birth—or immediately after eye opening—their perceptions are *not* those of an adult. Neural coding in a newborn differs from that of an adult, and many of the differences are caused by the adult's visual experiences. People blind from birth who have their vision restored as adults can learn to make their way through the visual world. But if only *one* eye has been blind from birth, that eye may never "learn" to see. Thus, the visual effects of **monocular deprivation** (blindness in one eye) differ from those of **binocular deprivation** (blindness in both eyes).

Binocular Deprivation

If adults are only temporarily blinded, they still have normal perceptions once their vision is restored. The same is not true of people blind from birth who suddenly have their vision restored (Hubel, 1979; Riesen, 1950; Wiesel, 1982). Immediately afterward, they still act blind. Although with time, experience, and training, they can learn to see, their vision is never completely normal.

Early visual deprivation has more profound effects than does deprivation begun later in life, after the sensitive and critical periods have gone by. The sensitive/critical period includes the first three months after eye opening in cats. Monkeys are most sensitive during the first six weeks of life, but some sensitivity to deprivation persists throughout the first year. In humans, the sensitive period may extend throughout the first five to even ten years of life (Wiesel, 1982).

Effects on anatomy, visually guided behaviors, and visual coding.   The effects of being blind during the sensitive and critical periods have been explored in both cats and monkeys. Binocular visual deprivation is usually achieved either by suturing the eyelids shut or by rearing the animal in the dark. The suturing procedure does not deprive the eye of all light (as you can see by shutting your own eyelids), and so the two procedures do not always produce similar effects; we will discuss the differences later. The effects of suturing in animals may be analogous to the effects that cataracts have on humans. In both procedures, the animal is binocularly deprived during its development, and then the properties of its visual system are explored.

The anatomy and physiology of the lateral geniculate are more affected by binocular deprivation than the retina is, and the cortex is even more affected (Hirsch, 1985; Hubel, 1979; Singer, 1985; Sherman & Spear, 1982; Wiesel, 1982). In the cat, the number of Y-cells in the geniculate is decreased by binocular deprivation, but there is little effect on the number of Y types of retinal ganglion cells. The physiology and coding responses of individual cells also show that geniculate cells are more severely affected by binocular deprivation than are retinal ganglion cells (Sherman & Spear, 1982).

After binocular deprivation, cortical cells respond abnormally to visual stimuli. In cats, the cells that respond to light often have very abnormal properties (Sherman & Spear, 1982). Their receptive fields are often nonspecific; only 10% to 20% of cells maintain normal orientational coding. Even in the few orientation-sensitive cells, the inhibitory parts of their receptive fields are often weak or even totally absent. This abnormal coding of visual information could well explain the inability of these cats to see normally. Binocular deprivation causes less disruption of orientation coding in monkeys than in cats, but in both species an abnormally large number of visually unresponsive cells are found after deprivation (Hubel, 1979; Wiesel, 1982).

Deprivation causes similar coding deficits in other visual cortical areas of the cat. For example, in the suprasylvian cortex (above the sylvian fissure), binocular deprivation decreases the number of cells responding to visual stimuli from 90% to 25% (Spear, Tong, & Sawyer, 1983). Directional selectivity is lost, and the cells have abnormally large visual fields with no surround inhibition. Similar abnormalities occur in Area II cells (Singer & Tretter, 1976).

Binocularity is disrupted by binocular deprivation in both cats and monkeys—though in slightly different ways in each species. Although some cortical cells responsive to either eye can be found after deprivation in both cats and monkeys, the normal interaction of left and right eye input is disrupted. In monkeys, very few cells could be driven by both eyes—only by one eye or by the other (Wiesel, 1982). These monocularly driven cells were organized into normal-looking dominance columns. Binocularly deprived cats have fewer-than-normal numbers of cells responding to both eyes. The cells that are found in deprived cats do not show normal sensitivity to retinal disparity, the cue for three-dimensional vision (Sherman & Spear, 1982; Wiesel, 1982). Also, the binocular cells tend to be those with nonspecific receptive fields; the cells with some degree of orientational tuning tend to be strictly monocular. Finally, cats reared in the dark have no ocular dominance columns, a lack further suggesting abnormalities in binocular coding.

Effects on synaptic connections.   The following research provides dramatic demonstrations of how the visual system can be "rewired" by developmental deprivation.

Cells within the visual cortex have different kinds of inputs and interconnections after binocular deprivation (Michalski, Kossut, Chmielowska, & Turlejski, 1984). By recording from several cells simultaneously, these researchers were able to compare responses of a pair of cells in a binocularly deprived cat with a pair in a normally reared cat. The cells in the deprived cortex were less likely to share a common afferent input (34% as opposed to 61%). Further, more inhibitory interconnections among cortical cells were found in the deprived cortex.

Binocular deprivation also changes the *type* of stimulus to which visual cells will respond. Visual deprivation increases the number of superior colliculus cells in cats responding to *auditory* stimuli (from 11% to 42%) (Rauschecker & Harris, 1983). In normally reared monkeys, all Area 19 cells (see Figure 7-11) respond *only* to visual stimuli. After bilateral lid suture, 20% of those cells responded *only* to *somatosensory* stimuli. This effect may explain why these monkeys appear functionally blind but can still move about actively by using somatosensory stimuli (Hyvärinen, Carlson, & Hyvärinen, 1981).

Some retinal cells do normally project to the somatosensory system in newborns, at least in hamsters. These connections are usually lost during development, but they can be induced to remain and even to become functional (Frost & Metin, 1985). The lateral geniculate and superior colliculus were lesioned unilaterally in newborn hamsters, destroying the normal targets for retinal cells on the lesioned side of the brain. At the same time, the somatosensory nucleus in the thalamus had its normal input removed. Under these conditions, retinal cells retain their projections to somatosensory thalamic cells even in adults, and visual stimuli will reliably evoke neural responses in the somatosensory cortex. The visual receptive fields in the somatosensory cortex even showed evidence of being topographically organized! If the same were true of cats and monkeys, the abnormal responses seen after deprivation might come from anomalous connections that, because of deprivation, developmental process fail to eliminate.

Dark rearing versus suture: Recovery effects.   When vision is first restored to binocularly deprived cats, they act as though they were blind. Some vision recovers with training, but the extent of the recovery depends on whether suturing or dark rearing was used and whether vision is restored to both eyes or only to one eye. For example, allowing the animal to use both eyes after the deprivation period does not produce as much recovery either in visual acuity or in single-unit coding properties as does allowing the use of only one eye (Mower, Caplan, & Letsou, 1982).

More visual recovery occurs in dark-reared than in bilaterally sutured cats (cats with both eyes sewn shut). Cells in

dark-reared cats given some visual experience later recovered about half of their normal level of orientational sensitivity (no recovery of directional sensitivity occurred) (Cynader, Berman, & Hein, 1976). Similarly, cats that have been deprived by dark rearing can eventually perform visual-motor tasks, whereas there is very little behavioral recovery in cats deprived by suture (Mower, Caplan, & Letsou, 1982). Behavioral and physiological recovery in bilaterally sutured cats may require extensive and specialized discrimination training, done under conditions carefully monitored to reduce stress.

The difference between dark rearing and bilateral suture suggests that the total absence of light prolongs the sensitive period. In one study, dark-reared and normally reared cats were allowed to see for a time out of only one eye. Then recordings from single cells in the visual cortex were made during various kinds of visual stimulation (Cynader, 1983). Cats that were monocularly deprived after spending their critical period in a normal visual environment showed no effect of that eye closure. But even after two years in the dark, cells in those cats were still sensitive to the effects of monocular deprivation. The period of subsequent monocular deprivation significantly reduced the number of cells responding to the completely deprived eye and thus further reduced binocularity.

This prolonged sensitive period rapidly terminates after visual experience. After six weeks in a normal visual environment, dark-reared cats were no longer sensitive to monocular deprivation. Even six hours of visual exposure may eliminate the sensitivity of a dark-reared cat to monocular deprivation (Mower, Christen, & Caplan, 1983).

In summary, dark rearing may keep the visual system in a state sensitive to visual input. This circumstance may explain why the dark-reared animal can show greater recovery effects. Even an extremely brief period of vision can terminate sensitivity. If the synaptic basis for the differences between the effects of dark rearing and binocular suture could be discovered, we might better understand how experience can affect brain coding mechanisms.

Monocular Deprivation

Monocular deprivation more profoundly affects visual coding than does binocular deprivation. If one eye is closed during the entire sensitive/critical period in monkeys, cats, or humans, that organism will be permanently blind in that one eye. In humans, the earlier and the longer the period of deprivation, the poorer visual acuity will be in the deprived eye (Wiesel, 1982). The monocular deprivation could have been caused by abnormalities in the lens or focusing muscles or by cataracts.

Two studies recently investigated humans monocularly deprived throughout the sensitive/critical period. The studies explored what the vision of these people is like when the deprivation is ended (as by corneal surgery). People with the most severe (earliest and longest-lasting) monocular deprivation can see almost nothing through the previously deprived eye. Such a person cannot even see diffuse spatial patterns through that eye, although that person *is* able to detect changes in luminance level over time (temporal patterns) (Hess, France, & Tulunay-Keesey, 1981). Even less severely deprived people, when shown a visual straight-line pattern, see broken, irregular, curved, and twisted lines (Hess, 1982). Perhaps in partial compensation, monocularly deprived humans may have better-than-normal acuity in the nondeprived eye (Freeman & Bradley, 1980).

Doctors have tried to increase recovery from monocular deprivation for a person still in his or her sensitive/critical period by covering the "good" eye and forcing the person to use the previously deprived, or "bad," eye. This procedure is modeled in lower animals by **reverse suture**. One eye is sutured shut during part of the sensitive/critical period, and then that eye is opened and the other eye is closed for varying periods of time.

Effects on anatomy, visually guided behaviors, and visual coding.   In cats, the retina of the deprived eye again shows little effect of deprivation, but the geniculate is markedly affected (Sherman & Spear, 1982). In the geniculate, as Figure 12-13 illustrates, input from the left and right eyes goes to different layers. The A layer receives input from the retinal ganglion cells of one eye and the A_1 layer from the other eye. Cells in the A layer connected to the deprived eye have much smaller cell bodies than do cells in the contralateral A layer. Y-cells are much less likely to be found in the deprived layer, and even the normal-looking X-cells show abnormally poor responses to spatial variations in visual inputs.

If kittens are raised with monocular deprivation throughout the sensitive/critical period, only about 5% to 10% of visual cortical cells respond to *any* input from the deprived eye (Sherman & Spear, 1982). The few cells that do respond are grossly abnormal. They show little or no orientation or directional selectivity, and they have only weak and inconsistent responses to any kind of visual stimulus. Cells with complex receptive fields are more affected by deprivation than are cells with simple receptive fields (Wilson & Sherman, 1977). Thus, binocularity is reduced more by monocular than by binocular deprivation.

One study recorded from cells undergoing a change in binocularity due to monocular deprivation (Tsumoto & Freeman, 1981). Anesthetized kittens were studied during the peak of the sensitive/critical period for effects of monocular

deprivation. Responses from individual cells were extensively recorded and classified with respect to binocularity. Then one of each kitten's eyes was shut for from 15 to 20 minutes while the other eye was visually stimulated. Afterward, the responses of that same cell were measured again. That cell's responses to the deprived eye decreased. This study established that a given cell's responses are changed by experience: it is not always the case that binocularity shifts just by making some nonresponsive cells active and some active cells nonresponsive.

The ocular dominance columns of monocularly deprived animals match their behavior and cellular physiology (Sherman & Spear, 1982). Normally cells in a given geniculate layer project to several dominance columns in layer IV of the visual cortex. The spread of axons from a geniculate cell in a normally reared adult looks like the pattern seen in Figure 12-14b. This pattern develops with experience, since it is not seen in the visually deprived kitten (Figure 12-14a). In the monocularly deprived cat, axon terminals coming from a non-deprived geniculate-layer cell show no evidence of any ocular dominance columns: there are no empty patches representing dominance columns for the other eye. The segregation of input from left and right eyes, causing left and right ocular dominance columns, is eliminated by monocular deprivation.

Similar effects are seen in monocularly deprived monkeys (Hubel, 1979; Wiesel, 1982). The geniculate layers receiving input from the deprived eye shrink, and cells in those layers are smaller than normal. As Figure 12-15 shows, few cortical cells respond to input from the previously deprived eye. In normally reared monkeys, only layer IV cells are strictly monocular. Cells in the other layers of a particular column have binocular inputs, but will prefer the eye to which the layer IV cells are sensitive. Predictably, the ocular dominance columns receiving input from the deprived eye are narrowed and shrunken, and the columns receiving input from the other eye are enlarged, as Figure 12-16 illustrates.

Recovery mechanisms.   If monocular deprivation is continued throughout the sensitive/critical period, no recovery is produced by simply exposing the organism to normal visual experiences through the previously deprived eye. Even reverse suture done after the sensitive/critical period will have little impact. The earlier during the sensitive/critical period the reverse suture is done, the more nearly complete the recovery will be.

One treatment increases the input a previously deprived eye has to the cortex even *after* the sensitive/critical period. Describing this treatment illustrates some of the ways deprivation works, but, as you will see, this procedure is usually not clinically relevant! Removing the previously nondeprived eye

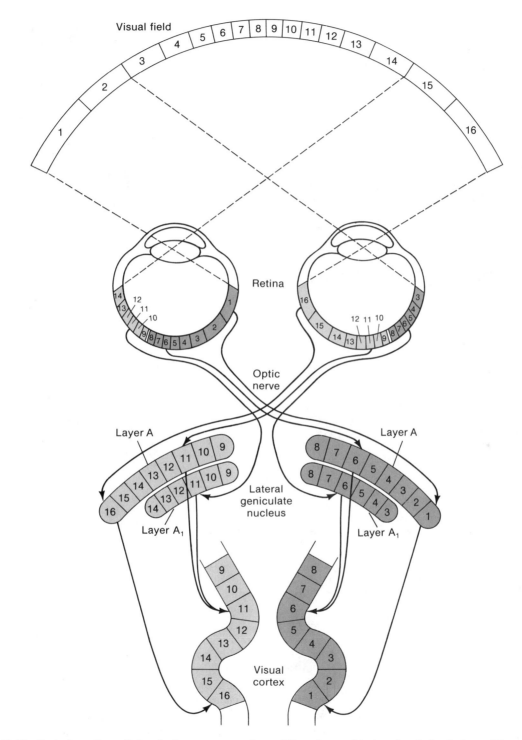

Figure 12-13 Retinal ganglion cells from both eyes are mapped onto different layers of the lateral geniculate in the cat. Thus, monocular deprivation will affect only certain layers of cells in the geniculate.

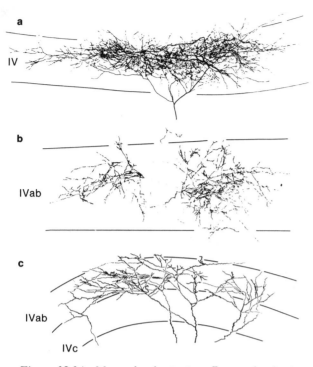

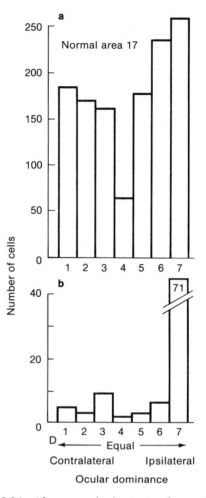

Figure 12-14 Monocular deprivation affects ocular dominance columns in the cat. These are patterns of aborization ("branchings" of the cell's dendritic "tree") of single geniculate axons in layer IV of the visual cortex. **a.** In a 17-day-old kitten the axon had been stained before columns formed; it aborizes profusely and uniformly over a disk-shaped area more than 2 mm in diameter. **b.** In the normal adult cat, the aborization is entirely within layer IVab and forms two patches separated by a terminal-free gap. This pattern presumably corresponds to the segregation of input from the two eyes in a columnar fashion. **c.** In a monocularly deprived cat, there is no terminal-free region: nondeprived geniculate axon branches are present in territory that normally belongs to the other eye.

Figure 12-15 After monocular deprivation, few cortical cells respond to the previously deprived eye. These are ocular dominance histograms in normal (**a**) and monocularly deprived (**b**) rhesus macaque monkeys. Cells in layer IVc are excluded. The deprived monkey had its right eye closed at the age of two weeks for 18 months. The letter D indicates the side of the histogram corresponding to dominance by the deprived eye. Cells in group 1 are driven exclusively by the contralateral eye and those in group 7 from the ipsilateral eye; those in group 4 respond to both eyes equally, and the remaining groups are intermediate.

produces recovery in the deprived eye in both monkeys and cats (Harwerth, Smith, Crawford, & von Noorden, 1984; Kratz & Lehmkuhle, 1983; Kratz, Spear, & Smith, 1976; Smith, 1981). The acuity of vision through that eye is dramatically increased. Removal of the nondeprived eye produces much more behavioral and physiological recovery than does reverse suture, and the number of cells responding to the previously deprived eye increases immediately after removal of the eye. Even in monocularly deprived humans, loss of the "good" eye can lead to almost immediate improvement in vision through the previously deprived eye. However, this effect depends on the degree and type of visual problem present before the loss.

The effects of eye removal suggest that neural activity driven by the "good" eye is actively inhibiting all input from the deprived eye. Only removal of the "good" eye — not just visual deprivation or reverse suture — eliminates this inhibition. Thus, retinal ganglion-cell activity, which normally continues even in the dark, inhibits any input from the "bad" eye. This inhibition occurs at the cortical level: removing the cor-

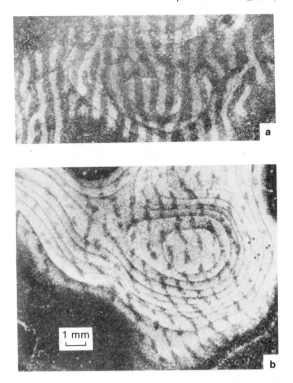

Figure 12-16 One way to visualize the effects of monocular deprivation on ocular dominance columns. During input from one eye, the cortex is radioactively labeled. **a.** The light stripes, representing the stimulated cell or labeled eye columns, are separated by gaps of the same width representing the other eye in the normally reared monkey. **b.** In the monocularly deprived monkey (having the right eye closed at two weeks for 18 months), the input from the normal eye is in the form of expanded bands that in places coalesce, obliterating the narrow gaps representing the columns connected to the previously closed eye.

Some procedures make things worse instead of facilitating recovery. If the monocular deprivation is not constant — if the open eye is alternated throughout the sensitive/critical period — then the eye opened for the greater total amount of time will dominate cells in the cortex. Instead of effecting recovery, a period of normal visual experience will *exaggerate* the deficits associated with the less-experienced eye (Tumosa, Nunberg, Hirsch, & Tieman, 1983).

Manipulating the Magnitude of the Monocular-Deprivation Effects

The differences in the effects of the various procedures show how visual coding normally develops and how it can develop abnormally after deprivation. In addition, some of these procedures are very much like those that facilitate memory (Chapter 11). Similar types of synaptic changes could be occurring in both the formation of memory traces and the changes in coding caused by various developmental experiences.

Effects of competition. Some research compares how deprivation affects various parts of the geniculate and cortex. Some areas of both the geniculate and the cortex normally receive input from both eyes. These are described as **binocular areas,** even though left- and right-eye cells are arranged in different layers in the geniculate and in different columns in the cortex. The **monocular areas** normally receive input from only one eye. For example, the far right visual field is not seen by the left eye (the nose is in the way), and so any part of the cortex or geniculate devoted to that visual-field area would be monocular (see in Figure 12-13).

By seeing how deprivation affects monocular and binocular areas, researchers can evaluate the effects of competition among afferents (Guillery, 1972, 1973; Sherman & Spear, 1982). For example, suppose that axons from two cells, one in the left and one in the right eye, made synaptic contact with the *same* postsynaptic cell in the neonatal geniculate or cortex. If one eye were deprived, axons coming from that eye might not be able to compete successfully with axons being stimulated by normal visual input. The synapses made by the inactive axon might regress and be replaced by synapses made by axons from the other eye.

Competition can explain why, when one eye is deprived, the dominance columns associated with the nondeprived eye are enlarged. Axons driven by cells in the nondeprived eye compete more successfully for synapses on the cortical cells, and so those columns enlarge. Competition was also used to explain some of the effects of removing a whisker barrel upon cortical somatosensory cells (Figures 12-11 and 12-12). If

tex also increases a cat's vision through a previously deprived eye (Sherman, 1974) (cats more than monkeys can show effective visual-motor activity even without a cortex).

Animals don't all recover equally after eye removal, and coding responses are not all equally affected. In the monkey, only spectral sensitivity shows some recovery (Harwerth et al., 1984). In cats, although more cells become responsive to the previously deprived eye, the ocular dominance columns remain abnormal (Yinon, Podell, & Goshen, 1984). Also among cats, the animal whose cortical cells showed the most input from the previously deprived eye was the one to show the greatest amount of behavioral-visual recovery after eye removal (Kratz & Lehmkuhle, 1983).

competition accounted for all effects of monocular deprivation, the monocular areas of the geniculate and the cortex should *not* be affected by deprivation of the eye to which they are connected.

In fact, many cells in the monocular portions of the geniculate or cortex are less affected by deprivation than are cells in the binocular portions (Guillery, 1972, 1973; Hirsch & Leventhal, 1983; Sherman & Spear, 1982; Wilson & Sherman, 1977). The anatomy and physiology of Y-cells are severely affected even in monocular segments, so competition is not the only mechanism causing deprivation effects (Sherman & Spear, 1982). In the cortex, monocular segment cells with complex receptive fields are affected. Therefore, normal visual input is required for the development of normal visual coding mechanisms even where competition is not possible.

Siamese cats provide another way to test the effects of competition. In Siamese cats (and in albino cats and rats), the pattern of retinal ganglion cell input to geniculate layers is disordered. One way in which the animals compensate for the disorder is by blocking the input of the "out-of-order" cells to the cortex. Consequently, many cells in the Siamese cat's cortex receive input from only one eye. So in Siamese, monocular deprivation affects cortical coding less than in other cats (Berman & Payne, 1982).

Given all the changes that occur even when competition cannot take place, it is not surprising that total blockage of neural activity coming from an eye can produce more severe effects than does simple closure of that eye. Injecting tetrodotoxin (which blocks depolarization-activated Na^+ channels: Chapter 3) into the optic nerve prevents any activity in that eye from reaching the geniculate or cortex. Such injections, when done during the sensitive/critical period, can make geniculate cells smaller and can create very abnormal responses to visual stimuli (Archer, Dubin, & Stark, 1982; Kuppermann & Kasamatsu, 1983).

Norepinephrine. Activity in the noradrenergic LC neurons may be important to developmental deprivation and recovery effects. Kasamatsu and Pettigrew (1979) destroyed LC cells (by intraventricular 6-OHDA injections) just before dark-reared kittens were monocularly exposed to light. Exposure of one eye increased the number of cortical cells responding to that eye much less than expected. Injecting NE onto the cortex of kittens previously given 6-OHDA injections *restored* the cortical response to monocular exposure (Kasamatsu, Pettigrew, & Ary, 1979, 1981). The kittens whose NE cells had been destroyed by 6-OHDA, but that were given NE just before the monocular exposure, still had most of their cells driven by the briefly exposed eye.

Even in cats with intact noradrenergic systems, NE perfusion interacts with visual experience. For example, microperfusions of NE onto the cortex during monocular deprivation, in cats who were past the sensitive/critical period, restored the ability of cortical cells to respond to that deprivation. Perfusing NE over the cortex of dark-reared kittens during a subsequent period of monocular exposure *increases* the degree to which input from the exposed eye acquires control over cortical cells. Stimulation of the mesencephalic reticular system during the period of monocular deprivation similarly accentuates the effect of that deprivation (Singer & Rauschecker, 1982). Finally, perfusing NE over the cortex of monocularly deprived kittens, which subsequently had both eyes opened while still in the sensitive/critical period, accelerated the recovery from deprivation.

The ability of a monocularly exposed eye to acquire input to cortical cells — and presumably the ability of activity from that eye to inhibit input coming from the other eye — requires that NE be present during the exposure period. Thus, "a critical amount of norepinephrine *is* necessary for the normal developmental plasticity of cerebral cortex" (Bear & Daniels, 1983, p. 415, emphasis theirs). NE may have these effects because it increases the signal-to-noise ratios in cells (Chapter 8). Singer (1985) has suggested that extracellular levels of Ca^{++} may also be involved. He found that extracellular levels of Ca^{++} in the visual cortex are decreased when dark-reared kittens are given a light stimulus at the same time as RF stimulation; either stimulus alone had no effect. Therefore, plasticity may involve opening electrically gated Ca^{++} channels in the membranes of affected neurons, an event that may require both afferent input and NE.

Summary of Visual Deprivation

Studies of binocular and monocular deprivation dramatically demonstrate that we have to learn to see. Depriving an organism of normal visual stimulation during the sensitive/critical period can produce permanent deficits — including blindness. Visual-cell responses to other types of sensory input are increased. Organisms can show dramatic recovery from binocular deprivation, particularly if the deprivation involved total darkness, as opposed to just the deprivation of pattern vision caused by suturing. But some subtle deficits in pattern vision seem to be permanent, not subject to recovery.

There are important species differences in the effects of binocular deprivation. The development of normal ocular dominance columns in the cat depends on the cat's having normal visual experiences during the sensitive/critical period, but some (abnormal) binocular input to cortical cells appears in those animals even after binocular deprivation. In the monkey, ocular dominance columns will develop despite the absence of visual input, but binocular input to cortical cells is lost after binocular deprivation.

Monocular deprivation can produce even more severe effects, at least with respect to the vision remaining in the deprived eye. In both cats and monkeys, monocular deprivation disrupts ocular dominance columns and the binocularity of input to cortical cells. If reverse suture is carried out early enough, some recovery can be produced. Monocular deprivation throughout the sensitive/critical period produces total blindness in the deprived eye. But removal of the "good" eye can restore some vision to the "bad" eye, suggesting that active inhibition of the input from the "bad" eye is part of the permanent deficit.

We have some clues about how visual experience changes visual coding mechanisms. Competition among axons for a given set of postsynaptic locations is part of the normal developmental process and accounts for some effects of deprivation. Normal activity coming from the sutured eye or from the eyes during dark rearing is also important: removal of that input produces even more dramatic coding effects. Normal NE is also required; increasing NE levels may facilitate developmentally induced changes in cortical coding mechanisms. Can these effects of NE and competition be related to the way that memory traces form in adult animals after special training?

Selective Exposure and Visual Coding

Developmental visual experiences can produce even more dramatic and important effects than changes in binocularity. The types of stimulus present during the sensitive/critical period can permanently change the way the brain codes and the way the organism perceives those stimuli.

Background and a Model

Visual cortical cells in the newborn mammal do not respond to visual stimuli exactly the way cells in the adult do, although some neurons in the newborn have some "adultlike" properties (Movshon & Van Sluyters, 1981; Pettigrew, 1978; Sherman & Spear, 1982; Wiesel, 1982; Wiesel & Hubel, 1974). First, the selectivity of cellular responses to varied line orientations is much greater in the adult. The cells that are orientation

selective in the newborn are only monocular, instead of binocular as in the adult. The preferred orientation is almost always horizontal or vertical in the newborn; fewer oblique orientation-sensitive cells are found in the newborn than in the adult. Finally, the young kitten has many cells that are not sensitive to orientation, and these cells are often binocular.

We do not know yet to what extent the changes from the immature to the mature responses depend on the presence of appropriate developmental visual stimulation. Researchers have reported directly contradictory results (see Sherman & Spear's 1982 discussion of some of these contradictions). As we have described, neither a monocularly nor a binocularly deprived cortex is entirely normal. Even more impressive, if visual deprivation is combined with selective exposure to only certain stimuli, the coding properties of the adult cortex can be drastically and permanently affected.

The following model of visual development is used to organize our discussion. It was derived from Pettigrew's (1978) and Grobstein and Chow's (1975) reviews of the visual developmental literature. This model is compatible with the neuron doctrine in Chapter 1.

1. **Genetics and the magnitude of the effects of experience.** First, *genetics specifies a range of possible interconnections. An individual's visual experiences work within this range to specify which connections will remain and which will disappear during the sensitive/critical period.* As we pointed out before, there is not enough information in the karyotype for all possible neural interconnections to be specified. However, genes could specify a *set* of possible connections, and the individual experiences of the organism could then determine which connections were "useful" and would remain. The other connections would atrophy, perhaps through disuse. Even at the cellular level, some kinds of visual cortical cells do and some do not require normal visual developmental experiences to have normal coding responses in the adult (Hirsch, 1985).

This first principle is not meant to exclude the possibility that some new connections, not present in the newborn, could be formed if the developing brain were subjected to certain types of stimulation. These new connections — or **instructive changes** — would be specified by the genes as potential ones, ones that could form in the presence of certain types of neural activity. Also, different strains of organisms, having different genes, may have different kinds of plasticity. As we have already described, cats and monkeys are differentially affected by binocular deprivation. Among cats, Siamese are less affected than others by monocular deprivation.

One striking example of species differences concerns the

effects of inverting the visual world. In lower species such as the frog, the visual world can be inverted by turning the eyeball upside down. The nerves will regrow and reform normal connections — but the world will now be projected wrong side up to the brain. The frog never learns to compensate and always tries to capture flying bugs by sending its tongue out toward the ground.

In contrast, even adult humans can compensate for inversion of their visual world. When people wear inverting prisms, at first everything looks upside down to them. Within a week or so of wearing the prisms, they can move normally about the world, and some objects will even look right side up (Gregory, 1973; Kuffler & Nicholls, 1976). (This adaptation to prisms probably requires actively moving about the environment while wearing them.)

2.   Variability in coding effects.   The principle of variability describes the ways in which effects can vary among cells. *Different types of coding mechanisms are differentially susceptible to specialized experiences and to the neural activities evoked by those experiences.* Thus, codes for orientation, color, and speed of movement and codes for stereoscopic vision, or binocular disparity, are differentially sensitive to experience. Sometimes the range of possible interconnections specified by genes may be so narrow that experience has little room in which to work. For other codes, the range may be so broad that the adult animal that was developmentally deprived of certain types of visual experiences in the sensitive/critical period may be unable to encode or to respond to those stimuli. Differential susceptibility also implies that different coding mechanisms may have different periods of sensitivity and may require a different exposure time.

3.   Exposure duration and consolidation versus recovery effects.   *Time can be critical to the effects of selective exposure.* How long an experience lasts determines how much it will affect brain coding mechanisms. Several hours of consolidation time may be required for the effects of the experience to be fully expressed (Pettigrew & Garey, 1974). For example, Peck and Blakemore (1975) gave binocularly deprived kittens a short period of monocular vision (1, 6, or 20 hours) during the sensitive/critical period. Then cortical-cell binocularity was tested either 2 or 8 hours after the monocular exposure or else after 2, 13, or 18 more days of continued binocular deprivation.

The effects of this selective experience on cortical binocularity can be seen in Figures 12-17 and 12-18. The **induction index** measures the monocularity of cortical input. The higher the number, the fewer cells responded to input from

both eyes. One hour of monocular experience produced no significant effects, but increasing the duration of exposure to 6 hours did change the binocularity of the cortex. And 20 hours of exposure had even more effect. With a 6-hour exposure period, the effects of selective exposure increased over time, as illustrated in Figure 12-18. Both the induction index and the extent to which cortical cells were sensitive to orientation increased over days since the exposure period. This pattern is reminiscent of the consolidation gradient revealed by using various amnesic agents (Chapter 11).

Sometimes consolidation and sometimes recovery occurs after the exposure period. Consistent with its definition in Chapter 11, "consolidation" refers to an increasing impact of selective-exposure effects on cortical coding as a function of the delay between exposure and single-unit recording. "Recovery," as previously described, refers to an increase in normal types of coding as a function of the time between selective exposure and single-unit recording.

Whether recovery or consolidation effects are seen depends on which deprivation procedures are used. Studies finding consolidation effects have generally exposed dark-reared kittens to some specific type of stimulus (Buisseret, Gary-Bobo, & Imbert, 1978; Peck & Blakemore, 1975; Pettigrew & Garey, 1974). Studies finding recovery have taken normally

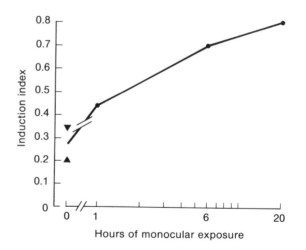

Figure 12-17   Increasing the duration of selective experience increases its effect on binocularity coding. The induction index is the number of monocular cells responding to the briefly exposed eye divided by the total number of visually responsive cells. Three experimental animals (●) had one eye opened for either 1, 6, or 20 hours at 29 days of age. The control animals either had 6 hours of binocular vision (▼) or were reared normally (▲). Single-unit responses to visual stimuli were recorded in the seventh week of life.

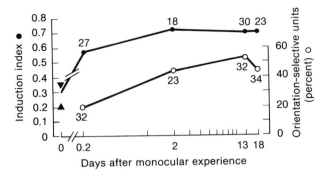

Figure 12-18 The effects of selective exposure can show a consolidation type of process. The induction index (left ordinate, solid circles; see caption for Figure 12-17) and the percentage of cells selective to line or bar orientation (right ordinate, open circles) are plotted for four kittens who had one eye opened for 6 hours at 29 days of age. Single-unit recordings were made at various times afterward. The induction indexes for two control subjects (triangles) are shown on the left side of the graph, for comparison. The number above each filled circle is the number of visually responsive cells in that sample; the one below each open circle is the total number of neurons studied.

reared kittens and exposed them briefly to some type of visually abnormal environment (Freeman & Olson, 1982; Levitt & Van Sluyters, 1982; Malach, Ebert, & Van Sluyters, 1984; Olson & Freeman, 1978; Tsumoto & Freeman, 1981). In this latter procedure, recovery is maximized by allowing the animal normal visual exposure during the recovery period. Some recovery also occurs even if the animal is kept in darkness between the selective-exposure experience and the single-unit recording.

As we noted before, a dark-reared brain may be different from a light-exposed brain. The dark-reared brain may be more sensitive not only to monocular exposure but also to selective-exposure effects. It also may be more likely to show consolidation effects.

4. Attention and play. *The effects of selective exposure on brain coding mechanisms may occur only if the animals are actively paying attention to the stimuli* (Hoyenga & Hoyenga, 1984; Singer, 1985). Just as the enrichment literature reported, animals only passively exposed to stimuli do not show changes in cortical coding responses. Furthermore, proprioceptive input from eye muscles may also be required; only if this input indicates that the organism's eyes are in focus may cortical changes take place. However, stimulation of the RF and the consequent release of NE may compensate for passivity. When RF stimulation is combined with selective expo-

sure, cortical coding characteristics change even in anesthetized cats (Singer, 1985).

Stereoscopic Coding

Binocularity of input to cortical cells is markedly affected by a period of monocular exposure. Since brain responses are affected, so is stereoscopic coding. Binocularity, or stereoscopic coding, can also be disrupted either by **alternating monocular deprivation** (reverse suture: opening first one eye and then the other alternately) or by presenting different stimuli to left and right eyes.

Alternating monocular deprivation. The effects of **unequal alternating monocular deprivation** have been compared with those of complete monocular deprivation lasting throughout the sensitive/critical period (Tieman, McCall, & Hirsch, 1983). In the alternating paradigm, not only is the deprivation alternated between eyes but one eye is usually given far less total experience than is the other eye—hence *unequal.* First, after unequal alternating exposure, the "disadvantaged" eye drives fewer cells, but the cells it does drive are found in all layers of the cortex. In contrast, the few cells driven by the "disadvantaged" eye after monocular deprivation are found only in layer IV. Second, even the cells driven by the "disadvantaged" eye after monocular exposure have unusual response properties (for example, they are unselective for speed of movement or line orientation). But the response properties of cells driven by the "disadvantaged" eye after alternating exposure are nearly normal.

Despite these differences, the two procedures can cause an equal decrease in binocularity. Thus, even the limited exposure given to the "disadvantaged" eye during the unequal alternating monocular period is sufficient to maintain some normal coding properties *other than* those for binocularity.

Equal alternating monocular deprivation also affects behaviorally measured perceptual responses (Blake & Hirsch, 1975). Kittens subjected to this procedure during the sensitive/critical period have normal vision through each eye, but they have severe deficits in binocular depth perception.

Different stimuli presented to each eye. Another way to disrupt binocularity is to give each eye a *different* type of selective-exposure experience. For research in this area, cats are usually reared with binocular deprivation except for a brief period of exposure. During light exposure, the cats wear goggles within which they can view stripes of different orientation (for example, vertical on the left side and horizontal on the right). Hirsch and his colleagues (Hirsch, Leventhal, McCall,

& Tieman, 1983) varied the types of exposure given to each eye. Both eyes were exposed to horizontal lines, both to vertical lines, or both to oblique lines—but to *different* oblique lines (45° and 135°)—or one eye was exposed to vertical and the other to horizontal lines (0° and 90°). Binocularity was equally reduced by all treatments. This equivalence of effects suggests that development of normal binocularity requires that both eyes view the *same external* world, both seeing the same change in stimuli associated with convergent eye movements.

Another type of binocular effect, **binocular transfer** (the ability to transfer information learned through one eye to performance with the other eye open), is also suppressed by this type of developmental environment (Hirsch, 1972). Cats were reared with one eye exposed to vertical and the other to horizontal lines. Later, as adults, the cats were given operant-discrimination training with one eye occluded. Then performance was tested with the trained eye occluded instead. The cats reared with their eyes looking at different stimuli had significantly poorer performance on this transfer task. It is as though the function of the interconnections of left and right visual brains were damaged by this developmental treatment.

Prismatically and surgically induced retinal disparity. Another way to reduce binocularity is to displace the visual field in one eye relative to that in the other. This can be done by placing a prism on one eye during the period of selective exposure, or by placing different prisms on each eye. Also, the experimenter can surgically interfere with the eye muscles so that one eye has a different squint from the other eye. These procedures seem to produce similar effects on binocularity.

Prismatically or surgically induced retinal disparity reduces the binocularity of cortical-cell visual responses. If the disparity is great enough, binocularity may be almost eliminated. In fact, the greater the prism-induced disparity between the corresponding images on the two retinas, the fewer binocularly excited cells can be found (Smith, Bennett, Harwerth, & Crawford, 1979). If only one eye is deviated, the receptive-field properties of cells driven by that eye will be abnormal (Chino, Shansky, Jankowski, & Banser, 1983). These cells show much lower selectivity and acuity and much larger receptive-field sizes (though directional selectivity is normal). But even the cells driven by the nondeviated eye have abnormal receptive-field characteristics. Thus, retinal disparity disrupts spatial coding in both eyes.

If the disparity between the retinal images on the left and right eyes is within a certain range, cortical coding for disparity may be able to adjust. Binocularity and stereoscopic vision will then be normal despite the disparity (Dürsteler & van der Heydt, 1983; Schlaer, 1971; Shinkman, Isley, & Rogers,

1983). This effect illustrates how experience can work within a range of genetically specified connections. At birth, retinal cells representing a range of possible binocular disparities are presumably all connected to the same cortical cell. Given normal visual experiences, the disparities and connections associated with normal stereoscopic vision remain and the others drop out. Given an abnormal disparity that is still within the range of connections present at birth, other connections drop out, leaving only connections that code for those particular disparities.

Effects seen in humans.   When one eye is deviated in relation to the orientational axis of the other eyeball, the human suffers from **strabismus.** This problem can be surgically corrected. But if it is not discovered and corrected early during the sensitive/critical period, stereoscopic vision can be permanently impaired. The long-term effects are most severe if the problem is not corrected between the ages of one and three (Banks, Aslin, & Letson, 1975; Levi, Harwerth, & Smith, 1979). Inhibitory types of binocular interconnections seem to be the most completely disrupted.

Orientational Coding

In some research, the organism is selectively exposed to only one line orientation at some point during the sensitive/critical period. Under some conditions, this selective exposure can permanently change the orientational coding of cortical cells and the ability to see lines of that particular orientation.

Original studies.   Two studies published in 1970 alerted researchers to these possibilities. Blakemore and Cooper (1970) reared kittens in the dark except for five hours each day. During that period, the kittens were placed, one at a time, in an upright plastic tube on the inside of which either horizontal or vertical lines had been painted. The kittens wore wide black collars that restricted their visual fields to the lines directly in front of them. This apparatus is illustrated in Figure 12-19.

When the kittens were five months old, this routine was stopped, and the kittens were then tested for several hours each day in a normal visual environment. At first they acted as though they were nearly blind, but normal visual motor responses quickly recovered. However, some deficits seemed permanent. The kittens acted as though they were virtually blind to contours perpendicular to the orientation they had experienced within the tube. A kitten reared with horizontal stripes would not react to or play with a vertically dangled rod, for example.

Figure 12-19 Apparatus used by Blakemore and Cooper to selectively expose kittens only to lines of a certain orientation. The visual display was an upright plastic tube. The kitten, wearing a black ruff so that it could not see its own body, stood on a glass plate supported in the middle of the cylinder. The stripes on the wall were illuminated from above by a spotlight and were of several different widths. For this diagram, the top cover and the spotlight were removed.

The receptive fields of cortical cells tested at $7\frac{1}{2}$ months of age showed similar deficits. Most cells were binocular and had distinct orientational preferences. However, the number of cells preferring various orientations was distinctly abnormal. Cells from vertically reared cats responded almost exclusively to vertical bars, and cells from horizontally reared cats responded almost exclusively to horizontal bars.

Hirsch and Spinelli (1970) used goggles for selective exposures. Kittens wore opaque goggles whenever they were not in total darkness. Within the goggles, each eye could see stripes of only one orientation, horizontal for one eye and vertical for the other. When these researchers later recorded from visual cortical cells in their cats, they found that many cells were nonselective for orientation. Furthermore, most cells were monocular and responded only to orientations to which that particular eye had been exposed.

Possible causes of effects. Selective exposure may change cortical orientational coding because of selective deprivation. Only cells receiving appropriate stimulation from the environment can maintain their connections with lower visual centers. Cells not stimulated because their preferred orientation is not present in the environment would become nonresponsive or nonselective. Some cells may acquire somewhat shifted orientational sensitivities, as long as the experienced line orientation is within the range of the interconnections specified by genetics for that cell (Rauschecker, 1982). Other cortical cells may actively inhibit input to cells coding for deprived line orientations.

Selective exposure (or deprivation) may have the effects it does because of a competition among nerve cells for targets to innervate. Those cortical cells whose selectivity matches the stimulus environment maintain their afferent input and the other types of cortical cell lose their input. For example, having each eye view *different* orientations increases the orientational selectivity of visual cortical cells (Gordon, Presson, Packwood, & Scheer, 1979).

In another study, kittens were dark reared until five weeks of age and then given monocular exposure to a normal visual environment for several days (Rauschecker & Singer, 1979).

Then the first eye was closed and the second eye opened. However, the second eye was fitted with a lens that distorted light rays in such a way that only lines of a single orientation would be in focus on the retina. When cells in the visual cortex were later tested, most were found to be binocular. But, more important, the only cells that were driven by the second eye were those sensitive to the orientation that had been in focus during the second eye's exposure period. Presumably those particular cells were the only ones that could successfully compete for afferent input.

Binocular disparity and selective-exposure effects. As we have said, the two pioneering research teams got somewhat different results. The difference was first attributed to the effects of binocular disparity. In the Blakemore and Cooper study, both eyes had the same experience, whereas in the Hirsch and Spinelli study, each eye was exposed to a different orientation.

A later study, using goggles, explicitly evaluated the role of binocular disparity (Hirsch et al., 1983). As we said earlier, either both eyes saw the same orientation or they saw different orientations. Binocular disparity had *no* effect on binocularity, the number of nonresponsive cells, or the degree of orientational selectively. However, one problem with this study is that both of the disparity conditions involved oblique lines. Oblique coding is more sensitive to experience (as we will describe) and so may change even without binocular disparity. Therefore the question remains open.

Orientational deprivation: Cells and behavior. The research done since 1970 has further explored the effects of selective exposure. As little as one hour of selective exposure can change orientational coding (Blakemore & Mitchell, 1973).

Deprivation affects behavior as well as cortical coding (Hirsch, 1972). In controlled behavioral tests, animals given selective exposure (in cylinders) are less able than control subjects to perform discriminations involving lines at right angles to the orientation to which they were exposed. Furthermore, these deficits persisted even after 30 months of normal visual exposure and visual-discrimination training (Muir & Mitchell, 1975). But in many cases, the behavioral effects seem small compared with the physiological effects. It may be the case, as has been suggested (Tees, Midgley, & Bruinsma, 1980), that behavioral preferences for certain types of stimulus may be more dramatically affected than is the capacity to discriminate among various line orientations. Rats given different developmental visual experiences have changed preferences for viewing certain kinds of visual stimulus arrays.

One important study measured both behavioral acuity and orientational coding in the same selectively reared cats. Even more impressive, the physiological recording was done blind by researchers who were not only in another laboratory but in another country (to eliminate the possibility of experimenter bias) (Blasdel, Mitchell, Muir, & Pettigrew, 1977). In this study, most kittens were given their selective exposure for two hours a day from 45 to 110 days of age. The kittens were kept in the dark both before selective exposure and for the other 22 hours of the day during the selective-exposure period. Thereafter, the cats were kept in the dark for another two months. Following from one to three years of normal visual experience and visual-discrimination training, the cats were shipped to the second laboratory for physiological recording.

Figure 12-20 summarizes the results. The first and second columns name and describe the selective-exposure conditions seen by each of the six cats. The third column describes the behavioral and the fourth column the physiological results. The behavioral sensitivity data rather closely matches the physiological orientational sensitivity data. In addition, all the cats given selective exposure showed a reduction in binocularity. The extended period of dark rearing before the selective exposure may have caused the reduction. Dark rearing can lead to strabismus, and strabismus reduces binocularity.

If kittens are selectively exposed to an environment without lines, their cells may be insensitive to orientation. One study gave kittens selective exposure to a cylinder that was covered with spots instead of lines (Van Sluyters & Blakemore, 1973). Another study selectively exposed kittens to a planetariumlike visual environment in which they saw only starlike spots of light (Pettigrew & Freeman, 1973). As Figure 12-21 illustrates, selective exposure to spots produces responses unlike those seen in either normally reared or dark-reared cats. Cells from the spot-reared kittens were insensitive to orientation, responding best to spots. Most cells were binocular.

We described earlier how avoidance training of young kittens can change somatosensory coding. Visual coding was also affected—even though the kittens were reared with *normal* visual experiences (Spinelli & Jensen, 1979). The kittens were placed in a sling for training. When a kitten dropped a forearm, that arm was shocked and horizontal lines were projected onto one eye. But as long as that arm was kept up, the kitten could avoid shock and vertical lines were projected onto the other eye. After training, the responses of visual cortical cells to visual stimuli were recorded. A shift toward monocularity was found, and most cells were driven by the eye stimulated during the shock. Most cells were sensitive to either horizontal or vertical lines; very few oblique edge detectors could be found. Furthermore, some cells showed effects never nor-

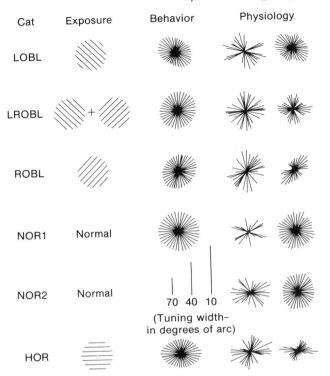

Cat	Exposure	Behavior	Physiology
LOBL			
LROBL			
ROBL			
NOR1	Normal		
NOR2	Normal	70 40 10 (Tuning width– in degrees of arc)	
HOR			

Figure 12-20   In one experiment, both the ability to discriminate among line orientations (behavioral) and the responses of cortical visual cells (physiological) were measured in the same cats, all of which had been given various kinds of selective exposure. The gratings on the left indicate the bar orientation the animal saw during its rearing. In the behavior column, the length of each line indicates the animal's relative ability to perceive gratings orientated at that angle. Lines at orientations other than 0°, 45°, 90°, and 135° were added, by extrapolation, to facilitate comparisons. Physiological data appears in the last two columns. Each line in the leftmost physiological column represents the responses of a single cell; the angle of the line corresponds to that cell's orientational preferences. The line's length is inversely related to the tuning width or the selectivity of that cell. The length of each line in the far-right column corresponds to the *proportion* of cells in the cat that were activated by that orientation.

mally seen: they responded to horizontal lines in one eye and to vertical lines in the other!

Thus, behavioral training seems to be particularly potent in changing cortical coding mechanisms. Training can even override a long time of exposure to a normal visual environment.

Under certain conditions, orientational coding even in an adult brain can be affected. For two weeks, adult cats were exposed to vertical stripes for one hour a day. The cats were maintained in the dark for the rest of the day (Creutzfeldt & Heggelund, 1975). This selective exposure *decreased* the frequency with which vertical sensitive cells could be found in the cortex. Thus, as was the case with the effects of enriched environments, the adult brain may show different *kinds* of changes in comparison with the brain of the immature animal.

The oblique effect.   Oblique coding is most sensitive to experience. Exposure to vertical or horizontal lines often totally eliminates oblique receptive fields (Hirsch & Spinelli, 1970). Selective exposure to diagonal lines does not eliminate horizontal or vertical receptive fields but only eliminates the type of field responding to the opposite tilt (Leventhal & Hirsch, 1975). In fact, even in the normally reared adult human or monkey, acuity is less for oblique than for horizontal or vertical lines. These differences in acuity are associated with differences in the numbers of each cell type found in the cortex (Mansfield, 1974). At least for cells whose receptive fields are in the fovea, far fewer oblique than vertical or horizontal edge detectors are found. Thus, oblique receptive fields are most sensitive to experience, and these fields may be relatively rare even in normally reared organisms.

Squint and astigmatism.   Squint also changes orientation coding. Squinting eyes do not receive the same visual image: the visual world is shifted on one eye in relation to the other. With squint either to the left or to the right, vertical edge detectors would be more affected by the input discrepancy than would horizontal edge detectors. Cats and monkeys can be reared with prisms that cause one or both eyes to squint either to the left or to the right (or both, one for each eye). Animals reared under such conditions have few vertical edge detectors (Harwerth, Smith, & Okundaye, 1983; Singer, Rauschecker & von Gruenau, 1979).

With an optically defective eyeball—or one having an **astigmatic** lens that blurs lines of all but a certain orientation— orientational sensitivity is altered. If this abnormality is not discovered and corrected early in development, the astigmatism will become permanent. Lines of a certain orientation will be perceived less clearly than lines of other orientations. Even when later provided with optically correcting lenses, human subjects who grew up with uncorrected astigmatism will have poor acuity for the line orientations that were blurred during their development (Mitchell & Wilkinson, 1974).

To reproduce this problem with experimental subjects, kittens are given selective exposure through astigmatic lenses. Later, their cortical cells respond only to the orientations that were in focus during rearing (Freeman & Pettigrew, 1973).

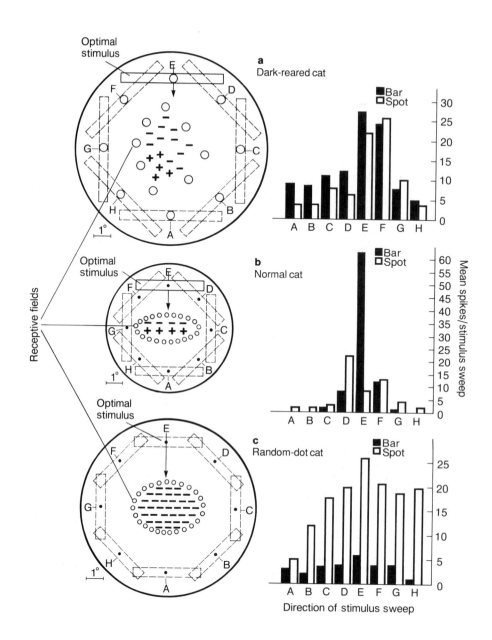

Figure 12-21 Selective exposure to spots changes orientational coding. This figure compares typical neurons from the visual cortex of three cats raised under different conditions: **a.** binocular deprivation; **b.** normal visual experience; **c.** seeing only randomly arranged light spots. Plus signs indicate on-responses and minus signs, off-responses. The neuron from the dark-reared cat responded variably, but preferred downward moving stimuli and responded as well to small spots as to lines. The normal cell preferred horizontal lines, corresponding to the shape of its receptive field, but the cell from the spot-reared cat had a circular-shaped receptive field. The histograms give the average number of responses that each cell made to a narrow bar and to a spot stimulus moved in each of the eight directions indicated (A–H).

Furthermore, if only one eye is given the astigmatic lens, that eye drives fewer cells on the cortex.

Not only will the abnormally few cells driven by the astigmatic eye favor the orientation that was in focus for that eye during rearing but the eye given normal visual experiences will show compensatory changes. This eye will have an *increased* number of cells favoring the orientations that were out of focus for the other eye (Cynader & Mitchell, 1977). If behavioral effects of this treatment are consistent with those found in other studies, this eye would have better acuity for those orientations. This compensation could be analogous to the increased acuity seen in the nondeprived eye of monocularly deprived humans (Freeman & Bradley, 1980).

Directional Coding

Cells in Areas I and II are sensitive to the direction of stimulus movement, and their sensitivity can be changed by selective exposure. First, not allowing the animal to see any moving stimuli at all during the sensitive/critical period reduces or even eliminates directional selectivity. To selectively deprive the animals just of movement, researchers can rear kittens in an environment illuminated only by stroboscopic flashes. The effect of this environment is illustrated in Figure 12-22. Unlike the dark-reared cats, the strobe-reared cats had normal orientational sensitivity. Directional sensitivity is nearly eliminated in both strobe- and dark-reared cats (Cynader & Chernenko, 1976). Although the lack of directional sensitivity cannot be reversed by later exposure to a normal visual environment, specialized training with directional discriminations may improve directional coding (Pasternak, Movshon, & Merigan, 1981). Again, specialized training very effectively changes cortical coding mechanisms.

Selective exposure to particular directions of movement can also change directional coding. Cells in animals selectively exposed to only one direction of movement preferentially respond to that direction instead of to other directions (Daw, Berman, & Ariel, 1978; Tretter, Cynader, & Singer, 1975).

Sensitivity of Coding Mechanisms

The research cited here documents the second principle of selective-exposure effects. Different codes are differentially plastic. As we have already pointed out, oblique receptive fields are more sensitive than are horizontal or vertical receptive fields.

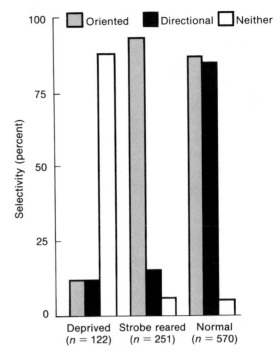

Figure 12-22 Directional coding of cortical cells can be changed by selective exposure. This figure shows the percentages of cells displaying orientational sensitivity, directional sensitivity, or neither, in cats reared either in the dark, in the presence of strobe lights, or in normal environments. For each group, *n* is the total number of cells studied in the various groups of cats.

Few effects on color coding.   Given the model, selective exposure should not affect color coding. The afferent connections can be completely specified by genetics, since appropriate connections would not vary according to the dimensions of the eyeball, for example. Thus, it is not surprising that light-deprived monkeys can show normal responses to color (Boothe, Teller, & Sackett, 1975).

But selective exposure to particular colors may have some impact on coding. Once again, preference may be more affected than capacity. Pigeons selectively exposed to only one color had normal color-discrimination ability as adults. These animals showed some tendency to learn faster if one of the colors to be discriminated included the one to which they had been exposed during rearing (Brenner, Spaan, Wortel, & Nuboer, 1983). In the ground squirrel, rearing in red light delays the development of adult-type color-coding mechanisms in the optic nerve in comparison with that of the normally reared or even the dark-reared squirrel (McCourt & Jacobs, 1983).

Daw, Berman, and Ariel (1978) contrasted ocularity coding with directional sensitivity. They exposed one eye of each kitten from $2\frac{1}{2}$ to 5 weeks of age to a rotating drum, the sides of which were painted with lines. Then that eye was shut, and the other eye was exposed to the drum moving in the *opposite* direction from 5 to 12 weeks of age. At that time, neural responses were tested. Most cells were driven by the eye opened second—but these cells preferred the direction of movement to which the kittens were first exposed. Thus, the sensitive period for ocularity is evidently later than the sensitive period for directional coding.

Tretter, Cynader, and Singer (1975) varied how long experimental kittens were selectively exposed to a rotating drum with stripes on it. Three hours of exposure was enough to change the orientational sensitivity of cells, but increasing the duration of exposure up to 12 hours increased the magnitude of the effect. However, directional sensitivity was changed only after 6 hours of exposure. Finally, although cortical cells are also selectively sensitive to the *velocity* of stimulus movement, this aspect of coding was *not* changed even by 12 hours of exposure to a particular velocity.

Complex objects.   Selective exposure can change the response of cortical cells to complex objects. Experiments of this type are most directly relevant to showing that we may have to learn how to perceive complex objects in our environments. Exposure to complex stimuli can facilitate an organism's performance in a subsequent discrimination task involving those stimuli (Hulse, Deese, & Egeth, 1975). Gibson and Walk (1956) raised rats with three-dimensional circles and triangles hanging from cardboard walls outside their cages. Subsequently, these rats learned a discrimination between circles and triangles faster than did control rats not previously exposed to those objects.

To demonstrate the coding effects, kittens were deprived of stimulation by having a hood placed over their heads except for a period of time each day when they were placed in a "play" box (Michalski, Kossut, & Zernicki, 1975; Zernicki & Michalski, 1974). Either a black three-dimensional cross or a black ping-pong ball was placed in the box. Later, single-cell responses to these stimuli were compared among selectively exposed kittens, completely deprived kittens, and normally reared kittens.

The effects of selective exposure depended on the brain area. In Areas I and II, cells in selectively exposed kittens showed stronger responses than cells in animals from the other two groups, but *only* to the complex object to which that

particular animal had been exposed. In Area III, cells in the selectively exposed animals had stronger responses to *both* types of complex object. Thus, Area III responses were affected by exposure, but the effects were not specific to the *type* of object to which the animal had been exposed.

Summary of the Effects of Specialized Experiences

Synaptic interconnections and cortical coding are sensitive to experience. Binocularity and stereoscopic coding can be changed by monocular deprivation, by alternating monocular deprivation, by squint, or by presenting different kinds of stimulus to each eye. The sensitive period for ocularity coding may be earlier than that for other types of coding. Oblique coding is more sensitive to experience than is horizontal or vertical coding, and orientational coding is more sensitive than directional coding. Velocity and color coding may be the least sensitive to experience. Even single-unit responses to complex objects can be altered by selective exposure.

Changes in cortical responses can often be directly related to changes in perception and/or preference both in humans and in animals trained to respond to a certain stimulus. What we see now may depend to a large extent on what we saw while growing up.

Synaptogenesis in the Brain

Experience may selectively change synaptic connections among neurons. The effects of environmental enrichment on brain microanatomy—the increases in spines and synapses—have been interpreted as being the visible effect of memories for that complex experience. The effects of visual deprivation and selective sensory deprivation on cortical coding imply that developmental experiences cause changes in synaptic connections—inactive synapses drop out and normally weak synapses are facilitated.

This last section describes some major areas of research directly concerned with synaptic changes. Synaptogenesis is a change in synaptic connections, emphasizing the formation of new synapses. These changes can be explored as a function of stage of development (time and/or experiences). But they also occur because of cell death. Lesions, age, and senility decrease the number of synapses present in the brain because of the death of neurons. Sometimes new synapses will form when other neurons die. This is **lesion-induced** or **reactive synaptogenesis.**

Changes during Development

Developmental changes in synaptogenesis can be studied as a function just of age, or they can be studied as a joint function of age and of selective exposure. Although the mechanisms responsible for these changes have not yet been explored on the molecular level, the changes in the types of brain protein found during development suggest that different genes are activated at different developmental stages (Chaudhari & Hahn, 1983).

Normal environments.   The rate of creating new synapses first increases and then decreases as a function of age. One period of increased synaptogenesis occurs just before birth in monkeys (Rakic & Riley, 1983). This fetal period reflects normal developmental processes, which include producing twice as many retinal axons in the prenatal monkey as are found in the neonate! Presumably only those prenatal axons that can form normal synaptic connections survive until birth.

In rodents such as the hamster and rat, this period of synaptogenesis continues for a while after birth. For example, both ipsilateral and contralateral projections from each eye are found at birth, but the ipsilateral ones tend to drop out, probably because of differential ganglion-cell death (Land & Lund, 1979; Sengelaub & Finlay, 1981).

A second period of synaptogenesis corresponds to the sensitive/critical period for visual experiences. This period occurs from 8 to 37 days after birth in cats (Cragg, 1975a) and from somewhere between 8 weeks and 6 months of age in monkeys (Boothe, Greenough, Lund, & Wrege, 1979; O'Kusky & Colonnier, 1982). After that period, the number of synapses declines: the adult has fewer synapses than does the young animal during the peak of its sensitive/critical period. Presumably the types of experience to which the developing animal is exposed affect *which* synapses are retained and which drop out. Certain types of environment may cause new and different types of synapses.

Sex hormones may also play a role in adult synaptogenesis. As Nottebohm found (Goldman & Nottebohm, 1983; Kolata, 1984; Paton & Nottebohm, 1984), testosterone injections given to adult female birds actually increase the number of cells in the brain area controlling singing behavior. These new cells respond to auditory stimuli and form functional circuits with other neurons.

The decrease in synaptic numbers associated with aging has been systematically studied. Aging animals have progressively

fewer cells in most (though not all) subcortical regions, as well as in the cortex and the cerebellum (Sabel & Stein, 1981). Loss of dopaminergic neurons may lead to the motor disorders of aging, and loss of cholinergic and noradrenergic cells may lead to learning and memory impairments (Gash, Collier, & Sladek, 1985).

Huttenlocher and his colleagues (Huttenlocher, 1979; Huttenlocher, de Courten, Garey, & Van der Loos, 1982) studied synaptogenesis in the human brain by examining brains of varying ages at autopsy. The number of synapses found in the frontal cortex is presented in Figure 12-23, and the number found in the visual cortex is shown in Figure 12-24. The number of synapses increases during early childhood, which is the sensitive/critical period for visual experiences in humans. After this early-childhood period, the number of synapses changes little until adolescence, when a decline occurs.

Aging processes may cause only a mild decrease in the number of synapses in the human brain. For example, after adolescence the numbers of synapses in the frontal and occipital areas of the human brain remain comparatively stable, with only a slight decline after age 60. Similarly, DeKosky and Bass (1982) found that older people (having a mean age of 74) had somewhat fewer synapses in their frontal cortex than did younger controls. Some synaptic losses may be caused by cell deaths. Age is associated with a significant decrease in the number of locus coeruleus cells, especially in the male human (Wree, Braak, Schleicher, & Zilles, 1980).

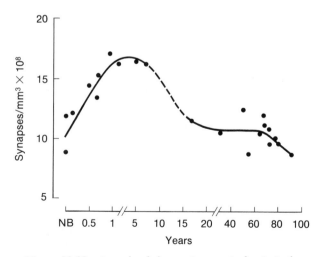

Figure 12-23 Age-related changes in synaptic density in the human brain. The number of synapses per mm³ of the cortex in the middle frontal gyrus is plotted. Note the decline between ages 5 and 15.

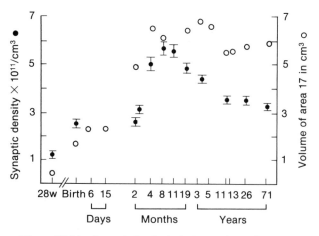

Figure 12-24 Synaptic density in the human brain changes as a function of age in all layers of Visual Area I (closed circles, left-hand scale). Each point represents the mean of several thousand counts; the vertical bars represent the standard errors of the mean of the 6 separate synapse counts made in the same brain. The open circles plot the volume of the right-hand Visual Area I (right-hand scale). Age is plotted on a logarithmic scale.

The hippocampus may be unique. The number of spines (and therefore presumably synapses) found in the brains of elderly humans (average age 79.6 years) was *greater* than that found in younger adults (average age 51.2 years) (Buell & Coleman, 1979). Maybe granule cells increase in adult human brains as well as in adult rat brains.

Senility.   Senility, and especially Alzheimer's disease (the relentlessly progressive and extreme form of senility: Chapter 11), involves even more dramatic synaptic deficits. Malfunctioning and dying cells are found in the nucleus basalis of Meynert in victims of Alzheimer's disease, a nucleus that is a major source of ACh axons projecting to the rest of the brain (Perry, Candy, Perry, Irving, Blessed, Fairbairn, & Tomlinson, 1982; Whitehouse, Price, Struble, Clark, Coyle, & DeLong, 1982). ACh cells may be destroyed throughout the brain; destruction of the ACh septal input to the hippocampus may cause the memory deficits associated with that disorder (Chapter 11).

Other types of cell are also destroyed. Senile patients show an extreme loss of cells in both the frontal cortex and the hippocampus (Buell & Coleman, 1979; DeKosky & Bass, 1982). Decreases in levels of NE and 5-HT are also found (Wurtman, 1985). The loss of locus coeruleus cells may even be greater than the loss of cholinergic basalis cells (Hardy et al.,

1985). Although the cause is unknown, Alzheimer's senility is presumably related to the loss of synaptic interconnections.

Abnormal environments.   Developmental changes in synaptogenesis may reflect how synaptic connections change through being used. More synapses are found in the neonate/fetus than in the adult (except in the hippocampus). Presumably this means that only the cells that make successful synaptic connections survive, and even then only the most-often-used synapses are retained. The less-often-used synapses may drop out during development. If so, changing the developmental environment — determining which synapses get used during the sensitive/critical period — should systematically change synaptogenesis.

Binocular deprivation causes systematic changes in synaptic interconnections in the visual cortex in cats and mice, but not in monkeys. Binocular deprivation decreases the number of synapses in cats by about 38% and decreases the number of vesicles found per synapse by about 40% to 45% (Cragg, 1975b; Sherman & Spear, 1982). Valverde (1971) found similar effects of binocular deprivation in the mouse. In mice, dark rearing causes a loss of dendritic spines in the apical shafts of layer V pyramidal cells. In contrast, dark rearing does not decrease the number of synapses present in the adult monkey (O'Kusky & Colonnier, 1982).

Different synapses may be differentially sensitive to experience. On the basis of his studies of visual deprivation and recovery in the mouse, Valverde (1971) hypothesized three types of synapse in the visual cortex. While one develops normally even in the total absence of normal visual inputs, the other two would require visual input to grow normally. The latter are split into two subtypes: those that develop normally only if visual input occurs during the sensitive/critical period and those that respond to visual input even after that period. This last type might be responsible for some behavioral and physiological recovery from effects of deprivation. Similarly, Boothe, Dobson, & Teller (1985) suggested that there were two types of synapse in the visual cortex of the monkey. One type decreased in frequency from the age of six months to adulthood and one did not. The synapses made by the direct afferents to the visual cortex might be the ones that decrease.

Until this point, we have discussed total numbers of synapses summed over large regions of the brain, but specific areas also show synaptogenesis. For example, the corpus callosum can be changed by developmental experiences. Shortly after birth, cells throughout Visual Areas I, II, and III are connected to cells on the other side of the brain, each to cells in its homologous area on that side; the connecting axons are in the corpus callosum. By a month later, only cells at the boundary between Areas I and II—cells whose receptive fields lie along the vertical meridian of the visual field—project to their counterparts on the other side (Innocenti, 1981). Thus, the connectivity between the left and right visual areas by means of the corpus callosum declines during development.

The extent of this decline can be manipulated by changing the environment during the sensitive/critical period. Binocular deprivation produces even more decrease in callosal axons. In contrast, monocular deprivation or monocular squint *prevents* some of this decline, so that kittens deprived this way grow up to have a projection of corpus callosum axons from one side to the other that is more extensive than in nondeprived control kittens (Cynader, Leporé, & Guillemot, 1981; Elberger, Smith, & White, 1983; Innocenti & Frost, 1979). This change could be compensating for the effects of monocular development. Would cutting the corpus callosum have more effects on monocularly deprived than on normally reared kittens?

Developmental synaptogenesis also occurs in the peripheral nervous system. Mammalian skeletal muscle fibers are first innervated by many motoneurons; all but a few are eliminated early in development. Elimination depends on muscular activity. Muscular paralysis prevents the loss, and chronic electrical stimulation of the muscles accelerates the loss (W. Thompson, 1983).

Damage to the neonatal brain can affect which connections remain and which drop out. As we have already noted, the anomalous projections of retinal cells to the somatosensory thalamus can be retained if the normal connections are damaged (Frost & Metin, 1985). Another example involves efferents from the frontal cortex that normally project only to the caudate on the same side of the brain. If the prefrontal cortex in a rhesus monkey is destroyed six weeks before birth, that monkey has a larger-than-normal *contralateral* projection from the normal frontal cortex to the caudate on the damaged side (Goldman, 1978).

Normally during the neonatal period, many retinal cells die out. For example, in the newborn rat or hamster, the retina projects to both the ipsilateral and contralateral superior colliculus, but most of the ipsilateral projections drop out. If one eye is removed at birth, cell death is reduced and the ipsilateral projections in the remaining eye do not drop out (Land & Lund, 1979; Sengelaub & Finlay, 1981). Also, if tetrodotoxin (which blocks action potentials: Chapter 3) is injected into one eye, the other eye retains its ipsilateral projections. If both eyes are injected, both eyes retain their ipsilateral connections (Fawcett, O'Leary, & Cowan, 1984).

The brain is obviously not static. Neural activity determines which connections remain and which drop out. Although dropout is more likely to happen during certain stages of development—times at which synapses are more sensitive to environmental effects—synaptic changes undoubtedly continue well into old age.

Changes in Synaptogenesis after Lesions

New synaptic connections can form after damage to the brain. Research in this area provides possibilities for future recovery of function after brain damage in humans, as well as hypotheses for a model of memory. Presumably this type of synaptogenesis reflects vestigial developmental plasticity as well as the types of plasticity normally responsible for learning and memory.

Recovery of function after brain damage. Functions and behaviors that cannot be observed immediately after brain damage sometimes recover over time—with or without specialized experiences or retraining exercises (see reviews of Finger, Walbran, & Stein, 1973; Goldman & Lewis, 1978; Stein, Finger, & Hart, 1983). The major factors affecting recovery are (1) the rate at which the lesions progress (**one-stage** versus **two-stage lesions**), (2) the types of experience given to the organism before and after the lesion, and (3) the organism's age at the time of the lesion.

Although there are exceptions, younger animals often show more recovery after brain damage. In adult humans, for example, damage to the verbal areas of the left hemisphere may cause permanent aphasia. The same damage might have caused no problems at all if it had occurred before language was acquired. Maybe the effects of age on developmental synaptogenesis also affect lesion-induced synaptogenesis.

However, the protective effects of youth are limited. The typical effects of certain kinds of brain damage may not appear during youth but may appear as the organisms age (Kennard, as cited by Stein, Finger, & Hart, 1983; Schallert, 1983). The loss of neurons during aging may cause the lesion effect to appear during old age. Also, in some cases of brain damage in young animals, new connections may be inappropriate and may lead to deficits and/or dysfunctional and abnormal behaviors (Devor, 1975; Kolb & Whishaw, 1985; Schneider, 1979).

"Slow" lesions usually create fewer behavioral deficits. In humans, this type of damage can come from a slowly growing brain tumor. In lower animals, it is mimicked by using a two-stage lesion process. That is, first one part of a structure is damaged and then, after some period of time, another part of the same structure is damaged. The resulting behavioral deficits are then compared with those occurring after one-stage lesions, in which the entire structure is destroyed at one time. Slowly growing lesions may produce fewer deficits because recovery can occur throughout the period of tumor growth or between the two lesion stages.

Experiences both before and after the lesion affect how much recovery occurs. Although there are exceptions, environmental enrichment before or after the lesions can alleviate some of their effects. Specific task training can also facilitate recovery. However, the benefits of specific training may depend on the type of motivation used (LeVere & Davis, 1977), the use of stimulating drugs (Feeney, Gonzalez, & Law, 1982), and the use of active as opposed to passive training procedures (Dru, Walker, & Walker, 1975).

Recovery could occur in several different ways. For example, depth perception in cats with bilateral visual cortical lesions recovers only if they are given visual experiences and high doses of amphetamine (Hovda & Feeney, 1985; Hovda, Sutton, & Feeney, 1985; Feeney & Hovda, 1985). First, the brain may gradually recover from the immediate effects of damage — rather like going into shock and then recovering. Another possibility is that the animal learns to use other parts of its brain to compensate for behavioral deficits. If its visual cortex has been removed, it may learn to use its nose and its tactile senses to find its way through a maze. Third, parts of the brain may take over functions once controlled by the damaged areas of the brain. This **vicarious functioning** may involve reorganizing neural networks (see, for example, Merzenich & Kaas, 1982). Fourth, the connections remaining in the damaged part of the brain may develop supersensitivity: an increased number and sensitivity of transmitter receptors in the postsynaptic membranes of the spared synapses (Chapter 4). Fifth — and we will explore this explanation in the rest of this section — new synapses may form.

Rules of lesion-induced synaptogenesis. Several recent reviews have extensively documented the extent to which new synapses can form following the removal of "old" ones by damage and neuronal death (Björklund & Stenevi, 1979; Cotman, Nieto-Sampedro, & Harris, 1981; Mendell, 1984). Discovery of the laws governing this type of synaptogenesis has implications not only for the treatment of brain-damaged people but also for the plasticity of brain coding functions.

In this kind of synaptogenesis, the new synapses are created by sprouting axons. Sometimes, even in adult mammals, when a nerve is cut (severing all its axons), the axons can regenerate and reinnervate the target organ or brain structure, as long as the cell bodies survive and scarring is somehow inhibited. In addition, the undamaged axons left in the lesioned area can sprout, and their new processes may eventually reinnervate the entire area once innervated by the destroyed nucleus or axon tract. A set of axons from a different but adjacent nerve tract can also sprout into the **denervated** area, forming completely new synapses. ("Denervation" refers to removal of synaptic input.)

The generalizations and conclusions about lesion-induced synaptogenesis listed in Table 12-1 come from Cotman, Nieto-Sampedro, and Harris (1981). This table describes some rules of synaptic replacement and specifies what responses to experimental lesions are expected. Most of these are well documented, but one is more tentative and is labeled as a "hypothesis." An area denervated by a lesion can have its number of synapses brought completely back to normal, but only if the sprouting axons come from cells that normally make synaptic connections with the denervated cells. There is a "dominance hierarchy." A certain type of axon may sprout and reinnervate a set of cells only if there has been a complete destruction of the more dominant types of input (cells that during development preferentially innervate that denervated area). A neuron in an adult may be reinnervated only if its genes and protein-synthesis apparatus were already producing the receptors for the transmitter used by the sprouting axons.

However, the sprouting axons do not necessarily reinnervate the same part of the denervated cells as did the lesioned axons. For example, suppose some cells were normally innervated by both NE and ACh axons, but the NE synapses were

Table 12-1   Conclusions about reactive synaptogenesis in adult vertebrates.

1. All the synaptic input lost after partial denervation can be completely restored by synaptogenesis, the new synapses coming from the sprouting of adjacent axons.
2. A sprouting axon will reinnervate a denervated zone only if its normal synaptic field overlaps that of a damaged afferent; the reinnervation occurs partly by reoccupying old synaptic sites and partly by creation of new sites.
3. Where a neuron receives more than one type of afferent, there is a hierarchy in the relative capacity of those afferents to grow in response to a lesion; some afferents will engage in synaptogenesis only if the more dominant type of afferent has been removed.
4. Sprouting and synaptogenesis cause only a quantitative increase or rearrangement of previously existing connections; new types of pathway are not created during reactive synaptogenesis.
5. Hypothesis: Presynaptic elements forming functional synapses during reactive synaptogenesis (and thus probably during spontaneous turnover and in the effects of experience) must use the same transmitter (or one functionally indistinguishable from it) as that used by the original, lesioned axons.

found on the basal and the ACh synapses on the apical dendrites. If the NE axons were lesioned, the ACh axons would sprout and more extensively cover the dendrites, including ones normally innervated by NE axons.

Much of this kind of research is done on the hippocampus (Chafetz, Evans, & Gage, 1982; Gage, Björklund, & Stenevi, 1983; Gage, Björklund, Stenevi, & Dunnett, 1983; see also the reviews of Cotman, Nieto-Sampedro, & Harris, 1981; Björklund & Stenevi, 1979). If part of the septal ACh input to the hippocampus is destroyed, other axons sprout and reinner-

vate the denervated area. This process is illustrated in Figure 12-25. Similarly, destruction of part of the NE input to the hippocampus also elicits sprouting and reinnervation of the synapses vacated by the lesioned, degenerated axons (see Figure 12-25). Destroying the NE input to the hippocampus causes the sympathetic axons innervating nearby blood vessels to sprout. The sprouting axons will reinnervate the areas normally innervated by the noradrenergic LC input to the hippocampus. This input follows the axon pathways of the granule cells.

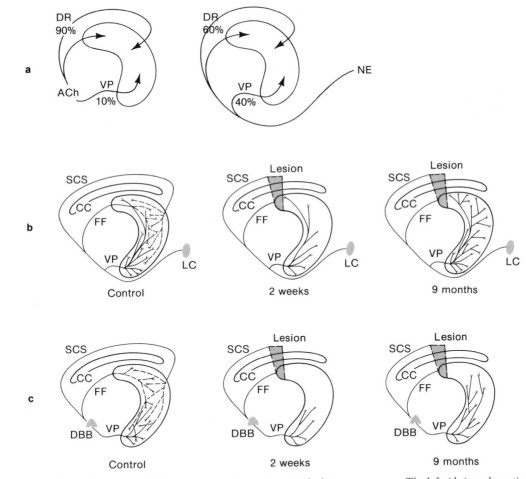

Figure 12-25   Different lesions create different reinnervation patterns in the hippocampus.   **a.** The left side is a schematic drawing of cholinergic (ACh) routes to the hippocampus. There is a dorsal route (DR) consisting of the supracollosal stria and the fimbria-fornix. The ventral cholinergic path (VP) has only about 10% as many fibers as does the DR. The right side shows paths to the hippocampus taken by neurons that use norepinephrine (NE); the dorsal route (DR) contributes about 60% of the total NE axons, and the ventral path (VP) about 40%.   **b.** NE input 2 weeks and 9 months after a unilateral fimbria-fornix lesion.   **c.** The cholinergic input 2 weeks and 9 months after a similar lesion. CC = corpus callosum; DBB = diagonal band of Broca and medial septum; FF = fimbria-fornix; LC = locus coeruleus; SCS = supracallosal stria.

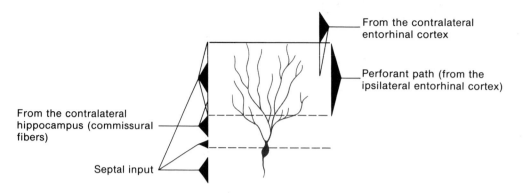

From the contralateral
entorhinal cortex

Perforant path (from the
ipsilateral entorhinal cortex)

From the contralateral
hippocampus (commissural
fibers)

Septal input

Figure 12-26   Another reinnervation pattern that can occur in a denervated hippocampus. The normal major afferent inputs to the dentate gyrus (filled triangles) are distributed in lamina, as illustrated. Removal of the perforant-path input results in an expansion of the terminal zones of the septal, commissural, and contralateral entorhinal inputs (open triangles).

Figure 12-26 illustrates another reinnervation pattern occurring in a denervated hippocampus. The input of the ipsilateral entorhinal cortex to the hippocampus (along the perforant path) was lesioned. Afterward, the other afferents to the granule cells sprouted and reinnervated some of the areas vacated by the degenerating perforant-path afferents. However, the sprouting and reinnervation seem to follow strict patterns. For example, only the septal input to the apical dendrites sprouts, and there is no sprouting of the septal input to the basal dendrites.

Sprouting occurs (at least at this level) only after brain damage. Researchers have suggested that trophic hormones are secreted after brain damage, and these hormones elicit the sprouting. For example, extracts from hippocampal cells have been found to secrete two distinct types of growth factor. One accelerates sprouting from NE sympathetic axons, and a separate one accelerates sprouting from ACh parasympathetic axons (Crutcher & Collins, 1982).

Reactive synaptogenesis and behavioral recovery.   Hippocampal reinnervation can be directly related to physiological and behavioral recovery from damage to hippocampal afferents. After damage to the NE input, once the sprouting of the sympathetic axons is complete, the spontaneous activity of dentate neurons returns to its normal low level (Barker, Howard, & Gage, 1984). Behavioral recovery occurs at about the same time (Chafetz, Evans, & Gage, 1982). Furthermore, after partial damage to hippocampal input, the sprouting and reinnervation of the remaining hippocampal axons occur at the time of behavioral recovery (Gage et al., 1983).

Synaptogenesis in other areas of the brain may also lead to behavioral recovery. For example, after the olfactory bulbs in

mice were removed, the olfactory neurons sprouted and directly reinnervated the olfactory cortex. After the sprouting and reinnervation, the mice again performed learned odor discriminations (Wright & Harding, 1982). (Another study used a less sensitive odor detection task and found no evidence of recovery: Butler, Graziadei, Graziadei, & Slotnick, 1984.) In one study, catecholaminergic fibers were cut in the area of the supraoptic nucleus in aged rats (Phelps & Sladek, 1984). The rats showed the decline in water intake and urine output expected after these lesions. However, at the time that supraoptic neurons were being reinnervated by sprouting catecholaminergic neurons, urine output and water consumption returned to normal.

Sometimes abnormal and dysfunctional connections will form. We already mentioned that this can happen after brain lesions in very young animals. Sympathetic axons sprout and innervate hippocampal cells not only after destruction of the NE input but also after medial septal lesions. In the latter case, the connections are obviously abnormal. These connections will impair the recovery of normal spatially guided behavior in rats (Harrell, Barlow, & Davis, 1983). Thus, lesion-induced sprouting can produce recovery, but if abnormal connections are created, abnormal behaviors instead of recovery occur.

Age and gender effects.   The degree to which sprouting and reinnervation will occur after brain damage is critically determined by the animal's age. The younger the lesioned animal, the greater the subsequent sprouting. This principle has been observed in several areas in rats: the sprouting of the remaining intact dorsal root axons after lesioning some of the dorsal root; the sprouting of 5-HT axons into the striatum after removal of its DA input; the sprouting of mossy fibers after

CA₃ lesions; and the reinnervation of the hippocampus after removal of the contralateral hippocampus (Hulsebosch & Coggeshall, 1983; Laurberg & Zimmer, 1980; McWilliams & Lynch, 1983, 1984; Stachowiak, Bruno, Snyder, Stricker, & Zigmond, 1984).

Age and gender effects can interact. If the cholinergic septal input to the hippocampus is lesioned, the growth of sympathetic NE axons into the denervated regions is greater in juvenile (13 days old) or adult females than in the same-aged males. However, in females, greater growth occurs 13 days after birth than at 3 days after birth or during adulthood. In males, the period of maximum growth occurs on the third day after birth (Loy & Milner, 1983; Milner & Loy, 1980). So age-dependent synaptogenesis after brain damage may be regulated by organizational and activational hormone levels.

Activity in the regenerating axons also regulates recovery (Schmidt & Edwards, 1983). This is important: it suggests that the environment may influence lesion-induced synaptogenesis just as it does developmental synaptogenesis. So both sex hormones and neural activity regulate both types of synaptogenesis.

Reinnervation of brain implants.   Finally, brain implants can be used to reinnervate denervated areas of the brain! Reinnervation can take place even in adults or aged organisms if some denervation of the neural structure adjacent to the implant occurred before the implant was made. In other words, a denervation hormone may facilitate sprouting and the innervation of an implant. Peripheral ganglia can survive implantation and reinnervate brain tissue even when the ganglia are removed from adult animals. However, the implants of mammalian cerebral tissue may have to come from young or even fetal animals (Björklund & Stenevi, 1979). Furthermore, although grafted neurons may survive, they may not always respond normally to internal and external stimuli, suggesting that the grafted cells did not get reinnervated by their normal afferents (Trulson, Hosseini, & Trulson, 1986).

Implanting brain-stem nuclei into a partially denervated hippocampus can reinnervate that structure, sometimes in a fashion closely paralleling the innervation pattern of the lesioned afferents. In this research, the entorhinal afferents to the hippocampus were removed, and the monoaminergic inputs had also been destroyed by treating the animal with specifically toxic drugs (such as 6-OHDA). Implants of noradrenergic LC neurons reinnervated the hippocampus in a pattern closely matching the normal pattern of NE innervation. Implants of 5-HT raphe cells or DA mesencephalic cells followed the normal pattern of 5-HT input — and presumably also the normal DA input (Schröder, Kammerer, & Matthies, 1982) — to the hippocampus.

These transplants can be used to restore behaviors and functions lost through brain damage, genetics, or age. In many of these studies, implants taken from areas of the fetal brain using other transmitters were without effect.

Brain damage.   The effects of hippocampal lesions can be reversed by brain grafts. Implanting septal tissue into the hippocampus can restore the maze-learning deficits usually caused by destroying the cholinergic, septal input to the hippocampus (Dunnett, Low, Iversen, Stenevi, & Björklund, 1982). This type of implant-induced recovery can even occur when the implants for the rat brain are taken from the septal area of neonatal *mice* (Daniloff, Bodony, Low, & Wells, 1985). In that study, the degree of behavioral recovery was directly related to the amount of cholinergic activity found after implants: the correlation was + .84. Removing NE input increases the spontaneous activity of hippocampal cells, but sprouting and reinnervating implants taken from the LC restore spontaneous activity to its normally low level (Björklund, Segal, & Stenevi, 1979).

Implants can also compensate for damage to other brain areas. Adult rats normally show deficits in spatial behavior after frontal cortex damage. However, frontal implants of tissue taken from a fetal frontal cortex reduce these deficits (Labbe, Firl, Mufson, & Stein, 1983). Implants of frontal cortex tissue into the occipital cortex can even reduce the visual deficits produced by bilateral occipital lesions in rats (Stein, Labbe, Attella, & Rakowsky, 1985). Damage to the striatum causes motor deficits, but grafting striatal neurons taken from fetal rats into the damaged area will significantly suppress the lesion-induced hyperactivity (Isacson, Brundin, Kelly, Gage, & Björklund, 1984). Destroying 5-HT neurons increases lordosis in female rats (see Chapter 9), but implanting fetal raphe cells into the hypothalamus suppresses that abnormal lordosis (Luine, Renner, Frankfurt, & Azmitia, 1984).

Implants of DA tissue have frequently been used. Substantia nigra implants taken from embryonic rats can restore self-stimulation behavior. This behavior is suppressed after the ascending DA tracts have been destroyed by 6-OHDA injections (Fray et al., 1983; Olds & Fobes, 1981). Destroying the nigrostriatal DA system can produce gross deficits in motor coordination and sensory processing in rats. All these deficits can be greatly reduced by implants of fetal brain tissue containing DA (Björklund, Stenevi, Dunnett, & Iversen, 1981; Perlow, Freed, Hoffer, Seiger, Olson, & Wyatt, 1979). These deficits in rats can even be reduced by grafting implants taken from the brains of embryonic mice (Björklund, Stenevi, Dunnett, & Gage, 1982). However, just as was the case with reinnervation by sprouting and regrowth, sometimes the graft-induced connections *cause* some problems even while ameliorating other problems (Dunnett, Whishaw, Jones, & Isacson, 1986).

Genetic defects.   Genetically caused deficits can also be alleviated by transplants of fetal brain tissue. The hypothalami of female mice of some strains do not secrete LHRH. Therefore, the pituitaries of these females do not produce LH or FSH. However, if these mice are given an implant of fetal preoptic cells, they do then have FSH and LH in their blood streams (Gibson, Charlton, Perlow, Zimmerman, Davies, & Krieger, 1984).

Aging.   Age-related deficits have been reversed by fetal implants. Even in aged brains, fetal implants form functional connections with their host brains (Gash, Collier, & Sladek, 1985). For example, female rats normally stop ovulating after 21 to 30 months of age (a rat menopause). Transplanting newborn hypothalamic neurons into the third ventricle causes corpora lutea (the egg follicles emptied by ovulation) to appear in their ovaries (Matsumoto, Kobayashi, Murakami, & Arai, 1984). Aging rats also show progressive deficits in their ability to learn a spatial task. Grafting fetal septal cells (ACh) into the hippocampi of aged rats significantly improved their performance (Gage, Björklund, Stenevi, Dunnett, & Kelly, 1984). The performance improvements caused by such septal grafts could be blocked by injecting an ACh antagonist, proving that the improvement involved ACh neurons (Gage & Björklund, 1986). Finally, aging rats develop motor deficits, but DA implants can relieve this problem (Gage, Dunnett, Stenevi, & Björklund, 1983).

Summary and Implications for the Effects of Experience on Coding

Synaptogenesis represents an exciting area for research. The brain retains its capacity for at least some synaptogenesis throughout life, and this allows neural connections and codes to be affected by developmental experiences. And the capacity for synaptogenesis may also be part of the way the adult brain responds to and encodes or remembers experiences. So many researchers believe that brain neurons are constantly breaking and reforming synaptic connections. The process is accelerated during certain early developmental stages and may be slowed by aging. This type of synaptogenesis may eventually be used to explain how developmental experiences change brain codes.

Brain damage can also accelerate synaptogenesis. This can lead to recovery, but it can also lead to inappropriate connections and maladaptive behaviors. Behavioral changes after brain lesions and lesion-induced synaptogenesis are both affected by the age of the animal and by its experiences.

The brain-implant literature seems to come directly from the pages of science fiction. If an area of the brain is denervated by genetics or damage or age, an implant taken from a fetal or neonatal brain that contains the appropriate types of neurons—neurons using the appropriate transmitter substance—can reduce behavioral and functional deficits.

Chapter Summary

We Learn to Perceive

No two adult organisms have had exactly the same developmental experiences. That means that no two adult organisms have exactly the same brain "wiring diagrams." This uniqueness may explain why psychologists find that early experiences durably affect adult personality and behavior patterns. Maybe quite literally, no two of us have exactly the same perceptions even when we are currently in exactly the same situation.

Organisms raised in an enriched environment have larger, heavier brains, and organisms raised in impoverished environments have smaller brains. Even more intriguing, the shapes of nerve cells are altered, as though the ways the brain processes information might have changed. These effects might account for the effects of enrichment on complex learning. Does enrichment attenuate the decline in the number of synapses that is normally seen in aging or developing brains?

The types of sensations to which the developing organism is exposed affect neural microanatomy and coding. The development of the visual, auditory, somatosensory, and olfactory systems may all be changed by experiences. Some types of visual coding develop normally even in deprived or abnormal environments, but other types of coding require normal sensory experiences, and abnormal experiences may create abnormal types of coding. As tested by behavior, the perceptions and preferences of these animals have been permanently altered. Do we perceive only what we learned to perceive during our childhoods? If so, is that because of the high levels of synaptic turnover found during that period?

Some effects appear consistently across many areas of research. Active interaction with the environment is required for the enrichment effects, and it also facilitates the effects of selective exposure and recovery after brain damage. NE is required for the enrichment effects, it increases the effects of selective experience on brain visual codes, and manipulations of peripheral or central NE levels affect memory retrieval (Chapter 11). Hippocampal cells show systematic changes in responses throughout learning. The hippocampus is also changed by enrichment experiences, and NE is involved in LTHP.

Brain implants may someday be routinely used to compensate for the denervation-produced deficits in behavior asso-ciated with aging, genes, and brain damage. Since mouse implants will work in brain-damaged rats, maybe labs will one day routinely culture fetal primate cells to be used by neurosurgeons in brain-damaged human patients. But this is not the only hope held out by future research. Studying the rules governing which axons sprout and when, and what types of synapse are formed where, on what types of denervated brain cells, may someday tell us how the brain normally remembers what happens to us. Will the reinnervation rules be the same as those regulating the effects that developmental and adult experiences have on brain codes?

PART SIX

Postscript and Prelude

CHAPTER

Single Cells and Mental Events

The implications of a psychobiological approach are both exciting and intriguing, holding out promises of surprising new advances. This chapter contains speculations, ideas, and hypotheses. You should use the material to trigger your own thinking. Where do *you* think the field is going? Have single-unit studies told us anything about consciousness and the mind? And what if the brain does not work the way the neuron doctrine says it does? How can you apply what you've learned to the problem of how the mind and brain interact? For example, the genetic basis of personality traits is now being recognized, and implants of male hypothalamic tissue into female brains cause masculine sexual behaviors. Juxtaposing these facts raises new questions like these: Will we ever be able to transplant a personality? If we could, what would that do to our world?

442

Consciousness

We return to the concept of consciousness, the center of the mind–brain dilemma described in Chapter 1. We will describe some interesting new approaches that might provide new ideas and some approaches that seem to be dead ends.

The Concept of Consciousness

Our consciousness of self creates the mind–body dilemma: how can our immaterial thoughts about ourselves, our wishes, and our desires affect brain neurons? Is there anything in what you have just learned that can tell us about the mind — either how the mind influences brain cells or how it is simply another way of viewing the activity of those cells? Or is the mind a conceptual mistake, the result of confusing physical structure (like computer hardware) with the rules of processing input (like the computer program or software)?

The concept of consciousness has several different meanings. "Consciousness" can be used to signify a readiness to perceive or to respond (in the sense of conscious and behaving versus unconscious and anesthetized, for example). "Consciousness" can refer to the content of an ongoing process, the process of being self-aware, and the nature of the thoughts contained in that stream of awareness. "Consciousness" can also mean being aware of oneself as an entity, and of being aware of being aware. Yates (1985) has described the content of awareness as a model of the world. Thus, consciousness consists not of sensations but rather of constructs, each being a model of a "real-world" event, object, or state of affairs hypothesized to exist in that way. Sensations themselves are not conscious; instead, constructs are created by consciousness to account for or explain a set of sensations. Much of what we have said about the difference between energies present in the physical world and a corresponding mental state or perception fits Yates's ideas.

Conscious mental events are not the only ones directly related to behaviors (Hoyenga & Hoyenga, 1984; Yates, 1985). Our beliefs and motives may influence the way we act, and we may often be entirely unaware of these motives or reasons for actions. We can nevertheless produce some conscious explanations (attributions) of our past behaviors. These seem to satisfy us, even though they may be completely in error.

Our conscious awareness of ourselves is **sequential** and **continuous** (though not uninterrupted). We are aware of thoughts succeeding each other, or of perceptions following other perceptions. Not only are we aware of thinking right now but we are aware of having thought just before the present

moment, and before that. Our serial stream of awareness is interrupted only by sleep and by any loss of consciousness. So our mind remembers what it was before — or does our brain do the remembering, and communicate those memories to our mind? Because of our memories, our self-consciousness has a strong sense of its own continuity.

However, that continuity can be distorted by the symbolic processes of the mind. Our minds use symbols to represent characteristics of the external world (such as "redness"), ideas (such as "freedom"), and our views of ourselves (for example, "competent and in control"). Our symbolic concepts of ourselves affect our memories. Some past memories are distorted and others suppressed to make the remembered past more consistent with the currently reconstructed self.

The symbols for ideas can even distort our view of the world. Causation is one such idea. Our minds evidently evolved in such a way that the idea of causation comes easily to us — at least once we pass a certain developmental age level. But our concepts are a representation of reality, and not reality itself. Reality is sequences of events, some of them always promptly following other events (such as falling after loss of support). In other pairs of events, one event only sometimes follows another, and the time between the events can vary from seconds to years. Among all these possible pairs of events, which ones are "real" causation?

In what other areas might our mind's symbols distort our perceptions of reality? Maybe it is true not only that the brain evolved with coding mechanisms that do not faithfully mimic reality but also that the mind so evolved (Stent, 1982; Wilson, 1976). Being able to think about causality may have facilitated the survival of our ancestors — for example, being able to control fire would involve being able to think causally. This example would be true whether the mind–brain complex were viewed dualistically or monistically.

Eccles's Evidence for a Mind

Chapter 1 described the debate between monism and dualism. In the most recently favored version of monism, the mind is identical to the brain: the mind is simply another way of experiencing brain functions. Conceptually, the idea might be in some ways analogous to physicists' ideas about the nature of light. Light sometimes has wavelike properties and sometimes particlelike properties. Thus, as seen through a psychobiologist's microelectrode, amplifier, and recorder, nerve cells have physical properties, but as seen through introspection, nerve cells have mindlike properties.

Eccles says that the brain and mind are two separate types of being. Not only does the mind influence neural activity but it also follows rules of its own in its own activity. But both these points of view suggest that studying consciousness might be a scientifically justifiable endeavor—it just happens to be one for which we have not yet generally agreed on the rules for research.

Eccles's main evidence for a mind, and therefore for a self-consciousness existing separately from (though entirely dependent on) the brain came from three sources (Popper & Eccles, 1977; Chapter 1; see also chapters by Eccles in the book he edited: 1982). One was the readiness potential, the slow build-up of negativity in the frontal and parietal cortex just before the beginning of a voluntary movement such as that of a finger in humans (Deecke, Scheid, & Kornhuber, 1969; Kornhuber, 1974). The second was the unity of self-consciousness in face of the apparent disunity of neural activity. The third was the "time tricks" that the mind plays with reality, to compensate for the time it takes a weak external stimulus to significantly influence brain activity (Libet, 1973; Libet et al., 1967). The mind "knows" about the time delay and "antedates" the weak stimulus so as to compensate for that delay.

But are these experiments conclusive evidence of a mind at work? Some alternative interpretations were pointed out by Wilson (1981). All that the readiness potential shows is that there may be some weak force involved, some force that requires time to build up, to become effective. But saying that the weak force is the mind does not contribute to a solution—how does even a weak nonphysical force affect synaptic activity?

Eccles borrows the principle of uncertainty from physics: the act of measuring the momentum of some subatomic particle changes its position, and so the measurement always contains some uncertainty. On a molar level (as opposed to a reductionist level), there could always be some uncertainty about the exact location of a synaptic vesicle. The mind could influence synaptic and thus neural activity if it could physically move a synaptic vesicle. But the random effects of uncertainty described by physicists are very different from the nonrandom effects of a self-conscious mind on neural activity described by Eccles.

The "time tricks" hypothesized by Eccles can be explained without assuming that an interactive mind is at work. In order to create a conscious sensation in humans, a train of stimuli to the brain, lasting about 0.5 sec, is required. Similarly, since consciousness of a weak stimulus presented to the skin can be blocked by stimulating the somatosensory cortex immediately after the stimulus, the weak natural stimulus must also need build-up time before conscious awareness occurs. But if the

skin stimulus is applied during cortical stimulation, the skin stimulus will be perceived as having occurred before the cortical stimulus—the "time trick." So a cortical stimulus requires time to reach consciousness, just as the skin stimulus does. The brain activity resulting from skin stimulation may well reach consciousness before the brain activity resulting from direct cortical stimulation does: no "time tricks."

Disposing of these arguments leaves us with the unity of conscious experience. No one can presently explain this. Talking about a separate mind only changes the problem and neither solves nor explains it. But identity theorists do not explain it either; they ignore it or talk about emergent properties.

Two Consciousnesses?

In Chapter 1 we also discussed the split-brain patients—people in whom the corpus callosum had been cut for treatment of epilepsy. Does this surgery create two separate consciousnesses occupying the same skull, as Sperry believes (1982)? Or does only one consciousness exist, limited to the left, verbal side (except in those cases in which verbal abilities occur in both halves of the cerebral hemispheres: LeDoux, Wilson, & Gazzaniga, 1977; Popper & Eccles, 1977)? Split-brain people do have the ability to shift control from left to right hemisphere for the performance of various tasks (Levy & Trevarthen, 1976). Is the "self" doing the shifting? Since control of the shift is subcortical, is the subcortex where the self-conscious mind originates?

One interesting study may shed some light on this question (Gott, Hughes, & Whipple, 1984). One woman with an intact corpus callosum can voluntarily select and maintain two very different states of consciousness at different times. She learned that skill at age 16, but she claims never to have heard anything about left-brain/right-brain research. Her ability to do this could have been learned or it could have come from a hereditary neural anomaly.

The researchers studied this woman during both states of consciousness. They attempted to infer the lateralization of states to either the left or right hemisphere by measuring task performances during each state, using tasks that in normal people involve different degrees of left or right hemispheric participation. The researchers claimed that State I came from left-hemisphere activation and State II from right-hemisphere activation, on the basis of associations with verbal functions. The woman had named her states. State I—the left, verbal hemisphere—was "me." State II—the right, nonverbal hemisphere—was only "it," even though "it" was associated with more pleasant affects and behaviors than was "me."

Thus, this woman, *if* she truly can separately activate left and right hemispheres, identifies only the left, verbal side as being "herself."

Animal Work: A Dead End?

Must all consciousness research be done with humans? Do animals ever have any form of self-consciousness? Rats can use stimuli from their own behavior (for example, washing a face produces sensations different from those produced by walking) as cues for discriminated operant responses (Beninger, Kendall, & Vanderwolf, 1974). Animals also have REM sleep. Do they then have dream images as we do, and does having dream images imply any form of self-consciousness? Maybe animals are conscious only in the sense of being aware of external events. They may not be self-conscious, in the sense of being able to perceive themselves as an object having a certain identity (Stent, 1982).

The most intriguing evidence for self-consciousness in animals comes from primate research. For example, primates will react to mirror images of themselves. If they have used a mirror before, and if their face is changed by make-up, they will look in the mirror and react to the change with excitement (Gallup, 1977). Interestingly enough, among primates, only orangutans and chimpanzees show these types of response — and only chimpanzees show the humanlike asymmetry in left-right temporal-lobe anatomy.

But animals must share the consciousness–unconsciousness continuum with us. Can we use that to explore consciousness?

Some studies used brain stimulation either as a CS for classical conditioning (for example, Doty, 1969; O'Brien & Quinn, 1982; Quinn & O'Brien, 1983) or as a discriminative stimulus in operant conditioning (for example, Bourassa & Swett, 1967, 1982; Stutz, Butcher, & Rossi, 1969; Swett & Bourassa, 1967, 1980). Some fascinating things have been learned about the nature of direct brain stimuli that can and cannot be used to control behavior. These paradigms can be studied with psychophysical procedures to measure what animals can and cannot detect about stimuli applied to their brains. Animals can detect stimulation of cutaneous nerves at intensities causing minimal changes in cortical evoked activity. The frequency of peripheral nerve stimulation does not affect its detectability, but CNS stimulation is more easily detected at higher than at lower stimulation frequencies. Animals have difficulty discriminating between stimulations in two different "reward" areas of their brains, but they can easily discriminate

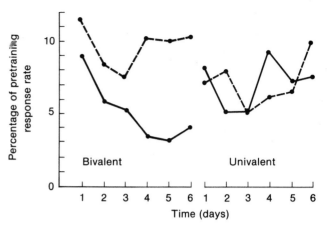

Figure 13-1 Animals' ability to differentiate between two electrical stimuli to the brain (in an operant-discrimination task) depends on the reinforcing properties of those brain stimuli, based on self-stimulation measures (Chapter 8). These graphs show the percentage of pretraining response rate made to one stimulus (the cue for responding; dashed line) compared with that made to the other stimulus (the cue for not responding; solid line) during six days of discrimination training. Thus, 100% would represent the response rate before discrimination training. "Bivalent" means that only one brain stimulus had reinforcing properties; "univalent" means that either *both* were reinforcing or *neither* brain stimulus was reinforcing.

between rewarding and nonrewarding stimulation (Figure 13-1).

However, detection or behavioral control does not necessarily imply conscious awareness. Human subjects can be controlled by stimuli of which they are unaware (see Underwood, 1983).

Dissociations of Behavior from Reported Awareness

At least three areas of research may provide promising leads for exploring and conceptualizing self-awareness and consciousness. All involve human subjects, and all involve procedures that apparently dissociate stimulus control of behavior from stimulus control of verbal statements of awareness.

Prosopagnosia. Prosopagnosia, described in Chapter 7, is an inability to visually recognize the faces of familiar people; it may be caused by certain bilateral cortical lesions. However, prosopagnosics may recognize people at some level but be unable to translate that recognition into conscious awareness

(Tranel & Damasio, 1985). Two prosopagnosic subjects were shown photographs of familiar and unfamiliar faces. The subjects were asked to rate verbally how familiar they felt each face was to them. Simultaneously, their autonomic responses to those faces were measured by recording changes in skin conductance (GSR, or galvanic skin responses, caused by activity in sweat glands). Both subjects were shown faces of familiar people whom they could not consciously recognize; yet their GSR responses to those familiar faces were significantly and consistently larger than their responses to unfamiliar faces. Thus, cortical damage may not have eliminated processing of facial stimuli, but it *did* impair conscious awareness of the product of that processing.

Amnesia. As described in Chapter 1, some forms of amnesia also show a dissociation between behavior and awareness (Cohen & Corkin, 1981; Cohen & Squire, 1980; Corkin et al., 1981; Nissen, Cohen, & Corkin, 1981). The patient who had suffered damage to both the left and right hippocampi cannot consciously remember anything that has happened to him since his surgery. However, he can learn perceptual-motor tasks, and even a mirror-reading verbal task, nearly normally, with good retention — all the while denying that he has ever seen those tasks before. So task stimuli are controlling his behaviors, but they are not controlling his verbal reports of remembering them.

This dissociation means that different brain circuits control those two aspects of task performance. In monkeys, the limbic system is involved in forming memory traces. Another set of brain circuits (a cortical-striatal circuit) may control "habit" formation, or conditioned responses (Bachevalier & Mishkin, 1984; Malamut, Saunders, & Mishkin, 1984). The cortical-striatal circuit may involve the kinds of behavioral control inaccessible to awareness in humans, whereas the cortical-limbic system may be crucial to awareness.

This same dissociation occurs in other states of amnesia. Patients during surgery are usually anesthetized and apparently unconscious. However, although they report themselves unable to remember what went on in the operating room during their surgery, their behaviors are affected by comments made during that time by the surgical personnel ("Most patients can 'hear'," 1984). Suggestions of having a speedy recovery with minimal pain *do* affect postoperative recovery. Amnesia created by ECS in humans shows similar effects (Squire, Cohen, & Zouzounis, 1984). Patients are given a task just before their ECS treatment (for depression). During the test 24 hours later, they deny having seen the task, but their behavior shows evidence of retention.

In contrast, Huntington's patients show the dissociation in the *opposite* direction (Martone, Butters, Payne, Becker, & Sax, 1984). Huntington's disease, a genetically caused type of dementia, also causes memory disorders. It is associated with damage to the basal ganglia. These patients could not learn a mirror reading task, but they *could* remember having seen the task before on each training day. Again, the dissociation may reflect differences in the striatal-cortical and limbic-system memory circuits.

"Blindsight." Humans with damage to some portion of their visual cortex have blind areas, or **scotomas,** in their visual fields. However, they can point to, and sometimes even identify, visual stimuli in their scotomas. At the same time, they often claim they are consciously unaware of any sensation (Weiskrantz, 1983; Weiskrantz et al., 1974; Zihl & Werth, 1984). When these patients are queried, they will sometimes report seeing "something" in the blind portion of their visual field (something that they can locate by pointing and discriminate from other stimuli with greater-than-chance levels of accuracy). They sometimes also say that the "something" is "indescribable." Stoerig, Hübner, and Pöppel (1985, p. 596) said of one of their subjects, "Over and over again he claimed that he had no sensation, that he was only guessing, and could hardly believe his performance was above chance." Zihl (1981) points out that this "blind-sight" is phenomenologically different from the vision that these same patients experience after recovery (the scotoma shrinks).

However, does the occurrence of blindsight mean that hippocampal or occipital lesions have destroyed the interface between subcortical brain activity and conscious awareness of sensations? Campion, Latto, and Smith (1983) critically reviewed the blindsight literature, and many of their cautions would be equally appropriate to the amnesia-consciousness literature. Often the method of measuring stimulus control of identification and discrimination behavior is very different from the method of measuring stimulus control of verbal reports of consciousness. Thus, the various methods could be differentially sensitive to (have differential ability to detect) functions degraded by brain damage, so what appears to be a discontinuous dissociation is really a continuum of abilities.

Recent blindsight research has attempted to control for these problems. The scotomic subject's own blind spot may be used as a control for biasing in verbal reports (see, for example, Stoerig, Hübner, & Pöppel, 1985). Stimuli presented to the blind spot produce no verbal reports of conscious sensation; subjects can neither point to nor identify such stimuli.

Some of the statements made by the blindsight patients during performance of their tasks are reminiscent of the responses of undamaged humans performing psychophysical absolute-threshold experiments. Their ability to identify trials on which the stimulus is present and those on which the stimulus is absent can be above chance, but they often say they don't ever consciously perceive anything. Is consciousness therefore a threshold type of phenomenon, requiring the synchronous firing of more neurons for consciousness than for performance? Or are the same cells involved in both, with consciousness requiring a faster firing rate (as described by the principle of degree of certainty in Table 1-1)? Or are entirely different sets of nerve cells, in different parts of the brain, involved in the two phenomena?

Single Nerve Cells and Illusions

Some fascinating new ideas about consciousness have come from recording the activities of individual cells. As described in Chapters 6 and 7, the coding functions of neurons cause them to respond to stimuli in ways that do not match the physically measurable energies present in the external world. Some cells in the "blob" parts of the visual cortex show color constancy. When the physical nature of the light reflected off an object back to the eye changes because the wavelengths striking the object changed, those cells continue to respond as though there had been no change in the physical stimulus. And we are consciously aware of an apple's still being "red" even when it is illuminated by very different lights.

A recent study provides an even more dramatic example of responses to absent stimuli. When human observers are exposed to stimuli like those in Figure 13-2, we see nonexistent "lines." Simplified versions of those figures, as shown in Figure 13-3, were presented to rhesus monkeys. The responses of single cells in Visual Areas I and II were recorded as illustrated (von der Heydt, Peterhans, & Baumgartner, 1984).

Cells in Area I (area 17) could not "see" those illusory lines, but cells in Area II (area 18) did. When the orientational sensitivity of these cells was measured, the researchers found that some cells were sensitive to real and illusory lines of ex-

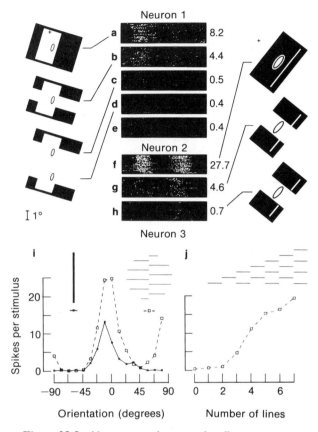

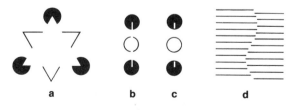

Figure 13-2 When a human sees these figures, she or he will perceive illusory contours at sites where the stimulus is homogeneous. Small alterations in the stimulus can have dramatic effects on the appearance of these contours (**c**).

Figure 13-3 Neurons can also respond to illusory contours. These are responses of neurons in Visual Area II of the monkey to stimuli producing illusory contours. The stimuli (insets) were moved back and forth across the cells' receptive fields several times. For neurons 1 and 2, the receptive fields are represented by elipses, and the monkey's fixation point is marked by crosses in a and f; the responses are represented by rows of dots. The average number of responses per stimulus is indicated on the right. Neuron 1 responded both to a real bar (**a**) and to an illusory contour (**b**). The cell did not respond to either half of the stimulus (**c** and **d**); (**e**) is spontaneous activity. Neuron 2 responded to a narrow bar (**f**) and to an illusory bar (**g**). The responses to the illusory bar were nearly abolished by intersecting lines (**h**). In neuron 3, the border between two abutting gratings elicited a strong response; the cell responded to both real and illusory gratings having the same orientation (**i**). When the lines inducing the contour were reduced to less than three, the cell's responses disappeared (**j**); compare the lines above the curve.

actly the same orientation. Any change in the stimulus that would weaken a human observer's perception of the illusory line also weakened the response to that illusory line.

Are small sets of such cells responding to lines that aren't there responsible for our conscious sensations of those lines? They certainly can*not* be coding for the physical aspects of the (nonexistent) stimulus. Can we then infer that consciousness can be created by the responses of a small set of cells?

Anxiety as Evidence of Human Self-Consciousness?

Earlier we mentioned the possibility that the mind — either separate from or identical to the brain — evolved under the same evolutionary pressures that affected brain coding mechanisms. Suppose that anxiety is present-day evidence of this in humans.

Animals can certainly show some forms of anxiety. But anxiety for far-future, and possible never-happening, events is peculiarly human. We are perfectly capable of worrying about a nuclear war. Maybe having this type of anxiety facilitated our ancestors' survival. Maybe, as a side-product, the human form of self-consciousness then evolved.

Many nonhibernating animals store food for the winter; their behavior is controlled by instinct and does not seem to involve any form of anxiety. But perhaps our human ancestors — some of them, at least — started worrying about what would happen if the winter were unusually long and unusually severe. These worriers then stored more food against a distant possibility that might never happen. But if it did happen, the worriers might have been the only ones to survive.

Worry can frequently motivate adaptive behaviors, and the adaptiveness of thinking about far-future possibilities could create self-awareness.

Summary and Implications of Consciousness

So far the study of single nerve cells in the brain seems far distant — both experimentally and conceptually — from any definition of consciousness and human self-awareness. We cannot even decide whether the brain is in any way separate from the mind or whether the two sides of our brain have separate forms of consciousness. In the latter case, the separate forms of consciousness would normally be inaccessible to us unless we had our corpus callosums cut or, like that woman, we could deliberately shift between the two states.

Research with animals, which cannot verbally report their conscious experiences, may not provide any clues about the human form of self-consciousness. But even research with humans is fraught with conceptual and technical difficulties, as witnessed by the amnesia and blindsight dissociation literature. Perhaps single-unit recordings and illusions may eventually

prove more productive. Until then, we are left with the puzzle: How do we relate your phenomenological experiences at this moment to what you have just learned about how nerve membranes and synapses function?

One disturbing possibility has to do with evolution and the symbolic properties of the mind discussed earlier. First our evolutionary history, and then our own personal developmental history, "fitted" the contents of the mind to our environments. Maybe our own brain is incapable of understanding the mind's relationship to the brain's physiology. If this inability comes from evolutionary history, it may be difficult for us ever to formulate the appropriate concepts. If the lack comes from developmental history, would a change in educational environments and books change how we conceptualize the mind?

Alternatives to the Neuron Doctrine

The neuron doctrine of Table 1-1 emphasizes single-cell recording and the idea that activity in a few cells represents a type of **quantum** (a single thing that cannot be broken down into component parts) of consciousness or a mental event. But what if this is not the case?

Consciousness and Global Patterns of Brain Activity

Many researcher-theorists, both monists and dualists, claim that global patterns of activity, occurring in cells throughout the brain, are the brain codes and the basis of consciousness. For example, Wilson (1976), an identity theorist, states that "the physical process which is consciousness is a totality of physical activity in a brain region. . . . We can speak, loosely, of spatial-temporal excitation patterns. . . ." (p. 577).

The book *Mind and Brain*, edited by Eccles (1982), contains several chapters written by people with similar viewpoints. According to Hydén (1982), memory is a particular spatiotemporal pattern of activity of brain cells, and if a particular pattern is repeated, the repetition or the "sum of differentiated activation in the three-dimensional brain is experienced as 'memory'" (p. 145). Zoologist Pringle (1982, p. 280) talks about synchronized oscillations of activity: "Consciousness occurs when complex time patterns spread over a sufficiently large region of space."

Eccles's interactive form of dualism represents one of the more sophisticated versions of such an idea. He discusses (1982) the columnar organization of the cortex, calling each column a module. According to him, "a spatio-temporal pattern of active modules. . . . will uniquely encode the information provided by sensory input. . . . It is postulated that such scintillating spatio-temporal patterns are read out by the mind in its performance of providing a unique perceptual experience" (p. 94).

Thus, many theorists explicitly deny the neuron doctrine. Stent (1982, p. 190) writes: "Somehow, for man the notion of the single cerebral nerve cell as the ultimate element of meaning seems worse than a gross oversimplification; it seems qualitatively wrong." (But he then goes on to say that this idea is, "so far at least, . . . the only neurologically coherent scheme that can be put forward.") To make these ideas testable, we need some idea of how these spatiotemporal patterns of activity can be a code.

Across-Fiber Coding

Erickson (1984) recently proposed one such theory. He attempted to avoid one of the basic conceptual-experimental difficulties faced by the neuron doctrine. If activity in a small set of cells is enough to create a conscious experience, how is the activity read? And by what? It almost seems as though there would have to be a "little person in the head" who regularly scanned the activity of all feature detectors and sent the result of each scan to consciousness.

Erickson uses the concept of across-fiber coding (Chapter 6). He says researchers should be looking *not* at how single cells respond to a variety of stimuli but at the way in which many cells respond to each stimulus in a certain set. His ideas are illustrated and contrasted with the neuron-doctrine ap-

proach in Figure 13-4. His proposed method of analysis would show how each different type of stimulus created a different *pattern* of activity across a particular set of cells.

This pattern would be the code for some aspect of the stimulus. The pattern would be transformed and eventually lead to a *pattern* of motor output. In this theory, each unique motive and memory would have its own pattern of brain activity, and that pattern would shape the stimulus input into a different *pattern* of appropriate efferent and motoneuron output.

Several other reviewers and theorists have described such motivational and motor patterns. For example, Isaacson (1980) describes the limbic system as being a neuromodulator of patterns of activity in other brain areas. Marr's theory of cerebellar function (1969) talks about "pieces of output" or **elemental movements.** An elemental movement may be a limb movement or a fine movement of one finger. But "every possible action can be represented as an ordered *pattern* of elemental movements" (p. 443, emphasis added).

These ideas run into some problems, especially in the area of memories, motives, and emotions. Erickson (1984) talks about this set of intervening variables (see definition in Chapter 1), which he describes as **intervening processes,** as though they were not only filters but also patterns of activity. If memories and motives are patterns of neural activity, do the patterns involve the same population of cells used for the stimulus input pattern and the motor output pattern? If so, there will be ambiguity. A given change in pattern could come either from a change in stimulus input or from a change in memory or motives or emotions. If there are at least three

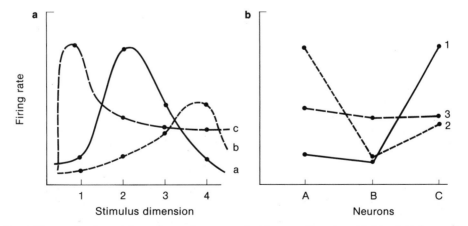

Figure 13-4 Across-fiber coding is one alternative to the neuron doctrine. **a.** Experimental data plotted according to the neuron doctrine: the responses of individual nerve cells (A–C) to various stimuli, very roughly redrawn from inverted characteristic-frequency curves taken from Figure 6-29. **b.** Across-fiber coding plot of the same data, taken from the points indicated by large dots in a. Here, the *pattern* of activity in many different neurons is emphasized for each of three different stimuli (1–3). See also Figures 6-22, 6-23, and 6-25.

different populations of cells (stimulus, motor, and motives/emotions/memories), how does the activity pattern in the memory-motive-emotion population affect the stimulus input pattern — and where does it do so? If there are different populations, the theory comes much closer to the neuron doctrine.

If Erickson's intervening processes act as a filter, how do we become consciously aware of those states and memories? Suppose that awareness involved comparing the stimulus input pattern with the pattern as it was altered by the intervening processes. If we use each pattern of *change* as a code for a particular type of intervening process, we are back to having some kind of "central readout agency," something that Erickson hoped his theory would make unnecessary.

Comparisons with the Neuron Doctrine

It may be helpful to point out similarities and differences between the across-fiber pattern theories and the neuron doctrine. Both theories could agree that motives, emotions, and memories could act like a filter. The filtering could affect the activity of many cells in many different areas of the brain. Things would look, smell, and feel quite different to us when our moods and motives changed or when we had salient memories associated with those stimuli.

The two theories have different ideas about what is required to create a conscious awareness of a certain internal state or of a certain memory. One theory emphasizes patterns of cortical — or even of whole-brain — activity, whereas the other talks about activity in a small, critical population of cells. For example, as Young (1979) points out with regard to learning, *"Many different parts of the brain contribute to learning, but each in a different and specific way. The critical changes may take place in one or a few places, but they are only made effectively with the essential cooperation of other parts. The whole nervous system is a densely interconnected unity"* (p. 805, emphases his). Thus, one comparatively small set of cells may be critical to the conscious awareness of one component of a memory, but normal activity in those cells may require the interacting influences of many other cells, all quite consistent with the neuron doctrine.

On the stimulus-input side, both theories can accept a peripheral across-fiber pattern code for sensory input, but they differ with regard to a central code. A theory like Erickson's never has the pattern code recoded into a labeled-line code. He says that the restrictive trigger features required by many cortical cells for firing mean "that the nervous system is instead re-arranging its information into the form most relevant for the species involved" (p. 239).

According to the neuron doctrine, all such across-fiber pattern codes would have to be recoded into labeled-line or place codes before a conscious sensation could occur. But are we then stuck with the "readout agency" problem? What is the nature of the little scanner person? Is it anything like Eccles's self-conscious mind? Or is it inherent in the mind-like properties that brain cells have as an intrinsic part of their complex physical properties?

Lateral inhibition presents another useful area of contrast between the two theories. In the spatial-pattern model, lateral inhibition is simply another part of the total pattern of brain activity associated with each conscious perception and eventually with motor output. In the neuron doctrine, lateral inhibition is *required* so that *only* the relevant neurons of the corresponding conscious percept are activated. Less strongly stimulated neurons will not be able to escape from that inhibition. Without lateral inhibition, our world, according to the neuron doctrine, really would be the "blooming, buzzing confusion" attributed to a newborn human's consciousness.

Lesion data also provide an area of contrast. Before dramatic behavioral effects of brain damage can be seen, almost *all* of a given brain area must be destroyed. This fact suggests considerable redundancy in neural coding of stimuli and responses and supports a spatial pattern rather than a neuron-doctrine theory. However, a percept may consist of many cognitively distinct *quanta* (irreducible mental entities), each corresponding to activity in its own small set of cells. Destruction of several sets of cells would degrade but would not eliminate the percept. Thus, the behavioral deficits resulting from subtotal damage to a brain structure should be subtle but measurable.

Summary of Alternatives

Obviously, the neuron doctrine is not the only way to explore the mind and the way consciousness is related to the physical properties of millions of complexly interconnected brain cells (as explored by microelectrodes and by microchemical and microanatomical techniques). Many brilliant and experienced neuroscientists have claimed that brain codes all involve patterns and that any given state of consciousness is simply a spatiotemporal pattern of activity throughout the brain. If so, the way to study the brain is not to examine the responses of single cells to various stimuli but to examine how the pattern of activity in hundreds of cells all over the brain varies when the stimulus is changed. The neuron doctrine states that significant information about brain functions and codes can come from recording from a select few brain cells.

Chapter Summary

Looking to the Future

This chapter reviewed issues of Chapter 1 in light of single-unit recording data, speculating about how these issues might someday be resolved. New techniques will of course be important, as will new applications of old techniques. Technology always changes the way we view the world. As Phillips, Zeki, and Barlow (1984, p. 356), put it, "The one certain thing about the future of cortical studies is that there will be surprises which will alter radically our way of thinking about the brain."

But as important as new technology will be, new ways of conceptualizing brain functions will be equally important, if not more so (Shuttlesworth, Neill, & Ellen, 1984). More models are needed if the fruits of new technology are to have any meaning.

Consciousness and alternatives to the neuron doctrine belong to the same set of problems. If the neuron doctrine is correct, how does the readout occur? How are the properties of consciousness we described created by the activities of nerve cells? Is a small set of cells sufficient, or is some pattern of activity across the whole brain required? Does only the verbal hemisphere create the kind of pattern necessary for awareness (or have the necessary sets of cells)? Or does the nonverbal hemisphere have its own type of consciousness? Did we become self-conscious when we developed symbolic ability, an ability that allowed us to anticipate far-distant and somewhat improbable events? Does the activity in a small set of cells, responding to an illusory line, provide proof of the neuron doctrine? Or are these cells just part of the overall pattern?

To prove the existence of a separate (but dependent) and interacting mind, we would have to show that nerve cells changed in ways that could not be explained by the laws of the physical universe. But will we ever know *everything* about the physical universe so that we can confidently rule out all possible physical causes? On the other hand, because of the princi-

ple of uncertainty, we can never simultaneously measure everything physically happening in and around a cell to rule out an interacting mind.

Thus, we are left with questions — and that is as it should be. Knowledge, we hope, makes successive questions ever more sophisticated, leading to ever more sophisticated answers. But having new questions — along with new ideas and new technology — is what makes the area of brain–mind research so exciting. Can we use the brain to understand itself? Will we have to train our brains in new directions to make this possible?

We can visualize the world of brain knowledge as consisting of two universes with an interface between them. One universe is that of the physical properties of the brain cell. From the point of view of the neuron doctrine, this universe is best studied by micro techniques: single-unit recordings, microanatomy, and microchemistry. But this universe follows the laws first discovered by the physicists and chemists: the so-called physical laws of the universe.

The second universe is that of the mind. Many areas of psychology explore this universe — though always indirectly. Psychophysics, cognitive psychology, and studies of expectancies in animals are all examples of how the laws and contents of the mental universe may be studied. It is usually assumed that this second universe also follows the physical laws of the universe. But that is not yet proved, and some people seem to be convinced that mental events follow some laws not discoverable through a study of the physical universe (which is *not* to say that things like ESP and telekinesis must therefore exist!).

Both these universes can be empirically and rigorously studied by currently available (and soon-to-be-developed) technology, both physical and psychological. However, the interface between the two universes — the mind–body problem, or how the universes interact with each other — remains unexplored: neither the technology nor the concepts currently exist to study it. *The interface is the mind's greatest mystery.*

REFERENCES

NOTE: The bold-print page number(s) at the end of each reference entry refer(s) to the page(s) in the book on which the referenced author's name(s) appear. Names in entries not followed by page numbers can be found in the Credit pages at the end of the book.

ABRAHAM, W. C., & GODDARD, G. V. (1983). Asymmetric relationships between homosynaptic long-term potentiation and heterosynaptic long-term depression. *Nature*, *305*, 717–719. **395**

ABRAMS, R., & TAYLOR, M. A. (1983). The genetics of schizophrenia: A reassessment using modern criteria. *American Journal of Psychiatry*, *140*, 171–175. **328**

ADAMEC, R. E., & STARK-ADAMEC, C. I. (1983). Limbic control of aggression in the cat. *Progress in Neuro-Psychopharmacology and Biological Psychiatry*, *7*, 505–512. **326**

ADAMEK, G. D., GESTELAND, R. C., MAIR, R. G., & OAKLEY, B. (1984). Transduction physiology of olfactory receptor cilia. *Brain Research*, *310*, 87–97. **150**

ADAMETZ, J. H. (1959). Rate of recovery of functioning in cats with rostral reticular lesions. *Journal of Neurosurgery*, *16*, 85–98. **35**

ADAMS, D. J., SMITH, S. J., & THOMPSON, S. H. (1980). Ionic currents in Molluscan soma. *Annual Review of Neuroscience*, *3*, 141–167. **59, 60**

ADAMS, W. B., & LEVITAN, I. B. (1982). Intracellular injection of protein kinase inhibitor blocks the serotonin-induced increase in K^+ conductance in *Aplysia* neuron R15. *Proceedings of the National Academy of Sciences, U.S.A.*, *79*, 3877–3880. **88**

ADELSON, E. H. (1982). The delayed rod afterimage. *Vision Research*, *22*, 1313–1328. **221**

ADRIAN, R. H., & BRYANT, S. H. (1974). On the repetitive discharge in myotonic muscle fibres. *Journal of Physiology*, *240*, 505–515. **128**

AGHAJANIAN, G. K. (1981). The modulatory role of serotonin on multiple receptors in brain. In B. L. Jacobs & A. Gelperin (Eds.), *Serotonin neurotransmission and behavior*. Cambridge, MA: MIT Press.

AGHAJANIAN, G. K., & ROGAWSKI, M. A. (1983). The physiological role of alpha-adrenoreceptors in the CNS: New concepts from single-cell studies. *Trends in Pharmacological Sciences*, *1*, 315–317.

AGHAJANIAN, G. K., & VANDERMAELEN, C. P. (1982). Alpha$_2$-adrenoreceptor-mediated hyperpolar-ization of locus coeruleus neurons: Intracellular studies in vivo. *Science*, *215*, 1394–1396. **89, 107**

AHERN, F. M., JOHNSON, R. C., WILSON, J. R., MCCLEARN, G. E., & VANDENBERG, S. G. (1982). Family resemblances in personality. *Behavior Genetics*, *12*, 261–280. **327**

AKAIKE, N. (1981). Sodium pump in skeletal muscle: Central nervous system-induced suppression by alpha-adrenoreceptors. *Science*, *213*, 1252–1254.

AKAIKE, N., NOMA, A., & SATO, M. (1976). Electrical responses of frog taste cells to chemical stimuli. *Journal of Physiology*, *254*, 87–107. **89, 151**

AKAISHI, T., & NEGORO, H. (1983). Effects of microelectrophoretically applied acetylcholine- and angiotensin-antagonists on the paraventricular neurosecretory cells excited by osmotic stimuli. *Neuroscience Letters*, *36*, 157–161. **254**

AKEMA, T., & KAWAKAMI, M. (1982). Sex difference and senile change in hypothalamic neuronal response to electrical stimulation of the limbic system in the rat. *Endocrinologica Japonica*, *29*, 683–693. **304**

AKISKAL, H. S. (1983). Diagnosis and classification of affective disorders: New insights from clinical and laboratory approaches. *Psychiatric Developments*, *2*, 123–160. **329**

ALBANI, C., & YOSHIKAMI, S. (1980). Two different mechanisms control the amplitude-intensity response and the dark current in retinal rods. *Federation Proceedings*, *39*, 2066. **218**

ALBERT, D. J., & WALSH, M. L. (1984). Neural systems and the inhibitory modulation of agonistic behavior: A comparison of mammalian species. *Neuroscience & Biobehavioral Reviews*, *8*, 5–24. **340**

ALBRECHT, D. G., DE VALOIS, R. L., & THORELL, L. G. (1980). Visual cortical neurons: Are bars or gratings the optimal stimuli? *Science*, *207*, 88–90. **212**

ALCARAZ, M., GUZMÁN-FLORES, C., SALAS, M., & BEYER, C. (1969). Effect of estrogen on the responsivity of hypothalamic and mesencephalic neurons in the female cat. *Brain Research*, *15*, 439–446. **315**

ALDENHOFF, J. B., GRUOL, D. L., RIVIER, J., VALE, W., & SIGGINS, G. R. (1983). Corticotropin releasing factor decreases postburst hyperpolarizations and excites hippocampal neurons. *Science*, *221*, 875–877. **358**

ALEKSANYAN, Z. A., BUREŠOVÁ, O., & BUREŠ, J. (1976). Modification of unit responses to gustatory stimuli by conditioned taste aversion in rats. *Physiology & Behavior*, *17*, 173–179. **261, 264**

ALKON, D. L. (1979). Voltage-dependent calcium and potassium ion conductances: A contingency mechanism for an associative learning model. *Science*, *205*, 810–816. **79, 396**

ALKON, D. L. (1982–1983). Regenerative changes of voltage-dependent Ca^{2+} and K^+ currents encode a learned stimulus association. *Journal of Physiology, Paris*, *78*, 700–706. **396**

ALKON, D. L. (1984). Calcium-mediated reduction of ionic currents: A biophysical memory trace. *Science*, *226*, 1037–1045. **396**

ALKON, D. L., ACOSTA-URQUIDI, J., OLDS, J., KUZMA, G., & NEARY, J. T. (1983). Protein kinase injection reduces voltage-dependent potassium currents. *Science*, *219*, 303–305. **88**

ALKON, D. L., LEDERHENDLER, I., & SHOUKIMAS, J. J. (1982). Primary changes of membrane currents during retention of associative learning. *Science*, *215*, 693–695. **396**

ALLEN, G. I., ECCLES, J., NICOLL, R. A., OSHIMA, T., & RUBIA, F. J. (1977). The ionic mechanisms concerned in generating the ipsps of hippocampal pyramidal cells. *Proceedings of the Royal Society of London, Series B*, *198*, 363–384. **80**

ALPERN, M., FALLS, H. F., & LEE, G. B. (1960). The enigma of typical total monochromacy. *American Journal of Ophthalmology*, *50*, 996–1011. **203**

ALTMAN, H. J., & QUARTERMAIN, D. (1983). Facilitation of memory retrieval by centrally administered catecholamine stimulating agents. *Behavioural Brain Research*, *7*, 51–63. **372, 375**

AMOORE, J. E. (1965). Psychophysics of odor. *Cold Spring Harbor Symposia*, *30*, 623–637. **135, 139**

AMOORE, J. E. (1969). A plan to identify most of the primary odors. In C. Pfaffmann (Ed.), *Olfaction and taste, III*. New York: Rockefeller Press. **150**

ANAND, B. K., CHHINA, G. S., SHARMA, K. N., DUA, S., & SINGH, B. (1964). Activity of single neurons in the hypothalamic feeding centers: Effect of glucose. *American Journal of Physiology*, *207*, 1146–1154. **255**

ANAND, B. K., & PILLAI, R. V. (1967). Activity of single neurones in the hypothalamic feeding centres: Effect of gastric distension. *Journal of Physiology*, *192*, 63–77. **257, 259**

ANDÉN, N.-E., DAHLSTRÖM, A, FUXE, K.,

LARSSON, K., OLSON, L., & UNGERSTEDT, U. (1966). Ascending monamine neurons to the telencephalon and diencephalon. *Acta Physiologica Scandinavica*, 67, 313–326.

ANDERSEN, P., SUNDBERG, S. H., SVEEN, O., & WIGSTRÖM, H. (1977). Specific long-lasting potentiation of synaptic transmission in hippocampal slices. *Nature*, 266, 736–737. **395**

ANDERSON, C. H. (1982). Changes in dendritic spine density in the preoptic area of the female rat at puberty. *Brain Research Bulletin*, 8, 261–265. **277, 307**

ANDERSON, D. K., RHEES, R. W., & FLEMING, D. E. (1985). Effects of prenatal stress on differentiation of the sexually dimorphic nucleus of the preoptic area (SDN-POA) of the rat brain. *Brain Research*, 332, 113–118. **303**

ANDERSON, G. H., & JOHNSTON, J. L. (1983). Nutrient control of brain neurotransmitter synthesis and function. *Canadian Journal of Physiology and Pharmacology*, 61, 271–281. **249**

ANDERSON, G. H., LEPROHON, C., CHAMBERS, J. W., & COSCINA, D. V. (1979). Intact regulation of protein intake during the development of hypothalamic or genetic obesity in rats. *Physiology & Behavior*, 23, 751–755. **253**

ANDERSON, J. L. (1983). Serotonin receptor changes after chronic antidepressant treatments: Ligand binding, electrophysiological, and behavioral studies. *Life Sciences*, 32, 1791–1801. **348**

ANDERSSON, B. (1978). Regulation of water intake. *Physiological Reviews*, 58, 582–603. **249**

ANDREW, R. J., & BRENNAN, A. (1984). Sex differences in lateralization in the domestic chick. *Neuropsychologia*, 503–509.

ANGELBECK, J. H., & DUBRUL, E. F. (1983). The effect of neonatal testosterone on specific male and female patterns of phosphorylated cytosolic proteins in the rat preoptic-hypothalamus, cortex and amygdala. *Brain Research*, 264, 277–283. **295**

ANISMAN, H. (1975). Time-dependent variations in aversively motivated behaviors: Nonassociative effects of cholinergic and catecholaminergic activity. *Psychological Review*, 82, 359–385. **335**

ANISMAN, H., GRIMMER, L., IRWIN, J., REMINGTON, G., & SKLAR, L. S. (1979). Escape performance after inescapable shock in selectively bred lines of mice: Response maintenance and catecholamine activity. *Journal of Comparative and Physiological Psychology*, 93, 229–241. **337**

ANISMAN, H., & SKLAR, L. S. (1979). Catecholamine depletion in mice upon reexposure to stress: Mediation of the escape deficits produced by inescapable shock. *Journal of Comparative and Physiological Psychology*, 93, 610–625. **332, 337, 338**

ANISMAN, H., & SKLAR, L. S. (1981). Social housing conditions influence escape deficits produced by uncontrollable stress: Assessment of the contribution of norepinephrine. *Behavioral and Neural Biology*, 32, 406–427. **332, 337, 338**

ANISMAN, H., & ZACHARKO, R. M. (1982). Depression: The predisposing influence of stress. *Behavioral and Brain Sciences*, 5, 89–137. **330, 333, 335**

ANTELMAN, S. M., & CAGGIULA, A. R. (1977). Norepinephrine-dopamine interactions and behavior. *Science*, 195, 646–653. **248, 268**

ANTELMAN, S. M., & CHIODO, L. A. (1981). Dopamine autoreceptor subsensitivity: A mechanism common to the treatment of depression and the induction of amphetamine psychosis? *Biological Psychiatry*, 16, 717–727. **356**

ANTELMAN, S. M., EICHLER, A. J., BLACK, C. A., & KOCAN, D. (1980). Interchangeability of stress and amphetamine in sensitization. *Science*, 207, 329–331. **338**

AOU, S., OOMURA, Y., LÉNÁRD, L., NISHINO, H., INOKUCHI, A., MINAMI, T., & MISAKI, H. (1984). Behavioral significance of monkey hypothalamic glucose-sensitive neurons. *Brain Research*, 302, 69–74. **257**

AOU, S., OOMURA, Y., & NISHINO, H. (1983). Influence of acetylcholine on neuronal activity in monkey ortitofrontal cortex during bar press feeding task. *Brain Research*, 275, 178–182.

AOU, S., OOMURA, Y., NISHINO, H., INOKU-CHI, A., & MIZUNO, Y. (1983). Influence of catecholamines on reward-related neuronal activity in monkey orbitofrontal cortex. *Brain Research*, 267, 165–170.

AOU, S., YOSHIMATSU, H., & OOMURA, Y. (1984). Medial preoptic neuronal responses to connatural females in sexually inactive male monkeys (*Macaca fuscata*). *Neuroscience Letters*, 44, 217–221.

ARAI, Y., & MATSUMOTO, A. (1978). Synapse formation of the hypothalamic arcuate nucleus during postnatal development in the female rat and its modification by neonatal estrogen treatment. *Psychoneuroendocrinology*, 3, 31–45. **297**

ARCHER, S. M., DUBIN, M. W., & STARK, L. A. (1982). Abnormal development of kitten retino-geniculate connectivity in the absence of action potentials. *Science*, 217, 743–745. **420**

ARENDASH, G. W., & GORSKI, R. A. (1982). Enhancement of sexual behavior in female rats by neonatal transplantation of brain tissue from males. *Science*, 217, 1276–1278. **297**

ARENDASH, G. W., & GORSKI, R. A. (1983). Effects of discrete lesions of the sexually dimorphic nucleus of the preoptic area or other medial preoptic regions on the sexual behavior of male rats. *Brain Research Bulletin*, 10, 147–154. **304**

ARIMATSU, Y. (1983). Short- and long-term influences of neonatal sex steroids on alpha-bungarotoxin binding capacity in the mouse amygdala. *Neuroscience*, 9, 873–877. **298**

ARIMATSU, Y., SETO, A., & AMANO, T. (1981). Sexual dimorphism in alpha-bungarotoxin binding capacity in the mouse amygdala. *Brain Research*, 213, 432–437. **298**

ARMSTRONG, C. M., & BEZANILLA, F. (1977). Inactivation of the sodium channel: II. Gating current experiments. *Journal of General Physiology*, 70, 567–590. **61**

ARMSTRONG, C. M., BEZANILLA, F., & ROJAS, E. (1973). Destruction of sodium conductance inactivation in squid axons perfused with pronase. *Journal of General Physiology*, 62, 375–391. **56**

ARNAULD, E., DUFY, B., PESTRE, M., & VINCENT, J. D. (1981). Effects of estrogens on the response of caudate neurons to microiontophoretically applied dopamine. *Neuroscience Letters*, 21, 325–331. **97, 313**

ARNOLD, A. P. (1980). Sexual differences in the brain. *American Scientist*, 68, 165–173. **297**

ARUSHANIAN, E. B., & BELOZERTSEV, Yu. B. (1978). The effect of amphetamine and caffeine on neuronal activity in the neocortex of the cat. *Neuropharmacology*, 17, 1–6. **240**

ARVIDSON, K., & FRIBERG, U. (1980). Human taste: Response and taste bud number in fungiform papillae. *Science*, 209, 807–808. **142, 151**

ÅSBERG, M., THORÉN, P., TRÄSKMAN, L., BERTILSSON, L., & RINGBERGER, V. (1976). "Serotonin depression"—a biochemical subgroup within the affective disorders? *Science*, 191, 478–480. **348**

ASH, K. O. (1968). Chemical sensing: An approach to biological molecular mechanisms using difference spectroscopy. *Science*, 162, 452–454. **150**

ASHMORE, J. F., & COPENHAGEN, D. R. (1980). Different postsynaptic events in two types of retinal bipolar cell. *Nature*, 288, 84–86.

ASSAF, S. Y., MASON, S. T., & MILLER, J. J. (1979). Noradrenergic modulation of neuronal transmission between the entorhinal cortex and the dentate gyrus of the rat. *Journal of Physiology, London*, 292, 52P. **395**

ASSAF, S. Y., & MILLER, J. J. (1978). Neuronal transmission in the dentate gyrus: Role of inhibitory mechanisms. *Brain Research*, 151, 587–592. **395**

ASTON-JONES, G. (1985). Behavioral functions of locus coeruleus derived from cellular attributes. *Physiological Psychology*, 13, 118–126. **236, 355, 376**

ASTON-JONES, G., & BLOOM, F. E. (1981a). Activity of norepinephrine-containing locus coeruleus neurons in behaving rats anticipates fluctuations in the sleep–waking cycle. *Journal of Neuroscience*, 1, 876–886. **236, 237, 355, 376**

ASTON-JONES, G., & BLOOM, F. E. (1981b). Norepinephrine-containing locus coeruleus neurons in behaving rats exhibit pronounced responses to non-noxious environmental stimuli. *Journal of Neuroscience*, 1, 887–900. **236, 355, 376**

ASTON-JONES, G., ENNIS, M., PIERIBONE, V. A., NICKELL, W. T., & SHIPLEY, M. T. (1986). The brain nucleus locus coeruleus: Restricted afferent control of a broad efferent network. *Science*, 234, 734–737. **240, 376**

ATRENS, D. M., WILLIAMS, M. P., BRADY, C. J., & HUNT, G. E. (1982). Energy balance and hypothalamic self-stimulation. *Behavioural Brain Research*, 5, 131–142. **266**

ATTARDI, B., GELLER, L. N., & OHNO, S. (1976). Androgen and estrogen receptors in brain cytosol from male, female, and testicular feminized (*tfm/y*) mice. *Endocrinology*, 98, 864–874. **288**

ATTARDI, B., & OHNO, S. (1976). Androgen and estrogen receptors in the developing mouse brain. *Endocrinology*, 99, 1279–1290. **281, 282, 284**

ATWEH, S. F., & KUHAR, M. J. (1983). Distribution and physiological significance of opioid receptors in the brain. *British Medical Bulletin*, 39, 47–52.

AVANZINO, G. L., CELASCO, G., COGO, C. E., ERMIRIO, R., & RUGGERI, P. (1983). Actions of microelectrophoretically applied glucocorticoid hormones on reticular formation neurones in the rat. *Neuroscience Letters*, 38, 45–49. **358**

AVISSAR, S., EGOZI, Y., & SOKOLOVSKY, M. (1981). Studies on muscarinic receptors in mouse and rat hypothalamus: A comparison of sex and cyclical differences. *Neuroendocrinology*, 32, 295–302. **309**

AYALA, F. J. (1978). The mechanisms of evolution. *Scientific American*, 239, 56–69. **120, 124**

AYOUB, D. M., GREENOUGH, W. T., & JURASKA, J. M. (1983). Sex differences in dendritic structure in the preoptic area of the juvenile macaque monkey brain.

Science, 219, 197–198. **300**

BACHEVALIER, J., & MISHKIN, M. (1984). An early and a late developing system for learning and retention in infant monkeys. *Behavioral Neurosciences, 98,* 770–778. **446**

BAEZ, L. A., BROWNING, R. A., & CUSATIS, M. (1980). Evaluation of body weight changes after selective serotonin depletion with 5,7-dihydrotryptamine. *Progress in Neuro-Psychopharmacology, 4,* 123–127. **248**

BAILEY, C. H., & CHEN, M. (1983). Morphological basis of long-term habituation and sensitization in *Aplysia. Science, 220,* 91–93. **360**

BAKER, H., JOH, T. H., RUGGIERO, D. A., & REIS, D. J. (1983). Variations in number of dopamine neurons and tyrosine hydroxylase activity in hypothalamus of two mouse strains. *Proceedings of the National Academy of Sciences, U.S.A., 77,* 4369–4373. **329**

BAKER, P. F. (1966). The nerve axon. *Scientific American, 214,* 74–82. **44, 53**

BAKER, P. F., HODGKIN, A. L., & SHAW, T. I. (1961). Replacement of the protoplasm of a giant nerve fibre with artificial solutions. *Nature, 190,* 885–887. **59**

BAKER, P. F., HODGKIN, A. L., & SHAW, T. I. (1962a). Replacement of the axoplasm of giant nerve fibres with artificial solutions. *Journal of Physiology, 164,* 330–354. **44, 53**

BAKER, P. F., HODGKIN, A. L., & SHAW, T. I. (1962b). The effects of changes in internal ionic concentrations on the electrical properties of perfused giant axons. *Journal of Physiology, 164,* 355–374. **44, 53**

BANCROFT, J. (1981). Hormones and human sexual behaviour. *British Medical Bulletin, 37,* 153–158. **291**

BANKS, M. S., ASLIN, R. N., & LETSON, R. D. (1975). Sensitive period for the development of human binocular vision. *Science, 190,* 675–677. **424**

BANNON, M. J., REINHARD, J. F., JR., BUNNEY, E. B., & ROTH, R. H. (1982). Unique response to antipsychotic drugs is due to absence of terminal autoreceptors in mesocortical dopamine neurones. *Nature, 296,* 444–446. **347**

BARDIN, C. W., & CATTERALL, J. F. (1981). Testosterone: A major determinant of extragenital sexual dimorphism. *Science, 211,* 1285–1294. **276, 277**

BARFIELD, R. J., GLASER, J. H., RUBIN, B. S., & ETGEN, A. M. (1984). Behavioral effects of progestin in the brain. *Psychoneuroendocrinology, 9,* 217–231. **281**

BARKER, D. J., HOWARD, A. J., & GAGE, F. H. (1984). Functional significance of sympathohippocampal sprouting: Changes in single cell spontaneous activity. *Brain Research, 291,* 357–363. **436**

BARLOW, H. B. (1972). Single units and sensation: A neuron doctrine for perceptual psychology? *Perception, 1,* 371–394. **3, 221**

BARLOW, H. B., FITZHUGH, R., & KUFFLER, S. W. (1957). Change of organization in the receptive fields of the cat's retina during dark adaptation. *Journal of Physiology, 137,* 338–354. **219**

BARLOW, R. B., JR., & KAPLAN, E. (1971). Limulus lateral eye: Properties of receptor units in the unexcised eye. *Science, 174,* 1027–1029.

BARNES, C. A. (1979). Memory deficits associated with senescence: A neurophysiological and behavioral study in the rat. *Journal of Comparative and Physiological Psychology, 93,* 74–104. **394**

BARR, G. A., AHN, H. S., & MAKMAN, M. H. (1983). Dopamine-stimulated adenylate cyclase in hypo-

thalamus: Influence of estrous cycle in female and castration in male rats. *Brain Research, 277,* 299–303. **313**

BARRACLOUGH, C. A., & CROSS, B. A. (1963). Unit activity in the hypothalamus of the cyclic female rat: Effect of genital stimuli and progesterone. *Journal of Endocrinology, 26,* 339–359. **312, 315**

BARRACLOUGH, C. A., LOOKINGLAND, K. J., & WISE, P. M. (1984). Role of the hypothalamic noradrenergic system in sexual differentiation of the brain. In M. Serio, M. Motta, M. Zanisi, & L. Martini (Eds.), *Sexual differentiation: Basic and clinical aspects.* New York: Raven. **298**

BARRACO, R. A., & FRANK, K. E. (1983). Temporal and pharmacological parameters of puromycin-induced amnesia. *Pharmacology, Biochemistry & Behavior, 18,* 809–815. **372**

BARRACO, R. A., & STETTNER, L. J. (1976). Antibiotics and memory. *Psychological Bulletin, 83,* 242–302. **372**

BARRETT, E. F., & BARRETT, J. N. (1976). Separation of two voltage-sensitive potassium currents, and demonstration of a tetrodotoxin-resistant calcium current in frog motoneurones. *Journal of Physiology, 255,* 737–774. **59, 60**

BARRIONUEVO, G., & BROWN, T. H. (1983). Associative long-term potentiation in hippocampal slices. *Proceedings of the National Academy of Sciences, U.S.A., 80,* 7347–7351. **395**

BARTOSHUK, L. M. (1979). Bitter taste of saccharin related to the genetic ability to taste the bitter substance 6-n-propylthiouracil. *Science, 205,* 934–935. **151, 253**

BARTUS, R. T. (1979). Physostigmine and recent memory: Effects in young and aged nonhuman primates. *Science, 206,* 1087–1089. **376**

BARTUS, R. T., DEAN, R. L., III, BEER, R., & LIPPA, A. S. (1982). The cholinergic hypothesis of geriatric memory dysfunction. *Science, 217,* 408–417. **376**

BATES, J. A. V. (1973). Electrical recording from the thalamus in human subjects. In A. Iggo (Ed.), *Handbook of sensory physiology: Vol. II. Somatosensory system.* New York: Springer-Verlag. **171**

BAUDRY, M., OLIVER, M., CREAGER, R., WIERASZKO, A., & LYNCH, G. (1980). Increase in glutamate receptors following repetitive electrical stimulation in hippocampal slices. *Life Sciences, 27,* 325–330. **396**

BAULIEU, E.-E. (1978). Cell membrane, a target for steroid hormones. *Molecular and Cellular Endocrinology, 12,* 247–254. **279**

BAUM, M. J. (1979). Differentiation of coital behavior in mammals: A comparative analysis. *Neuroscience & Biobehavioral Reviews, 3,* 265–284. **276, 277, 285, 291, 292**

BAYLOR, D. A., FUORTES, M. G. F., & O'BRYAN, P. M. (1971). Receptive fields of cones in the retina of the turtle. *Journal of Physiology, 214,* 265–294. **195, 197**

BAYLOR, D. A., & HODGKIN, A. L. (1973). Detection and resolution of visual stimuli by turtle photoreceptors. *Journal of Physiology, 234,* 163–198. **185, 194**

BAYLOR, D. A., & HODGKIN, A. L. (1974). Changes in time scale and sensitivity in turtle photoreceptors. *Journal of Physiology, 242,* 729–758. **218**

BAYLOR, D. A., HODGKIN, A. L., & LAMB, T. D. (1974). The electrical response of turtle cones to flashes and steps of light. *Journal of Physiology, 242,* 685–727. **218**

BAYLOR, D. A., LAMB, T. D., & YAU, K.-W. (1979a). The membrane current of single rod outer seg-

ments. *Journal of Physiology, 288,* 613–634. **218**

BAYLOR, D. A., LAMB, T. D., & YAU, K.-W. (1979b). Responses of retinal rods to single photons. *Journal of Physiology, 288,* 589–611. **194**

BEAR, M. F., & DANIELS, J. D. (1983). The plastic response to monocular deprivation persists in kitten visual cortex after chronic depletion of norepinephrine. *Journal of Neuroscience, 3,* 407–416. **420**

BEACH, F. A., JOHNSON, A. I., ANISKO, J. J., & DUNBAR, I. F. (1977). Hormonal control of sexual attraction in pseudohermaphroditic female dogs. *Journal of Comparative and Physiological Psychology, 91,* 711–715. **291**

BEATON, R., & MILLER, J. M. (1975). Single cell activity in the auditory cortex of the un-anesthetized, behaving monkey: Correlation with stimulus controlled behavior. *Brain Research, 100,* 543–562. **239, 383**

BEATTY, W. W. (1979). Gonadal hormones and sex differences in nonreproductive behaviors in rodents: Organizational and activational influences. *Hormones and Behavior, 12,* 112–163. **291, 301**

BEAUDET, A., & DESCARRIES, L. (1978). The monoamine innervation of rat cerebral cortex: Synaptic and nonsynaptic axon terminals. *Neuroscience, 3,* 851–860. **98**

BECKER, J. B., & RAMIREZ, V. D. (1981). Sex differences in the amphetamine stimulated release of catecholamines from rat striatal tissue in vitro. *Brain Research, 204,* 361–372. **309**

BÉGIN-HEICK, N., & HEICK, M. M. C. (1982). Adenylate cyclase activity in brown adipose tissue of the genetically obese *(ob/ob)* mouse. *Canadian Journal of Biochemistry, 60,* 910–916. **251**

BEIDLER, L. M. (1969). Innervation of rat fungiform papilla. In C. Pfaffmann (Ed.), *Olfaction and taste, III.* New York: Rockefeller Press. **142**

BEIDLER, L. M. (1975). Taste receptors. In R. Galun, P. Hillman, I. Parnas, & R. Werman (Eds.), *Sensory physiology and behavior.* New York: Plenum. **142**

BÉKÉSY, G. VON (1956). Current status of theories of hearing. *Science, 123,* 779–783. **149**

BÉKÉSY, G. VON (1964). Sweetness produced electrically on the tongue and its relation to taste theories. *Journal of Applied Physiology, 19,* 1105–1113. **151**

BÉKÉSY, G. VON (1966). Taste theories and the chemical stimulation of single papillae. *Journal of Applied Physiology, 21,* 1–9. **151**

BELL, C. C. (1981). An efference copy which is modified by reafferent input. *Science, 214,* 450–453. **176**

BENINGER, R. J., KENDALL, S. B., & VANDERWOLF, C. H. (1974). The ability of rats to discriminate their own behaviors. *Canadian Journal of Psychology/Review of Canadian Psychology, 28,* 79–91. **445**

BENNETT, E. L. (1976). Cerebral effects of differential experience and training. In M. R. Rosenzweig & E. L. Bennett (Eds.), *Neural mechanisms of learning and memory.* Cambridge, MA: MIT Press. **400, 403, 404, 406**

BENNETT, E. L., ROSENZWEIG, M. R., DIAMOND, M. C., MORIMOTO, H., & HEBERT, M. (1974). Effects of successive environments on brain measures. *Physiology & Behavior, 12,* 621–631. **404**

BENNETT, E. L., ROSENZWEIG, M. R., & WU, S.-Y. C. (1973). Excitant and depressant drugs modulate effects of environment on brain weight and cholinesterases. *Psychopharmacologia, 33,* 309–328. **402, 404**

BENNETT, J. P., MULDER, A. H., & SNYDER, S. H. (1974). Neurochemical correlates of synaptically active amino acids. *Life Sciences, 15,* 1045–1056. **98**

BENOFF, F. H., SIEGEL, P. B., & VAN KREY, H. P. (1978). Testosterone determinations in lines of chickens selected for differential mating frequency. *Hormones and Behavior, 10,* 246–250. **288**

BENSON, D. A., & HIENZ, R. D. (1978). Single-unit activity in the auditory cortex of monkeys selectively attending left vs. right ear stimuli. *Brain Research, 159,* 307–320. **239**

BENSON, T. E., RYUGO, D. K., & HINDS, J. W. (1984). Effects of sensory deprivation on the developing mouse olfactory system: A light and electron microscopic, morphometric analysis. *Journal of Neuroscience, 4,* 638–653. **410**

BEREITER, D. A., & BARKER, D. J. (1980). Hormone-induced enlargement of receptive fields in trigeminal mechanoreceptive neurons: I. Time course, hormones, sex and modality specificity. *Brain Research, 184,* 395–410. **315**

BEREITER, D. A., & JEANRENAUD, B. (1979). Altered neuroanatomical organization in the central nervous system of the genetically obese *(ob/ob)* mouse. *Brain Research, 165,* 249–260. **252**

BEREITER, D. A., & JEANRENAUD, B. (1980). Altered dendritic orientation of hypothalamic neurons from genetically obese *(ob/ob)* mouse. *Brain Research, 202,* 201–206. **252**

BEREITER, D. A., STANFORD, L. R., & BARKER, D. J. (1980). Hormone-induced enlargement of receptive fields in trigeminal mechanoreceptive neurons: II. Possible mechanisms. *Brain Research, 184,* 411–423. **315**

BERGER, P. A. (1981). Biochemistry and the schizophrenias: Old concepts and new hypotheses. *Journal of Nervous and Mental Disease, 169,* 90–99. **344**

BERGER, T. W. (1984). Long-term potentiation of hippocampal synaptic transmission affects rate of behavioral learning. *Science, 224,* 627–630. **394**

BERGER, T. W., CLARK, G. A., & THOMPSON, R. F. (1980). Learning-dependent neuronal responses recorded from limbic system brain structures during classical conditioning. *Physiological Psychology, 8,* 155–167. **390**

BERGER, T. W., RINALDI, P. C., WEISZ, D. J., & THOMPSON, R. F. (1983). Single-unit analysis of different hippocampal cell types during classical conditioning of rabbit nictitating membrane response. *Journal of Neurophysiology, 50,* 1197–1219. **392**

BERGER, T. W., & THOMPSON, R. F. (1978a). Neuronal plasticity in the limbic system during classical conditioning of the rabbit nictitating membrane response: I. The hippocampus. *Brain Research, 145,* 323–346. **390, 392**

BERGER, T. W., & THOMPSON, R. F. (1978b). Neuronal plasticity in the limbic system during classical conditioning of the rabbit nictitating membrane response: II. Septum and mammillary bodies. *Brain Research, 156,* 293–314. **391, 392**

BERGER, T. W., & THOMPSON, R. F. (1978c). Identification of pyramidal cells as the critical elements in hippocampal neuronal plasticity during learning. *Proceedings of the National Academy of Sciences, U.S.A., 75,* 1572–1576. **390, 392**

BERMAN, N., & PAYNE, B. R. (1982). Monocular deprivation in the Siamese cat: Development of cortical orientation and direction sensitivity without visual experience. *Experimental Brain Research, 46,* 147–150. **420**

BERNARD, B. K., & PAOLINO, R. M. (1974). Time-dependent changes in brain biogenic amine dynamics

following castration in male rats. *Journal of Neurochemistry, 22,* 951–956. **340**

BERMOND, B., MOS, J., MEELIS, W., VAN DER POEL, A. M., & KRUK, M. R. (1982). Aggression induced by stimulation of the hypothalamus: Effects of androgens. *Pharmacology, Biochemistry & Behavior, 16,* 41–45. **339**

BERNARDI, G., CHERUBINI, E., MARCIANI, M. G., MERCURI, N., & STANZIONE, P. (1982). Responses of intracellularly recorded cortical neurons to the iontophoretic application of dopamine. *Brain Research, 245,* 267–274. **97**

BERNSTEIN, J. (1902). Untersuchungen zur Thermodynamik der bioelektrischen Ströme. *Pflügers Archives, 92,* 521–562. **51**

BERRETTINI, W. H., NURNBERGER, J. I., JR., HARE, T. A., SIMMONS-ALLING, S., GERSHON, E. S., & POST, R. M. (1983). Reduced plasma and CSF gamma-aminobutyric acid in affective illness: Effect of lithium carbonate. *Biological Psychiatry, 18,* 185–194. **349**

BERRY, S. D., & THOMPSON, R. F. (1978). Prediction of learning rate from the hippocampal electroencephalogram. *Science, 200,* 1298–1300. **391**

BERTINO, M., BEAUCHAMP, G. K., RISKEY, D. R., & ENGELMAN, K. (1981). Taste perception in three individuals on a low sodium diet. *Appetite, 2,* 67–73. **264**

BEST, C. H., & TAYLOR, N. B. (1966). *The physiological basis of medical practice* (8th ed.). Baltimore: Williams & Wilkins.

BEST, M. R., & BEST, P. J. (1976). The effects of state of consciousness and latent inhibition on hippocampal unit activity in the rat during conditioning. *Experimental Neurology, 51,* 564–573. **389**

BEVAN, S., & RAFF, M. (1985). Voltage-dependent potassium currents in cultured astrocytes. *Nature, 315,* 229–232. **25, 27**

BEZANILLA, F., & ARMSTRONG, C. M. (1974). Gating currents of the sodium channels: Three ways to block them. *Science, 183,* 753–754. **56, 61**

BEZANILLA, F., & ARMSTRONG, C. M. (1977). Inactivation of the sodium channel: I. Sodium current experiments. *Journal of General Physiology, 70,* 549–566. **61**

BIEGON, A., & MCEWEN, B. S. (1982). Modulation by estradiol of serotonin receptors in brain. *Journal of Neuroscience, 2,* 199–205. **309**

BIEGON, A., RECHES, A., SNYDER, L., & MCEWEN, B. S. (1983). Serotonergic and noradrenergic receptors in the rat brain: Modulation by chronic exposure to ovarian hormones. *Life Sciences, 32,* 2015–2021. **309**

BILLINGS, A. G., & MOOS, R. H. (1984). Chronic and nonchronic unipolar depression: The differential role of environmental stressors and resources. *Journal of Nervous and Mental Disease, 172,* 65–75. **337**

BIOULAC, B., BENEZECH, M., RENAUD, B., NOEL, B., & ROCHE, D. (1980). Serotoninergic dysfunction in the 47,XXY syndrome. *Biological Psychiatry, 15,* 917–923. **341**

BIOULAC, B., & LAMARRE, Y. (1979). Activity of postcentral cortical neurons of the monkey during conditioned movements of a deafferented limb. *Brain Research, 172,* 427–437. **176, 230**

BISHOP, M. P., ELDER, S. T., & HEATH, R. G. (1963). Intracranial self-stimulation in man. *Science, 140,* 394–396. **263**

BJÖRKLUND, A., SEGAL, M., & STENEVI, U.

(1979). Functional reinnervation of rat hippocampus by locus coeruleus implants. *Brain Research, 170,* 409–426. **437**

BJÖRKLUND, A., & STENEVI, U. (1979). Regeneration of monoaminergic and cholinergic neurons in the mammalian central nervous system. *Physiological Reviews, 59,* 62–100. **434, 435, 437**

BJÖRKLUND, A., STENEVI, U., DUNNETT, S. B., & GAGE, F. H. (1982). Cross-species neural grafting in a rat model of Parkinson's disease. *Nature, 298,* 652–654. **438**

BJÖRKLUND, A., STENEVI, U., DUNNETT, S. B., & IVERSEN, S. D. (1981). Functional reactivation of the deafferented neostriatum by nigral transplants. *Nature, 289,* 497–499. **437**

BLACK, I. B. (1982). Stages of neurotransmitter development in autonomic neurons. *Science, 215,* 1198–1204. **126**

BLAKE, R., & HIRSCH, H. V. B. (1975). Deficits in binocular depth perception in cats after alternating monocular deprivation. *Science, 190,* 1114–1116. **423**

BLAKEMORE, C., & COOPER, G. F. (1970). Development of the brain depends on the visual environment. *Nature, 228,* 477–478. **424**

BLAKEMORE, C., & MITCHELL, D. E. (1973). Environmental modification of the visual cortex and the neural basis of learning and memory. *Nature, 241,* 467–468. **426**

BLANC, G., HERVÉ, D., SIMON, H., LISOPRAWSKI, A., GLOWINSKI, J., & TASSIN, J. P. (1980). Response to stress of mesocortico-frontal dopaminergic neurones in rats after long-term isolation. *Nature, 284,* 265–267. **332, 347**

BLASDEL, G. G., MITCHELL, D. E., MUIR, D. W., & PETTIGREW, J. D. (1977). A physiological and behavioural study in cats of the effect of early visual experience with contours of a single orientation. *Journal of Physiology, 265,* 615–636. **426**

BLASS, E. M., & EPSTEIN, A. N. (1971). A lateral preoptic osmosensitive zone for thirst in the rat. *Journal of Comparative and Physiological Psychology, 77,* 378–396. **254**

BLAUSTEIN, J. D., & FEDER, H. H. (1979). Cytoplasmic progestin-receptors in guinea pig brain: Characteristics and relationship to the induction of sexual behavior. *Brain Research, 169,* 481–497. **285**

BLAUSTEIN, J. D., RYER, H. I., & FEDER, H. H. (1980). A sex difference in the progestin receptor system of guinea pig brain. *Neuroendocrinology, 31,* 403–409. **285**

BLEIER, R., BYNE, W., & SIGGELKOW, I. (1982). Cytoarchitectonic sexual dimorphisms of the medial preoptic and anterior hypothalamic areas in guinea pig, rat, hamster, and mouse. *Journal of Comparative Neurology, 212,* 118–130. **303**

BLIER, P., & DE MONTIGNY, C. (1983). Electrophysiological investigations on the effect of repeated zimelidine administration on serotonergic neurotransmission in the rat. *Journal of Neuroscience, 3,* 1270–1278. **348, 355**

BLISS, T. V. P., & DOLPHIN, A. C. (1982). What is the mechanism of long-term potentiation in the hippocampus? *Trends in NeuroSciences, 5,* 289–290. **393, 395**

BLISS, T. V. P., & GARDNER-MEDWIN, A. R. (1973). Long-lasting potentiation of synaptic transmission in the dentate area of the unanaesthetized rabbit following stimulation of the perforant path. *Journal of Physiology, 232,* 357–374.

BLIZARD, D. A. (1981). The Maudsley Reactive and Nonreactive strains: A North American perspective. *Behavior Genetics, 11*, 469–489. **327**

BLOCH, V., & LAROCHE, S. (1981). Conditioning of hippocampal cells: Its acceleration and long-term facilitation by post-trial reticular stimulation. *Behavioural Brain Research, 3*, 23–42. **389**

BLOOM, F. E. (1981). Neuropeptides. *Scientific American, 245*, 148–168. **98, 168**

BLOUGH, D. S. (1955). Method for tracing dark adaptation in the pigeon. *Science, 121*, 703–704. **140**

BLUNDELL, J. E. (1977). Is there a role for serotonin (5-hydroxytryptamine) in feeding? *International Journal of Obesity, 1*, 15–42. **248**

BODIAN, D. (1978). Synapses involving auditory nerve fibers in primate cochlea. *Proceedings of the National Academy of Sciences, U.S.A., 75*, 4582–4586. **175**

BOGERTS, B., HÄNTSCH, J., & HERZER, M. (1983). A morphometric study of the dopamine-containing cell groups in the mesencephalon of normals, Parkinson patients, and schizophrenics. *Biological Psychiatry, 18*, 951–969. **346**

BOOTH, D. A. (1981). The physiology of appetite. *British Medical Bulletin, 37*, 135–140. **241**

BOOTHE, R., TELLER, D. Y., & SACKETT, G. P. (1975). Trichromacy in normally reared and light deprived infant monkeys *(Macaca nemestrina). Vision Research, 15*, 1187–1191. **429**

BOOTHE, R. G., DOBSON, V., & TELLER, D. Y. (1985). Postnatal development of vision in human and non-human primates. *Annual Review of Neurosciences, 8*, 495–545. **432**

BOOTHE, R. G., GREENOUGH, W. T., LUND, J. S., & WREGE, K. (1979). A quantitative investigation of spine and dendrite development of neurons in visual cortex (area 17) of *Macaca nemestrina* monkeys. *Journal of Comparative Neurology, 186*, 473–490. **431**

BORG, G., DIAMANT, H., STRÖM, L., & ZOTTERMAN, Y. (1967). The relation between neural and perceptual intensity: A comparative study on the neural and psychophysical response to taste stimuli. *Journal of Physiology, 192*, 13–20. **139, 168**

BORN, G., GRÜTZNER, P., & HEMMINGER, H. (1976). Evidenz für eine Mosaikstruktur der Netzhaut bei Konduktorinnen für Dichromasie. *Human Genetics, 32*, 189–196. **287**

BORSINI, F., & ROLLS, E. T. (1984). Role of noradrenaline and serotonin in the basolateral region of the amygdala in food preferences and learned taste aversion in the rat. *Physiology & Behavior, 33*, 37–43.

BOTTJER, S. W., & ARNOLD, A. P. (1984). Hormones and structural plasticity in the adult brain. *Trends in NeuroSciences, 7*, 168–171. **307**

BOUCHARD, C., SAVARD, R., DESPRÉS, J.-P., TREMBLAY, A., & LEBLANC, C. (1985). Body composition in adopted and biological siblings. *Human Biology, 57*, 61–75. **250**

BOUDREAU, J. C., BRADLEY, B. E., BEIRER, P. R., KRUGER, St., & TSUCHITANI, Ch. (1971). Single unit recordings from the geniculate ganglion of the facial nerve of the cat. *Experimental Brain Research, 13*, 461–488. **16**

BOUISSOU, M.-F. (1983). Androgens, aggressive behaviour and social relationships in higher mammals. *Hormone Research, 18*, 43–61. **291**

BOURASSA, C. M., & SWETT, J. E. (1967). Sensory

discrimination thresholds with cutaneous nerve volleys in the cat. *Journal of Neurophysiology, 30*, 515–529. **445**

BOURASSA, C. M., & SWETT, J. E. (1982). Behavioral detection of subcortical stimuli: Comparison of somatosensory and "motor" circuits. *Journal of Comparative and Physiological Psychology, 96*, 679–690. **445**

BOVET, D., BOVET-NITTI, F., & OLIVERIO, A. (1969). Genetic aspects of learning and memory in mice. *Science, 163*, 139–149. **373, 380**

BOWMAKER, J. K. (1981). Visual pigments and colour vision in man and monkeys. *Journal of the Royal Society of Medicine, 74*, 348–356. **202**

BOWNDS, M. D. (1980). Roles for calcium and cyclic nucleotides in visual transduction. *Federation Proceedings, 39*, 1814. **193**

BOYCOTT, B. B., & DOWLING, J. E. (1969). Organization of the primate retina: Light microscopy. *Philosophical Transactions of the Royal Society of London, Series B, 255*, 109–184. **183**

BOYCOTT, B. B., & KOLB, H. (1973). The horizontal cells of the rhesus monkey retina. *Journal of Comparative Neurology, 148*, 115–139. **183, 184**

BOYLE, B. P., & CONWAY, E. J. (1941). Potassium accumulation in muscle and associated changes. *Journal of Physiology, 100*, 1–63. **51**

BRAY, G. A. (1981). The inheritance of corpulence. In L. A. Cioffi, W. P. T. James, & T. B. Van Itallie (Eds.), *The body weight regulatory system: Normal and disturbed mechanisms*. New York: Raven Press. **250**

BRAY, G. A., & YORK, D. A. (1979). Hypothalamic and genetic obesity in experimental animals: An autonomic and endocrine hypothesis. *Physiological Reviews, 59*, 719–809. **251, 253**

BREEDLOVE, S. M., & ARNOLD, A. P. (1981). Sexually dimorphic motor nucleus in the rat lumbar spinal cord: Response to adult hormone manipulation, absence in androgen-insensitive rats. *Brain Research, 225*, 297–307. **301**

BREEDLOVE, S. M., & ARNOLD, A. P. (1983). Sex differences in the pattern of steroid accumulation by motoneurons of the rat lumbar spinal cord. *Journal of Comparative Neurology, 215*, 211–216. **284, 301**

BREEDLOVE, S. M., JACOBSON, C. D., GORSKI, R. A., & ARNOLD, A. P. (1982). Masculinization of the female rat spinal cord following a single neonatal injection of testosterone propinate but not estradiol benzoate. *Brain Research, 237*, 173–181. **301**

BRENNER, E., MIRMIRAN, M., UYLINGS, H. B. M., & VAN DER GUGTEN, J. (1983). Impaired growth of the cerebral cortex of rats treated neonatally with 6-hydroxydopamine under different environmental conditions. *Neuroscience Letters, 42*, 13–17. **402**

BRENNER, E., SPAAN, J. P., WORTEL, J. R., & NUBOER, J. F. W. (1983). Early colour deprivation in the pigeon. *Behavioural Brain Research, 8*, 343–350. **429**

BRIDGEMAN, B. (1973). Receptive fields in single cells of monkey visual cortex during visual tracking. *International Journal of Neuroscience, 6*, 141–152. **221**

BRILEY, M., LANGER, S. Z., & SETTE, M. (1981). Allosteric interaction between the ³H-imipramine binding site and the serotonin uptake mechanism. *British Journal of Pharmacology, 74*, 817P–818P. **354**

BRINDLEY, G. S., & LEWIN, W. S. (1968). The sensations produced by electrical stimulation of the visual cortex. *Journal of Physiology, 196*, 479–493. **217, 221**

BRITO, G. N. O., DAVIS, B. J., STOPP, L. C., &

STANTON, M. E. (1983). Memory and the septo-hippocampal cholinergic system in the rat. *Psychopharmacology, 81*, 315–320. **376**

BROADHURST, P. L. (1975). The Maudsley Reactive and Nonreactive strains of rats: A survey. *Behavior Genetics, 5*, 299–319. **327**

BROBECK, J. R. (1948). Food intake as a mechanism of temperature regulation. *Yale Journal of Biology and Medicine, 20*, 545–552. **243**

BROCK, L. G., COOMBS, J. S., & ECCLES, J. C. (1952). The recording of potentials from motoneurones with an intracellular electrode. *Journal of Physiology, 117*, 431–460.

BRODIE, J. D., CHRISTMAN, D. R., CORONA, J. F., FOWLER, J. S., GOMEZ-MONT, F., JAEGER, J., MICHEELS, P. A., ROTROSEN, J., RUSSELL, J. A., VOLKOW, N. D., WIKLER, A., WOLF, A. P., & WOLKIN, A. (1984). Patterns of metabolic activity in the treatment of schizophrenia. *Annals of Neurology, 15*, S166–S169.

BROIDA, J., & SVARE, B. (1983). Genotype modulates testosterone-dependent activity and reactivity in male mice. *Hormones and Behavior, 17*, 76–85. **288**

BROWN, D. A., & ADAMS, P. R. (1980). Muscarinic suppression of a novel voltage-sensitive K⁺-current in a vertebrate neurone. *Nature, 283*, 673–676. **60, 88, 90, 158**

BROWN, D. A., & CAULFIELD, M. P. (1979). Hyperpolarizing "alpha₂."-adrenoceptors in rat sympathetic ganglia. *British Journal of Pharmacology, 65*, 435–445. **98**

BROWN, D. A., CAULFIELD, M. P., & KIRBY, P. J. (1979). Relation between catecholamine-induced cyclic AMP changes and hyperpolarization in isolated rat sympathetic ganglia. *Journal of Physiology, 290*, 441–451. **90**

BROWN, D. A., & GRIFFITH, W. H. (1983a). Calcium-activated outward current in voltage-clamped hippocampal neurones of the guinea-pig. *Journal of Physiology, 337*, 287–301. **59**

BROWN, D. A., & GRIFFITH, W. H. (1983b). Persistent slow inward calcium current in voltage-clamped hippocampal neurones of the guinea-pig. *Journal of Physiology, 337*, 303–320. **59**

BROWN, D. D. (1981). Gene expression in eukaryotes. *Science, 211*, 667–674. **113, 126**

BROWN, E. L., & DEFFENBACHER, K. (1979). *Perception and the senses*. New York: Oxford University Press. **138, 172**

BROWN, G. W. (1979). The social etiology of depression: London studies. In R. A. Depue (Ed.), *The psychobiology of the depressive disorders*. New York: Academic Press. **337**

BROWN, M. C., NUTTALL, A. L., & MASTA, R. I. (1983). Intracellular recordings from cochlear inner hair cells: Effects of stimulation of the crossed olivocochlear efferents. *Science, 222*, 70–72. **175**

BROWN, T. H., & MCAFEE, D. A. (1983). Long-term synaptic potentiation in the superior cervical ganglion. *Science, 215*, 1411–1413. **393**

BROWN, T. J., & BLAUSTEIN, J. D. (1984). Supplemental progesterone delays heat termination and the loss of progestin receptors from hypothalamic cell nuclei in female guinea pigs. *Neuroendocrinology, 39*, 384–391. **280**

BROWNELL, W. E., BADER, C. R., BERTRAND, D., & DE RIBEAUPIERRE, Y. (1985). Evoked mechanical responses of isolated cochlear outer hair cells. *Science, 227*, 194–196. **167, 175**

BROWNING, M., DUNWIDDIE, T., BENNETT,

W., GISPEN, W., & LYNCH, G. (1979). Synaptic phosphoproteins: Specific changes after repetitive stimulation of the hippocampal slice. *Science, 203*, 60–62. **395**

BROZOSKI, T. J., BROWN, R. M., ROSVOLD, H. E., & GOLDMAN, P. S. (1979). Cognitive deficit caused by regional depletion of dopamine in prefrontal cortex of rhesus monkey. *Science, 205*, 929–932. **347**

BRUGGE, J. F., & MERZENICH, M. M. (1973). Responses of neurons in auditory cortex of the macaque monkey to monaural and binaural stimulation. *Journal of Neurophysiology, 36*, 1138–1158. **165, 168, 169, 171, 239**

BUBENIK, G. A., & BROWN, G. M. (1973). Morphologic sex differences in primate brain areas involved in regulation of reproductive activity. *Experientia, 29*, 619–624. **300**

BUCHSBAUM, M. S., CAPPELLETTI, J., BALL, R., HAZLETT, E., KING, A. C., JOHNSON, J., WU, J., & DELISI, L. E. (1984). Positron emission tomographic image measurement in schizophrenia and affective disorders. *Annals of Neurology, 15*, S157–S165.

BUCHSBAUM, M. S., COURSEY, R. D., & MURPHY, D. L. (1980). Schizophrenia and platelet monoamine oxidase: Research strategies. *Schizophrenia Bulletin, 6*, 375–384. **341**

BUELL, S. J., & COLEMAN, P. D. (1979). Dendritic growth in the aged human brain and failure of growth in senile dementia. *Science, 206*, 854–856. **432**

BÜHLER, E. M. (1980). A synopsis of the human Y chromosome. *Human Genetics, 55*, 145–175. **286**

BÜHRLE, C. P., & SONNHOF, U. (1985). The ionic mechanism of postsynaptic inhibition in motoneurones of the frog spinal cord. *Neuroscience, 14*, 581–592. **84, 85**

BUISSERET, P., GARY-BOBO, E., & IMBERT, M. (1978). Ocular motility and recovery of orientational properties of visual cortical neurones in dark-reared kittens. *Nature, 272*, 816–817. **422**

BUNNEY, B. S. (1984). Antipsychotic drug effects on the electrical activity of dopaminergic neurons. *Trends in NeuroSciences, 7*, 212–215. **356**

BUNNEY, B. S., & AGHAJANIAN, G. K. (1976a). d-amphetamine-induced inhibition of central dopaminergic neurons: Mediation by a striato-nigral feedback pathway. *Science, 192*, 391–393. **98, 356**

BUNNEY, B. S., & AGHAJANIAN, G. K. (1976b). Dopamine and norepinephrine innervated cells in the rat prefrontal cortex: Pharmacological differentiation using microiontophoretic techniques. *Life Sciences, 19*, 1783–1792. **356**

BUNNEY, B. S., & AGHAJANIAN, G. K. (1978). d-amphetamine-induced depression of central dopamine neurons: Evidence for mediation by both autoreceptors and a striato-nigral feedback pathway. *Archives of Pharmacology, 304*, 255–261. **356**

BUNNEY, B. S., & GRACE, A. A. (1978). Acute and chronic haloperidol treatment: Comparison of effects on nigral dopaminergic cell activity. *Life Sciences, 23*, 1715–1728. **356**

BURBAUD, P., GROSS, Ch., & BIOULAC, B. (1985). Peripheral inputs and early unit activity in area 5 of the monkey during a trained forelimb movement. *Brain Research, 337*, 341–346. **230**

BUREŠ, J., & BUREŠOVÁ, O. (1967). Plastic changes of unit activity based on reinforcing properties of extracellular stimulation of single neurons. *Journal of Neurophysiology, 30*, 98–113. **393**

BURGESS, P. R., & PERL, E. R. (1967). Myelinated afferent fibres responding specifically to noxious stimulation of the skin. *Journal of Physiology, 190*, 541–562. **163**

BURGOYNE, P. S., LEVY, E. R., & MCLAREN, A. (1986). Spermatogenic failure in male mice lacking H-Y antigen. *Nature, 320*, 170–172. **287**

BURKHART, C. A., CHERRY, J. A., VAN KREY, H. P., & SIEGEL, P. B. (1983). Genetic selection for growth rate alters hypothalamic satiety mechanisms in chickens. *Behavior Genetics, 13*, 295–300. **251**

BURNOD, Y., MATON, B., & CALVET, J. (1982). Short-term changes in cell activity of areas 4 and 5 during operant conditioning. *Experimental Neurology, 78*, 227–240. **383**

BURTON, M. J., ROLLS, E. T., & MORA, F. (1976). Effects of hunger on the responses of neurons in the lateral hypothalamus to the sight and taste of food. *Experimental Neurology, 51*, 668–677. **261, 264**

BUTLER, A. B., GRAZIADEI, P. P. C., GRAZIADEI, G. A. M., & SLOTNICK, B. M. (1984). Neonatally bulbectomized rats with new olfactory-neocortical connections are anosmic. *Neuroscience Letters, 48*, 247–254. **436**

CABANAC, M. (1979). Sensory pleasure. *Quarterly Review of Biology, 1979, 54*, 1–29. **264**

CADORET, R. J., CAIN, C. A., & CROWE, R. R. (1983). Evidence for gene-environmental interaction in the development of adolescent antisocial behavior. *Behavior Genetics, 13*, 301–310. **326**

CALDWELL, P. C., HODGKIN, A. L., KEYNES, R. D., & SHAW, T. I. (1960). The effects of injecting "energy-rich" phosphate compounds on the active transport of ions in the giant axons of *Loligo*. *Journal of Physiology, 152*, 561–590. **48**

CALDWELL, P. C., & KEYNES, R. D. (1960). The permeability of the squid giant axon to radioactive potassium and chloride ions. *Journal of Physiology, 154*, 177–189. **48, 51, 58**

CAMARDO, J. S., KLEIN, M., & KANDEL, E. R. (1981). Sensitization in *Aplysia*: Serotonin elicits a decrease in sensory neuron K^+ current not related to I/K early or I/K_{Ca++}. *Neuroscience Abstracts, 7*, 836. **60, 87**

CAMP, D. M., ROBINSON, T. E., & BECKER, J. B. (1984). Sex differences in the effects of early experience on the development of behavioral and brain asymmetries in rats. *Physiology & Behavior, 33*, 433–439. **301, 305**

CAMPBELL, E. A., COPE, S. J., & TEASDALE, J. D. (1983). Social factors and affective disorder: An investigation of Brown and Harris's model. *British Journal of Psychiatry, 143*, 548–553. **337**

CAMPBELL, F. W., & ROBSON, J. G. (1968). Application of Fourier analysis to the visibility of gratings. *Journal of Physiology, 197*, 551–566. **212**

CAMPFIELD, L. A., BRANDON, P., & SMITH, F. J. (1985). On-line continuous measurement of blood glucose and meal onset in free-feeding rats: The role of glucose in meal initiation. *Brain Research Bulletin, 14*, 605–616. **241**

CAMPION, J., LATTO, R., & SMITH, Y. M. (1983). Is blindsight an effect of scattered light, spared cortex, and near-threshold vision? *Behavioral and Brain Sciences, 6*, 423–486. **446**

CANDLAND, D. K. (1977). The persistent problems of emotion. In D. K. Candland, J. P. Fell, E. Keen, A. I. Leshner, R. M. Tarpy, & R. Plutchik (Eds.), *Emotion*. Monterey, CA: Brooks/Cole. **321, 324**

CANO, J., MACHADO, A., ROZA, C., & RODRI-

GUES-ECHANDIA, E. (1982). Effect of testosterone on serotonin and noradrenaline concentrations and taste bud cell number of rat circumvallate papilla. *Chemical Senses, 7*, 109–116. **315**

CAPLAN, A. I., & ORDAHL, C. P. (1978). Irreversible gene repression model for control of development. *Science, 201*, 120–130. **113, 126**

CARDINALI, D. P., VACAS, M. I., RITTA, M. N., & GEJMAN, P. V. (1983). Neurotransmitter-controlled steroid hormone receptors in the central nervous system. *Neurochemistry International, 5*, 185–192. **308**

CAREW, T. J., HAWKINS, R. D., & KANDEL, E. R. (1983). Differential classical conditioning of a defensive withdrawal reflex in *Aplysia californica*. *Science, 219*, 397–400. **396**

CARLEN, P. L., GUREVICH, N., & POLC, P. (1983). Low-dose benzodiazepine neuronal inhibition: Enhanced Ca^{2+}-mediated K^+-conductance. *Brain Research, 271*, 358–364. **344**

CARR, K. D., & COONS, E. E. (1982). Rats self-administer nonrewarding brain stimulation to ameliorate aversion. *Science, 215*, 1516–1517.

CARR, K. D., & SIMON, E. J. (1984). Potentiation of reward by hunger is opioid mediated. *Brain Research, 297*, 369–373.

CARROLL, P. T., & ASPRY, J.-A. M. (1980). Subcellular origin of cholinergic transmitter release from mouse brain. *Science, 210*, 641–642. **74**

CARTER, C. S., & DAVIS, J. M. (1977). Biogenic amines, reproductive hormones and female sexual behavior: A review. *Biobehavioral Reviews, 1*, 213–224. **310**

CASEY, K. L., & MORROW, T. J. (1983). Ventral posterior thalamic neurons differentially responsive to noxious stimulation of the awake monkey. *Science, 221*, 675–677. **163**

CASSENS, G., KURUC, A., ROFFMAN, M., ORSULAK, P. J., & SCHILDKRAUT, J. J. (1981). Alterations in brain norepinephrine metabolism and behavior induced by environmental stimuli previously paired with inescapable shock. *Behavioral Brain Research, 2*, 387–407. **332, 333**

CASTONGUAY, T. W., HARTMAN, W. J., FITZPATRICK, E. A., & STERN, J. S. (1982). Dietary self-selection and the Zucker rat. *Journal of Nutrition, 112*, 796–800. **253**

CATTERALL, W. A. (1984). The molecular basis of neuronal excitability. *Science, 223*, 653–661. **61**

CEDARBAUM, J. M., & AGHAJANIAN, G. K. (1978). Activation of locus coeruleus neurons by peripheral stimuli: Modulation by a collateral inhibitory mechanism. *Life Sciences, 23*, 1383–1392. **355**

CHAFETZ, M. D., EVANS, S., & GAGE, F. H. (1982). Recovery of function from septal damage and the growth of sympathohippocampal fibers. *Physiological Psychology, 10*, 391–398. **435, 436**

CHAMBON, P. (1981). Split genes. *Scientific American, 244*, 60–71. **120**

CHAN, L. (1976). Mechanisms of action of the sex steroid hormones. *New England Journal of Medicine, 294*, 1322–1328, 1430–1437.

CHAN, L., & O'MALLEY, B. W. (1976). Mechanism of action of the sex steroid hormones. *New England Journal of Medicine, 294*, 1322–1328, 1372–1381, 1430–1437. **278**

CHANDLER, S. H., CHASE, M. E., & NAKAMURA, Y. (1980). Intracellular analysis of synaptic mechanisms controlling trigeminal motoneuron activity during sleep and wakefulness. *Journal of Neurophysiology, 44,* 359–371. **235**

CHANDLER, S. H., NAKAMURA, Y., & CHASE, M. H. (1980). Intracellular analysis of synaptic potentials induced in trigeminal jaw-closer motoneurons by pontomesencephalic reticular stimulation during sleep and wakefulness. *Journal of Neurophysiology, 44,* 372–382. **235**

CHANDLER, W. K., & MEVES, H. (1965). Voltage clamp experiments on internally perfused giant axons. *Journal of Physiology, 180,* 788–820. **53, 54, 61**

CHANDLER, W. K., & MEVES, H. (1970). Evidence for two types of sodium conductance in axons perfused with sodium fluoride solution. *Journal of Physiology, 211,* 653–678. **53, 54**

CHANG, F.-L. F., & GREENOUGH, W. T. (1982). Lateralized effects of monocular training on dendritic branching in adult split-brain rats. *Brain Research, 232,* 183–202. **408**

CHAPMAN, J. (1966). The early symptoms of schizophrenia. *British Journal of Psychiatry, 112,* 225–251. **347**

CHARNEY, D. S., HENINGER, G. R., & REDMOND, D. E., JR. (1983). Yohimbine induced anxiety and increased noradrenergic function in humans: Effects of diazepam and clonidine. *Life Sciences, 33,* 19–29. **344**

CHARNEY, D. S., HENINGER, G. R., & STERNBERG, D. E. (1983). Alpha-2 adrenergic receptor sensitivity and the mechanism of action of antidepressant therapy: The effect of long-term amitriptyline treatment. *British Journal of Psychiatry, 142,* 265–275. **348, 349**

CHARNEY, D. S., MENKES, D. B., & HENINGER, G. R. (1981). Receptor sensitivity and the mechanism of action of antidepressant treatment: Implications for the etiology and therapy of depression. *Archives of General Psychiatry, 38,* 1160–1180. **346**

CHASE, M. H., CHANDLER, S. H., & NAKAMURA, Y. (1980). Intracellular determination of membrane potential of trigeminal motoneurons during sleep and wakefulness. *Journal of Neurophysiology, 44,* 349–358. **235**

CHASE, M. H., ENOMOTO, S., MURAKAMI, T., NAKAMURA, Y., & TAIRA, M. (1981). Intracellular potential of medullary reticular neurons during sleep and wakefulness. *Experimental Neurology, 71,* 226–233. **235**

CHASE, M. H., & MORALES, F. R. (1983). Subthreshold excitatory activity and motoneuron discharge during REM periods of active sleep. *Science, 221,* 1195–1198. **235**

CHAUDHARI, N., & HAHN, W. E. (1983). Genetic expression in the developing brain. *Science, 220,* 924–928. **431**

CHENOY-MARCHAIS, D. (1982). A Cl⁻ conductance activated by hyperpolarization in *Aplysia* neurones. *Nature, 299,* 359–361. **51**

CHEPKOVA, A. N., & SKREBITSKY, V. G. (1982). Effects of some adrenergic drugs and neuropeptides on long-term potentiation in hippocampal slices. In C. A. Marsan & H. Matthies (Eds.), *Neuronal plasticity and memory formation.* New York: Raven. **395**

CHEREK, D. R., LANE, J. D., FREEMAN, M. E., & SMITH, J. E. (1980). Receptor changes following shock avoidance. *Society for Neurosciences Abstracts, 6,* 543. **332**

CHEVILLARD, C., BARDEN, N., & SAAVEDRA, J. M. (1981). Estradiol treatment decreases type A and increases type B monoamine oxidase in specific brain stem areas and cerebellum of ovariectomized rats. *Brain Re-*

search, 222, 177–181. **309**

CHHINA, G. S., ANAND, B. K., SINGH, B., & RAO, P. S. (1971). Effect of glucose on hypothalamic feeding centers in deafferented animals. *American Journal of Physiology, 221,* 662–667. **255**

CHINO, Y. M., SHANSKY, M. S., JANKOWSKI, W. L., & BANSER, F. A. (1983). Effects of rearing kittens with convergent strabismus on development of receptive-field properties in striate cortex neurons. *Journal of Neurophysiology, 50,* 265–286. **424**

CHIODO, L. A., ANTELMAN, S. M., CAGGIULA, A. R., & LINEBERRY, C. G. (1980). Sensory stimuli alter the discharge rate of dopamine (DA) neurons: Evidence for two functional types of DA cells in the substantia nigra. *Brain Research, 189,* 544–549. **354**

CHIODO, L. A., & CAGGIULA, A. R. (1983). Substantia nigra dopamine neurons: Alterations in basal discharge rates and autoreceptor sensitivity induced by estrogen. *Neuropharmacology, 22,* 593–599. **309**

CHIU, S. Y. (1977). Inactivation of sodium channels: Second order kinetics in myelinated nerve. *Journal of Physiology, 273,* 573–596. **61**

CHIU, S. Y., RITCHIE, J. M., ROGART, R. B., & STAGG, D. (1979). A quantitative description of membrane currents in rabbit myelinated nerve. *Journal of Physiology, 292,* 149–166. **62**

CHOU, D. T., KHAN, S., FORDE, J., & HIRSH, K. R. (1985). Caffeine tolerance: Behavioral, electrophysiological and neurochemical evidence. *Life Science, 36,* 2347–2358. **236**

CHOUINARD, G., & JONES, B. D. (1980). Neuroleptic-induced supersensitivity psychosis: Clinical and pharmacologic characteristics. *American Journal of Psychiatry, 137,* 16–21. **346**

CHOW, K. L., & STEWART, D. L. (1972). Reversal of structural and functional effects of long-term visual deprivation in cats. *Experimental Neurology, 34,* 409–433.

CHRIST, D. D., & NISHI, S. (1971). Site of adrenaline blockade in the superior cervical ganglion of the rabbit. *Journal of Physiology, 213,* 107–117. **107**

CHRISTENSEN, L. W., & CLEMENS, L. G. (1974). Intrahypothalamic implants of testosterone or estradiol and resumption of masculine sexual behavior in long-term castrated male rats. *Endocrinology, 95,* 984–990. **280**

CHU, N.-S., & BLOOM, F. E. (1973). Norepinephrine-containing neurons: Changes in spontaneous discharge patterns during sleeping and waking. *Science, 179,* 908–910. **238, 355**

CHUNG, J. M., LEE, K. H., ENDO, K., & COGGESHALL, R. E. (1983). Activation of central neurons by ventral root afferents. *Science, 222,* 934–935. **156**

CHURCH, A. C., FLEXNER, J. B., FLEXNER, L. B., & RAINBOW, T. C. (1985). Blockade of peripheral beta-adrenergic receptors fails to suppress the cerebral spread of an engram in mice. *Pharmacology, Biochemistry & Behavior, 23,* 27–31. **374**

CIARANELLO, R. D., BARCHAS, R., KESSLER, S., & BARCHAS, J. D. (1972). Catecholamines: Strain differences in biosynthetic enzyme activity in mice. *Life Sciences, 11,* 565–572. **340**

CIARANELLO, R. D., LIPSKY, A., & AXELROD, J. (1974). Association between fighting behavior and catecholamine biosynthetic enzyme activity in two inbred mouse sublines. *Proceedings of the National Academy of Sciences, U.S.A., 71,* 3006–3008. **127, 340**

CICERONE, C. M. (1976). Cones survive rods in the

light-damaged eye of the albino rat. *Science, 194,* 1183–1185. **186**

CIDLOWSKI, J. A., & MULDOON, T. G. (1976). Sex-related differences in the regulation of cytoplasmic estrogen receptor levels in responsive tissues of the rat. *Endocrinology, 98,* 833–841. **282**

CLACK, J. W., OAKLEY, B., II, & STEIN, P. J. (1983). Injection of GTP-binding protein or cyclic GMP phosphodiesterase hyperpolarizes retinal rods. *Nature, 305,* 50–52. **194**

CLARK, C. R. (1984). The cellular distribution of steroid hormone receptors: Have we got it right? *Trends in Biochemical Sciences, 9,* 207–208. **279**

CLARK, J. T., SMITH, E. R., & DAVIDSON, J. M. (1984). Enhancement of sexual motivation in male rats by yohimbine. *Science, 225,* 847–849. **310**

CLARKE, P. B. S., PERT, C. B., & PERT, A. (1984). Autoradiographic distribution of nicotine receptors in rat brain. *Brain Research, 323,* 390–395. **95**

CLEMENS, L. G., HUMPHRYS, R. R., & DOHANICH, G. P. (1980). Cholinergic brain mechanisms and the hormonal regulation of female sexual behavior in the rat. *Pharmacology, Biochemistry & Behavior, 13,* 81–88. **310**

CLOPTON, B. M., & WINFIELD, J. A. (1976). Effect of early exposure to patterned sound on unit activity in rat inferior colliculus. *Journal of Neurophysiology, 39,* 1081–1089. **413**

COHEN, E., LIEBLICH, I., & GANCHROW, J. R. (1982). Saccharin preferences in prepubertal male and female rats: Relationship to self-stimulation. *Behavioral and Neural Biology, 36,* 88–93. **253**

COHEN, N. J., & CORKIN, S. (1981). The amnesic patient H.M.: Learning and retention of a cognitive skill. *Neuroscience Abstracts, 7,* 235. **13, 446**

COHEN, N. J., & SQUIRE, L. R. (1980). Preserved learning and retention of pattern-analyzing skill in amnesia: Dissociation of knowing how and knowing that. *Science, 210,* 207–210. **13, 446**

COHEN-PARSONS, M., VAN KREY, H. P., & SIEGEL, P. B. (1983). In vivo aromatization of [³H]testosterone in high and low mating lines of Japanese quail. *Hormones and Behavior, 17,* 316–323. **310**

COLE, A. E., & NICOLL, R. A. (1983). Acetylcholine mediates a slow synaptic potential in hippocampal pyramidal cells. *Science, 221,* 1299–1301. **91**

COLE, A. E., & SHINNICK-GALLAGHER, P. (1984). Muscarinic inhibitory transmission in mammalian sympathetic ganglia mediated by increased potassium conductance. *Nature, 307,* 270–271. **89, 90**

COLEMAN, D. L. (1978). Genetics of obesity in rodents. In G. A. Bray (Ed.), *Recent advances in obesity research: II.* London: Newman Publishing. **250**

COLLIER, H. O. J. (1980). Cellular site of opiate dependence. *Nature, 283,* 625–629. **99**

COMMINS, D., & YAHR, P. (1984a). Adult testosterone levels influence the morphology of a sexually dimorphic area in the Mongolian gerbil brain. *Journal of Comparative Neurology, 224,* 132–140. **303, 307**

COMMINS, D., & YAHR, P. (1984b). Lesions of the sexually dimorphic area disrupt mating and marking in male gerbils. *Brain Research Bulletin, 13,* 185–193. **304**

CONTI-TRONCONI, B. M., GOTTI, C. M., HUNKAPILLER, M. W., & RAFTERY, M. A. (1982). Mammalian muscle acetylcholine receptor: A supramolecular structure formed by four related proteins. *Science,*

218, 1227–1229. **80**

CONTRERAS, R. J. (1977). Changes in gustatory nerve discharges with sodium deficiency: A single unit analysis. *Brain Research, 121*, 373–378. **264**

COOMBS, J. S., ECCLES, J. C., & FATT, P. (1955). The specific ionic conductances and the ionic movements across the motoneuronal membrane that produce the inhibitory post-synaptic potential. *Journal of Physiology, 130*, 326–373. **48, 51, 80, 100**

COONS, E. E., & WHITE, H. A. (1977). Tonic properties of orosensation and the modulation of intracranial self-stimulation: The CNS weighting of external and internal factors governing reward. *Annals of the New York Academy of Sciences, 290*, 158–179.

COOPER, S. J. (1983). Benzodiazepine-opiate antagonist interactions in relation to feeding and drinking behavior. *Life Sciences, 32*, 1043–1051. **248**

COOPERSMITH, R., & LEON, M. (1984). Enhanced neural response to familiar olfactory cues. *Science, 225*, 849–851. **410**

COPENHAGEN, D. R., & OWEN, W. G. (1976). Functional characteristics of lateral interactions between rods in the retina of the snapping turtle. *Journal of Physiology, 259*, 251–282. **195**

COPPEN, A., SWADE, C., & WOOD, K. (1978). Platelet 5-hydroxytryptomine accumulation in depressive illness. *Clinical Chemical Acta, 87*, 165–168. **354**

CORBIER, P., KERDELHUÉ, B., PICON, R., & ROFFI, J. (1978). Changes in testicular weight and serum gonadotropin and testosterone levels before, during, and after birth in the perinatal rat. *Endocrinology, 103*, 1985–1991. **272**

CORBIER, P., ROFFI, J., RHODA, J., & KERDELHUÉ. (1984). Increased activity of the hypothalamo-pituitary axis in the rat at birth: Implications in the sexual differentiation of the brain? In M. Serio, M. Motta, M. Zanisi, & L. Martini (Eds.), *Sexual differentiation: Basic and clinical aspects* (Vol 11). New York: Raven. **272**

COREY, D. P., & HUDSPETH, A. J. (1979a). Response latency of vertebrate hair cells. *Biophysical Journal, 26*, 499–506. **153**

COREY, D. P., & HUDSPETH, A. J. (1979b). Ionic basis of the receptor potential in a vertebrate hair cell. *Nature, 281*, 675–677. **153**

CORKIN, S., SULLIVAN, E. V., TWITCHELL, T. E., & GROVE, E. (1981). The amnesic patient H.M.: Clinical observations and test performance 28 years after operation. *Neuroscience Abstracts, 7*, 235. **13, 446**

CORNWELL, P., & OVERMAN, W. (1981). Behavioral effects of early rearing conditions and neonatal lesions of the visual cortex in kittens. *Journal of Comparative and Physiological Psychology, 95*, 848–862. **403**

COSCINA, D. V., & STANCER, H. C. (1977). Selective blockade of hypothalamic hyperphagia and obesity in rats by serotonin-depleting midbrain lesions. *Science, 195*, 416–419. **248**

COSS, R. G., & GLOBUS, A. (1978). Spine stems on tectal interneurons in jewel fish are shortened by social stimulation. *Science, 200*, 787–790. **406**

COSTA, E., GUIDOTTI, A., & TOFFANO, G. (1978). Molecular mechanisms mediating the action of diazepam on GABA receptors. *British Journal of Psychiatry, 133*, 239–248. **344**

CÔTÉ, L. (1981). Basal ganglia, the extrapyramidal motor system, and diseases of transmitter metabolism. In E. R. Kandel & J. H. Schwartz (Eds.), *Principles of neural*

science. New York: Elsevier/North-Holland.

COTMAN, C. W., NIETO-SAMPEDRO, M., & HARRIS, E. W. (1981). Synapse replacement in the nervous system of adult vertebrates. *Physiological Reviews, 61*, 684–784. **434, 435**

COURSEY, R. D., BUCHSBAUM, M. S., & MURPHY, D. L. (1982). 2-year follow-up of subjects and their families defined as at risk for psychopathology on the basis of platelet MAO activities. *Neuropsychobiology, 8*, 51–56. **341**

CRAGG, B. G. (1975a). The development of synapses in the visual system of the cat. *Journal of Comparative Neurology, 160*, 147–166. **431**

CRAGG, B. G. (1975b). The development of synapses in kitten visual cortex during visual deprivation. *Experimental Neurology, 46*, 445–451. **432**

CRAIK, K. J. W. (1943). *The nature of explanation*. Cambridge: Cambridge University Press. **5**

CRANE, H. D., & PIANTANIDA, T. P. (1983). On seeing reddish green and yellowish blue. *Science, 221*, 1078–1080. **218**

CRASKE, B. (1977). Perception of impossible limb positions induced by tendon vibration. *Science, 196*, 71–73. **172**

CREESE, I., BURT, D. R., & SNYDER, S. H. (1976). Dopamine receptor binding predicts clinical and pharmacological potencies of antischizophrenic drugs. *Science, 192*, 481–483. **345**

CREUTZFELDT, O. D., & HEGGELUND, P. (1975). Neural plasticity in visual cortex of adult cats after exposure to visual patterns. *Science, 188*, 1025–1027. **427**

CRNIC, L. S. (1983). Effects of nutrition and environment on brain biochemistry and behavior. *Developmental Psychobiology, 16*, 129–145. **402, 403**

CROW, T. J. (1980). Molecular pathology of schizophrenia: More than one disease process? *British Medical Journal, 280*, 66–68. **327, 344**

CROW, T. J. (1985). The two-syndrome concept: Origins and current status. *Schizophrenia Bulletin, 11*, 471–486. **327, 344**

CROWLEY, W. R., O'DONOHUE, T. L., & JACOBOWITZ, D. M. (1978). Sex differences in catecholamine content in discrete brain nuclei of the rat: Effects of neonatal castration or testosterone treatment. *Acta Endocrinologica, 89*, 20–28. **298**

CROWLEY, W. R., O'DONOHUE, T. L., MUTH, E. A., & JACOBOWITZ, D. M. (1979). Effects of ovarian hormones on levels of luteinizing hormone in plasma and on serotonin concentrations in discrete brain nuclei. *Brain Research Bulletin, 4*, 571–574. **309**

CRUTCHER, K. A., & COLLINS, F. (1982). In vitro evidence for two distinct hippocampal growth factors: Basis of neuronal plasticity? *Science, 217*, 67–68. **436**

CUELLO, A. C., & SOFRONIEW, M. V. (1984). The anatomy of the CNS cholinergic neurons. *Trends in Neurosciences, 7*, 74–78. **95**

CURTIS, D. R., & ECCLES, J. C. (1959). The time courses of excitatory and inhibitory synaptic actions. *Journal of Physiology, 145*, 529–546. **100**

CYNADER, M. (1983). Prolonged sensitivity to monocular deprivation in dark-reared cats: Effects of age and visual experience. *Developmental Brain Research, 8*, 155–164. **415**

CYNADER, M., BERMAN, N., & HEIN, A. (1976). Recovery of function in cat visual cortex following prolonged deprivation. *Experimental Brain Research, 25*,

139–156. **415**

CYNADER, M., & CHERNENKO, G. (1976). Abolition of direction selectivity in the visual cortex of the cat. *Science, 193*, 504–505. **429**

CYNADER, M., LEPORÉ, F., & GUILLEMOT, J.-P. (1981). Inter-hemispheric competition during postnatal development. *Nature, 290*, 139–140. **433**

CYNADER, M., & MITCHELL, D. E. (1977). Monocular astigmatism effects on kitten visual cortex development. *Nature, 270*, 177–178. **429**

CYNADER, M., & REGAN, D. (1978). Neurones in cat parastriate cortex sensitive to the direction of motion in three-dimensional space. *Journal of Physiology, 274*, 549–569. **214**

DACHEUX, R. F., & MILLER, R. F. (1976). Photoreceptor-bipolar cell transmission in the perfused retina eyecup of the mudpuppy. *Science, 191*, 963–964.

DALLOS, P. (1981). Cochlear physiology. *Annual Review of Psychology, 32*, 153–190. **138, 147, 153**

DALLOS, P., & HARRIS, D. (1978). Properties of auditory nerve responses in absence of outer hair cells. *Journal of Neurophysiology, 41*, 365–383. **167**

DALLOS, P., SANTOS-SACCHI, J., & FLOCK, A. (1982). Intracellular recordings from cochlear outer hair cells. *Science, 218*, 582–584. **153**

DAMASIO, A. R. (1985). Prosopagnosia. *Trends in Neurosciences, 8*, 132–135. **217**

DANILOFF, J. K., BODONY, R. P., LOW, W. C., & WELLS, J. (1985). Cross-species embryonic septal transplants: Restoration of conditioned learning behavior. *Brain Research, 346*, 176–180. **437**

DARIAN-SMITH, I., SUGITANI, M., HEYWOOD, J., KARITA, K., & GOODWIN, A. (1982). Touching textured surfaces: Cells in somatosensory cortex respond both to finger movement and to surface features. *Science, 218*, 906–909. **171**

DARK, K. A., ELLMAN, G., PEEKE, H. V. S., GALIN, D., & REUS, V. I. (1984). Sex differences and symmetries of catecholamines: Relation to turning preferences. *Pharmacology, Biochemistry & Behavior, 20*, 327–330. **302**

DASTOLI, F. R., LOPIEKES, D. V., & DOIG, A. R. (1968). Bitter-sensitive protein from porcine taste buds. *Nature, 218*, 884–885. **151**

DASTOLI, F. R., & PRICE, S. (1966). Sweet-sensitive protein from bovine taste buds: Isolation and assay. *Science, 154*, 905–907. **151**

DAVIDSON, E. H., & BRITTEN, R. J. (1979). Regulation of gene expression: Possible role of repetitive sequences. *Science, 204*, 1052–1059. **113, 119, 126**

DAVIDSON, N. (1976). *Neurotransmitter amino acids*. New York: Academic Press. **98**

DAVIS, H. (1965). A model for transducer action in the cochlea. *Cold Spring Harbor Symposia, 30*, 181–190. **153**

DAVIS, H. P., & SQUIRE, L. R. (1984). Protein synthesis and memory: A review. *Psychological Bulletin, 96*, 518–559. **364, 365, 370, 372**

DAVIS, K. L., & YAMAMURA, H. I. (1978). Cholinergic underactivity in human memory disorders. *Life Sciences, 23*, 1729–1734. **376**

DAVIS, P. G., CHAPTAL, C. V., & MCEWEN, B. S. (1979). Independence of the differentiation of masculine and feminine sexual behavior in rats. *Hormones and Behavior, 12*, 12–19.

DAW, N. W. (1973). Neurophysiology of color vision.

Physiological Reviews, 53, 571–611. **203**

DAW, N. W., BERMAN, N. E. J., & ARIEL, M. (1978). Interaction of critical periods in the visual cortex of kittens. *Science, 199,* 565–567. **429, 430**

DE CEBALLOS, M. L., GUISADO, E., SANCHEZ-BLAZQUEZ, J., GARZON, J., & DEL RIO, J. (1983). Long-term social isolation in the rat induces opposite changes in binding to alpha₁- and alpha₂-adrenoreceptors in the brain and vas deferens. *Neuroscience Letters, 39,* 217–222. **332**

DE JONGE, F. H., & VAN DE POLL, N. E. (1984). Relationships between sexual and aggressive behavior in male and female rats: Effects of gonadal hormones. In G. J. De Vries, J. P. C. De Bruin, B. M. Uylings, & M. A. Corner (Eds.), *Sex differences in the brain.* New York: Elsevier. **293**

DE LACOSTE-UTAMSING, C., & HOLLOWAY, R. L. (1982). Sexual dimorphism in the human corpus callosum. *Science, 216,* 1431–1432. **302**

DE MONTIGNY, C. (1984). Electroconvulsive shock treatments enhance responsiveness of forebrain neurons to serotonin. *Journal of Pharmacology and Experimental Therapeutics, 228,* 230–234. **348**

DE MONTIGNY, C., & AGHAJANIAN, G. K. (1978). Tricyclic antidepressants: Long-term treatment increases responsivity of rat forebrain neurons to serotonin. *Science, 202,* 1303–1306. **348**

DE MONTIGNY, C., BLIER, P., & CHAPUT, Y. (1984). Electrophysiologically-identified receptors in the rat CNS. *Neuropharmacology, 23,* 1511–1520.

DE PEYER, J. E., CACHELIN, A. B., LEVITAN, I. B., & REUTER, H. (1982). Ca⁺⁺-activated K⁺ conductance in internally perfused snail neurons is enhanced by protein phosphorylation. *Proceedings of the National Academy of Sciences, U.S.A., 79,* 4207–4211. **88, 89**

DE TOLEDO-MORRELL, L., HOEPPNER, T. J., & MORRELL, F. (1979). Conditioned inhibition: Selective response of single units. *Science, 204,* 528–530. **383**

DE VALOIS, K. K., DE VALOIS, R. L., & YUND, E. W. (1979). Responses of striate cortex cells to grating and checkerboard patterns. *Journal of Physiology, 291,* 483–505. **214**

DE VALOIS, R. L., & ABRAMOV, I. (1966). Color vision. *Annual Review of Psychology, 17,* 337–361. **186**

DE VALOIS, R. L., & DE VALOIS, K. K. (1980). Spatial vision. *Annual Review of Psychology, 31,* 309–341. **206, 212**

DE VRIES, D. J., BEST, W., & SLUITER, A. A. (1983). The influence of androgens on the development of a sex difference in the vasopressinergic innervation of the rat lateral septum. *Developmental Brain Research, 8,* 377–380. **301**

DE VRIES, G. J., BUIJS, R. M., & SLUITER, A. A. (1984). Gonadal hormone actions on the morphology of the vasopressinergic innervation of the adult rat brain. *Brain Research, 298,* 141–145. **307**

DE VRIES, G. J., BUIJS, R. M., & SWAAB, D. F. (1981). Ontogeny of the vasopressinergic neurons of the suprachiasmatic nucleus and their extrahypothalamic projections in the rat brain—presence of a sex difference in the lateral septum. *Brain Research, 218,* 67–78. **301**

DE WEER, P. (1975). Aspects of the recovery process in nerve. In C. C. Hunt (Ed.), *Neurophysiology* (pp. 231–278). Baltimore: University Park Press. **89**

DE WIED, D., BOHUS, B., GISPEN, W. H., URBAN, I., & VAN WIMERSMA GREIDANUS, Tj. (1976). Hormonal influences on motivational, learning, and memory processes. In E. J. Sachar (Ed.), *Hormones, behavior and psychopathology.* New York: Raven. **358**

DEADWYLER, S. A., WEST, M. O., & ROBINSON, J. H. (1981). Entorhinal and septal inputs differentially control sensory-evoked responses in the rat dentate gyrus. *Science, 211,* 1181–1183. **384**

DEBOLD, J. F. (1978). Modification of nuclear retention of [³H]estradiol by cells of the hypothalamus as a function of early hormone experience. *Brain Research, 159,* 416–420. **282**

DEECKE, L., SCHEID, P., & KORNHUBER, H. H. (1969). Distribution of readiness potential, pre-motion positivity, and motor potential of the human cerebral cortex preceding voluntary finger movement. *Experimental Brain Research, 7,* 158–168. **444**

DEFRIES, J. C., GERVAIS, M. C., & THOMAS, E. A. (1978). Response to 30 generations of selection for open-field activity in laboratory mice. *Behavior Genetics, 8,* 3–13. **326**

DEFRIES, J. C., & PLOMIN, R. (1978). Behavioral genetics. *Annual Review of Psychology, 29,* 473–515. **115**

DEKOSKY, S. T., & BASS, N. H. (1982). Aging, senile dementia, and the intralaminar microchemistry of cerebral cortex. *Neurology, 32,* 1227–1233. **431, 432**

DELLA-FERA, M. A., BAILE, C. A., SCHNEIDER, B. S., & GRINKER, J. A. (1981). Cholecystokinin antibody injected in cerebral ventricles stimulates feeding in sheep. *Science, 212,* 687–689. **252**

DELONG, M. R. (1974). Motor functions of the basal ganglia: Single-unit activity during movement. In F. O. Schmitt & F. G. Worden (Eds.), *The neurosciences: Third study program.* Cambridge, MA: MIT Press. **34**

DEMAREST, K. T., MCKAY, D. W., RIEGLE, G. C., & MOORE, K. E. (1981). Sexual differences in tuberoinfundibular dopamine nerve activity induced by neonatal androgen exposure. *Neuroendocrinology, 32,* 108–113. **280, 298**

DENENBERG, V. H., & ROSEN, G. D. (1983). Interhemispheric coupling coefficients: Sex differences in brain neurochemistry. *American Journal of Physiology, 245,* R151–R153. **301**

DENNIS, S. G., & MELZACK, R. (1977). Pain-signalling systems in the dorsal and ventral spinal cord. *Pain, 4,* 97–132. **156, 175**

DEPUE, R. A., & MONROE, S. M. (1978). The unipolar–bipolar distinction in the depressive disorders. *Psychological Bulletin, 85,* 1001–1029. **329**

DESMEDT, J. E., & ROBERTSON, D. (1975). Ionic mechanism of the efferent olivo-cochlear inhibition studied by cochlear perfusion in the cat. *Journal of Physiology, 247,* 407–428. **175**

DESMOND, J. E., & MOORE, J. W. (1982). A brain stem region essential for the classically conditioned but not unconditioned nictitating membrane response. *Physiology & Behavior, 28,* 1029–1033. **392**

DESMOND, N. L., & LEVY, W. B. (1983). Synaptic correlates of associative potentiation/depression: An ultrastructural study in the hippocampus. *Brain Research, 265,* 21–30. **396**

DESMOND, N. L., & LEVY, W. B. (1986a). Changes in the numerical density of synaptic contacts with long-term potentiation in the hippocampal dentate gyrus. *Journal of Comparative Neurology, 253,* 466–475. **396**

DESMOND, N. L., & LEVY, W. B. (1986b). Changes in the postsynaptic density with long-term potentiation in the dentate gyrus. *Journal of Comparative Neurol-*ogy, *253,* 476–482. **396**

DETERRE, P., PAUPARDIN-TRITSCH, D., BOCKAERT, J., & GERSCHENFELD, H. M. (1981). Role of cyclic AMP in a serotonin-evoked slow inward current in snail neurones. *Nature, 290,* 783–785. **87, 88**

DETWILER, P. B., HODGKIN, A. L., & MCNAUGHTON, P. A. (1978). A surprising property of electrical spread in the network of rods in the turtle's retina. *Nature, 274,* 562–565. **185**

DEUTCH, A. Y., & MARTIN, R. J. (1983). Mesencephalic dopamine modulation of pituitary and central beta-endorphin: Relation to food intake regulation. *Life Sciences, 33,* 281–287. **252**

DEUTSCH, J. A. (1971). The cholinergic synapse and the site of memory. *Science, 174,* 788–794. **375**

DEVIETTI, T. L., & KIRKPATRICK, B. R. (1976). The amnesia gradient: Inadequate as evidence for a memory consolidation process. *Science, 194,* 438–440. **372**

DEVIVO, M., & MAAYANI, S. (1985). Inhibition of forskolin-stimulated adenylate cyclase activity by 5-HT receptor agonists. *European Journal of Pharmacology, 119,* 231–234.

DEVOR, M. (1975). Neuroplasticity in the sparing or deterioration of function after early olfactory tract lesions. *Science, 190,* 998–1000. **433**

DEWSON, J. H. (1968). Efferent olivocochlear bundle: Some relationships to stimulus discrimination in noise. *Journal of Neurophysiology, 31,* 122–130. **175**

DI PAOLO, T., BÉDARD, P. J., DUPONT, A., POYET, P., & LABRIE, F. (1982). Effects of estradiol on intact and denervated striatal dopamine receptors and on dopamine levels: A biochemical and behavioral study. *Canadian Journal of Physiology and Pharmacology, 60,* 350–357. **309**

DI PAOLO, T., DAIGLE, M., PICARD, V., & BARDEN, N. (1983). Effect of acute and chronic ¹⁷beta-estradiol treatment on serotonin and 5-hydroxyindole acetic acid content of discrete brain nuclei of ovariectomized rat. *Experimental Brain Research, 51,* 73–76. **309**

DI PAOLO, T., POYET, P., & LABRIE, F. (1982). Prolactin and estradiol increase striatal dopamine receptor density in intact, castrated and hypophysectomized rats. *Progress in Neuro-Psychopharmacology & Biological Psychiatry, 6,* 377–382. **309**

DIAMOND, D. M., & WEINBERGER, N. M. (1984). Physiological plasticity of single neurons in auditory cortex of the cat during acquisition of the pupillary conditioned response: II. Secondary field (AII). *Behavioral Neuroscience, 98,* 189–210. **226**

DIAMOND, M. (1984, November). A love affair with the brain. *Psychology Today,* pp. 62–73. **301**

DIAMOND, M. C., CONNOR, J. R., JR., ORENBERG, E. K., BISSELL, M., YOST, M., & KRUEGER, A. (1980). Environmental influences on serotonin and cyclic nucleotides in rat cerebral cortex. *Science, 210,* 652–654.

DIAMOND, M. C., DOWLING, G. A., & JOHNSON, R. E. (1981). Morphologic cerebral cortical asymmetry in male and female rats. *Experimental Neurology, 71,* 261–268. **301**

DIAMOND, M. C., MURPHY, G. M., JR., AKIYAMA, K., & JOHNSON, R. E. (1982). Morphologic hippocampal asymmetry in male and female rats. *Experimental Neurology, 76,* 553–565. **302**

DIAMOND, M. C., SCHEIBEL, A. B., MURPHY, G. M., JR., & HARVEY, T. (1985). On the brain of a scientist: Albert Einstein. *Experimental Neurology, 88*, 198–204. **404**

DIMITRIEVA, N., GOZZO, S., DIMITRIEV, Y., & AMMASSARI-TEULE, M. (1984). Mossy fiber distribution in four lines of rats: A correlative study with avoidance abilities and excitability thresholds. *Physiological Psychology, 12*, 30–34. **381**

DISTERHOFT, J. F., & SEGAL, M. (1978). Neuron activity in rat hippocampus and motor cortex during discrimination reversal. *Brain Research Bulletin, 3*, 583–588. **387, 388**

DOBELLE, W. H., MLADEJOVSKY, M. G., STENSAAS, S. S., & SMITH, J. B. (1973). A prosthesis for the deaf based on cortical stimulation. *Annals of Otolaryngology, 82*, 445–463. **165**

DOCKRAY, G. J. (1982). The physiology of cholecystokinin in brain and gut. *British Medical Bulletin, 38*, 253–258.

DOETSCH, G. S., & ERICKSON, R. P. (1970). Synaptic processing of taste-quality information in the nucleus tractus solitaris of the rat. *Journal of Neurophysiology, 33*, 490–507. **160, 161, 172, 173**

DOHANICH, G. P., BARR, P. J., WITCHER, J. A., & CLEMENS, L. G. (1984). Pharmacological and anatomical aspects of cholinergic activation of female sexual behavior. *Physiology & Behavior, 32*, 1021–1026. **298, 310**

DOHANICH, G. P., WITCHER, J. A., WEAVER, D. R., & CLEMENS, L. G. (1982). Alteration of muscarinic binding in specific brain areas following estrogen treatment. *Brain Research, 241*, 347–350. **298**

DÖHLER, K.-D. (1986). The special case of hormonal imprinting, the neonatal influence of sex. *Experientia, 42*, 759–769. **276**

DÖHLER, K.-D., COQUELIN, A., DAVIS, F., HINES, M., SHRYNE, J. E., & GORSKI, R. A. (1982). Differentiation of the sexually dimorphic nucleus in the preoptic area of the rat brain is determined by the perinatal hormone environment. *Neuroscience Letters, 33*, 295–298. **300**

DÖHLER, K.-D., COQUELIN, A., DAVIS, F., HINES, M., SHRYNE, J. E., & GORSKI, R. A. (1984). Pre- and postnatal influence of testosterone propinate and diethylstilbestrol on differentiation of the sexually dimorphic nucleus of the preoptic area in male and female rats. *Brain Research, 302*, 291–295. **300, 303**

DÖHLER, K.-D., HINES, M., COQUELIN, A., DAVIS, F., SHRYNE, J. E., & GORSKI, R. A. (1982). Pre- and postnatal influence of diethylstilboestrol on differentiation of the sexually dimorphic nucleus of the preoptic area of the female rat brain. *Neuroendocrinology Letters, 4*, 361–365. **300**

DÖHLER, K.-D., & WUTTKE, W. (1975). Changes with age in levels of serum gonadotropins, prolactin, and gonadal steroids in prepubertal male and female rats. *Endocrinology, 97*, 898–907. **272**

DOLPHIN, A. C., & GREENGARD, P. (1981). Serotonin stimulates phosphorylation of Protein I in the facial motor nucleus of rat brain. *Nature, 289*, 76–79. **88**

DONOVICK, P. J., BURRIGHT, R. G., & BEN-GELLOUN, W. A. (1979). The septal region and behavior: An example of the importance of genetic and experiential factors in determining effects of brain damage. *Neuroscience & Biobehavioral Reviews, 3*, 83–96. **12**

DORUS, E., PANDEY, G. N., SHAUGHNESSY, R., GAVIRIA, M., VAL, E., ERICKSEN, S., & DAVIS,

J. M. (1979). Lithium transport across red cell membrane: A cell membrane abnormality in manic-depressive illness. *Science, 205*, 932–934. **341**

DORUS, E., PANDEY, G. N., SHAUGHNESSY, R., & DAVIS, J. M. (1979). Low platelet monoamine oxidase activity, high red blood cell lithium ratio, and affective disorders: A multivariate assessment of genetic vulnerability to affective disorders. *Biological Psychiatry, 14*, 989–993. **349**

DOTY, R. W. (1969). Electrical stimulation of the brain in behavioral context. *Annual Review of Psychology, 20*, 289–230. **393, 445**

DOUGHTY, C., & MCDONALD, P. G. (1974). Hormonal control of sexual differentiation of the hypothalamus in the neonatal female rat. *Differentiation, 2*, 275–285. **276**

DOURISH, C. T., DAVIS, B. A., DYCK, L. E., JONES, R. S. G., & BOULTON, A. A. (1982). Alterations in trace amine and trace acid concentrations in isolated aggressive mice. *Pharmacology, Biochemistry & Behavior, 17*, 1291–1294. **332**

DOW, B. M., & GOURAS, P. (1973). Color and spatial specificity of single units in rhesus monkey foveal striate cortex. *Journal of Neurophysiology, 36*, 79–100. **207**

DOWLING, J. E. (1967a). The site of visual adaptation. *Science, 155*, 273–279. **219**

DOWLING, J. E. (1967b). Visual adaptation: Its mechanism. *Science, 157*, 584–585. **219**

DOWLING, J. E. (1977). Receptoral and network mechanisms of visual adaptation. *Neurosciences Research Program Bulletin, 15*, 1–12.

DOWLING, J. E., & BOYCOTT, B. B. (1966). Organization of the primate retina: Electron microscopy. *Proceedings of the Royal Society of London, Series B, 166*, 80–111. **183**

DOWLING, J. E., & EHINGER, B. (1975). Synaptic organization of the amine-containing interplexiform cells of the goldfish and cebus monkey retina. *Science, 188*, 270–273. **184**

DRAVNIEKS, A. (1982). Odor quality: Semantically generated multidimensional profiles are stable. *Science, 218*, 799–801. **139**

DRISCOLL, P., MARTIN, J. R., KUGLER, P., & BAETTIG, K. (1983). Environmental and genetic effects on food-deprivation induced stomach lesions in male rats. *Physiology & Behavior, 31*, 225–228. **327**

DRU, D., WALKER, J. P., & WALKER, J. B. (1975). Self-produced locomotion restores visual capacity after striate lesions. *Science, 187*, 265–266. **434**

DUBOIS, J. M. (1983). Potassium currents in the frog node of Ranvier. *Progress in Biophysics and Molecular Biology, 42*, 1–20. **60**

DUBOVSKY, S. L., & FRANKS, R. D. (1983). Intracellular calcium ions in affective disorders: A review and an hypothesis. *Biological Psychiatry, 18*, 781–797. **349**

DUCHAMP, A. (1982). Electrophysiological responses of olfactory bulb neurons to odour stimuli in the frog. A comparison with receptor cells. *Chemical Senses, 7*, 191–210. **160, 161, 168, 170**

DUDLEY, S. D. (1981). Prepubertal ontogeny of responsiveness to estradiol in female rat central nervous system. *Neuroscience & Biobehavioral Reviews, 5*, 421–435. **282**

DUFY, B., VINCENT, J.-D., FLEURY, H., DU PASQUIER, P., GOURDJI, D., & TIXIER-VIDAL, A. (1979). Membrane effects of thyrotropin-releasing hor-

mone and estrogen shown by intracellular recording from pituitary cells. *Science, 204*, 509–511. **279**

DUM, J., GRAMSCH, Ch., & HERZ, A. (1983). Activation of hypothalamic B-endorphin pools by reward induced by highly palatable food. *Pharmacology, Biochemistry & Behavior, 18*, 443–447.

DUN, N., & KARCZMAR, A. G. (1977). The presynaptic site of action of norepinephrine in the superior cervical ganglion of guinea pig. *Journal of Pharmacology and Experimental Therapeutics, 200*, 328–335. **107**

DUNANT, Y., & ISRAËL, M. (1985). The release of acetylcholine. *Scientific American, 252*, 58–66. **74**

DUNCAN, C. P. (1949). The retroactive effect of electroshock on learning. *Journal of Comparative and Physiological Psychology, 42*, 32–44. **368**

DUNLAP, J. L., GERALL, A. A., & CARLTON, S. F. (1978). Evaluation of prenatal androgen and ovarian secretions on receptivity in female and male rats. *Journal of Comparative and Physiological Psychology, 92*, 280–288. **277**

DUNN, A. J. (1980). Neurochemistry of learning and memory: An evaluation of recent data. *Annual Review of Psychology, 31*, 343–390. **370, 372, 373, 375, 377**

DUNNETT, S. B., LOW, W. C., IVERSEN, S. D., STENEVI, U., & BJÖRKLUND, A. (1982). Septal transplants restore maze learning in rats with fornix-fimbria lesions. *Brain Research, 251*, 335–348. **437**

DUNNETT, S. B., WHISHAW, I. Q., JONES, G. H., & ISACSON, O. (1986). Effects of dopamine-rich grafts on conditioned rotation in rats with unilateral 6-hydroxydopamine lesions. *Neuroscience Letters, 68*, 127–133. **438**

DÜRSTELER, M. R., & VAN DER HEYDT, R. (1983). Plasticity in the binocular correspondence of striate cortical receptive fields in kittens. *Journal of Physiology, 345*, 87–105. **424**

DVORAK, C. A., GRANDA, A. M., & MAXWELL, J. H. (1980). Photoreceptor signals at visual threshold. *Nature, 283*, 860–861. **194**

DYBALL, R. E. J., & POUNTNEY, P. S. (1973). Discharge patterns of supraoptic and paraventricular neurones in rats given a 2% NaCl solution instead of drinking water. *Journal of Endocrinology, 56*, 91–98. **254**

DYCK, P. J., MELLINGER, J. F., REAGAN, T. J., HOROWITZ, S. J., MCDONALD, J. W., LITCHY, W. J., DAUBE, J. R., FEALEY, R. D., GO, V. L., KAO, P. C., BRIMIJOIN, W. S., & LAMBERT, E. H. (1983). Not "indifference to pain" but varieties of hereditary sensory and autonomic neuropathy. *Brain, 106*, 373–390. **168**

DYER, R. G., MACLEOD, N. K., & ELLENDORFF, F. (1976). Electrophysiological evidence for sexual dimorphism and synaptic convergence in the preoptic and anterior hypothalamic areas of the rat. *Proceedings of the Royal Society of London, Series B, 193*, 421–440. **304**

DYER, R. G., PRITCHETT, C. J., & CROSS, B. A. (1972). Unit activity in the diencephalon of female rats during the oestrous cycle. *Journal of Endocrinology, 53*, 151–160. **312**

DZENDOLET, R., & MEISELMAN, H. L. (1967). Gustatory quality changes as a function of solution concentration. *Perception & Psychophysics, 2*, 29–33. **172**

EARLY, C. J., & LEONARD, B. E. (1977). The effects of testosterone and cyproterone acetate on the concentration of gamma-aminobutyric acid in brain areas of aggressive and nonaggressive mice. *Pharmacology, Biochemistry & Behavior, 6*, 409–413. **340**

EARLY, C. J., & LEONARD, B. E. (1978). GABA and gonadal hormones. *Brain Research, 155,* 27–34. **340**

ECCLES, J. C. (1953). *The neurophysiological basis of mind: The principles of neurophysiology.* Oxford: Clarendon Press. **3**

ECCLES, J. C. (1966). The ionic mechanisms of excitatory and inhibitory synaptic action. *Annals of the New York Academy of Sciences, 137,* 473–495. **80**

ECCLES, J. C. (1977). *The understanding of the brain* (2nd ed.). New York: McGraw-Hill. (Original work published 1973) **53, 70, 73, 78, 80, 100, 101, 104**

ECCLES, J. C. (Ed.). (1982). *Mind and brain: The many-faceted problems.* Washington, DC: Paragon House. **32, 444, 448**

ECCLES, J. C., FATT, P., & KOKETSU, K. (1954). Cholinergic and inhibitory synapses in a pathway from motor-axon collaterals to motoneuron. *Journal of Physiology, 126,* 524–562. **101**

ECKERT, M., & SCHMIDT, U. (1985). The influence of permanent odor stimuli on the postnatal development of neural activity in the olfactory bulbs of laboratory mice. *Developmental Brain Research, 20,* 185–190. **410**

EDWARDS, C. (1982). The selectivity of ion channels in nerve and muscle. *Neuroscience, 7,* 1335–1366. **49, 51, 61**

EDWARDS, D. J., SPIKER, D. G., KUPFER, D. J., FOSTER, G., NEIL, J. F., & ABRAMS, L. (1978). Platelet monoamine oxidase in affective disorders. *Archives of General Psychiatry, 35,* 1443–1446. **341**

EGOZI, Y., KLOOG, Y., & SOKOLOVSKY, M. (1986). Acetylcholine rhythm in the preoptic area of the rat hypothalamus is synchronized with the estrous cycle. *Brain Research, 383,* 310–313. **310**

EHRENSTEIN, G., & GILBERT, D. L. (1966). Slow changes of potassium permeability in the squid giant axon. *Biophysical Journal, 6,* 553–566. **61**

EHRHARDT, A. A. (1979). Psychosexual adjustment in adolescence in patients with congenital abnormalities of their sex organs. In H. L. Vallet & I. H. Porter (Eds.), *Genetic mechanisms of sexual development.* New York: Academic Press. **288, 291**

EHRHARDT, A. A., & MEYER-BAHLBURG, F. L. (1981). Effects of prenatal sex hormones on gender-related behavior. *Science, 211,* 1312–1318. **291**

EINON, D. (1980). Spatial memory and response strategies in rats: Age, sex and rearing differences in performance. *Quarterly Journal of Experimental Psychology, 32,* 473–489. **402, 407**

EISENSTEIN, E. M., ALTMAN, H. J., BARRACO, D. A., BARRACO, R. A., & LOVELL, K. L. (1983). Brain protein synthesis and memory: The use of antibiotic probes. *Federation Proceedings, 42,* 3080–3085. **372**

EKMAN, P., LEVENSON, R. W., & FRIESEN, W. V. (1983). Autonomic nervous system activity distinguishes among emotions. *Science, 221,* 1208–1210. **323**

EKMAN, P., & OSTER, H. (1979). Facial expressions of emotion. *Annual Review of Psychology, 30,* 527–554. **323**

ELBERGER, A. J., SMITH, E. L., III, & WHITE, J. M. (1983). Spatial dissociation of visual inputs alters the origin of the corpus callosum. *Neuroscience Letters, 35,* 19–24. **433**

ELIAS, M. (1981). Serum cortisol, testosterone, and testosterone-binding globulin responses to competitive fighting in human males. *Aggressive Behavior, 7,* 215–224. **292**

ELLIS, M. E. (1985). Amygdala norepinephrine involved in two separate long-term memory retrieval processes. *Brain Research, 342,* 191–195. **374**

ELLISON, G. D. (1977). Animal models of psychopathology: The low-norepinephrine and low-serotonin rat. *American Psychologist, 32,* 1036–1045. **248, 339**

EMMERS, R. (1969). Modulation of the activity of hypothalamic "feeding neurons" by stimulation of the gustatory nucleus of the cat thalamus. *The Physiologist, 12,* 215. **256, 260**

EMMETT-OGLESBY, M. W., LEWY, A. J., ALBERT, L. H., & SEIDEN, L. S. (1978). Role of lever responding and water presentation in altering rat brain catecholamine metabolism. *Journal of Pharmacology and Experimental Therapeutics, 204,* 406–415. **250, 332**

EMSON, P. C., LEE, C. M., & REHFELD, J. F. (1980). Cholecystokinin octapeptide: Vesicular localization and calcium dependent release from rat brain in vitro. *Life Sciences, 26,* 2157–2163.

ENDERSBY, C. A., & WILSON, C. A. (1974). The effect of ovarian steroids on the accumulation of ³H-labelled monoamines by hypothalamic tissue in vitro. *Brain Research, 73,* 321–331. **309**

ENGEL, J., AHLENIUS, S., ALMGREN, O., CARLSSON, A., LARSSON, K., & SÖDERSTEN, P. (1979). Effects of gonadectomy and hormone replacement on brain monoamine synthesis in male rats. *Pharmacology, Biochemistry & Behavior, 10,* 149–154. **309**

ENGELLENNER, W. J., GOODLETT, C. R., BURRIGHT, R. G., & DONOVICK, P. J. (1982). Environmental enrichment and restriction: Effects on reactivity, exploration and maze learning in mice with septal lesions. *Physiology & Behavior, 29,* 885–893. **12, 403**

ENGSTRÖM, B. (1983). Stereocilia of sensory cells in normal and hearing impaired ears. *Scandinavian Audiology,* Supplement 19.

ENROTH-CUGELL, C., & ROBSON, J. G. (1966). The contrast sensitivity of retinal ganglion cells of the cat. *Journal of Physiology, 187,* 517–552. **212**

EPSTEIN, A. N. (1982). The physiology of thirst. In D. W. Pfaff (Ed.), *The physiological mechanisms of motivation.* New York: Springer-Verlag. **249, 254**

ERICKSON, R. P. (1984). On the neural bases of behavior. *American Scientist, 72,* 233–241. **449**

ERICKSON, R. P., DOETSCH, G. S., & MARSHALL, D. A. (1965). The gustatory neural response function. *Journal of General Physiology, 49,* 247–263.

ERULKAR, S. C. (1972). Comparative aspects of spatial localization of sound. *Physiological Reviews, 52,* 237–360. **160, 163, 170–172**

ETGEN, A. M. (1981). Estrogen induction of progestin receptors in the hypothalamus of male and female rats which differ in their ability to exhibit cyclic gonadotropic secretion and female sexual behavior. *Biology of Reproduction, 25,* 307–313. **285**

ETGEN, A. M. (1984). Progestin receptors and the activation of female reproductive behavior: A critical review. *Hormones and Behavior, 18,* 411–430. **278, 291**

ETGEN, A. M. (1985). Effects of body weight, adrenal status, and estrogen priming on hypothalamic progestin receptors in male and female rats. *Journal of Neuroscience, 5,* 2439–2442. **285**

EUVRARD, C., LABRIE, F., & BOISSIER, J. R. (1979). Effect of estrogen on changes in the activity of striatal cholinergic neurons induced by DA drugs. *Brain Research, 169,* 215–220. **310**

EVANS, E. F., & WILSON, J. P. (1975). Cochlear tuning properties: Concurrent basilar membrane and single nerve fiber measurements. *Science, 190,* 1218–1221. **166**

EVARTS, E. V. (1966). Pyramidal tract activity associated with a conditioned hand movement in the monkey. *Journal of Neurophysiology, 29,* 1011–1027. **35**

EVARTS, E. V. (1967). Unit activity in sleep and wakefulness. In G. C. Quarton, T. Melnechuk, & F. O. Schmitt (Eds.), *The neurosciences: A study program.* New York: Rockefeller University Press. **241**

EVARTS, E. V. (1985, May). *Single cells and higher brain function.* Paper presented at the meeting of the Midwestern Psychological Association, Chicago. **93**

EVARTS, E. V., KIMURA, M., WURTZ, R. H., & HIKOSAKA, O. (1984). Behavioral correlates of activity in basal ganglia neurons. *Trends in NeuroSciences, 7,* 447–453. **34**

EVERITT, B. J., FUXE, K., HÖKFELT, T., & JONSSON, G. (1975). Role of monoamines in the control by hormones of sexual receptivity in the female rat. *Journal of Comparative and Physiological Psychology, 89,* 556–572. **310**

FABER, D. S., & KORN, H. (1982). Transmission at a central inhibitory synapse: I. Magnitude of unitary postsynaptic conductance change and kinetics of channel activation. *Journal of Neurophysiology, 48,* 654–678. **70, 73, 83, 84**

FADDA, F., ARGIOLAS, A., MELIS, M. R., TISSARI, A. H., ONALI, P. L., & GESSA, G. L. (1978). Stress-induced increase in 3,4-dihydrophenylacetic acid (DOPAC) levels in the cerebral cortex and in N. Accumbens: Reversal by diazepam. *Life Sciences, 23,* 2219–24. **344**

FAGAN, R. M. (1981). *Animal play behavior.* New York: Oxford University Press. **402**

FAIN, G. L. (1975a). Interactions of rod and cone signals in the mudpuppy retina. *Journal of Physiology, 252,* 735–769.

FAIN, G. L. (1975b). Quantum sensitivity of rods in the toad retina. *Science, 187,* 838–841. **194, 195**

FAIN, G. L. (1976). Sensitivity of toad rods: Dependence on wave-length and background illumination. *Journal of Physiology, 261,* 71–101. **218**

FAIN, G. L., GRANDA, A. M., & MAXWELL, J. H. (1977). Voltage signal of photoreceptors at visual threshold. *Nature, 265,* 181–183. **194**

FAIN, G. L., QUANDT, F. N., BASTIAN, B. L., & GERSCHENFELD, H. M. (1978). Contribution of a caesium-sensitive conductance increase to the rod photoresponse. *Nature, 272,* 467–469. **194, 218**

FAIN, G. L., QUANDT, F. N., & GERSCHENFELD, H. M. (1977). Calcium-dependent regenerative responses in rods. *Nature, 269,* 707–710. **194**

FAIRBANKS, L. A., & McGUIRE, M. T. (1985). Relationships of vervet mothers with sons and daughters from one through three years of age. *Animal Behaviour, 33,* 40–50. **292**

FANTINO, M. (1984). Role of sensory input in the control of food intake. *Journal of the Autonomic Nervous System, 10,* 347–358.

FATT, P., & KATZ, B. (1952). Spontaneous subthreshold activity at motor nerve endings. *Journal of Physiology, 117,* 109–128. **73**

FAUCHEUX, B. A., BOURLIÈRE, F., BAULON, A., & DUPUIS, C. (1981). The effects of psychosocial stress on urinary excretion of adrenaline and noradrenaline in 50- to 55- and 71- to 74-year-old men. *Gerontology, 27,* 313–325. **324**

FAUST, I. M., JOHNSON, P. R., & HIRSCH, J. (1977). Surgical removal of adipose tissue alters feeding behavior and the development of obesity in rats. *Science, 197,* 393–396. **242**

FAWCETT, J. W., O'LEARY, D. D. M., & COWAN, W. M. (1984). Activity and the control of ganglion cell death in the rat retina. *Proceedings of the National Academy of Sciences, U.S.A., 81,* 5589–5593. **433**

FEENEY, D. M., GONZALEZ, A., & LAW, W. A. (1982). Amphetamine, haloperidol, and experience interact to affect rate of recovery after motor cortex injury. *Science, 217,* 855–857. **434**

FEENEY, D. M., & HOVDA, D. A. (1985). Reinstatement of binocular depth perception by amphetamine and visual experience after visual cortex ablation. *Brain Research, 342,* 352–356. **214, 434**

FEENEY, D. M., & WIER, C. S. (1979). Sensory neglect after lesions of substantia nigra or lateral hypothalamus: Differential severity and recovery of function. *Brain Research, 178,* 329–346. **245, 248**

FEHR, F. S., & STERN, J. A. (1970). Peripheral physiological variations and emotion: The James-Lange theory revisited. *Psychological Bulletin, 74,* 411–424. **323**

FEIGL, H. (1958). The "mental" and the "physical." In H. Feigl, M. Scriven, & G. Maxwell (Eds.), *Minnesota studies in the philosophy of science: Vol II. Concepts, theories, and the mind–body problem* (pp. 370–497). Minneapolis: University of Minnesota Press. **7–9**

FENSTERMACHER, J. D. (1985). Current models of blood–brain transfer. *Trends in NeuroSciences, 8,* 449–453. **30**

FERCHMIN, P. A., BENNETT, E. L., & ROSENZWEIG, M. R. (1975). Direct contact with enriched environment is required to alter cerebral weights in rats. *Journal of Comparative and Physiological Psychology, 88,* 360–367. **401, 402**

FERCHMIN, P. A., & ETEROVIĆ, V. A. (1977). Brain plasticity and environmental complexity: Role of motor skills. *Physiology & Behavior, 18,* 455–461. **403, 405**

FERCHMIN, P. A., ETEROVIĆ, V. A., & LEVIN, L. E. (1980). Genetic learning deficiency does not hinder environment-dependent brain growth. *Physiology & Behavior, 24,* 45–50. **402, 403, 405**

FERGUSON-SEGALL, M., FLYNN, J. J., WALKER, J., & MARGULES, D. L. (1982). Increased immunoreactive dynorphin and leu-enkephalin in posterior pituitary of obese mice *(ob/ob)* and super-sensitivity to drugs that act at kappa receptors. *Life Sciences, 31,* 2233–2236. **254**

FERNSTROM, J. D. (1981). Dietary precursors and brain neurotransmitter formation. *Annual Review of Medicine, 32,* 413–425. **249**

FESENKO, E. E., KOLESNIKOV, S. S., & LYUBARSKY, A. L. (1985). Induction by cyclic GMP of cationic conductance in plasma membrane of retinal rod outer segment. *Nature, 313,* 310–313. **192, 194**

FIALA, B. A., JOYCE, J. N., & GREENOUGH, W. T. (1978). Environmental complexity modulates growth of granule cell dendrites in developing but not adult hippocampus of rats. *Experimental Neurology, 59,* 372–383. **409**

FIELDS, H. L., & HEINRICHER, M. M. (1985). Anatomy and physiology of a nociceptive modulatory sys-

tem. *Philosophical Transactions of the Royal Society of London, Series B, 308,* 361–374. **175**

FIFKOVÁ, E., & VAN HARREVELD, A. (1975). Morphological correlate of long-lasting potentiation of synaptic transmission in the dentate gyrus following stimulation of the entorhinal area. *Anatomical Record, 181,* 355–356.

FIFKOVÁ, E., & VAN HARREVELD, A. (1978). Changes in dendritic spines of the dentate molecular layer during conditioning. *Society for Neuroscience Abstracts, 4,* 257. **388, 396, 406**

FINGER, S., WALBRAN, B., & STEIN, D. G. (1973). Brain damage and behavioral recovery: Serial lesion phenomena. *Brain Research, 63,* 1–18. **433**

FINK, J. S., & REIS, D. J. (1981). Genetic variations in midbrain dopamine cell number: Parallel with differences in responses to dopaminergic agonists and in naturalistic behaviors mediated by central dopaminergic systems. *Brain Research, 222,* 335–349. **130, 329**

FINK, J. S., & SMITH, G. P. (1979a). Decreased locomotor and investigatory exploration after denervation of catecholamine terminal fields in the forebrain of rats. *Journal of Comparative and Physiological Psychology, 93,* 34–65. **329**

FINK, J. S., & SMITH, G. P. (1979b). L-Dopa repairs deficits in locomotor and investigatory exploration produced by denervation of catecholamine terminal fields in the forebrain of rats. *Journal of Comparative and Physiological Psychology, 93,* 66–73. **329**

FINKELSTEIN, J. A., CHANCE, W. T., & FISCHER, J. E. (1982). Brain serotonergic activity and plasma amino acid levels in genetically obese Zucker rats. *Pharmacology, Biochemistry & Behavior, 17,* 939–944. **252**

FINLAY, B. L., SCHILLER, P. H., & VOLMAN, S. F. (1976). Quantitative studies of single-cell properties in monkey striate cortex. IV. Corticotectal cells. *Journal of Neurophysiology, 39,* 1352–1361. **207, 212, 221**

FISCHETTE, C. T., BIEGON, A., & MCEWEN, B. S. (1983). Sex differences in serotonin 1 receptor binding in rat brain. *Science, 222,* 333–335. **309**

FISH, B. (1977). Neurobiologic antecedents of schizophrenia in children. *Archives of General Psychiatry, 34,* 1297–1313. **346**

FITZSIMONS, J. T. (1971). The physiology of thirst: A review of the extraneuronal aspects of the mechanisms of drinking. In E. Stellar & J. M. Sprague (Eds.), *Progress in physiological psychology* (Vol. 4). New York: Academic Press. **249**

FLEXNER, J. B., FLEXNER, L. B., & CHURCH, A. C. (1983). Studies on memory: The cerebral spread of an engram in mice as affected by inhibitors of dopamine beta-hydroxylase. *Pharmacology, Biochemistry & Behavior, 18,* 519–523. **374**

FLEXNER, L. B., CHURCH, A. C., FLEXNER, J. B., & RAINBOW, T. C. (1984). The effect of the beta-adrenergic receptor antagonist, propranolol, on the cerebral spread of a memory trace in mice. *Pharmacology, Biochemistry & Behavior, 21,* 633–639. **372, 374**

FLOCK, A., FLOCK, B., & ULFENDAHL, M. (1986). Mechanisms of movement in outer hair cells and a possible structural basis. *Archives of Otorhinolaryngology, 243,* 83–90. **167**

FLOCK, A., & STRELIOFF, D. (1984). Graded and nonlinear mechanical properties of sensory hairs in the mammalian hearing organ. *Nature, 310,* 597–599. **167**

FLOETER, M. K., & GREENOUGH, W. T. (1979).

Cerebellar plasticity: Modification of Purkinje cell structure by differential rearing in monkeys. *Science, 206,* 227–229. **408**

FLOOD, J. F., SMITH, G. E., & CHERKIN, A. (1984). Memory retention: Effect of prolonged cholinergic stimulation in mice. *Pharmacology, Biochemistry & Behavior, 20,* 161–163. **376**

FLOR-HENRY, P. (1979). On certain aspects of the localization of the cerebral systems regulating and determining emotion. *Biological Psychiatry, 14,* 677–698. **344**

FODOR, J. A. (1981). The mind–body problem. *Scientific American, 224,* 114–123. **7**

FOOTE, S. L., ASTON-JONES, G., & BLOOM, F. E. (1980). Impulse activity of locus coeruleus neurons in awake rats and monkeys is a function of sensory stimulation and arousal. *Proceedings of the National Academy of Sciences, U.S.A., 77,* 3033–3037. **236, 240, 254, 355**

FORD, J. J. (1983). Postnatal differentiation of sexual preference in male pigs. *Hormones and Behavior, 17,* 152–162.

FOREST, M. G., CATHIARD, A. M., & BERTRAND, J. A. (1973). Evidence of testicular activity in early infancy. *Journal of Clinical Endocrinology and Metabolism, 37,* 148–151. **272**

FOSSIER, P., BAUX, G., & TAUC, L. (1983). Possible role of acetylcholinesterase in regulation of postsynaptic receptor efficacy at a central inhibitory synapse of *Aplysia. Nature, 301,* 710–712. **85**

FOURMENT, A., HIRSCH, J. C., CHASTANET, M., & GUIDET, C. (1983). The effect of midbrain reticular stimulation upon perigeniculate neurons' activity during different states of the sleep–waking cycle in the cat. *Brain Research, 259,* 301–307.

FOWLER, C. J., TIPTON, K. F., MACKAY, A. V. P., & YOUDIM, M. B. H. (1982). Human platelet monamine oxidase—a useful enzyme in the study of psychiatric disorders? *Neuroscience, 7,* 1577–1594. **341**

FOY, M. R., CHIAIA, N. L., & TEYLER, T. J. (1984). Reversal of hippocampal sexual dimorphism by gonadal steroid manipulation. *Brain Research, 321,* 311–314. **307**

FOY, M. R., & TEYLER, T. J. (1983). 17-alpha-estradiol and 17-beta-estradiol in hippocampus. *Brain Research Bulletin, 10,* 735–739.

FRAY, P. J., DUNNETT, S. B., IVERSEN, S. E., BJÖRKLUND, A., & STENEVI, U. (1983). Nigral transplants reinnervating the dopamine-depleted neostriatum can sustain intracranial self-stimulation. *Science, 219,* 416–419. **267, 437**

FREEDMAN, R., ADLER, L. E., WALDO, M. C., PACHTMAN, E., & FRANKS, R. D. (1983). Neurophysiological evidence for a defect in inhibitory pathways in schizophrenia: Comparison of medicated and drug-free patients. *Biological Psychiatry, 18,* 537–551. **347**

FREEDMAN, R., & MARWAHA, J. (1980). Effects of acute and chronic amphetamine treatment on Purkinje neuron discharge in rat cerebellum. *Journal of Pharmacology and Experimental Therapeutics, 212,* 390–396. **356**

FREEMAN, R. D., & BRADLEY, A. (1980). Monocularly deprived humans: Nondeprived eye has supernormal vernier acuity. *Journal of Neurophysiology, 43,* 1645–1653. **412, 429**

FREEMAN, R. D., & OLSON, C. (1982). Brief periods of monocular deprivation in kittens: Effects of delay prior to physiological study. *Journal of Neurophysiology, 47,* 139–150. **423**

FREEMAN, R. D., & PETTIGREW, J. D. (1973). Alteration of visual cortex from environmental asymmetries. *Nature*, 246, 359–360. **427**

FRENCH, J. D. (1957). The reticular formation. *Scientific American*, 196, 54–60. **35**

FRIEDLANDER, M. J. (1982). Structure of physiologically classified neurones in the kitten dorsal lateral geniculate nucleus. *Nature*, 300, 180–183.

FRIEDMAN, M. I., & STRICKER, E. M. (1976). The physiological psychology of hunger: A physiological perspective. *Psychological Review*, 83, 409–431. **241**

FROME, F. S., PIANTANIDA, T. P., & KELLY, D. H. (1982). Psychophysical evidence for more than two kinds of cone in dichromatic color blindness. *Science*, 215, 417–419. **204, 205**

FROST, D. O., & METIN, C. (1985). Induction of functional retinal projections to the somatosensory system. *Nature*, 317, 162–164. **415, 433**

FRUMKES, T. E., MILLER, R. F., SLAUGHTER, M., & DACHEUX, R. F. (1981). Physiological and pharmacological basis of GABA and glycine action on neurons of mudpuppy retina: III. Amacrine-mediated inhibitory influences on ganglion cell receptive-field organization: A model. *Journal of Neurophysiology*, 45, 783–804. **198**

FUKUDA, M., ONO, T., NISHINO, H., & SASAKI, K. (1984). Independent glucose effects on rat hypothalamic neurons: An in vitro study. *Journal of the Autonomic Nervous System*, 10, 373–381. **255, 257**

FULLER, J. L., & THOMPSON, W. R. (1978). *Foundations of behavior genetics*. St. Louis: C.V. Mosby. **113, 115, 253, 288, 325–327**

FUORTES, M. G. F., SCHWARTZ, E. A., & SIMON, E. J. (1973). Colour-dependence of cone responses in the turtle retina. *Journal of Physiology*, 234, 199–216. **185**

FUSTER, J. M. (1984). Behavioral electrophysiology of the prefrontal cortex. *Trends in NeuroSciences*, 7, 408–414. **365, 383**

FUSTER, J. M., & JERVEY, J. P. (1982). Neuronal firing in the inferotemporal cortex of the monkey in a visual memory task. *Journal of Neuroscience*, 2, 361–375. **383**

GABRIEL, M., FOSTER, K., & ORONA, E. (1980). Interaction of laminae of the cingulate cortex with the anteroventral thalamus during behavioral learning. *Science*, 208, 1050–1052. **388**

GABRIEL, M., FOSTER, K., ORONA, E., SALTWICK, S. E., & STANTON, M. (1980). Neuronal activity of cingulate cortex, anteroventral thalamus, in hippocampal formation and discriminative conditioning: Encoding and extraction of the significance of conditional stimuli. In J. M. Sprague & A. N. Epstein (Eds.), *Progress in psychobiology and physiological psychology* (Vol. 9). New York: Academic Press. **367, 388**

GAGE, F. H., & BJÖRKLUND, A. (1986). Cholinergic septal grafts into the hippocampal formation improve spatial learning and memory in aged rats by an atropine-sensitive mechanism. *Journal of Neuroscience*, 6, 2837–2847. **438**

GAGE, F. H., BJÖRKLUND, A., & STENEVI, U. (1983). Reinnervation of the partially deafferented hippocampus by compensatory collateral sprouting from spared cholinergic and noradrenergic afferents. *Brain Research*, 268, 27–37. **435**

GAGE, F. H., BJÖRKLUND, A., STENEVI, U., & DUNNETT, S. B. (1983). Functional correlates of compensatory collateral sprouting by aminergic and cholinergic afferents in the hippocampal formation. *Brain Research*, 268, 39–47. **435**

GAGE, F. H., BJÖRKLUND, A., STENEVI, U., DUNNETT, S. B., & KELLY, P. A. T. (1984). Intrahippocampal septal grafts ameliorate learning impairments in aged rats. *Science*, 225, 533–535. **438**

GAGE, F. H., DUNNETT, S. B., STENEVI, U., & BJÖRKLUND, A. (1983). Aged rats: Recovery of motor impairments by intrastriatal nigral grafts. *Science*, 221, 966–969. **436**

GAGE, P. W. (1974). Movements of ions at synapses. *Proceedings of the Australian Physiological and Pharmacological Society*, 5, 18–22. **78, 80**

GAGE, P. W. (1976). Generation of end-plate potentials. *Physiological Review*, 56, 177–247. **78, 80, 85, 91**

GAGE, P. W., & ARMSTRONG, C. M. (1968). Miniature end-plate currents in voltage-clamped muscle fibre. *Nature*, 218, 363–365. **80**

GAITO, J. (1976). Molecular psychobiology of memory: Its appearance, contributions, and decline. *Physiological Psychology*, 4, 476–484. **377, 378**

GALAMBOS, R., & DAVIS, H. (1943). The response of single auditory-nerve fibers to acoustic stimulation. *Journal of Neurophysiology*, 6, 39–58. **163, 168**

GALLISTEL, C. R., SHIZGAL, P., & YEOMANS, J. S. (1981). A portrait of the substrate for self-stimulation. *Psychological Review*, 88, 228–273. **266**

GALLUP, G. G., JR. (1977). Self-recognition in primates: A comparative approach to the bidirectional properties of consciousness. *American Psychologist*, 32, 329–338. **445**

GAMBERT, S. R., GARTHWAITE, T. L., PONTZER, C. H., & HAGEN, T. C. (1980). Fasting associated with decrease in hypothalamic B-endorphin. *Science*, 210, 1271–1272. **248**

GANCHROW, J. R., LIEBLICH, I., & COHEN, E. (1981). Consummatory responses to taste stimuli in rats selected for high and low rates of self-stimulation. *Physiology & Behavior*, 27, 971–976. **253**

GANDELMAN, R. (1983). Gonadal hormones and sensory function. *Neuroscience & Biobehavioral Reviews*, 7, 1–17. **291**

GARDNER, E. B., BOITANO, J. J., MANCINO, N. S., D'AMICO, D. P., & GARDNER, E. L. (1975). Environmental enrichment and deprivation: Effects on learning, memory and exploration. *Physiology & Behavior*, 14, 321–327. **403**

GARTLER, S. M., & RIGGS, A. D. (1983). Mammalian X-chromosome inactivation. *Annual Review of Genetics*, 17, 155–190. **287**

GARVER, D. L., & DAVIS, J. M. (1979). Biogenic amine hypotheses of affective disorders. *Life Sciences*, 24, 383–394. **347, 348**

GASH, D. M., COLLIER, T. J., & SLADEK, J. R., JR. (1985). Neural transplantation: A review of recent developments and potential applications to the aged brain. *Neurobiology of Aging*, 6, 131–150. **431, 438**

GASTON, K. E., & GASTON, M. G. (1984). Unilateral memory after binocular discrimination training: Left hemisphere dominance in the chick? *Brain Research*, 303, 190–193. **20**

GAVISH, M., & SNYDER, S. H. (1981). Gamma-aminobutyric acid and benzodiazepine receptors: Copurification and characterization. *Proceedings of the National Academy of Sciences, U.S.A.*, 78, 1939–1942. **343**

GAZIRI, L. C. J., & LADOSKY, W. (1973). Monoamine oxidase variation during sexual differentiation. *Neuroendocrinology*, 12, 249–256. **296, 298**

GEINISMAN, Y., DE TOLEDO-MORRELL, L., & MORRELL, F. (1986). Aged rats need a preserved complement of perforated axospinous synapses per hippocampal neuron to maintain good spatial memory. *Brain Research*, 398, 266–275. **384, 394**

GEISELMAN, P. J., & NOVIN, D. (1982). The role of carbohydrates in appetite, hunger, and obesity. *Appetite: Journal for Intake Research*, 3, 203–223. **242**

GELENBERG, A. J., WOJCIK, J. D., & GROWDON, J. J. (1979). Lecithin for the treatment of tardive dyskinesia. In A. Barbeau, J. H. Growdon & R. J. Wurtman (Eds.), *Nutrition and the Brain* (Vol. 5). New York: Raven. **97**

GENT, J. F., & BARTOSHUK, L. M. (1983). Sweetness of sucrose, neohesperidin dihydrochalcone, and saccharin is related to genetic ability to taste the bitter substance 6-n-propylthiouracil. *Chemical Senses*, 7, 265–272. **253**

GEORGE, J. S., & HAGINS, W. A. (1983). Control of Ca^{2+} in rod outer segment disks by light and cyclic GMP. *Nature*, 303, 344–348. **194**

GERALL, A. A., DUNLAP, J. L., & HENDRICKS, S. E. (1973). Effect of ovarian secretions on female behavioral potentiality in the rat. *Journal of Comparative and Physiological Psychology*, 82, 449–465. **277**

GETCHELL, T. V. (1977). Analysis of intracellular recordings from salamander olfactory epithelium. *Brain Research*, 123, 275–286. **150, 151**

GETCHELL, T. V. (1986). Functional properties of vertebrate olfactory receptor neurons. *Physiological Reviews*, 66, 772–818. **150, 151, 173**

GETCHELL, T. V., MARGOLIS, F. L., & GETCHELL, M. L. (1984). Perireceptor and receptor events in vertebrate olfaction. *Progress in Neurobiology*, 23, 317–345. **150**

GHEZ, C., & FAHN, S. (1981). The cerebellum. In E. R. Kandel & J. H. Schwartz (Eds.), *Principles of neural science*. New York: Elsevier. **34**

GHRAF, R., MICHEL, M., HIEMKE, C., & KNUPPEN, R. (1983). Competition by monophenolic estrogens and catecholestrogens for high-affinity uptake of [^{3}H](—)-norepinephrine into synaptosomes from rat cerebral cortex and hypothalamus. *Brain Research*, 277, 163–168. **309**

GIBBONS, J. L., BARR, G. A., BRIDGER, W. H., & LEIBOWITZ, S. F. (1979). Manipulations of dietary tryptophan: Effects on mouse killing and brain serotonin in the rat. *Brain Research*, 169, 139–153. **340**

GIBBONS, J. L., BARR, G. A., BRIDGER, W. H., & LEIBOWITZ, S. F. (1981). L-tryptophan's effects on mouse killing, feeding, drinking, locomotion, and brain serotonin. *Pharmacology, Biochemistry & Behavior*, 15, 201–206. **248**

GIBBS, J., FAUSER, D. J., ROWE, E. A., ROLLS, B. J., ROLLS, E. T., & MADDISON, S. P. (1979). Bombesin suppresses feeding in rats. *Nature*, 282, 208–210.

GIBSON, E. J., & WALK, R. D. (1956). The effect of prolonged exposure to visually presented patterns on learning to discriminate them. *Journal of Comparative and Physiological Psychology*, 49, 239–242. **430**

GIBSON, M. J., CHARLTON, H. M., PERLOW, M. J., ZIMMERMAN, E. A., DAVIES, T. F., & KRIEGER, D. T. (1984). Preoptic area brain grafts in hypogonadal (hpg) female mice abolish effects of congenital hypothalamic gonadotropin-releasing hormone (GnRH) deficiency. *Endocrinology*, 114, 1938–1940. **438**

GIBSON, M. J., LIOTTA, A. S., & KRIEGER, D. T. (1981). The Zucker fa/fa rat: Absent circadian corticosterone periodicity and elevated beta-endorphin concentrations in brain and neurointermediate pituitary. *Neuropeptides, 1,* 349–362. **252**

GILAD, G. M., RABEY, J. M., & SHENKMAN, L. (1983). Strain-dependent and stress-induced changes in rat hippocampal cholinergic system. *Brain Research, 267,* 171–174. **107, 335**

GILBERT, C. D., & WIESEL, T. N. (1979). Morphology and intracortical projections of functionally characterized neurones in the cat visual cortex. *Nature, 280,* 120–125.

GILBERT, C. D., & WIESEL, T. N. (1983). Clustered intrinsic connections in cat visual cortex. *Journal of Neuroscience, 3,* 1116–1133.

GILLETTE, R., KOVAC, M. P., & DAVIS, W. J. (1982). Control of feeding motor output by paracerebral neurons in brain of *Pleurobranchaea californica. Journal of Neurophysiology, 47,* 885–908. **229**

GISPEN, W. H., PERUMAL, R., WILSON, J. E., & GLASSMAN, E. (1977). Phosphorylation of proteins of synaptosome-enriched fractions of brain during short-term training experience: The effects of various behavioral treatments. *Behavioral Biology, 21,* 358–363. **378**

GITTER, A. H., ZENNER, H. P., & FRÖMTER, E. (1986). Membrane potential and ion channels in isolated outer hair cells of guinea pig cochlea. *ORL, 46,* 68–75. **167**

GIULIAN, D., POHORECKY, L. A., & MCEWEN, B. S. (1973). Effects of gonadal steroids upon brain 5-hydroxytryptamine levels in the neonatal rat. *Endocrinology, 93,* 1329–1335. **295**

GLASS, I., & WOLLBERG, Z. (1983). Responses of cells in the auditory cortex of awake squirrel monkeys to normal and reversed species-specific vocalizations. *Hearing Research, 9,* 27–33. **172**

GLAVIN, G. B. (1985). Stress and brain noradrenaline: A review. *Neuroscience & Biobehavioral Reviews, 9,* 233–243. **335, 337**

GLENN, J. F., & ERICKSON, R. P. (1976). Gastric modulation of gustatory afferent activity. *Physiology & Behavior, 16,* 561–568. **264**

GLENN, L. L., & DEMENT, W. C. (1981). Membrane potential, synaptic activity, and excitability of hindlimb motoneurons during wakefulness and sleep. *Journal of Neurophysiology, 46,* 839–854. **235**

GLICK, S. D., WATERS, D. H., & MILLOY, S. (1973). Depletion of hypothalamic norepinephrine by food deprivation and interaction with D-amphetamine. *Research Communications in Chemical Pathology and Pharmacology, 6,* 775–778. **248**

GLICK, Z. (1982). Inverse relationship between brown fat thermogenesis and meal size: The thermostatic control of food intake revisited. *Physiology & Behavior, 29,* 1137–1140. **243**

GLICK, Z., TEAGUE, R. J., & BRAY, G. A. (1981). Brown adipose tissue: Thermic response increased by a single low protein, high carbohydrate meal. *Science, 213,* 1125–1127. **243**

GLOBUS, A., ROSENZWEIG, M. R., BENNETT, E. L., & DIAMOND, M. C. (1973). Effects of differential experience on dendritic spine counts in rat cerebral cortex. *Journal of Comparative and Physiological Psychology, 82,* 175–181. **406**

GOELET, P., CASTELLUCCI, V. F., SCHACHER, S., & KANDEL, E. R. (1986). The long and the short of long-term memory—a molecular framework. *Nature, 322,* 419–422. **377**

GOLD, G. H., & KORENBROT, J. I. (1980). Light-induced Ca efflux from intact rod cells in living retinas. *Federation Proceedings, 39,* 1814. **194**

GOLD, M. R., & MARTIN, A. R. (1982). Intracellular Cl⁻ accumulation reduces Cl⁻ conductance in inhibitory synaptic channels. *Nature, 299,* 828–830. **84**

GOLD, M. R., & MARTIN, A. R. (1983). Inhibitory conductance changes at synapses in the lamprey brainstem. *Science, 221,* 85–87.

GOLD, P. E., MCCARTY, R., & STERNBERG, D. B. (1982). Peripheral catecholamines and memory modulation. In C. A. Marsan & H. Matthies (Eds.), *Neuronal plasticity and memory formation.* New York: Raven. **374**

GOLD, P. E., & STERNBERG, D. B. (1978). Retrograde amnesia produced by several treatments: Evidence for a common neurobiological mechanism. *Science, 201,* 367–369. **374**

GOLD, P. E., & ZORNETZER, S. F. (1983). The mnemon and its juices: Neuromodulation of memory processes. *Behavioral and Neural Biology, 38,* 151–189. **373–376**

GOLD, R. M. (1973). Hypothalamic obesity: The myth of the ventromedial nucleus. *Science, 182,* 488–490. **243**

GOLDBERG, H. L., & FINNERTY, R. J. (1979). The comparative efficacy of buspirone and diazepam in the treatment of anxiety. *American Journal of Psychiatry, 136,* 1184–1187. **344**

GOLDBERG, S., BLUMBERG, S. L., & KRIGER, A. (1982). Menarche and interest in infants: Biological and social influences. *Child Development, 53,* 1544–1550. **291**

GOLDMAN, D. E. (1943). Potential, impedance, and rectification in membranes. *Journal of General Physiology, 27,* 37–60. **48**

GOLDMAN, L. (1976). Kinetics of channel gating in excitable membranes. *Quarterly Review of Biophysics, 9,* 491–526. **61**

GOLDMAN, P. S. (1978). Neuronal plasticity in primate telencephalon: Anomalous projections induced by prenatal removal of frontal cortex. *Science, 202,* 768–770. **433**

GOLDMAN, P. S., & LEWIS, M. E. (1978). Developmental biology of brain damage and experience. In C. W. Cotman (Ed.), *Neuronal plasticity.* New York: Raven. **433**

GOLDMAN, S. A., & NOTTEBOHM, F. (1983). Neuronal production, migration, and differentiation in a vocal control nucleus of the adult female canary brain. *Proceedings of the National Academy of Science, U.S.A., 80,* 2390–2394. **307, 431**

GOLDMAN-RAKIC, P. S. (1984). Modular organization of prefrontal cortex. *Trends in NeuroSciences, 7,* 419–424. **31**

GOLDSMITH, T. H. (1980). Hummingbirds see near ultraviolet light. *Science, 207,* 786–788. **203**

GOODBODY, A. E., & TRAYHURN, P. (1981). GDP binding to brown-adipose tissue mitochondria of diabetic-obese *(db/db)* mice. *Biochemical Journal, 194,* 1019–1022. **251**

GOODENOUGH, U. W., & LEVINE, R. P. (1970). The genetic activity of mitochondria and chloroplasts. *Scientific American, 223,* 22–29. **11, 124**

GOODMAN, R. L. (1978). The site of the positive feedback action of estradiol in the rat. *Endocrinology, 102,* 151–159. **280**

GOODMAN, R. R., KUHAR, M. J., HESTER, L., & SNYDER, S. H. (1983). Adenosine receptors: Autoradiographic evidence for their location on axon terminals of excitatory neurons. *Science, 220,* 967–969. **130**

GOODMAN, S. J. (1968). Visuo-motor reaction times and brain stem multiple-unit activity. *Experimental Neurology, 22,* 367–378. **239**

GOODWIN, F. K., & POST, R. M. (1983). 5-hydroxytryptamine and depression: A model for the interaction of normal variance with pathology. *British Journal of Clinical Psychology, 15,* 393S–405S. **339, 348, 354**

GOODWIN, G. M., DE SOUZA, R. J., & GREEN, A. R. (1985). Presynaptic serotonin receptor-mediated response in mice attenuated by antidepressant drugs and electroconvulsive shock. *Nature, 317,* 531–533. **354**

GOODWIN, G. M., MCCLOSKEY, D. I., MATTHEWS, P. B. C. (1972). Proprioceptive illusions induced by muscle vibration: Contribution by muscle spindles to perception? *Science, 175,* 1382–1384. **172**

GORDON, B., PRESSON, J., PACKWOOD, J., & SCHEER, R. (1979). Alteration of cortical orientation selectivity: Importance of asymmetric input. *Science, 204,* 1109–1111. **425**

GORDON, J. H., & PERRY, K. O. (1983). Pre- and postsynaptic neurochemical alterations following estrogen-induced striatal dopamine hypo- and hypersensitivity. *Brain Research Bulletin, 10,* 425–428. **309**

GORSKI, R. A. (1984). Sexual differentiation of brain structure in rodents. In M. Serio, M. Motta, M. Zanisi, & L. Martini (Eds.), *Sexual differentiation: Basic and clinical aspects.* New York: Raven. **304**

GORSKI, R. A. (1984). Critical role for the medial preoptic area in the sexual differentiation of the brain. In G. J. De Vries, J. P. C. De Bruin, H. B. M. Uylings, & M. A. Corner (Eds.), *Sex differences in the brain.* New York: Elsevier.

GORSKI, R. A. (1985). Sexual differentiation of the brain: Possible mechanisms and implications. The 13th J. A. F. Stevenson Memorial Lecture. *Canadian Journal of Physiology and Pharmacology, 63,* 577–594.

GORSKI, R. A., GORDON, J. H., SHRYNE, J. E., & SOUTHAM, A. M. (1978). Evidence for a morphological sex difference within the medial preoptic area of the rat brain. *Brain Research, 148,* 333–346.

GORSKI, R. A., HARLAN, R. E., & CHRISTENSEN, L. W. (1977). Perinatal hormonal exposure and the development of neuroendocrine regulatory processes. *Journal of Toxicology and Environmental Health, 3,* 97–121. **300**

GOTT, P., HUGHES, E. C., & WHIPPLE, K. (1984). Voluntary control of two lateralized conscious states: Validation by electrical and behavioral studies. *Neuropsychologia, 22,* 65–72. **444**

GOTTEFRIES, C. G. (1985). Critique: Transmitter deficits in Alzheimer's disease. *Neurochemistry International, 7,* 565–566. **376**

GOTTESMAN, I. I., & SHIELDS, J. (1976). A critical review of recent adoption, twin, and family history studies of schizophrenia: Behavioral genetics perspectives. *Schizophrenia Bulletin, 2,* 360–401. **344**

GOTTESMAN, I. I., & SHIELDS, J. (1982). *Schizophrenia: The epigenetic puzzle.* New York: Cambridge University Press. **327**

GOTTSCHALDT, K.-M., & VAHLE-HINZ, C. (1981). Merkel cell receptors: Structure and transducer function. *Science, 214,* 183–156. **152**

GOURAS, P., & ZRENNER, E. (1981). Color coding in primate retina. *Vision Research, 21*, 1591–1598. **199, 204**

GOVONI, S., & YANG, H.-Y. T. (1981). Sex differences in the context of beta-endorphin and enkephalin-like peptides in the pituitary of obese *(ob/ob)* mice. *Journal of Neurochemistry, 36*, 1829–1833. **252**

GOY, R. W. (1981). Differentiation of male social traits in female rhesus macaques by prenatal treatment with androgens: Variation in type of androgen, duration, and timing of treatment. In M. J. Novy & J. A. Resko (Eds.), *Fetal endocrinology.* New York: Academic Press. **276, 278, 291**

GOY, R. W., & JAKWAY, J. S. (1959). The inheritance of patterns of sexual behaviour in female guinea pigs. *Animal Behaviour, 7*, 142–149. **289**

GOY, R. W., MCEWEN, B. S. (1980). *Sexual differentiation of the brain.* Cambridge, MA: MIT Press. **276–278, 291, 293, 295**

GOY, R. W., & YOUNG, W. C. (1957). Strain differences in the behavioural responses of female guinea pigs to alpha-estradiol benzoate and progesterone. *Behavior, 10*, 340–354. **289**

GRANIT, R. (1968). The development of retinal neurophysiology. *Science, 160*, 1192–1196. **202**

GRANIT, R. A. (1982). Adaptability of the nervous system and its relation to chance, purposiveness, and causality. In J. Eccles (Ed.), *Mind and brain: The many-faceted problems.* Washington, DC: Paragon House.

GRANT, S. J., & REDMOND, D. E., JR. (1984). Neuronal activity of the locus ceruleus in awake *Macaca arctoides. Experimental Neurology, 84*, 701–708. **355**

GRAU, J. W., HYSON, R. L., MAIER, S. F., MADDEN, J., IV, & BARCHAS, J. D. (1981). Long-term stress-induced analgesia and activation of the opiate system. *Science, 213*, 1409–1411.

GRECKSCH, G., & MATTHIES, H. (1982). Involvement of hippocampal dopaminergic receptors in memory consolidation in rats. In C. A. Marsan & H. Matthies (Eds.), *Neuronal plasticity and memory formation.* New York: Raven. **375**

GREEN, E. J., GREENOUGH, W. T., & SCHLUMPF, B. E. (1983). Effects of complex or isolated environments on cortical dendrites of middle-aged rats. *Brain Research, 264*, 233–240. **402, 407**

GREENGARD, P. (1976). Possible role for cyclic nucleotides and phosphorylated membrane proteins in postsynaptic actions of neurotransmitters. *Nature, 260*, 101–108. **76, 86**

GREENGARD, P. (1978a). *Cyclic nucleotides, phosphorylated proteins, and neuronal function.* New York: Raven. **76, 86, 88, 90, 98**

GREENGARD, P. (1978b). Phosphorylated proteins as physiological effectors. *Science, 199*, 146–152. **76, 86**

GREENGARD, P., & KEBABIAN, J. W. (1974). Role of cyclic AMP in synaptic transmission in the mammalian peripheral nervous system. *Federation Proceedings, 33*, 1059–1067. **76, 86**

GREENOUGH, W. T. (1975). Experiential modification of the developing brain. *American Scientist, 63*, 37–46. **400, 401, 403, 404, 406, 407**

GREENOUGH, W. T. (1976). Enduring brain effects of differential experience and training. In M. R. Rosenzweig & E. L. Bennett (Eds.), *Neural mechanisms of learning and memory.* Cambridge, MA: MIT Press. **400, 401–404, 406, 407**

GREENOUGH, W. T., CARTER, C. S., STEERMAN, C., & DEVOOGD, T. J. (1977). Sex differences in dendritic patterns in hamster preoptic area. *Brain Research, 126*, 63–72. **300**

GREENOUGH, W. T., JURASKA, J. M., & VOLKMAR, F. R. (1979). Maze training effects on dendritic branching in occipital cortex of adult rats. *Behavioral and Neural Biology, 26*, 287–297. **408**

GREENOUGH, W. T., LARSON, J. R., & WITHERS, G. S. (1985). Effects of unilateral and bilateral training in a reaching task on dendritic branching of neurons in the rat motor-sensory forelimb cortex. *Behavioral and Neural Biology, 44*, 301–314. **408**

GREENOUGH, W. T., WOOD, W. E., & MADDEN, T. C. (1972). Possible memory storage differences among mice reared in environments varying in complexity. *Behavioral Biology, 7*, 717–722. **403**

GREENOUGH, W. T., YUWILER, A., & DOLLINGER, M. (1973). Effects of posttrial eserine administration on learning in "enriched"—and "impoverished"—reared rats. *Behavioral Biology, 8*, 261–272. **403**

GREGORY, E. (1975). Comparison of postnatal CNS development between male and female rats. *Brain Research, 99*, 152–156.

GREGORY, R. L. (1973). *Eye and brain: The psychology of seeing* (2nd ed.). New York: McGraw-Hill. **422**

GRIBKOFF, V. K., & ASHE, J. H. (1984). Modulation by dopamine of population responses and cell membrane properties of hippocampal CA1 neurons in vitro. *Brain Research, 292*, 327–338. **395**

GRIFFIN, W. S. T., ALEJOS, M., NILAVER, G., & MORRISON, M. R. (1983). Brain protein and messenger RNA identification in the same cell. *Brain Research Bulletin, 10*, 597–601.

GRINKER, J. A., DREWNOWSKI, A., ENNS, M., & KISSILEFF, H. (1980). Effects of d-amphetamine and fenfluramine on feeding patterns and activity of obese and lean Zucker rats. *Pharmacology, Biochemistry & Behavior, 12*, 265–275. **252**

GRIVELL, L. A. (1983). Mitochondrial DNA. *Scientific American, 248*, 78–89. **124**

GROBSTEIN, P., & CHOW, K. L. (1975). Receptive field development and individual experience. *Science, 190*, 352–358. **421**

GROSS, C. G., ROCHA-MIRANDA, C. E., & BENDER, D. B. (1972). Visual properties of neurons in inferotemporal cortex of the macaque. *Journal of Neurophysiology, 35*, 96–111. **217, 239**

GROSSMAN, S. P. (1979). The biology of motivation. *Annual Review of Psychology, 30*, 209–242. **241, 243, 245, 250**

GROVES, P. M. (1977). Possible mechanisms involved in the stereotyped behavior elicited by amphetamine. *Biological Psychiatry, 12*, 381–387. **356**

GRÜSSER, O.-J. (1984). Face recognition within the reach of neurobiology and beyond it. *Human Neurobiology, 3*, 183–190. **217**

GUILLERY, R. W. (1972). Binocular competition in the control of geniculate cell growth. *Journal of Comparative Neurology, 144*, 117–130. **419, 420**

GUILLERY, R. W. (1973). The effect of lid suture upon the growth of cells in the dorsal lateral geniculate nucleus of kittens. *Journal of Comparative Neurology, 148*, 417–422. **419, 420**

GUILLERY, R. W. (1974). Visual pathways in albinos. *Scientific American, 230*, 44–54.

GÜLDNER, F.-H. (1982). Sexual dimorphisms of axo-spine synapses and postsynaptic density material in the suprachiasmatic nucleus of the rat. *Neuroscience Letters, 28*, 145–150. **300**

GUR, R. C., GUR, R. E., OBRIST, W. D., HUNGERBUHLER, J. P., YOUNKIN, D., ROSEN, A. D., SKOLNICK, B. E., & REIVICH, M. (1982). Sex and handedness differences in cerebral blood flow during rest and cognitive activity. *Science, 217*, 659–661. **301, 302**

GUTHRIE, B. L., PORTER, J. D., & SPARKS, D. L. (1983). Corollary discharge provides accurate eye position information to the oculomotor system. *Science, 221*, 1193–1195. **222**

GUYTON, A. C. (1981). *Basic human neurophysiology* (3rd.). Philadelphia: Saunders. **33, 34, 155, 170, 172**

HABERLY, L. B. (1985). Neuronal circuitry in olfactory cortex: Anatomy and functional implications. *Chemical Senses, 10*, 219–238. **161, 171**

HABERT, R., & PICON, R. (1984). Testosterone, dihydrotestosterone and estradiol-17β levels in maternal and fetal plasma and in fetal testes in the rat. *Journal of Steroid Biochemistry, 21*, 193–198. **272**

HADFIELD, M. G. (1983). Dopamine: Mesocortical versus nigrostriatal uptake in isolated fighting mice and controls. *Behavioural Brain Research, 7*, 269–281. **340**

HAGBARTH, K.-E. (1983). Microelectrode exploration of human nerves: Physiological and clinical implications. *Journal of the Royal Society of Medicine, 76*, 7–15. **172, 175**

HAGEMENAS, F. C., & KITTINGER, G. W. (1972). The influence of fetal sex on plasma progesterone levels. *Endocrinology, 91*, 253–256. **272**

HAIER, R. J., BUCHSBAUM, M. S., MURPHY, D. L., GOTTESMAN, I. I., & COURSEY, R. D. (1980). Psychiatric vulnerability, monoamine oxidase, and the average evoked potential. *Archives of General Psychiatry, 37*, 340–345. **341**

HALL, C. J., & JENKINS, J. S. (1982). Effect of gonadal hormones on the incorporation of [³H]-lysine into proteins of human fetal brain. *Developmental Brain Research, 2*, 557–562. **295**

HALL, J. C. (1977). Portions of the central nervous system controlling reproductive behavior in *Drosophila melanogaster. Behavior Genetics, 7*, 291–312. **117**

HALPERN, B. P., & TAPPER, D. N. (1971). Taste stimuli: Quality coding time. *Science, 171*, 1256–1258. **141**

HAMBURG, M. D. (1971). Hypothalamic unit activity and eating behavior. *American Journal of Physiology, 220*, 980–985. **259**

HAMILTON, C. R., & VERMEIRE, B. A. (1982). Hemispheric differences in split-brain monkeys learning sequential comparisons. *Neuropsychologia, 20*, 691–698. **20**

HAMMER, R. P., JR. (1984). The sexually dimorphic region of the preoptic area in rats contains denser opiate receptor binding sites in females. *Brain Research, 308*, 172–176. **310**

HANCKE, J. L., & DÖHLER, K.-D. (1984). Sexual differentiation of female brain function is prevented by postnatal treatment of rats with the estrogen antagonist tamoxifen. *Neuroendocrinology Letters, 6*, 201–206. **304**

HANDA, R. J., CORBIER, P., SHRYNE, J. E., SCHOONMAKER, J. N., & GORSKI, R. A. (1985). Differential effects of the perinatal steroid environment on three sexually dimorphic parameters of the rat brain. *Biology of Reproduction, 32*, 855–864. **304**

HARACZ, J. L. (1982). The dopamine hypothesis: An overview of studies with schizophrenic patients. *Schizophrenia Bulletin, 8,* 438–468. **344, 345**

HARADA, Y., & TAKAHASHI, T. (1983). The calcium component of the action potential in spinal motoneurones of the rat. *Journal of Physiology, 335,* 89–100. **59, 60**

HARDIN, C. M. (1973). Sex differences in serotonin synthesis from 5-hydroxytryptophan in neonatal rat brain. *Brain Research, 59,* 437–439. **295**

HARDY, J., ADOLFSSON, R., ALAFUZOFF, I., BUCHT, G., MARCUSSON, J., NYBERG, P., PERDAHL, E., WESTER, P., & WINBLAD, B. (1985). Transmitter deficits in Alzheimer's disease. *Neurochemistry International, 7,* 545–563. **376, 432**

HARRELL, L. E., BARLOW, T. S., & DAVIS, J. N. (1983). Sympathetic sprouting and recovery of a spatial behavior. *Experimental Neurology, 82,* 379–390. **436**

HARSHMAN, R. A., HAMPSON, E., & BERENBAUM, S. A. (1983). Individual differences in cognitive abilities and brain organization: Part I. Sex and handedness differences in ability. *Canadian Journal of Psychology, 37,* 144–192. **295**

HARTZELL, H. C. (1981). Mechanisms of slow postsynaptic potentials. *Nature, 291,* 539–544. **76, 86**

HARVEY, A. R. (1980). A physiological analysis of subcortical and commissural projections of areas 17 and 18 of the cat. *Journal of Physiology, 302,* 507–534. **210**

HARWERTH, R. S., SMITH, E. L., III, CRAWFORD, M. L. J., & VON NOORDEN, G. K. (1984). Effects of enucleation of the nondeprived eye on stimulus deprivation amblyopia in monkeys. *Investigations in Ophthalmology and Visual Sciences, 25,* 10–18. **418, 419**

HARWERTH, R. S., SMITH, E. L., III, & OKUNDAYE, O. J. (1983). Oblique effects, vertical effects and meridional amblyopia in monkeys. *Experimental Brain Research, 53,* 142–150. **427**

HASKINS, J. T., & MOSS, R. L. (1983). Action of estrogen and mechanical vaginocervical stimulation on the membrane excitability of hypothalamic and midbrain neurons. *Brain Research Bulletin, 10,* 489–496. **280, 311–313, 315**

HAWKINS, R. D., ABRAMS, T. W., CAREW, T. J., & KANDEL, E. R. (1983). A cellular mechanism of classical conditioning in *Aplysia*: Activity-dependent amplification of presynaptic facilitation. *Science, 219,* 400–405. **396**

HAYASHI, M., HAYASHI, M. N., & SPIEGELMAN, S. (1963). Restriction of in vivo genetic transcription to one of the complementary strands of DNA. *Proceedings of the National Academy of Sciences, U.S.A., 50,* 664–672. **119**

HAYWARD, J. N. (1977). Functional and morphological aspects of hypothalamic neurons. *Physiological Review, 57,* 574–658. **254, 259**

HEATH, R. G. (1963). Electrical self-stimulation of the brain in man. *American Journal of Psychiatry, 120,* 571–577. **263, 268**

HEATH, R. G. (1972). Pleasure and brain activity in man. *Journal of Nervous and Mental Disease, 154,* 3–18. **263, 318**

HECHT, S., SHLAER, S., & PIRENNE, M. (1942). Energy, quanta, and vision. *Journal of General Physiology, 25,* 819–840. **179**

HECK, G. L., MIERSON, S., & DESIMONE, J. A. (1984). Salt taste transduction occurs through an amiloride-sensitive sodium transport pathway. *Science, 223,* 403–405. **151**

HEFFNER, H. E. (1983). Hearing in large and small dogs: Absolute thresholds and size of tympanic membrane. *Behavioral Neuroscience, 97,* 310–318. **152**

HEFFNER, H. E., & HEFFNER, R. S. (1984). Temporal lobe lesions and perception of species-specific vocalizations by macaques. *Science, 226,* 75–76. **20**

HEFFNER, T. G., HARTMAN, J. A., & SEIDEN, L. S. (1980). Feeding increases dopamine metabolism in the rat brain. *Science, 208,* 1168–1170. **245**

HEGMANN, J. P. (1975). The response to selection for altered conduction velocity in mice. *Behavioral Biology, 13,* 413–423. **128**

HEGMANN, J. P. (1979). A gene-imposed nervous system difference influencing behavioral covariance. *Behavioral Genetics, 9,* 165–175. **128**

HELMHOLTZ, H. VON (1962). *Hanbuch der physiolgischen Optik*, Vols. 1, 2, & 3. Reprinted as a Dover edition in 1962. (Original work published 1866) **202**

HENDRICKS, S. E., & DUFFY, J. A. (1974). Ovarian influences on the development of sexual behavior in neonatally androgenized rats. *Developmental Psychobiology, 7,* 297–303. **277**

HENDRICKS, S. E., & WELTIN, M. (1976). Effect of estrogen given during various periods of prepubertal life on the sexual behavior of rats. *Physiological Psychology, 4,* 105–110. **277**

HENKE, P. G. (1983). Unit-activity in the central amygdalar nucleus of rats in response to immobilization-stress. *Brain Research Bulletin, 10,* 833–837. **354**

HENKE, P. G. (1984). The bed nucleus of the stria terminalis and immobilization-stress: Unit activity, escape behaviour, and gastric pathology in rats. *Behavioural Brain Research, 11,* 34–45. **354**

HENON, B. K., & MCAFEE, D. A. (1983). The ionic basis of adenosine receptor actions on post-ganglionic neurones in the rat. *Journal of Physiology, 1983, 336,* 607–620. **90**

HENRY, G. H. (1977). Receptive field classes of cells in the striate cortex of the cat. *Brain Research, 133,* 1–28. **206, 207**

HENRY, J. L., & CALARESU, F. R. (1972). Topography and numerical distribution of neurons of the thoracolumbar intermediolateral nucleus in the cat. *Journal of Comparative Neurology, 144,* 205–214. **301**

HERING, E. (1964). *Outlines of a theory of the light sense* (L. M. Hurvich & D. Jameson, Trans.). Cambridge, MA: Harvard University Press. **202**

HERITAGE, A. S., STUMPF, W. E., SAR, M., & GRANT, L. D. (1980). Brainstem catecholamine neurons are target sites for sex steroid hormones. *Science, 207,* 1377–1379. **297**

HERMAN, J. P., GUILLONNEAU, D., DANTZER, R., SCATTON, B., SEMERDJIAN-ROUQUIER, L., & LE MOAL, M. (1982). Differential effects of inescapable footshocks and of stimuli previously paired with inescapable footshocks on dopamine turnover in cortical and limbic areas of the rat. *Life Sciences, 30,* 2207–2214. **332, 335**

HERRLING, P. L., & HULL, C. D. (1980). Iontophoretically applied dopamine depolarizes and hyperpolarizes the membrane of cat caudate neurons. *Brain Research, 192,* 441–462. **97**

HERVÉ, D., TASSIN, P. P., BARTHELEMY, C., BLANC, G., LAVIELLE, S., & GLOWINSKI, J. (1979). Difference in the reactivity of the mesocortical dopaminergic neurons to stress in the BALB/C and C57 BL/6 mice.

Life Sciences, 25, 1659–1664. **335**

HERVEY, G. R., & TOBIN, G. (1983). Luxuskonsumption, diet-induced thermogenesis and brown fat: A critical review. *Clinical Science, 64,* 7–18. **243**

HESS, R. F. (1982). Developmental sensory impairment: Amblyopia or tarachopia? *Human Neurobiology, 1,* 17–29. **416**

HESS, R. F., FRANCE, T. D., & TULUNAY-KEESEY, U. (1981). Residual vision in humans who have been monocularly deprived of pattern stimulation in early life. *Experimental Brain Research, 44,* 295–311. **416**

HEUSER, J. E. (1978). Quick-freezing evidence in favour of the vesicular hypothesis. *Trends in NeuroSciences, 1,* 80–82. **72, 74**

HEUSER, J. E., REESE, T. S., DENNIS, M. J., JAN, Y., JAN, L., & EVANS, L. (1979). Synaptic vesicle exocytosis captured by quick freezing and correlated with quantal transmitter release. *Journal of Cell Biology, 81,* 275–300. **74**

HEYM, J., STEINFELS, G. F., & JACOBS, B. L. (1984). Chloral hydrate anesthesia alters the responsiveness of central serotonergic neurons in the cat. *Brain Research, 291,* 63–72. **16**

HICKS, T. P. (1984). The history and development of microiontophoresis in experimental neurobiology. *Progress in Neurobiology, 22,* 185–240.

HILLE, B. (1978). Ionic channels in excitable membranes: Current problems and biophysical approaches. *Biophysical Journal, 22,* 283–294. **49, 51, 61**

HIMMS-HAGEN, J. (1985). Food restriction increases torpor and improves brown adipose tissue thermogenesis in *ob/ob* mice. *American Journal of Physiology, 248,* E531–E539. **251**

HIMMS-HAGEN, J., & DESAUTELS, M. (1978). A mitochondrial defect in brown adipose tissue of the obese *(ob/ob)* mouse: Reduced binding of purine nucleotides and a failure to respond to cold by an increase in binding. *Biochemical & Biophysical Research Communications, 83,* 628–634. **251**

HIMMS-HAGEN, J., TRIANDAFILLOU, J., & GWILLIAM, C. (1981). Brown adipose tissue of cafeteria-fed rats. *American Journal of Physiology, 241,* E116–E120. **243**

HINES, M. (1982). Prenatal gonadal hormones and sex differences in human behavior. *Psychological Bulletin, 92,* 56–80. **291**

HIRANO, T., BEST, P., & OLDS, J. (1970). Units during habituation, discrimination learning, and extinction. *Electroencephalography and Clinical Neurophysiology, 28,* 127–135. **387**

HIRSCH, H. V. B. (1972). Visual perception in cats after environmental surgery. *Experimental Brain Research, 15,* 405–423. **424, 426**

HIRSCH, H. V. B. (1985). The role of visual experience in the development of cat striate cortex. *Cellular and Molecular Neurobiology, 5,* 103–121. **400, 414, 421**

HIRSCH, H. V. B., & LEVENTHAL, A. G. (1983). Effects of monocular deprivation upon the binocularity of cells in area 18 of cat visual cortex. *Developmental Brain Research, 8,* 140–144. **420**

HIRSCH, H. V. B., LEVENTHAL, A. G., MCCALL, M. A., & TIEMAN, D. G. (1983). Effects of exposure to lines of one or two orientations on different cell types in striate cortex of cat. *Journal of Physiology, 337,* 241–255. **424, 426**

HIRSCH, H. V. B., & SPINELLI, D. N. (1970).

Visual experience modifies distribution of horizontally and vertically oriented receptive fields in cats. *Science, 168,* 869–871. **425, 427**

HIRSCH, J. C., FOURMENT, A., & MARC, M. E. (1983). Sleep-related variations of membrane potential in the lateral geniculate body relay neurons of the cat. *Brain Research, 259,* 308–312. **239**

HOBSON, J. A., & MCCARLEY, R. W. (1977). The brain as a dream state generator: An activation-synthesis hypothesis of the dream process. *American Journal of Psychiatry, 134,* 1335–1348.

HOBSON, J. A., MCCARLEY, R., FREEDMAN, R., & PIVIK, T. R. (1974). Time course of discharge rate changes by cat pontine brain stem neurons during sleep cycle. *Journal of Neurophysiology, 37,* 1297–1309. **238**

HOBSON, J. A., MCCARLEY, R. W., & WYZINSKI, P. W. (1975). Sleep cycle oscillation: Reciprocal discharge by two brainstem neuronal groups. *Science, 189,* 55–58. **233, 238**

HOCHERMAN, S., BENSON, D. A., GOLDSTEIN, M. H., JR., HEFFNER, H. E., & HIENZ, R. D. (1976). Evoked unit activity in auditory cortex of monkeys performing a selective attention task. *Brain Research, 117,* 51–68. **239**

HOCKMAN, C. H., & TALESNIK, J. (1971). Central nervous system modulation of baroceptor input. *American Journal of Physiology, 221,* 515–519. **175**

HODGKIN, A. L. (1964a). The ionic basis of nervous conduction. *Science, 145,* 1148–1154. **53, 54**

HODGKIN, A. L. (1964b). *The conduction of the nervous impulse.* Springfield, IL: Charles C Thomas. **53, 54**

HODGKIN, A. L. (1976). Chance and design in electrophysiology: An informal account of certain experiments on nerve carried out between 1934 and 1952. *Journal of Physiology, 263,* 1–21. **53, 54, 56**

HODGKIN, A. L., & HOROWICZ, P. (1959). The influence of potassium and chloride ions on the membrane potential of single muscle fibers. *Journal of Physiology, 148,* 127–160. **48, 49, 51, 53**

HODGKIN, A. L., & HUXLEY, A. F. (1952a). Currents carried by sodium and potassium through the membrane of the giant axon of *Loligo. Journal of Physiology, 116,* 449–472. **53, 54**

HODGKIN, A. L., & HUXLEY, A. F. (1952b). The components of membrane conductance in the giant axon of *Loligo. Journal of Physiology, 116,* 473–496. **53, 54**

HODGKIN, A. L., & HUXLEY, A. F. (1952c). The dual effect of membrane potential on sodium conductance in the giant axon of *Loligo. Journal of Physiology, 116,* 497–506. **53, 54**

HODGKIN, A. L., & HUXLEY, A. F. (1952d). A quantitative description of membrane current and its application to conduction and excitation in nerve. *Journal of Physiology, 117,* 500–544. **53, 54, 60**

HODGKIN, A. L., & KATZ, B. (1949). The effect of sodium ions on the electrical activity of the giant axon of the squid. *Journal of Physiology, 108,* 37–77. **48**

HOEBEL, B. G. (1979). Hypothalamic self-stimulation and stimulation escape in relation to feeding and mating. *Federation Proceedings, 38,* 2454–2461. **318**

HOEBEL, B. G. (1985). Integrative peptides. *Brain Research Bulletin, 14,* 525–528. **99, 265**

HOGAN, S., COSCINA, D. V., & HIMMS-HAGEN, J. (1982). Brown adipose tissue of rats with obesity-inducing ventromedial hypothalamic lesions. *American Journal of Physiology, 243,* E338–E344. **243**

HÖKFELT, T., JOHANSSON, O., LJUNGDAHL, A., LUNDBERG, J. M., & SCHULTZBERG, M. (1980). Peptidergic neurones. *Nature, 284,* 515–521. **98**

HÖKFELT, T., REHFELD, J. F., SKIRBOLL, L., IVEMARK, B., GOLSTEIN, M., & MARKEY, K. (1980). Evidence for coexistence of dopamine and CCK in meso-limbic neurones. *Nature, 285,* 476–478. **98, 168, 249**

HOLBROOKE, S. E., & MICHAEL, R. P. (1980). Depression by estrogen of electrical activity in the hypothalamic ventromedial nucleus of female cats. *Psychoneuroendocrinology, 5,* 13–24. **318**

HOLLOWAY, R. L., & DE LACOSTE, M. C. (1986). Sexual dimorphism in the human corpus callosum: An extension and replication study. *Human Neurobiology, 5,* 87–91. **302**

HONG, J. S., YOSHIKAWA, K., & LAMARTINIERE, C. A. (1982). Sex-related difference in the rat pituitary [Met5]-enkephalin level—altered by gonadectomy. *Brain Research, 251,* 380–383. **309**

HOPKINS, W. F., & JOHNSTON, D. (1984). Frequency-dependent noradrenergic modulation of long-term potentiation in the hippocampus. *Science, 226,* 350–352. **395**

HOPKINSON, D. A., & HARRIS, H. (1971). Recent work on isozymes in man. *Annual Review of Genetics, 5,* 5–32. **120**

HORN, G., & HILL, R. M. (1969). Modifications of receptive fields of cells in the visual cortex occurring spontaneously and associated with bodily tilt. *Nature, 221,* 186–188. **221**

HORN, J. P., & DODD, J. (1981). Monosynaptic muscarinic activation of K^+ conductance underlies the slow inhibitory postsynaptic potential in sympathetic ganglia. *Nature, 292,* 625–627. **90**

HORN, J. P., & DODD, J. (1983). Inhibitory cholinergic synapses in autonomic ganglia. *Trends in Neuro-Sciences, 6,* 180–184. **89, 90, 92**

HORN, J. P., & MCAFEE, D. A. (1979). Norepinephrine inhibits calcium-dependent potentials in rat sympathetic neurons. *Science, 204,* 1233–1235. **90, 98, 104**

HORN, J. P., & MCAFEE, D. A. (1980). Alpha-adrenergic inhibition of calcium-dependent potentials in rat sympathetic neurones. *Journal of Physiology, 301,* 191–204. **59, 60, 90, 107**

HOROWITZ, G. P., DENDEL, P. S., ALLAN, A. M., & MAJOR, L. F. (1982). Dopamine-beta-hydroxylase activity and ethanol-induced sleep time in selectively bred and heterogeneous stock mice. *Behavior Genetics, 12,* 549–561. **129**

HORTON, J. C., & HEDLEY-WHYTE, E. T. (1984). Mapping of cytochrome oxidase patches and ocular dominance columns in human visual cortex. *Philosophical Transactions of the Royal Society of London, Series B, 304,* 255–272. **215**

HORTON, J. C., & HUBEL, D. H. (1981). Regular patchy distribution of cytochrome oxidase staining in primary visual cortex of macaque monkey. *Nature, 292,* 762–764. **212**

HOVDA, D. A., & FEENEY, D. M. (1985). Holoperidol blocks amphetamine induced recovery of binocular depth perception after bilateral visual cortex ablation in cat. *Proceedings of the Western Pharmacological Society, 28,* 209–211. **214, 434**

HOVDA, D. A., SUTTON, R. L., & FEENEY, D. M. (1985, May). Asymmetry of bilateral visual cortex le-

sions affect amphetamine's ability to produce recovery of depth perception. Paper presented at the meeting of the Society for Neuroscience. **214, 434**

HOYENGA, K. B., & HOYENGA, K. T. (1979). *The question of sex differences: Psychological, cultural, and biological issues.* Boston: Little, Brown. **272, 274, 277, 285, 288, 291, 293, 294, 319, 326**

HOYENGA, K. B., & HOYENGA, K. T. (1982). Gender and energy balance: Sex differences in adaptations for feast and famine. *Physiology & Behavior, 28,* 545–563. **243, 245, 250–252, 271, 291, 293, 301**

HOYENGA, K. B., & HOYENGA, K. T. (1984). *Motivational explanations of behavior: Evolutionary, physiological, and cognitive ideas.* Monterey, CA: Brooks/Cole. **229, 241, 243, 258, 269, 274, 320, 321, 323, 324, 326, 329, 335, 338, 402, 423, 443**

HOYENGA, K. B., & WALLACE, B. (1978). Effects of stimulus size, intensity, color, and eye strain on autokinetic movement: An error signal and noise analysis. *Journal of General Psychology, 98,* 37–46. **222**

HOYENGA, K. B., & WALLACE, B. (1979). Sex differences in the perception of autokinetic movement of an afterimage. *Journal of General Psychology, 100,* 93–101. **222**

HOYENGA, K. B., & WALLACE, B. (1982). Illusory changes in a sound source and outflow theory. *Journal of General Psychology, 107,* 179–188. **176, 222**

HRUSKA, R. E. (1986). Elevation of striatal dopamine receptors by estrogen: Dose and time studies. *Journal of Neurochemistry, 47,* 1908–1915. **309**

HRUSKA, R. E., LUDMER, L. M., PITMAN, K. T., DE RYCK, M., & SILBERGELD, E. K. (1982). Effects of estrogen on striatal dopamine receptor function in male and female rats. *Pharmacology, Biochemistry & Behavior, 16,* 285–291. **309**

HRUSKA, R. E., & PITMAN, K. T. (1982). Distribution and localization of estrogen-sensitive dopamine receptors in the rat brain. *Journal of Neurochemistry, 39,* 1418–1423. **309**

HRUSKA, R. E., & SILBERGELD, E. K. (1980). Increased dopamine receptor sensitivity after estrogen treatment using the rat rotation model. *Science, 208,* 1466–1468. **313**

HUANG, Y. H. (1979). Chronic desipramine treatment increases activity of noradrenergic postsynaptic cells. *Life Sciences, 25,* 709–716. **355**

HUANG, Y. H., MAAS, J. W., & HU, G. H. (1980). The time course of noradrenergic pre- and postsynaptic activity during chronic desipramine treatment. *European Journal of Pharmacology, 68,* 41–47. **355**

HUBEL, D. H. (1959). Single unit activity in striate cortex of unrestrained cats. *Journal of Physiology, 147,* 226–238. **239**

HUBEL, D. H. (1960). Single unit activity in lateral geniculate body and optic tract of unrestrained cats. *Journal of Physiology, 150,* 91–104. **239**

HUBEL, D. H. (1979). The visual cortex of normal and deprived monkeys. *American Scientist, 67,* 532–543. **414, 416**

HUBEL, D. H. (1982). Evolution of ideas on the primary visual cortex, 1955–1978: A biased historical account. *Bioscience Reports, 2,* 435–469. **206, 207**

HUBEL, D. H., & LIVINGSTONE, M. S. (1981). Regions of poor orientation tuning coincide with patches of cytochrome oxidase staining in monkey striate cortex. *Society of Neurosciences Abstract, 7,* 367. **212**

HUBEL, D. H., & LIVINGSTONE, M. S. (1982). Cytochrome oxidase blobs in monkey area 17: Response properties and afferent connections. *Society of Neurosciences Abstract*, 8, 706.

HUBEL, D. H., & LIVINGSTONE, M. S. (1983). Blobs and color vision. *Canadian Journal of Physiology and Pharmacology*, 61, 1433–1441. **212, 215**

HUBEL, D. H., & WIESEL, T. N. (1959). Receptive fields of single neurons in the cat's striate cortex. *Journal of Physiology*, 148, 575–591. **206**

HUBEL, D. H., & WIESEL, T. N. (1962). Receptive fields, binocular interaction and functional architecture in the cat's visual cortex. *Science*, 160, 106–154. **206**

HUBEL, D. H., & WIESEL, T. N. (1965). Receptive fields and functional architecture in two nonstriate visual areas (18 and 19) of the cat. *Journal of Neurophysiology*, 28, 229–289. **206**

HUBEL, D. H., & WIESEL, T. N. (1970). Stereoscopic vision in macaque monkey. *Nature*, 225, 41–44. **214**

HUBEL, D. H., & WIESEL, T. N. (1974a). Sequence regularity and geometry of orientation columns in the monkey striate cortex. *Journal of Comparative Neurology*, 158, 267–294. **206**

HUBEL, D. H., & WIESEL, T. N. (1974b). Uniformity of monkey striate cortex: A parallel relationship between field size, scatter, and magnification factor. *Journal of Comparative Neurology*, 158, 295–306. **206**

HUBEL, D. H., & WIESEL, T. N. (1977). Functional architecture of macaque monkey visual cortex. *Proceedings of the Royal Society of London, Series B*, 198, 1–59. **206**

HUBEL, D. H., WIESEL, T. N., & STRYKER, M. P. (1977). Orientation columns in macaque monkey visual cortex demonstrated by the 2-deoxyglucose autoradiographic technique. *Nature*, 269, 328–330. **206, 209**

HUDSPETH, A. J. (1983). The hair cells of the inner ear. *Scientific American*, 248, 54–64. **153**

HUDSPETH, A. J. (1985). The cellular basis of hearing: The biophysics of hair cells. *Science*, 230, 745–752. **153, 167**

HUDSPETH, A. J., & COREY, D. P. (1977). Sensitivity, polarity, and conductance change in the response of vertebrate hair cells to controlled mechanical stimuli. *Proceedings of the National Academy of Sciences, U.S.A.*, 74, 2407–2411. **153**

HUDSPETH, A. J., & JACOBS, R. (1979). Stereocilia mediate transduction in vertebrate hair cells. *Proceedings of the National Academy of Sciences, U.S.A.*, 76, 1506–1509. **153, 174**

HULL, C. J. (1943). *Principles of behavior*. New York: Appleton-Century-Crofts. **229**

HULL, E. M., NISHITA, J. K., BITRAN, D., & DALTERIO, S. (1984). Perinatal dopamine-related drugs demasculinize rats. *Science*, 224, 1011–1013. **297, 310**

HULSE, S. H., DEESE, J., & EGETH, H. (1975). *The psychology of learning*. New York: McGraw-Hill. **430**

HULSEBOSCH, C. E., & COGGESHALL, R. E. (1983). Age related sprouting of dorsal root axons after sensory denervation. *Brain Research*, 288, 77–83. **437**

HUMPHREY, A. L., & HENDRICKSON, A. E. (1983). Background and stimulus-induced patterns of high metabolic activity in the visual cortex (area 17) of the squirrel and macaque monkey. *Journal of Neuroscience*, 3, 345–358. **212**

HUNT, T. (1983). Phosphorylation and the control of protein synthesis. *Philosophical Transactions of the Royal Society of London, Series B*, 302, 127–134. **378**

HURVICH, L. M., & JAMESON, D. (1956). Some quantitative aspects of an opponent colors theory. IV. A psychological color specification system. *Journal of the Optical Society of America*, 46, 416–421. **202**

HURVICH, L. M., & JAMESON, D. (1957). An opponent-process theory of color vision. *Psychological Review*, 64, 384–404. **202**

HUTCHISON, J. B., & STEIMER, T. (1984). Androgen metabolism in the brain: Behavioural correlates. In D. J. De Vries, J. R. C. De Bruin, H. B. M. Uylings, & M. A. Corner (Eds.), *Sex differences in the brain*. New York: Elsevier. **276, 293**

HUTTENLOCHER, P. R. (1979). Synaptic density in human frontal cortex—developmental changes and effects of aging. *Brain Research*, 163, 195–205. **431**

HUTTENLOCHER, P. R., DE COURTEN, C., GAREY, L. J., & VAN DER LOOS, H. (1982). Synaptogenesis in human visual cortex—evidence for synapse elimination during normal development. *Neuroscience Letters*, 33, 247–252. **431**

HYDE, J. S., & EBERT, P. D. (1976). Correlated response in selection for aggressiveness in female mice: I. Male aggressiveness. *Behavior Genetics*, 6, 421–427. **326**

HYDE, J. S., & SAWYER, T. F. (1979). Correlated characters in selection for aggressiveness in female mice: II. Maternal aggressiveness. *Behavior Genetics*, 9, 571–577. **326**

HYDÉN, H. (1978). Protein changes in neuronal membranes and synapses during learning. *Bioscience Communications*, 4, 185–204. **378**

HYDÉN, H. (1982). The brain, learning and values. In J. Eccles (Ed.), *Mind and brain: The many-faceted problems*. Washington, DC: Paragon House. **448**

HYDÉN, H., LANGE, P. W., & PERRIN, C. L. (1977). Protein pattern alterations in hippocampal and cortical cells as a function of training in rats. *Brain Research*, 119, 427–437. **378**

HYVÄRINEN, J., CARLSON, S., & HYVÄRINEN, L. (1981). Early visual deprivation alters modality of neuronal responses in area 19 of monkey cortex. *Neuroscience Letters*, 26, 239–243. **415**

IACONO, W. G. (1983). Psychophysiology and genetics: A key to psychopathology research. *Psychophysiology*, 20, 371–383. **346, 347**

IFUNE, C. K., VERMEIRE, B. A., & HAMILTON, C. R. (1984). Hemispheric differences in split-brain monkeys viewing and responding to videotape recordings. *Behavioral and Neural Biology*, 41, 231–235. **20**

IIMORI, K., TANAKA, M., KOHNO, Y., IDA, Y., NAKAGAWA, R., HOAKI, Y., TSUDA, A., & NAGASAKI, N. (1982). Psychological stress enhances noradrenaline turnover in specific brain regions in rats. *Pharmacology, Biochemistry & Behavior*, 16, 637–640. **333**

IKEDA, H., & SHEARDOWN, M. J. (1982). Acetylcholine may be an excitatory transmitter mediating visual excitation in "transient" cells with the periphery effect in the cat retina: Iontophoretic studies in vivo. *Neuroscience*, 7, 1299–1308. **198**

IMPERATO-MCGINLEY, J., PETERSON, R. E., & GAUTIER, T. (1984). Primary and secondary 5α-reductase deficiency. In M. Serio, M. Motto, M. Zanisi, & L. Martini (Eds.), *Sexual differentiation: Basic and clinical aspects*. New York: Raven. **277**

INABA, M., & KAMATA, K. (1979). Effect of estra-diol-17β and other steroids on noradrenaline and dopamine binding to synaptic membrane fragments of rat brain. *Journal of Steroid Biochemistry*, 11, 1491–1497. **309**

INGLIS, J., & LAWSON, J. S. (1982). A meta-analysis of sex differences in the effects of unilateral brain damage on intelligence test results. *Canadian Journal of Psychology*, 36, 670–683. **302**

INGLIS, J., RUCKMAN, M., LAWSON, J. S., MACLEAN, A. W., & MONGA, T. N. (1982). Sex differences in the cognitive effects of unilateral brain damage: Comparison of stroke patients and normal control subjects. *Cortex*, 18, 257–276. **302**

INGVAR, D. H. (1982). Mental illness and regional brain metabolism. *Trends in NeuroSciences*, 5, 199–202. **346**

INNOCENTI, G. M. (1981). Growth and reshaping of axons in the establishment of visual callosal connections. *Science*, 212, 824–827. **433**

INNOCENTI, G. M., & FROST, D. O. (1979). Effects of visual experience on the maturation of the efferent system to the corpus callosum. *Nature*, 280, 231–233. **433**

INSELMAN-TEMKIN, B. R., & FLYNN, J. P. (1973). Sex-dependent effects of gonadal and gonadotropic hormones on centrally-elicited attack in cats. *Brain Research*, 60, 393–410. **339**

IOVINO, M., MONTELEONE, P., BARONE, P., & STEARDO, L. (1983). Inhibition of septal hyperreactivity by testosterone and its reversion by an estrogen antagonist in weanling female rats. *Neuroscience Letters*, 40, 151–156. **301**

IP, N. Y., & ZIGMOND, R. E. (1984). Pattern of presynaptic nerve activity can determine the type of neurotransmitter regulating a postsynaptic event. *Nature*, 311, 472–474. **158**

IRIUCHIJIMA, J., & ZOTTERMAN, Y. (1960). The specificity of afferent cutaneous C fibres in mammals. *Acta Physiologica Scandinavica*, 49, 267–278. **163**

IRLE, E., & MARKOWITSCH, H. J. (1986). Afferent connections of the substantia innominata/basal nucleus of Meynert in carnivores and primates. *Journal für Hirnforschung*, 27, 343–367. **376**

IRWIN, L. N. (1978). Fulfillment and frustration: The confessions of a behavioral biochemist. *Perspectives in Biology and Medicine*, 21, 476–491.

ISAACSON, R. L. (1980). A perspective for the interpretation of limbic system function. *Physiological Psychology*, 8, 183–188. **12, 377, 449**

ISACSON, O., BRUNDIN, P., KELLY, P. A. T., GAGE, F. H., & BJÖRKLUND, A. (1984). Functional neuronal replacement by grafted striatal neurones in the ibotenic acid-lesioned rat striatum. *Nature*, 311, 458–460. **437**

ISHIBASHI, S., OOMURA, Y., OKAJIMA, T., & SHIBATA, S. (1979). Cholecystokinin, motilin and secretin effects on the central nervous system. *Physiology & Behavior*, 23, 401–403. **259**

ITO, M. (1972). Excitability of medial forebrain bundle neurons during self-stimulating behavior. *Journal of Neurophysiology*, 35, 652–664. **267**

ITO, M., & OLDS, J. (1971). Unit activity during self-stimulation behavior. *Journal of Neurophysiology*, 34, 263–273. **267**

ITO, M., & SEO, M. L. (1983). Avoidance of neonatal cortical lesions by developing somatosensory barrels. *Nature*, 301, 600–602. **171**

ITO, S.-I. (1982). Prefrontal unit activity of macaque

monkeys during auditory and visual reaction time tasks. *Brain Research, 247,* 39–47. **383**

IUVONE, P. M., GALLI, C. L., GARRISON-GUND, C. K., & NEFF, N. H. (1978). Light stimulates tyrosine hydroxylase activity and dopamine synthesis in retinal amacrine neurons. *Science, 202,* 901–902. **198**

IVERSEN, L. L. (1975). Dopamine receptors in the brain. *Science, 188,* 1084–1089. **97**

IVERSEN, L. L. (1982). Substance P. *British Medical Bulletin, 38,* 277–282. **168**

IVERSEN, L. L. (1984). Amino acids and peptides: Fast and slow chemical signals in the nervous system? *Proceedings of the Royal Society of London, Series B, 221,* 245–260. **86**

IWAI, E. (1985). Neuropsychological basis of pattern vision in macaque monkeys. *Vision Research, 25,* 425–439. **4**

IWASAKI, K., & SATO, M. (1984). Neural and behavioral responses to taste stimuli in the mouse. *Physiology & Behavior, 32,* 803–807. **133**

IZQUIERDO, I., ORSINGHER, O. A., & OGURA, A. (1972). Hippocampal facilitation and RNA build-up in response to stimulation in rats with a low inborn learning ability. *Behavioral Biology, 7,* 699–707. **394**

JACKLIN, C. N., MACCOBY, E. E., & DOERING, C. H. (1983). Neonatal sex-steroid hormones and timidity in 6–18-month-old boys and girls. *Developmental Psychobiology, 16,* 163–168. **277**

JACKLIN, C. N., MACCOBY, E., DOERING, C. H., & KING, D. R. (1984). Neonatal sex-steroid hormones and muscular strength of boys and girls in the first three years. *Developmental Psychobiology, 17,* 301–310. **277**

JACKSON, R. L., ALEXANDER, J. H., & MAIER, S. F. (1980). Learned helplessness, inactivity, and associative deficits: Effects of inescapable shock on response choice escape learning. *Journal of Experimental Psychology: Animal Behavior Processes, 6,* 1–20. **337**

JACOBS, B. L. (1986). Single unit activity of locus coeruleus neurons in behaving animals. *Progress in Neurobiology, 27,* 183–194. **236, 355, 376**

JACOBS, G. H. (1983). Differences in spectral response properties of LGN cells in male and female squirrel monkeys. *Vision Research, 23,* 461–468. **304**

JACOBSON, C. D., ARNOLD, A. P., & GORSKI, R. A. (1982). Steroid accumulation in the sexual dimorphic nucleus of the preoptic area (SN-POA). *Anatomical Record, 202,* 88A. **284**

JACOBSON, C. D., SHRYNE, J. E., SHAPIRO, F., & GORSKI, R. A. (1980). Ontogeny of the sexually dimorphic nucleus of the preoptic area. *Journal of Comparative Neurology, 193,* 541–548. **300, 303**

JACQUIN, M. F., HARRIS, R., & ZEIGLER, H. P. (1982). Dissociation of hunger and self-stimulation by trigeminal deafferentation in the rat. *Brain Research, 244,* 53–58. **266**

JAHR, C. E., NICOLL, R. A. (1982). Noradrenergic modulation of dendrodendritic inhibition in the olfactory bulb. *Nature, 297,* 227–229. **105**

JAKINOVICH, W., JR. (1983). Methyl 4,6-dichloror-4,6-dideoxy-alpha-D-galactopyranoside: An inhibitor of sweet taste responses in gerbils. *Science, 219,* 408–410. **151**

JAMESON, D., & HURVICH, L. M. (1955). Some quantitative aspects of an opponent colors theory. I. Chromatic responses and spectral saturation. *Journal of the Optical Society of America, 45,* 546–552. **202**

JAN, L. Y., JAN, Y. N., & BROWNFIELD, M. S. (1980). Peptidergic transmitters in synaptic boutons of sympathetic ganglia. *Nature, 288,* 380–382. **90**

JAN, Y. N., JAN, L. Y., & DENNIS, M. J. (1977). Two mutations of synaptic transmission in Drosophila. *Proceedings of the Royal Society, London, Series B, 198,* 87–108. **128**

JAN, Y. N., JAN, L. Y., & KUFFLER, S. W. (1979). A peptide as a possible transmitter in sympathetic ganglia of the frog. *Proceedings of the National Academy of Sciences, U.S.A., 76,* 1501–1505. **90**

JANOWSKY, A. J., OKADA, F., MANIER, D. H., APPLEGATE, C. G., SULSER, F., & STERANKA, L. R. (1982). Role of serotonergic input in the regulation of the beta-adrenergic receptor-coupled adenylate cyclase system. *Science, 218,* 900–901. **349**

JANOWSKY, D. S., & DAVIS, J. M. (1970). Progesterone-estrogen effects on uptake and release of norepinephrine. *Life Sciences, 9,* 525–531. **308**

JAROS, E., & JENKISON, M. (1983). Quantitative studies of the abnormal axon–Schwann cell relationship in the peripheral motor and sensory nerves of the dystrophic mouse. *Brain Research, 258,* 181–196. **128**

JÄRVILEHTO, T. (1977). Neural basis of cutaneous sensations analyzed by microelectrode measurements from human peripheral nerves—a review. *Scandinavian Journal of Psychology, 18,* 348–359. **168**

JEANMONOD, D., RICE, F. L., & VAN DER LOOS, H. (1981). Mouse somatosensory cortex: Alterations in the barrelfield following receptor injury at different early postnatal ages. *Neuroscience, 8,* 1503–1535. **410**

JEANNINGROS, R. (1982). Vagal unitary responses to intestinal amino acid infusions in the anesthetized cat: A putative signal for protein induced satiety. *Physiology & Behavior, 28,* 9–21. **152, 258**

JEEVES, M. A. (1984). The historical roots and recurring issues of neurobiological study of face perception. *Human Neurobiology, 3,* 191–196. **217**

JENKINS, J. S., & HALL, C. J. (1977). Metabolism of [¹⁴C]testosterone by human foetal and adult brain tissue. *Journal of Endocrinology, 74,* 425–429. **284**

JENKINS, T. C., & HERSHBERGER, T. V. (1978). Effect of diet, body type and sex on voluntary intake, energy balance and body composition of Zucker rats. *Journal of Nutrition, 108,* 124–136. **243**

JENSEN, G. D., BOBBITT, R. A., & GORDON, B. N. (1967). Sex differences in the development of independence of infant monkeys. *Behaviour, 30,* 1–14. **292**

JOFFE, J. M. (1965a). Genotype and prenatal and premating stress interact to affect adult behavior in rats. *Science, 150,* 1844–1845. **117**

JOFFE, J. M. (1965b). Effect of foster-mothers' strain and pre-natal experience on adult behaviour in rats. *Nature, 200,* 815–816. **117**

JOFFE, J. M. (1969). *Prenatal determinants of behavior.* Oxford: Pergamon Press. **337**

JOHANSSON, R. S., & VALLBO, A. B. (1983). Tactile sensory coding in the glabrous skin of the human hand. *Trends in NeuroSciences, 6,* 27–32. **3, 168, 170**

JOHN, E. R., TANG, Y., BRILL, A. B., YOUNG, R., & ONO, K. (1986). Double-labeled metabolic maps of memory. *Science, 233,* 1167–1175. **365**

JOHNSON, D. F., & PHOENIX, C. H. (1978). Sexual behavior and hormone levels during the menstrual cycles of rhesus monkeys. *Hormones and Behavior, 11,* 160–174. **291**

JOHNSTONE, J. R. (1981). Basic problems of cochlear physiology. *Trends in NeuroSciences, 1,* 106–108. **165, 172**

JONES, D. G., & SMITH, B. J. (1980). Morphological analysis of the hippocampus following differential rearing in environments of varying social and physical complexity. *Behavioral and Neural Biology, 30,* 135–147. **406**

JONES, E. G., BURTON, H., & PORTER, R. (1975). Commissural and cortico-cortical "columns" in the somatic sensory cortex of primates. *Science, 190,* 572–574. **156**

JONES, E. G., COULTER, J. D., & HENDRY, S. H. C. (1978). Intracortical connectivity of architectonic fields in the somatic sensory, motor and parietal cortex of monkeys. *Journal of Comparative Neurology, 181,* 291–348. **156, 176**

JORDAN, C. L., BREEDLOVE, S. M., & ARNOLD, A. P. (1982). Sexual dimorphism and the influence of neonatal androgen in the dorsolateral motor nucleus of the rat lumbar spinal cord. *Brain Research, 249,* 309–314. **?**

JOYCE, J. N. (1983). Multiple dopamine receptors and behavior. *Neuroscience & Biobehavioral Reviews, 7,* 227–256. **?**

JOYCE, J. N., MONTERO, E., & VAN HARTESVELDT, C. (1984). Dopamine-mediated behaviors: Characteristics of modulation by estrogen. *Pharmacology, Biochemistry & Behavior, 21,* 791–800. **313**

JURASKA, J. M. (1984). Sex differences in dendritic response to differential experience in the rat visual cortex. *Brain Research, 295,* 27–34. **292, 406**

JURASKA, J. M. (1984). Sex differences in developmental plasticity in the visual cortex and hippocampal dentate gyrus. In G. J. De Vries, J. P. C. De Bruin, H. B. M. Uylings, & M. A. Corner (Eds.), *Sex differences in the brain.* New York: Elsevier.

JURASKA, J. M., FITCH, J. M., HENDERSON, C., & RIVERS, N. (1985). Sex differences in the dendritic branching of dentate granule cells following differential experience. *Brain Research, 333,* 73–80. **406, 408**

JURASKA, J. M., GREENOUGH, W. T., ELLIOTT, C., MACK, K. J., & BERKOWITZ, R. (1980). Plasticity in adult rat visual cortex: An examination of several cell populations after differential rearing. *Behavioral and Neural Biology, 29,* 157–167. **402, 407, 408**

KAARS, C., & FABER, D. S. (1981). Myelinated central vertebrate axon lacks voltage-sensitive potassium conductance. *Science, 212,* 1063–1065. **62**

KAAS, J. H., NELSON, R. J., SUR, M., LIN, C.-S., & MERZENICH, M. M. (1979). Multiple representations of the body within the primary somatosensory cortex of primates. *Science, 204,* 521–523. **156**

KAMMERER, E., RAUCA, C., & MATTHIES, H. (1982). Cholinergic activity of the hippocampus and permanent memory storage. In C. A. Marsan & H. Matthies (Eds.), *Neuronal plasticity and memory formation.* New York: Raven. **375, 381**

KANDEL, E. R. (1976). *Cellular basis of behavior.* San Francisco: W. H. Freeman. **73, 229, 358**

KANDEL, E. R. (1981a). Brain and behavior. In E. R. Kandel & J. H. Schwartz (Eds.), *Principles of neural science.* New York: Elsevier/North-Holland. **3**

KANDEL, E. R. (1981b). Synaptic transmission: I. Postsynaptic factors controlling ionic permeability. In E. R. Kandel & J. H. Schwartz (Eds.), *Principles of neural science.* New York: Elsevier/North-Holland. **78**

KANDEL, E. R. (1981c). Synaptic transmission: II. Presynaptic factors controlling transmitter release. In E. R. Kandel & J. H. Schwartz (Eds.), *Principles of neural science*. New York: Elsevier/North-Holland. **73**

KANDEL, E. R. (1981d). Visual system: III. Physiology of the central visual pathways. In E. R. Kandel & J. H. Schwartz (Eds.), *Principles of neural science*. New York: Elsevier/North-Holland.

KANDEL, E. R. (1983). From metapsychology to molecular biology: Explorations into the nature of anxiety. *American Journal of Psychiatry, 140*, 1277–1293. **358, 359, 396**

KANKI, J. P., MARTIN, T. L., & SINNAMON, H. M. (1983). Activity of neurons in the anteromedial cortex during rewarding brain stimulation, saccharin consumption and orienting behavior. *Behavioural Brain Research, 8*, 69–84. **267**

KASAMATSU, T. (1970). Maintained and evoked unit activity in the mesencephalic reticular formation of the freely behaving cat. *Experimental Neurology, 28*, 450–470. **236**

KASAMATSU, T., & PETTIGREW, J. D. (1979). Preservation of binocularity after monocular deprivation in the striate cortex of kittens treated with 6-hydroxydopamine. *Journal of Comparative Neurology, 185*, 139–181. **420**

KASAMATSU, T., PETTIGREW, J. D., & ARY, M. (1979). Restoration of visual cortical plasticity by local microperfusion of norepinephrine. *Journal of Comparative Neurology, 185*, 163–181. **420**

KASAMATSU, T., PETTIGREW, J. D., & ARY, M. (1981). Cortical recovery from effects of monocular deprivation: Acceleration with norepinephrine and suppression with 6-hydroxydopamine. *Journal of Neurophysiology, 45*, 254–266. **420**

KASHIWAYANAGI, M., MIYAKE, J., KURIHARA, K. (1983). Voltage-dependent Ca^{2+} channel and Na^+ channel in frog taste cells. *American Journal of Physiology, 244*, C82–C88. **150**

KATO, G., & BAN, T. (1982). Central nervous system receptors in neuropsychiatric disorders. *Progress in Neuro-Psychopharmacology & Biological Psychiatry, 6*, 207–222. **345, 349**

KATO, J., ONOUCHI, T., OKINAGA, S., & TAKAMATSU, M. (1984). The ontogeny of cytosol and nuclear progestin receptors in male rat brain and its male-female differences. *Journal of Steroid Biochemistry, 20*, 147–152.

KATSUKI, Y. (1961). Neural mechanism of auditory sensation in cats. In W. A. Rosenblith (Ed.), *Sensory communication*. Cambridge, MA: MIT Press. **160**

KATZ, B., & MILEDI, R. (1967a). A study of synaptic transmission in the absence of nerve impulses. *Journal of Physiology, 192*, 407–436. **72**

KATZ, B., & MILEDI, R. (1967b). The timing of calcium action during neuromuscular transmission. *Journal of Physiology, 189*, 535–544. **72**

KATZ, B., & MILEDI, R. (1970). Membrane noise produced by acetylcholine. *Nature, 226*, 962–963. **78**

KATZ, B., & MILEDI, R. (1972). The statistical nature of the acetylcholine potential and its molecular components. *Journal of Physiology, 224*, 665–699. **78**

KATZ, H. B., & DAVIES, C. A. (1983). The separate and combined effects of early undernutrition and environmental complexity at different ages on cerebral measures in rats. *Developmental Psychobiology, 16*, 47–58. **402, 406**

KAWAKAMI, M., & OHNO, S. (1981). Estrogen-sensitive neurons with preoptic projection in the lower brain

stem of the female rat. *Endocrinologica Japonica, 28*, 677–684. **313**

KAYE, A. M. (1983). Enzyme induction by estrogen. *Journal of Steroid Biochemistry, 19*, 33–40. **278**

KEBABIAN, J. W., & CALNE, D. B. (1979). Multiple receptors for dopamine. *Nature, 277*, 93–96. **97**

KEENE, J. J. (1973a). Opposite medial thalamic unit responses to rewarding and aversive brain stimulation. *Experimental Neurology, 39*, 19–35. **267**

KEENE, J. J. (1973b). Reward-associated inhibition and pain-associated excitation lasting seconds in single intralaminar thalamic units. *Brain Research, 64*, 211–224. **267**

KEENE, J. J. (1975). Reward-associated excitation and pain-associated inhibition lasting seconds in rat medial pallidal units. *Experimental Neurology, 49*, 97–114. **267**

KEESEY, R. E., & POWLEY, T. L. (1975). Hypothalamic regulation of body weight. *American Scientist, 63*, 558–565. **243, 245**

KEHOE, J. S., & MARTY, A. (1980). Certain slow synaptic responses: Their properties and possible underlying mechanisms. *Annual Review of Biophysics and Bioengineering, 9*, 437–465. **60, 86**

KEIM, K. L., & SIGG, E. B. (1976). Physiological and biochemical concomitants of restraint stress in rats. *Pharmacology, Biochemistry & Behavior, 4*, 289–297. **335**

KELLY, D. D. (1981a). Physiology of sleep and dreaming. In E. R. Kandel & J. H. Schwartz (Eds.), *Principles of neural science*. New York: Elsevier/North-Holland. **232, 235, 238**

KELLY, D. D. (1981b). Disorders of sleep and consciousness. In E. R. Kandel & J. H. Schwartz (Eds.), *Principles of neural science*. New York: Elsevier/North-Holland. **129, 232**

KELLY, J., ALHEID, G. F., NEWBERG, A., & GROSSMAN, S. P. (1977). GABA stimulation and blockade in the hypothalamus and midbrain: Effects on feeding and locomotor activity. *Pharmacology, Biochemistry & Behavior, 7*, 537–541. **249**

KELLY, J. P. (1981). Visual system: II. Anatomy of the central visual pathways. In E. R. Kandel & J. H. Schwartz (Eds.), *Principles of neural science*. New York: Elsevier/North-Holland.

KELLY, J. S. (1982). Electrophysiology of peptides in the central nervous system. *British Medical Bulletin, 38*, 283–290. **98**

KELLY, M. J., MOSS, R. L., & DUDLEY, C. A. (1976). Differential sensitivity of preoptic-septal neurons to microelectrophoresed estrogen during the estrous cycle. *Brain Research, 114*, 152–157. **312**

KELLY, M. J., MOSS, R. L., & DUDLEY, C. A. (1977). The effects of microelectrophoretically applied estrogen, cortisol and acetylcholine on medial preoptic-septal unit activity throughout the estrous cycle of the female rat. *Experimental Brain Research, 1977, 30*, 53–64. **311, 312, 358**

KELLY, M. J., MOSS, R. L., & DUDLEY, C. A. (1978). The effects of ovariectomy on the responsiveness of preoptic-septal neurons to microelectrophoresed estrogen. *Neuroendocrinology, 25*, 204–211. **312**

KELLY, M. J., MOSS, R. L., DUDLEY, C. A., & FAWCETT, C. P. (1977). The specificity of the response of preoptic-septal area neurons to estrogen: 17alpha-estradiol versus 17beta-estradiol and the response of extrahypothalamic neurons. *Experimental Brain Research, 30*, 43–52. **311, 312**

KENDLER, K. S., & DAVIS, K. L. (1981). The genetics and biochemistry of paranoid schizophrenia and other paranoid psychoses. *Schizophrenia Bulletin, 7*, 689–709. **327, 346**

KENDRICK, K. M. (1983a). Effect of testosterone on medial preoptic/anterior hypothalamic neurone responses to stimulation of the lateral septum. *Brain Research, 262*, 136–142. **280, 312**

KENDRICK, K. M. (1983b). Electrophysiological effects of testosterone on the medial preoptic-anterior hypothalamus of the rat. *Journal of Endocrinology, 96*, 35–42. **280, 312**

KENDRICK, K. M., & DREWETT, R. F. (1979). Testosterone reduces refractory period of stria terminalis neurons in the rat brain. *Science, 204*, 877–879. **307, 313**

KENDRICK, K. M., & DREWETT, R. F. (1980). Testosterone-sensitive neurones respond to oestradiol but not to dihydrotestosterone. *Nature, 286*, 67–68. **313**

KENNEDY, B. G., & DE WEER, P. (1977). Relationship between Na:K and Na:Na exchange by the sodium pump of skeletal muscle. *Nature, 268*, 165–167. **51**

KENNEDY, D., CALABRESE, R. L., & WINE, J. J. (1974). Presynaptic inhibition: Primary afferent depolarization in crayfish neurons. *Science, 186*, 451–454. **103**

KENNEDY, G. C. (1953). The role of depot fat in the hypothalamic control of food intake in the rat. *Proceedings of the Royal Society, London, Series B, 140*, 578–592. **242**

KERR, F. W. L., TRIPLETT, J. N., JR., & BEELER, G. W. (1974). Reciprocal (push-pull) effects of morphine on single units in the ventromedian and lateral hypothalamus and influences on other nuclei: With a comment on methadone effects during withdrawal from morphine. *Brain Research, 74*, 81–103. **359**

KERR, L. M., & SPERELAKIS, N. (1983). Membrane alterations in skeletal muscle fibers of dystropic mice. *Muscle & Nerve, 6*, 3–13. **128**

KESNER, R. P. (1982). Brain stimulation: Effects on memory. *Behavioral and Neural Biology, 36*, 315–367. **371–373, 376**

KESNER, R. P., & ELLIS, M. E. (1983). Memory consolidation: Brain region and neurotransmitter specificity. *Neuroscience Letters, 39*, 295–300. **374, 375**

KESNER, R. P., & NOVAK, J. M. (1982). Serial position curve in rats: Role of the dorsal hippocampus. *Science, 218*, 173–175. **385**

KESSLER, J. A., ADLER, J. E., & BLACK, I. B. (1983). Substance P and somatostatin regulate sympathetic noradrenergic function. *Science, 221*, 1059–1061. **90, 108**

KESSLER, S. (1980). The genetics of schizophrenia: A review. *Schizophrenia Bulletin, 6*, 404–416.

KESSLER, S., ELLIOTT, G. R., ORENBERG, E. K., & BARCHAS, J. D. (1977). A genetic analysis of aggressive behavior in two strains of mice. *Behavior Genetics, 7*, 313–321. **326**

KEVERNE, E. B., EBERHART, J. A., YODYINGYUAD, U., & ABBOTT, D. H. (1984). Social influences on sex differences in the behaviour and endocrine state of talapoin monkeys. In G. J. De Vries, J. P. C. De Bruin, B. M. Uylings, & M. A. Corner (Eds.), *Sex differences in the brain*. New York: Elsevier. **293**

KEYNES, R. D. (1948). The leakage of radioactive potassium from stimulated nerve. *Journal of Physiology, 107*, 35P. **48, 53**

KEYNES, R. D. (1949). The movements of radioactive sodium during nervous activity. *Journal of Physiology, 109*, 13P. **48, 53**

KEYNES, R. D. (1951a). The leakage of radioactive potassium from stimulated nerve. *Journal of Physiology, 113*, 99–114. **48, 53**

KEYNES, R. D. (1951b). The ionic movements during nervous activity. *Journal of Physiology, 114*, 119–150. **48, 53**

KEYNES, R. D. (1979). Ion channels in the nerve-cell membrane. *Scientific American, 240*, 126–135. **48, 56, 61**

KHANNA, S., NAYAR, U., & ANAND, B. K. (1972). Effect of fenfluramine on the single neuron activities of the hypothalamic feeding centers. *Physiology & Behavior, 8*, 453–456. **257, 259**

KHANNA, S. M., & LEONARD, D. G. B. (1982). Basilar membrane tuning in the cat cochlea. *Science, 215*, 305–306. **166**

KIANG, N. Y. S., LIBERMAN, M. C., SEWELL, W. F., & GUINAN, J. J. (1986). Single unit clues to cochlear mechanisms. *Hearing Research, 22*, 171–182. **167, 175**

KIMURA, D. (1983). Sex differences in cerebral organization for speech and praxic functions. *Canadian Journal of Psychology, 37*, 19–35. **302**

KIMURA, D. (1985, November). Male brain, female brain: The hidden difference. *Psychology Today*, pp. 50–58. **302**

KIMURA, K., & BEIDLER, L. M. (1961). Microelectrode study of taste receptors of rat and hamster. *Journal of Cellular and Comparative Physiology, 58*, 131–139. **151**

KINE, D., VINSON, G., MAJOR, P., & KILPATRICK, R. (1980). Adrenal-gonad relationships. In I. Jones & I. Henderson (Eds.), *General, comparative and clinical endocrinology of the adrenal gland*. New York: Academic Press. **276**

KING, B. M., & FROHMAN, L. A. (1986). Hypothalamic obesity: Comparison of radio-frequency and electrolytic lesions in male and female rats. *Brain Research Bulletin, 17*, 409–413. **243, 245**

KING, W. J., & GREENE, G. L. (1984). Monoclonal antibodies localize oestrogen receptor in the nuclei of target cells. *Nature, 307*, 745–747. **279**

KIRCHHOFF, J., & GRÜNKE, W., & GHRAF, R. (1983). Estrogen induction of progestin receptors in pituitary, hypothalamic and uterine cytosol of androgenized female rats. *Brain Research, 275*, 173–177. **285**

KITADA, Y. (1984). Two different receptor sites for Ca^{2+} and Na^+ in frog taste responses. *Neurosciences Letters, 47*, 63–68. **151**

KITZES, L. M., FARLEY, G. R., & STARR, A. (1978). Modulation of auditory cortex unit activity during the performance of a conditioned response. *Experimental Neurology, 62*, 678–697. **239**

KLEIN, M., & KANDEL, E. R. (1980). Mechanism of calcium current modulation underlying presynaptic facilitation and behavioral sensitization in *Aplysia*. *Proceedings of the National Academy of Sciences, U.S.A., 77*, 6912–6916. **87, 104**

KLEMM, W. R., & SHERRY, C. J. (1982). Do neurons process information by relative intervals in spike trains? *Neuroscience & Biobehavioral Reviews, 6*, 429–437. **158**

KLÜVER, H., & BUCY, P. C. (1939). Preliminary analysis of functions of the temporal lobes in monkeys. *Archives of Neurology and Psychiatry, 42*, 979–1000. **325**

KNIGHT, P. L. (1977). Representation of the cochlea within the anterior auditory field (AAF) of the cat. *Brain Research, 130*, 447–467. **165, 171**

KNUDSEN, E. I. (1983). Early auditory experience aligns the auditory map of space in the optic tectum of the barn owl. *Science, 222*, 939–942. **413**

KNUDSEN, E. I., & KONISHI, M. (1978). Center-surround organization of auditory receptive fields in the owl. *Science, 202*, 778–780. **170**

KNUDSEN, E. I., KONISHI, M., & PETTIGREW, J. D. (1977). Receptive fields of auditory neurons in the owl. *Science, 198*, 1278–1280. **170, 171**

KOBAYASHI, H., & LIBET, B. (1970). Actions of noradrenaline and acetylcholine on sympathetic ganglion cells. *Journal of Physiology, 208*, 353–372. **107**

KOCSIS, J. D., & WAXMAN, S. G. (1980). Absence of potassium conductance in central myelinated axons. *Nature, 287*, 348–349. **62**

KOENIG, H., GOLDSTONE, A., & LU, C. Y. (1983). Polyamines regulate calcium fluxes in a rapid plasma membrane response. *Nature, 305*, 530–534. **279**

KOIKE, H., MANO, N., OKADA, Y., & OSHIMA, T. (1972). Activities of the sodium pump in cat pyramidal tract cells investigated with intracellular injection of sodium ions. *Experimental Brain Research, 14*, 449–462. **89**

KOKETSU, K., & OHTA, Y. (1976). Acceleration of the electrogenic Na^+ pump by adrenaline in frog skeletal muscle fibres. *Life Sciences, 19*, 1009–1014. **89**

KOKKINIDIS, L., & ANISMAN, H. (1980). Amphetamine models of paranoid schizophrenia: An overview and elaboration of animal experimentation. *Psychological Bulletin, 88*, 551–579. **338**

KOLATA, G. (1982). Brain receptors for appetite discovered. *Science, 218*, 460–461. **248**

KOLATA, G. (1984). New neurons form in adulthood. *Science, 224*, 1325–1326. **307, 431**

KOLATA, G. (1986). Maleness pinpointed on Y chromosome. *Science, 234*, 1076–1077. **287**

KOLB, H. (1970). Organization of the outer plexiform layer of the primate retina: Electron microscopy of Golgi-impregnated cells. *Philosophical Transactions of the Royal Society, Series B, 258*, 261–268. **183, 184**

KOLB, B., & WHISHAW, I. Q. (1985). Earlier is not always better: Behavioral dysfunction and abnormal cerebral morphogenesis following neonatal cortical lesions in the rat. *Behavioural Brain Research, 17*, 25–43. **433**

KOMISARUK, B. R., & OLDS, J. (1968). Neuronal correlates of behavior in freely moving rats. *Science, 161*, 810–813. **235, 254, 267**

KONNERTH, A., HEINEMANN, U., & YAARI, Y. (1984). Slow transmission of neural activity in hippocampal area CA1 in absence of active chemical synapses. *Nature, 307*, 69–71. **399**

KOOPMANS, H. S. (1981). The role of the gastrointestinal tract in the satiation of hunger. In L. A. Cioffi, W. P. T. James, & T. B. Van Itallie (Eds.), *The body weight regulatory system: Normal and disturbed mechanisms*. New York: Raven. **242, 249**

KORDAŠ, M. (1969). The effect of membrane polarization on the time course of the end-plate current in frog sartorius muscle. *Journal of Physiology, 204*, 493–502. **80**

KORENBROT, J. I. (1985). Signal mechanisms of phototransduction in retinal rod. *CRC Critical Reviews in Biochemistry, 17*, 223–256. **194**

KORENBROT, J. I., & CONE, R. A. (1972). Dark ionic flux and the effects of light in isolated rod outer segments. *Journal of General Physiology, 60*, 20–45.

KORN, H., MALLET, A., TRILLER, A. & FABER, D. S. (1982). Transmission at a central inhibitory synapse: II. Quantal description of release, with a physical correlate for binomial n. *Journal of Neurophysiology, 48*, 679–707. **70, 73**

KORNHUBER, H. H. (1974). Cerebral cortex, cerebellum, and basal ganglia: An introduction to their motor functions. In W. Schmitt (Ed.), *The neurosciences: Third study program*. Cambridge, MA: MIT Press. **9, 34, 444**

KOSHLAND, D. E., JR., GOLDBETER, A., & STOCK, J. B. (1982). Amplification and adaptation in regulatory and sensory systems. *Science, 217*, 220–225. **149**

KOSLOW, S. H., MAAS, J. W., BOWDEN, C. L., DAVIS, J. M., HANIN, I., & JAVAID, J. (1983). CSF and urinary biogenic amines and metabolites in depression and mania. *Archives of General Psychiatry, 40*, 999–1010. **348, 349**

KOW, K.-L., HARLAN, R. E., SHIVERS, B. D. & PFAFF, D. W. (1985). Inhibition of the lordosis reflex in rats by intrahypothalamic infusion of neural excitatory agents: Evidence that the hypothalamus contains separate inhibitory and facilitatory elements. *Brain Research, 341*, 26–34. **317**

KOW, L.-M., & PFAFF, D. W. (1982). Responses to medullary reticulospinal and other reticular neurons to somatosensory and brainstem stimulation in anesthetized or freely-moving ovariectomized rats with or without estrogen treatment. *Experimental Brain Research, 47*, 191–202. **313, 315**

KOW, L.-M., & PFAFF, D. W. (1985a). Actions of feeding-relevant agents on hypothalamic glucose-responsive neurons *in vitro*. *Brain Research Bulletin, 15*, 509–513.

KOW, L.-M., & PFAFF, D. W. (1985b). Estrogen effects of neuronal responsiveness to electrical and neurotransmitter stimulation: An in vitro study on the ventromedial nucleus of the hypothalamus. *Brain Research, 347*, 1–10. **256, 271, 317**

KRASNE, F. B., & BRYAN, J. S. (1973). Habituation: Regulation through presynaptic inhibition. *Science, 182*, 590–592. **176**

KRATZ, K. E., & LEHMKUHLE, S. (1983). Spatial contrast sensitivity of monocularly deprived cats after removal of the non-deprived eye. *Behavioural Brain Research, 7*, 261–266. **418, 419**

KRATZ, K. E., SPEAR, P. D., & SMITH, D. C. (1976). Postcritical-period reversal of effects of monocular deprivation on striate cortex cells in the cat. *Journal of Neurophysiology, 39*, 501–511. **418**

KRAUS, N., & DISTERHOFT, J. F. (1982). Response plasticity of single neurons in rabbit auditory association cortex during tone-signalled learning. *Brain Research, 246*, 205–215. **390**

KREY, L. C., BUTLER, W. R., & KNOBIL, E. (1975). Surgical disconnection of the medial basal hypothalamus and pituitary function in the rhesus monkey: I. Gonadotropin secretion. *Endocrinology, 96*, 1073–1087. **280**

KRNJEVIĆ, K. (1975). Acetylcholine receptors in vertebrate central nervous system. In L. L. Iversen, S. D. Iversen, & S. H. Snyder (Eds.), *Handbook of psychopharmacology* (Vol. 6). New York: Plenum. **95**

KRNJEVIĆ, K., PUIL, E., & WERMAN, R. (1978). EGTA and motoneuronal after-potentials. *Journal of Physiology, 275*, 199–223. **60**

KUBO, K., GORSKI, R. A., & KAWAKAMI, M. (1975). Effects of estrogen on neuronal excitability in the hippocampal-septal-hypothalamic system. *Neuroendocrinology, 18*, 176–191. **312**

KUBOTA, K., & FUNAHASHI, S. (1982). Direction-specific activities of dorsolateral prefrontal and motor cortex pyramidal tract neurons during visual tracking. *Journal of Neurophysiology*, 47, 362–376. **230**

KUBOTA, K., TONOIKE, M., & MIKAMI, A. (1980). Neuronal activity in the monkey dorsolateral prefrontal cortex during a discrimination task with delay. *Brain Research*, 183, 29–42. **383**

KUFFLER, S. W. (1952). Neurons in the retina: Organization, inhibition and excitation problems. *Cold Spring Harbor Symposium on Quantitative Biology*, 17, 281–292. **198**

KUFFLER, S. W., & NICHOLLS, J. G. (1976). *From neuron to brain*. Sunderland, MA: Sinauer Associates. **3, 29, 98, 422**

KUFFLER, S. W., NICHOLLS, J. G., & MARTIN, A. R. (1984). *From neuron to brain: A cellular approach to the function of the nervous system* (2nd ed.). Sunderland, MA: Sinauer Associates. **86**

KUFFLER, S. W., & YOSHIKAMI, D. (1975). The number of transmitter molecules in a quantum: An estimate from ionophoretic application of acetylcholine at the neuromuscular synapse. *Journal of Physiology*, 251, 465–482. **78, 85**

KUFFLER, S. W., & YOSHIKAMI, D. (1976). The distribution of acetylcholine sensitivity at the post-synaptic membrane of vertebrate skeletal twitch muscles: Ionophoretic mapping in the micron range. *Journal of Physiology*, 244, 703–730.

KUHAR, M. J., & MURRIN, C. L. (1978). Sodium-dependent, high affinity choline uptake. *Journal of Neurochemistry*, 30, 15–21. **107**

KÜHN, H. (1978). Light-regulated binding of rhodopsin kinase and other proteins to cattle photoreceptor membranes. *Biochemistry*, 17, 4389–4395. **192**

KUNG, C., CHANG, S.-Y., SATOW, Y., VAN HOUTEN, J., & HANSMA, H. (1975). Genetic dissection of behavior in *Paramecium*. *Science*, 188, 898–904. **117, 118, 128**

KUNO, M. (1971). Quantum aspects of central and ganglionic synaptic transmission in vertebrates. *Physiological Reviews*, 51, 647–678. **73, 74, 101**

KUPFERMANN, I. (1981). Hypothalamus and limbic system: I. Peptidergic neurons, homeostasis, and emotional behavior. In E. R. Kandel & J. H. Schwartz (Eds.), *Principles of neural science*. New York: Elsevier/North-Holland.

KUPFERMANN, I., & WEISS, K. R. (1982). Activity of an identified serotonergic neuron in free moving *Aplysia* correlates with behavioral arousal. *Brain Research*, 241, 334–337. **229**

KUPPERMANN, B. D., & KASAMATSU, T. (1983). Changes in geniculate cell size following brief monocular blockade of retinal activity in kittens. *Nature*, 306, 465–468. **420**

KUPRYS, R., & OLTMANS, G. A. (1982). Amphetamine anorexia and hypothalamic catecholamines in genetically obese mice (*ob/ob*). *Pharmacology, Biochemistry & Behavior*, 17, 271–282.

KUWADA, S., YIN, T. C. T., & WICKESBERG, R. E. (1979). Response of cat inferior colliculus neurons to binaural beat stimuli: Possible mechanisms for sound localization. *Science*, 206, 586–588. **171**

KWAN, H. C., MACKAY, W. A., MURPHY, J. T., & WONG, Y. C. (1985). Properties of visual cue responses in primate precentral cortex. *Brain Research*, 343, 24–35. **230**

KYRIACOU, C. P., & HALL, J. C. (1984). Learning and memory mutations impair acoustic priming of mating behaviour in *Drosophila*. *Nature*, 308, 62–65. **381**

LABBE, R., FIRL, A., JR., MUFSON, E. J., & STEIN, D. G. (1983). Fetal brain transplants: Reduction of cognitive deficits in rats with frontal cortex lesions. *Science*, 221, 470–472. **437**

LACKNER, J. R., & SHENKER, B. (1985). Proprioceptive influences on auditory and visual spatial localization. *Journal of Neuroscience*, 5, 579–583. **172**

LADOSKY, W., FIGUEIRÊDO, B. C., & SCHNEIDER, H. T. (1984). Hypothalamic nuclei catechol-O-methyl-transferase and the process of brain sexual differentiation. *Brazilian Journal of Medical Biological Research*, 17, 107–117. **297, 298**

LADOSKY, W., & GAZIRI, L. C. J. (1970). Brain serotonin and sexual differentiation of the nervous system. *Neuroendocrinology*, 6, 168–174. **295, 298**

LADOSKY, W., & SCHNEIDER, H. T. (1981). Changes in hypothalamic catechol-O-methyl-transferase during sexual differentiation of the brain. *Brazilian Journal of Medical Biological Research*, 14, 409–413. **298**

LAGAMMA, E. F., ADLER, J. E., & BLACK, I. B. (1984). Impulse activity differentially regulates [Leu]enkephalin and catecholamine characters in the adrenal medulla. *Science*, 224, 1102–1104. **323**

LAING, D. G., & PANHUBER, H. (1978). Neural and behavioral changes in rats following continuous exposure to an odor. *Journal of Comparative Physiology*, 124, 259–265. **410**

LAING, D. G., & PANHUBER, H. (1980). Olfactory sensitivity of rats reared in an odorous or deodorized environment. *Physiology & Behavior*, 25, 555–558. **410**

LAING, D. G., PANHUBER, J., PITTMAN, E. A., WILLCOX, M. E., & EAGLESON, G. K. (1985). Prolonged exposure to an odor or deodorized air alters the size of the mitral cells in the olfactory bulb. *Brain Research*, 336, 81–87. **410**

LAM, D. M.-K., LASATER, E. M., & NAKA, K.-I. (1978). Gamma-aminobutyric acid: A neurotransmitter candidate for cone horizontal cells of the catfish retina. *Proceedings of the National Academy of Sciences, U.S.A.*, 75, 6310–6313. **197**

LAMB, T. D. (1981). The involvement of rod photoreceptors in dark adaptation. *Vision Research*, 21, 1773–1782. **218**

LAMB, T. D., & SIMON, E. J. (1977). Analysis of electrical noise in turtle cones. *Journal of Physiology*, 272, 435–468. **194, 218**

LAND, E. H. (1959). Experiment in colour vision. *Scientific American*, 5, 84–90. **181**

LAND, E. H. (1974). The retinex theory of colour vision. *Proceedings of the Royal Institute of Great Britain*, 47, 23–58. **181**

LAND, P. W., & LUND, R. D. (1979). Development of the rat's uncrossed retinotectal pathway and its relation to plasticity studies. *Science*, 205, 698–700. **431, 433**

LANDAU, E. M., SMOLINSKY, A., & LASS, Y. (1973). Post-tetanic potentiation and facilitation do not share a common calcium-dependent mechanism. *Nature New Biology*, 244, 155–157. **110**

LANDFIELD, P. W. (1977). Different effects of post-trial driving or blocking of the theta rhythm on avoidance learning in rats. *Physiology & Behavior*, 18, 439–445. **373**

LANE, J. D., SANDS, M. P., SMITH, J. E., & CHEREK, D. R. (1980). Receptor changes following conditioned emotional response. *Society for Neurosciences Abstracts*, 6, 543. **332**

LANGER, S. Z., JAVOY-AGID, F., RAISMAN, R., BRILEY, M., & AGID, Y. (1981). Distribution of specific high-affinity binding sites for [^{3}H]imipramine in human brain. *Journal of Neurochemistry*, 37, 267–271. **354**

LANGER, S. Z., ZARIFIAN, E., BRILEY, M., RAISMAN, R., & SECHTER, D. (1982). High-affinity ^{3}H-imipramine binding: A new biological marker in depression. *Pharmacopsychiatria*, 15, 4–10. **354**

LAPIERRE, Y. D., KNOTT, V. J., & GRAY, R. (1984). Psychophysiological correlates of sodium lactate. *Psychopharmacology Bulletin*, 20, 50–57. **324**

LAROCHE, S., BERGIS, O. E., & BLOCH, V. (1983). Posttrial reticular facilitation of dentate multiunit conditioning is followed by an increased long-term potentiation. *Society for Neurosciences Abstracts*, 9, 645. **394**

LAROCHE, S., & BLOCH, V. (1982). Conditioning of hippocampal cells and long-term potentiation: An approach to mechanisms of posttrial memory facilitation. In C. A. Marsan & H. Matthies (Eds.), *Neuronal plasticity and memory formation*. New York: Raven. **389**

LAROCHE, S., FALCOU, R., & BLOCH, V. (1983). Post-trial reticular facilitation of associative changes in multiunit activity: Comparison between dentate gyrus and entorhinal cortex. *Behavioral Brain Research*, 9, 381–387. **389**

LAURBERG, S., & ZIMMER, J. (1980). Lesion-induced rerouting of hippocampal mossy fibers in developing but not in adult rats. *Journal of Comparative Neurology*, 190, 627–650. **437**

LAVIELLE, S., TASSIN, J.-P., THIERRY, A.-M., BLANC, G., HERVÉ, D., BARTHELEMY, C., & GLOWINSKI, J. (1978). Blockade by benzodiazepines of the selective high increase in dopamine turnover induced by stress in mesocortical dopaminergic neurons of the rat. *Brain Research*, 168, 585–594. **335, 344**

LAVOND, D. G., MCCORMICK, D. A., & THOMPSON, R. F. (1984). A nonrecoverable learning deficit. *Physiological Psychology*, 12, 103–110. **392**

LE MAGNEN, J. (1983). Body energy balance and food intake: A neuroendocrine regulatory mechanism. *Physiological Reviews*, 63, 314–386. **241**

LECONTE, P., & HENNEVIN, E. (1981). Post-learning paradoxical sleep, reticular activation and noradrenergic activity. *Physiology & Behavior*, 26, 587–594. **374**

LEDOUX, J. E., WILSON, D. H., & GAZZANIGA, M. S. (1977). A divided mind: Observations on the conscious properties of the separated hemispheres. *Annals of Neurology*, 2, 417–421. **444**

LEE, K. S., SCHOTTLER, F., OLIVER, M., & LYNCH, G. (1980). Brief bursts of high-frequency stimulation produce two types of structural change in rat hippocampus. *Journal of Neurophysiology*, 44, 247–258. **396**

LEIBOWITZ, S. F. (1976). Brain catecholaminergic mechanisms for control of hunger. In D. Novin, W. Wyrwicka, & G. Bray (Eds.), *Hunger: Basic mechanisms and clinical implications*. New York: Raven. **248, 254**

LEIBOWITZ, S. F. (1985). Brain neurotransmitters and appetite regulation. *Psychopharmacology Bulletin*, 21, 412–418. **248, 254**

LEIBOWITZ, S. F., WEISS, G. F., YEE, F., & TRETTER, J. B. (1985). Noradrenergic innervation of the paraventricular nucleus: Specific role in control of carbohydrate ingestion. *Brain Research Bulletin*, 14, 561–567.

References

246, 248, 249, 254, 256, 268

LEMBECK, F., DONNERER, J., & COLPAERT, F. C. (1981). Increase of substance P in primary afferent nerves during chronic pain. *Neuropeptides*, 1, 175–180. **168**

LEMOS, J., NOVAK-HOFER, I., & LEVITAN, I. B. (1981). Serotonin effects on protein phosphorylation within a single living nerve cell. *Neuroscience Abstracts*, 7, 932. **88**

LEMOS, J. R., NOVAK-HOFER, I., & LEVITAN, I. B. (1982). Serotonin alters the phosphorylation of specific proteins inside a single living nerve cell. *Nature*, 298, 64–67. **88**

LEONARD, B. E. (1982). Current status of the biogenic amine theory of depression. *Neurochemistry International*, 4, 339–350. **348**

LESTER, H. A. (1977). The response to acetylcholine. *Scientific American*, 236, 107–118. **78, 85**

LETTVIN, J. Y., MATURANA, H. R., MCCULLOCH, W. S., & PITTS, W. H. (1959). What the frog's eye tells the frog's brain. *Proceedings of the Institute of Radio Engineers*, 47, 1940–1951. **159**

LEVAY, S., HUBEL, D. H., & WIESEL, T. N. (1975). The pattern of ocular dominance columns in macaque visual cortex revealed by a reduced silver stain. *Journal of Comparative Neurology*, 159, 559–576.

LEVENTHAL, A. G., & HIRSCH, H. V. B. (1970). Cortical effect of early selective exposure to diagonal lines. *Science*, 190, 902–904. **427**

LEVERE, T. E., & DAVIS, N. (1977). Recovery of function after brain damage: The motivational specificity of spared neural traces. *Experimental Neurology*, 57, 883–899. **434**

LEVI, D. M., HARWERTH, R. S., & SMITH, E. L., III. (1979). Humans deprived of normal binocular vision have binocular interactions tuned to size and orientation. *Science*, 206, 852–854. **424**

LEVIN, B. E., COMAI, K., O'BRIEN, R. A., & SULLIVAN, A. C. (1982). Abnormal brown adipose composition and beta-adrenoreceptor binding in obese Zucker rats. *American Journal of Physiology*, 243, E217–E224. **251**

LEVIN, B. E., & SULLIVAN, A. C. (1979). Catecholamine levels in discrete brain nuclei of seven month old genetically obese rats. *Pharmacology, Biochemistry & Behavior*, 11, 77–82. **252**

LEVIN, B. E., TRISCARI, J., & SULLIVAN, A. C. (1981). Defective catecholamine metabolism in peripheral organs of genetically obese Zucker rats. *Brain Research*, 224, 353–366. **251**

LEVINE, A. S., & MORLEY, J. E. (1982). Purinergic regulation of food intake. *Science*, 217, 77–79.

LEVINE, M. W., & SHEFNER, J. M. (1981). *Fundamentals of sensation and perception*. Reading, MA: Addison-Wesley.

LEVITAN, I. B., DE PEYER, J. E., CACHELIN, A. B., & REUTER, H. (1982). Calcium-activated potassium conductance in internally perfused snail neurons is enhanced by protein phosphorylation. *Neuroscience Abstracts*, 79, 566. **88, 89**

LEVITT, D. R., & TEITELBAUM, P. (1973). Somnolence, akinesia, and sensory activation of motivated behavior in the lateral hypothalamic syndrome. *Proceedings of the National Academy of Sciences, U.S.A.*, 72, 2819–2823. **245**

LEVITT, F. B., & VAN SLUYTERS, R. C. (1982). Recovery of binocular function in kitten visual cortex. *Journal of Neurophysiology*, 48, 1336–1346. **423**

LEVITT, P., & NOEBELS, J. L. (1981). Mutant mouse tottering: Selective increase of locus ceruleus axons in a defined single-locus mutation. *Proceedings of the National Academy of Sciences, U.S.A.*, 78, 4630–4634. **130**

LEVY, J., & TREVARTHEN, C. (1976). Metacontrol of hemispheric function in human split-brain patients. *Journal of Experimental Psychology: Human Perception and Performance*, 2, 299–312. **444**

LEVY, W. B., & STEWARD, O. (1979). Synapses as associative memory elements in the hippocampal formation. *Brain Research*, 175, 233–245. **395**

LEWIS, D. J. (1979). Psychobiology of active and inactive memory. *Psychological Bulletin*, 86, 1054–1083. **365, 370–372**

LEWIS, D. J., BREGMAN, N. J., & MAHAN, J. J., JR. (1972). Cue-dependent amnesia in rats. *Journal of Comparative and Physiological Psychology*, 81, 243–247. **370**

LEWIS, R. S., & HUDSPETH, A. J. (1983). Voltage- and ion-dependent conductances in solitary vertebrate hair cells. *Nature*, 304, 538–541. **150, 167**

LEYSEN, J. E., DE CHAFFOY DE COURCELLES, D., DE CLERCK, F., NIEMEGEERS, C. J. E., & VAN NUETEN, J. M. (1984). Serotonin-S₂ receptor binding sites and functional correlates. *Neuropharmacology*, 23, 1493–1501.

LIANG, K. C., BENNETT, C., & MCGAUGH, J. L. (1985). Peripheral epinephrine modulates the effects of post-training amygdala stimulation on memory. *Behavioral Brain Research*, 15, 93–100. **374**

LIBERMAN, M. C. (1982). Single-neuron labeling in the cat auditory nerve. *Science*, 216, 1239–1241. **16, 147**

LIBERTUN, C., TIMIRAS, P. S., & KRAGT, C. L. (1973). Sexual differences in the hypothalamic cholinergic system before and after puberty: Inductory effect of testosterone. *Neuroendocrinology*, 12, 73–85. **298, 309**

LIBET, B. (1973). Electrical stimulation of cortex in human subjects, and conscious sensory aspects. In A. Iggo (Ed.), *Handbook of sensory physiology: Vol. II. Somatosensory system* (pp. 743–790). New York: Springer-Verlag. **9, 171, 172, 444**

LIBET, B. (1979). Which postsynaptic action of dopamine is mediated by cyclic AMP? *Life Sciences*, 24, 1043–1058. **86, 90, 98**

LIBET, B., ALBERTS, W. W., WRIGHT, E. W., JR., & FEINSTEIN, B. (1967). Responses of human somatosensory cortex to stimuli below threshold for conscious sensation. *Science*, 158, 1597–1600. **9, 171, 172, 444**

LIBET, B., ALBERTS, W. W., WRIGHT, E. W., JR., LEWIS, M., & FEINSTEIN, B. (1975). Cortical representation of evoked potentials relative to conscious sensory responses, and of somatosensory qualities — in man. In H. H. Kornhuber (Ed.), *The somatosensory system*. New York: Springer-Verlag.

LIEBURG, I., & MCEWEN, B. S. (1977). Brain cell nuclear retention of testosterone metabolites, 5,alpha-dihydrotestosterone and estradiol-17beta, in adult rats. *Endocrinology*, 100, 588–597. **284**

LIEBLICH, I., COHEN, E., & BEILES, A. (1978). Selection for high and for low rates of self-stimulation in rats. *Physiology & Behavior*, 21, 843–849. **253**

LIEBLICH, I., COHEN, E., GANCHROW, J. R., BLASS, E. M., & BERGMANN, F. (1983). Morphine tolerance in genetically selected rats induced by chronically elevated saccharine intake. *Science*, 221, 871–873. **253**

LILLY, R., CUMMINGS, J. L., BENSON, F., &

FRANKEL, M. (1983). The human Klüver-Bucy syndrome. *Neurology*, 33, 1141–1145. **325**

LINCOLN, D. W. (1967). Unit activity in the hypothalamus, septum and preoptic area of the rat: Characteristics of spontaneous activity and the effect of oestrogen. *Journal of Endocrinology*, 37, 177–189. **312**

LINCOLN, D. W., & CROSS, B. A. (1967). Effect of oestrogen on the responsiveness of neurones in the hypothalamus, septum and preoptic area of rats with light-induced persistent oestrus. *Journal of Endocrinology*, 37, 191–203. **315**

LINCOLN, J. S., MCCORMICK, D. A., & THOMPSON, R. F. (1982). Ipsilateral cerebellar lesions prevent learning of the classically conditioned nictitating membrane/eyelid response. *Brain Research*, 242, 190–193.

LINDSAY, P., & NORMAN, D. (1977). *Human information processing: An introduction to psychology* (2nd ed.). New York: Academic Press.

LINDSLEY, D. B., SCHREINER, L. H., KNOWLES, W. B., & MAGOUN, H. W. (1950). Behavioral and EEG changes following chronic brain stem lesions in the cat. *Electroencephalography and Clinical Neurophysiology*, 2, 483–498. **35**

LINGJAERDE, O. (1983). The biochemistry of depression. *Acta Psychiatrica Scandinavica* (Suppl. 302), 36–51. **348**

LIPP, H.-P., SCHWEGLER, H., & DRISCOLL, P. (1984). Postnatal modification of hippocampal circuitry alters avoidance learning in adult rats. *Science*, 225, 80–82.

LIPPA, A. S., KLEPNER, C. A., YUNGER, L., SANO, M. C., SMITH, W. V., & BEER, B. (1978). Relationship between benzodiazepine receptors and experimental anxiety in rats. *Pharmacology, Biochemistry & Behavior*, 9, 853–856. **343**

LIPTON, S. A. (1983). cGMP and EGTA increase the light-sensitive current of retinal rods. *Brain Research*, 265, 41–48. **193**

LIPTON, S. A., OSTROY, S. E., & DOWLING, J. E. (1977). Electrical and adaptive properties of rod photoreceptors in *Bufo marinus*: I. Effects of altered extracellular Ca²⁺ levels. *Journal of General Physiology*, 70, 747–770.

LIPTON, S. A., RASMUSSEN, H., & DOWLING, J. E. (1977). Electrical and adaptive properties of rod photoreceptors in *Bufo marinus*: II. Effects of cyclic nucleotides and prostaglandins. *Journal of General Physiology*, 70, 771–791. **193, 194**

LISKOWSKY, D. R., & POTTER, L. T. (1985). D-2 dopamine receptors in the frontal cortex of rat and human. *Life Sciences*, 36, 1551–1559.

LITTERIA, M. (1977). Inhibitory action of neonatal estrogenization on the incorporation of [³H]lysine into proteins of specific limbic and paralimbic neurons of the adult rat. *Brain Research*, 127, 164–167. **295**

LIVINGSTONE, M. S., & HUBEL, D. H. (1981). Effects of sleep and arousal on the processing of visual information in the cat. *Nature*, 291, 554–561. **239, 240**

LIVINGSTONE, M. S., & HUBEL, D. H. (1983). Specificity of cortico-cortical connections in monkey visual system. *Nature*, 304, 531–534. **162**

LIVINGSTONE, M. S., & TEMPEL, B. L. (1983). Genetic dissection of monamine neurotransmitter synthesis in *Drosophila*. *Nature*, 303, 67–70. **129**

LJUNGBERG, T., & UNGERSTEDT, U. (1976). Reinstatement of eating by dopamine agonists in aphagic dopamine denervated rats. *Physiology & Behavior*, 16,

References

277–283. **246**

LLINÁS, R. R. (1982). Calcium in synaptic transmission. *Scientific American*, 247, 56–65. **72, 73**

LLOYD, C. (1980). Life events and depressive disorder reviewed: II. Events as precipitating factors. *Archives of General Psychiatry*, 37, 541–548. **337**

LOEWENSTEIN, W. R. (1959). The generation of electric activity in a nerve ending. *Annals of the New York Academy of Sciences*, 81, 367–387. **152**

LOEWENSTEIN, W. R. (1960). Biological transducers. *Scientific American*, 203, 98–108. **152**

LOEWENSTEIN, W. R., & RATHKAMP, R. (1958). The sites for mechano-electric conversion in a Pacinian corpuscle. *Journal of General Physiology*, 41, 1245–1265. **152**

LOLLEY, R. N., & RACZ, E. (1982). Calcium modulation of cyclic GMP synthesis in rat visual cells. *Vision Research*, 22, 1481–1486. **194**

LONG, G. M., & BEATON, R. J. (1982). The case for peripheral persistence: Effects of target and background luminance on a partial-report task. *Journal of Experimental Psychology: Human Perception and Performance*, 8, 383–391. **221**

LORDEN, J. F. (1979). Differential effects on body weight of central 6-hydroxydopamine lesions in obese (*ob/ob*) and diabetes (*db/db*) mice. *Journal of Comparative and Physiological Psychology*, 93, 1085–1096. **252**

LÖSSNER, B., JORK, R., KRUG, M., & MATTHIES, M. (1982). Protein synthesis in rat hippocampus during training and stimulation experiments. In C. A. Marsan & H. Matthies (Eds.), *Neuronal plasticity and memory formation*. New York: Raven. **375, 381**

LOUIS-SYLVESTRE, J. (1984). Meal size: Role of reflexly induced insulin release. *Journal of the Autonomic Nervous System*, 10, 317–324. **242**

LOY, R., & MILNER, T. A. (1980). Sexual dimorphism in extent of axonal sprouting in rat hippocampus. *Science*, 208, 1282–1284. **301, 307, 437**

LOY, R., & MILNER, T. A. (1983). Neonatal steroid treatment alters axonal sprouting in adult hippocampus: Sexually dimorphic development of cholinergic target neurons. *Birth defects: Original Articles Series*, 19, 417–423. **301, 307**

LUINE, V. N., KHYLCHEVSKAYA, R. I., & MCEWEN, B. S. (1975). Effect of gonadal hormones on enzyme activities in brain and pituitary of male and female rats. *Brain Research*, 86, 283–292. **296**

LUINE, V. N., RENNER, K. J., FRANKFURT, M., & AZMITIA, E. C. (1984). Facilitated sexual behavior reversed and serotonin restored by raphe nuclei transplanted into denervated hypothalamus. *Science*, 226, 1436–1439. **437**

LUKOFF, D., SNYDER, K., VENTURA, J., & NUECHTERLEIN, K. H. (1984). Life events, familial stress, and coping in the developmental course of schizophrenia. *Schizophrenia Bulletin*, 10, 258–292. **337**

LUZZATTO, L., USANGA, E. A., BIENZLE, U., ESAN, G. F. J., & FASUAN, F. A. (1979). Imbalance in X-chromosome expression: Evidence for a human X-linked gene affecting growth of hemopoietic cells. *Science*, 205, 1418–1420. **287**

LYNCH, G., & BAUDRY, M. (1984). The biochemistry of memory: A new and specific hypothesis. *Science*, 224, 1057–1063. **394, 396**

LYNCH, G., LARSON, J., KELSO, S., BARRIONUEVO, G., & SCHOTTLER, F. (1983). Intracellular injections of EGTA block induction of hippocampal long-term potentiation. *Nature*, 305, 719–721. **395**

LYNCH, G. S., DUNWIDDIE, T., & CRIBKOFF, V. (1977). Heterosynaptic depression: A postsynaptic correlate of long-term potentiation. *Nature*, 266, 737–739. **395**

MACCOBY, E. E., DOERING, C. H., JACKLIN, C. N., & KRAEMER, H. (1979). Concentrations of sex hormones in umbilical-cord blood: Their relation to sex and birth order of infants. *Child Development*, 50, 632–642. **272**

MACDERMOTT, A. B., & WEIGHT, F. F. (1982). Action potential repolarization may involve a transient, Ca^{++}-sensitive outward current in a vertebrate neurone. *Nature*, 300, 185–188. **60**

MACHNE, X., CALMA, I., & MAGOUN, H. W. (1955). Unit activity of central cephalic brain stem in EEG arousal. *Journal of Neurophysiology*, 18, 547–558. **235**

MACKAY, A. V. P., IVERSEN, L. L., ROSSOR, M., SPOKES, E., BIRD, E., ARREGUI, A., CREESE, I., & SNYDER, S. H. (1982). Increased brain dopamine and dopamine receptors in schizophrenia. *Archives of General Psychiatry*, 39, 991–997. **345–347**

MACLEAN, P. D. (1970). The limbic brain in relation to the psychoses. In P. Black (Ed.), *Physiological correlates of emotion*. New York: Academic Press. **35, 324**

MACLEAN, P. D. (1975). Sensory and perceptive factors in emotional functions of the triune brain. In L. Levi (Ed.), *Emotions: Their parameters and measurement*. New York: Raven. **35, 324**

MACLEAN, P. D. (1985). Brain evolution relating to family, play, and the separation call. *Archives of General Psychiatry*, 42, 405–417. **35, 324**

MACLENNAN, A. J., & MAIER, S. F. (1983). Coping and the stress-induced potentiation of stimulant stereotypy in the rat. *Science*, 219, 1091–1093. **338**

MACLUSKY, N. J., LIEBERBURG, I., KREY, L. C., & MCEWEN, B. E. (1980). Progestin receptors in the brain and pituitary of the bonnet monkey (*Macaca radiata*): Differences between the monkey and the rat in the distribution of progestin receptors. *Endocrinology*, 106, 185–191. **285**

MACLUSKY, N. J., LIEBERBURG, I., & MCEWEN, B. S. (1979). Development of steroid receptor systems in the rodent brain. In T. H. Hamilton, J. H. Clark, & W. A. Sadler (Eds.), *Ontogeny of receptors and reproductive hormone action*. New York: Raven. **282**

MACVICAR, B. A. (1984). Voltage-dependent calcium channels in glial cells. *Science*, 226, 1345–1347. **25, 27**

MADDISON, S. (1977). Intraperitoneal and intracranial cholecystokinin depress operant responding for food. *Physiology & Behavior*, 19, 819–824.

MADISON, D. V., & NICOLL, R. A. (1982). Noradrenaline blocks accommodation of pyramidal cell discharge in the hippocampus. *Nature*, 299, 636–638. **90, 158, 240**

MAENO, T. (1966). Analysis of sodium and potassium conductances in the procaine end-plate potential. *Journal of Physiology*, 183, 592–606. **80**

MAGGI, A., & PEREZ, J. (1984). Progesterone and estrogens in rat brain: Modulation of GABA (gamma-aminobutyric acid) receptor activity. *European Journal of Pharmacology*, 103, 165–168. **310**

MAGGI, A., U'PRICHARD, D. C., & ENNA, S. J. (1980). Beta-adrenergic regulation of alpha$_2$-adrenergic receptors in the central nervous system. *Science*, 207, 645–647. **107**

MAGNAVACCA, C., & CHANEL, J. (1979). Modulation des réponses du bulbe olfactif à l'odeur du mâle. Étude de l'activité multiunitaire chez la ratte au cours du cycle oestral. *Journal of Physiology, Paris*, 75, 815–824. **315**

MAIER, S. F. (1984). Learned helplessness and animal models of depression. *Progress in Neuro-Psychopharmacology & Biological Psychiatry*, 8, 435–446. **331, 336, 338**

MAIER, S. F., & SELIGMAN, M. E. P. (1976). Learned helplessness: Theory and evidence. *Journal of Experimental Psychology: General*, 105, 3–46. **331, 337**

MAJ, M., ARIANO, M. G., PIROZZI, R., SALVATI, A., & KEMALI, D. (1984). Platelet monoamine oxidase activity in schizophrenia: Relationship to family history of the illness and neuroleptic treatment. *Journal of Psychiatric Research*, 18, 131–137. **339, 341**

MAJ, J., MOGILNICKA, E., & KORDECKA, A. (1979). Chronic treatment with antidepressant drugs: Potentiation of apomorphine-induced aggressive behaviour in rats. *Neurosciences Letters*, 13, 337–341.

MALACH, R., EBERT, R., & VAN SLUYTERS, R. C. (1984). Recovery from effects of brief monocular deprivation in the kitten. *Journal of Neurophysiology*, 51, 538–551. **423**

MALAMUD, N. (1967). Psychiatric disorder with intracranial tumors of limbic system. *Archives of Neurology*, 17, 113–123. **325**

MALAMUT, B. L., SAUNDERS, R. C., & MISHKIN, M. (1984). Monkeys with combined amygdalo-hippocampal lesions succeed in object discrimination learning despite 24-hour intertrial intervals. *Behavioral Neuroscience*, 98, 759–769. **446**

MALPELI, J. G., SCHILLER, P. H., & COLBY, C. L. (1981). Response properties of single cells in monkey striate cortex during reversible inactivation of individual lateral geniculate laminae. *Journal of Neurophysiology*, 46, 1102–1119. **188**

MANOSEVITZ, M., & JOEL, U. (1973). Behavioral effects of environmental enrichment in randomly bred mice. *Journal of Comparative and Physiological Psychology*, 85, 373–382. **403**

MANSFIELD, R. J. W. (1974). Neural basis of orientation perception in primate vision. *Science*, 186, 1133–1135. **427**

MANSKY, T., & WUTTKE, W. (1983). Glutamate in hypothalamic and limbic structures of diestrous, proestrous, ovariectomized and ovariectomized estrogen-treated rats. *Neuroscience Letters*, 38, 51–56. **309**

MARC, R. E., & SPERLING, H. G. (1977). Chromatic organization of primate cones. *Science*, 196, 454–456.

MARCUS, J., MACCOBY, E. E., JACKLIN, C. N., & DOERING, C. H. (1985). Individual differences in mood in early childhood: Their relation to gender and neonatal sex steroids. *Developmental Psychobiology*, 18, 327–340. **277**

MARG, E. (1973). Recording from single cells in the human visual cortex. In R. Jung (Ed.), *Visual centers in the brain: Handbook of sensory physiology, VII/3, Central visual information*. New York: Springer-Verlag. **217**

MARG, E., ADAMS, J. E., & RUTKIN, B. (1968). Receptive fields of cells in the human visual cortex. *Experientia*, 24, 348–350. **217**

MARGULES, D. L. (1970a). Alpha-adrenergic receptors in hypothalamus for the suppression of feeding behavior by satiety. *Journal of Comparative and Physiological Psy-*

chology, 73, 1–12. **248, 268**

MARGULES, D. L. (1970b). Beta-adrenergic receptors in hypothalamus for learned and unlearned taste aversions. *Journal of Comparative and Physiological Psychology, 73, 13–21.* **248, 268**

MARGULES, D. L. (1978). Molecular theory of obesity, sterility and other behavioral and endocrine problems in genetically obese mice *(ob/ob). Neuroscience & Biobehavioral Reviews, 2, 231–233.* **248**

MARGULES, D. L. (1979). Beta-endorphin and endoloxone: Hormones of the autonomic nervous system for the conservation or expenditure of bodily resources and energy in anticipation of famine or feast. *Neuroscience & Biobehavioral Reviews, 3, 155–162.* **248**

MARGULES, D. L., & DRAGOVICH, J. (1973). Studies on phentolamine-induced overeating and finickiness. *Journal of Comparative and Physiological Psychology, 84, 644–651.* **248, 268**

MARGULES, D. L., & LICHTENSTEIGER, W. (1978). Environmental events that modify the catecholamine fluorescence of the A2 cell bodies in nucleus tractus solitarii. *Journal of Comparative and Physiological Psychology, 92, 713–719.* **248**

MARGULES, D. L., MOISSET, B., LEWIS, M. J., SHIBUYA, H., & PERT, C. B. (1978). Beta-endorphin is associated with overeating in genetically obese mice *(ob/ob)* and rats *(fa/fa). Science, 202, 988–991.* **252**

MARIANI, A. P. (1982). Biplexiform cells: Ganglion cells of the primate retina that contact photoreceptors. *Science, 216, 1134–1136.* **184**

MARR, D. (1969). A theory of cerebellar cortex. *Journal of Physiology, London, 202, 437–471.* **449**

MARRONE, B. L., & FEDER, H. H. (1977). Characteristics of [³H]estrogen and [³H]progestin uptake and effects of progesterone on [³H]estrogen uptake in brain, anterior pituitary and peripheral tissues of male and female guinea pigs. *Biology of Reproduction, 17, 42–57.* **283**

MARSHALL, J. F. (1978). Comparison of the sensorimotor dysfunctions produced by damage to lateral hypothalamus or superior colliculus in the rat. *Experimental Neurology, 58, 203–217.* **245**

MARSHALL, K. C., & ENGBERG, I. (1979). Reversal potential for noradrenaline-induced hyperpolarization of spinal motor neurons. *Science, 205, 422–425.* **89**

MARTIN, G. E., & MYERS, R. D. (1975). Evoked release of [¹⁴C]norepinephrine from the rat hypothalamus during feeding. *American Journal of Physiology, 229, 1547–1555.* **248**

MARTIN, G. K., LAND, T., & THOMPSON, R. F. (1980). Classical conditioning of the rabbit *(Oryctolagus cuniculus)* nictitating membrane response, with electrical brain stimulation as the unconditioned stimulus. *Journal of Comparative and Physiological Psychology, 94, 216–226.* **390**

MARTIN, J. H. (1981). Somatic sensory system: II. Anatomical substrates for somatic sensation. In E. R. Kandel & J. H. Schwartz (Eds.), *Principles of neural science.* New York: Elsevier/North-Holland. **155**

MARTIN, J. T., & BAUM, M. J. (1986). Neonatal exposure of female ferrets to testosterone alters sociosexual preferences in adulthood. *Psychoneuroendocrinology, 11, 167–176.* **256, 291**

MARTIN, M. R., & DICKSON, J. W. (1983). Lateral inhibition in the anteroventral cochlear nucleus of the rat: A microiontophoretic study. *Hearing Research, 9, 35–41.* **160, 170**

MARTONE, M., BUTTERS, N., PAYNE, M., BECKER, J. T., & SAX, D. S. (1984). Dissociations between skill learning and verbal recognition in amnesia and dementia. *Archives of Neurology, 41, 965–970.* **446**

MARTRES, M.-P., BOUTHENET, M.-L., SOKOLOFF, P., & SCHWARTZ, J.-C. (1985). Widespread distribution of brain dopamine receptors evidenced with [¹²⁵I]iodosulpride, a highly selective ligand. *Science, 228, 752–755.*

MARWAHA, J., HOFFER, B., PITTMAN, R., & FREEDMAN, R. (1980). Age-related electrophysiological changes in rat cerebellum. *Brain Research, 201, 85–97.* **356**

MARX, J. L. (1983). Synthesizing the opioid peptides. *Science, 220, 395–397.* **126**

MASON, S. T., & FIBIGER, H. C. (1979). I. Anxiety: The locus coeruleus disconnection. *Life Sciences, 25, 2141–2147.* **355**

MASTERTON, R. B., & BERKLEY, M. A. (1974). Brain function: Changing ideas on the role of sensory, motor, and association cortex in behavior. *Annual Review of Psychology, 25, 277–312.* **31**

MATSUMOTO, A., & ARAI, Y. (1980). Sexual dimorphism in "wiring pattern" in the hypothalamic arcuate nucleus and its modification by neonatal hormonal environment. *Brain Research, 190, 238–242.* **300**

MATSUMOTO, A., & ARAI, Y. (1981a). Effect of androgen on sexual differentiation of synaptic organization in the hypothalamic arcuate nucleus: An ontogenetic study. *Neuroendocrinology, 33, 166–169.* **300**

MATSUMOTO, A., & ARAI, Y. (1981b). Neuronal plasticity in the deafferented hypothalamic arcuate nucleus of adult female rats and its enhancement by treatment with estrogen. *Journal of Comparative Neurology, 197, 197–205.* **307**

MATSUMOTO, A., & ARAI, Y. (1983a). Sex difference in volume of the ventromedial nucleus of the hypothalamus in the rat. *Endocrinologica Japonica, 30, 277–280.* **300**

MATSUMOTO, A., & ARAI, Y. (1983b). Sexual dimorphism in the ventromedial nucleus of the hypothalamus. *Neuroscience Letters Supplement, 13, S17.* **300**

MATSUMOTO, A., KOBAYASHI, S., MURAKAMI, S., & ARAI, Y. (1984). Recovery of declined ovarian function in aged female rats by transplantation of newborn hypothalamic tissue. *Proceedings of the Japan Academy, 60, 73–76.* **438**

MATSUO, R., SHIMIZU, N., & KUSANO, K. (1984). Lateral hypothalamic modulation of oral sensory afferent activity in nucleus tractus solitarius neurons of rats. *Journal of Neuroscience, 4, 1201–1207.* **264**

MATTHEWS, J. W., BOOTH, D. A., & STOLERMAN, I. P. (1978). Factors influencing feeding elicited by intracranial noradrenaline in rats. *Brain Research, 141, 119–128.* **248**

MAUNSELL, J. H. R., & VAN ESSEN, D. C. (1983). Functional properties of neurons in middle temporal visual area of the macaque monkey: II. Binocular interactions and sensitivity to binocular disparity. *Journal of Neurophysiology, 49, 1148–1167.* **214**

MAYER, D. J., & PRICE, D. D. (1982). A physiological and psychological analysis of pain: A potential model of motivation. In D. W. Pfaff (Ed.), *The physiological mechanisms of motivation.* New York: Springer-Verlag. **163, 168**

MAYER, J., DICKIE, M. M., BATES, M. W., & VITALE, J. J. (1951). Free selection of nutrients by heredi-

tarily obese mice. *Science, 113, 745–747.* **253**

MAZUR, A., & LAMB, T. A. (1980). Testosterone, status, and mood in human males. *Hormones and Behavior, 14, 236–246.* **292**

MCAFEE, D. A., HENON, B. K., WHITING, G. J., HORN, J. P., YAROWSKY, P. J., & TURNER, D. K. (1980). The action of cAMP and catecholamines in mammalian sympathetic ganglia. *Federation Proceedings, 39, 2997–3002.* **89**

MCAFEE, D. A., & YAROWSKY, P. J. (1979). Calcium-dependent potentials in the mammalian sympathetic neurone. *Journal of Physiology, 290, 507–523.* **60**

MCBRIDE, W. J., FLINT, R. S., CIANCONE, M. T., & MURPHY, J. M. (1983). In vitro release of endogenous monamines and amino acids from several CNS regions of the rat. *Neurochemical Research, 8, 245–257.* **98**

MCCARTHY, J. C. (1979). Normal variation in body fat and its inheritance. In M. F. W. Festing (Ed.), *Animal models of obesity.* New York: Oxford University Press. **251**

MCCLURKIN, J. W., & MARROCCO, R. T. (1984). Visual cortical input alters spatial tuning in monkey lateral geniculate nucleus cells. *Journal of Physiology, 348, 135–152.* **221**

MCCORMICK, D. A., & PRINCE, D. A. (1985). Two types of muscarinic response to acetylcholine in mammalian cortical neurons. *Proceedings of the National Academy of Sciences, U.S.A., 1985, 82, 6344–6348.*

MCCORMICK, D. A., & THOMPSON, R. F. (1984). Cerebellum: Essential involvement in the classically conditioned eyelid response. *Science, 223, 296–299.* **392**

MCCOURT, M. E., & JACOBS, G. H. (1983). Effects of photic environment on the development of spectral response properties of optic nerve fibers in the ground squirrel. *Experimental Brain Research, 49, 443–452.* **430**

MCEWEN, B. S. (1978). Sexual maturation and differentiation: The role of the gonadal steroids. *Progress in Brain Research, 48, 291–307.* **284**

MCEWEN, B. S. (1981). Neural gonadal steroid actions. *Science, 211, 1303–1311.* **306**

MCEWEN, B. S., BIEGON, A., FISCHETTE, C. T., LUINE, V. N., PARSONS, B., & RAINBOW, T. C. (1984). Sex differences in programming of responses to estradiol in the brain. In M. Serio, M. Motta, M. Zanisi, & L. Martini (Eds.), *Sexual differentiation: Basic and clinical aspects.* New York: Raven. **298**

MCGAUGH, J. L., & HERZ, M. J. (1972). *Memory consolidation.* San Francisco: Albion. **368, 369, 371, 373**

MCGAUGH, J. L., MARTINEZ, J. L., JENSEN, R. A., HANNAN, T. J., VASQUEZ, B. J., MESSING, R. B., LIANG, K. C., BREWTON, C. B., & SPIEHLER, V. R. (1982). Modulation of memory storage by treatments affecting peripheral catecholamines. In C. A. Marsan & H. Matthies (Eds.), *Neuronal plasticity and memory formation.* New York: Raven. **364, 374**

MCGLONE, J. (1980). Sex differences in human brain asymmetry: A critical survey. *Behavioral and Brain Sciences, 3, 215–227.* **302**

MCLAREN, A., SIMPSON, E., TOMONARI, K., CHANDLER, P., & HOGG, H. (1984). Male sexual differentiation in mice lacking H-Y antigen. *Nature, 312, 552–555.* **286**

MCLAUGHLIN, C. L., & BAILE, C. A. (1981). Obese mice and the satiety effects of cholecystokinin, bombesin and pancreatic polypeptide. *Physiology & Behavior, 26, 433–437.* **252**

MCLAUGHLIN, C. L., BAILE, C. A., DELLA-

FERA, M. A., & KASSER, T. G. (1985). Meal-stimulated increased concentrations of CCK in the hypothalamus of Zucker obese and lean rats. *Physiology & Behavior, 35,* 215–220.

MCLEAN, S., & HOEBEL, B. G. (1982). Opiate and norepinephrine-induced feeding from the paraventricular nucleus of the hypothalamus are dissociable. *Life Sciences, 31,* 2379–2382. **248**

MCMAHAN, U. J., & KUFFLER, S. W. (1971). Visual identification of synaptic boutons on living ganglion cells and of varicosities in postganglionic axons in the heart of the frog. *Proceeding of the Royal Society of London, Series B, 177,* 485–508.

MCNAUGHTON, B. L., BARNES, C. A., & O'KEEFE, J. (1983). The contributions of position, direction, and velocity to single unit activity in the hippocampus of freely-moving rats. *Experimental Brain Research, 52,* 41–49. **216, 384**

MCNAUGHTON, B. L., DOUGLAS, R. M., & GODDARD, G. V. (1978). Synaptic enhancement in fascia dentata: Cooperativity among coactive elements. *Brain Research, 157,* 277–293. **394, 395**

MCWILLIAMS, J. R., & LYNCH, G. (1983). Rate of synaptic replacement in denervated rat hippocampus declines precipitously from the juvenile period to adulthood. *Science, 221,* 572–574. **437**

MCWILLIAMS, J. R., & LYNCH, G. (1984). Synaptic density and axonal sprouting in rat hippocampus: Stability in adulthood and decline in late adulthood. *Brain Research, 294,* 152–156. **437**

MEDNICK, S. A., SCHULSINGER, F., TEASDALE, T. W., SCHULSINGER, H., VENABLES, P. H., & ROCK, D. R. (1978). Schizophrenia in high-risk children: Sex differences in predisposing factors. In G. Serban (Ed.), *Cognitive defects in the development of mental illness.* New York: Brunner/Mazel. **327**

MEECH, R. W. (1978). Calcium-dependent potassium activation in nervous tissues. *Annual Review of Biophysics and Bioengineering, 7,* 1–18.

MEECH, R. W., & STANDEN, N. B. (1975). Potassium activation in *Helix aspersa* neurones under voltage clamp: A component mediated by calcium influx. *Journal of Physiology, 249,* 211–239. **60**

MEFFORD, I. N., BAKER, T. L., BOEHME, R., FOUTZ, A. S., CIARANELLO, R. D., BARCHAS, J. D., & DEMENT, W. C. (1983). Narcolepsy: Biogenic amine deficits in an animal model. *Science, 220,* 629–632. **129**

MEI, N. (1978). Vagal glucoreceptors in the small intestine of the cat. *Journal of Physiology, 282,* 485–506. **152**

MELTZER, H. Y., ARORA, R. C., BABER, R., & TRICOU, B. J. (1981). Serotonin uptake in blood platelets of psychiatric patients. *Archives of General Psychiatry, 38,* 1322–1326. **354**

MELZACK, R., & WALL, P. D. (1965). Pain mechanisms: A new theory. *Science, 150,* 971–979. **175**

MENDELL, L. M. (1984). Modifiability of spinal synapses. *Physiological Review, 64,* 260–324. **434**

MENDLEWICZ, J., & BARON, M. (1981). Morbidity risks in subtypes of unipolar depressive illness: Differences between early and late onset forms. *British Journal of Psychiatry, 139,* 463–466. **329**

MENKES, D. B., RASENICK, M. M., WHEELER, M. A., & BITENSKY, M. W. (1983). Guanosine triphosphate activation of brain adenylate cyclase: Enhancement by long-term antidepressant treatment. *Science, 219,* 65–

67. **348**

MENZIES, K. D., DRYSDALE, D. B., & WAITE, P. M. E. (1982). Effects of prenatal progesterone on the development of pyramidal cells in the rat cerebral cortex. *Experimental Neurology, 77,* 654–667. **277**

MERIKANGAS, K. R. (1982). Assortative mating for psychiatric disorders and psychological traits. *Archives of General Psychiatry, 39,* 1173–1180. **327**

MERZENICH, M. M., & KAAS, J. H. (1980). Principles of organization of sensory-perceptual systems in mammals. In J. M. Sprague & A. N. Epstein (Eds.), *Progress in psychobiology and physiological psychology* (Vol. 9). New York: Academic Press. **434**

MERZENICH, M. M., & KAAS, J. H. (1982). Reorganization of mammalian somatosensory cortex following peripheral nerve injury. *Trends in NeuroSciences, 5,* 434–436. **156**

MERZENICH, M. M., KNIGHT, P. L., & ROTH, C. L. (1975). Representation of cochlea within primary auditory cortex in the cat. *Journal of Neurophysiology, 38,* 231–249. **165, 171**

MERZENICH, M. M., MICHELSON, R. P., PETTIT, C. R., SCHINDLER, R. A., & REID, M. (1973). Neuronal encoding of sound sensation evoked by electrical stimulation of the acoustic nerve. *Annals of Otolaryngology, 82,* 486–503. **165, 172**

MEYER, D. K., & KRAUSS, J. (1983). Dopamine modulates cholecystokinin release in neostriatum. *Nature, 301,* 338–340.

MEYER, D. R. (1972). Access to engrams. *American Psychologist, 27,* 124–133. **370**

MEYER, D. R. (1984). The cerebral cortex: Its roles in memory storage and remembering. *Physiological Psychology, 12,* 81–98. **365, 368**

MEYER, J. S. (1985). Biochemical effects of corticosteroids on neural tissue. *Physiological Review, 65,* 946–1020. **358**

MEYER-BAHLBURG, H. F. L., & EHRHARDT, A. A. (1982). Prenatal sex hormones and human aggression: A review, and new data on progestogen effects. *Aggressive Behavior, 8,* 39–62. **291**

MICHAEL, C. R. (1978a). Color vision mechanisms in monkey striate cortex: Dual-opponent cells with concentric receptive fields. *Journal of Neurophysiology, 41,* 572–588. **207**

MICHAEL, C. R. (1978b). Color vision mechanisms in monkey striate cortex: Simple cells with dual opponent-color receptive fields. *Journal of Neurophysiology, 41,* 1233–1249.

MICHAEL, C. R. (1978c). Color-sensitive complex cells in monkey striate cortex. *Journal of Neurophysiology, 41,* 1250–1266.

MICHAEL, C. R. (1979). Color-sensitive hypercomplex cells in monkey striate cortex. *Journal of Neurophysiology, 42,* 726–744. **207**

MICHAEL, C. R. (1981). Columnar organization of color cells in monkey's striate cortex. *Journal of Neurophysiology, 46,* 587–604. **214**

MICHAEL, R. P., HOLBROOKE, S. E., & WELLER, C. (1977). Telemetry and continuous energy analysis of hypothalamic EEG changes in female cats during intromission by the male. *Psychoneuroendocrinology, 2,* 287–301. **318**

MICHAEL, R. P., & REES, H. D. (1982). Autoradiographic localization of ³H-dihydrotestosterone in the proptic area, hypothalamus, and amygdala of a male rhesus monkey.

Life Sciences, 30, 2087–2093. **284**

MICHALSKI, A., KOSSUT, M., CHMIELOWSKA, J., & TURLEJSKI, K. (1984). Crosscorrelation analysis of intracolumnar neuronal connectivity in area 17 of binocularly deprived cats. *Acta Neurobiologica Experimentalis, 43,* 1–15. **415**

MICHALSKI, A., KOSSUT, M., & ZERNICKI, B. (1975). Single-unit responses to natural objects in area 19 of cats with different early visual experiences. *Acta Neurobiologica Experimentalis, 35,* 77–83. **430**

MICHELL, R. H., KIRK, C. J., JONES, L. M., DOWNES, C. P., & CREBA, J. A. (1981). The stimulation of inositol lipid metabolism that accompanies calcium mobilization in stimulated cells: Defined characteristics and unanswered questions. *Philosophical Transactions of the Royal Society of London, Series B, 296,* 123–137. **86**

MIDDLEBROOKS, J. C., DYKES, R. W., & MERZENICH, M. M. (1980). Binaural response-specific bands in primary auditory cortex (AI) of the cat: Topographical organization orthogonal to isofrequency contours. *Brain Research, 181,* 31–48. **171**

MIGEON, B. R., SHAPIRO, L. J., NORUM, R. A., MOHANDAS, T., AXELMAN, J., & DABORA, R. L. (1982). Differential expression of steroid sulphatase locus on active and inactive human X chromosome. *Nature, 299,* 838–840. **287**

MIKAMI, A., ITO, S.-I., & KUBOTA, K. (1982). Modifications of neuron activities of the dorsalateral prefrontal cortex during extrafoveal attention. *Behavioural Brain Research, 5,* 219–223. **239**

MIKAMI, A., KUBOTA, K. (1980). Inferotemporal neuron activities and color discrimination with delay. *Brain Research, 182,* 65–78. **383**

MILJANICH, G. P., SCHWARTZ, S., & DRATZ, E. A. (1980). The structure of retinal rod photoreceptor membranes. *Federation Proceedings, 39,* 2068. **191**

MILLAN, M. J., PRZEWŁOCKI, R., JERLICZ, M., GRAMSCH, Ch., HÖLLT, V., & HERZ, A. (1981). Stress-induced release of brain and pituitary beta-endorphin: Major role of endorphins in generation of hyperthermia, not analgesia. *Brain Research, 208,* 325–338. **332**

MILLER, J. C. (1983). Sex differences in dopaminergic and cholinergic activity and function in the nigro-striatal system of the rat. *Psychoneuroendocrinology, 8,* 225–236. **309, 310**

MILLER, J. D., FARBER, J., GATZ, P., ROFFWARG, H., & GERMAN, D. C. (1983). Activity of mesencephalic dopamine and non-dopamine neurons across stages of sleep and waking in the rat. *Brain Research, 273,* 133–141. **237, 377**

MILLER, J. D., SANGHERA, M. K., & GERMAN, D. C. (1981). Mesencephalic dopaminergic unit activity in the behaviorally conditioned rat. *Life Sciences, 29,* 1255–1263. **237, 377**

MILLER, J. M., SUTTON, D., PFINGST, B., RYAN, A., BEATON, R., & GOUREVITCH, G. (1972). Single cell activity in the auditory cortex of rhesus monkeys: Behavioral dependency. *Science, 177,* 449–451. **239**

MILLER, R. F., DACHEUX, R. F., & FRUMKES, T. E. (1977). Amacrine cells in *Necturus* retina: Evidence for independent gamma-aminobutyric acid- and glycine-releasing neurons. *Science, 198,* 748–750. **198**

MILLER, R. R., & SPRINGER, A. D. (1971). Temporal course of amnesia in rats after electroconvulsive shock. *Physiology & Behavior, 6,* 229–233. **369**

MILLER, W. H., & NICOL, G. D. (1979). Evidence

that cyclic GMP regulates membrane potential in rod photoreceptors. *Nature, 280,* 64–66. **194**

MILNER, B. (1962). Les troubles de la memoire accompagnant des lesions hippocampique bilaterales. In P. Passouant (Ed.), *Physiologie de l'hippocampe.* Paris: Centre Nationale de Recherche Scientifique. **13**

MILNER, T. A., & LOY, R. (1980). Interaction of age and sex in sympathetic axon ingrowth into the hippocampus following septal afferent damage. *Anatomica Embryologica, 161,* 159–168. **437**

MINK, J. W., SINNAMON, H. M., & ADAMS, D. B. (1983). Activity of basal forebrain neurons in the rat during motivated behaviors. *Behavioural Brain Research, 8,* 85–108. **251, 318**

MIRMIRAN, M., & UYLINGS, H. B. M. (1983). The environmental enrichment effect upon cortical growth is neutralized by concomitant pharmacological suppression of active sleep in female rats. *Brain Research, 261,* 331–334. **402**

MIRMIRAN, M., VAN DEN DUNGEN, H., & UYLINGS, H. B. M. (1982). Sleep patterns during rearing under different environmental conditions in juvenile rats. *Brain Research, 233,* 287–298. **402**

MISSLIN, R., ROPARTZ, P., UNGERER, A., & MANDEL, P. (1978). Nonreproducibility of the behavioural effects induced by scotophobin. *Behavioural Processes, 3,* 45–56. **378**

MISU, Y., & KUBO, T. (1983). Presynaptic beta-adrenoceptors. *Trends in NeuroSciences, 4,* 506–508.

MITCHELL, D. E., & WILKINSON, F. (1974). The effect of early astigmatism on the visual resolution of gratings. *Journal of Physiology, 243,* 739–756. **427**

MITCHELL, G. D. (1968). Attachment differences in male and female infant monkeys. *Child Development, 39,* 611–620. **292**

MITCHELL, G., & BRANDT, E. M. (1970). Behavioral differences related to experience of mother and sex of infant in the rhesus monkey. *Developmental Psychology, 3,* 149. **292**

MITTWOCH, U. (1986). Males, females and hermaphrodites. *Annals of Human Genetics, 50,* 103–121. **287**

MIYAHARA, S., & OOMURA, Y. (1982). Inhibitory action of the ventral noradrenergic bundle on the lateral hypothalamic neurons through alpha-noradrenergic mechanisms in the rat. *Brain Research, 234,* 459–463. **256, 259**

MIZUKAMI, S., NISHIZUKA, M., & ARAI, Y. (1983). Sexual difference in nuclear volume and its ontogeny in the rat amygdala. *Experimental Neurology, 79,* 569–575. **300**

MOGENSON, G. J., JONES, D. L., & YIM, C. Y. (1980). From motivation to action: Functional interface between the limbic system and the motor system. *Progress in Neurobiology, 14,* 69–97. **230**

MOGENSON, G. J., & PHILLIPS, A. G. (1976). Motivation: A psychological construct in search of a physiological substrate. In J. M. Sprague & A. N. Epstein (Eds.), *Progress in psychobiology and physiological psychology* (Vol. 6). New York: Academic Press.

MOGILNICKA, M. E., & KORDECKA, A. (1979). Chronic treatment with antidepressant drugs: Potentiation of apomorphine-induced aggressive behaviour in rats. *Neuroscience Letters, 13,* 337–341.

MOGUILEWSKY, M., & RAYNAUD, J.-P. (1979). Estrogen-sensitive progestin-binding sites in the female rat brain and pituitary. *Brain Research, 164,* 165–175. **285**

MOISES, H. C., WOODWARD, D. J., HOFFER, B. J., & FREEDMAN, R. (1979). Interactions of norepinephrine with Purkinje cell responses to putative amino acid neurotransmitters applied by microiontophoresis. *Experimental Neurology, 64,* 493–515. **240**

MOLLICA, A., MORUZZI, G., & NAQUET, R. (1953). Décharges reticulaires induites par la polarisation du cervelet: Leur rapportes avec le tonus postural et la réaction d'éveil. *Journal of Electroencephalography and Clinical Neurophysiology, 5,* 571–584. **235**

MONEY, J. (1980). Endocrine influences and psychosexual status spanning the life cycle. In H. M. Van Praag (Ed.), *Handbook of biological psychiatry: Part III. Brain mechanisms and abnormal behavior — genetics and neuroendocrinology.* New York: Marcel Dekker. **272**

MONEY, J., & EHRHARDT, A. A. (1972). *Man and woman, boy and girl.* Baltimore: Johns Hopkins University Press. **292**

MONTAROLO, P. G., GOELET, P., CASTELLUCCI, V. F., MORGAN, J., KANDEL, E. R., & SCHACHER, S. (1986). A critical period for macromolecular synthesis in long-term heterosynaptic facilitation in *Aplysia. Science, 234,* 1249–1254. **396**

MONTERO, M. T., GUILLAMÓN, A., AZUARA, M. C., AMBROSIO, E., SEGOVIA, S., & ORENSANZ, L. M. (1983). Sex differences in the protein content of membrane fractions from several regions of the rat central nervous system. *IRCS Medical Science, 11,* 317. **295**

MONTI, J. M. (1982). Catecholamines and the sleep–wake cycle: I. EEG and behavioral arousal. *Life Sciences, 30,* 1145–1157. **235**

MONTI, J. M. (1983). Catecholamines and the sleep–wake cycle: II. REM sleep. *Life Sciences, 32,* 1401–1415. **235**

MOODY, T. W., PERT, C. B., RIVIER, J., & BROWN, M. R. (1978). Bombesin: Specific binding to rat brain membranes. *Proceedings of the National Academy of Sciences, U.S.A., 75,* 5372–5376.

MOORE, C. L. (1982). Maternal behavior of rats is affected by hormonal condition of pups. *Journal of Comparative and Physiological Psychology, 96,* 123–129. **292**

MOORE, C. L. (1984). Maternal contributions to the development of masculine sexual behavior in laboratory rats. *Developmental Psychobiology, 17,* 347–356. **292**

MOORE, C. L. (1985). Another psychobiological view of sexual differentiation. *Developmental Review, 5,* 18–55. **292**

MOORE, J. W. (1979). Information processing in space–time by the hippocampus. *Physiological Psychology, 7,* 224–232. **384**

MOORE, R. Y., & BLOOM, F. E. (1978). Central catecholamine neuron systems: Anatomy and physiology of the dopamine systems. *Annual Review of Neuroscience, 1,* 129–169. **97, 98, 339**

MOORE, R. Y., & BLOOM, F. E. (1979). Central catecholamine neuron systems: Anatomy and physiology of the norepinephrine and epinephrine systems. *Annual Review of Neuroscience, 2,* 113–168. **97, 98, 339**

MORA, F., ROLLS, E. T., & BURTON, M. J. (1976). Modulation during learning of the responses of neurons in the lateral hypothalamus to the sight of food. *Experimental Neurology, 53,* 508–519. **383**

MORAN, J., & DESIMONE, R. (1985). Selective attention gates visual processing in the extrastriate cortex. *Science, 229,* 782–784. **239**

MOREAU, J.-L., COHEN, E., & LIEBLICH, I.

(1984). Ventral tegmental self-stimulation, sensory reactivity and pain reduction in rats selected for high and low rates of lateral hypothalamic self-stimulation. *Physiology & Behavior, 33,* 825–830. **253, 265**

MORELL, P., & NORTON, W. T. (1980). Myelin. *Scientific American, 242,* 88–117. **64**

MOREST, D. K., & BOHNE, B. A. (1983). Noise-induced degeneration in the brain and representation of inner and outer hair cells. *Hearing Research, 9,* 145–151. **16, 147**

MORGAN, D. G., & ROUTTENBERG, A. (1981). Brain pyruvate dehydrogenase: Phosphorylation and enzyme activity altered by a training experience. *Science, 214,* 470–471. **377**

MORLEY, J. E. (1980). The neuroendocrine control of appetite: The role of the endogenous opiates, cholecystokinin, TRH, gamma-amino-butyric-acid and the diazepam receptor. *Life Sciences, 27,* 355–368. **248**

MORLEY, J. E., & LEVINE, A. S. (1982). The role of the endogenous opiates as regulators of appetite. *American Journal of Clinical Nutrition, 35,* 757–761. **248**

MORLEY, J. E., LEVINE, A. S., YIM, G. K., & LOWY, M. T. (1983). Opioid modulation of appetite. *Neuroscience & Biobehavioral Reviews, 7,* 281–305. **99, 248**

MORRELL, J. I., & PFAFF, D. W. (1982). Characterization of estrogen-concentrating hypothalamic neurons by their axonal projections. *Science, 217,* 1273–1276. **317**

MOSS, R. L., & DUDLEY, C. A. (1984). Molecular aspects of the interaction between estrogen and the membrane excitability of hypothalamic nerve cells. In G. J. De Vries, J. P. C. De Bruin, H. B. M. Uylings, & M. A. Corner (Eds.), *Sex differences in the brain.* New York: Elsevier. **279**

MOSS, R. L., & LAW, O. T. (1971). The estrous cycle: Its influence on single unit activity in the forebrain. *Brain Research, 30,* 435–438. **312**

Most patients can "hear" while under anesthesia. (1984, May 4). *Chicago Tribune.* **446**

MOUNTAIN, D. C. (1980). Changes in endolymphatic potential and crossed olivocochlear bundle stimulation alter cochlear mechanics. *Science, 210,* 71–72. **175**

MOUNTCASTLE, V. B. (1975). The view from within: Pathways to the study of perception. *Johns Hopkins Medical Journal, 136,* 109–131. **4, 5, 8, 31, 156, 171, 173, 176, 230**

MOUNTCASTLE, V. B., LYNCH, J. C., GEORGOPOULOS, A., SAKATA, H., & ACUNA, C. (1975). Posterior parietal association cortex of the monkey: Command functions for operations within extrapersonal space. *Journal of Neurophysiology, 38,* 871–908. **176, 230**

MOUNTCASTLE, V. B., & POWELL, T. P. S. (1959). Neural mechanisms subserving cutaneous sensibility, with special reference to the role of afferent inhibition in sensory perception and discrimination. *Bulletin of the Johns Hopkins Hospital, 105,* 201–232. **160, 170**

MOUNTCASTLE, V. B., TALBOT, W. H., SAKATA, H., & HYVÄRINEN, J. (1969). Cortical neuronal mechanisms in flutter-vibration studied in unanesthetized monkeys: Neuronal periodicity and frequency discrimination. *Journal of Neurophysiology, 32,* 452–484. **158**

MOVSHON, J. A., & VAN SLUYTERS, R. C. (1981). Visual neural development. *Annual Review of Psychology, 32,* 477–522. **421**

MOWER, G. D., CAPLAN, C. J., & LETSOU, G. (1982). Behavioral recovery from binocular deprivation in the cat. *Behavioral Brain Research, 4,* 209–215. **415**

MOWER, G. D., CHRISTEN, W. G., & CAPLAN, C. J. (1983). Very brief visual experience eliminates plasticity in the cat visual cortex. *Science, 221,* 178–180. **415**

MOYER, K. E. (1976). *The psychobiology of aggression.* New York: Harper & Row. **324, 339, 340**

MUIR, D. W., & MITCHELL, D. E. (1975). Behavioral deficits in cats following early selected visual exposure to contours of a single orientation. *Brain Research, 85,* 459–477. **426**

MUKHAMETOV, L. M., RIZZOLATTI, G., & TRADARDI, V. (1970). Spontaneous activity of neurones of nucleus reticularis thalami in freely moving cats. *Journal of Physiology, 210,* 651–667.

MULDER, A. H., WARDEH, G., HOGENBOOM, F., & FRANKHUYZEN, A. L. (1984). Kappa- and delta-opioid receptor agonists differentially inhibit striatal dopamine and acetylcholine release. *Nature, 308,* 278–280. **99**

MÜLLER, U., & SCHINDLER, H. (1983). Testicular differentiation—a developmental cascade: Morphogenetic effects of H-Y antigen and testosterone in the male mammalian gonad. *Differentiation, 23,* S99–S103. **286**

MUMFORD, J. M., & BOWSHER, D. (1976). Pain and protopathic sensibility: A review with particular reference to the teeth. *Pain, 2,* 223–243.

MURAKAMI, M., SHIMODA, Y., NAKATANI, K., MIYACHI, E., & WATANABE, S. (1982a). GABA-mediated negative feedback from horizontal cells to cones in carp retina. *Japanese Journal of Physiology, 32,* 911–926. **197**

MURAKAMI, M., SHIMODA, Y., NAKATANI, K., MIYACHI, E., & WATANABE, S. (1982b). GABA-mediated negative feedback and color opponency in carp retina. *Japanese Journal of Physiology, 32,* 927–935. **197**

MURPHY, D. L., BELMAKER, R. H., BUCHSBAUM, M., MARTIN, N. F., CIARANELLO, R., & WYATT, R. J. (1977). Biogenic amine-related enzymes and personality variations in normals. *Psychological Medicine, 7,* 149–157. **341**

MURPHY, K. M., & MITCHELL, D. E. (1986). Bilateral amblyopia after a short period of reverse occlusion in kittens. *Nature. 323,* 536–538.

MYERS, R. D., & MCCALEB, M. L. (1980). Feeding: satiety signals from intestine trigger brain's noradrenergic mechanism. *Science, 209,* 1035–1037. **248, 257, 258**

MYERS, R. D., MCCALEB, M. L., & HUGHES, K. A. (1979). Is the noradrenergic "feeding circuit" in hypothalamus really an olfactory system? *Pharmacology, Biochemistry & Behavior, 10,* 923–927. **248**

NACHMAN, M. (1959). The inheritance of saccharin preference. *Journal of Comparative and Physiological Psychology, 52,* 451–457. **253**

NAKAHAMA, H., YAMAMOTO, M., AYA, K., SHIMA, K., & FUJII, H. (1983). Markov dependency based on Shannon's entropy and its application to neural spike trains. *IEEE Transactions on Systems, Man, and Cybernetics, SMC-13,* 692–701. **135, 158**

NAKAYAMA, T. (1986). Neuronal activities related to thermoregulation. *Yale Journal of Biology and Medicine, 59,* 189–195. **256**

NAKAYAMA, T., & IMAI-MATSUMURA, K. (1984). Response of glucose-responsive ventromedial hypothalamic neurons to scrotal and preoptic thermal stimulation in rats. *Neuroscience Letters, 45,* 129–134. **256**

NAMBA, H., & SOKOLOFF, L. (1984). Acute administration of high doses of estrogen increases glucose utilization throughout brain. *Brain Research, 291,* 391–

394. **311**

NATHANS, J., PIANTANIDA, T. P., EDDY, R. L., SHOWS, T. B., & HOGNESS, D. S. (1986). Molecular genetics of inherited variation in human color vision. *Science, 232,* 203–210. **202, 203**

NATHANS, J., THOMAS, D., & HOGNESS, D. S. (1986). Molecular genetics of human color vision: The genes encoding blue, green, and red pigments. *Science, 232,* 193–202. **193, 202, 203, 205**

NATHANSON, J. A. (1977). Cyclic nucleotides and nervous system function. *Physiological Reviews, 57,* 157–256. **86, 88**

NEGRO-VILAR, A., & OJEDA, S. R. (1981). Hypophysiotropic hormones of the hypothalamus. *International Review of Physiology, 24,* 97–156.

NEHER, E., & SAKMANN, B. (1976). Single-channel currents recorded from membrane of denervated frog muscle fibres. *Nature, 260,* 799–802. **78**

NELSON, D. W., & PROSSER, C. L. (1981). Intracellular recordings from thermosensitive preoptic neurons. *Science, 213,* 787–789. **135**

NELSON, R. (1977). Cat cones have rod input: A comparison of the response properties of cones and horizontal cell bodies in the retina of the cat. *Journal of Comparative Neurology, 172,* 109–136. **184**

NELSON, R., LÜTZOW, A. V., KOLB, H., & GOURAS, P. (1975). Horizontal cells in cat retina with independent dendritic systems. *Science, 189,* 137–139. **184**

NEMITZ, J. W., & GOLDBERG, S. J. (1983). Neuronal responses of rat pyriform cortex to odor stimulation: An extracellular and intracellular study. *Journal of Neurophysiology, 49,* 188–203. **161, 167, 170**

NESTOROS, J. N. (1980). Ethanol specifically potentiates GABA-mediated neurotransmission in feline cerebral cortex. *Science, 209,* 708–710. **343**

NEUMEYER, C. (1985). An ultraviolet receptor as a fourth receptor type in goldfish color vision. *Naturwissenschaften, 72,* 162–163. **186, 203**

NEURINGER, A., & CAMPBELL, N. (1983). Eating as a function of body weight and of hours of deprivation. *Physiology & Behavior, 30,* 863–866. **243**

NICOL, S. E., & GOTTESMAN, I. I. (1983). Clues to the genetics and neurobiology of schizophrenia. *American Scientist, 71,* 398–404.

NICOLAÏDIS, S. (1969). Early systemic responses to orogastric stimulation in the regulation of food and water balance: Functional and electrophysiological data. *Annals of the New York Academy of Sciences, 157,* 1176–1203. **255**

NICOLL, R. A., & ALGER, B. E. (1981). Synaptic excitation may activate a calcium-dependent potassium conductance in hippocampal pyramidal cells. *Science, 212,* 957–959. **98**

NIENHUYS, T. G. W., & CLARK, G. M. (1978). Frequency discrimination following the selective destruction of cochlear inner and outer hair cells. *Science, 199,* 1356–1357. **167**

NIIJIMA, A. (1969). Afferent impulse discharges from glucoreceptors in the liver of the guinea-pig. *Annals of the New York Academy of Sciences, 157,* 690–700. **152**

NIKI, H., & WATANABE, M. (1979). Prefrontal and cingulate unit activity during timing behavior in the monkey. *Brain Research, 171,* 213–224. **230**

NISBETT, R. E. (1972). Hunger, obesity, and the ventromedial hypothalamus. *Psychological Review, 79,*

433–453. **243, 245**

NISHIZUKA, M., & ARAI, Y. (1981a). Sexual dimorphism in synaptic organization in the amygdala and its dependence on neonatal hormone environment. *Brain Research, 213,* 31–38. **280, 300**

NISHIZUKA, M., & ARAI, Y. (1981b). Organizational action of estrogen on synaptic pattern in the amygdala: Implications for sexual differentiation of the brain. *Brain Research, 213,* 422–426. **280, 300**

NISHIZUKA, M., & ARAI, Y. (1982). Synapse formation in response to estrogen in the medial amygdala developing in the eye. *Proceedings of the National Academy of Sciences, U.S.A., 79,* 7024–7026.

NISSEN, M. J., COHEN, N. J., & CORKIN, S. (1981). The amnesic patient H.M.: Learning and retention of perceptual skills. *Neuroscience Abstracts, 7,* 235. **13, 446**

NOCK, B., & FEDER, H. H. (1981). Neurotransmitter modulation of steroid action in target cells that mediate reproduction and reproductive behavior. *Neuroscience & Biobehavioral Reviews, 5,* 437–447. **308**

NORDEEN, E. J., & YAHR, P. (1982). Hemispheric asymmetries in the behavioral and hormonal effects of sexually differentiating mammalian brain. *Science, 218,* 391–393. **276, 280, 293**

NORDEEN, E. J., & YAHR, P. (1983). A regional analysis of estrogen binding to hypothalamic cell nuclei in relation to masculization and defeminization. *Journal of Neuroscience, 3,* 933–941. **276, 281, 283**

NORGREN, R. (1970). Gustatory responses in the hypothalamus. *Brain Research, 21,* 63–77. **260, 261, 264, 267**

NORGREN, R., & GRILL, H. (1982). Brain-stem control of ingestive behavior. In D. W. Pfaff (Ed.), *The physiological mechanisms of motivation.* New York: Springer-Verlag. **227**

NORMANN, R. A., & PERLMAN, I. (1979a). Evaluating sensitivity changing mechanisms in light-adapted photoreceptors. *Vision Research, 19,* 391–394. **218**

NORMANN, R. A., & PERLMAN, I. (1979b). The effects of background illumination on the photoresponses of red and green cones. *Journal of Physiology, 286,* 491–507. **218**

NOTTEBOHM, F. (1981). A brain for all seasons: Cyclical anatomical changes in song control nuclei of the canary brain. *Science, 214,* 1368–1370. **307**

NOWAK, L. M., & MACDONALD, R. L. (1983). Muscarine-sensitive voltage-dependent potassium current in cultured murine spinal cord neurons. *Neuroscience Letters, 35,* 85–91. **60, 88, 89, 91**

NOYES, R., CLANCY, J., CROWE, R., HOENK, P. R., & SLYMEN, D. J. (1978). The familial prevalence of anxiety neurosis. *Archives of General Psychiatry, 35,* 1057–1059. **327**

NUTTALL, A. L., BROWN, M. C., MASTA, R. I., & LAWRENCE, M. (1981). Inner hair cell responses to the velocity of basilar membrane motion in the guinea pig. *Brain Research, 211,* 171–174. **153**

OADES, R. D. (1985). The role of noradrenaline in tuning and dopamine in switching between signals in the CNS. *Neuroscience & Biobehavioral Reviews, 9,* 261–282. **97, 98, 339**

OAKLEY, B., & BENJAMIN, R. M. (1966). Neural mechanisms of taste. *Physiological Reviews, 46,* 199–211. **161, 167**

O'BRIEN, D. F. (1982). The chemistry of vision. *Science, 218,* 961–966.

O'BRIEN, J. H., & QUINN, K. J. (1982). Central mechanisms responsible for classically conditioned changes in neuronal activity. In C. D. Woody (Ed.), *Conditioning*. New York: Plenum. **193, 445**

ODEN, B. G., CLOHISY, D. J., & FRANCOIS, G. R. (1982). Interanimal transfer of learned behavior through injection of brain RNA. *Psychological Record, 32,* 281–290. **378**

O'DOWD, D. K. (1983). RNA synthesis dependence of action potential development in spinal cord neurons. *Nature, 303,* 619–621. **115**

OGAWA, H., SATO, M., & YAMASHITA, S. (1973). Variability in impulse discharges in rat chorda tympanic fibers in response to repeated gustatory stimulations. *Physiology & Behavior, 11,* 469–479. **162, 174**

ÖGREN, S. O., ARCHER, T., & JOHANSSON, C. (1983). Evidence for a selective brain noradrenergic involvement in the locomotor stimulant effects of amphetamine in the rat. *Neuroscience Letters, 43,* 327–331. **338**

OHNO, S. (1979). *Major sex-determining genes.* New York: Springer-Verlag. **286–288**

OHNO, S. (1980). Two major regulatory genes for mammalian sex determination and differentiation. *Genetica, 52/53,* 267–273. **286, 287**

O'KEEFE, J. (1976). Place units in the hippocampus of the freely moving rat. *Experimental Neurology, 51,* 78–109. **384**

O'KEEFE, J. (1979). A review of the hippocampal place cells. *Progress in Neurobiology, 13,* 419–439. **216, 381, 384**

O'KEEFE, J., & NADEL, L. (1978). *The hippocampus as a cognitive map.* Oxford: Oxford University Press. **384**

OKULICZ, W. C., EVANS, R. W., & LEAVITT, W. W. (1981). Progesterone regulation of the occupied form of nuclear estrogen receptors. *Science, 213,* 1503–1505. **281**

O'KUSKY, J., & COLONNIER, M. (1982). Postnatal changes in the number of neurons and synapses in the visual cortex (area 17) of the macaque monkey: A stereological analysis in normal and monocularly deprived animals. *Journal of Comparative Neurology, 210,* 291–306. **431, 433**

OLDS, J. (1958a). Effects of hunger and male sex hormone on self-stimulation of the brain. *Journal of Comparative and Physiological Psychology, 51,* 320–324. **263, 265, 266**

OLDS, J. (1958b). Satiation effects in self-stimulation of the brain. *Journal of Comparative and Physiological Psychology, 51,* 675–678.

OLDS, J., DISTERHOFT, J. F., SEGAL, M., KORNBLITH, C. L., & HIRSH, R. (1972). Learning centers of rat brain mapped by measuring latencies of conditioned unit responses. *Journal of Neurophysiology, 35,* 202–219. **387**

OLDS, J., & MILNER, P. (1954). Positive reinforcement produced by electrical stimulation of septal area and other regions of rat brain. *Journal of Comparative and Physiological Psychology, 47,* 419–427. **262**

OLDS, M. E. (1974a). Effect of intraventricular norepinephrine on neuron activity in the medial forebrain bundle during self-stimulation behavior. *Brain Research, 80,* 461–477. **267**

OLDS, M. E. (1974b). Unit responses in the medial forebrain bundle to rewarding stimulation in the hypothalamus. *Brain Research, 80,* 479–495. **267**

OLDS, M. E., & FOBES, J. L. (1981). The central

basis of motivation: Intracranial self-stimulation studies. *Annual Review of Psychology, 32,* 523–574. **263–265, 437**

OLSEN, K. L., & WHALEN, R. E. (1980). Sexual differentiation of the brain: Effects on mating behavior and [³H]-estradiol binding by hypothalamic chromatin in rats. *Biology of Reproduction, 22,* 1068–1072. **283**

OLSEN, K. L., & WHALEN, R. E. (1981). Hormonal control of the development of sexual behavior in androgen-insensitive *(tfm)* rats. *Physiology & Behavior, 27,* 883–886. **288**

OLSEN, K. L., & WHALEN, R. E. (1984). Dihydrotestosterone activates male mating behavior in castrated King-Holtzman rats. *Hormones and Behavior, 18,* 380–392. **293**

OLSON, C. R., & FREEMAN, R. D. (1978). Monocular deprivation and recovery during sensitive period in kittens. *Journal of Neurophysiology, 41,* 65–74. **423**

OLTMANS, G. A. (1983). Norepinephrine and dopamine levels in hypothalamic nuclei of the genetically obese mouse *(ob/ob)*. *Brain Research, 272,* 369–373. **252**

ONDO, J., MANSKY, T., & WUTTKE, W. (1982). In vivo GABA release from the medial preoptic area of diestrous and ovariectomized rats. *Experimental Brain Research, 46,* 69–72. **310**

ONO, T., OOMURA, Y., SUGIMORI, M., NAKAMURA, T., SHIMIZU, N., KITA, H., & ISHIBASHI, S. (1976). Hypothalamic unit activity related to lever pressing and eating in the chronic monkey. In D. Novin, W. Wyrwicka, & G. Bray (Eds.), *Hunger: Basic mechanisms and clinical implications.* New York: Raven. **257, 259**

ONO, T., SASAKI, K., NAKAMURA, K., & NORGREN, R. (1985). Integrated lateral hypothalamic neural responses to natural and artificial rewards and cue signals in the rat. *Brain Research, 327,* 303–306. **260, 268**

OOMURA, Y. (1976). Significance of glucose, insulin, and free fatty acid on the hypothalamic feeding and satiety neurons. In D. Novin, W. Wyrwicka, & G. Bray (Eds.), *Hunger: Basic mechanisms and clinical implications.* New York: Raven. **255, 256**

OOMURA, Y., KIMURA, K., OOYAMA, H., MAENO, T., IKI, M., & KUNIYOSHI, M. (1964). Reciprocal activities of the ventromedial and lateral hypothalamic areas of cats. *Science, 143,* 484–485. **257**

OOMURA, Y., NAKAMURA, T., SUGIMORI, M., & YAMADA, Y. (1975). Effect of free fatty acid on the rat lateral hypothalamic neurons. *Physiology & Behavior, 14,* 483–486. **256**

OOMURA, Y., ONO, T., & OOYAMA, H. (1970). Inhibitory action of the amygdala on the lateral hypothalamic area in rats. *Nature, 228,* 1108–1110. **257**

OOMURA, Y., ONO, T., OOYAMA, H., & WAYNER, M. J. (1969). Glucose and osmosensitive neurones of the rat hypothalamus. *Nature, 222,* 282–284. **254, 255**

OOMURA, Y., OOYAMA, H., NAKA, F., YAMAMOTO, T., ONO, T., & KOBAYASHI, N. (1969). Some stochastical patterns of single unit discharge in the cat hypothalamus under chronic conditions. *Annals of the New York Academy of Sciences, 157,* 666–689. **259**

OOMURA, Y., OOYAMA, H., SUGIMORI, M., NAKAMURA, T., & YAMADA, Y. (1974). Glucose inhibition of the glucose-sensitive neurone in the rat lateral hypothalamus. *Nature, 247,* 282–286. **255**

OOMURA, Y., OOYAMA, H., YAMAMOTO, T., & NAKA, F. (1967). Reciprocal relationship of the lateral and ventromedial hypothalamus in the regulation of food intake.

Physiology & Behavior, 2, 97–115. **257**

OOMURA, Y., YOSHIMATSU, H., & AOU, S. (1983). Medial preoptic and hypothalamic neuronal activity during sexual behavior of the male monkey. *Brain Research, 266,* 340–343. **318**

ORMAN, S., & FLOCK, A. (1983). Active control of sensory hair mechanics implied by susceptibility to media that induce contraction in muscle. *Hearing Research, 11,* 261–266. **167, 175**

ORONA, E., & GABRIEL, M. (1983a). Multiple-unit activity of the prefrontal cortex and mediodorsal thalamic nucleus during acquisition of discriminative avoidance behavior in rabbits. *Brain Research, 263,* 295–312. **388**

ORONA, E., & GABRIEL, M. (1983b). Multiple-unit activity of the prefrontal cortex and mediodorsal thalamic nucleus during reversal of discriminative avoidance behavior in rabbits. *Brain Research, 263,* 313–329. **388**

OROSCO, M., JACQUOT, C., & COHEN, Y. (1981). Brain catecholamine levels and turnover in various models of obese animals. *General Pharmacology, 12,* 267–271. **252**

ORSINI, J.-C. (1982). Androgen influence on lateral hypothalamus in the male rat: Possible behavioral significance. *Physiology & Behavior, 29,* 979–987. **312**

ORSINI, J.-C., BARONE, F. C., ARMSTRONG, D. L., & WAYNER, M. J. (1985). Direct effects of androgens on lateral hypothalamic neuronal activity in the male rat: I. A microiontophoretic study. *Brain Research Bulletin, 15,* 293–297. **312**

ØSTERBERG, G. (1935). Topography of the layer of rods and cones in the human retina. *Acta Ophthalmica, 6*(Suppl. 6), 1–103.

OSTROW, D. G., HALARIS, A., DEMET, D., GIBBONS, R. G., & DAVIS, J. M. (1982). Ion transport and adrenergic function in major affective disorder. *Biological Psychiatry, 17,* 971–980. **349**

OWENS, D. G. C., JOHNSTONE, E. C., CROW, T. J., FRITH, C. D., JAGOE, J. R., & KREEL, L. (1985). Lateral ventricular size in schizophrenia: Relationship to the disease process and its clinical manifestations. *Psychological Medicine, 15,* 27–41. **328, 344**

OZEKI, M. (1971). Conductance change associated with receptor potentials of gustatory cells in rat. *Journal of General Physiology, 58,* 688–699. **151, 173**

PACKMAN, P. M., BOSHANS, R. L., & BRAGDON, M. J. (1977). Quantitative histochemical studies of the hypothalamus: Dehydrogenase enzymes following androgen sterilization. *Neuroendocrinology, 23,* 330–340. **296**

PADJEN, A. L., & SMITH, P. A. (1983). The role of the electrogenic sodium pump in the glutamate afterhyperpolarization of the frog spinal cord. *Journal of Physiology, 336,* 433–451. **59, 60**

PAGER, J. (1974). A selective modulation of olfactory input suppressed by lesions of the anterior limb of the anterior commissure. *Physiology & Behavior, 13,* 523–526. **264**

PAGER, J., GIACHETTI, I., HOLLEY, A., & LE MAGNEN, J. (1972). A selective control of olfactory bulb electrical activity in relation to food deprivation and satiety in rats. *Physiology & Behavior, 9,* 573–579. **264**

PAINTAL, A. S. (1954). A study of gastric stretch receptors: Their role in the peripheral mechanism of satiation of hunger and thirst. *Journal of Physiology, 126,* 255–270. **152**

PAK, R. C. K., TSIM, K. W. K., & CHENG, C. H. K. (1985). The role of neonatal and pubertal gonadal hormones in regulating the sex dependence of the hepatic microsomal testosterone 5-reductase activity in the rat. *Journal of Endocrinology*, 106, 71–79. **277**

PAK, W. L., OSTROY, S. E., DELAND, M. C., & WU, C.-F. (1976). Photoreceptor mutant of *Drosophila*: Is protein involved in intermediate steps of phototransduction? *Science*, 194, 956–959. **127**

PAK, W. L., & PINTO, L. H. (1976). Genetic approach to the study of the nervous system. *Annual Review of Biophysics and Bioengineering*, 5, 397–448. **113, 117, 127, 129**

PALFAI, T., BROWN, O. M., & WALSH, T. J. (1978). Catecholamine levels in the whole brain and the probability of memory formation are not related. *Pharmacology, Biochemistry & Behavior*, 8, 717–721. **374**

PALFAI, T., & WALSH, T. J. (1979). The role of peripheral catecholamines in reserpine-induced amnesia. *Behavioral and Neural Biology*, 27, 423–432. **374**

PALKOVITS, M., RAISMAN, R., BRILEY, M., & LANGER, S. Z. (1981). Regional distribution of [³H]imipramine binding in rat brain. *Brain Research*, 210, 493–498. **354**

PANG, S. F., & TANG, F. (1984). Sex differences in the serum concentrations of testosterone in mice and hamsters during their critical periods of neural sexual differentiation. *Journal of Endocrinology*, 100, 7–11. **272**

PANKSEPP, J. (1974). Hypothalamic regulation of energy balance and feeding behavior. *Federation Proceedings*, 33, 1150–1164. **243**

PANKSEPP, J., & MEEKER, R. (1976). Suppression of food intake in diabetic rats by voluntary consumption and intrahypothalamic injection of glucose. *Physiology & Behavior*, 16, 763–770. **255**

PAPEZ, J. W. (1937). A proposed mechanism of emotion. *Archives of Neurology and Psychiatry*, 38, 725–743. **324**

PAPIR-KRICHELI, D., & FELDMAN, S. (1981). Response of medial septal neurons to the iontophoretic application of glucocorticoids. *Experimental Neurology*, 73, 801–811. **358**

PAPIR-KRICHELI, D., & FELDMAN, S. (1983). Modifications in single cell activity in the rat midbrain during the iontophoretic application of cortisol. *Experimental Neurology*, 79, 576–581. **358**

PARLEE, M. B. (1983). Menstrual rhythms in sensory processes: A review of fluctuations in vision, olfaction, audition, taste, and touch. *Psychological Bulletin*, 93, 539–548. **291**

PARROTT, R. F., & BALDWIN, B. A. (1981). Operant feeding and drinking in pigs following intracerebroventricular injection of synthetic cholecystokinin octapeptide. *Physiology & Behavior*, 26, 419–422.

PARSONS, B., RAINBOW, T. C., & MCEWEN, B. S. (1984). Organizational effects of testosterone via aromatization on feminine reproductive behavior and neural progestin receptors in rat brain. *Endocrinology*, 115, 1412–1417. **282**

PARSONS, D. W., TER MAAT, A., & PINSKER, H. M. (1983). Selective recording and stimulation of individual identified neurons in freely behaving *Aplysia*. *Science*, 221, 1203–1206. **229**

PASTERNAK, T., MOVSHON, J. A., & MERIGAN, W. H. (1981). Creation of direction selectivity in adult strobe-reared cats. *Nature*, 292, 834–836. **429**

PATON, J. A., & NOTTEBOHM, F. N. (1984). Neurons generated in the adult brain are recruited into

functional circuits. *Science*, 225, 1046–1048. **307, 431**

PATRICK, J., & HEINEMANN, S. (1982). Outstanding problems in acetylcholine receptor structure and regulation. *Trends in NeuroSciences*, 5, 300–302. **80, 86**

PATTERSON, M. M., BERGER, T. W., & THOMPSON, R. F. (1979). Neuronal plasticity recorded from cat hippocampus during classical conditioning. *Brain Research*, 163, 339–343. **390**

PATTERSON, P. H., POTTER, D. D., & FURSHPAN, E. J. (1981). The chemical differentiation of nerve cells. *Scientific American*, 244, 48–59. **115, 126**

PAUL, L. A., FRIED, I., WATANABE, K., FORSYTHE, A. B., & SCHEIBEL, A. B. (1981). Structural correlates of seizure behavior in the Mongolian gerbil. *Science*, 213, 924–926. **130**

PAUL, S. M., AXELROD, J., SAAVEDRA, J. M., & SKOLNICK, P. (1979). Estrogen-induced efflux of endogenous catecholamines from the hypothalamus in vitro. *Brain Research*, 178, 499–505. **309**

PAUL, S. M., HULIHAN-GIBLIN, B., & SKOLNICK, P. (1982). (+)-Amphetamine binding to rat hypothalamus: Relation to anorexic potency of phenylethylamines. *Science*, 218, 487–490. **248**

PAUL, S. M., REHAVI, M., SKOLNICK, P., BALLENGER, J. C., & GOODWIN, F. K. (1981). Depressed patients have decreased binding of tritiated imipramine to platelet serotonin "transporter." *Archives of General Psychiatry*, 38, 1315–1317. **354**

PAUL, S. M., & SKOLNICK, P. (1982). Comparative neuropharmacology of antianxiety drugs. *Pharmacology, Biochemistry & Behavior*, 17, 37–41. **343, 344**

PAULSEN, R., & BENTROP, J. (1983). Activation of rhodopsin phosphorylation is triggered by the limirhodopsin-metarhodopsin I transition. *Nature*, 302, 417–419. **192**

PAYNE, B. R., ELBERGER, A. J., BERMAN, N., & MURPHY, E. H. (1980). Binocularity in the cat visual cortex is reduced by sectioning the corpus callosum. *Science*, 207, 1097–1099. **210**

PEARLMAN, C. (1983). Impairment of environmental effects on brain weight by adrenergic drugs in rats. *Physiology & Behavior*, 30, 161–163. **402**

PEARSON, J., BRANDEIS, L., & CUELLO, A. C. (1982). Depletion of substance P-containing axons in substantia gelatinosa of patients with diminished pain sensitivity. *Nature*, 295, 61–63. **168**

PECK, C. K., & BLAKEMORE, C. (1975). Modification of single neurons in the kitten's visual cortex after brief periods of monocular visual experience. *Experimental Brain Research*, 22, 57–68. **422**

PENFIELD, W. (1947). Some observations on the cerebral cortex of man. *Proceedings of the Royal Society of London*, 134, 329–347. **217**

PENFIELD, W., & BOLDREY, E. (1937). Somatic motor and sensory representation in the cerebral cortex of man as studied by electrical stimulation. *Brain*, 60, 389–443. **230**

PEPER, K., BRADLEY, R. J., & DREYER, F. (1982). The acetylcholine receptor at the neuromuscular junction. *Physiological Reviews*, 62, 1271–1340. **78, 80, 85**

PEPER, K., & MCMAHAN, U. J. (1972). Distribution of acetylcholine receptors in the vicinity of nerve terminals on skeletal muscle of the frog. *Proceedings of the Royal Society of London, Series B*, 181, 431–440.

PEPPER, C. M., & HENDERSON, G. (1980). Opiates and opioid peptides hyperpolarize locus coeruleus

neurons in vitro. *Science*, 209, 394–396. **99**

PÉREZ-CRUET, J., TAGLIAMONTE, A., TAGLIAMONTE, P., & GESSA, G. L. (1972). Changes in brain serotonin metabolism associated with fasting and satiation in rats. *Life Sciences*, 11, 31–39. **296**

PERKINS, M. N., ROTHWELL, N. J., STOCK, M. J., & STONE, T. W. (1981). Activation of brown adipose tissue thermogenesis by the ventromedial hypothalamus. *Nature*, 289, 401–402. **245**

PERLOW, M. J., FREED, W. J., HOFFER, B. J., SEIGER, A., OLSON, L., & WYATT, R. J. (1979). Brain grafts reduce motor abnormalities produced by destruction of nigrostriatal dopamine system. *Science*, 204, 643–647. **437**

PEROUTKA, S. J. (1984). 5-HT₁ receptor sites and functional correlates. *Neuropharmacology*, 23, 1487–1492.

PEROUTKA, S. J., LEBOVITZ, R. M., & SNYDER, S. H. (1981). Two distinct central serotonin receptors with different physiological functions. *Science*, 212, 827–829. **98**

PERRETT, D. I., ROLLS, E. T., & CAAN, W. (1982). Visual neurones responsive to faces in the monkey temporal cortex. *Experimental Brain Research*, 47, 329–342. **217**

PERRETT, D. I., SMITH, P. A. J., POTTER, D. D., MISTLIN, A. J., HEAD, A. S., MILNER, A. D., & JEEVES, M. A. (1984). Neurones responsive to faces in the temporal cortex: Studies of functional organization, sensitivity to identity and relation to perception. *Human Neurobiology*, 3, 197–208. **217**

PERRETT, D. I., SMITH, P. A. J., POTTER, D. D., MISTLIN, A. J., HEAD, A. S., MILNER, A. D., & JEEVES, M. A. (1985). Visual cells in the temporal cortex sensitive to face view and gaze direction. *Proceedings of the Royal Society of London, Series B*, 223, 293–317. **217**

PERRY, E. K., MARSHALL, E. F., BLESSED, G., TOMLINSON, B. E., & PERRY, R. H. (1983). Decreased imipramine binding in the brains of patients with depressive illness. *British Journal of Psychiatry*, 142, 188–192. **354**

PERRY, R. H., CANDY, J. M., PERRY, E. K., IRVING, D., BLESSED, G., FAIRBAIRN, A. F., & TOMLINSON, B. E. (1982). Extensive loss of choline acetyltransferase activity is not reflected by neuronal loss in the nucleus of Meynert in Alzheimer's disease. *Neuroscience Letters*, 33, 311–315. **432**

PERSKY, H., DREISBACH, L., MILLER, W. R., O'BRIEN, C. P., KHAN, M. A., LIEF, H. I., CHARNEY, N., & STRAUSS, D. (1982). The relation of plasma androgen levels to sexual behaviors and attitudes of women. *Psychosomatic Medicine*, 44, 305–319. **293**

PERUMAL, R., GISPEN, W. H., GLASSMAN, E., & WILSON, J. E. (1977). Phosphorylation of proteins of synaptosome-enriched fractions of brain during short-term training experience: Biochemical characterization. *Behavioral Biology*, 21, 341–357. **377**

PETERS, D. A. V. (1982). Prenatal stress: Effects on brain biogenic amine and plasma corticosterone levels. *Pharmacology, Biochemistry & Behavior*, 17, 721–725. **337**

PETERS, D. A. V. (1986). Prenatal stress: Effect on development of rat brain serotonergic neurons. *Pharmacology, Biochemistry & Behavior*, 24, 1377–1382. **337**

PETERS, R. H., GUNION, M. W., & WELLMAN, P. J. (1979). Influence of diet palatability on maintenance feeding behavior in rats with dorsolateral tegmental damage. *Physiology & Behavior, 23,* 685–692. **243**

PETERSON, D. A. V. (1982). Prenatal stress: Effects on brain biogenic amine and plasma corticosterone levels. *Pharmacology, Biochemistry & Behavior, 17,* 721–725.

PETERSON, R. E., IMPERATO-MCGINLEY, J., GAUTIER, T., & STURLA, E. (1979). Hereditary steroid 5alpha-reductase deficiency: A newly recognized cause of male pseudohermaphroditism. In H. L. Vallet & I. H. Porter (Eds.), *Genetic mechanisms of sexual development.* New York: Academic Press. **288, 291**

PETTIGREW, J. D. (1978). The paradox of the critical period for striate cortex. In C. W. Cotman (Ed.), *Neuronal plasticity.* New York: Raven. **421**

PETTIGREW, J. D., & FREEMAN, R. D. (1973). Visual experience without lines: Effect on developing cortical neurons. *Science, 182,* 599–601. **426**

PETTIGREW, J. D., & GAREY, L. J. (1974). Selective modification of single neuron properties in the visual cortex of kittens. *Brain Research, 66,* 160–164. **422**

PETTY, F., & SHERMAN, A. D. (1982). A neurochemical differentiation between exposure to stress and the development of learned helplessness. *Drug Development Research, 2,* 43–45. **332, 334, 338**

PETTY, F., & SHERMAN, A. D. (1983). Learned helplessness induction decreases *in vivo* cortical serotonin release. *Pharmacology, Biochemistry & Behavior, 18,* 649–650. **332, 334, 337**

PFAFF, D. W. (1966). Morphological changes in the brains of adult male rats after neonatal castration. *Journal of Endocrinology, 36,* 415–416.

PFAFF, D. W. (1980). *Estrogens and brain function.* New York: Springer-Verlag. **280, 315–317**

PFAFF, D. W. (1982). Motivational concepts: Definitions and distinctions. In D. W. Pfaff (Ed.), *The physiological mechanisms of motivation.* New York: Springer-Verlag. **229**

PFAFF, D. W., & GREGORY, E. (1971). Olfactory coding in olfactory bulb and medial forebrain bundle of normal and castrated male rats. *Journal of Neurophysiology, 34,* 208–216. **315, 318**

PFAFF, D. W., & MCEWEN, B. S. (1983). Actions of estrogens and progestins on nerve cells. *Science, 219,* 808–814. **278, 306, 309**

PFAFF, D. W., & PFAFFMANN, C. (1969). Olfactory and hormonal influences on the basal forebrain of the male rat. *Brain Research, 15,* 137–156. **312, 313, 315, 318**

PFAFF, D. W., SILVA, M. T. A., & WEISS, J. M. (1971). Telemetered recording of hormone effects on hippocampal neurons. *Science, 172,* 394–395. **358**

PFAFFMANN, C. (1959). The afferent code for sensory quality. *American Psychologist, 14,* 226–232. **161, 167**

PFAFFMANN, C., FRANK, M., BARTOSHUK, L. M., & SNELL, T. C. (1976). Coding gustatory information in the squirrel monkey chorda tympani. In J. M. Sprague & A. N. Epstein (Eds.), *Progress in psychobiology and physiological psychology* (Vol. 6). New York: Academic Press. **133, 161, 163, 168**

PFAFFMANN, C., FRANK, M., & NORGREN, R. (1979). Neural mechanisms and behavioral aspects of taste. *Annual Review of Psychology, 30,* 283–325. **142, 163, 170, 171**

PFAFFMANN, C., NORGREN, R., & GRILL, H. J. (1977). Sensory affect and motivation. *Annals of the New York Academy of Sciences, 290,* 18–34. **264**

PHELPS, C. J., & SLADEK, J. R., JR. (1984). Plasticity of catecholaminergic neurons in aged rat brain: Reinnervation and functional recovery after axotomy. *Brain Research Bulletin, 13,* 727–736. **436**

PHILLIPS, A. G., & DEOL, G. (1973). Neonatal gonadal hormone manipulation and emotionality following septal lesions in weanling rats. *Brain Research, 60,* 55–64. **301**

PHILLIPS, A. G., & MOGENSON, G. J. (1968). Effects of taste on self-stimulation and induced drinking. *Journal of Comparative and Physiological Psychology, 66,* 654–660. **265**

PHILLIPS, C. G., ZEKI, S., & BARLOW, H. B. (1984). Localization of function in the cerebral cortex. *Brain, 107,* 327–361. **451**

PHOENIX, C. H., & CHAMBERS, K. C. (1982). Sexual behavior in adult gonadectomized female pseudohermaphrodite, female, and male rhesus macaques (*Macaca mulatta*) treated with estradiol benzoate and testosterone propionate. *Journal of Comparative and Physiological Psychology, 96,* 823–833. **291**

PHOENIX, C. H., JENSEN, J. N. & CHAMBERS, K. C. (1983). Female sexual behavior displayed by androgenized female rhesus macaques. *Hormones and Behavior, 17,* 146–151. **291**

PIERCEY, M. F., SCHROEDER, L. A., FOLKERS, K., XU, J.-C., & HORIG, J. (1981). Sensory and motor functions of spinal cord substance P. *Science, 214,* 1361–1362. **168**

PIETRAS, R. J., & SZEGO, C. M. (1977). Specific binding sites for oestrogen at the outer surfaces of isolated endometrial cells. *Nature, 265,* 69–72. **279**

PILLARD, R. C., & WEINRICH, J. D. (1986). Evidence of familial nature of male homosexuality. *Archives of General Psychiatry, 43,* 808–812. **286**

PIMENTEL, E. (1978a). Cellular mechanisms of hormone action: I. Transductional events. *Acta Cientifica Venezolana, 29,* 73–82. **278**

PIMENTEL, E. (1978b). Cellular mechanisms of hormone action: II. Posttransductional events. *Acta Cientifica Venezolana, 29,* 147–157. **278**

PINEL, J. P. J. (1970). Two types of ECS-produced disruption of one-trial training in the rat. *Journal of Comparative and Physiological Psychology, 72,* 272–277.

PLOMIN, R., DEFRIES, J. C., & MCCLEARN, G. E. (1980). *Behavioral genetics: A primer.* San Francisco: W. H. Freeman. **112, 113, 115, 116, 121, 126, 127, 129, 326, 327, 380**

POGGIO, G. F., BAKER, F. H., MANSFIELD, R. J. W., SILLITO, A., & GRIGG, P. (1975). Spatial and chromatic properties of neurons subserving foveal and parafoveal vision in rhesus monkey. *Brain Research, 100,* 25–59. **207**

PÖPPEL, E., HELD, R., & DOWLING, J. E. (1977). Neuronal mechanisms in visual perception. *Neurosciences Research Progress Bulletin, 15.* **219**

POPPER, K. R., & ECCLES, J. C. (1977). *The self and its brain.* New York: Springer International. **8, 9, 32, 444**

PORITSKY, R. (1969). Two and three dimensional ultrastructure of boutons and glial cells on the motoneuronal surface in the cat spinal cord. *Journal of Comparative Neurology, 135,* 423–452.

POST, R. M. (1980). Intermittent versus continuous stimulation: Effect of the time interval on the development of sensitization or tolerance. *Life Sciences, 26,* 1275–

1282. **348**

POTEGAL, M., PERUMAL, A. S., BARKAI, A. I., CANNOVA, G. E., & BLAU, A. D. (1982). GABA binding in the brains of aggressive and non-aggressive female hamsters. *Brain Research, 247,* 315–324. **340**

POWLEY, T. L. (1977). The ventromedial hypothalamic syndrome, satiety, and a cephalic phase hypothesis. *Psychological Review, 84,* 89–126. **243**

PRADO DE CARVALHO, L., & ZORNETZER, S. F. (1981). The involvement of the locus coeruleus in memory. *Behavioral and Neural Biology, 31,* 173–186. **374**

PRANGE, A. J., WILSON, I. C., LYNN, C. W., ALLTOP, L. B., & STIKELEATHER, R. A. (1974). L-tryptophan in mania: Contribution to a permissive hypothesis of affective disorders. *Archives of General Psychiatry, 30,* 56–62. **348**

PRESCOTT, R. G. W. (1966). Estrous cycle in the rat: Effects on self-stimulation behavior. *Science, 152,* 796–797. **318**

PRIBRAM, K. H., LASSONDE, M. C., & PTITO, M. (1981). Classification of receptive field properties in cat visual cortex. *Experimental Brain Research, 43,* 119–130. **207, 214**

PRICE, L. H., CHARNEY, D. W., & HENINGER, G. R. (1984). Three cases of manic symptoms following yohimbine administration. *American Journal of Psychiatry, 141,* 1267–1268. **150, 349**

PRICE, S. (1984). Mechanisms of stimulation of olfactory neurons: An essay. *Chemical Senses, 8,* 341–354.

PRICE, S., & DESIMONE, J. A. (1977). Models of taste receptor cell stimulation. *Chemical Senses and Flavor, 2,* 427–456. **151, 152, 173**

PRINGLE, J. W. S. (1982). The mechanism of knowledge: Limits to prediction. In J. Eccles (Ed.), *Mind and brain: The many-faceted problems.* Washington, DC: Paragon House. **448**

PRITCHARD, R. M. (1961). Stabilized images on the retina. *Scientific American, 204,* 72–78. **218**

PRITCHARD, T. C., & SCOTT, T. R. (1982a). Amino acids as taste stimuli: I. Neural and behavioral attributes. *Brain Research, 253,* 81–92. **151, 161, 167**

PRITCHARD, T. C., & SCOTT, T. R. (1982b). Amino acids as taste stimuli: II. Quality coding. *Brain Research, 253,* 81–92. **141, 151, 161**

PROSEN, C. A., MOODY, D. B., STEBBINS, W. C., HAWKINS, J. E., JR. (1981). Auditory intensity discrimination after selective loss of cochlear outer hair cells. *Science, 212,* 1286–1288. **167**

PRZEWŁOCKA, B., STALA, L., & SCHEEL-KRÜGER, J. (1983). Evidence that GAGA in the nucleus dorsalis raphé induces stimulation of locomotor activity and eating behavior. *Life Sciences, 1979, 25,* 937–946.

PRZEWŁOCKI, R., LASÓN, W., KONECKA, A. M., GRAMSCH, C., HERZ, A., & REID, L. D. (1983). The opioid peptide dynorphin, circadian rhythms, and starvation. *Science, 219,* 71–73. **248**

PUCILOWSKI, O., & KOSTOWSKI, W. (1983). Aggressive behaviour and the central serotonergic systems. *Behavioural Brain Research, 9,* 33–48. **339, 340**

QUIG, D. W., LAYMAN, D. K., BECHTEL, P. J., & HACKLER, L. R. (1983). The influence of starvation and refeeding on the lipoprotein lipase activity of skeletal muscle and adipose tissue of lean and obese Zucker rats. *Journal of Nutrition, 113,* 1150–1156. **251**

QUINN, K. J., & O'BRIEN, J. H. (1983). Cortical

motor neuron activity in the cat during classical conditioning with central stimulation as the CS and the US. *Behavioral Neuroscience, 97,* 28–41. **445**

QUINN, W. G., SZIBER, P. P., & BOOKER, R. (1979). The *Drosophila* memory mutant amnesiac. *Nature, 277,* 212–214. **381**

RAAIJMAKERS, W. G. M. (1982). High-affinity choline uptake in hippocampal synaptosomes and learning in the rat. In C. A. Marsan & H. Matthies (Eds.), *Neuronal plasticity and memory formation.* New York: Raven. **375, 381**

RACINE, R. J., MILGRAM, N. W., & HAFNER, S. (1983). Long-term potentiation phenomena in the rat limbic forebrain. *Brain Research, 260,* 217–231. **393**

RACINE, R. J., WILSON, D. A., GINGELL, R., & SUNDERLAND, D. (1986). Long-term potentiation in the interpositus and vestibular nuclei in the rat. *Experimental Brain Research, 63,* 158–162. **393**

RAINBOW, T. C., BIEGON, A., & MCEWEN, B. S. (1982). Autoradiographic localization of imipramine binding in rat brain. *European Journal of Pharmacology, 77,* 363–364. **354**

RAINBOW, T. C., HOFFMAN, P. L., & FLEXNER, L. B. (1980). Studies of memory: A reevaluation in mice of the effects of inhibitors on the rate of synthesis of cerebral proteins as related to amnesia. *Pharmacology, Biochemistry & Behavior, 12,* 79–84. **372**

RAINBOW, T. C., PARSONS, B., & MCEWEN, B. S. (1982). Sex differences in rat brain oestrogen and progestin receptors. *Nature, 300,* 648–649. **280**

RAINBOW, T. C., SNYDER, L., BERCK, D. J., & MCEWEN, B. S. (1984). Correlation of muscarinic receptor induction in the ventromedial hypothalamic nucleus with the activation of feminine sexual behavior by estradiol. *Neuroendocrinology, 39,* 476–480. **297, 298**

RAINEY, J. M., FROHMAN, C. E., FREEDMAN, R. R., POHL, R. B., ETTEDGUI, E., & WILLIAMS, M. (1984). Specificity of lactate infusion as a model of anxiety. *Psychopharmacology Bulletin, 20,* 45–49. **324**

RAISMAN, G., & FIELD, P. M. (1973). Sexual dimorphism in the neuropil of the preoptic area of the rat and its dependence on neonatal androgen. *Brain Research, 54,* 1–29. **299, 300**

RAKIC, P., & RILEY, K. P. (1983). Overproduction and elimination of retinal axons in the fetal rhesus monkey. *Science, 219,* 1441–1446. **431**

RAMIREZ, V. D., KOMISARUK, B. R., WHITMOYER, D. I., & SAWYER, C. H. (1967). Effects of hormones and vaginal stimulation on the EEG and hypothalamic units in rats. *Journal of Physiology, 212,* 1376–1384. **312**

RASMUSSEN, K., & JACOBS, R. L. (1985). Locus coeruleus unit activity in freely moving cats is increased following systemic morphine administration. *Brain Research, 344,* 240–248. **16**

RASMUSSON, D. D., TURNBULL, B. G., & LEECH, C. K. (1985). Unexpected reorganization of somatosensory cortex in a raccoon with extensive forelimb loss. *Neuroscience Letters, 55,* 167–172. **413**

RASTAN, S., KAUFMAN, M. H., HANDYSIDE, A. H., & LYON, M. F. (1980). X-chromosome inactivation in extra-embryonic membranes of diploid parthenogenetic mouse embryos demonstrated by differential staining. *Nature, 288,* 172–173. **287**

RATLIFF, F., (1972). Contour and contrast. *Scientific American, 226,* 90–101. **201**

RATLIFF, F., & HARTLINE, H. K. (1959). The responses of *Limulus* optic nerve fibers to patterns of illumination on the receptor mosaic. *Journal of General Physiology, 42,* 1241–1255. **200, 201**

RATLIFF, F., MILKMAN, N., & RENNERT, N. (1983). Attenuation of Mach bands by adjacent stimuli. *Proceedings of the National Academy of Sciences, U.S.A., 80,* 4554–4558. **201**

RAUCA, Ch., KAMMERER, E., & MATTHIES, H. (1980). Choline uptake and permanent memory storage. *Pharmacology, Biochemistry & Behavior, 13,* 21–25. **375, 381**

RAUSCHECKER, J. P. (1982). Instructive changes in the kitten's visual cortex and their limitation. *Experimental Brain Research, 48,* 301–305. **425**

RAUSCHECKER, J. P., & HARRIS, L. R. (1983). Auditory compensation of the effects of visual deprivation in the cat's superior colliculus. *Experimental Brain Research, 50,* 69–83. **415**

RAUSCHECKER, J. P., & SINGER, W. (1979). Changes in the circuitry of the kitten visual cortex are gated by postsynaptic activity. *Nature, 280,* 58–60. **425**

RAVIOLA, E., & GILULA, N. B. (1973). Gap junctions between photoreceptor cells in the vertebrate retina. *Proceedings of the National Academy of Sciences, U.S.A., 70,* 1677–1681. **184**

READY, D. F., HANSON, T. E., & BENZER, S. (1976). Development of the *Drosophila* retina, a neurocrystalline lattice. *Developmental Biology, 53,* 217–240. **117**

REBEC, G. V., & BASHORE, T. R. (1982). Comments on "Amphetamine Models of Paranoid Schizophrenia": A precautionary note. *Psychological Bulletin, 92,* 403–409. **338**

REBILLARD, G., RYALS, B. M., & RUBEL, E. W. (1982). Relationship between hair cell loss on the chick basilar papilla and threshold shift after acoustic overstimulation. *Hearing Research, 8,* 77–81. **167**

RECHTSCHAFFEN, A., GILLILAND, M. A., BERGMANN, B. M., & WINTER, J. B. (1983). Physiological correlates of prolonged sleep deprivation in rats. *Science, 221,* 182–184. **232, 235**

REDDY, V. V. R., RAJAN, R., & DALY, M. J. (1980). Estrogen metabolism in neural tissues of six-day-old rats. *Brain Research, 197,* 443–452. **277, 282**

REDMOND, D. E., & HUANG, Y. H. (1979). II. New evidence for a locus coeruleus–norepinephrine connection with anxiety. *Life Sciences, 25,* 2149–2162. **344, 355**

REDMOND, D. E., MURPHY, D. L., & BAULU, J. (1979). Platelet monoamine oxidase activity correlates with social affiliative and agonistic behaviors in normal rhesus monkeys. *Psychosomatic Medicine, 41,* 87–100. **341**

REES, H. D., & MICHAEL, R. P. (1983). Autoradiographic localization of ³H-dihydrotestosterone in the thalamus and brain stem of a male rhesus monkey. *Neuroendocrinology Letters, 5,* 55–61. **284**

REES, S., GÜLDNER, F.-H., & AITKIN, L. (1985). Activity dependent plasticity of postsynaptic density structure in the ventral cochlear nucleus of the rat. *Brain Research, 325,* 370–374. **413**

REICH, H., RUPPRECHT, U., STUMPF, H., & STOCK, G. (1983). Modulation of unit activity in the amygdala of unrestrained cats during the sleep–waking cycle. *Neuroscience Letters, 35,* 209–214.

REID, L. D., KONECKA, A. M., PRZEWŁOCKI,

R., MILLAN, M. H., MILLAN, M. J., & HERZ, A. (1982). Endogenous opioids, circadian rhythms, nutrient deprivation, eating and drinking. *Life Sciences, 31,* 1829–1832. **248**

REISENZEIN, R. (1983). The Schachter theory of emotion: Two decades later. *Psychological Bulletin, 94,* 239–264. **323**

RENNER, K. J., BIEGON, A., & LUINE, V. N. (1985). Sex differences in long-term gonadectomized rats: Monamine levels and [³J]nitroimipramine binding in brain nuclei. *Experimental Brain Research, 58,* 198–201. **298**

RESKO, J. A., ELLINWOOD, W. E., PASZTOR, L. M., & BUHL, A. E. (1980). Sex steroids in the umbilical circulation of fetal rhesus monkeys from the time of gonadal differentiation. *Journal of Clinical Endocrinology and Metabolism, 50,* 900–905. **272**

RESKO, J. A., PLOEM, J. G., & STADELMANN, H. L. (1975). Estrogens in fetal and maternal plasma of the rhesus monkey. *Endocrinology, 97,* 425–430. **272**

RESTAK, R. M. (1979). *The brain: The last frontier.* New York: Doubleday (Warner Books Edition). **2**

REVIAL, M. F., SICARD, G., DUCHAMP, A., & HOLLEY, A. (1982). New studies on odour discrimination in the frog's olfactory receptor cells. I. Experimental results. *Chemical Senses, 7,* 175–190. **151, 161, 167**

REYES, F. I., BORODITSKY, R. S., WINTER, J. S. D., & FAIMAN, C. (1974). Studies on human sexual development: II. Fetal and maternal serum gonadotropin and sex steroid concentrations. *Journal of Clinical Endocrinology and Metabolism, 38,* 612–617. **272**

REYMANN, K. G., RÜTHRICH, H., LINDENAU, L., OTT, T., & MATTHIES, H. (1982). Monosynaptic activation of the hippocampus as a conditioned stimulus: Behavioral effects. *Physiology & Behavior, 29,* 1007–1012. **394**

RHODE, W. S. (1978). Some observations on cochlear mechanics. *Journal of the Acoustical Society of America, 64,* 158–176. **166**

RIBLET, L. A., ALLEN, L. E., HYSLOP, D. K., TAYLOR, D. P., & WILDERMAN, R. C. (1980). Pharmacologic activity of buspirone, a novel non-benzodiazepine antianxiety agent. *Federation Proceedings, 39,* 752. **344**

RICCIO, D. C., & RICHARDSON, R. (1984). The status of memory following experimentally induced amnesias: Gone, but not forgotten. *Physiological Psychology, 12,* 59–72. **365, 368, 371**

RIESEN, A. H. (1950). Arrested vision. *Scientific American, 183,* 16–19. **414**

RIGDON, G. C., & PIRCH, J. H. (1986). Nucleus basalis involvement in conditioned neuronal responses in the rat frontal cortex. *Journal of Neuroscience, 6,* 2535–2542. **383**

RINGO, J., WOLBARSHT, M. L., WAGNER, H. G., CROCKER, R., & AMTHOR, F. (1977). Trichromatic vision in the cat. *Science, 198,* 753–754. **186**

RITTER, R. C., & EPSTEIN, A. N. (1975). Control of meal size by central noradrenergic action. *Proceedings of the National Academy of Sciences, U.S.A., 72,* 3740–3743.

ROBERTS, D. C. S., & FIBIGER, H. C. (1977). Evidence for interactions between central noradrenergic neurons and adrenal hormones in learning and memory. *Pharmacology, Biochemistry & Behavior, 7,* 191–194. **375**

ROBERTS, G. W., FERRIER, I. N., LEE, Y., CROW, T. J., JOHNSTONE, E. C., OWENS, D. G.,

BACARESE-HAMILTON, A. J., MCGREGOR, G., O'SHAUGHNESSEY, D., POLAK, J. M., & BLOOM, S. R. (1983). Peptides, the limbic lobe and schizophrenia. *Brain Research*, 288, 199–211. **346**

ROBERTSON, H. A., MARTIN, I. L., & CANDY, J. M. (1978). Differences in benzodiazepine receptor binding in Maudsley reactive and non-reactive rats. *European Journal of Pharmacology*, 50, 455–457. **343**

ROBINSON, D. L., & WURTZ, R. H. (1976). Use of an extraretinal signal by monkey superior colliculus neurons to distinguish real from self-induced movement. *Journal of Neurophysiology*, 39, 852–870. **222**

ROBINSON, D. S., SOURKES, T. L., NIES, A., HARRIS, L. S., SPECTOR, S., BARTLETT, D. L., & KAYE, I. S. (1977). Monoamine metabolism in human brain. *Archives of General Psychiatry*, 34, 89–92. **309**

ROBINSON, J. A., & BRIDSON, W. E. (1978). Neonatal hormone patterns in the macaque: I. Steroids. *Biology of Reproduction*, 19, 773–778. **272**

ROBINSON, T. E., BECKER, J. B., & PRESTY, S. K. (1982). Long-term facilitation of amphetamine-induced rotational behavior and striatal dopamine release produced by a single exposure to amphetamine: Sex differences. *Brain Research*, 253, 231–241. **313, 338**

RODBELL, M. (1980). The role of hormone receptors and GTP-regulatory proteins in membrane transduction. *Nature*, 284, 17–22. **99**

RODIECK, R. W. (1973). *The vertebrate retina: Principles of structure and function*. San Francisco: W. H. Freeman. **184, 221**

RODRIGUEZ, M., CASTRO, R., HERNANDEZ, G., & MAS, M. (1984). Different roles of catecholaminergic and serotoninergic neurons of the medial forebrain bundle on male rat sexual behavior. *Physiology & Behavior*, 33, 5–11. **297, 310**

ROFFLER-TARLOV, S., & GRAYBIEL, A. M. (1984). Weaver mutation has differential effects on the dopamine-containing innervation of the limbic and nonlimbic striatum. *Nature*, 307, 62–66. **347**

ROLLS, B. J., WOOD, R. J., & ROLLS, E. T. (1980). Thirst: The initiation, maintenance, and termination of drinking. In J. M. Sprague & A. N. Epstein (Eds.), *Progress in psychobiology and physiological psychology* (Vol. 9). New York: Academic Press. **249, 250**

ROLLS, E. T. (1971a). Contrasting effects of hypothalamic and nucleus accumbens septi self-stimulation on brain stem single unit activity and cortical arousal. *Brain Research*, 31, 275–285. **266, 267**

ROLLS, E. T. (1971b). Involvement of brainstem units in medial forebrain bundle self-stimulation. *Physiology & Behavior*, 7, 297–310. **267**

ROLLS, E. T. (1972). Activation of amygdaloid neurones in reward, eating and drinking elicited by electrical stimulation of the brain. *Brain Research*, 45, 365–381. **267**

ROLLS, E. T. (1977). Neuronal activity during natural and brain stimulation reward. In R. D. Hall, F. E. Bloom, & J. Olds (Eds.), Neuronal and neurochemical substrates of reinforcement. *Neurosciences Research Progress Bulletin*, 15, 231–277. **267, 268**

ROLLS, E. T., BURTON, M. J., & MORA, F. (1976). Hypothalamic neuronal responses associated with the sight of food. *Brain Research*, 111, 53–66. **261**

ROLLS, E. T., & COOPER, S. J. (1973). Activation of neurones in the prefrontal cortex by brain-stimulation reward in the rat. *Brain Research*, 60, 351–368. **267**

ROLLS, E. T., JUDGE, S. J., & SANGHERA, M. K.

(1977). Activity of neurones in the inferotemporal cortex of the alert monkey. *Brain Research*, 130, 229–238.

ROLLS, E. T., SANGHERA, M. K., & ROPER-HALL, A. (1979). The latency of activation of neurones in the lateral hypothalamus and substantia innominata during feeding in the monkey. *Brain Research*, 164, 121–135. **261**

ROMSOS, D. R., CHEE, K. M., & BERGEN, W. G. (1982)—. Protein intake regulation in adult obese *(ob/ob)* and lean mice: Effects of nonprotein energy source and of supplemental tryptophan. *Journal of Nutrition*, 112, 505–513. **253**

ROMSOS, D. R., & FERGUSON, D. (1982). Self-selected intake of carbohydrate, fat, and protein by obese *(ob/ob)* and lean mice. *Physiology & Behavior*, 28, 301–305. **253**

ROOS, A., RYDENHAG, R., & ANDERSSON, S. (1983). Activity in cortical cells after stimulation of tooth pulp afferents in the cat: Intracellular analysis. *Pain*, 16, 49–60. **226**

ROPER, S. (1983). Regenerative impulses in taste cells. *Science*, 220, 1311–1312. **150**

ROSE, D. (1974). The hypercomplex cell classification in the cat's striate cortex. *Journal of Physiology*, 242, 123P–125P. **207**

ROSE, J. E., BRUGGE, J. F., ANDERSON, D. J., & HIND, J. E. (1967). Phase-locked response to low-frequency tones in single auditory nerve fibers of the squirrel monkey. *Journal of Neurophysiology*, 30, 769–793. **163**

ROSE, J. E., GROSS, N. B., GEISLER, C. D., & HIND, J. E. (1966). Some neural mechanisms in the inferior colliculus of the cat which may be relevant to localization of a sound source. *Journal of Neurophysiology*, 29, 288–314. **172**

ROSE, S. P. R. (1981). What should a biochemistry of learning and memory be about? *Neuroscience*, 6, 811–821.

ROSENTHAL, D. (1980). Genetic aspects of schizophrenia. In H. M. Van Praag (Ed.), *Handbook of biological psychiatry: Part III. Brain mechanisms and abnormal behavior—genetics and neuroendocrinology*. New York: Marcel Dekker.

ROSENZWEIG, M. R., & BENNETT, E. L. (1972). Cerebral changes in rats exposed individually to an enriched environment. *Journal of Comparative and Physiological Psychology*, 80, 304–313. **400**

ROSENZWEIG, M. R., BENNETT, E. L., & DIAMOND, M. C. (1972). Cerebral effects of differential experience in hypophysectomized rats. *Journal of Comparative and Physiological Psychology*, 79, 56–66. **400, 402, 404**

ROSS, R. A., JUDD, A. B., PICKEL, V. M., JOH, T. H., & REIS, D. J. (1976). Strain-dependent variations in number of midbrain dopaminergic neurones. *Nature*, 264, 654–656. **329**

ROTH, R. A., & CASSELL, D. J. (1983). Insulin receptor: Evidence that it is a protein kinase. *Science*, 219, 299–301. **242**

ROTHWELL, N. J., & STOCK, M. J. (1979). A role for brown adipose tissue in diet-induced thermogenesis. *Nature*, 281, 31–35. **243**

ROTHWELL, N. J., & STOCK, M. J. (1983). Luxuskonsumption, diet-induced thermogenesis and brown fat: The case in favour. *Clinical Science*, 64, 19–23. **243**

ROTMAN, A., ZEMISHLANY, A., MUNITZ, H., & WIJSENBEEK, H. (1982). The active uptake of serotonin by platelets of schizophrenic patients and their families: Possibility of a genetic marker. *Psychopharmacology*,

77, 171–174.

ROUTTENBERG, A. (1968). The two-arousal hypothesis: Reticular formation and limbic system. *Psychological Review*, 75, 51–80. **225**

ROUTTENBERG, A. (1971). Stimulus processing and response execution: A neurobehavioral theory. *Physiology & Behavior*, 6, 589–596. **225**

ROUTTENBERG, A. (1972). Intracranial chemical injection and behavior: A critical review. *Behavioral Biology*, 7, 601–641. **250**

ROUTTENBERG, A., & HUANG, Y. H. (1968). Reticular formation and brainstem unitary activity: Effects of posterior hypothalamic and septal-limbic stimulation at reward loci. *Physiology & Behavior*, 3, 611–617. **266**

ROWE, M. H., & STONE, J. (1977). Naming of neurones: Classification and naming of cat retinal ganglion cells. *Brain, Behaviour, and Evolution*, 14, 185–216. **188, 206**

ROWLAND, L. P. (1981). Blood-brain barrier, cerebrospinal fluid, brain edema, and hydrocephalus. In E. R. Kandel & J. H. Schwartz (Eds.), *Principles of neural science*. New York: Elsevier/North-Holland. **29, 30**

RUBIN, B. S., & BARFIELD, R. J. (1983). Induction of estrous behavior in ovariectomized rats by sequential replacement of estrogen and progesterone to the ventromedial hypothalamus. *Neuroendocrinology*, 37, 218–224. **280**

RUPNIAK, N. M. J., JENNER, P., & MARSDEN, C. D. (1983). The effect of chronic neuroleptic administration on cerebral dopamine receptor function. *Life Sciences*, 32, 2289–2311. **346**

RUSHTON, W. A. H. (1965). Visual adaptation. *Proceedings of the Royal Society of London, Series B*, 162, 20–46. **218**

RUSHTON, W. A. H. (1972). Pigments and signals in colour vision. *Journal of Physiology*, 220, 1P–31P. **203, 223**

RUSHTON, W. A. H. (1975). Visual pigments and color blindness. *Scientific American*, 232, 64–74. **203**

RUSSELL, I. J. (1983). Origin of the receptor potential in inner hair cells of the mammalian cochlea—evidence for Davis' theory. *Nature*, 301, 334–336. **150, 153**

RUSSELL, I. J., & SELLICK, P. M. (1977). Tuning properties of cochlear hair cells. *Nature*, 267, 858–860. **153**

RUSSELL, I. J., & SELLICK, P. M. (1978). Intracellular studies of hair cells in the mammalian cochlea. *Journal of Physiology*, 284, 261–290. **153**

RUSSELL, I. J., & SELLICK, P. M. (1983). Low-frequency characteristics of intracellularly recorded receptor potentials in guinea-pig cochlear hair cells. *Journal of Physiology*, 338, 179–206. **153**

RUSSELL, J. M., & BROWN, A. M. (1972). Active transport of chloride by the giant neuron of the *Aplysia* abdominal ganglion. *Journal of General Physiology*, 60, 499–518. **83**

RUSSO, A. F., & KOSHLAND, D. E., JR. (1983). Separation of signal transduction and adaptation functions of the aspartate receptor in bacterial sensing. *Science*, 220, 1016–1020. **149**

RÜTHRICH, H., MATTHIES, H., & OTT, T. (1982). Long-term changes in synaptic excitability of hippocampal cell populations as a result of training. In C. A. Marsan & H. Matthies (Eds.), *Neuronal plasticity and memory formation*. New York: Raven. **394**

RYAN, A. (1975). Effects of behavior performance on single-unit firing patterns in the inferior colliculus of the

Rhesus monkey: Additional observations. *Journal of the Acoustical Society of America*, 58(Suppl. 1), S65. **240**

RYAN, A., DALLOS, P., & MCGEE, T. (1979). Psychophysical tuning curves and auditory thresholds after hair cell damage in the chinchilla. *Journal of the Acoustical Society of America*, 66, 370–378. **167**

SABEL, B. A., & STEIN, D. G. (1981). Extensive loss of subcortical neurons in the aging rat brain. *Experimental Neurology*, 73, 507–516. **431**

SAITO, T., & KONDO, H. (1978). Ionic mechanisms underlying the center and surround responses of on-center bipolar cells in the carp retina. *Sensory Processes*, 2, 350–358.

SAITO, A., SANKARAN, H., GOLDFINE, I. D., & WILLIAMS, J. A. (1980). Cholecystokinin receptors in the brain: Characterization and distribution. *Science*, 208, 1155–1156.

SAITO, A., WILLIAMS, J. A., & GOLDFINE, I. D. (1981a). Alterations of brain cerebral cortex CCK receptors in the *ob/ob* mouse. *Endocrinology*, 109, 984–986. **252**

SAITO, A., WILLIAMS, J. A., & GOLDFINE, I. D. (1981b). Alterations in brain cholecystokinin receptors after fasting. *Nature*, 289, 599–600. **249**

SAITO, A., WILLIAMS, J. A., WAXLER, S. H., & GOLDFINE, I. C. (1982). Alterations of brain cholecystokinin receptors in mice made obese with goldthioglucose. *Journal of Neurochemistry*, 39, 525–528. **252**

SAKUMA, Y. (1984). Influences of neonatal gonadectomy or androgen exposure on the sexual differentiation of the rat ventromedial hypothalamus. *Journal of Physiology*, 349, 273–286. **300**

SAKUMA, Y., & PFAFF, D. W. (1979). Facilitation of female reproductive behavior from mesencephalic central gray in the rat. *American Journal of Physiology*, 237, 285–290. **280**

SAKUMA, Y., & PFAFF, D. W. (1980). Convergent effects of lordosis-relevant somatosensory and hypothalamic influences on central gray cells in the rat mesencephalon. *Experimental Neurology*, 70, 269–281. **317**

SALGANIK, R. I., PARVEZ, H., TOMSONS, V. P., & SHUMSKAYA, I. A. (1983). Probable role of reverse transcription in learning: Correlation between hippocampal RNA-dependent DNA synthesis and learning ability in rats. *Neuroscience Letters*, 36, 317–322. **378, 381**

SALKOFF, L. (1983). *Drosophila* mutants reveal two components of fast outward current. *Nature*, 302, 249–251. **59, 60, 128**

SALKOFF, L., & WYMAN, R. (1981). Genetic modification of potassium channels in *Drosophila Shaker* mutants. *Nature*, 293, 228–230. **128**

SALZBERG, B. M., DAVILA, H. V., & COHEN, L. B. (1973). Experimental creation of unusual neuronal properties in visual cortex of kitten. *Nature*, 246, 506–509.

SANES, D. H., & CONSTANTINE-PATON, M. (1983). Altered activity patterns during development reduce neural tuning. *Science*, 221, 1183–1185. **413**

SANES, D. H., & CONSTANTINE-PATON, M. (1985). The sharpening of frequency tuning curves requires patterned activity during development in the mouse, *Mus musculus. Journal of Neuroscience*, 5, 1152–1166. **413**

SANGAMESWARAN, L., & DE BLAS, A. L. (1985). Demonstration of benzodiazepine-like molecules in the mammalian brain with a monoclonal antibody to benzodiazepines. *Proceedings of the National Academy of Sciences, U.S.A.*, 82, 5560–5564. **343**

SANGER, D. J. (1981). Endorphinergic mechanisms

in the control of food and water intake. *Appetite: Journal for Intake Research*, 2, 193–208. **248**

SANGHERA, M. K., ROLLS, E. T., & ROPER-HALL, A. (1979). Visual responses of neurons in the dorsolateral amygdala of the alert monkey. *Experimental Neurology*, 63, 610–626.

SAR, M., & STUMPF, W. E. (1981). Central noradrenergic neurones concentrate ³oestradiol. *Nature*, 289, 500–502. **297**

SASAKI, K., ONO, T., MURAMOTO, K.-I., NISHINO H., & FUKUDA, M. (1984). The effects of feeding and rewarding brain stimulation on lateral hypothalamic unit activity in freely moving rats. *Brain Research*, 322, 201–211. **259, 267**

SATAKE, N., & MORTON, B. E. (1979). Scotophon A causes dark avoidance in goldfish by elevating pineal N-acetylserotonin. *Pharmacology, Biochemistry & Behavior*, 10, 449–456. **378**

SATO, T. (1980). Recent advances in the physiology of taste cells. *Progress in Neurobiology*, 14, 25–67. **150, 151, 167, 173**

SATO, T., & BEIDLER, L. M. (1975). Membrane resistance change of the frog taste cells in response to water and NaCl. *Journal of General Physiology*, 66, 735–763.

SATO, H., & KAYAMA, Y. (1983). Effects of noradrenaline applied iontophoretically on rat superior collicular neurons. *Brain Research Bulletin*, 10, 453–457. **240**

SAVAGEAU, M. M., & BEATTY, W. W. (1981). Gonadectomy and sex differences in the behavioral responses to amphetamine and apomorphine of rats. *Pharmacology, Biochemistry & Behavior*, 14, 17–21. **313**

SCARAVILLI, F. (1983). Reduced substance P in hereditary sensory neuropathy in the mf rat. *Brain Research*, 263, 147–150. **168**

SCHALLERT, T. (1983). Sensorimotor impairment and recovery of function in brain-damaged rats: Reappearance of symptoms during old age. *Behavioral Neuroscience*, 97, 159–164. **433**

SCHEIBEL, M. E., & SCHEIBEL, A. B. (1958). Structural substrates for integrative patterns in the brain stem reticular core. In H. J. Jasper, L. D. Proctor, R. S. Knighton, W. C. Noshay, & R. T. Costello (Eds.), *Reticular formation of the brain*. Boston: Little, Brown.

SCHEIN, S. J., BENNETT, M. V. L., & KATZ, G. M. (1976). Altered calcium conductance in pawns, behavioural mutants of *Paramecium aurelia. Journal of Experimental Biology*, 65, 699–724. **128**

SCHICK, R. R., YAKSH, T., & GO, V. L. W. (1986). An intragastric meal releases the putative satiety factor cholecystokinin from hypothalamic neurons in cats. *Brain Research*, 370, 349–353. **249**

SCHIFFMAN, H., & FALKENBERG, P. (1968). The organization of stimuli and sensory neurons. *Physiology & Behavior*, 3, 197–201. **160, 161**

SCHILLER, P. H., FINLAY, B. L., & VOLMAN, S. F. (1976a). Quantitative studies of single-cell properties in monkey striate cortex: I. Spatiotemporal organization of receptive fields. *Journal of Neurophysiology*, 39, 1288–1319. **212**

SCHILLER, P. H., FINLAY, B. L., & VOLMAN, S. F. (1976b). Quantitative studies of single-cell properties in monkey striate cortex: II. Orientation specificity and ocular dominance. *Journal of Neurophysiology*, 39, 1320–1333. **212**

SCHILLER, P. H., FINLAY, B. L., & VOLMAN, S. F. (1976c). Quantitative studies of single-cell properties

in monkey striate cortex: III. Spatial frequency. *Journal of Neurophysiology*, 39, 1334–1351. **212, 214**

SCHILLER, P. H., FINLAY, B. L., & VOLMAN, S. F. (1976d). Quantitative studies of single-cell properties in monkey striate cortex: V. Multivariate statistical analyses and models. *Journal of Neurophysiology*, 39, 1362–1374. **212**

SCHINDLER, A. E. (1976). Steroid metabolism in foetal tissues: IV. Conversion of testosterone to 5,alpha-dihydrotestosterone in human foetal brain. *Journal of Steroid Biochemistry*, 7, 97–100. **284**

SCHLAER, R. (1971). Shift in binocular disparity causes compensatory change in the cortical structure of kittens. *Science*, 173, 638–641. **424**

SCHLAGER, G., FREEMAN, R., & EL SEOUDY, A. A. (1983). Genetic study of norepinephrine in brains of mice selected for differences in blood pressure. *Journal of Heredity*, 74, 97–100. **129**

SCHLESINGER, K., LIPSITZ, D. U., PECK, P. L., & PELLEYMOUNTER, M. A. (1983). Substance P reversal of electroconvulsive shock and cycloheximide-induced retrograde amnesia. *Behavioral and Neural Biology*, 39, 30–39. **372**

SCHMIDT, J. T., & EDWARDS, D. L. (1983). Activity sharpens the map during the regeneration of the retinotectal projection in goldfish. *Brain Research*, 269, 29–39. **437**

SCHMITT, M. (1973). Influences of hepatic portal receptors on hypothalamic feeding and satiety centers. *American Journal of Physiology*, 225, 1089–1095. **259**

SCHNEIDER, G. E. (1979). Is it really better to have your brain lesion early?: A revision of the "Kennard Principle." *Neuropsychologia*, 17, 557–583. **433**

SCHNEIDER, J. E., LYNCH, C. B., & GUNDAKER, C. L. (1983). The influence of exogenous progesterone on selected lines of mice divergent for maternal nesting. *Behavior Genetics*, 13, 247–256. **288**

SCHNEIDER, J. E., LYNCH, C. B., POSSIDENTE, B., & HEGMANN, J. P. (1982). Genetic association between progesterone-induced and maternal nesting in mice. *Physiology & Behavior*, 29, 97–105. **288**

SCHOLES, J. H. (1975). Colour receptors, and their synaptic connexions, in the retina of a cyprinid fish. *Philosophical Transactions of the Royal Society, Series B*, 270, 8–118. **185**

SCHOLFIELD, S. N. (1978). A depolarizing inhibitory potential in neurons of the olfactory cortex in vitro. *Journal of Physiology*, 275, 547–557. **84, 85**

SCHOOLER, C., ZAHN, T. P., MURPHY, D. L., & BUCHSBAUM, M. S. (1978). Psychological correlates of monoamine oxidase activity in normals. *Journal of Nervous and Mental Disease*, 166, 177–186. **341**

SCHRADER, W. T. (1984). New model for steroid hormone receptors? *Nature*, 308, 17–18. **279**

SCHRÖDER, H., KAMMERER, E., & MATTHIES, H. (1982). Biochemical evidence for dopaminergic transmission in the rat hippocampus. In C. A. Marsan & H. Matthies, (Eds.), *Neuronal plasticity and memory formation*. New York: Raven. **384, 437**

SCHULTZ, J. E., SIGGINS, G. R., SCHOCKER, F. W., TÜRCK, M., & BLOOM, F. E. (1981). Effects of prolonged treatment with lithium and tricyclic antidepressants on discharge frequency, norepinephrine responses and *beta* receptor binding in rat cerebellum: Electrophysiological and biochemical comparison. *Journal of Pharmacology and Experimental Therapeutics*, 216, 28–38. **349, 356**

SCHWARTZ, E. A. (1975a). Rod–rod interaction in the retina of the turtle. *Journal of Physiology, 246,* 617–638. **194**

SCHWARTZ, E. A. (1975b). Cones excite rods in the retina of the turtle. *Journal of Physiology, 246,* 639–651. **185, 194**

SCHWARTZ, J. H. (1981). Chemical basis of synaptic transmission. In E. R. Kandel & J. H. Schwartz (Eds.), *Principles of neural science.* New York: Elsevier/North-Holland. **80, 86, 93, 98**

SCHWARTZ, M. (1978). *Physiological psychology* (2nd ed.). Englewood Cliffs, NJ: Prentice-Hall.

SCHWARTZ, R. D., & KELLAR, K. J. (1983). Nicotinic cholinergic receptor binding sites in the brain: Regulation in vivo. *Science, 220,* 214–216. **107**

SCHWARTZ, S. M., BLAUSTEIN, J. D., & WADE, G. N. (1979). Inhibition of estrous behavior by progesterone in rats: Role of neural estrogen and progestin receptors. *Endocrinology, 105,* 1078–1082. **281, 285**

SCHWARTZKROIN, P. A. (1975). Characteristics of CA1 neurons recorded intracellularly in the hippocampus in vitro slice preparation. *Brain Research, 85,* 423–436. **393**

SCHWEGLER, H., & LIPP, H.-P. (1981). Is there a correlation between hippocampal mossy fiber distribution and two-way avoidance in mice and rats? *Neuroscience Letters, 23,* 25–30. **38, 130, 383, 384**

SCHWEGLER, H., & LIPP, H.-P. (1983). Hereditary covariations of neuronal circuitry and behavior: Correlations between the proportions of hippocampal synaptic fields in the regio inferior and two-way avoidance in mice and rats. *Behavioral Brain Research, 7,* 1–38. **383, 384**

SCHWEGLER, H., LIPP, H.-P., VAN DER LOOS, H., & BUSELMAIER, W. (1981). Individual hippocampal mossy fiber distribution in mice correlates with two-way avoidance performance. *Science, 214,* 817–819. **130, 383, 384**

SCLAFANI, A., & KLUGE, L. (1974). Food motivation and body weight levels in hypothalamic hyperphagic rats: A dual lipostat model of hunger and appetite. *Journal of Comparative and Physiological Psychology, 86,* 28–46. **243, 245**

SCOTT, J. W., & PFAFFMANN, C. (1967). Olfactory input to the hypothalamus: Electrophysiological evidence. *Science, 158,* 1592–1594. **260**

SCOTT, T. R., JR., & ERICKSON, R. P. (1971). Synaptic processing of taste-quality information in thalamus of the rat. *Journal of Neurophysiology, 34,* 868–884. **162, 173**

SCRIMA, L., COREY, D. T., & CHOO, A. F. (1982). Interanimal transferability of taste aversion learning for 0.1% saccharin. *International Journal of Neuroscience, 16,* 135–142. **378**

SCUVÉE-MOREAU, J. J., & DRESSE, A. E. (1979). Effect of various antidepressant drugs on the spontaneous firing rate of locus coeruleus and dorsal raphe neurons of the rat. *European Journal of Pharmacology, 57,* 219–225. **355**

SEAL, J., GROSS, C., & BIOULAC, B. (1982). Activity of neurons in area 5 during a simple arm movement in monkeys before and after deafferentation of the trained limb. *Brain Research, 250,* 229–243. **176, 230**

SEDVALL, G., FYRÖ, B., GULLBERG, B., NYBÄCK, H., WIESEL, F.-A., & WODE-HELGODT, B. (1980). Relationships in healthy volunteers between concentrations of monoamine metabolites in cerebrospinal fluid and family history of psychiatric morbidity. *British Journal*

of Psychiatry, 136, 366–374. **348**

SEEMAN, P., & LEE, T. (1975). Antipsychotic drugs: Direct correlation between clinical potency and presynaptic action on dopamine neurons. *Science, 188,* 1217–1219. **345**

SEEMAN, P., ULPIAN, C., BERGERON, C., RIEDERER, P., JELLINGER, K., GABRIEL, E., REYNOLDS, G. P., & TOURTELLOTTE, W. W. (1984). Bimodal distribution of dopamine receptor densities in the brains of schizophrenics. *Science, 225,* 728–731. **346**

SEGAL, M. (1973). Dissecting a short-term memory circuit in the rat brain: I. Changes in entorhinal unit activity and responsiveness of hippocampal units in the process of classical conditioning. *Brain Research, 64,* 281–292. **387, 388**

SEGAL, M. (1977). Excitability changes in rat hippocampus during conditioning. *Experimental Neurology, 55,* 67–73. **394**

SEGAL, M. (1985). Mechanisms of action of noradrenaline in the brain. *Physiological Psychology, 13,* 172–178. **97, 98, 236, 240, 376**

SEGAL, M., & BLOOM, F. E. (1976). The action of norepinephrine in the rat hippocampus: IV. The effects of locus coeruleus stimulation on evoked hippocampal unit activity. *Brain Research, 107,* 513–525. **240, 395**

SEGAL, M., DISTERHOFT, J. F., & OLDS, J. (1972). Hippocampal unit activity during classical aversive and appetitive conditioning. *Science, 175,* 792–794. **388**

SEGAL, M., & OLDS, J. (1972). Behavior of units in hippocampal circuit of the rat during learning. *Journal of Neurophysiology, 15,* 680–690. **387**

SEGUNDO, J. P., MOORE, G. P., STENSAAS, L. J., & BULLOCK, T. H. (1963). Sensitivity of neurones in *Aplysia* to temporal pattern of arriving impulses. *Journal of Experimental Biology, 40,* 643–667. **158**

SEIDMAN, L. J. (1983). Schizophrenia and brain dysfunction: An integration of recent neurodiagnostic findings. *Psychological Bulletin, 94,* 195–238.

SELLICK, P. M., & RUSSELL, I. J. (1980). The responses of inner hair cells to basilar membrane velocity during low frequency auditory stimulation in the guinea pig cochlea. *Hearing Research, 2,* 439–445. **153**

SELLIN, L. C., & SPERELAKIS, N. (1978). Decreased potassium permeability in dystrophic mouse skeletal muscle. *Experimental Neurology, 62,* 605–617. **128**

SELMANOFF, M. K., BRODKIN, L. D., WEINER, R. I., & SIITERI, P. K. (1977). Aromatization and 5,alpha-reduction of androgens in discrete hypothalamic and limbic regions of the male and female rat. *Endocrinology, 101,* 841–848. **284**

SELMANOFF, M. K., GOLDMAN, B. D., MAXSON, S. C., & GINSBURG, B. E. (1977). Correlated effects of the Y-chromosome of mice on developmental changes in testosterone levels and intermale aggression. *Life Sciences, 20,* 359–365. **288**

SELYE, H. (1978). *The stress of life.* New York: McGraw-Hill Paperback. (Original work published 1976) **324**

SELYE, H. (1980). The stress concept today. In I. K. Kutash, L. B. Schlesinger, & associates (Eds.), *Handbook on stress and anxiety.* San Francisco: Jossey-Bass. **324**

SENGELAUB, D. R., & FINLAY, B. L. (1981). Early removal of one eye reduces normally occurring cell death in the remaining eye. *Science, 213,* 573–574. **431, 433**

SESSIONS, G. R., KANT, G. J., & KOOB, G. F.

(1976). Locus coeruleus lesions and learning in the rat. *Physiology & Behavior, 17,* 853–859. **374**

SESSLER, F. M., & SALHI, M. D. (1983). Convergences on lateral preoptic neurons of internal and external stimuli related to drinking. *Neuroscience Letters, 36,* 151–155. **255**

SETHY, V. H., & HARRIS, D. W. (1982). Role of beta-adrenergic receptors in the mechanism of action of second-generation antidepressants. *Drug Development Research, 2,* 403–406. **349**

SEYDOUX, J., ROHNER-JEANRENAUD, F., ASSIMACOPOULOS-JEANNET, F., JEANRENAUD, B., & GIRARDIER, L. (1981). Functional disconnection of brown adipose tissue in hypothalamic obesity in rats. *Pflügers Archiv, 390,* 1–4. **243**

SHAPIRO, B. H., & GOLDMAN, A. S. (1979). New thoughts on sexual differentiation of the brain. In H. L. Vallet & I. H. Porter (Eds.), *Genetic mechanisms of sexual development.* New York: Academic Press. **288**

SHAPIRO, B. H., GOLDMAN, A. S., BONGIOVANNI, A. S., & MARINO, J. M. (1976). Neonatal progesterone and feminine sexual development. *Nature, 264,* 795–796. **272**

SHAPIRO, L. J., MOHANDAS, T., WEISS, R., & ROMEO, G. (1979). Non-inactivation of an X-chromosome locus in man. *Science, 204,* 1224–1226. **287**

SHEARD, M. H., ZOLOVICK, A., & AGHAJANIAN, G. K. (1972). Raphe neurons: Effect of tricyclic antidepressant drugs. *Brain Research, 43,* 690–694. **355**

SHEKIM, W. O., HODGES, K., HORWITZ, E., GLASER, R. D., DAVIS, L., & BYLUND, D. B. (1984). Psychoeducational and impulsivity correlates of platelet MAO in normal children. *Psychiatry Research, 11,* 99–106. **341**

SHEPARD, P. D., & GERMAN, D. C. (1984). A subpopulation of mesocortical dopamine neurons possesses autoreceptors. *European Journal of Pharmacology, 98,* 455–456. **347, 358**

SHEPHERD, G. M. (1978). Microcircuits in the nervous system. *Scientific American, 238,* 92–103. **105**

SHEPHERD, G. M. (1983). *Neurobiology.* New York: Oxford Press. **28, 86, 142, 156, 174, 229**

SHERIDAN, P. J. (1983). Androgen receptors in the brain: What are we measuring? *Endocrine Reviews, 4,* 171–178. **283, 284**

SHERIDAN, P. J., & WEAKER, F. J. (1982). Androgen receptor systems in the brain stem of the primate. *Brain Research, 235,* 225–232. **281, 284**

SHERMAN, A. D., & PETTY, F. (1980). Neurochemical basis of the action of antidepressants on learned helplessness. *Behavioral and Neural Biology, 30,* 119–134. **338**

SHERMAN, A. D., & PETTY, F. (1982). Additivity of neurochemical changes in learned helplessness and imipramine. *Behavioral and Neural Biology, 35,* 344–353. **332**

SHERMAN, A. D., & PETTY, F. (1984). Learning helplessness decreases [³H]imipramine binding in rat cortex. *Journal of Affective Disorders, 6,* 25–32. **332, 348**

SHERMAN, A. D., SACQUITNE, J. L., & PETTY, F. (1982). Specificity of the learned helplessness model of depression. *Pharmacology, Biochemistry & Behavior, 16,* 449–454. **338**

SHERMAN, G. F., GALABURDA, A. M., & GESCHWIND, N. (1982). Neuroanatomical asymmetries in non-human species. *Trends in NeuroSciences, 5,* 429–

431. **20**

SHERMAN, G. F., GARBANATI, J. A., ROSEN, G. C., HOFMANN, M., YUTZEY, D. A., & DENENBERG, V. H. (1983). Lateralization of spatial preference in the female rat. *Life Sciences, 33*, 189–193. **302**

SHERMAN, S. M. (1974). Monocularly deprived cats: Improvement of the deprived eye's vision by visual decortication. *Science, 186*, 267–269. **419**

SHERMAN, S. M. (1985). Functional organization of the W-, X-, and Y-cell pathways in the cat: A review and a hypothesis. In J. M. Sprague & A. N. Epstein (Eds.), *Progress in psychobiology and physiological psychology* (Vol. 11). New York: Academic Press. **188, 200, 214**

SHERMAN, S. M., & SPEAR, P. D. (1982). Organization of visual pathways in normal and visually deprived cats. *Physiological Reviews, 62*, 738–855. **199, 200, 212, 414, 416, 419–421, 432**

SHERWIN, B. B., GELFAND, M. M., & BRENDER, W. (1985). Androgen enhances sexual motivation in females: A prospective, crossover study of sex steroid administration in the surgical menopause. *Psychosomatic Medicine, 47*, 339–351. **293**

SHIMAZU, T., & TAKAHASHI, A. (1980). Stimulation of hypothalamic nuclei has differential effects on lipid synthesis in brown and white adipose tissue. *Nature, 284*, 62–63. **245**

SHIMIZU, N., OOMURA, Y., NOVIN, D., GRIJALVA, C. V., & COOPER, P. H. (1983). Functional correlations between lateral hypothalamic glucose-sensitive neurons and hepatic portal glucose-sensitive units in rats. *Brain Research, 265*, 49–54. **248, 256, 259**

SHINKMAN, P. G., ISLEY, M. R., & ROGERS, D. C. (1983). Prolonged dark rearing and development of interocular orientation disparity in visual cortex. *Journal of Neurophysiology, 49*, 717–729. **424**

SHOLL, S. A., GOY, R. W., & UNO, H. (1982). Differences in brain uptake and metabolism of testosterone in gonadectomized, adrenalectomized male and female rhesus monkeys. *Endocrinology, 111*, 806–813. **284**

SHORT, R. V. (1978). Sex determination and differentiation of the mammalian gonad. *International Journal of Andrology* (Suppl. 2), 21–28. **286**

SHRENKER, P., & MAXSON, S. C. (1982). The Y chromosomes of DBA/1Bg and DBA/2Bg compared for effects on intermale aggression. *Behavior Genetics, 12*, 429–434. **288**

SHUTTLESWORTH, D., NEILL, D., & ELLEN, P. (1984). The place of physiological psychology in neuroscience. *Physiological Psychology, 12*, 3–7. **451**

SIEGEL, J. M. (1979). Behavioral functions of the reticular formation. *Brain Research Reviews, 1*, 69–105. **238, 269**

SIEGELBAUM, S. A., CAMARDO, J. S., & KANDEL, E. R. (1982). Serotonin and cyclic AMP close single K$^+$ channels in *Aplysia* sensory neurones. *Nature, 229*, 413–417. **60, 87, 104, 358**

SIGGINS, G. R., OLIVER, A. P., HOFFER, B. J., & BLOOM, F. E. (1971). Cyclic adenosine monophosphate and norepinephrine: Effects on transmembrane properties of cerebellar Purkinje cells. *Science, 171*, 192–194.

SIMERLY, R. B., SWANSON, L. W., HANDA, R. J., & GORSKI, R. A. (1985). Influence of perinatal androgen on the sexually dimorphic distribution of tyrosine hydroxylase-immunoreactive cells and fibers in the anteroventral periventricular nucleus of the rat. *Neuroendocrinology, 40*, 501–510. **300, 309**

SIMMONDS, M. A. (1983). Multiple GABA receptors and associated regulatory sites. *Trends in Neurosciences, 6*, 279–281.

SIMMONS, F. B., EPLEY, J. M., LUMMIS, R. C., GUTTMAN, N., FRISHKOPF, L. S., HARMON, L. D., & ZWICKER, E. (1965). Auditory nerve: Electrical stimulation in man. *Science, 148*, 104–106. **165**

SIMMONS, M. A. (1985). The complexity and diversity of synaptic transmission in the prevertebral sympathetic ganglia. *Progress in Neurobiology, 24*, 43–93. **69, 89–91**

SIMON, H., SCATTON, B., & LE MOAL, M. (1980). Dopaminergic A10 neurones are involved in cognitive functions. *Nature, 286*, 150–151. **347**

SIMON, N. G. (1979). The genetics of intermale aggressive behavior in mice: Recent research and alternative strategies. *Neuroscience & Biobehavioral Reviews, 3*, 97–106. **326**

SIMONS, D. J., DURHAM, D., & WOOLSEY, T. A. (1984). Functional organization of mouse and rat SmI barrel cortex following vibrissal damage on different postnatal days. *Somatosensory Research, 1*, 207–245. **410**

SIMPKINS, J. W., KALRA, S. P., & KALRA, P. S. (1983). Variable effects of testosterone on dopamine activity in several microdissected regions in the preoptic area and medial basal hypothalamus. *Endocrinology, 112*, 665–669. **309**

SIMSON, P. G., WEISS, J. M., HOFFMAN, L. J., & AMBROSE, M. J. (1986). Reversal of behavioral depression by infusion of an alpha$_2$-adrenergic agonist into the locus coeruleus. *Neuropharmacology, 25*, 385–389. **334**

SINGER, W. (1985). Central control of developmental plasticity in the mammalian visual cortex. *Vision Research, 25*, 389–396. **414, 420, 423**

SINGER, W., & RAUSCHECKER, J. P. (1982). Central core control of developmental plasticity in the kitten visual cortex: II. Electrical activation of mesencephalic and diencephalic projections. *Experimental Brain Research, 47*, 223–233. **420**

SINGER, W., RAUSCHECKER, J., & VON GRUENAU, M. (1979). Squint affects striate cortex cells encoding horizontal image movements. *Brain Research, 170*, 182–186. **427**

SINGER, W., & TRETTER, F. (1976). Receptive-field properties and neuronal connectivity in striate and parastriate cortex of contour-deprived cats. *Journal of Neurophysiology, 39*, 613–630. **414**

SINGER, W., TRETTER, F., & CYNADER, M. (1975). Organization of cat striate cortex: A correlation of receptive-field properties with afferent and efferent connections. *Journal of Neurophysiology, 38*, 1080–1098. **221**

SINNAMON, H. M., CROMARTY, A. S., & MILLER, C. A. (1979). Response of medial telencephalic neurons to stimulation in reinforcing sites in the medial forebrain bundle and ventral tegmental area. *Physiology & Behavior, 22*, 555–562. **267**

SKELTON, R. W., MILLER, J. J., & PHILLIPS, A. G. (1985). Long-term potentiation facilitates behavioral responding to single-pulse stimulation of the perforant path. *Behavioral Neuroscience, 99*, 603–620. **394**

SKOFF, R., & MONTGOMERY, I. N. (1981). Expression of mosaicism in females heterozygous for Jimpy. *Brain Research, 212*, 175–181. **287**

SKOLNICK, P., & DALY, J. W. (1974). Norepinephrine-sensitive adenylate cyclases in rat brain: Relation to behavior and tyrosine hydroxylase. *Science, 184*, 175–177. **329**

SLAUGHTER, M. M., & MILLER, R. F. (1983). An excitatory amino acid antagonist blocks cone input to sign-conserving second-order retinal neurons. *Science, 219*, 1230–1232. **195**

SLOB, A. K., HUIZER, T., & VAN DER WERFF TEN BOSCH, J. J. (1986). Ontogeny of sex differences in open-field ambulation in the rat. *Physiology & Behavior, 37*, 313–315. **277**

SLOB, A. K., OOMS, M. P., & VREEBURG, J. T. M. (1980). Prenatal and early postnatal sex differences in plasma and gonadal testosterone and plasma luteinizing hormone in female and male rats. *Journal of Endocrinology, 87*, 81–87. **272**

SMITH, C. U. M. (1970). *The brain: Towards an understanding*. New York: G. P. Putnam's Sons. **9**

SMITH, D. C. (1981). Functional restoration of vision in the cat after long-term monocular deprivation. *Science, 213*, 1137–1139. **418**

SMITH, D. V., VAN BUSKIRK, R. L., TRAVERS, J. B., & BIEBER, S. L. (1983a). Gustatory neuron types in hamster brain stem. *Journal of Neurophysiology, 50*, 522–540. **163**

SMITH, D. V., VAN BUSKIRK, R. L., TRAVERS, J. B., & BIEBER, S. L. (1983b). Coding of taste stimuli by hamster brain stem neurons. *Journal of Neurophysiology, 50*, 541–558. **163**

SMITH, E. L., III, BENNETT, M. J., HARWERTH, R. S., & CRAWFORD, M. L. J. (1979). Binocularity in kittens reared with optically induced squint. *Science, 204*, 875–877. **424**

SMITH, G. P. (1982). Satiety and the problem of motivation. In D. W. Pfaff (Ed.), *The physiological mechanisms of motivation*. New York: Springer-Verlag. **227**

SMITH, G. P., JEROME, C., CUSHIN, B. J., ETERNO, R., & SIMANSKY, K. J. (1981). Abdominal vagotomy blocks the satiety effect of cholecystokinin in the rat. *Science, 213*, 1036–1037.

SMITH, H. V. (1972). Effects of environmental enrichment on open-field activity and Hebb-Williams problem solving in rats. *Journal of Comparative and Physiological Psychology, 80*, 163–168. **403**

SMITH, L. T. (1974). The interanimal transfer phenomenon: A review. *Psychological Bulletin, 81*, 1078–1095. **378**

SMITH, P. K. (1982). Does play matter? Functional and evolutionary aspects of animal and human play. *Behavioral and Brain Sciences, 5*, 139–184. **402**

SNYDER, S. H. (1980). Brain peptides as neurotransmitters. *Science, 209*, 976–983. **98, 99, 168**

SNYDER, S. H. (1984). Drug and neurotransmitter receptors in the brain. *Science, 224*, 22–31. **98, 99**

SNYDER, S. H., KATIMS, J. J., ANNAU, Z., BRUNS, R. F., & DALY, J. W. (1981). Adenosine receptors and behavioral actions of methylxanthines. *Proceedings of the National Academy of Sciences, U.S.A., 78*, 3260–3264. **90**

SÖDERSTEN, P. (1984). Sexual differentiation: Do males differ from females in behavioral sensitivity to gonadal hormones? In G. J. De Vries, J. P. C. De Bruin, B. M. Uylings, & M. A. Corner (Eds.), *Sex differences in the brain*. New York: Elsevier. **293**

SÖDERSTEN, P., HENNING, M., MELIN, P., & LUDIN, S. (1983). Vasopressin alters female sexual behaviour by acting on the brain independently of alterations in blood pressure. *Nature, 301*, 608–610. **307**

SOKOLICH, W. G., HAMERNIK, R. P., ZWIS-

LOCKI, J. J., & SCHMIEDT, R. A. (1976). Inferred response polarities of cochlear hair cells. *Journal of the Acoustical Society of America*, 59, 963–974. **153**

SOLOMON, P. R. (1979). Temporal versus spatial information processing theories of hippocampal function. *Psychological Bulletin*, 86, 1272–1279. **384**

SOLOMON, P. R., SOLOMON, S. C., SCHAAF, E. V., & PERRY, H. E. (1983). Altered activity in the hippocampus is more detrimental to classical conditioning than removing the structure. *Science*, 220, 329–331. **14**

SOMJEN, G. (1975). *Sensory coding in the mammalian nervous system*. New York: Plenum. (Original work published 1972) **138, 139, 154, 174, 175**

SOVIJARI, A. R. A., & HYVÄRINEN, J. (1974). Auditory cortical neurons in the cat sensitive to the direction of sound source movement. *Brain Research*, 73, 455–471. **172**

SPEAR, P. D., TONG, L., & SAWYER, C. (1983). Effects of binocular deprivation on responses of cells in cat's lateral suprasylvian visual cortex. *Journal of Neurophysiology*, 49, 366–382. **414**

SPERRY, R. W. (1969). A modified concept of consciousness. *Psychological Review*, 76, 532–536. **1, 5, 8**

SPERRY, R. W. (1980). Mind-brain interactionism: Mentalism, yes; dualism, no. *Neuroscience*, 5, 105–206. **8**

SPERRY, R. W. (1982). Some effects of disconnecting the cerebral hemispheres. *Science*, 217, 1223–1226. **8, 444**

SPINELLI, D. N., & JENSEN, F. E. (1979). Plasticity: The mirror of experience. *Science*, 203, 75–78. **410, 426**

SPRINGER, S. P., & DEUTSCH, G. (1981). *Left brain, right brain*. San Francisco: W. H. Freeman. **20, 32**

SQUIRE, L. R., COHEN, N. J., & ZOUZOUNIS, J. A. (1984). Preserved memory in retrograde amnesia: Sparing of a recently acquired skill. *Neuropsychologia*, 22, 145–152. **446**

STACHOWIAK, M. K., BRUNO, J. P., SNYDER, A. M., STRICKER, E. M., & ZIGMOND, M. J. (1984). Apparent sprouting of striatal serotonergic terminals after dopamine-depleting brain lesions in neonatal rats. *Brain Research*, 291, 164–167. **437**

STANES, M. D., & BROWN, C. P., & SINGER, G. (1976). Effect of physostigmine on Y-maze discrimination retention in the rat. *Psychopharmacologia*, 46, 269–272. **375**

STANLEY, J. C., DEFRANCE, J. F., & MARCHAND, J. E. (1979). Tetanic and posttetanic potentiation in the septohippocampal pathway. *Experimental Neurology*, 64, 445–451.

STANLEY, M., VIRGILIO, J., & GERSHON, S. (1982). Tritiated imipramine binding sites are decreased in the frontal cortex of suicides. *Science*, 216, 1337–1339. **354**

STAUNTON, D. A., MAGISTRETTI, P. J., KOOB, G. F., SHOEMAKER, W. J., & BLOOM, F. E. (1982). Dopaminergic supersensitivity induced by denervation and chronic receptor blockade is additive. *Nature*, 229, 72–74. **107**

STEEL, K. P. (1983). The tectorial membrane of mammals. *Hearing Research*, 9, 327–359. **145**

STEFFEN, H., & VAN DER LOOS, H. (1980). Early lesions of mouse vibrissal follicles: Their influence on dendrite orientation in the cortical barrelfield. *Experimental Brain Research*, 40, 419–431.

STEIN, D. G., FINGER, S., & HART, T. (1983). Brain damage and recovery: Problems and perspectives.

Behavioral and Neural Biology, 37, 185–222. **13, 433**

STEIN, D. G., LABBE, R., ATTELLA, M. J., & RAKOWSKY, H. A. (1985). Fetal brain tissue transplants reduce visual deficits in adult rats with bilateral lesions of the occipital cortex. *Behavioral and Neural Biology*, 44, 266–277. **437**

STEIN, J. F. (1986). Role of the cerebellum in the visual guidance of movement. *Nature*, 323, 217–221. **34**

STEINFELS, G. F., HEYM, J., STRECKER, R. E., & JACOBS, B. L. (1983). Response of dopaminergic neurons in cat to auditory stimuli presented across the sleep–waking cycle. *Brain Research*, 277, 150–154. **236, 237, 377**

STELLAR, J. R., BROOKS, F. H., & MILLS, L. E. (1979). Approach and withdrawal analysis of the effects of hypothalamic stimulation and lesions in rats. *Journal of Comparative and Physiological Psychology*, 93, 446–466. **265**

STENT, G. S. (1964). The operon: On its third anniversary. *Science*, 144, 816–820. **113, 126**

STENT, G. S. (1982). Culturalism and biology. In J. Eccles (Ed.), *Mind and brain: The many-faceted problems*. Washington, DC: Paragon House. **443, 445, 448**

STEPHENSON, F. A. (1986). A new endogenous benzodiazepine receptor ligand? *Trends in NeuroSciences*, 9, 143–144. **343**

STERIADE, M., OAKSON, G., & ROBERT, N. (1982). Firing rates and patterns of midbrain reticular neurons during steady and transitional states of the sleep–waking cycle. *Experimental Brain Research*, 46, 37–51. **236**

STERLING, P. (1977). Principles of central nervous system organization. In A. Frazer & A. Winokur (Eds.), *Biological Bases of Psychiatric Disorders* (pp. 3–22). New York: Spectrum.

STERN, J. J., CUDILLO, C. A., & KRUPER, J. (1976). Ventromedial hypothalamus and short-term feeding suppression by caerulein in male rats. *Journal of Comparative and Physiological Psychology*, 90, 484–490.

STEVENS, C. F. (1977). Study of membrane permeability changes by fluctuation analysis. *Nature*, 270, 391–396. **61, 77, 85**

STEVENS, C. F. (1979). The neuron. *Scientific American*, 241, 55–65. **50**

STEVENS, J. K., MCGUIRE, B. A., & STERLING, P. (1980). Toward a functional architecture of the retina: Serial reconstruction of adjacent ganglion cells. *Science*, 207, 317–319.

STEVENS, J. R. (1973). An anatomy of schizophrenia? *Archives of General Psychiatry*, 29, 177–189. **346, 347**

STEVENS, J. R. (1982). Neuropathology of schizophrenia. *Archives of General Psychiatry*, 39, 1131–1139.

STEVENS, S. S. (1961). To honor Fechner and repeal his law. *Science*, 133, 80–86. **139**

STEVENS, S. S. (1962). The surprising simplicity of sensory metrics. *American Psychologist*, 17, 29–39. **139**

STEVENS, S. S. (1970). Neural events and the psychophysical law. *Science*, 170, 1043–1050. **139**

STOCKMEIER, C. A., MARTINO, A. M., & KELLAR, K. J. (1985). A strong influence of serotonin axons on beta-adrenergic receptors in rat brain. *Science*, 230, 323–325. **354**

STOERIG, P., HÜBNER, M., & PÖPPEL, E. (1985). Signal detection analysis of residual vision in a field defect due to a postgeniculate lesion. *Neuropsychologia*, 23,

589–599. **446**

STOLK, J. M., & NISULA, B. C. (1979). Genetic influences on catecholamine metabolism. In R. A. Depue (Ed.), *The psychobiology of the depressive disorders*. New York: Academic Press. **129, 330**

STONE, E. A. (1983). Reduction in cortical beta adrenergic receptor density after chronic intermittent food deprivation. *Neuroscience Letters*, 40, 33–37.

STONE, E. A. (1983). Problems with current catecholamine hypotheses of antidepressant agents: Speculations leading to a new hypothesis. *Behavioral and Brain Sciences*, 6, 535–577. **330, 332, 349**

STONE, E. A., & MCCARTY, R. (1983). Adaptation to stress: Tyrosine hydroxylase activity and catecholamine release. *Neuroscience & Biobehavioral Reviews*, 7, 29–34. **332, 336, 337**

STONE, E. A., & PLATT, J. E. (1982). Brain adrenergic receptors and resistance to stress. *Brain Research*, 237, 405–414. **330, 332**

STOOF, J. C., & KEBABIAN, J. W. (1981). Opposing roles for D-1 and D-2 dopamine receptors in efflux of cyclic AMP from rat neostriatum. *Nature*, 294, 366–368. **97**

STOTT, D. H. (1973). Follow-up study from birth of the effects of prenatal stresses. *Developmental Medicine and Child Neurology*, 15, 770–787. **337**

STOTT, D. H. (1977, May 19). Children in the womb: The effects of stress. *New Society*, pp. 329–331. **337**

STOTT, D. H., & LATCHFORD, S. A. (1976). Prenatal antecedents of child health, development and behavior: An epidemiological report of incidence and association. *Journal of Child Psychiatry*, 15, 161–191. **337**

STRAUS, E., & YALOW, R. S. (1979). Cholecystokinin in the brains of obese and nonobese mice. *Science*, 203, 68–69. **252**

STRECKER, R. E., STEINFELS, G. F., & JACOBS, B. L. (1983). Dopaminergic unit activity in freely moving cats: Lack of relationship to feeding, satiety, and glucose injections. *Brain Research*, 260, 317–321. **254**

STRICKER, E. M., & ZIGMOND, M. J. (1976). Recovery of function after damage to central catecholamine-containing neurons: A neurochemical model for the lateral hypothalamic syndrome. In J. M. Sprague & A. N. Epstein (Eds.), *Progress in Physiological Psychology* (Vol. 8). New York: Academic Press. **245, 254**

STRINGER, J. L., & GUYENET, P. G. (1983). Elimination of long-term potentiation in the hippocampus by phencyclidine and ketamine. *Brain Research*, 258, 159–164. **110**

STRUMWASSER, F. (1958). Long-term recording from single neurons in brain of unrestrained mammals. *Science*, 127, 469–470.

STUCKEY, J. A., & GIBBS, J. (1982). Lateral hypothalamic injection of bombesin decreases food intake in rats. *Brain Research Bulletin*, 8, 617–621.

STUDY, R. E., & BARKER, J. L. (1981). Diazepam and (—)-pentobarbital: Fluctuation analysis reveals different mechanisms for potentiation of gamma-aminobutyric acid responses in cultured central neurons. *Proceedings of the National Academy of Sciences, U.S.A.*, 78, 7180–7184. **343**

STUMPF, W. E., & SAR, M. (1976). Steroid hormone target sites in the brain: The differential distribution of estrogen, progestin, androgen and glucocorticosteroid. *Journal of Steroid Biochemistry*, 7, 1163–1170. **280, 284**

STUMPF, W. E., & SAR, M. (1978). Anatomical

distribution of estrogen, androgen, progestin, corticosteroid and thyroid hormone target sites in the brain of mammals: Phylogeny and ontogeny. *American Zoologist, 18,* 435–445. **280, 281, 284**

STUNKARD, A. J., FOCH, T. T., & HRUBEC, Z. (1986). A twin study of human obesity. *Journal of the American Medical Association, 256,* 51–54. **250**

STUNKARD, A. J., SØRENSEN, T. I. A., HANIS, C., TEASDALE, T. W., CHAKRABORTY, R., SCHULL, W. J., & SCHULSINGER, F. (1986). An adoption study of human obesity. *New England Journal of Medicine, 314,* 193–198. **250**

STUTZ, R. M., BUTCHER, R. E., & ROSSI, R. (1969). Stimulus properties of reinforcing brain shock. *Science, 163,* 1081–1082. **445**

SULKOWSKI, A. (1983). Psychobiology of schizophrenia: A neo-Jacksonian detour. *Perspectives in Biology and Medicine, 26,* 205–218. **347**

SUR, M., WALL, J. T., & KAAS, J. H. (1981). Modular segregation of functional cell classes within the postcentral somatosensory cortex of monkeys. *Science, 212,* 1059–1061. **156, 171**

SURANYI-CADOTTE, B. E., WOOD, P. L., NAIR, N. P. V., & SCHWARTZ, G. (1982). Normalization of platelet [³H]imipramine binding in depressed patients during remission. *European Journal of Pharmacology, 85,* 357–358. **354**

SUTHERLAND, E. W., ØYE, I., & BUTCHER, R. W. (1965). The action of epinephrine and the role of the adenyl cyclase system in hormone action. *Recent Progress in Hormone Research, 21,* 623–646. **86**

SUTHERLAND, R. C., MARTIN, M. J., MCQUEEN, J. K., & FINK, G. (1983). Water deprivation results in increased 2-deoxyglucose uptake by paraventricular neurones as well as pars nervosa in Wistar and Brattleboro rats. *Brain Research, 271,* 101–108. **254**

SVARE, B., & BROIDA, J. (1982). Genotypic influences on infanticide in mice: Environmental, situational and experiential determinants. *Physiology & Behavior, 28,* 171–175. **326**

SVENSSON, T. H., & USDIN, T. (1978). Feedback inhibition of brain noradrenaline neurons by tricyclic antidepressants: Alpha-receptor mediation. *Science, 202,* 1089–1091. **355**

SWAAB, D. F., & FLIERS, E. (1985). A sexually dimorphic nucleus in the human brain. *Science, 228,* 1112–1115. **300, 303**

SWAAB, D. F., FLIERS, E., & PARTIMAN, T. S. (1985). The suprachiasmatic nucleus of the human brain in relation to sex, age and senile dementia. *Brain Research, 342,* 37–44. **300**

SWENSON, R. M., & VOGEL, W. H. (1983). Plasma catecholamine and corticosterone as well as brain catecholamine changes during coping in rats exposed to stressful footshock. *Pharmacology, Biochemistry & Behavior, 18,* 689–693. **332**

SWERUP, C. (1983). On the ionic mechanisms of adaptation in an isolated mechanoreceptor—an electrophysiological study. *Acta Physiologica Scandinavica* (Suppl. 520). **174**

SWETS, J. A., TANNER, W. P., JR., & BIRDSALL, T. G. (1961). Decision processes in perception. *Psychological Review, 68,* 301–340. **137**

SWETT, J. E., & BOURASSA, C. M. (1967). Comparison of sensory discrimination thresholds with muscle and cutaneous nerve volleys in the cat. *Journal of Neuro-*

physiology, *30,* 530–545. **445**

SWETT, J. E., & BOURASSA, C. M. (1980). Detection thresholds to stimulation of ventrobasal complex in cats. *Brain Research, 183,* 313–328. **445**

SWINDALE, N. V. (1981). Absence of ocular dominance patches in dark-reared cats. *Nature, 290,* 332–333.

TALLMAN, J. F., PAUL, S. M., SKOLNICK, P., & GALLAGER, D. W. (1980). Receptors for the age of anxiety: Pharmacology of the benzodiazepines. *Science, 207,* 274–281. **341, 343, 344**

TAM, S.-P., HACHÉ, R. J. G., & DEELEY, R. G. (1986). Estrogen memory effect in human hepatocytes during repeated cell division without hormone. *Science, 234,* 1234–1237. **278**

TANABE, T., IINO, M., & TAKAGI, S. F. (1975). Discrimination of odors in olfactory bulb, pyriform-amygdaloid areas, and orbitofrontal cortex of the monkey. *Journal of Neurophysiology, 38,* 1284–1296. **160, 161, 163, 170**

TANABE, T., YARITA, H., IINO, M., OOSHIMA, Y., & TAKAGI, S. F. (1975). An olfactory projection area in orbitofrontal cortex of the monkey. *Journal of Neurophysiology, 38,* 1269–1283. **156**

TANAKA, Y., ASANUMA, A., & YANAGISAWA, K. (1980). Potentials of outer hair cells and their membrane properties in cationic environments. *Hearing Research, 2,* 431–438. **153**

TANNA, V. L., WINOKUR, G., ELSTON, R. C., & GO, R. C. P. (1977). A genetic linkage study in support of the concept of depression spectrum disease. *Alcoholism: Clinical and Experimental Research, 1,* 119–123.

TANNER, W. P., JR., & SWETS, J. A. (1954). A decision-making theory of visual detection. *Psychological Review, 61,* 401–409. **137**

TANOUYE, M. A., FERRUS, A., & FUJITA, S. C. (1981). Abnormal action potentials associated with the *Shaker* complex locus of *Drosophila. Proceedings of the National Academy of Sciences, U.S.A., 78,* 6548–6552. **128**

TAPANAINEN, J., HUHTANIEMI, I., KOIVISTO, M., KUJANSUU, E., TUIMALA, R., & VIHKO, R. (1984). Hormonal changes during the perinatal period: FSH, prolactin and some steroid hormones in the cord blood and peripheral serum of preterm and fullterm female infants. *Journal of Steroid Biochemistry, 20,* 1153–1156. **272**

TARPY, R. M. (1977). The nervous system and emotion. In D. K. Candland, J. P. Fell, E. Keen, A. I. Leshner, R. M. Tarpy, & R. Plutchik (Eds.), *Emotion.* Monterey, CA: Brooks/Cole. **323, 324**

TASKER, R. R., ORGAN, L. W., & HAWRYLYSHYN, P. (1980). Visual phenomena evoked by electrical stimulation of the human brain stem. *Applied Neurophysiology, 43,* 89–95. **217**

TAUC, L. (1982). Nonvesicular release of neurotransmitter. *Physiological Reviews, 62,* 857–893. **74**

TAYLOR, D. P., RIBLET, L. A., STANTON, H. C., EISON, A. S., EISON, M. S., & TEMPLE, D. L., JR. (1982). Dopamine and antianxiety activity. *Pharmacology, Biochemistry & Behavior, 17,* 25–35. **344**

TEES, R. C. (1967). Effects of early auditory restriction in the rat on adult pattern discrimination. *Journal of Comparative and Physiological Psychology, 63,* 389–393. **413**

TEES, R. C., MIDGLEY, G., & BRUINSMA, Y. (1980). Effect of controlled rearing on the development of stimulus-seeking behavior in rats. *Journal of Comparative and Physiological Psychology, 94,* 1003–1018. **407, 426**

TEITELBAUM, P., & EPSTEIN, A. N. (1962). The lateral hypothalamic syndrome: Recovery of feeding and drinking after lateral hypothalamic lesions. *Psychological Review, 69,* 74–90. **245**

TEITELBAUM, P., SCHALLERT, T., & WHISHAW, I. Q. (1983). Sources of spontaneity in motivated behavior. In E. Satinoff & P. Teitelbaum (Eds.), *Handbook of behavioral neurobiology* (Vol. 6). New York: Plenum. **229, 245**

TEITELBAUM, P., & STELLAR, E. (1954). Recovery from failure to eat produced by hypothalamic lesions. *Science, 20,* 894–895. **245**

TEPPERMAN, F. S., HIRST, M., & GOWDEY, C. W. (1981). Hypothalamic injection of morphine: Feeding and temperature responses. *Life Sciences, 28,* 2459–2467. **248**

TER HAAR, M. B., & MACKINNON, P. C. B. (1973). Changes in protein content and in vivo incorporation of the [³⁵S]methionine into protein of discrete brain areas of the rat over puberty: Sexual differences. *Brain Research, 60,* 209–218. **295**

TERASAWA, E., & TIMIRAS, P. S. (1968). Electrical activity during the estrous cycle of the rat: Cyclic changes in limbic structures. *Endocrinology, 83,* 207–216. **277**

TERMAN, G. W., SHAVIT, Y., LEWIS, J. W., CANNON, J. T., & LIEBESKIND, J. C. (1984). Intrinsic mechanisms of pain inhibition: Activation by stress. *Science, 226,* 1270–1277. **168, 175, 176, 324, 337**

TEYLER, T. J., & DISCENNA, P. (1984). Long-term potentiation as a candidate mnemonic device. *Brain Research Reviews, 7,* 15–28. **393**

TEYLER, T. J., VARDARIS, R. M., LEWIS, D., & RAWITCH, A. B. (1980). Gonadal steroids: Effects on excitability of hippocampal pyramidal cells. *Science, 209,* 1017–1019. **313**

THOENEN, H., & EDGAR, D. (1982). The regulation of neuronal gene expression. *Trends in NeuroScience, 5,* 311–313. **115, 126**

THOMPSON, D. A., PÉNICAUD, L., & WELLE, S. L. (1984). Alpha₂-adrenoreceptor stimulation inhibits thermogenesis and food intake during glucoprivation in humans. *American Journal of Physiology, 247,* R560–R566.

THOMPSON, R. F. (1967). *Foundations of physiological psychology.* New York: Harper & Row. **7**

THOMPSON, R. F. (1986). The neurobiology of learning and memory. *Science, 233,* 941–947. **365, 366**

THOMPSON, R. F., in collaboration with D. A. McCormick, D. G. Lavond, G. A. Clark, R. E. Kettner, & M. D. Mauk. (1983). The engram found?: Initial localization of the memory trace for a basic form of learning. In J. M. Sprague & A. N. Epstein (Eds.), *Progress in psychobiology and physiological psychology* (Vol. 10). New York: Academic Press. **367, 390–392**

THOMPSON, R. F., BERGER, T. W., BERRY, S. D., HOEHLER, F. K., KETTNER, R. E., & WEISZ, D. J. (1980). Hippocampal substrate of classical conditioning. *Physiological Psychology, 8,* 262–279. **384, 390, 391**

THOMPSON, W. (1983). Synapse elimination in neonatal rat muscle is sensitive to pattern of muscle use. *Nature, 302,* 614–616. **433**

TIEMAN, D. G., MCCALL, M. A., & HIRSCH, H. V. B. (1983). Physiological effects of unequal alternating monocular exposure. *Journal of Neurophysiology, 49,* 804–818. **423**

TIPLADY, B., KILLIAN, J. J., & MANDEL, P.

(1976). Tyrosine hydroxylase in various brain regions of three strains of mice differing in spontaneous activity, learning ability, and emotionality. *Life Sciences, 18*, 1065–1070. **129, 340**

TIZABI, Y., MASSARI, V. J., & JACOBOWITZ, D. M. (1980). Isolation induced aggression and catecholamine variations in discrete brain areas of the mouse. *Brain Research Bulletin, 5*, 81–86. **340**

TOLHURST, D. J., MOVSHON, J. H., & DEAN, A. F. (1983). The statistical reliability of signals in single neurons in cat and monkey visual cortex. *Vision Research, 23*, 775–785. **3**

TOLLEFSON, G. D., & SENOGLES, S. (1982). A cholinergic role in the mechanism of lithium in mania. *Biological Psychiatry, 18*, 467–479. **349**

TOMITA, T. (1965). Electrophysiological study of the mechanisms subserving color coding in the fish retina. *Cold Spring Harbor Symposia, 30*, 559–566. **189**

TONG, Y. C., CLARK, G. M., BLAMEY, P. J., BUSBY, P. A., & DOWELL, R. C. (1982). Psychophysical studies for two multiple-channel cochlear implant patients. *Journal of the Acoustical Society of America, 71*, 153–160. **165**

TOOTELL, R. B., SILVERMAN, M. S., & DE VALOIS. R. L. (1981). Spatial frequency columns in primary visual cortex. *Science, 214*, 813–815. **214**

TOOTELL, R. B. H., SILVERMAN, M. S., DE VALOIS, R. L., & JACOBS, G. H. (1983). Functional organization of the second cortical visual area in primates. *Science, 220*, 737–739. **214**

TOOTELL, R. B. H., SILVERMAN, M. S., SWITKES, E., & DE VALOIS, R. L. (1982). Deoxyglucose analysis of retinotopic organization in primate striate cortex. *Science, 218*, 902–904.

TORAN-ALLERAND, C. D. (1976). Sex steroids and the development of the newborn mouse hypothalamus and preoptic area in vitro: Implications for sexual differentiation. *Brain Research, 106*, 407–412. **296**

TORAN-ALLERAND, C. D. (1980). Sex steroids and the development of the newborn mouse hypothalamus and preoptic area in vitro: II. Morphological correlates and hormonal specificity. *Brain Research, 189*, 413–427. **296**

TORAN-ALLERAND, C. D. (1984). On the genesis of sexual differentiation of the central nervous system: Morphogenetic consequences of steroidal exposure and possible role of alpha-fetoprotein. In G. J. De Vries, J. R. C. De Bruin, H. B. M. Uylings, & M. A. Corner (Eds.), *Sex differences in the brain.* New York: Elsevier. **276**

TORAN-ALLERAND, C. D., HASHIMOTO, K., GREENOUGH, W. T., & SALTARELLI, M. (1983). Sex steroids and the development of the newborn mouse hypothalamus and preoptic area in vitro: III. Effects of estrogen on dendritic differentiation. *Developmental Brain Research, 7*, 97–101. **296**

TOREBJÖRK, H. E., & OCHOA, J. L. (1980). Specific sensations evoked by activity in single identified sensory units in man. *Acta Physiologica Scandinavica, 110*, 445–447. **168**

TORGERSEN, S. (1983). Genetics of neurosis: The effects of sampling variation upon the twin concordance ratio. *British Journal of Psychiatry, 142*, 126–132. **327**

TORREY, E. F., YOLKEN, R. H., & WINFREY, C. J. (1982). Cytomegalovirus antibody in cerebrospinal fluid of schizophrenic patients detected by enzyme immunoassay. *Science, 216*, 892–894. **347**

TOYAMA, K., KOMATSU, Y., & SHIBUKI. K.

(1984). Integration of retinal and motor signals of eye movements in striate cortex cells of the alert cat. *Journal of Neurophysiology, 51*, 649–665. **222**

TOYODA, J., NOSAKI, H., & TOMITA, T. (1969). Light-induced resistance changes in single photoreceptors of *Necturus* and *Gekko*. *Vision Research, 9*, 453–463. **189**

TOZZI, W., SALE, P., & ANGELUCCI, L. (1980). Transfer of information with brain extracts from donors to recipients in passive-avoidance behavior. *Pharmacology, Biochemistry & Behavior, 12*, 7–21. **378**

TRACEY, D. (1978). Joint receptors—changing ideas. *Trends in NeuroSciences, 1*, 63–65.

TRANEL, D., & DAMASIO, A. R. (1985). Knowledge without awareness: An autonomic index of facial recognition by prosopagnosics. *Science, 228*, 1453–1454. **214, 446**

TRAYHURN, P., GOODBODY, A. E., & JAMES, W. P. T. (1982). A role for brown adipose tissue in the genesis of obesity?: Studies on experimental animals. *Proceedings of the Nutrition Society, 41*, 127–131. **243**

TRETTER, F., CYNADER, M., & SINGER, W. (1975). Modification of direction selectivity of neurons in the visual cortex of kittens. *Brain Research, 84*, 143–149. **429, 430**

TRIANDAFILLOU, J., & HIMMS-HAGEN, J. (1983). Brown adipose tissue in genetically obese *(fa/fa)* rats: Response to cold and diet. *American Journal of Physiology, 244*, E145–E150. **251**

TRILLER, A., & KORN, H. (1982). Transmission at a central inhibitory synapse: III. Ultrastructure of physiologically identified and stained terminals. *Journal of Neurophysiology, 48*, 708–736. **70, 73**

TRULSON, M. E. (1985). Activity of dopamine-containing substantia nigra neurons in freely moving cats. *Neuroscience & Biobehavioral Reviews, 9*, 283–297. **237**

TRULSON, M. E., & CRISP, T. (1984). Role of norepinephrine in regulating the activity of serotonin-containing dorsal raphe neurons. *Life Sciences, 35*, 511–515. **354**

TRULSON, M. E., CRISP, T., & TRULSON, V. M. (1983). Dopamine-containing substantia nigra units are unresponsive to changes in plasma glucose levels induced by dietary factors, glucose infusions or insulin administration in freely moving cats. *Life Sciences, 32*, 2555–2564. **237, 238, 254, 377**

TRULSON, M. E., CRISP, T., & TRULSON, V. M. (1984). Activity of serotonin-containing nucleus centralis superior (raphe medianus) neurons in freely moving cats. *Experimental Brain Research, 54*, 33–44. **237**

TRULSON, M. E., & HENDERSON, L. J. (1984). Buspirone increases locus coeruleus noradrenergic neuronal activity in vitro. *European Journal of Pharmacology, 106*, 195–197. **354, 355**

TRULSON, M. E., HOSSEINI, A., & TRULSON, T. J. (1986). Serotonin neuron transplants: Electrophysiological unit activity of intrahippocampal raphe grafts in freely moving cats. *Brain Research Bulletin, 17*, 461–468. **437**

TRULSON, M. E., & JACOBS, B. L. (1979). Raphe unit activity in freely moving cats: Correlation with level of behavioral arousal. *Brain Research, 163*, 135–150. **236, 237, 354, 376**

TRULSON, M. E., & PREUSSLER, D. W. (1984). Dopamine-containing ventral tegmental area neurons in freely moving cats: Activity during the sleep-waking cycle and effects of stress. *Experimental Neurology, 83*, 367–377.

237, 238, 354

TRULSON, M. E., & TRULSON, T. J. (1986). Buspirone decreases the activity of serotonin-containing neurons in the dorsal raphe in freely-moving cats. *Neuropharmacology, 25*, 1263–1266. **354**

TRULSON, M. E., & TRULSON, V. M. (1983). Chloral hydrate anesthesia blocks the excitatory response of dorsal raphe neurons to phasic auditory and visual stimuli in cats. *Brain Research, 265*, 129–133. **16, 236, 237, 376**

TRZEBIATOWSKA-TRZECIAK, O. (1977). Genetical analysis of unipolar and bipolar endogenous affective psychoses. *British Journal of Psychiatry, 131*, 478–485.

TSUANG, M. T., WINOKUR, G., & CROWE, R. R. (1980). Morbidity risks of schizophrenia and affective disorders among first degree relatives of patients with schizophrenia, mania, depression and surgical conditions. *British Journal of Psychiatry, 137*, 497–504. **328**

TSUMOTO, T., & FREEMAN, R. D. (1981). Ocular dominance in kitten cortex: Induced changes of single cells while they are recorded. *Experimental Brain Research, 44*, 347–351. **416, 423**

TUMOSA, N., NUNBERG, S., HIRSCH, H. V. B., & TIEMAN, S. B. (1983). Binocular exposure causes suppression of the less experienced eye in cats previously reared with unequal alternating monocular exposure. *Investigations in Ophthalmology and Visual Sciences, 24*, 496–506. **419**

TUNNICLIFF, G., WIMER, C. C., & WIMER, R. R. (1973). Relationships between neurotransmitter metabolism and behaviour in seven inbred strains of mice. *Brain Research, 61*, 428–434. **129**

TURNER, A. M., & GREENOUGH, W. T. (1985). Differential rearing effects on rat visual cortex synapses: I. Synaptic and neuronal density and synapses per neuron. *Brain Research, 329*, 195–203. **406**

TURNER, B. B., & WEAVER, D. A. (1981). Glucocorticoid binding in the brain is sex dependent. *Neuroscience Abstracts, 7*, 723. **301**

TURNER, B. B., & WEAVER, D. A. (1985). Sexual dimorphism of glucocorticoid binding in rat brain. *Brain Research, 343*, 16–23. **300, 301**

UEDA, H., GOSHIMA, Y., & MISU, Y. (1983). Presynaptic mediation of alpha$_2$-, beta$_1$- and beta$_2$adrenoceptors of endogenous noradrenaline and dopamine release from slices of rat hypothalamus. *Life Sciences, 38*, 371–376.

UNDERWOOD, G. (1983). Verbal reports and visual awareness. *Behavioral and Brain Sciences, 3*, 463–464. **445**

UNGAR, G. (1972). Molecular approaches to neural coding. *International Journal of Neuroscience, 3*, 193–200. **378**

UNGAR, G. (1974). Peptides and memory. *Biochemical Pharmacology, 23*, 1553–1558. **378**

UPHOUSE, L. (1980). Reevaluation of mechanisms that mediate brain differences between enriched and impoverished animals. *Psychological Bulletin, 88*, 215–232. **401, 402, 404**

URCA, G., SEGEV, S., & SARNE, Y. (1985). Footshock-induced analgesia: Its opioid nature depends on the strain of rat. *Brain Research, 329*, 109–116. **176**

URETSKY, E., & MCCLEARN, R. A. (1969). Effect of hippocampal isolation on retention. *Journal of Comparative and Physiological Psychology, 68*, 1–8. **384**

UTTAL, W. R. (1969). Emerging principles of sensory coding. *Perspectives in Biology and Medicine, 12*, 344–368. **154**

UTTAL, W. R. (1973). *The psychobiology of sensory coding.* New York: Harper & Row. **2, 3, 9, 138, 139, 149, 154, 163, 165**

VAADIA, E., GOTTLIEB, Y., & ABELES, M. (1982). Single-unit activity related to sensorimotor association in auditory cortex of a monkey. *Journal of Neurophysiology, 48,* 1201–1213. **383**

VAGUE, J. (1983). Testicular feminization syndrome: An experimental model for the study of hormone action on sexual behavior. *Hormone Research, 18,* 62–68. **288**

VALE, J. R., RAY, D., & VALE, C. A. (1972). The interaction of genotype and exogenous neonatal androgen: Agonistic behavior in female mice. *Behavioral Biology, 7,* 321–333. **288**

VALE, J. R., RAY, D., & VALE, C. A. (1973). The interaction of genotype and exogenous neonatal androgen and estrogen: Sex behavior in female mice. *Developmental Psychobiology, 6,* 319–327. **288**

VALENSTEIN, E. S. (1968). Steroid hormones and the neuropsychology of development. In R. L. Isaacson (Ed.), *The neuropsychology of development.* New York: Wiley. **301**

VALENSTEIN, E. S. (1973). *Brain control.* New York: Wiley. **263**

VALENSTEIN, E. S., LIEBLICH, I., DINAR, R., COHEN, E., & BACHUS, S. (1982). Relation between eating evoked by lateral hypothalamic stimulation and tail pinch in different rat strains. *Behavioral and Neural Biology, 34,* 271–282.

VALLBO, A. B. (1981). Sensations evoked from the glabrous skin of the human hand by electrical stimulation of unitary mechanosensitive afferents. *Brain Research, 215,* 359–363.

VALLBO, A. B., HAGBARTH, K.-E., TOREBJÖRK, H. E., & WALLIN, B. G. (1979). Somatosensory, proprioceptive, and sympathetic activity in human peripheral nerves. *Physiological Reviews, 59,* 919–957. **168**

VALLI, P., ZUCCA, G., & CASELLA, C. (1979). Ionic composition of the endolymph and sensory transduction in labyrinthine organs. *Acta Otolaryngology, 87,* 466–471. **153**

VALVERDE, F. (1971). Rate and extent of recovery from dark rearing in the visual cortex of the mouse. *Brain Research, 33,* 1–11. **433**

VAN ATTA, L., & SUTIN, J. (1971). The response of single lateral hypothalamic neurons to ventromedial nucleus and limbic stimulation. *Physiology & Behavior, 6,* 523–536. **257**

VAN DIJK, A., GILLESSEN, D., MÖHLER, H., & RICHARDS, J. G. (1981). Autoradiographical localization of cholecystokinin-receptor binding in rat brain and pancreas in vitro using ^{3}H-CCK$_8$ as radioligand. *British Journal of Pharmacology, 74,* 858P. **251**

VAN EDEN, C. G., UYLINGS, H. B. M., & VAN PELT, J. (1984). Sex-difference and left-right asymmetries in the prefrontal cortex during postnatal development in the rat. *Developmental Brain Research, 12,* 146–153.

VAN KAMMEN, D. P., MANN, L. S., STERNBERG, D. E., SCHEININ, M., NINAN, P. T., MARDER, S. R., VAN KAMMEN, W. B., RIEDER, R. O., & LINNOILA, M. (1983). Dopamine-beta-hydroxylase activity and homovanillic acid in spinal fluid of schizophrenics with brain atrophy. *Science, 220,* 974–977. **346**

VAN KREY, H. P., SIEGEL, P. B., BALANDER, R. J., & BENOFF, F. H. (1983). Testosterone aromatization in high and low mating lines of Gallinaceous birds.

Physiology & Behavior, 31, 153–157. **289**

VAN PRAAG, H. M. (1982). Depression, suicide and the metabolism of serotonin in the brain. *Journal of Affective Disorders, 4,* 275–290. **339, 348**

VAN SLUYTERS, R. C., & BLAKEMORE, C. (1973). Experimental creation of unusual neuronal properties in visual cortex of kitten. *Nature, 246,* 506–508. **426**

VANDERMAELEN, C. P., MATHESON, G. K., WILDERMAN, R. C., & PATTERSON, L. A. (1986). Inhibition of serotonergic dorsal raphe neurons by systemic and iontophoretic administration of buspirone, a non-benzodiazepine anxiolytic drug. *European Journal of Pharmacology, 129,* 123–130. **354**

VELLEY, L., CHAMINADE, C., ROY, M. T., KEMPF, E., & CARDO, B. (1983). Intrinsic neurons are involved in lateral hypothalamic self-stimulation. *Brain Research, 268,* 79–86. **266**

VENABLES, P. H. (1981). Psychophysiology of abnormal behaviour. *British Medical Bulletin, 37,* 199–203. **347**

VERTES, R. P. (1979). Brain stem gigantocellular neurons: Patterns of activity during behavior and sleep in the freely moving rat. *Journal of Neurophysiology, 42,* 214–228. **235**

VERTES, R. P. (1984). Brainstem control of the events of REM sleep. *Progress in Neurobiology, 22,* 241–288. **232, 233, 235, 236**

VIDAL, C., JORDAN, W., & ZIEGLGÄNSBERGER, W. (1986). Corticosterone reduces the excitability of hippocampal pyramidal cells in vitro. *Brain Research, 383,* 54–59. **358**

VINCENT, J. D., ARNAULD, E., & BIOULAC, B. (1972). Activity of osmosensitive single cells in the hypothalamus of the behaving monkey during drinking. *Brain Research, 44,* 371–384. **254, 255**

VIRSU, V. (1978). Retinal mechanisms of visual adaptation and afterimages. *Medical Biology, 56,* 84–96. **218, 219**

VITO, C. C., & FOX, T. O. (1982). Androgen and estrogen receptors in embryonic and neonatal rat brain. *Developmental Brain Research, 2,* 97–110. **282**

VIZI, E. S. (1978). Na$^+$-K$^+$-activated adenosine triphosphatase as a trigger in transmitter release. *Neuroscience, 3,* 367–384. **72, 218**

VODYANOY, V., & MURPHY, R. B. (1983). Single-channel fluctuations in bimolecular lipid membranes induced by rat olfactory epithelial homogenates. *Science, 220,* 717–719. **150**

VOM SAAL, F. S. (1981). Variation in phenotype due to random intrauterine positioning of male and female fetuses in rodents. *Journal of Reproduction and Fertility, 62,* 633–650. **294**

VOM SAAL, F. S. (1983). Variation in infanticide and parental behavior in male mice due to prior intrauterine proximity to female fetuses: Elimination by prenatal stress. *Physiology & Behavior, 30,* 675–681. **294, 340**

VON DER HEYDT, R., PETERHANS, E., & BAUMGARTNER, G. (1984). Illusory contours and cortical neuron responses. *Science, 224,* 1260–1262. **447**

VON ECONOMO, C. (1929). *The cytoarchitectonics of the human cerebral cortex.* London: Oxford University Press.

VUONG, T. M., CHABRE, M., & STRYER, L. (1984). Millisecond activation of transducin in the cyclic nucleotide cascade of vision. *Nature, 311,* 659–661. **193**

WACHTEL, S. S. (1977). H-Y antigen and the ge-

netics of sex determination. *Science, 198,* 797–799. **286**

WALD, G. (1964). The receptors of human color vision. *Science, 145,* 1007–1016. **202–204**

WALD, G. (1965). Receptor mechanisms in human vision. *Proceedings of the 13th International Physiological Congress, Tokyo,* 69–79. **203**

WALKER, J. L., & BROWN, H. M. (1977). Intracellular ionic activity measurements in nerve and muscle. *Physiological Review, 57,* 729–778. **51, 83**

WALL, P. D. (1977). The presence of ineffective synapses and the circumstances which unmask them. *Philosophical Transactions of the Royal Society of London, Series B, 278,* 361–373. **365**

WALLACE, B., & HOYENGA, K. B. (1975). Outflow theory and autokinetic movement: Color, viewing angle, and dark adaptation. *American Journal of Psychology, 88,* 107–115. **222**

WALLACE, B., & HOYENGA, K. B. (1978a). Prismatically induced eye strain and autokinetic direction frequency. *Journal of General Psychology, 98,* 15–21. **222**

WALLACE, B., & HOYENGA, K. B. (1978b). Autokinetic movement of an induced afterimage. *Journal of General Psychology, 98,* 173–178. **222**

WALLIN, B. G., & FAGIUS, J. (1986). The sympathetic nervous system in man: Aspects derived from microelectrode recordings. *Trends in NeuroSciences, 9,* 63–66. **23**

WALOGA, G., & PAK, W. L. (1976). Horizontal cell potentials: Dependence on external sodium ion concentrations. *Science, 191,* 964–966. **195**

WALSH, L. L. (1982). Strain and sex differences in mouse killing by rats. *Journal of Comparative and Physiological Psychology, 96,* 278–283. **326**

WALSH, R. N. (1981). Effects of environmental complexity and deprivation on brain anatomy and histology: A review. *International Journal of Neuroscience, 12,* 33–51. **406**

WALSH, R. N., BUDTZ-OLSEN, O. E., PENNY, J. E., & CUMMINS, R. A. (1969). The effects of environmental complexity on the histology of the rat hippocampus. *Journal of Comparative Neurology, 137,* 361–366. **406**

WALSH, R. N., CUMMINS, R. A., BUDTZ-OLSEN, O. E., & TOROK, A. (1972). Effects of environmental enrichment and deprivation on rat frontal cortex. *International Journal of Neuroscience, 4,* 239–242. **405**

WALTERS, E. T., & BYRNE, J. H. (1983). Associative conditioning of single sensory neurons suggests a cellular mechanism for learning. *Science, 219,* 405–407. **396**

WALTERS, E. T., CAREW, T. J., & KANDEL, E. R. (1979). Classical conditioning in *Aplysia californica. Proceedings of the National Academy of Sciences, U.S.A., 76,* 6675–6679. **358**

WAREMBOURG, M. (1977). Topographical distribution of estrogen-concentrating cells in the brain and pituitary of the squirrel monkey. *Neuroscience Letters, 5,* 315–319. **281**

WARR, W. B., & GUINAN, J. J., JR. (1979). Efferent innervation of the organ of Corti: Two separate systems. *Brain Research, 173,* 152–155. **175**

WARREN, J. M., ZERWECK, C., & ANTHONY, A. (1982). Effects of environmental enrichment on old mice. *Developmental Psychobiology, 15,* 13–18. **402–404**

WATANABE, M. (1986a). Prefrontal unit activity during delayed conditional go/no-go discrimination in the monkey. I. Relation to the stimulus. *Brain Research, 382,* 1–14. **365, 383**

WATANABE, M. (1986b). Prefrontal unit activity

during delayed conditional go/no-go discrimination in the monkey. II. Relation to go and no-go responses. *Brain Research*, 382, 15–27. **365, 383**

WATERHOUSE, B. D., & WOODWARD, D. J. (1980). Interaction of norepinephrine with cerebrocortical activity evoked by stimulation of somatosensory afferent pathways in the rat. *Experimental Neurology*, 67, 11–34. **240**

WATERS, B. G., & LAPIERRE, Y. D. (1982). Current psychopharmacogenetic strategies in primary affective disorders. *Progress in Neuro-Psychopharmacology & Biological Psychiatry*, 6, 675–679.

WATKINS, L. R., & MAYER, D. J. (1982). Organization of endogenous opiate and nonopiate pain control systems. *Science*, 216, 1185–1192. **168, 175, 176**

WATSON, A. B., BARLOW, H. B., & ROBSON, J. G. (1983). What does the eye see best? *Nature*, 302, 419–422. **212**

WATSON, J. D., & CRICK, F. H. C. (1953a). Genetical implications of the structure of deoxyribonucleic acid. *Nature*, 171, 964–967. **118**

WATSON, J. D., & CRICK, F. H. C. (1953b). Molecular structures of nucleic acids: A structure for deoxyribose nucleic acids. *Nature*, 171, 737–738. **118**

WEBB, A. C. (1976a). The effects of changing levels of arousal on the spontaneous activity of cortical neurones: I. Sleep and wakefulness. *Proceedings of the Royal Society of London, Series B*, 194, 225–237. **231**

WEBB, A. C. (1976b). The effects of changing levels of arousal on the spontaneous activity of cortical neurones: II. Relaxation and alarm. *Proceedings of the Royal Society of London, Series B*, 194, 239–251. **231**

WEBER, G., & WEIS, S. (1986). Morphometric analysis of the human corpus callosum fails to reveal sex-related differences. *Journal für Hirnforschung*, 27, 237–240. **302**

WEBSTER, W. G. (1973). Assumptions, conceptualizations, and the search for the functions of the brain. *Physiological Psychology*, 1, 346–350. **4**

WEIGHT, F. F. (1974). Physiological mechanisms of synaptic modulation. In F. O. Schmitt & F. G. Worden (Eds.), *The neurosciences: Third study program* (pp. 929–941). Cambridge, MA: MIT Press. **104, 110**

WEIGHT, F. F., & VOTAVA, J. (1970). Slow synaptic excitation in sympathetic ganglion cells: Evidence for synaptic inactivation of potassium conductance. *Science*, 170, 755–758. **77, 78, 88**

WEINSTEIN, G. W., HOBSON, R. R., & DOWLING, J. E. (1967). Light and dark adaptation in the isolated rat retina. *Nature*, 215, 134–138. **219**

WEINSTEIN, S. (1968). Intensive and extensive aspects of tactile sensitivity as a function of body, sex, and laterality. In D. R. Kenshalo (Ed.), *The skin senses*. Springfield, IL: Charles C Thomas. **138**

WEISKRANTZ, L. (1972). Behavioural analysis of the monkey's visual system. *Proceedings of the Royal Society of London, Series B*, 182, 427–455. **178**

WEISKRANTZ, L. (1983). Evidence and scotomata. *Behavioral and Brain Sciences*, 3, 464–467. **446**

WEISKRANTZ, L., WARRINGTON, E. K., SANDERS, M. D., & MARSHALL, J. (1974). Visual capacity in the hemianopic field following a restricted occipital ablation. *Brain*, 97, 709–728. **13, 446**

WEISS, G. F., & LEIBOWITZ, S. F. (1985). Efferent projections from the paraventricular nucleus mediating alpha₂-noradrenergic feeding. *Brain Research*, 347, 225–238. **248, 254**

WEISS, J. M., GLAZER, H. I., POHORECKY, L. A., BAILEY, W. H., & SCHNEIDER, L. H. (1979). Coping behavior and stress-induced behavioral depression: Studies of the role of brain catecholamines. In R. A. Depue (Ed.), *The psychobiology of depressive disorders*. New York: Academic Press. **332, 333**

WEISS, J. M., GOODMAN, P. A., LOSITO, B. G., CORRIGAN, S., CHARRY, J. M., & BAILEY, W. H. (1981). Behavioral depression produced by an uncontrollable stressor: Relationship to norepinephrine, dopamine, and serotonin levels in various regions of rat brain. *Brain Research Reviews*, 3, 167–205. **332, 333**

WEISS, J. M., SIMSON, P. G., HOFFMAN, L. J., AMBROSE, M. J., COOPER, S., & WEBSTER, A. (1986). Infusion of adrenergic receptor agonists and antagonists into the locus coeruleus and ventricular system of the brain. *Neuropharmacology*, 25, 367–384. **334**

WEISS, S., SEBBEN, M., KEMP, D. E., & BOCKAERT, J. (1986). Serotonin 5-HT₁ receptors mediate inhibition of cyclic AMP production in neurons. *European Journal of Pharmacology*, 120, 227–230.

WEISSMAN, M. M., WICKRAMARATNE, P., MERIKANGAS, R., LECKMAN, J. F., PRUSOFF, B. A., CARUSO, K. A., KIDD, K. K., & GAMMON, D. (1984). Onset of major depression in early adulthood. *Archives of General Psychiatry*, 41, 1136–1143. **329**

WEISZ, J., & WARD, I. L. (1980). Plasma testosterone and progesterone titers of pregnant rats, their male and female fetuses, and neonatal offspring. *Endocrinology*, 106, 306–316. **272**

WELSHONS, W. V., LIEBERMAN, M. E., & GORSKI, J. (1984). Nuclear localization of unoccupied oestrogen receptors. *Nature*, 307, 747–749. **279**

WERBLIN, F. S. (1973). The control of sensitivity in the retina. *Scientific American*, 228, 70–79.

WERBLIN, F. S., & DOWLING, J. E. (1969). Organization of the retina of the mudpuppy, *Necturus maculosus*: II. Intracellular recording. *Journal of Neurophysiology*, 32, 339–355.

WERZ, M. A., & MACDONALD, R. L. (1982). Heterogeneous sensitivity of cultured dorsal root ganglion neurones to opioid peptides selective for mu- and delta-opiate receptors. *Nature*, 299, 730–732.

WEST, R. W., & GREENOUGH, W. T. (1972). Effect of environmental complexity on cortical synapses of rats: Preliminary results. *Behavioral Biology*, 7, 279–284. **406**

WESTFALL, T. C. (1977). Local regulation of adrenergic neurotransmission. *Physiological Reviews*, 57, 659–727. **107, 108**

WESTLEY, B. R., & SALAMAN, D. F. (1976). Role of oestrogen receptor in androgen-induced sexual differentiation of the brain. *Nature*, 262, 407–408. **281, 283**

WESTLEY, B. R., & SALAMAN, D. F. (1977). Nuclear binding of the oestrogen receptor of neonatal rat brain after injection of oestrogens and androgens: Localization and sex differences. *Brain Research*, 119, 375–388. **284**

WEVER, E. J. (1949). *Theory of hearing*. New York: Wiley. **164**

WHALEN, R. E., EDWARDS, D. A., LUTTGE, W. G., & ROBERTSON, R. T. (1969). Early androgen treatment and male sexual behavior in female rats. *Physiology & Behavior*, 4, 33–39. **278**

WHALEN, R. E., & MASSICCI, J. (1975). Subcellular analysis of the accumulation of estrogen by the brain of male and female rats. *Brain Research*, 89, 255–264. **283**

WHITE, F. J., & WANG, R. Y. (1983a). Differential effects of classical and atypical antipsychotic drugs on A9 and A10 dopamine neurons. *Science*, 221, 1054–1057. **357, 358**

WHITE, F. J., & WANG, R. Y. (1983b). Comparison of the effects of chronic haloperidol treatment on A9 and A10 dopamine neurons in the rat. *Life Sciences*, 32, 983–993. **357, 358**

WHITE, F. J., & WANG, R. Y. (1984). A10 dopamine neurons: Role of autoreceptors in determining firing rate and sensitivity to dopamine agonists. *Life Sciences*, 34, 1161–1170. **347, 358**

WHITE, M. M., & BEZANILLA, F. (1985). Activation of squid axon K⁺ channels: ionic and gating current studies. *Journal of General Physiology*, 85, 539–554. **61**

WHITEHOUSE, P. J., PRICE, D. L., STRUBLE, R. G., CLARK, A. W., COYLE, J. T., & DELONG, M. R. (1982). Alzheimer's disease and senile dementia: Loss of neurons in the basal forebrain. *Science*, 215, 1237–1239. **432**

WHITFIELD, I. C., & EVANS, E. G. (1965). Responses of auditory cortical neurons to stimuli of changing frequency. *Journal of Neurophysiology*, 28, 655–672.

WIEDERHOLD, M. L. (1970). Variations in the effects of electric stimulation of the crossed olivocochlear bundle on cat single auditory-nerve-fiber responses to tone bursts. *Journal of the Acoustical Society of America*, 48, 966–977. **175**

WIELAND, S. J., FOX, T. O., & SAVAKIS, C. (1978). DNA-binding of androgen and estrogen receptors from mouse brain: Behavior of residual androgen receptor from *Tfm* mutant. *Brain Research*, 140, 159–164. **288**

WIESEL, T. N. (1982). Postnatal development of the visual cortex and the influence of environment. *Nature*, 299, 583–591. **414–416, 421**

WIESEL, T. N., & HUBEL, D. H. (1966). Spatial and chromatic interactions in the lateral geniculate body of the rhesus monkey. *Journal of Neurophysiology*, 29, 1115–1156. **199**

WIESEL, T. N., & HUBEL, D. H. (1974). Ordered arrangement of orientation columns in monkeys lacking visual experience. *Journal of Comparative Neurology*, 158, 307–318. **421**

WILKINSON, M., BHANOT, R., WILKINSON, D. A., & BRAWER, J. R. (1983). Prolonged estrogen treatment induced changes in opiate, benzodiazepine and B-adrenergic binding sites in female rat hypothalamus. *Brain Research Bulletin*, 11, 279–281. **309, 310**

WILL, B. E. (1977). Neurochemical correlates of individual differences in animal learning capacity. *Behavioral Biology*, 19, 143–171. **129, 381**

WILLIAMS, J. T., EGAN, T. M., & NORTH, R. A. (1982). Enkephalin opens potassium channels on mammalian central neurones. *Nature*, 299, 74–77. **99**

WILSON, C. L., BABB, T. L., HALGREN, E., & CRANDALL, P. H. (1983). Visual receptive fields and response properties of neurons in human temporal lobe and visual pathways. *Brain*, 106, 473–502. **217**

WILSON, D. A., SULLIVAN, R. M., & LEON, M. (1985). Odor familiarity alters mitral cell response in the olfactory bulb of neonatal rats. *Developmental Brain Research*, 22, 314–317. **410**

WILSON, D. F., & SKIRBOLL, L. R. (1974). Basis for posttetanic potentiation at the neuromuscular junction. *American Journal of Physiology*, 227, 92–95. **110**

WILSON, D. L. (1976). On the nature of consciousness of and of physical reality. *Perspectives in Biology and Medicine, 19,* 568–581. **443, 448**

WILSON, J. A. (1981). Eccles's physiological evidence for a self-conscious mind. *Brain, Behavior and Evolution, 18,* 33–40. **9, 444**

WILSON, J. R., & SHERMAN, S. M. (1976). Receptive-field characteristics of neurons in cat striate cortex: Changes with visual field eccentricity. *Journal of Neurophysiology, 39,* 512–533.

WILSON, J. R., & SHERMAN, S. M. (1977). Differential effects of early monocular deprivation on binocular and monocular segments of cat striate cortex. *Journal of Neurophysiology, 40,* 891–903. **416, 420**

WILSON, P. D., ROWE, M. H., & STONE, J. (1976). Properties of relay cells in cat's lateral geniculate nucleus: A comparison of W-cells with X- and Y-cells. *Journal of Neurophysiology, 39,* 1193–1209.

WILSON, W. E., & AGRAWAL, A. K. (1979). Brain regional levels of neurotransmitter amines as neurochemical correlates of sex-specific ontogenesis in the rat. *Developmental Neuroscience, 2,* 195–200. **296**

WIMER, R. E., & WIMER, C. (1985). Three sex dimorphisms in the granule cell layer of the hippocampus in house mice. *Brain Research, 328,* 105–109. **301**

WINOKUR, G. (1979). Familial (genetic) subtypes of pure depressive disease. *American Journal of Psychiatry, 136,* 911–913.

WINOKUR, G. (1982). The development and validity of familial subtypes in primary unipolar depression. *Pharmacopsychiatria, 15,* 142–146. **329**

WINSON, J., & ABZUG, C. (1977). Gating of neuronal transmission in the hippocampus: Efficacy of transmission varies with behavioral state. *Science, 196,* 1223–1225. **389**

WISE, S. P., & MAURITZ, K.-H. (1985). Set-related neuronal activity in the premotor cortex of rhesus monkeys: Effects of changes in motor set. *Proceedings of the Royal Society of London, Series B, 223,* 331–354. **230**

WITELSON, S. F. (1985). The brain connection: The corpus callosum is larger in left-handers. *Science, 229,* 665–668. **302**

WITSCHY, J. K., MALONE, G. L., & HOLDEN, L. D. (1984). Psychosis after neuroleptic withdrawal in a manic-depressive patient. *American Journal of Psychiatry, 141,* 105–106. **346**

WOLGIN, D. L., & TEITELBAUM, P. (1978). Role of activation and sensory stimuli in recovery from lateral hypothalamic damage in the cat. *Journal of Comparative and Physiological Psychology, 92,* 474–500. **245, 246**

WONG, D. F., WAGNER, H. N., TUNE, L. E., DANNALS, R. F., PEARLSON, G. D., LINKS, J. M., TAMMINGA, C. A., BROUSSOLLE, E. P., RAVERT, H. T., WILSON, A. A., TOUNG, J. K. T., MALAT, J., WILLIAMS, J. A., O'TUAMA, L. A., SNYDER, S. H., KUHAR, M. J., & GJEDDE, A. (1986). Positron emission tomography reveals elevated D_2 dopamine receptors in drug-naive schizophrenics. *Science, 234,* 1558–1562. **345**

WOODS, S. C., & PORTE, D., JR. (1976). Insulin and the set-point regulation of body weight. In D. Novin, W. Wyrwicka, & G. Bray (Eds.), *Hunger: Basic mechanisms and clinical implications.* New York: Raven.

WOODRUFF, M. L., & BOWNDS, M. D. (1979). Amplitude, kinetics, and reversibility of a light-induced decrease in guanosine 3',5'-cyclic monophosphate in frog photoreceptor membranes. *Journal of General Physiology, 73,* 629–653. **192**

WOODRUFF, M. L., BOWNDS, P., GREEN, S. H., MORRISEY, J. L., & SHEDLOVSKY, S. (1977). Guanosine 3',5'-cyclic monophosphate and the in vitro physiology of frog photoreceptor membranes. *Journal of General Physiology, 69,* 667–679. **192**

WOODWARD, D. J., MOISES, H. C., WATERHOUSE, B. D., HOFFER, B. J., & FREEDMAN, R. (1979). Modulatory actions of norepinephrine in the central nervous system. *Federation Proceedings, 38,* 2109–2116. **240**

WOODY, C. D., & ENGEL, J., JR. (1972). Changes in unit activity and thresholds to electrical microstimulation at coronal-pericruciate cortex of cat with classical conditioning of different facial movements. *Journal of Neurophysiology, 35,* 230–241. **383**

WOOLLEY, D. E., HOPE, W. G., GIETZEN, D. W., THOMPSON, M. T., & CONWAY, S. B. (1982). Bromocriptine increases ³H-estradiol uptake in brain and pituitary of female, but not of male, gonadectomized adrenalectomized rats. *Proceedings of the Western Pharmacological Society, 25,* 437–441. **308**

WORDEN, F. G., CHILDS, B., MATTHYSSE, S., & GERSHON, E. S. (1976). Frontiers of psychiatric genetics. *Neurosciences Research Progress Bulletin, 14.*

WREE, A., BRAAK, H., SCHLEICHER, A., & ZILLES, K. (1980). Biomathematical analysis of the neuronal loss in the aging human brain of both sexes, demonstrated in pigment preparations of the pars cerebellaris loci coerulei. *Anatomy and Embryology, 160,* 105–109. **301, 431**

WRIGHT, J. W., & HARDING, J. W. (1982). Recovery of olfactory function after bilateral bulbectomy. *Science, 216,* 322–324. **436**

WRIGHT, L. L., & SMOLEN, A. J. (1983a). Effects of 17-beta-estradiol on developing superior cervical ganglion neurons and synapses. *Developmental Brain Research, 6,* 299–303. **301**

WRIGHT, L. L., & SMOLEN, A. J. (1983b). Neonatal testosterone treatment increases neuron and synapse numbers in male rat superior cervical ganglion. *Developmental Brain Research, 8,* 145–153. **301**

WU, C.-F., GANETZKY, B., HAUGLAND, F. N., & LIU, A.-X. (1983). Potassium currents in *Drosophila*: Different components affected by mutations of two genes. *Science, 220,* 1076–1078. **128**

WURTMAN, R. J. (1983, May 21). Nutrition: The changing scene. *Lancet,* 1145–1147. **248, 254**

WURTMAN, R. J. (1985). Alzheimer's disease. *Scientific American, 252,* 62–74. **376, 432**

WURTMAN, R. J., & FERNSTROMM, J. C. (1975). Control of brain monoamine synthesis by diet and plasma amino acids. *American Journal of Clinical Nutrition, 28,* 638–647. **249**

WYATT, R. J., POTKIN, S. G., KLEINMAN, J. E., WEINBERGER, D. R., LUCHINS, D. J., & JESTE, D. V. (1981). The schizophrenia syndrome: Examples of biological tools for subclassification. *Journal of Nervous and Mental Disease, 169,* 100–112. **328, 341, 346**

XENAKIS, S., & SCLAFANI, A. (1982). The dopaminergic mediation of a sweet reward in normal and VMH hyperphagic rats. *Pharmacology, Biochemistry & Behavior, 16,* 293–302. **246**

YAGI, K. (1973). Changes in firing rates of single preoptic and hypothalamic units following an intravenous administration of estrogen in the castrated female rat. *Brain Research, 53,* 343–352. **307, 312**

YAMADA, Y. (1979). Effects of testosterone on unit activity in rat hypothalamus and septum. *Brain Research, 172,* 165–168. **312**

YAMADA, Y., & NISHIDA, E. (1978). Effects of estrogen and adrenal androgen on unit activity of the rat brain. *Brain Research, 142,* 187–190. **307, 311, 312**

YAMAMOTO, T. (1984). Taste responses of cortical neurons. *Progress in Neurobiology, 23,* 273–315. **161–163, 167**

YAMAMOTO, T., YUYAMA, N., KATO, T., & KAWAMURA, Y. (1984). Gustatory responses of cortical neurons in rats. I. Response characteristics. *Journal of Neurophysiology, 51,* 616–635. **161**

YAMAMOTO, T., YUYAMA, N., KATO, T., & KAWAMURA, Y. (1985a). Gustatory responses of cortical neurons in rats. II. Information processing of taste quality. *Journal of Neurophysiology, 53,* 1356–1369. **161, 162**

YAMAMOTO, T., YUYAMA, N., KATO, T., & KAWAMURA, Y. (1985b). Gustatory responses of cortical neurons in rats. III. Neural and behavioral measures compared. *Journal of Neurophysiology, 53,* 1370–1386. **161, 162, 171**

YANAI, J. (1979). Strain and sex differences in the rat brain. *Acta Anatomica, 103,* 150–158.

YATES, J. (1985). The content of awareness is a model of the world. *Psychological Review, 92,* 249–284. **443**

YAU, K.-W., & NAKATANI, K. (1984). Electrogenic Na-Ca exchange in retinal rod outer segment. *Nature, 311,* 661–663. **193**

YENI-KOMSHIAN, G. H., & BENSON, D. A. (1976). Anatomical study of cerebral asymmetry in the temporal lobe of humans, chimpanzees, and rhesus monkeys. *Science, 192,* 387–389.

YEO, C. H., HARDIMAN, M. J., & GLICKSTEIN, M. (1984). Discrete lesions of the cerebellar cortex abolish the classically conditioned nictitating membrane response of the rabbit. *Behavioural Brain Research, 13,* 261–266. **392**

YEOMAN, R. R., & TERASAWA, E. (1984). An increase in single unit activity of the medial basal hypothalamus occurs during the progesterone-induced luteinizing hormone surge in the female rhesus monkey. *Endocrinology, 115,* 2445–2452. **312**

YINON, U., PODELL, M., & GOSHEN, S. (1984). Deafferentation of the visual cortex: The effect on cortical cells in normal and in early monocularly deprived cats. *Experimental Neurology, 83,* 486–494. **419**

YOSHIKAMI, S., GEORGE, J. S., & HAGINS, W. A. (1980). Light-induced calcium fluxes from outer segment layer of vertebrate retinas. *Nature, 286,* 395–398. **194**

YOSHIKAMI, S., & HAGINS, W. A. (1980). Kinetics of control of the dark current of retinal rods by Ca^{++} and by light. *Federation Proceedings, 39,* 1814. **194**

YOSHIKAWA, K., & HONG, J.-S. (1983). Sex-related difference in substance P level in rat anterior pituitary: A model of neonatal imprinting by testosterone. *Brain Research, 273,* 362–365. **298**

YOSHIMURA, M., & NORTH, R. A. (1983). Substantia gelatinosa neurones hyperpolarized in vitro by enkephalin. *Nature, 305,* 529–530. **99**

YOUNG, D. N., ELLISON, G. D., & FEENEY, D. M. (1971). Electrophysiological correlates of selective attention: Modality specific changes in thalamocortical evoked potentials. *Brain Research, 28,* 501–510. **239**

YOUNG, J. K. (1982). A comparison of hypothalami of rats and mice: Lack of gross sexual dimorphism in the mouse. *Brain Research, 239,* 231–239. **278, 293, 300, 303**

YOUNG, J. Z. (1979). Learning as a process of selection and amplification. *Journal of the Royal Society of Medicine, 72,* 801–814. **450**

YOUNG, S. N., SMITH, S. E., PIHL, R. O., & ERVIN, F. R. (1985). Tryptophan depletion causes a rapid lowering of mood in normal males. *Psychopharmacology, 87,* 173–177. **354**

YOUNG, T. (1802). On a theory of light and colours. *Philosophical Transactions of the Royal Society,* 12–48. **202**

YOUNG, W. S., III, & KUHAR, M. J. (1980). Noradrenergic alpha$_1$ and alpha$_2$ receptors: Light microscopic autoradiographic localization. *Proceedings of the National Academy of Sciences, U.S.A., 77,* 1696–1700. **107**

YU, W.-H. A. (1982). Sex difference in the regeneration of the hypoglossal nerve in rats. *Brain Research, 238,* 404–406. **306**

ZACHARKO, R. M., BOWERS, W. J., KOKKINIDIS, L., & ANISMAN, H. (1983). Region-specific reductions of intracranial self-stimulation after uncontrollable stress: Possible effects on reward processes. *Behavioural Brain Research, 9,* 129–141. **332**

ZAJONC, R. B. (1985). Emotion and facial efference: A theory reclaimed. *Science, 228,* 15–21. **323**

ZARZECKI, P., STRICK, P. L., & ASANUMA, H. (1978). Input to primate motor cortex from posterior parietal cortex (area 5): II. Identification from antidromic stimulation. *Brain research, 157,* 331–335. **230**

ZEKI, S. (1980). The representation of colours in the cerebral cortex. *Nature, 284,* 412–418. **215**

ZEKI, S. (1983). Colour coding in the cerebral cortex: The responses of wavelength-selective and colour-coded cells in monkey visual cortex to changes in wavelength composition. *Neuroscience, 9,* 767–781. **215, 216**

ZEMAN, W., & KING, F. A. (1958). Tumors of the septum pellucidum and adjacent structures with abnormal affective behavior: An anteriormidline structure syndrome. *Journal of Nervous and Mental Disease, 127,* 490–502. **325**

ZERBIN-RÜDIN, E. (1980). Genetics of affective psychoses. In H. M. Van Praag (Ed.), *Handbook of biological psychiatry: Part III. Brain mechanisms and abnormal behavior—genetics and neuroendocrinology.* New York: Marcel Dekker.

ZERNICKI, B., & MICHALSKI, A. (1974). Single-unit responses to natural objects in visual areas 17 and 18 of cats reared under different visual experiences. *Acta Neurobiologica Experimentalis, 34,* 697–712. **430**

ZIEGLGÄNSBERGER, W., & BAYERL, H. (1976). The mechanism of inhibition of neuronal activity by opiates in the spinal cord of cat. *Brain Research, 115,* 111–128. **91, 99**

ZIEGLGÄNSBERGER, W., & CHAMPAGNAT, J. (1979). Cat spinal motoneurones exhibit topographic sensitivity to glutamate and glycine. *Brain Research, 160,* 95–104. **98**

ZIHL, J. (1981). Recovery of visual functions in patients with cerebral blindness. *Experimental Brain Research, 44,* 159–169. **446**

ZIHL, J., & WERTH, R. (1984). Contributions to the study of "blindsight": I. Can stray light account for saccadic localization in patients with postgeniculate field defects? *Neuropsychologica, 22,* 1–11. **446**

ZIMBARDO, P. G., ANDERSEN, S. M., & KABAT, S. M. (1981). Induced hearing deficit generates experimental paranoia. *Science, 212,* 1529–1531. **347**

ZIMMERBERG, B., GLICK, S. D., & JERUSSI, T. P. (1974). Neurochemical correlates of a spatial preference in rats. *Science, 185,* 623–625. **302**

ZIPSER, B., & BENNETT, M. V. L. (1976). Interaction of electrosensory and electromotor signals in lateral line lobe of a mormyrid fish. *Journal of Neurophysiology, 39,* 713–721. **176**

ZOLA-MORGAN, S., SQUIRE, L. R., & MISHKIN, M. (1982). The neuroanatomy of amnesia: Amygdala-hippocampus versus temporal stem. *Science, 218,* 1337–1339. **385**

ZUCKER, R. S., & LARA-ESTRELLA, L. O. (1983). Post-tetanic decay of evoked and spontaneous transmitter release and a residual-calcium model of synaptic facilitation at crayfish neuromuscular junctions. *Journal of General Physiology, 81,* 355–372. **110**

ZUCKERMAN, M. (1984). Sensation-seeking: A comparative approach to a human trait. *The Behavioral and Brain Sciences, 7,* 413–471. **329, 341**

ZWISLOCKI, J. J. (1980). Five decades of research on cochlear mechanics. *Journal of Acoustical Society of America, 67,* 1679–1685. **167**

ZWISLOCKI, J. J., & KLETSKY, E. J. (1979). Tectorial membrane: A possible effect on frequency analysis in the cochlea. *Science, 204,* 639–641. **167**

INDEX

CREDITS

CHAPTER 1. 8, Figure 1-4 adapted from the *The Self and Its Brain*, by K. R. Popper and John C. Eccles. © by Sir Karl Popper and Sir John Eccles, 1977. **10,** Figure 1-5 adapted from "Distribution of Readiness Potential, Pre-motion Positivity, and Motor Potential of the Human Cerebral Cortex Preceding Voluntary Finger Movement," by L. Deecke, P. Scheid, and H. H. Kornhuber, *Experimental Brain Research*, 1969, 7, 158–168. Copyright 1969 by Springer Verlag. Reprinted by permission. **12,** Figure 1-6 from Marvin Schwartz, *Physiological Psychology*, 2nd Edition, © 1978, p. 5. Reprinted by permission of Prentice-Hall, Inc., Englewood Cliffs, New Jersey. **16,** Figure 1-8 adapted from "Effects of Room Acoustics on Evoked Auditory Potential," by J. T. Marsh, F. G. Worden, and L. Hicks, *Science*, 1962, 137, 280–282. Copyright © 1962 by the American Association for the Advancement of Science. Reprinted by permission.

CHAPTER 2. 27, Figure 2-5 adapted from *Neurobiology*, by G. M. Shepherd. Copyright 1983 by Oxford University Press. **32–33,** Figure 2-10 from *The Cytoarchitectonics of the Human Cerebral Cortex*, by C. Von Economo. Copyright 1929 by Oxford University Press, London.

CHAPTER 3. 46, Table 3-1 adapted from *The Understanding of the Brain*, 2nd Edition by J. C. Eccles. Copyright 1977, 1973 by McGraw-Hill Book Company. **50,** Figure 3-4 adapted from "The Effects of Injecting 'Energy-Rich' Phosphate Compounds on the Active Transport of Ions in the Giant Axons of Liligo," by P. C. Caldwell, A. L. Hodgkin, R. D. Keynes, and T. I. Shaw, *Journal of Physiology*, 1960, 152, 561–590. Copyright 1960 by The Physiological Society. Reprinted by permission of the author. **53,** Figure 3-6 reprinted by permission from "Replacement of the Protoplasm of a Giant Nerve Fibre with Artificial Solutions," by P. F. Baker, A. L. Hodgkin, and T. I. Shaw, *Nature*, Vol. 299, pp. 583–591. Copyright 1982 Macmillan Journals Limited. **54,** Figure 3-7 adapted from "The Effects of Changes in Internal Ionic Concentrations on the Electrical Properties of Perfused Giant Axons," by P. F. Baker, A. L. Hodgkin, and T. I. Shaw, *Journal of Physiology*, 1962, 164, 330–354. **55** and **57,** Figures 3-9a, 3-9c, and 3-10 adapted from "A Quantitative Description of Membrane Current and Its Application to Conduction and Excitation in Nerve," by A. L. Hodgkin and A. F. Huxley, *Journal of Physiology*, 1952, 117, pp. 500–554. **55,** Figure 3-9b adapted from A. L. Hodgkin, *The Conduction of the Nervous Impulse*, 1964. Courtesy of Charles C Thomas, Publisher, Springfield, Illinois.

CHAPTER 4. 73, Figure 4-3 adapted from "Calcium in Synaptic Transmission," by R. R. Llinas, *Scientific American*, 1982, 247, 56–65. Copyright 1982 by W. H. Freeman. **74,** Figure 4-4 adapted from "Quick-Freezing Evidence in Favour of the Vesticular Hypothesis," by J. E. Heuser, *Trends in Neurosciences*, 1978, 1, 80–82. Copyright 1978 by Elsevier Biomedical Press. Adapted by permission. **75,** Figure 4-5 adapted from "Synaptic Vesicle Exocytosis Captured by Quick Freezing and Correlated with Quantal Transmitter Release," by J. E. Heuser, T. S. Reese, M. J. Dennis, Y. Jan, L. Jan, and L. Evans, *Journal of Cell Biology*, 1979, 81, 275–300. **78,** Figure 4-8 adapted from "Slow Synaptic Excitation in Sympathetic Ganglion Cells: Evidence for Synaptic Inactivation of Potassium Conductance," by F. Weight, et al., *Science*, 1970, 170, 755–758. Copyright 1970 by the American Association for the Advancement of Science. Reprinted by permission. **79,** Figure 4-9 adapted by permission from "The Statistical Nature of the Acetycholine Potential and Its Molecular Components," by B. Katz and R. Miledi, *Nature*, 1970, Vol. 226, 962–963. Copyright 1970 by Macmillan Journals Limited. **79,** Figure 4-10 adapted by permission from "Single-Channel Currents Recorded from Membrane of Denervated Frog Muscle Fibres," by E. Neher and B. Sakmann, *Nature*, 1976, 260, 787–789. Copyright 1976 by Macmillan Journals Limited. **81,** Figure 4-11a from "The Distribution of Acetylcholine Sensitivity at the Post-Synaptic Membrane of Vertebrate Skeletal Twitch Muscles: Ionophoretic Mapping in the Micron Range," by S. W. Kuffler and D. Yoshikami, *Journal of Physiology*, 1976, 244, 703–730. **87,** Figure 4-15 from "The Specific Ionic Conductances and the Ionic Movements across the Motoneuronal Membrane That Produce the Inhibitory Post-Synaptic Potential," by J. S. Coombs, J. C. Eccles, and P. Fatt, *Journal of Physiology*, 1955, 130, 326–373. **92, 102,** and **103,** Figures 4-19, 4-24, and 4-25a through 4-25d from *The Understanding of the Brain*, 2nd Edition by John C. Eccles. Copyright 1973, 1977 by John C. Eccles. All rights reserved. Reprinted by permission of McGraw-Hill Book Company. **108** and **109,** Figures 4-29 and 4-30 from "Local Regulation of Adrenergic Neurotransmission," by T. C. Westfall, *Physiological Review*, 1977, 57, 659–727. Copyright 1977 by the American Physiological Society. Reprinted by permission.

CHAPTER 5. 112, Figure 5-1 Photo courtesy of Dr. Margery Shaw. **116,** Figure 5-2 from "Response to 30 Generations of Selection for Open-Field Activity in Laboratory Mice," by J. C. DeFries, M. C. Gervais, and E. A. Thomas, *Behavior Genetics*, 1978, 8, 3–13. Copyright © 1978 by Plenum Publishing Corporation. All rights reserved. Reprinted by permission. **120,** Table 5-1 from *Behavioral Genetics: A Primer*, by R. Plomin, J. C. DeFries, and G. E. McClearn, © 1980, W. H. Freeman, New York. **121,** Figure 5-6 from "The Mechanisms of Evolution," by F. J. Ayala, *Scientific American*, 1978, 239, 56–69.

CHAPTER 6. 138, Table 6-2 from *Perception and the Senses*, by E. L. Brown and K. Deffenbacher, © 1979 Oxford University Press, New York. **140**, Figures 6-3a, 6-3b, and 6-3c from *Sensory Coding in the Mammalian Nervous System*, by G. Somjen, © 1972 by Plenum Press, New York, a Division of Plenum Publishing Corporation. Reprinted by permission. **140**, Figure 6-3d adapted from "The Surprising Simplicity of Sensory Metrics," by S. S. Stevens, 1962, *17*, 29–39. Copyright 1962 by the American Psychological Association. **141**, Table 6-3 adapted from "Neural Events and the Psychophysical Law," by S. S. Stevens, *Science*, 1970, *170*, 1043–1050. **143**, Figures 6-6a, 6-6b, and 6-6c from "Innervation of Rat Fungiform Papilla" by L. M. Biedler. In C. Pfaffman (Ed.), *Olfactum and Taste*, 1969, Rockefeller Press. Reprinted by permission. **148**, Figures 6-12a, 6-12b, and 6-12c from "Structure of the Hairs on Cochlear Sensory Cells," by H. Engstrom and B. Engstrom, *Hearing Research*, 1978, *1*, 49–66. **156, 158**, and **160**, Figures 6-16, 6-19, and 6-21 adapted from "Principles of Organization of Sensory-Perceptual Systems in Mammals," by M. M. Merzenich and J. H. Kaas, *Progress in Psychobiology and Physiological Psychology*, Vol. 9. Copyright © 1980 by Academic Press, Inc. **161** and **162**, Figures 6-23a, 6-23b, 6-23c, 6-23d, and 6-24 adapted from "Coding Gustatory Information in the Squirrel Monkey Chorda Tympani," by C. Pfaffman, M. Frank, M. Bartoshuk, and T. C. Snell. In J. M. Sprague and A. N. Epstein (Eds.), *Progress in Psychobiology and Physiological Psychology*, Vol. 6. Copyright 1976 by Academic Press. Reprinted by permission. **162** and **163**, Figures 6-25 and 6-26 adapted with permission from "The Organization of Stimuli and Sensory Neurons," by H. Schiffman and P. Falkenberg, *Physiology and Behavior*, 1968, *3*, 197–200. Copyright 1968 Pergamon Press, Ltd. **164**, Figures 6-27a, 6-27b, and 6-27c adapted from "Synaptic Processing of Taste-Quality Information in Thalamus of the Rat," by T. R. Scott and R. P. Erickson, *Journal of Neurophysiology*, 1971, *34*, 868–884. Copyright 1971 by the American Physiological Society. Reprinted by permission. **166**, Figures 6-29a through 6-29f from "Neural Mechanisms of Auditory Sensation in Cats," by Y. Katsuki, in W. A. Rosenblith (Ed.), *Sensory Communication*. Copyright 1961 by MIT Press. Reprinted by permission. **167**, Figure 6-30 adapted from "Basic Problems of Cochlear Physiology," by J. R. Johnstone, *Trends in Neurosciences*, 1981, *1*, 106–108. Copyright 1981 by Elsevier Publications. Reprinted by permission. **167**, Figure 6-31 adapted with permission from "Recent Advances in the Physiology of Taste Cells," by T. Sato, *Progress in Neurobiology*, 1980, *14*, 25–67. Copyright 1980 by Pergamon Press, Ltd. (Original from "Electrical Responses of Frog Taste Cells to Chemical Stimuli," by N. Akaike, A. Noma, and M. Sato, *Journal of Physiology*, 1976, *254*, 87–107, Cambridge University Press.) **174**, Figure 6-36 adapted with permission from "Recent Advances in the Physiology of Taste Cells," by T. Sato, *Progress in Neurobiology*, 1980, *14*, 25–67. Copyright 1980 by Pergamon Press, Ltd. (Original from "Electrical Responses of Frog Taste Cells to Chemical Stimuli," by N. Akaike, A. Noma, and M. Sato, *Journal of Physiology*, 1976, *254*, 87–107, Cambridge University Press.)

CHAPTER 7. 180, Figure 7-1 from "Contour and Contrast," by F. Ratliff, *Scientific American*, 1972, *226*, 90–101. Reprinted by permission of Floyd Ratliff. **180**, Figure 7-2 adapted from *Perception and the Senses*, by E. Brown and K. Deffenbacher, Copyright 1979 by Oxford University Press. **184**, Figure 7-7 from "Organization of the Primate Retina: Electron Microscopy," by J. E. Dowling and B. B. Boycott, *Proceedings of the Royal Society of London*, Series B, 1966, *166*, 80–111. Reprinted by permission of the authors. **186**, Figure 7-9 from "The Control of Sensitivity in the Retina," by F. S. Werblin, *Scientific American*, 1973, *228*, 70–79. Copyright 1973 by Frank S. Werblin. **190**, Figure 7-14 from "Toward a Functional Architecture of the Retina: Serial Reconstruction of Adjacent Ganglion Cells," by J. K. Stevens, et al., *Science*, 1980, *207*, 317–319. Copyright 1980 by the American Association for the Advancement of Science. Reprinted by permission. **191** and **192**, Figures 7-15 and 7-16 adapted by permission from "Morphology and Intracortical Projections of Functionally Characterized Neurons in the Cat Visual Cortex," by C. D. Gilberg and T. N. Weisel, *Nature*, 1979, *280*, 12–25. Copyright ©

1979 Macmillan Journals Limited. **192**, Figure 7-17 from *The Vertebrate Retina*, by R. W. Rodieck. Copyright © 1973 W. H. Freeman Company. Used by permission. **196**, Figures 7-22 and 7-23 from "Responses of Retinal Rods to Single Photons," by D. A. Baylor, T. D. Lamb, and K. W. Yau, *Journal of Physiology*, 1979, *288*, 589–611. Copyright 1979 by the Physiological Society of England. Reprinted by permission. **196**, Figures 7-24a and 7-24b from "Organization of the Retina of the Mudpuppy *Necturus maculosus*, II. Intracellular Recording," by F. S. Werblin and J. E. Dowling, *Journal of Neurophysiology*, 1969, *32*, 339–355. Copyright 1969 by the American Physiological Society. Reprinted by permission. **199**, Figure 7-27 from "Limulus Lateral Eye: Properties of Receptor Units in the Unexcised Eye," by R. B. Barlow Jr., and E. Kaplan, *Science*, 1971, *174*, 1027–1036. Copyright © 1971 by the American Association for the Advancement of Science. Reprinted by permission. **201**, Figure 7-28 adapted from "The Responses of Limulus Optic Nerve Fibers to Patterns of Illumination on the Receptor Mosaic," by F. Ratliff and H. K. Hartline, *Journal of General Physiology*, 1959, *42*, 1241–1255. **202**, Figures 7-29a and 7-29b adapted from "Contour and Contrast," by F. Ratliff, *Scientific American*, 1972, *226*, 90–101. Reprinted by permission of the author. **203**, Figure 7-30 from "The Receptors of Human Color Vision," by G. Wald, *Science*, 1964, *145*, 1007–1016. **204**, Figure 7-31 adapted from "Chromatic Organization of Primate Cones," by R. Marc and H. G. Sperling, *Science*, 1977, *196*, 454–456. Copyright 1977 by the American Association for the Advancement of Science. Adapted by permission. **207**, Figure 7-33 adapted from "Receptive Fields, Binocular Interaction and Functional Architecture in the Cats's Visual Cortex," by D. H. Hubel and T. N. Wiesel, *Journal of Physiology*, 1962, *160*, 106–154. **208**, Figure 7-34 adapted from "Visual System III: Physiology of the Central Visual Pathways," by E. R. Kandel. In E. R. Kandel and J. H. Schwartz (Eds.), *Principles of Neural Science*, 1981, Elsevier/North-Holland. **210**, Figure 7-36 adapted from "Receptive Fields and Functional Architecture in Two Nonstriate Visual Areas (18 and 19) of the Cat," by D. H. Hubel and T. N. Wiesel, *Journal of Neurophysiology*, 1965, *28*, 229–289. Copyright 1965 by the American Physiological Society. Reprinted by permission. **211**, Figure 7-38a and 7-38b from "Deoxyglucose Analysis of Retinotopic Organization in Primate Striate Cortex," by R. Tottell, et al., *Science*, 1982, *281*, 902–904. Copyright 1982 by the American Association for the Advancement of Science. Reprinted by permission. **211**, Figures 7-39a and 7-39b from "Orientation Columns in Macaque Monkey Visual Cortex Demonstrated by the 2-deoxyglucose Autoradiographic Technique," by D. H. Hubel, T. N. Wiesel, and M. P. Stryker, *Nature*, 1977, *269*, 328–330. Copyright © 1977 by Macmillan Journals Limited. Reprinted by permission. **212**, Figures 7-40a and 7-40b adapted from "The Pattern of Ocular Dominance Columns in Macaque Visual Cortex Revealed by a Reduced Silver Strain," by S. LeVay, D. H. Hubel, and T. N. Wiesel, *Journal of Comparative Neurology*, 1975, *195*, 559–576. Copyright 1975 by Alan R. Liss, Inc. Reprinted by permission. **213**, Figure 7-41 from *Fundamentals of Sensation and Perception*, by M. W. Levine and J. M. Shefner. Copyright 1981 by Addison-Wesley Publishing Company, Inc. **215**, Figures 7-42a and 7-42b from "The Representation of Colours in the Cerebral Cortex," by S. Zeki, *Nature*, 1980, *284*, 412–418. Copyright © 1980 by Macmillan Journals Limited. Reprinted by permission. **216**, Figure 7-43 adapted from "Place Units in the Hippocampus of the Freely Moving Rat," by J. O'Keefe, 1976, *13*, 419–439. Copyright 1976 by Academic Press. Reprinted by permission of the author. **219**, Figure 7-44 adapted from *Perception and the Senses*, by E. L. Brown and K. Deffenbacher. Copyright 1979 by Oxford University Press. **220**, Figures 7-45a and 7-45b from "The Site of Visual Adaptation," by J. E. Dowling, *Science*, 1967, *155*, 273–279. Copyright 1967 by the American Association for the Advancement of Science.

CHAPTER 8. 231, Figure 8-1 from *Neurobiology*, by G. M. Shepherd, Oxford University Press, © 1983. **232**, Figure 8-2 reprinted by permission of the publisher from "Physiology of Sleep and Dreaming," by Dennis D. Kelley, in E. R. Kandel and J. H. Schwartz (Eds.), *Principles of Neural Science*.

Copyright 1981 by Elsevier Science Publishing Co., Inc. **234,** Figure 8-4 adapted with permission from *Progress in Neurobiology,* 22, R. P. Vertes, "Brainstem Control of the Events of REM Sleep," copyright 1984, Pergamon Press, Ltd. **234, 236,** and **237,** Figures 8-5, 8-7a, 8-7b, and 8-9 reprinted by permission of the publisher from "Physiology of Sleep and Dreaming," by D. D. Kelley, in E. R. Kandel and J. H. Schwartz (Eds.), *Principles of Neural Science.* Copyright 1981 by Elsevier Science Publishing Co., Inc. **238,** Figure 8-10 adapted from "Raphe Unit Activity in Freely Moving Cats: Correlation with Level of Behavioral Arousal," by M. E. Trulson and B. L. Jacobs, *Brain Research,* 1979, *163,* 135–150. © Elsevier North-Holland Biomedical Press. Reprinted by permission. **239,** Figure 8-11 adapted from "Recovery of Function after Damage to Central Catecholamine-Containing Neurons: A Neuro-Chemical Model for the Laberial Hypothalmic Syndrome," by E. M. Stricker and M. J. Zigmond, in J. M. Sprague and A. N. Epstein (Eds.), *Progress in Physiological Psychology.* Copyright 1976 by Academic Press. Reprinted by permission. **241** and **242** Figures 8-12 and 8-13 adapted from "The Physiological Psychology of Hunger: A Physiological Perspective," by M. I. Friedman and E. M. Stricker, *Psychological Review,* 1976, 83, 409–431. Copyright 1976 by the American Psychological Association. Reprinted by permission. **256,** Figure 8-19 adapted from "Significance of Glucose, Insulin, and Free Fatty Acid on the Hypothalamic Feeding and Satiety Neurons," by Y. Oomura. In N. W. Wyrwicka and G. Bray (Eds.), *Hunger: Basic Mechanisms and Clinical Implications,* Raven Press, New York, 1976. **257,** Tables 8-3 and 8-4 from "Significance of Glucose, Insulin, and Free Fatty Acid on the Hypothalamic Feeding and Satiety Neurons," by Y. Oomura, in D. Novin, W. Wyrwicka, and G. Bray (Eds.), *Hunger: Basic Mechanisms and Clinical Implications,* copyright 1976 Raven Press, New York. **258, 259, 260, 261,** and **262,** Figures 8-20 through 8-24 from "Some Stochastical Patterns of Single Unit Discharge in the Cat Hypothalamus under Chronic Conditions," by Y. Oomura, H. Ooyama, F. Naka, T. Yamamoro, T. Ono, and N. Kobayashi, *Annals of the New York Academy of Science,* 1969, *157,* 666–689. Copyright 1969 by The New York Academy of Sciences. Reprinted by permission of authors. **263,** Figure 8-25a adapted from "Hypothalamic Self-Stimulation and Stimulation Escape in Relation to Feeding and Mating," *Federation Proceedings,* 1979, *38,* 2454–2461. **263,** Figure 8-25b adapted from *Neurobiology,* by G. M. Shepherd, Oxford University Press, © 1983. **266,** Figure 8-26 adapted from "A Portrait of the Substrate for Self-Stimulation," by C. R. Gallistel, P. Shizgal, and J. S. Yoemans, *Psychological Review,* 1981, 83, 228–273. Copyright 1981 by the American Psychological Association. Reprinted by permission.

CHAPTER 9. **273,** Table 9-1 from *Motivational Explanations of Behavior,* by K. B. Hoyenga and K. T. Hoyenga. Copyright © 1979 by Wadsworth, Inc. Reprinted by permission of the authors. **275,** Figure 9-3 from "Action of Estrogen and Mechanical Vaginocervical Stimulation on the Membrane Excitability of Hypothalamic and Midbrain Neurons," by J. T. Haskins and R. L. Moss, *Brain Research Bulletin,* 1983, *10,* 489–496. Copyright 1983 by Ankho International, Inc. Reprinted by permission of the author. **275,** Figure 9-4 reprinted by permission of Elsevier Science Publishing Co., Inc. from "Mood, Sexuality, Hormones and the Menstrual Cycle. I. Changes in Mood and Physical State: Description of Subjects and Method," by D. Sanders, P. Warner, T. Backstrom, and J. Bancroft, *Psychosomatic Medicine,* December, 1983, *45,* Copyright © 1983 by the American Psychosomatic Society, Inc. **278,** Table 9-2 modified from "Differentiation of Coital Behavior in Mammals: A Comparative Analysis," by M. J. Baum, *Neuroscience and Behavioral Reviews,* 1979, 3, 265–284, and *Sexual Differentiation of the Brain,* by R. W. Goy and B. S. McEwen, 1980, MIT Press, Cambridge, Massachusetts. **282,** Figure 9-7a from "Androgen and Estrogen Receptors in Embryonic and Neonatal Rat Brain," by C. Vito and T. O. Fox, *Developmental Brain Research,* 1982, 2, 97–110. Copyright by Elsevier/North-Holland Biomedical Press. Reprinted by permission. **282,** Figure 9-7b from "The Ontogeny of Cytosol and Nuclear Progestin Receptors in Male Rat Brain and Its Male-Female Differences," by J. Kato, T. Onouchi, O. Shoichi, and M. Takamatsu,

Journal of Steroid Biochemistry, 1984, 20, 147–152. Copyright 1984 by Pergamon Press, Inc. Reprinted by permission. **283,** Figure 9-8 reprinted by permission from *Nature,* 300, 648–649. Copyright 1982 by Macmillan Journals Limited. **284,** Table 9-4 from "Androgen Receptors in the Brain: What Are We Measuring?" by P. J. Sheridan, *Endocrine Reviews,* 1983, 4, 171–178. **285,** Table 9-5 from "Aromatization and 5a-Reduction of Androgens in Discrete Hypothalamic and Limbic Regions of the Male and Female Rat," by M. K. Selmanoff, L. D. Brodkin, R. I. Weiner, and P. K. Siiteri, *Endocrinology,* 1977, *101,* 841–848. **286,** Figures 9-9a and 9-9b from Progestin Receptors in the Brain and Pituitary of the Bonnet Monkey *(Macaca radiata):* Differences between the Monkey and the Rat in the Distribution of Progestin Receptors," by N. J. MacLusky, I. Lieburburg, L. C. Krey, and B. S. McEwen, *Endocrinology,* 1980, *106,* 185–191. Copyright 1980 by The Endocrine Society. Reprinted by permission. **289,** Table 9-6 created from Tables 1 and 2 of "The Interaction of Genotype and Exogenous Neonatal Androgen and Estrogen: Sex Behavior in Female Mice," by J. R. Vale, D. Ray, and C. A. Vale, *Developmental Psychology,* 1972, 6, 319–327, John Wiley & Sons, Inc. **296,** Figure 9-10 from "On the Genesis of Sexual Differentiation of the Central Nervous System: Morphogenic Consequences of Steroidal Exposure and Possible Role of Alpha-fetoprotein," by C. D. Toran-Alleran. In G. J. DeBrier, J. R. C. De Bruin, H. B. M. Hylings, and M. A. Corner (Eds.), *Sex Differences in the Brain.* Copyright 1984 by Elsevier Science Publishers, B. V., Amsterdam. **299,** Figure 9-11 adapted from "Hypothalamic Nuclei Catechol-o-Methyl-Transferase and the Process of Brain Sexual Differentiation," by W. Ladosky, B. C. Figueiredo, and H. T. Schneider, *Brazilian Journal of Medical Biological Research,* 1984, 17, 107–117. **299,** Figure 9-12 from "Alteration of Muscarinic Binding in Specific Brain Areas Following Estrogen Treatment," by G. P. Dohanich, J. A. Witcher, D. R. Weaver, and L. G. Clemens, *Brain Research,* 1982, *241,* 347–350. Copyright 1982 by Elsevier Science Publishers, B. V., Amsterdam. Reprinted by permission. **303,** Figure 9-13 adapted from "Experiential Modification of the Developing Brain," by W. T. Greenough, *American Scientist,* 1975, 63, 37–46. Copyright 1976 by the Scientific Research Society. Reprinted by permission. **303,** Figure 9-14 from "Sexual Dimorphism in 'Wiring Pattern' in the Hypothalamic Arcuate Nucleus and Its Modification by Neonatal Hormonal Environment," by A. Matsumoto and Y. Arai, *Brain Research,* 1980, *190,* 238–242. Copyright 1980 by Elsevier Science Publishers, B. V., Amsterdam. Reprinted by permission. **304,** Figure 9-15 from "Sexual Dimorphisms of Axo-Spine Synapses and Postsynaptic Density Material in the Suprachiasmatic Nucleus of the Rat," by F. H. Guldner, *Neuroscience Letters,* 1982, 28, 145–150. Copyright 1982 by Elsevier/North-Holland Scientific Publishers, Ltd. Reprinted by permission. **305,** Figure 9-16 from "Sexual Differentiation of Brain Structure in Rodents," by R. A. Gorski. In M. Serio, M. Motta, M. Zanisi, and L. Martini (Eds.), *Sexual Differentiation: Basic and Clinical Aspects.* Copyright 1984 by Raven Press, New York. Reprinted by permission. **306,** Figure 9-17 from "Sexual Dimorphism in Synaptic Organization in the Amygdala and Its Dependence on Neonatal Hormone Environment," by M. Nishizuka and Y. Arai, *Brain Research,* 1981, *212,* 31–38. Copyright 1981 by Elsevier North-Holland Biomedical Press. Reprinted by permission. **308,** Figure 9-18a, 9-18b, and 9-18c from "Gonadal Steroids: Effects on Excitability of Hippocampal Pyramidal Cells," by T. J. Teyler, R. M. Vardaris, D. Lewis, and A. B. Rawitch, *Science,* 1980, *209,* 1017–1019. Copyright 1980 by the American Association for the Advancement of Science (AAAS). Reprinted by permission. **311,** Figure 9-19 from "Sex Differences in Serotonin Receptor Binding in Rat Brain," by C. T. Fischette et al., 1983, *222,* p. 333. Copyright 1983 by the American Association for the Advancement of Science (AAAS). Reprinted by permission. **314,** Figures 9-20a and 9-20b from "Effects of Estrogen and Adrenal Androgen on Unit Activity of the Rat Brain," by Y. Yamada and E. Nishida, *Brain Research,* 1978, *142,* 187–190. Copyright 1978 by Elsevier Science Publishers, B. V., Amsterdam. Reprinted by permission. **314,** Figure 9-20c from "The Specificity of the Response of Preoptic-Septal Area Neurons to Estrogen: 17 *α*-Estradiol Versus 17 *β*-Estradiol and the Response of Extrahypothalamic Neurons," by M. J. Kelly, R. L. Moss, C. A. Dudley, and C. P. Fawcett, *Experimental Brain Research*, 1977, *30*, 43–52. Copyright 1977 by Springer Verlag. Reprinted by permission. **316,** Figure 9-21 adapted from *Estrogens and Brain Function*, by D. W. Pfaff. Copyright 1980 by Springer-Verlag. Reprinted by permission. **317,** Figure 9-22 adapted from *Estrogens and Brain Function*, by D. W. Pfaff. Copyright 1980 by Springer-Verlag. Reprinted by permission.

CHAPTER 10. 329, Figure 10-3 modified from "The Development and Validity of Familial Subtypes in Primary Unipolar Depression," by G. Winokur, *Pharmacopsychiatria*, 1982, *15*, 142–146. **333, 334, 335,** and **336,** Figures 10-6, 10-7, 10-8, and 10-10 adapted from "Coping Behavior and Stress-Induced Behavioral Depression: Studies of the Role of Brain "Catecholomines," by J. M. Weiss, H. I. Glaxer, L. A. Pohorecky, W. H. Bailer, and L. H. Schneider. In R. A. Depue (Ed.), *The Psychology of Depressive Disorders*. Copyright 1976 by Academic Press. Reprinted by permission. **342,** Table 10-4 from "Sensation Seeking: A Comparative Approach to a Human Trait," by M. Zuckerman, *The Behavioral and Brain Sciences*, 1984, *7*, 413–471, Cambridge University Press. **343,** Table 10-5 adapted from "Platelet Monoamine Oxidase Activity Correlates with Social Affiliative and Agonistic Behaviors in Normal Rhesus Monkeys," by D. E. Redmon, Jr., D. L. Murphy, and J. Baulus, *Psychosomatic Medicine*, 1979, *41*, 87–100. **345,** Figure 10-11 reprinted with permission from "Dopamine and Antianxiety Activity," by D. P. Taylor, L. A. Riblet, H. C. Stanton, A. S. Elson, and D. L. Temple, Jr., in *Pharmacology, Biochemistry and Behavior*, 1982, *17*, 25–35. Copyright 1982 Pergamon Press, Ltd. **346,** Table 10-6 modified from "Schizophrenia and Brain Dysfunction: An Integration of Recent Neurodiagnositc Findings," by L. J. Seidman, *Psychological Bulletin*, 1983, *94*, 195–238, and "The Domamine Hypothesis: An Overview of Studies with Schizophrenic Patients," by J. L. Haracz, *Schizophrenic Bulletin*, 1982, *8*, 438–468. **348** and **349,** Figures 10-12 and 10-13 adapted from "Relationships in Healthy Volunteers between Concentrations of Monoamine Metabolites in Cerebrospinal Fluid and Family History of Psychiatric Morbidity," by G. Sedvall, B. Fyron, B. Gullberg, H. Nyback, F. Wiesel, and B. Wode-Helgodt, *British Journal of Psychiatry*, 1980, *136*, 366–374. Copyright 1980 by the British Journal of Psychiatry. Reprinted by permission. **350, 351, 352,** and **353,** Tables 10-8 and 10-9 adapted from "Receptor Sensitivity and the Mechanism of Action of Antidepreseant Treatment: Implications for the Etiology and Therapy of Depression," by D. S. Charney, D. B. Menkes, and G. R. Heninger, *Archives of General Psychiatry*, 1981, *38*, 1160–1180. **359,** Figure 10-15 from "Classical Conditioning in *Aplysia californica*," by E. T. Walters, T. J. Carew, and E. R. Kandel, *Neurobiology*, 1979, *76*, 6675–6679. **359,** Figure 10-16 adapted from "From Metapsychology to Molecular Biology: Explorations Into the Nature of Anxiety," by E. R. Kandel, *American Journal of Psychiatry*, 1983, *140*, 1277–1293. Copyright 1983 by the American Psychiatric Association. Reprinted by permission. **360** and **361,** Figures 10-17, 10-18, 10-19, and 10-20 adapted from "From Metapsychology to Molecular Biology: Explorations Into the Nature of Anxiety," by E. R. Kandel, *American Journal of Psychiatry*, 1983, *140*, 1277–1293. Copyright 1983 by the American Psychiatric Association. Reprinted by permission.

CHAPTER 11. 369, Figure 11-1 adapted from "The Retroactive Effect of Electroshock on Learning," by C. P. Duncan, *Journal of Comparative and Physiological Psychology*, 1949, *42*, 32–44. **369,** Figure 11-2 adapted from "Two Types of ECS-Produced Disruption of One-Trial Training in the Rat," by J. P. J. Pinel, *Journal of Comparative and Physiological Psychology*, 1970, *72*, 272–277. **370,** Figure 11-3 adapted from "Temporal Course of Amnesia in Rats after Electroconvulsive Shock," by R. R. Miller and A. D. Springer, *Physiology and Behavior*, 1971, *6*, 229–233. Copyright 1971 by Pergamon Press. **375,** Figure 11-6 adapted from "Effect of Physostigmine on Y-Maze Discrimination Retention in the Rat," by M. D. Stanes and C. P. Brown, *Psychopharmacologia*, 1976, *46*, 269–276. Copyright 1976 by Springer Verlag. **377,** Table 11-1 modified from "What Should a Biochemistry of Learning

and Memory Be About?" by S. P. R. Rose, *Neuroscience*, 1981, *6*, 811–821. **379** and **380,** Figures 11-7 and 11-8 adapted from "Protein Pattern Alterations in Hippocampal and Cortical Cells as a Function of Training in Rats," by H. Hyden, P. W. Lange and C. L. Perrin, *Brain Research*, 1977, *119*, 427–437. Copyright 1977 by Elsevier Science Publishers, B. V., Amsterdam. Reprinted by permission. **386,** Figure 11-10a, 11-10b, and 11-10c adapted from "17-α-Estradoil and 17-β-Estradoil in Hippocampus," by M. R. Foy and T. J. Teyler, *Brain Research Bulletin*, 1983, *10*, 735–739. Copyright 1983 by Ankho International. Reprinted by permission. **387,** Figure 11-11 adapted from "Serial Position Curve in Rats: Role of the Dorsal Hippocampus," by R. Kesner and J. Novak, *Science*, 1982, *218*, 173–175. Copyright 1982 by the American Association for the Advancement of Science. Reprinted by permission. **389,** Figure 11-12 from *Introduction to Physiological Psychology*, by T. L. Bennett. Copyright 1982, Wadsworth, Inc. **390** and **392,** Figures 11-13 and 11-15 adapted from "The Engram Found? Initial Localization of the Memory Trace for a Basic Form of Associative Learning," by R. F. Thompson. In J. M. Sprague and A. N. Epstein (Eds.), *Progress in Psychobiology and Physiological Psychology*. Copyright 1983 by Academic Press. Reprinted by permission of the author. **391,** Figure 11-14 adapted from "Neuronal Plasticity in the Limbic System during Classical Conditioning of the Rabbit Nictitating Membrane Response. I. The Hippocampus," by T. W. Berger and R. F. Thompson, *Brain Research*, 1978, *145*, 323–346. Copyright 1978 by Elsevier Science Publishers, B. V., Amsterdam. Reprinted by permission. **394,** Figure 11-16 adapted from "What Is the Mechanism of Long-Term Potentiation in the Hippocampus?" by T. V. P. Bliss and A. C. Dolphin, *Trends in Neurosciences*, 1982, *5*, 289–290. Copyright 1982 by Elsevier Biomedical Press, Amsterdam. Adapted by permission. **397,** Figure 11-18 adapted from "Regenerative Changes of Voltage-Dependent Ca+ and K+ Currents Encode a Learned Stimulus Association," by D. L. Alkon, *Journal of Physiology*, Paris, 1982–1983, *78*, 700–706.

CHAPTER 12. Figure 12-1a from "Experiential Modification of the Developing Brain," by W. T. Greenough, *American Scientist*, 1975, *63*, 37–46. Figure 12-1b from "Direct Contact with Enriched Environment Is Required to Alter Cerebral Weights in Rats," by P. A. Frechmin, E. L. Bennett, and M. R. Rosenzweig, *Journal of Comparative and Physiological Psychology*, 1975, *88*, 360–367. Figure 12-1c adapted from "Environmental Enrichment and Deprivation: Effects on Learning, Memory and Exploration," by E. B. Gardner, J. J. Boitano, N. S. Mancino, and D. P. D'Amico, *Physiology and Behavior*, 1975, *14*, 321–327. **403,** Figure 12-2 from "Possible Memory Storage Differences among Mice Reared in Environments Varying in Complexity," by W. T. Greenough, W. E. Wood, and T. C. Madden, *Behavioral Biology*, 1972, *7*, 717–722. Copyright 1972 by Academic Press. Reprinted by permission. **405,** Figures 12-4 and 12-5 reprinted with permission from "Effects of Successive Environments on Brain Measures," by E. L. Bennett, M. R. Rosenzweig, M. C. Diamond, and H. M. and M. Hebert, *Physiology and Behavior*, 1974, *12*, 621–631. Copyright 1974 Pergamon Press, Ltd. **408,** Figure 12-8 adapted from "Experiential Modification of the Developing Brain," by W. Greenough, *American Scientist*, 1975, *63*. Copyright 1975 by the Scientific Research Society. Reprinted by permission. **409,** Figures 12-9 and 12-10 from "Sex Differences in Developmental Plasticity in the Visual Cortex and Hippocampal Dentate Gyrus," by J. M. Juraska. In G. J. DeVries, J. P. C. DeBruin, H. B. M. Uylings, and M. A. Corner (Eds.), *Sex Differences in the Brain*. Copyright 1984 Elsevier Science Publishing Co. Reprinted by permission of the author. **411** and **412,** Figures 12-11 and 12-12 reprinted with permission from "Mouse Somatosensory Cortex: Alterations in the Barrelfield Following Receptor Injury at Different Early Postnatal Ages," by D. Jeanmonod, F. L. Rice, and H. Van der Loos, *Neuroscience*, 1981, *6*, 1503–1535. Copyright 1981 Pergamon Press, Ltd. **418,** and **419,** Figures 12-14, 12-15, and 12-16 reprinted by permission from "Postnatal Development of the Visual Cortex and the Influence of Environment," by T. N. Wiesel, *Natura*, 1982, *299*, 583–591. Copyright © 1982 Macmillan Journals Limited. **422** and **423** Figure 12-17 and 12-18 from "Modification of Single Neurons in the Kitten's

Visual Cortex after Brief Periods of Monocular Visual Experience," by C. K. Peck and C. Blakemore, *Experiential Brain Research*, 1975, 22, 57–68. Copyright 1975 by Springer-Verlag. **427,** Figure 12-20 adapted from "A Physiological and Behavioural Study in Cats of the Effect of Early Visual Experience with Contours of a Single Orientation," by G. G. Blasdel, D. E. Mitchell, D. W. Muir, and J. D. Pettigrew, *Journal of Physiology*, 1977, 265, 615–636. **428,** Figure 12-21 adapted from "Visual Experience without Lines: Effect on Developing Cortical Neurons," by J. D. Pettigrew and R. D. Freeman, *Science*, 1973, 182, 599–601. Copyright 1973 by the American Association for the Advancement of Science. **429,** Figure 12-12 adapted from "Abolition of Direction Selectivity in the Visual Cortex of the Cat," by M. Cynader and G. Chernenko, *Science*, 193, 504–555. Copyright 1976 by the American Association for the Advancement of Science. Reprinted by permission. **431** and **432,** Figures 12-23 and 12-24 adapted from "Synaptogenesis in Human Visual Cortex — Evidence for Synapse Elimination During Normal Development," by P. R. Huttenlocher, C. deCourten, L. J. Garey, and H. Van der Loos, *Neuroscience Letters*, 1982, 33, 247–252. Copyright 1982 Elsevier Scientific Publishers, Ireland, Ltd. Adapted by permission. **434,** Table 12-1 adapted from "Synapse Replacement in the Nervous System of Adult Vertebrates," by C. W. Cotman, M. Nieto-Sampedro and E. W. Harris, *Physiological Reviews*, 1981, 61, 684–784. **435,** Figure 12-25 from "Reinnervation of the Partially Deafferented Hippocampus by Compensatory Collateral Sprouting from Spared Cholinergic and Noradrenergic Afferents," by F. H. Gage, A. Bjorklund, and U. Stenevi, *Brain Research*, 1983, 268, 27–37. Copyright 1983 by Elsevier Science Publishers, B. V., Amsterdam. Reprinted by permission.

CHAPTER 13. 445, Figure 13-1 adapted from "Stimulus Properties of Reinforcing Brain Shock," by R. M. Stutz, R. E. Butcher, and R. Rossi, *Science*, 1969, 182, 599–601. Copyright 1969 by the American Association for the Advancement of Science.